A Dictionary of Japan in English
英語で案内する日本の伝統・大衆文化辞典

森口 稔 [編著]

William S. Pfeiffer [英文校閲]

三省堂

© Sanseido Co., Ltd. 2018
Printed in Japan

編著者

森口　稔

英文校閲

William S. Pfeiffer

執筆者

池田　千鶴　　　井上　亜依　　　金指　　崇

三舛畑春香　　　森口　朗

執筆協力

川内　規会　　　小山　敏子　　　白水　盛博

鈴木三千代　　　関山　健治　　　田中美和子

福本　明子　　　町田佳世子　　　森口　武

調査協力

高梨　成三　　　藤田　理子

装丁

下野ツヨシ

装画

永島　壮矢

はじめに

　日本は，かつて，自らを「神国」と呼び，Japan as Number One と持ち上げられて有頂天になり，「もう，欧米から学ぶものは何もない」という言葉まで聞こえた時代もあった。しかし，昨今は，経済力や技術力において，往年ほどの国際社会における勢いが感じられなくなってきた。その巻き返しのためか，政府は「クール・ジャパン」をキーワードに観光立国を喧伝し，各地の経済も「おもてなし」を合い言葉として，インバウンド観光客の増加に期待を寄せている。事実，和食，マンガ・アニメ，忍者など，日本文化は海外に幅広く浸透しつつある。

　しかしながら，そういった様々な日本文化を幅広く，かつ，手軽に説明している辞書は，現在のところほとんど見当たらない。日本文化を英語で説明する類の書籍は数多く出版されているにもかかわらず，1冊で網羅している辞書が存在しない状況と言える。こういった背景を踏まえ，本書を世に送り出したい。

　本書を一言で説明するならば，日本に関する様々な項目を扱った和英辞典＋英文百科事典である。その特徴は，次の8点である。

(1) 日本に関する項目を網羅的に収録：日本を紹介する際に，誰しも思いつくのは，上述した和食やアニメに加え，神社仏閣，着物，文楽・歌舞伎・能，茶道・華道などである。しかし，日本独自の文化はそれに留まらない。古代から現代までの歴史の流れを踏まえ，かつ，現在の日本の姿を知るためにも，政治・経済，科学技術，スポーツ，動植物，自然，生活など，広範囲の分野をカバーする項目を収録した。たとえば，「日経平均株価」「ノルディック複合」「フォッサマグナ」なども見出し項目にしている。

(2) 各分野の詳細項目を収録：日本全般を紹介する書籍で，「忍者」「寺院」「茶道」などが記載されていない書籍はほとんどないだろう。しかし，そういった大項目ではなく，その内部の詳細な用語にまで踏み込んでいる書籍はあまり見かけない。本書では，たとえば，忍者の武器である「苦無」，仏像の「二十八部衆」，茶道の「貴人立て」など，少しマニアックと思われる用語も独立した項目として収録している。

(3) 固有名詞を収録: 上記とも関連するが, 固有名詞も積極的に収録した。織田信長, 鑑真, 関孝和, アーネスト・フェノロサなどの歴史上の人物, 『古事記』『今昔物語』『奥の細道』などの作品名, 東京都庁, 日本経済団体連合会, 徳川美術館などの機関・施設, JR, 日本経済新聞などの交通やマスコミ関連企業などもカバーしている。

(4) 見出し項目の英訳: 各項目の語義は, 上述した和英辞典的要素として, その見出し項目の英訳から始めている。説明的になりすぎず, 数語の英単語だけで表現するように努めた。

(5) 長すぎない説明と参照指示: 見出し項目の英訳の後には, 20語から100語程度の百科的説明を加えた。また, 関連する項目は, 本文内のスモールキャピタル (小型大文字) や矢印等によって参照できるように配慮した。

(6) 類義項目の違いの説明: 類似の項目がある場合, できる限り, その違いを説明するように努めた。たとえば, 「浪人」と「浪士」, 「浄土教」と「浄土宗」, 「仲人」と「媒酌人」などの違いは, それぞれの説明を比較すれば理解できるようにしたつもりである。

(7) 日本語の長音のローマ字表記: 日本語の長音のローマ字表記については, 現在, 一般化されているものとは異なる方法を, 敢えて採用した。現在, 日本語の「太郎」をローマ字表記する際, Taro と書くことが多い。そうでない場合も, せいぜい, Tarō と, o の上に長音記号を付加する程度であり, 「たろう」をそのままアルファベットにすることは比較的少ない。しかし, 本書では, 以下の理由から, Tarou と表記している。まず, 数多くの日本語を扱う場合, 長音と短音を区別して表記しなければ, 混乱を招くためである。たとえば, 本書では「近江」「臣」「大臣」のいずれをも見出し項目として記載している。もし, 「おう」「お」「おお」のすべてを o と表記すれば, それぞれが omi, omi, oomi となり, 混乱は必至となる。それならば ō と表記すれば良いのではないかという意見もあるかもしれないが, 今後, 世界中の多くの人々が日本語の長音を書こうとする場合, 一々, 長音記号を打つのは煩雑きわまりない。加えて, 電子化された際の表示の問題がある。今後も様々な電子機器が発達した際, 常に長音記号の表示が可能かという不安感は拭えない。さらに, 外国人の日本語学習の点からも, 「近江」はOumi と表記されるべきだろう。仮に, 「近江」を Omi と覚えた外国人学習者がワープロに向かうとき, Omi と打てば「臣」が表示されてしまうことに

なる。ただ，英語化していると思われる表現や，施設などについて，運営している団体などが正式な英文名称をつけている場合には，特に当該項目内においては上記の原則から外れ，可能な限りその名称を採用した。

⑻ 分野表示：すべての項目に，1つまたは2つの分野表示を加えた。2つの分野が付加されている項目は，その2つが重なっている場合も，その2つのどちらにも適応できる場合もある。たとえば，「仏教・美術」という分野が付加されている項目は，仏像や仏画などであることが多い。一方，「シテ」は「能・狂言」という分野が付加されているが，この場合は，能の用語でもあり狂言の用語でもあることを示す。

　本書の企画構想は2012年辺りから始めたが，その後，出版に至るまでに多くの方々のお世話になった。心からお礼申し上げたい。まず，執筆者や執筆協力者，さらに，英文校閲をしていただいた恩師のウィリアム・S・ファイファー先生。また，本書の企画を取り上げていただいた三省堂の山本康一氏や側面からサポートいただいた坂本淳氏，中でも，遅れがちになる執筆に辛抱強く付き合い，最後の最後まで面倒を見ていただいた西垣浩二氏には，感謝の言葉も尽きない。

　編纂を開始した当初は，常に，「日本とは何か」を意識しながら見出し項目を収集したが，カバーし切れていない項目も多々あるし，候補に挙げながら力及ばず記載を断念した項目もある。また，編纂に際しては多くの参考文献に当たったが，誤解や記載ミスが起きているとすれば，編者の力不足というほかはない。ご指摘いただければ，今後の糧としたい。

　最後になるが，本書の英語名はA Dictionary of Japan in Englishであり，仲間内ではこれを略してDOJIEとし「どうじ」と呼んでいる。簡単な雑用を言いつければ，飛んできてささっと片付けてくれる小さな子ども。多くの文献を調べずとも，とりあえずの説明ができる手軽な辞書。本書に対してそんなイメージを持っていただければ，この上ない幸いである。

2018年5月

森口　稔

本書の使い方

1 見出し語

日本史, 伝統文化, 宗教, 寺社仏閣, 政治, 現代文化, 精神性など, さまざまな分野からなる見出し語約 8,600 項目を立項した。

1.1 配列

和英形式で, 日本語の読み方のあいうえお順に配列した。

見出し語の読みを太字のひらがな, 一般的な表記をその後に漢字などで示した。表記が何種類かある場合には, カンマ(,)で区切って示した。

　　例: **てんぷら**　天麩羅, 天婦羅

長音符(ー)については, 長音符を直前の文字に含まれる母音に置き換えて配列した。

　　例: **すぴいどすけえと**　スピードスケート

同じかなが続く場合は, 原則として以下の順で配列した

　　(1) ひらがな→カタカナ→漢字
　　(2) 清音→濁音→半濁音
　　(3) 直音→促音・拗音
　　(4) 接頭語→接尾語
　　(5) 漢字の画数が少ないもの→多いもの
　　(6) 記述量の多いもの→少ないもの

1.2 空見出し

別の言い方・読み方のある語については, 主項目を参照させる空見出しを立項した。その際に, 必要に応じ振り仮名を付した。

　　例: **そうず**　添水〖建築〗 ⇨鹿威(しおど)し

　　　　しん　辛〖干支〗 ⇨辛(かのと)

1.3 語義番号

当該見出し語に意味が複数ある場合には, **(1)**, **(2)** のように語義番号を付し, 見出しをまとめて表示した。ただし, 読みが同一でも日本語表記が異なる場合には, まとめておらず別項目として立項している。

例：**あかえい** 赤鱝 **(1)** 〖妖怪〗a gigantic stingray-like monster... **(2)** 〖食べ物・魚〗a stingray...

2 分野表示

見出し語とその一般的日本語表記に続けて，当該語がどのような分野に属するのかを示すレーベルを，〔　〕に入れて見出し語の読み・表記に続いて示した。複数の分野にまたがる場合は中黒(·)を用いて併記した。

例：**ねんぐまい** 年貢米〔農業・行政〕

3 英文解説

可能な限り，冒頭に見出し語の数語訳を付し，その後に文化・百科的な背景解説を加えた。解説に関しては，冗長を排し，できるだけその語の理解に必要十分と思われる要点を的確に示せるよう，コンパクトにまとめた。その一環として，説明文の主語が見出し語と一致する場合は，主語を省略し，動詞句から始めた。

例：**すはまざ** 州浜座〔仏教・美術〕a sandy beach pedestal. Is used for the image of a deva or a priest...

3.1 イタリック体

日本語以外の外国語(サンスクリット語や学名のラテン語など)については，イタリック体で示した。また，書籍名や，絵画などの一部芸術作品名についても，イタリック体で示した。短編の作品などについては，" "に囲って示した。

3.2 日本語

英文説明中に表れる日本語に関しては，' 'に囲って示した。ただし，固有名詞，英語化している日本語に関しては，その限りでない。スモールキャピタル体については 6.3 を参照。

4 ローマ字表記の原則

4.1 ローマ字表

ローマ字に関しては，さまざまなかたちでの表記が行われており，統一を図るのには困難を極めた。本書では，基本的にヘボン式に順じ，以下の形式で表記している。

あ a	い i	う u	え e	お o	が ga	ぎ gi	ぐ gu	げ ge	ご go
か ka	き ki	く ku	け ke	こ ko	ざ za	じ ji	ず zu	ぜ ze	ぞ zo
さ sa	し shi	す su	せ se	そ so	だ da	ぢ di	づ du	で de	ど do
た ta	ち chi	つ tsu	て te	と to	ば ba	び bi	ぶ bu	べ be	ぼ bo
な na	に ni	ぬ nu	ね ne	の no	ぱ pa	ぴ pi	ぷ pu	ぺ pe	ぽ po
は ha	ひ hi	ふ fu	へ he	ほ ho					
ま ma	み mi	む mu	め me	も mo					
や ya		ゆ yu		よ yo					
ら ra	り ri	る ru	れ re	ろ ro					
わ wa	ゐ wi		ゑ we	を wo					

4.2 拗音・促音・撥音

拗音は「直前の子音字＋hないしはy＋当該拗音の母音字」で示した。促音は直後の子音字を重ねて示した。撥音はnで示したが，直後に母音やや行音が続く場合には，(')を挿入してナ行音との区別を試みた。

　　例：**しょうじ** shouji　　　　**にっぽんばし** Nipponbashi

　　　　のれん noren　　　　　　**まんようしゅう** Man'youshuu

4.3 長音符

長音符については，長音記号（ ¯ ）やhは用いずに仮名書きをそのままローマ字に遷した。例えば，「とう」はtohやtōではなくtou，「しゅう」はshūではなくshuuを用いて示した。

　　例：**さとうえいさく** Satou Eisaku　　　　**おおいちょう** ooichou

4.4 接尾的要素

…寺，…川のように，固有名詞に付いてその性質を表す語が後続する場合は，ハイフン(-)につないで示す場合がある。ただし，後続語も含めて固有名詞化している場合は，ハイフンを略して示す。英文としてのわかりやすさのため，"Sengaku Temple" ではなく "Sengaku-ji Temple" のように「寺」を示す要素を重複して示した場合がある。

例：Jouchi-ji Temple 　　 Mt. Sakura-jima 　　 Arakawa River

5 ローマ字表記の例外

5.1 英語化しているものについて

原則として，英英辞典に立項されている，ないしは英語化した表現が報道・学会などで一般化している日本語については，4 の原則によらず英語として一般化した表記を用いた。例えば，以下のようなものが挙げられる。

将棋 shogi	横綱 yokozuna	安土 Azuchi
会津 Aizu	能 noh	小豆 adzuki

5.2 慣例によるもの

一部の地名，施設・団体名などについては，4 の原則によらず慣例に従って表記した。例えば，以下のようなものが挙げられる。

東京 Tokyo	京都 Kyoto	大阪 Osaka	日光 Nikko
北海道 Hokkaido	東北 Tohoku	九州 Kyushu	
東海道新幹線 Tokaido Shinkansen		東武鉄道 Tobu Railway	
山陽新幹線 San'yo Shinkansen		朝日新聞 Asahi Shimbun	
上越新幹線 Joetsu Shinkansen		慶應義塾大学 Keio University	

5.3 固有名詞の正式名称

寺社名など各種施設などについて，独自に発行しているパンフレットやウェブサイトにおいて，正式名称を英文にて示しているものについては，当該項目においてはローマ字表記も 4 の原則によらずその正式名称に合わせて表示した。ただし，当該の寺社名などがほかの項目で取り上げられている場合には，4 の原則に従って表記している。

例：善光寺 Zenkoji Temple（正式名称のため Zenkou-ji としない）

※ただし,「善光寺式阿弥陀三尊」では a Triad of the Amitabha Buddha in the Zenkou-ji style

5.4 英文書名などの場合

書籍などが英訳されて出版されている場合には, 4 の原則によらずその正式書名を用いた。

例: 高野聖 *The Saint of Mount Koya* (正式書名のため Kouya としない)

5.5 スモールキャピタルの場合

上記 5.1〜5.4 について, スモールキャピタルで表された参照を示す表現のなかに出現する場合は, 例外扱いとせずに 4 で示した原則に従って表記している。詳しくは 6.3 を参照。

6 参照

当該項目に関しての理解を深めるために, 適宜関連項目などに参照指示を送った。以下の 3 種類の参照がある。

6.1 → 項目の末尾に, →に続けて関連項目への参照指示を付した。複数ある場合はセミコロン (;) で区切って示した

例: **にんなじ 仁和寺** 〚寺院〛Ninna-ji Temple. ... Was designated a World Heritage Site in 1994. →真言宗; 阿弥陀三尊

6.2 ↔ 項目の末尾に, ↔に続けて対語・反意語への参照指示を付した。

例: **にぎみたま 和御霊** 〚神道〛a peaceful divine spirit. ↔荒御霊(あらみたま)

6.3 スモールキャピタル

英文解説内において, 参照先の語を示すためにスモールキャピタル体で表示をした。スモールキャピタル体の部分は 4 の原則に従って表記されているので, ひらがなに読み替えて当該項目を参照されたい。

例: **にょにんこうや 女人高野** 〚仏教〛another name for MUROU-JI Temple in Nara Pref. or JISON-IN Temple in Wakayama Pref...
※「むろうじ」と「じそんいん」に対する参照指示となる

分野表示レーベル一覧

遊び	弓道	災害
アニメ	教育	祭礼
遺跡	狂言	魚
医療	行政	作品
色	行政機関	酒
氏族	漁業	茶道
映画	距離	山岳
干支	キリスト教	寺院
音楽	軍事	時刻
温泉	経済	史跡
絵画	芸術	施設
外交	芸道	自然
海洋	芸能	思想
科学技術	ゲーム	時代
家具	結婚	漆器
河川	研究機関	社会
学校	言語	宗教
華道	剣術	柔道
歌舞伎	建築	祝日
貨幣	碁	城郭
髪	公害	正月
官位	工芸	将棋
玩具	考古	少数民族
冠婚葬祭	交通	商標
漢字	香道	浄瑠璃
企業	国名	職業
企業名	湖沼	植物
技術	古墳	食文化
気象	米	助数詞
ギャンブル	暦	食器
旧国名	娯楽	書道

書名	島名	文様
神社	都道府県	ヤクザ
神道	人形	ゆるキャラ
人文学	忍者	妖怪
神話	年中行事	落語
寿司	能	礼儀作法
スポーツ	農業	湾
相撲	農林水産	
政治	飲み物	
精神性	俳句	
セックス	履物	
禅	博物館	
戦争	橋	
船名	犯罪	
組織	半島	
大道芸	ビジネス	
旅	美術	
食べ物	武器	
単位	服飾	
団体名	武士	
地名	武術	
彫刻	仏教	
調味料	風呂	
通過儀礼	文具	
通信	文芸	
庭園	文書	
鉄道	文楽	
テレビ	法律	
伝説	マスコミ	
天皇	漫画	
道具	民間信仰	
陶磁器	民芸	
動物	民話	

あ

**ああねすとさとお　アーネスト・サ
トー**〖外交〗Ernest Mason Satow.
1843-1929. A British diplomat.
Came to Japan first in 1862 and
stayed for 25 years in total, though
sometimes went back to Britain.
His works include *A Diplomat in
Japan*.

**ああねすとふぇのろさ　アーネス
ト・フェノロサ**〖美術〗Ernest
Francisco Fenollosa. 1853-1908. An
American philosopher and art historian who came to Japan in 1878
and left in 1890. Taught at Tokyo
Imperial Univ. and founded Tokyo
Fine Arts School, the present Tokyo Univ. of the Arts, in cooperation with Okakura Tenshin.

あいうえおじゅん　アイウエオ順〖言
語〗⇨五十音順

あいがも　合鴨〖食べ物・動物〗a
crossbreed between a wild and
domestic ducks. Edible and sometimes used in organic farming to
control pests and weeds.

あいきどう　合気道〖武術〗a martial
art derived from jujitsu. Its main
technique is throwing, utilizing
the vulnerability of the opponent's
joints. →柔術

あいきょうげん　間狂言〖芸能〗an
interlude performed by a KYOUGEN
actor during a Noh play.

あいくおう　阿育王〖仏教〗⇨アショ
カ王

あいこくふじんかい　愛国婦人会
〖軍事・団体名〗Patriotic Women's
Association. 1901-1942. Was organized to help families of the war
dead and disabled veterans.

あいさいべんとう　愛妻弁当〖食
文化〗a boxed meal prepared by
one's wife.

あいすもなか　アイス最中〖食べ物〗
wafer-wrapped ice cream. Does not
contain adzukibeans. →最中

あいぜんみょうおう　愛染明王〖仏
教〗Wisdom King of Passion.
Ragaraja. Has a ferocious face,
three eyes, a red body, and six
arms. One hand holds a bow, and
another hand holds an arrow, like
Cupid. →明王

あいちけん　愛知県〖都道府県〗Aichi
Pref. Its capital is Nagoya City.
Is located in central Japan, facing
the Pacific Ocean. Its area is 5,164
km^2. The cultures of Eastern and
Western Japan are blended here.
Its industrial area includes Toyota
City, with its automobile industry,
and Seto City, with its ceramic in-
dustry. Used to be called Owari and
Mikawa.

あいづ　会津〖地名〗western
Fukushima Pref. Used to be the
sphere of the Aizu feudal domain in
the Edo period.

あいづじょう　会津城〖城郭〗Aizu
Castle, also called Tsuruga Castle.
The original structure was built
in 1384 by Ashina Naomori and

became the headquarters of pro-shogunate forces during the Battle of Aizu. The present structure was restored in 1965. →会津戦争

あいづせんそう　会津戦争〔戦争〕 Battle of Aizu. A major battle in the Boshin War. The pro-shogunate forces of allied feudal domains fought with the new government forces in 1868. →戊辰（ぼしん）戦争

あいづぬり　会津塗〔漆器〕 Aizu lacquerware. Is produced in the Aizu area of Fukushima Pref. and decorated mainly with dust particles of gold or silver. Originated in the late 16th century.

あいづやいち　会津八一〔文芸〕 1881 -1956. A poet, calligrapher, and art historian, born in Niigata Pref.

あいづやき　会津焼〔陶磁器〕 Aizu ware. Porcelain manufactured in the Aizu area of Fukushima Pref. Originated in the mid-17th century.

あいどる　アイドル〔芸能〕 a pop idol. A popular young entertainer.

あいなめ　鮎魚女〔食べ物・魚〕 a rock trout or greenling. *Hexagrammos otakii*. About 30 cm long. Its color is yellowish or greenish-brown. Lives in coastal waters all over Japan except Hokkaido.

あいなめさい　相嘗祭〔祭礼〕 a festival to celebrate the harvesting. People thank 71 deities by offering new rice in November of the traditional calendar.

あいにえのまつり　相嘗の祭〔祭礼〕 ⇨相嘗祭（あいなめさい）

あいぬ　アイヌ〔少数民族〕 indig-enous minority people in Hokkaido. Traditionally, they used to live mostly on hunting and fishing. Some anthropologists say that Ainu is offspring of Joumon people.

あいぬご　アイヌ語〔少数民族・言語〕 the language of the Ainu people. Relationship to other languages, including Japanese, is unknown. Nearly extinct.

あいぬしんぽう　アイヌ新法〔少数民族・法律〕 ⇨アイヌ文化振興法

あいぬぶんかしんこうほう　アイヌ文化振興法〔少数民族・法律〕 Act on the Promotion of Ainu Culture, and Dissemination and Enlightenment of Knowledge about Ainu Tradition, etc.

あいのだけ　間ノ岳〔山岳〕 Mt. Aino. Is located on the border of Yamanashi and Shizuoka Prefs. The height is 3,189 m, the fourth highest in Japan. One of Shirane Sanzan.

あいぼし　相星〔相撲〕 having the same number of wins as the opponent.

あいもとはし　愛本橋〔橋〕 Aimoto Bridge. Is located in northeastern Toyama Pref. The original one, constructed in the Edo period, was a huge drawbridge and considered one of the three extraordinary bridges in Japan, but it was washed away by heavy rains in 1969. The present bridge was built in 1972. →錦帯橋（きんたいきょう）; 猿橋

あうん　阿吽〔仏教〕 beginning and ending. In Sanskrit alphabet, *a* (a)

is the first sound, and *hum* (un) is the last sound; therefore, 'a' is interpreted as the cause of everything, and 'un' is its effect.

あうんのこきゅう 阿吽の呼吸 〖精神性〗 ideal combination or ideal teamwork. When one member does something, the other member responds or supports perfectly without verbal communication. It is as if one would learn everything up to the end 'un' (Sanskrit *hum*) by only hearing the first thing 'a.'

あえごろも 和え衣〖食文化〗 a seasoning or dressing for AE-MONO. Tofu, ground radish, mustard, miso, etc. are used.

あえもの 和え物〖食べ物〗 vegetable or seafood salad dressed with miso, vinegar, sesame, tofu paste, etc. Popular examples are spinach dressed with sesame and octopus dressed with vinegared miso.

あおい 葵〖植物〗 a plant in the mallow family. *Asarum caulescens*. The design of its leaves was used as a family crest of the Tokugawa clan.

あおいまつり 葵祭 〖祭礼〗 Hollyhock Festival. One of the three great festivals in Kyoto, held at two Kamo Shrines on May 15. Participants wear nobles' costumes from the 9th to 12th centuries, and some ride on ox-drawn carriages. The parade starts from the Kyoto Imperial Palace, goes to Shimogamo Shrine, and ends at Kamigamo Shrine. →賀茂神社

あおうめ 青梅〖食べ物・植物〗 green fruit of the Japanese plum. Is used to make pickles or an alcohol beverage.

あおうめづけ 青梅漬け 〖食べ物〗 pickled green fruit of the Japanese plum.

あおきがはらじゅかい 青木が原樹海〖植物・地名〗 Aokigahara Sea of Trees. Is located at the base of Mount Fuji. The large forest was formed on the lava plateau created by the eruption of Mt. Fuji in 864. Is sometimes called "Suicide Forest" because many people commit suicide in this forest.

あおきしげる 青木繁〖絵画〗 1882–1911. painter born in Fukuoka Pref. Although he was influenced by European arts, many of his works were related to Japanese myth or legends. His works include *A Gift of the Sea* and *Paradise under the Sea*, both displayed at Ishibashi Museum of Art in Fukuoka Pref.

あおさ 石蓴〖調味料・植物〗 a sea lettuce. *Ulva*. Powder of dried sea lettuce is sprinkled on OKONOMIYAKI or TAKOYAKI.

あおざかな 青魚〖食べ物・魚〗 bluefish. Fish with blue backs, including sardines and mackerels. Is called hikarimono, meaning glittering thing, in sushi restaurants.

あおじそ 青紫蘇〖食べ物・植物〗 a green perilla. *Perilla frutescens*. Eaten as a condiment.

あおだいしょう 青大将〖動物〗 rat snake. *Elaphe climacophora*. Dark-green or blue-gray, 1.5 to 2 m long, and lives near human residences.

あおたがい 青田買い **(1)**〔農業〕 buying a paddy field in advance, anticipating the harvest. **(2)**〔職業〕 company's promise to employ prospective job-seekers, mostly college students, in advance of the ordinary job-hunting season. Is also called 'aota-gari' by mistake.

あおたがり 青田刈り〔農業〕 reaping rice before it becomes ripe. → 青田買い

あおたけふみ 青竹踏み〔医療・生活〕 bamboo treading. Good health is promoted by treading on bamboo cut in half with one's bare feet. Stimulate shiatsu points in the sole.

あおだたみ 青畳〔家具〕 a brand-new tatami. So called because the color of a new tatami is pale blue-green.

あおづけ 青漬け〔食べ物〕 green pickles. Mainly composed of leaf mustard called takana.

あおねぎ 青葱〔食べ物・植物〕 a green Welsh onion. Is used as ingredient or garnish in many kinds of cuisine.

あおのどうもん 青の洞門〔交通・地名〕 a tunnel dug by human hands. Is located in northwestern Ooita Pref. A priest named Zenkai spent about 30 years digging the 80-meter-long tunnel in the 18th century.

あおのり 青海苔〔調味料・植物〕 green laver. *Enteromorpha*. Dried in small flakes and sprinkled on food when eaten.

あおばじょう 青葉城〔城郭〕 ⇨仙台城

あおぶさ 青房〔相撲〕 a blue tassel. Hung at the northeastern corner of a suspended roof above a sumo ring. Has two meanings: the spring season or a blue dragon. →赤房；黒房；白房；青竜(せいりゅう)

あおふどう 青不動〔仏教・絵画〕 Blue Immovable Wisdom King. Nickname for the pictured Immovable Wisdom King at Shouren-in Temple in Kyoto. Is depicted on a silk screen from the mid-11th century. A National Treasure. →不動明王；三不動

あおもりけん 青森県〔都道府県〕 Aomori Pref. Is located at the northern end of Honshuu. Is 9,645 km^2 in area. Its capital is Aomori City. Famous for apple production and has many tourist spots such as Lake Towada, the Oirase River, and Mt. Osore. Used to be a part of Mutsu.

あおもりし 青森市〔地名〕 Aomori City. The capital of Aomori Pref., located in its central part. Famous for the Nebuta Festival, Asamushi hot springs, and Sannai Maruyama Site. →青森佞武多(ねぶた)祭り；浅虫温泉；三内丸山遺跡

あおもりねぶたまつり 青森佞武多祭り〔祭礼〕 Lantern Float Festival in Aomori on August 2nd to 7th. Many of giant lantern floats depicting heroes from stories are in the parade, and jumping dancers called 'haneto' dance between the lanterns.

あおやぎ 青柳 〖食べ物〗 the meat of a trough shell. Is used for sushi or tempura. →馬鹿(ばか)貝

あおりいか 障泥烏賊 〖食べ物・動物〗 a bigfin reef squid or oval squid. *Sepioteuthis lessoniana*. About 45 cm long. Eaten as sashimi or surume.

あか 閼伽 〖仏教〗 water served for the Buddha. Originally a Sanskrit word. It is said that the English word "aqua" has the same etymology as this word.

あかあたま 赤頭 〖妖怪〗 Red head. Mythic figure that looks like a four- or five-year-old boy and has Herculean strength but is harmless. Was said to appear in Tottori Pref.

あかいしさんみゃく 赤石山脈 〖山岳〗 the Akaishi Mountains. Are located on the border of Nagano, Yamanashi, and Shizuoka Prefs. The highest peak is Mt. Kita.

あかいしだけ 赤石岳 〖山岳〗 Mt. Akaishi. Is located on the border of Nagano and Shizuoka Prefs. The height is 3,120 m. The name 'Akaishi' means "red stone" because of the color of the rocks on the mountainside. A major peak of the Akaishi Mountains. →赤石山脈

あかえい 赤鱏 (**1**) 〖妖怪〗 a gigantic stingray-like monster. More than 12 km long. In the Edo period, fishermen sometimes landed on the back of this creature by mistake, thus wrecking their ship. (**2**) 〖食べ物・魚〗 a stingray. *Dasyatis akajei*. Is usually eaten boiled with soy sauce and sugar. Its grilled fin goes well with sake.

あかえび 赤海老 〖食べ物・動物〗 a whiskered velvet shrimp. *Metapenaeopsis barbata*. Literally means "red shrimp." About 10 cm long and edible.

あかがい 赤貝 〖食べ物・動物〗 an ark shell. *Scapharca broughtonii*. Eaten as sushi or sashimi.

あかかげ 赤影 〖忍者〗 the hero of a ninja manga and TV drama, *A Masked Ninja, Akakage*, written by Yokoyama Mitsuteru. Akakage literally means "red shadow," and he wears a red mask.

あかかぶ 赤蕪 〖食べ物・植物〗 red or purple root of a turnip, radish, or beet.

あかがみ 赤紙 〖戦争〗 a red call-up paper for military service during World War II.

あかぎさん 赤城山 〖山岳〗 Mt. Akagi. A volcano, located in Gunma Pref. The height is 1,828 m. Famous for a story about the yakuza, Kunisada Chuji. One of the three famous mountains in Gunma, which are called JOUMOU SANZAN.

あかしかいきょう 明石海峡 〖海洋〗 Akashi Strait. Is located between Awaji Island and Honshu. Connects the Inland Sea with Osaka Bay. Is about 4 km wide. Octopuses and sand lances are caught there. →玉筋魚(いかなご)

あかしかいきょうおおはし 明石海峡大橋 〖橋〗 Akashi-Kaikyo

Bridge. Was constructed over the Akashi Channel between Akashi City and Awaji Island in 1998. Its length is 3,911 m, making it the world's largest suspension bridge. →本州四国連絡橋

あかしし 明石市 〖地名〗 Akashi City. Is located just in front of Awaji Island, Hyougo Pref., at exactly 135 degrees east longitude, which is designated the standard meridian of Japan. Famous for AKASHI-YAKI. → 明石海峡大橋

あかじそ 赤紫蘇 〖食べ物・植物〗 a red perilla. *Perilla frutescens*. Is used to color pickled plums.

あかじた 赤舌 〖妖怪〗 Red tongue. A legendary monster that helped solve the water-rights dispute in Aomori Pref. in the Edo period.

あかしやき 明石焼き 〖食べ物〗 ball-shaped soft scrambled egg with octopus inside. Dipped into broth when eaten. A local food of Akashi City.

あかせん 赤線 〖娯楽〗 red-light district. Lieterally means "red-line" because this area was enclosed by a red line on a police map. Prostitutes used to be permitted in this area as special measures. Official red-light district were abolished in 1958.

あがた 県 〖政治〗 a local political unit under the Yamato administration in ancient times. Incorporated into the administration system established by the Taika Reform of 645. →大和朝廷；大化の改新

あかだし 赤出し 〖食べ物〗 reddish-brown miso soup. Dark-brown miso produced in Aichi Pref. is also used.

あがたぬし 県主 〖官位〗 a chief of AGATA, an ancient local political unit.

あかちょうちん 赤提灯 〖酒〗 a small and inexpensive Japanese-style tavern or pub. A red lantern is hung in front, beside the entrance. →居酒屋

あかなめ 垢嘗め 〖妖怪〗 dirt licker. Mystic figure that licks dirt in a bath tub at night. People kept the bath tub clean so that Akaname might not appear.

あかねいろ 茜色 〖色〗 madder, or dark yellowish-red. The color of dyestuff made from madder roots.

あがのがわ 阿賀野川 〖河川〗 the Agano River. Flows from Aizu Basin in Fukushima Pref. to northern Niigata Pref. The length is 210 km and is the tenth longest river in Japan.

あがのやき 上野焼 〖陶磁器〗 Agano ware. Pottery manufactured in the Agano area of Fukuoka Pref. at the one of the Enshuu Seven Kilns. Started by a Korean potter in the 16th century. →遠州七窯

あかはだやき 赤膚焼 〖陶磁器〗 Akahada ware. Pottery manufactured in Nara city at the one of the Enshuu Seven Kilns. Decorated with reddish-gray glaze and painting. Is said to have started in the 16th century. →遠州七窯

あかひげ 赤髭 〖医療・映画〗 *Red Beard*. A Novel and a movie about

a humane compassionate in the Edo period. The novel was written by Yamamoto Shuugorou in 1958, entitled *Akahige shinryou-tan*. The movie was directed by Kurosawa Akira in 1965.

あかふくもち 赤福餅〔食べ物〕 rice cake covered with strained, sweet adzuki paste. A local specialty of Ise, Mie Pref.

あかぶさ 赤房〔相撲〕 red tassel. Hung at the southeastern corner of a suspended roof above a sumo ring. Has two meanings: the summer season or a mythical red phoenix. →青房；黒房；白房；朱雀(ば)

あかふどう 赤不動〔仏教・絵画〕 Red Immovable Wisdom King. Nickname for the pictured Immovable Wisdom King, at Myouou-in in Mt. Kouya, Wakayama Pref. Is depicted on a silk screen around the 12th to 13th centuries. →三不動

あかべこ 赤べこ〔民芸〕 a papier-mâché red ox or cow with a wagging head. Is produced in eastern Fukushima Pref. 'Beko' means ox or cow in that area.

あかほん 赤本 **(1)**〔教育〕 a red-covered book for a student who is studying for the entrance exam for a specified university. Contains questions on exams for the university from the past several years. 'Akahon' for 375 universities were published as of 2013. **(2)**〔文芸〕 red-covered books from the 17th to 18th centuries. Contain illustrated stories for children. →草双紙(をぞうし)

あかまつ 赤松〔植物〕 a Japanese red pine. *Pinus densiflora*. Matsutake mushrooms grow beside it. Is also called me-matsu, female pine tree. ↔黒松

あかみそ 赤味噌〔食べ物〕 reddish-brown miso. Takes a long time for mature and is a little salty compared with white miso.

あがり 上がり〔食文化〕 hot green tea. Is served at the end of the meal at a sushi bar or a traditional style restaurant, usually in a large cup.

あがりがまち 上がり框〔建築〕 a piece of wood attached to the edge of the floor at the front entrance of a house. Separates the lower floor of the vestibule from the higher level of the first floor. Guests take off shoes here before entering the home.

あかりぐち 明り口〔華道〕 direction from which the sunlight enters in when a flower is arranged.

あがりゆ 上がり湯〔風呂〕 clean hot water to rinse oneself before getting out of the bath.

あかんこ 阿寒湖〔湖沼〕 Lake Akan. A volcanic dammed lake located in eastern Hokkaido. The area is 13 km^2. The maximum depth is 45 m, and the surface is 420 m above sea level. Famous for round green algae called marimo.

あき 安芸〔地名〕 old name of western Hiroshima Pref.

あきあじ 秋味〔食べ物・魚〕 a salmon swimming up a river to lay

eggs in autumn.

あきさめ 秋雨 〖気象〗 fall rain. In Japan, it rains much in September or October because of the autumn rain front.

あきさめぜんせん 秋雨前線 〖気象〗 autumn rain front. Appears along the south coast of Japan from mid-September to mid-October and brings a long rain.

あきしのでら 秋篠寺 〖寺院〗 Akishino-dera Temple. Is located in Nara City. Was founded in 776 at the behest of Emperor Kounin. Famous for the image of Gigei-ten, the deity of arts who is sometimes called Muse of the East. Its main building was constructed in the Kamakura period and is a National Treasure. →光仁(こうにん)天皇

あきたいぬ 秋田犬 〖動物〗 an Akita dog. Large-sized, brown or white, short-haired, and quiet. A protected animal, native to Akita Pref.

あきたかんとうまつり 秋田竿灯祭り 〖祭礼〗 Lantern Festival in Akita City that takes place from August 3rd to 5th. Local youths parade while balancing a long bamboo pole with several cross bars from which hang many lanterns.

あきたけん 秋田県 〖都道府県〗 Akita Pref. Its capital is Akita City. Is located on the coast of the Sea of Japan, between Aomori and Yamagata Prefs. Its area is 1,612 km². Famous for the production of rice and Japanese cedar. Lake Tazawa is 423 m deep, making it the deepest lake in Japan. Lake Hachirougata used to be the second largest lake in Japan, but 80% of it has been reclaimed by drainage. Used to be a part of Dewa.

あきたけん 秋田犬 〖動物〗 ⇨秋田犬(いぬ)

あきたこまち あきたこまち 〖食べ物・植物〗 a sort of hybrid rice, invented in Akita Pref. Its main feature is a springy texture.

あきたし 秋田市 〖地名〗 the capital of Akita Pref., located in its western part and facing the Sea of Japan. Famous for the Kantou Festival. →秋田竿灯(かんとう)祭り

あきたしんかんせん 秋田新幹線 〖鉄道〗 connects Morioka Station in Iwate Pref. with Akita Station. Started service in 1997. The express KOMACHI is the only train that runs on the Akita Shinkansen.

あきつしま 秋津島 〖地名〗 an ancient name of Japan.

あきのななくさ 秋の七草 〖植物〗 the seven flowers of autumn in a lunar calendar. Hagi (bush clover), susuki (pampas grass), kudzu, nadeshiko (pink), ominaesi (maiden flower), fujibakama (boneset), and kikyo (Chinese bellflower). ↔春の七草

あきのみやじま 安芸の宮島 〖地名〗 ⇨宮島

あきばけい 秋葉系 〖精神性〗 an Aki-habara-type computer geek. Loves techno subculture and frequently visits an electric town such as Akihabara in Tokyo or Nipponbashi in Osaka.

あきばしょ 秋場所〖相撲〗 Autumn Sumo Tournament. Is held at a sumo arena named Kokugikan in Tokyo in September.

あきばじんじゃ 秋葉神社 〖神社〗 Akiba Shrine. Was established in present Shizuoka Pref. in 709. Enshrines HINOKAGUTSUCHI NO KAMI, a deity of fire. The head shrine of other Akiba Shrines all over Japan.

あきはばら 秋葉原〖地名〗 a manga and IT area in the center of Tokyo city proper. Also called Akiba.

あぎょう 阿形〖仏教〗 the open-mouth form of a Guardian King at a temple. Represents the beginning of everything in the universe. →仁王(のう)

あきよしだい 秋吉台〖地名〗 largest limestone plateau in Japan. Famous for karst topography. Is located in western Yamaguchi Pref.

あきよしどう 秋芳洞〖地名〗 largest limestone cave in Japan. Developed under the Akiyoshidai plateau. Is also called Shuuhou-dou.

あくたがわしょう 芥川賞 〖文芸〗 Akutagawa Prize. A biannual prize for a newer novelist, oriented toward serious literary stories. Was established by KIKUCHI KAN in a magazine, named *Bungei Shunjuu*, in 1935 to commemorate the life of AKUTAGAWA RYUUNOSUKE. The Naoki Prize was established at the same time. →直木賞

あくたがわりゅうのすけ 芥川龍之介 〖文芸〗 1892-1927. Novelist born in Tokyo. His 1916 work, *The Nose*, was recognized by Natsume Souseki and made him well known. Committed suicide at the age of 35. His other works include *Hell Screen* in 1918, *In a Grove* in 1922, and *Kappa* in 1927. →地獄変; 鼻; 河童

あくにんしょうきせつ 悪人正機説 〖仏教〗 doctrine that insists even evil people are the object of salvation. The essence of the True Pure Land sect. A famous phrase is "A good person is to be saved. Needless to say about an evil person," because one of the Amitabha Buddha's vows is to save them. This phrase is written in the collection of sayings of the sect founder, SHINRAN. →歎異抄(たんにしょう)

あくび 欠 〖漢字〗 the radical of "yawn." A kanji containing this radical is usually related to breathing or opening the mouth. The radical is placed in the right part of a kanji, such as in 歌 or 欧.

あぐら 胡座 〖生活〗 cross-legged sitting. In an informal occasion, Japanese males often sit cross-legged on a floor when there is no chair. ↔正座

あくろおう 悪路王 〖少数民族〗 a derogatory name of ATERUI, who was a leader of people living in Northern Japan in ancient times.

あげ 揚げ〖食べ物〗 ⇨油揚げ

あげく 揚げ句〖文芸〗 the last two lines in a linked poem, RENGA. Contains fourteen syllables. ↔発句

あげだしどうふ 揚げ出し豆腐〔食べ物〕 fried tofu in broth. Sometimes chopped Welsh onion or ground radish is added.

あげだま 揚げ玉〔食べ物〕 a deep-fried batter ball. Is sprinkled on soba or udon. →天かす

あけちみつひで 明智光秀 〔武士〕 1528?-1582. A high-ranking warrior in the Warring States period. Though serving ODA NOBUNAGA, Mitsuhide destroyed his master and was defeated afterwards by TOYOTOMI HIDEYOSHI. →本能寺の変

あげちれい 上知令〔政治〕 Land Requisition Orders. Part of the Tenpou Reforms. Were not realized because of strong opposition and caused the downfall of its leader, Mizuno Tadakuni. →天保の改革

あげまき 揚巻〔髪〕 a hairstyle for a boy in ancient times. The hair was parted on the right and left sides and done up in loops.

あげまく 揚幕〔芸能〕 a curtain at the entrance to an elevated walkway on the stage. Opens up when an actor comes into or goes out of a kabuki or Noh stage.

あけむつ 明け六つ〔時刻〕 the sixth time in the morning in the Edo period. Around 6 a.m. ↔暮れ六つ

あげもの 揚げ物〔食べ物〕 deep-fried dishes. Typical examples are tempura or fried chicken called KARA-AGE.

あこうぎし 赤穂義士〔武士〕 ⇨赤穂浪士

あこうし 赤穂市〔地名〕 Akou City. Is located in southern Hyougo Pref. Famous for salt extraction and the revenge episode by the forty-seven masterless samurai.

あこうろうし 赤穂浪士〔武士〕 forty-seven masterless samurai from the Akou feudal domain. Killed KIRA YOSHINAKA in 1702 to avenge the death of their lord, ASANO NAGANORI. →忠臣蔵

あざいながまさ 浅井長政 〔武士〕 1545-1573. A feudal lord in the north of present Shiga Pref. Betrayed his brother-in-law, ODA NOBUNAGA, and was destroyed by Nobunaga. After his death, his eldest daughter married TOYOTOMI HIDEYOSHI, who succeeded Nobunaga's position and unified the nation. Nagamasa's third daughter married TOKUGAWA HIDETADA, who became the third shogun of the Tokugawa shogunate.

あさぎいろ 浅黄色〔色〕 pale yellow or light yellow.

あさぎいろ 浅葱色〔色〕 light greenish-blue. The pale color of Welsh onion leaves.

あさくさ 浅草〔地名〕 the name of sightseeing spot in northeastern Tokyo. Famous for Sensou-ji Temple, a shopping street called Nakamise, and a large red lantern hung from the Kaminari-mon Gate.

あさくさじんじゃ 浅草神社 〔神社〕 Asakusa Shrine. Is located in Tokyo. Famous for SANJA-MATSURI in May.

あさくさのり 浅草海苔 〔食べ物〕 purple laver. *Porphyra tenera*. Dried laver is used for various Japanese cuisines such as sushi or onigiri. → 味付け海苔；焼き海苔

あさくらよしかげ 朝倉義景 〔武士〕 1533-1573. A feudal lord in present Fukui Pref. After a long-lasting conflict, made peace with uprisings by devotees of the True Pure Land sect in Buddhism, called Ikko-ikki. In alliance with AZAI NAGAMASA, fought against ODA NOBUNAGA and was defeated.

あさじあえ 朝地和え 〔食べ物〕 a boiled green vegetable dressed with ground sesame seeds.

あさつき 浅葱 〔植物・食べ物〕 chives. *Allium schoenoprasum* var. *foliosum*. Eaten as a condiment.

あさづけ 浅漬け 〔食べ物〕 a lightly pickled vegetable. Is preserved in salt or rice-bran paste for a short period. ↔古漬け

あさのたくみのかみ 浅野内匠守 〔武士〕 ⇨浅野長矩（ながのり）

あさのながのり 浅野長矩 〔武士〕 1667-1701. A feudal lord of the Ako fief. Attacked Kira Yoshinaka in 1701 with a dagger in Edo Castle, because he thought Kira insulted him. On the next day, Naganori was commanded to commit hara-kiri by the shogunate. This affair led to the revenge by the 47 masterless samurai from Ako. →赤穂浪士

あさひかせい 旭化成 〔企業名〕 Asahi Kasei Corporation. A comprehensive manufacturer of chemicals and fibers. Its predecessor, Asahi Fabric, was established in 1922. Famous for its marathon team.

あさひかわし 旭川市 〔地名〕 Asahikawa City. The second largest city in Hokkaido, located in its central part. Asahiyama Zoo is popular across the country.

あさひしんぶん 朝日新聞 〔企業名〕 The Asahi Shimbun. One of the five major newspapers. Founded in 1879 and had a circulation of over seven million as of 2010.

あさひなたかし 朝比奈隆 〔音楽〕 1908-2001. A conductor born in Tokyo. Established present Osaka Philharmonic Orchestra in 1949.

あさひやき 朝日焼き 〔陶磁器〕 Asahi ware. Pottery manufactured in the Uji area of Kyoto Pref. One of the Enshuu Seven Kilns. Started in the 16th or 17th century. →遠州七窯

あさひやまどうぶえん 旭山動物園 〔娯楽・施設〕 Asahiyama Zoo. Is located in Asahikawa City of Hokkaido, making it the northernmost zoo in Japan. One of the most popular zoos in Japan.

あさま あさま 〔鉄道〕 the express train on Hokuriku Shinkansen. Is named after Mt. Asama, an active volcano on the border between Nagano and Gunma Prefs. Connects Tokyo with Nagano within two hours, while stopping at all of four stations in Nagano Pref. from Karuizawa to Nagano.

あさまさんそうじけん 浅間山荘事件 〚犯罪〛 an incident in 1972, in which five members of a terrorist group, the United Red Army, occupied a mountain villa, Asama Sansou, while taking a hostage. → 連合赤軍

あさまじんじゃ 浅間神社 〚神社〛 ⇨ 浅間(せん)神社

あさまやま 浅間山 〚山岳〛 Mt. Asama. An active volcano on the border of Gunma and Nagano Prefs. The height is 2,568 m. Erupted violently in 1783 and caused the Tenmei Famine.

あさむしおんせん 浅虫温泉 〚温泉〛 a hot spring in northeastern Aomori Pref. Has been used since the Kamakura period.

あさり 浅利 〚食べ物・動物〛 a Japanese littleneck clam. *Ruditapes philippinarum*. The shell length is about 4 cm. Is put into miso soup, steamed with sake, or boiled with rice.

あし 脚 〚漢字〛 a lower-part radical of a kanji character. For example, four dots in the lower part of 点, or 心 in the lower part of 思. →部首

あじ 鯵 〚食べ物・魚〛 a horse mackerel. *Trachurus japonicus*. About 30 cm long. Living in Japanese waters, along the Korean Peninsula and in the East China Sea. Is used for various cuisines such as fried fish, chopped sashimi, sushi, or dried fish.

あしあらいやしき 足洗い屋敷 〚妖怪〛 Mansion of Foot-Washing Monster. A giant foot and leg appears late at night, kicking down the ceiling, and requests to be washed.

あしいれこん 足入れ婚 〚冠婚葬祭〛 a kind of trial marriage before the modern era. For a certain period, the future bride worked at her future husband's home during the daytime and went back to her parent's home at night.

あしかががっこう 足利学校 〚教育〛 Ashikaga School. There are varying opinions about who founded it and when. Possibly existed as recently as the 13th century. Taught warriors, priests, and doctors in present Gunma Pref. until the Meiji period.

あしかがたかうじ 足利尊氏 〚武士〛 1305-1358. The 1st Muromachi Shogun. Helped Emperor Godaigo when the Emperor raised his forces against the Kamakura shogunate from 1331 to 1333. But he started the Northern Court by parting with the Emperor in 1336 and established the Muromachi shogunate in 1338. →後醍醐(ごだいご)天皇; 鎌倉幕府; 北朝; 室町幕府

あしかがばくふ 足利幕府 〚武士・政治〛 ⇨室町幕府

あしかがよしまさ 足利義政 〚武士〛 1436-1490. The 8th Muromachi Shogun, from 1449 to 1473. First planned to give his position as shogun to his younger brother, but changed his mind and decided to make his son the next shogun after his wife, HINO TOMIKO, bore the son. This issue became a cause of the Ounin War. Built the Silver Pavilion. →応仁の乱；東山(ひがしやま)文化；銀閣

あしかがよしみつ 足利義満 〖武士〗 1358-1408. The 3rd Muromachi Shogun, from 1368 to 1394. Unified the Northern and Southern Courts in 1392, built the Golden Pavilion in 1397, and started tally trade with the Ming in China in 1401. →南北朝時代；北山(きたやま)文化；金閣

あしがらやま 足柄山 〖山岳〗 the Ashigara Mountains. Are located on the border of Kanagawa and Shizuoka Prefs. It is said that a boy with superhuman strength, KINTAROU, lived there.

あしがる 足軽 〖武士〗 temporary foot soldier in medieval times, or a samurai of the lowest rank in the Edo period.

あじさい 紫陽花 〖植物〗 a hydrangea. *Hydrangea macrophylla Otaksa*. About 1.5 m high. Is used for decorative purposes. Native to Japan.

あしずりみさき 足摺岬 〖地名〗 Cape Ashizuri. Is located in southwestern Kouchi Pref., on the southernmost end of Shikoku, facing the Pacific Ocean. Its 80-meter-high cliffs are covered by subtropical flowers.

あしだ 足駄 〖服飾〗 pair of high wooden sandals. Worn on rainy days. Also worn by cooks, students, or TENGU.

あしたのじょお 明日のジョー 〖漫画〗 *Tomorrow's Joe*. A boxing manga, written by KAJIWARA IKKI and illustrated by Chiba Tetsuya. Was published serially in a boy's magazine, *Shounen Magajin*, from 1967 to 1973. Its TV anime program started in 1970.

あしたば 明日葉 〖植物〗 a "tomorrow leaf." *Angelica keiskei*. Its leaves are edible as tempura or boiled cuisine.

あしづかい 足遣い 〖文楽〗 a leg puppeteer in bunraku. Operates the legs of a puppet. →三人遣い

あじつけのり 味付け海苔 〖食べ物〗 seasoned dried laver. Is seasoned with soy sauce and mirin. ↔焼き海苔

あしで 葦手 〖書道・絵画〗 reed-style calligraphy. Characters, especially hiragana, are transformed to become small parts of a painting. The painting usually depicts waterside scenery.

あしとり 足取り 〖相撲〗 leg pick. A technique to throw down the opponent by holding up one of his legs.

あしながてなが 足長手長 〖妖怪〗 ⇨ 手長足長

あしなずちてなずち 足名椎・手名椎 〖神話〗 parents of Kushinada Hime, wife of the God of Storms. Ashinazuchi is her father, and Tenazuchi is her mother. →須佐之男命(すさのおのみこと)

あしなみじっかじょう 足並み十箇条 〖忍者〗 ten styles of walking steps. *True Path of the Ninja*

(SHOUNIN-KI) says a ninja has to learn all of them: stealthy step, rub step, tight step, flying step, one step, big step, little step, small step, proper step, and normal step.

あしのこ 芦ノ湖 〖湖沼〗 Lake Ashi. A popular sightseeing spot located in the Hakone area of Kanagawa Pref. The area is 7 km². The surface is 725 m above sea level. Good for viewing Mt. Fuji.

あじのもと 味の素 〖調味料・商標〗 an umami seasoning. The main ingredient is monosodium glutamate. A registered trade mark.

あしばらい 足払い 〖柔道〗 a foot sweep. A technique to trip the opponent from the outside while he or she is moving.

あしはらのなかつくに 葦原の中つ国 〖神話〗 Central Land of Reeds. Another name of Japan in mythology. The earthly land was located between the High Celestial Plain, Takamagahara, and the Land of Darkness, Yomi no kuni.

あしび 馬酔木 〖植物〗 ⇨馬酔木(あせび)

あしへん 足偏 〖漢字〗 a left-side radical meaning "foot." Kanji examples with this radical include 跡 (trace), 跳 (jump), and 路 (street).

あじゃり 阿闍梨 〖仏教〗 a status in esoteric Buddhism, given to a priest who has finished certain ascetic practices.

あしゆ 足湯 〖風呂〗 an open footbath. A free footbath open to the public. May be found in some spa towns.

あしゅくにょらい 阿閦如来 〖仏教〗 Buddha with No Wrath. *Aksobhya Tathagata*. The east Buddha in the Diamond Realm of esoteric Buddhism. →金剛界曼荼羅(こんごうかいまんだら)

あしゅら 阿修羅 〖仏教〗 *Asura*. A benevolent divine, incorporated from Indian mythology into Buddhism. Has three heads and six arms. The most famous one is at KOUFUKU-JI Temple. →八部衆

あしょかおう アショカ王 〖仏教〗 King Asoka. ?-232 B.C.? A king of ancient India who protected Buddhism. Is also called Aiku-ou. →阿育王

あじろ 網代 **(1)** 〖工芸〗 a piece of wickerwork. Is made of split bamboo or wood and used for fences, walls, ceilings, etc. **(2)** 〖漁業〗 a wickerwork trap for catching fish. Is placed in a river or pond so that fish should naturally swim into it.

あじろがさ 網代笠 〖服飾〗 a hat woven with shaved bamboo. Worn by a Buddhist monk or a pilgrim.

あじろてんじょう 網代天井 〖建築〗 a lattice-pattern ceiling. Is often used for a teahouse.

あすか 明日香 〖地名〗 Asuka Village. Is located in central Nara Pref. Has many ancient historic sites such as several tumuli and the Asuka-dera Temple.

あすかじだい 飛鳥時代 〖時代〗 the Asuka period, from the latter half of the 6th century to the first half of the 7th century. The capital moved around in southern Nara Pref., and

Prince Shoutoku carried out political reforms during the period. →聖徳太子

あすかでら 飛鳥寺 〖寺院〗 Asuka-dera Temple. Is located in central Nara Pref. Was founded in 596 by Soga no Umako. The principal image, Asuka Great Buddha, was built in 606 by Kuratsukuri no Tori and is said to be the oldest Buddhist sculpture made in Japan.

あすかぶんか 飛鳥文化 〖時代〗 the Asuka culture. Was based on Buddhism and strongly influenced by the culture of the Six Dynasties in China, which came to Japan via the Korean Peninsula. Cultural assets of Houryuu-ji Temple are typical examples of the Asuka culture.

あずき 小豆 〖食べ物・植物〗 an adzuki bean. *Vigna angularis*. An edible small red bean, mainly used for sweets or boiled with rice.

あずきあらい 小豆洗い 〖妖怪〗 Adzuki-Washing Goblin. Makes a sound like washing adzuki by a river. Sometimes sings a song which refers to eating human flesh.

あずきいろ 小豆色 〖色〗 dark red. The color of an adzuki bean.

あずまうた 東歌 〖文芸〗 a short poem in ancient Eastern Japan. Is anonymous and folkish and uses dialect. Such poems are contained in the *Anthology of Myriad Leaves* (Man'youshuu), and the *Collection of Ancient and Modern Japanese Poetry* (Kokinwakashuu).

あずまおとこにきょうおんな 東男

に京女 〖精神性〗 a man from Edo and a woman from Kyoto. It is said that a manly Edoite and a womanly Kyoto girl would make an ideal couple.

あずまや 四阿 〖建築〗 a small garden hut without walls, similar to a gazebo.

あぜくらづくり 校倉造り 〖建築〗 the building style of a log storehouse. Its walls are made of triangular or rectangular timbers in sections, and it has a high floor and no pillars. Shousou-in of Toudai-ji Temple is famous for this style.

あせび 馬酔木 〖植物〗 a Japanese andromeda. *Pieris japonica*. When a horse eats the leaves of this plant, its legs will be numbed.

あぜみち 畔道 〖農業・交通〗 an unpaved path between rice paddies.

あそさん 阿蘇山 〖山岳〗 Mt. Aso. An active volcano in Kumamoto Pref. The height is 1,592 m. Its caldera is 18 km from east to west and 24 km from north to south, making it one of the largest calderas in the world.

あそん 朝臣 〖官位〗 a title of a high-ranking noble. Is added to the family name such as "Fujiwara no ason."

あだうち 仇討 〖武士・精神性〗 revenge for a killed lord or a family member. Was officially permitted and regarded as an ethical deed for samurai in the Edo period. Is sometimes a motif in literature or drama.

あたけぶね 安宅船 〖軍事〗 a large

battleship in the Warring States period. The Tokugawa shogunate prohibited other feudal lords from building this type of ship.

あたごじんじゃ 愛宕神社 〖神社〗 Atago Shrine. Is located in Kyoto City. Is consecrated to deities of fire prevention. The head shrine of about 800 Atago Shrines all over Japan.

あだちがはら 安達ケ原 〖地名〗 a local area famous for a legend of a female ogre, located in Nihonmatsu City, Fukushima Pref.

あたみおんせん 熱海温泉 〖温泉〗 a hot spring in eastern Shizuoka Pref. Was discovered around the 5th century. One of the largest spa resorts in Japan.

あたりめ 当たりめ 〖食べ物・言語〗 a substitute word for "surume," dried squid. The sound of "suru" may be associated with a Japanese verb, "suru," which means "to lose money." →忌(い)み言葉

あつあげ 厚揚げ 〖食べ物〗 thick deep-fried tofu. Is grilled and eaten with soy sauce and ginger, or boiled in broth with other ingredients. →おでん

あつかん 熱燗 〖酒〗 hot sake. The temperature is about 55 degrees centigrade. →燗酒(かんざけ); 銚子; 猪口(ちょこ)

あつたじんぐう 熱田神宮 〖神社〗 Atsuta Shrine. Is located in Nagoya City. Enshrines Atsuta no Ookami, the Sun Goddess, the God of Storms, Yamato Takeru, etc.

The object of worship is Kusanagi no Tsurugi, the sacred sword, one of the Three Sacred Treasures of the Imperial Family. A short dagger made in the 14th century is a National Treasure.

あづちじょう 安土城 〖城郭〗 Azuchi Castle. Was built in 1576 by ODA NOBUNAGA and destroyed in 1582 after he killed himself at HONNOU-JI Temple. Some parts of its stone walls remain in Shiga Pref.

あっちむいてほい あっち向いてホイ 〖ゲーム〗 "Look there, now" game. Played by two people. First, they do rock-paper-scissors to decide the offense and defense. The offense points at the face of the defense with an index finger, saying 'Acchi muite, hoi!' (Look there, now!). Upon saying "hoi," the offense points in one of the four directions: up, down, left, or right, and the defense has to look in a direction he or she likes. If the defense looks in the same direction where the offense points, the offense wins. If not, they do rock-paper-scissors again.

あづちももやまじだい 安土桃山時代 〖時代〗 the Azuchi-Momoyama period, from 1568 to 1603. ODA NOBUNAGA entered Kyoto as the ruler of Japan in 1568. After his death, one of his vassals, TOYOTOMI HIDEYOSHI, acquired political power. After the death of Hideyoshi, TOKUGAWA IEYASU won the Battle of Sekigahara in 1600 and established the Tokugawa shogunate in present Tokyo in 1603.

あづまかがみ 吾妻鏡 〖文芸・作品〗 a chronicle describing events from 1180 to 1266 related to the Kamakura shogunate. Was compiled in the late 13th or early 14th century. The compiler is unknown.

あつみきよし 渥美清〖映画〗 1928–1996. A movie star born in Tokyo. Played the main act in the movie series, *It's Tough Being a Man*. His real name was Tadokoro Yasuo. → 男はつらいよ

あつもの 羹 〖食べ物〗 hot soup containing meat or vegetables. Literally means "hot thing."

あつやきたまご 厚焼き卵 〖食べ物〗 ⇨卵焼き

あて 当て 〖酒・食べ物〗 ⇨つまみ

あてじ 当て字 〖漢字〗 a kanji character that does not correspond to the original sound or meaning. The former example is 明日, which sounds 'asu' and means "tomorrow." The latter example is 目出度い, which sounds 'medetai' and means "auspicious."

あてみ 当て身 〖武術〗 a technique of hitting a vital part of one's opponent in jujitsu.

あてるい 阿弖流為 〖少数民族〗 ?–802. A leader of people living in Northern Japan, called Ezo, in the Heian period. Defeated the Imperial force in 789, but surrendered to a general, SAKANOUE NO TAMURAMARO in 802. Was executed in the capital, though Tamuramaro

appealed for mercy.

あてわざ 当て技 〖柔道〗 a technique of hitting a vital part of one's opponent. Is prohibited in modern judo.

あど アド 〖狂言〗 the partner to the main character called SHITE in a Noh farce. Corresponds to WAKI in a Noh play.

あとざ 後座 〖能〗 the rear stage where musicians (HAYASHI-KATA) are seated.

あとやく 後厄 〖宗教〗 the year after an unlucky age. In the traditional approach to age counting, these years are 26 and 43 for men and 20 and 34 for women. →厄年；前厄

あな ANA 〖交通・企業名〗 ⇨全日本空輸

あなかんむり 穴冠〖漢字〗 a crown radical meaning "hole." Is used in kanji such as 空(sky) and 突(pierce).

あなぐもじぐも 穴蜘蛛地蜘蛛 〖忍者〗 a technique for sneaking up on someone by digging a tunnel in the ground.

あなご 穴子 〖食べ物・魚〗 a conger eel. *Conger myriaster*. Is usually broiled and dipped in salty-sweet sauce. Eaten as sushi or a bowl of rice called donburimono.

あなりつ 阿那律〖仏教〗 *Aniruddha*. One of the Ten Great Disciples of the Historical Buddha. Also his cousin. Foremost among the disciples in attentiveness. →十大弟子

あなんだ 阿難陀〖仏教〗 *Ananda*. One of the Ten Great Disciples of the Historical Buddha. Foremost among the disciples in memorizing the Buddha's teachings. →十大弟子

あにそん アニソン 〖アニメ・音楽〗 abbreviation of "animation song." An opening or closing song of an anime TV series or an anime movie.

あにめ アニメ 〖アニメ〗 anime. Originally the shortened form of an English word "animation." Many manga have been converted to anime.

あねがわのたたかい 姉川の戦い 〖戦争〗 Battle of Anegawa. Took place in present northern Shiga Pref. on July 30, 1570. ODA NOBUNAGA and TOKUGAWA IEYASU defeated AZAI NAGAMASA and ASAKURA YOSHIKAGE.

あねさまにんぎょう 姉様人形 〖玩具〗 a paper or cloth doll wearing a bridal costume.

あのうしゅう 穴太衆 〖建築〗 a group of stonemasons from Anou, an area in southern Shiga Pref., on the coast of Lake Biwa. They often were employed by feudal lords to build a castle in the Warring States period.

あびじごく 阿鼻地獄 〖仏教〗 Hell of Avici. The worst of Eight Great Hells. Those who have committed a serious sin such as patricide fall into this hell.

あびせたおし 浴びせ倒し 〖相撲〗 backward force-down. A technique pushing down one's opponent on his back by placing one's own weight on him.

あぶくまがわ 阿武隈川 〖河川〗 the Abukuma River. Flows from southern Fukushima Pref. to Sendai Bay of Miyagi Pref. Its length is 239 km, making it the sixth longest river in Japan.

あぶなえ 危な絵 〖絵画〗 softly pornographic ukiyo-e. Is considered an intermediate art form between general ukiyo-e and hardcore pornographic ukiyo-e, shunga.

あぶらあげ 油揚げ 〖食べ物〗 thin deep-fried tofu. Is used as an ingredient of miso soup or for wrapping INARI-ZUSHI.

あぶらすまし 油澄まし 〖妖怪〗 a harmless goblin in Kumamoto Pref. It is said that he appeared when an old lady talked about him to her grandson while walking on a mountain path.

あぶらな 油菜 〖食べ物・植物〗 Chinese colza. *Brassica campestris* var. *nippo-oleifera*. Oil is extracted from its seeds, and its leaves are edible.

あべかわもち 安倍川餅 〖食べ物〗 a toasted rice cake dusted with soybean flour and sugar. Is named after the Abe River in Shizuoka City.

あべこうぼう 安倍公房 〖文芸〗 1924 -1993. A surrealistic novelist born in Tokyo. His works include *The Crime of S. Karma* in 1951, *The Woman in the Dunes* in 1962, and *The Face of Another* in 1964.

あべのせいめい 安倍清明 〖妖怪〗 921-1005. A yin-yang master born in present Osaka. His mother was said to be a fox named Kuzu-no-ha gitsune. →陰陽師(おんみょうじ)

あべのなかまろ 阿倍仲麻呂 〖外交〗 698-770. A scholar, who went to Tang China and failed to come back to Japan. Served the Tang emperor and died there.

あべのはるかす あべのハルカス 〖施設〗 Abeno Harukas. Is located in Osaka City. Its height is 300 m, making it the tallest building in Japan. Contains stations, department stores, an observation deck, a hotel, an art museum, and offices.

あべのひらふ 阿倍比羅夫 〖軍事〗 ?-? A warrior in ancient age. Attacked Ezo in the mid-7th century and was defeated by Sinra in the Battle of Baekgang-gu in the Korean Peninsula, in 663. →白村江(はくそんこう)の戦い

あべのやすな 安倍保名 〖妖怪〗 ?-? The father of a famous yin-yang master, Abe no Seimei, in the Heian period. A legend says that he married a female fox named Kuzu-no-ha gitsune.

あべべびきら アベベ・ビキラ 〖スポーツ〗 Abebe Bikila. 1932-1973. A marathon runner from Ethiopia. Won the gold medal in the Tokyo Olympic Games in 1964.

あほうぐすり 阿呆薬 〖忍者〗 poison made from hemp. *The Book of Ninja* (BANSENSHUUKAI) says it causes temporary insanity or cardiac arrest.

あぼしんのう 阿保親王 〖政治〗 792 -842. A son of Emperor Heizei. Father of Ariwara no Narihira. →在原業平

あほだらきょう 阿呆陀羅経 〖娯楽〗 a satirical song resembling sutra chanting. Performed on the street by a fake monk in the Edo period.

あま 尼 〖仏教〗 a nun. Shaves her head and lives in a Buddhist convent. →比丘尼(びくに)

あま 海女 〖漁業〗 a woman diver. Dives without oxygen tanks to collect shell fish, seaweed, cultured pearl, sea urchin, etc.

あまいろ 亜麻色 〖色〗 ecru or flaxen color.

あまえ 甘え 〖精神性〗 dependence and attachment to another person or other people. Often is exhibited unconsciously. May be related to Japanese groupism.

あまえのこうぞう 甘えの構造 〖書名〗 *The Anatomy of Dependence*. Written by Doi Takeo in 1971. The Japanese title literally means "structure of dependence."

あまえび 甘海老 〖食べ物・動物〗 a pink shrimp. *Pandalus eous*. About 12 cm long. Lives in the Sea of Japan or Northern Pacific. Eaten as sushi or sashimi.

あまくさしょとう 天草諸島 〖島名〗 the Amakusa Islands. Are located mainly in western Kumamoto Pref. and partly in Kagoshima Pref. The main islands are Kami and Shimo. Consist of more than 100 islands. There are several historic spots related to hidden Christians. →隠れキリシタン

あまくさしろう 天草四郎 〖キリスト教〗 1621-1638. A Christian born in present Kumamoto Pref. The leader of the Shimabara Uprising. His real name is Masuda Tokisada. →島原の乱

あまくだり 天下り 〖職業・政治〗 literally means "descent from heaven." A term indicating that government officials can easily find good jobs in private companies after retirement just because they have been government officials, even though they are useless.

あまぐり 甘栗 〖食べ物〗 sweet roasted chestnuts. Are sweetened with sugar or syrup.

あまこはるひさ 尼子晴久 〖武士〗 1514-1562. A feudal lord who lived around present-day Shimane Pref. Fought with the Mouri and Oo'uchi clans. →毛利元就(もとなり); 大内義隆

あまざけ 甘酒 〖飲み物〗 a sweet, hot beverage made from fermented rice or sake lees. Not classified as an alcoholic beverage because of its low alcohol content, though the name literally means "sweet sake."

あまじお 甘塩 〖調味料〗 lightly salted. Usually refers to the taste of salmon.

あまず 甘酢 〖調味料〗 sweetened vinegar. Is used to season meat or to pickle vegetables.

あまだい 甘鯛 〖食べ物・魚〗 a tilefish. *Branchiostegidae*. About 30-50 cm long. Living in the sea bottom of Southern Japan. Eaten grilled or dried.

あまちゃ 甘茶 〖飲み物・植物〗 hortensia. *Hydrangea macrophylla* var. *thunbergii*. Sweet tea made from dried leaves. Is poured onto a small Buddhist image on Buddha's birthday, April 8. →灌仏会(かんぶつえ)

あまつかみ 天つ神 〖神話〗 a heavenly deity residing in or coming from the High Celestial Plain (TAKAMAGAHARA). For example, AMENO MINAKANUSHI NO KAMI, IZANAGI NO MIKOTO, AMATERASU OOMIKAMI, etc. ↔国つ神

あまでら 尼寺 〖仏教〗 a Buddhist convent. It is said that the first one in Japan was established in Asuka in the 6th century.

あまてらすおおみかみ 天照大神 〖神話〗 the Sun Goddess. A daughter of IZANAGI NO MIKOTO. Ruling the High Celestial Plain (TAKAMAGAHARA) and enshrined in the Grand Shrine of Ise. →伊勢神宮

あまど 雨戸 〖建築〗 a storm shutter. A traditional one is a wooden sliding door. In normal weather, it is contained in a flat case beside the window or door. →戸袋

あまなつ 甘夏 〖食べ物・植物〗 a sweet summer orange, or sweet Watson pomelo. *Citrus natsudaidai*. Not so sour, compared with an ordinary Watson pomelo (NATSU-MIKAN).

あまなっとう 甘納豆 〖食べ物〗 half-dried sweet beans with icing. Adzuki, cowpeas, green beans, etc. are used as ingredients.

あまに 甘煮 〖食べ物〗 food boiled with sweet taste. Is seasoned with sugar, mirin, and soy sauce.

あまのいわと 天岩戸 〖神話〗 the Gate of the Celestial Rock Cave.

The Sun Goddess hid herself in the cave and closed the gate after she became infuriated at the villainy of her brother, the God of Storms. → 天照大神（あまてらすおおみかみ）；天鈿女命（あめのうずめのみこと）；手力男命（たぢからおのみこと）

あまのがわ 天の川 〖民話〗 the Milky Way. Literally means the "Heaven River." In a legend introduced from ancient China, Vega (ORIHIME) and Altair (HIKOBOSHI) cross the river to meet each other once a year on July 7th. →七夕

あまのさけ 天野酒 〖酒〗 sake brewed at Amano-san Kongou-ji Temple in Osaka in the Muromachi period. It is said that Toyotomi Hideyoshi loved it.

あまのじゃく 天邪鬼 〖妖怪・仏教〗 a small devil. Can read the human mind and is good at mimicry. Trodden under foot by the Four Guardian Kings. →四天王

あまのはしだて 天橋立 〖地名〗 one of the Three Famous Views of Japan, and a Special Place of Scenic Beauty in Kyoto Pref. A sandbank stretches about 3 km in Miyadu Bay along the Sea of Japan. The view from Mt. Nariai toward the north is excellent. *View of Amano-Hashidate* drawn by SESSHUU in the early 16th century is a National Treasure. →日本三景

あまのり 甘海苔 〖食べ物〗 ⇨浅草海苔

あまびえ アマビエ 〖妖怪〗 a shining mermaid. Is covered with scales except for the face and head. Was said to appear in Kumamoto Pref. in the Edo period and made a prediction about the year's harvest.

あまみおおしま 奄美大島 〖島名〗 Amami-ooshima Island, in Kagoshima Pref. Is located southward off Kyushu Island. Its area is 712 km^2. Sugar cane, papayas, and pineapples are cultivated. The fabric called Ooshima tsumugi is a local specialty.

あまみそ 甘味噌 〖調味料〗 lightly salted miso. Sweeter than ordinary miso. ↔辛味噌

あまめはぎ あまめはぎ 〖妖怪〗 a demon who remonstrates people's laziness. Was said to appear in Ishikawa Pref. Similar to Namahage in Akita Pref.

あみがさ 編笠 〖服飾〗 a hat woven with sedge or rush. Has been used since the Heian period.

あみきり 網切 〖妖怪〗 a net-cutting goblin. Cuts a mosquito or fishing net unseen at night.

あみだくじ 阿弥陀籤 〖生活〗 lattice-pattern lottery. Each participant selects an end of a vertical line of a lattice pattern, traces vertical and horizontal lines alternatively, and reaches the opposite end of another vertical line. There is usually a prize or prizes at one of the opposite ends of the vertical lines.

あみださんぞん 阿弥陀三尊 〖仏教〗 the Triad of the Amitabha Buddha. Combination of the Amitabha Buddha and the two attendant bodhisattvas: KANNON BOSATSU,

Avalokitesvara, on the left, and SEISHI BOSATSU, *Mahasthamaprapta*, on the right. →阿弥陀如来

あみだにょらい 阿弥陀如来 〖仏教〗 Amitabha Buddha. The Buddha of Infinite Light, or Infinite Life. *Amitabha Tathagata*. Vowed to save all living things and resides in the Western Pure Land. →極楽往生; 浄土宗; 浄土真宗

あみだらいごう 阿弥陀来迎 〖仏教〗 the advent of Amitabha Buddha. Amitabha comes down to welcome the soul of a dying person to the Western Pure Land. There remain many pictures of this subject. →阿弥陀如来; 西方極楽浄土

あみもと 網元 〖漁業〗 a fishery manager. Possesses fishing nets and boats and employs fishermen.

あめいろ 飴色 〖色〗 amber. Transparent honey-yellow. The color of traditional candy.

あめかんむり 雨冠 〖漢字〗 rain crown radical. A kanji character with this radical usually has a meaning related to rain, such as snow(雪), thunder(雷), or cloud (雲).

あめだす AMeDAS 〖気象・科学技術〗 Automated Meteorological Data Acquisition System. Weather information is automatically transmitted from about 1,300 points throughout Japan to the Meterological Agency. Started operation in 1974.

あめつちのことば 天地の詞 〖言語〗 a training material for learning to read and write in the 9th or 10th century. Consists of 48 letters without overlapping. →伊呂波歌(いろは うた)

あめのうずめのみこと 天鈿女命 〖神話〗 a female deity of dancing. Danced fanatically in semi nudity to provoke laughter among deities gathered in front of AMA NO IWATO when the Sun Goddess hid herself behind there. →天照大神(あまてらす おおみかみ); 猿田彦

あめのおしほみみのみこと 天之忍穂耳命 〖神話〗 a son of the Sun Goddess (AMATERASU OOMIKAMI), and the father of NINIGI NO MIKOTO. Born when Amaterasu and the God of Storms (SUSANOO NO MIKOTO) asked divine judgment concerning Susanoo's belligerence. When Amaterasu ordered him to descend from the High Celestial Plain to the Central Land of Reeds, he refused the order and recommended that his son should descend. Is worshipped as a deity of agriculture.

あめのこやねのみこと 天児屋命 〖神話〗 the ancestor of the Fujiwara clan. Recited a ritual prayer when the Sun Goddess hid herself in the Celestial Rock Cave. →天岩戸(あまの いわと); 藤原氏

あめのみなかぬしのかみ 天之御中主神 〖神話〗 the first-born deity who appeared during the creation of the world. →造化(ぞうか)三神

あめのむらくものつるぎ 天叢雲剣 〖神話・天皇〗 the Sacred Sword. One of the Three Sacred Treasures of the Imperial Family. Was found in the tail of YAMATA NO OROCHI. Is also called 'Kusanagi no tsurugi,' the Grass-Mowing Sword, because YAMATO TAKERU NO MIKOTO mowed the burning grass with it to get out of danger. →三種の神器

あめのわかひこ　天若日子　〖神話〗 a deity dispatched from the High Celestial Plain to the Central Land of Reeds before NINIGI NO MIKOTO was dispatched. However, he betrayed the Plain and did not conquer the Land, so he was killed by an arrow TAKAMIMUSUHI NO KAMI threw from the Plain. →天孫降臨

あめふりこぞう　雨降り小僧　〖妖怪〗 a rain kid. Was said to appear in a field when it was raining, putting an umbrella on his head.

あやとり　綾取り　〖遊び〗 cat's cradle. Similar games can be found all over the world.

あやめ　菖蒲　〖植物〗 a blood iris. *Iris sanguinea.* Grows on sunny dry grassland. Reddish or bluish purple flowers bloom in early summer.

あゆ　鮎　〖食べ物・魚〗 a sweetfish. *Plecoglossus altivelis.* Lives in a river, is spindle-shaped and 20-30 cm long, with a black-green back and silver belly. Often eaten grilled with salt, or as sushi.

あら　粗　〖食文化〗 fish head and bones after being trimmed. Is used to make soup stock.

あら　鰔　〖食べ物・魚〗 a sawedged perch. *Niphon spinosus.* About 80 cm long. Lives along Southern Japan to the Philippines. Eaten as

SASHIMI or NABEMONO.

あらい　洗い　〖食べ物〗 sashimi rinced in icy water. Usually eaten in summer. A carp and a sea bass are popular ingredients. Traditionally, carps are eaten mostly in mountainous regions, where saltwater fishes are hard to obtain.

あらいはくせき　新井白石　〖武士〗 1657-1725. A Confucian scholar and statesman, born in Edo. Served the 6th Tokugawa Shogun, Ienobu.

あらいはり　洗い張り　〖服飾〗 to unsew, wash, starch, press, and dry a kimono.

あらかん　阿羅漢　〖仏教〗 an arhat. An enlightened Buddhist priest. These priests are sometimes depicted in a group of sixteen or five hundred. →十六羅漢；五百羅漢

あらぎょう　荒行　〖宗教〗 rigorous religious exercises, such as standing under a waterfall or walking on fire. Done in some Buddhist sects and in mountain asceticism.

あらこ　粗粉　〖食べ物〗 coarse-grain rice flour. An ingredient of a dry confectionery (HIGASHI).

あらごと　荒事　〖歌舞伎〗 the valiant style of kabuki plays. The hero is usually a samurai or a demon and uses exaggerated posing, movement, makeup, and costume to express his bravery and wildness. →和事；実事

あらじお　粗塩　〖調味料〗 unrefined salt. Is used not only for seasoning but also for scattering on a sumo ring.

あらしやま 嵐山〖地名〗a sightseeing spot in western Kyoto City. One can enjoy visiting spotted temples and shrines, walking through bamboo forests, and viewing cherry blossoms in spring and maple leaves in fall.

あらばしり 新走り〖酒〗the first flow of sake after a fermented mixture is squeezed.

あらひとがみ 現人神〖天皇〗a living god. From ancient times until the end of World War II, this term was used to refer to Emperors.

あらぼとけ 新仏〖仏教〗a newly departed soul. Is called so when worshipped in the first Bon Festival after the person's death.

あらまきじゃけ 新巻鮭〖食べ物〗a salty salmon, with its guts removed, and tied up with a thick straw rope.

あらみたま 荒御霊〖神道〗a violent divine spirit. Sometimes causes natural disasters. ↔和御霊(にぎみたま)

あららぎ アララギ〖文芸〗the name of a tanka magazine based on real life. Aspired to achieve the style of the *Anthology of Myriad Leaves* (MAN'YOUSHUU). Was first published in 1909 by Warabi Shin'ichirou. Editors included ITOU SACHIO and SAITOU MOKICHI. The final issue was published in 1997.

あららぎ 蘭〖植物〗⇨檪(いちい)

あられ 霰〖食べ物〗a bite-sized rice cracker. Is usually seasoned with salt or soy sauce, and sometimes red pepper. Sometimes is rolled with dried laver. →おかき

あられそば 霰蕎麦〖食べ物〗buckwheat noodles with adductors of surf clams (BAKAGAI).

ありあけかい 有明海〖地名〗Ariake Sea. A bay surrounded by Nagasaki, Saga, Fukuoka, and Kumamoto Prefs. Famous for a mudskipper and a natural phenomenon of flickering lights called SHIRANUI.

ありしまたけお 有島武郎〖文芸〗1878-1923. A novelist born in Tokyo. Helped to start the literary magazine *Shirakaba*. Committed a double suicide with a married woman. His works include *Descendants of Cain* in 1917 and *A Certain Woman* in 1919. →カインの末裔(まつえい); 或(あ)る女

ありたやき 有田焼〖陶磁器〗Arita ware. Porcelain produced in Arita, Saga Pref. Was the first porcelain made in Japan by a Korean potter, Ri Sampei, in 1616. Became popular after a potter, Kakiemon, decorated it with orange red. Is also called Imari ware because it was shipped from the port of Imari.

ありのみ 有の実〖植物・食べ物〗the substitute word for 'nashi,' meaning "pear." The word 'nashi' tends to be avoided, especially on an auspicious occasion, because it has the same pronunciation as another word meaning "nothing." →忌み言葉

ありまおんせん 有馬温泉〖温泉〗a hot spring in southern Hyougo Pref. Is referred to in the *Chronicles*

of Japan (NIHONSHOKI), compiled in the 8th century. Effective in treating neuralgia, arthritis, and other diseases.

ありまのみこ 有間皇子〔政治〕 640 -658. Prince of Emperor Kotoku. Was executed on suspicion of treason by Emperor Tenji.

ありわらのなりひら 在原業平 〔文芸〕 825-880. One of the Six Immortal Poets, one of the Thirty-six Immortal Poets, and a grandson of Emperor Heizei. About 90 of his tanka are contained in the *Collection of Ancient and Modern Japanese Poetry* (KOKINWAKASHUU). Is said to have been a handsome playboy. →六歌仙; 三十六歌仙

あるおんな 或る女〔文芸・作品〕 *A Certain Woman*. A novel published in parts from 1911 to 1919 by ARISHIMA TAKEO. Describes the life of a woman who had a personal awakening, resisted tradition, and died unhappily.

あるきみこ 歩き巫女〔神道〕 a wandering female shaman. Evoked the spirits of the dead, with no affiliation with a Shinto shrine or sect. An aruki-miko in the lowest rank sometimes made a living by prostitution.

あわ 粟〔植物・食べ物〕 foxtail millet. *Setaria italica*. Used to be eaten as a staple food in some areas. Nowadays, it is still used as an ingredient for sweets or alcohol beverages.

あわ 安房〔旧国名〕 the old name for southern Chiba Pref.

あわ 阿波〔旧国名〕 the old name for Tokushima Pref.

あわおこし 粟粗粉 〔食べ物〕 a crispy crushed-rice cookie. Is made of rice that has been crushed into millet-like size. Contains ginger and sesame. 'Awa' literally means "millet," but present-day 'awa okoshi' does not contain millet. A specialty of Osaka. →岩粗粉(いわおこし)

あわおどり 阿波踊り〔祭礼〕 Awa Bon Dance. Many people parade dancing in groups with rather free postures to the accompaniment of up-tempo music. A famous phrase is "Dancing fools and watching fools. If we're fools anyway, why don't we dance?"

あわじしま 淡路島〔島名〕 Awaji Island, in Hyougo Pref. The area is 592 km^2, making it the largest island in the Inland Sea. Onions, oranges, or loquats are cultivated. →瀬戸内海

あわせ 袷〔服飾〕 a kimono with a lining. Worn from autumn to spring.

あわせじょうゆ 合わせ醤油〔調味料〕 soy sauce blended with other seasonings such as mirin, citrus juice, or bonito broth.

あわせみそ 合わせ味噌 〔調味料〕 blended miso. For example, a mixture of red and white miso.

あわび 鮑〔動物・食べ物〕 an abalone. *Haliotis*. Its meat is edible, and its shell is used for mother-of-pearl inlay. →熨斗鮑(のしあわび)

あわもり 泡盛〔酒〕 spirits distilled

in Okinawa Pref. Are made from rice or millet. Popular types have alcohol content of 30%, milder ones less than 25%, and some of the aged ones more than 40%.

あん 餡 〔食べ物〕 **(1)** sweet paste made of adzuki beans, sweet potato, chestnut, squash, or egg yolk. →餡子 **(2)** thick kudzu sauce. Is dressed on fried food or noodles. →餡掛け

あんあみよう 安阿弥様 〔仏教・彫刻〕 Kaikei style of the standing Amitabha Buddha. Was named because KAIKEI, a sculptor in the Kamakura period, embraced the faith of Amitabha.

あんか 行火 〔家具〕 a foot and hand warmer. Contains a charcoal fire and sometimes is covered with futon.

あんかけ 餡掛け 〔食べ物〕 food dressed with a thick kudzu sauce such as an-kake udon or an-kake tofu. →餡 **(2)**

あんかんてんのう 安閑天皇 〔天皇〕 Emperor Ankan. ?-? The 27th, on the throne around the 6th century. The first prince of Emperor Keitai. →継体(けいたい)天皇

あんきも 鮟肝 〔食べ物〕 liver of anglerfish. Is boiled with salt, sliced and dipped in soy sauce, or dressed with miso when eating.

あんぎゃ 行脚 〔仏教・旅〕 a pilgrimage of a monk. The purpose is to discipline himself. →巡礼

あんぐう 行宮 〔天皇・旅〕 a temporary palace when an Emperor was on a trip.

あんこ 餡子 〔食べ物〕 sweet adzuki paste. Is used for traditional sweets such as OHAGI as an ingredient. →餡 **(1)**

あんこうてんのう 安康天皇 〔天皇〕 Emperor Ankou. ?-? The 20th Emperor. A son of Emperor Ingyou. Is said to be one of the Five Kings of Wa. →倭(わ)の五王

あんころもち 餡ころ餅 〔食べ物〕 a rice cake covered with sweet adzuki paste. Usually strained adzuki paste is used.

あんざいしょ 行在所 〔天皇・旅〕 ⇨ 行宮(あんぐう)

あんじゅ 安寿 〔芸能〕 a heroine of *Sansho the Steward*. Killed herself to let her younger brother, ZUSHIOU, flee from SANSHOU-DAYUU, who forced them to work as slaves. →山椒大夫(さんしょうだゆう)；厨子王(ずしおう)；森鴎外

あんせい 安政 〔時代〕 an era name from 1854 to 1860. Toward the end of the Edo period.

あんせいのおおじしん 安政の大地震 〔災害〕 the Ansei Great Earthquake. Occurred on October 2 in 1855 and killed approximately 7,000 people.

あんせいのたいごく 安政の大獄 〔政治〕 the Ansei Purge from 1858 to 1859 by II NAOSUKE. Terribly oppressed those who advocated revering the Emperor and expelling the foreigners and killed eight leaders of the new ideology, including YOSHIDA SHOUIN.

あんちんきよひめ 安珍・清姫 〔民

話〕 a legend told at Doujou-ji Temple in Wakayama Pref. A girl named Kiyohime fell in love with a monk named Anchin, who stayed at her parents' house. Anchin escaped from her and hid himself inside a temple bell, but Kiyohime transformed herself into a serpent and burned him to death. →道成(どうじょう)寺

あんどうひろしげ 安藤広重 〔絵画〕 1797-1858. An ukiyo-e artist born in Edo. Firstly painted portraits of kabuki actors and beautiful women, but around 1830 shifted to landscape pictures. His works include *Fifty-Three Relay Stations of the Tokaido Highway*.

あんどうももふく 安藤百福 〔食べ物〕 1910-2007. A businessman born in Taiwan. Invented instant noodles named Chicken Ramen and founded Nisshin Food Products.

あんどおなつ あんドーナツ 〔食べ物〕 an adzuki doughnut. A fried bread with sweet adzuki paste inside.

あんとくてんのう 安徳天皇 〔天皇〕 Emperor Antoku. 1178-1185. The 81st, on the throne from 1180 to 1185. A grandson of Taira no Kiyomori, who had absolute political power. Drowned himself in the Battle of Dan-no-ura. →壇ノ浦の戦い; 建礼門院

あんどん 行燈 〔家具〕 a paper-covered lamp with square wooden frames. The wick, in oil on a small plate inside, is lit. Popular in the Edo period, but became obsolete after a kerosene lamp was introduced.

あんとんへえしんく アントン・ヘーシンク 〔スポーツ〕 Anthonius Geesink. 1934-2010. A judoist from the Netherlands. Won the gold medal in the open-weight class of the Tokyo Olympic Games in 1964.

あんぱん 餡パン 〔食べ物〕 adzuki bread. A bun with sweet adzuki paste inside. It was invented in 1874 by a bakery, Kimura-ya, in Tokyo.

あんぱんまん アンパンマン 〔アニメ〕 Adzuki Bread Man. Popular series of picture books, comics, and anime for young children. Its underlying theme is "a hero should save hungry people."

あんま 按摩 〔医療〕 massage or a massager. This business was monopolized by visually impaired persons in the Edo period, providing them with some social security.

あんまん 餡饅 〔食べ物〕 a Chinese-style adzuki bun. Containing sweet adzuki paste inside and steamed when served. Said to have been invented in Japan, imitating Chinese baos. →中華饅頭

あんみつ 餡蜜 〔食べ物〕 agar cubes and cut fruits in syrup, covered with adzuki paste. →蜜豆

あんやこうろ 暗夜行路 〔文芸・作品〕 *Dark Night's Passing*. A novel published in parts from 1921 to 1937 by Shiga Naoya. Describes the mental development of the hero, who was born as the result of adultery between his mother and grandfather.

い

い 亥〖干支〗 the twelfth of the Chinese zodiac signs. Means "boar." Recently the years 1983, 1995, and 2007 were boar years. Indicates the north-northwest in direction and around 10 p.m. for hours.

いあい 居合い〖武術〗 a martial art of drawing a sword and cutting down one's opponent in one motion. It is difficult for the opponent to predict the motion.

いいだこ 飯蛸〖食べ物・動物〗 a webfoot octopus. *Octopus ocellatus*. About 20 cm long from the top of the head to the end of the arms. Literally means "rice octopus" because its roe looks like rice when boiled.

いいなおすけ 井伊直弼〖政治〗 1815 -1860. An interim super prime minister of the Tokugawa shogunate, born in present Shiga Pref. Signed U.S.-Japan Treaty of Amity and Commerce, without imperial authorization, and conducted the Ansei Purge. Was assassinated near Sakurada Gate of Edo Castle by masterless samurai from the Mito domain. →日米修好通商条約；安政の大獄

いえ 家〖精神性〗 a family. In traditional culture, the name and lineage of a family were to be passed to the eldest son from generation to generation, and a family functioned as a smallest unit in the society. Though 'ie' was based on blood relationship, people sometimes adopted a son to maintain the family line. This concept of 'ie' started in medieval times, developed in early modern times, and ended after World War II.

いえい 遺影〖冠婚葬祭〗 a formal photo of a deceased person. Is often placed in front of a family altar or put on the wall of the room where a family altar is placed.

いえがたはにわ 家形埴輪〖考古〗 a clay image in the shape of a house, put on a tumulus. Is 26-170 cm in height. The oldest one was made in the 4th century and found in the Hiraoyamashiro Tumulus in Saitama Pref.

いえずすかい イエズス会〖キリスト教〗 The Society of Jesus, established in Paris in 1534 by Spanish Christians. One of their missionaries, Francis Xavier, arrived in Japan in 1549. →ザビエル

いえもと 家元〖芸道〗 the head of a school of traditional arts such as flower arrangement, tea ceremony, and Noh play. Has exclusive priviledge to issue a teaching license in these arts or to admit the grade.

いおまんて イオマンテ〖少数民族・祭礼〗 the Bear Festival of Ainu. A bear is regarded as a deity in the Ainu culture. A young bear is brought up and killed so that its soul can be sent back to the country of the gods.

いおり 庵 〖建築〗 a hermitage, made of wood and often thatched.

いおんびん イ音便 〖言語〗 a phonetic change from 'ki, gi, shi' to 'i' in a word or an inflection. For example, a continuative of 'kaku' (write) used to be 'kakite,' but the phonetic change occurred so that it became 'kaite.' →音便

いか 烏賊 〖食べ物・動物〗 a cuttlefish, or a squid. *Sepiida* or *Teuthida*. Eaten in various ways such as deep-fried, grilled, dried, or raw as sashimi or sushi.

いが 伊賀 〖忍者・旧国名〗 the old name of western Mie Pref. The homeland of Iga ninja.

いがいちょう 居開帳 〖仏教〗 exhibition of a secret Buddhist image at the home temple. ↔出開帳 →開帳

いかそうめん 烏賊素麺 〖食べ物〗 noodle-like, thin-stripped raw squid. Eaten by dipping in soy sauce or in dipping sauce for noodles.

いかどっくり 烏賊徳利 〖酒〗 a bottle-shaped dried squid. Is used as a bottle for hot sake, to enjoy the flavor of squid.

いかなご 玉筋魚 〖食べ物・魚〗 a sand lance. *Ammodytes personatus*. About 20 cm long. Young fish are caught near Awaji Island in spring and boiled down in soy, sugar, and ginger.

いがにんじゃ 伊賀忍者 〖忍者〗 a generic name for ninjas belonging to several schools in the Iga area in present Mie Pref. One of the most well-known ninja groups, along with Kouka ninjas. Is noted for excellent physical skills by undergoing special training. It is said that Iga ninjas were more "business-like" because their employment was contract-based, while Kouka ninjas had more loyal attachement to a feudal lord who employed them. Although it is often said that Iga were hostile to Kouka, they sometimes cooperated with each other. After Oda Nobunaga attacked Iga from 1578 to 1581, the group was dismissed, and Iga ninjas scattered to locations all over Japan. →甲賀忍者

いがのかげまる 伊賀の影丸 〖忍者・漫画〗 Kage-maru from Iga. A ninja manga written by Yokoyama Mitsuteru. Appeared serially in a boy's magazine, *Weekly Manga Sunday* (Shounen Sandee), from 1961 to 1966.

いかのしおから 烏賊の塩辛 〖食べ物〗 strips of salted and fermented squid.

いかほおんせん 伊香保温泉 〖温泉〗 a hot spring in central Gunma Pref. Hot spring inns and restaurants are lined up along the stone stairways. The spring is said to be effective in preventing and treating women's diseases and sterility.

いがもの 伊賀者 〖忍者〗 ⇨伊賀忍者

いかやき イカ焼き 〖食べ物〗 **(1)**

a grilled squid. Is seasoned with soy sauce and ginger. **(2)** a squid pancake. Is seasoned with teriyaki sauce. Mainly eaten in the Kansai area.

いがやき 伊賀焼〔陶磁器〕 Iga ware. Ceramics produced in the present Iga area, Mie Pref. Is said to have been started to meet farmers' demands in the 8th century. Prospered in the 16th century. Its simple and quiet beauty was projected on flower vases with handles in the 17th century and on casseroles today.

いがりゅう 伊賀流〔忍者〕 ⇨伊賀忍者

いがりゅうせんりぜんそうのほう 伊賀流千里善走之法〔忍者〕 secret technique of Iga ninja to run a long distance.

いがりゅうにんじゃはくぶつかん 伊賀流忍者博物館〔忍者・博物館〕 Ninja Museum of Iga-ryu. Is located in Iga City, Mie Pref. Visitors can enjoy observing traps and fake hallways at a ninja house, using ninja tools, and watching a demonstration show.

いかんそくたい 衣冠束帯〔服飾〕 male court costume first used in the 10th century. Originally 'sokutai' was formal and 'ikan' less formal. Is now worn by Shinto priests and by members of the Imperial family at an Imperial ceremony.

いき 粋〔精神性〕 an aesthetic sense that values being sophisticated, stylish, casual, smart, and considerate. Is related to dress, language or behavior. Originated as a clever way of amusement at a red-light district. Then became regarded as an ideal manner by merchants and artisans living in Edo from the late 18th to 19th centuries, but the concept still exists. The antonym of 'iki' is 'yabo' in Japanese.

いき 壱岐〔島名〕 Iki Island, in Nagasaki Pref. Is located northward off Kyushu Island. Its area is 134 km². Was an important port of call between Japan and the Korean Peninsula. Local specialties include tobacco, beef, squid, and sea urchin.

いきづくり 活き造り〔食文化〕 sashimi prepared while the fish is still alive. The sliced meat is placed in its original position as if the fish were alive.

いぐさ 藺草〔建築・植物〕 a common rush, a grass-like marsh plant. *Juncus effusus*. Is used to cover the surface of a tatami mat.

いくら イクラ〔食べ物〕 separated salmon roe seasoned with soy sauce or salt. Orange or reddish color, round, and 5 to 7 mm in diameter. Popular sushi topping. When served in a bowl on top of rice, it is called Ikura-don.

いけいようし イ形容詞〔言語〕 i-adjective. The infinitive form ends with 'i,' like 'samui'(cold), 'takai'(high), or 'utsukushii'(beautiful). ↔ナ形容詞

いけがみそねいせき 池上曽根遺

跡〖考古〗 the Ikegami Sone Ruins. Are located in southwestern Osaka Pref. Remains of residences, graves, and wells in the Yayoi period have been excavated. A large wooden building and a well have been restored. A survey revealed that a pillar of the building had been logged in 52 B.C.

いけす 生簀〖食文化〗 a fishtank or small pool to temporarily preserve fish before eating.

いけづくり 活け造り〖食文化〗 ⇨活き造り

いけなみしょうたろう 池波正太郎〖文芸〗 1923-1990. A writer of period and historic novels born in Tokyo. His works include *Detective Records of Heizou the Demon* (Onihei hankachou) and *Master Assassin Baian* (Shikakenin Baian). The former deals with a historical person named Hasegawa Heizou (1745-1795), who worked as a chief of special police in the Edo period. The story was adopted as a TV series, movie, drama, and cartoon. The latter was translated into English. He won the 43rd Naoki Prize for *Confusion* (Sakuran) at the age of 37. Is also known as a gastronome and a film reviewer.

いけのたいが 池大雅〖絵画〗 1723-1776. A painter and calligrapher born in Kyoto. Established an original and fluid style by merging the tradition of Japanese-style painting with the conventions of Western painting. Also perfected the Japanese style of nanga, which originated in China. His works include *Folding Screen with the Painting of a Pavilion and a Landscape* (Roukaku Sansuizu Byoubu) and *Album of Ten Conveniences and Ten Pleasures* (Juuben Juugyuu Gasatsu), which is a collaboration with Yosa Buson.

いけのぼうりゅう 池坊流〖華道〗 Ikenobo. The oldest and largest school of Japanese flower arrangement. Was founded in the late 15th century by Ikenobou Senkei.

いけばな 生け花, 活け花〖華道〗 Japanese traditional flower arrangement. Developed as an ornament for an alcove called TOKONOMA in the early Muromachi period. Several schools were established, including IKENOBOU-RYUU, OHARA-RYUU, and MISHOU-RYUU. Styles of arranging flowers are also various, such as SEIKA, MORIBANA, and bunjin-ike.

いご 囲碁〖碁〗 ⇨碁

いこう 衣桁〖服飾・家具〗 a clotheshorse, mainly for kimono.

いこつ 遺骨〖冠婚葬祭〗 ashes. As a Japanese Buddhist custom, the family of the deceased brings ashes to its home after cremation and keeps them until the 49th day after death. On that day, the family has a memorial service and places the ashes in the grave.

いざかや 居酒屋〖酒〗 a traditional-style pub. Generally serves Japanese-style drinks such as sake or a spirit called SHOUCHUU and food such as SASHIMI and YAKITORI, as well as beer and salad. Usually not very expensive.

いさき 伊佐木〖食べ物・魚〗 a grunt. *Parapristipoma trilineatum*. About 30 cm long. Tasty in summer. Lives along the coast of central Honshuu and southward.

いざなぎけいき 伊弉諾景気 〖経済〗 the Izanagi Boom. Continued from November 1965 to July 1970, owing to the plant and equipment investment. Was nicknamed after IZANAGI NO MIKOTO, a male deity who created Japan in the myth, because it was said to be the greatest business boom since the age of Izanagi, breaking the record set by the Iwato Boom from 1958 to 1961. During this period, Japan's GNP doubled and became the second largest next to the United States. →神武景気；岩戸景気

いざなぎじんぐう 伊弉諾神宮 〖神社〗 Izanagi Shrine. Is located in Awaji Island of Hyougo Pref. Enshrines IZANAGI NO MIKOTO and IZANAMI NO MIKOTO, two deities who are a married couple. In the myth, Awaji is the first island they produced after they got married. The *Chronicles of Japan* (NIHONSHOKI) notes Izanagi died here after giving birth to the Sun Goddess (AMATERASU OOMIKAMI) and the God of Storms (SUSANOO NO MIKOTO) and living out his remaining years. →多賀大社

いざなぎのみこと 伊邪那岐命

〖神話〗 the husband of the first couple in mythology. The husband and wife bore several islands and deities. After visiting the Land of Darkness to see his dead wife, he bore the Sun Goddess (AMATERASU OOMIKAMI), Tsukuyomi, and the God of Storms (SUSANOO NO MIKOTO).

いざなみのみこと 伊邪那美命 〖神話〗 the wife of the first couple in mythology. The husband and wife bore several islands and deities. After bearing the God of Fire (HINOKAGUTSUCHI NO KAMI), she died from burning.

いさみあし 勇み足〖相撲〗 stepping out of the ring by mistake.

いざやべんださん イザヤ・ベンダサン 〖人文学〗 Isaiah Ben-Dasan. The pen name of a social critic, YAMAMOTO SHICHIHEI, who wrote *The Japanese and the Jews*.

いざよい 十六夜〖暦〗 the sixteenth night in a month in the traditional calendar. The next night after the full moon.

いざよいにっき 十六夜日記〖文芸・作品〗 *Diary of the Waning Moon*. A travel diary written around 1280 by the nun Abutsu. Describes her travel from Kyoto to Kamakura to resolve a dispute between her biological child and stepchild regarding an inheritance.

いしいらんしんぐきょうてい 石井・ランシング協定 〖外交〗 Lansing-Ishii Agreement. A 1917 agreement between Japan and the United States. Was signed by Ishii

Kikujiro, special envoy of Japan, and Robert Lansing, the U.S. secretary of state to President Woodrow Wilson. It promoted an open-door policy toward China, while supporting China's territorial rights. The agreement unwittingly led to later imperialistic moves in Manchuria by Japan.

いしうす 石臼 〖食文化・家具〗 a stone mill. Is used to grind flour, buckwheat, and other materials.

いしおき 石置き 〖忍者〗 cryptography to describe letters with pebbles.

いしがき 石垣 〖建築〗 a stone outer wall. Was used for the foundation of a castle in early-modern times.

いしがきいちご 石垣苺 〖食べ物・植物〗 stone-wall strawberries. Are grown in Shizuoka Pref.

いしがきじま 石垣島 〖島名〗 Ishigaki Island. Is part of Okinawa Pref., located at the end of the Ryuukyuu Islands. Is 410 km from the prefectural capital, Naha City, while the distance from Taiwan is about 270 km. Its area is 223 km^2. Famous for coral reefs.

いしかりがわ 石狩川 〖河川〗 the Ishikari River. Flows from Mt. Ishikari in Mt. Taisetu National Park in Hokkaido to the Sea of Japan. Its length is 268 km, making it the third longest river in Japan.

いしかりなべ 石狩鍋 〖食べ物〗 a one-pot dish containing salmon, vegetables, and tofu. Is seasoned with soy sauce or miso. A local cuisine of Hokkaido.

いしかりわん 石狩湾 〖湾〗 Ishikari Bay. Is located on the midwest coast of Hokkaido and surrounded by Cape Ofuyu in the north and Cape Shakotan in the south.

いしかわけん 石川県 〖都道府県〗 Ishikawa Pref. Its capital is Kanazawa City. Is located in central Japan, facing the Sea of Japan. Its area is 4,185 km^2. In addition to many historic sites in Kanazawa, visitors can relax at several hot spas such as Katayamadu, Yamanaka, and Wakura, and can sit on the world's longest garden bench in Hakui. The Noto Peninsula offers the experience of the Wajima ware production and a beautiful view of terraced rice fields. Kutani ware is also famous. Used to be called Kaga and Noto.

いしかわごえもん 石川五右衛門 〖犯罪〗 ?-1594. A chief of robbers. His birthplace still remains unknown. Was boiled to death with his son by the order of Toyotomi Hideyoshi because of repetitive crimes he committed. Appears in several stories of kabuki or joururi. →五右衛門風呂

いしかわたくぼく 石川啄木 〖文芸〗 1886-1912. A poet born in Iwate Pref. Composed poems about his poor and lonely life. His works include *A Handful of Sand* in 1910 and *Sad Toys* in 1912. →一握(いちあく)の砂

いしぐみ 石組み 〖庭園〗 disposition

of natural rocks in a traditional garden.

いしだばいがん 石田梅巌 〖教育〗 1685-1744. A philosopher born in present Kyoto Pref. After studying Shintoism, Buddhism, and Confucianism while working as a businessman, established his own system of ethics, Heart Learning.

いしだみつなり 石田三成 〖武士〗 1560-1600. A feudal lord born in present Shiga Pref. One of the five magistrates in the Toyotomi administration. After the death of Toyotomi Hideyoshi, fought against Tokugawa Ieyasu in the Battle of Sekigahara in 1600 as the leader of the West squad and lost. →関ヶ原の戦い

いしづちやま 石鎚山 〖山岳〗 Mt. Ishiduchi, located in Ehime Pref. Is 1982 m in height, the highest mountain in Western Japan.

いじどうくん 異字同訓 〖漢字〗 ⇨同訓異字

いしどうろう 石灯籠 〖宗教・庭園〗 a stone lantern. Its form was introduced from China along with Buddhism. Is now put in the precincts of a Buddhist temple, a Shinto shrine, or a Japanese-style garden. →灯籠

いじのあざまろ 伊治砦麿 〖少数民族〗 ?-? The leader of a rebellion in 780, by Ezo, an indigenous people of Northern Japan. Served the central government, the Imperial Court, before the rebellion.

いしぶたいこふん 石舞台古墳 〖古墳〗 the Ishibutai Tumulus. Is located in Asuka Village, Nara Pref., and dates back to the 7th century. Used to be square- or rectangular-shaped though the covering mound has been lost and the huge stone burial chamber is exposed. Is said to be the tomb of SOGA NO UMAKO, a leader of a powerful clan named Soga.

いしへん 石偏 〖漢字〗 a left-side radical meaning "stone." Examples with this radical include 砂(sand), 磁(magnet), and 研(polish).

いじめ 虐め 〖教育〗 bullying in school. The educational administration and school teachers have been struggling to solve the problem, but they rarely have perceived the situation correctly. Many students are still suffering from it.

いしやきいも 石焼き芋 〖食べ物〗 a sweet potato baked in hot stones or pebbles. Mainly eaten in winter.

いしゃなてん 伊舎那天 〖仏教〗 a guardian deity of Buddhism. *Isana*. Guards the northeast as one of the Twelve Devas. Is sometimes identified with Siva in the Indian mythology. →十二天

いしやまでら 石山寺 〖寺院〗 Ishiyama-dera Temple. Affiliated with the Mimuro school of the Shingon sect of Buddhism. Is located in Ootsu City, Shiga Pref. Is said to have been founded in the mid-8th century by the priest ROUBEN. The main hall and the two-storied pagoda are National Treasures. It is said that MURASAKI SHIKIBU wrote *The Tale of Genji* in its main hall. →真言宗；源氏物語

いしやまほんがんじ 石山本願寺〘寺院〙 Ishiyama Hongan-ji Temple. The head temple of the True Pure Land sect of Buddhism, which existed at the location of the present Osaka Castle. Was founded in 1496 by the priest RENNYO. In 1570, the head priest KENNYO had a conflict with a feudal lord, ODA NOBUNAGA, and started to fight. In 1580, Kennyo surrendered, and the temple buildings were destroyed. →浄土真宗；大坂城

いじんかん 異人館〘外交・建築〙 a traditional Western-style residence. Was resided in by Westerners who came to Japan mainly in the late 19th century. Ones in Koube City, Hyougo Pref. are famous.

いしんでんしん 以心伝心〘精神性〙 mind-to-mind communication. Communication in which a person senses what his or her partner is thinking, without verbal communication.

いしんぽう 医心方〘医療・書名〙 the oldest existing medical book in Japan. A doctor named Tanba no Yoriyasu extracted significant parts from more than 100 Chinese medical books, and compiled them into 30 volumes in 984.

いず 伊豆〘旧国名〙 the old name for eastern Shizuoka Pref., particularly the Izu Peninsula.

いずし 飯寿司〘食べ物〙 lactic fermented food. Contains rice, fish, and vegetables. Eaten in Northern Japan.

いずしょとう 伊豆諸島〘島名〙 the Izu Islands in Tokyo Pref. Are located off the eastern coast of the Izu Peninsula, spreading over 600 km from north to south. The largest island is Ooshima with an area of 91 km^2. There are nine inhabited islands. The Japan Current flows rapidly between these islands. Ooshima and Miyake-jima have very active volcanoes. On and around some of the islands, visitors enjoy bird watching, fishing, diving, and swimming with dolphins. Until the early 19th century, the islands were the place to which criminals were exiled.

いずのおどりこ 伊豆の踊子〘文芸・作品〙 *The Izu Dancer*. A novel published in 1926 by KAWABATA YASUNARI. Depicts the romance between a dancing girl and an elite student who met each other in Izu, in eastern Shizuoka Pref.

いずみ 和泉〘旧国名〙 the old name for southwestern Osaka Pref.

いずみきょうか 泉鏡花〘文芸〙 1873-1939. A novelist born in Ishikawa Pref. His mysterious and romantic works include *The Saint of Mount Koya* (KOUYA-HIJIRI) in 1900 and *Demon Lake* in 1913.

いずみしきぶ 和泉式部〘文芸〙 ?-? A poet from the 10th to 11th centuries. A daughter of an aristocrat. Composed many passionate poems. Her works include *The Izumi Shikibu Diary* (IZUMI SHIKIBU NIKKI). →和泉式部日記

いずみしきぶにっき　和泉式部日記〖文芸・作品〗 *The Izumi Shikibu Diary.* Was written around 1007 by a female poet, IZUMI SHIKIBU. Since Izumi Shikibu is mentioned in the third person, some researchers say the work was written by another person. Thus it is also called the *Izumi Shikibu Story.* Describes her love with Atsumichi, the fourth prince of Emperor Reizen, from 1003 to 1004.

いずも　出雲〖旧国名・神話〗 the old name of eastern Shimane Pref. Many stories in Japanese mythology are set in this area.

いずもたいしゃ　出雲大社〖神社〗 Izumo Grand Shrine. Is said to have been founded in the mythical age and is located in northeast Shimane Pref. Enshrines OOKUNINUSHI NO KAMI. Its main building is rebuilt every sixty years. →縁結び；神在月(かみありづき)

いずものおくに　出雲の阿国〖歌舞伎〗 ?–? a female dancer from the 16th to 17th centuries. Is said to have been born in Izumo, present Shimane Pref. Began to perform a kind of revue dancing in Kyoto in 1603, applying peculiar manners and customs of kabuki-mono. Her dancing style laid the foundation for the present kabuki. →歌舞伎者

いずもふどき　出雲風土記〖神話・書名〗 *Record of Izumo Province.* Although there exist several Records of Provinces called FUDOKI, Izumo Fudoki is the sole Fudoki existing in a complete form.

いせ　伊勢〖旧国名〗 the old name for most of Mie Pref.

いせえび　伊勢海老〖食べ物・動物〗 a spiny lobster. *Panulirus japonicus.* About 30 cm long but lacks large claws. Is used in an auspicious occasion as an expensive food choice.

いせこう　伊勢講〖神道・旅〗 a mutual financing group for the Ise Shrine pilgrimage. Was started in the Muromachi period and became popular in the Edo period. Members saved up money and dispatched their representatives to the Ise Shrine. →伊勢神宮

いせじんぐう　伊勢神宮〖神社〗 Ise Jingu, or the Ise Shrine. Is located in eastern Mie Pref. Consists of the Inner Shrine, NAIKUU, and the Outer Shrine, GEKUU. Buildings of plain wood are rebuilt every 20 years. →式年遷宮(しきねんせんぐう)

いせしんとう　伊勢神道〖神道〗 Ise Shintoism, preached in the Kamakura period by a Shinto priest, Watarai Ieyuki, at the Ise Shrine. Is opposed to the syncretism between Shintoism and Buddhism, which was popular in those days. Claimed that Japan was a nation of deities and that the Ise Shrine was the root of all shrines.

いせまいり　伊勢参り〖神道・旅〗 a pilgrimage to the Ise Shrine. Became popular among ordinary people in the Edo period.

いせものがたり 伊勢物語 〖文芸・作品〗 *The Tale of Ise*. A collection of short stories formed around poems. Probably written in the 10th century. Describes the life and loves of a man, who seems to be a poet and a grandson of Emperor Heizei, ARIWARA NO NARIHIRA. The author is unknown.

いせわん 伊勢湾 〖地名〗 Ise Bay. Is located on the south coast of Aichi Pref. and the northeast coast of Mie Pref. Is surrounded by the Atsumi Peninsula in the east and the Shima Peninsula in the west.

いせわんたいふう 伊勢湾台風 〖災害〗 the Ise Bay Typhoon. Came ashore on Wakayama Pref. on September 26, 1959. More than 5,000 people were killed or missing.

いぜんけい 已然形 〖言語〗 a conjugation for a fixed condition in old Japanese. Corresponds to the conditional form in modern Japanese.

いぞう 椅像 〖彫刻〗 a Buddhist sculpture having a seat on a pedestal. Many such sculptures were produced in the late 7th century. → 座像；立像

いそのかみじんぐう 石上神宮 〖神社〗 Isonokami Jingu Shrine. Is located in northern Nara Pref. Enshrines Futsu no mitama no ookami, which is the deification of the sword owned by Takemikaduchi no onokami and is also the tutelary deity of the Mononobe clan, who was in charge of military affairs in the Yamato Court. Its worship hall and seven-branched sword are National Treasures.

いそべまき 磯部巻き 〖食べ物〗 ⇨磯辺焼き

いそべやき 磯辺焼き 〖食べ物〗 grilled rice cake wrapped with dried laver. Is seasoned with soy sauce.

いそほものがたり 伊曽保物語 〖文芸〗 Japanese translation from *Aesop's Fables*. Was published in 1593. Contains 70 stories. The translator is unknown.

いたいいたいびょう イタイイタイ病 〖公害〗 ouch-ouch disease. A pollution-related disease that plagued the areas along Jintsuu River in Toyama Pref. in the mid-20th century. Its cause was cadmium in industrial waste.

いたいじ 異体字 〖漢字〗 a variant kanji. Although its form is different, its pronunciation and meaning are the same as the standard kanji. For example, 烟 is a variant of 煙; the pronunciation is 'en,' and the meaning is "smoke."

いたがきたいすけ 板垣退助 〖政治〗 1837-1919. A politician born in Kouchi Pref. Was known as the leader of the Freedom and People's Rights Movements and received overwhelming public support. Survived an assassination attempt targeted at him in 1882. Founded the first party cabinet together with OOKUMA SHIGENOBU, who served as the prime minister, and took the position of the home secretary in 1898. →自由民権運動；隈板(わいはん)内閣

いたこ イタコ〔宗教〕 a necromancer in the Tohoku region. Many of them are blind women. A festival of necromancy at Mt. Osore-zan in July is famous. →恐山

いたせくすありす イタ・セクスアリス〔文芸〕 ⇨キタ・セクスアリス

いただきます 頂きます〔食文化・言語〕 a greeting phrase immediately before eating or drinking. Literally means "I'll have it." The main verb 'itadaku' is an honorific expression of "eat." ↔ご馳走(ちそう)様でした

いだてん 韋駄天〔仏教〕 a guardian deity for temple buildings. *Skanda*. One of the eight generals under *Virudhaka* (ZOUCHOU-TEN). Is said to run very fast.

いたどこ 板床〔建築〕 a decorative alcove with a wooden floor. Is not covered with tatami mats. →床の間

いたどり 虎杖〔植物〕 a native Japanese knotweed shrub. *Fallopia japonica*. The name literally means "pain puller." Is used to prepare herbal teas and to treat various maladies. Was brought to Europe in the late Edo period by Philippe Franz von Siebold, a German doctor who served as physician and scientist at the Dutch trading post of Deshima. It has become a major invasive plant species in the West, especially in the United Kingdom.

いたのまかせぎ 板の間稼ぎ〔犯罪〕 stealing, or one who steals, at a public bath.

いたば 板場〔食文化〕 **(1)** a kitchen of a traditional-style restaurant. **(2)** ⇨板前

いたび 板碑〔仏教〕 a stone plate erected to the memory of a dead person. The top is triangle-shaped. Under it, a Sanskrit character, a Buddhist picture, the name of the erector, and the erection date are inscribed. Was popular from the 13th to 16th centuries, mainly in the Kantou region.

いたまえ 板前〔食文化・職業〕 a professional cook of traditional Japanese cuisine. It is said that it takes several years to stand on his or her own as a respectable itamae.

いたみくうこう 伊丹空港〔交通〕 ⇨大阪国際空港

いため 板目〔建築〕 lumber whose wooden grain is not straight and parallel. ↔柾目(まさめ)

いたわさ 板わさ〔食べ物〕 slices of steamed fish paste. Eaten with grated WASABI and soy sauce. →蒲鉾(かまぼこ)

いちあくのすな 一握の砂〔文芸・作品〕 *A Handful of Sand*. An anthology of poems by ISHIKAWA TAKUBOKU, published in 1910. Provides impressions of everyday life. Contains 551 poems.

いちい 櫟〔植物〕 a Japanese yew tree. *Taxus cuspidata*. Its fruit is edible, and the wood is used for furniture. A wooden scepter, called SHAKU, was made of this wood. Also called 'araragi.'

いちこ 市子 〚宗教〛 a female medium. The spirit of a dead person possesses her and communicates with a living person.

いちごいちえ 一期一会 〚茶道・精神性〛 Literally means "one time, one meeting." An important concept in tea ceremony. Implies that you should treasure every encounter because it will never happen again. Is based on the words by Yamanoue Souji, a disciple of a great tea master, SEN NO RIKYUU.

いちごがり 苺狩り 〚食文化〛 strawberry picking for pleasure. There are farms where people can enjoy this pastime.

いちごだいふく 苺大福〚食べ物〛 a soft rice cake containing sweet adzuki paste and strawberries.

いちじゅういっさい 一汁一菜 〚食文化〛 a traditional simple meal containing rice, soup, and just one dish. →一汁三菜

いちじゅうさんさい 一汁三菜 〚食文化〛 a traditional meal containing rice, soup, and three dishes. Three dishes include grilled food, boiled food, and vinegared raw food. →一汁一菜

いちぜんめし 一膳飯〚冠婚葬祭〛 a bowl of rice for the dead. Is penetrated with a chopstick and placed beside the pillow of the dead person.

いちぜんめしや 一膳飯屋 〚食文化〛 a simple and cheap restaurant.

いちのぜん 一の膳 〚食文化〛 the first-served set of dishes in a traditional full course of Japanese cuisine. Is placed right in front of each peron on a square tray with legs. Consists of rice, soup, pickles, grilled food, boiled food, and vinegared raw food. →本膳料理；二の膳；三の膳

いちのとり 一の酉 〚暦〛 the first "cock" day of the Chinese zodiac signs in November. A fair is held at the Ootori Shrines all over Japan. →酉の市；十二支

いちのみや 一の宮 〚神社〛 the first-ranked shrine in a province (KUNI). The term remains as a place name in several provinces.

いちばんだいご 一番太鼓 〚芸能・相撲〛 drum beating to notify the audience that the show would start for performing arts such as KABUKI or traditional storytelling called RAKUGO.

いちばんだし 一番出汁 〚調味料〛 the first soup stock made from kelp and dried bonito. Is used for mild tasting dish such as clear hot soup or steamed savory custard. →出汁；吸い物；茶碗蒸し

いちふじにたかさんなすび 一富士、二鷹、三茄子 〚精神性〛 Mt. Fuji is gold, a hawk is silver, and an eggplant is bronze. It is said to be a good omen if one of them appears in the first dream of a year.

いちぼくづくり 一木造り〚仏教・彫刻〛 carving technique for a sculpture, using a single section of a tree trunk. Was popular around the 9th century. The inside of the sculpture is hollowed out to prevent the wood from cracking when it dries up. Examples include the Healing Buddha at JINGO-JI Temple in Kyoto, and the Eleven-headed Bodhisattva of Mercy at DOUGAN-JI Temple in Shiga Pref. ↔寄木造り →内刳(うちぐ)り

いちまつもよう 市松模様〚文様〛 a black and white checked pattern. Is often used for arts and crafts or architecture. Its name came about because a kabuki actor, Ichimatsu, used it in the Edo period.

いちみとうがらし 一味唐辛子〚調味料〛 red chili pepper. Literally means "one-taste pepper" because it is not mixed with other spices, as opposed to the seven-spice chili pepper called SHICHIMI TOUGARASHI.

いちやづけ 一夜漬け〚食文化〛 an overnight pickled vegetable. Is dipped in salt or vinegar for just one night.

いちやぼし 一夜干し〚食文化〛 fish dried outdoors for just one night.

いちょう 銀杏〚植物〛 a maidenhair tree. *Ginkgo biloba*. Its seed called GINNAN is edible. Originally came from China.

いちょうぎり 銀杏切り〚食文化〛 cutting a vegetable in a fan shape. Literally means "gingko cutting." A carrot or white radish is cut into four lengthwise pieces and is then sliced widthwise. Each piece looks like a leaf of a gingko tree.

いちょうまげ 銀杏髷〚髪〛 a top-knot of which the folded-back part

has the shape of a gingko leaf.

いちりづか 一里塚〚交通〛 a mile-stone mound. Was placed about every 4 km along main highways in the Edo period.

いちりんざし 一輪挿し〚華道〛 flower arrangement with a single flower.

いっかんばり 一閑張り〚茶道・漆器〛 a lacquerware technique to paste paper in layers on a wooden or bamboo frame.

いっき 一揆〚政治〛 an uprising in medieval and early modern times. →一向一揆；百姓一揆

いっきのみ 一気飲み〚酒〛 drinking a glassful of alcohol without pausing. Used to be popular among college students, but now the popularity of this custom is declining because it might cause acute alcohol poisoning.

いっきゅうそうじゅん 一休宗純〚仏教〛 1394-1481. A Zen priest, born in Kyoto. Is said to be a son of Emperor Gokomatsu. Was well-known for his eccentricities and spirit of defiance. Became the chief priest of Daitoku-ji Temple. His famous anecdotes about his boyhood were fictitious.

いつくしま 厳島〚地名〛 ⇨宮島

いつくしまじんじゃ 厳島神社〚神社〛 Itsukushima Shrine. Is located on Miyajima Island, Hiroshima Pref. Enshrines Ichikishima-hime and two other deities, who have been said to guard sea navigation. Famous for the Great Torii standing in the sea. The buildings and sutras dedicated by the Taira clan are National Treasures. A World Heritage Site.

いっこういっき 一向一揆 〖仏教・政治〗 uprisings by devotees of the True Pure Land sect. Occurred mainly in present Ishikawa, Fukui, Aichi, Mie, and Osaka Prefs. from the mid-15th to toward the end of the 16th centuries. Ended with the battle between ODA NOBUNAGA and the ISHIYAMA HONGAN-JI Temple. → 浄土真宗

いっこうしゅう 一向宗 〖仏教〗 another name for the True Pure Land sect. This name had been used from the early 14th to the later 19th centuries by other sects.

いっさいきょう 一切経 〖仏教〗 ⇨大蔵(だい)経

いっしそうでん 一子相伝 〖芸道・武術〗 succession of secret techniques in various arts and scholarship such as martial arts, flower arrangement, and traditional mathematics. Is passed on to only one child. Usually the eldest son.

いっしゅうき 一周忌 〖仏教〗 the first anniversary of a person's death. The memorial service is held on this day. →〜回忌

いっしょうびん 一升瓶 〖酒〗 a 1.8 liter bottle, mainly used for sake. A king-sized sake bottle. →四合(ちごう)瓶

いっすんぼうし 一寸法師 〖民話〗 the hero named One-Inch Boy in a fairy tale. He rode on a wooden soup bowl as a boat, using a chop-stick as an oar, and went to Kyoto to serve a court noble. Traveled to an island to exterminate demons living there and acquired the magical mallet that realizes the wish of its bearer. Thanks to the mallet, he became an ordinary-sized gentleman, and married a daughter of a nobleman.

いっせんようしょく 一銭洋食 〖食べ物〗 a cheap, savory pancake. Was popular in the first half of the 20th century. Is an original form of OKO-NOMIYAKI.

いったんもめん 一反木綿 〖妖怪〗 ten-meter-long cotton monster. Long cotton cloth dwelled in by a spirit. Flies through the air at night and tries to wrap itself around a human face or mouth to choke the person. Its folktale has been told in Kagoshima Pref.

いってきます 行ってきます 〖言語〗 a greeting phrase uttered by a person who is leaving his or her home place. Literally means "I'm going and will come back." ↔行ってらっしゃい

いってらっしゃい 行ってらっしゃい 〖言語〗 a greeting phrase uttered to a person who is leaving his or her home place. Literally means "Go and come back." ↔行ってきます

いっとうさんらい 一刀三礼 〖仏教・彫刻〗 praying to three treasures with every stroke. It is said that a sculptor of a Buddhist image worshipped three treasures—

the Buddha, dharma, and monks—
every time he made a stroke of a
chisel on the wood.

いっとうぼり 一刀彫り〚彫刻〛 flat-
plane carving. Featuring a rough-
finishing style as if the sculpture is
carved with only one knife. Began
around the 17th century. Dolls or
toys using this technique are mainly produced in Nara.

いっとうりゅう 一刀流〚剣術〛 a
school of swordsmanship established at the beginning of the Edo
period by ITOU ITTOUSAI. Later
spawned several famous branch
schools such as the Hokushin Ittou
school and influenced modern
sports-oriented swordsmanship.

いっとき 一刻〚生活〛⇨～刻

いっぱんさんが 一般参賀〚天皇〛
congratulatory visit to the Imperial
Palace by the general public. Is
held on January 2nd and the birthday of the current Emperor as an
official Imperial event.

いっぺん 一遍〚仏教〛1239-1289.
A priest of Pure Land Buddhism,
born in present Ehime Pref.
Founded the Ji sect and traveled
all over Japan, spreading Odori
nenbutsu, which is the prayer to
Buddha while chanting sutra and
dancing at the same time. →時宗

いっぽん 一本〚柔道〛a full point in
judo or karate match. A player who
gets ippon in the match will be immediately judged the winner.

いっぽんざし 一本差し〚ヤクザ〛
euphemism for yakuza in the Edo
period. Literally means "to carry
just one sword." Official samurai
carried two swords, long and short
ones, in those days, but yakuza carried only one. ↔二本差し

いっぽんじめ 一本締め〚生活・言語〛
a ceremonial hand-clapping. People
clap hands just once in unison
immediately after the ceremony
leader gives a shout. →手締め

いっぽんぜおい 一本背負い〚柔道・
相撲〛 one-armed shoulder throw.

いっぽんせんこう 一本線香〚仏
教・冠婚葬祭〛 a single joss stick.
Is stood up on the very day when
someone dies.

いといがわしずおかこうぞうせん
糸魚川静岡構造線〚自然〛Itoigawa-
Shizuoka Tectonic Line. A huge
fault, extending from Itoigawa City
in Niigata Pref. through Matsumoto
City and Lake Suwa in Nagano
Pref. to Shizuoka City in Shizuoka
Pref. Forms the western edge of
the great central rift called Fossa
Magna.

いとういっとうさい 伊藤一刀斎〚剣
術〛 ?-? An expert swordsman in
the 16th to 17th centuries, born in
Izu, present Shizuoka Pref. Is said
to have had 33 matches in his lifetime without any defeats.

いとうさちお 伊藤左千夫〚文芸〛
1864-1913. A tanka poet and novelist born in Chiba Pref. Studied
under Masaoka Shiki, edited a
tanka magazine, *Araragi*, and established a style resembling that of
the *Anthology of Myriad Leaves*

(MAN'YOUSHUU).

いとうじゃくちゅう 伊藤若冲 〔絵画〕 1716-1800. A painter born in Kyoto. Painted mainly animals and plants, especially domestic fowls in a decorative style with strong colors. His works include *Colorful Realm of Living Beings* in the Imperial Household Collection.

いとうひろぶみ 伊藤博文 〔政治〕 1841-1909. A statesman born in present Yamaguchi Pref. Joined the anti-shogunate movement. After the shogunate returned political power to the Emperor, established the cabinet and was inaugurated as the first prime minister of Japan. Was assassinated in China by a Korean young man, who opposed the annexation of Korea to Japan.

いとこんにゃく 糸蒟蒻 〔食べ物〕 noodle-like strips of konjac. Are used as an ingredient for sukiyaki or a beef bowl.

いどし 亥年〔暦〕 ⇨亥(いのしし)年

いとづくり 糸作り 〔食文化〕 thin-stripped sashimi. A squid or a half-beak is sometimes cut in this style.

いとへん 糸偏 〔漢字〕 a left-side radical meaning "thread." Examples with this radical include 細(thin), 紡(spin), and 絹(silk).

いなかけ 稲掛け〔農業〕 ⇨稲(いね)掛け

いなかまんじゅう 田舎饅頭〔食べ物〕 a thin-skinned bun stuffed with a chunky sweet adzuki paste.

いなかみそ 田舎味噌〔調味料〕 miso made with molded barley.

いなぎ 稲木〔農業〕 ⇨稲(いね)掛け

いなさく 稲作〔農業〕 rice cultivation. Started in the Yayoi period.

いなせ 鯔背〔精神性〕 to be chivalrous, gallant, dashing, stylish, and frank. Refers to a young man in a traditional Japanese situation.

いなだ 鰍〔食べ物・魚〕 a young yellowtail. About 40 cm long. →鰤(ぶり); 出世魚

いなば 因幡〔旧国名〕 the old name for eastern Tottori Pref.

いなばのしろうさぎ 因幡の白兎 〔神話〕 the mythic White Hare of Inaba. Cheated sharks into floating in a line to cross the sea from Oki Island to Inaba. However, his trick failed, and he was skinned by the sharks. Ookuninushi no kami, passing by, taught him how to cure the injury.

いなり 稲荷 〔神道〕 a deity of cereals. Another name for Ukanomitama no kami, a son of the God of Storms (SUSANOO NO MIKOTO), according to the *Records of Ancient Matters* (KOJIKI). Has also been worshipped as a deity of commerce since the Edo period. A fox is regarded as a messenger of Inari though there are several theories about the connection between Inari and a fox.

いなりじんじゃ 稲荷神社〔神社〕 an INARI shrine. It is said that there are more than 30,000 Inari shrines throughout Japan. The head shrine is FUSHIMI INARI Shrine.

いなりずし 稲荷寿司 〔寿司〕 fox sushi. Vinegared rice mixed with

saulty and sweet-flavoured sesame or chopped shiitake mushrooms is stuffed in salty and sweet flavored thin fried tofu. Is named because it is said that thin fried tofu is the favorite food of a fox, which is the messenger of a cereal deity called INARI.

いなりやまこふん 稲荷山古墳 〖史跡〗 the Inariyama Tumulus. A keyhole-shaped burial mound located in northern Saitama Pref. Dates back to the 5th century and is the oldest in that area. An iron sword with 115 letters referring to Emperor Yuuryaku was discovered there. Visitors can climb to the top of the tumulus. →埼玉古墳群

いなわしろこ 猪苗代湖 〖湖沼〗 Lake Inawashiro. Is located at the southern foot of Mt. Bandai in central Fukushima Pref. The area is 103 km², making it the fourth largest lake in Japan. Visitors can enjoy aquatic sports such as yachting and wakeboarding.

いぬ 戌 〖干支〗 the eleventh of the Chinese zodiac signs. Means "dog." Recently the years 1982, 1994, and 2006 were dog years. Indicates the west-northwest in direction and around 8 p.m. for hours.

いぬあわせ 犬合わせ 〖娯楽〗 ⇨闘犬

いぬい 乾 〖生活〗 the northwest. The direction between INU (dog) and I (boar).

いぬくぼう 犬公方 〖武士・政治〗 the derogative nickname of the 5th Tokugawa shogun, TOKUGAWA TSUNAYOSHI. He enacted notorious Edicts on Compassion for Living Things. →生類憐(しょうるい／あわれ)みの令

いぬどし 戌年 〖暦〗 the year of the dog in the Chinese zodiac signs. The years 1994, 2006, and 2018 are years of the dog. →干支; 戌

いぬばしり 犬走り 〖忍者〗 a running technique using four limbs. Literally means "dog running." Was used in places where a ninja could not stand up, such as under a floor.

いぬぼうかるた 犬棒歌留多 〖ゲーム〗 the "dog-bar" matching card game. The proverb beginning from 'i' on a reading card is 'inu mo arukeba bou ni ataru,' which means "A dog bumps into a bar when walking." This phrase implies "Forwardness causes trouble."

いぬぼうさき 犬吠埼 〖地名〗 Cape Inubou. Is located at the eastern tip of Chiba Pref., facing the Pacific Ocean. Famous as the place where visitors can see the year's first sunrise at the earliest time in Japan, except in the remote islands and high mountains.

いぬやまじょう 犬山城 〖城郭〗 Inuyama Castle. Is located in northwestern Aichi Pref. Was constructed in 1537 by Oda Nobuyasu, an uncle of ODA NOBUNAGA. Has the oldest existing donjon in Japan. Is designated a National Treasure.

いぬやらい 犬矢来 〖建築〗 a low fence made of bent bamboo strips. Covers the lower part of the outer walls of a traditional house.

いね 稲 〖植物〗 rice. *Oryza sativa* var. *japonica*. Has been cultivated since the Yayoi period and has been the staple food for Japanese. Has round and short grains, differing from Indian rice.

いねかけ 稲掛け 〖農業〗 a rice-hanging bar. Peasants hang rice plants on the bar to dry after reaping.

いのうえやすし 井上靖 〖文芸〗 1907-1991. A novelist born in Hokkaido. His works include *The Bullfight* in 1949, *The Samurai Banner of Furin Kazan* in 1954, *Ice Crag* and *The Roof Tile of Tempyo* in 1957, and *Tun-Huang* in 1959.

いのうただたか 伊能忠敬 〖科学技術〗 1745-1818. A geologist, born in present Chiba Pref. Surveyed lands all over Japan and drew a precise map of the nation.

いのこく 亥の刻 〖時刻〗 the hour of the boar in the old hour system. Around 10 p.m., or between 9 p.m. to 11 p.m. →〜刻(こく)

いのししどし 亥年 〖暦〗 the year of the boar in the Chinese zodiac signs. The years 1995, 2007, and 2019 are years of the boar. →干支; 亥(い)

いはい 位牌 〖仏教〗 a memorial tablet. Is inscribed with the posthumous Buddhist name of the deceased and is enshrined in the family altar. →戒名

いはつ 衣鉢 〖仏教〗 **(1)** three rectangular sashes, called KESA, and a bowl for religious mendicancy. Are handed over from a teacher priest to his disciple. →袈裟(けさ); 托鉢(たくはつ) **(2)** the essential teaching that a teacher priest imparts to his disciple in Zen Buddhism.

いばらきけん 茨城県 〖都道府県〗 Ibaraki Pref. Is located in Eastern Japan, facing the Pacific Ocean. Is 6,097 km^2 in area. Its capital is Mito City. Two large lakes, Kasumigaura and Kitaura, are along the Tone River. Because of the vast and fertile farmland, melon, chestnut, nappa cabbage, green pepper, and rice are produced in large quantities. Used to be called Hitachi.

いばらきどうじ 茨木童子 〖妖怪〗 a demon who appeared at Rajoumon in Kyoto. Had an arm cut off by a samurai named WATANABE NO TSUNA. Later it tried to get it back, changing its appearance to that of a woman. →鬼

いはらさいかく 井原西鶴 〖文芸〗 1642-1693. A novelist and haiku poet born in Osaka. Depicted the life of merchants, artisans, and samurai in realistic novels such as *The Eternal Storehouse of Japan*, *The Life of an Amorous Man*, and *Transmission of the Martial Arts*. As a haiku poet, set a record of creating 23,500 haiku in one day. →好色一代男; 日本(にほん)永代蔵; 矢数俳諧(やかずはいかい)

いぶすきおんせん 指宿温泉 〖温泉〗 a hot spring in southern Kagoshima Pref. Effective in treating neuralgia, rheumatism, and gastrointestinal disorders. Famous for sand bathing called 'sunamushi,' during which visitors are buried up to their necks in warm sand.

いぶせますじ 井伏鱒二 〖文芸〗 1898-1993. A novelist born in Hiroshima. Wrote novels with his distinctive humor and pathos. His works include *Salamander* in 1929 and *Black Rain* in 1966.

いぼだい 疣鯛 〖食べ物・魚〗 a Japanese butterfish, a melon seed, or a wart perch. *Psenopsis anomala*. Is about 30 cm long. Mainly eaten in summer.

いまかがみ 今鏡 〖書名〗 *The Mirror of the Present*. The author is unknown. A chronology written in 1170 or later. Describes the history from 1025 to 1170. One of the Four Mirrors. →四鏡(しきょう)

いまがわやき 今川焼 〖食べ物〗 a round-shaped hot muffin containing adzuki. Is sometimes called 'kaiten-yaki' or 'ooban-yaki.' Its name varies from region to region.

いまがわよしもと 今川義元 〖武士〗 1519-1560. A feudal lord born in present Shizuoka Pref. Ruled most part of present Shizuoka Pref. and the eastern part of present Aichi Pref., and temporarily held Tokugawa Ieyasu as a strategic hostage. Was defeated at Okehazama in 1560 by Oda Nobunaga and was decapitated by a vassal of the Oda family named Yoshikatsu Mouri. →桶狭間(おけはざま)の戦い

いまにしきんじ 今西錦司 〖科

学技術〗 1902-1992. An ecologist, cultural anthropologist, and mountain climber born in Kyoto. Obtained Ph.D. in science at Kyoto Imperial University, the present Kyoto University, in 1939. Studied primates and was known as the founding father of primate research in Japan. Later became a professor emeritus at Kyoto University and Gifu University. Established the Habitat Segregation Theory, which is not based on the natural selection of Darwinism but rather on coexistence.

いまみやえびすじんじゃ 今宮戎神社 〖神社〗 Imamiya Ebisu Shrine. Is located in Osaka City and enshrines the Sun Goddess, the God of Storms, Kotoshiro nushi, and other deities. Famous for its Ebisu Festival. →十日戎(とおかえびす)

いまよう 今様 〖音楽〗 a song popular in the 12th century. Is based on four phrases with seven or five syllables.

いまりやき 伊万里焼 〖陶磁器〗 ⇨有田焼

いみことば 忌み言葉 〖宗教・言語〗 **(1)** a taboo word. **(2)** a substitute for a taboo word. Examples include ATARIME, which means "dried squid."

いもあん 芋餡 〖食べ物〗 sweet-potato paste. Is widely used in traditional sweets.

いもじょうちゅう 芋焼酎 〖酒〗 a Japanese spirit distilled from sweet potatoes. A local favorite of

Kagoshima Pref. Its alcohol content is about 25 to 35% ABV.

いもにかい 芋煮会 〖食文化〗 an outdoor party to eat taro stew. Is popular in Yamagata Pref.

いもようかん 芋羊羹 〖食べ物〗 a sweet potato bar. Sweet potato is steamed, mashed, and combined with sugar.

いもり 井守 〖動物〗 a Japanese newt. *Triturus pyrrhogaster*. An amphibian about 10 to 20 cm long. The back is black, and the belly is red with black spots.

いもりのくろやき 井守の黒焼き 〖医療〗 charred newt powder. Is said to have been an aphrodisiac.

いもんぶくろ 慰問袋 〖軍事〗 a sac containing letters, food, and daily necessities. Was sent to a soldier in a battleground from the Russo-Japanese War to World War Ⅱ.

いよ 伊予 〖旧国名〗 the old name for Ehime Pref.

いよ 壱与 〖政治〗 235-? The successor of Queen HIMIKO in Yamatai. After Himiko's death, a king was enthroned, but a civil war broke out. Then Iyo became queen at the age of 13. She was called a wonder child because of magical powers since her childhood. Information about her and Yamatai is still largely unknown. Is sometimes called Toyo.

いよかん 伊予柑 〖食べ物〗 an Iyo orange. *Citrus iyo*. Is mainly produced in Ehime Pref., which used to be called Iyo.

いよまんて イヨマンテ 〖少数民族・祭礼〗 ⇨イオマンテ

いりえたいきち 入江泰吉 〖芸術〗 1905-1992. A photographer born in Nara. Mainly took photos of landscapes, architecture, and Buddhist sculptures in Nara. All his works are kept at Irie Taikichi Memorial Museum of Photography in Nara.

いりおもてやまねこ 西表山猫 〖動物〗 an Iriomote cat. *Mayailurus iriomotensis*. Lives in the Iriomote Island, Okinawa Pref. A Special Natural Monument.

いりこ 炒り子 〖調味料〗 ⇨煮干し

いりごま 煎り胡麻 〖食文化〗 roasted sesame seeds. Are often ground. Are sprinkled over various foods.

いりでっぽうにでおんな 入り鉄砲に出女 〖交通・軍事〗 a rigorous inspection on "incoming guns and outgoing women." The Tokugawa shogunate prohibited feudal lords from bringing guns into Edo. Also, the shogunate forced feudal lords' wives and children to live in Edo, as a kind of hostage, and prohibited them from going back to their homeland, as a measure against possible rebellion.

いりまめ 煎り豆 〖食べ物〗 roasted beans, especially soybeans.

いりもやづくり 入母屋造り 〖建築〗 a building style that has a small gable at the top of a hip roof. Is often seen on a temple building and sometimes on a private house. →寄棟(むね)造り；切妻(つま)造り

いれずみ 刺青 〖服飾〗 a tattoo.

Probably originated in ancient times. Has been used as punishment or ornamentation. Some public baths and hot springs today deny admittance of a tattooed person.

いろぐすり 色釉 〖陶磁器〗 color glaze. Is used to paint on ceramics.

いろとめそで 色留袖 〖服飾〗 a formal kimono with a colored background for a married woman. Is decorated with five family crests. →留袖

いろなおし 色直し〖冠婚葬祭〗 ⇨お色直し

いろはうた 伊呂波歌〖言語・音楽〗 a recitation poem to memorize kana syllables. Beginning with 'i,' 'ro,' and 'ha,' uses all 47 kana and each just once. Was invented around the 10th century or later. Its content is said to be a translation of a Buddhist sutra.

いろはがるた 伊呂波歌留多 〖ゲーム〗 a proverb-matching card game. Uses 48 reading cards and 48 pick-up cards. On a reading card, a proverb beginning with one of 47 hiragana or a kanji 京, meaning "capital," is written. A pick-up card contains a picture matching one of 48 proverbs. One player reads aloud a proverb on a reading card, and other players pick out the matching card among picture cards spread on the floor.

いろむじ 色無地〖服飾〗 a kimono in a single color without patterns. Some 'iro-muji' are decorated with one, three, or five family crest(s).

People decide which one to wear, depending on the formality of the occasion. The one with one family crest is informal, and the one with five family crests is the most formal.

いろもの 色物 〖芸能〗 various acts in traditional vaudeville, with the exception of RAKUGO or storytelling, which is considered the main act. →寄席

いろり 囲炉裏 〖建築〗 an open sunken hearth at a traditional-style house. Is square-shaped, with one side about 1 meter long. Is used for room heating and cooking. A kettle or a pot is hung over the hearth, using a hook suspended from the ceiling. →自在鉤(ﾌﾟｶﾘ)

いわいばし 祝箸 〖食器〗 a pair of special chopsticks for festive occasions. Are not lacquered and are tapered at both ends while ordinary chopsticks are lacquered and have only one tapered end.

いわおこし 岩粔籹 〖食べ物〗 a hard crushed-rice cookie. Is made of rice that has been crushed into sand size and contains ginger and sesame. A specialty of Osaka. →粟粔籹

いわき 磐城 〖旧国名〗 the old name for eastern Fukushima Pref.

いわくら 磐座〖神道〗 a deity's seat. Usually a huge rock with a flat top. It is said that a religious service at the rock was conducted in ancient times before Shinto shrines became common.

いわくらともみ 岩倉具視 〖政治〗 1825-1883. A statesman and imperial official, born in present Kyoto Pref. Was influential in bringing about the Meiji Restoration, whereby the Emperor replaced the shogun as the nation's leader. Led an 1871-1873 diplomatic and cultural mission to the United States and Europe, to study the Western system that could help Japan's modernization and to seek changes in unfair treaties, with Western countries, that Japan was forced to sign at the beginning of the Meiji period. Initiated process to establish the Meiji constitution.

いわさきやたろう 岩崎弥太郎 〖経済〗 1835-1885. A businessman born in Kouchi Pref. The founder of Mitsubishi Zaibatsu. Also founded Mitsubishi Nautical School, which is the present Tokyo University of Marine Science and Technology. He paid employees a "bonus," an extra seasonal pay besides regular wages, for the first time in Japan.

いわし 鰯 〖食べ物・魚〗 a sardine. *Sardinops melanosticta*. About 25 cm long. Migrates from the East China Sea to Sakhalin. Is edible and also used as fertilizer or livestock feed. →潤目(うるめ)鰯；片口(かたくち)鰯

いわしみずはちまんぐう 石清水八幡宮 〖神社〗 Iwashimizu Hachimangu. Was established in 859 in southern Kyoto Pref. Enshrines Emperor Oujin, Empress Consort Jinguu, and Princess Ookami.

Bamboo in the vicinity was used by Thomas Edison for electric bulb.

いわじゅくいせき 岩宿遺跡 〖史跡〗 the Iwajuku Ruins. Are located in eastern Gunma Pref. Chipped stone tools were excavated in 1946, and Japanese Paleolithic culture was confirmed for the first time.

いわしろ 岩代 〖旧国名〗 the old name of the western half of Fukushima Pref.

いわたおび 岩田帯 〖生活〗 a maternity sash for a pregnant woman. Is worn in the fifth month of pregnancy to keep warm and maintain the position of the fetus.

いわたけ 岩茸 〖食べ物〗 a rock tripe. *Umbilicaria esculenta*. An edible lichen. Grows on rocks in the mountain.

いわてけん 岩手県 〖都道府県〗 Iwate Pref. Its capital is Morioka City. Is located in northeastern Japan, on the coast of the Pacific Ocean. Its area is 15,275 km^2, which makes it the second largest prefecture. With a subarctic climate, it has many snow resorts in its mountain areas. Its inland areas are famous for stock farming and forestry. With the Tohoku Shinkansen starting operation in 1982, and with the attraction of factories that followed, it is now famous for car and flash memory production. Its coastal areas were severely damaged by a tsunami after the Great East Japan Earthquake in 2011. However, they still produce brown seaweed and abalones in large quantities. The old temples and gardens in Hiraizumi in its southern region represent the Buddhist Pure Land sect. They were designated a World Heritage Site in 2011. Used to be called Rikuchu.

いわてさん 岩手山〘山岳〙 Mt. Iwate. A volcano located in north-western Iwate Pref. Is 2,038 m, the highest mountain in the Tohoku region.

いわとけいき 岩戸景気〘経済〙 the Iwato Boom. Continued from July 1958 to December 1961, owing to technological innovation. Was nick-named after the event of AMA NO IWATO, "the Gate of the Celestial Rock Cave," in Japanese mytholo-gy, because it was said to be the greatest business boom since that event, beyond the Jinmu Boom from 1954 to 1957. During this pe-riod, TV sets, refrigerators, and washing machines, which were called "Three Status Symbols for a Modern Family," rapidly became popular among ordinary citizens. → 神武景気; 伊弉諾(いざなぎ)景気

いわな 岩魚〘食べ物・魚〙 a Japanese charr. *Salvelinus leucomaenis*. About 30 cm long. Inhabits in mountain streams and is popular among anglers.

いわなざけ 岩魚酒〘酒〙 heated sake with a charr. A grilled charr is dipped into heated sake, and only the sake is drunk. The charr is not to be eaten.

いわみ 石見〘旧国名〙 the old name for western Shimane Pref.

いわみぎんざん 石見銀山 **(1)**〘史跡〙 Iwami Ginzan Silver Mine. The silver was discovered in the 14th century. Its remains are located in Shimane Pref. Was designated a World Heritage Site in 2007. **(2)** 〘生活〙 a rat poison used in the Edo period. Arsenic from Iwami Ginzan Silver Mine was used for it.

いん 印〘仏教〙 ⇨印相

いん 院〘政治〙 **(1)** the palace of a retired Emperor. **(2)** the title of a retired Emperor. For example, Emperor Gotoba is called Gotoba-in when a reference is to his title after retirement.

いんかん 印鑑〘生活〙 a seal. Is usu-ally engraved with a family name, but a registered seal sometimes has both family and given names. Is stamped on various documents such as a contract, an application form, or a curriculum vitae.

いんきょ 隠居〘生活・落語〙 a retired old man. Lives a slow life after quitting the job and handing over the position of the head of a family. Often appears as an advisor for the neighborhood in a RAKUGO story.

いんぎょうてんのう 允恭天皇〘天皇〙 Emperor Ingyou. ?-? The 19th Emperor. The fourth son of Emperor Nintoku. Is said to be one of the Five Kings of Wa. →倭(わ)の五王

いんげん 隠元〘仏教〙 Yinyuan.

1592-1673. A Chinese Zen priest who came from Ming to Japan in 1654. Founded the Manpuku-ji Temple in Uji, Kyoto Pref., in 1661. It is said that he introduced green beans to Japan. →隠元豆

いんげんまめ 隠元豆 〚食べ物・植物〛 green beans, or French beans. *Phaseolus vulgaris*. Are said to have been introduced from China by a Ming priest named Yinyuan. →隠元

いんしょひとくのほう 陰文秘匿之法 〚忍者〛 a cryptograph technique using diagonally rolled paper. A communicator wrote a letter vertically on paper obliquely rolled on a bar, and the receiver used the identical bar to decipher it.

いんすたんとらあめん インスタントラーメン 〚食べ物〛 instant ramen. Dried noodles, seasoning, and ingredients are packed together and can be cooked in a few minutes.

いんせい 院政 〚政治〛 a political administration by a retired Emperor. Was began in 1086 by Ex-Emperor Shirakawa and continued until the Joukyuu War in 1221, in which Ex-Emperor Gotoba attempted to overthrow the Kamakura shogunate and failed.

いんぜん 院宣 〚政治〛 the document of an order issued by a retired Emperor.

いんそう 印相 〚仏教〛 a symbolic form and position of hands and fingers of a Buddhist image, called *mudra* in Sanskrit. It is fixed, to some extent, as to which Buddhist image takes which *mudra*. →施無畏(せむい)印；与願(よがん)印；智拳(ちけん)印；九品往生(くほんおうじょう)

いんにく 印肉 〚生活〛 ⇨朱肉

いんにん 隠忍 〚忍者〛 the invisible tactics of a ninja. Fulfilled his or her duty without being seen by anyone. For example, hiding under the floor. A ninja conducted either visible or invisible tactics according to the situation. ↔陽忍

いんのしま 因島 〚軍事・島名〛 Innoshima Island, in Hiroshima Pref. The area is 40 km². Was a base camp of a marine warrior group named the Murakami clan. →水軍

いんぱ 院派 〚彫刻〛 the In school of Buddhist sculpture from the 12th to 13th centuries. The names of many sculptors in this school begin with 'In,' such as Inkei. It is said that the style of this school is conservative compared to the Kei school style. Its examples are seen at Sanjuusangen-dou Temple in Kyoto. →慶派(けいは)；円派(えんぱ)

いんぽん 院本 〚文楽〛 a complete text of a dramatic narrative called JOURURI.

いんようごぎょうせつ 陰陽五行説 〚宗教〛 the Theory of Yin-Yang and the Five Elements. A kind of cosmology introduced from ancient China. Preaches that everything can be explained by binary oppositional principles, namely yin and yang, and that everything derives from five elements, namely wood, fire, earth, metal, and water.

いんようどう 陰陽道〔宗教〕 ⇨陰陽(おんみょう)道

いんれき 陰暦〔暦〕 ⇨太陰暦

いんろう 印籠〔工芸〕 a small portable container for samurai. Has a flat and round rectangular shape and is lacquered, often adorned with inlay of mother-of-pearl or dust of gold. Was used as a seal case in the Muromachi period and then became used as a pillbox in the Edo period.

う 卯 〖干支〗 the fourth of the Chinese zodiac signs. Means "hare." Recently the years 1987, 1999, and 2011 were hare years. Indicates the east in direction and around 6 a.m. for hours.

う 鵜 〖動物〗 a cormorant. *Phalacrocoracidae*. A large water bird of dark color. Exists all over the world. Is used for fishing. →鵜飼

ういこうぶり 初冠 〖通過儀礼〗 the coming-of-age ceremony for a male in ancient times. Wore an official cap for the first time.

うぃりあむあだむず ウィリアム・アダムズ 〖外交〗 ⇨三浦按針(あんじん)

ういろう 外朗 〖食べ物〗 sweet rice jelly. There are several kinds of 'uirou' such as green tea and adzuki flavors. Is popular in the Tokai region, such as Aichi Pref.

うえすぎけんしん 上杉謙信 〖武士〗 1530-1578. A feudal lord governing around present-day Niigata and Toyama Prefs. Fought several times with TAKEDA SHINGEN in present Nagano and Yamanashi Prefs. The Battles of Kawanaka-jima, from 1553 to 1564 are famous. Died from a stroke during the conflict with Oda Nobunaga.

うえすぎようざん 上杉鷹山 〖武士〗 1751-1822. A feudal lord of the Yonezawa domain in present Yamagata Pref. Reformed the domain's finances, promoted industries, and founded an official school of the domain.

うえだあきなり 上田秋成 〖人文学〗 1734-1809. A scholar of Japanese classics and novelist, born in Osaka. Wrote books about the floating world, UKIYO-ZOUSHI. Also wrote fictional stories based on historical events and folktales called YOMIHON. His works include *Tales of Moonlight and Rain*. →雨月物語

うえだびん 上田敏 〖文芸〗 1874-1916. A poet and scholar of English literature born in Tokyo. His major work is *Kaichouon*, a collection of translations of French poems, in 1905.

うえの 上野 〖地名〗 an area in the northeast part of Tokyo City proper. Famous for the Ueno Zoo, Kan'ei-ji Temple, several museums, and the bronze statue of SAIGOU TAKAMORI. A semi-open-air market district called Ameya-yokochou is in its southern part. Its eastern and northern parts are a working class area where a large number of homeless people live.

うえむらなおみ 植村直巳 〖スポーツ〗 1941-1984. A mountaineer and adventurer born in Hyougo Pref. Conquered the summits of the highest mountains in five continents—Mont Blanc in Europe, Kilimanjaro in Africa, Aconcagua in South America, Everest in Asia, and McKinley in North America—for the first time in the world. Also successfully reached the North Pole by dog sledge.

うぉしゅれっと ウォシュレット〔家具〕 Washlet. A trademark. Is used to wash one's bottom with warm water after defecation.

うおすき 魚鋤〔食べ物〕 a sukiyaki-style, one-pot dish of fish. Seafood and vegetables are simmered with broth in a shallow pan.

うおぬまし 魚沼市〔地名〕 Uonuma City. Is located in southeastern Niigata Pref. Famous for high-grade rice, KOSHIHIKARI. Has heavy snow in winter.

うおへん 魚偏〔漢字〕 ⇨魚（さかな）偏

うかい 鵜飼〔漁業〕 cormorant fishing, or a cormorant fisher. The fisher lets the cormorants swallow the fish, but the bird cannot gulp it down because of a rope around its neck. Then, the fisher forces the cormorant to disgorge the fish.

うかみ 斥候〔忍者〕 an ancient ninja. Is referred to in the *Chronicles of Japan* (NIHONSHOKI), but the details are unknown.

うがやふきあえずのみこと 鵜葺草葺不合命〔神話〕 a son of HOORI NO MIKOTO and TOYOTAMA HIME. Was brought up by his aunt, TAMAYORI HIME, got married to her after growing up, and fathered Emperor Jinmu. →神武天皇

うかんむり ウ冠〔漢字〕 a crown radical in the shape of ウ (u).

Originally meant "roof." Kanji with this radical include 家（house）, 客（guest）, 宝（treasure）, 室（room）, 害（damage）, 宮（palace）, 宿（accommodation）, 寒（cold）, 富（rich）, and 実（fruit）.

うきあし 浮足〔忍者〕 the floating step. A walking technique on fallen leaves, stepping down on the tip of one's toes first.

うきぐも 浮雲〔文芸・作品〕 *Drifting Clouds*. A novel published in parts from 1887 to 1889 by FUTABATEI SHIMEI. Was written in the spoken style and is said to be the first modern realistic novel in Japan.

うきこ 浮粉〔食文化〕 refined wheat or rice powder. Is used to cook cake.

うきだすき 浮き襷〔忍者〕 floats worn across one's chest.

うきだま 浮き玉〔忍者〕 a float made from animal intestines. Was used when swimming across a moat.

うきはし 浮橋〔忍者〕 a floating bridge. Is made of bamboo boards, two ropes, and four iron stakes. Its shape is like a ladder. One person swims across the water to fix the stakes.

うきみどう 浮御堂〔寺院〕 the popular name of Mangetsu-ji Temple. Literally means "floating hall." Is built above the surface of Lake Biwa in Shiga Pref. One of the Eight Views of Lake Biwa.

うきよえ 浮世絵〔絵画〕 pictures of the floating world. Developed

from genre paintings and depicted aspects of entertainment quarters, kabuki actors, sumo wrestlers, beautiful women, and landscapes from the 17th to 19th centuries. Although many ukiyo-e were woodblock prints, some were painted by hand. Had a great influence on French artists in the 19th century, especially the Impressionists.

うきよぞうし 浮世草子 〖文芸〗 books of the floating world in Kyoto and Osaka from the 17th to 18th centuries. Contain realistic popular novels depicting everyday life. Are said to have started with *The Life of an Amorous Man* by IHARA SAIKAKU. →好色一代男

うぐい 鯎 〖魚〗 a Japanese dace, or big-scaled redfin. *Tribolodon hakonensis*. About 30 cm long. Is a target for pleasure fishing and edible.

うぐいす 鶯 〖動物〗 a Japanese bush warbler. *Cettia diphone*. Is considered a bird that announces the advent of spring. Its chirping has been enjoyed for a long time by Japanese people.

うぐいすあん 鶯餡 〖食べ物〗 sweet paste of green peas. Is named after the green color of a Japanese bush warbler, UGUISU.

うぐいすばり 鶯張り 〖建築〗 a floorboard squeaking like a Japanese bush warbler. Chirps when walked on so that an intruder could be easily detected. One at Chion-in Temple in Kyoto is well-known.

うぐいすまめ 鶯豆 〖食べ物〗 sweet-boiled green peas. Is named after the green color of a Japanese bush warbler, UGUISU.

うぐいすもち 鶯餅 〖食べ物〗 rice cake filled with adzuki paste and sprinkled with green soy flour. Is shaped like a Japanese bush warbler and eaten in spring. Instead of rice cake, a rice-flour confection like Turkish delight is sometimes used.

うけい 誓約 〖神道〗 judgment according to divine will. Term used for divination in ancient times. →神盟探湯(くかたち)

うげつものがたり 雨月物語 〖文芸・作品〗 *Tales of Moonlight and Rain*. A collection of nine supernatural stories written in 1768 by UEDA AKINARI.

うけみ 受け身 〖柔道〗 technique of falling safely in judo. Decreases the shock of being thrown by hitting the floor. A novice in judo has to master it before starting to learn the throwing technique.

うご 羽後 〖旧国名〗 the old name for most of Akita Pref. and northern Yamagata Pref.

うこっけい 烏骨鶏 〖動物・食べ物〗 a silky fowl. *Gallus gallus domesticus*. Its skin, meat, and bones are black, while the feathers are silky white. Its eggs and meat are considered delicacies.

うこん 鬱金 〖植物〗 turmeric. *Curcuma longa*. Is used as spice such as curry powder, as dye, or as herbal medicine.

うざく 鰻ざく〔食べ物〕 chopped grilled eel with sliced cucumber. Is flavored with sake, soy sauce, and vinegar.

うさじんぐう 宇佐神宮〔神社〕 Usa Shrine. The head shrine of the Hachiman Shrines throughout Japan, located in northern Oita Pref. Enshrines Emperor Oujin, Empress Consort Jinguu, and Princess Ookami. Its main building is a National Treasure.

うさはちまん 宇佐八幡〔神社〕 ⇨宇佐神宮

うし 丑〔干支〕 the second of the Chinese zodiac signs. Means "cow." Recently the years 1985, 1997, and 2009 were cow years. Indicates the north-northeast in direction and around 2 a.m. for hours.

うじ 氏〔政治〕 a clan. A social and political group whose family members insisted that they had common ancestors in ancient times. The leaders of this group conducted religious rights for their tutelary deity or deities. The Imperial and other powerful clans formed the Yamato coalition government.

うしあわせ 牛合わせ〔娯楽〕 ⇨闘牛

うしおじる 潮汁〔食べ物〕 thin soup containing fish or shellfish boiled in salt water.

うしおに 牛鬼〔妖怪〕 a mythic huge spider with the head of an ox. Is said to have appeared along the seashore in Western Japan and attacked people. Story of its appear-

ance vary from region to region.

うじがみ 氏神〔神道〕 a tutelary deity of a clan or a local community. It was originally an ancestor worshipped as a deity or a deity deeply related to a clan, but it has become a guardian spirit since medieval times. →産土神(うぶすながみ)

うじがみじんじゃ 宇治上神社〔神社〕 Ujigami Shrine. Is located in southern Kyoto Pref. Enshrines Emperor Oujin, Emperor Nintoku, and Ujinowakiiratsuko, a son of Oujin and younger brother of Nintoku. Its main sanctuary building is one of the oldest Shinto structures and a National Treasure.

うじきんとき 宇治金時〔食べ物〕 shaved ice topped with green tea syrup and sweet adzuki beans.

うじこ 氏子〔神道〕 a parishioner of a local Shinto shrine. Resides in the area under the protection of a tutelary deity and participates in the local festival. →氏神

うじし 宇治市〔地名〕 Uji City. Is located in southern Kyoto Pref. One of the settings for *The Tale of Genji*. Has Byoudou-in and Manpuku-ji Temples. Famous for tea production.

うじしゅういものがたり 宇治拾遺物語〔文芸・作品〕 *A Collection of Tales from Uji*. Contains 197 narratives, many of which are related to Buddhism. Was written in the early 13th century. Its editor is unknown.

うじじゅうじょう 宇治十帖〔文芸・作品〕 "The Ten Uji Chapters."

The last part of *The Tale of Genji*. Is set in Uji, in southern Kyoto Pref., after the hero, Genji, is dead. Describes the life of Kaoru, the false son of Genji.

うじちゃ 宇治茶 〔飲み物〕 the generic term for tea produced in the Uji area, Kyoto Pref. Its cultivation is said to have started in the Kamakura period. Most varieties are high-grade.

うしどし 丑年 〔暦〕 the year of the cow in the Chinese zodiac signs. The years 1997, 2009, and 2021 are years of the cow. →干支; 丑

うしとら 丑寅 〔生活〕 the northeast. The direction between USHI, (cow) and TORA (tiger). Is said to be an ill-omened direction in the Yin-Yang Way, and is also called KIMON, which means "demon's gate." Although the idea comes from China, there are several theories to explain the origin. One possibility is that a typical demon is horned like a cow, wearing a loincloth made of tiger skin.

うしのこくまいり 丑の刻参り 〔宗教〕 a curse ritual established in the Edo period. The petitioner sticks long nails into a figure of the enemy made with straw at a Shinto shrine around 2 a.m. The petitioner wears a white costume and puts three lit candles on an iron crown. The nails are around 15 cm long so that the petitioner could nail down the figure onto a sacred tree at the shrine. The petitioner must per-

form this ritual for seven nights in a row without being noticed by others. When the curse is successful, the enemy will die with pains in the same part of the body where the straw figure has been nailed.

うしのひ 丑の日 〔暦〕 ⇨土用の丑の日

うしへん 牛偏 〔漢字〕 a left-side radical meaning "cow." However, several kanji containing this radical such as 物 (thing) or 特 (special) do not have meanings related to a cow. Kanji with a cow-related meaning include 牧 (pasturage) and 犠 (sacrifice).

うしみつどき 丑三つ時 〔時刻・宗教〕 the dead of night. The third quarter of the Ox hour in the traditional Japanese time system. Around 2 to 2:30 a.m. in the present time system.

うしょう 鵜匠 〔漁業〕 a cormorant fisherman or fisherwoman. Takes care of cormorants, wears a unique costume, and uses about ten cormorants when fishing.

うしろみごろ 後ろ身頃 〔服飾〕 the back cloth of the main part of a kimono. ↔前身頃

うす 臼 〔食文化〕 (**1**) a mortar. Glutinous rice is pounded into a rice cake with a mallet in a wooden mortar. (**2**)⇨挽き臼

うすあげ 薄揚げ 〔食べ物〕 thin deep-fried tofu. A dialect of the Kansai region.

うすい 雨水 〔暦〕 one of the 24 seasonal nodes in the traditional calendar. Around February 19 in the current calendar. Means "rain water has warmed up, and plants begin to bud." →二十四節気(にじゅうしせっき)

うすかわまんじゅう 薄皮饅頭 〖食べ物〗 a thin-skin bun stuffed with sweet adzuki paste. There are some variations from region to region.

うすきせきぶつ 臼杵石仏 〖仏教・彫刻〗 Usuki Stone Buddhas. Are located in Ooita Pref. Many Buddhist images are carved in niches of cliffs. This group of Buddhas is designated a National Treasure.

うすぎぬ 薄絹 〖服飾〗 thin silk fabric.

うすくちしょうゆ 薄口醤油 〖調味料〗 thin-colored soy sauce. Although the color is not very dark, contains more salt than ordinary soy sauce, KOIKUCHI SHOUYU. Is often used in the Kansai region.

うすざん 有珠山 〖山岳〗 Mt. Usu. An active volcano located in southwestern Hokkaido. The height is 732 m. Has several parasitic volcanos including Shouwa Shinzan formed in 1943.

うずしお 渦潮 〖自然〗 a tidal whirlpool. Those in the Naruto Strait between the Shikoku and Awaji Islands are famous. Are created by fast tidal currents and the consequent differences in water levels.

うすたあそおす ウスターソース 〖調味料〗 Worcester sauce. Was adopted from Worcestershire sauce in England, but is now popular in Japan.

うすちゃ 薄茶 〖茶道〗 thin powdered green tea. Is used in a casual tea ceremony. ↔濃茶

うすばた 薄端 〖華道〗 a wide-mouthed vase of thin metal. The mouth part is detachable.

うずまさえいがむら 太秦映画村 〖映画・施設〗 ⇨東映太秦映画村

うずめび 埋め火 〖忍者〗 a land mine.

うすやきせんべい 薄焼き煎餅 〖食べ物〗 a thin rice cracker. Is tasted with salt or soy sauce.

うずら 鶉 〖食べ物・動物〗 a Japanese quail. *Coturnix japonica*. The body length is about 20 cm, and the wing length is about 10 cm. Is bred for its meat and eggs.

うずらがくれ 鶉隠れ 〖忍者〗 a hiding technique imitating a quail. A ninja stooped and squatted down while whispering a mantra for the deity of heat haze called MARISHI-TEN.

うぜん 羽前 〖旧国名〗 the old name for most parts of Yamagata Pref.

うそかえしんじ 鷽替神事 〖祭礼〗 a bullfinch exchange rite. Pronunciation of the Japanese word meaning bullfinch, 'uso,' is the same as that of the word "lie." People exchange their bullfinch figures with each other or dedicate them to the shrine and buy a new one to transform their troubles into fiction. Is held at several Tenjin shrines throughout Japan.

うたあわせ 歌合せ 〖文芸〗 a tanka

competition. Two teams compose poems on the same topic, and the judge decides the winner. Was popular in the 9th to 14th centuries.

うたい 謡〖能〗 chanting a Noh text.

うだいじん 右大臣〖官位〗 the minister of the right. Was positioned next to the minister of the left in the Grand Council of State in ancient times. →左大臣; 太政官

うたいもの 唄い物〖音楽〗 a generic term for traditional songs such as IMAYOU, SAIBARA, and NAGAUTA,

うたかい 歌会〖文芸〗 a meeting to compose rhyming poems and to critique each other.

うたかいはじめ 歌会始 〖文芸・天皇〗 Imperial New Year's Poetry Reading. The present event started in 1869. On the theme announced in the previous year, the Imperial family composes rhyming poems, TANKA, while the general citizenry send its own tanka to the Imperial Household Agency.

うたがき 歌垣〖セックス・祭礼〗 an ancient group ritual for mating. People sang, danced, and made love freely.

うたがわくにさだ 歌川国貞 〖絵画〗 1786-1865. An ukiyo-e artist born in Edo. Famous for pictures depicting kabuki actors. His works include *One Hundred Beautiful Women at Famous Places in Edo*. Is also called Utagawa Toyokuni III.

うたがわくによし 歌川国芳〖絵画〗 1797-1861. An ukiyo-e artist born in Edo. Famous for pictures depict-

ing warriors. His works include *Benkei*, a warrior monk.

うたがわとよくに 歌川豊国〖絵画〗 (1) 1769-1825. An ukiyo-e artist born in Edo. Started his career with portraits of beautiful women, then became popular for painting kabuki actors. His works include *Actors on Stage*. (2) ⇨歌川国貞

うたがわとよはる 歌川豊春 〖絵画〗 1735-1814. An ukiyo-e artist born in present Ooita Pref. Learned the Kanou school in Kyoto, moved to Edo, and founded the Utagawa school. His works include *Perspective View of Moon Viewing in Mid-Autumn*.

うたがわは 歌川派〖絵画〗 the Utagawa school of ukiyo-e. Was founded by UTAGAWA TOYOHARU and became popular in the 19th century.

うたがわひろしげ 歌川広重〖絵画〗 ⇨安藤広重

うだつ 梲〖建築〗 (1) a small wall for fire prevention on a row house. Was considered as a symbol of financial prosperity. Thus the expression 'udatsu ga agaranai,' which literally means "udatsu is not raised," refers to the condition of unsuccessfulness. (2) a short pillar between a beam and ridgepole.

うだてんのう 宇多天皇 〖天皇〗 Emperor Uda. 867-931. The 59th, on the throne from 887 to 897. Attempted to restrain the power of the Fujiwara clan by promoting SUGAWARA NO MICHIZANE.

うたまくら 歌枕 〖文芸〗 a famous place described in traditional poetry. Examples are Mt. Kagu and Tatsuta River in Nara Pref., Ousaka in Shiga Pref., and Suma in Hyougo Pref.

うたまろ 歌麿 〖絵画〗 ⇨喜多川歌麿

うたものがたり 歌物語 〖文芸〗 a collection of short stories formed around poems. Developed in the 10th century.

うちあわび 打ち鮑 〖生活〗 ⇨熨斗鮑 (のしあわび)

うちいり 討ち入り 〖武士〗 the attack by 47 masterless samurai on Kira Yoshinaka. →忠臣蔵

うちいわい 内祝い 〖生活〗 a family celebration. Or a present that the celebrating family gives to other people.

うちうらわん 内浦湾 〖湾〗 Uchiura Bay. Is also called Funka Bay, meaning Eruption Bay. It is said that a British captain named it in 1796 when seeing Mt. Usu smoking from the crater. Is located on the eastern side of the Oshima Peninsula of Hokkaido, facing the Pacific Ocean. Salmon, righteye flounder, and squid are caught there.

うちかぎ 打ち鉤 〖忍者〗 bundled iron hooks. →鉤縄

うちかけ 打ち掛け 〖服飾〗 a long and gorgeous-colored bridal robe worn over a kimono in a wedding banquet. A bride often changes from a white robe into this one during the banquet. →白無垢(しろむく)

うちがけ 内掛け 〖相撲〗 an inside leg trip. One hooks his leg on the inside of the opponent's leg and pulls it.

うちぐり 内刳り 〖仏教・彫刻〗 a hollow section in a wooden sculpture. Its purpose is to reduce the weight of the sculpture and to prevent the wood from cracking when it dries. →一木造り

うちこ 打粉 (1)〖食文化〗 flour for noodle making. Prevents the dough from sticking to the board when the dough is stretched to form the noodle shape. (2)〖武器〗 sword powder. Is used to remove old oil on the sword surface.

うちこわし 打ち壊し 〖政治・経済〗 an urban riot by the poor in the Edo period. Was mainly triggered by a famine and occurred nearly 200 times. Poor people attacked merchants and public officials.

うちでのこづち 打出の小槌 〖民話〗 a good-luck mallet. A kind of cornucopia. Can realize wishes of the owner. In the story of the One-Inch Boy, the dwarf hero becomes an ordinary-sized gentleman thanks to this mallet. →一寸法師

うちとそと ウチとソト 〖精神性〗 the inside and outside of a community. It is said that Japanese people tend to distinguish the inside from the outside of a community, in any social unit such as family, school, corporation, village, prefecture, or nation. This differentiation awareness is an essential concept of

Japanese culture and is reflected in several features such as architecture or language.

うちなあぐち 沖縄口 〖言語〗 the term to mean "the Okinawa dialect" in the Okinawa dialect. →琉球方言

うちぼり 内堀 〖城郭〗 an inner moat. Was dug within a castle precinct. ↔外堀

うちまた 内股 〖柔道〗 inner thigh throw.

うちみず 打水 〖生活〗 sprinkling water on a street or in a garden. During the summer, people sprinkle water in front of their house or in the garden to cool things off.

うちむらかんぞう 内村鑑三 〖キリスト教〗 1861-1930. A writer, magazine editor, and Christian philosopher, born in Edo. Founded the Nonchurch Movement, or 'Mukyokai,' the most famous indigenous Christian organization in Japan. Wrote in both English and Japanese. Major works include *How I Became a Christian* and *Japan and the Japanese*. Argued strongly for a Japanese-style Christianity free of Western customs.

うちゆ 内湯 〖温泉〗 a bath inside a hot spring inn. This term is contrasted with a bath outside an inn, SOTOYU.

うちゅうこうくうけんきゅうかいはつきこう 宇宙航空研究開発機構 〖科学技術・研究機関〗 Japan Aerospace Exploration Agency (JAXA). Was established in 2003. Its head-quarters is in Choufu, Tokyo, which is open for visitors to study.

うちゅうせんかんやまと 宇宙戦艦ヤマト 〖アニメ〗 *Space Battleship Yamato*. A science fiction anime in which the remains of World War II battleship Yamato have been transformed into a spaceship, which travels to another planet called Iscandar to save the earth while fighting against the enemy, Gamilas.

うちわ 団扇 〖生活〗 a round fan with a handle. Paper is pasted on a thin flat frame.

うちわえび 団扇海老 〖食べ物・動物〗 a fan lobster. *Ibacus ciliatus*. About 15 cm long. Edible but with few fleshy parts.

うちわだいこ 団扇太鼓 〖音楽・仏教〗 a hand drum. Is used in the Nichiren sect while chanting a phrase, "NAMU MYOUHOU RENGE KYOU."

うづき 卯月 〖暦〗 April in the traditional calendar. Means "deutzia month" because a deutzia flower blooms in this month. →旧暦；卯の花

うっちゃり 打っ遣り 〖相撲〗 a backward pivot throw. A technique to throw the opponent at the edge of the ring by leaning back and twisting one's own upper body.

うつのみやし 宇都宮市 〖地名〗 Utsunomiya City. The capital of Tochigi Pref. Is located in its central part. The Oushuu and Nikko Highways fork at this city. Famous for Chinese-style dumplings. →奥州街道; 日光街道

うつほものがたり 宇津保物語 〔文芸・作品〕 *The Tale of the Hollow Tree*. Was written probably in the late 10th century. The author is unknown. Describes musical life of zither players and love affairs in the imperial court.

うでくらべ 腕くらべ 〔文芸・作品〕 *Rivalry: A Geisha's Tale*. A novel published in parts from 1916 to 1917 by NAGAI KAFUU. Describes life in a red-light district, focusing on a geisha girl.

うど 独活 〔食べ物・植物〕 a Japanese spikenard, or mountain asparagus. *Aralia cordata*. A herbaceous perennial plant growing about 1.5 m tall. Young buds are edible.

うとん 雨遁 〔忍者〕 the ninja escaping technique using rain. One of the ten heaven-class escaping techniques.

うどん 饂飩 〔食べ物〕 thick white noodles made from wheat flour. Eaten hot in broth or eaten cold after being dipped in a soy-sauce-flavored sauce. When served hot, is usually topped with thinly chopped green onions. Other common toppings include a tempura, deep-fried tofu pockets seasoned with mirin and soy sauce, or a thin-sliced steamed fish paste in a halfmoon shape. Red pepper is added to taste. Is said to have been introduced from China in the Nara period and became popular in the Edo period. Is now a nationwide favorite, especially in Western Japan. There are many local varieties, of which the Sanuki-udon in Kagawa Pref. may be the most famous.

うどんこ 饂飩粉 〔食べ物〕 wheat flour used in making thick white noodles, UDON. The wheat is usually domestically produced.

うどんすき 饂飩鋤 〔食べ物〕 suki-yaki with thick white noodles. →饂飩

うなぎ 鰻 〔食べ物・魚〕 a Japanese eel. *Anguilla japonica*. Is 40 to 50 cm in length. Spawns roe in deep water near Okinawa. Within one year after incubation, young fish goes up a river. The popular cuisine is UNAGI NO KABAYAKI.

うなぎのかばやき 鰻の蒲焼 〔食べ物〕 grilled eel with thick sauce. The sauce is made from soy sauce and mirin. In the East Japan style, the eel is cut open on the back, grilled and steamed, and dipped in sauce. In the West Japan style, the eel is cut open at the abdomen, dipped in the sauce, and grilled.

うなぎのねどこ 鰻の寝床 〔建築〕 a narrow and deep house or place. Literally means "bed of an eel." It is said that many traditional residences in Kyoto had this style.

うなじゅう 鰻重 〔食べ物〕 grilled eel served over rice in a lacquered box. At some restaurants, the two pieces of grilled eel are served; one is on top of the rice and the other is placed inside the rice.

うなづきおんせん 宇奈月温泉 〖温泉〗 a hot spring in northeastern Toyama Pref. A tourist base for sightseeing around Kurobe Canyon.

うなどん 鰻丼 〖食べ物〗 a bowl of rice topped with grilled eel. Is customarily eaten to regain energy and stamina. Also eaten to overcome the summer heat on the day known as the Midsummer Day of the Ox (DOYOU NO USHI NO HI), which falls around the end of July on the traditional calendar.

うに 雲丹 〖食べ物・動物〗 a sea urchin. *Echinoidea*. Its ovary is eaten raw or as an ingredient of sushi.

うねめ 采女 〖天皇・官位〗 a maid-in-waiting at the low rank of the Imperial court in ancient times. Though assigned chores, some maids-in-waiting obtained power when winning an Emperor's favor.

うのはな 卯の花 **(1)**〖食べ物〗⇨雪花菜(おから) **(2)**〖植物〗 a deutzia. *Deutzia crenata*. This flower has five white petals and blooms in early summer.

うばい 優婆夷 〖仏教〗 a female lay adherent to Buddhism. Has vowed to worship the Three Treasures in Buddhism and to observe the Five Precepts. ↔優婆塞(うばそく) →三宝(さんぼう); 五戒

うばがい 姥貝 〖食べ物・動物〗 a Sakhalin surf clam. *Spisula sachalinensis*. Eaten raw or dried.

うばすてやま 姥捨山 〖民話・山岳〗 a mountain where old people are abandoned in folklore. It is said a son tried to abandon his father ac-cording to the order of the lord, but he stopped doing so for some reason. Later the wisdom of the father saved the country. There are several versions of the story.

うばそく 優婆塞 〖仏教〗 a male lay adherent to Buddhism. Has vowed to worship the Three Treasures in Buddhism and to observe the Five Precepts. ↔優婆夷(うばい) →三宝(さんぼう); 五戒

うばり 優波離 〖仏教〗 *Upali*. One of the Ten Great Disciples of the Historical Buddha. Foremost among the disciples in observing the precepts. →十大弟子

うぶすながみ 産土神 〖神道〗 a tutelary deity of one's local community. Though originally different, ubu-suna-gami and UJI-GAMI have been confused since medieval times.

うぶめ 産女, 姑獲鳥 〖妖怪〗 a ghost of a woman who died during delivery. Appears with her baby and asks a person to hold the baby. Is transformed into a monster bird in some folktales.

うま 午 〖干支〗 the seventh of the Chinese zodiac signs. Means "horse." Recently the years 1990, 2002, and 2014 were horse years. Indicates the south in direction and around noon for hours.

うまき 鰻巻き 〖食べ物〗 an omelet with grilled eel.

うまじるし 馬印 〖軍事〗 a banner to indicate the location of a full general in the battlefield. Was placed near the horse of the general. Is said to have started in the mid-16th century. A banner with the image of a bottle gourd for TOYOTOMI HIDEYOSHI is famous.

うまどし 午年 〖暦〗 the year of the horse in the Chinese zodiac signs. The years 1990, 2002, and 2014 are years of the horse. →干支; 午

うまに 旨煮 〖食べ物〗 meat, fish, and vegetables simmered in the sauce flavored with sugar, soy sauce, and mirin.

うまのあし 馬の脚 〖歌舞伎〗 an actor who plays legs of a horse in kabuki. Also means "a poor actor" because a low-class actor usually plays it.

うまへん 馬偏 〖漢字〗 a left-side radical meaning "horse." Kanji with this radical include 駅(station), 馳 (gallop), 駐(stay), and 騎(riding). → 偏; 部首

うまみ 旨味 〖食文化〗 umami. A good taste though not sweet, salty, bitter, or sour. Its main component is glutamic acid.

うみうなぎ 海鰻 〖食べ物・魚〗 **(1)** another name for conger eel, ANAGO. **(2)** a generic name for a seawater fish whose shape is similar to eel. For example, conger eel, moray, or sea snake.

うみさちひこ 海幸彦 〖神話〗 another name for Hoderi no mikoto. Made his living by fishing in the sea, but fought with YAMASACHIHIKO, one of his brothers, because Yamasachihiko lost Umisachihiko's fishing hook.

うみねこ 海猫 〖動物〗 a black-tailed gull. *Larus crassirostris*. Literally means "sea cat" because its cry is similar to that of a cat. Some of its breeding sites in Aomori and Shimane Prefs. are designated Natural Monuments.

うみのひ 海の日 〖祝日〗 Marine Day. The third Monday in July. A national holiday to express thanks for the blessings of the sea and best wishes for the prosperity of Japan as a maritime nation. Was ordained in 1996.

うみびらき 海開き 〖暦〗 the opening of ocean beaches for sea bathing. Usually a ceremony is held, and facilities such as parking lots, public showers, and lavatories open on this day.

うみぶどう 海葡萄 〖食べ物・植物〗 green caviar, or sea grapes. *Caulerpa lengillifera*. An edible seaweed popular in Okinawa.

うみぼうず 海坊主 〖妖怪〗 a giant sea monk. Was said to be a vengeful spirit of a drowned sailor and to moan loudly.

うみほたる 海蛍 〖動物〗 a sea firefly. *Vargula hilgendorfi*. A crustacean. The shell is about 8 mm long, and the body is about 3 mm long. Emits blue luminescence at night.

うめ 梅 〖植物〗 Japanese plum or Japanese apricot. *Prunus mume*. Was introduced from China in ancient times. There are more than 300 varieties, and some of their fruits are used for pickles and alcohol beverages.

うめきゅう 梅キュウ〔食べ物〕 cucumber with the flesh of pickled plum.

うめこぶちゃ 梅昆布茶 〔飲み物〕 kelp tea with the flavor of salted plum.

うめさおただお 梅棹忠夫〔科学技術〕 1920-2010. An ethnologist and anthropologist born in Kyoto. Studied zoology first at Kyoto Imperial University, but moved to ethnology and anthropology after participating in academic explorations led by IMANISHI KINJI. One of his works, *An Ecological View of History: Japanese Civilization in the World Context*, presented a parallel theory of evolution of Japanese and Western civilizations. Became the first director of the National Museum of Ethnology in 1974. →国立民族学博物館

うめしゅ 梅酒〔酒〕 plum liqueur. Can be privately made from plum fruits, sugar crystals, and Japanese spirits.

うめず 梅酢〔食べ物〕 plum vinegar. Sour liquid oozed from pickled plums.

うめぼし 梅干し〔食べ物〕 a salted or pickled plum. Is usually round-shaped and varies from smooth to very wrinkled. Tastes salty and extremely sour due to its high citric acid content, but sweeter versions exist, as well. As popular pickles, is served for breakfast or eaten in rice balls for lunch, often without removing the pit.

うらかみてんしゅどう 浦上天主堂 〔キリスト教・建築〕 Urakami Cathedral, or St. Mary's Cathedral. Is located in Nagasaki City. The construction of the original cathedral started in 1895 and was completed in 1914. After its destruction by the atomic bomb in 1945, the present cathedral was rebuilt in 1959.

うらしまたろう 浦島太郎 〔民話〕 the hero of a fairy tale similar to Rip van Winkle. Tarou helped a turtle, which invited him to the Sea God's Palace. He spent three years with a beautiful princess, Otohime, at the palace. When Tarou determined it was time to go home, Otohime presented him with a box, but she told him not to open it. He came back to his village and found that 300 years had passed. When he opened the box, mysterious smoke rose, and he became a gray-haired old man.

うらじろ 裏白〔植物〕 a forked fern. *Gleichenia japonica*. The back of the leaves is white. Is used for the New Year ornament.

うらせんけ 裏千家〔茶道〕 the Urasenke school. One of the three SENKE schools in tea ceremony.

うらながや 裏長屋〔生活・建築〕 a row house along a backstreet. Residents are usually not very rich. →長屋

うらぼんえ 盂蘭盆会 〔仏教・暦〕 Bon Festival. *Ullambana*. Is held

on August 13 to 15, or July in some regions. Relatives get together to welcome the spirits of ancestors who come home. Is based on an East Asian Buddhist legend that says that a disciple of Buddha, Mogallana, conducted a religious service for his dead mother.

うらみごろ 裏身頃〔服飾〕 the inner cloth of the main part of a kimono. ↔表身頃

うるうづき 閏月〔暦〕 an intercalary month. Is sometimes inserted in a lunar calendar to adjust the connection between seasons and dates. The frequency of its use varies, according to the type of lunar calendar.

うるか 潤香〔食べ物〕 salted guts and roe of freshwater trout. Is served with Japanese sake.

うるし 漆〔植物・美術〕 a sumac or lacquer tree. *Rhus vernicinflua*. Sometimes irritates the skin. Its resinous sap, lacquer, is used for lacquerware.

うるしえ 漆絵〔絵画〕 (1) a picture painted with lacquer. The lacquer is mingled with pigments for colors. (2) ukiyo-e with lacquer black. Lacquer was used for black portions, such as those portraying shiny hair.

うるしこうげい 漆工芸〔工芸〕 ⇨漆器

うるしぬり 漆塗り〔工芸〕 ⇨漆器

うるちまい 粳米〔食べ物〕 ordinary rice. This term is used to distinguish ordinary rice from glutinous rice used for rice cake.

うるめいわし 潤目鰯〔食べ物・魚〕 a round herring. *Etrumeus teres*. About 30 cm long. Contains less fat than an anchovy or sardine and is dried to eat.

うわえ 上絵 (1)〔工芸〕 pictures or patterns on the glaze of pottery. (2)〔服飾〕 pictures or patterns dyed on white cloth.

うわおび 上帯〔服飾〕 the outermost sash for a kimono. Can be tied in many different ways.

うわぐすり 上薬〔工芸〕 glaze. Is put on pottery to improve its appearance and strength and to prevent water absorption.

うわてだしなげ 上手出し投げ〔相撲〕 a pulling overarm throw. A technique to throw the opponent by grasping his belt over his arm and turning outside one's own body.

うわてなげ 上手投げ〔相撲〕 an overarm throw. A technique to throw the opponent by grasping the belt over the arm.

うわばき 上履き〔履物〕 indoor footgear. In most Japanese schools, students and teachers must change their shoes upon entering the building.

うわばみ 蟒蛇〔民話・動物〕 a serpent in folklore. So big as to swallow a man in a gulp. Also means a heavy drinker because a serpent swallows or drinks a lot.

うわまえ 上前〔服飾〕 the outer fold of a kimono.

うんぎょう 吽形〔仏教〕 the closed-mouth form of a Guardian King at a temple. Represents the end of everything in the universe. →仁王

うんけい 運慶 〖彫刻〗 ?–1223. A sculptor of Buddhist images and a leader of the Kei school. His works include *Great Sun Buddha* at ENJOU-JI Temple, *Two Guardian Kings* at the south main gate of TOUDAI-JI Temple, and the portraits of MUJAKU and SESHIN at KOUFUKU-JI Temple, all of which are located in Nara Pref. →慶派(ケイ)

うんげん 繧繝 〖文様〗 a coloring technique with stripes. Narrow areas in several different colors are placed side by side. This technique was mainly used for Buddhist art and architecture from the 8th to 12th centuries.

うんざ 運座 〖文芸〗 a meeting where writers compose haiku on the same topic and critique each other's work.

うんしゅうみかん 温州蜜柑 〖食べ物〗 a satsuma. *Citrus unshiu*. The most common orange in Japan. Is mainly produced in Wakayama, Ehime, and Shizuoka Prefs.

うんじょう 運上 〖交通〗 miscellaneous taxes in the Edo period.

うんすい 雲水 〖仏教〗 **(1)** an ascetic monk wandering various provinces. **(2)** a trainee monk of Zen Buddhism.

うんぜんだけ 雲仙岳 〖山岳〗 Mt. Unzen. Is an active volcano, located in the center of the Shimabara Peninsula in southeastern Nagasaki Pref. Consists of eight peaks, with Mt. Heiseishin-zan being the highest (1,495 m). Erupted several times from 1990 to 1996, and more than 40 lives were lost in the pyroclastic flow. Unzen Volcanic Area Geopark is one of Japan's first geoparks, designated in 2009.

うんりゅうがた 雲竜型 〖相撲〗 Unryuu style of a ring-entering ceremony for sumo champion. In the ceremony, he claps his hands, stomps on the ground, rises his upper body and stomps on the ground again. In the Unryuu style, he places the left hand in front of his chest and stretches the right hand in the air.

え

えいえいおう えい、えい、おー〖言語〗 a battle cry meaning "Go, go, go," or "hip, hip, hooray." It is said to have been chanted before or after a battle in medieval times. It is also said that the commander shouted the first two 'ei,' and his soldiers answered 'ou.' The origin or the details of the usage are unknown.

えいおう 叡王〖将棋〗 King of Wisdom. One of the eight titles in professional shogi. The best-of-seven title match, 'eiou-sen,' takes place annually from March to May. Before it was promoted to a title match in 2017, the Eiou (human) of the year fought against the champion (AI) of the matches among shogi programs.

えいかいわがっこう 英会話学校〖言語・教育〗 an English conversation school. Teachers are usually native speakers of English with no background of TESOL or linguistics and little experience studying a foreign language themselves.

えいきゅうせんぱん Ａ級戦犯〖政治〗 a class-A war criminal. After World War II, 28 suspects were prosecuted by the Allies for crimes against peace at the International Military Tribunal for the Far East.
→極東国際軍事裁判

えいけん 英検〖言語〗 ⇨実用英語技能検定

えいさあ エイサー〖祭礼〗 Bon dancing in Okinawa. The name comes from the yell, 'eisah,' during the dance and songs.

えいさい 栄西〖仏教〗 1141-1215. A Zen priest, born in present Okayama Pref. Went to Sung twice to study Zen and founded the Rinzai sect. →臨済宗

えいたいくよう 永代供養〖仏教〗 the system of perpetual memorial services. If a person requests a temple and pays the ritual cost during his or her lifetime, or if the bereaved family requests and pays, the temple takes care of the grave and holds memorial services on several anniversaries of a person's death, especially the 13th, 17th, and 33th.

えいたいばし 永代橋〖建築〗 Eitai Bridge. Spans the Sumida River in Tokyo. The original one was built in 1698. In 1702, forty-seven masterless samurai from Akou feudal domain crossed this bridge after their act of vengeance. In 1807, the bridge collapsed under the weight of a huge festival crowd, and about 1,500 people died. →赤穂浪士

えいひれ 鱏鰭〖食べ物〗 dried fin of a ray. Often eaten with mayonnaise and red pepper. Goes well with sake.

えいへいじ 永平寺〖寺院〗 Eiheiji Temple. The head temple of

the Soutou sect, located in Fukui Pref. Was founded in 1244 by a Zen priest DOUGEN. Even today, many monks train themselves there in ascetic practices. →曹洞宗

えいほうじ 永保寺〖寺院〗 Eihou-ji Temple. Affiliated with the Rinzai sect. Is located in southern Gifu Pref. Was founded in 1314 by a Zen priest MUSOU SOSEKI. The Kannon Hall and the Founder's Hall are National Treasures. →開山(かいさん)堂

えいんがきょう 絵因果経〖仏教・絵画〗 the *Illustrated Sutra of the Cause and Effect*. Describes the life of the Historical Buddha, *Sakyamuni*, as well as his previous incarnations. The upper half of the scroll paper provides the illustration, and the lower half provides the text of the sutra. The work has several editions, the first of which was created in the 8th century. →過去現在因果経

ええじゃないか ええじゃないか〖神道・政治〗 "It's all right" Movement. This frenzied popular movement occurred in 1867, arising from the tradition of the mass pilgrimage to the Ise Shrine. Shouting 'Eejanaika!,' which means "It's all right," a horde of people danced wildly on the street and burgled wealthy households and merchants. →御蔭(おかげ)参り

えがみなみお 江上波夫〖人文学〗 1906-2002. An Oriental historian and archaeologist born in Yamaguchi Pref. After researching

at the University of Tokyo, became the first director of the Ancient Orient Museum in 1978. Proposed the Horse-Rider Theory, claiming that nomads from north-eastern Asia conquered Japan and established the nation.

えき 易〖宗教〗 the Yi divination. Is based on the *Book of Divination* among the ancient Chinese *Five Classics*. Is said to have been introduced from China around the 6th century. →四書五経

えきしゃ 易者〖宗教〗 a fortune-teller using the Yi divination. Uses 50 bamboo sticks called 'zeichiku' and 6 wooden square sticks called 'sangi.'

えきじん 疫神〖宗教〗 ⇨疫病(やくびょう)神

えきでん 駅伝〖スポーツ〗 a long-distance relay race. Each runner hands a cloth sash, called TASUKI, to the next runner, instead of a baton. Started in Japan in 1917. The first race was run between Kyoto and Tokyo.

えきなか 駅ナカ〖鉄道・ビジネス〗 a shopping area inside a railroad station.

えきべん 駅弁〖食べ物〗 a box meal sold at railroad stations. People can buy local food at the station and enjoy it on the train.

えこう 回向〖仏教〗 a memorial service, or a prayer for the dead.

えこういん 回向院〖寺院〗 Ekou-in Temple. Affiliated with the Pure Land sect. Is located in Sumida-ku, Tokyo. Was founded in 1657 to hold a memorial service for the victims of a destructive fire called MEIREKI NO TAIKA. Fund-raising sumo matches were held there in 1768, which is the origin of present-day professional sumo. →勧進相撲

えことば 絵詞〖絵画・書道〗 **(1)** text written in a picture scroll. **(2)**⇨絵巻物

えし 絵師〖絵画〗 a professional painter or drawer.

えじ 衛士〖軍事〗 a guard of the Imperial Palace in ancient times. Was recruited from local provinces.

えしき 会式〖仏教〗 a memorial service for Nichiren in the Nichiren sect. Is held on the anniversary of his death.

えしゃじょうり 会者定離〖仏教〗 a word that suggests the transience of life, that we meet other people only to discover that we have to part ways later.

えしんそうず 恵心僧都〖仏教〗 ⇨源信

えすごろく 絵双六〖娯楽〗 ⇨双六

えぞ 蝦夷〖政治〗 people living in Northern Japan in ancient times. Were not submissive to the authority of the central government, Imperial Court. Were gradually driven north.

えぞうし 絵草紙〖文芸〗 ⇨草双紙

えぞち 蝦夷地〖地名〗 the old generic name for Hokkaido, Sakhalin, and the Kuril Islands.

えた 穢多〖政治・職業〗 an outcaste group in medieval and early modern times. Was mainly engaged in leather works, public security, and public cleaning. Was severely discriminated against. The Meiji government abolished the caste system in 1871. →被差別部落

えたじま 江田島〖軍事・島名〗 Eta Island. Is located in southwestern Hiroshima Pref. Its area is 30 km^2. The Naval Academy was located there from 1888 to 1945.

えだまめ 枝豆〖食べ物〗 green soybeans. Are harvested while still green and boiled in salted water. People pop the beans out of their shells upon eating. Go well with beer.

えちご 越後〖旧国名〗 the old name of Niigata Pref.

えちごじし 越後獅子〖大道芸〗 a traditional street performance by a child or children wearing the lion-shaped headgear in olden times. They danced while beating small drums or stood on their hands. Originated from Echigo, present Niigata Pref.

えちぜん 越前〖旧国名〗 the old name of Fukui Pref.

えつけ 絵付け〖陶磁器・絵画〗 painting on ceramics.

えっちゅう 越中〖旧国名〗 the old name of Toyama Pref.

えっちゅうふんどし 越中褌〖服飾〗 a G-string for men. Is fastened by an about-one-meter-long cord at the waist. Was popular before Western-style underpants became common among Japanese people.

えと 干支〖干支〗 **(1)** combination

of ten trunks, JIKKAN, with twelve branches, JUUNISHI. Any and all years have this combination of a trunk with a branch. Although there are 120 combinations of trunks with branches, half of them are allotted to 60-year cycles, and the rest are not related to years. For example, 2004, 1944, and 1884 were all the year of 甲申 kinoe SARU, while there is no year of 甲丑 kinoe USHI. **(2)** twelve branches, or twelve signs of the Chinese zodiac. →十二支

えど 江戸 〖地名〗 the old name of Tokyo. Was used until the city was renamed at the Meiji Restoration in 1868. Was a castle town around Edo Castle, where the Tokugawa shogunate was based. In the 17th century during the Edo period, it grew to be one of the largest cities in the world.

えど 穢土 〖仏教〗 the Impure Land. Namely, this world. ↔浄土

えどうぃんらいしゃわあ エドウィ ン・ライシャワー 〖人文学〗 ⇨ライ シャワー

えどかのう 江戸狩野 〖絵画〗 the Kanou sub-school in Edo. The Kanou school of painting, founded around the 15th century, was divided into two sub-schools in the 17th century, when some painters were officially employed by the Tokugawa shogunate in Edo. Painters moving to Edo included KANOU TAN'YUU. →狩野派; 京狩野

えどがろう 江戸家老 〖武士・政治〗 an Edo chief vassal of a feudal lord in the Edo period. Lived in Edo and was in charge of communication and negotiation with the Tokugawa shogunate. ↔国家老; 参勤交代

えどがわらんぽ 江戸川乱歩 〖文芸〗 1894-1965. Pen name of a novelist, Hirai Tarou, born in Mie Pref. Chose his pen name after his favorite novelist, Edgar Allen Poe, with which the pen name sounds quite similar. Wrote some of the earliest detective fiction in Japan. His works include *The Two-sen Copper Coin* in 1923, *The Psychological Test* in 1925, and *The Man Traveling with the Brocade Portrait* in 1929. His action mystery series of Detective Akechi Kogorou versus the Man of Twenty Faces was immensely popular among Japanese children.

えとき 絵解き 〖絵画〗 oral explanation of a picture. In ancient and medieval times, a specialized priest explained the contents of a narrative picture at a temple. Later became a kind of street performance.

えどこもん 江戸小紋 〖服飾〗 a fine pattern originating from the formal costume for samurai in the Edo period.

えどししゅく 江戸四宿 〖交通〗 the four post-station towns in Edo. Include Senju-shuku on Nikko Kaidou and Oushuu Kaidou, Itabashi-shuku on Nakasendou, Naitou Shinjuku on Koushuu Kaidou, and Shinagawa-shuku on

Toukaidou. These are the post towns closest to Nihon-bashi on each route.

えどじだい 江戸時代 〚時代〛 the Edo period, from 1603 to 1867. TOKUGAWA IEYASU established the shogunate in Edo, present Tokyo. The seclusion policy was adopted, and feudalism was established. Arrival of an American naval officer, Matthew Perry, in 1853 triggered the opening of the country. The shogunate returned political power to the Emperor in 1867.

えどじょう 江戸城 〚城郭〛 Edo Castle. Was first constructed in 1457 by Oota Doukan and reconstructed several times. Became the resident castle for the Tokugawa shoguns in 1590. The donjon was burned down during the Meireki Conflagration in 1657. Became the Imperial Palace after the Meiji Restoration in 1868.

えどっこ 江戸っ子 〚精神性〛 an Edoite. A merchant or artisan who was born and brought up in EDO. Is said to have been vigorous, frank, thoughtless, short-tempered, and conceited.

えどとうきょうはくぶつかん 江戸東京博物館 〚施設〛 Edo-Tokyo Museum. Exhibits historical and cultural materials and replicas related to Edo and Tokyo from the time Tokugawa Ieyasu entered Edo in the 15th century until the present day.

えどばくふ 江戸幕府 〚武士・政治〛

⇨徳川幕府

えどはんてい 江戸藩邸 〚武士・政治〛
⇨江戸屋敷

えどまえ 江戸前 〚食文化〛 Edo-style cuisine. Literally means "in front of Edo" because Edoites preferred fresh fish captured in present Tokyo Bay. This term is now mainly used for sushi.

えどまちぶぎょう 江戸町奉行 〚武士・官位〛 the feudal commissioner who governed EDO under the Tokugawa shogunate. Was in charge of judicature, administration, and police.

えどもじ 江戸文字 〚言語〛 Edo-style calligraphy. Was invented in the Edo period and is now used in a kabuki theater, a theater for comic storytelling, or a sumo ranking table.

えどやしき 江戸屋敷 〚武士・政治〛 an Edo residence of a feudal lord. The Tokugawa shogunate ordered each feudal lord to make his legitimate wife and children live in Edo.

えとろふとう 択捉島 〚島名〛 Iturup Island. Is located northward off Hokkaido. Its area is 3,183 km², making it the largest island among the Kuril Islands. Has been under Russian rule since 1945.

えのき 榎 〚植物〛 a hackberry. *Celtis sinensis* var. *japonica*. Grows until 20 m. Can be found all over Japan except Hokkaido. Was planted as a milestone marker in the Edo period.

えのしま 江の島 〚島名〛 Enoshima

Island. The area is 0.4 km². Is located off the coast of Shounan Beach in Fujisawa City in southern Kanagawa Pref. Is connected to the main part of the city by a 600 m-long bridge. Visitors can walk, cycle, or drive across the bridge. Marine sports such as sailing and surfing are popular.

えのもとたけあき 榎本武揚 〖政治〗 1836-1908. A statesman born in Edo. Led ex-shogunal vassals and resisted the Meiji government, locating his headquarters at a Western-style, star-shaped fortress called Goryoukaku in Hokkaido. Later he surrendered. After the war, was recruited as an Hokkaido development official and held various posts such as minister of education and minister of foreign affairs. →箱館戦争

えばもよう 絵羽模様 〖服飾〗 a design technique for a tailored kimono. Since the patterns are dyed after the kimono is temporarily tailored, the patterns flow over the wearer's body, shoulders, and sleeves as if they have been painted on a canvas. This technique is used for high-ranking kimonos.

えびす 恵比寿 〖宗教〗 the deity of business and fishing. One of the Seven Deities of Good Fortune. Is depicted as a middle-aged stout man carrying a fishing rod and a sea bream, wearing a cap, and growing a goatee and mustache. Also, is sometimes identified with HIRUKO, the first son of IZANAGI NO MIKOTO, while sometimes identified with KOTOSHIRONUSHI NO KAMI, a son of OOKUNINUSHI NO KAMI. The word 'Ebisu' may also mean "foreigner."

えびすこう えびす講 〖ビジネス〗 an Ebisu party. Is held on October 20th in the lunar calendar by merchants who prayed for their property to a deity of business called EBISU.

えびすじんじゃ 戎神社 〖神社〗 an Ebisu Shrine. There are many Ebisu Shrines throughout Japan, and there are several ways to depict 'Ebisu' in kanji: 戎, 恵比寿, 恵美須, 蛭子, etc. EBISU is identified with HIRUKO in some shrines, while it is identified with KOTOSHIRONUSHI NO KAMI in other shrines.

えひめけん 愛媛県 〖都道府県〗 Ehime Pref. Its capital is Matsuyama City. Is located in western Shikoku, facing the Inland Sea. Its area is 5,677 km². Mt. Ishiduchi is the highest peak in Western Japan. Famous for the production of citrus fruits and a spa called DOUGO ONSEN. Was connected with Hiroshima Pref. via the Shimanami Expressway in 1999. Used to be called Iyo.

えびら 箙 〖武器〗 a quiver. Was carried on the back to hold arrows.

えぶみ 絵踏み 〖キリスト教・政治〗 ⇨ 踏み絵

えほう 恵方 〖宗教〗 a lucky direction. Changes from year to year. The deity of the New Year is located in this direction. →年神(とし); 恵方巻き

えほうまいり 恵方参り〖宗教・年中行事〗 visiting a Shinto shrine or Buddhist temple in the lucky direction during the New Year's holidays. →恵方

えほうまき 恵方巻き〖年中行事・寿司〗 a lucky sushi roll. Eaten on the day just before the beginning of spring in the traditional calendar. People eat the whole roll without cutting into pieces, facing the lucky direction of the year. Such customs started in the Osaka area.

えぼし 烏帽子〖服飾〗 a traditional high black cap. Was worn by adult noblemen or warriors. Is worn by Shinto priests at present.

えぼしおや 烏帽子親〖通過儀礼〗 a godfather in medieval times. Put a high black cap on a new adult's head in the coming-of-age ceremony and gave the person an adult name.

えま 絵馬〖神社・寺院〗 a votive picture tablet. Literally means "pictured horse." Is offered to a Shinto shrine or Buddhist temple when one prays to the deity or deities or when a prayer has been answered. Originally a living horse was offered. →神馬(しんめ)

えまきもの 絵巻物〖絵画〗 a picture scroll. The pictures are drawn, often together with text side by side, on joined sheets of paper. The combination of pictures and text explains Buddhist sutras, the origin of a temple or shrine, the biography of a high priest, or fictional or historical stories. Scenes get unfolded from right to left as the scroll is unrolled.

えみし 蝦夷〖政治〗 ⇨蝦夷(えぞ)

えみのおしかつ 恵美押勝〖政治〗 another name for FUJIWARA NO NAKAMARO, which was given by Emperor Junnin.

えむおおええ MOA〖宗教〗 ⇨世界救世教

えむおおええびじゅつかん MOA美術館〖美術・博物館〗 the MOA Museum of Art. MOA stands for Mokichi Okada Association, a kind of religious group. Was founded in 1982 and is located in Atami, Shizuoka Pref. Contains Japanese and Chinese art, including three National Treasures and 65 Important Cultural Properties. Of its collection, a painting, *Red and White Plum Blossoms*, by OGATA KOURIN, is the most famous. →世界救世教

えもじ 絵文字〖言語〗 a pictograph used for an email message.

えもん 衣文〖美術〗 the depiction of the pleats or wrinkles of a costume in a sculpture or painting. Its style differs from era to era.

えもんかけ 衣紋掛け〖服飾〗 ⇨衣桁(いこう)

えりもみさき 襟裳岬〖地名〗 Cape Erimo. Is located in Hokkaido and faces the Pacific Ocean. From the cape, a reef stretches about 1.5 km toward the south and is home to harbor seals. Famous for the strong wind blowing throughout the year. Popular New Year's sunrise viewing spot.

えるしいしい LCC 〖交通・企業〗 ⇨ 格安航空会社

えるとぅぅるるごうそうなんじけん エルトゥールル号遭難事件 〖交通・外交〗 the shipwreck of the Ottoman frigate Ertugrul. The battleship sank after hitting the reefs of the Kii Peninsula on September 16, 1890. More than 500 sailors died, though nearby residents saved the lives of 69.

えれきてる エレキテル 〖科学技術〗 an electric generator using friction. Was invented by Hiraga Gennai in the Edo period, and its name came from *electriciteit* in Dutch.

えんえんら 煙々羅 〖妖怪〗 ⇨煙羅煙羅(えんらえんら)

えんか 演歌 〖音楽〗 a melancholic popular ballad. Most of the melody is in a sad minor key, and the words are from the viewpoint of a broken-hearted woman.

えんがくじ 円覚寺 〖寺院〗 Engaku-ji Temple. A main temple of the Rinzai sect, ranked second among the Five Zen Temples of Kamakura, Kanagawa Pref. Was founded in 1282 by a Chinese Zen monk, Mugaku Sogen, who was invited to Japan by the then ruler of Japan, HOUJOU TOKIMUNE. Was built to spread the teaching of Zen Buddhism, to protect Japan, and to hold a memorial service for the victims of the Mongolian invasions in 1274 and 1281 regardless of their nationalities. The reliquary hall and the temple bell are National Treasures. →臨済宗; 元寇; 鎌倉五山; 舎利殿(しゃりでん)

えんがわ 縁側 **(1)** 〖建築〗 a porch, or a veranda. An external wooden corridor under the eaves of a house. Was considered as an interim space between the inside and outside of a house, and close house guests sometimes came here without permission. **(2)** 〖食べ物〗 flesh near the dorsal and anal fins of a flatfish. Eaten raw as SASHIMI or SUSHI.

えんぎ 延喜 〖時代〗 an era name from 901 to 923. In the early Heian period.

えんぎ 縁起 〖仏教〗 **(1)** the idea that everything originates from the connection with other things. **(2)** the history of a Buddhist temple or a Shinto shrine.

えんぎしき 延喜式 〖法律〗 a collection of governmental regulations. The contents include penal, administrative, and ceremonial procedures. Began to be compiled in 905 by Fujiwara no Tadahira by order of Emperor Daigo and was completed in 927. Still exists in almost perfect condition.

えんぎもの 縁起物 〖宗教〗 a good luck charm. Examples include a beckoning cat figure, a Dharma doll, and a small bamboo rake sold at Cock Fairs. →招き猫; 達磨(だるま);

酉(り)の市

えんきょりつうきん　遠距離通勤〔生活〕　long-distance commuting. Some people commute over two hours and more than 100 km from their home to their office.

えんきりでら　縁切寺〔仏教〕　the divorce temple. In the feudal era, it was very difficult for women to file for divorce with their husbands, so they took refuge in this temple when abused by their husbands. The women were allowed to become officially divorced after staying there for three years. There were two divorce temples in the latter half of the Edo period: Toukei-ji Temple in Kamakura, present Kanagawa Pref. and Mantoku-ji Temple in present Gunma Pref.

えんくう　円空〔彫刻〕　1632-1695. A Zen monk and sculptor of Buddhist images born in present Gifu Pref. Did much walking in areas from Kansai to Hokkaido and carved more than 4,000 images. Had a rough style of carving, intentionally keeping the chisel traces. Many of his works are scattered in Gifu and Aichi Prefs.

えんこさいよう　縁故採用〔職業〕　employing a worker through personal connections. Is regarded as being unfair.

えんじばんしょう　烟寺晩鐘〔絵画〕　Evening Gong at Qingliang Temple. One of the Eight Views of Xiaoxiang. →瀟湘(しょう)八景

えんしゅう　遠州〔地名〕　⇨遠江(とおとうみ)

えんしゅうななながま　遠州七窯〔工芸・茶道〕　Enshuu Seven Kilns. Includes Shitoro in Shizuoka, Zeze in Shiga, Asahi in Kyoto, Akahada in Nara, Kosobe in Osaka, Agano and Takatori in Fukuoka Prefs. It is said that Kobori Enshuu directed craftsmen to create tea ceremony utensils.

えんしょう　遠称〔言語〕　a demonstrative referring to a distant relation. Its first letter is あ(a) such as あれ(are), which means "that," and あちら(achira), which means "there." →近称; 中称; 不定称

えんじょうじ　円成寺〔寺院〕　Enjouji Temple. Affiliated with the Shingon sect. Is located in northern Nara Pref. Was founded in 756 at the behest of Emperors Shoumu and Kouken. The image of the Great Sun Buddha is the sculptor Unkei's early work, made in 1176, and is a National Treasure. →大日如来

えんだか　円高〔経済〕　yen appreciation, or strong yen. For example, one dollar was around 80 yen in 2012, compared to 120 yen per dollar in 2015. ↔円安

えんちん　円珍〔仏教〕　814-891. A priest of the Tendai sect, born in present Kagawa Pref. A grandnephew of Kuukai, the founder of the Shingon sect. Studied in Tang, and revived Onjou-ji Temple. →天台宗

えんとう　遠島〔犯罪〕　⇨島流し

えんどうしゅうさく　遠藤周作〔文

芸〗 1923-1996. A novelist born in Tokyo. Received Catholic baptism in his childhood and wrote novels that addressed the topic of Christianity in Japan as well as light essays. His works include *White Man* in 1955, *The Sea and Poison* in 1957, and *Silence* in 1966.

えんとうはにわ 円筒埴輪 〖考古〗 a cylindrical clay image put on a tumulus. Is 40-200 cm in height and 15-80 cm in diameter. It is estimated that there were over 20,000 cylindrical clay images at the Nintoku-ryo Tumulus.

えんにち 縁日 〖祭礼〗 a temple or shrine fair. Since many people visit a temple or shrine on the day of 'ennichi,' various street vendors, such as food sellers, prize game joints, and goldfish-scooping pools, open temporary shops at the precincts. Originally means "the day connected to a deity in Buddhism or Shintoism."

えんにん 円仁 〖仏教〗 794-864. A priest of the Tendai sect, born in present Tochigi Pref. Studied in Tang, brought 584 sutras to Japan, completed the theory of the Tendai sect, and wrote a travel diary in Tang. →天台宗; 入唐求法巡礼行記 (にっとうぐほうじゅんれいぎょうき)

えんのおづぬ 役小角 〖宗教〗 a mountain ascetic in the Nara period. Trained himself at Mt. Katsuragi in present Nara Pref., attained supernatural power, and established the way of mountain asceticism. →修験道

えんのぎょうじゃ 役行者 〖宗教〗 ⇨ 役小角(えんのおづぬ)

えんぱ 円派 〖彫刻〗 the En school of Buddhist sculpture from the 12th to 13th centuries. The names of sculptors in this school include 'en.' It is said that the style of this school is conservative compared to the Kei school style. Examples are seen at Sanjuusangen-dou Temple in Kyoto. →慶派(けいは); 院派(いんぱ)

えんぷん 円墳 〖考古〗 a round burial mound. Is dated from the 3rd to 7th centuries and seen all over Japan. The biggest existing 'enpun' is the Maruhakayama Tumulus in Saitama Pref.

えんぽきはん 遠浦帰帆 〖絵画〗 Sailing Ship Returning Home. One of the Eight Views of Xiaoxiang. → 瀟湘(しょうしょう)八景

えんま 閻魔 〖仏教〗 the Lord of Netherworld. *Yama*. Judges a human after death and decides whether he or she should go to the Western Pure Land or to hell.

えんまてん 閻魔天 〖仏教〗 another name for Enma when it is regarded as one of the Twelve Devas. Guards the southwest. →十二天

えんむすび 縁結び 〖宗教〗 matchmaking. People visit a shrine or temple to pray for finding a good partner or love. Izumo Grand Shrine is the most famous shrine for matchmaking.

えんやす 円安 〖経済〗 yen depreciation, or weak yen. For example, one dollar was around 120 yen in 2015, compared to 80 yen per dollar in 2012. ↔円高

えんらえんら 煙羅煙羅 〔妖怪〕 a mythical smoke-goblin. Smoke forms something like a human face or an animal. Just startles humans and is harmless. Is also called 'en'enra.'

えんりえど 厭離穢土 〔仏教〕 a phrase meaning to have disdain for this world, filthy with its earthly desires, and to desire to leave it. This phrase is often paired with GONGU JOUDO.

えんりゃくじ 延暦寺 〔寺院〕 Enryakuji Temple. The head temple of the Tendai sect, located in Mt. Hiei, northeast of Kyoto. Was founded in 788 by a priest named SAICHOU. Produced many great priests in the early Kamakura period, such as HOUNEN, SHINRAN, DOUGEN, EISAI, and NICHIREN. Was almost completely destroyed by ODA NOBUNAGA in 1571. Its main hall, named 'Konpon chuu-dou,' and several calligraphies are National Treasures. Was designated a World Heritage Site in 1994. →天台宗

お

お 御〜〔言語〕 a prefix to express respect. Is attached before an indigenous Japanese noun, verb, or adjective.

おあいそ 御愛想〔食文化〕 restaurant jargon to mean payment of a bill.

おい 笈〔宗教・旅〕 a portable box with short legs. A monk or pilgrim puts clothes, books, dishes, and Buddhist utensils in it and carries it on the back. →行脚; 山伏

おいえ 御家〔武士・政治〕 the honorific term for the family of a samurai's lord.

おいえそうどう 御家騒動〔武士・政治〕 an internal conflict in a feudal family in the Edo period. Was caused by an issue of inheritance or a struggle for power. Was often dramatized and became a motif of KABUKI or of storytelling called KOUDAN.

おいこん 追いコン〔酒・学校〕 ⇨追い出しコンパ

おいだしこんぱ 追い出しコンパ〔酒・学校〕 a farewell party for graduating senior students. Is usually held by members of club activities.

おいちょかぶ おいちょかぶ〔ゲーム〕 Japanese baccarat. Each resulting number is nicknamed. For example, 'kabu' means "nine," and 'oicho' means "eight."

おいてけぼり 置行堀〔妖怪〕 Leave-it-behind Moat. A man heard a voice say "Leave it behind" when going home after fishing along the moat. He found his fish basket empty when he checked it at home.

おいらせけいりゅう 奥入瀬渓流〔自然・地名〕 Oirase Mountain Stream. A part of the Oirase River flowing in eastern Aomori Pref. Along the stream is a natural trail continuing 14 km.

おいらん 花魁〔娯楽・セックス〕 a courtesan in the Edo period. Lived in a special area for licensed prostitution.

おいろなおし お色直し〔冠婚葬祭〕 the dress change by a bride and bridegroom. They usually change from official kimono to western costumes or from white western dresses to colorful costumes.

おいわ お岩〔歌舞伎・妖怪〕 the heroine of *The Ghost Story of Tokaido Yotsuya* (TOUKAIDOU YOTSUYA KAIDAN) by TSURUYA NANBOKU. After having her features made ugly and then being killed by the poison administered by her husband, she revenged him as a ghost.

おうい 王位〔将棋〕 Crown of Shogi. One of the eight titles in professional shogi. The best-of-seven title match, 'oui-sen,' takes place annually from July to August or September.

おうう 奥羽〔地名〕 another name for the Tohoku region. The first kanji 'ou'(奥) is derived from 'Michinoku'(陸奥), the eastern half of the Tohoku region, and the last kanji 'u'(羽) is derived from 'Dewa' (出羽), the western half of it.

おううえつれっぱんどうめい 奥羽越列藩同盟〖戦争〗 the alliance of feudal domains in northeastern Japan. Was formed in May 1868 by 31 feudal domains against the Meiji government and was defeated in September.

おううさんみゃく 奥羽山脈 〖山岳〗 the Ouu Mountains. Are one of the backbone mountain chains of Japan. Are also the longest chain of mountains. Starting from southern Aomori Pref., they run on the border between Iwate and Akita Prefs., between Miyagi and Yamagata Prefs., through Fukushima Pref., and to the north of Tochigi Pref., covering 500 km. The highest peak is Mt. Iwate.

おうざ 王座 **(1)** 〖碁〗 Throne, in the sense of "a special chair." One of the seven titles in professional GO. The best-of-five title match, 'ouza-sen,' takes place annually between October and December. **(2)** 〖将棋〗 one of the eight titles in professional shogi. The best-of-five title match takes place annually from September to October.

おうじ 王子〖神道〗 ⇨熊野王子
おうしゅう 奥州〖地名〗 ⇨陸奥(む)
おうしゅうかいどう 奥州街道 〖交通〗 the Oushuu Highway. **(1)** one of the five highways radiating

from Edo during the Edo period. Starting from Nihon-bashi, Edo, it ran through present Saitama, Ibaraki, and Tochigi Prefs., and terminated in Shirakawa, Fukushima Pref. Took roughly the same route as present Route 4. **(2)** the route from Edo to Hakodate during the Edo period, including the first definition of Oushuu Kaidou and the route crossing the channel between Honshu and Hokkaido.

おうじゅほうしょう 黄綬褒章〖政治〗 the Medal with Yellow Ribbon. Is "awarded to individuals who, through their diligence and perseverance, became public role models," says the Cabinet Office.

おうしょう 王将〖将棋〗 **(1)** a king. Is commonly called by its abbreviated form 'ou,' or its nickname 'ousama.' There are two kings in shogi, 'gyokushou' and 'oushou.' The player having the first move has the gyokushou, and the opponent has the oushou. **(2)** King of Shogi. One of the eight titles in shogi, named after the oushou piece. The best-of-seven title match, 'oushou-sen,' takes place annually from January to February or March.

おうじんてんのう 応神天皇〖天皇〗 ?-? Emperor Oujin. 15th, around the 5th century. His tumulus, the second largest in Japan, suggests the prosperity of the Yamato Court in his years.

おうじんてんのうりょう 応神天皇陵〖古墳〗 the Tumulus of Emperor

Oujin. Is located in central Osaka Pref. and dates back to the 5th century. Its length is 430 m, and its height is 36 m, making it the second-largest keyhole-shaped burial mound in Japan. Is surrounded by a single moat though it is presumed to have been double because of existing traces of the outer moat.

おうせいふっこ 王政復古 〖政治〗 the Restoration of Imperial Rule. An edict was issued on December 9, 1867, and the administrative power was returned to the Imperial Court.

おうちょうじだい 王朝時代 〖政治〗 the period when the country was governed by the Imperial Court. The Nara and Heian periods, especially Heian.

おうちょうぶんがく 王朝文学 〖文芸〗 literature in the Heian period. Especially refers to works written in KANA by women in the aristocratic class.

おうにんのらん 応仁の乱 〖戦争〗 the Ounin War. 1467-1477. The succession issue of the Muromachi shogunate, the conflict between two military governors, Hosokawa Katsumoto and Yamana Souzen, and other political problems intertwined and developed into an eleven-year war, mainly in Kyoto. The Muromachi shogunate completely lost authority, and the Warring States period began.

おうばくしゅう 黄檗宗 〖禅〗 the Oubaku sect of Zen Buddhism. Was founded by a Chinese priest, INGEN, in the Edo period. Keeps the Chinese style in architecture, rituals, and utensils. The head temple is MANPUKU-JI Temple in Uji City, southeastern Kyoto Pref.

おうみ 近江 〖旧国名〗 the old name of Shiga Pref.

おうみしょうにん 近江商人 〖職業〗 businessmen from present Shiga Pref. Active in many areas throughout Japan in the Edo period.

おうみはっけい 近江八景 〖絵画・自然〗 Eight Views of Lake Biwa. Is modeled after Eight Views of Xiaoxiang in China, which is a popular subject for an India ink painting. The eight views are Autumn Moon at Ishiyama, Evening Snow at Hira, Sunset at Seta, Returning Sailboat at Yabashi, Night Bell at Mii, Night Rain at Karasaki, Flying Geese at Katada, and Mountain Mist at Awadu. →瀟湘(しょう)八景

おうむしんりきょう オウム真理教 〖宗教〗 Aum Shinri-kyo, or Teaching of Supreme Truth. A fanatic millenarian sect formed in the 1980s by Asahara Shoko. Beliefs are based on a combination of asceticism, meditation, and disdain for the modern world. Brainwashed its followers and was responsible for the 1995 sarin gas attack in a Tokyo subway, which killed 12 people and injured thousands. Asahara and most other leading members were arrested, and Asahara was convicted of murder.

おうらいもの 往来物 〔教育〕 a generic term for fundamental textbooks for reading and writing. Were first compiled in the 11th century and were used until the 19th century.

おえしき 御会式 〔仏教〕 ⇨会式

おおあし 大足 〔忍者〕 Big step. One of the ten walking techniques described in the *True Path of Ninjya* (Shounin-ki).

おおあまのおうじ 大海人皇子 〔政治〕 another name for Emperor Tenmu (?–686) when he was young.

おおいがわ 大井川 〔河川〕 the Ooi River. Flows from the Akaishi Mountains in Shizuoka Pref. to Suruga Bay. The length is 160 km. For defensive reasons, the Tokugawa shogunate prohibited building a bridge on it or crossing it by ship. Thus travelers crossed it by riding on a litter or the shoulder of a professional carrier.

おおいしくらのすけ 大石内蔵助 〔武士〕 1659–1703. A samurai born in present Hyougo Pref. When serving the Akou domain as a chief vassal in 1701, his master, ASANO NAGANORI, was forced to commit hara-kiri for attacking another feudal lord, KIRA YOSHINAKA, in the Edo Castle. Ooishi avenged his master's death by killing Kira, leading other 46 Akou ex-vassals in 1702.

おおいたけん 大分県 〔都道府県〕 Ooita Pref. Its capital is Ooita City. Is located in northeastern Kyushu, facing the Inland Sea. Its area is 6,339 km^2. In addition to many spas such as BEPPU ONSEN and YUFUIN, visitors can enjoy a glorious view of YABAKEI, Usa Shrine, stone Buddhas carved on cliffs at Usuki, and historic sites of unique Buddhist culture in the Kunisaki Peninsula. The production of Japanese cedar woods, pine woods, SHIITAKE mushrooms, and citrus fruits is considerable. Used to be Bungo and a part of Buzen. →宇佐神宮; 臼杵石仏 (うすきせきぶつ)

おおいたし 大分市 〔地名〕 Ooita City. The capital of Ooita Pref. Is located in its central part, facing Beppu Bay. Mt. Takasaki is famous for the largest populations of wild monkeys in Japan.

おおいちょう 大銀杏 〔相撲〕 a large-ginkgo-leaf topknot. Is allowed only for high-ranking sumo wrestlers. →銀杏髷 (いちょうまげ)

おおうちがり 大内刈り 〔柔道〕 major inner reap.

おおうらてんしゅどう 大浦天主堂 〔キリスト教・建築〕 Ooura Cathedral. Is located in Nagasaki City. Was built in 1864 by French missionaries, Louis Furet and Bernard Petitjean. Was dedicated to the 26 Christian martyrs who were killed in 1596. Is the oldest existing Christian church building in Japan. A National Treasure.

おおえやましゅてんどうじ 大江山酒呑童子 〔妖怪〕 the leader of demons living in Mt. Ooe in present Kyoto Pref. Robbed women and treasures in Kyoto in the Heian period. According to legend, was exterminated by MINAMOTO NO YORIMITSU.

おおおかえちぜん 大岡越前 〖武士〗 1677-1751. A samurai born in Edo. In TV dramas, is described as a great feudal commissioner in the governance of Edo.

おおおかしょうへい 大岡昇平 〖文芸〗 1909-1988. A novelist born in Tokyo. His works include *Taken Captive* in 1948 and *Fires on the Plain* in 1951.

おおおく 大奥 〖政治・セックス〗 the inner palace of Edo Castle for the Tokugawa shogunate. Wives of a shogun and many female servants lived there. All men, excepting the shogun, were prohibited from entering.

おおおみ 大臣 〖官位〗 the top administrator in the ancient Imperial Court. Was abolished during the Taika Reform of 645 after the Soga clan, which inherited this position for three generation, was exterminated.

おおかがみ 大鏡 〖文芸・作品〗 *The Great Mirror*. The author is unknown. A story of biographical history probably written in the 12th century. Describes the prosperity of the Fujiwara clan from 850 to 1025, in dialogue form between two old men. One of the Four Mirrors. →藤原氏; 四鏡

おおかみ 狼 〖動物〗 ⇨日本狼

おおきびつひこ 大吉備津彦 〖神話〗 ⇨吉備津彦命 (きびつひこのみこと)

おおぎまちてんのう 正親町天皇 〖天皇〗 Emperor Oogimachi. 1517-1593. 106th, on the throne from 1557 to 1586. Succeeded to the throne in 1557, but could not hold the enthronement ceremony because of poverty. Held it in 1560, financially supported by ODA NOBUNAGA and TOYOTOMI HIDEYOSHI.

おおぎり 大喜利 〖落語〗 a comic show in which players produce a funny or witty response to a question posed by a host. When the answer is a big hit, the player gets a floor cushion. When his answer does not appeal to the host or audience, the player loses a floor cushion. The term 'oogiri' originally meant an additional piece after the day's program.

おおくにぬしのかみ 大国主神 〖神話〗 an offspring of SUSANOO NO MIKOTO. Famous for the episode of a white rabbit in Inaba and is enshrined in the Izumo Grand Shrine. He transferred his realm to NINIGI NO MIKOTO when Ninigi descended from TAKAMAGAHARA. →大黒天

おおくびえ 大首絵 〖絵画〗 an ukiyo-e for depicting a bust portrait. Was popular around 1800. The models were kabuki actors and beautiful women.

おおくぼとしみち 大久保利通 〖政治〗 1830-1878. A statesman born in present Kagoshima Pref. One of the key figures in the Meiji Restoration. Facilitated the Alliance of Satsuma and Choushuu to overthrow the Tokugawa shogunate. After the shogunate returned political power to the Emperor, made feudal lords return their land and people to the Emperor, abolished the feudal domain system, and established the prefectural system. Opposed to the Policy of Punishing Korea proposed by SAIGOU TAKAMORI and ITAGAKI TAISUKE. Was assassinated by discontented former samurai.

おおくましげのぶ　大隈重信　〘政治〙　1838-1922. A statesman and educator born in Saga Pref. As a statesman, worked as the prime minister twice. In 1882, established Constitutional Reform Party (Rikken Kaishinto), and became its first party leader. In 1898, formed Constitutional Politics Party (Kenseito), with Itagaki Taisuke and organized the first party cabinet called Waihan Cabinet, meaning "the cabinet of Ookuma and Itagaki." As an educator, was known as the founder and first president of Waseda University.

おおくらしゅうこかん　大倉集古館　〘美術・博物館〙　Okura Museum of Art. Was founded in 1917 and is located in Akasaka, Tokyo. Contains Japanese and East Asian art, including 3 National Treasures and 13 Important Cultural Properties. A Buddhist image, *Samantabhadra Riding on Elephant*, is famous.

おおごし　大腰　〘柔道〙　full hip throw.

おおごしょ　大御所　〘政治〙　a former shogun. TOKUGAWA IEYASU and TOKUGAWA IENARI were called so and kept political power even after retirement.

おおさか　大坂　〘地名〙　an old name for Osaka. Though its pronunciation is the same as present Osaka, the second kanji 坂 is different. It was replaced with the present kanji 阪 in the Meiji period.

おおさかこくさいくうこう　大阪国際空港　〘交通〙　Osaka International Airport. Is located in Itami City, Hyougo Pref., and is commonly known as Itami Airport (ITM). Opened in 1958 and has specialized in domestic flights since Kansai International Airport opened in 1994. From the airport, passengers can get to Osaka, Kyoto, and Kobe by bus. →関西国際空港

おおさかし　大阪市　〘地名〙　Osaka City. An ordinance-designated city, and the capital of Osaka Pref. Is located in its central part, facing Osaka Bay. According to the *Chronicles of Japan* (NIHONSHOKI), Emperor Oujin and Emperor Nintoku constructed their imperial palaces here in ancient times. One of the first historical structures on the current site of Osaka City was the SHITENNOU-JI Temple, founded in 593 by Prince Shoutoku. More recently, a priest named Rennyo founded the ISHIYAMA HONGAN-JI Temple there in 1496, and TOYOTOMI HIDEYOSHI built Osaka

Castle at the same site in 1593. During the Edo period, the city developed as an economic center. In addition to historic sites, visitors can enjoy eating OKONOMIYAKI, TAKOYAKI, and KUSHIKATSU. →難波宮 (なにわの みや);聖徳太子;大阪城;天下の台所

おおさかじめ　大阪締め〖言語・精神性〗 the traditional Osaka style of a ceremonial hand-clapping. People clap hands 7 times in unison, accompanied by key shouting. Consists of 2-2-3 pattern of hand-clapping. →手締め

おおさかじょう　大坂城〖城郭〗 Osaka Castle. The original structure was constructed in 1583 by Toyotomi Hideyoshi. After being destroyed in the Summer Campaign in Osaka in 1615, was repaired several times. During the Edo period, a hereditary feudal lord was appointed as the manager of this castle by the Tokugawa shogunate to govern the Osaka area and watch the outside feudal lords in Kyushu, Chuugoku, and Shikoku. The present reinforced concrete architecture was reconstructed in 1931 by Osaka City.

おおさかじょうだい　大阪城代〖官位〗 the manager of Osaka Castle. A hereditary feudal lord was appointed by the Tokugawa shogunate to govern the Osaka area and watch outside feudal lords in Western Japan. →譜代(だい)大名;外様(ざま)大名

おおさかずし　大阪寿司〖食べ物〗 Osaka-style sushi. Mainly pressed sushi such as BATTERA.

おおさかだいがく　大阪大学〖教育〗 Osaka University. Its roots were two private schools in the Edo period, KAITOKUDOU and TEKIJUKU, and it was founded in 1931 as the 6th imperial university. Has three campuses in northern Osaka Pref.

おおさかてんまんぐう　大阪天満宮〖神社〗 Osaka Temmangu Shrine. Is located in Osaka City and enshrines SUGAWARA NO MICHIZANE, worshipped as a deity of study. Famous for the TENJIN-MATSURI Festival.

おおさかなつのじん　大坂夏の陣〖戦争〗 the Summer Campaign in Osaka. Tokugawa Ieyasu attacked Osaka Castle in 1615 to kill Toyotomi Hideyori, the son of Toyotomi Hideyoshi, and Chacha, a wife of Toyotomi Hideyoshi. In so doing, he completely unified the country. →大坂冬の陣

おおさかばんぱく　大阪万博〖経済・科学技術〗 Expo '70. The 1970 Japan World Exposition. Was held from March 14 to September 13 in Osaka, and was the first world expo in Asia. Seventy-seven countries and 34 companies participated, and more than 64 million people visited. The site is now the Expo '70 Commemorative Park.

おおさかふ　大阪府〖都道府県〗 Osaka Pref. Its capital is Osaka City, an ordinance-designated city.

Its area is 1,894 km^2, making it the second smallest prefecture. Developed from ancient times and has many historic sites such as Nintoku-ryo Tumulus, Shitennou-ji Temple, Sumiyoshi Grand Shrine, and Osaka Castle. Now functions as the industrial and cultural center of Western Japan. Used to be Izumi, Kawachi, and the eastern part of Settsu.

おおさかふゆのじん　大坂冬の陣 〖戦争〗 the Winter Campaign in Osaka. TOKUGAWA IEYASU attacked Osaka Castle in 1614, where Toyotomi Hideyori, the son of TOYOTOMI HIDEYOSHI, and Chacha, a wife of Toyotomi Hideyoshi, lived. When the Toyotomi side surrendered, Ieyasu promised not to bury the moats, but actually he did. This led to the ruin of the Toyotomi family in the next battle called OOSAKA NATSU NO JIN.

おおさかまちぶぎょう　大坂町奉行 〖官位〗 the feudal commissioner that governed Osaka citizens under the Tokugawa shogunate. Was in charge of judicature, administration, and the police.

おおさかわん　大阪湾 〖湾〗 Osaka Bay. Is located between Awaji Island and Osaka Plain at the east end of the Inland Sea. Ship traffic is heavy because of the Osaka and Koube Ports. Used to be called Chinu no umi.

おおさんしょううお　大山椒魚 〖動物〗 a Japanese giant salamander. *Megalobatrachus japonicus*. Lives in clear streams in Western Japan. Is about 1.5 m long, to making it the largest amphibian in the world.

おおしおへいはちろう　大塩平八郎 〖政治〗 1793-1837. A samurai born in Osaka. A platoon commander under a feudal commissioner that governed Osaka. Also a scholar of the Wang Yang-ming school. Raised a rebellion in 1837. →大塩平八郎 の乱

おおしおへいはちろうのらん　大塩 平八郎の乱 〖戦争〗 the Rebellion of OOSHIO HEIHACHIROU. Occurred in Osaka in 1837. A retired officer and philosopher, Ooshio Heihachirou, suggested that the feudal commissioner's office had to save people when famine struck, but his view was rejected. He rose up together with his disciples, colleagues, and peasants and destroyed storehouses to give rice to the people. However, the rebellion was suppressed within one day.

おおしこうちのみつね　凡河内 躬恒 〖文芸〗 ?-? A poet in the early Heian period. Compiled the *Collection of Ancient and Modern Japanese Poetry* (KOKINWAKASHUU) in 905, together with Ki no Tsurayuki and two other poets. One of the Thirty-six Immortal Poets. → 三十六歌仙

おおしまつむぎ　大島紬 〖服 飾〗 a textile produced in Amami Ooshima Island in Kagoshima Pref. Is woven by hand with colored spun silk threads.

おおしまなぎさ 大島渚 〔映画〕 1932-2013. A movie director born in Okayama Pref. His works include *In the Realm of the Senses* in 1976 and *Merry Christmas, Mr. Lawrence* in 1983.

おおすみ 大隅 〔旧国名〕 the old name of eastern Kagoshima Pref.

おおずもう 大相撲 〔相撲〕 Grand Sumo Tournament. Is run by the Japan Sumo Association (Nihon Sumo Kyokai).

おおぜき 大関 〔相撲〕 a sumo wrestler at the second highest rank in the Grand Sumo Tournament. If he loses more matches than he wins in two consecutive tournaments, he goes down to the third rank called SEKIWAKE.

おおそとがり 大外刈り 〔柔道〕 major outer reap. A technique to lean the opponent's body backwards, take a position on his or her side, and sweep the opponent's leg by swinging one's own leg from front to rear.

おおたく 大田区 〔地名〕 Oota City. One of the 23 cities in central Tokyo, located in its southern part. Its business center is in the Kamata area. The Buddhist temple, Ikegami Honmon-ji, is a landmark in its central part. Across the Tama River is Kanagawa Pref. Haneda Airport is located in its bayside area. Has been known for small and medium-sized manufacturing businesses, such as nori seaweed

production and straw work before World War II. More recently, metalworking started in small factories that do subcontracting work for larger companies. However, such traditional ways of doing business in this city are in decline.

おおたけべら 大竹箆 〔忍者〕 an indoor trick used by ninja. In this trick, a large piece of bamboo hit the enemy's face when he or she opened the door.

おおだち 大太刀 〔武器〕 an extra-long sword. Is longer than 90 cm. →刀；太刀

おおたどうかん 太田道灌 〔武士〕 1432-1486. A warlord in the Kantou region. Built the original Edo Castle in 1457.

おおつえ 大津絵 〔絵画〕 Ootsu painting. Has countrified, humorous, and light brushwork. Was sold as a souvenir around Ootsu in present Shiga Pref. from the 17th to 19th centuries.

おおつきふみひこ 大槻文彦 〔言語〕 1847-1928. A Japanese philologist and lexicographer born in Edo. Compiled a Japanese dictionary called *Daigenkai*, which had a great influence on later dictionaries.

おおつし 大津市 〔地名〕 Ootsu City. The capital of Shiga Pref. Is located in its southwestern part. An imperial capital was placed here in the 7th century by Emperor Tenji. Has many shrines and temples such as Enryaku-ji, Onjou-ji, and Ishiyama-dera. Seven of Eight Views of Lake

Biwa can be observed in this city. →近江八景

おおつづみ 大鼓 〖能・音楽〗 a large hand drum. Is used in traditional music. The diameter of the head is about 23 cm, and the length is about 30 cm. The player places it on the left side of the lap and hits it with the right hand.

おおてもん 大手門 〖城郭・建築〗 the main gate of a castle. The castle tower usually cannot be seen straight from this gate, for defensive reasons. ↔搦(から)め手門

おおとの 大殿 〖武士・政治〗 Literally means "great lord." When a current lord was old and had a young adult successor, he was called 'oo-tono.' When a retired lord was still alive, he was also called 'oo-tono.' ↔若殿

おおともそうりん 大友宗麟 〖武士〗 1530-1587. A Christian feudal lord born in present Ooita Pref. Governed northern Kyushu and dispatched the mission of four boys to the Pope, in cooperation with two other feudal lords, Oomura Sumitada and Arima Harunobu.

おおとものおうじ 大友皇子 〖天皇〗 Prince Ootomo. 648-672. A son of Emperor Tenji. Was defeated in the Jinshin War of 671. Though the *Chronicles of Japan* (NIHONSHOKI) does not refer to him, the Meiji Government admitted that he was an Emperor and gave him a posthumous name, Koubun. →壬申(じん)の乱

おおとものくろぬし 大伴黒主 〖文芸〗 ?-? One of the Six Immortal Poets. His ten tanka are contained in the *Collection of Ancient and Modern Japanese Poetry* (KOKINWAKASHUU). His biographical details are unknown. →六歌仙

おおとものたびと 大伴旅人 〖文芸〗 665-731. A poet and statesman. Served as the director of the Dazaifu Government Office in present Fukuoka Pref. Contributed about 80 poems to the *Anthology of Myriad Leaves* (MAN'YOUSHUU). The father of OOTOMO NO YAKAMOCHI.

おおとものやかもち 大伴家持 〖文芸〗 718?-785. A poet and statesman. Is thought of as a compiler of the *Anthology of Myriad Leaves* (MAN'YOUSHUU). Contributed 473 poems to it, which is the most among all the poets. The son of OOTOMO NO TABITO.

おおとりじんじゃ 大鳥神社 〖神社〗 an Ootori Shrine. There are several Ootori Shrines, mainly around the Kantou region. Enshrine a legendary hero in Japanese mythology named YAMATO TAKERU NO MIKOTO.

おおとりたいしゃ 大鳥大社 〖神社〗 Ootori Grand Shrine. The head shrine of the Ootori Shrines throughout Japan, located in Sakai, Osaka Pref. Enshrines two deities: a legendary hero in Japanese mythology named YAMATO TAKERU NO MIKOTO, and the ancestor of the local clan in the vicinity.

おおとろ 大トロ 〖食べ物〗 highly

fatty meat of tuna. Is taken from the forward ventral sections.

おおなむちのかみ 大己貴神〖神話〗⇨大国主神(おおくにぬしの かみ)

おおなめまつり 大嘗祭〖天皇・祭礼〗⇨大嘗(だいじょう)祭

おおなるときょう 大鳴門橋〖橋〗 Oonaruto Bridge. Is a suspension bridge connecting Awaji Island in Hyougo Pref. with Naruto City in Tokushima Pref. Was opened to traffic in 1985. Is 876 m long. The whirlpools below the bridge are a popular tourist attraction. →渦潮

おおのじょう 大野城〖城郭〗 Oono Fortress. A Paekche-style mountain fortress in present Fukuoka Pref. Was constructed in 665 to defend the government office called DAZAIFU. Only the ruins remain.

おおのやすまろ 太安万侶〖文芸〗 ?-723. A bureaucrat who recorded the imperial genealogy and mythology, which HIEDA NO ARE recited, and that was included in the *Records of Ancient Matters* (KOJIKI) in 711. Also assisted with the compilation of the *Chronicles of Japan* (NIHONSHOKI).

おおば 大葉〖植物・食べ物〗 a leaf of a beefsteak plant. Is served with sashimi.

おおはらえ 大祓〖神道〗 Grand Purification. Is held at a Shinto shrine or the Imperial Court in July and December to remove uncleanness from all people.

おおはらびじゅつかん 大原美術館〖美術・博物館〗 the Ohara

Museum of Art. Was established in Kurashiki, Okayama Pref., in 1930. Stores Egyptian art, Western paintings such as *Annunciation* by the Spanish painter, El Greco, modern pottery, and Japanese paintings including works by Kojima Torajirou, who also collected many of the art works in this museum.

おおばん 大判〖貨幣〗 a large oval gold coin. Was imprinted with the characters meaning ten RYOU but did not necessarily have the literal value. Was often used as a gift or bonus during the Edo period. →小判

おおばんとう 大番頭〖職業〗 a general manager at a shop in the Edo period. Directed other clerks and apprentices such as BANTOU, TEDAI, and DECCHI.

おおばんやき 大判焼き〖食べ物〗⇨ 今川焼

おおふりそで 大振袖〖服飾〗 a kimono with very long sleeves. Is worn by unmarried young women at a formal ceremony.

おおぼけこぼけ 大歩危小歩危〖地名〗 two gorges along the Yoshino River. Are located on the border between Tokushima and Kouchi Prefs. In Ooboke Gorge, many odd-looking gigantic rocks are exposed. Visitors can enjoy cruising, kayaking, and rafting. Koboke Gorge is located a few kilometers downstream and is also famous for kayaking and rafting.

おおまんどころ 大政所〖政治〗 the

mother of a regent or a supreme adviser to an Emperor. Especially referred to the mother of TOYOTOMI HIDEYOSHI in the 16th century.

おおみそか 大晦日〖暦〗December 31st, or New Year's Eve. People prepare for welcoming the New Year, eat buckwheat noodles, and listen to temple bell tolling.

おおみねさん 大峰山〖山岳・宗教〗the Oomine Mountains. Are located in central Nara Pref. Have been a training place for mountain asceticism. Were designated a World Heritage Site in 2004. →修験道

おおみやびと 大宮人〖天皇・職業〗a courtier at the Imperial Court.

おおみわじんじゃ 大神神社〖神社〗Oomiwa Shrine. Is located in northern Nara Pref. Is dedicated to Oomononushi no kami but has no main sanctuary building because the deity dwells in Mt. Miwa behind the shrine. It is said that this is the oldest form of a shrine.

おおむこう 大向こう〖芸能〗seats right in front of the stage in a theater. It is said that many of the audiences in these seats were connoisseurs of performing arts.

おおむらじ 大連〖官位〗the top administrator in the ancient Imperial Court. Was abolished after the Mononobe clan was exterminated in 587 by the Soga clan.

おおめつけ 大目付〖官位〗a super-inspector or censor in the Tokugawa shogunate. Observed all political affairs and oversaw feudal lords under the command of a minister called ROUJUU.

おおもときょう 大本教〖宗教〗a Shinto-related new religion. Established in 1892 by Deguchi Nao. The headquarters is located in Kameoka, Kyoto Pref.

おおものぬしのかみ 大物主神〖神話〗the deity enshrined in OOMIWA JINJA. The *Records of Ancient Matters* (KOJIKI) says he is a collaborator of OOKUNINUSHI NO KAMI while the *Chronicles of Japan* (NIHONSHOKI) says he is the peaceful divine spirit of dead Ookuninushi. He is also worshipped as a deity of brewing sake.

おおもりかいづか 大森貝塚〖史跡〗Oomori Shell Mound. Was discovered in 1877 by an American zoologist, E. S. Morse. Japanese archaeology started with the excavation of this shell mound.

おおやまつみのかみ 大山津見神〖神話〗the great deity of mountains. A son of IZANAGI NO MIKOTO and IZANAMI NO MIKOTO, and the father of KONOHANA NO SAKUYA HIME.

おおわだつみのかみ 大綿津見神〖神話〗the great deity of oceans. The father of Toyotama-hime and Tamayori-hime. Helped Yamasachi-hiko look for a fishing hook borrowed from Umisachihiko.

おおわにおんせん 大鰐温泉〖温泉〗a hot spring in southern Aomori Pref. Was supposedly discovered in the 12th century. Effective in treating neuralgia and rheumatism. Is close to a ski slope.

おかえりなさい お帰りなさい〖言語〗 a greeting phrase uttered to a person who has just come back. Equivalent to English "Welcome back." ↔ただいま帰りました

おかき おかき〖食べ物〗 a rice cracker. One of the popular confections. Rice cakes cut thin are dried, baked or fried, and seasoned to become 'okaki.' Mostly flavored with soy sauce or salt, but some of them are topped with sugar and taste sweet.

おかぐら 御神楽〖神道・音楽〗 ⇨神楽

おかくらてんしん 岡倉天心〖美術〗 1862-1913. A scholar, art critic, and curator, born in present Yokohama City. Attended a mission school run by Curtis Hepburn, and studied under an American art historian, Ernest Fenollosa, at Tokyo Imperial University. Helped introduce Western ideas to Japan, while also advocating the preservation of national art and culture. In the early 1900s, became a curator of the Asian collection at the Boston Museum of Fine Arts. Main works in English include *The Ideals of the East* in 1903, *The Awakening of Japan* in 1904, and *The Book of Tea* in 1906.

おかげさまで 御蔭様で〖言語〗 "owing to someone's help" or "thanks to good luck." This phrase is uttered even when the speaker does not feel grateful.

おかげまいり 御蔭参り〖神道〗 mass pilgrimage to the Ise Shrine. Spontaneously occurred about every 60 years in the Edo period: namely, the years 1650, 1705, 1771, and 1830. For example, more than two million people visited Ise in 1771, and more than four million in 1830. →ええじゃないか

おがさわらしょとう 小笠原諸島〖島名〗 the Bonin Islands, in Tokyo Pref. Are located in the Pacific Ocean, about 1,200 km south of central Tokyo. Consist of about 30 islands, including Chichi-jima and Haha-jima Islands. Are said to have been discovered by a feudal warrior named Ogasawara Sadayori in 1593. Were under American rule from 1945 to 1968.

おがさわらりゅうれいほう 小笠原流礼法〖礼儀作法〗 Ogasawara-ryu Etiquette. The courtesy and rules of the Ogasawara school. Was established in the Muromachi period, spread in the Edo period, and is still in use at present.

おかしらつき 尾頭付き〖食文化〗 a fish served with head and tail. Usually a sea bream. Is served particularly at celebratory occasions.

おかず 御数〖食文化〗 a dish accompanying rice. Includes both main and side dishes.

おかずぱん おかずパン〖食べ物〗 bread containing fried noodles, curry roux, scrambled eggs, a croquette, etc. Is like a sandwich.

おがたけんざん 尾形乾山 〖芸術〗 1663-1743. A potter and painter, born in Kyoto. The younger brother of a painter, OGATA KOURIN. Learned pottery making under a leading potter, NONOMURA NINSEI. His work varies from raku ware to Kyoto ceramics in a decorative style. Sometimes Kenzan made ceramics, and Kourin painted on them. A British potter, Bernard Leach, who lived in Japan in the 20th century, earned the title of Ogata Kenzan VII.

おがたこうあん 緒方洪庵 〖科学技術〗 1810-1863. A Dutch scholar, doctor, and educator, born in present Okayama Pref. Founded a private school of Dutch learning, named Tekijuku, which produced many important figures of the Meiji Restoration. Also published the first book of pathology in Japan and made an effort to spread vaccinations against smallpox.

おがたこうりん 尾形光琳 〖絵画〗 1658-1716. A painter and designer of handicrafts born in Kyoto. Learned the Kanou school first, was influenced by TAWARAYA SOUTATSU, and founded the Rin school. His works include *Irises* at the Nezu Museum in Tokyo and *Red and White Plum Blossoms* at the MOA (Mokichi Okada Association) Museum of Art in Shizuoka Pref.

おかっぴき 岡っ引き 〖犯罪・職業〗 ⇨目明し

おかでら 岡寺 〖寺院〗 Oka-dera Temple. Affiliated with the Shingon sect. Is located in central Nara Pref. Was founded in 663 by a priest named Gien. The principal object of devotion is the Omnipotent Bodhisattva of Mercy (NYOIRIN-KANNON), which is the largest clay figure in Japan. The image of Gien in this temple is a National Treasure.

おかばしょ 岡場所 〖娯楽・セックス〗 an unauthorized prostitution area in the Edo period. Was located at Fukagawa, Shinagawa, or Shinjuku in Edo. →吉原

おかぼ 陸稲 〖農業・植物〗 dryland rice, or upland rice. Is less tasty than ordinary rice.

おかみ 女将 〖職業〗 the hostess of a traditional inn or restaurant. Manages the customer relations and often holds the rights of administration.

おかめ 阿亀 〖芸能〗 a mask of a round-faced woman with a flat nose and plump cheeks. Appears on the stage of BUNRAKU and Noh farce. In a musical comedy for a Shinto ritual, plays the fool with a funny-faced man, HYOTTOKO. Is said to come from AME NO UZUME in the myth.

おかめそば お亀蕎麦 〖食べ物〗 buckwheat noodles in broth topped with steamed fish paste, dried laver, sliced shiitake mushroom, etc. The toppings are shaped like a woman's face.

おかもち 岡持ち 〖食文化〗 a food

delivery box. Has a lid and a handle.

おかもとたろう 岡本太郎 〖美術〗 1911-1996. A painter and sculptor born in Tokyo. Took part in Abstraction-Creation in Paris. One of his most famous works is *Tower of the Sun*, which was built at Expo '70, the world's fair held in Osaka in 1970.

おかやまけん 岡山県 〖都道府県〗 Okayama Pref. Is located in Western Japan, facing the Inland Sea. Is 7,113 km^2 in area. Its capital is Okayama City. Produces grapes and peaches. Used to be Bizen, Bicchuu, and Mimasaka.

おかやまし 岡山市 〖地名〗 Okayama City. The capital of Okayama Pref. Is located in its central part, facing the Inland Sea. Developed as a castle town of the Ikeda clan. Famous for the Kouraku-en park.

おから 雪花菜 〖食べ物〗 tofu waste, or soy pulp. Is good for health and beauty. Is usually cooked with some vegetables like carrots, seasoned with soy source, sugar, and sake. Is also called 'unohana' or 'kirazu.'

おきあがりこぼし 起き上がり小法師 〖人形〗 a small tumbler doll. Originally a local toy at Aizu in Fukushima Pref.

おきいし 置き石 **(1)**〖庭園〗 a garden stone that serves as an ornament. **(2)**〖碁〗 a stone for handicap. A weaker player sets more than one stone in advance before the go-game begins.

おきく お菊 〖妖怪〗 the heroine of a ghost story entitled SARA-YASHIKI.

おきくるみ オキクルミ 〖少数民族・宗教〗 a hero in the Ainu mythology. Is said to be the ancester of Ainu.

おきしょとう 隠岐諸島 〖島名〗 the Oki Islands. Belong to Shimane Pref. Are located about 45 to 90 km northward off Shimane in the Sea of Japan. Consist of about 180 islands. Were a penal colony, where Emperor Gotoba and Emperor Godaigo were exiled.

おきたそうじ 沖田総司 〖剣術〗 1844 -1868. An expert swordsman. Belonged to a special police unit for guarding Kyoto, called SHINSENGUMI. Though extremely strong, died of tuberculosis.

おきづけ 沖漬け 〖食べ物〗 squid or fish pickled in soy sauce. Literally means "offshore pickles" because it was originally made on the boat immediately after being caught.

おきながたらしひめ 息長足媛 〖天皇〗 another name for JINGUU KOUGOU.

おきなます 沖膾 〖食べ物〗 raw fish sliced on a boat on which the fish has been caught.

おきなわけん 沖縄県 〖都道府県〗 Okinawa Pref. Its capital is Naha City. Is located between Kyushu and Taiwan in the Pacific Ocean. Consists of the Okinawa Islands, the Miyako Islands, the Yaeyama Islands, and other islands. Its area is 2,276 km^2. In the 82-day Battle of Okinawa in 1945, there were huge casualties on both sides, including civilians. Was under American rule from 1945 to 1972 after the war. Most of the U.S. military bases in Japan are in this prefecture. Visitors can enjoy a unique culture and places of historical interest such as Shuri Castle and the remains of Nakijin Castle, in addition to its subtropical climate. Used to be the Ryuukyuu Kingdom. →首里城；今帰仁城（なきじん）

おきなわじま 沖縄島 〔島名〕 Okinawa Island. The main land of Okinawa Pref. Is located in the central part of the Southwest Islands between Kyushu and Taiwan. Its area is 1,208 km^2.

おぎのぎんこ 荻野吟子〔医療〕 1851 -1913. The first woman who passed the examination for medical practitioners and became a doctor.

おきのしま 隠岐の島〔島名〕 ⇨隠岐諸島

おきのしまいせき 沖ノ島遺跡 〔史跡〕 the Okinoshima Ruins. Are located on Okinoshima Island, Fukuoka Pref. Are supposedly a ritual site related to marine transportation. Remains from the 4th to 10th centuries, such as mirrors, accessories, and swords, have been excavated. Were designated a World Heritage Site in 2017.

おきばな 置き花〔華道〕 a flower or flowers arranged in a container on an alcove floor.

おきや 置屋 〔娯楽・セックス〕 a geisha agency. Retains geisha and dispatches them upon request.

おぎゅうそらい 荻生徂徠〔人文学〕 1666-1728. A Confucianist born in Edo. Advised the shogun to severely punish forty-seven masterless samurai from Ako, who avenged the death of their lord. →赤穂浪士

おくいぞめ お食い初め〔通過儀礼〕 ⇨食い初め

おくざしき 奥座敷〔建築〕 a traditional-style tatami room towards the back of a house. This term often metaphorically refers to a spa near an urban area. For example, a spa called Jouzankei is the 'okuzashiki' of Sapporo in Hokkaido. →座敷

おくしゃ 奥社 〔神社〕 an innermost shrine. Is placed far behind the main shrine and enshrines the same deity as the main shrine.

おくじょちゅう 奥女中〔武士・生活〕 a housemaid working for a shogun or feudal lord in the Edo period.

おくつき 奥津城〔冠婚葬祭・神道〕 a Shinto-style grave. Its shape is different from a Buddhist one. For example, the top may be like a pyramid, or the entire form may be like a small shrine.

おくのいん 奥ノ院〔寺院・神社〕 an innermost sanctum. Is placed far behind the main building, deep inside a Buddhist temple or Shinto shrine. Sometimes contains the image of the founder.

おくのほそみち 奥の細道 〔文芸・

作品』 *The Narrow Road to the Interior*. A travel diary with haiku written in 1702 by Matsuo Bashou. He walked around Northern Japan with his disciple in 1689.

おくみ 衽〘服飾〙 a front gusset below the collar of a kimono.

おくやみ お悔み〘冠婚葬祭・言語〙 ⇨ 悔やみ

おぐらあん 小倉餡〘食べ物〙 mixture of sieved sweet adzuki paste and sweet simmered adzuki grains.

おぐらひゃくにんいっしゅ 小倉百人一首〘文芸・娯楽〙 ⇨百人一首

おくりがな 送り仮名〘漢字〙 a kana or kanas added next to a kanji to define how it is read.

おくりだし 送り出し〘相撲〙 push-out from behind. A sumo technique of pushing out the opponent from behind, with or without holding his belt.

おくりび 送り火〘仏教〙 a fire to send off the spirits of the ancestors. Is lit at the house gate on the last evening of the Bon Festival. ↔迎え火 →盂蘭盆会(うらぼんえ)

おくりぼん 送り盆〘仏教〙 the last day of the Bon Festival. The spirits of the ancestors depart their homes. →盂蘭盆会(うらぼんえ)

おくるみ 御包み〘服飾〙 swaddling cloth for a baby to protect against the cold.

おけ 桶〘生活〙 a wooden tub or pail. Some are deep, and others are shallow, depending on their use. Sometimes has a lid or a handle. →寿司桶；天水桶；湯桶

おけはざまのたたかい 桶狭間の戦い〘戦争〙 Battle of Okehazama. In 1560, Oda Nobunaga made a surprise attack on Imagawa Yoshimoto, who led a massive army on the way to Kyoto. This victory became the first step for Nobunaga to unify the nation.

おけらまいり おけら参り 〘祭礼〙 visiting the Okera Festival. 'Okera' is a herb burnt in the festival, and people bring back the fire at the end of a hand-held cord to light a candle on the home altar. The festival is held at Yasaka Shrine in Kyoto from December 31 to January 1.

おこげ お焦げ〘食べ物〙 crisp bits of burnt rice. Stick to the bottom when rice is boiled in a ceramic or iron pot.

おこし 粔籹〘食べ物〙 a crisp rice cookie. There are several types such as awa-okoshi, iwa-okoshi, and kaminari-okoshi.

おこぜ 虎魚〘食べ物・魚〙 ⇨鬼虎魚(おに
おこぜ)

おこそずきん 御高祖頭巾〘服飾〙 a headscarf. Was worn against the cold weather from the 18th to 19th centuries.

おこのみやき お好み焼き〘食べ物〙 a Japanese-style savory pancake. Has a variety of ingredients, such as cabbage, bean sprouts, green onions, seafood, and pork. Is brushed with a kind of teriyaki sauce and sprinkled with dried bonito flakes and the powder of dried sea lettuce.

おこもり 御籠り〔神道・仏教〕 voluntary confinement in a shrine or temple. The duration varies from one night to one thousand days, and the purposes vary. Examples include prayer, ascetic practice, or purification before a ritual.

おこわ お強〔食べ物〕 glutinous rice steamed with adzuki. Is sometimes cooked with other beans, edible wild plants, or seafood.

おさえこみ 抑え込み〔柔道〕 holding techniques. Include kamishihou-gatame, yokoshihou-gatame, and KESA-GATAME.

おざきこうよう 尾崎紅葉〔文芸〕 1867–1903. A novelist born in Tokyo. Dropped out of Tokyo Imperial Univ. Is said to be realistic, in contrast to his contemporary, Kouda Rohan, who is said to be idealistic. His works include *The Golden Demon*. →金色夜叉(こんじきやしゃ)

おざしき お座敷〔娯楽〕 a banquet to which a geisha or other entertainer is called. This term is used by a geisha or entertainer.

おしあゆ 押し鮎〔食べ物〕 a salted sweetfish. Eaten at the New Year celebration.

おしいれ 押入れ〔生活・建築〕 a traditional closet with sliding doors. Is usually 180 cm wide and 90 cm deep, namely the same size as a TATAMI mat, and has two tiers.

おしえ 押し絵〔美術〕 an embossed picture. Usually depicts flowers, birds, or persons in color.

おしき 折敷〔食文化・神道〕 a square wooden tray with rims. Is used for a Shinto ritual or tea ceremony cuisine.

おじぎ お辞儀〔礼儀作法〕 a bow. Japanese people often bow for various purposes such as greeting, gratitude, favor, and apology. Depending on the degree of courtesy, the angle of the upper body differs. The deeper the bow, the greater the degree of courtesy or deference.

おしずし 押し寿司〔食べ物〕 pressed sushi. Vinegared rice and fish are pressed into a rectangular wooden frame and cut into a bite-sized pieces. Was started in Osaka.

おしたおし 押し倒し〔相撲〕 frontal push-down. A sumo technique of pushing down the opponent.

おしだし 押し出し〔相撲〕 frontal push-out. A sumo technique of pushing out the opponent without holding his belt.

おしちや お七夜〔通過儀礼〕 ⇨七夜

おしどり 鴛鴦 **(1)**〔動物〕 a mandarin duck. *Aix galericulata*. A pair of them is considered a symbol for the affection of a couple. **(2)**〔髪〕 a traditional hairstyle for a young daughter of a merchant in early modern times.

おしぶた 押し蓋〔食文化〕 a lid to press down the pickles in a jar.

おしぼり お絞り〔食文化〕 a small wet towel for guests to wipe their hands at a meal. Cold in summer and hot in other seasons. Is often put on a special tray at a restaurant.

おじや おじや〔食べ物〕 ⇨雑炊

おじゅけん お受験〔教育〕 taking an entrance exam. This term is often used to ridicule the case in which a small child at a rich family takes an entrance exam for a famous kindergarten or elementary school.

おしょう 和尚〔仏教〕 a senior priest. This pronunciation, 'oshou,' is used only in Zen Buddhism and the Pure Land sect. Although they use the same kanji, the Tendai and Kegon sects pronounce 'kashou,' and the Hossou and Shingon sects pronounce 'wajou.' →和上(じょう)

おしょうばん お相伴〔食文化〕 to have a meal together with one's superior.

おしらさま オシラサマ〔宗教〕 pair of deities of sericulture in northeastern Japan. The single ends of two mulberry rods about 30 cm long are carved into faces and wrapped with layers of cloth.

おしらす お白洲〔犯罪〕 ⇨白洲

おしん おしん〔テレビ〕 *Oshin*. A serialized TV drama aired from April 1983 to March 1984. Depicts the life of a woman born into a poor farm family. Recorded a yearly average audience rating of 52.6%, which was considered high.

おしんこ お新香〔食べ物〕 pickled vegetables. Originally refers to lightly pickled ones. →浅漬け

おぜ 尾瀬〔地名〕 an area with a marshland on the border between Fukushima and Gunma Prefs. Is located at the altitude of 1,400 m, at the foot of Mt. Hiuchi-ga-take (2,356 m) in Fukushima Pref. The plants such as white skunk cabbages called 'mizu-bashou' and yellow alpine lilies called 'Nikko-kisuge' are popular among hikers. It is said that the song named *Natsu no Omoide* made Oze well-known when it was first broadcast on NHK in 1949. Accessible by bus, with a 2.5-hour ride from Joumou Kougen Station on Joetsu Shinkansen, or with a 2-hour ride from Aizukougen Ozeguchi Station on Yagantetsudou Railway and Aizu Railway. A direct bus service connects Oze with Tokyo or Shinjuku Stations in 4 to 6 hours.

おせいぼ 御歳暮〔生活〕 a year-end gift. People send gifts as a token of gratitude in December to those who have given great support.

おせちりょうり 御節料理 〔食文化〕 special dishes served during the first three days of the New Year. A variety of ingredients are artistically arranged in a set of three-tiered lacquered boxes called JUUBAKO. The first tier, 'ichi-no-juu,' holds various hors d'oeuvre, such as boiled fish paste in red and white, salmon and herring roes, red and white pickles, black beans, and sweet potatoes mixed with chestnuts. The second tier, 'ni-no-juu,' holds grilled fish and meat such as broiled sea bream, salmon, prawns, chicken, etc. The third tier, 'san-no-juu,' holds boiled vegetables such as Japanese radish, taro potatoes, lotus roots, bamboo shoots, and lily bulbs. Historically there used to be the fourth and fifth tiers, but nowadays three-tiered boxes are most common.

おそなえ 御供え〘仏教・神道〙 an offering to a Buddha, a deity, or a deceased spirit. Usually food, alcohol, or flowers are offered.

おそれざん 恐山〘山岳〙 Mt. Osore. An active volcano, located in the center of the Shimokita Peninsula in northeastern Aomori Pref. Its height is 828 m. It is said that many necromancers called ITAKO call up the spirits of the dead at this location.

おたいこ 御太鼓〘服飾〙 a way of fastening the decorative broad sash for a female kimono, which looks like a drum.

おだきゅうでんてつ 小田急電鉄〘鉄道〙 Odakyu Electric Railway. Connects Tokyo city proper with western and southern Kanagawa Pref., by use of three lines and 70 stations. Is well-known for its limited express trains, called the Romancecar which runs from its Shinjuku terminal in Tokyo to holiday spots such as Odawara, Hakone, Enoshima, and the Tanzawa Mountains. Other express and local trains are mainly for commuters. Near Shinjuku, it shares tracks with one of the Tokyo Metro lines. At the other end of the Odakyu main line is Odawara,

where Romancecar continues on the Hakone Tozan Railway to take tourists directly to the hot spring resorts in Hakone.

おたく お宅〘精神性〙 a geek. Has plenty of knowledge about specific fields in pop culture such as anime or TV games. Is usually not good at communication with those who are not interested in his or her field.

おだのぶなが 織田信長〘武士〙 1534 -1582. A feudal lord born in present Aichi Pref. Attempted to unify medieval Japan. First, defeated IMAGAWA YOSHIMOTO at Okehazama in present Aichi Pref. in 1560. In alliance with TOKUGAWA IEYASU, defeated AZAI NAGAMASA and ASAKURA YOSHIKAGE at Anegawa in present Shiga Pref. in 1570. Burned Enryaku-ji Temple in 1571. Purged the 15th Muromachi shogun, Ashikaga Yoshiaki, in 1573. Defeated TAKEDA KATSUYORI at Nagashino in present Aichi Pref. in 1575. Killed himself at Honnou-ji Temple in Kyoto by the rebellion of his vassal, AKECHI MITSUHIDE.

おたびしょ 御旅所〘神道〙 a temporary station of a deity. A portable shrine stops here while being carried around the parish on festival days.

おたふく 阿多福〘芸能〙 ⇨阿亀(おかめ)

おたふくまめ お多福豆〘食べ物〙 a boiled and sweetened broad bean. Traditionally has been said to bring happiness because its round-shape evokes the face of a plump woman, named 'otafuku,' which means "a lot of happiness."

おたま 御玉 〚食文化〛 a ladle.

おだまきむし 小田巻き蒸し 〚食べ物〛 cup-steamed savory custard with thick wheat noodles. Was originally high-class cuisine in the Kansai region.

おだまこと 小田実 〚文芸〛 1932 -2007. A novelist and literature critic born in Osaka. In 1965, established a civic movement group, 'Beheiren,' whose English name is "Citizen's Federation for Peace in Vietnam." His works include *H: A Hiroshima Novel* in 1981.

おたまや 御霊屋 〚宗教〛 ⇨御霊屋（みたまや）

おだみきお 織田幹雄 〚スポーツ〛 1905-1998. An athlete born in Hiroshima. Participated the triple jump at the Amsterdam Olympic Games in 1928 and won the first Olympic gold medal ever received by a Japanese athlete.

おだわらちょうちん 小田原提灯 〚生活〛 a cylindrical foldable paper lantern. Was invented in Odawara, present Kanagawa Pref., in the 16th century.

おち オチ 〚落語〛 a punchline uttered at the end of the traditional comic story called RAKUGO. There are several types, such as a pun, a riddle, and even a gesture without words. Is also called 'sage.'

おちあゆ 落ち鮎 〚魚〛 a sweetfish going downstream for spawning in autumn.

おちくぼものがたり 落窪物語 〚文芸・作品〛 *The Tale of the Lady Ochikubo*. Was written in the late 10th century. Consists of four volumes. The author is unknown. The heroine, Lady Ochikubo, was ill-treated by her stepmother, but she finally got married happily.

おちむしゃ 落ち武者 〚武士〛 a defeated fugitive from a war.

おちゃうけ お茶請け 〚食文化〛 ⇨茶請（ちゃうけ）

おちゅうげん お中元 〚年中行事〛 a summer gift. People send a gift as a token of gratitude in July to those who have given great support.

おちゅうど 落人 〚武士〛 a defeated warrior in hiding. There are several legends throughout Japan that Taira fugitives from the war with the Minamoto clan in the 12th century lived in a village far from populous areas. →平家

おつ 乙 〚干支〛 ⇨乙（きのと）

おつかれさまでした お疲れ様でした 〚精神性・言語〛 "It has been a hard time." This phrase is used after people finish working, studying, exercising, or practicing, or as they prepare to go home.

おづやすじろう 小津安二郎 〚映画〛 1903-1963. A film director born in Tokyo. His works include *Tokyo Story* (Tokyo monogatari) in 1953 and *Taste of Pacific Saury* (Sanma no aji) in 1962.

おてだま お手玉 〚遊び〛 beanbags, or a child's game with beanbags. The player throws two or three beanbags and catches them in turn, usually while singing a song.

おてつき 御手付き 〖遊び〗 to pick up a wrong card in a matching card game called KARUTA.

おてふき 御手拭 〖食文化〗 a wet hand towel or paper towel. Is often served before meal at a restaurant or on a luxurious train car.

おてまえ 御点前〖茶道〗 ⇨手前

おでん おでん 〖食べ物〗 stew in a light soy-sauce-flavored broth. Consists of several ingredients such as boiled eggs, white radish, konjac, deep-fried tofu, and processed fish cakes. Is popular in winter.

おとおし お通し 〖食文化〗 an hors d'oeuvre at a traditional-style pub. Is automatically served immediately after a customer takes a seat. Its price is added to the customer's bill, although it is not ordered.

おとぎぞうし 御伽草子 〖文芸〗 a group of popular short stories from the 14th to 16th centuries. Many of them are fanciful or instructive. Examples are ISSUN-BOUSHI and URASHIMA TAROU.

おとこざか 男坂 〖交通〗 a steeper slope leading to a shrine or temple on a hill. Is shorter but harder. Literally means "male slope." ↔女坂

おとこはつらいよ 男はつらいよ〖映画・作品〗 a series of Tora-san films. Literally means "It's tough being a man." The kind but bumbling folk hero, Tora-san, who comes from Shibamata in Katsushika, Tokyo, wanders throughout Japan as a street vendor. He always comes across an attractive woman, loses in love, and returns home. The leading actor is ATSUMI KIYOSHI, and the director is Yamada Youji. Forty-eight episodes in more than 20 years were produced, and the series was recognized as the longest movie series in the world by the *Guinness Book of Records*.

おとこやまはちまんぐう 男山八幡宮 〖神社〗 ⇨石清水(いわしみず)八幡宮

おとしざし 落とし差し 〖武器〗 wearing a sword casually at the belt. The sword hangs down diagonally or almost vertically.

おとしだま お年玉 〖年中行事〗 a New Year gift of money. Is usually handed in a special envelope from parents or relatives to children.

おとしだまつきねんがはがき お年玉付き年賀はがき 〖年中行事〗 ⇨年賀はがき

おとたちばなひめ 弟橘媛〖神話〗 a wife of YAMATOTAKERU NO MIKOTO. It is said she pacified the wrath of the ocean god by throwing herself into the sea when Yamatotakeru went across the present Tokyo bay. After her death, the sea became calm.

おとひめ 乙姫 〖民話〗 the heroine of a fairy tale similar to Rip van Winkle. Welcomed the hero named Tarou at the Sea God's palace, to which a turtle had invited him. When Tarou went home, Otohime presented him with a box. When he opened the box, mysterious smoke arose from it, and he became a gray-haired old man.

おどりぐい 踊り食い〖食文化〗 eating live seafood such as ice gobies, shrimps, and squids, while still moving. →素魚(しらうお)

おどりじ 踊り字〖言語〗 a symbol for repeating the prior character or characters. For example, "people" can be translated into 人々, with the second character being a repetition symbol. In other words, 人々 is equal to 人人, but usually the former is used.

おどりねんぶつ 踊念仏 〖仏教〗 prayers to Buddha or chants of sutra while dancing. Were begun by a priest, KUUYA, and became popular among ordinary people from the 10th to 13th centuries. →念仏

おなりもん 御成門〖建築〗 a special gate for the shogun. When entering a feudal lord's mansion or a large temple, the shogun used this gate. Other people were not allowed to pass through it.

おに 鬼〖妖怪〗 a demon. Has horns like a bull, fangs like a tiger, and a human body in red or blue skin. Wears a loincloth made of tiger skin and carries an iron rod. Is usually harmful but sometimes is helpful to people, using superhuman powers in various stories such as folktales or legends.

おにおこぜ 鬼虎魚〖魚〗 a devil stinger, or Japanese goblinfish. *Inimicus japonicus*. Eaten as sashimi or soup ingredients in winter.

おにがらやき 鬼殻焼き〖食べ物〗 a roasted lobster or prawn with its shell on. Is seasoned with soy sauce and mirin.

おにがわら 鬼瓦〖建築〗 a ridge-end tile of a house roof. Often has a demon face to keep away evil spirits.

おにぎり お握り〖食べ物〗 a rice ball. Often has a triangular shape. Is usually wrapped in dried laver or sprinkled with sesame seeds. Sometimes has a filling such as a pickled plum or salty salmon.

おにこうべおんせん 鬼首温泉〖温泉〗 hot springs in northern Miyagi Pref. Famous for geysers.

おにころし 鬼殺し〖酒〗 a brand name of sake. Literally means "demon killer," suggesting that it is so tasty that even a demon would drink too much and be drunk. Many brewers use this name for their sake because the first brewer did not register it as a trade mark.

おにのせんたくいた 鬼の洗濯板〖地名〗 sea-eroded rock formation named "Devil's Washboard." Surrounds Aoshima Island in Miyazaki Pref. Was designated a Natural Monument in 1934.

おにはそとふくはうち 鬼は外！福は内！〖年中行事・言語〗 ⇨福は内！鬼は外！

おにばば 鬼婆〖妖怪〗 a mythic ogress, or a demon hag. The one living in Adachigahara, Fukushima Pref., ate the flesh of passing travelers.

おにわばん 御庭番〔忍者〕 a secret agent under a Tokugawa shogun in the Edo period. Was established by TOKUGAWA YOSHIMUNE and placed under the direct control of the shogun. The official job was to guard the garden of Edo Castle, but the agent sometimes reported observations about Edo and secretly inspected other provinces.

おのだひろお 小野田寛郎 〔戦争〕 1922-2014. An army soldier born in Wakayama Pref. Did not believe that Japan surrendered in World War II and continued to hide himself for 30 years in an island in the Philippines.

おののいもこ 小野妹子〔外交〕 ?-? The first diplomat in ancient times. Was dispatched to the Sui dynasty in China in 607 by Prince Shoutoku. →聖徳太子

おののこまち 小野小町〔文芸〕 ?-? One of the Six Immortal Poets and one of the Thirty-six Immortal Poets. Her 17 tanka are contained in the *Collection of Ancient and Modern Japanese Poetry* (KOKIN-WAKASHUU). Is said to have been a woman of great beauty who appeared in many legends. →六歌仙；三十六歌仙

おのみちし 尾道市〔地名〕 Onomichi City. Is located in southeastern Hiroshima Pref. Is called "the City of Slopes," because of its many slopes, even near the coast. Is also called "the City of Literature" and "the City of Movies," because it is the setting for many novels and movies. Famous writers such as HAYASHI FUMIKO and SHIGA NAOYA once lived here. Has many temples on its hillside and many islands in the Inland Sea. Navel oranges and figs are produced in large quantities. Is the starting point of the Shimanami Expressway.

おはぎ お萩〔食べ物〕 a glutinous rice ball coated with sweet adzuki paste. Some are covered with sesame or soybean flour. The same food used to be called 'ohagi' in the vernal equinoctial week and 'botamochi' in the autumnal equinoctial week.

おはぐろ 鉄漿〔生活・服飾〕 dark-brown liquid to blacken teeth. Was made by putting an iron tip into strong tea with a little sake. This custom was mainly for women, though it was done by men in medieval times. It was prohibited after the Meiji Restoration.

おはじき お弾き〔遊び〕 a finger-flicking game, or the small glass disk used in the game. Is mainly played by girls.

おばすてやま 姨捨て山〔民話〕 ⇨姥(うば)捨て山

おばな 尾花〔植物〕 ⇨すすき

おばまし 小浜市〔地名〕 Obama City. Is located in western Fukui Pref., facing the Sea of Japan. Developed as a port town leading to Kyoto and has many shrines and temples. The Water-Sending Ceremony, called OMIZU-OKURI, is held at Jinguu-ji Temple on March 2, during which the sacred water poured into an adjacent river is said to be drawn up at Toudai-ji Temple in Nara. The main hall and the pagoda at Myoutsuu-ji Temple are National Treasures.

おはらい お祓い〚神道〛 purification or exorcism. Is performed by a Shinto priest. Generally, people provide a fee. Occasions for requesting the ceremony include reaching an unlucky age and buying a car, in hopes that good fortune and good health will result.

おはらりゅう 小原流〚華道〛 Ohara School of Ikebana. Was founded in 1912 by Ohara Unshin, who had belonged to the Ikenobo school.

おばんざい 御番菜〚食文化〛 Kyoto-style, home-cooked dishes. Have been cooked at home in Kyoto for a long time. Recipes passed down through the generations feature seasonal ingredients.

おび 帯〚服飾〛 a decorative broad sash tightened around the waist when wearing a kimono. Has wide variations depending on the wearer, kimono, and situations.

おびあげ 帯揚げ〚服飾〛 long cloth to support an obi knot and to adjust its shape when a woman wears a kimono. The wearer rolls a small cushion called OBIMAKURA and places it underneath an obi on the back.

おびいた 帯板〚服飾〛 a small board slipped between the front folds of an obi or placed on the abdomen so that an obi should not be wrinkled.

おびいわい 帯祝い〚生活〛 a ceremony to wish an easy delivery in the fifth month of pregnancy. The pregnant woman wears a special sash called IWATA-OBI.

おびじ 帯地〚服飾〛 cloth for an obi.

おびじめ 帯締め〚服飾〛 a cord to keep the shape and position of an obi. Is fastened on the surface of the obi.

おびしん 帯芯〚服飾〛 thick cotton cloth inside an obi to maintain its shape.

おひたし 御浸し〚食べ物〛 a boiled vegetable dipped in sauce. Dried bonito flakes or sesame seeds are sometimes sprinkled on it. Various vegetables are used, depending on the season.

おひつ お櫃〚食器〛 a wooden tub to serve boiled rice. Some are made of unvarnished wood, and some are lacquered. →米櫃

おびどめ 帯留め〚服飾〛 an ornamental accessory for a kimono. An obi cord called OBI-JIME is passed through it.

おびな 男雛〚年中行事・人形〛 a doll of an Emperor. Is displayed side by side with an Empress doll on the top tier of a platform during the Girls' Festival in March.

おひなさま 御雛様〚年中行事・人形〛 ⇨雛人形

おひねり 御捻り〚生活〛 a monetary gift or tip wrapped in twisted white paper.

おびひも 帯紐〚服飾〛 a generic

term for an obi and small items to fasten it when wearing a kimono.

おびまくら 帯枕 〖服飾〗 a small cushion to support an obi knot and to adjust its shape when a woman wears a kimono. Is rolled with the long cloth called OBIAGE and is placed underneath an obi on the back.

おひゃくどまいり お百度参り 〖宗教〗 ⇨百度参り

おひろめ 御披露目 〖芸能・ビジネス〗 a public announcement of celebration. For example, a kabuki actor holds a ceremony to announce his succession to a stage name.

おふせ 御布施 〖仏教〗 gratuity to a monk, a nun, or a temple. Sometimes is food.

おへんろさん お遍路さん 〖仏教〗 ⇨ 遍路

おほおつくぶんか オホーツク文化 〖時代〗 Okhotsk Culture. People lived by hunting and fishing in the coastal areas of northern and eastern Hokkaido, southern Sakhalin Island, and the southern Kuril Islands from the 6th to 11th centuries. Is said to have been influenced by continental cultures and belongs to a different group from cultures in Japan proper. →縄文文化；擦文(ᵉ)文化

おぼろ 朧 〖食べ物〗 minced and simmered fish. Is seasoned with salt and sugar and is sometimes colored with food red. Pale flesh fish is often used.

おぼろどうふ 朧豆腐 〖食べ物〗 half-curdled tofu. Is mostly served cold with soy sauce.

おぼん お盆 〖仏教〗 ⇨盂蘭盆会(ᵘ ᵃ ᵇ); 盆休み

おまいり お参り 〖仏教・神道〗 visiting a person's grave, a Buddhist temple, or a Shinto shrine.

おまかせ おまかせ 〖食文化〗 a chef's choice course. Is sometimes offered at a traditional restaurant or sushi bar. The guest does not have to choose from the menu, and various types of food are served.

おまち 雄町 〖酒・植物〗 a kind of rice for sake. A chief producing area is Okayama Pref. →酒米(ᵉ ᵃ)

おまもり お守り 〖神道・仏教〗 a talisman. Is covered with decorative cloth and sold at a Shinto shrine or Buddhist temple. Inside is a small wooden tablet with a name or an image of the Buddha or deity, mantra, etc.

おみ 臣 〖政治・言語〗 a title given to a high-ranking clan in ancient times. Was attached after the clan name such as 'Soga no omi.'

おみおつけ 御御御付け 〖食べ物〗 a polite term for miso soup. →味噌汁

おみき 御神酒 〖神道・酒〗 sake offered to a Shinto deity. Is usually drunk afterward by those who have attended the ritual.

おみくじ お御籤 〖神社・寺院〗 a fortune slip. People draw it at a Shinto shrine or Buddhist temple and tie it to a branch of a tree in the precinct after it is read. The best fortune is called 'daikichi,' while the worst is called 'daikyou.'

おみこし 御神輿 〚神道〛 ⇨神輿

おみずおくり お水送り 〚仏教〛 the Water-Sending Ceremony. Is held on March 2 at Jinguu-ji Temple in Obama, Fukui Pref. It is said that the sacred water poured into the nearby Onyu River is drawn up in the Water-Drawing Ceremony, called OMIZU-TORI, held at Toudai-ji Temple in Nara.

おみずとり お水取り 〚仏教〛 the Water-Drawing Ceremony. Is held from the late night of March 12th to the early morning of the 13th at Nigatsu-dou of the Toudai-ji Temple. Monks extend large torches from the terrace of the hall, draw water from the well named Wakasa-i, and offer it to the Eleven-headed Bodhisattva of Mercy in the hall. →お水送り

おみなえし 女郎花 〚植物〛 a maiden flower. *Patrinia scabiosaefolia*. Small yellow flowers bloom from summer to autumn. One of the seven flowers in autumn. →秋の七草

おむすび おむすび 〚食べ物〛 ⇨おにぎり

おむそば オムそば 〚食べ物〛 stir-fried noodles flavored with Worcester sauce and covered with a thin omelette.

おむらいす オムライス 〚食べ物〛 ketchup-flavored fried rice wrapped in a thin omelette. Is said to have been invented at a restaurant named Rengatei in Tokyo or at Hokkyokusei in Osaka. Both are still in operation.

おめみえいじょう 御目見え以上 〚武士〛 a rank of samurai who is allowed to meet the shogun, in the Edo period.

おもあど 主アド 〚狂言〛 the major partner of the main character in a play when there are two partners. →アド

おもがし 主菓子 〚茶道〛 unbaked sweets served with thick powdered green tea. →濃茶

おもづかい 主遣い 〚文楽〛 a main puppeteer in BUNRAKU. Operates the head and the right arm of a puppet. →三人遣い

おもてせんけ 表千家 〚茶道〛 the Omotesenke school. One of the three SENKE schools in tea ceremony.

おもてなし おもてなし 〚精神性・ビジネス〛 cordial hospitality, or a hearty welcome. This term has become very popular in the sightseeing business, after being used as a catchphrase in a presentation to invite the 2020 Olympic Games to Tokyo.

おもてみごろ 表身頃 〚服飾〛 the outer cloth of the main part of a kimono. ↔裏身頃

おもや 母屋 〚建築〛 the main building of a large residence. ↔離れ

おもゆ 重湯 〚食べ物〛 liquid of rice gruel for a sick person.

おやかた 親方 〚職業〛 a master or boss in a traditional artisan society or a sumo stable.

おやき 御焼き〚食べ物〛 a round-shaped muffin containing various kinds of ingredients such as sweet adzuki or pickles of turnip leaves.

おやこどん 親子丼〚食べ物〛 a bowl of rice topped with soy sauce and sugar, seasoned chicken, egg, and vegetables. 'Oyako' means parents and children. Is named after the two ingredients, chicken and egg, because they are parents and children.

おやしお 親潮〚海洋〛 the Kuril current. A large cold current around Japan. Literally means "parent seawater" because it has abundant plankton that helps create fine fishing grounds. Starts in the Bering Sea and flows along the coast of northeastern Japan toward the south. ↔黒潮

おやじぎゃぐ 親父ギャグ〚言語・遊び〛 a sick joke or unfunny pun. Literally means "middle-aged man's joke" because many older men like it.

おやつ お八つ〚食文化〛 a snack. 'Yatsu' means "eight," which referred to three o'clock in a traditional time-counting because people eat snacks around three p.m.

おやぶん 親分〚精神性〛 a boss. Often refers to a boss of gangsters called yakuza.

おやま 女形〚歌舞伎〛 ⇨女形(おんながた)

おゆわり お湯割り〚酒〛 ⇨湯割り

おりがみ 折り紙 **(1)**〚遊び〛 origami, or the art of folding paper. People can make various objects such as a crane, a warrior's helmet, a boat, and a wallet by folding a piece of square colored paper, usually without cutting or pasting. **(2)**〚芸術・武器〛 a certificate of authenticity for paintings, calligraphy, ceramics, and swords.

おりぐちしのぶ 折口信夫〚人文学〛 1887-1953. A researcher of Japanese literature and folklore, born in Osaka Pref. Developed the folklore study under YANAGITA KUNIO. Also composed poems himself.

おりたたみじゅうじしゅりけん 折り畳み十字手裏剣〚忍者〛 a foldable, cross-shaped shuriken. Its blade parts can be folded.

おりづめ 折詰〚食文化〛 foods packed in a wooden box. Are catered for luncheon meetings, school events, and ceremonial occasions such as the coming of age, marriage, funeral, and memorial service. Usually contains food for one person and can be taken out.

おりづる 折り鶴〚遊び〛 a paper crane. The most popular ORIGAMI. →千羽鶴

おりひめ 織姫〚伝説〛 Vega. Literally means "weaving girl." In a Chinese legend, fell in love with Hikoboshi (Altair) and was allowed to meet him, crossing the Milky Way only on the day of the Star Festival, July 7. →七夕

おりべやき 織部焼〚陶磁器〛 Oribe ware. Pottery produced in eastern Gifu Pref. in the late 16th century.

Named after FURUTA ORIBE, a tea master. Famous for its unique design and style. Glaze colors and its combination produce diverse patterns of Oribe ware.

おれいまいり お礼参り〖仏教・神道〗 revisiting a temple or shrine to offer thanks. People visit a temple or shrine again when their wish from the last visit is realized.

おろしあえ 卸し和え〖食べ物〗 vegetable, mushroom, or seafood salad dressed with grated white radish.

おろしがね 卸し金〖食文化〗 a flat grater for vegetables. →大根卸し；紅葉卸

おろししょうが 卸し生姜〖調味料〗 grated ginger. Is added to various foods such as chilled tofu, grilled eggplant, and thin wheat noodles like vermicell.

おろしそば 卸し蕎麦〖食べ物〗 cold buckwheat noodles topped with grated spicy white radish.

おろち 大蛇〖神話・動物〗 a monster serpent. Appears in legend and myth. →八岐大蛇(やまたの おろち)

おわり 尾張〖旧国名〗 the old name of western Aichi Pref.

おんきゅう 温灸〖医療〗 indirect moxibustion. To avoid the scar of moxibustion, some other items such as salt, garlic, or soybean paste are inserted between moxa and skin, or moxa is put in a special container.

おんぎょうじゅつ 隠形術〖忍者〗 techniques for hiding oneself. →観音隠れ；ウズラ隠れ

おんしゅうのかなたに 恩讐の彼方に〖文芸・作品〗 *Beyond the Pale of Vengeance*. A short story published in 1919 by KIKUCHI KAN. To make amends for his previous wrongdoings, a priest, Ryoukai, who used to be a robber, digs a tunnel at a dangerous spot, for travelers to pass through it safely. Although a young man whose father was killed by Ryoukai came for revenge, the young man ultimately did not kill Ryoukai.

おんじょうじ 園城寺〖寺院〗 Onjo-ji Temple. Is also called Miidera. The head temple of the Jimon school of the Tendai sect, located in southern Shiga Pref. Is said to have been founded in the 7th century and revived in the 9th century by a priest named ENCHIN. Possesses several National Treasures including the main hall, a portrait of Enchin, and a painting of the Immovable Wisdom King, called KI-FUDOU.

おんすいせんじょうべんざ 温水洗浄便座〖家具〗 a toilet seat with an automatic bidet. Washes one's bottom with warm water after defecation.

おんせん 温泉〖風呂〗 a hot spring, or a spa. Many spas are scattered throughout the country, and people enjoy staying at a hot spring inn that serves traditional-style dinner and breakfast. Some hot springs are effective in treating chronic diseases. Famous spas include Arima in Hyougo Pref., Kusatsu in Gunma

Pref., Gero in Gifu Pref., Shirahama in Wakayama Pref., Dougo in Ehime Pref., and Beppu in Ooita Pref.

おんせんたまご　温泉卵〖食べ物〗 a half-boiled egg in broth.

おんせんのもと　温泉の素　〖風呂〗 spa-inspired bath products. Do not necessarily copy the qualities or features of a hot spring, but have some effects such as recovery from exhaustion and relaxation of muscles and joints.

おんせんりょかん　温泉旅館〖風呂・旅〗　a hot spring inn. Has a hot spring inside the grounds, which is called UCHIYU.

おんたけさん　御嶽山〖山岳〗　Mt. Ontake. Is an active volcano located between Nagano and Gifu Prefs., near the southern tip of the North Alps. Is 3,067 m high. A phreatic eruption of groundwater occurred in September 2014, and 58 lives were lost. It was Japan's worst volcanic accident after World War II.

おんだんしつじゅんきこう　温暖湿潤気候〖自然〗 a temperate humid climate. All areas excepting Hokkaido and high mountaneous regions have this climate.

おんどのせと　音戸の瀬戸〖地名〗 a channel in Kure City in southern Hiroshima Pref., between Honshuu Island and Kurahashi Island. Taira no Kiyomori is said to have opened the waterway in 1167, and it was used for maritime trade between Japan and the Sung dynasty. Is now a busy waterway because the ferries connecting Hiroshima City with Matsuyama City in Ehime Pref. regularly go through this narrow channel, which is only 90 m wide.

おんながた　女形〖歌舞伎〗 a female impersonator. In kabuki, a female role has been played by a male actor since female actors were banned from playing on the stage by the Tokugawa shogunate in 1629. Is also called 'oyama.' The leading actor of 'onnagata' in a theatrical troupe is called 'tate-oyama,' and an actor who plays only female roles is called 'ma-onnagata.'

おんなざか　女坂　〖交通〗　a less steep slope leading to a shrine or temple on a hill. Is longer but gentler. Literally means "female slope." ↔男坂

おんなへん　女偏〖漢字〗 a left-side radical meaning "woman." Kanji examples with this radical include 婦(lady), 姉(elder sister), and 姫 (princess).

おんばしらまつり　御柱祭〖神社・祭礼〗　Sacred Pillar Festival. Is held at Suwa Grand Shrines in Nagano Pref. in the spring of the Years of the Tiger and the Monkey. Eight large fir logs are cut down in the mountain, drawn to the Upper and Lower Shrines, and erected in the four corners of the two shrines. Logs are about 15 m long, and all work is done by human power, not machines. →諏訪大社

おんびん 音便 〚言語〛 a phonetic change in a part of a word or an inflection. Occurred in the history of the Japanese language. For example, the te-form of 'yomu'(read) used to be 'yomite,' but the phonetic change occurred and it became 'yonde.'

おんみつ 隠密 〚政治〛 a secret agent in the Muromachi and Edo periods. Served a feudal lord or shogun with intelligence work. Some of them were ninja. An example is ONIWABAN of the Tokugawa shogunate.

おんみょうじ 陰陽師 〚妖怪・宗教〛 a yin-yang master. Worked as a diviner, astrologist, and exorcist based on the yin-yang way. Disappeared after the Meiji Restoration. →陰陽道

おんみょうどう 陰陽道 〚妖怪・宗教〛 the yin-yang way. Magic technique based on the Theory of Yin-Yang and the Five Elements, which were introduced from ancient China. Was popular in the Heian period. →陰陽五行説

おんようじ 陰陽師 〚妖怪・宗教〛 ⇨ 陰陽師(おんみょうじ)

おんよみ 音読み〚漢字〛 a Chinese-style pronunciation of a kanji. Some kanji have more than one 'on' pronunciations. For example, a kanji 日 is read as 'nichi' or 'jitsu,' both of which are 'on' pronunciation. ↔訓読み

おんりえど 厭離穢土 〚仏教〛 ⇨厭離穢土(えんりえど)

か

かい 甲斐〖地名〗 the old name for Yamanashi Pref.

かいあわせ 貝合わせ〖ゲーム〗 a clamshell matching game. The insides of paired shells are painted with similar pictures.

がいえん 外苑〖神社・庭園〗 the outer garden of the Imperial Palace or a Shinto shrine. ↔内苑

かいえんたい 海援隊〖企業名〗 a trading company established in 1865 by SAKAMOTO RYOUMA. Had about 20 members but disbanded after Ryouma was assassinated.

かいかせんげん 開花宣言〖植物〗 the announcement of the first opening of cherry blossoms. Is issued regularly by the Japan Meteorological Agency. →気象庁

かいかどん 開化丼〖食べ物〗 a bowl of rice topped with egg, sliced onion, and beef or pork. 'Kaika' means "social progression immediately after the Meiji Restoration." Is named because beef, pork, and onion were not eaten before the Restoration.

かいき 開基〖仏教〗 (**1**) the founding of a Buddhist temple or sect. (**2**) the founder of a Buddhist temple or sect. Sometimes refers to a financial supporter of the founding.

かいき 開器〖忍者〗 the generic term for tools for infiltration. Includes a pointed hand saw (SHIKORO), a two-pronged drill (TSUBOKIRI), a drill, and a chisel. →忍器(にんき)

かいき ～回忌〖冠婚葬祭・仏教〗 an anniversary of a person's death. A memorial service is usually held on the 2nd, 6th, 12th, and 32nd anniversaries. However, the 2nd anniversary is called the 3rd round, 'san-kaiki,' because the day of the person's death is counted as the first anniversary. →一周忌(いっしゅうき)

かいぐんへいがっこう 海軍兵学校〖軍事〗 the Naval Academy. Was established to train naval officers in Tokyo in 1876, was moved to the Etajima Island in Hiroshima in 1888, and was abolished in 1945.

かいけい 快慶〖彫刻〗 ?-? A sculptor of Buddhist images from the 11th to 12th centuries. Belonged to the same studio as UNKEI in the Kei school and established the original Annami style exemplified in the standing Amitabha Buddha at TOUDAI-JI Temple. Deeply believed in Pure Land Buddhism as a pupil of CHOUGEN. His works include the *Amitabha Triad* at JOUDO-JI Temple in Hyougo Pref. and *Hachiman as a Buddhist Monk* at Toudai-ji Temple. →慶派(けいは)；安阿弥様(あんなみよう)

かいけいけんさいん 会計検査院〖行政機関〗 Board of Audit. One of the Japanese state organizations. Examines the legitimacy of expenses of the national government. Also examines local governments and private enterprises that receive national subsidies or grants.

かいけん 懐剣 〖武器〗 a dagger. Was kept in a kimono for self-protection during feudal periods.

かいげん 改元 〖暦〗 a change of an era name. An era name used to be changed when an auspicious sign was observed, a disaster occurred, or a new Emperor ascended the throne. After the Meiji Restoration in the 19th century until the end of the 20th century, it had been changed only when a new Emperor was enthroned. →元号

かいげんくよう 開眼供養 〖仏教〗 the consecration ceremony for a new Buddhist painting or statue. When a priest paints in the pupils of the eyes in this ceremony, the Buddha spirit is said to enter the image and the image becomes an object of worship.

かいこ 蚕 〖服飾・動物〗 a silkworm. A caterpillar of a silkmoth. Eats mulberry leaves. Silk is produced from its cocoon. →桑

かいこく 開国 〖外交〗 the opening of the country. After the national seclusion, Japan started to exchange and trade with foreign countries in 1854. This term was used mainly in the 19th century. ↔ 鎖国

がいこくぶぎょう 外国奉行 〖外交・官位〗 a feudal commissioner of foreign affairs. Was established in 1858 when the U.S.-Japan Treaty of Amity and Commerce was con-

cluded. →日米修好通商条約

かいごほけん 介護保険 〖医療・行政〗 nursing care insurance. A person aged 40 or over has to have it.

かいこまがたけ 甲斐駒ヶ岳 〖山岳〗 Mt. Kai Komagatake. Is located in the Southern Alps, on the border between Yamanashi and Nagano Prefs. The height is 2,967 m. Is abbreviated to Kai Koma among mountaineers to distinguish it from other mountains named Komagatake, such as 'Kiso Komagatake,' 'Oshima Komagatake,' and 'Aizu Komagatake.'

かいさん 開山 〖仏教〗 (1) the founding of a Buddhist temple or sect. (2) the founder of a Buddhist temple or sect.

かいさんどう 開山堂 〖仏教〗 a hall to enshrine the image of the founder of a sect or temple. This term is often used in Zen Buddhism. →祖師堂

かいし 懐紙 〖茶道〗 a paper napkin. In a tea ceremony, a guest takes a cake from the cake box and puts it on a 'kaishi' before eating the cake.

かいしゃく 介錯 〖武士〗 beheading a person who is committing hara-kiri, to assist him in dying.

かいしょ 楷書 〖書道〗 the block style of calligraphy. Each stroke is drawn precisely. →行書；草書

かいしらね 甲斐白根 〖山岳〗 ⇨北岳

がいじん 外陣 〖宗教・建築〗 ⇨外陣 (じん)

かいせいじょ 開成所 〖学校〗 a

school to teach foreign languages, natural sciences, and military science. Was established in 1863 by the Tokugawa shogunate. After the Meiji Restoration, the new government revived the school, which later became the University of Tokyo.

かいせきぜん 会席膳 〚食文化〛 a small dinner tray for a traditional banquet. Is individually set for each guest.

かいせきりょうり 会席料理 〚食文化〛 cuisine for a traditional-style banquet, served on an individual lacquer tray. Rice, miso soup, and pickles are usually served at the end of the course. Originally developed in haiku parties during the Edo period.

かいせきりょうり 懐石料理 〚食文化〛 cuisine for the tea-ceremony, served before drinking tea. The present form was said to be perfected by SEN NO RIKYUU in the 16th century. 'Kaiseki' means "a warm stone inside the kimono bosom," with which a Zen monk was said to have warmed himself.

かいせん 廻船 〚交通〛 a cargo ship, or transportation using a cargo ship. Developed in medieval times and became quite active in the Edo period. There were several routes such as ones between Edo and Osaka or between Osaka and coastal areas of the Sea of Japan.

かいぜん 改善 〚ビジネス〛 an approach to work that involves continuous, incremental improvements in every process, as opposed to radical changes. Originated in Japan but has been used widely in other countries, in all kinds of organizations but especially in business and industry.

かいせんどんや 廻船問屋 〚ビジネス〛 a cargo ship agency in the Edo period. Some of these agencies also traded local commodities in addition to shipping.

かいそ 開祖 〚仏教〛 the founder of a Buddhist sect.

かいそくれっしゃ 快速列車 〚鉄道〛 a rapid train. Generally stops more frequently than an express train, but passes some stations on its route. No extra fee is needed to get on it. Is operated by JR and many major private railway companies.

かいたいしんしょ 解体新書 〚医療・書名〛 the first translation of a book of Western medical science. The source book was *Ontleedkundige Tafelen* in the Netherlands.

かいだん 戒壇 〚仏教〛 an ordination platform. A monk was given the commandments on the three-tiered platform with a two-storied pagoda. A Chinese priest, GANJIN, created it at Todai-ji Temple for the first time in 754.

かいだんいん 戒壇院 〚仏教・建築〛 a temple building containing an ordination platform.

かいだんどう 戒壇堂 〚仏教・建築〛 ⇨戒壇院

かいだんばなし 怪談噺 〚落語〛 a ghost story in RAKUGO, traditional

comic storytelling. Developed in the late 19th century.

かいちょう 開帳 〖仏教〗 exhibition of a secret Buddhist image to the public. A secret image is usually housed in an ornamented double-door chest and thus cannot be seen. →厨子(ｽﾞ)

かいづか 貝塚 〖史跡〗 a kitchen midden, or a shellmound. Was made in the Joumon period.

かいてん 回天 〖武器〗 the name of a human-driven torpedo. Literally means "moving heaven and earth." Its length was 14.8 m, and its maximum speed was 30 kiloknot. A human operated this torpedo like a small submarine and crashed into an enemy ship at the risk of his life. Was used toward the end of World War II but militarily achieved very little.

かいてんうち 回転打ち 〖忍者〗 a spinning throw technique of a small knife. With this technique, one can throw a knife at very high speed, though with some loss of accuracy.

かいてんずし 回転寿司〖食文化〗 a conveyor belt sushi restaurant, or rotating sushi bar. A customer picks up his or her favorite sushi plates circulating on a conveyor belt. The price is rather reasonable, compared with an ordinary sushi restaurant. Is said to have started in Osaka around 1958.

かいてんやき 回転焼き 〖食べ物〗 ⇨ 今川焼

かいどう 街道 〖交通〗 a highway. Sometimes means a historical highway. →五街道

かいとくどう 懐徳堂 〖学校〗 a private school established in 1726 by Osaka merchants. Had a liberal academic atmosphere and admitted both samurai and common people.

かいばらえきけん 貝原益軒 〖人文学〗 1630-1714. A herbalist and Confucian samurai born in present Fukuoka Pref. His work, *Japanese Secret of Good Health* (Youjoukun), is still popular today.

かいふうそう 懐風藻 〖文芸・作品〗 *Fond Recollections of Poetry*. The oldest anthology of Chinese-style poems, compiled in 751. The compiler is unknown. Contains 120 poems by 64 poets.

かいへん 貝偏 〖漢字〗 a left-side radical meaning "shellfish." Since shells were used as money in ancient times, this radical is used for kanji related to money such as 財(property) and 貯(saving). →偏; 部首

かいほうゆうしょう 海北友松 〖絵画〗 1533-1615. A painter born in a samurai household in present Shiga Pref. Learned painting techniques under the Kanou school. His works include *Eight Drinking Hermits* at the Kyoto National Museum and *Dragon and Clouds* at Kennin-ji Temple in Kyoto.

かいまき 掻巻 〖家具〗 a kimono-shaped padded quilt. A sleeper wears it under the top futon.

かいみょう 戒名〖仏教〗 a Buddhist

name given to a person after death. Is inscribed on the gravestone and the memorial tablet. There are several ranks of this name, depending on the amount of money paid to the temple. →位牌(はい)

がいむしょう 外務省 〔外交・行政機関〕 Ministry of Foreign Affairs. Was established in 1869.

かいゆうしきていいえん 回遊式庭園 〔庭園〕 a landscape garden with a circular path. People can enjoy various views while strolling along the path around a pond. Examples include KENROKU-EN in Ishikawa Pref. and KOISHIKAWA KOURAKU-EN in Tokyo.

かいらくえん 偕楽園 〔庭園〕 a park in Mito, Ibaraki Pref. Was completed in 1842 under the order of Tokugawa Nariaki. Famous for the beauty of its plums. One of the three most beautiful gardens in Japan. →日本三名園

かいりつ 戒律 〔仏教〕 the precepts in Buddhism. 'Kai' indicates the voluntary readiness to observe the rules, while 'ritsu' indicates the need for external rules.

かいりゅうおうじ 海龍王寺 〔寺院〕 Kairyuouji Temple. Was founded in 731 by Empress Koumyou and is located in Nara. The five-story miniature pagoda is a National Treasure.

かいろ 懐炉 〔生活〕 a pocket body warmer. Used to be a small metal case containing burning ash, but disposable paper type is popular these days.

かいろせんげん カイロ宣言 〔外交〕 Cairo Declaration. An agreement resulting from the November 1943 Cairo Conference called by U.S. President Franklin Roosevelt and attended by him, by British Prime Minister Winston Churchill, and by Chinese President Chiang Kai-shek. The written statement pledged to continue the war against Japan, to take from Japan all land it had acquired since 1914, to return various domains to China, and to restore the independence of Korea. Besides affirming aims for the end of the war, the Cairo Conference was intended to establish firm relations between China and the United States.

かいわれだいこん 貝割れ大根 〔食べ物〕 white radish sprouts. Taste somewhat spicy and are sometimes used as a topping in various dishes such as salad and soup.

かいんのまつえい カインの末裔 〔文芸・作品〕 *Descendants of Cain.* A novel published in 1917 by ARISHIMA TAKEO. Describes the life of a wild tenant farmer who struggled against the harsh natural environment in Hokkaido.

かえりてん 返り点 〔漢字〕 a mark to make the text of Chinese classics easy to read in the order of Japanese. Is attached at the lower left corner on a kanji. →訓点

かえりにゅうまく 帰り入幕 〔相撲〕 the re-promotion in professional

sumo wrestling. This term is used when a wrestler who used to be in the top division has fallen into the second division and then has come back to the top division.

かえるまた 蟇股〔建築〕 a frog-leg strut in a structure. Supports the load between two horizontal beams. Looks like a frog spreading its legs.

かえんこうはい 火炎光背〔仏教〕 a flame-type halo. Decorates the back of a Wisdom King such as FUDOU MYOUOU.

かえんだいこ 火炎太鼓〔音楽〕 a large decorative drum with flame-like ornaments. Is played in court music called GAGAKU.

かえんどき 火焔土器〔考古〕 earthenware with a flame-shaped rim. Was created mainly along the Shinano River in present Niigata Pref. in the mid-Joumon period.

かおう 花押〔文書〕 a pictorial signature, or written seal. Is placed at the end of a document or the corner of a painting.

かおみせ 顔見世〔歌舞伎〕 a lineup performance in Tokyo in November and in Kyoto in December. Most of the major kabuki actors appear. In the Edo period, this term meant the first performance with a new lineup of actors. Was an important event to introduce all the actors in a kabuki theatrical troupe.

かおもじ 顔文字〔言語〕 an emoticon. A different emoticon from the Western counterpart is used to show the same feeling. For example, a smiley face is written as (＾ ＾), not ;-).

かおるだいしょう 薫大将〔文芸〕 the hero of "Ten Uji Chapter" in *The Tale of Genji*. Though the son of Genji in name, he is actually the son of another man. →源氏物語

かが 加賀〔旧国名〕 the old name for the central and southern parts of Ishikawa Pref.

かかい 歌会〔文芸〕 ⇨歌会(うた)

ががく 雅楽〔天皇・音楽〕 court music. Was originally introduced from the continent in the Nara and Heian periods. Has since been performed at the Imperial Court and Shinto shrines.

かがみいた 鏡板〔能〕 the back wall of a Noh stage. Is painted with a stylized pine tree.

かがみのま 鏡の間〔能〕 a mirror room attached to a Noh stage. Is behind the curtain at the end of the bridge called HASHI-GAKARI. Performers wait here for their turn on stage.

かがみびらき 鏡開き **(1)**〔食文化・正月〕 rice-cake cutting. Round rice cake offered to the New Year deity is cut and eaten usually on January 11th. **(2)**〔酒・冠婚葬祭〕 sake-cask opening. A sake cask is opened by cracking its lid with a wooden hammer. Is seen at auspicious ceremonies such as wedding parties.

かがみもち 鏡餅〔食べ物・正月〕 round rice cakes offered to the New Year deity.

かがみわり 鏡割り 〖食文化・正月〗
⇨鏡開き

かがやき かがやき 〖鉄道〗 the fastest express train on Hokuriku Shinkansen. Literally means "glitter." Runs between Tokyo and Kanazawa Station in Ishikawa Pref. via Joetsu and Hokuriku Shinkansen. Connects the two stations in 2.5 hours. All Kagayaki trains are reservation-only.

かがゆうぜん 加賀友禅 〖服飾〗 textile dyed in the yuuzen style in Kanazawa, Ishikawa Pref. Is characterized by its shading technique. Different from yuuzen in Kyoto. Does not use gold leaves or embroidery. →友禅染め

かかりじょし 係り助詞 〖言語〗 a binding particle. Expresses emphasis, limitation, or addition. Some binding particles specify the form of the predicate. →係り結び; 助詞

かかりむすび 係り結び 〖言語〗 binding the predicate. When a binding particle is added, the form of the predicate is specified. →係り助詞

かがわけん 香川県 〖都道府県〗 Kagawa Pref. Is located in northeastern Shikoku, facing the Island Sea. Is 1,877 km^2 in area, the smallest of all the prefectures. Its capital is Takamatsu City. Is generally warm and dry and has many ponds, in preparation for the droughts. Famous for thick wheat noodles, salt, rice, oranges, and olive production. Has Shoudo Island and the Naoshima Islands in the Inland Sea, the Sanuki Mountains in its southern part, and the KOTOHIRA-GUU Shrine and Mannou Pond in its central part. The Great Seto Bridge connects its northern part with Okayama Pref. Used to be called Sanuki. →讃岐饂飩(さぬき)

かき 柿 〖食べ物・植物〗 a persimmon. *Diospyros kaki.* Native to China. Bears orange-colored edible fruits in autumn. The wood can be used for furniture.

かき 火器 〖忍者〗 a tool using fire. Its main purposes are destruction, communication, and illumination. The Iga and Kouka areas are abundant in materials for fire powder such as moxa, camphor, and horse dung. In addition, people around these areas had high skills in producing fire powder because there lived many skilled experts who came from China or Korea.

かき 花器 〖華道〗 a flower container for flower arrangement. Includes vases, bowls, and baskets.

がき 餓鬼 〖仏教〗 (**1**) a starving ghost. In Sanskrit, *preta.* Is always suffering from hunger and thirst and appears to be all skin and bones with a swelled belly. (**2**) the Realm of Starving Ghosts in reincarnation. →六道; 輪廻(りんね)

かきあげ 掻き揚げ 〖食べ物〗 a tempura of various ingredients, such as small shrimps, shellfish, and chopped vegetables.

かぎかっこ 鉤括弧 〖言語〗 「　」.

Encloses text that is said by someone, is quoted, refers to the title of a magazine article, or is emphasized.

かきごおり かき氷〖食べ物〗 shaved ice. Is usually served with flavored syrup, or sometimes with assorted toppings. One of the Japanese summer desserts. When 'kakigoori' is made, a special hand-cranked kit or electric machine is used to spin a block of ice over a shaving blade.

かきぞめ　書き初め　〖書道・正月〗 New Year calligraphy. Was practiced with India ink on January 2nd.

かきたまじる　掻き玉汁　〖食べ物〗 clear soup containing beaten egg.

かきつばた 杜若〖植物〗　a water iris, or rabbit-ear iris. *Iris laevigata*. Grows in shallow water and marshy ponds. Dark-purple flowers bloom in early summer.

かぎなわ 鉤縄〖忍者〗　a portable iron hook with rope. Was used to climb to a high place or was stretched so that an enemy would trip and fall.

かきのたね 柿の種〖食べ物〗 spicy rice crackers that look like persimmon seeds.

かきのはずし　柿の葉寿司　〖寿司〗 sushi wrapped with persimmon leaves. A specialty of Nara.

かきのもとのひとまろ　柿本人麻呂 〖文芸〗　?-708? A court poet. Served Empress Jitou and Emperor Monmu. Contributed 86 poems to the *Anthology of Myriad Leaves* (Man'youshuu).

かぎばしご 鉤梯子〖忍者〗 a ladder with hooks. Was used to climb to a high place.

かきはん 書き判〖文書〗 ⇨花押(ホゥ)

かきぴい 柿ピー〖食べ物〗 combination of small, spicy rice crackers and peanuts.

かきぶね 牡蠣船〖食文化〗 an oyster boat. People eat oyster cuisine on the boat moored at the edge of a river. Is popular in Hiroshima and Osaka.

かきもち 欠き餅〖食べ物〗 a thinly sliced rice cake. Is grilled and dipped into soy sauce.

かぎょうへんかくかつよう　カ行変格活用　〖言語〗　the irregular conjugation of a verb 'kuru,' which means "to come."

かくあんどん 角行燈〖家具〗　a square paper lantern. The modern version uses an LED lamp in it.

かくおび 角帯〖服飾〗 a sash for man's kimono. A little stiffer and narrower than woman's sash.

かくかい 角界〖相撲〗　the sumo world. Is called so because the Japanese word, sumo, can be written as 角力.

かくぎょう 角行〖将棋〗 a bishop. Is commonly called by its abbreviated form, 'kaku.' A bishop who has been promoted is called RYUUMA, or simply 'uma.'

かくしあじ 隠し味〖食文化〗 subtle seasoning to enrich the flavor of a dish. Is put into a dish in addition to the main seasoning. For example, a small amount of honey is sometimes added when cooking curry.

がくしゅうかんじ 学習漢字〔漢字・教育〕 ⇨教育漢字

がくしゅうじゅく 学習塾 〔教育〕 an after-school learning center, or a cram school. Aims to reinforce the academic ability of students at elementary, junior-high, and senior-high schools. Some students go to 'juku' to prepare for entrance examinations, and others go for remedial learning. The teaching styles can be classified into two: the group learning type and the individual tutoring type.

かくじょし 格助詞〔言語〕 a postpositional particle to indicate a case. For example, 'ga' indicates that the noun immediately before it has the nominative case, and 'no' indicates that the noun has the genitive case. →助詞

かくすう 画数〔漢字〕 the number of strokes to write a kanji. Is used as a clue when looking up a kanji in a kanji dictionary. →漢和辞典

がくせいふく 学生服 〔教育・服飾〕 a uniform for Japanese school-children of junior and senior high schools, sometimes of elementary schools and universities. Traditionally, stand-up collar jackets are worn by boys, and sailor-style suits by girls, but blazer jackets and pants/skirts are getting popular nowadays. →学ラン；セーラー服

かくそで 角袖〔服飾〕 an overcoat for men's kimono. Literally means "square sleeve."

かぐつちのかみ 迦具土神〔神話〕 ⇨火之迦具土(ﾋﾉｶｸﾞｯﾁﾉ)神

かくて 角手〔忍者〕 a thorned finger ring. Was attached on each finger and used like brass knuckles.

かくていしんこく 確定申告〔ビジネス・行政〕 a final declaration of tax. Most full-time employees do not have to complete it. Business owners, free-lancers, employees with high salaries, and employees working for more than one company have to declare their income and deductions from mid-February to mid-March every year.

がくどうそかい 学童疎開〔戦争・教育〕 the evacuation of school children toward the end of World War II. School children took refuge in a rural or suburban area from a big city. Some children depended on their relatives, while other children evacuated to temples or inns.

がくとしゅつじん 学徒出陣〔戦争・教育〕 students' participation in World War II. Students who were 20 years old or higher and majored in subjects other than science, technology, and pedagogy were forced to leave for the battlefront in 1943.

かくに 角煮〔食べ物〕 simmered cubic meat or fish. Usually pork, tuna, or bonito is simmered in soy sauce, mirin, and other seasonings.

がくばつ 学閥〔精神性・ビジネス〕 a school clique. It was said that being in a school clique later had a strong influence on promotions within organizations.

がくもんのすすめ　学問ノススメ
〖教育・書名〗 *An Encouragement of Learning*. A collection of treatises published from 1872 to 1876 by FUKUZAWA YUKICHI. By opposing discrimination based on feudal hierarchy, he advocated egalitarianism and insisted on the significance of practical science.

かくやすこうくうがいしゃ　格安航空会社 〖交通・企業〗 a low-cost carrier. Includes Jetstar, Peach Aviation, Vanilla Air, and Air Asia.

かぐやひめ　香具姫 〖民話〗 Princess Kaguya. The heroine of *The Tale of the Bamboo Cutter* (TAKETORI MONO-GATARI).

かぐら　神楽 〖神道〗 music and dance in a Shinto ritual. There are two kinds of kagura: 'mi-kagura' and 'sato-kagura.' Mi-kagura is performed at the Imperial Court, based on a tradition since the Heian period, while sato-kagura is performed in a festival of a local community.

がくらん　学ラン 〖教育・服飾〗 an informal name for a school uniform for male students.

かくりんじ　鶴林寺 〖寺院〗 Kakurin Temple. Is said to have been founded at the end of the 6th century by Prince Shoutoku and is located in Hyougo Pref. Its main building and the Prince Shotoku Hall are National Treasures.

がくれきしゃかい　学歴社会 〖教育・経済〗 an education-conscious so-ciety. In such a society, educational background is respected more than social class, family line, or financial power. In Japan, it is said that the name of the university from which a person has graduated is respected more than his or her academic achievement at the university, or the name of the graduate school he or she attended.

かくれきりしたん　隠れキリシタン 〖キリスト教〗 a hidden Christian in the Edo period. Believed in Christianity during the period of the prohibition of Christianity imposed by the Tokugawa shogunate.

かくれざと　隠れ里 〖民話〗 a Utopia far away from human habitation. Is described in folktales.

かくれみの　隠れ蓑 〖民話〗 an invisible cape. Hides the figure of a wearer. Is possessed by a supernatural being called TENGU.

かくれみののじゅつ　隠蓑の術 〖忍者〗 a stealth technique that involves someone hiding in baggage. A female ninja was employed as a maid by an enemy and had a large parcel sent to her, in which another ninja hid himself or herself.

かくれんぼ　隠れん坊 〖遊び〗 hide-and-seek. This term began to be used in the 19th century.

かくん　家訓 〖生活・精神性〗 a family precept. Was inherited from generation to generation. Is very rare at present.

かけい　筧 〖庭園〗 ⇨懸け樋(かけひ)

かげうた　陰唄 〖歌舞伎〗 a background song in kabuki.

かけうどん 掛け饂飩〔食べ物〕 plain thick wheat noodles in hot broth. No topping or only chopped green onion, if any, is added.

かけえり 掛け襟〔服飾〕 an outer collar sewn on a kimono to keep the kimono clean.

かけこみでら 駆け込み寺〔仏教〕 ⇨ 縁切寺

かけじく 掛け軸〔絵画・書道〕 a hanging scroll. A painting or calligraphy is mounted on cloth or paper and attached to rods at both ends, to be hung on the wall of a decorative alcove in a traditional room. → 床の間

かげぜん 陰膳〔食文化〕 a meal prepared at home for a person even though he or she is away. The family prepares the meal at the person's seat to wish for his or her safe return.

かけそば 掛け蕎麦〔食べ物〕 plain buckwheat noodles in hot broth. Either no topping or only chopped green onion is added.

かけづつ 掛け筒〔華道〕 a cylindrical vase hung on a wall or pillar.

かけながし 掛け流し〔温泉〕 ⇨源泉 掛け流し

かけばな 掛け花〔華道〕 a flower or flowers arranged in a container hung on a wall or pillar.

かけひ 懸け樋〔庭園〕 a water pipe in a traditional garden, extending from the water source to a washbasin. Is usually made of wood or bamboo.

かけぶとん 掛け布団〔家具〕 a top futon. Covers a sleeper. ↔敷布団

かげま 陰間〔セックス・娯楽〕 a gay prostitute in the Edo period.

かげむしゃ 影武者〔武士・政治〕 a double for a warlord. Pretended to be the warlord to deceive the enemy and sometimes died in place of the lord.

かけむしろ 掛け筵〔建築〕 a straw-mat curtain. Is hung down as a partition in a room.

かけもの 掛物〔絵画・書道〕 ⇨掛け 軸

かげろうにっき 蜻蛉日記〔文芸・作品〕 *The Gossamer Years*. A diary written in or after 974 by the mother of Fujiwara no Michitsuna. Describes her unstable marriage life and her maternal love of her son from 954 to 974. Influenced later diary literature and *The Tale of Genji*.

かご 駕籠〔交通〕 a palanquin, or covered litter. Became popular in the Edo period. The passenger box was hung down from a horizontal pole carried by two bearers.

かごかき 駕籠かき〔交通・職業〕 a palanquin bearer. A pair of bearers carried a palanquin.

かこげんざいいんがきょう 過去 現在因果経〔仏教〕 the Sutra of the Past and Present Causes and Effects. Describes the past incarnation and the actual life in this world of the Historical Buddha. →絵因果 経

かごしまけん 鹿児島県〔都道府

県〕 Kagoshima Pref. Is located in southwestern Japan. Is composed of the southern part of Kyushu Island, Tanegashima Island, Yaku Island, and the Amami Islands. Is 9,187 km^2 in area. Its capital is Kagoshima City. Has a warm and rainy climate, and a sub-tropical climate on Amami islands. The whole prefecture is often hit by typhoons. Half of its area on Kyushu Island is on the Shirasu Plateau, a kind of pyroclastic plateau. Sweet potatoes, soybeans, and oilseed rape are produced in large quantities on the plateau. Also famous for Japanese spirits called SHOUCHUU made from sweet potatoes, deep-fried patties of fish paste containing vegetable bits, and pork. Historically, a drifting ship from Portugal introduced guns to Tanegashima Island in 1543. The use of guns dramatically changed war tactics in the Warring States period. In 1549, Francis Xavier landed on Kagoshima and started his two-year mission of preaching Christianity in Western Japan. Used to be called Oosumi and Satsuma.

かごしまし 鹿児島市 〔地名〕 Kagoshima City. Is the capital of Kagoshima Pref., located in its central part, facing Kagoshima Bay. Much of its land comprises commercial, industrial, or residential areas. Sakura-jima Island is located in the east of the city, accessible by ferry from the city center on the west side of the bay. Because of the beautiful view of Sakura-jima Island, the city is sometimes compared to Naples in Italy with its view of Mt. Vesuvius. A warrior and politician, SAIGOU TAKAMORI, who was active in the Meiji Restoration, was born and died in this city in the 19th century. There are some monuments and buildings commemorating or related to him, such as Shiroyama Park, Nanshuu Shrine, and the ruins of Shigakkou, the private school he ran. Other sightseeing spots include Kagoshima Castle, Sengan-en Park, and Io World Kagoshima Aquarium.

かごしまわん 鹿児島湾 〔湾〕 Kagoshima Bay. Is located between the Oosumi and Satsuma Peninsulas in Kagoshima Pref. Inside the bay is an active volcano on Sakura-jima Island. Is also called Kinkou-wan.

がごぜ 元興寺 〔妖怪〕 the monster that appeared at Gangou-ji Temple in ancient times. It is said that the hairs of the monster still exist at the temple. The first YOUKAI (monsters and goblins) in Japanese history.

かこちょう 過去帳 〔仏教〕 the death register at a temple. Includes the secular name, the posthumous Buddhist name, the date of death, and the age when the person died.

かごめかごめ かごめかごめ 〔遊び〕 the bird-in-the-cage game. A child

sits down on the heels in a circle, with eyes closed. Other children walk around while singing 'kagome, kagome.' When they stop walking and singing, the child in the center guesses who is just behind him or her.

かさ 笠〖生活〗 a lampshade headgear with a chin strap. Is often woven with sedge, bamboo, or rush. There are several styles such as ami-gasa, fukaami-gasa, jin-gasa, suge-gasa, ajiro-gasa, sando-gasa, and manjuu-gasa.

かさじぞう 笠地蔵〖民話〗 "A Lampshade Headgear Jizou." A folk tale. A poor old man made five lampshade headgears and tried to sell them on a cold day, but no one bought them. On his way back, he saw six monk-shaped Buddhist statues, called Jizou, in snow. Feeling sorry for them, he put the five headgears on the heads of five statues. He covered the head of the last statue with his own towel. That night, the six statues presented the poor man with a variety of food and daily goods. The details of the story vary, depending on the region.

かさねもち 重ね餅〖食べ物〗 a doubled rice cake. One is placed on top of the other.

かさばけ 傘化け〖妖怪〗 ⇨唐傘

かざりぎり 飾り切り〖食文化〗 cutting vegetables into beautiful shapes such as flowers or maple leaves.

がさん 画賛〖絵画・書道〗 text written on a blank space in a picture. Was written by an acquaintance or patron of the painter or by the owner of the picture in later times.

かじいもとじろう 梶井基次郎〖文芸〗 1901-1932. A novelist born in Osaka. His style is highly sensitive. His works mainly include short stories such as "Lemon." Died from lung desease.

かしおり 菓子折り〖食文化〗 a box of sweets. People bring it when visiting someone's home or send it as an expression of appreciation or apology.

かじか 鰍〖食べ物・魚〗 a fluvial sculpin. *Cottus pollux*. Lives in a clean mountain stream. About 15 cm long and edible.

かしき 菓子器〖茶道〗 a vessel for sweets. Sweets are served before drinking tea in the tea ceremony.

かじき 旗魚〖食べ物・魚〗 (**1**) a marlin. *Istiophoridae*. (**2**) a swordfish. *Xiphias gladius*. Though they are different species, both (1) and (2) have a spear-like snout and are eaten as sashimi.

かしこどころ 賢所〖天皇・建築〗 the hall enshrining the Sacred Mirror in the Imperial Palace. →八咫の鏡 (やたの かがみ)

かしはらじんぐう 橿原神宮〖神社〗 Kashihara Shrine. Was founded in northwestern Nara Pref. in 1890 to commemorate the 2,550th year after the first Emperor Jinmu ascended the throne. Enshrines Jinmu and his wife. It is said that he ascended the throne on the site of the present precinct of the shrine on February 11th, which is a national holiday, National Foundation Day. →神武天皇；建国記念日

かしまじんぐう 鹿島神宮 【神社】 Kashima Shrine. Is located in northern Ibaraki Pref. Enshrines TAKEMIKADUCHI NO ONOKAMI, a deity of thunder and martial arts. Was widely worshipped by warriors. Houses the oldest uncurved sword in Japan, which is a National Treasure.

かしまだち 鹿島立ち 【旅・神道】 a departure for a journey. Is said to have originated from a myth that deities at Kashima and Katori Shrines set out to conquer the country or from a tradition that ancient soldiers prayed for a safe journey at Kashima Shrine. →鹿島神宮；香取神宮；防人(さきもり)

かじゃ 冠者 【冠婚葬祭】 **(1)** a young man who has finished the coming-of-age ceremony in olden days. **(2)** a young male servant in olden days.

かしゃけん 火車剣 【忍者】 a star-shaped throwing knife with a fire fuse. Was used for illumination or time-delayed arson.

かじゅつ 火術 【忍者】 ninja technique using fire. This technique was frequently used because a ninja was usually operating during the night and was good at developing firearms.

がしょう 賀正 【正月・言語】 "Happy New Year!" Is written in a new year card or poster.

かじょうほうそう 過剰包装 【ビジネス・精神性】 excessive packaging at a shop. For example, a small cake is wrapped in a soft paper, a dozen of them are placed on a plastic tray and covered with a plastic cover, and the case is put in a paper bag at a department store.

かしわ 柏 【植物】 a Japanese emperor oak. *Quercus dentata*. The leaves are used for wrapping a rice cake containing sweet adzuki paste, called KASHIWAMOCHI.

かしわで 柏手 【神道】 handclapping to worship a Shinto deity or deities. Usually, hands are clapped twice. →二礼二拍手一礼

かしわもち 柏餅 【食べ物】 a rice cake wrapped in an oak leaf. Contains sweet adzuki paste or miso paste. Is mainly eaten around the Boys' Festival on May 5. Symbolizes prosperity of descendants because it is widely believed that an oak leaf would never die until the young leaf grows.

かじわらいっき 梶原一騎 【漫画】 1936-1988. A story writer for manga. His real name was Takamori Asao. His works include a baseball manga, *Star of the Giants* (KYOJIN NO HOSHI), and a boxing manga, *Tomorrow's Joe* (ASHITA NO JOO).

かしん 家臣 【武士】 a vassal of a feudal load or a shogun.

かじん 歌人 【文芸】 a TANKA poet.

かすがたいしゃ 春日大社 【神社】 Kasuga Grand Shrine. Is located in

Nara City and enshrines four tutelary deities of the Fujiwara clan, including TAKEMIKADUCHI NO ONO-KAMI. Deer inhabiting its precinct have been regarded as sacred messengers from the deities. →藤原氏

かすがづくり 春日造り〖神社・建築〗 Kasuga style of Shinto architecture. The entrance is on the gable side. A pent roof is added to the gable end to cover the stairs leading to the entrance. The main sanctuary buildings of Kasuga Grand Shrine have this style. →本殿; 春日大社

かずさ 上総〖地名〗 the old name for central Chiba Pref.

かすじる 粕汁〖食べ物〗 sake lees soup. Is made of sake lees and white miso, simmered with salmon and various root vegetables. Is popular on a cold winter day.

かすづけ 粕漬け〖食べ物〗 vegetables, fish, or meat pickled in sake lees.

かすてら カステラ〖食べ物〗 a Japanese sponge cake. Is made of sugar, flour, eggs, and starch syrup. Its origin was a cake brought in by Portuguese merchants in the 16th century, and is now known as a specialty of Nagasaki Pref. Its name is derived from Portuguese 'Pão de Castela,' meaning "bread from Castile."

かずのこ 数の子〖食べ物〗 salted herring roe. Is often eaten during the New Year's holidays. Symbolizes prosperity of descendants because it has many eggs.

かすみがうら 霞ヶ浦〖湖沼〗 Lake Kasumigaura. Located in Ibaraki Pref. The area is 168 km^2, making it the second largest lake in Japan after Lake Biwa. The maximum depth is 7 m, and the surface is almost at sea level.

かずらもの 鬘物〖能〗 a Noh play whose main character is female.

かすり 絣〖文様・服飾〗 a splashed pattern, or fabric with splashed patterns. Threads are dyed before weaving.

かぜ 風〖落語・言語〗 jargon indicating a folding fan in rakugo society.

かせいぶんか 化政文化〖時代〗 the Kasei culture, in the latter Edo period. Was developed by townspeople in Edo, present-day Tokyo. Its main feature is stylishness and decadence. →元禄文化

かせんねん 迦旃延〖仏教〗 *Katyayana*. One of the Ten Great Disciples of the Historical Buddha. Foremost among the disciples in debating the Dharma. →十大弟子

かぞえどし 数え年〖通過儀礼〗 traditional age counting. A person is considered to be one year old at birth, and two years old on the first January 1 after one's birth. After that, a year is added to one's age each January 1, without affecting one's actual birth day designation.

かぞく 華族〖官位〗 the nobility before the end of World War II. Includes former feudal lords and those who contributed greatly to the Meiji Restoration. Imitating

European examples, the titles such as marquis, count, viscount, and baron were given.

かぞくそう 家族葬 〔冠婚葬祭〕 a private funeral service. Only family and relatives attend. The cost is rather low. This type of funeral is getting popular mainly in urban areas.

かぞくぶろ 家族風呂 〔風呂〕 a public bath for family use at an inn. Is sometimes available at a spa.

かた 型 〔武術〕 a form of combat based on established techniques. Is repeatedly practiced against imaginary opponents.

かたうた 片歌 〔文芸〕 an ancient rhyming poem in three lines with 5, 7, and 7 syllables in each line. Only 11 poems are included in *Records of Ancient Matters* (KOJIKI), and only six poems in the *Chronicles of Japan* (NIHONSHOKI). The *Anthology of Myriad Leaves* (MAN'YOUSHUU) contains none.

かたかな 片仮名 〔言語〕 an angular letter to represent a syllable, or the writing system using it. Was invented from part of a kanji. Is mainly used to write loanwords or to reflect onomatopoeia.

かたきうち 敵討ち 〔武士〕 ⇨仇討〔あだうち〕

かたぎぬ 肩衣 〔服飾〕 a long stiff vest for a samurai. Was worn on ceremonial occasions.

かたくちいわし 片口鰯 〔食べ物・魚〕 a Japanese anchovy. *Engraulis japonica*. About 15 cm. Young fish are eaten in several ways such as CHIRIMEN JAKO, SHIRASU-BOSHI, and GOMAME.

かたくりこ 片栗粉 〔食文化〕 dogtooth violet starch. Is often substituted for potato starch. Is used to thicken broth in various dishes or as a sweetening ingredient.

かたぐるま 肩車 〔柔道〕 shoulder wheel. Lifting the opponent on one's own shoulder and throwing the person forward.

かたしろ 形代 〔神道〕 a human-shaped piece of paper. People move their impurities into this slip by stroking it and then wash it down the river as a scapegoat.

かたたがえ 方違え 〔宗教〕 avoiding an ill-omened compass direction for departure in the Heian period. If the destination was in an ill-omened direction, court nobles first went in another direction, stayed somewhere at night, and then left for the original destination.

かたな 刀 〔武器〕 ⇨日本刀

かたなかくし 刀隠し 〔忍者〕 an underfloor storage compartment for swords.

かたなかけ 刀掛け 〔武器〕 a sword rest. There are two types: a sword is placed vertically with one type, and a sword is placed horizontally with the other type.

かたなかじ 刀鍛冶 〔武器・職業〕 a swordsmith. Appeared in ancient times and developed at the period when the military class was gaining power.

かたながり 刀狩り〔武器・政治〕 the sword hunt. Toyotomi Hideyoshi issued this decree in 1588 to prohibit farmers and priests from possessing weapons. Clearly distinguished the military class from others and established the foundation of the feudal system.

かだのあずままろ 荷田春満〔人文学〕 1669-1736. A scholar of Japanese classics and poet, born in Kyoto. Advocated Restoration Shintoism, and researched *Records of Ancient Matters* (KOJIKI), *Chronicles of Japan* (NIHONSHOKI), and *Anthology of Myriad Leaves* (MAN'YOUSHUU). The teacher of KAMO NO MABUCHI. →国学

かたびら 帷子〔服飾〕 unlined summer kimono made of hemp or silk. →経帷子（きょうかたびら）; 鎖帷子（くさりかたびら）

かたみ 形見〔精神性〕 a memorial object that has been used or possessed by a person before his or her death. Is often presented to a person who was close to the person who has died.

かためわざ 固め技〔柔道〕 the grappling techniques. Include holding, choking, and armlock techniques.

かたやきせんべい 堅焼煎餅〔食べ物〕 (**1**) a very hard rice cracker. Has soy sauce flavor. (**2**) a very hard flour cookie. Is said to have been eaten as preserved food by ninja in IGA, Mie Pref.

かたやまづおんせん 片山津温泉〔温泉〕 a hot spring in western Ishikawa Pref. Its hot water is salty. Was discovered in 1653 and became popular in the Meiji period. Can be accessed by bus, with a 10-minute ride from JR Kaga-onsen Station.

かたりべ 語部〔言語〕 an ancient storyteller, or narrator. Served the Imperial Court by reciting myth and legends.

かだん 歌壇〔文芸〕 the community of TANKA poets.

かちかちやま かちかち山 〔民話〕 "The Farmer and The Badger." A folk tale. An old farmer lived with his wife, but an evil-minded badger killed her. A hare, the sole friend of the farmer, avenged her death.

かちぐり 勝ち栗〔食べ物〕 a dried and peeled chestnut. Eaten at a celebratory occasion. The former part of this term, 'kachi,' is associated with "victory."

かちこし 勝ち越し〔相撲〕 winning more times than losing. In the top division of the Grand Sumo Tournament, sumo wrestlers have 15 bouts. Low-rank wrestlers sometimes set a goal of winning more times than losing. ↔負け越し

かちなのり 勝ち名乗り〔相撲〕 calling the name of a winner, by the referee called GYOUJI. While calling, the referee points at the winner with a black fan called GUNBAI.

かちぼし 勝ち星〔相撲〕 a win. Is marked with a white circle on the scoresheet, which is called 'hoshi-tori-hyou.'

がちゃっく ガチャック 〔文具〕 Gachuck. Trade mark of a paper

clipper. Is also called Paper Shark. Was invented in 1980 in Japan.

がちゃぽん ガチャポン 〖遊び〗 a capsuled goods vending machine. A capsule contains a small article such as a figurine, key chain, or cell phone straps. The price ranges from 100 to 500 yen. Since it is a kind of blind box, a person cannot always get what he or she wants. Is also called Gashapon or Gacha.

かちょうが 花鳥画 〖絵画〗 a painting of flowers and birds. Was most popular from the 14th to 18th centuries. Insects were sometimes added.

かちょうせいど 家長制度 〖生活〗 a patriarchal system. Used to be the conventional family system of the samurai class in the Edo period and was officially adopted from 1898 to 1947 by the government. The family leader had the right to command all other members. The eldest son in the direct line usually became the next leader.

かちょうふうげつ 花鳥風月 〖精神性・自然〗 the beauties of nature. Literally means "flower, bird, wind, and moon." Also refers to art, such as poems or paintings, that appreciates the beauty of nature.

かちわり かち割り 〖食べ物〗 bite-sized crushed ice. Is sometimes topped with various syrups and is eaten in summer.

かつ 喝 〖仏教・精神性〗 a shout to scold a trainee in Zen Buddhism.

かつお 鰹 〖食べ物・魚〗 a bonito, or a skipjack tuna. *Euthynnus pelamis*, or *Katsuwonus pelamis*. About 1 m long. Eaten in several ways such as dried and shaved, slightly roasted, and boiled. →鰹節；叩き

かつおぎ 鰹木 〖神道・建築〗 an ornamental short log placed across the ridge of a Shinto shrine roof. The number of logs is different from shrine to shrine. →千木(ぎ)

かつおだし 鰹出汁 〖調味料〗 soup stock made from dried bonito.

かつおぶし 鰹節 〖調味料〗 dried bonito. Is usually shaved into flakes. Contains abundant inosinic acid, which is a constituent of UMAMI, and is used for making soup stock. The flakes are sprinkled on many dishes such as tofu, grilled eggplant, or savory pancake called OKONOMIYAKI. →出汁；冷奴(ひややっこ)；焼き茄子(ぎ)

かつかいしゅう 勝海舟 〖武士〗 1823-1899. A samurai and politician born in Edo. As a vassal of the Tokugawa shogunate, negotiated with the leader of an anti-shogunate troops, SAIGOU TAKAMORI, and peacefully surrendered the Edo Castle, which was the headquarters of the Tokugawa shogunate. After the Meiji Restoration, made an effort to recover the honor of the last shogun, TOKUGAWA YOSHINOBU, and to reemploy the shogun's retainers.

かつかれえ カツカレー 〖食べ物〗 curry and rice with a pork, chicken, or beef cutlet.

がっき 学期 〖教育〗 a school term. Many primary and secondary

schools use a three-term system, with the new academic year starting in April. In higher education, the semester system is common.

かつぎょりょうり　活魚料理　〔食文化〕　fresh fish cuisine. Strictly speaking, fish should have been alive immediately before preparation. A restaurant that serves such cuisine usually has a small fishtank called IKESU.

がっこうきゅうしょく　学校給食〔教育〕　a school lunch. Is provided according to the School Lunch Law promulgated in 1954. Its taste used to be awful, but it is now quite good.

がっこうぼさつ　月光菩薩　〔仏教〕　Bodhisattva of Moonlight. *Candraprabha*. An attendant to the Healing Buddha on the right in a triad. Is not worshipped separately. →薬師如来(にょらい);日光菩薩

かっこんとう　葛根湯〔医療〕　a traditional Chinese medicine for cold and inflammation. Is made from kudzu root, ginger root, ephedra, jujube, and other herbs.

かつしかほくさい　葛飾北斎　〔絵画〕　1760-1849. An ukiyo-e painter born in Edo. Incorporated techniques of several schools such as Kanou, Rin, and Tosa, as well as the Western style. Had influence on French Impressionism. Changed his own name more than twenty times and moved more than ninety times. His works include *Thirty-six Views of Mt. Fuji* and *Hokusai Manga*.

がっしょう　合掌　〔仏教〕　putting the palms together to worship the Buddha or Buddhist deities. Is also used when making a request or an apology, or before and after eating.

がっしょうづくり　合掌造り〔建築〕　a traditional style of a private house with a huge, steep, thatched roof. Usually has three or four floors. The second, third, and fourth were used for silkworm culture, while the first was used as living quarters. Many houses in this style are seen at Gokayama in Toyama Pref. and Shirakawa-gou in Gifu Pref.

かっちゅう　甲冑　〔武器〕　a helmet and armor. Had more openings, compared with the European counterpart.

かってぐち　勝手口　〔建築〕　**(1)** a kitchen door of a private house.　**(2)** ⇨茶道口

がってん　月天　〔仏教〕　Deva of the Moon. *Candra*. One of the Twelve Devas. Guards the moon. →十二天

かつどん　カツ丼〔食べ物〕　a bowl of rice topped with a pork cutlet, egg, and sliced onions.

かっぱ　河童　**(1)**〔妖怪〕　a water imp. Appears in Japanese folklore, and its name literally means "river child." Is about one meter tall and has a beak, bobbed hair, a plate on the head containing water, webbed limbs, and a shell on the back. Lives in a river and, when the water on the plate on its head is dried up, it dies. Loves cucumbers and sumo wrestling.　**(2)**〔文芸・作品〕

Kappa. A novel published in 1927 by AKUTAGAWA RYUUNOSUKE. The title means "a water imp." A crazy man insists that he visited the country of water imps.

かっぱまき 河童巻き 〖食べ物〗 a sushi roll containing cucumber. Its name comes from a story about a water imp, KAPPA, who loves cucumbers.

かっぷめん カップ麺 〖寿司〗 instant noodles in a plastic handleless cup. Is served hot in soup with freeze-dried meat and vegetables.

かっぽう 割烹 〖食文化〗 (1) traditional-style cooking. The first kanji 割 means "cutting," and the second kanji 烹 means "boiling." (2) a traditional-style restaurant.

かっぽうぎ 割烹着 〖食文化〗 a sleeved Japanese apron. Can be put on over either a kimono or Western-style clothes.

かっぽうりょうりや 割烹料理屋 〖食文化〗 a traditional-style restaurant.

かっぽうりょかん 割烹旅館 〖食文化・旅〗 a traditional-style inn that specializes in its cuisine.

かっぽざけ かっぽ酒 〖食文化・酒〗 sake or Japanese spirits warmed in a bamboo container. Bamboo flavor oozes into the liquor.

かっぽれ 活惚れ 〖芸能〗 a comical dance and song. The player dances while singing "kappore, kappore." Was invented in the 19th century.

かつら 桂 〖植物〗 a katsura tree. *Cercidiphyllum japonicum*. The wood is used for architecture, furniture, and the boards of a board game such as GO or SHOUGI.

かつらこごろう 桂小五郎 〖武士〗 1833-1877. A samurai and politician born in present Yamaguchi Pref. The leader of the Choushuu domain during the Meiji Restoration. After the Meiji Restoration, changed his name to Kido Takayoshi and became a core member of the new government. Drafted several major policies such as "Return of the lands and people to the Emperor," "Abolition of feudal domains and the establishment of prefectures," and "Equality of people in all social classes."

かつらべいちょう 桂米朝 〖落語〗 Katsura Beichou the third. 1925 -2015. A comic storyteller born in Manchuria. Was designated a Living National Treasure in 1996. His real name was Nakagawa Kiyoshi. →重要無形文化財保持者

かつらむき 桂剥き 〖食文化〗 to peel a vegetable, such as white raddish or carrot, into a long slice.

かつらりきゅう 桂離宮 〖建築・庭園〗 the Katsura Imperial Villa. Was built around 1620 to 1624. Is located in Kyoto. Has been famous worldwide since a German architect, Bruno Taut, highly praised it. Especially beautiful are its landscape gardens and its architecture, which is in the style of a tea-ceremony room. To visit the Villa, one has to apply for permission to the Imperial Household Agency.

かつれきもの 活歴物 〖歌舞伎〗 a drama in kabuki that is faithful to historical fact. A subcategory of JIDAIMONO. Was written only in the early Meiji period.

かていけい 仮定形 〖言語〗 the conditional form of a verb. Precedes a conjunctive particle 'ba.'

かてん 火天 〖仏教〗 Deva of Fire. *Agni*. One of the Twelve Devas. Guards the southeast. →十二天

かでんしょ 花伝書 〖能・書名〗 ⇨風姿花伝(ふうしかでん)

かどう 華道, 花道 〖華道〗 the way of flower arrangement. →生け花

かどう 歌道 〖文芸〗 the art and manner for composing and interpreting traditional rhyming poems.

かとうあらため 火盗改め 〖犯罪・官位〗 ⇨火付け盗賊改め

かとうまど 花頭窓 〖建築〗 a bell-shaped window. Is often used in a temple building.

かとくそうぞく 家督相続 〖法律〗 the succession to the position as family head in the patriarchal system. Was usually done by the eldest son in the direct line. Was abolished when the Civil Law Act was revised in 1947.

かどばん 角番 〖相撲〗 a do-or-die bout or tournament for a sumo wrestler at the second highest rank, called OOZEKI. He is demoted if he loses.

かどまつ 門松 〖正月〗 a New Year's decoration, made from pine branches, bamboo, and straw. Is used in pairs, one on each side of the front gate or door of a house. The pine tree is a symbol of longevity.

かとりじんぐう 香取神宮 〖神社〗 Katori Shrine. Is located in northern Chiba Pref. Enshrines FUTSUNUSHI NO KAMI, a deity of military arts. Was widely worshipped by warriors. Houses a mirror with a sea animal and grapevine design, which is a National Treasure.

かとりせんこう 蚊取り線香 〖生活〗 a mosquito-repellent coil. Is made from pyrethrum and burned during summer nights.

かとん 火遁 〖忍者〗 escape technique using fire. One of the five major techniques. Uses fires and runs away in the confusion caused by fire.

かな 仮名 〖言語〗 a letter to represent a syllable, or writing system using syllables. A rounded type is called HIRAGANA, and an angular type is called KATAKANA.

かながわけん 神奈川県 〖都道府県〗 Kanagawa Pref. Its capital is Yokohama City. Is located on the south of Tokyo. Its area is 2,416 km². Sightseeing spots include Mt. Hakone, Enoshima Island, Kamakura City, Yokohama City, and the Tanzawa Mountains. Used to be Sagami and part of Musashi.

かなかんじへんかん 仮名漢字変換 〖言語〗 the kana-kanji conversion. When writing Japanese on a computer, people first type in hiragana and then change it to kanji by pressing a key.

かなざわし 金沢市 〖地名〗 Kanazawa City. The capital of Ishikawa Pref. Is located in its central part, facing the Sea of Japan. Developed as a castle town of the Maeda clan. Famous for Kanazawa Castle, traditional townscape of samurai mansions, and the KENROKU-EN park. Produces the Kutani ware, lacquerware, and the KAGA-YUUZEN textile. Is connected to Tokyo by Hokuriku Shinkansen.

かなざわはっけい 金沢八景 〖地名〗 Eight Views of Kanazawa. Is modeled on Eight Views of Xiaoxiang in China, which is a popular theme for an India ink painting. The eight views are Autumn Moon at Seto, Evening Snow at Uchikawa, Sunset at Nojima Island, Returning Sailboat at Ottomo, Night Bell at Shoumyou-ji Temple, Night Rain at Koizumi, Flying Geese at Hirakata, and Mountain Mist at Suzaki. Note that this Kanazawa is a part of Yokohama City in Kanagawa Pref., not Kanazawa City in Ishikawa Pref. →瀟湘(しょう)八景

かなぞうし 仮名草子 〖文芸〗 KANA books in the 17th century. Cover wide variety of literature including entertainment, religious and ethical instructions, and practical information. Are said to be a precursor to books of the floating world, UKIYO-ZOUSHI.

かなでほんちゅうしんぐら 仮名手本忠臣蔵 〖芸能〗 *The Treasury of Loyal Retainers*. A program of KABU-KI or BUNRAKU. Its story is based on the revenge incident by forty-seven masterless samurai from the Akou feudal domain. →赤穂浪士(ろうし)

かなめいし 要石 〖神道・災害〗 the foundation stone at Kashima Shrine. Is said to press down upon a huge catfish, whose violent motion then causes an earthquake.

かにかまぼこ 蟹蒲鉾 〖食べ物〗 imitation-crab fish cake. Is shaped to resemble crab leg meat. Its ingredient is white fish, not crab.

かにこうせん 蟹工船 〖文芸・作品〗 *The Crab Cannery Ship*. A proletarian novel published in 1929 by KOBAYASHI TAKIJI. Describes the situation of exploited laborers and their rebellion on a crab cannery ship.

かにみそ 蟹味噌 〖食べ物〗 crab butter. The internal organs of a crab. Has a strong flavor and is sometimes mixed with Japanese sake.

かね 鐘 〖仏教〗 ⇨釣鐘

かね 鉄漿 〖服飾〗 ⇨お歯黒

かねつきどう 鐘突き堂 〖仏教・建築〗 ⇨鐘楼(しょうろう)

かねへん 金偏 〖漢字〗 a left-side radical meaning "metal." Is used in kanji such as 鉄(iron), 針(needle), and 鉱(mine). →偏；部首

かのうえいとく 狩野永徳 〖絵画〗 1543-1590. A painter born in Kyoto. A grandson of KANOU MOTONOBU. Was sponsored by ODA NOBUNAGA and TOYOTOMI HIDEYOSHI and painted pictures on the wall of their castles and residences.

Reflected the magnificent style of this era and the prosperity of the Kanou school. His works include *Cypress Tree* at the Tokyo National Museum and *Birds and Flowers* at Daitoku-ji Temple in Kyoto. →狩野派

かのうけい 可能形 〖言語〗 the potential form of a verb. Indicates that the subject has the ability of doing.

かのうさんせつ 狩野山雪 〖絵画〗 1590-1651. A painter born in present Okayama Pref. Studied under KANOU SANRAKU and got married to his daughter. His style was strongly decorative as well as intellectual. His works include *Old Plum* at the Metropolitan Museum of Art in New York.

かのうさんらく 狩野山楽 〖絵画〗 1559-1635. A painter born in present Shiga Pref. Was discovered by TOYOTOMI HIDEYOSHI and became a disciple of KANOU EITOKU. His style was decorative and magnificent. His works include *Dragon and Tiger* at Myoushin-ji Temple in Kyoto.

かのうじごろう 嘉納治五郎 〖柔道〗 1860-1938. A judoist and educator born in Hyougo Pref. Established modern judo by combining forms of traditional jujitsu. →柔術

かのうたんゆう 狩野探幽 〖絵画〗 1602-1674. A painter born in Kyoto. A grandson of KANOU EITOKU. Went to Edo to get hired by the Tokugawa shogunate as one of its official painters. Different from the magnificent style of his predecessors, his style was elegant and refined. Founded the Edo Kanou school. His works include *Four Elegant Pastimes* at Nagoya Castle and pictures on sliding screens at Honbou of Daitoku-ji Temple in Kyoto. →狩野派

かのうなおのぶ 狩野尚信 〖絵画〗 1607-1650. A painter born in Kyoto. A younger brother of KANOU TAN'YUU. Went to Edo and got hired by the Tokugawa shogunate as one of its official painters. His works include *Eight Views of Xiaoxiang* at the Tokyo National Museum. →狩野派；瀟湘(しょう)八景

かのうは 狩野派 〖絵画〗 the Kanou school of painting. Was founded in Kyoto by KANOU MASANOBU around the 15th century and continued to occupy the major position in Japanese painting until the 19th century. Was divided into two sub-schools, Edo Kanou and Kyou Kanou, in the 17th century. The former was officially employed by the Tokugawa shogunate. →御用絵師(ごよう)

かのうほうがい 狩野芳崖 〖絵画〗 1828-1888. A painter born in present Yamaguchi Pref. Based on the tradition of the Kanou school, sought a new type of Japanese-style paintings together with OKAKURA TENSHIN and Ernest Fenollosa and made an effort to establish the Tokyo Fine Arts School.

His works include *Avalokiteshvara as a Merciful Mother* at Tokyo University of the Arts.

かのうまさのぶ 狩野正信 〖絵画〗 1434-1530. A painter born in Izu, present Shizuoka Pref. Founder of the Kanou school. His works include *Zhou Maoshu Appreciating Lotuses* at the Kyushu National Museum.

かのうもとのぶ 狩野元信 〖絵画〗 1476-1559. A painter born in Kyoto. Was hired by the Muromachi shogunate as its official painter. Merging the Japanese and Chinese styles, solidified the foundation of the Kanou school in its second generation. His works include pictures on sliding screens at Daisen-in of Daitoku-ji Temple in Kyoto. →狩野派

かのえ 庚 〖干支〗 the seventh item of JIKKAN. Literally means "yang of metal" or "the elder brother of metal." Its Chinese-style pronunciation is 'kou.' →十干(じっかん)

かのこしぼり 鹿の子絞り 〖服飾〗 fawn tie-dying. Produces a pattern resembling the one on a fawn, which is translated to 'kanoko' in Japanese.

かのこもち 鹿の子餅 〖食べ物〗 a "fawn" rice cake. Is made from rice, beans, sugar, and other ingredients. There are several versions, depending on shops or areas. A picture of a deer is printed on some cakes, while others depict specks on deer skin with beans.

かのと 辛 〖干支〗 the eighth item of JIKKAN. Literally means "yin of metal" or "the younger brother of metal." Its Chinese-style pronunciation is 'sin.' →十干(じっかん)

かばいて 庇い手 〖相撲〗 protecting the opponent from injury. When two sumo wrestlers fall down together, the upper wrestler touches the ground first to protect his opponent. In this case, the upper wrestler wins.

かばね 姓 〖政治・言語〗 a title to indicate the rank or profession of a clan in ancient times. Was attached after the clan name. Includes OMI, MURAJI, atai, obito, and miyatsuko.

かばやき 蒲焼き 〖食べ物〗 ⇨鰻の蒲焼

かひ 歌碑 〖文芸〗 a monument inscribed with a rhyming poem, TANKA. Is usually constructed at a place related to the poet or the motif of the poem. →句碑

かぶ カブ 〖娯楽〗 ⇨おいちょかぶ

かぶ 蕪 〖食べ物・植物〗 a turnip. *Brassica campestris*. Is pickled or simmered for eating.

がぶ ガブ 〖文楽〗 a mechanism to drastically change the face of a female puppet to a demoniac expression.

かぶき 冠木 〖神社・建築〗 a crossbeam at the top of a gate or TORII.

かぶき 歌舞伎 〖歌舞伎〗 kabuki. A traditional form of Japanese drama, combined with music, dance, and mime. Is said to have been started by a female dancer, IZUMO NO OKUNI, in the 17th century. Is now performed only by male actors and is characterized by elaborate costumes, striking makeup, exaggerated gestures, and stylized dances.

かぶきざ　歌舞伎座　〖歌舞伎〗 Kabukiza Theater. The principal theater for KABUKI in Tokyo. Was opened in 1889. Holds kabuki performances every month. Was ravaged by fire, natural disaster, and war, and was rebuilt three times.

かぶきもの　傾奇者〖精神性・服飾〗 a rough dandy from the 16th to 17th centuries. Dressed in flamboyant clothing and behaved in a peculiar manner, believing it was fashionable.

かぶきもん　冠木門〖建築〗 a traditional gate without a roof. A crossbeam is put on the two pillars.

かぶきやくしゃ　歌舞伎役者〖歌舞伎〗 a kabuki actor. There is no kabuki actresses.

かぶせるほてる　　カプセルホテル 〖旅〗 a capsule hotel. One guest sleeps in each sleeping module called a capsule, which is equipped with a bed, TV, alarm, and lighting.

かぶと　兜〖武器〗 a warrior's helmet. Was made of iron or leather and used together with a suit of armor. The design was different from period to period. →鎧(よろい)

かぶとちょう　兜町〖ビジネス・地名〗 the name of the town where the Tokyo Stock Exchange is located.

かぶとに　兜煮〖食べ物〗 the boiled head of a sea bream. Is seasoned with soy sauce, mirin, and gingers.

かぶとやき　兜焼き〖食べ物〗 the grilled head of a sea bream. Is flavored with salt or seasoned in teriyaki style. Other fish such as tuna or yellow tail are sometimes used.

かぶなかま　株仲間〖経済〗 a guild in the Edo period. Was approved by the shogunate or feudal governments, which intended to control the economy.

かぶら　蕪〖食べ物・植物〗 ⇨蕪(かぶ)

かぶらや　鏑矢〖武器〗 a whistling arrow. Was used on a battlefield as a signal or to threaten the enemy.

かほう　家宝〖生活〗 a family treasure. A valuable object handed down in a family for generations.

かぼちゃ　南瓜〖食べ物・植物〗 a pumpkin. *Cucurbita*. Eaten in various ways such as in tempura and simmered food. Traditionally eaten on a winter solstice day to wish for health and longevity.

かま　釜〖食文化〗 **(1)** a pot for steaming rice. Is attached with two short wings to hang on a kitchen range called KAMADO. **(2)** a teakettle. Is used in the tea ceremony.

かま　窯〖陶磁器〗 a kiln to fire ceramics. Began to be used in Japan when Sue ware was introduced in ancient times. →須恵器(すえき)

かまあげうどん　釜揚げ饂飩〖食べ物〗 thick wheat noodles served in the hot water used for boiling them. Are dipped in sauce when eaten.

がまいかだ　蒲筏〖忍者〗 a portable raft made of cattails and tree

branches. Can be easily dismantled and reassembled.

かまいたち 鎌鼬〔気象〕 an atmospheric phenomenon, literally meaning "sickle weasel." A local temporary vacuum caused by a whirlwind, sometimes cutting human skin sharply. This phenomenon occurred in present Nagano and Niigata Prefs. The cut was believed to be done by a mysterious weasel in olden times.

かまえ 構〔漢字〕 an enclosure radical. Literally means "structure." For example, the 門 shaped part of 間 and 行 shaped part of 術 are enclosure radicals.

かまくら かまくら〔年中行事〕 a children's festival of snow shelter. Is held in Akita Pref. in mid-January. Children make an igloo-like shelter with snow, in which they enshrine the deity of water and eat rice cake.

かまくらござん 鎌倉五山〔仏教〕 Five Zen Temples of Kamakura: Kenchou-ji Temple, Engaku-ji Temple, Jyufuku-ji Temple, Jyochi-ji Temple, and Jyoumyou-ji Temple. They are all in the Rinzai sect and were built during the Kamakura period. →京都五山

かまくらし 鎌倉市〔地名〕 a city located southwest of Yokohama City, Kanagawa Pref. Is surrounded on three sides by mountains and on one side by the sea. Used to be the capital of the Kamakura shogunate, which lasted from around 1185 to 1333.

かまくらじだい 鎌倉時代〔時代〕 the Kamakura period, from around 1185 to 1333. MINAMOTO NO YORITOMO, the leader of the samurai at that time, established the shogunate and placed the seat of the government in Kamakura in present Kanagawa Pref. →鎌倉幕府

かまくらだいぶつ 鎌倉大仏〔仏教・彫刻〕 the Great Buddha of Kamakura. A National Treasure. Retains the original form and sits in the precinct of Koutoku-in in Kamakura City, Kanagawa Pref. Its height is 11.31 m (18.05 m including the platform) and its weight is 121 tons.

かまくらばくふ 鎌倉幕府〔武士・政治〕 the Kamakura shogunate. Was established by MINAMOTO NO YORITOMO, the leader of the samurai at that time. The Kamakura shogunate was the first time that the government was run by the samurai instead of the Emperor or his aristocracy.

かまくらぶんか 鎌倉文化〔時代〕 the Kamakura culture. Was developed by the samurai in the Kamakura period. Was deeply influenced through trade by the cultures of Sung (960-1279) and Yuan (1279-1368) in China. Its features were simple and masculine, completely different from the culture of the Heian period. It was in this era that ZEN Buddhism was brought into, and became widespread, throughout Japan.

かまくらぼり 鎌倉彫 〔工芸〕
Kamakura lacquerware. Is produced in Kamakura, chiseled in hardwood, and repeatedly lacquered in black and vermilion.

かましき 釜敷 〔茶道〕 a caldron mat. The host or hostess places the teakettle on it during the tea ceremony, while adding charcoal.

かまじるし 窯印 〔陶磁器〕 a potter's mark. Is put mainly on the bottom of ceramics to indicate who made or owned them.

かまだし 窯出し 〔陶磁器〕 to unload burnt ceramics from a kiln. The last step in making ceramics.

かまち 框 〔建築〕 a general term for the frame of a window, door, SHOUJI (sliding paper door), etc. Also indicates the rail of a threshold floor or an alcove. →上り框

かまど 竈 〔食文化〕 a kitchen range made from soil, stones, or bricks. Has been regarded as sacred and also has symbolized a family.

かまどがみ 竈神 〔宗教〕 a deity or deities of the cooking stove. Is enshrined around KAMADO, a kitchen range, where fire is used. Is sometimes called KOUJIN.

がまのあぶらうり 蝦蟇の油売り 〔大道芸〕 a street vendor selling toad-oil as medicine in the Edo period by chanting a familiar sales pitch. The sales pitch can be now heard only in fictional stories such as RAKUGO, comic storytelling.

かまぼこ 蒲鉾 〔食べ物〕 steamed fish paste, or a fish cake. Its ingredient is the white meat of fish such as sardines and walleye pollacks. Is cut into slices when eaten. Is served with horseradish and soy sauce or put in noodles as a topping. One of the popular fish cakes is imitation crab meat, called KANI-KAMABOKO.

かまぼこいた 蒲鉾板 〔食文化〕 a board attached to steamed fish paste.

かまめし 釜飯 〔食べ物〕 pot rice. Seasoned rice is boiled with a variety of ingredients such as meat, shrimp, and vegetables in a small pot. Is sometimes cooked in an earthen pot.

かまもと 窯元 〔陶磁器〕 **(1)** a ceramic atelier. **(2)** the master at the ceramic atelier.

かみ 神 〔宗教〕 a deity. Different from monotheistic beliefs such as Christianity, Islam, and Judaism, Japanese Shintoism has many deities. Buddhism also has several Buddhas and Bodhisattvas, in addition to many deities assimilated from other religions in India, China, and Japan.

かみ ～守 〔官位〕 the Lord of ～. A title of a high-ranking samurai. Though a place name or a profession was put in part of the "～," the person whose title was "the Lord of ～" was not actually in charge of managing of the place or profession. For example, 'Higo no kami' means "the Lord of Higo," but he actually did not administer the Higo area, which is present Kumamoto Pref.

かみありづき 神在月〖暦・神道〗 another name for October, but only in Shimane Pref. in the traditional calendar. Means "a month when deities are present" because all deities flock to Izumo, the eastern part of Shimane, from all over Japan. →神無月(かんなづき)

かみいずみひでつな 上泉秀綱 〖剣術〗 ?-1573. An expert swordsman born in present Nara Pref. Is also called Nobutsuna or Ise-no-kami. Founded the Shinkage school. His disciples include YAGYUU MUNEYOSHI, the founder of the Yagyuu school.

かみいちだんかつよう 上一段活用 〖言語〗 a verb conjugation in which the consonant of the stem end is always 'i.' Examples include 'miru' (to look) and 'okiru'(to wake up).

かみがき 神垣〖神道〗 ⇨玉垣

かみかくし 神隠し〖民話〗 the divine kidnap. People in olden times thought that when a child was missing, he or she had been spirited away by a supernatural being.

かみかぜ 神風〖軍事・自然〗 a divine wind. In the Mongolian invasions of 1274 and 1281, strong typhoons destroyed the invading fleet off Kyushu. These typhoons were called 'kamikaze,' a term that was applied to suicide attacks by Japanese pilots during World War II. → 元寇

かみかぜとっこうたい 神風特攻隊 〖軍事〗 Kamikaze Special Attack Force, which involved suicide attacks on enemy ships during World War II. The first attack was conducted at the Battle of Leyte Gulf in October 1944. More than 2,000 kamikaze soldiers died by the end of the war.

かみがた 上方〖地名〗 the Kansai region. Mainly refers to Kyoto and Osaka in reference to their culture.

かみがもじんじゃ 上賀茂神社〖神社〗 Kamigamo Shrine. Is located in the northern part of Kyoto City. The formal name is Kamo-wake-ikazuchi Jinja. Enshrines Kamo-wakeikazuchi no kami, a deity of thunder. The main building and the emergency building, 'Gonden,' are National Treasures. The whole shrine was designated a World Heritage Site in 1994. →賀茂神社；下鴨神社；葵(あおい)祭

かみかんむり 髪冠〖漢字〗 a crown radical meaning "hair." Is used in kanji such as 髪(hair) and 髭(mustache). →冠

かみきり 紙切り〖芸能〗 the stage performance of silhouette cutting. The performer promptly cuts a piece of paper into a silhouette, in response to requests from the audience.

かみざ 上座〖礼儀作法〗 the seat for an upper-ranking person in a room. In a traditional room, the seat in front of the alcove is 'kami-za.' ↔下座

かみしばい 紙芝居 〖娯楽〗 a picture-story show. Entertained children on a street in the early and mid-20th century. A storyteller told a story, showing a series of picture cards. The child audience had to buy cheap food as a fee to enjoy the show.

かみしも 裃 〖服飾〗 a formal costume for samurai in the Edo period. Consists of a long stiff vest called KATAGINU, a kimono with family crests, and loose-legged pleated trousers called HAKAMA.

かみすき 紙漉き 〖職業〗 making traditional paper. →和紙

かみだな 神棚 〖神道〗 a home Shinto altar. Is a kind of miniature shrine placed on a high shelf and enshrines a talisman. The number of households having 'kamidana' is decreasing these days. →箱宮(ほこみや)

かみて 上手 〖芸能〗 the right side on the stage when viewed from the audience. ↔下手

かみなべ 紙鍋 〖食文化〗 an individual-sized hot-pot dish cooked in fireproof paper. A kind of Japanese stew. Is mainly eaten in a cold season. Its ingredients are vegetables, seafood, meat, and other items according to taste.

かみなりおこし 雷粔籹 〖食べ物〗 a crispy roasted rice cake. Its name comes from KAMINARI-MON, Thunder Gate, at Sensou-ji Temple in Tokyo. A specialty of Tokyo.

かみなりもん 雷門 〖寺院・建築〗 Thunder Gate. The main gate of the SENSOU-JI Temple in Tokyo. Its name comes from the thunder deity statue placed at the gate. A huge red lantern is hung in the center of the gate. →雷神

かみのく 上の句 〖文芸〗 the first 17 syllables in a short rhyming poem, TANKA. ↔下の句

かみむすひのかみ 神皇産霊神 〖神話〗 the third-born deity who appeared in the creation of the world in Japanese mythology. Had the power of creation.

かみやしき 上屋敷 〖武士〗 a feudal lord's residence in Edo. The Tokugawa shogunate required feudal lords to live in Edo and in their homeland in alternate years. ↔下屋敷 →参勤交代

かむいがいでん カムイ外伝 〖忍者・漫画〗 *Kamui the Lone Ninja*. A ninja manga, written by Shirato Sanpei. Was published irregularly in a boys' manga magazine, *Weekly Manga Sunday* (Shounen Sandee), from 1965 to 1967.

かむいでん カムイ伝 〖忍者・漫画〗 *The Legend of Kamui: A Genuine Ninja Story*. A ninja manga, written by Shirato Sanpei. Was published serially in a manga magazine, *Monthly Manga Garo* (Gekkan Manga Garo), from 1964 to 1971.

かむやまといわれひこ 神日本磐余彦 〖神話〗 another name for Emperor Jinmu. →神武天皇

かめ 亀 〖動物〗 a turtle. Is considered to be an auspicious animal, like a crane, because of its longevity. Appears in some fairy tales such as "Urashima Tarou."

かめがおかいせき 亀ヶ岡遺跡 〖遺跡〗 the Kamegaoka Ruins. Were found in the early Edo period. Are located in Tsugaru City, Aomori Pref. Clay figures, earthen ware, and jades of the late Joumon period were excavated.

がめら ガメラ〖映画・動物〗 Gamera. A monster like a gigantic turtle in Daiei films. Debuted in 1965 and has appeared in several monster series. Though a monster itself, it usually fights with other evil monsters to help humans.

かも 鴨〖食べ物・動物〗 a wild duck. *Anas platyrhynchos*. Eaten as an ingredient in a one-pot dish, called 'kamonabe,' and in noodles such as KAMO-NANBAN.

かもい 鴨居 〖建築〗 a grooved wooden lintel for sliding screens. Several sliding screens are inserted and move along the groove. ⇨敷居 (しきい)(2)

かもしか 羚羊〖動物〗 ⇨日本羚羊

かもじんじゃ 賀茂神社 〖神社〗 Kamo Shrines. Two shrines located in the northern part of Kyoto City. Kamo-wakeikazuchi Jinja is commonly known as Kamigamo Shrine, and Kamo-mioya Jinja is commonly known as Shimogamo Shrine. In the Hollyhock Festival, the parade starts from the Kyoto Imperial Palace and goes to Shimogamo Shrine, then Kamigamo Shrine. Both shrines were designated a World Heritage Site in 1994.

かもなんばん 鴨南蛮 〖食べ物〗 buckwheat noodles served with cooked wild duck and green onions on top.

かものちょうめい 鴨長明 〖文芸〗 1155-1216. A poet born in Kyoto. His father was a Shinto priest, but he failed to become a Shinto priest and became a Buddhist monk instead. His works include an essay, *An Account of My Hut.* →方丈記

かものまぶち 賀茂真淵〖思想〗 1697 -1769. A scholar of Japanese classics and a poet, born in present Shizuoka Pref. Advocated reactionism and researched the *Anthology of Myriad Leaves* (MAN'YOUSHUU). A disciple of Kada no Azumamaro and the teacher of Motoori Norinaga. →国学

かもん 家紋 〖精神性・文様〗 a family crest. Is often put on a formal kimono. Aristocrats began to use it in the Heian period and warriors put it on their flags, armor, or helmets, and partition curtains in the Warring States period. Merchants and artisans also came to have their own family crests in the Edo period.

かや 茅 〖植物〗 a generic term for grasses for thatching roof. Includes sedge and Japanese pampas grass. →茅葺(かやぶ)き

かや 蚊帳 〖家具〗 a mosquito net. Is hung from the ceiling to prevent mosquitos from coming in on summer nights. People sleep inside the net.

かやくうどん 加薬饂飩 〔食べ物〕 thick wheat noodles with various toppings. Toppings are different from restaurant to restaurant; for example, chopped green onions, fish paste, seaweed, and mushrooms.

かやくごはん 加薬御飯 〔食べ物〕 rice cooked with vegetables and meat or fish.

かやぶき 茅葺 〔建築〕 a traditional thatching technique with sedge or Japanese pampas grass. Though rare these days, some private homes still have this type of roof, especially in the countryside.

かゆ 粥 〔食べ物〕 rice gruel or rice porridge. Mainly eaten in the event of ill health, especially gastrointestinal malfunction.

からあげ 唐揚げ 〔食べ物〕 deep-fried food without batter. The main ingredient is thinly covered with flour or dogtooth violet starch and is deep fried, not using batter. Chicken is popular.

からえ 唐絵 〔絵画〕 a Chinese picture. From the 9th to 12th centuries, this term referred to a picture imported from China or a painting whose theme was Chinese. Around the 13th century and later, it referred to a picture in the Sung or Yuan dynasty or a picture in Chinese style. →漢画

からおけ カラオケ 〔音楽〕 karaoke. Literally means "empty orchestra." People sing along back-up song tracks played with a machine. Was invented in Koube in the 1970s and performed at bars or clubs. Is now also popular in many other countries.

からおけぼっくす カラオケボックス 〔音楽〕 a karaoke booth. A small group can use a private room equipped with a karaoke machine.

からおり 唐織 〔服飾〕 a textile imported from China, or a Chinese-style textile manufactured in Japan. After being introduced from China, was further refined in the Nishijin area of Kyoto in the 16th century. Many different-colored silk yarns are weaved into decorative designs, as if they were embroidered. Its beauty makes it suitable for bridal and Noh costumes.

からかさ 唐傘 〔妖怪〕 an umbrella goblin. Had one eye, one leg, and a long tongue, and wore a wooden sandal. One of the most famous haunted objects, called TSUKUMO-GAMI.

からかみ 唐紙 〔生活〕 thick paper with colorful patterns or gold paint. Was originally imported from China. Is now used for sliding doors or wall paper.

からくさもよう 唐草模様 〔美術〕 an arabesque design. Was introduced from China to Japan in ancient times.

からくさもん 唐草文 〔文様〕 arabesque, or foliage scrolls. Spread from Greece or Persia through China to Japan.

からくりぎえもん からくり儀右衛門〖科学技術〗⇨田中久重

からくりにんぎょう からくり人形〖科学技術・人形〗a mechanical doll. Moves by a coil spring or hydraulic power. Developed in early modern times, influenced by mechanical developments in China and Europe.

からこにんぎょう 唐子人形〖人形〗a child doll in a Chinese-style costume.

からさわだけ 涸沢岳〖山岳〗Mt. Karasawa. Is located 1 km north of Mt. Oku Hotaka, the highest peak of the Northern Alps, which are on the border between Nagano and Gifu Prefs. Is 3,110 m high, the eighth highest peak in Japan.

からしあえ 辛し和え〖食べ物〗vegetable or seafood dressed with miso, vinegar, soy sauce, and mustard.

からしじょうゆ 辛子醤油〖調味料〗mustard soy sauce. Mustard is mixed with soy sauce. Is often used to season vegetables.

からしな 芥子菜〖調味料・植物〗mustard greens, leaf mustard, or a brown mustard. *Brassica juncea*. The leaves are used for pickles, and the seeds are used for spice.

からしめんたいこ 辛子明太子〖食べ物〗spicy cod roe. Is seasoned with chili powder. Is used in various dishes such as in the filling for rice balls and as an ingredient for pasta.

からしれんこん 辛子蓮根〖食べ物〗deep-fried lotus root with mustard. A specialty of Kumamoto Pref.

からすがい 烏貝〖動物〗a freshwater mussel. *Cristaria plicata*. The shell is used for shellwork.

からすてんぐ 烏天狗〖妖怪〗a raven bogeyman in legend. Has a crow-like beak and a pair of wings to fly.

からすみ 烏魚子〖食べ物〗roe of a striped mullet. Goes well with sake. A specialty of Nagasaki.

からつやき 唐津焼〖陶磁器〗Karatsu ware. Pottery produced around Karatsu City, Saga Pref. Is said to have been started by Korean potters, who came to Japan during TOYOTOMI HIDEYOSHI's invasions of Korea in 1592 and 1597.

からつゆ 空梅雨〖気象〗a rainy season with less rain. The rainy season is usually from June to July. →梅雨

からて 空手〖武術〗karate. A type of Chinese kung fu that was introduced to Okinawa and revised there. In a usual bout, blows and kicks must be stopped immediately before contact.

からはふ 唐破風〖建築〗a Chinese-style gable. The central part is convex, and the right and left parts are concave. In spite of its name, this style was invented in Japan.

からびつ 唐櫃〖生活〗a four- or six-legged Chinese-style large chest with a cover. Contained clothes, books, and armor in olden times.

からふと 樺太〖外交・地名〗Sakhalin, Russia. An island located to the north of Hokkaido. Its area is 76,400 km^2. Although Japan and Russia had repeated territorial negotiations, all of Sakhalin became part of Russia after World War II.

からぼり 空堀 〖建築〗 a dry moat. The moat intentionally is left without water.

からまつ 唐松 〖植物〗 a Japanese larch. *Larix leptolepis*. The wood is used for architecture.

からみそ 辛味噌 〖調味料〗 **(1)** strongly salty miso. ↔甘味噌 **(2)** spicy miso.

からめてもん 搦め手門 〖城郭〗 the rear gate of a castle. Was designed for the lord of the castle to escape in case of emergency. ↔大手門

からもん 唐門 〖建築〗 a gate with a Chinese-style gable. Examples are seen at Sanpou-in of DAIGO-JI Temple and DAITOKU-JI Temple in Kyoto. →唐破風(からはふ)

からよう 唐様 〖建築〗 ⇨禅宗様

がらん 伽藍 〖仏教・建築〗 a temple building. Derived from the abbreviation of a Sanskrit word, *samgharama*.

がらんはいち 伽藍配置 〖仏教・建築〗 a layout of temple buildings. The layout plan varied from period to period, and from sect to sect.

がり ガリ 〖寿司〗 sushi jargon for ginger. →生姜(しょうが)

かりぎぬ 狩衣 〖服飾〗 literally means "hunting costume." Was used as informal men's dress for court nobles in the Heian period, and formal men's dress for warriors in later periods. Is worn by

Shinto priests in modern times.

かりしゅうげん 仮祝言 〖冠婚葬祭〗 a preliminary wedding. Is privately held within family or relatives.

かりていも 訶梨帝母 〖仏教〗 ⇨鬼子母神(きしじん)

かりばかま 狩袴 〖服飾〗 a loose-legged long-pleated pair of trousers for hunting. Was worn over a kimono by a man.

かりゆしうえあ かりゆしウェア 〖服飾〗 an Okinawa-style aloha shirt. 'Kariyushi' means "being auspicious."

かりん 花梨 〖植物〗 **(1)** a quince. *Cydonia oblonga*. Arrived in Japan in the early Edo period. Eaten as jam or drunk as liquor. **(2)** *Chaenomeles sinensis*. The wood is used as a pillar in a decorative alcove.

かりんとう 花林糖 〖食べ物〗 deep-fried brown sugar snacks. Are crispy and tasty, though they look awful.

かるいざわ 軽井沢 〖地名〗 a resort in the mountains in northeastern Nagano Pref. Developed as a post town on NAKASENDOU in the Edo period. Later in 1886, the Canadian missionary Alexander Shaw introduced it as a summer resort. Today, it is popular among visitors with its many hotels, shops, museums, and tennis courts. Near its central part is Karuizawa Station on Hokuriku Shinkansen, which connects Karuizawa with Tokyo in 70 minutes.

かるかん 軽羹〔食べ物〕 a steamed spongy cake of rice powder and grated yam. A specialty of Kagoshima Pref.

かるさん 軽衫〔服飾〕 a loose pair of trousers with rather tight cuffs. Were used as a working wear in the 18th and 19th centuries.

かるた 歌留多〔ゲーム〕 a traditional matching card game. One player reads aloud a text on a reading card, and other players pick out the matching card among pick-up cards spread out on the floor. Is usually played on New Year's holidays. The name comes from a Portuguese word, 'carta,' which means "card."

かるら 迦楼羅〔仏教〕 *Garuda*. A legendary gigantic bird in Indian mythology. Was incorporated into Buddhism. Eats dragons. One of the Eight Devas that guard Buddhism. →八部衆

かれい 鰈〔魚〕 a right-eye flounder. *Pleuronectidae*. Eaten dried, grilled, simmered, or as sashimi.

かれえうどん カレー饂飩〔食べ物〕 thick white noodles in a curry broth.

かれえこ カレー粉〔調味料〕 curry powder. Consists of various spices such as pepper, ginger, turmeric, coriander, and cinnamon. Was introduced from India through the United Kingdom to Japan in the 19th century.

かれえちゃあはん カレー炒飯〔食べ物〕 ⇨ドライカレー(**2**)

かれえぱん カレーパン〔食べ物〕 a curry bread. Contains curry and is often deep-fried.

かれえらいす カレーライス〔食べ物〕 curry and rice. One of the most popular dishes in Japan. Popular ingredients are stir-fried carrots, onions, potatoes, and meat. These ingredients are seasoned with curry roux, and the mixture is served with rice. Very different from Indian curry.

かれさんすい 枯山水〔庭園・寺院〕 a dry landscape garden. Is mainly composed of rocks and sand, with no water. Represents mountains, rivers, and the spiritual world of Buddhism. Developed in the Muromachi period. Famous examples include the gardens in the RYOUAN-JI Temple and the DAITOKU-JI Temple.

かろう 家老〔武士・官位〕 a chief vassal of a feudal lord in the Edo period. Those living in the feudal domain were called KUNI-GAROU, and those living in Edo were called EDO-GAROU.

かろうし 過労死〔経済・医療〕 karoshi. Death from overwork. Also includes suicide from overwork-related stress is included.

かわいい カワイイ〔精神性〕 an adjective whose sense includes "cute," "lovely," or/and "sweet," but it does not end there. Sometimes implies "imperfect" or "separate from reality." Some typical "kawaii things" are YURUKYARA and Hello Kitty.

かわいかんじろう 河井寛次郎 〚陶磁器〛 1890-1966. A potter born in Shimane Pref. Was impressed by the works of Bernard Leach and joined the folk-arts movement started by YANAGI MUNEYOSHI.

かわかみてつはる 川上哲治 〚スポーツ〛 1920-2013. A professional baseball player born in Kumamoto Pref. Played for the Yomiuri Giants from 1938 to 1958. Was the Central League batting champion five times, the RBI leader three times, and the home run king twice. After retiring, won the Japan Series nine times consecutively as manager of the Yomiuri Giants. →日本シリーズ

かわぐちこ 河口湖 〚湖沼〛 Lake Kawaguchi. One of the Fuji Five Lakes in southeastern Yamanashi Pref. The area is 6.1 km². The surface is 833 m above sea level, and the maximum depth is 15 m. Windsurfing, camping, and sports fishing are popular. Visitors can enjoy the view of cherry blossoms in April, autumn leaves in November, and Mt. Fuji all year round, as well as hot springs. Is the most popular of the five lakes among tourists, partly because of its easy access from central Tokyo by bus or train, each taking 2 hours. There is also seasonal direct train service from Narita Airport on weekends. →富士五湖

かわさきだいし 川崎大師 〚寺院〛 Kawasaki Daishi Heikenji Temple. A main temple of the Shingon sect, founded in the early 12th century by a priest named Sonken. Is located in Kawasaki City, Kanagawa Pref. Is often visited by people who would like to have unluckiness exorcized when they are at an unlucky age. →真言宗; 厄除け

かわたけもくあみ 河竹黙阿弥 〚歌舞伎〛 1816-1893. A playwright of kabuki, born in Edo. Mainly wrote social dramas that depict everyday life of townspeople in the Edo period. His works include *Sannin Kichisa Kuruwa no Hatsugai*, commonly known as *Sannin Kichisa*. Wrote a new style of drama, namely social drama and drama faithful to historical fact.

かわち 河内 〚地名〛 old name for the eastern Osaka Pref.

かわちおんど 河内音頭 〚音楽〛 a rhythmical narrative song for the Bon Festival dancing. Developed in the Kawachi area, Osaka Pref., in the 19th century. →盆踊り

かわなかじまのたたかい 川中島の戦い 〚戦争〛 Battles of Kawanakajima. Two feudal lords, TAKEDA SHINGEN and UESUGI KENSHIN fought each other five times in the mid-16th century in present Nagano Pref.

かわばたやすなり 川端康成 〚文芸〛 1899-1972. A novelist born in Osaka. Was awarded the Nobel Prize for Literature in 1968, the first in Japan. Killed himself in 1972. His works include *The Izu Dancer* in 1926, *Snow Country* in

1935, *Thousand Cranes* in 1951, and *The Sound of the Mountain* in 1954.

かわむらずいけん 河村瑞賢 〔経済〕 1618-1699. A businessman born in Ise city, present Mie Pref. Made a huge profit in the timber business after the Meireki Conflagration in Edo in 1657. Developed the sea route between Osaka and ports along the Sea of Japan and the sea route between Edo and present Yamagata Pref.

かわや 厠 〔生活〕 an old term for "lavatory."

かわゆか 川床 〔食文化・娯楽〕 ⇨納涼床

かわら 瓦 〔建築〕 a roof tile. Was introduced from China in ancient times, together with Buddhist architecture.

かわらけ 土器 〔陶磁器〕 unglazed earthenware, especially a sake cup.

かわらせんべい 瓦煎餅 〔食べ物〕 a sweet cracker in the shape of a roof tile. Is made from flour, eggs, and sugar.

かわらばん 瓦版 〔文書〕 a commercial newssheet in the Edo period. The seller read aloud selected passages to attract people on the street.

かわらもの 河原者 〔芸能〕 the untouchable in medieval times. Literally means "people of the riverside." Their occupations included butchers, gardeners, sanitation workers, and actors.

かわりごろも 変わり衣 〔忍者〕 a technique of disguise. Since the reverse side of a ninja costume has a totally different color from the outside surface, a ninja easily disguised himself or herself by reversing the costume.

かん 漢 〔国名〕 the Han dynasty. Is divided into the Earlier Han from 202 B.C. to A.D. 8, and the Later Han from 25 to 220. Na-koku in Japan sent an envoy to Han in 57 and was presented a gold seal. Wielded great influence on ancient Japan.

かん 燗 〔酒〕 to heat or warm sake. →燗酒

かん 鐶 〔茶道〕 a pair of metal rings with which to carry a teakettle.

かん ～貫 〔単位〕 a unit to measure weight, which is rarely used today. One kan is about 3.75 kg, and 1,000 monme is one kan.

かんあみ 観阿弥 〔能〕 1333-1384. A Noh actor and playwright born in Iga, present Mie Pref. The father of Zeami and the founder of the Kanze school of Noh. His philosophy is written in Zeami's work, *The Flowering Spirit: Classic Teachings on the Art of Noh* (Fuushikaden).

かんいじゅうにかい 冠位十二階 〔官位〕 the system of twelve court ranks. Was invented in 603 by Prince Shoutoku. Its intention was to recruit or promote skilled people, not based on their family background but on their ability or their achievements, but it was not fully successful. Each court rank was distinguished by a colored cap.

かんえい 寛永 〖時代〗 an era name from 1624 to 1644 in the early Edo period. The government began to mint coins circulated in the Edo period during this era.

かんえいじ 寛永寺 〖寺院〗 Kan'ei-ji Temple. Affiliated with the Tendai sect. Was founded in 1625 by TENKAI and is located in the northeastern part of Tokyo. Its establishment was financially supported by TOKUGAWA IEMITSU. Almost all buildings were destroyed by fire in the Boshin Civil War of 1868, and its precinct became Ueno Park after the Meiji Restoration. →戊辰(ﾎ ｼﾝ)戦争

かんえいつうほう 寛永通宝 〖貨幣〗 a coin with a square hole in the center. Was first minted in 1636 and circulated during the Edo period.

かんおうかい 観桜会 〖年中行事〗 a cherry blossom viewing party hosted by the Emperor. Was held at Shinjuku Gyoen National Garden in Tokyo. Started in 1881 and ended in 1938.

かんおん 漢音 〖漢字〗 the Han-dynasty style pronunciation of a kanji. Some kanji have two Chinese-style pronunciations, besides a Japanese-style pronunciation. For example, 生, which means life, has two Chinese-style pronunciations: 'sei' and 'shou.' The first pronunciation is in the Han style, while the last pronunciation is in the Wu style, GO-ON. The latter

came to Japan earlier than the former. ↔呉音(ﾟ ｵﾝ)

かんが 漢画 〖絵画〗 a Chinese-style ink painting in medieval and early-modern times. This style modeled itself on the paintings in the Sung and Yuan dynasties. Paintings of the Kanou school are also sometimes called 'kanga.' →唐絵(ﾟ ｴ); 狩野(ﾟ ﾉ)派

かんかんせったい 官官接待 〖政治〗 the entertaining of official servants by other official servants. In many cases, prefectural official servants entertain national government officers who have authorization powers.

かんぎくかい 観菊会 〖天皇〗 a chrysanthemum appreciation party hosted by the Emperor. Was held at Shinjuku Gyoen National Garden in Tokyo. Started in 1880 and ended in 1937.

かんきてん 歓喜天 〖仏教〗 the deity of wealth, conjugal harmony, and child birth. *Ganapati* or *Ganesa*. Has two kinds of appearance: one is as a human with an elephant head, and the other is as a man and woman embracing each other. Is also called 'Shou-ten.'

かんきょうしょう 環境省 〖行政機関〗 Ministry of the Environment. Started in 2001 based on the previous Environment Agency.

かんぐん 官軍 〖軍事〗 the Imperial army. Often refers to the army of the new government in the Meiji Restoration.

かんげつかい 観月会 〖自然〗 a moon-viewing party. Is held at the night of the full moon. Is sometimes hosted by a temple or a shrine.

かんご 漢語 〖漢字〗 a kanji word read in the Chinese-style pronunciation. Some were introduced from China and became loanwords in Japanese. There are many homophones among 'kango.' ↔大和言葉

かんごうしゅうらく 環濠集落 〖考古〗 a moated village in ancient times. There are several reasons for the moat such as promoting drainage and defense and establishing a boundary.

かんこうちょう 観光庁 〖行政機関〗 Japan Tourism Agency. An external agency of the Ministry of Land, Infrastructure, Transport and Tourism. Was established in 2008, with the aim of revitalizing regional economies through tourism and promoting international mutual understanding.

かんごうぼうえき 勘合貿易 〖経済〗 the tally trade. Was carried out with the Ming dynasty from 1401 to 1547. Japan exported copper, sulfur, gold, and swords, and imported copper coins, raw silk, and silk textiles.

かんこくへいごう 韓国併合 〖外交〗 the annexation of Korea to Japan. Japan colonized Korea in 1910 as a result of the Russo-Japanese War. It continued until the end of World War II.

かんこんそうさい 冠婚葬祭 〖冠婚葬祭〗 wedding ceremonies and funerals. This term used to refer to four kinds of ceremonies: coming of age, marriage, funerals, and ancestral worship.

かんさいこくさいくうこう 関西国際空港 〖交通〗 Kansai International Airport (KIX). Is located on an artificial island 5 km off the coast in the southeastern part of Osaka Bay. Opened in 1994 and is open 24 hours a day. From the airport, passengers can get to Osaka and Kyoto mainly by train, including the Airport Express HARUKA. →大阪国際空港

かんさいちほう 関西地方 〖地名〗 the Kansai region. Consists of six prefectures in south-central Honshuu, namely, Shiga, Kyoto, Osaka, Hyougo, Nara, and Wakayama. Sometimes, Mie or Fukui Pref. is added to the list. Is used almost interchangeably with KINKI CHIHOU, but 'Kansai chihou' is used in less formal contexts. Literally means "the region to the west of the tollgates," in contrast to KANTOU CHIHOU meaning "the region to the east of the tollgates." The tollgates used to be in Fukui, Gifu, and Mie Prefs.

かんざけ 燗酒 〖酒〗 heated sake. Is usually served in a small ceramic bottle and is drunk with a tiny ceramic cup. Is called by different names based on its heated temperature: HITOHADA, NURUKAN, JOUKAN,

and ATSTUKAN. ↔冷や酒 →銚子；猪
口(ちょこ)

かんざし 簪 〖服飾〗 an ornamental hairpin. A woman sometimes wears it when dressed in a kimono.

かんざんじっとく 寒山拾得 〖絵画〗 Han-shan and Shi-de. Two legendary priests in the Tang period (618–907) of China. A popular subject in Zen pictures. Often, Han-shan reads a sutra, and Shi-de holds a broom. It is said that they were reincarnations of *Manjusri* and *Samantabhadra*. Examples are contained in the Tokyo National Museum, the MOA (Mokichi Okada Association) Museum of Art, and other museums. →文殊菩薩(もんじゅぼさつ)；普賢菩薩(ふげんぼさつ)

かんし 漢詩 〖文芸〗 classic Chinese poetry. Imitating its style, Japanese also composed kanshi, using Chinese characters and standard formats. →絶句；律詩(りっし)

かんじ 漢字 〖漢字〗 a kanji, or a Chinese character. One of the four letter types used in the Japanese language: HIRAGANA, KATAKANA, kanji, and alphanumeric characters. Japan did not have its own writing system before Chinese characters were introduced in ancient times. Hiragana and katakana, which were phonograms, were invented from kanji, which is an ideogram.

かんじかなまじりぶん 漢字仮名交じり文 〖漢字〗 a text written with KANJI, HIRAGANA, and KATAKANA. The standard writing system in modern Japanese.

かんじき 樏 〖生活〗 traditional snowshoes. Round-shaped, different from modern racket-like snowshoes.

かんじけんてい 漢字検定 〖漢字・教育〗 the Japan Kanji Aptitude Test. There are ten grades and several pre-stage grades. The highest level is the first grade, and the lowest is the tenth grade.

かんじざいぼさつ 観自在菩薩 〖仏教〗 ⇨観音菩薩

かんしつ 乾漆 〖仏教〗 a sculpture technique using dry lacquer. There are two variations of this technique: one for a hollow sculpture and the other for a wood-core sculpture. →脱活(だっかつ)乾漆；木心(もくしん)乾漆

がんじつ 元日 〖正月〗 New Year's Day. January 1. A national holiday. Many people visit a Shinto shrine or Buddhist temple and celebrate the New Year with family by eating special dishes. →初詣；御節(おせち)料理

かんじゃ 冠者 〖冠婚葬祭〗 ⇨冠者(かじゃ)

かんじゃ 間者 〖軍事〗 an old term for a "spy." Was used until the end of the 19th century.

かんじゅ 貫首 〖仏教〗 the chief priest of a main temple of a sect or a large temple. →住職；管長

かんじょうぶぎょう 勘定奉行 〖官位〗 a feudal commissioner of finance under the Tokugawa shogunate. Administered financial matters and tax collection.

かんじん 勧進〖仏教〗 calling for donations to build or repair temple or shrine buildings. Originally meant "preaching Buddhism and inviting people to become a Buddhist."

がんじん 鑑真〖仏教〗 Jianzhen. 688 -763. A Chinese priest. Came to Japan in 753, introduced the Ritsu sect, and founded the TOUSHOUDAI-JI Temple.

かんしんじ 観心寺〖寺院〗 Kanshin-ji Temple. Affiliated with the Shingon sect. Is located in southern Osaka Pref. Is said to have been established by EN NO ODUNU and revived by the priest KUUKAI and his two disciples. The main hall, the image of the Bodhisattva of Mercy with Wish-fulfilling Jewel and Dharma Ring, and the inventory of property are National Treasures.

かんじんずもう 勧進相撲〖相撲〗 a sumo event to raise money for temple or shrine buildings. Is said to have been started around the 14th century and has later become a professional event. →勧進

かんじんちょう 勧進帳 **(1)**〖宗教〗 a proposal document to call for donations to build or repair temple or shrine buildings. **(2)**〖歌舞伎〗 the title of a kabuki program that describes the runaway trip of MINAMOTO NO YOSHITSUNE and his retainers.

かんす 鑵子〖茶道〗 ⇨茶釜

かんせい 寛政〖時代〗 an era name from 1789 to 1801 in the mid-Edo period. MATSUDAIRA SADANOBU implemented political reform in this era.

かんせいのかいかく 寛政の改革〖政治〗 Kansei Reform. Was conducted from 1787 to 1793 by MATSUDAIRA SADANOBU. Promoted simple frugality, cancelled samurai's debts, controlled sake brewing and publication, and stored rice for emergencies. However, it was very unpopular with the merchant class and eventually failed.

かんぜおんじ 観世音寺〖寺院〗 Kanzeon-ji Temple. Affiliated with the Tendai sect. Is located in DAZAIFU City, Fukuoka Pref. Was established in the 8th century by Emperor Tenji, who prayed for the repose of the soul of his mother, Empress Saimei. Had one of the three great ordination platforms called KAIDAN. Its temple bell is a National Treasure. →天智天皇

かんぜおんぼさつ 観世音菩薩〖仏教〗 ⇨観音菩薩

かんせつわざ 関節技〖柔道〗 an armlock technique. Many of such techniques are forbidden in a match.

かんだまつり 神田祭〖祭礼〗 Kanda Festival. Is held at KANDA MYOUJIN on May 15. One of the Three Great Festivals in Edo.

かんだみょうじん 神田明神〖神社〗 Kanda Shrine. Is located in Tokyo. Enshrines OONAMUCHI NO KAMI, SUKUNAHIKONA NO MIKOTO, and TAIRA NO MASAKADO. →神田祭

がんだむ ガンダム〘アニメ〙 ⇨機動戦士ガンダム

がんだれ 雁垂れ〘漢字〙 an upper-to-left radical of a KANJI. An abbreviated form of 雁(wild goose). Is used in kanji such as 原(field), 厚(thick), and 灰(ash).

がんたん 元旦〘正月〙 New Year's morning. The morning of January 1. →元日

かんちゅうみまい 寒中見舞〘暦・文書〙 a card of midwinter greetings. Is sent from January 5 or 6 until February 3. Those who have not sent New Year's greetings because they are in mourning often send this card instead.

かんちょう 管長〘仏教〙 the head administrator of a sect. →貫首(かんじゅ)

かんづくり 寒造り〘酒〙 brewing sake in winter. Also refers to the sake brewed in winter.

かんつばき 寒椿〘植物〙 a sasanqua camellia. *Camellia sasanqua.* Blooms bright pink flowers from the end of November to the beginning of February.

かんていりゅう 勘亭流〘書道〙 the thick and round style of calligraphy. Is used in a poster or in an actor's list of kabuki.

かんてん 寒天〘食べ物〙 agar-agar. Is made from seaweed and often used as an ingredient of sweets.

がんどう 龕灯〘犯罪〙 ⇨強盗提灯(がんどうちょうちん)

かんとうい 貫頭衣〘服飾〙 an ancient poncho. Was worn by women, according to "The Record of Japan" in the *History of Wei* (GISHI WAJIN-DEN).

かんとうさんち 関東山地〘地名〙 the Kantou Mountains. Are located on the border between the Kantou region and the Chuubu region. On the Kantou side are Gunma, Saitama, Tokyo, and Kanagawa Prefs., and on the Chuubu side are Nagano and Yamanashi Prefs. Are divided by the upper reaches of the Sagami River. In the northern half are the Chichibu Mountains, and in the southern half the Tanzawa Mountains. The highest peak is Mt. Kitaokusenjou-dake in the Chichibu Mountains, which is 2,601 m high.

かんとうしょう 敢闘賞〘相撲〙 Fighting Spirit Prize. Is given to a wrestler, excepting two higher-ranking wrestlers called YOKODUNA and OOZEKI, who has shown a great fighting spirit and enlivened the sumo tournament. The criteria of awarding the prize differs according to each case; for example, it may be given to a wrestler who has won more than 10 times among 15 bouts though he has failed to win the tournament, or to a rookie wrestler who has yielded good results.

かんとうだいしんさい 関東大震災〘災害〙 the Great Kanto Earthquake. Occurred at 11:58 on September 1, 1923, and struck the entire Kantou region. The epicenter was in Sagami Bay on Kanagawa Pref. The magnitude was 7.9, and the maximum seismic intensity was 6. About 140,000 people were found dead or were missing. →震度

かんとうだき 関東炊き〖食べ物〗 a Kansai dialect for ODEN, stew in broth lightly flavored with soy sauce.

かんとうちほう 関東地方 〖地名〗 the Kantou region. Is located in Eastern Japan, facing the Pacific Ocean. Consists of Ibaraki, Tochigi, Gunma, Saitama, Chiba, Tokyo, and Kanagawa Prefs.

がんどうちょうちん 強盗提灯〖犯罪〗 a portable search light in the Edo period. Illuminated one direction, owing to a reflector and a rotating candle stand that kept a candle upright.

かんとうへいや 関東平野 〖地名〗 Kantou Plain. The largest plain in Japan. Is located in Eastern Japan, facing the Pacific Ocean. Parts of Ibaraki, Tochigi, Gunma, Saitama, Chiba, Tokyo, and Kanagawa Prefs. are on the plain. Consists of plateaus covered with a volcanic loam layer.

かんとうまつり 竿灯祭り〖祭礼〗 ⇨ 秋田竿灯祭り

かんどころ 勘所〖音楽〗 a position on the fingerboard to be pressed in playing a stringed instrument such as SHAMISEN and KOTO.

かんなづき 神無月〖暦〗 October in the traditional calendar. Means "no deity month" because it is said that all deities flock to Izumo, eastern Shimane Pref., from all over Japan in this month. →旧暦；神在月 (かみあり づき)

かんなべ 燗鍋〖酒〗 a flat kettle to heat sake. Is often made of bronze.

かんぬし 神主〖神道〗 the general term for a Shinto priest. Wears a kind of kimono and HAKAMA, a pleated skirt. The color of the dress is different, depending on the priest's rank. →宮司(ぐうじ)；禰宜(ねぎ)；笏(しゃく)

がんねん 元年〖暦〗 the first year of a new era. For example, the year 1926 was 'gannen' of the Shouwa era, and the year 1989 was 'gannen' of the present era, Heisei.

かんのあけ 寒の明け〖暦〗 the end of mid-winter.

かんのいり 寒の入り 〖暦〗 the beginning of mid-winter. Around January 5 or 6.

かんのわのなのこくおういん 漢委奴国王印〖外交・考古〗 a gold seal engraved with 漢委奴国王, which means "the King of Na in Japan, under the Han dynasty." Was discovered in present Fukuoka Pref. in 1784. Is probably identified with a seal that the emperor of Han bestowed to the king of Na in 57, which was referred to in the *History of the Later Han*. →奴国(なこく)

かんのんがくれ 観音隠れ〖忍者〗 a hiding technique that involves stopping the motion behind an object while covering one's face with sleeves. The face has to be covered to conceal its brightness and to eliminate the wind and sound of breathing.

かんのんぼさつ 観音菩薩 〖仏教〗 Kuan-Yin or Guanyin. Bodhisattva of Mercy. *Avalokiteshvara*. Transforms him/herself to assist those who are seeking salvation. One of the Amitabha Triad. →阿弥陀三尊 (あみださんそん)

かんぱく 関白 〖官位〗 a supreme adviser to an Emperor. The position started in the 9th century and ended in the 19th century. When an Emperor was young, a regent called SESSHOU helped him; when an Emperor became an adult, 'kanpaku' helped him. Through history, the Fujiwara clan monopolized this position, excepting TOYOTOMI HIDEYOSHI and Toyotomi Hidetsugu, who became kanpaku in the 16th century. →藤原氏

かんぱち 間八 〖食べ物・魚〗 a greater amberjack. *Seriola dumerili*. Lives near Japan, in the East China Sea, and around Hawaii. About 1.5 m long and edible.

かんばんほうしき 看板方式 〖経済・科学技術〗 the just-in-time production system. Aims at minimize the stock of parts in assembling automobiles. Was devised by Toyota Motor Corporation.

がんぴ 雁皮 〖植物〗 there is no common English name. *Wikstroemia sikokiana*, or *Diplomorpha sikokiana*. Grows in a mountainous area of Western Japan. A raw material for traditional paper.

かんぴょう 干瓢 〖食べ物〗 dried strips of a bottle gourd. Are soaked in water for eating. Are often used for a sushi roll or five-item sushi. →巻き寿司；五目寿司

かんぶつ 乾物 〖食文化〗 dried food for preservation. Includes dried fish, dried seaweed, and dried mushrooms.

かんぶつえ 灌仏会 〖仏教・年中行事〗 the Birthday Festival for the Historical Buddha on April 8. People pour fragrant water or hydrangea tea on a small statue of the Buddha. This rite is associated with a story that two dragons poured fragrant water on the Historical Buddha when he was born. →誕生仏

かんぶり 寒鰤 〖食べ物・魚〗 a yellowtail caught in a cold season. →鰤

かんぶん 漢文 〖漢字〗 Chinese classics. Modern high school students study Chinese classics in a Japanese class because formal documents in Japan were written in the Chinese language in ancient times.

かんぶんくんどく 漢文訓読 〖漢字〗 reading the text of Chinese classics as Japanese. Special reading marks to indicate how to read the sentences are often added. →訓点

かんぽうい 漢方医 〖医療〗 a doctor of traditional Chinese medical science. →漢方薬

かんぽうやく 漢方薬 〖医療〗 traditional Chinese medicine. Most materials are herbs though some are made from animals or minerals.

Is said to have been introduced into Japan around the 5th century.

かんみどころ 甘味処 〖食文化〗 a sweets parlor. Serves traditional sweets such as rice dumpling and sweet adzuki soup.

かんむてんのう 桓武天皇 〖天皇〗 Emperor Kanmu. 737-806. The 50th, on the throne from 781 to 806. Relocated the capital to Kyoto in 794.

かんむり 冠 〖漢字〗 a crown radical. Forms the upper part of a kanji. For example, the ワ shaped part of 冠 and ウ shaped part of 字 are crown radicals.

かんめん 乾麺 〖食べ物〗 dried noodles. Are boiled in water when eaten, like dried pasta.

がんもどき 雁擬き 〖食べ物〗 a fried bean curd cake with chopped vegetables and other ingredients. Is usually cooked in stewed dishes.

かんもんかいきょう 関門海峡 〖地名〗 Kanmon Straits. Are located between Honshuu and Kyushu Islands and connect the Sea of Japan with the Inland Sea. Large cargo ships between Osaka and Korea or China go through the straits. On the Honshuu side is Shimonoseki City in Yamaguchi Pref., and on the Kyushu side is Kita Kyushu City in Fukuoka Pref. Between the two cities are underground tunnels for trains, cars, and pedestrians and a bridge for cars on the expressway. →関門トンネル

かんもんとんねる 関門トンネル 〖施設〗 the Kanmon tunnels. Connect Shimonoseki in Yamaguchi Pref. with Kitakyuushuu in Fukuoka Pref. There are two tunnels: one is for trains, and the other is for cars in the upper part and pedestrians in the lower part. The railroad tunnel was the first undersea tunnel in Japan, completed in 1944.

がんりゅうじま 巌流島 〖島名〗 Ganryuu Island. Is located at the western tip of Yamaguchi Pref., near the Kanmon straits. The famous duel between two sword masters, MIYAMOTO MUSASHI and Sasaki Kojirou, took place on this island in 1612.

かんれい 管領 〖官位〗 an assistant to a shogun in the Muromachi period. After the mid-Muromachi period, this post was occupied by one of the three clans: Shiba, Hosokawa, and Hatakeyama.

かんれき 還暦 〖通過儀礼〗 the age of 61, using the traditional approach to age counting. People usually celebrate when a person turns 60, in the modern approach to age counting. 'Kanreki' literally means "one cycle of a calendar." That is, a 60-year cycle, which combines the ten trunks, JIKKAN, with the twelve branches, JUUNISHI, is completed. As a metaphor to show that he or she is born again, the 60-year-old person wears a red sleeveless jacket, mimicking the clothes of a baby. → 数え年

かんろ 寒露 〖暦〗 one of the 24 seasonal nodes in the traditional calendar. Around October 8th. Ice forms for the first time in northern areas around this period. →二十四節気(にじゅうしせっき)

かんろに 甘露煮 〖食べ物〗 caramelized fish. Is grilled, dried, and then simmered with soy sauce, mirin, and sugar. Usually consists of a freshwater fish such as sweet fish and goby. →鮎(あゆ); 沙魚(はぜ)

かんわじてん 漢和辞典 〖漢字〗 a kanji dictionary. The user can look up meanings, sounds, radicals, stroke counts, and etymologies of kanji.

き

き 己〖干支〗 ⇨己(つち)

き 癸〖干支〗 ⇨癸(みずのと)

ぎ 魏〖国名〗 Wei. A Chinese dynasty from 220 to 265. Is referred to in *Romance of the Three Kingdoms*. "The Record of Japan" in the *History of Wei* referred to prehistorical Japan. →魏志倭人伝(ぎしわじんでん)

きあい 気合〖精神性〗 **(1)** strong will and concentration to do the best. **(2)** a shout given to oneself to strengthen one's willingness to attain success.

きあけ 忌明け〖冠婚葬祭〗 the end of the mourning period. In Japanese Buddhism, it is sometimes said that the mourning period is over on the 49th day from a person's death.

きい 紀伊〖地名〗 the old name for Wakayama Pref. and southwestern Mie Pref.

きいさんち 紀伊山地〖地名〗 the Kii Mountains. Extend over most of the Kii Peninsula. Include several sightseeing spots such as Kumano, YOSHINO, and Mt. Kouya. The highest peak is Mt. Hakkou-ga-take, which is 1,915 m high.

きいすいどう 紀伊水道〖地名〗 the Kii Channel. Is surrounded by Wakayama and Tokushima Prefs., and Awaji Island in Hyougo Pref. To its south is the Pacific Ocean, and to its north is Osaka Bay.

きいちほうげん 鬼一法眼〖武術〗 a legendary diviner, astrologist, and exorcist. It is said that his treasured book on tactics was stolen by MINAMOTO NO YOSHITSUNE, a military commander in the 12th century.

きいっぽん 生一本〖酒〗 undiluted sake.

きいと 生糸〖服飾〗 raw silk. Has not been boiled to be made smooth.

きいはんとう 紀伊半島〖半島〗 the Kii Peninsula. Projecting into the Pacific Ocean, and extending over Mie, Nara, and Wakayama Prefs. Most of it is mountainous. The coastline is irregular, creating many good harbors.

ぎえん 義淵〖仏教〗 ?-728. A priest born in present Nara Pref. The teacher of GENBOU and GYOUKI.

きえんれい 棄捐令〖武士・法律〗 an order to eliminate the debts of each samurai to any merchants. Was issued in 1789 and 1843. →寛政の改革

きおう 棋王〖将棋〗 Shogi King. One of the eight titles in shogi. The best-of-five title match, 'kiou-sen,' takes place annually from February to March.

きおりもの 生織物〖服飾〗 a textile made of raw silk.

ぎおん 祇園〖地名〗 an entertainment area in eastern Kyoto. There are many traditional high-class restaurants and teahouses, where GEISHA girls entertain their guests.

ぎおんしょうじゃ 祇園精舎 〖仏

教・施設】 the Jetavana Monastery. *Jetavana-vihara*. Was donated to the Historical Buddha by a rich merchant named Sudatta.

ぎおんまつり 祇園祭 〖祭礼〗 Gion Festival. Is held at Yasaka Shrine in Kyoto from July 1st to 31st. Many beautiful floats parade through the city on the 17th. One of the Three Great Festivals in Kyoto. →京都三大祭

ぎがく 伎楽 〖芸能〗 a masque pantomime accompanied by music in ancient times. Is said to have come from India through China and Korea to Japan.

ぎがくめん 伎楽面 〖芸能・彫刻〗 a mask for ancient music pantomime. There exist several masks at Toudai-ji Temple, which are said to be the oldest in the world.

きかつがん 飢渇丸 〖忍者〗 an anti-hunger pill.

きき 記紀 〖神話・書名〗 *Records of Ancient Matters* (Kojiki) and *Chronicles of Japan* (Nihonshoki). Two of Japan's oldest chronicles, which include mythology.

ききざけ 利き酒 〖酒〗 tasting sake to assess its quality. The color, fragrance, and flavor are evaluated.

ききづつ 聞き筒 〖忍者〗 an eavesdrop cylinder. Was used to listen in to the enemy's communications.

ききょう 桔梗 〖植物〗 a balloon flower, or a Chinese bellflower. *Platycodon grandiflorum*. One of the seven flowers of autumn in a lunar calendar. →秋の七草

きく 菊 〖植物〗 a chrysanthemum. *Chrysanthemum morifolium*. Is said to have been imported from China in ancient times. The variety was invented in the Edo period. Since 1871, has symbolized the Imperial family.

きくちかん 菊池寛 〖文芸〗 1888-1948. A novelist and playwright born in Kagawa Pref. Started a literary magazine, *Bungei Shunjuu*, in 1923 and created the Akutagawa and Naoki Prizes in 1935. His works include *Return of the Father* in 1917 and *Beyond the Pale of Vengeance* in 1919. →芥川(あくたがわ)賞；直木賞；父帰る；恩讐の彼方に

きくとかたな 菊と刀 〖書名〗 *The Chrysanthemum and the Sword*. A study on Japanese culture written in 1946 by an American anthropologist, Ruth Benedict.

きくな 菊菜 〖植物・食べ物〗 ⇨春菊

きくにんぎょう 菊人形 〖植物・人形〗 a chrysanthemum doll. Life-sized figures, decorated with chrysanthemum flowers, reproduce a historical scene.

きくのごもん 菊の御紋 〖天皇〗 the Imperial crest which displays a chrysanthemum. Has sixteen open petals.

きくのせっく 菊の節句 〖暦〗 ⇨重陽(ちょうよう)の節句

ぎげいてん 伎芸天 〖仏教〗 Deity of the Arts. Is said to have been born from the hairline of the Hindu deity, *Siva*, which is called Daijizai-ten in Japanese Buddhism.

きげんせつ 紀元節〖天皇〗 the anniversary of the enthronement of the first Emperor Jinmu. February 11th was prescribed as this day and designated a National Holiday in 1873 but was abolished in 1948. The same day was designated National Foundation Day in 1966. →建国記念日

きご 季語〖文芸〗 a season word. Is used in HAIKU to imply a season. For example, "frost" is a season word for winter.

きごう 揮毫〖書道〗 calligraphy or drawing in India ink by a famous person. In many cases, the person has responded to a request.

きこくしじょ 帰国子女〖教育〗 a returnee student. A child who has lived abroad for some reason, such as a parent's job, and has returned to Japan. Though their foreign language skills are appreciated, returnee students sometimes have difficulty integrating back into Japan.

きざみこんぶ 刻み昆布〖食べ物〗 shredded kelp seasoned with salt or soy sauce.

きざみのり 刻み海苔〖食べ物〗 shredded dried laver. Is sprinkled on noodles or tofu, or scattered on sushi.

きさらぎ 如月〖暦〗 February in the traditional calendar. Means "to wear double layers of clothing (because it is cold)." →旧暦

きし 棋士〖碁・将棋〗 a professional player of GO or SHOUGI.

きじ 雉〖動物〗 a green pheasant.

Phasianus versicolor. Was designated Japan's national bird in 1947. Its meat is edible. In a folk tale called "MOMOTAROU," is a servant to the hero, Peach Boy.

ぎし 義士〖武士〗 an ethical or righteous samurai.

きじし 木地師〖工芸〗 ⇨木地屋（きじや）

きじむなあ キジムナー〖妖怪〗 an old banyan tree sprite in Okinawa. Its appearance is like a little boy with red hair or a red face.

きしめん きしめん〖食べ物〗 flat wheat noodles. Are generally 1 mm thick and 7 to 8 mm wide. Has a smooth and soft texture and easily picks up soup, comparing with UDON. A specialty of Aichi Pref.

きしもじん 鬼子母神〖仏教〗 Goddess of Children and Easy Childbirth. *Hariti*. As a female demon, she captured and ate little children, but, after the Historical Buddha temporarily concealed one of her own children for disciplinary purposes, she embraced the Buddhist faith and became a deity. The image holds a child and has a pomegranate in hand.

きじや 木地屋〖工芸〗 a woodcraft smith. Shapes wood into daily tableware with a turning lathe or other tools. After this process, the tableware is lacquered by a lacquerware artisan. →塗り師

きじやき 雉焼き〖食べ物〗 grilled chicken flavored with soy sauce, mirin, and spices. Bonito or tuna is sometimes used. Although 'kiji'

means "pheasant," its meat is rarely used.

きじゅ 喜寿〖通過儀礼〗 the age of 77, using the traditional approach to age counting. People usually celebrate when a person turns 76, in the modern approach to age counting. 'Kiju' literally means "glad age," because when 77 is written vertically in KANJI (七十七), it looks like 喜 in a cursive style, which means "gladness." →数え年

きしゅう 紀州〖地名〗 ⇨紀伊

きじょ 鬼女〖妖怪〗 an ogress. A female monster who eats people.

きしょうちょう 気象庁〖自然・行政機関〗 Meteorological Agency. An external bureau of the Ministry of Land, Infrastructure, Transport and Tourism. By providing meteorological information, aims to prevent and mitigate natural disasters, to maintain and strengthen transportation, to help industries prosper, and to improve public welfare.

きしょうてんけつ 起承転結〖文芸〗 the four-phase structure in Chinese classic poems: introduction, development, turn, and conclusion. Is applied to a four-frame comic strip that appears in newspapers.

きじょうゆ 生醤油〖調味料〗 unprocessed soy sauce. Soy sauce is often sterilized with heat or is supplemented with water or seasonings, but 'kijouyu' is not.

ぎしわじんでん 魏志倭人伝〖書名〗 "The Record of Japan" in the *History of Wei*. Consists of about 2,000 Chinese characters and describes the location, society, customs, products, and political system of Japan in the 3rd century. A country named YAMATAI-KOKU existed within the area that later became Japan.

きじんだて 貴人立て〖茶道〗 tea making for a noble person. The tea master places a tea bowl on a small stand when making tea for a noble person, because it is considered rude to put the tea bowl directly on the floor.

きせい 棋聖 **(1)**〖碁〗 Board Game Saint. One of the seven titles in professional GO. The name is a combination of 'ki,' meaning go and shogi, and 'sei,' literally meaning a saint. The best-of-seven title match, 'kisei-sen,' takes place annually from January to February or March. The winner of this title match in 2015 got a prize of over 40,000,000 yen, the highest of all the go titles. **(2)**〖将棋〗 one of the eight titles in professional shogi. The best-of five title match takes place annually from June to July.

きせいらっしゅ 帰省ラッシュ〖暦・交通〗 the homecoming rush in a holiday season. A great number of people return from urban areas to their hometowns to visit their parents or relatives. Occurs during the so-called Golden Week from the end of April to the beginning of May, during the Bon holidays in mid-August, and during the year-end and New Year's holidays.

きせる 煙管〖娯楽〗 a traditional tobacco pipe. Has a long body with a small cup at the end. Is said that its name comes from a Khmer word "khsier."

きせんほうし 喜撰法師〖文芸〗 ?–? One of the Six Immortal Poets. Only one tanka in the *Collection of Ancient and Modern Japanese Poetry* (KOKINWAKASHUU) is identified as his work. →六歌仙

きそ 木曽〖地名〗 southwestern Nagano Pref. The area in Kiso Valley, along the upper reaches of the Kiso River. Famous for Japanese cypresses.

きそがわ 木曽川〖河川〗 the Kiso River. Flows from Mt. Hachimori in western Nagano Pref. into Ise Bay in Mie Pref. Is 227 km long, making it the eighth longest river in Japan. Along it are many sightseeing places such as Nezame no toko, Ena Vally, and Japan Rhine.

きぞくいん 貴族院〖政治〗 House of Peers. The Upper House in the Imperial Diet from 1890 to 1947. Were not to be dissolved, and the term of many Diet members was lifelong.

きそこまがたけ 木曽駒ヶ岳〖山岳〗 Mt. Kiso Komagatake. Is located in the Central Alps, in southern Nagano Pref. Is 2,956 m high. Is also called 'Kiso Koma' among mountaineers.

きそさんみゃく 木曽山脈〖地名〗 the Kiso Mountains. Lie in south-

western Nagano Pref. The highest peak is Mt. Kiso Komagatake, which is 2,956 m high.

きそば 生蕎麦〖食べ物〗 genuine buckwheat noodles. Are made from only buckwheat, without wheat flour.

きそよしなか 木曽義仲〖武士〗 1154 –1184. A warlord born in present Nagano Pref. Defeated a troop of the Taira clan and entered Kyoto. However, conflicted with Monastic Ex-Emperor Goshirakawa in Kyoto and was destroyed by his cousin, MINAMOTO NO YOSHITSUNE.

きたあるぷす 北アルプス〖地名〗 the Northern Alps. Another name for the Hida Mountains.

きたおおじろさんじん 北大路魯山人〖陶磁器〗 1883–1959. A potter and calligrapher born in Kyoto. Also opened a traditional-style luxury restaurant as a gourmet.

きだおれ 着倒れ〖精神性〗 bankruptcy by dressing up. Refers to the nature of Kyoto people, who is said to care greatly about their appearance and spend accordingly. ↔ 食い倒れ

きたかみがわ 北上川〖地名〗 the Kitakami River. Flows from Mt. Nanashigure in northern Iwate Pref. into the Pacific Ocean in Miyagi Pref. Is 249 km long, making it the fifth longest river in Japan. Used to flow into Ishinomaki Bay in Miyagi Pref. Functioned as the main artery for water transportation in the east Tohoku region during the Edo period.

きたがわうたまろ 喜多川歌麿 〖絵画〗 1753-1806. An ukiyo-e painter. Birthplace unknown. Famous for portraits of beautiful women. His works include *Women at Various Hours of the Day*.

きたきゅうしゅうし 北九州市 〖地名〗 an ordinance-designated city in Fukuoka Pref., located in its northeastern part and facing the Sea of Japan. Its growth has been based on heavy industry.

きたざとしばさぶろう 北里柴三郎 〖医療〗 1853-1931. A bacteriologist born in Kumamoto Pref. After graduating from the Univ. of Tokyo, studied bacteriology under Robert Koch in Germany. Became the first head of the medical department at Keio Univ.

きただけ 北岳 〖山岳〗 Mt. Kita. Is located in Yamanashi Pref. Is 3,193 m high, making it the second highest mountain in Japan and also the highest as a non-volcano mountain. One of the Three Mountains of Shirane.

きだち 木太刀 〖剣術〗 ⇨木刀

きたちょうせんらちもんだい 北朝鮮拉致問題 〖外交〗 the issue of North Korea's abduction of Japanese citizens. North Korean spies kidnapped Japanese people and forcefully brought them to North Korea several times from the 1970s to 1980s. Only five abductees came back to Japan, which occurred in 2002.

きたのてんまんぐう 北野天満宮 〖神社〗 Kitano Tenmangu Shrine. One of the two head shrines, together with Dazaifu Tenmangu Shrine. Is located in Kyoto City. Enshrines SUGAWARA NO MICHIZANE, as a deity of study. The main building, built by TOYOTOMI HIDEYORI, and the Illustrated Scroll on the Origin of Kitano Tenjin are National Treasures.

きたばたけちかふさ 北畠親房 〖武士〗 1293-1354. A court noble and warlord. Assisted Emperor Godaigo in political and military affairs.

きたはち 喜多八 〖文芸〗 ⇨弥次さん・喜多さん

きたまえぶね 北前船 〖交通・経済〗 a north-route cargo ship, or transportation using a north-route cargo ship. Developed in the 18th and 19th centuries. Commuted between Osaka and Northern Japan through the Sea of Japan and the Inland Sea. →廻船(かいせん)

きたまくら 北枕 〖仏教〗 lying with one's head northward. A dead person is laid with his or her head to the north after the manner that the Historical Buddha passed away.

きたまちぶぎょう 北町奉行 〖武士・官位〗 the northern feudal commissioners in the Edo period. There were two feudal commissioners to govern the Edo commoners, and they were alternately on duty for a month. The one whose office was in the north was called 'kita machi-bugyou.' ↔南町奉行 →江戸町奉行

きたみさんち 北見山地〔地名〕 the Kitami Mountains. Run parallel to the coastline in northeastern Hokkaido. The highest peak is Mt. Teshio, which is 1,558 m high.

きたやまぶんか 北山文化 〔時代〕 the Kitayama culture in the 14th century. Was named after the Kitayama area in Kyoto, where ASHIKAGA YOSHIMITSU constructed the Golden Pavilion. The cultures of the noble court and the warriors were fusing into one. India ink paintings and Chinese-style literature written by priests, called GOZAN BUNGAKU, developed under the cultural influence from the Ming dynasty. Noh was completed by ZEAMI and KAN'AMI. ↔東山文化 →金閣

ぎだゆうぶし 義太夫節〔音楽〕 a school of dramatic narrative recited to a shamisen accompaniment. Originated in the 17th century by Takemoto Gidayuu and later connected to BUNRAKU.

きち 吉〔神社・寺院〕 good fortune. A message on a fortune slip availabe at a Shinto shrine or Buddhist temple. ↔凶 →お神籤（おみくじ）; 大吉

きちじつ 吉日〔宗教〕 an auspicious day. For example, a day of "great peace" called TAIAN.

きちゅう 忌中〔冠婚葬祭〕 the mourning period. Forty-nine days after a person's death. His or her family keeps away from celebrations during this period. →喪中（もちゅう）

きちんやど 木賃宿〔旅〕 a cheap inn. This term was obsolete before World War II.

きっくぼくしんぐ キックボクシング〔スポーツ〕 kickboxing. Was devised in Japan, based on Muay Thai, Thai-style martial arts.

きっこうもん 亀甲紋〔文様〕 a tortoiseshell pattern, or honeycomb pattern. Has been broadly used in textiles, lacquerware, or metalware.

ぎっしゃ 牛車〔交通〕 a two-wheeled ox-drawn cart with a roof. Was used as a court noble's transportation in the Heian period.

きっしょうてん 吉祥天〔仏教〕 Goddess of Beauty, Prosperity, and Happiness. *Srimahadevi*. Or, *Laksmi*. Is depicted as a Chinese noble woman with a wish-fulfilling jewel in the left hand. Is considered to be a daughter of KISHIMOJIN and the wife of BISHAMON-TEN.

きっちょう 吉兆〔宗教〕 an auspicious omen. ↔凶兆

きつね 狐〔動物・宗教〕 a fox. *Vulpes vulpes*. Often bewitches a human in a fairy tale. Is also considered to be a servant of a deity of cereals, INARI, and to love thin deep-fried tofu.

きつねうどん 狐饂飩〔食べ物〕 thick white wheat noodles in hot soup with thin deep-fried tofu. 'Kitsune' means "fox." It is said that thin deep-fried tofu is a favorite food of foxes.

きつねがくれ 狐隠れ〔忍者〕 a fox-like hiding technique. A ninja

would enter water with the head above the surface and would cover the head with waterweeds, lotus leaves, or tree leaves. Since a fox enters water to remove its own odor when escaping from hunting dogs, this technique was named after the "fox."

きつねけん 狐拳 〖遊び〗 a three-cornered gesture game. By positioning the hands, a player shows one of the three symbols: a fox, a village mayor, or a rifle. A fox, indicated by placing both open hands on the head, wins a village mayor, indicated by placing both hands on the laps. A village mayor wins a rifle, indicated by imitating the posture of holding a rifle with both hands. A rifle wins a fox.

きつねつき 狐憑き 〖宗教〗 fox possession. A person in an abnormal psychic state was said to be possessed by a fox spirit.

きつねのよめいり 狐の嫁入り 〖気象〗 a sun shower. Literally means "fox wedding." Although there are several explanations of the etymology, most of them are related to the supernatural power that a fox was said to have.

きつねび 狐火 〖妖怪〗 foxfire. It is said that fire breathed out by a fox was seen in the mountains at night.

きてぃ キティ 〖服飾・ビジネス〗 ⇨ハローキティ

きど 木戸 〖建築〗 **(1)** a simple wooden door. Is placed at the entrance of a garden. **(2)** the entrance to a theater in the Edo period.

きどうせんしがんだむ 機動戦士ガンダム 〖アニメ〗 *Mobile Suit Gundam*. A space war anime produced by an anime production company, Sunrise Inc. Began to be broadcast in 1979, and its sequel appeared later.

きどたかよし 木戸孝允 〖政治〗 1833 -1877. Another name for KATSURA KOGOROU.

きとらこふん キトラ古墳 〖古墳〗 the Kitora tumulus. Is located in Asuka Village, Nara Pref. Is considered to have been built in the 7th to 8th centuries. The pictures of animal deities symbolizing four directions, called SHIJIN, were found in 1983.

きない 畿内 〖地名〗 a generic term for five provinces around the Imperial castle. YAMASHIRO, YAMATO, KAWACHI, IZUMI, and SETTSU.

きながし 着流し 〖服飾〗 men's casual style of kimono. A short coat called HAORI or loose-legged pleated trousers called HAKAMA are not worn.

きなこ 黄粉 〖調味料〗 roasted soybean flour. Is mainly mixed with sugar and sprinkled on baked rice cake.

きなこもち 黄粉餅 〖食べ物〗 rice cake coated with sweetened soybean flour.

きぬおりもの 絹織物 〖服飾〗 a generic term of silk textile. Includes CHIRIMEN, HABUTAE, and TSUMUGI.

きぬごしどうふ 絹濾し豆腐 〖食べ物〗 soft tofu. Literally means "tofu strained through silk," but actually it is not. Is named after "silk" because of its smoothness. ↔木綿豆腐

きぬさや 絹莢 〖食べ物・植物〗 ⇨莢豌豆(さやえんどう)

きぬた 砧 〖生活〗 a platform on which to beat cloth with a mallet in the old days. The cloth was beaten to be soft and glossy.

きね 杵 〖食文化〗 a mallet. Is used to pound glutinous rice into rice cake.

きねんさい 祈年祭 〖天皇〗 an Imperial festival to pray for a rich harvest. Was held on February 4th in the traditional calendar.

きねんぶつ 記念物 〖行政〗 a Monument. Includes living things, places, and architecture with scientific, historical, scenic, or artistic value. Is defined by the Law for the Protection of Cultural Properties.

ぎのうしょう 技能賞 〖相撲〗 Technique Prize. Is given to a wrestler, excepting YOKODUNA and OOZEKI, who has demonstrated excellent techniques in a sumo tournament.

きのえ 甲 〖干支〗 the first item of JIKKAN. Literally means "yang of wood" or "the elder brother of wood." Its Chinese-style pronunciation is 'kou,' which was used to refer to the first rank in grading because 'kinoe' is the first item among 'jikkan.'

きのさきおんせん 城崎温泉 〖温泉〗 a hot spring in northern Hyougo Pref. Is said to have been discovered in the 8th century, when a wounded stork was found bathing. Later, it developed as a resort with seven public baths. A novel, *At Kinosaki*, written in 1917 by Shiga Naoya, made the place even more famous. Can be accessed directly by JR limited express from Kyoto, Osaka, and Koube, each taking 2.5 to 3 hours. →城の崎にて

きのさきにて 城崎にて 〖文芸・作品〗 *At Kinosaki*. A novel published in 1917 by SHIGA NAOYA. The hero discusses his view of life and death while observing the death of small animals.

きのしたけいすけ 木下恵介 〖映画〗 1912-1998. A film director born in Shizuoka Pref. His works include *Twenty-four Eyes* in 1954 and *The Ballad of Narayama* in 1958.

きのつらゆき 紀貫之 〖文芸〗 868/872(?)-945. A poet, writer, and literary theorist. Compiled the *Collection of Ancient and Modern Japanese Poetry* (KOKINWAKASHUU) in 905, together with three other poets. Wrote the oldest diary literature, *The Tosa Diary*, around 935, under the pretense of being a woman. His work had a huge impact on literature later in the Heian period. One of the Thirty-six Immortal Poets. →三十六歌仙

きのと 乙 〖干支〗 the second item of JIKKAN. Literally means "yin of wood" or "the younger brother of wood." Its Chinese-style pronunciation is 'otsu,' which was used to refer to the second rank in grading because 'kinoto' is the second item among 'jikkan.'

きのとものり 紀友則 〔文芸〕 ?-? A poet in the early Heian period. Compiled the *Collection of Ancient and Modern Japanese Poetry* (KOKIN-WAKASHUU) in 905, together with his cousin, KI NO TSURAYUKI, and two other poets. One of the Thirty-six Immortal Poets. →三十六歌仙

きのめあえ 木の芽和え 〔食べ物〕 salad with buds of prickly ash and white miso. Bamboo shoots or squid are also used as ingredients.

きはちじょう 黄八丈 〔服飾〕 a textile with stripes or a check pattern on yellow background. Is woven with spun silk thread. A specialty on Hachijou Island in Tokyo.

きび 黍 〔食べ物・植物〕 common millet. *Panicum miliaceum*. Can be an ingredient of dumplings or cake. Is also used as livestock feed. Was introduced from the Korean Peninsula in ancient times.

きび 吉備 〔旧国名〕 the old name for present Okayama Pref. and eastern Hiroshima Pref.

きびだんご 黍団子 〔食べ物〕 sweet millet dumplings. Used to be the local specialty in Okayama Pref. Now made from rice flour and is similar to Turkish delight.

きびつじんじゃ 吉備津神社 〔神社〕 Kibitsu Shrine. Is located in southern Okayama Pref. and enshrines KIBITSUHIKO NO MIKOTO. The main building and the oratory are National Treasures.

きびつひこのみこと 吉備津彦命 〔神話〕 a son of the 7th Emperor Kourei. Subjugated a demon named Ura. It is said that his story was the model of a folktale, "MOMOTAROU."

きびなご 吉備奈仔 〔食べ物・魚〕 a banded blue sprat. *Spratelloides gracilis*. Eaten in various ways, for example as sashimi, in tempura, and as dried fish. Popular in Kagoshima Pref.

きびのまきび 吉備真備 〔政治〕 695 -775. A statesman and scholar born in present Okayama Pref. After studying in Tang for about 20 years, came back and obtained political power as a result of a conspiracy with Tachibana no Moroe and Genbou. Was demoted and sent to present Fukuoka Pref. after FUJIWARA NO NAKAMARO gained political power. Revisited Tang and became the Minister of the Right after Nakamaro fell.

きびょうし 黄表紙 〔文芸〕 yellow-cover books from the 18th to 19th centuries. Contain illustrated stories for adults. →草双紙(そうし)

きふ 棋譜 〔将棋〕 the record of SHOUGI or GO.

ぎふけん 岐阜県 〔都道府県〕 Gifu Pref. Its capital is Gifu City. Is located in central Japan, adjacent to Aichi Pref. and six other prefectures. Its area is 10,621 km^2. The residential and industrial areas are on the Noubi Plain in its southern part, called Mino. Its northern part, called Hida, located between the North Alps and Central Alps, is mountainous and has heavy snowfall in winter. Used to be known for paper and sword making. Has produced cutlery in Seki City in its southern part, and Mino ware in its southeastern part. The battlefield of Sekigahara is at its southwestern end. Gujou, in its central part, is famous for its all-night dancing event held annually in August. In its northern part, the historic villages in Shirakawa-gou were designated a World Heritage Site in 1995, together with Gokayama in Toyama Pref. Used to be called Mino and Hida.

ぎふし 岐阜市 〔地名〕 Gifu City. Is the capital of Gifu Pref., located in its southwest part. Has long been famous for cormorant fishing in the Nagara River, and the production of lanterns and umbrellas. The Dousan Festival and the Gifu Festival are held in April, and the Gifu Nobunaga Festival in October. Two of them are held in memory of the lords who governed the area in the Warring States period in the mid-16th century. After Saitou Dousan was killed in a battle, ODA NOBUNAGA governed the area, gave it the current name Gifu in 1567, and set out on his quest to unify all of Japan.

ぎふじょう 岐阜城 〔城郭〕 Gifu Castle. Was constructed in another name at the beginning of the 13th century. Was obtained, renovated, and renamed as Gifu Castle in 1567 by ODA NOBUNAGA. Was abandoned in 1601 and reconstructed in 1956.

ぎふちょうちん 岐阜提灯 〔生活〕 a Gifu paper lantern. Is oval-shaped and painted with colorful pictures, and has a tassel on the bottom.

きふどう 黄不動 〔仏教・絵画〕 Yellow Immovable Wisdom King. Nickname for the pictured Immovable Wisdom King at Onjouji Temple in Shiga Pref. It is said that a priest, Enchin, was inspired and painted the figure on a silk screen in 838. A National Treasure. A duplication of the painting is at Manshu-in in Kyoto. →不動明王

きへいたい 奇兵隊 〔軍事〕 the Irregular Militia. Was organized in 1863 by TAKASUGI SHINSAKU of the Choushuu domain. Recruited soldiers from both samurai and common people. Was actively involved in the shogunate's second punitive expedition and the Boshin Civil War. →長州征伐；戊辰戦争

きへん 木偏 〔漢字〕 a left-side radical meaning "tree." Is used in kanji such as 机(desk), 松(pine tree), 材(wood), and 村(village). →偏；部首

ぎぼし 擬宝珠 〔建築〕 an ornament on the top of a handrail post of a bridge. Also decorates a post of a handrail along an outer corridor of a shrine or temple building.

きまりて 決まり手〚相撲〛 a technique for finishing a bout.

きみあん 黄身餡〚食べ物〛 sweet bean paste with egg yolk. Is used in various sweets such as 'Hakata Toorimon' in Fukuoka Pref. and 'Poemu' in Ehime Pref.

きみがよ 君が代〚天皇・音楽〛 the Japanese national anthem. Means "the eternal world under Japanese Emperors."

ぎむきょういく 義務教育〚教育〛 compulsory education. Six years at elementary school and three years at junior high school. Senior high school is not included in compulsory education in Japan.

きめこみにんぎょう 木目込み人形〚人形〛 a wooden doll on which colorful cloth is pasted. Is said to have been invented in Kyoto in the mid-18th century.

きもすい 肝吸い〚食べ物〛 clear hot soup with eel liver. Is served with broiled eel over rice in a lacquered box.

きもの 着物〚服飾〛 a kimono. An ankle-length loose robe with wide sleeves. Is tied at the waist with a broad sash called OBI. The present style became popular in the Edo period. There are many kinds of kimono such as FURISODE and TOMESODE.

きもん 鬼門〚宗教〛 the ill-omened direction, which is the northeast. It is said that an evil spirit comes in and goes out in the Yin-Yang Way. Even today, some people care about the direction and say, for example, that the entrance of a building should not be located in the northeast.

きゃはん 脚絆〚忍者・服飾〛 a gaiter made of cloth in olden times. Was also called 'habaki.'

きゃぷてんつばさ キャプテン翼〚漫画〛 *Captain Tsubasa*. A soccer manga, written by Takahashi Youichi. Was published serially in a boy's manga magazine, *Weekly Shonen Jump* (Shounen Janpu), from 1981 to 1988.

きゃら 伽羅〚植物・香道〛 the best quality of aloeswood. Is used for its aroma. →沈香(じんこう)

きゃらぶき 伽羅蕗〚食べ物〛 stalks of butterbur boiled with soy sauce, sake, and sugar. A kind of preserved food.

きやりうた 木遣り歌〚音楽〛 a work song when a group carries a heavy log or rock.

きゅう 灸〚医療〛 moxibustion. A traditional method to treat disease by burning substance made from dried mugwort, called MOGUSA, on vital points of the skin.

きゅう ～級(「段」の下の)〚武術・書道〛 a grade under DAN, reffering to advanced classes. The first grade is highest, and above the first grade is the first dan, called SHODAN.

きゅうかこくじょうやく 九か国条約〚外交〛 Nine-Power Treaty. A February 1922 treaty that resulted from the Washington Conference and that was signed by Belgium,

China, France, Great Britain, Italy, Japan, the Netherlands, Portugal, and the United States. Signatories agreed to respect the independence and territorial integrity of China. They also agreed that all nine nations would have equal access to China with respect to commerce. The treaty lacked enforcement provisions and thus, for example, failed to prevent Japanese aggression in China in the 1930s.

ぎゅうき 牛鬼〖妖怪〗 ⇨牛鬼(うしおに)

きゅうじたい 旧字体〖漢字〗 the traditional form of a kanji. Usually a bit complicated, compared with the current form. For example, 駅 meaning "station" was once written as 驛.

きゅうしゅうこくりつはくぶつかん 九州国立博物館〖施設〗 Kyushu National Museum. Was founded in Fukuoka Pref. in 2005. Its aim is to "understand Japanese culture from the Asian point of view."

きゅうしゅうさんち 九州山地〖地名〗 the Kyushu Mountains. Are located on the border between Kumamoto and Miyazaki Prefs., with the northern tip in Ooita Pref. and southern tip in Kagoshima Pref. Its highest peak is Mt. Sobo at 1,756 m, on the border between Ooita and Miyazaki Prefs. Mt. Aso and Mt. Kirishima are not included.

きゅうしゅうしんかんせん 九州新幹線〖鉄道〗 Kyushu Shinkansen. Connects HAKATA Station in Fukuoka Pref. with Kagoshima-Chuuou Station in Kagoshima Pref. Started service in 2004 between Shin-Yatsushiro in Kumamoto Pref. and Kagoshima-Chuuou. The extended route between Hakata and Shin-Yatsushiro started service in 2011. The fastest super express, Mizuho, takes 80 minutes from Hakata to Kagoshima-Chuuou. Other express trains are named Sakura and Tsubame.

きゅうしゅうちほう 九州地方〖地名〗 the Kyushu region. Consists of all the seven prefectures on Kyushu Island, namely, Fukuoka, Saga, Nagasaki, Ooita, Kumamoto, Miyazaki, and Kagoshima Prefs., as well as Okinawa Pref.

きゅうしゅうばしょ 九州場所〖相撲〗 the November Grand Sumo Tournament. Is held at Fukuoka Kokusai Center.

きゅうしょうがつ 旧正月〖暦〗 New Year's holidays in the traditional calendar. Around the end of January or the beginning of February.

きゅうしょく 給食〖教育〗 ⇨学校給食

きゅうす 急須〖食器〗 a small teapot with a handle. Is used to make green tea, brown rice tea, etc.

ぎゅうたん 牛タン〖食べ物〗 beef tongue. Is grilled in the Korean style or put into a stew or curry. Sendai City is famous for beef tongue.

きゅうていこくだいがく 旧帝国大学〖教育〗 ⇨帝国大学

きゅうどう 弓道〔武術〕 Japanese archery. Values not only technique but also manners and courtesy.

ぎゅうどん 牛丼〔食べ物〕 a beef bowl. Is a simple meal of simmerd thin-sliced beef and onion on top of a bowl of rice. Is popular as fast food, so there are several 'gyudon' chains throughout Japan.

ぎゅうなべ 牛鍋〔食べ物〕 an old name for SUKIYAKI. Was used mainly in the Tokyo area in the 19th century.

ぎゅうひ 求肥〔食べ物〕 a rice flour confection like Turkish delight. Becomes translucent by kneading rice flour with sugar or starch syrup for a long time.

きゅうびのきつね 九尾の狐〔妖怪〕 an imaginary fox with nine tails. Appeared in Chinese mythology and was introduced to Japan.

きゅうぼん 旧盆〔暦〕 Bon Festival in the traditional calendar.

ぎゅうめし 牛飯〔食べ物〕 ⇨牛丼

きゅうり 胡瓜〔食べ物・植物〕 a cucumber. Is mainly eaten in summer and is prepared in various ways like vinegared sliced cucumbers and Japanese-style cucumber pickles.

きゅうりまき 胡瓜巻き〔寿司〕 ⇨かっぱ巻き

きゅうりもみ 胡瓜揉み〔食べ物〕 sliced cucumber seasoned with salt and vinegar.

きゅうれき 旧暦〔暦〕 the traditional calendar. Is based on the lunisolar calendar, which was used until 1872. ↔新暦 →太陰太陽暦

きょう 凶〔神社・寺院〕 bad fortune. A message on a fortune slip available at a Shinto shrine or Buddhist temple. ↔吉 →お神籤(くじ); 大凶

きょう 〜京〔政治〕 the suffix meaning "capital." Before Kyoto was fixed as the Imperial Capital in 794, the capital was moved several times.

ぎょう 行〔書道・芸術〕 the simplified and flowing style in various traditional arts such as calligraphy, paintings, and tea ceremony. Literally means "line" or "training." Is a kind of intermediate between the basic and fully depicted style, called SHIN, and the simplified or flowing style, called SOU.

きょういくかんじ 教育漢字〔漢字・教育〕 a kanji to be taught in elementary school. Is also called 'gakushuu kanji.' About 1,000 kanji are included.

きょういくちょくご 教育勅語〔教育・天皇〕 the Imperial Rescript on Education. Was issued in 1890 by Emperor Meiji and became the fundamental principle of Japanese moral education. Was no longer in effect as of 1948.

きょうおうごこくじ 教王護国寺〔寺院〕 ⇨東寺

きょうか 狂歌〔文芸〕 a comical, witty, or satirical poem in the TANKA format. Was popular around the 18th century, but is now obsolete.

きょうかく 侠客〔ヤクザ〕 a eulogistic name for YAKUZA.

きょうかたびら 経帷子〔仏教・服飾〕

a white kimono for a dead person. Sutra or Sanskrit letters are written on it. →帷子

きょうかのう 京狩野 〖絵画〗 the Kanou sub-school in Kyoto. The Kanou school of painting founded around the 15th century was divided into two sub-schools in the 17th century, when some painters were officially employed by the Tokugawa shogunate in Edo. Painters remaining in Kyoto included KANOU SANRAKU and KANOU SANSETSU. →狩野派；江戸狩野

ぎょうがまえ 行構え 〖漢字〗 an enclosure radical related to "going" or "street." Is used in kanji such as 街 (street) and 術 (method). →構え；部首

きょうかん 経巻 〖仏教〗 a scroll of sutra.

きょうぎ 経木 〖食文化〗 a paper-thin wooden board. Is used to make a lunch box or to wrap food. Formerly it was used as a surface on which sutras were written.

ぎょうき 行基 〖仏教〗 668-749. A priest born in present Osaka Pref. Constructed roads, bridges, and river banks, together with ordinary people. Although the government oppressed his activities at first, Emperor Shoumu approved of him. Gyouki helped the foundation of Todai-ji Temple.

きょうげん 狂言 〖狂言〗 a Noh farce. Developed from the comical elements of a performing art, called SARUGAKU, in ancient to medieval times. The development of its style was completed in the Muromachi period. Was originally performed in the interlude of Noh plays.

きょうげんし 狂言師 〖狂言〗 a performer of Noh farce.

ぎょうこう 行幸 〖天皇〗 a term for the Emperor's trips away from the Imperial Palace.

ぎょうざ 餃子 〖食べ物〗 jiao-zi. A crescent-shaped dumpling stuffed with minced pork and vegetables, especially garlic. Originally came from China. Though it's usually boiled in China, is mainly eaten pan-fried in Japan.

きょうさく 警策 〖禅〗 a striking rod for Zen meditation. About 1.2 m long, flat, and wooden. A meditator is struck with it when becoming sleepy or when asking to be struck for motivational purposes.

きょうじ 脇侍 〖仏教〗 ⇨脇侍（わきじ）

ぎょうじ 行司 〖相撲〗 a sumo referee. Wears traditional costumes, has a special fan called GUNBAI, and judges the bout in the sumo ring.

きょうしゃ 香車 〖将棋〗 a lance. Is commonly called by its abbreviated form, 'kyou,' or by its nickname, 'yari.' Like a rook, it can go forward for any number of squares, but unlike a rook, it cannot move sideways or backwards. When it is promoted to 'nari-kyo,' it moves like a KINSHOU.

ぎょうしょ 行書 〖書道〗 the semi-cursive style of calligraphy. Strokes are somewhat simplified. →楷書；

草書

きょうす 香子〘将棋〙 ⇨香車（ｷｮｳｼｬ）

きょうぞう 経蔵〘仏教・建築〙 a storehouse for Buddhist scriptures in a temple.

きょうそく 脇息〘生活〙 a portable armrest. Is used when a person sits on a tatami mat.

きょうちょう 凶兆〘宗教〙 a menacing omen. ↔吉兆

きょうてん 経典〘仏教〙 a Buddhist sutra, or a sacred book of Buddhism. Many such books were translated from Sanskrit to Chinese.

きょうどがんぐ 郷土玩具〘玩具〙 a toy unique to each local community. Examples include a papier-mâché tiger, a KOKESHI doll, and a DARUMA doll.

きょうとぎていしょ 京都議定書〘政治・自然〙 Kyoto Protocol to the United Nation's Framework Convention on Climate Change. Was adopted at the Kyoto Conference on Global Warming in 1997.

きょうどげいのう 郷土芸能〘芸能〙 a traditional performing art handed down in a local community from generation to generation. Is often performed at a local festival.

きょうとこくりつはくぶつかん 京都国立博物館〘施設〙 Kyoto National Museum. Was founded in Kyoto City in 1897. Mainly stores fine art in and after the Heian period.

きょうとござん 京都五山〘仏教〙 Five Zen Temples of Kyoto: TEN-RYUU-JI, SHOUKOKU-JI, KENNIN-JI, TOUFUKU-JI, and Manju-ji Temples. NANZEN-JI Temple was ranked as the leader among these five temples. This ranking was fixed in the early Muromachi period, when temples were cultural centers. →鎌倉五山

きょうとごしょ 京都御所〘天皇〙 the Kyoto Imperial Palace. The official residence of Emperors until 1869, when the capital was relocated to Tokyo. Is managed by the Imperial Household Agency.

きょうとさんだいまつり 京都三大祭〘祭礼〙 Three Great Festivals in Kyoto. The Aoi Festival of the two Kamo Shrines, the Gion Festival of the Yasaka Shrine, and the Festival of Ages of the Heian Shrine.

きょうとし 京都市〘地名〙 Kyoto City. The capital of Kyoto Pref. and an ordinance-designated city. Is located in southeastern Kyoto Pref. Had been the capital of Japan from 794 to 1868 until the capital was relocated to Tokyo. Is extremely rich in points of scenic and historic interest, such as KINKAKU-JI, DAITOKU-JI, YASAKA JINJA, NIJOU-JOU, and KYOUTO GOSHO. Also, several famous festivals such as AOI-MATSURI, GION-MATSURI, and JIDAI-MATSURI are held in the city, and it is home to many universities such as Kyoto University and Doshisha University.

きょうとしょしだい 京都諸司代〘官位〙 Kyoto governor under the

Tokugawa shogunate. Administered the affairs of the Imperial Court, processed justice in the adjacent provinces, managed the feudal commissioners called MACHI-BU-GYOU, and watched over the feudal domains in Western Japan.

きょうとだいがく 京都大学 〖教育〗 Kyoto University. Was founded as the second Imperial university in 1897. As of 2016, six among 25 Japanese Nobel Prize winners graduated from Kyoto University.

きょうとふ 京都府 〖都道府県〗 Kyoto Pref. Is located in central Japan, facing the Sea of Japan. Is 4,613 km^2 in area. Its capital is Kyoto City. The climates are different in its northern and southern parts. In addition to Kyoto City, has several sightseeing spots such as AMA NO HASHIDATE in the northern part and BYOUDOU-IN Temple in the southern part. Used to be Yamashiro, Tango, and most of Tanba.

きょうどりょうり 郷土料理 〖食文化〗 traditional local cuisine. Examples include KIRITANPO in Akita, WANKO-SOBA in Iwate, ISHIKARI-NABE in Hokkaido, FUKAGAWA-MESHI in Tokyo, HITSUMABUSHI in Aichi, HOU-TOU in Yamanashi, FUNA-ZUSHI in Shiga, KAKINOHA-ZUSHI in Nara, SHIPPOKU RYOURI in Nagasaki, and GOOYA CHANPURUU in Okinawa.

きょうにんぎょう 京人形 〖人形〗 a traditional doll made in Kyoto. Is wooden and dressed up.

きょうのきだおれおおさかのくいだおれ 京の着倒れ、大阪の食い倒れ 〖精神性〗 "Kyotoites ruin themselves by dressing too much, Osakaians ruin themselves by eating too much." A phrase describing the stereotype about the different natures of people from Kyoto and Osaka.

きょうはしんとう 教派神道 〖神道〗 Sect Shintoism. In and after 1882, the government authorized 13 Shinto sects. Each sect had its own founder and religious centers, different from Jinja Shintoism or State Shintoism. →神社神道；国家神道

きょうほう 享保 〖時代〗 an era name from 1716 to 1736 in the mid-Edo period. Tokugawa Yoshimune, the 8th Tokugawa shogun, led some impressive reforms.

きょうほうのかいかく 享保の改革 〖政治〗 Kyouhou Reform. Was conducted from 1716 to 1745 by TOKUGAWA YOSHIMUNE. Promoted simple frugality, cancelled samurai's debts, initiated an appeal box called MEYASU-BAKO, recommended development of new rice fields, and raised the land tax. However, its effects were short-lived because of a famine and the decline in the price of rice.

きょうまい 京舞 〖芸能〗 traditional dance originated in Kyoto. Is elegantly performed to a song accompanied by SHAMISEN. It is said that Noh dancing is inspired by the style of kyoumai.

きょうもん 経文〔仏教〕 a sutra, or the text of a sutra. Many sutras were translated from Sanskrit to Chinese.

きょうやき 京焼〔工芸〕 Kyo ware. Ceramics manufactured in Kyoto in and after the Edo period, including KIYOMIZU-YAKI. The typical style was evident in the work of NONOMURA NINSEI.

きょうゆうぜん 京友禅〔服飾〕 textile dyed in the Yuuzen style in Kyoto. ↔加賀友禅

きょうりょうり 京料理〔食文化〕 traditional Kyoto cuisine. Uses soup stock made from fish and kelp, is beautifully displayed and tastes bland. Its ingredients are mainly seasonal vegetables, because Kyoto is located far away from the sea and not blessed with fresh seafood.

ぎょえい 御詠〔天皇〕 a poem composed by a member of the Imperial family.

ぎょえん 御苑〔天皇〕 an Imperial garden.

ぎょくおんほうそう 玉音放送〔天皇〕 the radio broadcast of the Emperor's speech to announce the end of World War II. Was on air at noon on August 15th, 1945.

ぎょくがん 玉眼〔仏教・彫刻〕 inlaid crystal eyes. A technique for depicting eyes in a wooden Buddhist sculpture. The oldest example is those of Amitabha Buddha at Chougaku-ji Temple in Nara, which was carved in 1151. ↔彫眼(ちょうがん)

きょくじつき 旭日旗〔軍事〕 the rising sun flag. The military flag of the Imperial Japanese Army and Navy until 1945, and is still employed by Maritime Self Defense Forces. 16 red lines radiate from the sun disc in the center.

きょくじつしょう 旭日章〔政治〕 Order of the Rising Sun. Was established in 1875 as the first national order. Is "bestowed upon individuals in recognition of their services to the nation or public," according to the Cabinet Office.

ぎょくしょう 玉将〔将棋〕 a king. Is commonly called by its abbreviated form, 'gyoku.' →王将 (**1**)

きょくすいのえん 曲水の宴〔文芸〕 a poetry party along a stream in the Heian period. A participant composed a poem while a sake cup was floating in front of him or her along the stream. Was held on March 3rd in the Imperial Palace or by court nobles.

ぎょくだい 玉代〔娯楽〕 a charge for geisha entertainment.

きょくていばきん 曲亭馬琴〔文芸〕 1767-1848. A popular novelist born in Edo. Wrote books for entertainment called YOMI-HON. His works include *The Eight Dog Chronicles*. →南総里見八犬伝

きょくとうこくさいぐんじさいばん 極東国際軍事裁判〔外交・戦争〕 International Military Tribunal for the Far East. Was held from 1946 to 1948 after Japan surrendered in World War II. The Japanese military leaders were judged to have committed "a crime against peace," not on "a crime against humanity" that Nazis were judged to have committed. Is also called the Tokyo Trial.

ぎょくへん 玉編 〖漢字〗 ⇨玉偏(たま)

ぎょくろ 玉露 〖飲み物〗 highest-quality green tea. Is brewed with lukewarm water, from 40 to 50 degrees centigrade. Tastes faintly sweet.

きょじょう 居城 〖城郭〗 a resident castle of a feudal lord. A lord sometimes had several castles in medieval and early-modern times, at one of which he lived.

きょじんのほし 巨人の星 〖漫画〗 *Star of the Giants*. A baseball manga, written by Kajiwara Ikki and illustrated by Kawasaki Noboru. Was published serially in a boy's magazine, *Shounen Magajin*, from 1966 to 1971. Its TV anime started in 1968, and the sequel appeared in 1976.

ぎょそんせきしょう 漁村夕照 〖絵画〗 Fishing Village in the Evening Glow. One of the Eight Views of Xiaoxiang. →瀟湘(しょうしょう)八景

ぎょたく 魚拓 〖娯楽〗 a fish impression printed with India ink. Is taken to record the size of the fish and the time and place of fishing.

ぎょにくそおせえじ 魚肉ソーセージ 〖食べ物〗 fish sausage. Is mainly made from ground meat of Alaskan pollack, with lard added.

ぎょばん 魚版 〖仏教〗 a fish-shaped wooden gong. Is sounded to let monks know the time of meals.

きよひめ 清姫 〖民話〗 ⇨安珍(あんちん)・清姫

きよみずでら 清水寺 〖寺院〗 Kiyomizu-dera Temple. Affiliated with the Hossou sect. Was founded in 798 by a priest, Enchin, with financial support by a military commander, SAKANOUE NO TAMURAMARO. Is located in Kyoto City. The main hall with a stage built out on a cliff is a National Treasure. The entire temple was designated a World Heritage Site in 1994.

きよみずやき 清水焼 〖陶磁器〗 Kiyomizu ware. Started in Kyoto in the 18th century. Is painted with colorful pictures. →京焼

きよめ 清め 〖宗教〗 purification. Uses salt, water, incantation, or other special tools such as NUSA. The methods are different from religion to religion, or sect to sect.

きよめのしお 浄めの塩 〖冠婚葬祭・相撲〗 salt for purification. People are given a packet containing salt when attending a funeral. They sprinkle the salt on themselves when coming home. A sumo wrestler also purifies the sumo ring with salt before every bout.

きよもとぶし 清元節 〖音楽〗 a school of dramatic narrative recited to a shamisen accompaniment. Originated in the 19th century by Kiyomoto Enjudayuu. Was popular in the late 19th century.

きらいばし 嫌い箸 〖食文化〗 bad chopstick etiquette. →刺し箸；舐

(はし)り箸；迷い箸；寄せ箸；渡し箸

きらこうずけのすけ 吉良上野介〖武士〗 ⇨吉良義央(よしなか)

きらず 雪花菜〖食べ物〗 another name for OKARA.

きらよしなか 吉良義央〖武士〗 1641 -1702. A direct shogunal vassal born in Edo. Managed ceremonies in the shogunate and taught ceremonial rules to the feudal lord, ASANO NAGANORI. However, Naganori thought Yoshinaka was insulting him and attacked Yoshinaka with a dagger. Naganori was ordered to commit hara-kiri for that behavior. Yoshinaka was killed later by vassals of Naganori. →忠臣蔵

きり 桐〖植物〗 a princess tree, or an empress tree. *Paulownia tomentosa*. Is used for wooden sandals called GETA and a chest of drawers called TANSU.

ぎり 義理〖精神性〗 socially expected duty, or binding obligation. Is based on a human relation such as supervisor-subordinate, teacher-student, and mutually supporting colleagues. To neglect 'giri' is considered to be strongly against moral. Is sometimes contrasted with NINJOU, natural human emotion.

きりえ 切り絵〖美術〗 paper cutting. Is created by cutting out the form to be depicted and mounting it on background paper.

きりかね 截金〖美術〗 gold leaf cut like strings. Is pasted on a painting or surface of a sculpture to represent lines or patterns.

きりさめ 霧雨〖気象〗 misty rain. The diameter of a raindrop is less than 0.5 mm, according to the Japan Meteorological Agency.

きりしたん 切支丹 〖キリスト教〗 the term to refer to a Christian or Christianity from the 16th to 19th centuries. Came from a Portuguese word, Christao.

きりしたんせいさつ 切支丹制札 〖キリスト教・政治〗 an official announcement board to prohibit Christianity. Was put up a few times during the Edo period.

きりしたんだいみょう キリシタン大名〖キリスト教〗 a Christian feudal lord from the late 16th to the early 17th centuries. Vanished after Christianity was banned in the mid-17th century. Examples are Takayama Ukon and Konishi Yukinaga in Osaka and Ootomo Sourin in Kyushu.

きりしまおんせん 霧島温泉〖温泉〗 a group of hot springs in eastern Kagoshima Pref., at the foot of the Kirishima Mountains. Was discovered in the early 18th century. In 1866, SAKAMOTO RYOUMA and his wife visited one of the hot springs, Einoo Hot Spring. Their trip is known as the first honeymoon in Japan.

きりすときょう キリスト教〖キリスト教〗 Christianity. Was introduced to Japan in 1549 by Saint Francis Xavier and later prohibited in the Edo period. Though only about 1%

of the population are Christians at present, Christmas parties and Christian-style weddings are popular. Several universities such as Sophia Univ. and Doshisha Univ. have connections to the Christian Church.

きりたんぽ きりたんぽ 〖食べ物〗 a cylindrical rice cake. Is usually skewered and baked with miso or used as dumplings in soup. A specialty of Akita Pref.

ぎりちょこ 義理チョコ 〖食べ物・精神性〗 chocolate obligatorily given to a man by a woman on Valentine's Day. Women at a workplace or school give small chocolates to all of their male colleagues and friends as a matter of courtesy. →バレンタインデー

きりづまづくり 切妻造り 〖建築〗 a building style with a gable roof. Is the most common style of Japanese architecture. →入母屋(いりもや)造り；寄棟(よせむね)造り

きりづみおんせん 霧積温泉 〖温泉〗 a hot spring in western Gunma Pref. Was discovered in the 13th century. Around 1900, many famous politicians and writers visited there and stayed at one of the many inns. However, the area was severely damaged by a landslide in 1910. At present, there is only one inn with a hot spring.

きりど 切り戸 **(1)** 〖建築〗 a wicket door attached to a large swinging door gate. **(2)** 〖能〗 a sliding side door on a Noh stage.

ぎりにんじょう 義理人情 〖精神性〗 a term for the socially expected duty and the natural human emotion. The former is based on a specific human relation and implies a kind of moral force. The latter is more universal and is usually regarded as more heartfelt. These two feelings sometimes conflict to each other.

きりび 切り火 〖宗教〗 flint sparks used for purification. Flint was struck when a person departed for a journey or a test.

きりぼしだいこん 切り干し大根 〖食べ物〗 thinly sliced and dried strips of white radish. Are often simmered with carrots to make a typical side dish at home.

きりもち 切り餅 〖食べ物〗 rice cakes cut into rectangles. Are eaten mainly in the Kantou region.

きりん 麒麟 〖動物〗 a kylin, a qilin, or a chi lin. An auspicious, imaginary animal in Chinese legend. Has a horn, the body of a deer, hooves of a horse, and a tail of an ox. Emits five-colored lights from the whole body. Is said to have appeared as a precursor before a saint appears in this world.

きん ～斤 〖単位〗 a unit to measure weight. About 600g. One 'kin' is 160 MONME. This unit system is rarely used today.

きんいっぷう 金一封 〖生活・ビジネス〗 a money gift contained in an envelope. This term is used when the exact amount is not shown.

きんいん 金印 〖考古〗 ⇨漢委奴
(かんの)(わのなの)国王印

きんかいわかしゅう 金槐和歌集
〖文芸・作品〗 *The Golden Pagoda-Tree Collection of Japanese Poetry*. An anthology compiled in 1213 by MINAMOTO NO SANETOMO, the second son of Minamoto no Yoritomo, who founded the Kamakura shogunate. Contains 663 poems.

きんかくし 金隠し 〖生活〗 the front cover of a squat-style lavatory pan.

きんかくじ 金閣寺 (1) 〖寺院〗 the Temple of the Golden Pavilion. Is located in Kyoto. The three-story pavilion, gilt inside and outside, was built as a villa in 1397 by ASHIKAGA YOSHIMITSU. The pavilion was burned down in 1950 as a result of arson and rebuilt in 1955. The official name is ROKUON-JI. The whole temple was designated a World Heritage Site in 1994. (2) 〖文芸・作品〗 *The Temple of the Golden Pavilion*. A novel published in 1956 by MISHIMA YUKIO, based on a true story. The hero set fire to the Golden Pavilion for a mysterious reason.

ぎんかくじ 銀閣寺 〖寺院〗 the Temple of the Silver Pavilion. Is located in Kyoto. Originally a villa of ASHIKAGA YOSHIMASA built toward the end of the 15th century. The two-story pavilion was planned to be covered with silver leaf, but the project was not accomplished because Yoshimasa died. The official name is JISHOU-JI. The whole temple was designated a World Heritage Site in 1994.

きんがしんねん 謹賀新年 〖正月〗 "I Wish You A Happy New Year." Is often written on a new year's card or poster, but it is not to be spoken aloud.

ぎんがてつどうのよる 銀河鉄道の夜 〖文芸・作品〗 *Night on the Galactic Railroad*. A children's story published in 1941, after the author, Miyazawa Kenji, died in 1933. A boy dreams that he gets on the Galactic Railroad and goes around constellations together with his friend. After waking up, he is told that the friend has died.

きんかん 金柑 〖植物〗 a kumquat. *Fortunella*. Eaten after being simmered in a syrup.

きんきしょが 琴棋書画 〖絵画〗 four elegant pastimes. A popular subject of paintings in East Asia. The four pastimes are zither, go, calligraphy, and painting.

きんきちほう 近畿地方 〖地名〗 the Kinki region. Consists of seven prefectures in south-central Honshuu, namely, Mie, Shiga, Kyoto, Osaka, Hyougo, Nara, and Wakayama. Is used almost interchangeably with KANSAI CHIHOU, but 'Kinki chihou' is used in more formal and official contexts. However, some people dislike the sound of 'Kinki' because it is similar to the English word "kinky." For that reason, Kinki Daigaku changed its official English name from "Kinki

University" to "Kindai University."

きんきにほんてつどう 近畿日本鉄道 〖鉄道〗 Kintetsu Railway. A private railway company that serves Aichi, Mie, Kyoto, Osaka, and Nara Prefs. Holds 16 lines and 281 stations. Its length is 501 km, which makes it Japan's largest private railway company. Has several terminals in Nagoya, Kyoto, Osaka, and Nara. Is well known for its limited express trains, such as Urban Liner, which runs from Osaka to Nagoya, and Ise-Shima Liner, which runs from Osaka or Nagoya to holiday spots in the Ise-Shima area.

きんぎょ 金魚 〖魚〗 a goldfish. *Carassius auratus*. An ornamental fresh-water fish. Native to China, was introduced to Japan in the early 16th century.

きんぐぎどら キングギドラ 〖映画〗 King Ghidorah. The strongest among enemy monsters of Godzilla. Has a pair of wings, three dragon-like heads, and two tails. Gold-colored and 100 m high.

ぎんこう 吟行 〖文芸〗 a trip a poet takes to explore subjects to be used for HAIKU or TANKA.

ぎんざ 銀座 〖地名〗 a luxurious shopping and entertaining area in the center of Tokyo city proper. Many famous department stores, bars, and restaurants are located there, and many of them are quite pricey.

きんし 金鵄 〖神話・動物〗 a golden kite. In the Japanese mythology, when Emperor Jinmu was on campaign, a golden kite settled on the tip of his bow and flashed like lightning to dazzle his enemies.

きんしたまご 錦糸玉子 〖食べ物〗 omelet strips. Are often topped on scattered sushi or ramen noodles served cold.

きんしょう 近称 〖言語〗 a demonstrative pronoun referring to a nearby thing, place, or person. Its first letter is 'ko' such as in 'kore' (this), 'kono' (this), and 'koko' (here). →中称；遠称；不定称

きんしょう 金将 〖将棋〗 a gold officer. A piece that Western chess does not have. Is commonly called by its abbreviated form, 'kin.' Moves one square forward, diagonally forward, sideways, and backward. Cannot be promoted.

ぎんしょう 銀将 〖将棋〗 a silver officer. A piece that Western chess does not have. Is commonly called by its abbreviated form, 'gin.' Moves one square forward, diagonally forward, and diagonally backward, to 5 places in total. When it is promoted to 'narigin,' it moves like a KINSHOU.

ぎんじょうしゅ 吟醸酒 〖酒〗 a high-quality sake. Is brewed at low temperatures from rice polished to 60% or less of its original weight.

きんじょうてんのう 今上天皇 〖天皇〗 a generic term for the current Emperor. The specific name of each Emperor is given posthumously.

きんせい 近世 〔時代〕 the early-modern times. Consist of the Azuchi-Momoyama (1573-1603) and Edo periods (1603-1867) in Japanese chronology.

きんせいしょきふうぞくが 近世初期風俗画 〔絵画〕 early modern genre painting. Depicts manners and customs of Kyoto and its suburbs. Originated from the Tosa-style genre painting around the 16th century, was later promoted mainly by the Kanou school, and developed among town painters in Edo in the 17th century. →土佐派

きんだい 近代 〔時代〕 modern times. Consists of the Meiji (1868-1912), Taishou (1912-1926), and early Shouwa (1926-1989) periods in Japanese chronology. Namely, from 1868 to 1945.

きんたいきょう 錦帯橋 〔橋〕 Kintaikyo Bridge. A wooden arch bridge that crosses the Nishiki River in Iwakuni City in eastern Yamaguchi Pref. Was originally built in 1673. Its five sequential arches add up to the total length of 175 m. Can be accessed by bus, from either Shin-Iwakuni Station on San'yo Shinkansen or Iwakuni Station on the JR lines.

きんだいちきょうすけ 金田一京助 〔言語〕 1882-1971. A Japanese philologist and lexicographer born in Iwate Pref. Completed foundational research on the Ainu language and epic poetry. The father of KINDAICHI HARUHIKO.

きんだいちはるひこ 金田一春彦 〔言語〕 1913-2004. A Japanese philologist and lexicographer born in Tokyo. Researched accents and dialects of the Japanese language. A son of KINDAICHI KYOUSUKE.

きんたろう 金太郎 〔民話〕 Golden Boy. The hero of a folk tale, modeled on the childhood of a real samurai, SAKATA NO KINTOKI. In the folk tale, he was a son of a mountain crone, had Herculean strength, and played together with animals in the forest, wearing a bib with the kanji meaning "gold." After growing up, he met a samurai, MINAMOTO NO YORIMITSU, became his retainer, and assisted him in exterminating demons.

きんたろうあめ 金太郎飴 〔食べ物〕 a Golden Boy candy bar. The face of the Golden Boy appears wherever the bar is cut.

きんちゃく 巾着 〔生活〕 a pouch with a drawstring, made of cloth or leather. Was used mainly in the Edo period for holding coins, a seal, a talisman, or medicine.

きんちゅうならびにくげしょはっと 禁中並公家諸法度 〔政治〕 Laws for the Imperial and Court Officials. Were enacted in 1615 by the Tokugawa shogunate to regulate the Imperial Court and nobility.

きんつば 金鍔 〔食べ物〕 confection of sweetened adzuki beans wrapped in thin wheat-flour dough. Was originally shaped like a sword guard, but is now cuboid.

きんでい 金泥 〔美術〕 gold paint. Is used for paintings and Buddhist images. Looks a little darker, compared to gold leaf. →金箔

きんてつ 近鉄 〔鉄道〕 ⇨近畿日本鉄道

きんときまめ 金時豆 〔食べ物・植物〕 red kidney beans. One of the French beans.

きんとん 金団 〔食べ物〕 mashed sweet potatoes, or white pea beans. Are often mixed with chestnuts. →栗金団

きんとん 禽遁 〔忍者〕 an escaping technique using birds. A ninja shook a tree on which many birds were perched and got away while the chasers were upset at the noise of the birds.

ぎんなん 銀杏 〔植物・食べ物〕 a ginkgo nut. Is prepared and eaten in several ways such as grilled on a skewer or put in cup-steamed savory custard called CHAWAN-MUSHI.

きんのう 勤王 〔天皇〕 reverence for the Emperor. Was a political belief in the mid-19th century.

きんのうのしし 勤王の志士 〔政治〕 an ambitious samurai with respect for the Emperor. In response to social disorders toward the end of the Tokugawa shogunate in the 19th century, many of them expressed their respect for the Emperor and also resigned from their feudal domains.

きんぱく 金箔 〔美術〕 gold leaf. Is used to decorate the surface of Buddhist images and paintings on sliding doors, folding screens, and walls. Is produced by beating gold into a paper-thin leaf.

きんばん 勤番 〔武士〕 the duty of local samurai in Edo or Osaka.

きんびょうぶ 金屏風 〔家具〕 a gilted folding screen. Is usually placed as background on the stage in a ceremony such as a wedding or graduation.

きんぴら 金平 〔食べ物〕 chopped burdock roots, and sometimes carrots, cooked in sugar and soy sauce and seasoned with chili pepper.

きんぷせんじ 金峯山寺 〔寺院〕 Kinpusen-ji Temple. Was said to be founded by EN NO ODUNU and is located in Yoshino, Nara Pref. Has been a training center for mountain ascetics since medieval times. The gate of the Two Guardian Kings and the main hall are National Treasures. →修験道

ぎんぶら 銀ブラ 〔娯楽〕 a stroll on GINZA, a fancy and flourishing shopping district in Tokyo. Something like strolling on Fifth Avenue in New York City.

きんぼし 金星 〔相撲〕 a surprise victory over a top-level sumo wrestler by a lower-rank wrestler. Strictly speaking, it refers only to a victory over a YOKODUNA by a MAE-GASHIRA.

きんまきえ 金蒔絵 〔美術〕 lacquerware sprinkled with golden dust. →蒔絵

きんみずひき 金水引 〔生活〕 gold

paper cords on an envelope for money gift. Is used on an auspicious occasion. →水引

きんめいてんのう 欽明天皇 〖天皇〗 Emperor Kinmei. 510?–571. The 29th, on the throne from 531 to 571. During his reign, Buddhism was introduced from Paekche, present southwestern Korea.

きんめだい 金目鯛〖魚〗 a splendid alfonsino. *Beryx splendens*. Eaten simmered in thick broth, or as sashimi.

きんゆうちょう 金融庁 〖行政〗 Financial Services Agency. One of the Japanese state organizations. Was reformed from the Financial Supervisory Agency in 2000. Aims to protect depositors and investors and to facilitate finance.

きんらん 金襴〖服飾〗 brocade with patterns woven from gold yarn.

きんらんどんす 金襴緞子 〖服飾〗 satin cloth with golden patterns. Is usually used for a bridal costume.

きんろうかんしゃのひ 勤労感謝の日 〖祝日〗 Labor Thanksgiving Day, November 23. A national holiday to set a high value on labor, to celebrate production, and to express thanks for everyone's hard work. This day has traditionally been the day of the Imperial festival of the rice harvest. Was ordained in 1948. →新嘗(にいなめ)祭

く 区〖行政〗 **(1)** one of the 23 special cities in Tokyo. Has its own municipal government, and its head is elected by popular vote. **(2)** an administrative district of an ordinance-designated city such as Osaka and Sapporo. Has no government and is, in effect, administrated by the city. Its head is appointed by the mayor. Although the Japanese term for (1) and (2) is the same, in most cases "city" is used for (1), and "ward" is used for (2), as an English translation.

く 句〖文芸〗 **(1)** a structural unit in a traditional rhyming poem. **(2)** the abbreviated term for HAIKU.

〜く 〜句〖文芸〗 a counting suffix for haiku. →〜首(しゅ)

くいあわせ 食い合わせ〖食文化〗 ⇨ 食べ合わせ

くいぞめ 食い初め〖食文化〗 ceremony for weaning. Literally means "eating for the first time." Is held on the 100th day after childbirth. Actually, the parents only pretend to feed a baby with ordinary food, using special tableware for the ceremony.

くいだおれ 食い倒れ〖食文化・精神性〗 bankruptcy by eating. Refers to the nature of Osaka people, who love to eat. ↔着倒れ

ぐいのみ ぐい飲み〖酒〗 a small cup for cold sake. Larger than CHOKO, a tiny sake cup. Its capacity is about 50 to 100 cc.

くうかい 空海〖仏教〗 774-835. A priest and the founder of the Shingon sect, born in present Kagawa Pref. Introduced esoteric Buddhism from China in 806, built the KONGOUBU-JI Temple in Mt. Kouya in 816, was given the TOU-JI Temple in Kyoto by Emperor Saga in 823, and built the first educational institute to teach the common people, named 'Shugeishuchiin,' in 828. Also a great calligrapher. Is known by his posthumous name, Koubou Daishi.

ぐうじ 宮司〖神道〗 a chief priest of a Shinto shrine. →神主；禰宜(ねぎ)

くうすう 古酒, クースー〖酒〗 old spirits in Okinawa Pref. Refers to spirits, called AWAMORI, that have matured for more than three years.

くうそくぜしき 空即是色〖仏教〗 a term meaning that emptiness is nothing but a materialistic object. This emptiness enables everything in the universe to exist. The term is included in the Heart Sutra. →般若心経(はんにゃしんぎょう)；色即是空

くうぼあかぎ 空母赤城〖軍事〗 Aircraft Carrier Akagi. A flagship of the Japanese Navy before World War II. Was constructed in 1927 and was sunk at the Battle of Midway in 1942.

くうや 空也〖仏教〗 902-972. A Buddhist priest who invented ODORI

NENBUTSU, the style of chanting prayers while dancing. Constructed roads and bridges, provided education to ordinary people, and founded the Rokuharamitsu-ji Temple.

くえ　九絵〚食べ物・魚〛　a long-tooth grouper, or a kelp grouper. *Epinephelus moara*. About 1 m long. Eaten as sashimi or in one-pot dish.

くおんじ　久遠寺〚寺院〛　Minobusan Kuonji. The head temple of the Nichiren sect, located in south-western Yamanashi Pref. Was founded in 1274.

くかい　句会〚俳句〛　a meeting to compose rhyming HAIKUS and for the writers to critique each other.

くかたち　盟神探湯〚宗教〛　judgment with boiling water in ancient times. The suspect was first forced to put his or her hand into boiling water. If the hand became burned, he or she was judged guilty. If it did not, he or she is judged not guilty.

くがたち　盟神探湯〚宗教〛　⇨盟神探湯(くかたち)

くぎかくし　釘隠し〚建築〛　an ornament to cover a nail head. Is often used at the crossing part of a column and a horizontal bar in a traditional mansion.

くきしゅうぞう　九鬼周造〚人文学〛　1888-1941. A philosopher born in Tokyo. Analyzed the Japanese mentality and aesthetics by using existentialism. His works include *Reflections on Japanese Taste: the Structure of Iki* in 1930.

くぐつ　傀儡〚芸能〛　a puppet or a puppeteer in the Heian period. These people wandered around various places in a group and performed puppetry. The men in the group also hunted, and the women practiced prostitution. A part of their puppetry later developed into NINGYOU JOURURI.

くげ　公家〚天皇〛　a court noble. This term was used as the antonym for BUKE, meaning samurai, after the first samurai government, or shogunate, was established.

くげしょはっと　公家諸法度〚天皇・法律〛　⇨禁中並(きんちゅうならびに)公家諸法度

くさいち　草市〚仏教・植物〛　a market to sell flowers or goods for the Bon Festival. Is held from the evening of July 12th to the morning of July 13th.

くさかんむり　草冠〚漢字〛　a crown radical meaning "grass." Is used in kanji such as 花(flower), 芝(turf), 芽(bud), 茎(stem), and 芋(potato). →冠；部首

くさぞうし　草双紙〚文芸〛　illustrated volumes of popular novels from the 17th to 19th centuries. On each page, text was written in HIRAGANA in the blank space around the illustrations. There were several types such as yellow-cover or red-cover books. →黄表紙；赤本

くさだんご　草団子〚食べ物〛　a rice-flour dumpling containing mugwort leaves.

くさつおんせん　草津温泉〚温泉〛　a hot spring in western Gunma Pref.

Effective in treating skin diseases, gastrointestinal malfunctions, and neuralgia. Has several sports facilities including ski slopes. One of the three most famous hot springs in Japan. →日本三名泉

くさなぎのつるぎ 草薙剣 〖神話〗 ⇨ 天叢雲剣(あめのむらくものつるぎ)

くさまくら 草枕 〖文芸・作品〗 *The Grass Pillow*. A novel published in 1906 by NATSUME SOUSEKI. Presents the author's view of the arts by describing an exchange between a painter and an inn's hostess.

くさもち 草餅 〖食べ物〗 a rice cake flavored with the mugwort herb. Has traditionally been eaten during the Doll Festival on March 3rd.

くさや くさや 〖食べ物〗 dried fish with a unique smell. A horse mackerel or flying fish is soaked in fermented sauce and sundried. A specialty of the Izu islands.

くさりかたびら 鎖帷子 〖忍者〗 chain mail. Was worn under a kimono during battle by samurai or ninja.

くさりがま 鎖鎌 〖忍者・武器〗 a weapon composed of a sickle, a chain, and a weight. The handle of the sickle is about 60 cm long, the blade about 20 cm long, and the chain 1 to 4 m long. The user holds the sickle in one hand while swinging the chain in a circular motion with the other hand.

くじ 九字 〖忍者・宗教〗 ⇨臨兵闘者皆陣列在前(りんびょうとうしゃかいじんれつざいぜん)

くしかつ 串カツ 〖食べ物〗 a bite-sized cutlet on a bamboo skew. Common ingredients are pork and onion or green onion, but eggs of a Japanese quail, lotus roots, and asparagus are also tasty ingredients. At restaurants in Shinsekai, Osaka, one can eat as much garnished cabbage as one likes for a set price.

くしなだひめ 櫛名田比売 〖神話〗 the wife of the God of Storms, SUSANOO NO MIKOTO. She was saved by Susanoo before being sacrificed to YAMATA NO OROCHI.

くしもとちょう 串本町 〖地名〗 Kushimoto Town. Is located in southern Wakayama Pref. South of it is Cape Shiono-misaki, the southernmost point of Honshuu. The coastal areas and wetlands have been designated a Ramsar site. Scuba diving is popular.

くじゃくみょうおう 孔雀明王 〖仏教〗 the Peacock Wisdom King. *Mahamayuri*. Has four arms and sits on a peacock. Swallows evil spirits like a peacock swallows a poisoned snake. Paintings of it are stored at the Tokyo National Museum and Ninna-ji Temple in Kyoto.

くじゅうくりはま 九十九里浜 〖地名〗 Kujuukuri Beach. Is located in northeastern Chiba Pref., facing the Pacific Ocean. Is 66 km long, making it the longest sandy beach in Japan that is open to the public. Has a relatively straight coastline, shaped like an arc. Farming and marine sports are popular.

くじら 鯨 〔食べ物・動物〕 a whale. *Cetacea*. The species whose length is shorter than 5 m is called 'iruka,' which means "dolphin." The meat was eaten popularly, the oil was used for lamps or soaps, and the baleen was used for rulers, before commercial whaling was banned.

くじらじゃく 鯨尺 〔服飾〕 a ruler used when sewing a kimono. Used to be made from whalebone.

くじらまく 鯨幕 〔冠婚葬祭〕 a curtain with broad black-and-white stripes. Is used for a funeral.

くず 葛 〔植物〕 kudzu, or arrowroot. *Pueraria lobata*. One of the seven flowers of autumn. Its root is used for medicine or as a material of starch. →秋の七草

くずあん 葛餡 〔食べ物〕 thick sauce made from kudzu starch. Is seasoned with soy sauce or sugar.

くずきり 葛切り 〔食べ物〕 kudzu starch noodles. Syrup is poured on them when they are eaten.

ぐすく 城久 〔城郭〕 the term for any castle in the Ryuukyuu Islands. More than 200 were built from the 12th to 16th centuries.

くすこのへん 薬子の変 〔政治〕 the Revolt of Kusuko. A political event that occurred in the early 9th century. A lover of Retired Emperor Heijou, named Fujiwara no Kusuko, attempted to obtain political power together with her elder brother, Nakanari. However, she was defeated by the Emperor Saga and then committed suicide.

くずしじ 崩し字 〔言語〕 a cursive characters. Both kana and kanji characters can be written in this style. Nowadays most Japanese people find it difficult to read such cursive characters.

くすのき 楠 〔植物〕 a camphor tree. *Cinnamomum camphora*. Grows to more than 20 m high. The wood is used to make insect repellent or for furniture or building material.

くすのきまさしげ 楠木正成 〔武士〕 1294?-1336. A warlord born in present Osaka Pref. Assisted Emperor Godaigo in conquering the Kamakura shogunate by fighting against the shogunate troops at the Akasaka and Chihaya Castles in southern Osaka Pref. Was defeated in present Koube by ASHIKAGA TAKAUJI, who later established the Muromachi shogunate.

くずのはぎつね 葛の葉狐 〔妖怪・動物〕 a female white fox in a legend. Lived in a forest, called Shinoda, in southern Osaka Pref. Was helped by a human, ABE NO YASUNA, married him, and bore ABE NO SEIMEI, a prominent ghost buster. The story was introduced into kabuki and joururi.

くすみもりかげ 久隅守景 〔絵画〕 ?-? A painter in the early Edo period. Learned under the Kanou school but was expelled later. His works include *Family Enjoying the Evening Cool* at the Tokyo National Museum.

くずもち 葛餅 〔食べ物〕 a kudzu

starch cake. As it's eaten, syrup is poured on it, or soybean flour mixed with sugar is sprinkled on it.

くずゆ 葛湯〖食べ物〗 thick hot water that contains sugar and kudzu starch. Is drunk to heat the body and is good for digestion.

ぐそく 具足〖武士〗 ⇨甲冑（かっちゅう）

ぐそくに 具足煮〖食べ物〗 a boiled lobster or crab with its shell on. Is called so because the shell is compared to 'gusoku,' which means "armor."

くたにやき 九谷焼〖陶磁器〗 Kutani ware. Porcelain originally produced in Kutani village, Ishikawa Pref. First produced in the late 1600s by Goto Saijiro, who had been apprenticed to a master in Arita, where Japan's porcelain-making started. Typically includes bold designs and combinations of colors such as gold, red, purple, blue, and green.

くだら 百済〖国名〗 Paekche. Existed in western Korea from the 4th century to 663. Exported many continental cultural features, including Buddhism, to Japan. When Tang in China and Sinra in eastern Korea attacked it in 660, Japan tried to help Paekche but was defeated in the Battle of Baekgang-gu, and Paekche collapsed in 663. Many people came to settle in Japan and were leaders in the cultural scene in ancient Japan. An area where Paekche people settled in Osaka is still called 'Kudara.' →新羅（しらぎ）；白村江（はくそんこう）の戦い

くちいれや 口入屋〖ビジネス〗 an employment agent. A somewhat derogatory term. Now obsolete.

くちなし 梔子〖植物〗 a common gardenia, or cape jasmine. *Gardenia jasminoides*. Is used as dyestuff.

くちへん 口偏〖漢字〗 a left-side radical meaning "mouth." Is used in kanji such as 呼(call), 吸(absorb), and 叫(shout). →偏；部首

くちよせ 口寄せ〖宗教〗 invoking the soul of a dead person and letting it talk through the medium's mouth. →イタコ

くつがた 沓形〖仏教・建築〗 ⇨鴟尾（しび）

くっしゃろこ 屈斜路湖〖湖沼〗 Lake Kussharo. Is located in eastern Hokkaido. Its area is 79.3 km^2. The deepest point is 117.5 m. The name comes from the Ainu language. Is part of Akan National Park.

くつわむし 轡虫〖動物〗 a giant katydid. *Mecopoda nipponensis*. Chirps a little noisily.

くてん 句点〖言語〗 a period. Marks the end of a sentence. Is represented as 。 and often called 'maru,' which means "circle."

くどく 功徳〖仏教〗 a good deed that leads a person deserving a future reward in Buddhism.

くない 苦無〖忍者・武器〗 a double-bladed knife. Was used as a weapon and also as a tool to dig up the ground, to destroy a fence, to climb a stone outer wall, and to strike sparks. Its size varies from 20 to 50

cm.

くないちょう　宮内庁　〖天皇・行政〗
Imperial Household Agency. One of the Japanese state organizations. "Takes charge of state matters concerning the Imperial House" and "assists His Majesty in receiving foreign ambassadors and ministers and performing ceremonial functions," according to its official website.

くないちょうごようたし　宮内庁御用達　〖天皇・経済〗 a merchant or company that supplies goods to the Imperial Household Agency. The official system to approve merchants and companies started in 1891 and was abolished in 1954.

くなこく　狗奴国　〖国名〗 a nation that is said to have existed toward the south of YAMATAI-KOKU in the 3rd century. Its king was male, and it was hostile to Yamatai.

くなしりとう　国後島　〖地名〗 Kunashir Island. Is located northward off Hokkaido. Its area is 1,499 km^2. Has been under Russian rule since 1945.

くに　国　〖行政〗 a province. An old administrative unit. There used to be 58 provinces and 3 islands when they were first established in the 7th century, but later the size and number of the units were slightly changed. The province system was abolished in the Meiji Restoration of 1868, and the prefectural system was established.

くにがまえ　国構え　〖漢字〗 an enclosure radical related to "surrounding" or "circulation." Is used in kanji such as 国(country) and 回(turning). →構え；部首

くにがろう　国家老　〖官位〗 a local chief vassal of a feudal lord in the Edo period. Lived in the feudal domain and was in charge of its administration when the lord was required to stay in Edo. ↔江戸家老 →参勤交代

くにきだどっぽ　国木田独歩　〖文芸〗 1871-1908. A poet and novelist born in Chiba Pref. Was influenced by the British poet, Wordsworth, and published a collection of short stories named *Musashino* in 1901.

くにきょう　恭仁京　〖政治〗 Kuni Capital. Was located in southwestern Kyoto Pref. from 740 to 744. Before its construction was finished, the capital moved to Naniwa-kyou in Osaka.

くにさきはんとう　国東半島　〖半島〗 the Kunisaki Peninsula. Is located in northeastern Ooita Pref. and extends into the Inland Sea, extending around a volcano, Mt. Futago. Buddhist culture flourished from the 8th to 12th centuries, and a great number of Buddhist images were engraved using volcanic rocks.

くにさだちゅうじ　国定忠治〖ヤクザ〗 1810-1850. A yakuza born in present Gunma Pref. Was regarded as a hero after death and appeared as a character in KABUKI and KOUDAN, which is the rhythmical storytelling of historical episodes or fiction.

くにつかみ 国つ神 〖神話〗 a genius loci. Deities who ruled lands before the descent of NINIGI NO MIKOTO. Include OOKUNINUSHI NO KAMI, Sarutahiko, and ASHINAZUCHI TENAZUCHI. ↔天(￰)つ神

くにともてっぽうかじ 国友鉄砲鍛冶 〖武器〗 a gunsmith at Kunitomo Village. Kunitomo Village in present Shiga Pref. was famous for gun manufacturing from the 16th to 19th centuries.

くぬぎ 櫟 〖植物〗 a sawtooth oak. *Quercus acutissima*. Its fruits are called 'donguri,' which means "acorns."

くのいち くノー 〖忍者〗 a female ninja. Was named after a kanji, 女, which means "woman" and can be disassembled into く (ku), ノ (no), and 一 (ichi).

くひ 句碑 〖文芸〗 a monument inscribed with a haiku. Is usually constructed at a place related to the poet or to the motif of the poem. →歌碑

くびなげ 首投げ 〖相撲〗 a head throw. Throwing down the opponent by holding his head.

くぶんでん 口分田 〖政治〗 a personally granted rice field. Was allotted to commoners under the centralized administration system, called RITSURYOU-SEI, in the 7th century. Its owner had to pay 3% of the harvest as tax.

くぼう 公方 〖天皇・武士〗 originally, the Emperor. In and after the Kamakura period, referred to a shogun.

くほんいん 九品印 〖仏教〗 nine types of symbolic forms and positions of Amitabha's hands and fingers. There are nine ranks of rebirth in the Western Pure Land, and the form and position of the hands and fingers indicate the rank. →印相

くほんおうじょう 九品往生 〖仏教〗 the nine ranks of rebirth in the Western Pure Land. The rank is determined by the practice of a person's lifetime. The image of Amitabha takes one of the nine types of symbolic forms. The position of the hands and fingers indicates the rank. →印相

くまそ 熊襲 〖少数民族〗 an ancient tribe in Kyushu. Is mentioned in the *Records of Ancient Matters* (KOJIKI), and the *Chronicles of Japan* (NIHONSHOKI). Rebelled against the Yamato Court and was defeated by YAMATO TAKERU NO MIKOTO.

くまで 熊手 〖生活・宗教〗 a bamboo rake. Originally, a tool to sweep fallen leaves to clean a garden or street. A small bamboo rake with ornaments is sold at a Shinto festival, called TORI NO ICHI, as a good luck charm for gaining good fortune.

くまどり 隈取り 〖歌舞伎〗 a make-up to exaggerate the character or expression of a role. Depicts muscles or prominences on the face, using red, blue, or black lines.

Is used in JIDAIMONO, a historical drama.

くまの 熊野 〖地名〗 an area extending over the southern parts of Wakayama and Mie Prefs. Famous for the Three Great Shrines of Kumano. →熊野三山

くまのい 熊の胆 〖医療〗 dried gallbladder of a bear. Is used as a gastrointestinal drug in traditional Chinese medicine.

くまのおうじ 熊野王子 〖神道〗 a local shrine along the Kumano pilgrimage. Pilgrims held various rituals at Ouji on the way to the Three Great Shrines of Kumano, but not on the way back. →熊野三山

くまのこどう 熊野古道 〖交通〗 Old Pilgrimage Routes to Kumano. The Kumano area, which has the Three Great Shrines, can be reached in several ways. The integrated routes were designated a World Heritage Site in 2004. →熊野三山；高野山

くまのさんざん 熊野三山 〖神道〗 Three Great Shrines of Kumano: KUMANO HONGUU TAISHA, KUMANO HAYATAMA TAISHA, and KUMANO NACHI TAISHA. Kumano has been a mecca of mountain asceticism since medieval times, and all three shrines were a popular pilgrimage for ordinary people from the 12th to 17th centuries. It was said that pilgrims walked in a line like ants. The whole area was designated a World Heritage Site in 2004. →修験道

くまのじんじゃ 熊野神社 〖神社〗 a Kumano Shrine. There are more than 3,000 Kumano Shrines throughout Japan. Usually enshrines Ketsumimiko no ookami, Kumano Hayatama no ookami, or Kumano Fusumi no ookami, who are enshrined in the Three Great Shrines of Kumano. →熊野三山

くまのなちたいしゃ 熊野那智大社 〖神社〗 Kumano Nachi Taisha. Is located in southeastern Wakayama Pref. Enshrines Kumano Fusumi no ookami, who is identified with IZANAMI NO MIKOTO. Nachi Waterfall has been worshipped as a god. →熊野三山；熊野古道；那智(さん)の滝

くまのはやたまたいしゃ 熊野速玉大社 〖神社〗 Kumano Hayatama Taisha. Is located in southeastern Wakayama Pref. Enshrines Kumano Hayatama no ookami and Kumano Fusumi no ookami, who are identified with a married divine couple, Izanagi and Izanami. Sculptures of deities are National Treasures. →熊野三山；熊野古道

くまのほんぐうたいしゃ 熊野本宮大社 〖神社〗 Kumano Hongu Taisha. Hongu Taisha means "original grand shrine." The head shrine of the Kumano Shrines throughout Japan, located in southeastern Wakayama Pref. Enshrines Ketsumimiko no ookami, who is identified with SUSANOO NO MIKOTO, the God of Storms. →熊野三山；熊野古道

くままつり 熊祭り 〖少数民族・祭礼〗

⇨イオマンテ

くまもとけん 熊本県 〖都道府県〗
Kumamoto Pref. Is located in central Kyushu in Western Japan. Is 7,409 km^2 in area. The capital is Kumamoto City, located in its northern part, on the coast of the Ariake Sea. Off the coast are the Amakusa Islands, facing the East China Sea. In its eastern part is Mt. Aso, which has Japan's second largest caldera after the one around Lake Kussharo in Hokkaido. In Hitoyoshi City in southern Kumamoto Pref. is Aoi Aso Shrine. Its five buildings have been designated National Treasures. Was hit by two great earthquakes in April 2016, both with a magnitude of 7, but has made a steady recovery. Used to be called Higo.

くまもとし 熊本市 〖地名〗 Kumamoto City. An ordinance-designated city and the capital of Kumamoto Pref., located in its northern part. Developed as a castle town of the Katou clan after 1600, and of the Hosokawa clan after 1632. Rice, melons, watermelons, eggplants, and satsuma mandarin oranges are produced in large quantities. Purple laver and littleneck clams are grown in the Ariake Sea. In addition to the Kyushu Shinkansen and some train lines, the city is served efficiently by trams and buses. In particular, Kumamoto Koutsuu Center is one of Japan's largest bus terminals.

くまもとじょう 熊本城 〖城郭〗
Kumamoto Castle. Is located in the center of Kumamoto City. Was first built in 1467, but it was Katou Kiyomasa who greatly expanded it from 1601 to 1607. During the Satsuma rebellion in 1877, the Satsuma army besieged the castle, but its steep stone walls and the well-organized defense by the Imperial army, with the help of conscripts, prevented it from being taken. Was severely damaged in the 2016 Kumamoto Earthquake, but it is expected that it will have been fully repaired by 2036.

くまもん くまもん 〖ゆるキャラ〗 a relaxing mascot character of Kumamoto Pref. It first appeared in March 2011, when Kyushu Shinkansen started operating.

くみて 組手 〖武術〗 sparring, or freestyle fighting in karate. Two participants fight each other under some specified rules, applying basic sparring techniques.

くみやしき 組屋敷 〖武士・建築〗 a residence of a police officer under a feudal commissioner in the Edo period.

くもがたひじき 雲形肘木 〖建築〗 ⇨ 雲肘木(ひじ)

くもすけ 雲助 〖交通〗 a pair of violent and vulgar palanquin bearers in the Edo period. →駕籠(かご)

くものうえびと 雲の上人 〖天皇〗 the nobles at the Imperial Court in olden times.

くもひじき 雲肘木 〖建築〗 a cloud-shaped horizontal short bar to support a beam or an eave.

くやみ 悔やみ〖冠婚葬祭・言語〗condolence.

くよう 供養〖仏教〗a Buddhist ritual. Usually refers to a memorial service for the souls of the dead. Other cases include the eye-opening ceremony for a new Buddhist image, called KAIGEN KUYOU, and a memorial ceremony for needles, called HARI KUYOU. →永代(えいたい)供養；追善供養

くようとう 供養塔〖仏教・建築〗a stone monument where one prays for the calm rest of a dead soul. Many such monuments are shaped like pagodas, but some are Buddhist statues or stone panels with epitaphs.

くら 蔵〖建築〗⇨土蔵

くらあく クラーク〖教育〗William Smith Clark. 1826-1886. An American educator, Civil War hero, and lay Christian. Was recruited in 1876 to teach ethical training and agricultural methods at Sapporo Agricultural College. Based the ethical education of his students on the Bible. Led many of his students to become Christians. Returned to the U.S. after less than a year in Japan. His parting words to his students—"Boys, be ambitious!"—are well-known in Japan to this day.

くらしきし 倉敷市〖地名〗Kurashiki City. Is located in southern Okayama Pref. Famous for the Historical Quarters, where there

are several museums such as the Ohara Museum of Art are lined.

くらたひゃくぞう 倉田百三〖文芸〗1891-1943. A playwright and critic born in Hiroshima Pref. His works include *The Priest and the Disciples* in 1916.

くらつくりのとり 鞍作止利〖彫刻〗?-? A sculptor of Buddhist images in the 7th century. His ancestors came from the Korean Peninsula. His works include the Triad of the Historical Buddha at Houryuu-ji Temple and the Historical Buddha at Asuka-dera Temple.

ぐらばあてい グラバー邸〖建築〗the Glover Mansion. Is located in Nagasaki. Was built as the residence of a British businessman, Thomas B. Glover, in 1863. Is said to be the first Western-style house built by a Japanese carpenter.

くらべうま 競べ馬〖スポーツ〗a horse race in ancient times. Was held as an imperial ceremony.

くらま 鞍馬〖地名〗a sightseeing spot in a northern suburban area of Kyoto City. Visitors can enjoy autumnal red leaves, traditional-style restaurants, hot springs, and the Kurama-dera Temple.

くらもと 蔵元〖酒〗a brewery of sake, soy sauce, or soybean paste.

くらやしき 蔵屋敷〖武士・経済〗a business office of a shogun, feudal lord, and direct vassal of the shogun in the Edo period. Stored and traded rice and other local specialties. Many of such offices were located in Osaka.

くり 庫裡〖仏教・建築〗 the kitchen or residential part of a Buddhist temple. →寺務所(ｼﾞﾑ)

ぐりいんしゃ グリーン車〖交通〗 a first-class train car. A JR express train has this type of car, which is marked with a logo of a green four-leaved clover.

くりからもんもん 倶利伽羅紋紋〖ヤクザ・服飾〗 **(1)** a colorful dragon tattooed on the back. **(2)** a person with such a tattoo.

くりきんとん 栗金団 〖食べ物〗 mashed sweet potato with sweetened chestnuts. Is mainly eaten on New Year's holidays because the yellow color of chestnuts is associated with gold coins.

くりごはん 栗ご飯〖食べ物〗 rice cooked with chestnuts.

くりすます クリスマス〖キリスト教・娯楽〗 Christmas. Though only 1% of the population is Christian in Japan, most Japanese people hold a Christmas party just for fun. In particular, young people consider Christmas Eve as special and tend to spend it with their sweetheart. →キリスト教

くりまんじゅう 栗饅頭〖食べ物〗 a steamed chestnut bun. Looks like an actual chestnut because of its colors and shape and includes a real chestnut in it.

くりようかん 栗羊羹 〖食べ物〗 sweet adzuki-paste jelly including pieces of chestnuts.

くりん 九輪〖仏教・建築〗 nine rings on top of a pagoda roof.

くるまけん 車剣〖忍者〗 a three-dimensional throwing knife. The points of six blades from a regular octahedron.

くるまとらじろう 車寅次郎〖映画〗 ⇨フーテンの寅

くるまひき 車引き〖交通・職業〗 ⇨人力車夫

くるまへん 車偏〖漢字〗 a left-side radical meaning "wheel." Is used in kanji such as 軌(track), 転(rolling), and 軸(axle). →偏；部首

くるまや 俥屋〖交通〗 ⇨人力車夫

くるわ 廓〖セックス・娯楽〗 a red-light district in olden times.

くるわ 曲輪〖建築〗 a section of a castle. Is surrounded by walls or earthwork.

くれむつ 暮れ六つ〖時刻〗 the sixth time in the afternoon in the Edo period. Around 6 p.m. ↔明け六つ

くれよんしんちゃん クレヨンしんちゃん〖アニメ・作品〗 *Crayon Shin-chan*. A manga and anime series created by Yoshito Usui. The story follows the daily life and adventures of the five-year-old Shinnosuke Nohara and his family, friends, and neighbors. The manga was published serially in two magazines from 1990 to 2010, and its anime began in 1992.

くろいあめ 黒い雨 〖文芸・作品〗 *Black Rain*. A novel published in parts from 1965 to 1966 by IBUSE MASUJI. Describes the tragedy in everyday life in Hiroshima immediately after the atomic bomb was dropped in 1945.

くろうどどころ 蔵人所 〖行政〗 the document office for the Imperial Court. Was established in 810 by Emperor Saga and was abolished in the 19th century. →令外官(りょうげのかん)

くろおび 黒帯 〖武術〗 a black belt. Is worn by a martial artist who displays advanced techniques. →段

くろかわおんせん 黒川温泉 〖温泉〗 the name of a hot spring in north-eastern Kumamoto Pref. Effective in treating rheumatism and incisions.

くろげわぎゅう 黒毛和牛 〖動物・食べ物〗 Japanese black cattle. Produce high-quality beef.

くろこ 黒子 〖歌舞伎・文楽〗 a stage assistant in black costume. Assists on stage with a kabuki or bunraku performance. Audience assumes that he is invisible.

くろさわあきら 黒沢明 〖映画〗 1910-1998. A film director born in Tokyo. His works include *Rashomon* in 1950, *Seven Samurai* in 1954, and *Kagemusha* in 1980.

くろしお 黒潮 〖海洋〗 the Japan current. The largest warm current around Japan. Literally means "black seawater" because it looks blackish. Starts toward the east of the Philippine Islands and flows along the southern coast of Japan, from southwest to northeast. Has had a great influence on Japanese climate and culture. ↔親潮

くろしょいん 黒書院 〖建築〗 literally means "black study room." Its meaning is different among facilities. For example, 'kuro-shoin' at Nijou Castle in Kyoto was used as the meeting room for the shogun and feudal lords, while the one at Hongan-ji Temple in Kyoto was used as the study room for the head priest. ↔白書院

くろだかんべえ 黒田官兵衛 〖武士〗 1546-1604. A warlord. Is said to have been born in present Shiga Pref. Was good at constructing a castle and devising tactics. Served ODA NOBUNAGA, TOYOTOMI HIDEYOSHI, and TOKUGAWA IEYASU; was favored especially by Toyotomi Hideyoshi.

くろだせいき 黒田清輝 〖絵画〗 1866-1924. A Western-style painter born in Kagoshima Pref. Introduced Impressionism to Japan. Used a naked model for the first time in Japan. His works include *The Lakeside* and *Reading*, stored at the Tokyo National Museum.

くろとめそで 黒留袖 〖服飾〗 a formal kimono for a married woman with a black background. Is decorated with five duplicates of her family crests. →留袖

くろはばき 黒脛巾 〖忍者〗 the name for a ninja group under a feudal lord, DATE MASAMUNE, in the 16th to 17th centuries. Literally means "black gaiter." Its actual existence is doubtful.

くろぶさ 黒房 〖相撲〗 a black tassel. Hung at the northwestern corner of a suspended roof above the sumo ring. In this case, black indicates winter or an animal deity called GENBU, which is the black turtle-and-snake. →青房; 赤房; 白房; 玄武(げんぶ)

くろふね 黒船 〖外交〗 a Western black warship. Visited Japan to open the country in the 19th century. The first example was four American warships under Commodore Perry in 1853. Frightened Japanese people as a symbol of Western power.

くろぼし 黒星 〖相撲〗 a defeat mark. Literally means "black star." Is symbolized by a black dot in the list of tournament records, BANDUKE. ↔白星

くろまぐろ 黒鮪 〖食べ物・魚〗 a bluefin tuna. *Thunnus orientalis*. A Japanese favorite mainly eaten as sashimi and sushi. Is also called 'hon-maguro.'

くろまつ 黒松 〖植物〗 a Japanese black pine. *Pinus thunbergii*. Grows near a coastal area and has honeycomb patterns on the surface.

くろまめ 黒豆 〖食べ物・植物〗 simmered black soybeans. Are eaten on New Year's Day to offer a wish for good health.

くろみす 黒御簾 〖歌舞伎〗 ⇨下座(げざ)⑴

くろみずひき 黒水引 〖冠婚葬祭〗 black paper cords on an envelope that includes a gift of money. Is used on mournful occasions. →水引

くろもじ 黒文字 〖茶道〗 a short wooden stick with the bark of the

tree on one side. Is used to eat sweets during the tea ceremony.

くわ 桑 〖植物〗 mulberry. *Morus bombycis*. The leaves are feed for silkworm cultures.

くわい 慈姑 〖食べ物・植物〗 an arrowhead bulb. *Sagittaria trifolia* var. *sinensis*. Often eaten during the New Year's holidays.

くわいれしき 鍬入れ式 〖農業・建築〗 a ceremony of breaking new ground with a hoe. When starting a large construction project, higher-rank people related to the new construction actually break ground with a hoe. For example, the chair of an executive committee, the president of a related company, or the orderer of the construction join.

ぐんかんまあち 軍艦マーチ 〖軍事・音楽〗 Warship March. Was composed in 1897 by Setoguchi Fujiyoshi. Used to be popular as background music in a pachinko parlor.

ぐんかんまき 軍艦巻 〖寿司〗 a battleship sushi. The bite-sized rice piece is topped with seafood such as sea urchin or salmon roe, and the side of the piece is wound with purple laver. Its shape looks like a battleship.

ぐんせん 軍扇 〖軍事〗 a folding fan for a warlord to command in a battlefield around the 16th century. The sticks are lacquered black. The sun, moon, and stars are painted on the paper.

ぐんだりみょうおう 軍荼利明王

〔仏教〕 Wisdom King of Coiling Female Snakes. *Kundali*. One of the Five Great Wisdom Kings. Originally a female deity in Hinduism. One-faced, three-eyed, and eight-armed. Is decorated with snake accessories such as necklaces, earrings, and bracelets.

くんてん 訓点 〔漢字〕 a mark to make the text of Chinese classics easy to read as Japanese. Indicates the reading order or pronunciation or adds a postpositional particle. → 漢文

くんどく 訓読 〔漢字〕 **(1)**⇨漢文訓読 **(2)**⇨訓読み

ぐんばい 軍配 〔相撲〕 a fan of a warlord or a sumo referee. Was used by a warlord around the 16th century to conduct his troops. Is used by a sumo referee at present to indicate a winner in the bout. Is usually lacquered black.

ぐんまけん 群馬県 〔都道府県〕 Gunma Pref. Is located in central Japan, in the northwestern part of the Kantou region. Is 6,362 km² in area. Its capital is Maebashi City. Has thunder frequently in summer and is windy in winter. There is a great difference in temperature in summer between its northern mountainous areas and southern flat land. Has three national parks, namely, Nikko, Oze, and Joushin'etsu Kougen, and popular hot springs such as Kusatsu and Ikaho. Famous for konjac and cabbage production. Car ownership ratio per household is the highest of all the prefectures. Tomioka Silk Mill in its southwestern part was designated a World Heritage Site in 2014. Used to be called Kouzuke.

くんよみ 訓読み 〔漢字〕 a Japanese-style pronunciation of a kanji. A kanji usually has only one 'kun' pronunciation. ↔音読み

くんれいしきろおまじ 訓令式 ローマ字 〔言語〕 the statutory system of writing Japanese in the Roman alphabet. Some sounds are expressed differently from the Hepburn system. For example, ふ is written as 'hu' in the statutory system, while it is written as 'fu' in the Hepburn system. ↔ヘボン式 ローマ字

け

け 褻 〖精神性〗 the concept referring to daily ordinary life. On the days of 'ke,' people wear ordinary clothes, eat ordinary food, and do their routine work. Was contrasted with the concept of a special occasion, called HARE, by a folklorist, YANAGITA KUNIO.

げいあみ 芸阿弥 〖絵画〗 1431–1485. A painter, curator, and art advisor for the Muromachi shogunate. Was good at India ink paintings. His works include *Viewing Waterfall* at the Nezu Museum in Tokyo. His father, Nouami, and his son, Souami, also served in the same position for the shogunate.

けいおう 慶応 〖時代〗 an era name from 1865 to 1868, toward the end of the Edo period.

けいおうぎじゅくだいがく 慶應義塾大学 〖学校〗 Keio University. Was founded in 1858 by FUKUZAWA YUKICHI. Has six campuses in Tokyo, Yokohama, and Fujisawa in Kanagawa Pref.

けいおうでんてつ 京王電鉄 〖鉄道〗 Keio Corporation. One of the 16 major private railway operators of Japan that serves central and southwestern Tokyo. Has seven lines and 69 stations. Connects its terminals Shinjuku and Shibuya with residential areas such as Choufu, Tama, and Hachiouji Cities. All trains on the Keio New Line continue on the Toei Shinjuku Subway Line to eastern Tokyo. Although it primarily serves commuters, some of its trains are for those who visit holiday spots such as Mt. Takao in Hachiouji, Tokyo Racecourse in Fuchuu, Tama Zoological Park in Hino, and the indoor theme park called Sanrio Puroland in Tama City.

げいぎ 芸妓 〖娯楽・職業〗 ⇨芸者

けいきゅう 京急 〖鉄道〗 ⇨京浜急行電鉄

けいぐ 敬具 〖言語〗 a conclusive greeting in a letter. Equivalent to "Sincerely yours." When a letter begins with the word HAIKEI, the letter has to be concluded with this word.

けいご 敬語 〖言語〗 the honorific language. Includes three types of honorific expressions: to show respect, to show humbleness, and to show courtesy to the listener or reader. Usually these three types are used in combination. →尊敬語；謙譲語；丁寧語

げいこ 芸子 〖娯楽・職業〗 the word meaning GEISHA in the Kansai dialect.

けいこうてんのう 景行天皇 〖天皇〗 Emperor Keikou. ?–? The 12th Emperor. Dispatched his son, YAMATO TAKERU NO MIKOTO, to conquer EMISHI and KUMASO.

けいこそうけん 稽古総見 〖相撲〗

the periodic open training session. Is held before a Tokyo tournament by the Yokozuna Deliberation Council. Is joined by almost all wrestlers in the two upper-rank division of the Grand Sumo Tournament.

けいさいえいせん 渓斎英泉 〔絵画〕 1790-1848. An ukiyo-e painter born in Edo. Main subjects were decadent and erotic women, as well as landscapes. His works include *Floating World Beauties Through the Twelve Months* at the Edo-Tokyo Museum.

けいざいさんぎょうしょう 経済産業省 〔行政機関〕 Ministry of Economy, Trade and Industry. METI. Was founded in 2001 by reforming the Ministry of International Trade and Industry.

けいさく 警策 〔禅〕 ⇨警策(きょうさく)

けいさつよびたい 警察予備隊 〔軍事〕 National Police Reserve. Existed from 1950 to 1952. Japan was disarmed after its defeat in World War II. When the United States participated in the Korean War in 1950, Japan did not have the military power to address any possible domestic disturbance that might take place. To fill that military void, the National Police Reserve was formed. It became the National Safety Forces in 1952, and then the Ground Self-Defense Force in 1954.

げいしゃ 芸者 〔娯楽・職業〕 a geisha. At a banquet, professionally entertains men with skillful conversation and traditional dancing and singing, dressed in a kimono. Is also called 'geigi.'

けいせいでんてつ 京成電鉄 〔鉄道〕 Keisei Electric Railway. One of the 16 major private railway operators of Japan, serving eastern Tokyo and northwestern Chiba Pref. Has seven lines and 66 stations. Connects its terminal Keisei Ueno with the residential areas such as Ichikawa, Funabashi, Chiba, and Narita Cities. A part of the Keisei Main Line, Narita Line, and Oshiage Line is on the route for the direct train service from Narita Airport to Haneda Airport via the Tokyo metropolitan area.

けいたい 敬体 〔言語〕 a courteous language style. Examples include ending a sentence with "desu" or "masu." ↔常体

けいだい 境内 〔神社・寺院〕 precincts of a Buddhist temple or Shinto shrine. →参道

けいたいてんのう 継体天皇 〔天皇〕 Emperor Keitai. 450-531. The 26th, on the throne from 507 to 531. Came from present Fukui Pref.

けいちつ 啓蟄 〔暦〕 one of the 24 seasonal nodes in the traditional calendar. Around March 6 in the current calendar. Means "insects come out of the ground." →二十四節気(にじゅうしせっき)

けいちょう 慶長 〔時代〕 an era name from 1596 to 1615, from the Azuchi-Momoyama to early Edo period. A great earthquake hit Kyoto in 1596. Toyotomi Hideyoshi invaded Korea in 1597.

けいちょうのえき 慶長の役 〖戦争〗
⇨文禄・慶長の役

けいは 慶派 〖彫刻〗 the Kei school of Buddhist sculpture. Was the most popular in the Kamakura period. Names of the many sculptors in this school include 'kei,' such as UNKEI, KAIKEI, and Tankei. →院派；円派

けいはんでんきてつどう 京阪電気鉄道 〖鉄道〗 Keihan Electric Railway. One of the 16 major private railway operators of Japan, serving Shiga, Kyoto, and Osaka Prefs. Has six train lines and 87 stations, of which 42 are on its main line between Demachi-Yanagi in Kyoto and Yodoya-bashi in Osaka. In addition, it operates a cable car system up to the top of Mt. Otokoyama in Kyoto Pref. Keishin Line offers a through service system in combination with Kyoto's Subway Tozai Line. Popular sightseeing spots along its routes include Mt. Hiei, Fushimi Inari Taisha Shrine, Byoudou-in Temple, and Osaka Castle.

けいひ 桂皮 〖医療・調味料〗 cinnamon. Is used as a condiment or traditional Chinese medicine.

げいひんかん 迎賓館 〖外交・建築〗 State Guest House. Is also called Akasaka Palace. Was originally built as the Imperial Palace for the Crown Prince in 1909. Is now the official lodgings of the national government for foreign visitors. Is open to the public for several days in a year.

けいひんきゅうこうでんてつ 京浜急行電鉄 〖鉄道〗 Keikyu Corporation. One of the 16 major private railway operators of Japan, serving southeastern Tokyo and eastern Kanagawa Pref. Has five lines and 73 stations. Connects Shinagawa and Yokohama Stations with the areas along Tokyo Bay and in the Miura Peninsula such as Kawasaki, Yokosuka, and Miura Cities. A part of Keikyu Main Line and Keikyu Airport Line is on the route for the direct train service from Haneda Airport to Narita Airport via the Tokyo metropolitan area.

けいま 桂馬 〖将棋〗 a knight. Is commonly called by its abbreviated form, 'kei.' Unlike a knight in Western chess, it only moves forward to two places, not sideways or backward. When it is promoted to 'nari-kei,' it moves like a KINSHOU, losing the unique movement of a knight.

けいようし 形容詞 〖言語〗 an adjective. Is also called i-adjective, contrasted with na-adjective, in Japanese pedagogy to foreign people, because its dictionary form ends with 'i.' →イ形容詞；ナ形容詞

けいようどうし 形容動詞 〖言語〗 a nominal adjective. Literally means "adjectival verb." Is also called na-adjective, in Japanese pedagogy to foreign people, because its dictionary form ends with 'na.' →ナ形容詞

げいよしょとう 芸予諸島 〔島名〕 Geiyo Islands. Are located in the mid-western part of the Inland Sea. Spread over Hiroshima and Ehime Prefs.

けいらく 経絡 〔医療〕 a meridian in Chinese medicine. Connects vital points on the body surface with internal organs, so that vital energy can flow through it.

けいれつ 系列 〔経済〕 a keiretsu, or a corporate family. Members are strongly linked together by cross-shareholdings or by continuous transactions.

けいろうのひ 敬老の日 〔祝日〕 Respect-for-the-Aged Day. The third Monday in September. A national holiday to respect senior citizens and celebrate their longevity. Was ordained in 1966.

けがに 毛蟹 〔食べ物・動物〕 a horse-hair crab, or hair crab. *Erimacrus isenbeckii*. Is caught around Hokkaido. Is considered tasty.

けがれ 穢れ 〔精神性〕 the concept referring to dirtiness or impurity. Though death is a typical example of 'kegare,' something related to blood such as child birth, menstruation, or meat processing were also regarded as 'kegare.' Some theories discuss the relation of 'kegare' with KE, which means "ordinary life," and HARE, which means "auspicious occasion."

げきが 劇画 〔漫画〕 a story manga.

Emphasizes a narrative and realistic depiction. Examples include *Manual of Ninja Arts* by Shirato Sanpei, *Star of the Giants* by Kajiwara Ikki, and *Silent Service* by Kawaguchi Kaiji.

げくう 外宮 〔神道〕 the Outer Shrine of Ise. Enshrines Toyouke no Oomikami, the deity of grains. Is also called Toyouke-daijinguu. →伊勢神宮；内宮（ﾅｲｸｳ）

げこくじょう 下剋上 〔武士・政治〕 the social climate of the Warring States period, in which the low-rank people overcame the high-rank one and acquired power.

けごんしゅう 華厳宗 〔仏教〕 the Kegon sect. One of the Six Sects of Nara. Was introduced from China in 736 by a Chinese priest, Dousen. Emphasizes the connections among all things in the universe. The head temple is the TOUDAI-JI Temple in Nara. →南都六宗

けごんのたき 華厳の滝 〔地名〕 Kegon Falls. Are located in Nikko in Tochigi Pref., between Lake Chuuzenji and the Daiya River. Consist of the main falls with a height of 97 m and some 12 other falls. Were discovered by the priest Shoudou in the 9th century. Its name, 'Kegon,' is a Buddhist term, which refers to a sutra or sect. Are famous for autumn colors seen from the viewing spot accessed by an elevator. Some limited express trains that run from Asakusa to Tobu Nikko are named Kegon.

Can be accessed by bus from Tobu Nikko or JR Nikko Station.

けさ 袈裟〖仏教・服飾〗 a rectangular sash for a monk. A monk hangs it from the left shoulder down to the right armpit.

げざ 下座〖歌舞伎〗 (**1**) the box for accompanists. Is placed behind a black curtain on the left of the audience. (**2**) music played in kabuki.

けさがため 袈裟固め〖柔道〗 a scarf hold. A hold technique that involves leaning over the opponent's side and holding the neck and one arm.

げさく 戯作〖文芸〗 a generic term for popular novels or stories from the 18th to 19th centuries. Includes KI-BYOUSHI, SHARE-BON, KOKKEI-BON, NINJOU-BON, and YOMI-HON.

げし 夏至〖暦〗 the summer solstice. One of the 24 seasonal nodes in the traditional calendar. Around June 21 in the current calendar. → 二十四節気(にじゅうしせっき)

けじめ ケジメ〖精神性〗 a clear-cut manner of responding ethically to a controversy or sensitive matter. For example, if a company causes a scandal, the president resigns for 'kejime.'

けしょうじお 化粧塩〖調味料〗 decoration salt. Is sprinkled on easily burnable portions, such as a tail and fin of a fish, to keep them from being tanned.

けしょうまわし 化粧回し〖相撲〗 a decorative apron worn by a sumo wrestler in the ring-entering ceremony called DOHYOU-IRI. Is usually colorfully designed and richly embroidered. Is only presented to high-ranking wrestlers, called SEKI-TORI, by their patrons.

けしょうみず 化粧水〖相撲〗 ⇨力水

げじん 外陣〖宗教・建築〗 the outer space in the main building of a Buddhist temple or Shinto shrine. General visitors worship here because they are not admitted into the inner sanctum. ↔内陣

けずりぶし 削り節〖調味料〗 dried fish flakes. Used as a condiment, or for making soup stock. The most popular are bonito flakes, while sardines or horse mackerels are sometimes used. →鰹節

げた 下駄〖履物〗 a pair of rectangular wooden sandals with two supports under the sole. People sometimes wears geta when they wear a kimono.

けたぐり 蹴たぐり〖相撲〗 a pulling inside ankle sweep. A technique of sweeping the opponent's front leg from the inside and pulling down his arm.

げだつ 解脱〖仏教〗 the deliverance. Relief from reincarnation. Is considered to be equivalent to nirvana and is thought of as an ultimate goal in Buddhism. In this condition, the soul is perfectly free from earthly desires or sufferings. →涅槃(ねはん)

げたばこ 下駄箱〖生活〗 a shoe cupboard. Is set just inside of the front door of a house or building. People take off and store their shoes while they are in the house or building.

けっかい 結界〔宗教〕 a religious sanctuary where priests are protected against evil spirits and where they train themselves.

けっかふざ 結跏趺坐〔仏教〕 the full lotus position for sitting. A meditator places both of his or her feet on the opposite thighs. If it is too difficult, he or she may take the half-lotus position, HANKA-FUZA.

けっこんひよう 結婚費用〔冠婚葬祭〕 wedding expenses. As of 2016, the average was more than 4 million yen including the ceremony, banquet, honeymoon, and durable goods for the new household, according to a survey in the bridal industry.

けっこんひろうえん 結婚披露宴〔冠婚葬祭〕 a wedding banquet after a marriage ceremony. Usually a pair of wedding witnesses, called BAISHAKUNIN, introduce the new couple to the attendants, some of whom make congratulatory speeches. The wedding banquet is gorgeous and entertaining, while the marriage ceremony is religious and solemn.

げっとん 月遁〔忍者〕 an escaping technique using the moon. A ninja got away immediately after the moon went behind a cloud.

げにん 下忍〔忍者〕 a low-skilled ninja. According to *The Book of Ninja* (BANSENSHUUKAI), ninjas were divided into three ranks: high, me-

dium, and low. In modern fictions, 'genin' is ranked at the lowest level of a ninja organization and carries out the spy activity under a medium-ranked ninja. →上忍；中忍

けびいし 検非違使〔軍事〕 an ancient police. Was established in 810 by Emperor Saga. Its power declined when samurai gained power in the administration.

けひじんぐう 気比神宮〔神社〕 Kehi Shrine. Is located in central Fukui Pref. Enshrines Izasawake no mikoto, YAMATOTAKERU NO MIKOTO, etc. Is said to have been founded during the reign of Emperor Monmu (697-707).

けぶつ 化仏〔仏教〕 a small image of a Buddha on the head of a Bodhisattva.

けまり 蹴鞠〔スポーツ〕 ancient football. Is said to have started in the 7th century and to have become popular in the 12th century. The players made a circle and kicked a ball back and forth into the air without letting it fall on the ground.

けむりだし 煙出し〔建築〕 a vent for kitchen smoke. A small roof covering the vent is placed on top of the main roof.

けものへん 獣偏〔漢字〕 a left-side radical meaning "animal." Is used in kanji such as 狩 (hunt), 狂 (mad), 狐 (fox), and 猫 (cat). →偏；部首

けやき 欅〔植物〕 a Japanese zelkova. *Zelkova serrata*. Grows about 30 m high. The grain is beautiful, and the wood is used for building material.

けやり 毛槍 〔武士〕 a long spear decorated with feathers on its tip. Was carried at the head of the procession when a feudal lord went to and from Edo in the Edo period. → 大名行列

げろおんせん 下呂温泉 〔温泉〕 a hot spring in eastern Gifu Pref. Effective in treating rheumatism and neuralgia. Footbaths are also available, free of charge. One of the three most famous hot springs in Japan. →日本三名泉

けん 県 〔政治〕 a prefecture. A local autonomous public entity containing cities or villages. There are 43 'ken' in Japan. →都道府県

けん 〜間 〔単位〕 a unit of length. About 1.8 meters. Six SHAKU equal one 'ken.'

げん 元 〔外交〕 Yuan. The Mongol dynasty from 1271 to 1368. Attacked Japan twice in 1274 and 1281.

げんかい 言海 〔言語・書名〕 *Sea of Words*. The first modern dictionary of the Japanese language. Was compiled in 1886 by Ootsuki Fumihiko.

げんかいなだ 玄界灘 〔地名〕 the Sea of Genkai. Is located north off Fukuoka Pref.

けんかく 剣客 〔剣術〕 ⇨剣豪

けんぎゅうせい 牽牛星 〔伝説〕 ⇨彦星(ぼし)

けんごう 剣豪 〔剣術〕 an expert swordsman. Examples are TSUKA-HARA BOKUDEN, ITOU ITTOUSAI, KA-MIIZUMI HIDETSUNA, YAGYUU JUUBEE, MIYAMOTO MUSASHI, and Sasaki Kojirou.

げんこう 元寇 〔戦争〕 Mongol Invasions of Japan. The Yuan dynasty attacked northern Kyushu twice, in 1274 and 1281. The former is called Bun'ei no eki, and the latter is called Kouan no eki. Although the campaign failed in both cases because of violent weather, this event propelled the decline of the Kamakura shogunate.

げんごう 元号 〔時代・暦〕 an era name, or the name of a subset of a period. For example, the Edo period from 1603 to 1867 includes many eras such as Kan'ei (1624-1628), Genroku (1688-1708), and Tenpou (1830-1843). The origin dates back to the Han dynasty of China. The first Japanese era was Taika from 645 to 650. An era name used to be changed when an auspicious sign was observed, a disaster occurred, or a new Emperor ascended the throne. After the Meiji Restoration in the 19th century, it has been changed only when a new Emperor was enthroned. ↔西暦

けんこうほうし 兼好法師 〔文芸〕 ⇨ 吉田兼好

けんこくきねんび 建国記念日 〔暦〕 National Foundation Day. February 11. A national holiday. Is based on the myth in the *Chronicles of Japan* (NIHONSHOKI), which says the first Emperor, Jinmu, was enthroned on

this day. Was ordained in 1966. →
日本書紀；神武天皇；紀元節

けんざん 剣山 〖華道〗 a pinholder,
or frog. Consists of a metal plate
topped with projecting spikes. Is
used to fix branches or stems of
flowers.

げんざんみよりまさ 源三位頼政 〖武
士〗 ⇨源頼政

げんじ 源氏 〖氏族〗 the Minamoto
clan. The offspring of the Emperor
Seiwa. Became warriors around the
10th century, conflicted with the
Taira clan in the struggle for power
in the 12th century. MINAMOTO
NO YORITOMO established the first
shogunate in Kamakura, present
Kanagawa Pref., in 1185. ↔平氏

げんじな 源氏名 〖娯楽・言語〗 a generic term for a professional name
of a prostitute, a geisha, or a night-
club hostess. Was originally named
after the chapter name of *The Tale
of Genji* (GENJI MONOGATARI).

げんしばくだん 原子爆弾 〖武器〗 an
atomic bomb. One using uranium,
named Little Boy, was dropped at
Hiroshima on August 6th, 1945.
The other using plutonium, named
Fat Man, was dropped on Nagasaki
on August 9th.

げんじものがたり 源氏物語 〖文
芸〗 *The Tale of Genji*. A long
story written in the 11th century
by Murasaki Shikibu. The main
part describes the glorious life and
loves of the hero, Hikaru Genji,
while the last part describes the
melancholy of the aristocracy in
that era, establishing the son of
Hikaru Genji as the hero. Is said
to be the culmination of classic
Japanese literature. Also had a
great influence on later literature
as one of the two greatest female
works in the Heian period, together with *The Pillow Book*, by Seishounagon. →枕草子

げんじものがたりえまき 源氏物語
絵巻 〖絵画〗 *Illustrated Handscroll
of The Tale of Genji*. Was produced
in the 12th century. Some parts
of the scroll are contained at The
Tokugawa Art Museum in Nagoya,
and other parts are at the Gotoh
Museum in Tokyo. A National
Treasure. →徳川美術館；五島美術
館

げんしゅ 原酒 〖酒〗 primitive sake.
Is to be filtered, pasteurized, aged,
and bottled before shipping.

けんじゅつ 剣術 〖武術〗 swords-
manship. A swordsman held a
single-edged long sword with both
hands. Several schools were born
in the Muromachi period and developed in the Edo period. The
current style as a sport is called
KENDOU.

けんじょ 見所 〖能〗 the audience
seats in a Noh theater.

けんじょうご 謙譲語 〖言語〗 an
honorific expression to show humility. Can express the humbleness
of not only the speaker or writer
but also people associated with
them. This type of honorific expression of a verb is made by con-

jugating the word end and adding the set of a prefix 'o' and an auxiliary 'suru.' Some verbs and nouns such as "go" "say," "my son" or "my book" have specific forms to show humility. For example, "go," is translated to 'iku' in everyday language, while it is translated to 'mairu' in 'kenjou-go.'

げんしりょくはつでんしょ 原子力発電所〖科学技術〗 a nuclear power plant. As of the 2016 fiscal year, nuclear power accounted for only 1.7% of total electric output in Japan. Meanwhile, the anti-nuclear movement is quite active.

げんしん 源信〖仏教〗 942-1017. A priest born in present Nara Pref. His main work, *Essentials of Salvation* (Oujou-youshuu), had great influence on the later priests of Japanese Pure Land Buddhism, such as HOUNEN and SHINRAN, as the originator of Japanese Pure Land Buddhism. Is also called Eshin-souzu. →浄土教

けんすい 建水〖茶道〗 a rinse-water container. Water is placed in it after washing a teacup or tea whisk.

けんずいし 遣隋使〖外交〗 an envoy to the Sui dynasty (581-618) in China. The first envoy, ONO NO IMOKO, was dispatched in 607 by Prince Shoutoku.

げんせんかけながし 源泉掛け流し〖温泉〗 a term for when water from a hot spring is poured directly into a bathtub, without altering the natural condition of the water.

けんぞく 眷属〖仏教〗 an attendant of a main Buddhist image. For example, the Twelve Divine Generals for the Healing Buddha, or the Twenty-eight Devas for the Thousand-armed Kuan-Yin. →十二神将；二十八部衆

げんぞく 還俗〖仏教〗 the return of a Buddhist monk or nun to secular life.

けんだい 見台〖音楽・落語〗 a small table on which to rest a piece music. In the Kansai region, is sometimes tapped with small clappers by a comic storyteller, to add sound effects.

げんだいかなづかい 現代仮名遣い〖言語〗 the modern orthography for kana. Was ordained in 1946. In this system, most kana are written based on the modern pronunciation, which is different from the historical orthography for kana. ↔歴史的仮名遣い

げんだいにほんごかきことばきんこうこおばす 現代日本語書き言葉均衡コーパス〖言語〗 Balanced Corpus of Contemporary Written Japanese (BCCWJ) by the National Institute for Japanese Language and Linguistics. Contains about 105,000,000 words. Is open to the public.

けんだつば 乾闥婆〖仏教〗 *Gandharva*. Serves Indra by playing music in Indian mythology. Was incorporated into Buddhism. One of the Eight Devas who guard Buddhism. →八部衆

けんだま 剣玉 〖遊び〗 a bilboquet. Combines a cup-and-ball game with a ring-and-pin game. Was introduced from China in the Edo period.

げんたんせいさく 減反政策 〖政治〗 the rice acreage reduction policy. Aims at the maintenance of rice price by reducing rice production and promoting the production of other crops. Started in 1971. Subsidies were provided to farmers who reduced their rice acreage. In 2004, the goal was changed from price maintenance to stockpiling of rice. In 2018, this policy is to be abandoned.

けんちょう 県庁 〖行政・施設〗 a prefectural government, or the office of the government. Is located in the capital of each prefecture. The prefectural government of Osaka or Kyoto is called FUCHOU, the government of Hokkaido is called DOUCHOU, and the Tokyo metropolitan government is called TOCHOU.

けんちょうじ 建長寺 〖寺院〗 Kenchou-ji Temple. A main temple of the Rinzai sect, ranked first among the Five Zen Temples of Kamakura, Kanagawa Pref. Was founded in 1253 by a Chinese Zen master, Rankei Douryuu. The temple bell, the picture of the founder, and several other parts of the temple are designated National Treasures. The temple garden is designated a historic site and is a place of scenic beauty.

けんちょうしょざいち 県庁所在地 〖行政〗 the capital of a prefecture. Some capitals such as Fukushima and Nara have the same name as the prefectures while others such as Sendai in Miyagi Pref. and Takamatsu in Kagawa Pref. have different names.

けんちんじる けんちん汁 〖食べ物〗 kenchin-jiru soup. Is originally a dish in vegetarian cuisine for Buddhist monks. Has two different stories of its origin. One says that it is named after the Kenchou-ji Temple in Kamakura because it is widely believed that it was eaten by the monks of Kenchou-ji Temple. The other says that the name comes from the word related to Chinese-style vegetarian cuisine.

けんとう 献灯 〖宗教〗 **(1)** offering a lantern to a temple or shrine. **(2)** a votive lantern.

けんどう 剣道 〖剣術〗 kendo. Japanese-style fencing, derived from swordsmanship of the samurai. Contestants wear protectors and hold bamboo swords with both hands. →剣術

けんとうし 遣唐使 〖外交〗 an envoy to the Tang dynasty (618–907) in China. Started in 630 and was abolished in 894 according to the proposal by SUGAWARA NO MICHIZANE. Was dispatched more than 10 times and brought back the advanced culture and political institutions of Tang.

げんな 元和 〖時代〗 an era name

from 1615 to 1624 in the early Edo period. In the first year, the Summer Campaign in Osaka occurred and the Toyotomi clan was exterminated by TOKUGAWA IEYASU. →大坂夏の陣

けんにょ 顕如〖仏教〗1543-1592. A priest of the True Pure Land sect, born in Osaka. Fought against ODA NOBUNAGA from 1570 to 1580. Was given land in Kyoto by TOYOTOMI HIDEYOSHI, where NISHI HONGAN-JI Temple exists today. →浄土真宗

けんにんじ 建仁寺〖寺院〗Kenninji. A main temple of the Kenninji school of the Rinzai sect. Ranked third among the Five Zen Temples of Kyoto in the Muromachi period. Was founded in 1202 by a priest EISAI, with financial support from Minamoto no Yoriie. The pictures of Wind and Thunder Gods painted by TAWARAYA SOUTATSU are National Treasures. →臨済宗

げんばく 原爆〖武器〗⇨原子爆弾

げんばくどおむ 原爆ドーム〖施設〗Atomic Bomb Dome. Is located in Hiroshima City. The atomic bomb exploded right above this building on August 6th, 1945. Was designated a World Heritage Site in 1995.

げんぱつ 原発〖科学技術・施設〗⇨原子力発電所

けんぶ 剣舞〖芸能〗a sword dance. Is performed to song-like recitation of a Chinese-style poem.

げんぶ 玄武〖宗教・動物〗the black turtle-and-snake. The animal deity that symbolizes the north. The snake winds itself around the turtle. →四神(しん); 青竜(せいりゅう); 白虎(びゃっこ); 朱雀(すざく)

げんぷく 元服〖冠婚葬祭〗a ceremony for a boy's coming of age in olden days. Was held between the ages of 11 and 17. A boy would change his infant name to an adult name at the ceremony.

げんぶんいっち 言文一致〖言語〗writing texts using the spoken language. Japanese written texts were different from the daily spoken language until the 19th century. A movement to unify the two styles occurred in the mid-19th century, and official documents finally began to use spoken styles after World War II.

げんぺい 源平〖氏族〗the Minamoto and the Taira clans. Two head clans of warriors in the 12th century. They competed against each other, and the Minamoto destroyed the Taira in 1185. →源氏; 平氏

げんぺいとうきつ 源平藤橘〖氏族〗the four honorable clans: Minamoto, Taira, Fujiwara, and Tachibana.

げんぼう 玄昉〖仏教〗?-746. A priest born in present Nara Pref. After studying in the Tang dynasty for about 20 years, came back and obtained political power in conspiracy with TACHIBANA NO MOROE and KIBI NO MAKIBI. Was demoted to the Kanzeon-ji Temple in present Fukuoka Pref. after FUJIWARA NO

NAKAMARO gained political power.

けんぽうきねんび　憲法記念日
〖暦〗 Constitution Memorial Day. May 3. A national holiday. The Constitution of Japan became effective on this day in 1947. Was ordained in 1948.

けんぽうだいきゅうじょう　憲法第九条 〖法律〗 Article 9 of the Constitution. Prescribes the renunciation of war. →日本国憲法

けんぽん　絹本 〖絵画・書道〗 painting or writing on silk cloth. ↔紙本(ほん)

げんまい　玄米 〖植物〗 unpolished brown rice. Abundant with Vitamin B1. Chaff has been removed.

げんまいず　玄米酢 〖調味料〗 vinegar made from unpolished brown rice.

げんまいちゃ　玄米茶 〖飲み物〗 green tea with roasted unpolished brown rice. Small amount of salt is sometimes added.

けんむのしんせい　建武の新政 〖政治〗 the Kenmu Restoration. Emperor Godaigo, assisted by ASHIKAGA TAKAUJI and other warriors, overthrew the Kamakura shogunate and restored the Imperial political power in 1333. However, the administration treated the court nobles favorably; therefore, the warrior class was dissatisfied and disaffected toward the new regime. As a result, Emperor Godaigo fled to Yoshino in 1336, marking the beginning of the period of the Northern and Southern Courts. →南北朝時代

げんめいてんのう　元明天皇 〖天皇〗 Empress Genmei. 661-721. The 43rd, on the throne from 707 to 715. A daughter of Emperor Tenji and the mother of Emperors Monmu and Genshou. Ordered to compile the *Records of Ancient Matters* (KOJIKI).

けんれいもんいん　建礼門院 〖政治〗 1155-1213. A wife of Emperor Takakura, the mother of Emperor Antoku, and the daughter of TAIRA NO KIYOMORI. Dived into the sea in the Battle of Dan no ura, holding her son, Emperor Antoku. However, only she was saved and lived in seclusion at JAKKOU-IN Temple in Kyoto.

げんろく　元禄 〖時代〗 an era name from 1688 to 1704 in the middle of Edo period. →元禄文化

けんろくえん　兼六園 〖庭園〗 a park in Kanazawa, Ishikawa Pref. Was completed in 1822 under the order of the feudal lord in its area, Maeda Narinaga. Famous for a stone lantern beside a pond and for snow suspenders called yukiduri. One of the three most beautiful gardens in Japan. →日本三名園

げんろくそで　元禄袖 〖服飾〗 a short and roundish sleeve of a kimono.

げんろくぶんか　元禄文化 〖時代〗 the Genroku culture, in the earlier Edo period, from the late 17th to early 18th centuries. Was developed by townspeople in Kyoto and Osaka. Its features are popularity and gorgeousness. ↔化政文化

こ

ご 碁〚碁〛 a territory board game. Two players place white and black small stones alternatively on the board to capture their own territories. →碁石

こあがり 小上がり〚食文化〛 a small tatami floor in a traditional restaurant. Is sometimes screened from the table-and-chair floor. Is also sometimes partitioned for small separate groups.

こい 鯉〚魚〛 a carp. *Cyprinus carpio*. Its fillet is sliced and chilled in iced water when eating. In a Chinese legend, a carp becomes a dragon after swimming up a waterfall in the upper part of the Yellow River.

こいぐち 鯉口〚武器〛 the opening of a sword sheath. Is called so because its appearance is like a mouth of carp.

こいくちしょうゆ 濃口醤油〚調味料〛 ordinary soy sauce. Literally means "thick soy sauce." This term is used to distinguish it from "thin soy sauce," USUKUCHI SHOUYU.

こいこく 鯉濃〚食べ物〛 strong miso soup containing round slices of a carp.

ごいし 碁石〚遊び〛 a GO stone. A game player can use 180 white stones while the opponent can use 181 black stones.

こいしかわこうらくえん 小石川後楽園〚庭園〛 a landscape garden with a circular path, located in Bunkyou-ku, Tokyo. Was completed in 1669 under the order of the Mito Tokugawa family. Is designated a Special Historic Site and a Special Place of Scenic Beauty.

こいずみやくも 小泉八雲 〚文芸〛 Lafcadio Hearn. 1850-1904. A writer who was born in Greece and immigrated to America in 1869. Moved to Japan in 1889, where he spent the rest of his life. Became a citizen of Japan and a professor of English literature at the University of Tokyo. Some of his books include *Glimpses of an Unfamiliar Japan* (1894), *In Ghostly Japan* (1899), *Japanese Miscellany* (1901), and *Japan: An Attempt at Interpretation* (1904).

こいちゃ 濃茶〚茶道〛 thick powdered green tea. Is drunk in a formal tea ceremony, in which a bowl of tea is circulated and consumed. ↔薄茶

こいのたきのぼり 鯉の滝昇り〚宗教〛 a carp swimming up a waterfall. A Chinese legend says a carp would become a dragon after swimming up a waterfall in the upper reaches of the Yellow River. This expression is sometimes figuratively used to refer to someone's rapid promotion.

こいのぼり 鯉幟〚年中行事〛 a carp-shaped streamer. A set includes a

simple streamer, a black carp, and a red carp. Are often hoisted before and on May 5 to celebrate the Boys' Festival.

こいも 小芋 〚食べ物〛 a young tuber of taro.

ごいんきょ 御隠居 〚落語〛 a retired old man. Often appears as an advisor to a stupid young man called YOTAROU in a traditional comic storytelling called RAKUGO.

こう 甲 〚干支〛 ⇨甲(きのえ)

こう 庚 〚干支〛 ⇨庚(かのえ)

こう 香 〚仏教・茶道〛 incense. Is related to traditional culture in various ways. Is said to have been introduced into Japan together with Buddhism in the 6th century. Court nobles perfumed their clothes by burning incense. The host of a tea ceremony now burns incense to welcome guests. →香道(こうどう)

ごう 業 〚仏教〛 karma. Human actions, whether good or bad, to be completed in one's life. Deeds in this life are the result of actions in previous lives and the cause of actions in future lives.

ごう ～合 〚酒・単位〛 a unit to measure the volume of rice or sake. One gou is about 180 cc, and ten gou is one SHOU.

こうあん (禅の)公案 〚仏教〛 a koan. A question without a fixed answer used in Zen meditation. For example, "Does a dog have potential Buddhahood?" The answer may be either "yes" or "no." The point is not the answer but instead one's mental attitude when answering.

こうあんのえき 弘安の役 〚戦争〛 ⇨元寇

こうえつ 光悦 〚芸術〛 ⇨本阿弥光悦(ほんあみこうえつ)

こうがい 笄 〚服飾〛 **(1)**⇨簪(かんざし) **(2)** a long hairpin shaped like a chopstick. Is put in the hair horizontally to pin up a woman's hair. Originally a tool to push up a strand of hair.

こうかにんじゃ 甲賀忍者 〚忍者〛 a generic term for ninjas belonging to several schools in the Kouka area in what is present Shiga Pref. Is the most well-known ninja group, ranking beside IGA NINJA. Is said to have come from mountainous warrior groups in this area. Maintained its autonomy with a council system. Was good at using medicine and poison. Although it is often said that Kouka was hostile to Iga, they sometimes cooperated with each other.

こうかのさとにんじゅつむら 甲賀の里・忍術村 〚忍者・博物館〛 Koka Ninja Village. Is located in Kouka, Shiga Pref. Visitors can tour a house full of ninja gadgets, see an exhibit of archives and weapons, and partake in barbecue. →甲賀流忍術屋敷

こうかりゅうにんじゅつやしき 甲賀流忍術屋敷 〚忍者・博物館〛 Kouka-ryuu Ninjutsu House. Is located in Kouka, Shiga Pref. Was a real ninja house built in the 17th or 18th century. Visitors can see various tricks devised in the house. →甲賀

の里・忍術村

こうぎ 公儀 〖武士・政治〗 the Imperial Court, or the shogunate.

こうぎおんみつ 公儀隠密〖武士〗 a spy dispatched by the shogunate in the Edo period.

こうきこうれいしゃ 後期高齢者 〖行政〗 a senior citizen aged 75 or over. Receives various services from national and local governments.

こうきょ 皇居〖天皇〗 the Imperial Palace. Was moved from Kyoto to Tokyo in 1868. Some parts are open for tourists.

こうぎょくてんのう 皇極天皇 〖天皇〗 Empress Kougyoku. 594-661. The 35th, on the throne from 642 to 645. The wife of Emperor Jomei, and the mother of Emperors Tenji and Tenmu. Although she retired, she gained the throne again after her brother Emperor Koutoku died. →斉明(さいめい)天皇

こうくり 高句麗〖国名〗 Koguryo. Emerged around A.D. 1 in northern Korea and was destroyed in 668 by the allied forces of Tang and Shilla. Was sometimes written as 高麗, KOMA, in Japanese archives. →新羅(しらぎ); 唐

こうけんてんのう 孝謙天皇〖天皇〗 Empress Kouken. 718-770. The 46th, on the throne from 749 to 758. After retiring, had an intimate relation with Priest DOUKYOU and acceeded to the throne again as Emperess Shoutoku.

こうごう 香合〖茶道〗 an incense container. Is made of lacquered wood, porcelain, metal, or seashells. The incense is burned inside.

こうごう 皇后〖天皇〗 an Empress Consort. The legitimate wife of an Emperor.

こうこうやきゅう 高校野球 〖スポーツ〗 high school baseball. The national spring and summer tournaments held at Hanshin Koshien Stadium in Hyougo Pref. are very popular throughout Japan.

こうこく 皇国〖天皇・思想〗 a nation governed by an Emperor. Japan called herself this name before and during World War II.

こうこくしかん 皇国史観〖天皇・思想〗 the Emperor-centered historiography. Insists that the history of Japan has been formed with "the unbroken line of the Imperial family," as a central feature of Japanese culture. Only few people supported this concept after World War II.

こうごたい 口語体〖言語〗 the modern style of written Japanese. Literally means "spoken style" because it is based on the spoken language, while the old style of written Japanese was far from the spoken style. ↔文語体

ごうこん 合コン〖娯楽〗 a matchmaking party between male and female groups.

こうざ 高座〖落語〗 the stage for traditional comic storytelling, RAKUGO.

こうさつ 高札〖行政〗 an official

notice board in the Edo period. Was hung at an intersection or square.

こうさんじ 高山寺 〖寺院〗 Kosanji. A temple of esoteric Buddhism in the northern part of Kyoto. A priest, Myoue, revived an old temple in 1206. Although it is popularly called 'Kouzan-ji,' the second syllable of its official name is 'sa,' not 'za.' Scrolls of Animal Caricatures, a portrait of Myoue, and Sekisui Hall are National Treasures. The whole temple was designated a World Heritage Site in 1994.

ごうざんぜみょうおう 降三世明王 〖仏教〗 Wisdom King of Conquering-Three-World. *Trailokyavijaya*. One of the Five Great Wisdom Kings. Removes earthly desires in the past, the present, and the future. Four-faced, with three eyes on each face, and eight-armed. Tramps on Siva, whose Buddhist name is Daijizai-ten, and his wife Uma. Has several arms in his hands, such as a bow and arrow, a sword, and a rope.

こうし 孔子 〖思想〗 Confucius. 552 B.C.-479 B.C. A Chinese philosopher and the founder of Confucianism. The record of his words and deeds, *The Analects of Confucius* (RONGO), had a great influence on Japanese culture.

こうし 格子 〖建築・服飾〗 a lattice. Traditional architecture uses the lattice structure for doors, windows, and walls. The lattice pattern is also used on a kimono.

こうじ 糀, 麹 〖食文化〗 mold-covered rice, wheat, and soybeans for making brewed products, such as SAKE, MISO, and soy sauce. →麹菌; 醤油

ごうし 郷士 〖武士〗 a squire, or a peasant samurai in the Edo period. Lived in a rural community and engaged in agriculture, though his status was that of a samurai.

こうしえん 甲子園 〖スポーツ・施設〗 a baseball stadium in southeastern Hyougo Pref. The home field of a professional baseball team, the Hanshin Tigers. High-school baseball tournaments are also held there in spring and summer. These are very popular throughout Japan.

こうじきん 麹菌 〖食文化〗 a mold. *Aspergillus oryzae*. Breaks down starches in steamed rice or soybeans into fermentable sugars.

こうしつ 皇室 〖天皇〗 the Imperial family. Includes the Emperor, the Empress Consort, the Empress Dowager, princes, and princesses.

こうしつてんぱん 皇室典範 〖天皇〗 Imperial House Act. The current version was enacted in 1947. Defines the right of the Imperial succession, the Imperial family, and the regency.

こうしど 格子戸 〖建築〗 a door in a framework with crossing wooden bars.

こうしゃくし 講釈師 〖芸能〗 ⇨講談師

こうしゅう 甲州 〖地名〗 ⇨甲斐

こうしゅうかいどう 甲州街道 〖交

通』 the Koushuu Highway in the Edo period. Connected Edo with Shimo-Suwa in present Nagano Pref. with 38 relay stations. Went through present Kanagawa and Yamanashi Prefs., and merged into NAKASEN DOU at Shimo-Suwa.

こうじゅほうしょう 紅綬褒章 〖政治〗 the Medal with Red Ribbon. Is "awarded to individuals who have risked their own lives to save others," according to the Cabinet Office. →褒章

こうしょくいちだいおとこ 好色一代男 〖文芸・作品〗 *The Life of an Amorous Man*. Was written in 1682 by IHARA SAIKAKU. Describes many love affairs of the hero, Yonosuke, including parodies on *The Tale of Genji* and *The Tale of Ise*. →源氏物語；伊勢物語

こうじん 荒神 〖神道・仏教〗 ⇨三宝荒神

こうしんえつちほう 甲信越地方 〖地名〗 the generic name for Kai, Shinano, and Echigo. Present Yamanashi, Nagano and Niigata Prefs., respectively.

こうしんしんこう 庚申信仰 〖宗教〗 the belief related to the day of 'koushin,' or 'kanoe-saru' in a traditional Chinese calendar. It was said in Taoism that a bug living in a human body went out to the Lord of Heaven to report the human's sin while he or she was asleep. So, people sat up all night on the day of 'kanoe-saru' to keep the bug inside his or her body. This belief

was imported to Japan in the Heian period. It was later connected with Buddhism, especially a Buddhist deity, the Blue-faced Diamond Demon called 'Shoumen kongou.'

こうじんだにいせき 荒神谷遺跡 〖考古〗 the Koujindani Ruins. Was found in 1983. Is located in Izumo City, Shimane Pref. Contained 358 bronze swords, 6 bell-shaped bronze vessel, and 16 socketed bronze spearheads of the Yayoi period.

こうしんづか 庚申塚 〖仏教〗 a standing stone sacred to Blue-faced Diamond Demon, called 'Shoumen kongou.' Three monkeys are often carved in relief because the second character 申 is also pronounced 'saru,' which means "monkey."

こうずけ 上野 〖旧国名〗 the old name of Gunma Pref. Is also called Joushuu.

こうせいろうどうしょう 厚生労働省 〖行政〗 Ministry of Health, Labor and Welfare. Started in 2001 by unifying the Ministry of Health and Welfare with the Ministry of Labor.

こうせき 皇籍 〖天皇〗 membership registered as a member of the Imperial family.

こうそ 皇祖 〖天皇〗 the ancestors of the Emperor. Include AMATERASU OOMIKAMI and Emperor Jinmu.

こうぞ 楮 〖植物〗 paper mulberry. *Broussonetia kazinoki*. Grows in a mountainous area of Western Japan. A raw material for traditional paper.

こうぞく 皇族 〖天皇〗 the Emperor's relatives. Include the Empress Consort, the Empress Dowager, princes, and princesses.

こうた 小唄 〖音楽〗 a traditional short ballad sung to shamisen accompaniment. Popular in the 19th to early 20th centuries.

こうたいごう 皇太后 〖天皇〗 an Empress Dowager. The living mother of a current Emperor.

こうたいし 皇太子 〖天皇〗 the Crown Prince. The first candidate is the first son of the Emperor under the current law. Is also called 'Touguu.'

こうたいしひ 皇太子妃 〖天皇〗 the Crown Princess. The wife of a crown prince.

こうだろはん 幸田露伴 〖文芸〗 1867 -1947. A novelist born in Tokyo. Is said to have been idealistic, in contrast to his contemporary, Ozaki Kouyou, who is said to have been realistic. His works include *Pagoda*. →五重塔

こうだん 講談 〖芸能〗 traditional rhythmical storytelling of historical episodes or fiction. Started in the 17th century by the reading aloud of the *Record of Great Peace* (TAIHEIKI), a war chronicle in the late 14th century. Was called 'koushaku' at that time. Was popular from the 18th to the early 20th centuries.

こうだんし 講談師 〖芸能〗 a professional storyteller of historical episodes. Recites the episodes rhythmically, sometimes humorously, using a table and a special folding fan.

こうちがり 小内刈り 〖柔道〗 minor inner reap. To sweep the opponent's lower leg in the air toward him- or herself with a leg.

こうちけん 高知県 〖都道府県〗 Kouchi Pref. Is located in the southern part of Shikoku, facing the Pacific Ocean. 7,103 km^2 in area. The capital is Kouchi City. Nearly 90% of its land is mountainous. Famous for pure and clear rivers such as the Shimanto and the Niyodo, where camping and canoeing are popular. On Kouchi Plain, eggplant, green peppers, tomatoes, pomelos, and citrons are grown in large quantities, thanks to the warm climate. Its frigate tuna catch is larger than that of any other prefecture. Is often hit by a typhoon. Used to be called Tosa.

こうちこうみん 公地公民 〖政治〗 the concept that all the land and people are the Imperial property. The centralized administration system in ancient times, called RITSU-RYOU-SEI, was based on this idea.

こうちし 高知市 〖地名〗 Kouchi City. The capital of Kouchi Pref., located in its central part. Developed as a castle town of the Yamanouchi clan in the Edo period. Sightseeing spots include Kouchi Castle, Harimaya Bridge, and Katsura Beach.

こうでん 香典 〔冠婚葬祭〕 condolence money. Is offered to the family of the deceased by mourners. A new unfolded banknote should not be used.

こうでんがえし 香典返し 〔冠婚葬祭〕 a small return gift for condolence money. Is offered to mourners by the family of the deceased.

こうでんぶくろ 香典袋 〔冠婚葬祭〕 a special envelope for condolence money. The mourner's name is written on the front.

こうてんぼせつ 江天暮雪 〔絵画〕 River and Sky in Evening Snow. One of the Eight Views of Xiaoxiang. →瀟湘(しょうしょう)八景

こうどう 香道 〔芸道〕 incense ceremony. An aesthetic pastime of enjoying the fragrance from burning aromatic wood. The custom of burning aromatic wood came to Japan, together with Buddhism, in the 6th century and became very popular in the 17th century. Attracts fewer people at present, compared with the tea ceremony and the art of flower arrangement.

こうどう 講堂 〔仏教・建築〕 the lecture hall of a Buddhist temple. A priest lectures on sutras or preaches a doctrine in this building. In a Zen temple, the lecture hall is called HATTOU.

こうとくいん 高徳院 〔寺院〕 Kotoku-in. A Buddhist temple of the Pure Land sect located in Kamakura, Kanagawa Pref. Famous for the Great Buddha of Kamakura, which is 11.3 m high and weighs around 121 tons. Is designated a National Treasure. It is still unknown when and by whom it was built. →鎌倉大仏

こうとくてんのう 孝徳天皇 〔天皇〕 Emperor Koutoku. 597-654. The 36th, on the throne from 645 to 654. Implemented the Taika Reform of 645 and relocated the capital from Asuka in Nara to Osaka in 646.

こうどけいざいせいちょう 高度経済成長 〔経済〕 rapid economic growth. Japanese annual economic growth was more than 10% on average from the 1960s to the first oil crisis in 1973.

こうなご 小女子 〔食べ物・魚〕 ⇨玉筋魚(いかなご)

こうにんじょうがんぶんか 弘仁・貞観文化 〔時代〕 the Kounin and Jougan culture, in the 9th century. This term is mainly used in art history. During this period the arts were strongly influenced by esoteric Buddhism. Existing examples include the sculpture of the Healing Buddha at JINGO-JI Temple and the picture of the Blue Immovable Wisdom King at SHOUREN-IN Temple, both of which are located in Kyoto.

こうにんてんのう 光仁天皇 〔天皇〕 Emperor Kounin. 709-781. The 49th, on the throne from 770 to 781. Reformed several administrative systems because they placed much emphasis on Buddhism.

こうのもの 香の物〖食文化〗 ⇨漬物

こうはい 光背〖仏教〗 a halo on a Buddhist image. There are several types: a single circle that is only behind the head, double circles behind the whole body, and a ship-shaped flame behind the whole body.

こうばい 紅梅〖植物〗 a Japanese plum tree with red flowers. A painting by OGATA KOURIN that depicts 'koubai' and a white-flowering plum, HAKUBAI, is a National Treasure, stored at the MOA Museum of Art in Shizuoka Pref.

こうはく 紅白〖色〗 red and white. **(1)** This combination is used for dividing a team into two subgroups to compete with each other in practice. Originates from a historical fact that the Taira clan used red banners, while its rival, the Minamoto clan, used white banners in battles around the 12th century. →紅白歌合戦；紅白試合；源平 **(2)** This combination suggests celebration. There are several theories to explain this connection. One possibility is that red is associated with a baby and white is associated with death. Thus, the combination represents the lifetime of a human. →紅白蒲鉾(かまぼこ)；紅白饅頭(まんじゅう)

こうはくうたがっせん 紅白歌合戦〖テレビ〗 Red and White Year-end Song Festival. A singing contest between two teams: the red team of female singers and the white team of male singers. Has been broadcast annually by NHK on New Year's Eve since 1951.

こうはくかまぼこ 紅白蒲鉾〖食べ物〗 red and white steamed fish paste. Is usually eaten for celebrations or happy events such as for New Year's holidays. →紅白；蒲鉾

こうはくじあい 紅白試合〖スポーツ〗 a practice game between two subgroups of one team. Is also called 'kouhakusen' or 'genpeisen.' →紅白

こうはくぼう 紅白帽〖教育〗 a red and white hat. A part of a gym suit at elementary schools. Is reversible so that one side can be red and the other side can be white. Is sometimes worn to distinguish the two different teams in an athletic meeting or a physical education class.

こうはくまんじゅう 紅白饅頭〖通過儀礼・食べ物〗 red and white buns stuffed with sweet adzuki paste. Are distributed to participants in an auspicious ceremony such as wedding or commencement.

こうばん 交番〖犯罪・行政〗 a police box. In most communities, there are several police officers deployed per shift. They assist residents when needed and patrol the vicinity.

こうひつ 硬筆〖文具〗 a general term for a writing instrument with a hard tip, such as a pen or a pencil. The term does not include a writing brush, which has a soft tip. ↔毛筆

こうぶがったい 公武合体〖政治〗

the political movement that pushed for the union of the Imperial Court and the shogunate. Was supported by the shogunate, Satsuma, Tosa, and other feudal domains. As a result, the 14th shogun, Tokugawa Iemochi, married Princess Kazunomiya, a sister of Emperor Koumei, in 1861. However, the Satsuma domain converted to the faction that wanted to overthrow the shogunate. Thus this movement failed.

こうふくじ 興福寺 〖寺院〗 Kohfukuji. The head temple of the Hossou sect, located in Nara City. One of the Seven Great Temples of Nara. Its predecessor, Yamashina-dera, was founded in Kyoto in the 7th century by Kagami no ookimi, a wife of FUJIWARA NO KAMATARI. Was moved to Nara and renamed as Kohfuukji in 710 by FUJIWARA NO FUHITO. Has many National Treasures related to its architecture, sculptures, and calligraphy. Was designated a World Heritage Site in 1998. →華厳(ごん)宗

こうふくのかがく 幸福の科学 〖宗教〗 Happy Science. New religion established by Oukawa Ryuuhou in 1986. "The exploration of the Right Mind" and the practical expansion of "the principles of Happiness" make up its fundamental doctrine. There are followers in over 100 countries worldwide.

こうふし 甲府市 〖地名〗 Koufu City. The capital of Yamanashi Pref., located in its central part. Developed as a castle town under TAKEDA SHINGEN in the 16th century. Winemaking is now flourishing there.

こうぶだいがっこう 工部大学校 〖科学技術・教育〗 the Imperial College of Engineering. The predecessor of the Faculty of Engineering at the present University of Tokyo. Was established in 1877 and contributed to founding and expanding the foundation of Japanese industries.

こうぶんてんのう 弘文天皇 〖天皇〗 Emperor Koubun. 648-672. The 39th, on the throne from 671 to 672. Was defeated in the Jinshin War by OOAMA NO OUJI. →壬申(じん)の乱

こうべし 神戸市 〖地名〗 Koube City. Is an ordinance-designated city and the capital of Hyougo Pref., located in its southeastern part. The Rokkou Mountains run through the center of the city from east to west, and to its south is Osaka Bay. Historically, the Fukuhara area in the city was briefly the capital of Japan in 1180, when TAIRA NO KIYOMORI used the seaport for trade with the Sung dynasty. The Kitano area is famous for its foreign residences from the Meiji period, as it attracted many Westerners since the opening of Koube Port in 1868. Japan's first beef restaurant opened in 1869, and Japan's first aquarium in 1897. The Hanshin-Awaji Earthquake of magnitude 7.3 occurred in 1995. Its port functions as a container port and manufacturing center.

こうぼ 酵母 〖酒〗 yeast. Converts sugar into alcohol and carbon dioxide.

こうぼうだいし 弘法大師 〖仏教〗 ⇨ 空海

ごうまいん 降魔印 〖仏教〗 the mudra for exorcising the devil. The image is sitting, with the right hand hung down from the right knee, and the palm turned inwards.

こうみょうこうごう 光明皇后 〖天皇〗 Empress Consort Koumyou. 701-760. The wife of Emperor Shoumu, a daughter of FUJIWARA NO FUHITO, and the mother of Empress Kouken. Was the first Empress Consort to come from outside the Imperial family. Established social welfare facilities to save orphans and sick people.

ごうめ ～合目 〖山岳〗 a stage when climbing a mountain. The route from the foot to the top is divided into ten stages, and the top is regarded as the tenth stage.

こうめいてんのう 孝明天皇 〖天皇〗 Emperor Koumei. 1831-1866. The 121st, on the throne from 1846 to 1866. First took the position of expelling foreigners. Later attempted the union of the Imperial Court and the shogunate and required his sister, Kazu no miya, get married to the 14th Tokugawa shogun, Tokugawa Iemochi. → 攘夷(じょう)論; 公武合体

こうめいとう 公明党 〖政治〗 Komeito. A political party established in 1964, based on a new religion group named Souka Gakkai.

こうもくてん 広目天 〖仏教〗 one of the Four Guardian Kings. *Virupaksa*. Defends the west and usually carries a writing brush and a scroll.

こうやさん 高野山 〖仏教・地名〗 Mt. Kouya. A generic term for a peneplain about 1,000 m high in northeastern Wakayama Pref. The priest KUUKAI founded the KONGOUBU-JI Temple here in the 9th century. The site contains a great deal of Buddhist art, including several National Treasures. Sightseers can stay overnight at a temple called SHUKUBOU. Is easily accessible from Osaka by the Nankai Line. Was designated a World Heritage Site in 1994.

こうやどうふ 高野豆腐 〖食べ物〗 freeze-dried tofu. A kind of preserved food. Is spongy and absorbs flavors well. Is often served as a vegetarian dish. Is commonly said to have been invented at a temple on Mt. Kouya during the Edo period.

こうやひじり 高野聖 〖文芸・作品〗 *The Saint of Mount Koya*. A novel published in 1900 by IZUMI KYOUKA. A priest from Mt. Kouya gets lost in the Hida Mountains and comes across a devilish, enchanting, and beautiful woman.

こうようぐんかん 甲陽軍鑑 〖軍事・

書名〗 a book of military science compiled in the 17th century. Is mainly based on the events and the way of thinking of TAKEDA SHINGEN.

こうらい 高麗〖国名〗 Koryo. A dynasty on the Korean Peninsula from 918 to 1392. Joined the Mongol Invasions to Japan in the 13th century. Suffered from Japanese pirates, called WAKOU, in the 14th century.

こうらいにんじん 高麗人参〖医療・植物〗 a Korean ginseng. *Panax ginseng*. Is native to China and Korea and used as a tonic in traditional Chinese medicine.

こうらくえん 後楽園〖庭園〗 a park in Okayama City, Okayama Pref. Was completed in 1700 under the order of the feudal lord in its area, Ikeda Tsunamasa. Red-crowned cranes have been kept there since the Edo period. One of the three most beautiful gardens in Japan. Note that it is different from KOISHIKAWA KOURAKU-EN in Tokyo. →日本三名園

こうらざけ 甲羅酒〖酒〗 hot sake in a crab shell. After the eating of the inside of the shell, the shell is grilled and sake is poured in it. Thus the flavor of the crab can be enjoyed while drinking the sake.

こうり 行李〖生活〗 a wicker container with a lid. Is used to hold clothes. Is woven from bamboo or willow.

ごうりき 強力〖山岳・ビジネス〗 a mountain porter. Also guides climb-

ers.

こうりゅうじ 広隆寺〖寺院〗 Kouryuu-ji Temple. Is said to have been founded in 603 by Hata no Kawakatsu under the order of Prince Shoutoku. Is located in the northwestern part of Kyoto City. The wooden image of Maitreya Bodhisattva was designated the first National Treasure. →聖徳太子

こうりゅうじみろくぼさつはんかぞう 広隆寺弥勒菩薩半跏像〖仏教・彫刻〗 Maitreya Bodhisattva at Kouryuu-ji Temple in Kyoto. Was produced with Japanese red pine in the early 7th century. Sits with the right foot resting on the left thigh and the left leg hanging down. The height is about 120 cm. Was designated the first National Treasure.

こうれいかしゃかい 高齢化社会〖生活〗 an aging society. As of 2017, the average life expectancy was 81 for males and 87 for female in Japan. It is estimated that senior citizens will reach 40% of the population by the year 2050.

こうろ 香炉〖仏教〗 an incense burner. Originally one of the utensils associated with Buddhism. The burner comes in various shapes based on its specific purpose, such as resting in an alcove or perfuming clothes.

ごえいか 御詠歌〖仏教・音楽〗 a Buddhist pilgrim hymn. Is chanted to the accompaniment of a little bell.

ごえもんぶろ 五右衛門風呂〖風呂〗

an iron bathtub. Is heated directly from beneath. The bather sits on the floating wooden lid, causing it to sink, because the bottom of the bathtub is too hot to sit on directly. Is said to have been named after Ishikawa Goemon, a robber in the 16th century, who was boiled to death.

ごおや ゴーヤ〔食べ物・植物〕 a go-oya, or bitter melon. *Momordica charantia*. Is also called 'nigauri' or 'tsurureishi.' →ゴーヤチャンプルー

ごおやちゃんぷるう ゴーヤチャンプルー〔食べ物〕 bitter melon stir-fried with pork or luncheon meat, tofu, and other vegetables. Is a local cuisine of Okinawa.

こおりどうふ 凍り豆腐〔食べ物〕⇨ 高野豆腐

ごおるでんういいく ゴールデンウィーク〔暦〕 "Golden Week." A holiday-studded week from the end of April to the beginning of May. Includes Shouwa Day on April 29, Constitution Day on May 3, Greenery Day on May 4, and Children's Day on May 5.

こおれるおんがく 凍れる音楽〔仏教・建築〕 "Frozen music." The nickname for the East Pagoda at YAKUSHI-JI Temple in Nara City. It is said that an American art historian, Ernest Fenellosa, originated the term to describe the pagoda's rhythmic appearance and beauty.

ごおん 呉音〔漢字〕 the Wu-dynasty style of pronunciation of a kanji. Some kanji have two Chinese-style pronunciations, besides a Japanese-style pronunciation. For example, 生, which means life, has two Chinese-style pronunciations: 'shou' and 'sei.' The former pronunciation is in the Wu style, while the latter pronunciation is in the Han style, kan-on. The former came to Japan earlier than the latter. The Wu style pronunciation is frequently used in Buddhist terminology. ↔漢音

ごかい 五戒〔仏教〕 the Five Precepts in Buddhism. Not to kill living things, not to steal, not to commit adultery, not to tell a lie, and not to drink alcohol.

ごかいちょう 御開帳〔仏教〕⇨開帳

ごかいどう 五街道〔交通〕 Five major highways in the Edo period. The starting point for all of them was Nihonbashi in Edo. TOUKAIDOU led to Kyoto, NAKASENDOU led to Kyoto by another route, NIKKOU KAIDOU led to Nikko, OUSHUU KAIDOU led to Aomori, and KOUSHUU KAIDOU led to Koufu.

ごかこくじょうやく 五か国条約〔外交〕 Five-Power Treaty. A February 1922 treaty, also known as the Washington Naval Treaty, that resulted from the Washington Conference and that was signed by France, Great Britain, Italy, Japan, and the United States. Was intended to reduce the number of large warships in the Pacific. Signatories determined that the agreed-upon scrapping of large ships would result in the following ratio of the number of ships: 5 for Great Britain and the United States, 3 for Japan, and 1.67 for France and Italy. All five parties also agreed to stop building new ships for ten years; and Great Britain, Japan, and the United States agreed to maintain the current status of bases. The treaty expired in 1936.

ごかじょうのごせいもん 五箇条の御誓文〚政治〛 Imperial Covenant with Five Articles. Included the fundamental policies of the Meiji government. Was issued on March 14, 1868, in the name of Emperor Meiji.

こかた 子方〚歌舞伎・能〛 a part for a child actor in a Noh play. In some programs, a child actor plays a role of an adult.

ごがたき 碁敵〚遊び〛 a rival in playing the GO game.

ごがつにんぎょう 五月人形〚人形〛 a doll for the Boys' Festival on May 5th. An armored samurai or the Plague-Queller called SHOUKI is popular.

ごがつびょう 五月病〚精神性〛 May melancholy. Some first-year students or employees who entered the school or company in April would fall into an unstable psychological condition in May.

ごかのしょう 五家荘〚地名〛 an area in southeastern Kumamoto Pref. Is said to have been a hidden village of defeated Heike fugitives from the war with the Minamoto clan in the 12th century. Is located along the upper reaches of the Kawabe River, which is a branch of the Kuma River, deep in the Kyushu Mountains. Until the 19th century, the people made their living in the traditional way, by making woodwork products and developing slash-and-burn agriculture. It was not until the late 20th century that some national and prefectural routes were constructed and the area began to be known as a tourist spot.

ごかやま 五箇山〚地名〛 an area in southwestern Toyama Pref. Is said to have been a hidden village of fugitives from the war between the Minamoto and Taira clans in the 12th century. An extremely snowy and mountainous region, in the upper reaches of the Shou River. Famous for a traditional architectural style, gasshou-dukuri, in which the house roofs are steep enough to shed snow easily. A traditional dance that uses a small percussion instrument called a kokiriko is well preserved by the local people. The historic villages of Shirakawa-gou and Gokayama were designated a World Heritage Site in 1995.

こき 古稀〚通過儀礼〛 the age of 70, using the traditional approach to age counting. People usually celebrate when a person turns 69, in the modern approach to age counting. The word 'koki,' which literally means "old and rare," comes from a phrase in a Chinese classic poem written by Du Fu, "A person at the age of 70 has been rare since ancient times."

ごぎょう 御形 〖植物〗 a Jersey cudweed. Another name of HAHA-KO-GUSA. One of the seven herbs of spring in a lunar calendar. →春の七草

こきんわかしゅう 古今和歌集 〖文芸・作品〗 *Collection of Ancient and Modern Japanese Poetry*. The first imperial anthology of poetry. Was compiled in 905 at Emperor Daigo's command by Ki no Tsurayuki, Ki no Tomonori, Ooshikouchi no Mitsune, and Mibu no Tadamine. Contains 1,095 poems in 20 volumes. The poetry style is elegant and delicate.

こく 国～ 〖言語〗 a kanji sometimes meaning "Japanese," "domestic," or "national." For example, a class that deals with Japanese language for Japanese native speakers is called 'kokugo,' which literally means "national language," at the elementary, junior high, or senior high school level.

こく ～石 〖単位〗 (**1**) a unit to measure the volume of rice. Approx. 180 liters. One 'koku' equals ten TO. (**2**) a unit to measure the volume of timber or the load of a ship. Approx. equals 0.28 m³.

こくいのさいしょう 黒衣の宰相 〖仏教・政治〗 a minister in black robes. A cynical nickname to refer to a priest who had a strong influence on politics because a priest's robe is black. Examples include TENKAI and KONCHI-IN SUUDEN.

こくう 穀雨 〖暦〗 one of the 24 seasonal nodes in the traditional calendar. Around April 20 in the current calendar. Means "spring rain soaks grains." →二十四節気(にじゅうしせっき)

こくうぞうぼさつ 虚空蔵菩薩 〖仏教〗 Bodhisattva of Space Repository, or Bodhisattva of Space Womb. *Akasa-garbha*. Has a sword to symbolize immeasurable wisdom on the right hand. Has a wish-filling jewel on the left hand. A picture stored at the Tokyo National Museum and five sculptures enshrined at the Jingo-ji Temple in Kyoto are National Treasures.

こくがく 国学 〖人文学〗 study of Japanese classics. Explores thoughts and spirits indigenous to Japan by studying texts such as the *Records of Ancient Matters* (KOJIKI), *Chronicles of Japan* (NIHONSHOKI), *Anthology of Myriad Leaves* (MAN'YOUSHUU), and other classics written before Buddhism and Confucianism strongly influenced Japanese culture. Was begun in the 17th century by Keichuu, was established by KADA NO AZUMAMARO, KAMO NO MABUCHI, and MOTOORI NORINAGA around the 18th century, and was taken over by HIRATA ATSUTANE in the 19th century.

こくがくしゃ 国学者 〖人文学〗

scholars of Japanese classics in the Edo period. →国学

こくぎかん 国技館〔相撲〕 a sumo arena operated by the Japan Sumo Association. Was first built in 1909. The present arena was built in 1985 at the Ryougoku area in Tokyo. The Sumo Museum, a restaurant, and food stores are housed in the same building.

こくご 国語〔言語〕 the Japanese language. Literally means "national language." This term is also used as the name of a school subject when teaching the Japanese language to Japanese people. →日本語

こくごがく 国語学〔言語〕 Japanese linguistics. Literally means "research of national language." Is now usually called 'nihongo-gaku.'

こくさいこうりゅうききん 国際交流基金〔外交〕 Japan Foundation. Was founded in 1972 as an agent of the government to promote Japanese culture abroad. In 2003 became an independent unit with the Foreign Ministry. Has headquarters in Tokyo, an office in Kyoto, and offices in 21 other countries. Promotes the study of the Japanese language, cultural exchanges, and the study of Japanese culture overseas.

こくさいにほんぶんかけんきゅうせんたあ 国際日本文化研究センター 〔人文学・研究機関〕 International Research Center for Japanese Studies. Was founded in Kyoto in 1987. Mainly conducts inter-disciplinary research on various fields about Japanese culture and also provides post-graduate education.

こくし 国司〔官位〕 a provincial governor in ancient times. Aristocrats were dispatched from the Imperial Court to a local province. However, the system became merely nominal because the Kamakura shogunate placed its military governors called SHUGO at the end of the 12th century.

こくし 国師〔仏教・官位〕 Most Reverend Priest. This title was given by the Imperial Court. The first example was Shouichi Kokushi in 1312.

こくじ 国字〔漢字〕 **(1)** a kanji invented in Japan. Has no Chinese-style pronunciation. Examples are 峠(mountain pass), 畑(cultivated land), and 辻(intersection). **(2)** a letter to represent a syllable. HIRAGANA and KATAKANA.

こくちょう 国鳥〔動物〕 a national bird. The national bird of Japan is a green pheasant. →雉(き)

こくていこうえん 国定公園〔娯楽・行政〕 a quasi-national park. Is designated by the national government and managed by the respective prefectural government. →国立公園

こくてつ 国鉄〔交通〕 ⇨日本国有鉄道

こくどこうつうしょう 国土交通省〔交通・行政機関〕 Ministry of Land, Infrastructure, Transport and Tourism. Was started in 2001 by unifying the Ministry of Construction, the Ministry of Transport, the National Land Agency, and the Hokkaido Development Agency.

こくふうぶんか 国風文化 〔精神性〕 the Japanese-style aristocratic culture from the 10th to 12th centuries. Although Japan was eager to adopt aspects of Chinese culture from the 7th to 9th centuries, the culture unique to Japan developed after abolishing envoys to the Tang dynasty in 894.

こくぶんがく 国文学 〔文芸〕 **(1)** Japanese literature. Is sometimes called 'nihon bungaku' to distinguish from the research of it. **(2)** the research of Japanese literature.

こくぶんがくけんきゅうしりょうかん 国文学研究資料館〔文芸・研究機関〕 National Institute of Japanese Literature. Was founded in western Tokyo in 1972. Researches Japanese literature and collects its original texts.

こくぶんがくし 国文学史 〔文芸〕 the history of Japanese literature.

こくぶんがくしゃ 国文学者 〔文芸〕 a scholar of Japanese literature.

こくぶんじ 国分寺〔仏教・政治〕 a term for provincial temples. They were built in 66 provinces and on three islands: Iki, Tsushima, and Tane, according to the imperial order of Emperor Shoumu in the 8th century. Each temple had a seven-story pagoda. The head temple was the Toudai-ji Temple. The Kokubunji System deteriorated around the 11th century, but some temples still survive as independent temples.

こくぶんにじ 国分尼寺 〔仏教・政治〕 a provincial nunnery. Was built in each province according to the order of Emperor Shoumu in the 8th century. The head nunnery was Hokke-ji Temple in present Nara. →国分寺

こくべつしき 告別式〔冠婚葬祭〕 a formal term for "funeral." →葬式

こくほう 国宝〔芸術〕 a National Treasure. As of September 2017, 1,101 items including fine arts, crafts, architecture, calligraphy, and archaeological materials have been designated as such by the Minister of Education, Culture, Sports, Science and Technology under the Law for the Protection of Cultural Properties. →文化財保護法

こくみんえいよしょう 国民栄誉賞 〔行政〕 People's Honor Award. Was established in 1977. Is bestowed to a person or a group that is loved and respected by many people and has inspired bright hopes in the society. The recipients include a baseball player, Ou Sadaharu, a film director, Kurosawa Akira, a manga artist, Hasegawa Machiko, a singer, Misora Hibari, a sumo wrestler, Taihou, and a climber and adventurer, Uemura Naomi, among others.

こくみんがっこう 国民学校 〔教育〕 a national elementary school. The government converted conventional elementary schools to national elementary schools in April 1941. The latter were more nationalistically focused and were abolished in March 1947 after World War II.

こくみんのしゅくじつ 国民の祝日 〖暦〗 a national holiday. Sixteen holidays are ordained by law. New Year's Day (January 1), Coming-of-Age Day (2nd Monday in January), National Foundation Day (February 11), Vernal Equinox Day (March 20 or 21), Shouwa Day (April 29), Constitution Memorial Day (May 3), Greenery Day (May 4), Children's Day (May 5), Marine Day (3rd Monday in July), Mountain Day (August 11), Respect for the Aged Day (3rd Monday in September), Autumnal Equinox Day (September 22 or 23), Health Sports Day (2nd Monday in October), Culture Day (November 3), Labor Thanksgiving Day (November 23), and Emperor's Birthday (December 23; as of 2017).

こくら 小倉 〖地名〗 the western area of Kitakyuushuu City. Has a station of San'yo Shinkansen, where the fastest train, Nozomi, stops.

ごくらく 極楽 〖仏教〗 Paradise. Refers to the Western Pure Land. Is preached in Pure Land Buddhism. →西方極楽浄土

ごくらくおうじょう 極楽往生 〖仏教〗 to die peacefully and be reborn in the Western Pure Land. →西方極楽浄土

ごくらくじ 極楽寺 〖寺院〗 Goku-raku-ji Temple. A Buddhist temple of the Shingon Ritsu sect located in Kamakura, Kanagawa Pref. Was founded in 1259 by a priest, Ninshou. Its foundation was financially supported by a samurai, Houjou Shigetoki.

こくりつかがくはくぶつかん 国立科学博物館 〖科学技術・研究機関〗 National Museum of Nature and Science. Was founded in 1877 in Ueno, Tokyo.

こくりつこうえん 国立公園 〖法律・自然〗 a national park. Is designated, preserved, and managed by the national government. According to the Ministry of the Environment, its objectives are "to protect Japan's exceptional natural sites and preserve them for future generations so the latter can experience these with the same sense of wonder and joy as our generation."

こくりつこくごけんきゅうしょ 国立国語研究所 〖言語・研究機関〗 National Institute for Japanese Language and Linguistics. One of the National Institutes for the Humanities. Was founded in 1948 in Tokyo.

こくりつみんぞくがくはくぶつかん 国立民族学博物館 〖人文学・研究機関〗 National Museum of Ethnology. One of the National Institutes for the Humanities. Was founded in 1974 in Osaka.

こくりつれきしみんぞくはくぶつか

ん 国立歴史民俗博物館 〖人文学・研究機関〗 National Museum of Japanese History. One of the National Institutes for the Humanities. Was founded in 1983 in Chiba.

ごくろうさま ご苦労様 〖精神性・言語〗 "You are a hard worker." Is uttered to show appreciation for someone's job. Should not be uttered to a superior or an elder.

ごけ 碁笥 〖碁〗 a container for go-stones with a lid. Is made of wood and is round-shaped.

こけし 木形 〖民芸〗 a handcrafted wooden doll with a cylindrical-shaped body, a round head, and no limbs. A specialty of the Tohoku region.

こけでら 苔寺 〖寺院〗 Moss Temple. The nickname for the SAIHOU-JI Temple in Kyoto.

ごけにん 御家人 〖武士〗 **(1)** a direct vassal of a shogun in the Kamakura period. **(2)** a low-level vassal of a shogun in the Edo period. Was not qualified to see the shogun directly.

こけらぶき 杮葺き 〖建築〗 a thatching technique with wood shingles of Japanese cypress or cedar. Examples include the Golden Pavilion in Kyoto and MUROU-JI Temple in Nara Pref.

ごこう 後光 〖仏教〗 ⇨光背(ぶ)

ごこく 五穀 〖農業・食文化〗 five main cereals. Rice, barley, foxtail millet, common millet, and beans. →米；粟(勢)；黍(勢)

ごこくじんじゃ 護国神社 〖神社〗 a "defense of the nation" shrine.

Is located in each prefecture excepting Kanagawa and Tokyo. Enshrines the war dead, Self-Defense Forces officials, police officers, and fire fighters who died on duty. →靖国神社；自衛隊

ごこくほうじょう 五穀豊穣 〖精神性・宗教〗 an abundant crop. Is often prayed for in a Shinto rite.

ごごんぜっく 五言絶句 〖文芸〗 a Chinese-style classic poem, consisting of four lines with five characters.

ごごんりっし 五言律詩 〖文芸〗 a Chinese-style classic poem, consisting of eight lines with five characters.

ござ 茣蓙，蓙 〖生活〗 a mat made of rush. Is spread on the floor to sit on.

ござしょ 御座所 〖天皇〗 a room for the Emperor or other Imperial family members. Is called so, for example, when a room has been used at a temple or a hotel.

こさつ 古刹 〖寺院〗 a temple with an old history.

こざとへん 阜偏 〖漢字〗 a left-side radical meaning "hill." Is used in kanji such as 防(defense), 限(limit), and 降(descend). →偏；部首

ござん 五山 〖仏教〗 five high-ranked Zen temples. →鎌倉五山；京都五山

ごさんけ 御三家 **(1)** 〖武士〗 the three major branches of the Tokugawa clan: Owari, Kii, and Mito. Descended from last three sons of TOKUGAWA IEYASU. Were ranked the highest among feudal lords in the Edo period. **(2)**〖精神性〗 three prominent figures in a certain field. For example, the 'go-sanke' of Tokyo's private boys' junior high schools are Kaisei, Azabu, and Musashi.

ごさんねんのえき　後三年の役　〖戦争〗 the Later Three Years' War. From 1083 to 1087. MINAMOTO NO YOSHIIE, who was dispatched to the Tohoku region as the regional lord, interfered the internal dispute of a local clan, named Kiyohara. Yoshiie assisted the head of another local clan, Fujiwara no Kiyohira, and destroyed the Kiyohara clan. After this war, Kiyohira obtained the power in the Tohoku region, and the Minamoto clan strengthened its power in the Kantou region. →前九年の役

ござんぶんがく　五山文学　〖文芸〗 Chinese-style literature written by priests at the Five Zen Temples of Kyoto or Five Zen Temples of Kamakura. Was written from the 14th to 16th centuries. →京都五山; 鎌倉五山

こじ　居士　〖仏教〗 a title attached to a man's posthumous Buddhist name. ↔大姉(だいし)

こしあげ　腰揚げ　〖服飾〗 tucking in a kimono at the waist to adjust the length.

こしあん　漉し餡　〖食べ物〗 sieved sweet adzuki paste. After being boiled, adzuki beans are strained to remove the skin and supplemented with sugar. ↔粒餡

こじき　古事記　〖神話・書名〗 *Records of Ancient Matters*. Japan's oldest chronicle, in three volumes. Was compiled at the behest of Emperor Genmei in 712 by Oono Yasumaro, who transcribed the oral recitation by Hieda no Are. Covers events from the creation of heaven and earth to the time of Empress Suiko. →日本書紀; 元明天皇; 推古天皇

こしきえいほう　古式泳法　〖スポーツ〗 the traditional swimming method. Its techniques include swimming with armor, fighting with a sword while swimming, and shooting arrows while crossing a river. The style was established in the 17th century. The Japan Swimming Federation officially recognizes 12 schools of the traditional method.

ごしきまい　五色米　〖忍者〗 five-colored rice grains. Yellow, red, blue, purple, and black grains were used for communication. The arrangement of the grains and the combination of the colors functioned as a cryptogram to convey a message to allies. A bird or insect would not eat the rice colored by dyeing powder.

こしぐるま　腰車　〖柔道〗 a hip wheel throw. The technique to put an opponent on the waist and throw.

こしだかしょうじ　腰高障子　〖建築〗 a sliding screen with a wooden panel. The panel is about 60 to 80 cm high. The upper part is made of a latticed wooden frame and trans-

こしだま 腰玉〔忍者〕⇨浮き球

こしたんれい 越淡麗〔酒・植物〕 a kind of rice for sake. A chief producing area is Niigata Pref. →酒米（さかまい）

こしひかり コシヒカリ〔食べ物・植物〕 a name of rice cultivars. One of the most popular types of rice. Was invented in Fukui Pref. in 1956.

こしひも 腰紐〔服飾〕 a waist cord on a woman's kimono. Is fastened under the OBI to keep the kimono and the underwear stable.

こしびょうぶ 腰屏風〔家具〕 a waist-high folding screen. Usually consists of two panels. →屏風

こしまき 腰巻〔服飾〕 woman's underwear for the lower body. Is wound around the waist when wearing a kimono.

こしみの 腰蓑〔服飾〕 a short cape covering the lower body. Was made of straw or sedge and used by hunters and fishermen.

こしもと 腰元〔職業〕 a maid for a socially high-ranked lady in early modern times.

こしゃまいんのたたかい コシャマインの戦い〔戦争・少数民族〕 a large-scale rebellion by Ainu. Occurred in southern Hokkaido from 1456 to 1458.

こしゅ 古酒〔酒〕 a long-aged sake. Generally refers to sake aged three years or more. The color is a little dark, and the flavor is strong. Since the market is small, the price is rather high.

ごしゅいんちょう 御朱印帳〔寺院・神社〕⇨朱印帳

ごじゅうおんじゅん 五十音順〔言語〕 the order in a table of the Japanese syllabary. The first one is 'a,' and the last one is 'wa.'

ごじゅうおんず 五十音図〔言語〕 a table of the Japanese syllabary. Literally means "fifty sounds table." Consists of five rows representing vowels and ten columns representing consonants, including the null consonant.

ごじゅうのとう 五重塔 **(1)**〔仏教・建築〕 a five-storied pagoda. One of the major wooden buildings in a Buddhist temple. Has high resistance to earthquakes. Although the first floor is usually decorated as a room, the higher floors are just empty spaces with the framework exposed. The oldest one is at Houryuu-ji Temple in Nara Pref., and the highest one is at Tou-ji Temple in Kyoto. →塔 **(2)**〔文芸・作品〕 *Pagoda*. A novel published in parts from 1891 to 1892 by KOUDA ROHAN. Describes the conflict between two carpenters in building a five-storied pagoda.

ごしゅん 呉春〔絵画〕 1752–1811. A painter born in Kyoto. Studied painting and haiku under Yosa Buson, then painting under Maruyama Oukyo. Later invented his own urbane and witty style. His works include *Willow with Heron and Other Birds* at the Kyoto

National Museum.

ごしょ 御所〖天皇〗 the Imperial Palace. The permanent or temporary residence of the Emperor. Is now located in Tokyo and Kyoto.

こしょう 小姓〖武士〗 a page boy for a shogun or a feudal lord. Started in the Muromachi period.

こしょうがつ 小正月〖暦〗 January 15th, or the three days from January 14th to 16th. Means "Little New Year."

ごじょうごよくのことわり 五情五欲の理〖忍者〗 to utilize five emotions and five desires when manipulating others. The five emotions are gladness, anger, sadness, pleasure, and fear. The five desires are appetite, sexual desire, desire for money, desire for fame, and desire for refinement.

ごしょぐるま 御所車〖交通〗 ⇨牛車(ぎっしゃ)

ごしょにんぎょう 御所人形 〖人形〗 a baby-type dress-up doll. Has a large round head and is finished in white with seashell powders. Was invented in Kyoto in the early 18th century. Was used as a gift in return from the Imperial family to feudal lords.

ごじら ゴジラ〖映画〗 Godzilla. A dinosaur-like monster in films. Its name was coined by blending an English word "gorilla" and a Japanese word 'kujira,' which means "whale." Debuted in 1954 and has appeared in many films in Japan and overseas such as *King Kong vs. Godzilla* in 1962, *Terror of Mechagodzilla* in 1975, *The Return of Godzilla* in 1984, and *Shin Godzilla* in 2016.

ごしらかわてんのう 後白河天皇〖天皇〗 Emperor Goshirakawa. 1127–1192. The 77th, on the throne from 1155 to 1158. After stepping down from the throne, became a monastic ex-Emperor. →後白河法皇

ごしらかわほうおう 後白河法皇〖天皇〗 Monastic Ex-Emperor Goshirakawa. Retired from the throne in 1158 and became a priest in 1169. After stepping down from the throne, tried to keep administrative power and is said to have schemed behind the scenes during the war between the Minamoto and Taira clans. Frequently visited several temples and shrines such as Toudai-ji Temple and the Three Great Shrines of Kumano. Compiled an anthology of popular songs called RYOUJINHISHOU.

ごしんえい 御真影〖天皇〗 a polite term to refer to a profile photo of the Emperor and Empress. Was used until the end of World War II.

ごしんたい ご神体〖神道〗 ⇨神体

ごずてんのう 牛頭天王〖神道・仏教〗 the bull-head deity. It is said that he was originally the guardian of the Jetavana Monastery in ancient India. In Japan, was identified with the God of Storms in Shintoism and is enshrined as a plague-preventing deity at Yasaka Shrine in Kyoto. →祇園精舎(ぎおんしょうじゃ)；須佐之男命

(すきのおの みこと)；八坂神社

こすぷれ コスプレ〔娯楽・服飾〕 cosplay. An abbreviation for "costume play." The player wears a costume to turn into a character in manga or anime. Has been getting popular since the 1990s.

ごすろり ゴスロリ 〔娯楽・服飾〕 Gothic and Lolita. Women's fashion with decadent, demonic, but girlish image.

ごすんくぎ 五寸釘〔生活・科学技術〕 an about 15-cm-long nail.

ごせい 碁聖〔碁〕 Saint of Go. One of the seven titles in professional GO. The name is a combination of 'go' and 'sei,' literally meaning "saint." The best-of-five title match, 'gosei-sen,' takes place annually from July to August.

ごせいばいしきもく 御成敗式目 〔法律〕 the Formulary of Adjudications. The first legal code for the samurai. Was promulgated in 1232 by the Kamakura shogunate under the shogun's regent, Houjou Yasutoki.

こせき 戸籍〔行政〕 family registration. The Imperial Court publicly clarified and recorded the relationship of individual citizens in the 7th century, as part of the centralized administration system called RITSURYOU-SEI. Though it was not conducted in the Heian period, the Meiji government in the 19th century introduced it again to revise the Tokugawa version of the registration.

こせきしょうほん 戸籍抄本〔行政〕 an official partial copy of a family register.

こせきとうほん 戸籍謄本〔行政〕 an official whole copy of a family register.

ごぜんかいぎ 御前会議 〔天皇〕 a council attended by the Emperor. Was held from the Meiji period until the end of World War II in 1945. Its members include ministers and military leaders.

ごぜんじるこ 御膳汁粉 〔食べ物〕 sweet soup of sieved adzuki beans. Contains rice cake.

ごぜんそば 御膳蕎麦 〔食べ物〕 high-quality white buckwheat noodles.

こそあど こそあど〔言語〕 a generic term for demonstratives referring to the close, intermediate, distant, and indefinite relations. Each begins with 'ko,' 'so,' 'a,' and 'do,' respectively.

ごぞうろっぷ 五臓六腑〔医療〕 five vital organs and six digestive organs in Chinese medicine. The five vital organs are the heart, liver, lungs, spleen, and kidney. The six digestive organs are the large intestine, small intestines, stomach, gallbladder, urinary bladder, and 'sanshou,' which is unknown.

こそで 小袖〔服飾〕 a kimono with short sleeves and small sleeve openings. The origin of the modern kimono. Began to be worn in the Heian period.

こそでのて 小袖の手〔妖怪〕 hands

extended from a kimono. It is said that the kimono is haunted by a young prostitute.

こそとがり 小外刈り〖柔道〗 minor outer reap.

こだい 古代〖時代〗 ancient times. Consists of the Tumulus (3rd to 7th centuries), Asuka (592-710), Nara (710-794), and Heian periods (794-1185) in Japanese chronology.

ごだいごてんのう 後醍醐天皇〖天皇〗 Emperor Godaigo. 1288-1339. The 96th, on the throne from 1318 to 1339. Was once exiled to Oki Island in 1331 by the Kamakura shogunate, but defeated them and restored the Imperial political power in 1333. →建武の新政

ごだいみょうおう 五大明王〖仏教〗 Five Great Wisdom Kings. FUDOU MYOUOU is positioned in the center, GOUZANZE MYOUOU is in the east, GUNDARI MYOUOU is in the south, DAIITOKU MYOUOU is in the west, and KONGOU-YASHA MYOUOU is in the north. An example of this group is seen at Toji Temple in Kyoto.

ごたいろう 五大老〖武士〗 five ministers of the government of TOYOTOMI HIDEYOSHI in the late 16th century. Include TOKUGAWA IEYASU, Maeda Toshiie, Ukita Hideie, Mouri Terumoto, and Kobayakawa Takakage. After Takakage died, Uesugi Kagekatsu was appointed.

こたつ 炬燵〖家具〗 a low table with a heater underneath. Consists of a top board, futon, four-legged wooden frame, and heater. In winter, people sit around it with their legs under the futon.

こだま こだま〖鉄道〗 the express train on Tokaido and San'yo Shinkansen. Stops at every station on its route. Its name, meaning "echo," has been used since 1964, when Japan's first Shinkansen started operation. There are more non-reserved cars on Kodama than Nozomi or Hikari. Takes 4 hours from Tokyo to Shin-Osaka, and 5 hours from Shin-Osaka to Hakata in Fukuoka Pref.

こだま 木霊〖妖怪〗 a spirit of a tree. It was said that an echo would come back in the mountains because 'kodama' provides answers.

こたん コタン〖少数民族〗 a village or community of Ainu.

ごだんかつよう 五段活用〖言語〗 a verb conjugation in which the vowel of the stem end varies among 'a,' 'i,' 'u,' 'e,' and 'o.' For example, the verb 'iku' (go) takes one of the following forms: ika, iki, iku, ike, or iko.

ごちそうさまでした 御馳走様でした〖食文化・言語〗 "It was wonderful food." Is uttered by a person who has just finished eating or drinking. ↔頂きます

ごちにょらい 五智如来〖仏教〗 Five Wisdom Buddhas. Are worshipped in esoteric Buddhism. The arrangement and selection of the five in the Mandala of the Diamond Realm are different from that in the Womb Realm, though the Great Sun

Buddha is centered in both. →金剛界曼荼羅(こんごうかいまんだら)；胎蔵界曼荼羅(たいぞうかいまんだら)

こつあげ 骨上げ〖冠婚葬祭〗 to pick up ashes of a deceased person. After cremation, the family members put the bones into a cinerary urn by using chopsticks.

こっか 国花 〖政治・植物〗 the national flower. Is not officially decided, but a cherry blossom or chrysanthemum is considered to symbolize Japan.

こっか 国歌〖政治・音楽〗 ⇨君が代

こづか 小柄〖武器〗 a small dagger attached to a sword sheath.

こっかい 国会 〖政治〗 Diet. The legislative body of Japan. Is regarded as the highest body of national rights by the Constitution of Japan. Consists of the House of Representatives and the House of Councilors. Members of the House of Representatives have a term of office for four years, but they lose their status or seniority each term because the House is dissolved. Members of the House of Councilors are not dissolved for six years. In deciding the budget and laws, the House of Representatives has priority over the House of Councilors.

こっかいぎじどう 国会議事堂〖政治・建築〗 National Diet Building. Construction began in 1920 and was completed in 1936. The right wing is for the House of Councilors, and the left wing is for the House of Representatives.

こっかこうあんいいんかい 国家公安委員会〖行政機関・犯罪〗 National Public Safety Commission. An external agency of the Cabinet Office. Supervises, controls, and administers the police.

こっかしんとう 国家神道〖政治・神道〗 State Shintoism. Was founded as a kind of theocracy or state religion immediately after the Meiji Restoration in the 19th century. The government considered State Shintoism not as a religion and ranked it above religions such as Sect Shintoism, Buddhism, and Christianity. In State Shintoism, the Emperor was worshipped as the offspring of the Sun Goddess. It was abandoned in 1945 according to an order from the occupation army. →神道指令；神社神道

こっけいぼん 滑稽本 〖文芸〗 humorous books in the 19th century. Realistically describe the life of townspeople in Edo.

こつざけ 骨酒〖酒〗 ⇨岩魚酒

こつつぼ 骨壺 〖宗教〗 a cinerary urn. After cremation, family members put the deceased person's bones into the urn by using chopsticks.

こつづみ 小鼓〖音楽〗 a small hand drum. Is used in traditional music. The diameter of the head is about 20 cm, and the whole length is about 25 cm. The player places it on the left shoulder and hits it with the right hand.

こつぶつ 骨仏 〖仏教〗 a Buddhist image made from human ashes. As a kind of memorial service, ashes of thousands of the deceased are ground and mingled with other materials to produce Buddhist images. One at Isshin-ji Temple in Osaka is famous.

こて 籠手 **(1)**〖剣術〗 a gauntlet used in KENDOU. Is divided into two parts, one for the thumb and the other for all four fingers. Covers hands and forearms. **(2)**〖剣術〗 a kendo technique to strike on the gauntlet. **(3)**〖弓道〗 an elbow cover. Is attached on the left arm when shooting an arrow.

こてなげ 小手投げ 〖相撲〗 an armlock throw. A sumo technique of throwing down the opponent by holding his arm below the elbow.

ごてんい 御典医 〖医療・武士〗 a doctor serving for a shogun or feudal lord in the Edo period.

こてんらくご 古典落語 〖落語〗 classic comic storytelling. The stories were mainly written in the Edo period.

こと 琴 〖音楽〗 a traditional 13-stringed zither. Was introduced from China in the Nara period. Is about 180 cm long and 30 cm wide. The player attaches plectrums on the thumb, the index finger, and the middle finger of the right hand.

ことう 古刀 〖武器〗 an old sword. Was made from the 9th to 16th centuries. A sword made before the 9th century is called 'joukotou.' ↔

新刀

ごとうちけんてい ご当地検定 〖人文学〗 a certification exam on knowledge about a local area. Provides questions on the history, geography, sightseeing, food, dialect, and other items in a specific area. Many areas such as Tokyo, Kyoto, Osaka, Sapporo, and Koube have such exams.

ごとうびじゅつかん 五島美術館 〖美術・博物館〗 The Gotoh Museum. Was established in Tokyo in 1960. Stores fine art of Japan and East Asia.

ごとうれっとう 五島列島 〖島名〗 the Gotou Islands. Are located off the west coast of Kyushu Island, in western Nagasaki Pref. in the East China Sea. Consist of 140 islands. The main island is Fukue Island, which has an airport. Some descendants of Christians who survived the persecution from the 17th to 19th centuries, called "kakure kirishitan," still live on the islands. Famous for the production of oysters, sea urchins, and natural camellia oil.

ごとく 五徳 **(1)**〖茶道・家具〗 a tripod or tetrapod kettle rest. Is placed over a floor-level brazier or a sunken hearth. A kettle is placed on it. **(2)**〖家具〗 a kettle rest for modern gas ranges.

ことじ 琴柱 〖音楽〗 a string support on a traditional zither called KOTO. Can be moved to adjust the pitch.

ことしろぬしのかみ 事代主神 〖神

話】 a son of OOKUNINUSHI NO KAMI. Recommended that Ookuninushi should transfer his realm to NINIGI NO MIKOTO. Is identified with EBISU of SHICHIFUKUJIN in a folk belief.

ことだま 言霊 〖言語・精神性〗 the supernatural power of language. It was believed that what was orally expressed would become real.

ことづめ 琴爪 〖音楽〗 plectra for playing a 13-stringed zither, called KOTO. Are attached on the thumb, the indicate finger, and the middle finger of the right hand.

ごとばてんのう 後鳥羽天皇 〖天皇〗 Emperor Gotoba. 1180-1239. The 82nd, on the throne from 1183 to 1198. After retiring, kept political power. Although he tried to overthrow the Kamakura shogunate, he failed and was exiled to Oki Island, where he passed away. Issued the command to compile the *New Collection of Ancient and Modern Japanese Poetry* (SHIN-KOKINWAKA-SHUU). →承久(じょうきゅう)の乱

ことばへん 言葉偏 〖漢字〗 ⇨言偏(ごんべん)

ことひらぐう 金刀比羅宮 〖神社〗 Kotohira-gu, or Konpira Shrine. Is located in western Kagawa Pref. Enshrines OOMONONUSHI NO KAMI and Emperor Sutoku, but used to be dedicated to Konpira Daigongen, a guardian of sailors. Famous for long stone stairways.

ことふるぬし 琴古主 〖妖怪〗 a goblin of a 13-stringed zither called KOTO. It is said that a spirit dwells in an instrument, which is transformed to a goblin after being used for many years.

ことほぞんほう 古都保存法 〖法律〗 Ancient Capitals Preservation Law. Came into force in 1966.

こどものひ こどもの日 〖祝日〗 Children's Day. May 5. A national holiday to show respect for children and to enhance their happiness. Is also celebrated as the Boys' Festival. Was ordained in 1948. →端午の節句

ごとんのじゅつ 五遁の術 〖忍者〗 five techniques for escape. Utilize water, metal, earth, fire, and trees.

こなきじじい 子泣き爺 〖妖怪〗 Baby-crying Old Man. Though he looks like an old man, cries loudly like a baby. If someone holds him up, 'Konaki jijii' gets heavier and heavier, sticking to the holder tightly.

こなべだて 小鍋立て 〖食文化〗 a small one-pot dish. Is served for one or two person(s).

こなもん 粉物 〖食べ物〗 food of lightly fried batter. Literally means "powder thing" because it is made from flour. Usually refers to a Japanese-style savory pancake called OKONOMIYAKI and an octopus ball called TAKOYAKI.

ごにんぐみ 五人組 〖行政〗 a five-household neighborhood association for commoners in the Edo period. The Tokugawa shogunate required the associations to prevent crimes, help each other in case of disasters, and provide mutual aid on collective responsibility.

ごにんばやし 五人囃子 〔暦・玩具〕 dolls of five court musicians. Are displayed on the third tier of a platform on which the dolls called 'hina ningyou' are set. These dolls are for the Girls' Festival, called HINA-MATSURI held on March 3rd.

こぬかあめ 粉糠雨 〔気象〕 a drizzle. Literally means "rice bran rain." Fineness of the drizzle drops may be metaphorically associated with fineness of rice bran.

このしろ 鮗 〔食べ物・魚〕 a dotted gizzard shad. *Konosirus punctatus*. About 25 cm long. Is marinated with vinegar and eaten as sushi. A young fish shorter than about 10 cm is called KOHADA.

このはどん 木の葉丼 〔食べ物〕 a bowl of rice with sliced steamed fish paste, egg, and vegetables. Similar to OYAKO-DON, but uses thin-sliced fish paste instead of chicken meat. Is popular in the Kansai region.

このはなのさくやひめ 木花之佐久夜毘売 〔神話〕 the deity of Mt. Fuji. The wife of NINIGI NO MIKOTO, a daughter of OOYAMATSUMI NO KAMI, and the mother of HODERI NO MIKO-TO, HOSUSERI NO MIKOTO, and HOORI NO MIKOTO.

このめあえ 木の芽和え 〔食べ物〕 ⇨ 木(ੋ)の芽和え

このわた 海鼠腸 〔食べ物〕 salted entrails of sea cucumber. Good with sake.

こはぜ 鞐 〔服飾〕 the clasp for an ankle-length sock called TABI, with a separate section for the big toe. Fastens the sock behind the ankle so that it fits the foot.

こはだ 小鰭 〔魚〕 young dotted gizzard shad. Is marinated with vinegar and eaten as sushi. →鮗(ੋ)

こばち 小鉢 〔食文化〕 various food placed in a small bowl and served at a traditional-style restaurant. Often is traditional salad or vinegared food.

こばなし 小噺 〔落語〕 a short funny story. Is sometimes performed as an introduction to a traditional comic storytelling, RAKUGO.

こばやしいっさ 小林一茶 〔文芸〕 1736-1827. A haiku poet born in present Nagano Pref. After wandering throughout Japan, he came back to his home village. Reflecting his somewhat unprivileged walk of life, composed haiku with a rebellious tone and cynical style, using colloquialisms and dialects. His works include *The Spring of My Life* (Oraga Haru).

こばやしたきじ 小林多喜二 〔文芸〕 1903-1933. A proletarian novelist born in Akita Pref. Was tortured to death by the Special Higher Police, which suppressed thought, expression, and political activities. His works include *The Crab Cannery Ship* (Kani-kousen) in 1929. →特高警察

こばん 小判 〔貨幣〕 a small oval gold coin. Circulated with the value

of one RYOU during the Edo period.
→大判

ごばん 碁盤 〖遊び〗 a 'go' board.
The 'go' stones are placed on intersections of 19 lines drawn vertically and horizontally.

ごひゃくまんごく 五百万石 〖酒・植物〗 a kind of rice for sake. Is produced mainly in Niigata Pref. →酒米(さかまい)

ごひゃくらかん 五百羅漢 〖仏教〗 five hundred arhats. It is said that this group image depicts five hundred saints who gathered to compile the Buddhist scriptures after Buddha's death. →十六羅漢

こびょうし 小拍子 〖落語〗 small clappers. Are used to make sound effects during a comic storytelling called RAKUGO in the Kansai area. Sounds are made by hitting a small desk in front of the storyteller. →見台

こぶ 昆布 〖食べ物・植物〗 ⇨昆布(こんぶ)

ごふ 護符 〖神道・仏教〗 ⇨お守り

ごふく 呉服 〖服飾〗 **(1)** the generic term for textile used for a kimono. **(2)** silk textile. This term is used when contrasting textiles made of other materials.

こぶし 小節 〖音楽〗 a decorative vibrato. Is used when singing a traditional folk song called MIN'YOU or a melancholic ballad called ENKA.

こぶじめ 昆布締め 〖食文化〗 salted fish sandwiched between sheets of kelp. Was originally a specialty of Toyama Pref.

こぶじゅつ 古武術 〖武術〗 premodern martial arts. Are said to have been more practical than modern martial arts such as judo and kendo, which have become a kind of sport. Include jujitsu and NINJUTSU. →柔術

こぶちゃ 昆布茶 〖飲み物〗 kelp tea. Is prepared by pouring hot water into thinly sliced or powdered dry kelp.

ごぶつぜん 御仏前 〖仏教〗 the offering placed in front of a memorial tablet of the deceased.

こぶとりじじい 瘤取り爺 〖民話〗 "Old Man With the Lump." An old man had a big lump on his cheek. When he came across a banquet of demons, he performed a great dance. As a reward, the demons removed his lump.

こぶまき 昆布巻き 〖食べ物〗 rolled kelp with fish or meat in it. Is mainly served as New Year's food.

こふん 古墳 〖考古〗 a tumulus. A burial mound for a leading person in ancient times. Its shape is various such as a circle, square, and keyhole. The period when many tumuli were constructed is called KOFUN JIDAI, which means "the Tumulus period."

こぶん 子分 〖精神性〗 a henchman. Often refers to an underling in gangster organizations called YAKUZA.

こぶん 古文 〖教育・言語〗 classical Japanese. Texts written in or before the Edo period.

ごふん 胡粉 〖美術〗 seashell powder. Is used as white paint on a picture or sculpture.

こふんじだい 古墳時代〖時代〗 the Tumulus period. From the late 3rd to 7th centuries. Hierarchical societies were born, unification of the country progressed, and large tumuli were built throughout Japan.

ごへい 御幣〖神道〗 ⇨幣(〜)

ごぼう 牛蒡〖食べ物・植物〗 a burdock. *Arctium lappa*. The root is usually boiled and used as an ingredient for several cuisine.

こぼりえんしゅう 小堀遠州〖茶道〗 1579-1647. A tea master, garden designer, architect, and potter born in present Shiga Pref. Studied the tea ceremony under FURUTA ORIBE and established his own school. His works include the tea ceremony room and the garden at a sub-temple of DAITOKU-JI Temple, named Kohou-an, and the garden at a sub-temple of NANZEN-JI Temple, named Konchi-in.

こま 駒〖将棋〗 a piece. There are 8 types of pieces, and each player starts a game with a total of 20: a king, a rook, a bishop, 2 golds, 2 silvers, 2 knights, 2 lances, and 9 pawns. →王将；玉(〜)将；飛車；角行；金将；銀将；桂馬；香車；歩

こま 独楽〖遊び〗 a spinning top. Some are spun by a hand, and others are spun with a string. Were imported to Japan in ancient times.

こま 高麗〖国名〗 **(1)** another name for Koguryo. →高句麗(〜) **(2)** another name for Koryo. →高麗(〜)

ごま 胡麻〖食べ物・植物〗 sesame.

Sesamum indicum. Its seed is edible and used in various ways such as being roasted, ground, or pasted.

ごま 護摩〖仏教〗 a fire ritual in esoteric Buddhism. In Sanskrit, *homa*. A priest burns small wood sticks in front of the Immovable Wisdom King or Wisdom King of Passion to pray for health, happiness, or exorcism.

ごまあえ 胡麻和え〖食べ物〗 a vegetable salad dressed with ground sesame.

こまい 氷下魚〖食べ物・魚〗 a saffron cod. *Eleginus gracilis*. Is often dried to be eaten.

こまいぬ 狛犬〖神社〗 a pair of stone guardian dogs. Is placed at the entrance of a Shinto shrine or in front of the main building. Although its name is 'inu,' meaning "dog," each dog's appearance is like a lion. Usually the right one opens its mouth, while the left one's mouth is closed. →神社；阿吽(〜)

こまがたけ 駒ヶ岳〖山岳〗 **(1)**⇨甲斐駒ヶ岳 **(2)**⇨木曽駒ヶ岳

こまきながくてのたたかい 小牧長久手の戦い〖戦争〗 Battle of Komaki and Nagakute. TOKUGAWA IEYASU and TOYOTOMI HIDEYOSHI fought each other in present Aichi Pref. in 1584.

こまげた 駒下駄〖履物〗 a pair of low wooden clogs. The sole portion and the supporting portion are both carved from a single piece of wood.

ごまだれ 胡麻垂れ〖調味料〗 creamy sesame sauce. Is made from sesame, soy sauce, and mirin. Is used for salad, cold noodles, one-pot dish, and other various others.

ごまだん 護摩壇〖仏教〗 an altar for a fire ritual in esoteric Buddhism.

こまち こまち〖鉄道〗 the express train on the Tohoku and Akita Shinkansen. Is named after the beauty Ono no Komachi from Akita Pref. in the 9th century. Most Komachi trains connect Tokyo and Akita within 4 hours. All Komachi trains have only reserved seats.

こまつさきょう 小松左京 〖文芸〗 1931-2011. A pioneer novelist of modern Japanese science fiction. His works include *Virus: the Day of Resurrection* (Fukkatsu no Hi) in 1964 and *Japan Sinks* (Nihon Chinbotsu) in 1973.

こまつな 小松菜〖植物〗 Japanese mustard spinach. *Brassica campestris* var. *perviridis*. Similar to turnip leaves. Is said to be native to Tokyo. Is boiled or stir-fried.

ごまどうふ 胡麻豆腐 〖食べ物〗 sesame tofu. A vegetarian dish for Buddhist monks. Is made from sesame and kudzu. Is shaped like tofu.

こまどり 駒鳥〖動物〗 a Japanese robin. *Erithacus akahige*. Though a different species, it looks like a European robin.

ごまみそ 胡麻味噌〖調味料〗 miso with ground sesame. Is used as seasoning for various cuisine.

ごまめ 鱓〖食べ物〗 dried young anchovies simmered with soy sauce,

mirin, and sugar. Eaten as a New Year cuisine.

こまものや 小間物屋〖ビジネス〗 a notions store. Deals in cosmetics, accessories, and daily necessities.

ごみ 五味 〖食文化〗 five tastes. Sweetness, saltiness, sourness, bitterness, and spiciness.

こむすび 小結〖相撲〗 a sumo wrestler at the fourth highest rank in the Grand Sumo Tournament. Next to SEKIWAKE, and above MAEGASHIRA.

こむそう 虚無僧〖仏教〗 a pilgrim monk of the Fuke sect in Zen Buddhism. Had hair, wore a full-face cylindrical straw hat, and walked around playing a vertical bamboo flute called SHAKUHACHI.

こむらじゅたろう 小村寿太郎 〖外交〗 1855-1911. A diplomat and politician born in present Miyazaki Pref. After graduating from the current University of Tokyo, studied law at Harvard University. Played a central role in signing the Portsmouth Treaty after the Russo-Japanese War.

こめ 米〖食べ物〗 rice. Was introduced into Japan probably from the 3rd to 1st centuries B.C. and was used as currency before the Meiji Restoration in 1868. Though its consumption is decreasing, is still the staple food for the Japanese and is used for brewing sake and making traditional cake or crackers. Also plays an important role in religions, especially Shintoism.

こめず 米酢〖調味料〗 rice vinegar.

こめだわら 米俵 〖食文化〗 a cylindrical straw sack of rice. Contains about 60kg or 72 liters of rice.

こめぬか 米糠 〖食文化・生活〗 rice bran. Is used in various ways such as for making plant fertilizer, body soap, and pickles.

こめびつ 米櫃 〖食器〗 a chest to store raw rice at home. Administration of the rice chest was once an important job for a house wife. →御櫃(おひつ)

こめへん 米偏 〖漢字〗 a left-side radical meaning "rice." Is used in kanji such as 粉(powder), 粒(grain), 糖(sugar), and 糧(food). →偏; 部首

こもかぶり 薦被り 〖酒〗 a sake cask wrapped in a straw mat. Usually contains 72 liters. Is opened with a wooden hammer in a ceremonial occasion.

ごもくごはん 五目御飯〖食べ物〗 ⇨加薬(かやく)御飯

ごもくずし 五目寿司〖食べ物〗 five-item sushi. Is not in a cake shape, different from ordinary sushi. Although the name means "five-item," it actually has more items including vinegared rice, various vegetables, seafood, and other ingredients.

ごもくならべ 五目並べ 〖碁〗 gobang, or five in a row. Players alternatively place stones. The person who makes an unbroken row of five stones either horizontally, vertically, or diagonally, wins.

こもだる 菰樽〖酒〗 ⇨薦(こも)被り

こもちこんぶ 子持昆布 〖食べ物〗 herring roe on kelp. Is sometimes served as a sushi toppings.

こもん 小紋 〖服飾〗 a fine pattern spread over a whole kimono.

こやすじぞう 子安地蔵 〖仏教〗 Jizou Bodhisattva for an easy childbirth. Its figure usually holds a baby in his arm or has children on his lap.

ごようえし 御用絵師〖絵画〗 an official painter employed by the shogunate or a feudal lord. Mainly refers to a painter in the Kanou school in the Edo period.

ごようおさめ 御用納め 〖ビジネス〗 the last business day of a year at national and municipal government offices. Usually December 28th. ↔御用始め

ごようきき 御用聞き 〖犯罪・職業〗 ⇨目明し

ごようたし 御用達 〖ビジネス〗 a company that supplies goods to the Imperial Household Agency or other significant customers.

ごようてい 御用邸〖天皇・建築〗 an Imperial villa. There are three villas: Hayama, Kanagawa Pref.; Nasu, Tochigi Pref.; and Suzaki, Shizuoka Pref. →離宮(りきゅう)

ごようはじめ 御用始め 〖ビジネス〗 the first business day of a year at national and municipal government offices. Usually, January 4th. ↔御用納め

ごらいこう ご来光〖山岳・宗教〗 the sunrise seen from the top of a high mountain. May have been related to mountain or sun worship in ancient times.

ごり 鮴 〖魚〗 a local name for a freshwater goby, HAZE. Mainly used in the Hokuriku area.

ごりやく 御利益 〖仏教・神道〗 a divine favor as a return for worship.

こりゅう 古流 〖華道〗 the old school of flower arrangement. Started in the mid-Edo period.

ごりょう 御陵 〖天皇・冠婚葬祭〗 a tumulus of an Emperor or an Empress Consort.

ごりょうかく 五稜郭 〖城郭〗 a Western-style star-shaped fortress, built in HAKODATE, Hokkaido, in 1864. During the Battle of Hakodate from 1868 to 1869, ex-shogunal vassals, led by ENOMOTO TAKEAKI, resisted the new government at this fort. Is now a park famous for cherry blossom viewing. →箱館戦争

こりょうりや 小料理屋 〖食文化〗 a Japanese-style small restaurant. Serves casual a la carte dishes.

ごりんとう 五輪塔 〖仏教〗 a small five-story stone pagoda. From the bottom to the top, consists of the cuboid to symbolize "earth," the sphere to symbolize "water," the pyramid to symbolize "fire," the hemisphere to symbolize "wind," and the short and thick teardrop to symbolize "emptiness." Has been used as a gravestone since the Kamakura period.

ごりんのしょ 五輪書 〖武術・書名〗 *A Book of Five Rings*. Was written in 1643 by Miyamoto Musashi, an expert swordsman. Teaches the techniques and spirit of swordsmanship.

ごれんじゃあ ゴレンジャー 〖娯楽〗 Power Rangers. Red, blue, yellow, green, and pink rangers cooperatively fight enemies. Originated from a Japanese TV drama for children.

ころう 鼓楼 〖仏教・建築〗 a drum tower. Is situated on the opposite side of the belfry in temple precincts. Is two-storied, and the first floor sometimes has a trapezoidal shape. A drum used to be beaten to chime the hours.

ころっけ コロッケ 〖食べ物〗 a croquette. Contains mashed potato and a little minced beef and is often sold at a butcher shop. Different from the French counterpart, as it does not contain fish.

ころぼっくる コロポックル 〖妖怪〗 korpokkur, or koro-pok-guru. A small fairy under a butterbur leaf. Appears in folktales of the AINU people in Hokkaido.

ころも 衣 〖食べ物〗 a coating of batter.

ころもがえ 衣替え 〖服飾〗 a seasonal change of a uniform. Company employees or school students change from a winter uniform into a summer one on June 1st. They change it again on October 1st.

ころもへん 衣偏 〖漢字〗 a left-side radical meaning "clothes." Is used in kanji such as 袖(sleeve), 裾

(hem), and 裸 (naked). →偏；部首

こわめし 強飯 〖食べ物〗 ⇨おこわ

こんがらどうじ 矜羯羅童子 〖仏教〗 *Kimkara*. An attendant of the Immovable Wisdom King. Often puts the palms of his hands together.

ごんぐじょうど 欣求浄土〖仏教〗 a phrase meaning to wish to be reborn in the Western Pure Land. This phrase is often paired with ENRI EDO.

ごんげん 権現〖仏教・神道〗 a Shinto deity as an avatar of a Buddha or Bodhisattva. This idea is based on the theory of original reality and manifested traces. →本地垂迹(ほんじすいじゃく)説；蔵王権現

ごんげんづくり 権現造り〖神道・建築〗 Gongen style of Shinto architecture. The main sanctuary building and the oratory are connected by a paved room. The main building of Toushouguu Shrine in Nikko has this style. →本殿；日光東照宮

こんごうかいまんだら 金剛界曼荼羅〖仏教〗 Mandala of the Diamond Realm. Consists of nine small mandalas in three columns with three rows, each of which has circles with Buddhas and Bodhisattvas in it. The Diamond Realm represents the power of the Great Sun Buddha.

こんごうぐみ 金剛組 〖企業〗 the oldest company in the world. Was founded in present Osaka in 578 by an artisan from Paekche. The company's first job was to construct SHITENNOU-JI Temple, and it has been specializing in building temples and shrines for more than 1,400 years.

こんごうしょ 金剛杵 〖仏教〗 a dumbbell-shaped weapon in ancient India. Literally means "diamond mallet." In Sanskrit, *vajra*. Is used as a symbol to destroy earthly desire in the service of esoteric Buddhism. Is held by the image of a guardian king called NIOU.

こんごうはんにゃきょう 金剛般若経〖仏教〗 Diamond Wisdom Sutra. Important in Zen Buddhism.

こんごうぶじ 金剛峰寺 〖寺院〗 Kongobuji Temple. The head temple of the Shingon sect, founded in 816 by KUUKAI with financial support from Emperor Saga. Is located in Mt. Kouya in Wakayama Pref. and has many National Treasures including a pagoda, pictures, and sculptures. Was designated a World Heritage Site in 2004. →真言宗

こんこうみょうさいしょうおうきょう 金光明最勝王経〖仏教〗 Sovereign Kings Golden Light Sutra. Was regarded as a sutra for pacification and protection of the nation in the Nara period.

こんごうやしゃみょうおう 金剛夜叉明王〖仏教〗 Wisdom King of Diamond Demon. *Vajrayaksa*. One of the Five Great Wisdom Kings. Originally a demon in Hinduism. Defeats a devil with a weapon called kongousho, which literally means "diamond mallet." Three-faced and six-armed. Five-eyed on the main face. Has several weapons in its hands, such as a sword and a bow.

こんごうりきし 金剛力士〖仏教〗 ⇨ 仁王(におう)

こんじきどう 金色堂 〖寺院〗 Golden Hall. The gilt mausoleum for the Fujiwara clan. Was built at CHUUSON-JI Temple in Iwate Pref. in 1124.

こんじきやしゃ 金色夜叉〖文芸・作品〗 *The Golden Demon*. A novel published in parts from 1897 to 1902 by OZAKI KOUYOU. Describes romance and financial matters between an elite student named Kan'ichi and his girlfriend named Omiya.

こんじゃくものがたり 今昔物語〖文芸・作品〗 *Tales of Times Now Past*. A collection of narratives written in the early 12th century. Consists of 31 volumes, of which 28 still exist, and contains about 1,000 tales. Each tale begins with the phrase, "Once upon a time."

こんじゅほうしょう 紺綬褒章〖政治〗 the Medal with Dark Blue Ribbon. Is "awarded to individuals who have made exceptionally generous financial contributions for the good of the public," according to the Cabinet Office. →褒章

こんだはちまんぐう 誉田八幡宮〖神社〗 Konda Hachiman Shrine. Is located beside the tumulus of Emperor Oujin in central Osaka. Enshrines Emperor Oujin. →応神天皇陵; 八幡宮

こんちいんすうでん 金地院崇伝〖仏教〗 1569-1633. A Zen priest born in Kyoto. Made an effort to revive the NANZEN-JI Temple and later had a strong influence on politics and diplomacy of the Tokugawa administration in the early Edo period. A political rival of TENKAI. →黒衣の宰相

こんでんえいねんしざいほう 墾田永年私財法〖法律〗 Law Permitting Permanent Ownership of Newly Cultivated Land. Was issued in 743. As a result, newly opened agricultural land increased, but it triggered the development of the manorial system.

こんどう 金堂〖仏教・建築〗 the main hall of a Buddhist temple. Contains the principal image of the temple. This term is mainly used in the Six Sects of Nara and esoteric Buddhism. →本堂; 南都六宗; 密教

こんどういさみ 近藤勇〖武士〗 1834-1868. The commander of special police for Kyoto, called SHINSENGUMI, born in present Tokyo. After being defeated in the Boshin Civil War, was captured and executed.

こんとん 金遁〖忍者〗 an escaping technique utilizing metal.

こんにちは 今日は〖言語〗 "Good afternoon," or "Hello." Literally means "Today is." Is uttered to a person when the speaker sees him or her for the first time on a day during the daytime.

こんにゃく 蒟蒻, 菎蒻 〖食べ物・植物〗 konjac, or devil's tongue. Is made by adding limewater to powdered konjac potato and boiling it to congeal. Has the texture of jelly, has almost no calories, and is high in fiber. Is often used as diet food.

こんばんは 今晩は 〖言語〗 "Good evening," or "Hello." Literally means "This evening is." Is uttered to a person when the speaker sees him or her for the first time on a day in the evening.

こんぴら 金毘羅 **(1)**〖仏教〗 a guardian deity of sailors. *Kumbhira*. The deification of a crocodile living in the Ganges River, India. **(2)**〖神社〗 another name for KOTOHIRA-GUU Shrine.

こんぶ 昆布 〖食べ物・植物〗 kelp, or kombu. *Laminaria*. Grows to be several feet long off the coast of Northern Japan. Contains monosodium glutamate, a constituent of umami, and is used for making soup stock. Is boiled in salt or soaked in vinegar and thinly scraped for eating. →出汁(だ); 塩昆布; とろろ昆布

こんぶだし 昆布出汁 〖調味料〗 soup stock made from kelp.

こんぺいとう 金平糖 〖食べ物〗 a pointed sugar candy. Is pea-sized and colorful. Its etymology is related to "confeito" in Portuguese.

ごんべん 言偏 〖漢字〗 a left-side radical meaning "language." Is used in kanji such as 語(word), 話 (speech), and 読(reading). →偏;

部首

さ

さあびすざんぎょう　サービス残業〔経済〕overtime work without extra pay. Has become a social problem because many employees are forced into this situation.

さい　〜歳〔助数詞〕a counting suffix for age. There are two ways to count the age: traditional and modern. →数え年

さいかいどう　西海道〔地名〕Saikaidou, an administrative district before the Meiji Restoration in 1868. Consists of all seven prefectures on Kyushu Island, namely, Fukuoka, Saga, Nagasaki, Kumamoto, Ooita, Miyazaki, and Kagoshima.

さいかく　西鶴〔文芸〕⇨井原西鶴

さいぎょう　西行〔文芸〕1118-1190. A priest and poet. Was named Satou Norikiyo before becoming a priest at age 23. Walked around the Tohoku, Chuugoku, and Shikoku regions and composed about 2,000 tanka.

さいきょうづけ　西京漬け〔食べ物〕fish pickled in sweet Kyoto-style miso. A Spanish mackerel (SAWARA), salmon (SAKE), and chub mackerel (SABA) are popular.

さいきょうみそ　西京味噌〔調味料〕sweet white miso. Is made in Kyoto, using a good deal of malted rice (KOUJI).

さいきょうやき　西京焼き〔食べ物〕grilled fish pickled in a sweet Kyoto-style miso. →西京漬け

ざいけ　在家〔仏教〕a lay adherent of Buddhism. ↔出家 →優婆塞(うばそく)；優婆夷(うばい)

さいごうたかもり　西郷隆盛〔政治〕1827-1877. A statesman born in Kagoshima. Founded the Satsuma-Choushuu Alliance and made the Edo Castle surrender without firing a shot. After the Meiji Restoration, took a position as a high-ranking official in the new government, but resigned it and went back to Kagoshima in 1873 because of a political disturbance related to the Policy of Punishing Korea. Was defeated in the Satsuma Rebellion and killed himself in 1877. →征韓論；西南戦争

さいごくさんじゅうさんかしょ　西国三十三カ所〔仏教〕Thirty-three Holy Places around the Kansai region. It is said that pilgrimages to these holy places began in the 10th century, when Monastic Ex-emperor Hanayama took the journey here, and became popular in the Edo period. All temples at the holy places enshrine the Bodhisattva of Mercy. →観音菩薩

さいじき　歳時記〔文芸〕a glossary of season words for HAIKU.

さいじょう　斎場　**(1)**〔冠婚葬祭〕a funeral hall.　**(2)**〔宗教〕a holy place to worship a deity.

さいじん　祭神〔神道〕a deity worshipped at a shrine. The deity is

sometimes a deified person, such as Emperor Meiji enshrined at Meiji Shrine.

ざいす 座椅子〖家具〗 a floor chair. Is often folding and used on tatami mats.

さいせん 賽銭〖宗教〗 an offertory when worshipping at a Shinto shrine or Buddhist temple. People usually toss a coin, not a bill, into the offertory box before the prayer.

さいせんばこ 賽銭箱〖宗教〗 an offertory box. Is placed in front of the main building or the worship hall of a Shinto shrine or Buddhist temple.

さいだいじ 西大寺〖寺院〗 Saidai-ji Temple. The head temple of the Shingon-Ritsu sect, located in Nara City. One of the Seven Great Temples of Nara. Was founded in 765, according to the Imperial order by Emperor Shoutoku. Pictures of the Twelve Devas are National Treasures. →南都七大寺

さいたまけん 埼玉県 〖都道府県〗 Saitama Pref. Is located in central Japan, just north of Tokyo. Its area is 3,798 km². The capital, Saitama City, is located in its southeast part, which is within the Tokyo metropolitan area. Much of its land is on the Kantou Plain, including two large rivers, the Tone River and the Arakawa River. Rivers make up 4% of its area, higher than any other prefecture. Produces green onions, spinach, and broccoli. In its west are the Chichibu Mountains. Used to be part of Musashi.

さいたまし さいたま市 〖地名〗 Saitama City. The capital of Saitama Pref. and an ordinance-designated city. Is located in its southeastern part. Much of the city is populous residential areas, and its economy relies heavily on commercial businesses. Tohoku, Joetsu, and Hokuriku Shinkansen trains stop at Oomiya Station. Soccer is particularly popular, not only among the supporters of two professional teams based in the city, Urawa Red Diamonds and Omiya Ardija, but also among schoolchildren. Saitama Super Arena is the second largest indoor arena in the world after Philippine Arena in Bocaue, the Philippines.

さいちょう 最澄〖仏教〗 766?-822. A priest born in present Shiga Pref. Learned the Buddhism in the Tang dynasty and introduced the teachings of the Tendai sect to Japan. Founded ENRYAKU-JI Temple in Mt. Hiei, near Kyoto. →天台宗；比叡山

さいでんすてっかあ サイデンステッカー〖文芸〗 Edward George Seidensticker. 1921-2007. A well-known American translator of Japanese literature and cultural historian of Japan. Served in the U.S. Diplomatic Corps in Japan after World War II. Later studied at the University of Tokyo and taught at Sophia University. Completed translations of authors such as Mishima Yukio, Kawabata Yasunari, and Tanizaki Jun'ichirou. Other works include a biography of Nagai Kafuu, *Kafu the Scribbler*, and a two-volume history of Tokyo, *Low City, High City and Tokyo Rising*.

さいとうひでさぶろう 斉藤秀三郎 〔言語〕 1866-1929. An English philologist and lexicographer born in Miyagi Pref. Compiled *Saito's Idiomological English-Japanese Dictionary* and *Saito's Japanese-English Dictionary*.

さいとうもきち 斉藤茂吉 〔文芸〕 1882-1953. A tanka poet and psychiatrist born in Yamagata Pref. Studied under Itou Sachio. Edited a tanka magazine, *Araragi*. His second son was a novelist, Kita Morio.

さいとばるこふんぐん 西都原古墳群 〔考古〕 Saitobaru Burial Mounds. Are located in central Miyazaki Pref. Were built in the 4th to 6th centuries. The Saitobaru Tomb Area contains 319 tombs: 31 keyhole, 2 rectangular, and 286 circular types.

ざいにちかんこくちょうせんじん 在日韓国・朝鮮人 〔少数民族〕 Korean people living in Japan. Their nationality is Korean, but many of them speak Japanese as their first language. Most of their ancestors came to Japan when Korea was a colony of Japan before and during World War II.

ざいにちべいぐんきち 在日米軍基地 〔軍事〕 a U.S. military base in Japan. Exists by virtue of the U.S.-Japan Security Treaty. Since the bases were built under the Allied Occupation after World War II, the anti-base movement has continued to be a social and political issue in Japan.

さいのかわら 賽の河原 〔仏教・民間信仰〕 the riverside of the River of Three Crossings. Is sometimes translated as Children's Limbo. A child who has died before his or her parents repeatedly tries to make a small pagoda to pray for their parents by piling up stones, but a demon destroys it before finishing. Finally, Jizou Bodhisattva appears to save the child. This story is not included in any Buddhist sutra and is considered to be folklore. →三途の川; 地蔵菩薩

さいばし 菜箸 〔食文化〕 a pair of long chopsticks for cooking and serving. Usually about 30 cm long.

ざいばつ 財閥 〔経済〕 a financial and industrial conglomerate. With its own bank or holding company as the center, consisted of companies in major industries such as trading, manufacturing, mining, and transportation. Was usually organized around a single clan and had a close relationship with the national government. Mitsui, Mitsubishi, Sumitomo, and Yasuda were called four great zaibatsu. All conglomerates were dissolved after World War II.

ざいばつかいたい 財閥解体 〔経済〕 dissolution of ZAIBATSU. Financial and industrial conglomerates were liquidated under the order of the General Headquarters of the Supreme Commander for the Allied Powers after World War II.

さいばら　催馬楽〖音楽〗 a song in the 9th to 10th centuries. Ancient folksongs were arranged in the Chinese or Korean style in the Heian period.

さいほうごくらくじょうど　西方極楽浄土〖仏教〗 the Western Pure Land. The paradise of Amitabha Buddha, ten billion Buddha lands away from this world. In the belief of Pure Land Buddhism, a dead soul is reborn in this paradise. ↔東方瑠璃光(るり)浄土　→阿弥陀如来(あみだにょらい)

さいほうじ　西芳寺〖寺院〗 Saihou-ji Temple. A temple of the Rinzai sect located in Kyoto City. Was founded between 729 and 749 by a priest, GYOUKI, and is commonly known as Moss Temple (Koke-dera). Was designated a World Heritage Site in 1994. Advance application is necessary for visiting.

さいほうじょうど　西方浄土〖仏教〗 ⇨西方極楽浄土

ざいむしょう　財務省〖行政機関〗 Ministry of Finance. MOF. Established in 2001 by reorganizing the former Ministry of Finance and changing its Japanese name from 'Ookura-shou' to 'Zaimu-shou.'

さいめいてんのう　斉明天皇〖天皇〗 Empress Saimei. 594–661. The 37th, on the throne from 655 to 661. The wife of Emperor Jomei,

the mother of Emperors Tenji and Tenmu, and a sister of Emperor Koutoku. Was also enthroned earlier, from 642 to 645, under the name Empress Kougyoku. Dispatched troops to assist Paekche in 661, but they were defeated.

さえきゆうぞう　佐伯祐三〖絵画〗 1898–1928. A painter born in Osaka. Graduated from Tokyo Fine Arts School, present Tokyo University of the Arts. Went to France and painted many street scenes of Paris.

さえのかみ　塞の神〖宗教〗 ⇨道祖神

さお　～棹〖助数詞〗 a counting suffix for chests of drawers called TANSU.

ざおう　蔵王〖地名〗 an area on the border between Miyagi and Yamagata Prefs. The highest point is Mt. Kumano (1,841 m) in the Ouu Mountains. Near its peak is a crater lake called Okama. On the Yamagata side is a huge snow resort, famous for its rime-covered trees seen in mid-winter, and hot springs. →樹氷

ざおうごんげん　蔵王権現〖仏教・神道〗 the principal deity of mountain asceticism. Was perceived by En no Odunu in Mt. Kinpusen in present Nara Pref. The image usually stands only on the left foot, raising up the right hand and the right foot in the air, and placing the left hand on the waist. →修験道；金峯山(きんぷせん)寺

さおとめ　早乙女〖農業〗 a girl transplanting rice sprouts to serve the deity of rice fields. →田植え；田の神

さかいし 堺市 〔地名〕 Sakai City. An ordinance-designated city. Is located next to, and just south of, Osaka City, facing Osaka Bay. Developed as the autonomous center of foreign trade from the 14th to 16th centuries and later produced guns. The culture of the townspeople was robust, including the tea ceremony. Has Mozu Burial Mounds including the Tumulus of Emperor Nintoku. →仁徳天皇陵

さかき 榊〔神道・植物〕 sacred evergreen. *Cleyera japonica*. Its twigs are often used in Shinto rituals.

さかきりょう 榊料〔神道〕 a condolence gift of money at a Shinto-style funeral. Is offered to the chief mourner by participants.

さかぐちあんご 坂口安吾 〔文芸〕1906-1955. A novelist born in Niigata Pref. His works include *The Idiot* and *Discourse on Decadence*, both in 1946.

さがけん 佐賀県〔都道府県〕 Saga Pref. Its capital is Saga City. Is located in western Kyushu, between Fukuoka and Nagasaki Prefs. Its area is 2,440 km². Karatsu City, located in the northern part, includes the pine field called Niji-no-matsubara, with one million Japanese black pine trees. Karatsu is also famous for producing ceramics. In the western part of the prefecture are Imari City and Arita Town, famous for porcelain

production. In its eastern part are the Yayoi Ruins, where many prehistoric artifacts such as bronze mirrors and iron and wooden tools have been found. Used to be part of Hizen. →吉野ヶ里遺跡

さかさふじ 逆さ富士 〔山岳・絵画〕 an upside-down image of Mt. Fuji reflected on the water. The contrast between the real figure and the upside-down reflection of Mt. Fuji is a popular theme for paintings and photos.

さがし 佐賀市 〔地名〕 Saga City. The capital of Saga Pref, located in its central part and facing the Ariake Sea. Developed as the capital town of the Nabeshima clan in the Edo period.

さかたさんきち 坂田三吉 〔将棋〕1870-1946. A professional shogi player born in Sakai City, Osaka. Studied shogi by himself and was isolated in the shogi society. His life became the theme of a drama, a movie, and a song.

さかたのきんとき 坂田金時 〔武士〕?-? A samurai in the late Heian period. Served MINAMOTO NO YORIMITSU to exterminate demons. Became a legend as KINTAROU. →大江山酒呑童子(おおえやま・しゅてんどうじ)

さかだる 酒樽〔酒〕 a sake cask. Its capacity varies from 18 to 72 liters. Some types are wrapped with a straw mat. →〜斗；薦(こも)被り

さがてんのう 嵯峨天皇 〔天皇〕Emperor Saga. 786-842. The 52nd, on the throne from 809 to 823. The second prince of Emperor Kanmu. Established the police system and the document office for the Imperial Court. One of the Three Great Calligraphers. →検非違使 (けびいし); 蔵人所; 三筆

さかな (酒の)肴 〖酒〗 accompaniment to sake. Used to be fish in many cases; that's why 'sakana' means either "fish" or "side dish to go with sake."

さかなへん 魚偏〖漢字〗 a left-side radical meaning "fish." Is used in kanji such as 鮭(salmon), 鱗(scale), and 鮨(sushi).

さがにんぎょう 嵯峨人形〖人形〗 a wooden colored doll made in the Saga area of Kyoto. Was popular in the Edo period.

さかのうえのくも 坂の上の雲 〖文芸・作品〗 *Clouds above the Hill.* A historical novel published in parts from 1968 to 1973 by SHIBA RYOUTAROU. Describes the Russo-Japanese War and the lives of three young men in that era.

さかのうえのたむらまろ 坂上田村麻呂〖軍事〗 758-811. A military commander. Made an military expedition to conquer indigenous people called EZO in northeastern Japan several times and defeated their leader, ATERUI. Gave financial support to build KIYOMIZU-DERA Temple in 798.

さかばしら 逆柱 an upside-down pillar. **(1)**〖建築〗If a pillar is used at a house in the direction opposite to a growing tree, it is said to become a goblin and haunt the house. **(2)**〖宗教〗A pillar is intentionally used upside down at the Youmei Gate of the TOUSHOUGUU Shrine in Nikko to avoid perfection.

さかまい 酒米〖酒〗 rice good for brewing sake. Contains a high percentage of starch and less protein. Examples are YAMADA NISHIKI, Gohyakuman-goku, and Miyama Nishiki.

さかまんじゅう 酒饅頭〖食べ物〗 a steamed white sake bun including adzuki paste. Is made from wheat flour and sake. Smells slightly like sake.

さがみ 相模〖旧国名〗 the old name of Kanagawa Pref.

さがみてつどう 相模鉄道 〖鉄道〗 Sagami Railway. Serves cities in eastern Kanagawa Pref. such as YOKOHAMA, Yamato, and Ebina. Is the smallest among the 16 major private railway operators of Japan.

さがみわん 相模湾〖湾〗 Sagami Bay. Is located on the western coast of Kanagawa Pref. and surrounded by the Miura Peninsula in the east and Cape Manaduru in the west. Offers good fishing grounds because of a branch of the Japan Current.

さかむし 酒蒸し〖食文化〗 food steamed with Japanese sake. Crams or other shellfish are mainly used. Is often served in spring because crams are in season.

さかもときゅう 坂本九 〖音楽〗 1941-1985. A singer born in

Kanagawa Pref. Released a single record "Sukiyaki" in the U.S. in 1963, which sold more than one million copies and won the Gold Award. Died in an airplane accident.

さかもとりょうま 坂本竜馬 〖政治〗 1835-1867. An ambitious and business-minded samurai born in present Kouchi Pref. While learning swordsmanship in Edo, was influenced by the thought of the Emperor loyalists. After studying the art of navigation under a shogun's retainer, KATSU KAISHUU, organized Japan's first modern trading company, named Kameyama Shachuu, in Nagasaki in 1865. Mediated the Satsuma-Choushuu Alliance in 1866 and formulated the proposal that led to the resignation of the last shogun, TOKUGAWA YOSHINOBU, in 1867. Was assassinated in Kyoto that year. The assassins are still unknown. →薩長連合

さかやき 月代 〖武士・髪〗 the shaved front and top part of male's head. Had been popular since early modern times until the Meiji Restoration.

さきがち 先勝 〖暦〗 ⇨先勝(せんしょう)

さきたまこふんぐん 埼玉古墳群 〖考古〗 Sakitama Burial Mounds. Are located in Gyouda City, Saitama Pref. Consists of more than 30 tumuli, including the Inariyama Tumulus, where an iron sword with 115 letters referring to Emperor Yuuryaku was excavated. →雄略天皇

さぎちょう 左義長 〖祭礼〗 ⇨どんど焼き

さきづけ 先付 〖食文化〗 an appetizer served at the beginning of a meal. Mainly for drinking sake.

さきまけ 先負 〖暦〗 ⇨先負(せんぶ)

さきもり 防人 〖軍事〗 name for a soldier that guarded northern Kyushu in ancient times. Such soldiers were called up mainly from the eastern provinces.

さきもりのうた 防人の歌 〖文芸〗 a poem sung by an ancient soldier. Many such poems are contained in the *Anthology of Myriad Leaves* (MAN'YOUSHUU). Soldiers were called up mainly from the eastern provinces and dispatched to guard northern Kyushu. Many of the poems describe the sorrow of being separated from their family or the pain of traveling.

さぎょうへんかくかつよう サ行変格活用 〖言語〗 the irregular conjugation of a verb 'suru,' which means "to do."

さくら さくら 〖鉄道〗 the express train on Kyushu Shinkansen. Its name, meaning "cherry blossom," symbolizes the nation of Japan and has been used for many express trains since Taishou era. Connects Hakata in Fukuoka Pref. with Kagoshima-Chuuou in 1.5 hours. Some Sakura express trains go through to San'yo Shinkansen, connecting Shin-Osaka and Kagoshima-Chuuou within 4.5 hours.

さくら 桜 〚植物〛 a cherry tree or cherry blossom. *Prunus*. The national flower of Japan. Has been loved since ancient times by the Japanese and used as names of people, places, companies, and products, to name a few.

さくらえび 桜海老 〚動物・食べ物〛 a sakura shrimp, or small spotted pink shrimp. *Sergia lucens*. About 4 to 5 cm long. Is caught in Suruga Bay of Shizuoka Pref. Eaten dried, sometimes raw.

さくらじま 桜島 〚島名〛 Mt. Sakura-jima. A very active volcano in Kagoshima Bay in Kagoshima Pref. Its highest peak is Kita-dake, which is 1,117 m high. When it erupted in 1914, its lava filled the strait and connected the volcano with the Oosumi Peninsula.

さくらぜんせん 桜前線 〚自然〛 the cherry blossom front. The places where cherry trees bloom at the same time form a east-west line on the Japanese Archipelago, which moves from south to north.

さくらだもんがいのへん 桜田門外の変 〚政治〛 Sakurada Gate Incident. The ad hoc super prime minister, Iı Naosuke, was assassinated in 1860. Masterless samurai from the Mito domain, who insisted that Japan should revere the Emperor and expel the barbarians, killed Naosuke outside the Sakurada Gate of Edo Castle because he signed the Harris Treaty without Imperial authorization.

さくらにく 桜肉 〚食べ物〛 horse meat. Literally means "cherry blossom meat" because of its pink color.

さくらふぶき 桜吹雪 〚自然〛 cherry blossom petals falling like a blizzard in a wind.

さくらます 桜鱒 〚食べ物・魚〛 a cherry salmon. *Oncorhynchus masou*. About 60 cm long. After living in a river for one or two years, goes down to the sea. Eaten as sashimi, or grilled with salt.

さくらもち 桜餅 〚食べ物〛 a round thin pink-colored rice cake with adzuki bean paste inside, wrapped in a salted cherry leaf. Eaten in spring.

さくらゆ 桜湯 〚飲み物〛 hot beverage with salted cherry blossoms. Is made by pouring boiled water over cherry blossoms preserved with salt.

さぐりばし 探り箸 〚食文化〛 to grope for one's favorite food in a dish with chopsticks. Is regarded as bad etiquette, known as KIRAIBASHI.

さけ 酒 〚酒〛 **(1)** sake, or rice wine. Has numerous variations in its ingredients, the rate of polishing, the way of processing, and the temperature when drinking. →酒米(さかまい); 純米酒; 吟醸酒; 生酒; 燗酒; 冷酒 **(2)** a generic term for an alcoholic beverage including beer, whiskey, and SHOUCHUU. To distinguish traditional sake from other liquor, a word 'nihon-shu' is used for traditional sake.

さけ 鮭〖食べ物・魚〗 a salmon, especially chum salmon. *Oncorhynchus keta*. About 90 cm long. Eaten as sashimi, sushi, grilled fish, and an ingredient in a one-pot dish called ISHIKARI-NABE, among other ways.

さげ 下げ〖落語〗 ⇨オチ

さげお 下げ緒〖武器〗 a sword strap. Was used by a samurai or ninja to attach the sword to the belt.

さげおななじゅつ 下げ緒七術〖忍者〗 seven techniques of using a sword strap. Namely, YOUJIN-NAWA, TABI-MAKURA, YARI-DOME, TSURI-GATA-NA, ZA-SAGASHI, NONAKA NO JINBARI, and binding the enemy.

さけかす 酒粕〖食文化〗 sake-strained lees. Is white and smells sake. Is used in cooking foods such as a soup called KASUJIRU, which includes vegetables and fish, and pickles called KASUDUKE.

さこく 鎖国〖外交〗 the national isolation, or the national seclusion. The Tokugawa shogunate banned the departure of Japanese people to foreign countries and controlled the entry of foreigners and foreign trade, except for the trade with the Netherlands, China, and Korea. This policy started in 1639 and ended in 1854. ↔開国

ささ 笹〖植物〗 bamboo grass. *Sasa*. Is not clearly distinguished from TAKE, bamboo. Sometimes, it is called 'take' when talking about its stem, while it is called 'sasa' when talking about its leaves.

さざえ 栄螺〖食べ物・動物〗 a horned turban shell. *Turbo cornutus*. The flesh is edible, and the shell is used for shellwork.

さざえさん サザエさん〖漫画〗 Mrs. Sazae. A family-life four-frame manga and anime. Was written and illustrated by Hasegawa Machiko. Was first published in a local paper of Fukuoka, later in a national newspaper, Asahi Shimbun. The TV anime started in 1969 and is still on the air, as of 2017. It has been broadcast every Sunday from 6:30 to 7:00 p.m. and contains three vignettes.

さざえさんしょうこうぐん サザエさん症候群〖精神性〗 Mrs. Sazae syndrome, or Sunday evening blues. Since a long-running anime, SAZAE-SAN, is broadcast every Sunday from 6:30 to 7:00 p.m., the melancholy felt Sunday evening after the show is over is called such.

ざさがし 座探し〖忍者〗 the technique to find an enemy in a dark place. The sword, the sheath, and the sword strap are used in combination. One of the seven techniques of using a sword strap. →下げ緒七術

ささかまぼこ 笹蒲鉾〖食べ物〗 steamed fish paste shaped like a bamboo grass leaf. A specialty of SENDAI City in Miyagi Pref. →蒲鉾

ささきのぶつな 佐々木信綱〖文芸〗 1872-1963. A poet and scholar

of Japanese literature, born in Mie Pref. Studied the *Anthology of Myriad Leaves* (MAN'YOUSHUU).

ささぐり 座探り〖忍者〗 ⇨座探し

ささにしき ササニシキ〖食べ物・植物〗 a brand name of one of the rice cultivars. Used to be the second most popular brand of rice, which was mainly produced in Miyagi Pref., but its yield amount drastically decreased due to cold weather in 1993.

ささぶね 笹船〖玩具〗 a toy boat made of a bamboo grass leaf.

ささめゆき 細雪〖文芸・作品〗 *The Makioka Sisters*. A novel published in parts from 1943 to 1948 by TANIZAKI JUN'ICHIROU. Describes the life of four beautiful sisters in an upper-class family in Osaka. Publication was temporarily forbidden by military authorities.

ささんか 山茶花〖植物〗 a sasanqua camellia. *Camellia sasanqua*. Bears white or pink flowers from October to December.

ざしき 座敷〖建築〗 a traditional-style tatami room. Is usually partitioned by sliding doors and sometimes has a decorative alcove and different-levelled shelves. →畳; 襖(ふすま); 床の間; 違い棚

ざしきろう 座敷牢〖建築〗 a private cell for confinement. In premodern days, a mentally or physically disabled or badly behaved family member was locked in this room to avoid contact with outer society.

ざしきわらし 座敷童〖妖怪〗 a

home guardian child. Was believed to live in an old house in Northern Japan. Regardless of its mischievous behavior, the family members wanted the guardian child in their house because they believed the family would decline if the guardian child left.

さしこ 刺し子, 刺子〖服飾〗 quilting of cotton clothes. Is a robust fabric and used for durable goods such as judo wear and kitchen towels.

さして 差し手〖相撲〗 **(1)** a technique to insert an arm under the opponent's armpit. **(2)** the arm inserted under the opponent's armpit.

さしばし 刺し箸〖食文化〗 to skewer one's food with a chopstick in order to pick it up. Is regarded as bad etiquette, known as KIRAI-BASHI.

さしばし 指し箸〖食文化〗 to point at something or someone with a chopstick. Is regarded as bad etiquette, known as KIRAI-BASHI.

さしみ 刺身〖食べ物〗 sashimi, or sliced raw fish. Is dipped in soy sauce with WASABI or grated ginger. Is always included in a traditional full-course meal. Sea bream, tuna, yellowtail, squid, and scallop are popular.

さしもの 指し物〖軍事〗 ⇨旗指物(はたさしもの)

さしものし 指物師〖職業〗 a joiner. Makes boxes, cabinets, desks, or chairs by fabricating wooden boards.

ざす 座主〖仏教〗 **(1)** the abbot of

a large Buddhist temple. **(2)** the head priest of the Tendai sect.

さすけ サスケ〖忍者・漫画〗 *Sasuke*. A ninja manga, written and illustrated by Shirato Sanpei. Was published serially in a boys' manga magazine, *Shounen*, from 1961 to 1966.

さすまた 刺股〖武器〗 a bident, or a two-pronged weapon with a long shaft. Was used to catch a criminal in the Edo period.

ざぜん 座禅〖仏教〗 Buddhist meditation. One of the ascetic practices. To sit in the full lotus position called KEKKA-FUZA and to try to be free from all ideas and thoughts. Is implemented mainly in Zen Buddhism.

ざぞう 座像〖彫刻〗 a sculpture sitting directly on a pedestal. →立像(りつ); 椅像(いぞう)

さだいじん 左大臣〖政治〗 Minister of the Left. Administered affairs of state when no one was appointed as the Grand Minister of State in ancient times. →太政(だじょう)大臣

ざたく 座卓〖家具〗 a low table. People sit around it directly on the floor without chairs.

さたみさき 佐多岬〖地名〗 Cape Sata. Is located at the end of the Oosumi Peninsula in southeastern Kagoshima Pref., on the southernmost end of Kyushu Island, facing the Pacific Ocean. King sago palm trees, called SOTETSU, grow in abundance.

さだみさきはんとう 佐田岬半島〖半島〗 the Sada-misaki Peninsula. Is located in western Ehime Pref., at the western tip of Shikoku Island. Separates the Inland Sea from the Pacific Ocean. Extends into the sea in a straight line for 40 km and is known as the thinnest peninsula in Japan.

さっかあ サッカー〖スポーツ〗 soccer. Was introduced to Japan in 1873 and is now very popular. The Japan Professional Football League opened in 1993. Japan made the first appearance in the World Cup in 1998, and co-hosted it with Korea in 2002.

さつき 皐月〖暦〗 May in the traditional calendar. The sound is said to come from "rice sprout month" because rice sprouts are transplanted from nursery beds into a rice field in this month, though the first kanji character does not match the sound. →旧暦; 田植え

さつきばれ 五月晴れ〖気象〗 fine weather in May.

さつじん 殺陣〖武士・芸能〗 ⇨殺陣(たて)

さっちょうどうめい 薩長同盟〖政治〗 Satsuma-Choushuu Alliance. A political and military alliance between the Satsuma and Choushuu domains, which was arranged by SAKAMOTO RYOUMA and concluded in 1866. The representatives of Satsuma were SAIGOU TAKAMORI and Komatsu Tatewaki, and the one for Choushuu was KATSURA KOGOROU.

さっちょうとひ 薩長土肥 〖政治〗

Satsuma, Choushuu, Tosa, and Hizen. Four big feudal domains in the 19th century. Played a central role in the Meiji Restoration. Present Kagoshima, Yamaguchi, Kouchi, and Saga Prefs.

さっぽろおりんぴっく　札幌オリンピック〖スポーツ〗 the Sapporo Olympics. The 11th Winter Olympics held from February 3rd to 11th in 1972. 35 nations participated, and 35 events were contested in 6 sports. Japan swept the ski jumping 70 m event for gold, silver, and bronze. For this Olympics, the subway line was constructed in the urban area of Sapporo.

さっぽろし　札幌市〖地名〗 Sapporo City. The capital of Hokkaido and an ordinance-designated city. Famous for the Snow Festival, beer, ramen, and a mutton barbecue called JINGISUKAN-NABE. Hosted the Winter Olympic Games in 1972.

さっぽろのうがっこう　札幌農学校〖教育・施設〗 Sapporo Agricultural School. Was established in 1876 to foster human resources for the development of Hokkaido and produced Uchimura Kanzo (Christian thinker), Nitobe Inazo (educator), etc. The first vice-principal was William Smith Clark from the U.S. In 1918, became the Imperial University of Hokkaido and later Hokkaido University in 1947.

さっぽろゆきまつり　さっぽろ雪祭り〖祭礼〗 Sapporo Snow Festival. Held annually in February in downtown Sapporo as its main venue. Enormous snow statues (15 m high, using 2,500 tons of snow) attract more than two million visitors each year from all over Japan and overseas. Started in 1950 with only six snow statues. Now features more than 200 large and medium-sized snow statues.

さつま　薩摩〖旧国名〗 the old name of western Kagoshima Pref.

さつまあげ　薩摩揚げ〖食べ物〗 round-shaped deep fried fish paste. Contains chopped vegetables. Is widely said that it came from China through present Okinawa to Satsuma, present Kagoshima Pref., and became widespread in Japan. Is served as a topping for UDON noodle or as an ingredient of soy-flavored stew called ODEN.

さつまいも　薩摩芋〖食べ物・植物〗 sweet potato. *Ipomoea batatas*. Is named after the production district, Satsuma, which is present Kagoshima Pref.

さつまはん　薩摩藩〖政治〗 the Satsuma domain. Governed present Kagoshima Pref., part of Miyazaki Pref., and Okinawa Pref. in the Edo period. Its feudal lords were from the Shimadu clan. Played the leading role in the Meiji Restoration in the late 19th century. Produced SAIGOU TAKAMORI and OOKUBO TOSHIMICHI.

さつまやき　薩摩焼〖陶磁器〗 Satsuma ceramic ware. Has been produced in Kagoshima Pref. since the early Edo period. Its production was started by Korean potters, who were fetched by the feudal lord of this area after Toyotomi Hideyoshi invaded Korea in 1592.

さつもんぶんか 擦文文化 〔考古〕 Satsumon Culture. Developed in Hokkaido and the northern Tohoku region from the 8th to 12th centuries. People lived mainly by fishing. Was influenced by the culture of central Honshuu Island and created unique earthen ware with a scratches pattern on its surface. Was later replaced by the Ainu Culture. →土師器(はじ); アイヌ

さといも 里芋 〔食べ物・植物〕 taro. *Colocasia esculenta*. The subterranean stems are edible.

さどう 茶道 〔茶道〕 tea ceremony. Was begun by Murata Jukou, succeeded by TAKENO JOUOU, and completed by SEN NO RIKYUU. Later divided into three major Sen-ke schools: OMOTE-SENKE, URA-SENKE, and Mushakouji-senke. Other great tea masters include HON'AMI KOUETSU, KOBORI ENSHUU, and FURUTA ORIBE. The tea ceremony is now thought of as mental and etiquette training as well as integrating arts including architecture, gardening, paintings, calligraphy, and crafts. Used to be called 'chadou.'

ざとう 座頭 〔職業〕 a visually disabled person with the appearance of a monk in the Muromachi and Edo periods. Played musical instruments such as SHAMISEN or Japanese lute called BIWA or gave massage or acupuncture to maintain a livelihood.

さとうえいさく 佐藤栄作 〔政治〕 1901-1975. A politician born in Yamaguchi Pref. A prime minister from 1964 to 1972. Won the Nobel Peace Prize in 1974.

さどうぐち 茶道口 〔茶道・建築〕 the entrance for the host to the tea-ceremony room. Guests use the other entrance. →躙(にじ)り口

さとお サトー 〔外交〕 ⇨アーネスト・サトー

さどおけさ 佐渡おけさ 〔音楽〕 a folk song for the Bon Festival dancing in Sado Island, Niigata Pref.

さとがえり 里帰り 〔生活〕 a visit to one's parents' home or hometown. Is usually made during the New Year's holidays and Bon holidays in mid-August.

さどがしま 佐渡島 〔地名〕 Sado Island. An S-shaped island off the coast of Niigata Pref. in the Sea of Japan. Its area is 855 km². Because it is located near the boundary between warm and cold currents, many fish are caught, and plants native to Hokkaido and those native to Okinawa can both be seen. From the 17th to 20th centuries, it was famous for the production of gold. After all the mines were closed by the late-20th century, it attracted visitors with the ruins of mines and with the temples that Emperor Juntoku and the Buddhist monk Nichiren visited while they were exiled to this island in the 13th century. In its center is a plain where rice is grown in abundance. Oysters are cultivated in Mano Bay and Lake Kamo.

さとへん　里偏 〖漢字〗 a left-side radical meaning "rural area." Is used in kanji such as 野（field）. → 偏；部首

さとみとん　里見弴 〖文芸〗 1888-1983. A novelist born in Kanagawa Pref. The youngest brother of Arishima Takeo. His works include *The Compassion of Buddha* in 1923.

さとやま　里山 〖自然〗 a natural environment of hills, forests, and rivers, close to a residential area. Is utilized to gather firewood or edible wild plants.

さとり　サトリ 〖妖怪〗 a mind-reading goblin. Is not harmful but mischievously tells a person what he or she is thinking.

さとり　悟り 〖仏教〗 enlightenment, or spiritual awakening. One who has attained enlightenment and is released from a continuous round of transmigration is called Buddha.

さなえ　早苗 〖農業〗 a rice sprout. Is transplanted from a nursery bed for seedlings to a rice field.

さなだのぶゆき　真田信幸 〖武士〗 1566-1658. A warlord born in present Nagano or Gunma Pref. The son of SANADA MASAYUKI. At the Battle of Sekigahara and the Winter and Summer Campaigns in Osaka,

he took the side of TOKUGAWA IEYASU, while his father and younger brother were on the opposite side. →関ヶ原の戦い；大坂冬の陣；大坂夏の陣

さなだまさゆき　真田昌幸 〖武士〗 1547-1611. A warlord born in present Nagano Pref. The father of SANADA NOBUYUKI and SANADA YUKIMURA. Served TAKEDA SHINGEN, TOKUGAWA IEYASU, and TOYOTOMI HIDEYOSHI. At the Battle of Sekigahara in 1600, he blocked the troops of TOKUGAWA HIDETADA, who intended to join the Battle of Sekigahara. →関ヶ原の戦い

さなだゆきむら　真田幸村 〖武士〗 1567-1615. A warlord. The son of SANADA MASAYUKI. At the Battle of Sekigahara in 1600, he helped his father block the troops of TOKUGAWA HIDETADA, who intended to join the Battle of Sekigahara. Took the side of TOYOTOMI HIDEYORI and died in the Summer Campaign in Osaka. →関ヶ原の戦い；大坂冬の陣；大坂夏の陣

さぬき　讃岐 〖旧国名〗 the old name of Kagawa Pref.

さぬきうどん　讃岐饂飩 〖食べ物〗 Sanuki UDON noodles. A specialty of Kagawa Pref., whose old name is Sanuki. Thicker than other udon noodles.

さば　鯖 〖動物・食べ物〗 a chub mackerel. *Scomber japonicus*. About 40 cm long. Lives throughout the world. Eaten salted and vinegared, simmered, grilled, or as sushi.

さばかいどう 鯖街道 〚食文化・交通〛 Mackerel Road. Was used to transport fish, particularly mackerel, from Wakasa Bay in present Fukui Pref. to Kyoto, before trains and automobiles began to be used.

さばく 佐幕 〚政治〛 the political idea to support the Tokugawa shogunate in the 19th century. ↔倒幕

さばずし 鯖寿司 〚食べ物〛 pressed sushi of chub mackerel. →押し寿司

さはちりょうり 皿鉢料理 〚食文化〛 large-plate banquet cuisine in Kouchi Pref. Different kinds of food such as sashimi, sushi, and grilled, simmered, and vinegared dishes are decoratively arranged on a large plate.

さび サビ 〚調味料〛 a sushi jargon meaning WASABI, Japanese horseradish.

さび 寂 〚精神性〛 elegant simplicity, or beauty through a sense of quietness and antiquity. Originally a HAIKU term.

ざびえる ザビエル 〚キリスト教〛 ⇨ フランシスコ・ザビエル

さびぬき サビ抜き 〚調味料〛 a sushi jargon meaning sushi without WASABI, Japanese horseradish.

ざぶとん 座布団 〚家具〛 a square floor cushion. One side is about 60 cm long.

さみせん 三味線 〚音楽〛 ⇨三味(しゃ)線

さみだれ 五月雨 〚暦・気象〛 rain in May in the traditional calendar. Falls intermittently and can last for days at a time.

さむえ 作務衣 〚仏教・服飾〛 work wear for a Zen priest. Is usually made of cotton and dyed with indigo.

さむらい 侍 〚武士〛 a warrior, or a swordsman. Originally, a retainer who had weapons and served a nobleman in the Heian period. Later a member of a military class.

さむらいどころ 侍所 〚政治〛 **(1)** a guard station of a residence for high-ranking aristocrats in the Heian period. **(2)** an office to administer high-ranking vassals under the Kamakura and Muromachi shogunates.

さや (刀の)鞘 〚武器〛 a sheath. Is sometimes decorated with mother-of-pearl inlay or gold or silver dust.

さやえんどう 莢豌豆 〚食べ物〛 snow peas. Pods are rather flat and contain very small peas. The whole pod is edible.

さやまいけ 狭山池 〚湖沼〛 Sayama Pond. Is located in southern Osaka Pref. The oldest artificial pond for irrigation in Japan.

さより 細魚 〚食べ物・魚〛 a Japanese halfbeak. *Hyporhamphus sajori*. About 30 cm long. Eaten grilled or dried, as sushi, sashimi, or as an ingredient of clear soup.

さらうどん 皿饂飩 〚食べ物〛 fried noodles with various toppings like vegetables and seafood. A specialty of Nagasaki City. Though the name includes the word UDON, which is thick wheat noodles, 'sara-udon' is thin.

さらし 晒し 〚服飾〛 ⇨晒(さら)し木綿

さらしあん 晒餡 〖食べ物〗 adzuki powder. Is used for instant sweet adzuki soup or adzuki-bean jelly after being mixed with water and sugar. →汁粉(ˡˢ); 羊羹(ˡˢ)

さらしなにっき 更級日記 〖文芸・作品〗 *As I Crossed a Bridge of Dreams*. A diary written around 1060 by a daughter of a low-ranking aristocrat, Sugawara no Takasue. Describes her life from 1020, when her family went back to Kyoto from present Chiba, the place of her father's assignment, to 1058, when her husband died.

さらしねぎ 晒葱 〖調味料〗 chopped and washed green onion. Is not very spicy and is used as a condiment.

さらしもめん 晒し木綿 〖服飾〗 bleached cotton cloth. Is soft, permeable, and tough. Has been used for underwear, baby wear, and towels.

さらそうじゅ 沙羅双樹 〖仏教・植物〗 a sal. *Shorea robusta*. Native to northern India, not Japan. It is said that, when the Historical Buddha passed away, two sals grew in each of the four directions from the Buddha's body. →涅槃(ˡˢ)図

さらやしき 皿屋敷 〖妖怪〗 "Plate Mansion." A traditional ghost story. A housemaid named O-kiku broke one of the ten dishes that were her master's family treasure and committed suicide or was killed by the master. Her ghost appeared and counted dishes until the ninth one.

The story has several variations and is performed in kabuki and bunraku.

さらりいまん サラリーマン 〖職業〗 a company employee. Usually refers to a white-collar worker. Though the term "salaryman" was coined in Japan, it is defined in some English dictionaries as "a Japanese white-collar worker."

さる 申 〖干支〗 the ninth of the Chinese zodiac signs. Means "monkey." Recently the years 1992, 2004, and 2016 were monkey years. Indicates the west-southwest in direction and around 4 p.m. for hours.

ざるうどん 笊饂飩 〖食べ物〗 chilled thick white noodles topped with shredded dry purple laver sheet. Is served on a woven bamboo tray called ZARU and eaten by dipping it into special broth with condiments such as WASABI, grated ginger, or chopped green onion. Mainly eaten in summer.

さるがく 猿楽 〖芸能〗 a performing art from ancient to medieval times. Was originally introduced from Tang China in the 8th century. Included comical mimicry, acrobatics, songs, dance, and drama. Later developed to Noh and Noh farce called KYOUGEN.

さるかにがっせん 猿蟹合戦 〖民話〗 "The Battle of Crab and Monkey." A folktale. A monkey cheats a crab out of a persimmon and kills the crab. A child of the crab avenges its mother's death with the help of a bee, a chestnut, and a mortar.

さるさわのいけ 猿沢の池 〔湖沼〕 Sarusawa Pond. An artificial pond, on the edge of Nara Park in Nara City. The scene of this pond with the moon and the five-storied pagoda of KOUFUKU-JI Temple as an adjacent feature, has been chosen as one of the Eight Views of Nara. Famous for its many legends and seven wonders.

さるすべり 百日紅 〔植物〕 a crape myrtle. *Lagerstroemia indica*. Literally means "monkey slipping" because the surface of the trunk is too smooth for a monkey to climb up.

ざるそば 笊蕎麦 〔食べ物〕 chilled buckwheat noodles topped with shredded dry purple laver sheet. Is served on a woven bamboo tray called ZARU, and eaten by dipping it into special broth with condiments such as WASABI or chopped green onion.

さるたひこ 猿田彦 〔神話〕 a tall local deity with a long nose. Guided NINIGI NO MIKOTO, who had descended from the High Celestial Plain.

さるどし 申年 〔暦〕 the year of the monkey in Chinese zodiac signs. The years 1992, 2004, and 2016 are years of the monkey. →干支；申(る)

さるとびさすけ 猿飛佐助 〔忍者〕 ?–? A legendary ninja. Learned ninjutsu in KOUKA, present Shiga Pref., and served a warlord, SANADA YUKIMURA, in present Nagano Pref.

さるのこしかけ 猿の腰掛 〔植物〕 a shelf fungus, or bracket fungus. *Polyporaceae*. Corrodes timbers but can be used as medicine. Literally means "monkey's chair."

さるはし 猿橋 〔橋〕 a bridge in Ootsuki City in eastern Yamanashi Pref. Literally means "Monkey Bridge." Was originally built in the 7th or 8th century. Later in the 17th or 18th century, the wood blocks were combined as if some monkeys used their bodies in collaboration to let another monkey cross the river on them. It was on the busy route of the Koushuu Highway in the Edo period. Today, it is labeled as one of the three most odd-looking bridges.

さるまわし 猿回し 〔娯楽〕 the street performance using a monkey. Was originally shown during the New Year's holidays.

ざれい 座礼 〔礼儀作法〕 a bow when sitting on a tatami mat. The procedure is as follows: [1] Formally sit on a tatami mat, [2] softly place both palms on the mat, with the tips of both index fingers touching each other, and [3] bow until the head is close to the mat.

さろまこ サロマ湖 〔湖沼〕 Lake Saroma. The largest lagoon in Hokkaido, located in its northeastern part, facing the Sea of Okhotsk. Also the largest lake in Hokkaido, and the third largest lake in Japan. The area is 152 km². Scallop and oyster production is famous.

さわがに 沢蟹 〔動物〕 a Japanese

freshwater crab, or a small river crab. *Geothelphusa dehaani*. Eaten deep fried. The shell width is about 2.5 cm.

さわちりょうり 皿鉢料理 〖食文化〗 ⇨皿鉢(ほち)料理

さわら 鰆 〖食べ物・魚〗 a Japanese Spanish mackerel. *Scomberomorus niphonius*. About 1 m long. Eaten grilled, pickled in a sweet Kyoto-style miso. →西京漬け

さん 讃 〖書道・美術〗 ⇨画賛

さんあみ 三阿弥 〖絵画〗 the generic name of three painters from the 15th to 16th centuries: NOUAMI, GEIAMI, and SOUAMI. Father, son, and grandson.

さんいんどう 山陰道 〖地名〗 (1) an administrative district before the Meiji Restoration in 1868. Consisted of present Kyoto, northern Hyougo, Tottori, and Shimane Prefs., including the Oki Islands. (2) the main route from Kyoto to Yamaguchi along the Sea of Japan before 1868.

さんえん 三猿 〖精神性〗 three wise monkeys. One covering its eyes, one its ears, and one its mouth, with both hands. Each figure, respectively, means to see, to hear, and to speak no evil. Example at Toushouguu Shrine in Tochigi Pref. is famous. →日光東照宮

さんがい 三界 〖仏教〗 the three worlds: the world of desire (YOKKAI), the world of being with form (SHIKIKAI), and the world of formless beings (MUSHIKIKAI).

さんかいき 三回忌 〖冠婚葬祭〗 the second anniversary of a person's death. The memorial service is held. →一周忌；～回忌

さんかく △ 〖教育〗 a triangle mark. Means partial points in the grading of exams.

さんがく 散楽 〖芸能〗 ancient performing arts including acrobatics, magic, comical mimicry, and drama. Was introduced from Tang China in the 8th century and later became SARUGAKU.

さんがく 算額 〖科学技術〗 a mathematical tablet. Traditional Japanese mathematicians described mathematical problems on votive wooden tablets and dedicated the tablets to shrines or temples in the Edo period. →和算

さんかくこおなあ 三角コーナー 〖家具〗 a small triangle container for kitchen garbage. Fits into the corner of a kitchen sink and drains the garbage through many small holes in it.

さんかくぶちしんじゅうきょう 三角縁神獣鏡 〖考古〗 an ancient mirror with a triangular rim, decorated with gods and animals in relief. Usually 20 to 23 cm in diameter. Is excavated in a tumulus built from the late 3rd to 4th centuries.

さんがにち 三が日 〖正月〗 the three days of January 1st to 3rd. People visit a shrine or temple to pray for the new year and visit relatives or friends for new year greetings. Many businesses are closed.

さんかん 三関 〔交通〕 three toll-gates placed in the Heian period. 'Fuwa no seki' in Gifu Pref., 'Arachi no seki' between present Shiga and Fukui Prefs., and 'Suzuka no seki' in present Mie Pref.

さんかんしおん 三寒四温 〔暦・自然〕 three cold days and four warm days. It is said that it will get warmer in early spring, repeating this pattern.

さんぎいん 参議院 〔政治〕 House of Councilors. The term for its members is six years, and it is not to be dissolved.

さんぎょうぎじゅつそうごうけんきゅうじょ 産業技術総合研究所 〔科学技術・研究機関〕 National Institute of Advanced Industrial Science and Technology. AIST. Was established in 2001. The headquarters is located in Tokyo.

さんきょく 三曲 〔音楽〕 an ensemble of three traditional instruments: SHAMISEN, a 13-stringed zither called KOTO, and a vertical bamboo flute called SHAKUHACHI.

ざんぎり 散切り 〔髪〕 a cropped hairstyle. Men cut off their topknots after the Meiji Restoration. Was regarded as a symbol of Western-oriented civilization. →文明開化

ざんぎりもの 散切物 〔歌舞伎〕 a social drama in kabuki in the early Meiji era. A subcategory of SEWAMONO. Reflected the social environment after the Meiji Restoration. ZANGIRI is a male cropped hairstyle,

symbolizing Western-oriented civilization in the late 19th century.

さんきんこうたい 参勤交代 〔武士・政治〕 the system of periodic residence of feudal lords in Edo. The Tokugawa shogunate, which intended to weaken the financial power of feudal lords, made them live in Edo and their homeland in alternate years. The legitimate wife and her children had to live full-time in Edo as hostages.

さんくつほう 三屈法 〔仏教〕 tribanga. The way that a Buddhist image bends the waist and the neck sideways.

さんけえ ３Ｋ 〔ビジネス・精神性〕 a 3D job. Has three features of three Japanese words: 'kitsui' (demanding), 'kitanai' (dirty), and 'kiken' (dangerous). Such jobs are avoided by modern Japanese people.

さんげん 三弦 〔音楽〕 another name for SHAMISEN.

さんごくかんしょう 三国干渉 〔外交〕 the Triple Intervention. Russia, France, and Germany strongly requested Japan in 1895 to retrocede the Liaodong Peninsula to China, which Japan won in the Sino-Japanese War from 1894 to 1895.

さんごくどうめい 三国同盟 〔外交〕 ⇨日独伊三国同盟

さんさい 山菜 〔食べ物・植物〕 edible wild plants. Include bracken (warabi), mountain asparagus (UDO), and royal fern (ZENMAI).

さんさいおこわ 山菜おこわ 〔食べ物〕

glutinous rice steamed with edible wild plants such as bracken, mountain asparagus, and royal ferns.

さんさいそば 山菜蕎麦 〖食べ物〗 hot buckwheat noodles with edible wild plants such as bracken, mountain asparagus, and royal ferns.

さんざし 山査子 〖医療・植物〗 a hawthorn. *Crataegus cuneata*. Bears white flowers in spring. The fruits can be used for medicinal purposes.

さんざる 三猿〖精神性〗 ⇨三猿(ざる)

さんさんくど 三三九度 〖冠婚葬祭〗 to sip sake nine times in a Shinto-style marriage ceremony. The bride and the groom sip sake three times poured in a small plate. They repeat it three times with different plates.

さんさんななびょうし 三三七拍子 〖精神性〗 a cheering hand-clapping in the 3-3-7 rhythm.

さんしせいらん 山市晴嵐 〖絵画〗 Mountain Village Veiled in Mist on a Fine Day. One of the Eight Views of Xiaoxiang. →瀟湘(しょうしょう)八景

さんじっこくぶね 三十石船 〖交通〗 a 30-koku ship, or a 2-ton ship. KOKU is a unit to measure the load of a ship, and 1 KOKU equals about 0.28 m^3. The vessel plied the Uji River and the Yodo River between Kyoto and Osaka to carry passengers and commercial products such as sake and rice, up to 2 tons. Was in operation in the Edo and Meiji periods. In 1998 it was revived as a vessel for sightseeing in Kyoto.

さんじゃくおび 三尺帯 〖服飾〗 a one-meter-long sash for children's kimono.

さんじゃまつり 三社祭 〖祭礼〗 Sanja Festival. Is held at Asakusa Shrine in Tokyo on the third Saturday and Sunday in May.

さんじゅ 傘寿 〖通過儀礼〗 the age of 80 in the traditional approach to age counting. People usually celebrate it when a person turns 79, in the modern approach to age counting. 'Sanju' literally means "umbrella age," because when 80 is written vertically in kanji (八十), it looks like 傘 in a cursive style, which means "umbrella." →数え年

さんじゅうさんかんのん 三十三観音〖仏教〗 thirty-three forms of the Bodhisattva of Mercy. Sometimes refers to a set of 33 temples, each of which enshrines the Bodhisattva of Mercy. →観音

さんじゅうさんげんどう 三十三間堂 〖仏教・建築〗 Sanjusangen-do Temple. The common name of Rengeou-in. This name means a hall with thirty-three spaces between columns. Affiliated with the Tendai sect and is located in Kyoto. Was founded by Taira no Kiyomori at the behest of Ex-emperor Goshirakawa. Enshrines 1,000 statues of the Thousand-armed Bodhisattva of Mercy and the Twenty-eight Devas. →千手観音; 二十八部衆

さんじゅうにそうはちじっしゅごう 三十二相八十種好 〖仏教〗 thirty-two major and eighty minor physical characteristics of the Buddha. Includes the protruding head, white bristles between eyebrows, flatfeet, long fingers, etc. →肉髻（にっけい）; 白毫（びゃくごう）

さんじゅうのとう 三重塔 〖仏教・建築〗 a three-story pagoda. One of the major wooden buildings in a Buddhist temple. The oldest one is at Hokki-ji Temple in Nara Pref. →塔

さんじゅうろっかせん 三十六歌仙 〖文芸〗 Thirty-six Immortal Poets. Thirty-six master poets selected by Fujiwara no Kintou in the 11th century. Include Kakinomoto no Hitomaro, Ootomo no Yakamochi, Yamabe no Akahito, Sarumaru dayuu, Ki no Tsurayuki, Mibu no Tadamine, Ariwara no Narihira, and Ono no Komachi.

さんしゅのじんぎ 三種の神器 〖神話〗 the Three Sacred Treasures of the Imperial Family: a comma-shaped jewel, a mirror, and a sword. Symbolize the legitimacy and authority of the Emperor. →八尺瓊（やさかに）の勾玉（まがたま）; 八咫（やた）の鏡; 天叢雲剣（あめのむらくものつるぎ）

ざんしょ 残暑 〖暦〗 the lingering summer heat. The heat in the autumnal season of the traditional calendar. →立秋

さんしょう 山椒 〖調味料・植物〗 a prickly ash, or a Japanese pepper. *Zanthoxylum piperitum*. Its dried fruit skin is powdered and used as spice. The bud is put on a dish or floated on a soup for aroma.

さんしょう 三賞 〖相撲〗 the three special prizes in the Grand Sumo Tournament. Namely, Fighting Spirit Prize (KANTOU-SHOU), Technique Prize (GINOU-SHOU), and Outstanding Performance Prize (SHUKUN-SHOU).

さんじょうさねとみ 三条実美 〖政治〗 1837-1891. A court noble and statesman, born in Kyoto. Cooperated with the Choushuu domain and took the side of the pro-Emperor camp. →長州藩; 尊皇攘夷（そんのうじょうい）

さんしょうだゆう 山椒大夫 〖文芸・作品〗 *Sansho the Steward*. A short novel published in 1915 by MORI OUGAI. Describes the sufferings of an elder sister and a younger brother, who were enslaved by an inhumane and greedy millionaire, and the success story of the younger brother after he escaped.

さんじょうてんのう 三条天皇 〖天皇〗 Emperor Sanjou. 976-1017. The 67th, on the throne from 1011 to 1016. The second prince of Emperor Reizei. Because of blindness, gave up the throne to Emperor Goichijou, a son of FUJIWARA NO MICHINAGA.

さんしょくだんご 三色団子 〖食べ物〗 a skewered set of three rice dumplings, each of a different color. Usually, pink, white, and green. Pink is colored with red food coloring, and green is colored with mugwort or food coloring.

さんしょくどん 三食丼 〖食べ物〗 a

three-colored rice bowl. Has three kinds of toppings on the rice. For example, soy-flavored minced meat, scrambled eggs, and a green vegetable such as spinach.

ざんしょみまい 残暑見舞い〖暦・文書〗 a card of late summer greetings. Is sent after August 8. →暑中見舞い

さんしん 三線〖音楽〗 a shamisen in the Okinawa area. Is covered with snake skin. Is also called 'jabisen.'

さんすいが 山水画〖絵画〗 a landscape painting. One of the main categories of East Asian painting. Was introduced into Japan from China around the 7th or 8th century and later developed its own unique features. →山水屏風(さんすいびょうぶ)；水墨画；詩画軸(しが)；瀟湘(しょうしょう)八景

さんずいへん 三水偏〖漢字〗 a left-side radical meaning "water." Is used in kanji such as 池(pond), 汗(sweat), and 沈(to sink).

さんすけ 三助〖風呂〗 a bathhouse attendant. Worked at a public bathhouse in olden times. Boiled water, scrubbed the guest's back, or gave the guest a massage.

さんずのかわ 三途の川〖仏教〗 River of Three Crossings. Is sometimes translated as the River Styx. People cross this river seven days after death. The way of crossing this river varies, depending on the sins committed during one's lifetime.

さんぜいっしんのほう 三世一身法〖法律〗 Law of Three Generations

or a Lifetime. Was issued to encourage new rice cultivation in 723. Allowed a person who irrigated the land and newly cultivated a rice field to possess the field privately for three generations. Allowed a person who newly cultivated a rice field by using existing irrigation to possess the field privately during his lifetime.

さんせき 三蹟〖書道〗 Three Great Calligraphers in the mid-Heian period. Ono no Toufuu, Fujiwara no Sukemasa, and Fujiwara no Yukinari. →三筆

さんぜんいん 三千院〖寺院〗 Sanzen-in Temple. A temple of the Tendai sect, located in Kyoto City. Was founded in between 782 and 806 by the founder of the Tendai sect, SAICHOU. Is now famous for beautiful colored leaves in autumn. Its chief priest used to come from the Imperial family. →天台宗

さんぜんせかい 三千世界〖仏教〗 the entire universe. 'Sanzen' in this word does not mean "three thousand" but "one thousand cubed." A small world spreads around Mt. Sumeru, one thousand small worlds form a middle world, and one thousand middle world form the great world, namely the entire universe. →須弥山(しゅみせん)

さんぞんけいしき 三尊形式〖仏教〗 a triad form of Buddhist images. Consists of a central image and two attendants. The Triad of Amitabha Buddha, the Triad of the Historical

Buddha, the Triad of the Healing Buddha are popular. →阿弥陀三尊；釈迦三尊；薬師三尊

さんだいじつろく 三代実録 〔政治・書名〕 ⇨日本三代実録

さんだいにんじゅつひでんしょ 三大忍術秘伝書 〔忍者〕 the three major ninjutsu books. *True Path of the Ninja* (SHOUNINKI) written in 1681 by Natori Masazumi, *The Book of Ninja* (BANSENSHUUKAI) written in 1676 by Fujibayashi Yasutake, and *The Secret Traditions of the Shinobi* (NINPIDEN) written in 1560 by Hattori Hanzou.

さんだいばなし 三題噺 〔落語〕 an impromptu story containing three topics. A storyteller makes up a story ad lib and performs it, incorporating any three topics offered by the audience.

さんだんきょう 三段峡 〔地名〕 Sandankyou Gorge. Is located in western Hiroshima Pref., along Oota River. From the footpath, visitors can see fresh green foliage in spring and red and yellow leaves in autumn along the cliffs and waterfalls. Can be accessed by bus, with a 70-minute ride from Hiroshima Station on San'yo Shinkansen.

さんだんめ 三段目 〔相撲〕 the third-lowest division in the Grand Sumo Tournament. Next to MAKU-SHITA and above JONIDAN.

さんどう 参道 〔寺院・神社〕 an approach to a Shinto shrine or Buddhist temple. The approach street to a famous shrine or temple is lined with souvenir shops or restaurants.

さんとうきょうでん 山東京伝 〔文芸〕 1761-1816. A popular novelist born in Edo. Wrote yellow-cover books, 'ki-byoushi,' and witty books, 'share-bon.' After being punished in the Kansei Reform in 1791, which restricted publishing, he wrote books for reading, 'yomi-hon.'

さんどうらく 三道楽 〔娯楽〕 ⇨飲む・打つ・買う

さんどがさ 三度笠 〔旅・服飾〕 a flat-top conic hat woven with sedge. Has a chin strap. Was used by a traveler or a courier in the Edo period.

さんないまるやまいせき 三内丸山遺跡 〔史跡〕 Sannai-Maruyama Site. Ruins of a large community in the early to the mid-Joumon period. Is located in western Aomori Pref.

さんにんかんじょ 三人官女 〔暦・玩具〕 dolls of three court ladies-in-waiting. Are displayed on the second tier of a platform for the Girls' Festival. →雛(ひな)祭り

さんにんづかい 三人遣い 〔文楽〕 the puppet operation by three people in bunraku. The main puppeteer, the left-arm puppeteer, and the leg puppeteer operate a puppet in cooperation. →主(おも)遣い；左遣い；足遣い

さんねいざか 産寧坂 〔地名〕 ⇨三年坂

さんねんざか 三年坂 〔地名〕 Sannen Slope. Is located in the Higashiyama area of Kyoto. Traditional shops line the path. Leads to Ninen Slope and is good for strolling. →二年坂

さんのうしんこう 山王信仰 〖神道〗 worship for Ooyamakui no kami. The deity is enshrined as the guardian of Mt. Hiei at Hiyoshi Grand Shrine in Shiga Pref. It is said that a monkey is a messenger of the deity. →日吉大社; 比叡山

さんのうじんじゃ 山王神社 〖神社〗 a Sannou Shrine. There are many Sannou Shrines throughout Japan. All of them enshrine the guardian of Mt. Hiei, Ooyamakui no kami. The head shrine is Hiyoshi Grand Shrine in Shiga Pref. →比叡山; 日吉大社

さんのうまつり 山王祭 〖祭礼〗 Sannou Festival. (**1**) Is held at Hie Shrine in Tokyo in mid-June. One of the two great festivals in Edo. →日枝(ｴﾀﾞ)神社 (**2**) Is held at Hiyoshi Grand Shrine in Shiga Pref. in April. →日吉大社

さんのぜん 三の膳 〖食文化〗 the third-served set of dishes in a full course of traditional Japanese cuisine. Is placed on the right side of the first-served tray. →本膳料理; 一の膳; 二の膳

さんのまる 三の丸 〖建築〗 the outermost section of a castle. Encloses the second outer section. →本丸; 二の丸

さんばいず 三杯酢 〖調味料〗 a mixture of vinegar, soy sauce, and mirin. Is used for vinegared seafood or cucumber.

さんぴつ 三筆 〖書道〗 Three Great Calligraphers in the early Heian period. Emperor Saga, KUUKAI, and Tachibana no Hayanari. →三蹟

さんふどう 三不動 〖仏教・絵画〗 Three Pictures of Immovable Wisdom Kings. Red Immovable Wisdom King at Myouou-in Temple of Mt. Kouya in Wakayama Pref., Blue Immovable Wisdom King at Shouren-in Temple in Kyoto, and Yellow Immovable Wisdom King at Onjou-ji Temple in Shiga Pref. →赤不動; 青不動; 黄不動; 不動明王

さんふらんしすここうわじょうやく サンフランシスコ講和条約 〖戦争〗 San Francisco Peace Treaty, or Treaty of Peace with Japan. Was concluded in San Francisco in 1951 between Japan and the Allied Powers of 48 nations, to officially end World War II, which had actually ended in 1945.

さんぽう 三方 〖宗教・家具〗 a small unlacquered wooden stand with three openings on the support. The three sides of the support have openings. The wood is usually HINOKI cypress. A sacred thing or offering to a deity is placed on it in a ceremony.

さんぽう 三宝 〖仏教〗 the Three Treasures in Buddhism. In Sanskrit, *triratna*. Buddha, dharma (the Law), and sangha (priests).

さんぽうこうじん 三宝荒神 〖仏教・神道〗 a deity of fire and kitchen stoves. Originally a deity to protect three Buddhist treasures: Buddha, dharma (the Law), and sangha (priests).

さんぽうしゅりけん 三方手裏剣 〔忍者〕 a throwing star with three striking points. →手裏剣

さんぼんじめ 三本締め〔精神性〕 a ceremonial 30-time hand-clapping. People clap hands in unison accompanied with key shouting. One round consists of 3-3-3-1 hand-clapping, and three rounds are repeated. →手締め

さんま 秋刀魚 〔動物・食べ物〕 a Pacific saury. *Cololabis saira*. About 30 cm. Often eaten grilled, especially in fall.

さんまい 三昧 **(1)**〔仏教〕 religious concentration. In Sanskrit, *samadhi*. To free the mind from earthly thoughts, be spiritually stable, and focus the mind on the object. **(2)** 〔冠婚葬祭〕 a public cemetery, or a grave.

さんもん 三門〔禅・建築〕 the front gate of a Zen temple. Literally means "three gates." Symbolizes the three stages that a person has to go through to be relieved from spiritual darkness. Is usually two-storied and contains the image of the Historical Buddha upstairs. → 山門

さんもん 山門 〔仏教・建築〕 the front gate of a temple. Literally means "mountain gate" because many temples used to be constructed on a mountain. Zen Buddhism uses a different kanji for 'sanmon.' →三門

さんもんは 山門派 〔仏教〕 the Sanmon school of the Tendai sect. The founder is ENNIN, and the head temple is ENRYAKU-JI Temple in Shiga Pref. They had opposed the Jimon sect at ONJOU-JI Temple since the 10th century. ↔寺門派

さんやく 三役 〔相撲〕 three high ranks in the Grand Sumo Tournament. OOZEKI, SEKIWAKE, and KOMUSUBI.

さんやくそろいぶみ 三役揃い踏み 〔相撲〕 the ritual leg-stomping by three high-ranking wrestlers: OOZEKI, SEKIWAKE, and KOMUSUBI. Is performed in the ring on the last day of the Grand Sumo Tournament.

さんようしんかんせん 山陽新幹線 〔鉄道〕 San'yo Shinkansen. Connects Shin-Osaka Station with Hakata Station in Fukuoka Pref. Started service in 1972. The fastest super express trains are Nozomi and Mizuho. Nozomi goes to Tokyo via Tokaido Shinkansen, and Mizuho to Kagoshima-Chuuou via Kyushu Shinkansen. Each takes 2.5 hours from Shin-Osaka to Hakata. Other express trains are named Hikari, Kodama, and Sakura.

さんようどう 山陽道 **(1)**〔地名〕 an administrative district before the Meiji Restoration in 1868. Consisted of present southern Hyougo, Okayama, Hiroshima, and Yamaguchi Prefs., including islands in the Inland Sea. **(2)**〔交通〕 the main route from Kyoto to Kyushu along the Inland Sea before 1868.

さんりく 三陸〖地名〗 Sanriku Coast. The coast of the Pacific Ocean in Aomori, Iwate, and northern Miyagi Prefs. 'Sanriku' literally means 'three provinces' which refers to the three provinces in the 19th century, each having 'riku' in its name, corresponding to the three prefectures listed above. Thanks to its location on the boundary between the warm and cold currents, a variety of fish and seaweed is produced off the coast. However, because of the irregular coastline called ria, the area has often been severely damaged by tsunami, as in the Meiji-Sanriku Earthquake in 1896 and the Great East Japan Earthquake in 2011.

さんりくてつどう 三陸鉄道 〖鉄道〗 Sanriku Railway. Is abbreviated Santetsu. Was established in 1984 with two lines along the Sanriku Coast in Iwate Pref. The northern line, Kita-Riasu Line, runs from Miyako to Kuji, and the southern line, Minami-Riasu Line, from Sakari to Kamaishi. Both lines were heavily damaged by the Great East Japan Earthquake and tsunami in 2011, but they fully restored operations in 2014. The railway's gradual restoration served as a symbol of the area's recovery.

さんりんぼう 三隣亡〖暦〗 a construction taboo day. It is said that, if a house begins to be built on this day, the house and the three adjacent houses will be destroyed by fire. The day of wild boar in January, April, July, or October, the day of tiger in February, May, August, or November, and the day of horse in March, June, September, or December correspond to it. →十二支

さんろう 参籠〖仏教・神道〗 ⇨御籠（おこも）り

し

しあつ 指圧 〖医療〗 shiatsu, or acupressure. A therapy of pressing particular parts of the body called TSUBO with thumbs and fingers.

しい 椎 〖植物〗 a Japanese chinquapin. *Castanopsis cuspidata*. Is used to cultivate shiitake mushrooms. Its wood is used for architecture, and its acorn is edible.

じいえいちきゅう ＧＨＱ 〖戦争〗 General Headquarters of the Supreme Commander for the Allied Powers (SCAP). Was placed at Yokohama in August 1945 and moved to Tokyo in September. Was dismissed in 1952 when the peace treaty with Japan came into effect.

しいさあ シーサー 〖宗教〗 a pair of pottery guardian dogs in Okinawa. Are placed on the roof or gate pillars of a house.

しいざかな 強肴 〖食文化〗 side dish that accompanies a main dish during the tea ceremony. →懐石料理

しいたけ 椎茸 〖植物・食べ物〗 a shiitake mushroom. *Lentinus edodes*. Grows on a broad-leaved tree such as an oak. The cap is dark brown. The most popular edible mushroom in Japanese cuisine.

しいぼると シーボルト 〖医療〗 Philipp Franz von Siebold. 1796 -1866. A German physician and botanist who joined the Dutch military and served at the trading island of Dejima from 1823-1829, pretending to be a Dutchman. Was permitted by the shogunate to start a school of medicine near Nagasaki. Learned much about the Japanese culture and flora from his students and also advanced medical knowledge in Japan. Was expelled from the country in 1829 for securing a map of Northern Japan, but he continued his study of Asia back in Europe. Returned to Japan in 1859 when the ban on him was lifted. Wrote several works on Japan including *Fauna Japonica* in 5 volumes from 1833 to 1850.

しいぼるとじけん シーボルト事件 〖外交〗 Siebold Incident. Siebold, a German doctor who worked for a Dutch trading company, tried to take Japanese maps out of the country in 1828. He was expelled from the country and was forbidden from re-entry. The astromer Takahashi Kageyasu, who had given the maps, received a death sentence and died in prison. Many other people involved were arrested.

じうた 地唄 〖音楽〗 a traditional song accompanied by SHAMISEN, mainly sung in Kyoto and Osaka. Has been handed down by blind musicians since the 17th century.

じうたい 地謡 〖能〗 a chorus in a Noh or Noh farce. The words describe the scene or the character's psychology.

じぇいあある ＪＲ 〔鉄道〕 JR, or Japan Railway. In 1987, the Japan National Railway (JNR), being in huge debt, was privatized as JR and was divided into seven companies. JR Hokkaido, JR East, JR Central, JR West, JR Shikoku, and JR Kyushu operate passenger trains in each region. All these passenger JR companies except JR Shikoku have at least one Shinkansen line. JR Freight operates the freight trains.

じぇいしいへぼん Ｊ･Ｃ･ヘボン 〔言語〕 ⇨ヘボン

じえいたい 自衛隊 〔軍事〕 the Self-Defense Forces of Japan. Was established in 1954. Belongs to the Ministry of Defense and consists of Ground, Maritime, and Air Self-Defense Forces.

じぇいりいぐ Ｊリーグ 〔スポーツ〕 Japan Professional Football League. Is usually called J. League. Was established in 1991 and consists of three divisions, J1, J2, and J3.

じぇとろ JETRO 〔経済〕 JETRO, or Japan External Trade Organization. Government-related trade organization founded in 1958. Original purpose was to encourage the exporting of goods and services from Japan. In recent years its focus has expanded to promote direct investment in Japan and to assist firms of small and medium size with their export goals. Has headquarters in Tokyo, many other offices in Japan, and offices in over 50 other countries.

じえん 慈円 〔仏教〕 1155-1225. A priest of the Tendai sect born in Kyoto. Wrote *Gukanshou*, literally meaning "Jottings of a Fool," which is a 7-volume work on Japanese history. Is also known as a poet.

しお 塩 〔調味料・宗教〕 salt. Is not only used for cooking but also has been considered to have purifying power. For example, sumo wrestlers sprinkle salt on the ring before a bout, and people sprinkle salt on themselves when coming home from a funeral. 浄めの塩; 盛り塩

しおから 塩辛 〔食べ物〕 salted fish guts. Roes and fish flesh are pickled in salt and fermented by enzymes, resulting in tasty combinations of amino acids. The most popular shiokara is made from squid.

しおこうじ 塩麹 〔調味料〕 salted rice mold. Recently has become popular. Can be used instead of salt in a variety of cooking, for example, to marinate meat, fish, and vegetables before they are fried or grilled.

しおこぶ 塩昆布 〔食べ物〕 thin-stripped or square-cut kelp seasoned with salt or soy sauce. Sometimes contains dried bonito, sesame, or perilla. Eaten with various food like rice balls.

しおざけ 塩鮭 〔食べ物〕 salted salmon. The internal organs have been removed.

しおせんべい 塩煎餅 〔食べ物〕 a rice cracker seasoned with soy

sauce. →煎餅

しおのみさき 潮岬 〔地名〕 Cape Shionomisaki. Is located in Kushimoto Town in southern Wakayama Pref., on the southernmost end of the Main Island of Japan, facing the Pacific Ocean. Is a rich fishing ground, and visitors can enjoy the view of tropical fish from a semi-submarine style boat or a glass window in Kushimoto Marine Park.

しおのみち 塩の道 〔食文化・交通〕 a salt road. Was used for transporting salt from a coastal area to an inland area. Chikuni Kaidou, from Niigata to Nagano Prefs. (120 km), and Akiba Kaidou, from Shizuoka to Nagano Prefs. (200 km), are famous.

しおばらい 塩払い 〔宗教〕 salt sprinkling for purification. When coming home from a funeral, people sprinkle salt on oneself or each other because salt is considered to have purification power.

しおもみ 塩揉み 〔食べ物〕 sprinkling salt on a raw vegetable and fish and rubbing it in. A cooking process to dehydrate ingredients and make them more tasty.

しおやき 塩焼き 〔食べ物〕 grilled fish or meat with salt.

じおりがさ 地降傘 〔忍者〕 a technique of jumping down from a height, using one's clothes as a parachute. It's not clear if the technique had any effect on the jump.

しおりど 枝折り戸 〔建築〕 a simple door made of bamboos or branches. Is used for an entrance to a traditional-style garden.

しか 鹿 〔動物・神道〕 a Japanese deer. *Cervus nippon*. Is regarded as a sacred messenger from the deities at Kasuga Grand Shrine in Nara. On the other hand, wild deer eat farm products throughout Japan, and the total amount of damage reached 6 billion yen as of 2015. Local governments and the Ministry of Agriculture, Forestry and Fisheries now recommend eating its meat, which is sometimes called MOMIJI, autumnal red maples. →春日大社

じかくだいし 慈覚大師 〔仏教〕 ⇨円仁(えんにん)

しがけん 滋賀県 〔都道府県〕 Shiga Pref. Its capital is Ootsu City. Is located in Western Japan, adjacent to Kyoto to the east. Its area is 4,017 km². The capital, Ootsu City, is located in its southwestern part, facing Lake Biwa. Ootsu was Japan's capital from 667 to 672. Its places of scenic beauty are known as Oumi Hakkei. Kouka, a homeland of ninja, is located in southern Shiga. Is known for rice and beef production, but has gradually turned from farmland to an industrial area, particularly in its southern part. Used to be called Oumi.

しがじく 詩画軸 〔絵画〕 a poetry and painting scroll. A Chinese-style poem, related to the subject of the painting, is written on an

India ink painting. Developed in the Muromachi period. Examples include *Newly Risen Moon above the Brushwood Gate* at Fujita Museum.

しかせんべい 鹿煎餅〘動物・食べ物〙 a deer cookie. A tourist can buy and feed it to deer at Nara Park in Nara City.

じかたび 地下足袋〘服飾〙 a pair of rubber-soled and split-toed footgear. Is mainly worn by construction workers.

しがなおや 志賀直哉〘文芸〙 1883 –1971. A novelist born in Miyagi Pref. Started the literary magazine *Shirakaba*, together with Mushanokouji Saneatsu. His works include *A Dark Night's Passing* (AN'YA KOURO) from 1921 to 1937 and *At Kinosaki* (KINOSAKI NITE) in 1917.

しがらきのみや 紫香楽宮 〘政治〙 Shigaraki Palace in present Shiga Pref. Emperor Shoumu resided here in 745 and vowed to construct the Great Buddha.

しがらきやき 信楽焼 〘陶磁器〙 Shigaraki ware. Stoneware produced in southern Shiga Pref. Is said to have originated in 742 with roof tiles by the order of Emperor Shomu. Was most popular in the 16th century with the tea ceremony. Has characteristics of a coarse-grained surface and natural glazing, and is famous for raccoon dog figures. →狸(たぬき)

しがん 此岸〘仏教〙 this world of ignorance, illusion, and anguish.

Literally means "this shore," regarding the world of nirvana as the other shore. ↔彼岸(ひがん)

しかんたざ 只管打坐〘禅〙 single-minded sitting in meditation. A teaching of the Soutou sect to attain enlightenment. To concentrate on just sitting without thinking. →曹洞宗

じき 磁器〘陶磁器〙 porcelain. Is fired at 1,200 or higher degrees Celsius. Is translucent and not water-absorbent. Was introduced from China and began to be made with Arita ware in Japan in the 17th century.

しきい 敷居〘建築〙 **(1)** a threshold. **(2)** a grooved wooden sill for sliding screens. Several sliding screens are inserted and move along the groove. ↔鴨居(かもい)

しきかい 色界〘仏教〙 the world of beings with form. Exists under the world of formless beings, called MUSHIKIKAI. The beings have no desire but are still bound by materialistic forms.

しきがみ 式神〘宗教〙 a servant spirit used by a yin-yang master.

しききん 敷金〘生活〙 rental security deposit. Is paid to the landlord by a tenant in addition to the rent when moving in a house or an apartment. Is paid back if there is no problem with the realty when the tenant moves out. →礼金

じきさん 直参〘武士〙 a direct shogunal vassal or retainer in the Edo period. Those who had the privilege to see the shogun were called HATAMOTO and those who did not have it were called GOKENIN. Received an annual stipend of 10,000 KOKU or less of rice. Those who received more than 10,000 were called DAIMYOU.

しきし 色紙〔精神性〕 an almost square-shaped white cardboard. Its size is about 20 cm in length and 17 cm in width. Is used to write a signature, poetry, or short messages or to draw a picture.

しきしま 四季島〔鉄道〕 Train Suite Shiki-shima. One of Japan's most luxurious cruise trains, operated by JR East. Has 2-day to 4-day courses, starting from Tokyo, going through the points of interest in the Hokkaido, Tohoku, Kantou, and Chuubu regions.

しきしま 敷島〔地名〕 a name for present Nara or for Japan in ancient times.

じきしん 直臣〔武士〕 a direct vassal or retainer in medieval and early modern times.

しきそくぜくう 色即是空〔仏教〕 a term meaning that all materialistic objects are nothing but emptiness. As well, everything in the universe exists only in relation to everything else, and its essence is vanity. The term is included in the Heart Sutra. →般若心経；空即是色(くうそくぜしき)

しきていさんば 式亭三馬 〔文芸〕 1776-1822. A popular novelist born in Edo. His works include *The Bathhouse of the Floating World* (Ukiyo-buro) and *The Barbershop of the Floating World* (Ukiyo-doko).

じきどう 食堂〔仏教・建築〕 the dining hall of a Buddhist temple. Although it was one of the major buildings of an ancient temple, monks came to have meals in another building, KURI, in and after medieval times.

しきねんせんぐう 式年遷宮 〔神社・建築〕 periodic rebuilding of a Shinto shrine. After rebuilding of the shrine, the sacred object is moved into the new building. Its fundamental principle is revival of a deity. The most famous example is one held at the Ise Shrine every 20 years. →伊勢神宮

しきのう 式能〔能〕 a ceremonial Noh play. Was performed in an auspicious event for the shogunate.

しきぶとん 敷布団〔家具〕 a bottom futon. Is spread on the tatami floor, and the sleeper lies on it. ↔掛布団

しきみ 樒 〔植物・冠婚葬祭〕 a Japanese anise tree. *Illicium anisatum*. Is offered to the spirit of the departed in a funeral. Its fruits are poisonous.

しぎやき 鴫焼き〔食べ物〕 ⇨茄子田楽(なすでんがく)

じきゃく 次客〔茶道〕 the second guest at a tea ceremony. Enters the tea room next to the main guest.

しきょう 四鏡〔文芸〕 the Four Mirrors. The generic term for four historical stories whose names include "mirror." →今鏡；大鏡；増鏡；水鏡

しぎょうしき 始業式〖教育〗 term-opening ceremony. Is held by most elementary and secondary schools on the first day of each academic term. Usually in early April for the spring term, in late August for the fall semester, and in early January for the winter term.

しきり 仕切り〖相撲〗 crouching for the initial charge. Wrestlers touch the ground with their fists in front of the center line on their side. During 'shikiri,' wrestlers adjust breathing, think over tactics, and glare fiercely at the opponent.

しぎん 詩吟〖文芸・音楽〗 song-like recitation of a Chinese-style poem in a unique Japanese way. Is said to have started at a school called SHOUHEIKOU in Edo in the 19th century.

じぐち 地口〖落語〗 a word play, mainly based in a proverb.

しぐれ 時雨〖気象〗 a shower in early winter.

しぐれに 時雨煮〖食べ物〗 seafood or beef preserves made with mirin, ginger, and soy sauce.

しこ 四股〖相撲〗 stomping as warm-up before a bout. Also has ritual meaning to suppress evil spirits. A wrestler laterally raises his leg high and stomps it on the ground. He repeats the same motion with the other leg.

しごう 諡号〖言語〗 a posthumous name for an Emperor, a nobleman, or a priest.

じごく 地獄〖仏教〗 **(1)** a hell. In Sanskrit, *naraka*. The soul of a dead person who has done evil during his or her lifetime goes down to one of the 136 hells, according to his or her sin. Souls in a hell keep suffering from various torments. ↔ 極楽 **(2)** the Realm of Hells in reincarnation. →六道(ろくどう); 輪廻(りんね)

しこくさぶろう 四国三郎〖河川〗 a personified name of the Yoshino River. 'Saburou' literally means the third son. →吉野川

しこくさんち 四国山地〖地名〗 the Shikoku Mountains. Is the backbone mountain range of Shikoku. Starting from the west of Tokushima Pref., it runs on the border between Ehime and Kouchi Prefs. The highest peak is Mt. Ishizuchi.

しこくちほう 四国地方〖地名〗 the Shikoku region. Consists of Tokushima, Kagawa, Ehime, and Kouchi Prefs. in Western Japan. 18,298 km^2 in area. The northern prefectures, Kagawa and Ehime, have a warm and dry climate, but the other two, Tokushima and Kouchi, have an even warmer and rainy climate, and are often hit by a typhoon.

じこくてん 持国天〖仏教〗 one of the Four Guardian Kings, *Dhrtarastra*. He often brings a sword and defends the east.

しこくはちじゅうはっかしょ 四国八十八カ所〖仏教・旅〗 Eighty-eight Holy Places in Shikoku. Pilgrimage to the holy places is called HENRO, which began around the 12th century and was popular in the Edo period. It is said that a priest, KUUKAI, visited those holy places for ascetic practices. Most of them are along the seashore.

じごくへん 地獄変 〖文芸・作品〗 *Hell Screen*. A novel published in 1918 by AKUTAGAWA RYUUNOSUKE. An archduke orders a painter to paint the folding hell screen, and the painter lets his daughter be burned to death before his eyes.

しこたんとう 色丹島 〖島名〗 Shikotan Island. Is located northward off Hokkaido. Its area is 255 km^2. Has been under Russian rule since 1945.

しこつこ 支笏湖 〖湖沼〗 Lake Shikotsu. A caldera lake in southwestern Hokkaido, to the south of Sapporo City. Its surface area is 78.4 km^2, and its maximum depth is 363 m, which makes it the second deepest lake in Japan, after Lake Tazawa in Akita Pref. Is also Japan's northernmost ice-free lake. Can be accessed by bus from New Chitose Airport, with a 50-minute ride.

しごとおさめ 仕事納め 〖ビジネス〗 the last working day in a year. Around December 29 in many companies.

しごとはじめ 仕事始め 〖ビジネス〗 the first working day in a year. Around January 4 in many companies.

しこな 四股名 〖相撲〗 the ring name of a professional sumo wrestler.

しこみ 仕込み 〖酒〗 preparation for brewing sake. Water, steamed rice, molded rice called KOUJI, and yeast are put in a vat for preparation.

しこみづえ 仕込み杖 〖武器〗 a sword stick. A sword is hidden in the guise of a stick.

しころ しころ 〖忍者〗 a pointed hand saw to cut through metal or wood.

しころ 錏 〖武器〗 a neck guard. Layered leather strips or metal plates are attached to the back and sides of a helmet.

じざいかぎ 自在鉤 〖家具〗 an adjustable pot hanger. Is hung from the ceiling over the sunken hearth in the floor, called IRORI.

しざいちょう 資材帳 〖寺院〗 an inventory of property of a Buddhist temple.

じざけ 地酒 〖酒〗 local sake. Sake brewed in local areas except Nada in Koube and Fushimi in Kyoto, where several large sake breweries are based.

じざむらい 地侍 〖武士〗 a powerful local samurai who also engaged in agriculture in medieval times.

しし 志士 〖武士〗 an ambitious samurai who tries to devote himself to the nation. Usually refers to a samurai who has respect for the Emperor at the end of the Edo period.

しし 獅子 〖動物〗 a lion. Though a wild lion does not inhabit Japan, an imaginary creature similar to a lion was painted in pictures or curved as guardians of a Shinto shrine.

ししおどし 鹿威し 〘庭園〙 a deer-scarer. Makes clapping sound at few-minute intervals to drive away birds and animals. Water flows into a short bamboo cylinder, which slants downward when being filled. The water flows out, which makes a clapping sound by striking a stone underneath when turning back.

ししとう 獅子唐 〘調味料〙 a small sweet green pepper. *Capsicum annuum* var. *angulosum*. Eaten stir-fried, simmered, or grilled.

ししなべ 猪鍋 〘食べ物〙 ⇨牡丹(ぼたん)鍋

ししまい 獅子舞い 〘宗教〙 a lion dance. One person wears the lion head, and the other puts on a curtain that is supposed to resemble a lion's body. Is performed at a festival or in the New Year's holidays.

しじみ 蜆 〘食べ物・動物〙 a Japanese freshwater clam, or a Japanese basket clam. *Corbiculidae*. The length of the shell is about 4 cm. Is put into miso soup.

じしゃ 寺社 〘寺院・神社〙 Buddhist temples and Shinto shrines. On a map, a temple is marked by the ancient swastika symbol, called MANJI, while a shrine is marked by a TORII.

じしゃぶぎょう 寺社奉行 〘官位・宗教〙 a political administrator over temples and shrines. Started in the Kamakura period. →奉行

ししゃも 柳葉魚 〘食べ物・魚〙 a surf smelt. *Spirinchus lanceolatus*. About 15 cm long. Eaten dried and grilled. One that has roe inside is popular.

じじゅう 時宗 〘仏教〙 the Ji sect of Pure Land Buddhism. Was founded by IPPEN in the Kamakura period. The head temple is SHOUJOUKOU-JI Temple in Kanagawa Pref.

しじゅうくにち 四十九日 〘仏教〙 the forty-ninth day after one's death. A memorial service is held on that day. In Japanese Buddhism, it is said that forty-nine days are needed after the death in this world before one would be reborn in the next world. Is also called 'manchuu'in.' →忌(き)明け

しじゅうしちし 四十七士 〘武士〙 ⇨赤穂浪士

しじゅく 私塾 〘教育〙 a private school. This term often refers to private schools established by scholars in early modern to modern ages, distinguished from official schools of the shogunate or feudal domains. →昌平坂学問所；藩校

しじゅほうしょう 紫綬褒章 〘行政〙 the Medal with Purple Ribbon. Is "awarded to individuals who have contributed to academic and artistic developments, improvements and accomplishments," says the Cabinet Office. →褒章

じしょうじ 慈照寺 〘寺院〙 Jishou-ji Temple. The official name of GINKAKU-JI, located in Kyoto. ASHIKAGA YOSHIMASA built the two-story pavilion and intended to cover it with silver leaf, but the project remained unfinished because of his death. Now a subsidiary temple of SHOUKOKU-JI Temple.

ししょごきょう 四書五経 〖人文学〗 Four Books and Five Classics. Authoritative works of Confucianism written in China before 300 B.C. The Four Books are *Great Learning*, *Doctrine of the Mean*, *Analects of Confucius*, and *Mencius*. The Five Classics are *Book of Divination*, *Book of Poetry*, *Book of Historical Documents*, *Book of Rites*, and *Spring and Autumn Annals*. Were used as textbooks at schools in the Edo period.

しじん 四神 〖宗教〗 animal deities symbolizing four directions. The blue dragon for the east, the white tiger for the west, the red phoenix for the south, and the black turtle-and-snake for the north. This idea was introduced from China in ancient times and is seen in many aspects of Japanese culture. →青竜(せいりゅう); 白虎(びゃっこ); 朱雀(すざく); 玄武(げんぶ)

じしん 地震 〖自然〗 an earthquake. Japan, located in the circum-Pacific seismic zone, has repeatedly experienced big earthquakes such as the Great Kanto Earthquake in 1923, the Great Hanshin and Awaji Earthquake in 1995, and the Great East Japan Earthquake in 2011. The seismic intensity called SHINDO is used to show the scale of an earthquake in addition to magnitude.

じしんかみなりかじおやじ 地震、雷、火事、親父 〖精神性〗 earthquake, thunder, fire, and father. A phrase used to refer to frightening things in olden days.

ししんでん 紫宸殿 〖天皇・建築〗 the Hall for Imperial Ceremonies. Is located in the Imperial Palace and faces south. The current building was built in 1855.

じしんばん 自身番 〖犯罪〗 a guard for crime and fire prevention. Townspeople took turns at this task during the Edo period.

じす JIS 〖科学技術〗 ⇨日本工業規格

しすいず 四睡図 〖絵画〗 The Four Sleepers. Feng-kan, Han-shan, and Shi-de are having a nap with a tiger. A popular theme among Zen pictures. The three people are legendary priests in the Tang period (618–907) of China. An example is seen at the Tokyo National Museum. →寒山拾得(かんざんじっとく)

しずおかけん 静岡県 〖都道府県〗 Shizuoka Pref. Is located in central Japan, facing the Pacific Ocean. Is 7,777 km^2 in area. The capital is Shizuoka City. The Izu Peninsula and Cape Omae-zaki protrude into the Pacific Ocean. Large rivers such as the Abe River, the Ooi River, and the Tenryuu River flow from the Akaishi Mountains in its northern part, but the Fuji River flows from the foot of Mt. Fuji in its northeastern part. Thanks to the warm and wet climate, green tea leaves and mandarin oranges are produced in abundance. Eels are cultivated in Lake Hamana. Mt. Fuji and the pine-covered area called Miho-no-matsubara were designated a World Heritage Site in 2013. Used to be called Izu, Suruga, and Tootoumi.

しずおかし 静岡市〖地名〗 Shizuoka City. An ordinance-designated city and the capital of Shizuoka Pref. Is located in its central part, facing Suruga Bay. Used to be called Sunpu. Famous for an archaeological site, Toro ruins.

しずがたけ 賤ヶ岳〖山岳〗 Mt. Shizu-ga-take. Is located in Nagahama City, Shiga Pref., to the north of Lake Biwa. Is 421 m high. Is famous for the Battle of Shizuga-take in 1583, where TOYOTOMI HIDEYOSHI defeated Shibata Katsuie. Hideyoshi's seven generals earned great fame and honor because of the victory, and that came to be called the "Seven Spears of Shizuga-take." Can be accessed by bus from JR Kinomoto Station, with a 6-minute ride.

しせいせいど 氏姓制度〖行政〗 the ancient political system that ranked clans (UJI) by titles (KABANE). Was abolished by the Taika Reform of 645.

じせいのく 辞世の句〖文芸〗 a rhyming poem as a swansong by a person in history. Written as haiku, tanka, or other forms.

しせき 史跡〖法律〗 a Historic Site. As of August 1, 2016, the Agency for Cultural Affairs designated 1,760 such sites. They include shell mounds, tumuli, sites of fortified capitals, sites of forts or castles, and monumental houses of high historical or scientific value.

しせきめいしょうてんねんきねんぶつ 史跡名勝天然記念物〖法律〗 Historic Sites, Places of Scenic Beauty, and Natural Monuments. Are designated based on the Law for the Protection of Cultural Properties.

しそ 紫蘇〖調味料・植物〗 a beefsteak plant. *Perilla frutescens* var. *crispa*. Is edible, is used to dye food, and is used as a condiment or in traditional Chinese medicine.

じぞうぼさつ 地蔵菩薩〖仏教〗 Jizou Bodhisattva, or the Bodhisattva of Earth Repository, or the Bodhisattva of Earth Womb. *Ksitigarbha*. Has been saving all living things in this world since the death of the Historical Buddha and will do so until the advent of the Future Buddha. Is depicted as a monk, often with a jingling rod in the right hand and a wish-fulfilling jewel in the left hand. → 錫杖(しゃくじょう); 如意宝珠 (にょいほうじゅ); 六地蔵; 賽(さい)の河原; 弥勒(みろく)如来

しぞく 士族〖政治〗 a family who used to be members of the samurai class before the Meiji Restoration. This title was abolished after World War II.

じそんいん 慈尊院 〔寺院〕 Jison-in Temple. Affiliated with the Shingon sect. Is located in northern Wakayama Pref. When founding the Kongoubu-ji Temple at Mt. Kouya in 816, KUUKAI placed an office at the foot of the mountain, which later became Jison-in. Its statue of Maitreya Bodhisattva is a National Treasure.

じだいげき 時代劇〔娯楽〕 a historical TV drama. Its story is usually fictional, and the background is the Edo period.

じだいしょうせつ 時代小説 〔文芸〕 a period novel. Fictionally describes ordinary people, including samurai, in the Edo period, but rarely depicts an actual historical event. →歴史小説

じだいまつり 時代祭り 〔祭礼〕 Festival of Ages. Is held at the Heian Shrine in Kyoto on October 22. Started in 1895 when the Heian Shrine was founded to celebrate the 1,100th anniversary of Kyoto as capital. Famous for the procession in which people wear the costume of each period from Heian to Meiji.

じだいもの 時代物 〔浄瑠璃・歌舞伎〕 a historical drama in kabuki. Depicts social life of Court nobles, priests, or warriors in and before the Edo period. A drama faithful to the historical fact is called KATSURE-KIMONO. Is more stylized compared to SEWAMONO, a social or domestic drama.

したおび 下帯〔服飾〕 ⇨ふんどし(1)

したきりすずめ 舌切り雀 〔民話〕 "Tongue-Cut Sparrow." A folk tale. An honest old man kept a sparrow, but the sparrow had its tongue cut by a dishonest old woman when it pecked at her starch. Later, the old man was rewarded while the old woman was punished.

したくべや 支度部屋 〔相撲〕 a dressing room. A wrestler warms up here before a bout.

しだし 仕出し 〔食文化・ビジネス〕 catering of traditional course cuisine. Food for each person is often packed individually in a wooden box. →出前

したじき 下敷き 〔書道〕 a felt sheet. Is placed under paper when a person writes characters on it with a brush and India ink.

しだしべんとう 仕出し弁当〔食文化〕 catered box lunch. Usually includes traditional cuisine.

したっぴき 下っ引き 〔犯罪〕 an assistant to a low-ranking criminal investigator, called MEAKASHI, in the Edo period.

したてなげ 下手投げ〔相撲〕 an underarm throw. A sumo technique of throwing the opponent by grasping his belt under his arm.

したまえ 下前〔服飾〕 the inner fold of a kimono.

したまち 下町 〔地名〕 a lowland area in a large city. Was an industrial area in the Edo period, where businessmen and craftsmen lived. Corresponds to the eastern part of Tokyo city proper such as Asakusa,

Kanda, and Fukagawa.

しだれざくら 枝垂桜 〖植物〗 a weeping cherry tree. *Prunus pendula*. Bears pink flowers in March.

しだれやなぎ 枝垂柳 〖植物〗 a weeping willow. *Salix babylonica*. Was introduced from China in ancient times.

しちごさん 七五三 〖通過儀礼〗 an event to celebrate the growth of children. Literally means "seven, five, three." When a boy is three or five years old and when a girl is three or seven years old, the parents dress them up and take them to a local Shinto shrine for blessing around November 15th.

しちごんぜっく 七言絶句 〖文芸〗 a Chinese-style classic poem, made up of four lines with seven characters.

しちごんりっし 七言律詩 〖文芸〗 a Chinese-style classic poem, made up of eight lines with seven characters.

しちしとう 七支刀 〖考古〗 the seven-branched sword. Has been handed down at Isonokami Jingu Shrine in Nara Pref. The inscription says that it was made in Paekche in the 4th century.

しちどうがらん 七堂伽藍 〖仏教・建築〗 the seven major buildings of a Buddhist temple. Originally included a pagoda, main hall, lecture hall, belfry, storehouse for scriptures, residential building for monks, and dining hall. The buildings vary depending on the era or sect. →塔；

金堂；講堂；経蔵；鐘楼(しょうろう)；僧坊；食堂(じきどう)

しちにんのさむらい 七人の侍 〖映画・作品〗 *Seven Samurai*. A samurai drama directed by Kurosawa Akira in 1954. Seven samurai protected a farm village from bandits, though four of them were killed in the battle with the bandits.

しちふくじん 七福神 〖宗教〗 the Seven Deities of Good Fortune. This group, including one female and six male deities, is worshipped in folklore, but their origins are related to Buddhism, Taoism, and Shintoism. The group is often depicted as being on a treasure ship. It is said that placing the deities' picture under one's pillow brings a pleasant first dream on the night of January 1st or 2nd. →大黒天；恵比須(えびす)；毘沙門(びしゃもん)天；弁財天；福禄寿(ふくろくじゅ)；寿(じゅ)老人；布袋(ほてい)；初夢；宝船

しちほうで 七方出 〖忍者〗 seven ways of a ninja disguising himself or herself. They include warriors, artisans, theatrical artists, merchants, street performers, monks, and mendicant Zen priests.

しちみとうがらし 七味唐辛子 〖調味料〗 seven-spice chili pepper. Includes raw hot pepper, prickly ash, Chinese pepper, dried citrus peel, black sesame, hemp seeds, and poppy seeds. The seven spices vary from area to area.

しちや 七夜 〖通過儀礼〗 the seventh night after a childbirth. People celebrate it and sometimes name the newborn baby on this day.

しちりき 篳篥〔音楽〕 ⇨篳篥(ひちりき)

しちりのわたし 七里の渡し〔交通〕 about 30 km ferry between present Nagoya and Kuwana in present Mie Pref. The only marine route on the TOUKAIDOU Highway in the Edo period.

しちりん 七輪〔食文化〕 a portable clay stove. Food is broiled over a burning charcoal. Its name, literally meaning "seven rin," indicates its portability. →厘

じちんさい 地鎮祭〔建築・神道〕 a Shinto ceremony to pacify the ground spirit. Is conducted before starting a construction project, even today.

じついん 実印〔生活〕 a registered seal. Is used on a significant occasion. A person can register only one specific seal with his or her municipal government. ↔認印 →印鑑

じっかん 十干〔干支〕 ten trunks. Each trunk represents a year or day of a traditional calendar, by being combined with the Chinese zodiac signs, juunishi. The number, ten, is the result of multiplying the two principles, yin and yang, by the five elements: wood, fire, earth, metal, and water. For example, the first trunk, kinoe, means "yang of wood," because 'ki' means "wood," 'e' means "elder brother," which is considered "yang," and 'no' between 'ki' and 'e' is a function

word. Although there are 120 combinations of 'jikkan' with 'juunishi,' half of them are allotted to the 60-year cycles, and the rest are not related to years. For example, 2004, 1944, and 1884 were all the year of 甲申 kinoe saru, while there is no year of 甲丑 kinoe ushi. Thus any and all years have the combination of 'jikkan' and 'juunishi.' →甲(きのえ); 乙(きのと); 丙(ひのえ); 丁(ひのと); 戊(つちのえ); 己(つちのと); 庚(かのえ); 辛(かのと); 壬(みずのえ); 癸(みずのと); 陰陽五行説; 還暦

しっき 漆器〔漆器〕 lacquerware or japan. Is made of wood, bamboo, or paper varnished with lacquer. A soup bowl or chopsticks are sometimes lacquered.

しっけん 執権〔武士・官位〕 a shogunal regent in the Kamakura period. Houjou Tokimasa, who was the father-in-law of MINAMOTO NO YORITOMO, first took the position in 1203. After that time, a member of the Houjou clan exclusively possessed the post and held the actual political power.

じつごと 実事〔歌舞伎〕 **(1)** a role of a hero who has the ability to judge, a strong sense of justice, and an excellent personality. **(2)** an action to realistically express the role.

しつしつざ 瑟瑟座〔仏教・美術〕 an abstracted rock pedestal. Is used for the image of the Immovable Wisdom King (FUDOU MYOUOU). Examples include the image at Tou-ji Temple in Kyoto. →台座

じって 十手〔武器〕 a forked iron

truncheon about 18 inches long. An Edo-period police officer used it to subdue criminals and to protect himself from sword attack.

しっぱく 漆箔 〖彫刻〗 the technique of gilding over lacquer on a sculpture. Very common among Buddhist sculptures.

じっぺんしゃいっく 十返舎一九 〖文芸〗 1765-1831. A popular novelist born in present Shizuoka Pref. Wrote yellow-cover books, KI-BYOUSHI, and humorous books, KOK-KEI-BON. His works include *Shank's Mare*. →東海道中膝栗毛

しっぽうやき 七宝焼き 〖陶磁器〗 cloissone, or enamel work on a metal backing.

しっぽくりょうり 卓袱料理 〖食べ物〗 Japanized Chinese or Western cuisine. The dishes are served in large plates, and diners help themselves. Is a local specialty of Nagasaki City because Nagasaki was the only place trading with China and the Netherlands in the Edo period, thus this mixed-style cuisine.

じつようえいごぎのうけんてい 実用英語技能検定 〖言語〗 Test in Practical English Proficiency. There are seven grades in different levels. The highest level is the first grade, and the lowest the fifth grade, with two pre-stages.

しつれいします 失礼します 〖言語〗 literally means "I'll be rude." Is uttered to mean "Excuse me," "Good-bye," "I'll come in," or "Let me do it."

して 仕手 〖能・狂言〗 (**1**) a protagonist, or a main character in a Noh play. Wears a special mask called NOUMEN, and plays the leading role, which is often a supernatural being such as a deity or ghost. (**2**) a main character in a Noh farce.

しで 紙垂 〖神道〗 a zigzag-shaped white paper strip. Is suspended from a sacred rice rope, SHIMENAWA, or attached to a sprig of holly wood, SAKAKI, as an offering to a god. It is said that its zigzag shape comes from lightning. →玉串

してつ 私鉄 〖交通〗 a private railway company. Refers to all the railway companies in Japan except JR and municipally owned subway companies. Many of them adopt the through-line service with each other. Sixteen of them are called 'oote shitetsu,' having a longer railway system, and carrying more passengers in a mega city. →相互乗り入れ

してばしら 仕手柱 〖能〗 the rear-left pillar on a Noh stage.

じてん 地天 〖仏教〗 Deva of Earth. *Prthivi*. One of the Twelve Devas. Guards the downward direction. Is said to have appeared from the earth as a witness when the Historical Buddha attained enlightenment. →十二天

してんのう 四天王 〖仏教〗 the Four Guardian Kings. JIKOKU-TEN, ZOUCHOU-TEN, KOUMOKU-TEN, and TAMON-TEN defend the east, south, west, and north, respectively.

してんのうじ　四天王寺　〚寺院〛 Shitennou-ji Temple. Is located in Osaka. Although all buildings in the precinct have been rebuilt, it is said that this is the oldest Buddhist temple in Japan, which Prince Shoutoku founded in 593.

じとう　地頭　〚武士・官位〛 a local administrator under the Kamakura shogunate. Administrated the land and collected taxes.

じとうてんのう　持統天皇　〚天皇〛 Empress Jitou. 645-702. The 41st, on the throne from 686 to 698. The second princess of Emperor Tenji, and the wife of Emperor Tenmu. Relocated the capital to Fujiwara-kyou in present Nara Pref.

しとみど　蔀戸　〚建築〛 a rotating wooden shutter with lattice. There are one-panel and two-panel types. The former is rotated up to the horizontal position when opened. The upper part of the latter is opened in the same way as the former, and the lower part can be removed.

じどり　地鶏　〚動物・食べ物〛 a chicken native to a local area. However, most 'jidori' are actually hybrids. Examples are Nagoya cochin and Hinai jidori.

しない　竹刀　〚剣術〛 a bamboo sword. Is made of four strips of bamboo, bound with leather. The string stretched on one side is considered as the back of the sword.

しなちく　支那竹　〚食べ物〛 ⇨メンマ

しなの　信濃　〚旧国名〛 the old name of Nagano Pref.

しなのがわ　信濃川　〚河川〛 the Shinano River. Flows from Mt. Kobushi in eastern Nagano Pref. into the Sea of Japan in Niigata City. Its upper reaches in Nagano Pref. are called the Chikuma River. Is 367 km long from the source of the Chikuma River, and the longest in Japan. The Chikuma and Sai Rivers meet on the plain of Kawanaka-jima near Nagano City, where two rival feudal lords, Takeda Shingen and Uesugi Kenshin, fought in the mid-16th century. In 1922, the Ookouzu Diversion Channel was completed, to save the Niigata Plains from floods. After World War II, many dams and hydroelectric power stations were built to supply electricity to the Kantou region.

しなんばん　指南番　〚武士〛 a swordsmanship instructor for the shogunate or a feudal domain in the Edo period.

しにせ　老舗　〚ビジネス〛 a shop, restaurant, inn, or company with a long tradition. There are more than 30,000 businesses with the history of 100 years or longer in Japan.

じぬしがみ　地主神　〚神道〛 the guardian deity of land or a mansion. Sometimes family ancestors are worshipped as jinushi-gami.

しのうこうしょう　士農工商　〚政治・職業〛 four hierarchical classes in the Edo period. Samurai, 'shi,' were ranked at the top; followed by farmers, 'nou,' as the second;

artisans, 'kou,' as the third; and merchants, 'shou,' at the bottom. In reality, however, merchants had the strongest economic power, especially toward the end of the period.

しのぎ 鎬〖武術〗 a low ridge on the side of a sword blade. Exists on either side.

しのび 忍び〖忍者〗 ⇨忍者

しのびあし 忍び足〖忍者〗 a silent walking method. To walk by raising the foot as if the walker draws the foot upward ('nukiashi') and by putting it down softly ('sashiashi') so that the little toe could touch the floor first.

しのびがえし 忍び返し〖忍者・建築〗 spikes on the top end of a wall to prevent burglars or ninja from breaking into a house.

しのびがたな 忍び刀〖忍者〗 a ninja sword. Is not curved, different from an ordinary samurai sword, and a little shorter than an ordinary sword. The handguard called TSUBA is large enough to serve as a foot tread when placing the sword upright against the wall and climbing it.

しのびくまで 忍び熊手〖忍者〗 an extendable rake. Consists of a grappling hook and telescoping bamboo pieces.

しのびしょうぞく 忍び装束〖忍者〗 ninja costume. Though many people imagine it was black, it actually was not. Its main feature, paradoxically, was that it had no specific features, so that it would not draw attention to itself.

しのびづつ 忍び筒〖忍者〗 a bamboo cylinder for eavesdropping. A ninja eavesdropped on a conversation by touching the cylinder onto the ceiling when he or she was in a loft or by touching it on the wall when he or she was in the next room.

しのびひでん 忍秘伝〖忍者〗 ⇨忍秘伝(ひでん)

しのびろくぐ 忍び六具〖忍者〗 six tools for ninja. They included a rope with a hook, a braided hat, a hand towel, medicine, a live charcoal, and writing utensils.

しのぶえ 篠笛〖音楽〗 a bamboo flute. Has 7 finger holes.

しのやき 志野焼〖陶磁器〗 Shino ware. White-glazed pottery produced in present Gifu Pref. in the late 16 century.

しばいぬ 柴犬〖動物〗 Shiba Inu. A small-sized brown dog native to Japan. Was originally kept for hunting, but now is used as a watchdog or as a pet.

しばがき 柴垣〖建築〗 a brushwood fence.

しばづけ 柴漬け〖食べ物〗 chopped vegetables pickled in salt with red leaves of perilla. Eaten mainly in summer. Summer vegetables such as cucumbers and eggplants are used as ingredients. Originally a specialty of Kyoto.

しばりょうたろう 司馬遼太郎〖文芸〗 1923-1996. A historical novelist born in Osaka. Wrote many historical novels and essays, based on his unique historical view. His works include *Ryoma Goes His Way* in 1966, *Last Shogun: the Life of Tokugawa Yoshinobu* in 1967, *Clouds above the Hill* in 1973, and *Kukai the Universal—Scenes from His Life* in 1975.

しはん 師範〚職業〛 an instructor of swordsmanship, arts, or study.

しはんだい 師範代〚職業〛 an assistant instructor of swordsmanship, arts, or study.

しはんとき 四半刻〚時刻〛 about half an hour. Literally means "a quarter of one TOKI," which was a unit to count time in olden times. One 'toki' was one sixth of the duration from sunrise to sunset.

しび 鴟尾〚仏教・建築〛 a ridge-end ornament for an ancient palace or temple building. Is shaped like a bird's tail or a shoe. Is said to have developed to SHACHIHOKO or ONIGAWARA in later ages.

じひ 慈悲〚仏教〛 compassion and mercy of Buddha or Bodhisattva toward living things. Is similar to supreme friendship.

しぶがき 渋柿〚植物〛 an astringent persimmon. Eaten dried.

しふく 仕覆〚茶道〛 a pouch for a tea caddy called CHAIRE. Is made of silk brocade or satin cloth.

じぶくろ 地袋〚建築〛 a small storage space below different-levelled shelves. Has sliding doors and a flat top. ↔天袋 →違い棚

しぶさわえいいち 渋沢栄一〚経済〛

1840-1931. A samurai and merchant born in present Saitama Pref. Although he was a shogunal vassal during the Edo period, he became a merchant in the Meiji period and founded many companies, which form the core of the Japanese economy such as the current Mizuho Bank, Kirin Brewery, Imperial Hotel, and Tokyo Marine & Nichido Fire.

じぶに 治部煮〚食べ物〛 duck meat simmered in soy sauce and broth soup. Is added to with vegetables and tastes creamy. A specialty of Kanazawa, Ishikawa Pref.

じぶり ジブリ〚アニメ〛 ⇨スタジオジブリ

しべりあよくりゅう シベリア抑留〚外交〛 detention in Siberia. Japanese captives caught by the Soviet Union at the end of World War II were forced to work in Siberia until 1950. About 62,000 died among 640,000 including civilians.

じほう 次鋒〚武術〛 the second fighter in a five-member team competition of martial arts such as judo. →先鋒；中堅；副将；大将

しほうしゅりけん 四方手裏剣〚忍者〛 a throwing star with four striking points. →手裏剣

しほうはい 四方拝〚天皇〛 a ritual of praying towards the four directions. Is performed at dawn on January 1 by the Emperor, for universal peace and an abundant crop.

しぼりぞめ 絞り染め〚服飾〛 tie-dyeing. When dyeing, some parts of the cloth are tied up with a thread. The tied-up parts are not dyed and become patterns.

しぼりたて 絞りたて〖酒〗 freshly pressed sake after brewing. Is not pasteurized and is put on the market from winter to early spring.

しほん 紙本〖絵画・書道〗 painting or writing on paper. ↔絹本(けん)

しまあじ 縞鯵〖食べ物・魚〗 a white trevally, or a striped yellow jack. *Pseudocaranx dentex*. About 1 m long. Is tasty in summer and eaten as suhi or sashimi.

しまい 仕舞〖能〗 a dance performed without a mask or elaborate costume, by a protagonist called SHITE. Is only accompanied by songs, not by instruments.

しまざきとうそん 島崎藤村〖文芸〗 1872-1943. A poet and novelist born in Gifu Pref. Started as a poet by publishing a collection of poems in 1897 and later published novels such as *The Broken Commandment* and *Before the Dawn*. →破戒; 夜明け前

しまだまげ 島田髷〖髪〗 a traditional hairstyle for an unmarried woman. Was popular in the Edo period.

しまづし 島津氏〖政治〗 the Shimadu clan. Had governed southern Kyushu since the 12th century and led the Meiji Restoration in the 19th century.

しまながし 島流し〖犯罪・行政〗 an exile, or a banishment, to an island. Even some Emperors were exiled in Japanese history.

しまなみかいどう しまなみ海道 〖交通〗 Shimanami Expressway. 'Kaidou' literally means "sea road." Was opened in 1999 and is 59.4 km long. Connects Onomichi, Hiroshima Pref. with Imabari, Ehime Pref. through nine bridges linking six islands between Honshuu and Shikoku. One of the three routes that connect Japan's main islands, Honshuu and Shikoku. Is popular among cyclists as the only route where one can cross the Inland Sea by bicycle.

しまねけん 島根県 〖都道府県〗 Shimane Pref. Its capital is Matsue City. Is located in Western Japan, facing the Sea of Japan. Its area is 6,708 km^2. Famous for freshwater clam, snow crab, and yellowtail production. In the Sea of Japan are the Oki Islands and Take-shima Island. The Iwami Ginzan Silver Mine, located in its central part, produced high-quality silver from the 16th to the early 20th centuries. Major locations in Japanese mythology are the Izumo Grand Shrine, in its northeastern part, as well as areas around the shrine. Used to be called Izumo, Iwami, and Oki.

しまばらのらん 島原の乱 〖戦争〗 Shimabara Uprising. About 38,000 peasants and Christians rose up, led by Amakusa Shirou, against the feudal lords in present Nagasaki and Kumamoto Prefs. in 1637. Was suppressed by the Tokugawa shogunate in 1638.

しまへび 縞蛇〚動物〛 a Japanese four-lined rat snake, or a Japanese striped snake. *Elaphe quadrivirgata*. About 1 m long. Native to Japan.

しまんとがわ 四万十川〚河川〛 the Shimanto River. Flows in southern Kouchi Pref., from the Shikoku Mountains, meandering through the woods, into the Pacific Ocean in Shimanto City. Is 196 km long, the longest river in Shikoku. Is called "the last clear stream of Japan." Famous for production of sweet fish, eel, and seaweed such as purple laver or sea lettuce. Visitors can enjoy camping, fishing, and canoeing. Is one of the few rivers in Japan with sinking bridges called 'chinka-bashi'. They are low water crossings without parapets, and in case of floods they are not easily washed away.

しまんろくせんにち 四万六千日〚仏教〛 ⇨千日参り(**1**)

しみんびょうどう 四民平等〚政治〛 the equality of all people in the four classes. The slogan of the modern status system claimed by the Meiji government. The four classes refer to samurai, peasants, artisans, and merchants. In the Edo period, however, these four were not clearly distinguished as classes. Ironically, the Meiji government first divided people into aristocrats, former samurai, former lower-class soldiers, and commoners.

じむしょ 寺務所〚寺院〛 a temple office. Deals with clerical jobs in a Buddhist temple. →庫裏(⅙)

しめかざり 注連飾り〚暦〛 a New Year's decoration of twisted straw hung above the entrance of a house. Indicates that the house is purified and ready for welcoming the deity of the New Year. Is made up of fern leaves, a bitter orange called DAIDAI, zigzag-shaped paper strips called SHIDE, etc.

しめさば 締め鯖〚食べ物〛 salted and vinegared mackerel. Is served in slices.

しめじ 占地〚食べ物〛 a shimeji mushroom. *Lyophyllum*. It is said that MATSUTAKE is the best for fragrance, and 'shimeji' is the best for taste.

しめすへん 示偏〚漢字〛 a left-side radical related to "deity." Is used in kanji such as 神(god), 祈(pray), and 祝(celebrate). →偏；部首

しめだいこ 締め太鼓〚音楽〛 a two-headed drum tunable with cords. Can be tuned by adjusting the cords penetrating the rim of both heads.

しめなわ 注連縄〚神道〛 sacred straw rope. Is hung at the entrance of the main building or gate in a Shinto shrine. Indicates the structure is a sanctuary. Usually zigzag-shaped white paper strips are suspended from the festoon. →紙垂(⅙)

しめわざ 絞め技〚柔道〛 choking techniques. To choke the opponent's neck with arms, legs, or the neckband.

しもいちだんかつよう 下一段活用 〖言語〗 a verb conjugation in which the consonant of the stem end is always 'e.' Examples include 'ukeru' (receive) and 'ageru' (raise).

しもうさ 下総 〖旧国名〗 the old name of northern Chiba Pref.

しもがもじんじゃ 下鴨神社 〖神社〗 Shimogamo Shrine. Is located in the northern part of Kyoto City. The formal name is Kamo-mioya Jinja. Enshrines Tamayori-hime no mikoto and Kamo Taketsunomi no mikoto. The former is the mother of Kamo-wakeikazuchi no kami, a deity of thunder enshrined at KAMIGAMO JINJA, and the latter is her father. The east and west main buildings are National Treasures. The whole shrine was designated a World Heritage Site in 1994. →賀茂神社；葵祭

しもざ 下座 〖礼儀作法〗 the seat for a lower-rank person in a room. In a traditional room, the seat close to the entrance is 'shimo-za.' ↔上座

しもざわかん 子母澤寛 〖文芸〗 1892-1968. A novelist born in Hokkaido. Wrote historical stories set at the end of the Edo period, such as *Oyakodaka*, a novel about Katsu Kokichi, the father of KATSU KAISHUU, a vassal of the shogun in the 19th century.

しもたや 仕舞屋 〖経済・建築〗 a residential house that was used as a shop.

しもつき 霜月 〖暦〗 November in the traditional calendar. Means "frost month" because frost arrives in this month. →旧暦

しもつけ 下野 〖地名〗 the old name for Tochigi Pref.

しもて 下手 〖芸能〗 the left side of the stage when viewed from the audience.

しものく 下の句 〖文芸〗 the last 14 syllables in a short rhyming poem, TANKA. ↔上の句

しものせきし 下関市 〖地名〗 Shimonoseki City. Is located in western Yamaguchi Pref., at the western tip of Honshuu, facing the Kanmon Straits. Famous for globefish production. Buckwheat noodles on a hot roof tile are another specialty. Is the location of some historic events such as the Battle of Dannoura in 1185, the duel between Miyamoto Musashi and Sasaki Kojirou in 1612, and the Battle of Shimonoseki in 1864.

しもふりにく 霜降り肉 〖食べ物〗 marbled beef. Literally means "frost-falling beef." Small fat spots are dotted in the lean beef as if it is covered with frost. Good for sukiyaki and is sometimes sent as a gift.

しもやしき 下屋敷 〖武士・生活〗 a secondary mansion of a local feudal lord in the suburban area of Edo. →上屋敷

じもんは 寺門派 〖仏教〗 the Jimon school of the Tendai sect. The founder was ENCHIN, and the head temple is ONJOU-JI Temple in Shiga Pref. The school had opposed the

Sanmon sect at Enryaku-ji Temple since the 10th century. ↔山門派

じゃいあんとばば ジャイアント馬場 〔スポーツ〕 1938-1999. A professional wrestler, 209 cm tall, born in Niigata Pref. His real name is Baba Shouhei. First became a professional baseball player and then turned to wrestling in 1960, on the recommendation of Rikidouzan. Established All Japan Pro-Wrestling and led the golden age of Japanese professional wrestling, together with Antonio Inoki.

しゃいんしょくどう 社員食堂 〔食文化・ビジネス〕 a company cafeteria. Provides food at reasonable prices. Some company cafeterias are open to the public.

しゃうぷかんこく シャウプ勧告 〔経済・行政〕 Shoup Recommendations. The core of the tax system developed for Japan after World War II by Carl S. Shoup, a Columbia University economist recruited by Douglas MacArthur. Approved by the Japanese Diet in 1950, the recommendations of Shoup and his team of economists simplified the previous tax code, created a more equitable tax structure, and paved the way for Japan's economic recovery. Later Shoup was honored by Emperor Shouwa for his work.

しゃかさんぞん 釈迦三尊 〔仏教〕 the Triad of the Historical Buddha. Combination of the Historical Buddha and the two attendant bodhisattvas: Monju Bosatsu, *Manjusri*, on the left, and Fugen Bosatsu, *Samantabhadra*, on the right. →釈迦如来

しゃかむに 釈迦牟尼 〔仏教〕 the Historical Buddha. Sakyamuni. 463 B.C.?-383 B.C.? The founder of Buddhism. His secular name was Siddhartha Gautama. Was born as a prince of the Sakya tribe in north India, married a woman, and fathered a son. Became a monk at the age of 29, attained enlightenment under a bo tree in Bodhgaya at the age of 35, and founded Buddhism. Preached his beliefs around the basin of the Ganges River and passed away at the age of 80. →仏教；悟り；涅槃(ねはん)

しゃきょう 写経 〔仏教〕 transcription of a sutra by hand. Has been considered a religious deed and was practiced also by lay people. A calligraphy brush and India ink are used.

しゃく 笏 〔服飾〕 a wooden scepter. About 40-cm-long thin panel, which Emperors or noblemen brought to ceremonies. Is sometimes used today in a Shinto ritual by a priest.

しゃく 酌 〔酒・精神性〕 pouring sake for others. It is regarded as a courtesy to pour sake when a superior or senior person's cup or glass is empty.

しゃく ～勺 〔単位〕 a unit of volume. About 18 cc. Ten 'shaku' equal one gou.

しゃく ～尺 〔単位〕 a unit of length. About 30 cm. Ten sun equal one 'shaku.' Ten 'shaku' equal one JOU.

じゃくさ JAXA〔科学技術〕 ⇨宇宙航空研究開発機構

しゃくしゃいんのたたかい シャクシャインの戦い　〔戦争・少数民族〕 Revolt of Shakushain. The Ainu people rose up against the Matsumae domain in Hokkaido in 1669. The leader, Shakushain, was deceived and killed at the meeting for reconciliation.

しゃくじょう 錫杖〔仏教〕 a jingling rod. Is carried by a priest. Several rings are hung at the top of a rod so that they make a sound when the carrier swings the rod or prods the ground with the rod.

しゃくそん 釈尊〔仏教〕 ⇨釈迦牟尼

じゃくちゅう 若冲〔絵画〕 ⇨伊藤若冲(じゃくちゅう)

しゃくなげ 石楠花〔植物〕 a rhododendron. *Rhododendron metternichii* var. *hondoense*. Bears white or light-purple flowers in April and May.

しゃくはち 尺八〔音楽〕 a vertical bamboo flute. Is about 56 cm long and has 5 finger holes.

しゃこ 蝦蛄〔食べ物・動物〕 a mantis shrimp, or squilla. *Oratosquilla oratoria*. Eaten as sushi.

しゃこうきどぐう 遮光器土偶〔考古〕 a snow-goggle clay figurine. Represents a woman with large buttocks and breasts and has a pattern on the trunk. Usually is missing part of the body, probably for religious reasons.

しゃし 社司〔神道〕 ⇨神主

じゃすだっく JASDAQ　〔経済〕 (**1**) Japan Securities Dealers Association Quotation System. A dealing system for the over-the-counter market.　(**2**) The stock market for venture capital companies.

しゃたく 社宅〔生活〕 a company-rent residence for an employee and the family. Often an apartment.

しゃちほこ 鯱〔城郭〕 a ridge-end ornament for a castle roof. Is shaped like an imaginary fish with a dragon face and a tail toward the sky.

しゃちゅう 社中〔芸道〕 a troupe or company of traditional musicians or poets.

しゃっかんほう 尺貫法〔単位〕 traditional weights and measures. The length is measured by SHAKU, about 30 cm, the capacity is measured by SHOU, about 1.8 liter, and the weight is measured by KAN, 3.8 kg.

しゃっく 赤口〔暦〕 ⇨赤口(しゃっこう)

しゃっけい 借景〔建築〕 landscape borrowing. A traditional garden sometimes makes use of beautiful scenery outside of it as background.

しゃっこう 赤口〔暦〕 a day of "red mouth" in the unofficial six-day calendar. People will have the worst fortune on this day, except around noon. The deity of red mouth rules this day. →六曜(ろくよう)

じゃっこういん 寂光院　〔寺院〕 Jakkoin Temple. A nunnery of the Tendai sect located in Kyoto City. Has been said to be founded in 594 by Prince Shoutoku. The daughter of TAIRA NO KIYOMORI, Kenreimon-in, lived here to pray for the soul of her son, Emperor Antoku, after the destruction of the Taira clan. Is known as a temple described in *The Tale of the Heike*. →平氏；安徳天皇

しゃでん 社殿〖神社〗 buildings of a Shinto shrine. Sometimes only refers to the main sanctuary building.

じゃのめ 蛇の目〖文様〗 a bull's eye, or two concentric circles.

じゃのめがさ 蛇の目傘〖生活〗 an umbrella with a bull's eye design.

じゃぱねすく ジャパネスク〖精神性〗 Japanesque. The Japanese style.

じゃぱんたいむず ジャパンタイムズ〖マスコミ〗 *The Japan Times*. Daily English-language newspaper founded in 1897 by Motosada Zumoto. Its original main goal was to give readers in Japan the chance to practice English skills and thereby acquire a more global perspective. Today it has both print and web editions, along with several related weekly publications, such as its students' edition. Is often read by visitors to Japan. Has a circulation close to 70,000 as of 2006 according to its Internet site.

じゃびせん 蛇皮線〖音楽〗 ⇨三線（さんしん）

しゃふ 車夫〖交通・ビジネス〗 ⇨人力車夫

しゃぶしゃぶ しゃぶしゃぶ〖食べ物〗 a hot-pot dish with parboiled thin-sliced beef and vegetables. An eater waves the beef around in the broth with chopsticks. The beef is thin enough to be parboiled and ready to eat as soon as its color changes. Fish is sometimes used instead of beef. Sesame sauce, called goma-dare, and soy sauce mixed with citrus vinegar, called PONZU, are the most popular sauces for shabu-shabu.

しゃみせん 三味線〖音楽〗 a shamisen. A traditional three-stringed musical instrument. Has a square body and is played by a gingko-leaf-shaped plectrum.

しゃむしょ 社務所〖神社〗 a shrine office. Deals with clerical jobs in a Shinto shrine.

しゃも 和人〖少数民族・言語〗 a word in the Ainu language, which refers to "the Japanese people."

しゃもじ 杓文字〖食器〗 a rice scoop made of wood or plastic. Is used to scoop rice from a rice cooker into a bowl.

しゃようぞく 社用族〖経済〗 business people who waste money on eating and drinking at the company's expense.

しゃらく 写楽〖絵画〗 ⇨東洲斎写楽（とうしゅうさいしゃらく）

しゃり 舎利 **(1)**〖仏教〗 Buddha's relics. Transliteration of Sanskrit *sarira*, which originally meant "body." The relics after cremation were distributed to his devotees, and stupas to contain them were constructed. **(2)**〖寿司〗 jargon for boiled white rice. Is called so because it looks like (1).

しゃりでん 舎利殿 〖仏教・建築〗 a hall enshrining the Buddha's relics. In Japan, however, jewels are used as a substitute for the relics.

しゃりとう 舎利塔 〖仏教・建築〗 a small pagoda containing the Buddha's relics. Jewels are actually used as a substitute for the relics in Japan.

しゃりほつ 舎利弗 〖仏教〗 *Sariputra*. One of the Ten Great Disciples of the Historical Buddha. Foremost among the disciples in wisdom. →十大弟子

じゃる JAL 〖交通・企業名〗 ⇨日本航空

しゃれぼん 洒落本 〖文芸〗 witty books in the late 18th century. Describe the activities of the pleasure quarters in a dialogue-style novel.

じゃんけん じゃん拳 〖娯楽〗 rock-paper-scissors. A method to decide who has priority to do something, like tossing a coin. The participants stretch one hand at a time in one of the three forms: rock, paper, or scissors. The rock beats the scissors, the scissors beat the paper, and the paper beats the rock.

じゃんぷ ジャンプ 〖スポーツ〗 ski jumping. As of 2017, Japan won three gold, five silver, and three bronze medals in the Winter Olympics.

しゅ ～首 〖文芸〗 a counting suffix used in rhyming poems, except haiku. →～句

しゅいんせんぼうえき 朱印船貿易 〖外交〗 foreign trade by licensed ships in the early 17th century. The ship had a warrant with a vermilion seal called 'shuin.'

しゅいんちょう 朱印帳 〖寺院・神社〗 a notebook for collecting official vermilion seals. Since each Buddhist temple or Shinto shrine uses a unique seal and adds its signature for a charge, some people collect them on the notebook for pleasure.

しゅう ～州 〖言語・地名〗 the suffix to make a nickname of an old province. For example, 遠江 Tootoumi, the western part of present Shizuoka Pref., was also called 遠州 Enshuu.

じゅういちめんかんのん 十一面観音 〖仏教〗 Eleven-headed Bodhisattva of Mercy. Three faces in the front express mercy, three on the left release anger, three on the right show fangs, one on the back laughs, and one on the tops expresses Buddhahood. Is said to save those who reside in the Realm of Bellicose Spirits (SHURA-DOU) in esoteric Buddhism. Famous examples include the ones at Dougan-ji Temple in Shiga Pref. and Shourin-ji Temple in Nara Pref. →観音

じゅういちめんせんじゅせんがんかんのん 十一面千手千眼観音 〖仏教〗 ⇨千手観音

しゅうがくりょこう 修学旅行 〖教育・旅〗 a school trip. Usually sixth graders at elementary, third graders at junior high, and second graders at high school participate. All students at one school go together and make two- or three-night stays. This custom started in the late 19th century.

しゅうぎ　祝儀〖礼儀作法〗**(1)** money gift of congratulation.　**(2)** a tip for an entertainer or craftsman.

しゅうぎいん　衆議院〖政治〗House of Representatives. The term of membership is four years. Can be dissolved by the Cabinet.

しゅうぎぶくろ　祝儀袋〖礼儀作法〗an envelop for a money gift.

じゅうぎゅうず　十牛図〖禅・絵画〗Series of Ten Bull Herding Pictures. Figuratively depict the process of attaining enlightenment in Zen Buddhism.

しゅうぎょうしき　終業式〖教育〗term-end ceremony. Is held by most elementary and secondary schools on the last day of the spring and fall terms. Usually around mid-July for the spring term and late December for the fall term. After the ceremony, a report card is given to the students, and they usually clean the whole school before vacation. →修了式

じゅうぐんいあんふ　従軍慰安婦〖戦争・外交〗a military comfort woman. Was forced into prostitution by Imperial troops before and during World War II. Not until the 1990s were facts on the issue acknowledged by the government, after records were found and published and after survivors came forth. However, there is still considerable controversy on topics such as the extent of involvement by the government, the actual number and ethnicity of comfort women, and the accuracy of descriptions of the issue in contemporary school textbooks.

しゅうげん　祝言〖結婚〗an old term referring to a marriage ceremony.

じゅうごや　十五夜〖暦〗the full-moon night of the 15th in a month in the traditional calendar. Often the most important example is considered to be August 15 in the traditional calendar (somewhere between mid-September and early October in the current calendar), when people enjoy viewing the moon. →月見

じゅうさんじゅうのとう　十三重塔〖仏教・建築〗a thirteen-story pagoda. Most of them are made of stone and are small compared with three- or five-story pagodas. →塔

じゅうさんぶつしんこう　十三仏信仰〖仏教・民間信仰〗belief in 13 Buddhist deities including Buddhas, Bodhisattvas, and a Wisdom King. They are worshipped in 13 memorial services, given from the 7th day after a person's death to the 32nd anniversary. For example, the Immovable Wisdom King is worshipped on the 7th day, the Historical Buddha on the 27th day, the Amitabha Buddha on the 2nd anniversary, and the

Great Sun Buddha on the 12th anniversary. →〜回忌

じゅうさんまいり 十三参り 〖仏教〗 a ritual in which a 13-year-old boy or girl visits Hourin-ji Temple in Kyoto to worship the Bodhisattva of Space Repository (KOKUUZOU BOSATSU), on March 13 in the traditional calendar.

しゅうじ 習字 〖書道〗 learning of calligraphy or penmanship. →書道

しゅうしけい 終止形 〖言語〗 the conclusive form. In the verb and i-adjective conjugation, takes the dictionary form. In the na-adjective, ends with 'da.'

じゅうしちじょうけんぽう 十七条憲法 〖法律〗 Seventeen-Article Constitution. Was invented in 604 by Prince Shoutoku. The first written law in Japan. Although named "constitution," its contents are a kind of ethical code based on Buddhism and Confucianism.

じゅうじゅつ 柔術 〖武術〗 jujitsu. A traditional weaponless martial arts established from the 16th to the 17th centuries. Modern judo was developed from jujitsu in the 19th century.

じゅうしょく 住職 〖仏教〗 the chief priest of a temple. The qualifications for 'juushoku' vary from sect to sect.

しゅうじょし 終助詞 〖言語〗 a postpositional particle at the end of a sentence. Indicates the speaker's attitude toward the proposition stated in the sentence. For ex-

ample, a sentence added on to with 'ka' becomes interrogative. →助詞

しゅうしん 修身 〖教育〗 moral training. The right way of living was taught as a subject in elementary schools before World War II. Was abolished under the Occupation by the General Headquarters of the Supreme Commander for the Allied Powers, which considered it to be ultra nationalistic. Was restored as moral education in another name called 'doutoku' in 1958.

しゅうしんこよう 終身雇用 〖企業・組織〗 lifetime employment. Most Japanese companies applied this system after World War II, but the system is in decline.

しゅうせんきねんび 終戦記念日 〖戦争・暦〗 the anniversary of the end of World War II. August 15.

じゅうだいでし 十大弟子 〖仏教〗 the Ten Great Disciples of the Historical Buddha. *Sariputra, Mogallana, Mahakasyapa, Subhuti, Purna, Katyayana, Aniruddha, Upali, Rahula,* and *Ananda.* Are mentioned in a sutra, *Vimalakirti-nirdesa-sutra.* →舎利弗(しゃりほつ)；目犍連(もくけんれん)；摩訶迦葉(まかしょう)；須菩提(すぼだい)；富楼那(ふるな)；迦旃延(かせんねん)；阿那律(あなりつ)；優波離(うばり)；羅睺羅(らごら)；阿難陀(あなんだ)

じゅうだん 十段 〖碁・将棋〗 Ten Dan. One of the seven titles in professional go. Though it literally means "the tenth grade," the title Ten Dan is a special rank, because professional go and shogi players without this title can proceed only to nine dan. The best-of-five title match, 'Juudan-sen,' takes place annually from March to April. Juudan-sen used to exist also in professional shogi, but it was renamed to Ryuuou-sen in 1987.

しゅうだんそかい 集団疎開 〖戦争〗 group evacuation. Usually refers to the evacuation of school children from urban to rural areas to avoid air raids during World War II.

じゅうどう 柔道 〖柔道〗 judo. Its techniques include throwing, grappling, and attacking vital points. Was developed as a sport by KANOU JIGOROU, based on jujitsu. Became a formal event at the Tokyo Olympic Games in 1964 for the first time. Overall, Japan has won more than 30 Olympic gold medals in judo. → 柔術

じゅうどうせいふくし 柔道整復師 〖柔道・医療〗 a judo healing practitioner. Has an official license to treat sprains, dislocations, fractures, torn muscles, and bruises. Different from an orthopedic surgeon. Is not a medical doctor. → 整骨院

じゅうななじょうのけんぽう 十七条の憲法 〖法律〗 ⇨ 十七(じゅうしち)条憲法

じゅうにし 十二支 〖干支〗 twelve branches, or twelve signs of the Chinese zodiac. Twelve animals are allotted to years, days, hours, and directions. They are mouse, ox, tiger, hare, dragon, snake, horse,

sheep, monkey, cock, dog, and boar, in that order. → 子(ね); 丑(うし); 寅(とら); 卯(う); 辰(たつ); 巳(み); 午(うま); 未(ひつじ); 申(さる); 酉(とり); 戌(いぬ); 亥(い); 十干(じっかん)

じゅうにしんしょう 十二神将 〖仏教〗 the Twelve Divine Generals. Guard the Healing Buddha. Famous examples are at SHIN'YAKUSHI-JI Temple in Nara. → 薬師如来

じゅうにてん 十二天 〖仏教〗 the Twelve Devas. Guardians of the eight directions, the heaven, the earth, the sun, and the moon. TAISHAKU-TEN, KA-TEN, ENMA-TEN, RASETSU-TEN, SUI-TEN, FUU-TEN, BISHAMON-TEN, ISHANA-TEN, BON-TEN, JI-TEN, NIT-TEN, and GAT-TEN. Famous examples are at Saidai-ji Temple in Nara.

じゅうにひとえ 十二単 〖服飾〗 a layered women's kimono. Was worn as formal wear by a court lady.

じゅうばこ 重箱 〖食器〗 a stackable lacquered food box with a lid. The New Year's special dishes are usually served in the tiered boxes. → 御節(おせち)料理

じゅうばこよみ 重箱読み 〖漢字〗 reading a two-kanji compound in a Chinese-style pronunciation for the first kanji and in a Japanese-style pronunciation for the second kanji. For example, in the word 重箱, which means "a stackable lacquered wooden food box," the first kanji 重 is pronounced as 'juu,' which is the Chinese-style pronunciation of the kanji. On the other hand, the second kanji 箱 is pronounced as 'bako,' which is the Japanese-style pronunciation of the kanji. →湯桶(ゆとう)読み

しゅうばつ 修祓〖神道〗 ⇨お祓(はら)い

しゅうぶつ　繍仏　〖仏教・美術〗 Buddhist embroidery. A topic concerning Buddhism is embroidered on textile fabrics. Was popular from ancient to medieval times. Examples are Embroidery of Long Life in Heaven at Chuguu-ji Temple in Nara and Embroidered Buddha at the Tokyo National Museum.

しゅうぶん　周文〖絵画〗　?–? A painter and priest at Shoukoku-ji Temple in Kyoto in the 15th century. Studied under Josetsu and was officially employed by the Ashikaga shogunate. Works attributed to him include *Reading in Bamboo Grove Study* at the Tokyo National Museum. →室町幕府

じゅうぶん　重文〖行政〗 ⇨重要文化財

しゅうぶんのひ　秋分の日　〖暦〗 Autumnal Equinox Day. September 22 or 23. A national holiday. Occurs in the middle of the autumnal equinoctial week. →彼岸(ひがん)**(1)**

しゅうほうどう　秋芳洞〖地名〗 ⇨秋芳(あき)洞

じゅうみんけんうんどう　自由民権運動〖政治〗 the Freedom and People's Rights Movement. Was initiated in 1874 by ITAGAKI TAISUKE to counter the politics governed by cliques of specific feudal domains. Demanded that the Diet be established. Later, the Liberal Party and Constitutional Reform Party were established, and the first party cabinet was formed in 1898. However, the movement soon fell into decline when the peasants' riots in Fukushima and Chichibu were put down. →藩閥政治

じゅうみんひょう　住民票〖行政〗 a certificate of residence. The name, birthday, gender, address, and other information of a person are recorded.

しゅうめい　襲名〖芸能〗　succession to a hereditary stage name. A succession ceremony is held in the community of performing arts such as kabuki, Noh, bunraku, and comic story telling called RAKUGO.

しゅうもんあらため　宗門改め〖宗教・政治〗 religion test or check by the Tokugawa shogunate. Was begun to suppress Christianity after the Shimabara Uprising from 1637 to 1638. →島原の乱

じゅうようぶんかざい　重要文化財〖芸術〗 an Important Cultural Property. As of August 2014, 12,936 items including fine arts, crafts, and architecture had been designated by the Minister of Education, Culture, Sports, Science and Technology under the Law for the Protection of Cultural Properties. →文化財保護法

じゅうようぶんかてきけいかん　重要文化的景観〖法律〗 an Important Cultural Landscape. As of August

2014, 43 items had been selected through application by prefectural or municipal governments under the Law for the Protection of Cultural Properties. →文化財保護法

じゅうようむけいぶんかざい　重要無形文化財〖法律〗　an Important Intangible Cultural Property. As of August 2014, 109 persons and 26 groups related to performing arts and craft techniques had been designated by the Minister of Education, Culture, Sports, Science and Technology under the Law for the Protection of Cultural Properties. →文化財保護法

じゅうようむけいぶんかざいほじしゃ　重要無形文化財保持者〖芸術〗　a holder of an Important Intangible Cultural Property. Is usually called 'ningen kokuhou,' which means "Living National Treasure."

じゅうよくごうをせいす　柔よく剛を制す〖柔道・精神性〗　Softness controls hardness well. Flexibility wins over rigidness. A motto of judo.

じゆうりつ　自由律〖文芸〗　free verse. Although a haiku generally has 5-7-5 syllables and a tanka 5-7-5-7-7 syllables, a free-verse haiku or tanka does not have this restriction.

じゅうりょう　十両〖相撲〗　the second division in professional sumo wrestling. Next to MAKUUCHI, and above MAKUSHITA.

じゅうりょうあげ　重量挙げ〖スポーツ〗　weight lifting. Was introduced to Japan in 1934. Miyake Yoshinobu won the gold medal at the Tokyo Olympics in 1964 and the Mexico City Olympics in 1968.

しゅうりょうしき　修了式〖教育〗　year-end ceremony. Is held by most elementary and secondary schools on the last day of the school year, usually around mid-March. →終業式

じゅうろくらかん　十六羅漢〖仏教〗　sixteen arhats. It is said that this group image depicts sixteen saints who vowed to protect the teachings of Buddhism. →五百羅漢

じゅうわりそば　十割蕎麦〖食べ物〗　soba noodle made with only buckwheat flour. Is thicker but breaks more easily than NIHACHI SOBA noodle, which is made from 80 percent buckwheat flour and 20 percent wheat flour. Is more fragrant because it doesn't use wheat flour.

じゅかい　受戒〖仏教〗　to receive the precepts in Buddhism and to vow to observe Buddhist teachings. →戒律

じゅがく　儒学〖人文学〗　the academic contents of Confucianism.

しゅがくいんりきゅう　修学院離宮〖庭園〗　the Shugakuin Imperial Villa. Was constructed in Kyoto by the order of Emperor Gomizunoo in 1659. Consists of three villas: Lower, Middle, and Upper. Visitors can enjoy the garden design combined with the surrounding natural scenery. To visit the villa, one has to apply for permission to the Imperial Household Agency.

じゅきょう 儒教 〖宗教〗 Confucianism. Was introduced to Japan in ancient times and had a great influence on Japanese culture. Examples include the Seventeen-Article Constitution, the ancient centralized administration system called RITSURYOU-SEI, and the education at official schools of feudal domains in the Edo period.

しゅぎょうそう 修行僧 〖仏教〗 a novice or a monk in ascetic practice.

じゅく 塾 〖教育〗 a cram school, or a private school outside the ordinary educational system. Many students in elementary, junior high, or high school go to 'juku' for entrance exams or for remedial learning. Its fee can be a financial burden for some households.

しゅくごう 宿業 〖仏教〗 deeds in previous lives, or *karma*. Determines fate in this life.

しゅくじつ 祝日 〖暦〗 ⇨国民の祝日

しゅくばまち 宿場町 〖交通〗 a post-station town with hotels and inns in the Edo period. Developed along the Five Highways radiating from Edo. →五街道

しゅくぼう 宿坊 〖仏教〗 a temple inn. Is available to general visitors. Mt. Kouya has many inns of this type.

しゅくんしょう 殊勲賞 〖相撲〗 Outstanding Performance Prize. Is given to a wrestler, excepting YOKODUNA and OOZEKI, who defeats a grand champion or a wrester who has won the tournament. The criteria are different, case by case.

しゅげいしゅちいん 綜芸種智院 〖仏教・学校〗 the first educational institute to teach Buddhism and Confucianism to the common people. Was founded in Kyoto in 828 by KUUKAI.

しゅげんじゃ 修験者 〖宗教〗 ⇨山伏(やまぶし)

しゅげんどう 修験道 〖宗教〗 mountain asceticism. Was founded by combining mountain worship with esoteric Buddhism in the Heian period, though it is said that the legendary founder, En no Odunu, lived in the Nara period. Holy mountains of 'Shugendou' include Katsuragi and Kinpusen in present Nara Pref., Kumano in present Wakayama Pref., and Hakusan in present Ishikawa Pref. →山伏(やまぶし)

しゅご 守護 〖官位〗 a military provincial governor under the Kamakura shogunate. Was assigned to maintain public order and control the vassals, with military power and police authority. Some of them obtained more power and became semi-independent provincial governors called SHUGO DAIMYOU, in the Muromachi period.

しゅごだいみょう 守護大名 〖政治〗 a semi-independent military governor with feudal power in the Muromachi period. Had feudal relationship with warriors living in his fief. Is distinguished from a military governor, called SHUGO, under the Kamakura shogunate. Many of them fell after the Ounin War from 1467 to 1477, and military feudal lords, called SENGOKU DAIMYOU, appeared instead.

しゅざん 珠算〖教育〗⇨そろばん

しゅじ 種子〖仏教〗a Sanskrit character representing a deity in esoteric Buddhism.

しゅしがく 朱子学〖人文学〗 the teachings of Zhu Xi, or Neo-Confucianism. Was advocated by the Tokugawa shogunate.

しゅじょう 衆生〖仏教〗 living things, or *sattva*. Especially refers to stray people should be saved.

しゅす 繻子〖服飾〗satin. Can be a material for kimono.

じゅず 数珠〖仏教〗 a Buddhist rosary. Is sometimes made up of 108 threaded beads that represent 108 earthly desires. People hang it around the hands with palms together to pray in a Buddhist ritual.

しゅぞうこうてきまい 酒造好適米〖米・植物〗⇨酒米(さかまい)

しゅぞうまい 酒造米〖米・植物〗⇨酒米(さかまい)

しゅっけ 出家〖仏教〗 a Buddhist monk. Or, to become a Buddhist monk. ↔在家

しゅっけとそのでし 出家とその弟子〖文芸・作品〗 *The Priest and the Disciples*. A drama published in 1916 by KURATA HYAKUZOU. Preaches the teaching of the True Pure Land sect of Buddhism by describing psychological conflicts among the priest SHINRAN and his disciples.

しゅっせうお 出世魚〖魚〗fish that changes names as it grows. Examples are a sea bass, a yellowtail, and a striped mullet. For example, a sea bass is called 'seigo' at first, then 'fukko,' and finally 'SUZUKI' when grown up. →鰤(ぶり)；鰡(ぼら)

しゅてんどうじ 酒呑童子〖妖怪〗⇨大江山酒呑童子(おおえやましゅてんどうじ)

しゅとう 酒盗〖食べ物〗 salted and fermented bonito intestines. A preserved food. Literally means "stealing sake" because one tends to drink too much when it is served with Japanese sake.

しゅとけん 首都圏〖地名〗 the National Capital Region. Consists of all seven prefectures in the Kantou region and Yamanashi Pref. Its area is 36,889 km^2, roughly equal to that of Kyushu Island. Is Japan's most populous area and has the largest metropolitan economy in the world. There are 23 special cities in central Tokyo. Five ordinance-designated cities, Yokohama, Kawasaki, Saitama, Chiba, and Sagamihara, are each divided into wards. Most cities and wards in the region are connected by the railway network, still expanding even today, or the Shuto Expressway and other expressways that radiate from central Tokyo.

しゅにく 朱肉〖文具〗 a vermilion ink pad. Is usually round-shaped.

しゅはり 守破離〖精神性〗 observation, destruction, and separation. Three stages in mastering martial arts, the tea ceremony, or other traditional performances. First, a pupil should follow the teacher's instruction and conventions. Second, the pupil should doubt and break them to create his or her own original teaching. Last, the pupil becomes a master and goes beyond existing rules or forms.

じゅばん 襦袢〖服飾〗 underwear for kimono. Is said to have derived from a Portuguese word, "gibao."

じゅひょう 樹氷〖自然〗 a rime-covered tree. Is also known as a snow monster. Water freezes against a tree, and ice forms on and between branches. When snow falls on the iced branches, the tree looks like a snow monster. One at the Zaou Snow Resort in Yamagata Pref. is famous.

じゅふくじ 寿福寺〖寺院〗 Jufuku-ji Temple. A temple of the Kenchou-ji school of the Rinzai sect, ranked third among the Five Zen Temples of Kamakura, Kanagawa Pref. Was founded in 1200 by a priest, EISAI, with financial support from HOUJOU MASAKO, the wife of MINAMOTO NO YORITOMO, the founder of the Kamakura shogunate, to pray for her husband's soul. Was designated a Historic Site of Japan in 1966.

しゅぼ 酒母〖酒〗 yeast starter for sake. Is made from the mixture of molded steamed rice, regular steamed rice, and water. →酵母; 麹(こう)

しゅぼだい 須菩提〖仏教〗 ⇨須菩提(すぼだい)

しゅみせん 須弥山〖仏教〗 Mt. Sumeru. An imaginary lofty mountain located in the center of the world. Indra lives on the top of the mountain, and the Four Guardian Kings live on the mountainside. The sun and the moon revolve around the mountain. →帝釈(たいしゃく)天; 四天王

しゅみだん 須弥壇〖仏教〗 a platform on which to place Buddhist images. Is said to imitate Mt. Sumeru, an imaginary high mountain located in the center of the world. →須弥(しゅみ)山

しゅもく 撞木〖仏教〗 **(1)** a T-shaped hammer to strike a gong. →磬(けい); 叩き鉦(がね) **(2)** a swinging beam to strike a temple bell. →釣鐘

しゅらどう 修羅道〖仏教〗 the Realm of Bellicose Spirits. Souls in this realm keep fighting each other. →六道; 輪廻(りんね)

しゅりけん 手裏剣〖忍者〗 a small knife or star-shaped throwing weapon with blades. The star-shaped type was thrown with a spin. There are several shapes of shuriken, such as cross and eight-pointed.

しゅりじょう 首里城〖城郭〗 Shuri Castle. Is located in Naha City in the south of Okinawa Island. Was constructed in the 14th century, under the heavy influence of

Chinese architecture. From the 14th to 19th centuries, functioned as the administrative center of the Kingdom of Ryuukyuu. After Japan annexed the Kingdom in 1879, was occupied by the Imperial Japanese Army. In 1945 during the Okinawa campaign of World War II, was completely destroyed. In the 1980s, its reconstruction started. In 2000, was designated a World Heritage Site. Visitors can see the reconstructed buildings including the main gate called Shurei-mon. Is within walking distance from Shuri Station on Okinawa City Monorail, commonly known as Yui Rail, which can be accessed from Naha Airport Station within 30 minutes.

しゅれいもん 守礼門 〔城郭・建築〕 Shureimon Gate. The main gate of Shuri Castle in Okinawa. Was built in the 16th century.

じゅろうじん 寿老人 〔宗教〕 the deity of longevity. One of the Seven Deities of Good Fortune. Is depicted as a long-headed old man accompanied by a deer, carrying a fan and a holy staff with a holy scroll attached on its top. Was worshipped as a manifestation of the southern polar star. Was originally identical to the deity FUKUROKUJU in China. →七福神

しゅん 旬 〔食文化〕 the best season for specific foodstuff such as fish, vegetables, or fruits. For example, 'shun' for bamboo shoots is March and April.

しゅんが 春画 〔絵画〕 a pornographic picture. Is also called 'makura-e,' meaning "pillow picture," or 'warai-e,' meaning "smile picture." Was produced by many ukiyo-e painters, such as KITAGAWA UTAMARO, KATSUSHIKA HOKUSAI, and KEISAI EISEN.

しゅんぎく 春菊 〔食べ物・植物〕 edible chrysanthemum. *Glebionis coronaria*. Is used as an ingredient of a hot-pot dish, salad, or marinated food. Tastes bitter.

じゅんきゅうれっしゃ 準急列車 〔鉄道〕 semi-express train. Stops more frequently than an express train, but passes some stations on its route. No extra fee is needed to get on it. Is operated by some major private railway companies like Tobu, Tokyu, Odakyu, Hankyu, and Kintetsu, but not by JR.

しゅんきんしょう 春琴抄 〔文芸・作品〕 *A Portrait of Shunkin*. A novel published in 1933 by TANIZAKI JUN'ICHIROU. Describes the love of a male disciple for his female master of musical instruments.

しゅんけいぬり 春慶塗 〔漆器〕 Shunkei lacquerware. The wood is colored red or yellow, and the transparent lacquer is applied for the last touch so that the wood grain is shown.

じゅんさい 蓴菜 〔食べ物・植物〕 a water shield. *Brasenia schreberi*. Young buds or leaves are eaten in a soup or seasoned with vinegar.

じゅんし 殉死 〔天皇・武士〕 the immolation of vassals on the death of their master. Was carried out either voluntarily or forcibly. Was forbidden in the 7th century, but was seen again in the 16th and 17th centuries. Even after the Tokugawa shogunate prohibited it in 1663, it still existed. When Emperor Meiji died, an army officer, Nogi Maresuke, and his wife committed suicide.

じゅんていかんのん 准胝観音 〖仏教〗 Pure One Bodhisattva of Mercy. Usually has three eyes and 18 arms. Is said to save those who reside in the Realm of Humans in esoteric Buddhism. Famous examples include the one at DAIHOUON-JI Temple in Kyoto. →観音；人間道

しゅんとう 春闘 〖ビジネス〗 spring labor offensive. Each spring, a labor union and company management negotiate about working conditions and wages. Some companies in the same industry collaborate with each other.

じゅんとくてんのう 順徳天皇 〖天皇〗 Emperor Juntoku. 1197–1242. The 84th, on the throne from 1210 to 1221. The third prince of Emperor Gotoba. Participated in his father's plan to destroy the Kamakura shogunate, gave up the throne to his son, and raised an army in 1221. However, was defeated, was exiled to Sado Island, and died there. →承久の乱

じゅんにんてんのう 淳仁天皇 〖天皇〗 Emperor Junnin. 733–765. The 47th, on the throne from 758 to 764. A grandson of Emperor Tenji. Was exiled to Awaji Island by Exempress Kouken and died there.

しゅんぶんのひ 春分の日 〖暦〗 Vernal Equinox Day. March 20 or 21. A national holiday. Occurs in the middle of the vernal equinoctial week. Was ordained in 1948. →彼岸(ひがん) **(1)**

しゅんぼう 皴法 〖絵画〗 a painting technique to depict mountains or rocks with strokes of India ink.

じゅんまいぎんじょうしゅ 純米吟醸酒 〖酒〗 pure rice high-quality sake. Is brewed at low temperatures from rice polished to 60% or less of its original weight and is not supplemented with brewing alcohol.

じゅんまいしゅ 純米酒 〖酒〗 pure rice sake. Sake is usually mingled with brewing alcohol, but this type of sake is fermented with rice enzyme only.

じゅんれい 巡礼 〖宗教〗 a pilgrimage. Famous destinations include Thirty-three Holy Places around the Kansai region and Eighty-eight Holy Places in Shikoku. →西国三十三カ所；四国八十八カ所

じょあん 如庵 〖茶道・建築〗 a hermitage for the tea ceremony, made in 1618 by a warlord, Oda Urakusai. Was originally built in the precinct of Kennin-ji Temple in Kyoto. Has been moved to Inuyama, Aichi Pref. A National Treasure.

しょいん 書院 〖建築〗 a study room

or a drawing room in traditional architecture.

しょいんづくり 書院造り 〖建築〗 the style of a warrior-class residence in early modern times. Had a study room or a drawing room with a decorative alcove and different-levelled shelves. The floors were covered with tatami mats. Today's Japanese style architecture for a general residence originated from this style. An existing example can be seen at Jishou-ji Temple in Kyoto. →床の間; 違い棚

しょう 笙 〖音楽〗 ⇨笙の笛

しょう ～升 〖酒・単位〗 a unit of liquid or rice. About 1.8 liters. Ten GOU equal one 'shou.' Ten 'shou' equal one TO.

じょう ～丈 〖単位〗 a unit of length. About 3 m. Ten SHAKU equal one 'jou.'

じょう ～畳 〖建築・単位〗 a unit of tatami mat to indicate a room size. One 'jou' is the area of 180 cm by 90 cm.

じょうい 攘夷 〖外交〗 to expel the barbarians, or anti-foreign sentiment. →攘夷論; 尊皇攘夷

しょういだん 焼夷弾 〖軍事〗 an incendiary bomb. The U.S. Air Force dropped them on major cities in Japan during World War II.

じょういろん 攘夷論 〖外交〗 the doctrine of expelling foreigners. The idea of trying to eliminate Westerners by military power spread among samurai in the 19th century. Originated from the words

in the Spring and Autumn period in China.

じょういん 定印 〖仏教・美術〗 the mudra for meditation. The Buddha is sitting down, the right hand is placed on the left hand, with the fingers stretched in front of the belly, and the tips of the thumbs contact each other.

じょうえいしきもく 貞永式目 〖政治〗 ⇨御成敗式目

じょうえつしんかんせん 上越新幹線 〖鉄道〗 Joetsu Shinkansen. Connects Tokyo with Niigata. Started service in 1982. The super express, Toki, takes 2 hours from Tokyo to Niigata. Another express is named Tanigawa. In winter seasons, direct Tanigawa trains from Tokyo to a snow resort called GALA Yuzawa in Niigata Pref. provide service to meet skiers' and snowboarders' needs.

しょうえん 荘園 〖政治・経済〗 a manor, or a private rice field owned by a noble, temple, or shrine from the 8th to 17th centuries. Started with the issue of Law Permitting Permanent Ownership of Newly Cultivated Land in 743. It was popular in the Heian period, but it tailed off because of the invasion by the warrior class. Disappeared when TOYOTOMI HIDEYOSHI conducted the land survey in the 17th century. →墾田永年私財法

しょうが 生姜 〖調味料・植物〗 ginger. *Zingiber officinale*. Is used in various ways such as a condiment for sushi or chilled noodles, seasoning for meat or fish, and ingredient of cake.

しょうがじょうゆ 生姜醤油 〖調味料〗 ginger-flavored soy sauce. Mirin or sake is sometimes added.

しょうかそんじゅく 松下村塾 〖教育〗 a private school located in present Hagi City, Yamaguchi Pref. from 1842 to 1892. A person in any social class was admitted. It is well-known that a political theorist, Yoshida Shouin, taught at this school from 1857 to 1858. His students, many of whom were active in the Meiji Restoration, include TAKASUGI SHINSAKU, ITOU HIROBUMI, Kusaka Genzui, and Yamagata Aritomo.

しょうがつ 正月 〖暦〗 New Year's holidays. The biggest event of the year in Japan. People usually celebrate it with family, relatives, or friends, eating special cuisine called OSECHI RYOURI and rice cake soup called ZOUNI. Children receive New Year's pocket money, OTOSHIDAMA, from family members.

しょうかどうべんとう 松華堂弁当 〖食べ物〗 tea ceremony dishes contained in a 30-cm-square lacquered box divided into four equal compartments. Was named after a priest, painter, and calligrapher, Shoukadou Shoujou, in the 17th century, who loved this type of box.

じょうかまち 城下町 〖政治・経済〗 a castle town. Developed around a resident castle of a feudal lord and functioned as the capital of his fief. Typical examples include Edo, Osaka, Kagoshima, Koufu, Odawara, and Yamaguchi.

しょうかん 小寒 〖暦〗 one of the 24 seasonal nodes in the traditional calendar. Around January 5 in the current calendar. Means "the coldness begins to be a little serious." →二十四節気(にじゅうし せっき)

じょうかん 上燗 〖酒〗 warm sake. The temperature is around 50 degrees centigrade. →燗酒；銚子；猪口(ちょこ)

しょうかんのん 聖観音 〖仏教〗 Holy Bodhisattva of Mercy. The standard form of Kannon. Is said to save those who reside in the Realm of Hells in esoteric Buddhism. Famous examples include the ones at YAKUSHI-JI Temple in Nara. →観音；地獄

しょうき 鍾馗 〖宗教〗 the Plague-Queller. Was imported from China. Appeared in the dream of a Chinese emperor, Xuan Zong, and subjugated an imp. The Plague-Queller grows a mustache, a beard, and whiskers, has saucer eyes, and holds a sword. His image is depicted on a banner or as a doll for the Boys' Festival in May.

しょうぎ 床几 〖軍事・生活〗 a portable folding chair.

しょうぎ 将棋 〖将棋〗 shogi, or Japanese chess. A board game played by two players with a board and pieces. Its object is to checkmate the opponent's king. Was introduced to Japan from India through China between the 6th and 11th centuries. One of the differences between the Japanese shogi and Western chess is that in shogi, if a player captures the opponent's piece, he or she can put it on the board again and use it as his or her own.

しょうぎたい 彰義隊 〖政治〗 a military unit of ex-vassals of the Tokugawa shogunate. About 3,000 samurai resisted the Meiji government and established their headquarters at Kan'ei-ji Temple in Ueno, Tokyo, in February 1868. They were destroyed by the government army in May.

しょうきち 小吉 〖宗教〗 small good fortune. A message on a fortune slip available at a Shinto shrine or Buddhist temple. →お神籤(ﾐﾌ); 吉

しょうぎばん 将棋盤 〖将棋〗 a shogi board, or a Japanese chess board. Has 81 squares (9×9). Unlike a Western chess board, it is not checkered.

しょうきゃく 正客 〖茶道〗 the main guest at a tea ceremony. Enters the tea room first and plays an important role such as asking the host about the utensil used at the ceremony.

じょうきゅうのらん 承久の乱 〖戦争〗 Joukyuu War in 1221. Ex-emperor Gotoba raised an army to destroy the Kamakura shogunate but was suppressed. Ex-emperors Gotoba, Tsuchimikado, and Juntoku were exiled. After this incident, the shogunate placed a local agency in Kyoto to watch the Imperial Court. As a result, the shogunate power was reinforced.

しょうきょうと 小京都 〖旅・建築〗 a "little Kyoto." It is a term for a small old city surrounded by mountains and having many temples and shrines. Examples include Kakunodate in Akita, Obama in Fukui, Tsuwano in Shimane, and Takehara in Hiroshima.

しょうぐん 将軍〖武士・官位〗 ⇨征夷大将軍

しょうけいもじ 象形文字〖言語〗 a hieroglyph. It is said that one of the origins of kanji is hieroglyphics.

しょうけんこうたいごう 照憲皇太后〖天皇〗 the Empress Dowager Shouken. 1850-1914. The wife of Emperor Meiji. Accompanied the Emperor at official events, hosted Imperial visits, such as that of U.S. President Ulysses S. Grant, strongly supported the Japanese Red Cross, and visited military hospitals. Unable to bear children, adopted the Emperor's eldest son, Yoshihito, by a concubine. Yoshihito became Emperor Taishou in 1912.

しょうこ 鉦鼓 〖音楽〗 **(1)** a round bronze percussion instrument in court music. **(2)** a round bronze percussion instrument at a Buddhist service.

しょうこう 焼香 〖冠婚葬祭〗 incense burning to pray for the dead at a Buddhist-style funeral or memorial service. All attendants perform it while a priest is chanting a sutra.

じょうこう 上皇 〖天皇〗 a retired Emperor, or an Ex-emperor. This term has been used in and after the Heian period, before which they were called DAJOU TENNOU. An Emperor who retired and became a priest was called HOUOU. →院政

しょうこくじ 相国寺 〖寺院〗 Shokoku-ji. A main temple of the Shokoku-ji school of the Rinzai sect, ranked second among the Five Zen Temples of Kyoto. Was founded in 1383 by MUSOU SOSEKI with financial support from ASHIKAGA YOSHIMITSU. The Temples of Golden and Silver Pavilions, KINKAKU-JI and GINKAKU-JI, are subsidiary temples of Shokoku-ji. →臨済宗

しょうごん 荘厳 〖仏教〗 ornaments of a Buddhist image, altar, or hall. Include the crown, jewels, halo, and canopy.

じょうざぶぶっきょう 上座部仏教 〖仏教〗 ⇨小乗仏教

じょうざんけいおんせん 定山渓温泉 〖温泉〗 a hot spring in Sapporo, Hokkaido. Its hot water is salty. Was opened in 1866 by a priest named Jouzan, who came from present Fukui Pref.

しょうざんしこう 商山四皓 〖絵画〗 Four Graybeards in Mt. Shang. A popular theme for an India ink painting. It is said that four Chinese hermits escaped wars of the Qin dynasty to live in Mt. Shang. An example is housed at the Tokyo National Museum.

しょうじ 障子 〖建築〗 a sliding screen made of a latticed wooden frame and translucent paper. Its lower part is a wooden board. Glass is sometimes fit into the middle part. Shouji in which frosted glass is used instead of translucent paper are now increasing in number.

しょうじがみ 障子紙 〖建築〗 paper for a sliding screen. Is tear-resistant, allows sunlight to pass through, and hardly fades in the sunlight.

じょうしきまく 定式幕 〖芸能〗 an official draw curtain for a kabuki stage. Is vertically striped with black, green, and orange.

じょうしゅ 城主 〖武士〗 a castle master, or the lord of a castle.

じょうしゅう 上州 〖地名〗 ⇨上野 (ﾉﾉﾉ)

しょうしゅうれいじょう 召集令状 〖軍事〗 a draft notification slip. Is also called 'akagami' because it was printed on red paper.

しょうしょ 小暑 〖暦〗 one of the 24 seasonal nodes in the traditional calendar. Around July 7 in the current calendar. Means "it begins to be hot." →二十四節気(にじゅうしせっき)

しょうじょう 猩猩 〖妖怪〗 an imaginary ape like an orangutan. Has long red hair, understands human languages, and loves sake. Became a title of a Noh song.

しょうじょうこうじ 清浄光寺

【寺院】 Shoujoukou-ji Temple. The head temple of the Ji sect in Kanagawa Pref. Was founded in 1324 by a priest, Donkai. The scroll painting of the life of a priest, IPPEN, is a National Treasure. Is also called Yugyou-ji, which means a temple for pilgrimage. →時宗

しょうしょうはっけい 瀟湘八景 【絵画】 Eight Views of Xiaoxiang. A popular theme for an India ink painting although the location is in China. The eight views are Mountain Village Veiled in Mist on a Fine Day (SANSHI-SEIRAN), Rain at Night on the Xiaoxiang (SHOUSHOU-YAU), Sailing Ship Returning Home (ENPO-KIHAN), Fishing Village in the Evening Glow (GYOSON-SEKISHOU), Wild Geese Descending on a Sandbank (HEISA-RAKUGAN), Harvest Moon over Lake Dongting (DOUTEI-SHUUGETSU), River and Sky in Evening Snow (KOUTEN-BOSETSU), and Evening Gong at Qingliang Temple (ENJI-BANSHOU). Is sometimes thought to be modeled after beautiful spots in Japan such as KANAZAWA HAKKEI or OUMI HAKKEI.

しょうじょうぶっきょう 小乗仏教 【仏教】 Hinayana Buddhism. Hinayana means "lesser vehicle." Was called so by its opposite party, Mahayana Buddhism, but is now usually called Theravada Buddhism. Theravada Buddhism, spread in South and Southeast Asia while Mahayana Buddhism spread in the Far East. ↔大乗仏教

しょうしょうやう 瀟湘夜雨 【絵画】 Rain at Night on the Xiaoxiang. One of the Eight Views of Xiaoxiang. →瀟湘(しょう)八景

しょうじんあげ 精進揚げ 【食べ物】 vegetable tempura. Uses various vegetables such as squash, beefsteak plants, green peppers, and eggplant, as well as mushrooms.

しょうじんおとし 精進落とし 【食文化・仏教】 (**1**) eating meat after abstaining from it. (**2**) a banquet immediately after a funeral or during the memorial service, on the forty-ninth day after a person's death.

じょうしんこ 上新粉 【食文化】 flour made from ordinary rice. Is used as an ingredient for traditional-style confectionery.

しょうじんりょうり 精進料理 【食文化】 Buddhist vegetarian cuisine. Ingredients include vegetables, seaweed, and tofu. Originally derived from the dietary restrictions of Buddhist priests, but is now eaten by lay people. The appearance of some food is similar to non-vegetarian food.

じょうせき 定石, 定跡 【碁・将棋】 an orthodox move in the games of GO or SHOUGI. Though the pronunciation is the same, the second kanji is different between them.

しょうせつ 小雪 【暦】 one of the 24 seasonal nodes in the traditional calendar. Around November 22 in the current calendar. Means "a little snow." →二十四節気(にじゅうしせっき)

しょうせつしんずい 小説神髄 【文

芸・作品』 *The Essence of the Novel.*
A literature critique published
in parts from 1885 to 1886 by
TSUBOUCHI SHOUYOU. The first modern
literature critique in Japan.

しょうそういん 正倉院 〖仏教・建築〗 the Treasure House of Toudai-ji Temple. Contains about 9,000 treasures including documents, stationery, musical instruments, furniture, Buddhist utensils, weapons, toys, accessories, and tableware. Most of them date back to the 8th century. The building is in the style of a log storehouse, called azekura-dukuri. A National Treasure.

じょうたい 常体 〖言語〗 an ordinary language style. A sentence ends with 'da,' 'dearu,' or a conclusive form. ↔敬体 →終止形

じょうだい 城代 〖武士・官位〗 **(1)** a deputy manager of a castle. **(2)** a manager of one of the four important castles under the Tokugawa shogunate: Osaka Castle, Sunpu Castle in present Shizuoka Pref., and Nijou and Fushimi Castles in Kyoto.

じょうだいがろう 城代家老 〖武士・官位〗 a chief vassal to manage a castle during the absence of a feudal lord in the Edo period. A deputy manager of a local castle. Feudal lords were forced to live in Edo and their homeland in alternate years. →参勤交代

しょうちく 松竹 〖映画・企業名〗 SHOCHIKU Co., Ltd. A company of motion pictures, theaters, and kabuki established in 1920. Has produced and distributed a great number of films. Shochiku films include *It's Tough Being a Man* (OTOKO WA TSURAIYO), *Departures* (Okuribito), and *A Silent Voice* (Koe no katachi).

しょうちくばい 松竹梅 〖精神性〗 pine, bamboo, and plum. Traditionally considered to be auspicious plants because they bear winter coldness. Often refers to food grades in a restaurant: top, medium, and bottom.

じょうちじ 浄智寺 〖寺院〗 Jouchi-ji Temple. A temple of the Engaku-ji school of the Rinzai sect, ranked fourth among the Five Zen Temples of Kamakura, Kanagawa Pref. Was founded in 1283 by a Chinese priest, Gottan Funei, with financial support by Houjou Morotoki, to pray for his father's soul. Is designated a National Historical Site of Japan. The main objects of worship inside the main hall are the three statues, Amitabha, Sakyamuni, and Maitreya, which represent the past, current, and future, respectively.

しょうちゅう 焼酎 〖酒〗 a Japanese spirit. Is distilled from sweet potato, rice, or wheat. Sometimes uses other materials. Its alcohol content is 20 to 45%. →泡盛

じょうちょう 定朝 〖彫刻〗 ?-1057. A sculptor of Buddhist images. Established the original elegant and graceful style of Buddhist sculpture. Was the first Buddhist sculptor to be honored with the title of hokkyou, which means a priest of the third highest rank. Owing to this bestowal, the social status of Buddhist sculptors improved. The sole example of his existing work is the Amitabha Buddha at Byoudou-in Temple, though his name and works are frequently referred to in archives.

しょうちょく 詔勅〔天皇・文書〕 a document to communicate an Imperial edict. Written in classical Chinese style.

しょうつきめいにち 祥月命日〔仏教〕 the anniversary of a person's death. People hold a memorial service on this day.

しょうてん 聖天〔仏教〕 ⇨歓喜天

じょうど 浄土〔仏教〕 the Pure Land. Typically indicates the Western Pure Land of Amitabha Buddha, but there are several Joudos such as the Eastern Pure Land of the Healing Buddha. ↔穢土(ど)→西方極楽浄土；東方瑠璃光(じょう)浄土

じょうどう 成道〔仏教〕 a Bodhisattva's enlightenment.

じょうとうしき 上棟式〔建築〕 ⇨棟上げ式

じょうどきょう 浄土教〔仏教〕 Pure Land Buddhism. Adherents desire to be saved by Amitabha Buddha and to be reborn in the Western Pure Land. Includes several sects such as the Pure Land sect, the True Pure Land sect, and the Ji sect. →浄土宗；浄土真宗；時宗

しょうとくたいし 聖徳太子〔仏教〕 574-622. Prince Shoutoku, a son of Emperor Youmei. Was also called Prince Umayado. Helped Empress Suiko, his aunt, as a regent. Invented the System of Twelve Court Ranks and the Seventeen-Article Constitution, dispatched the first envoy to the Sui dynasty in China, and founded several temples such as HOURYUU-JI and SHITENNOU-JI. →冠位十二階；十七(じゅう)条憲法；遣隋使

しょうとくてんのう 称徳天皇〔天皇〕 Empress Shoutoku. 718-770. The 48th, on the throne from 764 to 770. Was also enthroned earlier, from 749-758, under the name Empress Kouken. Favored the priest Doukyou. →孝謙(こう)天皇

じょうどじ 浄土寺〔寺院〕 Joudo-ji Temple. Affiliated with the Shingon sect. Is located in middle Hyougo Pref. Was founded around the 12th century by a priest named CHOUGEN. The Amitabha Triad by KAIKEI and the hall containing it are National Treasures.

じょうどしゅう 浄土宗〔仏教〕 the Pure Land sect. A sect of Pure Land Buddhism. Was founded in the 12th century by HOUNEN, the teacher of SHINRAN. Adherents desire to be reborn in the Western Pure Land by worshipping Amitabha Buddha and reciting "I put my faith in Amitabha Buddha."

Compared with the True Pure Land sect, the organization of the service is more systematic, though the doctrines are similar. The head temple is Chion-in Temple in Kyoto.

じょうどしんしゅう 浄土真宗 〖仏教〗 the True Pure Land sect. Was founded in the 13th century by SHINRAN, a disciple of HOUNEN. Adherents desire to be reborn in the Western Pure Land by worshipping Amitabha Buddha and reciting "I put my faith in Amitabha Buddha." Compared with the Pure Land sect, the organization of the service is less systematic, and the discipline is less rigorous, though the doctrines are similar. There are ten subsects, and two major subsects are the Honganji and Ootani schools. The head temple of the former is NISHI HONGAN-JI Temple, that of the latter is HIGASHI HONGAN-JI Temple, with both being in Kyoto.

しょうなごん 少納言 〖官位〗 a clerk of the Grand Council of State in ancient times. Ranked next to CHUU-NAGON.

しょうなん 湘南 〖地名〗 the name of a prominent resort area along Sagami Bay in southern Kanagawa Pref. Is located 50 km south of Tokyo city proper and has a warm and mild climate. It is said that Ishihara Shintarou's novel, *Season of Violence*, published in 1955, made the area popular. Is named after a scenic region in Hunan in southern China. Visitors can enjoy various marine sports, including diving, sail boating, windsurfing, and standup paddle boarding, thanks to long beaches and Enoshima Island.

しょうにん 上人 〖仏教〗 a honorific name for a priest of virtue or a high-ranking priest.

じょうにん 上忍 〖忍者〗 a high-skilled ninja. According to *The Book of Ninja*, ninjas were divided into three ranks by their skills. Examples of 'jounin' include Momochi Tanba, Hattori Hanzou Yasunaga, and Fujibayashi Nagato. In modern fictions, 'jounin' is usually the commander-in-chief for a ninja organization and administrates medium- and low-ranking ninjas. →萬川集海(ばんせんしゅうかい); 中忍; 下忍

しょうにんき 正忍記 〖忍者〗 *True Path of the Ninja*. One of the three major ninjutsu books. Was written in 1681 by Natori Masazumi, a military scientist of the Kishuu domain. Consists of 3 volumes and illustrates practical ninja skills and incantation. Does not depend on oral tradition, on which the other two major ninjutsu books are mainly based. →萬川集海(ばんせんしゅうかい); 忍秘伝(にんぴでん)

しょうねんさんでえ 少年サンデー 〖漫画〗 *Weekly Shonen Sunday*. A comic magazine for boys. Was first issued in March 1959 by Shogakukan Inc. Published many popular manga series such as

Tacchi and Urusei Yatsura.

しょうねんじゃんぷ 少年ジャンプ 〖漫画〗 *Weekly Shonen Jump*. A comic magazine for boys. Was first issued in July 1968 by Shueisha Inc. Published many popular manga series such as Kyaputen Tsubasa and Hadashi no Gen.

しょうねんまがじん 少年マガジン 〖漫画〗 *Weekly Shonen Magazine*. A comic magazine for boys. Was first issued in March 1959 by Kodansha Ltd. Published popular manga series such as Kyojin no Hoshi and Ashita no Joo.

しょうのふえ 笙の笛 〖音楽〗 a traditional mouth organ. Was primarily used in court music.

じょうはく 条帛 〖仏教・美術〗 a sash worn diagonally by a Bodhisattva or Wisdom King. Is said to come from a garment for noblemen in ancient India.

じょうびけし 定火消し 〖災害・職業〗 an official fire brigade for Edo under the Tokugawa shogunate. → 大名火消し；町火消し

しょうひぜい 消費税 〖行政・ビジネス〗 consumption tax. Was started at 3% in 1989 and is 8% as of 2017. Will be raised to 10% in the near future.

しょうぶ 菖蒲 〖植物〗 a sweet flag. *Acorus calamus*. Grows at the waterside. Light yellow flowers bloom in early summer. Is put into a bath at the Boys' Festival on May 5 to drive away malicious air.

じょうぶつ 成仏 **(1)** 〖仏教〗 to attain enlightenment. **(2)** 〖言語〗 to die.

しょうぶゆ 菖蒲湯 〖風呂〗 sweet flag bath. Is prepared at the Boys' Festival on May 5 to drive away malicious air.

しょうへいが 障屏画 〖絵画〗 a picture on sliding doors, folding screens, walls, or ceilings. →襖(ﾌｽﾏ)絵；杉戸絵；屏風(ﾋﾞｮｳﾌﾞ)絵

しょうへいこう 昌平黌 〖学校〗 ⇨昌平坂学問所

しょうへいざかがくもんじょ 昌平坂学問所 〖学校〗 a school opened inside the Confucian Sacred Hall at Yushima in 1797 by the Tokugawa shogunate. Taught the doctrines of Zhu Xi to samurai and was closed in 1871. →湯島聖堂

じょうへいてんぎょうのらん 承平・天慶の乱 〖政治〗 Jouhei and Tengyou Rebellions. Taira no Masakado rose against the Imperial Court in 935 and governed the present Kantou region but was suppressed in 940. Fujiwara no Sumitomo rose in present Ehime Pref., in cooperation with pirates of the Inland Sea in 939 but was subdued in 941.

しょうへきが 障壁画 〖絵画〗 a picture on sliding doors, walls, or ceilings. →襖(ﾌｽﾏ)絵；杉戸絵

じょうほうていきょうねっとわあくしすてむ 情報提供ネットワークシステム 〖行政〗 Cooperation Network System for Personal Information. A computer network system for exchanging personal information associated with a personal number (My Number) among administrative agencies. A personal number card was issued in 2016, and operation began in 2017.

しょうまん 小満〖暦〗 one of the 24 seasonal nodes in the traditional calendar. Around May 21 in the current calendar. Means "plants begin to grow." →二十四節気(にじゅうしせっき)

しょうみょう 小名〖政治〗 a feudal lord of a comparatively small domain in the Edo period.

しょうみょう 声明 〖仏教・音楽〗 sutra chanting by priests in a Buddhist ritual. Has a melody, sometimes with instrumental accompaniment. Its contents celebrate the virtue of the Buddha.

しょうみょう 称名〖仏教〗 to praise Buddha aloud. For example, to say "I put my faith in Amitabha Buddha." →南無阿弥陀仏

じょうみょうじ 浄妙寺 〖寺院〗 Joumyou-ji Temple. A temple of the Kenchou-ji school of the Rinzai sect, ranked fifth among the Five Zen Temples of Kamakura, Kanagawa Pref. Was founded in 1188 by a priest, Taikou Gyouyuu, with financial support from Ashikaga Yoshikane. Is the only one of the Five Zen Temples not founded by the Houjou family. Is designated a Historic Site of Japan.

しょうむてんのう 聖武天皇 〖天皇〗 Emperor Shoumu. 701-756. The 45th, on the throne from 724 to 749. The first prince of Emperor Monmu. Married a daughter of an aristocrat, FUJIWARA NO FUHITO. Patronized Buddhism, built the TOUDAI-JI Temple, and established the system of provincial temples. →光明皇后；国分寺

じょうもうさんざん 上毛三山 〖山岳〗 the Three Mountains in Gunma Pref., namely, Mt. Akagi, Mt. Haruna, and Mt. Myougi. 'Joumou' refers to Kouzuke, the old name of Gunma Pref.

じょうもんかいしん 縄文海進 〖自然〗 Holocene marine transgression. The sea level rose about 2 m around 6,000 years ago in the Joumon period.

じょうもんしきどき 縄文式土器〖考古〗 ⇨縄文土器

じょうもんじだい 縄文時代 〖時代〗 the Joumon period. From about 12000 B.C. to about 300 B.C. After the Old Stone Age and prior to the Yayoi period. 'Joumon' literally means "rope pattern," which the earthenware in this period has on its surface. →縄文文化；弥生時代

じょうもんすぎ 縄文杉 〖植物〗 a Japanese cedar in Yaku Island, Kagoshima Pref., which is more than 2,000 years old. →屋久島

じょうもんどき 縄文土器 〖考古〗 Joumon earthenware. 'Joumon' literally means "cord mark" because the earthenware often has such patterns on its surface. Was calcinated at around 500 degrees Celsius, is dark brown, and is unglazed.

じょうもんぶんか 縄文文化 〖時代〗 the Joumon culture. From about 12000 B.C. to about 300 B.C. People hunted, fished, and collected nuts and fruits, used earthenware and stoneware, and lived in pit dwellings. →縄文土器

しょうや 庄屋 〖農業・官位〗 a village mayor in the Edo period. This name was mainly used in Western Japan. →名主

しょうやく 生薬 〖医療〗 crude drugs. Living things or minerals are used in their natural state, or after being processed slightly.

しょうゆ 醤油 〖調味料〗 soy sauce. Unique to Japanese culinary culture. Is made from soybeans, wheat, and salt. Was invented probably around the 15th century and became popular in the Edo period. Thick soy sauce (KOIKUCHI SHOUYU) is popular in Eastern Japan, while thin soy sauce (USUKUCHI SHOUYU) is popular in Western Japan. Famous producing districts are Noda and Choushi in Chiba Pref., Tatsuno in Hyougo Pref., and Yuasa in Wakayama Pref.

しょうゆいれ 醤油入れ 〖食文化〗 a small soy sauce container. Is attached to delivered sushi. There are two types: fish-shaped and bottle-shaped.

じょうようかんじ 常用漢字 〖漢字〗 kanji for common use. Provides a kind of standard of kanji for daily use. In 1981, 1,945 kanji were designated for daily use by the government. In 2010, 196 kanji were added, and 5 kanji were deleted. Consequently, 2,136 kanji are now officially designated.

しょうようじゅりんぶんか 照葉樹林文化 〖考古・人文学〗 Laurel Forest Culture. Spread from the foot of the Himalaya Mountains, through northern Southeast Asia and southern China, to Western Japan. Common features include slash-and-burn agriculture, fermented food of soy beans, and tea drinking.

じょうよまんじゅう 薯蕷饅頭 〖食べ物〗 a round-shaped steamed yam bun including adzuki-paste filling. Is made of grated yam with sugar and fine-grade wheat flour. Its color is mainly white or red. Is served on celebratory occasions or at tea ceremonies.

じょうらく 上洛 〖政治〗 to go up to Kyoto. This term is usually used in a political context in medieval to early modern times. The subject is often a feudal lord.

しょうりゃくじ 正暦寺 〖寺院〗 Shouryaku-ji Temple. Affiliated with the Shingon sect. Is located in Nara City. Was founded in 992 in accordance with an imperial order of Emperor Ichijou. Is said to be the birthplace of refined sake. →清酒

しょうりょうだな 精霊棚 〖仏教〗 a temporary altar to welcome the spirits of the dead during the Bon Festival. A memorial tablet, called

IHAI, is set on it, and fruits or vegetables are offered.

しょうりょうながし 精霊流し 〖仏教〗 a Bon event of floating a tiny boat on a river or sea. People place a paper lantern or votive offerings on the boat to see off the spirits of the dead on the last day of the Bon Festival. →盂蘭盆会(うらぼんえ)

しょうりょうぶね 精霊舟〖仏教〗 a tiny boat to see off the spirits of the dead. Is made of straw or wood. →精霊流し

しょうりんじ 聖林寺 〖寺院〗 Shourin-ji Temple. A temple of the Shingon sect located in central Nara Pref. Was founded in 712 by Joue, a son of FUJIWARA NO KAMATARI. The Eleven-headed Bodhisattva of Mercy is a National Treasure.

しょうりんじけんぽう 少林寺拳法〖武術・仏教〗 a modern Japanese martial art based on Shaolin kung fu. Was founded in 1947 by Sou Doushin. The original Shaolin kung fu is said to have been introduced from India to Shaolin Temple in China by Bodhidharma, the founder of Zen Buddhism.

しょうるいあわれみのれい 生類憐みの令〖行政〗 Edicts on Compassion for Living Things. Were issued several times since 1685 by TOKUGAWA TSUNAYOSHI, the 5th shogun of the Tokugawa shogunate. Sometimes referred to as a typical example of governmental misrule.

じょうるり 浄瑠璃〖芸能〗 a dramatic narrative accompanied by a traditional three-stringed instrument called SHAMISEN. Started in the Muromachi period and was connected with a puppet show to form NINGYOU JOURURI in the Edo period.

しょうれんいん 青蓮院 〖寺院〗 Shouren-in Temple. A temple of the Tendai sect located in Kyoto City. Was founded in 1150 by SAICHOU, who founded the Tendai sect. Blue Immovable Wisdom King is a National Treasure. →天台宗

しょうろう 鐘楼〖仏教・建築〗 a belfry. Is lower than a bell tower in a Western church and often has no wall, just four pillars.

しょうろうながし 精霊流し〖仏教〗 ⇨精霊(しょうりょう)流し

じょうろく 丈六〖仏教〗 the size of a Buddhist sculpture. About 4.8 m high for a standing image, and about 2.4 m high for a sitting image.

しょうわじだい 昭和時代 〖時代〗 the Shouwa period, from 1926 to 1989. Japan started the war with China, which led to the Pacific War of World War II. During the high economic growth after the war, hosted two Olympic Games, in Tokyo in 1964 and in Sapporo in 1972, and the World's Fair in Osaka in 1970, also called Expo '70. →太平洋戦争；東京オリンピック；札幌オリンピック；大阪万博

しょうわしんざん 昭和新山 〖地名〗 Mt. Shouwa-shinzan. A volcanic lava dome in southwestern

Hokkaido. Is located to the east of its parent volcano Mt. Usu, and to the south of Lake Touya. Literally means "Shouwa New Mountain." In 1944, or the 19th year of the Shouwa period, lava broke through the wheat and vegetable fields. Later, the lava dome grew to be 200 m tall from the ground. At present, its peak is 398 m above the sea, but the dome is gradually shrinking.

しょうわてんのう 昭和天皇 〖天皇〗 Emperor Shouwa, or Emperor Hirohito. 1901-1989. The 124th, on the throne from 1926 to 1989. The son of Emperor Taisho and father of Emperor Akihito. During his long reign, the nation greatly expanded its military might, fought and lost World War II in the Pacific, recovered from the war during and after the Occupation, and grew into a major economic power with new democratic traditions.

しょうわのひ 昭和の日 〖祝日〗 Shouwa Day. April 29. A national holiday. Was celebrated as the birthday of Emperor Shouwa from 1926 to 1989.

しょか 書家 〖書道〗 ⇨書道家

しょぎょうむじょう 諸行無常 〖仏教〗 Everything is changing, and nothing is eternal. One of the fundamental thoughts of Buddhism. It is well known that *The Tale of the Heike* quotes this phrase. →平家物語

しょくいんしょくどう 職員食堂 〖食

文化・ビジネス〗 SHAIN SHOKUDOU for organizations besides companies, such as government offices and schools.

しょくじょせい 織女星 〖伝説〗 ⇨織姫

しょくにほんぎ 続日本紀 〖政治・書名〗 *Chronicles of Japan, Continued*. One of the Six National Histories. Was compiled in 797. Covers from 697 to 791. →六国史（りっこくし）

しょくにほんこうき 続日本後紀 〖政治・書名〗 *Later Chronicle of Japan, Continued*. One of the Six National Histories. Was compiled in 869. Covers from 833 to 850. →六国史（りっこくし）

しょくひんさんぷる 食品サンプル 〖食文化〗 plastic food imitation. Looks exactly like real food or drink. Is often displayed in front of a restaurant to help the customers decide what to eat or drink.

しょこう 諸侯 〖武士・政治〗 a feudal lord in the Edo period.

しょさごと 所作事 〖歌舞伎〗 a dance or dance drama in kabuki. Is also called 'furigoto' or 'keigoto'.

じょし 助詞 〖言語〗 a postpositional particle. Is added to an independent word or compound to indicate the relation among words or the speaker's attitude toward the proposition stated in the clause. The classification is different among several grammar theories. →格助詞；接続助詞；副助詞；終助詞

しょしだい 所司代 〖官位〗 ⇨京都所司代

しょしょ 処暑〔暦〕 one of the 24 seasonal nodes in the traditional calendar. Around August 23 in the current calendar. Means "the heat begins to be tempered." →二十四節気(にじゅうしせっき)

じょすうし 助数詞〔言語〕 a counting suffix. Different counting suffixes are added after numbers, based on the property of counted nouns. For example, when things with the property of being flat such as dishes or paper are counted, a suffix 'mai' is added after a number. Namely, one dish is 'ichi-mai,' two dishes are 'ni-mai,' and so on.

じょせいせんようしゃりょう 女性専用車両〔鉄道〕 the women-only car of a train. In some trains for commuters in and around the Tokyo, Osaka, and Nagoya areas, one of the cars is for the exclusive use of women, children, and the disabled. The car is usually less crowded than other cars of the same train.

じょせつ 如拙〔絵画〕 ?-? A painter and priest at Shoukoku-ji Temple in Kyoto from the end of the 14th century to the beginning of the 15th century. Learned the Sung and Yuan paintings and pioneered India ink painting in Japan. His works include *Catching a Catfish with a Gourd* at Taizouin Temple in Kyoto.

じょせん 除染〔災害〕 decontamination of radioactive substances.

しょたい 書体〔書道〕 a style of calligraphy. There are three styles: KAISHO, GYOUSHO, and SOUSHO.

しょだん 初段〔武術・書道〕 the first DAN. The starting grade in the senior class of martial arts or calligraphy above KYUU. A martial artist with 'shodan' or higher grades is permitted to fasten a black belt.

じょちゅうぎく 除虫菊〔生活・植物〕 a Dalmatian pyrethrum. *Chrysanthemum cinerariaefolium.* The material for insecticides and for a mosquito-repellent coil called KA-TORI-SENKOU.

しょちゅうみまい 暑中見舞い〔暦・文書〕 a card of mid-summer greetings. Is sent from July 7 until August 8.

しょっきり 初っ切り〔相撲〕 a series of comical bouts. Are performed as exhibitions by lower-ranking sumo wrestlers.

しょっつる 塩汁〔調味料〕 fish sauce made from sandfish or sardine. A specialty of Akita Pref.

しょどう 書道〔書道〕 Japanese calligraphy. The art of writing KANJI or KANA with a brush and India ink. Has three styles: KAISHO, GYOUSHO, and SOUSHO.

しょどうか 書道家〔書道〕 a professional calligrapher. Is also called 'shoka.'

しょなのか 初七日〔仏教・冠婚葬祭〕 the 7th day after one's death. The bereaved family holds a memorial service. It is said that the soul of the deceased crosses the River of Three Crossings, the Japanese counterpart to the River Styx. →法

事；三途の川

じょにだん 序二段 〖相撲〗 the second-lowest division in the Grand Sumo Tournament. Next to SAN-DANME, and above JONOKUCHI.

じょのくち 序の口 **(1)** 〖相撲〗 the lowest division in the Grand Sumo Tournament. **(2)** 〖生活〗 a starting point or the first stage. Derived from (1).

じょのまい 序の舞 **(1)** 〖歌舞伎〗 a soft musical accompaniment to kabuki. Uses a bamboo flute, a drum, and hand drums. Is played while actors go on and off stage or say their lines. **(2)** 〖能〗 an extremely slow and elegant dance of Noh. Starts with beating time with feet and gradually steps up the tempo.

じょはきゅう 序破急 〖能・精神性〗 introduction, expansion, and conclusion. The term refers to the principle of organization in traditional performing arts.

じょふく 徐福 〖民話〗 Xu Fu. ?–? A Chinese hermit wizard. It is said that he departed China to find an elixir of life under the command of Shi Huang-ti of the Qin dynasty, together with several thousand children. In legend, he landed on present Wakayama Pref., and Japanese people are the offspring of the children.

じょめいてんのう 舒明天皇 〖天皇〗 Emperor Jomei. 593–641. The 34th, on the throne from 629 to 641. A grandson of Emperor Bidatsu. Was helped to the throne by the head of a powerful clan, SOGA NO EMISHI.

じょや 除夜 〖暦〗 New Year's Eve.

じょやのかね 除夜の鐘 〖暦〗 temple bell tolling on the New Year's Eve. Is considered that when the temple bell is rung 108 times, people's 108 earthly desires, BONNOU, will be removed.

じょろう 女郎 〖セックス・娯楽〗 a prostitute in the Edo period.

じょろうぐも 女郎蜘蛛 〖動物〗 a silk spider, or a Joro spider. *Nephila clavata*. Is widely distributed in Japan, except Hokkaido.

じょんまんじろう ジョン万次郎 〖外交〗 ⇨中浜万次郎

しらあえ 白和え 〖食べ物〗 a cooked salad dressed with smashed tofu and white sesame.

しらうお 白魚 〖食べ物・魚〗 an icefish. *Salangichthys microdon*. Is about 10 cm long. Is translucent when it is alive and turns white after death. Is mainly eaten deep fried.

しらうめ 白梅 〖植物〗 ⇨白梅

しらえび 白海老 〖食べ物・魚〗 a glass shrimp. *Pasiphaea japonica*. Is about 5 to 8 cm long. Is translucent when it is alive and turns white after death. Eaten deep fried or as sushi or sashimi. A specialty of Toyama Pref.

しらかば 白樺 **(1)** 〖植物〗 a white birch. *Betula platyphylla* var. *japonica*. Grows wild in high mountains. **(2)** 〖文芸〗 a literary magazine whose title means "white birch." Was first published in 1910, mainly by MUSHANOKOUJI SANEATSU and SHIGA NAOYA. Publication ceased in 1923. Contributors include SATOMI TON, ARISHIMA TAKEO, KURATA HYAKUZOU, and TAKAMURA KOUTAROU.

しらかみさんち 白神山地 〖山岳〗 the Shirakami Mountains. Are located in Northern Japan, on the border between Aomori and Akita Prefs. The highest peak is Mt. Shirakami. Much of its area is covered with beech trees. Was designated a World Heritage Site in 1993.

しらかゆ 白粥 〖食べ物〗 plain gruel of rice. Contains no other ingredients.

しらかわごう 白川郷 〖地名〗 Shirakawa-gou area. Is located in northern Gifu Pref. An extremely snowy and mountainous region in the upper reaches of the Shou River. Famous for a traditional architectural style, GASSHOU-DUKURI, in which the house roofs are steep enough to shed snow easily. The historic villages of Shirakawa-gou and Gokayama were designated a World Heritage Site in 1995.

しらかわし 白河市 〖地名〗 Shirakawa City in the south of Fukushima Pref. Used to be the castle town of the Matsudaira clan.

しらかわてんのう 白河天皇 〖天皇〗 Emperor Shirakawa. 1053-1129. The 72nd, on the throne from 1072 to 1086. The first prince of Emperor Gosanjou. Continued to have political power for 43 years after retirement. →院政

しらぎ 新羅 〖国名〗 Silla. Emerged in eastern Korea in the 4th century and unified the Korean Peninsula in 668 after destroying Paekche and Koguryo in 668. Allying with Tang in China, attacked Paekche and defeated the allied force of Paekche and Japan at the Battle of Baekgang-gu. Was destroyed in 935 by Koryo. →百済(くだら); 高句麗(こうくり); 高麗(こうらい); 白村江の戦い

しらきづくり 白木造り 〖建築・工芸〗 the style of using unpainted or unvarnished wood for wooden furniture or structures.

しらこ 白子 〖食べ物・魚〗 milt. Milt of cod and angler fish is used for ingredients of soup. ↔真子(まこ)

しらさぎじょう 白鷺城 〖城郭〗 a nickname of Himeji Castle. →姫路城

しらす 白子 〖食べ物・魚〗 young fish of Japanese anchovy, sardine, or sand lance. The body is translucent. Eaten raw or dried.

しらす 白洲 〖犯罪〗 a law court in the Edo period. A suspect sat on the ground covered with white sands, and the judge sat on the building floor in front of it.

しらすだいち シラス台地 〖自然〗 Shirasu Plateau. A type of pyroclastic plateau. Is located in southern Kyushu Island, particularly in Kagoshima Pref. Sweet potatoes, Japanese white radish, soybeans, and canola flowers are grown.

しらすぼし 白子干し〔食べ物〕 baby anchovies boiled in salt water and dried soft.

しらたき 白滝〔食べ物〕 noodle-like strips of white konjac. Are often put in a one-pot dish. →鍋物

しらたま 白玉〔食べ物〕 a dumpling of glutinous rice flour. Eaten with sweet soybean flour sprinkled on it, adzuki paste covering it, or in soup.

しらたまこ 白玉粉〔食文化〕 flour made from glutinous rice. Is used for traditional-style confectioneries.

しらなみもの 白波物〔歌舞伎〕 a thief drama in kabuki or traditional storytelling called KOUDAN. Was prevalent in the late Edo period. The most representative works in kabuki are *The Three Kichisas and the New Year's First Visit to the Pleasure Quarters* (Sannin Kichisa kuruwa no hatsugai), *The Shiranami Five* (Shiranami gonin otoko), and *Nezumi Kozou* written by KAWATAKE MOKUAMI.

しらに 白煮〔食べ物〕 a dish simmered with salt and mirin. Does not use soy sauce for seasoning. White vegetables are used as ingredients.

しらぬい 不知火〔自然〕 flickering lights seen along the coasts of the Ariake Sea and Yatsushiro Sea in Kyushu. Occur because of abnormal light reflection.

しらぬいがた 不知火型〔相撲〕 Shiranui style of a ring-entering ceremony for a sumo champion. In the ceremony, he claps his hands, stomps on the ground, raises his upper body, and stomps on the ground again. In the Shiranui style, he stretches both hands in the air on his sides. →雲竜型

しらはまおんせん 白浜温泉〔温泉〕 a hot spring in central Wakayama Pref. Was discovered in ancient times and visited by at least 3 Emperors in the 7th and 8th centuries. Also called Nanki Shirahama Onsen.

しらひげじんじゃ 白髭神社〔神社〕 Shirahige Shrine. Is located in northwestern Shiga Pref., and enshrines SARUTAHIKO.

しらびょうし 白拍子〔芸能・セックス〕 a prostitute in the 12th century. Danced in a male costume such as hunting wear (SUIKAN) and a high black cap (TATE-EBOSHI) while singing popular songs.

しらやまひめじんじゃ 白山比咩神社〔神社〕 Shirayama-hime Shrine. The head shrine of the Hakusan Shrines throughout Japan. Is located in southern Ishikawa Pref. Originates from the worship of Mt. Hakusan, and enshrines Shirayama-hime no ookami. The double-edged dagger, named Yoshimitsu, is a National Treasure. →白山(はくさん)神社; 白山(はくさん)

しりからげ 尻からげ〔服飾〕 ⇨尻っぱしょり

しりっぱしょり 尻っぱしょり〔服飾〕 to tuck up the hem of a kimono. Was done by a man in olden times to allow his legs to move more freely.

しりとり 尻取り〖遊び・言語〗 a word chain game. A player has to say a word that begins with the final syllable of the word given by the previous player. A player is prohibited from saying the same word twice. The game ends when a player has said a word that ends with ん, 'n.'

しりはしょり 尻はしょり〖服飾〗 ⇨ 尻っぱしょり

しるこ 汁粉〖食べ物〗 sweet adzuki bean soup with rice cake or dumpling. Some types use sieved adzuki paste called KOSHIAN, and other types use chunky adzuki paste called TSUBUAN.

しるしばんてん 印半纏〖服飾〗 a traditional short coat for a craftsman. Includes the crest or name of the employer on the back and lapels.

しるばあしいと シルバーシート〖交通〗 ⇨優先座席

しるもの 汁物〖食文化〗 soup. Includes miso soup (MISOSHIRU), clear soup (SUIMONO), and sake lees soup (KASUJIRU).

しれとこはんとう 知床半島〖半島〗 the Shiretoko Peninsula. Protrudes into the Sea of Okhotsk from northeastern Hokkaido. Has many volcanos and hot springs. Its environment has not been destroyed by human activities, and diverse plants and animals inhabit it. Was designated a World Heritage Site in 2005.

しろあん 白餡〖食べ物〗 sweet paste made from white beans.

しろうお 素魚〖食べ物・魚〗 an ice goby. *Leucopsarion petersii*. Is about 5 cm long. Is translucent when it is alive and turns white after death. Eaten alive while still moving. →踊り食い

しろえび 白海老〖食べ物・魚〗 ⇨白(ﾗ)海老

しろざけ 白酒〖酒〗 sweet white sake. Contains less alcohol than ordinary sake and is drunk at the Girls' Festival in March.

しろしょいん 白書院〖建築〗 literally means "white study room." Its meaning is different among facilities. For example, the 'shiro-shoin' at Nijou Castle in Kyoto was used as the living room and bedroom for the shogun, while the one at Hongan-ji Temple in Kyoto was used as the official drawing room. ↔黒書院

しろしょうぞく 白装束〖服飾・武士〗 a white costume. Entire piece of clothing is white. Is used for a religious service. Was a costume for ritual suicide in the Edo period.

しろねぎ 白葱〖食べ物・植物〗 a long white onion. Is popular in the Kantou region.

しろぶさ 白房〖相撲〗 a white tassel. Hung at the southwestern corner of a suspended roof above the sumo ring. Means autumn and the white tiger. →青房; 赤房; 黒房; 白虎(ﾋﾞゃっこ)

しろへび 白蛇 〚動物〛 a white snake. The albino of a rat snake. Has been regarded as a messenger of a deity in some areas.

しろぼし 白星 〚相撲〛 a victory mark. Literally means "white star." Is symbolized by a white dot in the list of tournament records, BAN-DUKE. ↔黒星

しろみざかな 白身魚 〚食べ物〛 a fish with pale flesh. Examples are a sea bream, a flatfish, and a sea bass.

しろみそ 白味噌 〚食べ物〛 white miso. A little sweet. An example is SAIKYOU-MISO.

しろむく 白無垢 〚服飾〛 an all-white bridal kimono. A bride wears this garment in the marriage ceremony and changes the white robe into a gorgeously colored one, called UCHIKAKE, during the wedding banquet after the ceremony.

しわす 師走 〚暦〛 December. Was originally used in the traditional calendar, but is also often used in the current calendar. Means "priest or teacher running" because everyone is very busy in this month.

しん 辛 〚干支〛 ⇨辛(かのと)

しん 真 〚書道・芸術〛 the basic and fully depicted style of various traditional arts. Literally means "truth." →真・行・草

しん 清 〚国名〛 Chin. A Chinese dynasty from 1616-1912. The Sino-Japanese War raged from 1894 to 1895.

じん 壬 〚干支〛 ⇨壬(みずのえ)

しんいき 神域 〚神社〛 the precincts of a Shinto shrine.

しんうち 真打ち 〚落語〛 a master of comic storytelling called RAKUGO. This title is not used for storytellers in the Kansai region.

しんえん 神苑 〚神社・庭園〛 the precinct of a Shinto shrine, or the sacred garden in the precinct.

しんかげりゅう 新陰流 〚剣術〛 a school of swordsmanship established in the 16th century by KAMI-IZUMI HIDETSUNA. One of the best disciples is YAGYUU MUNEYOSHI, who later founded the Yagyuu school.

じんがさ 陣笠 〚服飾〛 a soldier's hat. A low-ranking soldier did not wear a helmet in a battle.

しんかん 神官 〚神社〛 a Shinto priest. →神主

しんかんせん 新幹線 〚鉄道〛 super express bullet train. There are 9 Shinkansen lines in Japan, namely, Tokaido, San'yo, Kyushu, Tohoku, Yamagata, Akita, Joetsu, Hokuriku, and Hokkaido Shinkansen. Runs at maximum speed of 260-320 km/h in most sections, and carries a total of 150 million passengers per year. Tokaido Shinkansen is the oldest of the nine, which started service in 1964, the year of the first Tokyo Olympics. The newest is Hokkaido Shinkansen, which started service in 2016. Japan's technology of constructing the network of high-speed railway lines was exported to Taiwan in 2007, and will be exported to India in 2023.

じんぎ 仁義 〚精神性〛 humanity

and justice. The idea of an ancient Chinese philosopher, Mencius (Moushi).

じんぎ 神器 〘神話〙 ⇨三種の神器

じんぎかん 神祇官 〘神道・行政〙 a government agency in charge of matters related to Shintoism. Was active in ancient times, deteriorated in medieval and early-modern times, and was revived in 1868.

じんぎすかんなべ ジンギスカン鍋 〘食べ物〙 Genghis Khan barbecue. Sliced lamb or mutton and various vegetables are grilled in a dome-shaped frying pan. Are dipped in special sauce before eating. Is popular in Hokkaido. Goes well with beer.

しんきゅういん 鍼灸院 〘医療〙 a clinic of acupuncture and moxibustion. →鍼灸院

しんきゅうし 鍼灸師 〘医療〙 a practitioner of acupuncture and moxibustion. Needs a national license different from that of a medical doctor.

しんぎょうそう 真・行・草 〘書道・芸術〙 three styles of various traditional arts including calligraphy, painting, tea ceremony, flower arrangement, and performing arts. 'Shin,' which means "truth," is the basic and fully depicted style. 'Sou,' which means "grass," is the simplified or flowing style. 'Gyou,' which means "line" or "training," is the intermediate style between 'shin' and 'sou.'

しんぐう 新宮 〘神社〙 a branch shrine. When a divine spirit at a shrine is newly enshrined at another shrine, the former is called HONGUU, and the latter is called shinguu.

じんぐう 神宮 〘神社〙 a high-ranking Shinto shrine. Although the shrine ranking system was abolished after World War II, some shrines are still using the names with jinguu, such as ATSUTA JINGUU. In a narrow sense, it only means the Ise Shrine. →伊勢神宮

じんぐうこうごう 神功皇后 〘天皇〙 Empress Consort Jinguu. The wife of Emperor Chuuai and the mother of Emperor Oujin. After the death of her husband, attacked Silla in the Korean Peninsula during her pregnancy. Came back to Japan and gave birth to her son. →仲哀(ちゅうあい)天皇；応神天皇

じんぐうじ 神宮寺 〘神道・仏教〙 a Buddhist temple attached to a Shinto shrine. Was built within the precincts of a shrine, based on the fusion of Shintoism and Buddhism. Was ruined or was separated from the shrine, after the Edict for Separation of Shintoism and Buddhism in 1868. →神仏習合；神仏分離

しんげい 真芸 〘芸術〙 ⇨芸阿弥(げいあみ)

しんけん 真剣 **(1)**〘剣術〙 a real sword. This term is used to distinguish it from a wooden or bamboo sword. **(2)**〘精神性〙 seriousness, earnestness, or sincerity. Derived from (1).

しんこ 新香〔食べ物〕 ⇨おしんこ

じんこう 沈香〔植物・香道〕 aloeswood, or agarwood. *Aquilaria agallocha*. Grows in tropical Asia up to 30 m high. Is used as aromatic wood. The best quality wood is called KYARA.

じんごうき 塵劫記〔科学技術・作品〕 *Inalterable Treatise*. A reference book of fundamental mathematics written in 1627 by YOSHIDA MITSUYOSHI.

しんこきんわかしゅう 新古今和歌集〔文芸・作品〕 *New Collection of Ancient and Modern Japanese Poetry*. The eighth imperial anthology of poetry. Was compiled in 1205 at the command of the retired Emperor Gotoba by Minamoto no Michitomo, Fujiwara no Ariie, FUJIWARA NO TEIKA, Fujiwara no Ietaka, Fujiwara no Masatsune, and Jakuren. Contains about 1,980 poems in 20 volumes. The poetry style is emotional and symbolic.

じんごじ 神護寺〔寺院〕 Jingo-ji Temple. A temple of the Shingon sect located in Kyoto City. Was founded in 824 by an aristocrat, WAKE NO KIYOMARO, and was revived in the early Kamakura period by a priest, MONGAKU, after being devastated temporarily. Is now famous for beautiful colored leaves in autumn.

しんこまき 新香巻〔寿司〕 a sushi roll of pickled vegetable. The vegetable is usually daikon, but the vegetables used are different from region to region.

しんこもち 糝粉餅〔食べ物〕 rice-flour dough. Is said to be a specialty at a hot spring in Toukamachi, Niigata Pref., but is now eaten throughout Japan.

しんごん 真言〔仏教〕 a mantra, or magic words in esoteric Buddhism. Literally means "true words." Each mantra is phonetically transliterated from Sanskrit into Chinese characters. Its contents vary, such as the name of Buddha or a Bodhisattva or their teaching.

しんごんしゅう 真言宗〔仏教〕 the Shingon sect. Was founded at the beginning of the 9th century by KUUKAI, who studied esoteric Buddhism in the Tang dynasty. The principal Buddha is the Great Sun Buddha. The head temple is KONGOUBU-JI Temple in Mt. Kouya, Wakayama Pref.

しんごんみっきょう 真言密教〔仏教〕 ⇨真言宗

しんさくらくご 新作落語〔落語〕 modern comic storytelling. Its subject matter is mainly contemporary issues or topics.

しんじ 信士〔仏教〕 a suffix of a man's posthumous name in Buddhism. The most common among such suffixes. People have to pay more money to a temple to raise the rank of the suffix. ↔信女

しんじいけ 心字池〔庭園〕 a pond shaped in a kanji, 心, meaning "heart." Is set in a traditional garden. Exists at Hongou Campus of the Univ. of Tokyo, Engaku-ji Temple in Kamakura, the Katsura Imperial Villa in Kyoto, etc.

しんじこ 宍道湖 〖湖沼〗 Lake Shinji. A brackish lake near the mouth of the Hii River in northeastern Shimane Pref. The area is 79 km². Famous for the production of freshwater clams. Was designated a Ramsar site in 2005, together with the neighboring lake, Naka Inlet, on the border between Tottori and Shimane Prefs. →中海（なかうみ）; ラムサール条約登録湿地

じんじゃ 神社 〖神社〗 a Shinto shrine. There are more than 80,000 shrines throughout Japan, and one shrine usually enshrines more than one deity. The various deities include nature deities, mythical ancestors of Imperial or local clans, and deified spirits of historical people. When visiting a shrine, people worship them according to a specific procedure, called NIREI NI-HAKUSHU ICHIREI. →神道; 稲荷; 天神; 八幡宮

じんじゃしんとう 神社神道 〖神道〗 Shrine Shintoism. The Meiji government divided Shintoism into non-religious Shrine Shintoism and religious Sect Shintoism. It ranked the former above the latter and protected all shrines. Since the end of World War II, the term has referred to various forms of worship, from worship of a local tutelary deity to that of the Ise Shrine. →教派神道; 国家神道

しんしゅ 新酒 〖酒〗 new sake. Is brewed with new rice and shipped the following spring.

しんしゅう 信州 〖地名〗 ⇨信濃

しんじゅう 心中 〖精神性〗 **(1)** a double lovers' suicide. Actual incidents became the theme of bunraku or kabuki stories in the Edo period. **(2)** a family suicide. A murder-suicide sometimes happens at present because a son or a daughter is too tired to care for a senile parent.

しんじゅうもの 心中物 〖文芸〗 a story about a double lovers' suicide in bunraku or kabuki. Is based on an actual incident.

しんじゅく 新宿 〖地名〗 the name of a very popular shopping and entertaining area in central Tokyo city proper. Is also an administrative center that includes the Tokyo Metropolitan Government Building, and an economic hub that includes the headquarters of many major companies. JR Shinjuku Station is the busiest JR station in terms of the number of passengers. BASUTA SHINJUKU, the newly opened bus terminal, is also gaining popularity among tourists.

しんじゅくぎょえん 新宿御苑 〖施設〗 Shinjuku Gyoen National Garden. Is located on the border between Shinjuku and Shibuya Cities in central Tokyo. Is 0.6 km² in area. Developed as an experimental agricultural center and a botanical garden, and was opened to the public in 1949. Has three areas with their own styles: a French Formal style, an English Landscape style, and a Japanese Traditional style. Attracts a great number of visitors when its 1,500 cherry trees are in full bloom from late March to late April.

しんじゅわんこうげき 真珠湾攻撃 〖戦争〗 Attack on Pearl Harbor. The surprise attack by Japanese Navy planes on the American naval base at Pearl Harbor in Hawaii, on December 7, 1941, in Hawaii-Aleutian Standard Time. The attack destroyed much of the U.S. Pacific fleet, killed over 2,000 military personnel and civilians, and led to an immediate declaration of war by the U.S. against Japan. While it was the precipitating event for war, tensions between Japan and the U.S. had been building for years.

しんじょ 真薯 〖食べ物〗 dumpling paste of ground shrimp, yam, and egg white. Eaten fried or steamed.

じんしんのらん 壬申の乱 〖戦争〗 Jinshin War. Was fought in 672 between OOAMA NO OUJI, a younger brother of Emperor Tenji, and Ootomo no ouji, a son of Emperor Tenji, both of whom tried to succeed the Imperial Throne. The former defeated the latter and became Emperor Tenmu the next year.

しんせかい 新世界 〖地名〗 the name of a retrospective entertainment area in Naniwa Ward in central Osaka City. Literally means "the new world." Modeled on Paris

and New York, was opened in 1912 at the site of an industrial exhibition held in 1903. Its symbolic tower, Tsuuten-kaku, was first built modeled on the Eiffel Tower, but the present tower, rebuilt in 1956, changed its design. From the 1960s to 1980s, it had a bad reputation as a place where blue-collar workers hung out in poverty. In the 1990s, however, it became popular as an area that conveys the atmosphere of the good old days of the Shouwa period.

しんせん 神饌 〖神道〗 food or drink offered to a deity or deities. Worshippers eat or drink it after the ritual. →直会(なおらい)

しんせんぐみ 新撰組 〖武士・政治〗 the Kyoto special police under the Tokugawa shogunate. Was founded in 1863 and led by KONDOU ISAMI. Suppressed the movement of "Revere the Emperor and expel the barbarians." Scattered away after being defeated in the Battle of Toba and Fushimi in 1868.

しんぜんけっこん 神前結婚 〖冠婚葬祭〗 a Shinto-style wedding. Is held at a shrine. Has been popular since the 19th century.

しんそう 真相 〖絵画〗 ⇨相阿弥(そうあみ)

しんそうさい 神葬祭 〖神道・冠婚葬祭〗 a Shinto-style funeral. Has been performed since the separation of Shintoism from Buddhism in the Meiji period.

しんそうとほ 深草兎歩 〖忍者〗 a special walking performed by

crouching and putting each foot on the back of each hand. A ninja can move silently with this walking method.

しんたい 神体 〔神道〕 a sacred object in Shintoism. The object is usually kept concealed in the main sanctuary building of a shrine. Examples of a sacred object include a tree, stone, mountain, sword, and mirror. →本殿

じんだいこ 陣太鼓 〔軍事〕 a battle drum. Was beaten to order troops forward or backward.

じんだいもじ 神代文字 〔言語・考古〕 fictional ancient characters. Some scholars insisted original Japanese characters had existed before kanji was introduced from China, but they are now considered to be fictitious.

じんたん 仁丹 〔食べ物〕 the trademark of an oral refrigerant. A small silver ball made from crude medicines such as cinnamon and menthol.

しんちとせくうこう 新千歳空港 〔交通〕 New Chitose Airport. The airport code is CTS. Is located in Chitose City, to the southeast of Sapporo. It is about 40 minutes from Sapporo Station by JR rapid train. Passengers can enjoy a hot spring at the New Chitose Airport Onsen.

しんちゃ 新茶 〔飲み物〕 green tea made with newly picked leaves.

しんでん 新田 〔農業〕 a newly developed rice field. Especially ones developed in the Edo period.

しんでんづくり 寝殿造り 〔建築〕 the style of aristocratic mansions in the Heian period. The main building facing south was located at the center of the complex. Three annexes linked by veranda corridors were located on the east, west, and north. The southern garden had a pond with a miniature island. Tatami mats were used only for places where noble people sat, not spread over the rooms.

しんど 震度 〔自然・災害〕 seismic intensity. Is ranked from zero to seven. When the Great East Japan Earthquake occurred in 2011, Kurihara City in Miyagi Pref. registered the maximum scale number of 7.

しんとう 新刀 〔武器〕 a sword made in and after the 17th century.

しんとう 神道 〔神道〕 Shintoism, or Shinto. Japanese indigenous pantheistic religion, based on worshipping nature and ancestors. Its holy place is a Shinto shrine called JINJA. Shintoism has been influenced by Buddhism, Confucianism, and Taoism. Typical examples of the influence from Buddhism are "the theory of original reality and manifested traces" (HONJISUIJAKU-SETSU) in the Heian period, and Dual Shintoism (RYOUBU SHINTOU) in the Kamakura period. As the anti-movement against foreign religions such as Buddhism and Confucianism, Restoration

Shintoism (FUKKO SHINTOU) appeared in the Edo period. The Meiji government founded State Shintoism (KOKKA SHINTOU) as a kind of theocracy, by closely connecting it to the Imperial system. At present, some of the Japanese new religions are based on Shintoism and generically are called Sect Shintoism (KYOUHA SHINTOU).

しんとうしれい 神道指令 〖神道・政治〗 the Shinto Directive. Was issued by the Supreme Commander of the Allied Powers to abolish state support for Shintoism. Its official title is "Abolition of Governmental Sponsorship, Support, Perpetuation, Control, and Dissemination of State Shinto." It is also called SCAPIN 448, which stands for the Supreme Commander for Allied Powers Instruction Note. →国家神道

しんにゅうまく 新入幕 〖相撲〗 a debut into the top division of professional sumo wrestling. Or, the sumo wrestler who has just debuted.

しんにょ 信女 〖仏教〗 a suffix of a woman's posthumous name in Buddhism. The most common among such suffixes. People have to pay more money to a temple to raise the rank of the suffix. ↔信士 (しんじ)

しんねんかい 新年会 〖酒〗 New Year's party. Friends or colleagues get together and eat and drink to celebrate the new year.

しんのう 親王 〖天皇・行政〗 **(1)** a legitimate prince, or a son of the eldest legitimate prince, according to the Imperial House Act. **(2)** a prince, or a brother of an Emperor, in ancient times. ↔内親王

しんのう 真能 〖芸術〗 ⇨能阿弥 (のうあみ)

じんばおり 陣羽織 〖軍事・服飾〗 a sleeveless coat for a warlord. Was worn on armor in a battlefield or camp.

しんぱん 親藩 〖武士・政治〗 a feudal domain of Tokugawa relatives. Examples are Owari, Kii, Mito, Echizen, and Aizu. Their family name was Tokugawa or Matsudaira. →譜代大名；外様大名

しんぷ 神符 〖神道〗 a talisman sold at a shrine. →お守り

しんぶつこんこう 神仏混淆 〖神道・仏教〗 ⇨神仏習合

しんぶつしゅうごう 神仏習合 〖神道・仏教〗 fusion of Shintoism and Buddhism. Began in the Nara period and ended with the order by the Meiji government in 1868 to separate them. →神宮寺；本地垂迹 (ほんじすいじゃく)説；神仏分離；神仏判然の令

しんぶつはんぜんのれい 神仏判然令 〖神道・仏教〗 the Shinto and Buddhism Separation Order. Was decreed in 1868 and triggered the movements to abolish Buddhism. →神仏分離；国家神道；廃仏毀釈 (はいぶつきしゃく)

しんぶつぶんり 神仏分離 〖神道・仏教〗 separation between Shintoism

and Buddhism. The government issued the order to reinforce the authority of Emperors as the offspring of the Sun Goddess. →神仏習合；国家神道；廃仏毀釈（はいぶつきしゃく）；神仏判然の令

じんべ 甚平 〘服飾〙 a traditional summer indoor suit for men. Has short sleeves and short pants. Is worn by fastening the attached cord.

しんぼく 神木 〘神道〙 a sacred tree in a Shinto shrine. Usually it is large or uniquely shaped. Sacred straw rope is hung around it, and a fence is put it around.

じんむけいき 神武景気 〘経済〙 the Jinmu Boom. Continued from December 1954 to June 1957, owing to the expansion of exports. Was nicknamed after the first Emperor Jinmu because it was said to be the greatest business boom since his era. During this period, economic activity exceeded the level before World War II, and the Economic White Paper said, "The postwar period is over." →神武天皇；岩戸景気；伊弉諾（いざなぎ）景気

じんむてんのう 神武天皇 〘天皇・神話〙 Emperor Jinmu. A legendary figure. An offspring of NINIGI NO MIKOTO. In a Japanese myth, departed from HYUUGA in Kyushu, where Ninigi had descended from the High Celestial Plain, towards the east. Ascended the throne as the first Emperor and passed away at the age of 127.

しんめ 神馬 〘神道・動物〙 a sacred horse. Was offered to a shrine as a vehicle for a deity. It was usually white. A tablet with a picture of a horse is offered instead of a living horse these days. →絵馬

しんめいづくり 神明造り 〘神社・建築〙 Shinmei style of Shinto architecture. The entrance is on the side where the roof line is parallel to the ground, not on the gable side. The pillars outside of each gable directly support the ridge. The main sanctuary buildings of the Ise Shrine have this style. →本殿；伊勢神宮

しんめいとりい 神明鳥居 〘神社〙 a Shinmei-style gateway to a Shinto shrine. Consists of two vertical columns and two horizontal bars without a vertical strut between the bars. A Shinto shrine whose building is in the Shinmei-style of architecture has this type of gate. ↔明神（みょうじん）鳥居 →鳥居；神明造り

じんや 陣屋 〘行政〙 a local office or residence of a magistrate or governor in his fief in the Edo period.

しんやくしじ 新薬師寺 〘寺院〙 Shin'yakushi-ji Temple. Affiliated with the Kegon sect. Is located in Nara City. Was founded in 747 by Empress Consort Koumyou, who prayed for her husband's recovery from eye disease. The Healing Buddha and the Twelve Divine Generals are National Treasures. →光明皇后；聖武（しょうむ）天皇；薬師如来；十二神将

しんようくみあい 信用組合〖ビジネス〗 a credit association, or a credit cooperative. A mutually helpful financial institution for small companies.

しんらん 親鸞〖仏教〗 1173-1262. A priest born in Kyoto. The founder of the True Pure Land sect. Regarded Hounen as his master. Since few books or materials concerning Shinran exist, details of his life remains unclear. →浄土真宗；歎異抄(たんにしょう)

じんりきしゃ 人力車 〖交通〗 a human-powered rickshaw. Was popular in the late 19th century. Is now available around some tourist spots such as Kyoto and Asakusa.

じんりきしゃふ 人力車夫〖交通・職業〗 a driver of a human-powered rickshaw.

しんれき 新暦〖暦〗 the current calendar. Is based on the solar calendar, which has been used since 1873. ↔旧暦

しんろく 神鹿〖神道・動物〗 a sacred deer. Is thought of as a servant or vehicle of a deity. Kasuga Grand Shrine in Nara is famous for deer. →春日大社

しんわ 神話〖神話〗 ⇨日本神話

す

す 酢 〖調味料〗 vinegar. Was introduced from China around the 4th century. Rice vinegar is common in Japan. Is often mixed with other seasoning such as soy sauce, sugar, or miso.

すあげ 素揚げ 〖食べ物〗 deep-fried food without batter or bread crumbs.

ずい 隋 〖国名〗 Sui. A Chinese dynasty from 581 to 619. Japan began to dispatch envoys in 607.

すいえん 水煙 〖仏教〗 openwork at the top of a pagoda roof. Literally means "water spray," although its design represents a flame, because water puts out fire. A famous example is one at the east pagoda at Yakushi-ji Temple in Nara City. → 相輪(ﾆ)

すいか Suica 〖鉄道〗 Suica. Stands for "Super Urban Intelligent CArd." Is a contactless, credit-card-sized smart card, widely used in urban and suburban areas in Japan for many purposes. Can be purchased at a JR East station for ¥2,000, and is rechargeable. Operates on a pre-pay basis. When it was launched in 2001, it was usable only when a passenger entered and exited the ticket gate at JR East stations in and around Tokyo. But later, it came to be used in other areas such as Sapporo, Sendai, Nagoya, Kyoto, Osaka, Kobe, Hiroshima, and Fukuoka, and at stations operated by non-JR railway companies. Is usable not only for riding a train but also for riding a bus, for purchasing goods at stores and vending machines, even outside the railway premises, and for using the keyless locker system. Offers inter-operability with other local smart cards such as PASMO, Kitaca, TOICA, ICOCA, and SUGOCA.

すいかつがん 水渇丸 〖忍者〗 an anti-thirst pill.

すいかん 水干 〖服飾〗 a hunting costume. Was first used as informal men's dress for common people in the Heian period and became formal men's dress for warriors in later periods. The tail of the upper garment was stuffed inside the loose-legged trousers, different from KARIGINU.

ずいがんじ 瑞巌寺 〖寺院〗 Zuigan-ji Temple. Affiliated with the Rinzai sect. Is located in middle Miyagi Pref. Was founded in 838 by the priest ENNIN. Used to be the family temple of the Date clan, a powerful feudal lord in Northern Japan. The main hall and the kitchen building, which were built under the sponsorship of DATE MASAMUNE, are National Treasures. →松島

すいき 水器 〖忍者〗 a tool used to cross the water. A ninja, who hated getting wet and exhausted, made a temporary tool with things on hand and broke it after using it to erase the traces. 'Suiki' incudes a floating bridge, a small straw raft, and a water spider.

ずいき 芋茎 〖食べ物・植物〗 leaf stalks of a taro. Eaten boiled or vinegared.

すいきんくつ 水琴窟 〖庭園〗 a water harp hollow. Is buried in a garden. Creates a pleasant sound by resonance when a person pours water on it and the water drips on the water in the buried jar.

すいぐん 水軍 〖軍事〗 a marine warrior group from ancient to early modern times. Managed marine transportation, sometimes cooperated with political administrations, and sometimes pirated other ships. The Kuki clan around present Mie Pref. and the Murakami clan in present Hiroshima Pref. are famous as 'suigun.'

すいげつかんのん 水月観音 〖仏教〗 Water-moon KANNON. One of the 33 forms of the Bodhisattva of Mercy. Is depicted as a figure looking at the moon reflected on the water.

すいこてんのう 推古天皇 〖天皇〗 Empress Suiko. 554-628. The 33rd, on the throne from 592 to 628. The third princess of Emperor Kinmei and the wife of Emperor Bidatsu. Appointed her nephew, Prince Shoutoku, as a regent. →聖徳太子

すいじゅつ 水術 〖武術〗 swimming as martial arts. For example, to swim in a suit of armor, to use weapons in the water, and to ride a horse in the water.

ずいじん 随身 〖政治〗 a guard for high-ranking court noble in the Heian period and later. Their number varied with the rank of the person they guarded.

ずいじんもん 隋身門 〖宗教〗 the gate of a Shinto shrine with the sculpture of two court guards.

すいせんにゅうし 推薦入試 〖教育〗 entrance exams upon recommendation. Students take entrance exams for high schools or universities, based on the recommendation by their schools. There are several different systems from school to school.

すいてん 水天 〖仏教〗 Water Deva. *Varuna*. One of the Twelve Devas. Guards the west.

すいでん 水田 〖農業〗 a paddy field, or a rice paddy. The total area is 241.8 hectares in Japan as of 2017, according to the Ministry of Agriculture, Forestry and Fisheries.

すいとう 水稲 〖農業〗 paddy rice, or wet-field rice.

すいとん 水団 〖食べ物〗 a soup with flour dumpling. Was eaten during a food shortage.

すいとん 水遁 〖忍者〗 escape techniques using water. One of five major techniques. Include swimming under water or making the enemy hallucinate that the ninja has plunged into water by throwing a large stone into pond with a splash.

→五遁

すいにんてんのう 垂仁天皇〔天皇〕 Emperor Suinin. ?–? The 11th. The third prince of Emperor Sujin, and the father of Emperor Keikou. Abolished the immolation of vassals on the death of their master, following the advice of NOMI NO SUKUNE. →殉死(じゅんし)

すいばん 水盤〔華道〕 a shallow container for arranging flowers.

すいはんき 炊飯器〔食文化〕 a rice cooker. Is powered by electricity or gas. The user only has to set rice and water in it.

すいびょう 水瓶〔仏教〕 a water container. One of the belongings of a monk or nun. Is also held by some kinds of Buddhist images such as the Eleven-headed Bodhisattva of Mercy. →十一面観音

ずいほうしょう 瑞宝章〔政治〕 Order of the Sacred Treasure.

すいぼくが 水墨画〔絵画〕 India ink painting. Was introduced from China in the Kamakura period. Represents the object, using the outline drawn with India ink or a light shade of the ink. Weak coloring is sometimes used.

すいもの 吸い物〔食べ物〕 a clear hot soup. Contains fish, chicken, or vegetables. Is usually in a lacquer bowl.

すうがくけんてい 数学検定〔教育〕 Practical Mathematics Proficiency Test. Is held three times a year. There are 14 levels, ranging from the test for college graduates to the one for preschool children.

ずうずうべん ずうずう弁〔言語〕 the Tohoku dialect. Is distinguished by its unique nasal sounds.

すうたい 素謡〔能・音楽〕 to chant a Noh song without dance or music. The singers sit in a formal way while singing.

すうでん 崇伝〔仏教〕 ⇨金地院(こんち いん) 崇伝

すうどん 素饂飩〔食べ物〕 a dialect word of the Kansai region, referring to plain thick wheat noodles in hot broth. →掛け饂飩

すうみついん 枢密院〔政治〕 the Privy Council. The highest advisory organ for the Emperor under the Constitution of the Empire of Japan. Was established in 1888 and abolished in 1947.

すえき 須恵器〔考古・陶磁器〕 sue ware. Hard and gray unglazed earthenware used from the 5th to the 12th centuries. Was fired stone-hard at around 1,200 degrees centigrade. The technique is said to have been introduced from the Korean Peninsula.

すえきち 末吉〔神社・寺院〕 good fortune to come. A message on a fortune slip available at a Shinto shrine or Buddhist temple. The message implies that the present fortune is not good but that it will become better in the future. →お神 籤(くじ)

すおう 周防〔旧国名〕 the old name of southeastern Yamaguchi Pref.

すがたずし 姿鮨〔食べ物〕 fish-shaped sushi. Keeps the original shape of a fish and is stuffed with vinegared rice.

すがたづくり 姿造り 〔食べ物〕 sashimi adorned with the head and tail of the fish. Is arranged on a plate to look like its original shape.

すがたに 姿煮 〔食べ物〕 a boiled whole fish. Keeps its original shape.

すがたやき 姿焼き 〔食べ物〕 a grilled whole fish. Keeps its original shape. Ones of sea bream and squid are popular.

すがわらのみちざね 菅原道真 〔政治〕 845-903. An aristocrat, scholar, and poet. Was favored by Emperor Uda, who tried to resist the powerful Fujiwara clan and proposed to abolish an official mission to Tang in 894. After Emperor Uda abdicated, Michizane was exiled to Dazaifu in present Fukuoka Pref. and died there. After his death, the government founded a shrine to pacify his vengeful spirit. →天神; 天満宮

すき 数寄 〔精神性〕 pursuit of elegance in the tea ceremony, flower arrangement, and poetry.

すぎ 杉 〔植物〕 a Japanese cedar. *Cryptomeria japonica*. An evergreen that grows about 50 m high. Some are more than 1,000 years old. Its timber is used for architecture and furniture. Causes pollen allergy these days.

すきい スキー 〔スポーツ〕 skiing. Was first taught in Japan in 1911 by an Austrian army officer, Theodor Edler von Lerch.

すぎたげんぱく 杉田玄白 〔医療〕 1733-1817. A medical doctor who translated a Dutch medical book, *Ontleedkundige Tafelen*, into Japanese.

すぎだま 杉玉 〔酒〕 a cedar leaf ball. A sake brewery hangs it under the eaves to announce that new sake is brewed.

すぎど 杉戸 〔建築〕 a sliding door made of Japanese cedar. The panel is often decorated with a painting of flowers and birds.

すぎどえ 杉戸絵 〔絵画〕 a picture on a sliding door made of Japanese cedar. Often a flower or a bird is depicted.

すきや 数寄屋 〔茶道・建築〕 an annex that is used mainly for the tea ceremony. Is equipped with a kitchen.

すきやき 鋤焼き 〔食べ物〕 sukiyaki, or a soy-flavored one-pot dish with sliced beef, tofu, vegetables, and mushrooms. Is cooked in a shallow pan at the table, seasoned with soy sauce, mirin, and sugar. Most people dip the hot food into raw egg before eating.

すきやづくり 数寄屋造り 〔建築〕 the style of a tea-ceremony room. Uses natural or natural-like materials. A famous example can be seen in the Katsura Detached Palace in Kyoto. →桂離宮

すくいなげ 掬い投げ 〔相撲〕 a beltless arm throw. A sumo technique

of throwing the opponent without grasping his belt.

すぐき 酢茎 〖食べ物〗 lacto-fermented pickles of turnip. A specialty of Kyoto.

すくなひこなのかみ 少名毘古那神 〖神話〗 a deity with a tiny build. A son of KAMIMUSUBI NO KAMI. Helped OOKUNINUSHI NO KAMI establish the Central Land of Reeds. Is worshipped as a deity of medicine or rice wine.

すげ 菅 〖植物〗 a sedge. *Carex*. Is used as material of a lampshade headgear (KASA), a rain cap (MINO), or flat-thonged sandals (ZOURI).

すげがさ 菅笠 〖服飾〗 a flat conic hat woven with sedge. Has a chin strap.

すけだち 助太刀 〖武士〗 help in a revenge or duel.

すけとうだら 介党鱈 〖食べ物・魚〗 an Alaska pollack, or a walleye pollack. *Theragra chalcogramma*. About 70 cm long. Eaten as fish paste or dried fish. Its roe is popular as TARAKO.

すけろく 助六 **(1)** 〖歌舞伎〗 a common name of a popular kabuki program, *Sukeroku: Flower of Edo* (Sukeroku yukari no edo zakura). **(2)** 〖歌舞伎〗 the name of its hero. Committed double suicide with a prostitute, Agemaki. **(3)** 〖寿司〗 a set of sliced sushi roll and fox sushi. Is named after the hero of a kabuki play, who committed double suicide with a prostitute, Agemaki. The first half of her name, 'age,'

means "thin fried tofu," which is a major ingredient of fox sushi. The last half of her name, 'maki,' means "sushi roll." →太巻き；稲荷寿司

すごろく 双六 〖遊び〗 a traditional board game similar to Indian pachisi, British Ludo, or American Life. Players move pieces forward a square by throwing a dice and try to reach the goal earlier than others.

すざく 朱雀 〖宗教・動物〗 the red phoenix. The animal deity that symbolizes the south. →四神(しん)；青竜(せいりゅう)；白虎(びゃっこ)；玄武(げんぶ)

すざくもん 朱雀門 〖天皇・建築〗 the south gate of Heijou and Heian Palaces. 'Suzaku' means "the red phoenix," which symbolizes the south.

すさのおのみこと 須佐之男命 〖神話〗 the God of Storms. A son of IZANAGI NO MIKOTO and younger brother of AMATERASU OOMIKAMI. After being exiled from the High Celestial Plain because of his violent behavior, he exterminated YAMATA NO OROCHI and married KUSHINADA HIME.

すし 鮨, 鮓, 寿司 〖食べ物〗 sushi. Originally, naturally fermented fish with rice such as NARE-ZUSHI. The present-style sushi was developed in the Edo period and includes numerous variations such as NIGIRI-ZUSHI, MAKI-ZUSHI, CHIRASHI-ZUSHI, MUSHI-ZUSHI, INARI-ZUSHI, and OSHI-ZUSHI, each of which uses different ingredients. →寿司屋

ずし 厨子 〖仏教〗 an ornamented double-door chest. Stores a Buddhist image or sutras. Is sometimes shaped like a palace or house.

ずしおう 厨子王 〖芸能〗 the hero of *Sansho the Steward*. Assisted by his elder sister ANJU, fled from SANSHOU-DAYUU, who kidnapped them and forced them to work as slaves. After growing up, Zushiou took revenge on Sanshou-dayuu.

すしおけ 寿司桶 〖食文化〗 a shallow wooden container to mingle rice with vinegar, sugar, and salt for sushi.

すじこ 筋子 〖食べ物〗 salted salmon roe. When separated, it is called IKURA.

すしや 寿司屋 〖食べ物・ビジネス〗 a sushi restaurant, or a sushi shop. Some sushi shops offer delivery services. A conveyor belt sushi bar, called KAITEN-ZUSHI, serves various kinds of sushi at reasonable prices.

すしゅんてんのう 崇峻天皇 〖天皇〗 Emperor Sushun. ?-592. The 32nd, on the throne from 587 to 592. Was helped to the throne by SOGA NO UMAKO, but later they confronted each other and the Emperor was assassinated.

すじょうゆ 酢醤油 〖調味料〗 vinegared soy sauce. Is used for vegetables or a Chinese-style pork bun.

すじんてんのう 崇神天皇 〖天皇〗 Emperor Sujin. ?-? The 10th. The second prince of Emperor Kaika. Some researchers say that he must be the first Emperor because he established the financial system of the Imperial Court.

すすき 薄 〖植物〗 a Japanese pampas grass, or eulalia. *Miscanthus sinensis*. Grows in colonies, and its height is 1 to 2 m. Is sometimes combined with the moon as a motif of a picture. One of the seven flowers of autumn. →秋の七草

すずき 鱸 〖魚〗 a Japanese sea bass. *Lateolabrax japonicus*. About 1 m long. Eaten in various ways such as grilled, deep-fried, or as sashimi.

すずきだいせつ 鈴木大拙 〖仏教〗 1870-1966. A Buddhist scholar born in Ishikawa Pref. His real name is Suzuki Teitarou. Wrote 23 books on Zen in English, among his approximately 100 books, and introduced Japanese Zen culture to the world.

すすきの 薄野 〖酒・地名〗 an entertainment area in the middle part of Sapporo City.

すずきはるのぶ 鈴木春信 〖絵画〗 1725-1770. An ukiyo-e painter born in Edo. Invented nishiki-e in 1765 and frequently painted portraits of beautiful ladies.

すずしろ 清白 〖植物〗 a giant white radish. An old name of DAIKON. *Raphanus sativus*. One of the seven herbs of spring in a lunar calendar. →春の七草

すずな 鈴菜 〖植物〗 a turnip. Another name of KABU. *Brassica campestris*. One of the seven herbs of spring in a lunar calendar. →春の

七草

すすはらい 煤払い 〔生活〕 a year-end house cleaning. Is done as preparation to welcome the New Year's deity.

すずむし 鈴虫 〔動物〕 a bell-ring cricket. *Homoeogryllus japonicus*. About 1.5 cm long. Chirps like a ringing bell.

すずめやき 雀焼き 〔食べ物〕 **(1)** teriyaki sparrow. **(2)** skewed teriyaki of small crucian carp.

すずり 硯 〔書道〕 an inkstone. Is used to rub down an India ink stick to make liquid ink.

すずりばこ 硯箱 〔書道〕 a case of a calligraphy kit. Contains an ink stick, an inkstone, and writing brushes.

すそ 裾 〔服飾〕 the hem or lower part of a kimono.

すそさばき 裾捌き 〔服飾〕 to walk elegantly so that the lower part of a kimono does not flap.

すそはらい 裾払い 〔相撲〕 a rear foot sweep. A technique to pull down the opponent backwards by sweeping his leg forward.

すそまわし 裾回し 〔服飾〕 the lining of the lower part of a kimono.

すたじおじぶり スタジオジブリ 〔アニメ〕 Studio Ghibli. A production company of anime movies, established in 1985. Its works include *My Neighbor Totoro* (Tonari no Totoro) in 1988, *Grave of the Fireflies* (Hotaru no Haka) in 1988, *Princess Mononoke* (Mononoke-hime) in 1997, and *Spirited Away* (Sen to Chihiro no Kamikakushi) in 2001.

すだち 酢橘 〔調味料・植物〕 *Citrus sudachi*. Is used as a condiment to add aroma and sour flavor.

ずだぶくろ 頭陀袋 〔仏教〕 a cloth sack. A monk fills it with sutras or tableware and hangs it from his neck.

すだれ 簾 〔生活・建築〕 a blind screen made of reeds or split bamboo. Is lowered to keep the sun out or to partition a room.

すづけ 酢漬け 〔調味料〕 fish or vegetable pickled with vinegar.

すっぱ 素破, 透破 〔忍者〕 a generic term for ninja working in Central and Western Japan. Often refers to ninja serving TAKEDA SHINGEN, a warlord in present Yamanashi Pref. He selected personnel for ninja among not only warriors but also merchants, artisans, and peasants and incorporated a 'suppa' system with 200 ninja.

すっぽん スッポン 〔食べ物・動物〕 a softshell turtle. *Trionyx sinensis japonicus*. Its meat is edible. Its blood is treasured as a kind of energy drink.

すててこ ステテコ 〔服飾〕 men's summer long underpants. Do not stick to the skin and are cool.

すとくてんのう 崇徳天皇 〔天皇〕 Emperor Sutoku. 1119-1164. The 75th, on the throne from 1123 to 1141. The first prince of Emperor Toba. After retirement, was defeated in the Hougen Disturbance and was exiled to Sanuki, present Kagawa Pref. →保元の乱

すなかけばばあ 砂掛け婆 〖妖怪〗 Sand-Sprinkling Old Woman. Sprinkles sand on a person who is walking in a lonely forest or under a shrine gate.

すなかぶり 砂被り 〖相撲〗 a ringside seat. The most expensive seat. Wrestlers might fall from the ring onto it.

すなぎも 砂肝 〖食べ物〗 a gizzard. A part of the stomach of a chicken. Eaten grilled or deep fried.

すなずり 砂摩り 〖食べ物〗 ⇨砂肝

すなぶろ 砂風呂 〖風呂〗 a sand bath. Sand is warmed by the vapor from a hot spring. The bather lies on the sand and is buried except for the head. Ibusuki in Kagoshima Pref. is famous for sand bathing.

すのこ 簀子 〖生活〗 a wooden or bamboo lattice.

すのもの 酢の物 〖食べ物〗 vinegared seafood or vegetables.

すはまざ 州浜座 〖仏教・美術〗 a sandy beach pedestal. Is used for the image of a deva or a priest. Examples include the Ten Great Disciples of the Historical Buddha at Koufuku-ji Temple in Nara. →台座

すぴいどすけえと スピードスケート 〖スポーツ〗 speed skating. As of 2018, Japan has won five gold medals in the Winter Olympics: Shimizu Hiroyasu and Nishitani Takafumi at Nagano in 1998 and Kodaira Nao, Takagi Nana, and

women's pursuit team at Peong Chang in 2018.

すべらかし 垂髪 〖髪〗 women's long hair tied at the back of the head. Hangs down long on the back.

すべりどめ 滑り止め 〖教育〗 a safety school. Many students take the entrance exam for a less desired school as insurance in case he or she fails the exam for the first choice.

すぼし 素干し 〖食べ物〗 to dry fish or seaweed in the shade, without seasoning.

すぼだい 須菩提 〖仏教〗 *Subhuti*. One of the Ten Great Disciples of the Historical Buddha. Foremost among the disciples in realizing emptiness. →十大弟子

すましじる 澄まし汁 〖食べ物〗 clear soup. Is seasoned with soy sauce, salt, and DASHI.

すみ 炭 〖生活・茶道〗 charcoal. Is used for cooking, deodorization, and the tea ceremony, but was also used for heating in the olden days.

すみ 墨 〖書道・美術〗 India ink. Is made from soot and glue and used for calligraphy and paintings.

すみえ 墨絵 〖絵画〗 ⇨水墨画

すみそ 酢味噌 〖調味料〗 mixture of miso, vinegar, and sugar. Is put on vegetables, seaweed, or fish.

すみぞめのころも 墨染の衣 〖仏教・服飾〗 black costume for a priest.

すみだがわ 隅田川 〖地名・河川〗 the Sumida River. Branches off the Arakawa River and runs through the eastern part of Tokyo city proper into Tokyo Bay. Is 23 km long. Famous for cherry blossoms, and its young cherry trees were sent to the U.S. in 1912. They were planted along the Potomac River in Washington, D.C.

すみだわら 炭俵 〚生活・茶道〛 a straw bag for charcoal.

すみつぼ 墨壺 〚科学技術・文具〛 a carpenter's device to draw a straight line. The user draws out a string that has absorbed ink on it and flips it to draw the line.

すみとり 炭斗 〚茶道〛 a charcoal container. The host or hostess brings it to the tea room and puts the charcoal from it into the hearth.

すみながし 墨流し 〚美術〛 **(1)** a pattern of India ink when it is dropped on the surface of water. **(2)** a technique of printing the ink floating pattern on paper.

すみのえのかみ 住吉神 〚神道〛 three deities of safe voyage. Soko-tsutsunoo-no-mikoto, born on the bottom of the sea, Nakatsutsunoo-no-mikoto, born in the sea, and Uwatsutsunoo-no-mikoto, born on the surface of the sea. Their father is IZANAGI NO MIKOTO.

すみびやき 炭火焼き 〚食文化〛 food grilled over charcoal.

すみません すみません 〚精神性・言語〛 "I'm sorry," "Excuse me," or "Thanks." This phrase is used to express apology or gratitude with a light heart, usually toward one's superior or a stranger.

すみやきごや 炭焼小屋 〚農林水産〛 a charcoal-burning hut.

すみよしじんじゃ 住吉神社 〚神社〛 a Sumiyoshi Shrine. There are many Sumiyoshi Shrines throughout Japan, usually near the sea or a lake. The shrines are consecrated to three deities of safe voyage, collectively called SUMINOE NO KAMI.

すみよしたいしゃ 住吉大社 〚神社〛 Sumiyoshi Grand Shrine. The head shrine of the Sumiyoshi Shrines throughout Japan, located in Osaka City. Enshrines three deities of safe voyage, collectively called SUMINOE NO KAMI, and Empress Consort Jinguu. Its four main buildings are National Treasures.

すみよしづくり 住吉造り 〚神社・建築〛 the Sumiyoshi style of Shinto architecture. The entrance is on the gable side. The inside is divided into two rooms. The main sanctuary buildings of Sumiyoshi Grand Shrine have this style. →本殿；住吉大社

すめし 酢飯 〚食べ物〛 vinegared rice. A principal ingredient for sushi.

すもう 相撲, 角力 〚相撲〛 sumo wrestling. The *Chronicles of Japan* (NIHONSHOKI), compiled in the 8th century, describes a bout between NOMI NO SUKUNE and TAIMA NO KEHAYA. Was continued as ritual in ancient times. Professional sumo was popular in the Edo period and is now called the Grand Sumo Tournament, which is held six times a year. →相撲取り；相撲部屋；国技館

すもうじんく 相撲甚句 〔相撲・音楽〕 a song of joys and sorrows of sumo wrestlers. Is sung on the occasion of exhibition bouts outside the regular tournaments.

すもうとり 相撲取り 〔相撲〕 a sumo wrestler. Professional wrestlers are divided into several ranks, from YOKODUNA to JONOKUCHI.

すもうべや 相撲部屋 〔相撲〕 a sumo stable. The master, who used to be a wrestler, trains professional wrestlers, entrusted by the Japan Sumo Association. A professional sumo wrestler has to belong to a stable.

すらむだんく スラムダンク 〔漫画〕 *Slam Dunk*. A basketball manga, written and illustrated by Takehiko Inoue. Was published serially in a boy's magazine, *Weekly Shonen Jump*, from 1990 to 1996.

すりあし 摺足 〔忍者・能〕 rub step. To walk by lifting one's feet off the ground very little.

すりこぎ 擂粉木 〔食文化〕 a wooden pestle. It is said that the wood of a prickly ash is good as its material.

すりし 刷師 〔絵画〕 a printer of woodblock painting.

すりばち 擂鉢 〔食文化〕 a pottery mortar. Closely spaced notches are on its inner surface.

すりみ 擂身 〔食べ物〕 ground fish. An ingredient of fish paste.

するが 駿河 〔旧国名〕 the old name for central Shizuoka Pref.

するがとらふ 駿河トラフ 〔地名〕 Suruga Trough. Stretches through the central part of Suruga Bay southward to the Nankai Trough. The Philippine Sea Plate sinks below earth here.

するがわん 駿河湾 〔湾〕 Suruga Bay. Is located off the coast of Shizuoka Pref., between the Izu Peninsula in the east and Cape Omae-zaki in the west. Is the deepest bay in Japan, measuring 2,500 m deep at its deepest point. Famous for tuna, bonito, and sakura shrimp production.

するめ 鯣 〔食べ物〕 dried squid. Sometimes seasoned with a mixture of soy sauce, mayonnaise, and red pepper. Goes well with sake.

ずわいがに ズワイガニ 〔食べ物・魚〕 a snow crab, or a queen crab. *Chionoecetes opilio*. Eaten boiled. Is called 'echizen-gani' in Fukui Pref. and 'matsuba-gani' in Shimane and Tottori Prefs.

すわこ 諏訪湖 〔湖沼〕 Lake Suwa. A fault lake located in central Nagano Pref., in the Kiso Mountains. The area is 13 km^2. The source of the Tenryuu River. The natural winter phenomenon called o-miwatari, literally meaning "God's Crossing," is a line of cracked ice on the lake's surface caused by temperature changes and considered to be a good omen. A popular fireworks festival takes place in August, with 40,000 fireworks displayed above the lake.

すわたいしゃ 諏訪大社 〖神社〗
Suwa Grand Shrine. Consists of the Kami-sha (Upper Shrine) and the Shimo-sha (Lower Shrine). Is located in middle Nagano Pref. Enshrines TAKEMINAKATA NO KAMI. The Sacred Pillar Festival is held every six years. →御柱(おんばしら)祭り

すん 〜寸 〖単位〗 a unit of length. About 3 cm. Ten 'sun' equal one SHAKU.

すんし 寸志 〖精神性・貨幣〗 a humble expression for monetary remuneration as token of the gratitude. Is usually put in an envelope with 寸志 written on the surface.

せ

ぜあみ 世阿弥〔能〕 1363-1443. A Noh actor and playwright. The son of KAN'AMI. Was sponsored by the third Ashikaga shogun, ASHIKAGA YOSHIMITSU. His works include *The Flowering Spirit: Classic Teachings on the Art of No* (FUUSHIKADEN).

せいいたいしょうぐん 征夷大将軍〔官位〕 a generalissimo, or shogun. The original role was as commander-in-chief to conquer the people who lived in the present Tohoku region and did not obey the Central Government of Japan. Ootomo no Otomaro was first appointed in 794. However, after Minamoto no Yoritomo obtained this position in 1192, this title became the title of the leader of warriors, who had political power.

せいおん 清音〔言語〕 the original pure sound of kana. Is not supplemented by voiced or p-sound markings.

せいか 生花〔華道〕 a style of flower arrangement consisting of three basic branches to symbolize heaven, earth, and humans. The entire shape forms a triangle. Is called 'shouka' in the Ikenobou school.

せいがいは 青海波〔文様〕 a pattern of blue ocean waves, or repeating blue scales.

せいかつほごほう 生活保護法〔法律〕 Public Assistance Act. Its purpose is "to guarantee a minimum standard of living as well as to promote self-support for all citizens who are living in poverty by providing the necessary public assistance," according to the Ministry of Justice.

せいがん 正眼〔剣術〕 the standard posture, in which the swordsman holds the sword right in front of the body and points it at the opponent's eyes.

せいがんとじ 青岸渡寺〔寺院〕 Seiganto-ji Temple. Is affiliated with the Tendai sect and located in southern Wakayama Pref. Is said to have been founded by an Indian priest. The first temple among Thirty-three Holy Places around the Kansai region. Was designated a World Heritage Site in 2004. → 西国三十三カ所

せいかんとんねる 青函トンネル〔交通〕 the Seikan tunnel. Connects Imabetsu in Aomori Pref. with Shiriuchi in Hokkaido. Was completed in 1988. The total length is 53.85 km, making it the longest railroad tunnel in the world.

せいかんろん 征韓論〔外交〕 the Policy of Punishing Korea. It is said that SAIGOU TAKAMORI and ITAGAKI TAISUKE insisted Japan should dispatch troops to anti-Japanese Korea at that time. IWAKURA TOMOMI and OOKUBO TOSHIMICHI, who came back from the inspection tour to Europe and America, disagreed about it, and Saigou and his followers resigned their public posts.

せいこ 西湖〔絵画・湖沼〕 Lake Xihu. Means "West Lake." Is located in Zhe-jiang Province in China. A popular theme for landscape pictures.

せいこうとうてい 西高東低〔気象〕 an atmospheric condition in which high pressure is in the west while low pressure is in the east. Is often observed in winter.

せいこついん 整骨院〔医療〕 an osteopathic clinic. A judo healing practitioner, not an orthopedic surgeon, treats sprains, dislocations, fractures, torn muscles, bruises, and other troubles of muscles or bones.

せいざ 正座〔生活〕 the formal way of sitting on a tatami mat. The person kneels on the floor, sits on the heels, and keeps the back upright. Is applied in formal settings such as the tea ceremony, a funeral, or martial arts training.

せいさつ 制札〔法律〕 a bulletin board containing an official announcement or prohibition. Was placed at the roadside or in the precincts of a temple or shrine. Began to be used in the Heian period and became popular in the Edo period.

せいじ 青磁〔陶磁器〕 celadon ware, or blueish-green glazed porcelain. Was developed in China. Production began in Japan in the Edo period. Sanda, Hyougo Pref.,

and Arita, Saga Pref., are famous.

せいしつ 正室〔結婚〕 the prime wife of an Emperor, a shogun, an aristocrat, or a feudal lord in olden days. ↔側室

せいしぼさつ 勢至菩薩〔仏教〕 Seishi Bodhisattva. *Mahasthamaprapta*. The right attendant in an Amitabha triad. Is said to save or retrieve people from an illusion by the light of wisdom. A small water vase is contained in the crown on his head. →阿弥陀三尊

せいしゅ 清酒〔酒〕 ordinary sake. Is refined and clear. Its alcoholic content is 15 to 20%.

せいじゅ 聖寿〔天皇〕 the age of an Emperor.

せいしゅんじゅうはちきっぷ 青春18切符〔交通〕 Seishun 18. Using this ticket, a passenger can ride on local and rapid JR trains throughout Japan, except for a reserved-seat car and express trains. Is sold as a five-ticket package during specific seasons in a year.

せいしょうなごん 清少納言〔文芸〕 ?-? A novelist and poet. Her works include *The Pillow Book*. Worked under a wife of Emperor Ichijou, named Teishi. →枕草子；一条天皇

せいじんのひ 成人の日〔暦〕 Coming-of-Age Day. The second Monday in January. A national holiday to encourage youth to be conscious of their duties as grown-ups and to learn to live independently. Was established in 1948.

せいたかどうじ 制多迦童子〔仏

教〕 *Cetaka*. An attendant of the Immovable Wisdom King. Often carries a diamond rod in his right hand.

ぜいちく 筮竹 〔宗教〕 a set of 50 bamboo sticks for fortune telling, based on the Yi divination. →易(_{えき})

せいどう 青銅 〔科学技術〕 bronze. Was introduced from China and used for bronze ware in the Yayoi period. Later, was also used for coins, sculptures, and temple bells.

せいどうか 青銅貨 〔経済〕 a bronze coin.

せいどうき 青銅器 〔考古〕 bronze ware. Began to be used in the Yayoi period. Includes bronze swords (DOUKEN) and bell-shaped ritual tools (DOUTAKU).

せいなんせんそう 西南戦争 〔戦争〕 Satsuma Rebellion. In 1877, ex-samurai in present Kagoshima Pref., who were dissatisfied with the Meiji government, rose in rebellion under the banner of SAIGOU TAKAMORI, one of the leaders of the Meiji Restoration. However, they were suppressed by government troops, and Saigou killed himself.

せいはくまいい 精白米 〔食文化〕 polished rice. People usually eat this type of rice. ↔玄米

せいふく 制服 〔服飾〕 a uniform. Many schools, from kindergarten to high school, and companies have their own uniforms.

せいぶてつどう 西武鉄道 〔交通〕 Seibu Railway. One of the 16 major private railway operators of Japan. Mainly serves western Tokyo and southern Saitama Pref. Its two main lines start from Shinjuku and Ikebukuro, and both go through Tokorozawa in Saitama Pref. Operates a through-line service with Tokyo Metro lines.

せいぼ 歳暮 〔生活〕 ⇨お歳暮

せいまい 精米 〔食文化〕 **(1)** to polish rice. To remove a hull, bran, and germ. **(2)**⇨精白米

せいまいぶあい 精米歩合 〔酒〕 rice polishing ratio. Rice is polished to remove the surface part such as rice bran before eating or brewing sake. The ratio of the weight of the rice after polishing to its weight before polishing is about 90%, for eating. The ratio is lower for brewing sake, depending on the quality of sake.

せいめい 晴明 〔暦〕 one of the 24 seasonal nodes in the traditional calendar. Around April 5 in the current calendar. Means "it is clear and bright." →二十四節気(_{にじゅうし}
_{せっき})

せいようじじょう 西洋事情 〔人文学・書名〕 *Conditions in the West*. A book published from 1866 to 1870 by FUKUZAWA YUKICHI. Introduces Western politics, economy, history, science, and other fields.

せいりゅう 青竜 〔宗教・動物〕 the blue dragon. The animal deity that symbolizes the east. →四神(_{しん}); 白虎(_{びゃっこ}); 朱雀(_{すざく}); 玄武(_{げんぶ})

せいりょうじ 清涼寺 〔寺院〕 Seiryou-ji Temple. Is also called 'Saga Shaka-dou,' which means

Buddha Chapel in Saga. Affiliated with the Joudo sect and is located in Kyoto City. Was founded by a priest named Jouzan to enshrine the image of the Historical Buddha brought back from China in 987 by his master, Chounen. The image of the Historical Buddha is a National Treasure. →清凉寺式釈迦如来

せいりょうじしきしゃかにょらい 清凉寺式釈迦如来 〖仏教・彫刻〗 a standing figure of the Historical Buddha in the Seiryou-ji style. Its characteristics are that the dress is high middle-necked, unlike other Buddhist images, and the wrinkles are almost symmetrical as in a concentric circle. The original statue was brought from the Northern Sung dynasty in 987 by a priest named Chounen. The copies of this type are contained at SAIDAI-JI Temple, TOUSHOUDAI-JI Temple, and other temples.

せいれいしていとし 政令指定都市 〖行政〗 an ordinance-designated city. Should have a population of at least 500 thousand. Has fiscal and administrative powers equivalent to a prefecture. As of 2016, 20 cities are also designated.

せいれき 西暦 〖暦〗 the Christian Era. The term began to be used in the 19th century in Japan.

せいろ 蒸籠 〖食文化〗 **(1)** a steaming basket. Is made of wood or bamboo and used to steam food. **(2)** ⇨ 盛り蕎麦

せいわてんのう 清和天皇 〖天皇〗 Emperor Seiwa. 850-880. The 56th, on the throne from 858 to 876. The ancestor of the Minamoto clan. →源氏

せえらあふく セーラー服 〖教育・服飾〗 a sailor-style uniform for girls in junior and senior high school, and sometimes elementary school. The lower part is not pants but a skirt.

せおいなげ 背負い投げ 〖柔道〗 a shoulder throw. A judo technique of lifting the opponent on the back and throwing him or her down on the front.

せおどあるうずべると セオドア・ルーズベルト 〖外交〗 Theodore Roosevelt. 1858-1919. The 26th U.S. President from 1901 to 1909. Was a strong believer in the importance of Japan in modern Asia. At Japan's suggestion, he mediated the 1905 peace negotiations in Portsmouth, New Hampshire, to end the Russo-Japanese War, and he won the Nobel Peace Prize for it. The Treaty of Portsmouth supported the presence of Japan in Manchuria and Korea and gave half of Sakhalin Island to Japan, while requiring no reparations from Russia. Later in his presidency, he concluded a 1907 "gentlemen's agreement" between Japan and the U.S. concerning Japanese immigration to the U.S. and the treatment of immigrants.

せかいいさん 世界遺産 〖政治〗 World Heritage. Japan has

17 Cultural Heritage Sites and 4 Natural Heritage Sites, as of 2017. Include Mt. Fuji, the Shirakami Mountains, Yaku Island, Itsukushima Shrine, Iwami Ginzan Silver Mine, Tomioka Silk Mill, and National Museum of Western Art.

せかいきゅうせいきょう 世界救世教 〖宗教〗 the World Messianity Church. Was founded in 1952 by Okada Mokichi. The headquarters are located in Atami, Shizuoka Pref. Constructed the Hakone Museum of Art in 1952 and the MOA Museum of Art in 1982, both in Shizuoka Pref.

せがき 施餓鬼 〖仏教〗 a Buddhist rite for souls in the Realm of Starving Ghosts. Is often conducted during the Bon Festival in summer.

せき 〜勺 〖単位〗 ⇨〜勺(しゃく)

せき 〜隻 〖助数詞〗 **(1)** a counting suffix for big ships. ↔艘(そう) **(2)** a counting suffix for folding screens. ↔双

せき 〜関 〖相撲〗 an honorific title for a sumo wrestler in a high rank.

せきがはらのたたかい 関ヶ原の戦い 〖戦争〗 Battle of Sekigahara. In 1600, TOKUGAWA IEYASU, who later established the Tokugawa shogunate, defeated ISHIDA MITSUNARI, a favorite retainer of TOYOTOMI HIDEYOSHI, at Sekigahara in present Gifu Pref.

せきしつ 石室 〖考古〗 a stone burial chamber found in a tumulus. There are two types of chambers: pit-type and tunnel-type, and the former is older than the latter. Inside a chamber are a coffin, which is made of wood, pottery, or stone, as well as accessories.

せきしょ 関所 〖交通〗 a barrier station, or checkpoint. Was installed along major highways and stopped travelers for inspection. The system was first established in ancient times and had been changing until ODA NOBUNAGA and TOYOTOMI HIDEYOSHI abolished it in early modern times. Was re-established by the Tokugawa shogunate and was abolished again in 1869 after the Meiji Restoration.

せきたかかず 関孝和 〖科学技術〗 1640?-1708. A mathematician born in present Gunma Pref. Researched the theory of equation, determinants, and geometry.

せきてい 石庭 〖庭園〗 a rock garden. The combination of sands and rocks in various sizes depicts a natural landscape, or sometimes a Buddhist world view.

せきてい 席亭 〖落語〗 a manager of traditional vaudeville theater.

せきとう 石塔 〖仏教〗 a pagoda made of stone. Is sometimes used as a gravestone.

せきとり 関取 〖相撲〗 a sumo wrestler in the top and second divisions. Is permitted to wear a large ginkgo-leaf topknot called OOICHOU. →幕内；十両

せきはん 赤飯 〖食べ物〗 red rice. Glutinous rice boiled with adzuki beans. Eaten on auspicious occasions such as a wedding ceremony.

せきひつ 石筆 〖科学技術・忍者〗 a wax pencil. Is used to write on a stone or iron plate, sometimes at construction sites, because it is not removed by high temperature or water. Was used as a communication tool by ninja and as a learning tool by elementary school children.

せきぶつ 石仏 〖仏教・彫刻〗 a Buddhist image made of stone. Examples include Usuki Stone Buddhas in Ooita Pref. →臼杵(うすき)石仏

せきわけ 関脇 〖相撲〗 a sumo wrestler at the third highest rank in the Grand Sumo Tournament. Next to OOZEKI and superior to KOMUSUBI.

せぐり 背刳り 〖彫刻〗 an indentation in the back of a wooden sculpture. Helps prevent cracking of the wood. Is covered so as not to be seen. →内刳り

ぜげん 女衒 〖職業〗 a dealer of prostitutes. Bought a poor girl and sold her to the owner of a red-light district in olden times.

せけんむねさんよう 世間胸算用 〖文芸・作品〗 *This Scheming World.* Was written in 1692 by IHARA SAIKAKU. Describes the life of ordinary people on December 31, the day of reckoning in a year.

せしゅ 施主 〖仏教〗 **(1)** ⇨喪主 **(2)** the person financially responsible for a funeral.

せしん 世親 〖仏教〗 *Vasubandhu.* 320?-400? An Indian priest. Established the "consciousness only" theory, YUISHIKI, together with his elder brother, MUJAKU. His statue is at KOUFUKU-JI Temple.

せっかんせいじ 摂関政治 〖政治〗 regency government. A regent called SESSHOU ruled the government when the Emperor was a young child or a woman. A supreme adviser called KANPAKU ruled the government when the Emperor was grown up. Position was occupied by the Fujiwara clan in the Heian period.

せっく 節句, 節供 〖暦〗 a seasonal festival. Five days were defined as 'sekku' in the Edo period, which were January 7, March 3, May 5, July 7, and September 9. Three of them, March 3, May 5, and July 7, are still celebrated as the Girls' Festival, the Boys' Festival, and the Star Festival, respectively.

ぜっく 絶句 〖文芸〗 a Chinese-style classic poem, made up of four lines. ↔律詩 →五言絶句; 七言絶句

せつげつか 雪月花 〖絵画〗 snow, moon, and flowers. Have been popular subjects in painting as seasonal beauties.

せっこついん 接骨院 〖医療〗 ⇨整骨院

せっしゃ 摂社 〖神社〗 an affiliated shrine. Enshrines a deity related to a deity of the head shrine. →本宮; 末社

せっしゅう 雪舟 〖絵画〗 1420-1506. A painter and priest born in present Okayama Pref. Studied under

SHUUBUN at SHOUKOKU-JI Temple in Kyoto. Visited China in 1467, came back in 1469, and lived in present Yamaguchi Pref. His style, learned from the Sung and Yuan paintings, was magnificent and unique in spatial representation, and it greatly influenced the latter generation of the India ink painters. His works include *View of Ama-no-hashidate* at the Kyoto National Museum and *Landscape with Ink Broken* at the Tokyo National Museum.

せっしょう 摂政〖官位〗 an Imperial regent. Ruled government when the Emperor was a young child or a woman. For example, Prince Shoutoku was the regent for Empress Suiko in the 7th century. →摂関政治

せっしょうかい 殺生戒〖仏教〗 the precept not to kill, in Buddhism. One of the five precepts. →五戒

せつぞくじょし 接続助詞〖言語〗 a conjunctive particle. Appears at the end of a clause and closes a subordinate clause.

せっそん 雪村〖絵画〗 1504-? A painter born in present Ibaraki Pref. Used to be a samurai and studied paintings under SESSHUU. His style was strong and dynamic. His works include *Hawks and Pines* at the Tokyo National Museum.

せった 雪駄〖履物〗 leather-soled sandals. Small metal plates are attached on the heel to protect it from wearing off.

せっちん 雪隠〖生活・建築〗 an old term meaning "lavatory." Comes from Zen Buddhism.

せっつ 摂津〖旧国名〗 the old name for northwestern Osaka and southwestern Hyougo Prefs.

せっぷく 切腹〖武士〗 hara-kiri. A samurai killed himself by cutting his stomach open with a sword as punishment, in despair, or to appeal something very strongly. Was often beheaded by another samurai while cutting the stomach.

せつぶん 節分〖暦・宗教〗 the day just before the beginning of spring in the traditional calendar. Usually February 3. People scatter parched soybeans to expel evil spirits and invite good luck. Some people set the head of a sardine and the twig of a holly tree at the entrance of the house to protect it from evil spirits. →豆撒き

せっぽう 説法〖仏教〗 a Buddhist sermon to preach the dharma.

せっぽういん 説法印〖仏教・美術〗 the mudra for preaching the dharma. Both hands are placed in front of the chest.

せつわぶんがく 説話文学〖文芸〗 narrative literature. The generic term for a collection of myth, legend, and folk tales. Examples include *Miraculous Stories from the Japanese Buddhist Tradition* (NIHON RYOUIKI) and *Tales of Times Now Past* (KONJAKU MONOGATARI).

せどうか 旋頭歌〖文芸〗 a short rhyming poem with six lines of 5, 7,

7, 5, 7, and 7 syllables each. Is seen mainly in the *Anthology of Myriad Leaves* (MAN'YOUSHUU).

せとうちしまなみかいどう 瀬戸内しまなみ海道〖交通〗 ⇨ しまなみ海道

せとおおはし 瀬戸大橋〖橋〗 Great Seto Bridge. Was built in 1988 above the 9.4 km-wide strait of the Inland Sea. Connects Kojima, Okayama Pref. with Sakaide, Kagawa Pref. Is used both for a motorway and a railway. One of the three routes that connect Japan's main islands, HONSHUU and SHIKOKU.

せとないかい 瀬戸内海〖海洋〗 the Inland Sea of Seto. About 2,000 islands are dotted between HONSHUU and SHIKOKU. Has been an important sea-lane between the Kansai and Kyushu regions since ancient times.

せともの 瀬戸物〖陶磁器〗 **(1)**⇨瀬戸焼 **(2)** the common term referring to ceramics. Is used mainly in the Kansai region and eastward.

せとやき 瀬戸焼〖陶磁器〗 Seto ware. Glazed ceramics produced in Seto in northern Aichi Pref. Started around the late 10th century and was popular in the 14th century. Later the main production site shifted to MINO, but Seto rose again in the 19th century. 'Setomono,' the generic term for ceramic, represents Seto ware's significant contribution in Japan.

ぜに 銭〖貨幣〗 a metal round coin

with a hole in the center. In the Edo period, it was used as small change since the value was low, as opposed to a KOBAN.

ぜにがたへいじとりものひかえ 銭形平次捕物控〖文芸・作品〗 *Coin-Throwing Detective, Zenigata Heiji.* Series of detective stories set in Edo, published in parts from 1931 to 1957 by NOMURA KODOU. The hero detective, Heiji, throws a coin at a criminal who tries to run away.

せむいいん 施無畏印 〖仏教・美術〗 the mudra for soothing fear. The right hand is raised in front of the shoulder, its palm is turned toward the front, and its fingers are stretched or slightly bent. Is usually combined with the mudra for fulfilling a wish, YOGAN-IN.

せり 芹〖植物〗 a Java water dropwort. *Oenanthe javanica*. One of the seven herbs of spring in a lunar calendar. →春の七草

せりいぐ セ・リーグ〖スポーツ〗 ⇨ セントラル・リーグ

せりだし 迫り出し〖歌舞伎〗 a mechanism to elevate actors or stage settings onto the stage. Is used when a scene has to be changed quickly.

ぜろせん ゼロ戦〖軍事〗 ⇨零式(れい)艦上戦闘機

せわもの 世話物〖歌舞伎・文楽〗 a social or domestic drama in kabuki or bunraku. Depicts everyday life of townspeople in the Edo period and the early Meiji period.

せん ～銭〖経済・単位〗 a unit of

money. One hundredth of a yen. Is not used in daily life but is used when talking about a wholesale price, stock price, or a foreign exchange rate.

ぜん 禅〖禅〗**(1)**⇨座禅 **(2)**⇨禅宗

ぜん 膳〖食文化〗a square tray with legs. Is used to serve dishes for one person.

ぜん ～膳〖食文化・助数詞〗a suffix counter for pairs of chopsticks. When counting chopsticks separately, the counter HON is used. → 助数詞

ぜんえいいけばな 前衛生け花〖華道〗avant-garde flower arrangement. Started after World War II. Uses metals, stones, seashells, feathers, etc.

ぜんが 禅画〖仏教・絵画〗Zen painting. Expresses the spirit of Zen philosophy.

せんがくじ 泉岳寺〖寺院〗Sengaku-ji Temple. Is located in Tokyo. Was founded in 1612 with financial support from TOKUGAWA IEYASU. Contains the graves of forty-seven masterless samurai from Akou and their ex-master, Asano Naganori. → 赤穂浪士

せんかくしょとう 尖閣諸島〖島名〗the Senkaku Islands. Part of the Ryuukyuu Islands. Uninhabited and about 400 km away from Okinawa Island.

ぜんがくれん 全学連〖政治〗All-Japan Federation of Students' Self-Governing Associations. Was formed with students' associa-

tions at 145 universities in 1948. Developed intense student movements such as the struggle against the revision of the U.S.-Japan Security Treaty during the 1960s and 1970s.

せんがち 先勝〖暦〗⇨先勝(せんしょう)

せんかんみかさ 戦艦三笠〖軍事・船名〗Battleship Mikasa. A flagship at the Battle of Tsushima during the Russo-Japanese War. Its displacement was 15,140 t. Is preserved at Yokosuka Port in Kanagawa Pref. → 日本海海戦

せんかんむさし 戦艦武蔵〖軍事・船名〗Battleship Musashi. One of the largest battleships in history, with a total length of 263 m, a width of 38.9 m, and a displacement of 64,000 t. It was made in Nagasaki in 1942 and was sunk in the Battle of Leyte Gulf in 1944.

せんかんやまと 戦艦大和〖軍事・船名〗Battleship Yamato. One of the largest battleships in history, with a total length of 263 m, a width of 38.9 m, and a displacement of 64,000 t. It was made in Kure in 1941 and was sunk at the south of Kyushu in 1945 by American carrier-borne aircraft.

せんきょうし 宣教師〖キリスト教〗a Christian missionary. The first example was Saint Francis Xavier, who came from Spain to Japan in 1549. Other examples include a Portuguese missionary, Luis Frois, and an American missionary, J. C. Hepburn. → フランシスコ・ザビエ

ル；ルイス・フロイス；ヘボン

ぜんきょうとう 全共闘〖政治〗 All-Campus Joint Struggle Committee. A supra-sect association within a university at the hey day of the student movement in the latter half of the 1960s. The groups at Nippon University and the University of Tokyo are famous.

せんぎり 千切り〖食べ物〗 vegetable shreds. Often refers to white radish, cabbage, or carrot. Literally means "cutting into 1,000 pieces."

せんぐう 遷宮〖神道〗 temporary move of a sacred object. When the sanctuary building is rebuilt or repaired, the sacred object is moved to the temporary building and is moved back afterward.

ぜんくねんのえき 前九年の役〖戦争〗 the Earlier Nine Years' War. From 1051 to 1062. The Abe clan in the Tohoku region rebelled, and the Imperial Court dispatched Minamoto no Yoriie and Yoshiie to subjugate them. Became a trigger for the Minamoto clan to obtain the power in Eastern Japan. →後三年の役

せんけ 千家〖茶道〗 the Sen family, or the Senke schools of the tea ceremony. There are three Senke schools derived from the 16th-century tea master, SEN NO RIKYUU: Omote-senke, Ura-senke, and Mushanokouji-senke.

せんげ 遷化〖仏教〗 death of a high priest.

せんげんじんじゃ 浅間神社〖神社〗 a Sengen Shrine, or an Asama Shrine. There are more than 1,000 Sengen Shrines in central and eastern Japan. Enshrines KONOHANA NO SAKUYA HIME, the deity of Mt. Fuji.

せんこう 線香〖娯楽〗 a joss stick. Is made by solidifying incense powder made from white sandalwood, clove tree, or eaglewood. Is usually about 15 to 30 cm long and takes 30 to 100 minutes to burn out.

ぜんこうじ 善光寺〖寺院〗 Zenkoji Temple. Independent from sects. Is located in Nagano City of Nagano Pref. It is said that a person named Honda Yoshimitsu enshrined an image of the Amitabha Buddha in 642, which was introduced from Paekche in 552. The temple name comes from another way of reading Yoshimitsu. The main hall, built in the 18th century, is a National Treasure. →善光寺式阿弥陀如来

ぜんこうじしきあみださんぞん 善光寺式阿弥陀三尊〖仏教・彫刻〗 a Triad of the Amitabha Buddha in the Zenkou-ji style. The bronze Amitabha Buddha and the two attendants stand on each lotus flower pedestal and share one nimbus. It is said that the original sculpture was brought from Paekche to Zenkou-ji Temple in present Nagano Pref. in 552. This style was popular from the 12th to the 13th centuries when Pure Land Buddhism was prosperous.

せんこうはなび 線香花火〖娯楽〗 a sparkler, or small fireworks like

joss sticks.

せんごくじだい 戦国時代 〖時代〗 the Warring States period. Started at the Ounin War from 1467 to 1477 and ended when ODA NOBUNAGA entered Kyoto to unite the nation in 1568. The latter half of the Muromachi period. →応仁の乱；室町時代

せんごくせん 千石船 〖交通〗 a large junk in the Edo period. 'Sengoku' means one thousand KOKU, which is a unit to count the volume of rice.

せんごくだいみょう 戦国大名 〖武士・政治〗 a feudal lord in the Warring States period. These lords governed their territory and fought against each other to swallow up the opponent's territory and, ultimately, to unite the entire nation. →戦国時代；戦国武将

せんごくぶしょう 戦国武将 〖武士・軍事〗 a warlord in the Warring States period. Fought under a feudal lord. Some of these warlords rebelled against their master. →戦国時代；戦国大名；下剋上(げこくじょう)

せんごくぶね 千石船 〖交通〗 ⇨千石船(せんごくせん)

せんざ 遷座 **(1)**〖神道〗 the transfer of a sacred object. It can happen because of an accident, such as a fire in a shrine building, or because of a seasonal transfer between two shrines. **(2)**〖天皇〗 the transfer of an Emperor.

ぜんざ 前座 〖落語〗 the lowest-ranking storyteller in the Tokyo area. Acts as a curtain raiser.

A novice storyteller has to go through probation before getting this position. A 'zenza' storyteller is promoted to the second-lowest rank, FUTATSUME, according to his or her skills. The rakugo community in the Osaka area does not have this system.

せんざい 前栽 〖庭園〗 a front garden with trees and flowers.

ぜんざい 善哉 〖食べ物〗 **(1)** sweet adzuki bean soup with rice cake or dumpling, using chunky adzuki paste called TSUBUAN. This term is used in the Kansai region. **(2)** thick adzuki paste with baked rice cake. This term is used in the Kantou region.

せんじゃふだ 千社札 〖宗教〗 a slip as a pilgrimage token. Is pasted on the pillars or ceiling of a Buddhist temple or Shinto shrine, with a pilgrim's name. Nowadays, it is forbidden to paste these slips in many temples and shrines. →千社参り

せんじゃまいり 千社参り 〖神道〗 a one-thousand-shrine pilgrimage. To visit one thousand Shinto shrines, or sometimes Buddhist temples, to pray to the deities and to paste a slip as a pilgrimage token on the building. →千社札

せんじゃもうで 千社詣で 〖神道〗 ⇨千社参り

せんしゅう 泉州 〖地名〗 ⇨和泉(いずみ)

ぜんしゅう 禅宗 〖仏教〗 Zen Buddhism. Aims to attain enlightenment through meditation. There are three Zen sects in Japan:

Rinzai, Soutou, and Oubaku. →臨済宗；曹洞宗；黄檗(おうばく)宗

ぜんしゅうよう 禅宗様〚建築〛 the Zen style of architecture. Was introduced from northern China together with Zen Buddhism in the 12th century. The typical example is at ENGAKU-JI Temple in Kamakura. Is also called 'kara-you,' which literally means "Tang style" though the dynasty in China in those days was Sung. ↔大仏様(だいぶつよう)

せんしゅうらく 千秋楽〚相撲・芸能〛 the last day of a sumo tournament or stage performance such as kabuki or BUNRAKU.

せんじゅかんのん 千手観音 〚仏教〛 Thousand-armed Bodhisattva of Mercy. Has an eye on the palm of each hand and also has eleven faces. One of the six forms of the Bodhisattva of Mercy. Is said to save those who reside in the Realm of Starving Ghosts in esoteric Buddhism. There are few examples of statues that actually have 1,000 arms in Japan, and most images have 42. Famous examples are in SANJUUSANGEN-DOU in Kyoto and TOUSHOUDAI-JI Temple in Nara. →観音；餓鬼道

せんしょう 先勝〚暦〛 a day of "early victory" in the unofficial six-day calendar. Everything should be done in a hurry. People will have good fortune in the morning and bad fortune in the afternoon. →六曜(ろくよう)

ぜんじょういん 禅定印〚仏教〛 the mudra for meditation. Both hands are in front of the navel on the crossed legs. One palm is placed on the other, both upward. Four fingers are stretched, and the tips of the thumbs touch.

せんじょうもんじだい 先縄文時代 〚時代〛 ⇨先土器時代

ぜんしんに 善信尼〚仏教〛 574 -? One of the first three Japanese nuns (Ezen-ni, Zenzou-ni) in the Asuka period. Went to Paekche on the Korean Peninsula in 588 and learned the commandments of Buddhism there. Lived in the Sakurai-ji Temple located in present Nara Pref. and contributed to the rise of Buddhism after coming back to Japan in 590.

せんす 扇子〚茶道・落語〛 a folding fan. Is used not only for cooling but also for ceremonies, dancing, and comic storytelling called RAKUGO. Was originally invented in Japan in ancient times and introduced through China to Europe. Often pictures or texts are depicted on it.

せんずいびょうぶ 山水屏風〚絵画〛 a folding screen or a pair of folding screens depicting a landscape. Was used in the Imperial Palace in the Heian period, but later came to be used for the ceremony of the Shingon sect of Buddhism in the Kamakura period. The oldest one is a National Treasure at the Kyoto National Museum.

せんそ 践祚〚天皇〛 the succession

to the throne. The Emperor receives the Three Sacred Treasures of the Imperial Family. This term is not used at present. →即位

せんそうえき 千宗易 〖茶道〗 ⇨千利休(せんのりきゅう)

せんそうじ 浅草寺 〖寺院〗 Sensou-ji Temple. Is also called 'Asakusa Kannon.' The head temple of the Shoukannon sect, located in Tokyo. Was founded in 645. It is said that the principal image, the Bodhisattva of Mercy, was salvaged with a net from the Sumida River in 628. A shopping street in the precincts, called NAKAMISE, is famous.

せんだいし 仙台市 〖地名〗 Sendai City. An ordinance-designated city, and the capital of Miyagi Pref. Is located in its eastern part and faces Sendai Bay. Since a feudal lord DATE MASAMUNE relocated to Sendai in 1600, it has developed as the capital town of the Date clan into the largest city in the Tohoku region. Japan's largest star festival is held in Sendai every August, attracting two million visitors. Famous for foods such as grilled beef tongue, steamed fish paste shaped like a bamboo leaf, and rice balls with sweet green paste.

せんだいじょう 仙台城 〖城郭〗 Sendai Castle. The main structure was constructed on Mt. Aobayama in 1602 by a feudal lord, DATE MASAMUNE. Buildings were burned down during World War II. The statue of Masamune riding on a horse now stands on the top of the mountain. Is also called Aoba Castle.

せんだいたなばたまつり 仙台七夕祭り 〖祭礼〗 Sendai Tanabata Festival. Though star festivals in other areas are usually held in July, in Sendai it is held at the beginning of August, based on a traditional calendar. It dates back to the 17th century and features colorful decorations around the central city and shopping districts. →七夕祭り；仙台

せんたいぶつ 千体仏 〖仏教〗 One Thousand Buddhas. A set of many small Buddhas painted or carved in the same size.

せんだいわん 仙台湾 〖湾〗 Sendai Bay. In its broad sense, it is the water surrounded by the Ojika Peninsula in northeastern Miyagi Pref. and Cape Unoo-saki in northern Fukushima Pref. Can be divided into three parts from north to south, namely, Ishinomaki Bay, Matsushima Bay, and Sendai Bay in its narrow sense. Oysters and laver are cultivated. Cruising in Matsushima Bay, windsurfing, sea kayaking, and scuba diving are popular.

せんだん 栴檀 〖植物〗 **(1)** a white cedar, a Persian lilac, a chinaberry, a bead tree, or an umbrella tree. *Melia azedarach*. The timber is used for furniture, and the fruit is used for medicine. **(2)**⇨白檀(びゃくだん)

せんちゃ 煎茶 〖飲み物〗 middle-quality green tea. Is made from

new buds of tea leaves. Is brewed with hot water, from 60 to 70 degrees centigrade.

ぜんつうじ 善通寺〚寺院〛 Zentsuji Temple. The head temple of the Zentsuu-ji school in the Shingon sect. Is said to have been founded in 807 by the priest Kuukai. Is located at his birthplace in Kagawa Pref.

せんていどき 尖底土器 〚考古〛 earthenware with a pointed bottom. Was used as a cookpot, mainly in the early Joumon period.

ぜんでら 禅寺〚寺院〛 a Zen temple. The style of architecture is slightly different from that of other sects. →禅宗様(ぜんしゅうよう)；法堂(はっ とう)；方丈(ほうじょう)；僧堂

せんと 遷都〚政治〛 relocation of the capital. The capital was frequently relocated in ancient times. Before it was fixed to Nara in 710, Osaka, Ootsu, Nagaoka, and other cities had been a capital.

せんとう 銭湯〚風呂〛 a public bath. Is separated by gender. A bather pays the fee at the entrance and takes the bath without a swimsuit. In some large public bath, called super sentou, a bather can enjoy a cold bath, a steam bath, an open-air bath, and a Jacuzzi in addition to ordinary baths.

せんとうごしょ 仙洞御所〚天皇・建 築〛 a palace for a retired Emperor. →上皇

せんどきじだい 先土器時代〚時代〛 the pre-ceramic period, or pre-earthenware period. The Paleolithic period in Japan, which preceded the Joumon period. Its culture was confirmed by the excavation of the Iwajuku Ruins in Gunma Pref.

せんとくん せんとくん 〚ゆるキャ ラ〛 a relaxing mascot character of Nara Pref. Was created in February 2008 to commemorate the 1,300th Anniversary of Nara Capital.

せんとちひろのかみかくし 千と 千尋の神隠し〚アニメ〛 *Spirited Away*. An anime film produced in 2001 by Studio Ghibli. A sullen ten-year-old girl, Chihiro, enters the spirit world, where she works for a public bathhouse. After finding a way to free herself, she returns to the human world.

せんとらるりいぐ セントラル・ リーグ〚スポーツ〛 Central League. One of the two professional baseball leagues. Was established in 1949. Includes six teams: Bay Stars, Carp, Dragons, Giants, Swallows, and Tigers.

せんなりびょうたん 千成瓢箪 〚武 士〛 a banner for TOYOTOMI HIDEYOSHI, a warlord in the 16th century. Its design uses a cluster of bottle gourds.

せんにちて 千日手〚将棋〛 endless repetition of the same moves. In this case the game is replayed from the beginning.

せんにちまいり 千日参り (1)〚仏教〛 to visit a temple on the connection day of the Bodhisattva of Mercy. By visiting on this day, the worshiper is granted the same degree of divine favor that he or she would have received by visiting 46,000 times during the rest of the year. Is also called 'shiman-rokusen-nichi.' **(2)**〖神道・仏教〗to visit a temple or shrine for a consecutive one thousand days.

せんにちもうで 千日詣で〖神道・仏教〗⇨千日参り

ぜんにほんくうゆ 全日本空輸〖交通・企業名〗 All Nippon Airways. The largest domestic air carrier. Was established in 1952.

せんにゅうじ 泉涌寺〖寺院〗 Sennyuu-ji Temple. The head temple of the Sennyuu-ji school of the Shingon sect. Originated from a thatched hermitage built by the priest KUUKAI in the 9th century and was revived in 1218 by the priest Shunjou. Became the family temple of the Imperial Household since the funeral of Emperor Shijou was held there in the 14th century.

せんにん 仙人〖宗教〗 a mountain hermit with magical powers and immortality. Is considered to be an ideal person in Taoism.

せんにんばり 千人針〖戦争・精神性〗a soldier's charm cloth with one thousand red stitches. Was begun in the Meiji era and became popular during World War II. Each stitch was sewn by a different woman.

せんのりきゅう 千利休〖茶道〗1522-1591. A tea master and the founder of the Senke school, born in present Sakai City, Osaka Pref.

Learned the tea ceremony under TAKENO JOUOU and perfected the tea ceremony, called WABICHA. Though having served ODA NOBUNAGA and TOYOTOMI HIDEYOSHI, incurred Hideyoshi's anger and was ordered to commit suicide.

ぜんぱ 善派〖彫刻〗 the Zen school of Buddhist sculpture. The names of sculptors in this school begin with 'Zen,' such as Zen'en. This 'Zen' has no relation with Zen Buddhism because the kanji character is different. →慶派; 院派; 円派

せんばこき 千歯こき〖農林水産〗 a threshing tool, or thousand-tooth rake. Was invented at the end of the 17th or the beginning of the 18th century. Is not used at present.

せんばづる 千羽鶴〖精神性〗 one thousand origami cranes strung together. Is often used as prayer for someone's recovery from sickness.

せんひめ 千姫〖政治〗 1597-1666. A daughter of TOKUGAWA HIDETADA and the wife of TOYOTOMI HIDEYORI. Was rescued from the castle in the Summer Campaign in Osaka in 1615.

せんぶ 先負〖暦〗 a day of "early defeat" in the unofficial six-day calendar. Everything should be done calmly. People will have bad fortune in the morning and good fortune in the afternoon. →六曜(るくよう)

せんぶつ 塼仏〖仏教・美術〗 relief of Buddhist images on an unglazed

clay tile. Examples include the work at OKA-DERA Temple in Nara Pref.

せんべい 煎餅 〖食べ物〗 **(1)** a Japanese-style cookie. Is made from sugar, flour, water, and egg. → 瓦 (かわ)煎餅 **(2)** a rice cracker. Is made from rice powder and seasoned with soy sauce or salt. →薄焼き煎餅；堅焼煎餅

せんべいぶとん 煎餅布団〖家具〗 a thin low-quality futon. Literally means "rice cracker futon."

せんべつ 餞別 〖生活〗 a farewell gift, or a parting gift. Often cash in Japan.

せんぽう 先鋒 〖武術〗 the first fighter in a five-member team competition of martial arts such as judo. →次鋒；中堅；副将；大将

ぜんぽうこうえんふん 前方後円墳 〖考古〗 a keyhole-shaped tumulus. Dates from the 3rd to the 7th centuries, and examples are seen all over Japan and in part of Korea. Is square-shaped at the one side and round-shaped at the other side. The 46 largest existing burial mounds are in this style.

せんぼんしゃかどう 千本釈迦堂 〖寺院〗 the common name for DAI-HOUON-JI Temple.

せんまい 饌米〖神道〗 washed rice offered to a deity. People eat it after offering.

ぜんまい 薇 〖食べ物・植物〗 a royal fern. *Osmunda japonica*. A coiled young leaf is edible.

せんまいづけ 千枚漬け 〖食べ物〗 pickles of thin-sliced turnip. Are seasoned with mirin, kelp, and red pepper. A specialty of Kyoto.

せんみょう 宣命〖天皇・文書〗 a document to communicate an Imperial edict. Is written with kanji that are used as phonograms.

せんみょうたい 宣命体〖言語〗 the style of Imperial edicts, called SEN-MYOU.

せんめんながしず 扇面流し図 〖絵画〗 a painting of fans floating on a stream. Depicts many folding fans in the background of a stream, often on a folding screen.

ぜんもんどう 禅問答〖仏教〗 a Zen riddle. Often cannot be understood by an ordinary person.

せんりゅう 川柳〖文芸〗 a comical, witty, or satirical poem in the HAIKU format. Does not contain a season word, as opposed to a haiku. Is still popular, and ordinary people often publish them in newspapers.

せんりょうぐんしれいぶ 占領軍司令部〖戦争・外交〗 ⇨連合国軍最高司令官総司令部

せんりょうばこ 千両箱 〖貨幣〗 a small wooden safe in the Edo period. Contained one thousand golden coins.

せんりん 戦輪〖忍者〗 a throwing metal ring. The outer edge is bladed to injure the enemy. Its origin is *chakram*, a throwing weapon in ancient India.

せんろっぽん 千六本〖食文化〗 ⇨千切り

そ

そう 宋 〖国名〗 Sung. A Chinese dynasty from 960 to 1279. Trade was active with Japan during this time. The former half from 960 to 1127 is called Northern Sung, and the latter half from 1127 to 1279 is called Southern Sung.

そう 草 〖書道・芸術〗 the simplified or flowing style of various traditional arts. Literally means "grass." →真・行・草

そう 惣 〖行政〗 an autonomous community of peasants. Was formed in the present Kansai region from the 13th to 16th centuries. Held a meeting, called 'yoriai,' to manage the land and water resources cooperatively and to punish violators of their own rules.

そう ～双 〖美術・助数詞〗 a counting suffix for pair of folding screens. ↔隻(せき)

そう ～艘 〖交通・助数詞〗 a counting suffix for small boats. ↔隻(せき)

そうあみ 相阿弥 〖絵画〗 ?-1525. A painter, curator, and art advisor for the Ashikaga shogunate. Was good at India ink paintings. His works include *Eight Views of Xiaoxiang* at the Kyoto National Museum. His grandfather, NOUAMI, and his father, GEIAMI, also served in the same position for the shogunate.

そうかがっかい 創価学会 〖宗教〗 Soka Gakkai, or Value-Creating Educational Society. Best known and largest new religion in Japan, with roots in Nichiren's teachings. Was founded in 1930 by Makiguchi Jozaburo, who mainly recruited followers from among teachers. Has supported many educational groups, runs a university, has been connected to a political party, and publishes magazines and a newspaper. Also operates in countries outside of Japan. According to a survey conducted by a publishing company, Diamond Inc., more than eight million households were believers as of 2009.

ぞうかさんしん 造化三神 〖神話〗 the first three deities in a Japanese myth: AME-NO MINAKANUSHI NO KAMI, TAKAMIMUSUHI NO KAMI, and KAMIMUSUHI NO KAMI. They appeared when chaos separated into the heavens and earth.

ぞうがん 象嵌 〖美術〗 the inlay technique for arts and crafts. Gold, silver, or mother of pearl is engraved on the surface of metal, ceramic, or wooden works.

そうぎょうはちまん 僧形八幡 〖仏教・神道〗 Hachiman deity with an appearance of a Buddhist priest. Has a rosary, called JUZU, in the left hand and a crosier, called SHAKUJOU, in the right hand. This image was created, based on HONJISUIJAKU-SETSU, the theory of original reality and manifested traces.

そうきょく 箏曲〔音楽〕 traditional music for a zither-like instrument called KOTO. Was begun in the Edo period.

そうけ 宗家〔芸道〕 ⇨家元

そうげつりゅう 草月流 〔華道〕 Sogetsu School. Was established as modern-style flower arrangement in 1927 by Teshigawara Soufuu.

そうげんが 宋元画〔絵画〕 paintings in the Sung and Yuan dynasties. Especially paintings imported from China in the Kamakura and Muromachi periods.

そうこう 霜降〔暦〕 one of the 24 seasonal nodes in the traditional calendar. Around October 23 in the current calendar. Means "frost begins to form." →二十四節気(にじゅうし せっき)

そうごう 相好〔仏教〕 ⇨三十二相八十種好

そうごうしょうしゃ 総合商社〔経済〕 a general trading company. Deals with numerous kinds of items from instant ramen to rockets. The largest examples are Mitsubishi Corporation, Sumitomo Corporation, and Mitsui & Co., Ltd.

そうごのりいれ 相互乗り入れ〔鉄道〕 the through-line service between different railroad companies. Saves the commuters the trouble of changing trains at a crowded terminal station at the busiest time.

そうざい 総菜〔食文化〕 a cuisine in a daily meal, eaten with rice.

そうざいや 総菜屋〔食文化〕 a food shop that sells house-cooked cuisine, such as salad, tempura, and simmered food, at reasonable prices.

そうしき 葬式〔冠婚葬祭〕 a funeral. Many Japanese hold a Buddhist-style funeral even though they may not believe in Buddhism. A funeral of the Imperial family is Shinto-style.

そうじゅつ 槍術〔武術〕 spearmanship. Is said to have appeared in the late 13th century.

そうしょ 草書〔書道〕 the cursive style of calligraphy. Strokes are very simplified. →楷書；行書

そうしょう 宗匠〔芸道・文芸〕 a master and instructor of poetry, tea ceremony, flower arrangement, etc.

そうじょう 僧正〔仏教〕 the title of the highest class of an official administrative priest. →大僧正；僧都(そうづ)；律師(りっし)

ぞうじょうじ 増上寺〔寺院〕 Zojoji. One of the seven main temples of the Pure Land sect, located close to Tokyo Tower. Was converted from the Shingon sect to the Pure Land sect in 1385 and became the family temple of the Tokugawa clan in 1590.

ぞうじょうてん 増長天〔仏教〕 ⇨増長(ぞうちょう)天

そうじょうへんじょう 僧正遍照〔文芸〕 816-890. One of the Six Immortal Poets, one of the Thirty-six Immortal Poets, and a grandson of Emperor Kanmu. His 35 tanka are contained in the *Collection of Ancient and Modern Japanese Poetry* (KOKINWAKASHUU). Became a priest after his master, Emperor Ninmei, passed away. →六歌仙；三十六歌仙

そうしょくこふん 装飾古墳 〖史跡〗 a decorated tumulus. The inside of the burial mound and the coffin are decorated with pictures or patterns. Was mainly created in northern Kyushu from the 5th to 6th centuries.

そうず 添水 〖建築〗 ⇨鹿威(しし)し

そうず 僧都 〖仏教〗 the title of the second highest class of an official priest. →僧正(そうじょう)；律師(りっし)

ぞうすい 雑炊 〖食べ物〗 rice porridge containing vegetables, bits of meat or fish, and eggs. Is seasoned with miso or soy sauce and sometimes eaten as a closer in hot-pot cooking.

そうたつ 宗達 〖絵画〗 ⇨俵屋宗達

そうたつこうりんは 宗達光琳派 〖絵画〗 ⇨琳派

ぞうちょうてん 増長天 〖仏教〗 One of the Four Guardian Kings. *Virudhaka*. Often carries a spear and defends the south. →四天王

そうてつ 相鉄 〖鉄道〗 ⇨相模鉄道

そうどう 僧堂 〖仏教・建築〗 a meditation hall at a Zen temple. Originally a living place for monks, which corresponds to SOUBOU in some other sects.

そうとうしゅう 曹洞宗 〖仏教〗 the Soutou sect. A sect of Zen Buddhism. Was introduced from the Sung dynasty to Japan in the 13th century by DOUGEN. Mainly spread among the common people while another Zen sect, RINZAI-SHUU, was popular among the ruling class. Emphasizes single-minded sitting in meditation. The two head temples are EIHEI-JI Temple in Fukui Pref. and Souji-ji Temple in Kanagawa Pref. →只管打坐(しかんたざ)

ぞうに 雑煮 〖食べ物〗 a rice cake soup. Usually contains produce of each region, such as vegetables, fish, chicken, etc. Eaten on the New Year's holidays.

そうびょう 宗廟 〖冠婚葬祭〗 a mausoleum for ancestors.

ぞうひょう 雑兵 〖軍事〗 a foot soldier, or an infantryman, mainly in the Muromachi period. Accompanied a samurai on horseback. Was in charge of shooting a gun, drawing a bow, raising a banner, or holding a horse in the battlefield.

ぞうぶつしょ 造仏所 〖仏教・彫刻〗 a temporary studio for producing Buddhist sculpture in the 8th and 9th centuries. Was established when a temple was being constructed and was removed after construction.

そうへい 僧兵 〖仏教・軍事〗 a monk soldier. Was armed and trained in martial arts under the pretext of protecting Buddhism. Large temples such as KOUFUKU-JI, ENRYAKU-JI, and ONJOU-JI had troops from the 11th to 16th centuries and put pressure on the government or fought with each other.

そうぼう 僧坊 〖仏教・建築〗 a

residential building for monks in a Buddhist temple. Is called SOUDOU in a Zen temple.

そうほんけ　総本家　(1)〖生活〗the head family. **(2)**〖ビジネス〗the originator of some business.

そうほんざん　総本山〖仏教〗a head temple. Each sect or subsect of Buddhism usually has a sole head temple that supervises main temples. Examples are CHION-IN of the Pure Land sect, KONGOUBU-JI of the Shingon sect, etc. →大本山

そうほんしゃ　総本社〖神道〗a general head shrine. A head shrine and branch shrines enshrine the same deity or deities. There is not a rigid vertical relationship between the head and branch shrines.

そうまとう　走馬灯〖生活〗⇨回り灯籠(どうろう)

そうむしょう　総務省　〖行政機関〗Ministry of Internal Affairs and Communications. MIC. Was established in 2001 by unifying the Management and Coordination Agency, the Ministry of Home Affairs, and the Ministry of Posts and Telecommunications.

そうめん　素麺〖食べ物〗very thin wheat noodles like vermicelli. Is preferred in summer, served cold, and dipped into a sauce before eating. Is sometimes used as ingredients in miso soup in winter. →煮麺(にゅうめん)

そうめんながし　素麺流し〖食文化〗⇨流し素麺

そうもん　総門〖仏教・建築〗⇨大門

そうやかいきょう　宗谷海峡〖海洋〗La Pérouse Strait, or the Souya Channel. Runs between Cape Souya and Sakhalin Island. The width is 43 km. The deepest point is about 70 m. Connects the Sea of Japan and the Sea of Okhotsk. →宗谷岬；樺太(からふと)

そうやみさき　宗谷岬〖地名〗Cape Souya. Is located in Hokkaido and is the northernmost cape of Japan. Faces the Souya Channel. On fine days, Sakhalin Island can be observed from the cape. →樺太(からふと)

ぞうり　草履〖履物〗thonged flat sandals. Used to be made of straw, common rush, or bamboo skin. Are now made of these traditional materials as well as cloth, leather, and other substances.

そうりょ　僧侶〖仏教〗a Buddhist priest, or a bonze. Shaves his or her head, except for the priests of the True Pure Land sect, and wears a special costume.

そうりん　相輪〖仏教・建築〗the decorative part on the top of a pagoda roof. Consists of seven parts: 'houju,' 'ryuusha,' 'suien,' 'kurin,' 'ukebana,' 'fukubachi,' and 'roban,' from the top to the bottom.

そおすかつどん　ソースかつ丼〖食べ物〗a bowl of rice topped with a pork cutlet and chopped cabbage. Special sauce is put on it. A specialty of Fukui Pref.

そかい　疎開〖軍事〗to evacuate from urban areas to rural areas to avoid an air raid. Was conducted during World War II.

そがし 蘇我氏 〖氏族〗 the Soga clan. Was powerful in ancient times, but was destroyed in the Taika Reform of 645. →蘇我馬子(そがの うまこ); 蘇我蝦夷 (そがの えみし); 蘇我入鹿(そがの いるか)

そがしょうはく 曾我蕭白 〖絵画〗 1730–1781. A painter born in Kyoto. Preferred eccentricity and painted weird human figures related to Taoism or Buddhism. His works include *Dragon and Clouds* at the Museum of Fine Arts, Boston.

そがのいるか 蘇我入鹿 〖政治〗 ?–645. A top administrator in the Imperial Court. The son of SOGA NO EMISHI. Held the reins of power under Empress Kougyoku and killed Yamashiro no Ooe, a son of Prince Shoutoku. Was assassinated by Prince Naka no Ooe, NAKATOMI NO KAMATARI, and their collaborators. →聖徳太子; 中大兄皇子(なかのおおえの おうじ); 大化の改新

そがのうまこ 蘇我馬子 〖政治〗 ?–626. A top administrator in the Imperial Court. The father of SOGA NO EMISHI. Helped introduce Buddhism to Japan. In 587 destroyed MONONOBE NO MORIYA, who had rejected Buddhism. Assassinated Emperor Sushun and assisted his niece in gaining the throne as Empress Suiko. →推古天皇

そがのえみし 蘇我蝦夷 〖政治〗 ?–645. A top administrator in the Imperial Court. The son of SOGA NO UMAKO, and the father of SOGA NO IRUKA. Backed up Emperor Jomei and held the reins of power. When Iruka was assassinated, killed himself.

そがは 曾我派 〖絵画〗 Soga school of Chinese-style ink painting. Was started by Soga Jasoku in the Muromachi period.

そくい 即位 〖天皇〗 the announcement to the whole country that an Emperor is enthroned. →践祚(せん そ)

そくおん 促音 〖言語〗 a geminate consonant. Is spelled as double consonants such as pp in 'Nippon,' which means "Japan." Since a geminate consonant is a phoneme, its presence affects the meaning of a word. For example, 'aka' means "red" while 'akka' means "getting worse."

ぞくぎいん 族議員 〖政治〗 a politician who serves the interests of a specific industry or organization.

ぞくじ 俗字 〖言語〗 an informal form of a kanji character. For example, a kanji that means "shame" should be spelled as 恥, but its informal form is 耻.

そくしつ 側室 〖政治〗 an official sub-wife of an Emperor, a shogun, an aristocrat, or a feudal lord in the past. One of their purposes in having a sub-wife or sub-wives was to retain the lineage by bearing male offspring. ↔正室

ぞくじょうもんぶんか 続縄文文化 〖時代〗 Post-Joumon Culture. People lived by hunting, fishing, and gathering in Hokkaido and the northern Tohoku region from approximately 2,500 years ago to the 7th century. Was influenced by the Yayoi Culture in Honshuu but did not cultivate rice because of the cold climate. Was later replaced by the Satsumon Culture. →縄文文化；弥生文化；擦文(ﾓﾝ)文化

そくしんじょうぶつ　即身成仏〖仏教〗attainment of Buddhahood while in the flesh. The fundamental doctrine of Shingon esoteric Buddhism.

そくしんぶつ　即身仏〖仏教〗a self-mummified priest, or a living Buddha. This type of priest ate or drank nothing, died in meditation, and became a mummy by his own will. There are several examples, mainly in the Tohoku region.

そくたい　束帯〖服飾〗official court costume for men. Began to be worn in the Heian period.

ぞくみょう　俗名〖仏教〗**(1)** a name before a person's death. After death, the bereaved family buys a posthumous name from a temple. →戒名 **(2)** a name as a lay person. A monk or nun is given a Buddhist name.

そくよう　粗供養〖仏教〗a small return gift to the mourners in a funeral or memorial service.

そしぞう　祖師像〖仏教・美術〗a portrait of the founder of a sect or temple. Is either a painting or a sculpture. Creation of such a portrait was especially popular in Zen and esoteric Buddhism.

そしどう　祖師堂〖仏教・建築〗a hall to enshrine the image of the founder of a sect or temple. The name differs from sect to sect. →開山堂

そせき　礎石〖建築〗a foundation stone. Supports a pillar on the ground. Provides historical information about buildings that no longer exist.

そつぎょうしき　卒業式〖教育〗commencement. Is usually held in late February or March. Is a very formal ceremony in Japan to award diplomas to students. Many students wear formal clothes, such as a school uniform, a suit, or a kimono, for the ceremony.

そつじゅ　卒寿〖通過儀礼〗the age of 90 in the traditional approach to age counting. People usually celebrate when a person turns 89, in the modern approach to age counting. 'Sotsuju' literally means "graduating age," because when 90(九十) is written vertically in KANJI, it looks like 卒 in a cursive style, which means "graduation." →数え年

そてつ　蘇鉄〖植物〗a king sago palm, or cycad. *Cycas revoluta*. Native to southern Kyushu and the Southwest Islands. Grows up to 3 m high.

そと　外, ソト〖精神性〗⇨ウチとソト

そとがけ　外掛け〖相撲〗an outside leg trip. A technique to trip the outside of the opponent's leg with one's leg while holding the opponent's body, and then to pull the opponent's leg toward oneself.

そとば 卒塔婆 〖仏教〗 a pagoda-shaped long wooden tablet erected beside a grave. Sanskrit characters, the posthumous name, or the date of the death may be written on it.

そとぼり 外堀 〖城郭〗 an outer moat. Was dug surrounding a castle precinct. ↔内堀

そとゆ 外湯 〖温泉〗 a public bath of a hot spring town. Is available at Kinosaki in Hyougo, Kusatsu in Gunma, Nozawa in Nagano, and other spas.

そなえもち 供え餅 〖宗教・食べ物〗 piled round rice cakes offered to a deity. The smaller rice cake is put on the larger one.

そねざきしんじゅう 曽根崎心中 〖文楽〗 *The Love Suicides at Sonezaki*. A puppet drama written by CHIKAMATSU MONZAEMON, based on a real love suicide in Osaka. Was first played in 1703.

そば 蕎麦 〖食べ物〗 buckwheat noodles. Eaten hot in broth or eaten cold after being dipped in a soy-flavored sauce. When served hot, are usually topped with thinly chopped green onions. Other common toppings include a tempura and a deep-fried batter ball. Red pepper is added according to taste. Buckwheat is native to Central Asia. It is said that a Korean priest introduced buckwheat noodles into Japan in the 17th century. Is now a nation-wide favorite, especially in Eastern Japan. →お亀蕎麦；掛け蕎麦；笊(ざる)蕎麦；十割蕎麦；狸(たぬき)蕎麦；茶蕎麦；年越し蕎麦；二八蕎麦；引っ越し蕎麦；盛り蕎麦；藪(やぶ)蕎麦；夜鳴き蕎麦；椀子(わんこ)蕎麦

そばうち 蕎麦打ち 〖食文化〗 preparation of buckwheat noodles. Buckwheat dough is kneaded, rolled out, and cut thinly to form noodles.

そばがき 蕎麦掻き 〖食べ物〗 cooked buckwheat dough. Eaten dipped in soy sauce or covered with sweet adzuki paste.

そばがら 蕎麦殻 〖生活〗 buckwheat chaff. Is stuffed in a traditional pillow.

そばこ 蕎麦粉 〖食文化〗 buckwheat flour.

そばつゆ 蕎麦汁 〖食文化〗 dipping sauce for buckwheat noodles. Is made from soy sauce, mirin, and dashi.

そばまんじゅう 蕎麦饅頭 〖食べ物〗 a dumpling made of buckwheat flour containing adzuki paste.

そばや 蕎麦屋 〖食文化〗 a buckwheat noodle restaurant. Besides buckwheat noodles, often serves thick white noodles, called UDON, and rice with toppings, called DONBURI-MONO.

そばゆ 蕎麦湯 〖飲み物〗 buckwheat hot water. Water in which buckwheat noodles have been boiled. After eating cold buckwheat noodles, people enjoy drinking the mixture of 'sobayu' and dip for buckwheat noodles. →蕎麦汁(つゆ)

そばようにん 側用人 〖武士・官位〗 a grand chamberlain, or an aide of the Tokugawa shogunate. Conveyed messages between the shogun and his ministers and had strong political power.

そふとてにす ソフトテニス〖スポーツ〗 ⇨軟式テニス

そふとぼおる ソフトボール〖スポーツ〗 softball. Was introduced to Japan in 1921. Japan won the gold medal at the Beijing Olympics in 2008.

そぼろ そぼろ〖食べ物〗 minced and cooked meat or fish. Is seasoned with soy sauce and sugar. Is often used for a three-colored rice bowl. →三色丼

そめいよしの 染井吉野〖植物〗 a Yoshino cherry, a Japanese flowering cherry, or a Potomac cherry. *Prunus* x *yedoensis*. The most common cherry tree in Japan. Was first sold at Somei in present Tokyo in the 19th century. Is not directly relevant to YOSHINO, Nara Pref., where mountain cherry trees are seen. →山桜

そめつけ 染付 〖陶磁器〗 white porcelain with blue patterns or pictures. After patterns or pictures are painted, the porcelain is baked with transparent glaze.

そめもの 染物〖服飾〗 dyed textiles.

そようちょう 租庸調 〖行政〗 ancient taxes. Are paid with rice and local specialties.

そらからちゃん ソラカラちゃん〖ゆるキャラ〗 Tokyo Skytree mascot. 'Sorakara' literally means "from the sky," and 'chan' is a suffix to express friendly feelings.

そろばん 算盤〖教育〗 an abacus. A person calculates by sliding beads in rows, which are penetrated with parallel sticks. Abacus schools were very popular before electronic calculators spread.

そんきょ 蹲踞〖相撲・剣術〗 a squat. Two fighters squat face to face immediately before a bout in sumo or kendo.

そんけいご 尊敬語 〖言語〗 an honorific expression to show respect to others. Can express respect not only to the listeners or readers but also to the third person in the topic. This type of honorific expression of a verb is made by conjugating the word end and adding an auxiliary 'rareru' or conjugating the word end and adding the set of a prefix 'o' and an auxiliary 'ninaru.' Some verbs such as "go," "say," or "eat" also have a specific forms to show respect. This type of honorific expression of a noun or adjective is made by adding a prefix 'o' or 'go.' Some nouns such as "your father" or "your company" also have a specific form to show respect.

そんのうじょうい 尊皇攘夷, 尊王攘夷 〖思想〗 "Revere the Emperor and expel the barbarians." Although this concept was combined with the movement to overthrow the Tokugawa shogunate and also facilitated the Meiji Restoration, the Meiji government promoted the policy of Europeanization.

た

たい 鯛 〖食べ物・魚〗 a sea bream. *Pagrus major*, or *Chrysophrys major*. About 1 m long. Is often eaten on auspicious occasions. Eaten in various ways, such as sashimi, sushi, grilled, and simmered. →鯛飯

たいあん 大安 〖暦〗 a day of "great peace" in the unofficial six-day calendar. Everything works well on this day. Often couples hold their weddings on this day. →六曜(るく)

だいあんじ 大安寺 〖寺院〗 Daian-ji Temple. One of the Seven Great Temples of Nara. Is located in Nara City and affiliated with the Shingon sect. Was founded in 617 at the request of Prince Shoutoku. Used to be called Daikandai-ji, meaning "great national temple," but declined after medieval times.

たいいくのひ 体育の日 〖暦〗 Health Sports Day. The second Monday in October. A national holiday to enjoy sports and foster sound body and mind. Was ordained to commemorate the Tokyo Olympics in 1964.

だいいとくみょうおう 大威徳明王 〖仏教〗 Wisdom King of Great Virtue and Authority. *Yamantaka*. One of the Five Great Wisdom Kings. Destroys harmful evils. Six-faced, six-armed, and six-legged. Has several weapons in his hands, such as a sword and a spear, and rides on an ox.

たいいんたいようれき 太陰太陽暦 〖暦〗 the lunisolar calendar. Is based on the waxing and waning of the moon and, according to the solar motion, is adjusted by placing seven intercalary months in each of 19 years. The traditional calendar of Japan used this system from ancient times until 1872.

たいいんれき 太陰暦 〖暦〗 the lunar calendar. Includes the lunisolar calendar in a broad sense. Strictly speaking, the calendar Japanese used until 1872 was the lunisolar one, though most people do not distinguish between the lunar and lunisolar calendars. ↔太陽暦 →太陰太陽暦

だいえい 大映 〖映画・企業名〗 Daiei Film Co. Ltd. A motion picture company established in 1945. Went bankrupt in 1971. Was revived in 1974 and was taken over by Kadokawa. Daiei films include *Rashoumon* directed by Kurosawa, *Zatoichi: The Blind Swordsman* series starring Katsu Shintarou, and the *Gamera* series.

たいおとし 体落とし 〖柔道〗 a body drop. A technique to extend one's leg, trip the opponent, and pull down him or her.

たいか 大化 〖時代〗 The era from 645 to 650. The first subset of a period, which is called GENGOU. The Taika Reform was implemented during this era.

だいがく 大学〖教育〗 a university or a college. As of 2016, Japan had 777 universities, including 86 national, 91 municipal or prefectural, and 600 private ones. The university attendance rate of high school graduates was 52.6% as of 2017. Annual tuition fees were about 540 thousand yen at public universities and about 1 million yen at private universities in average, though the tuition at private universities varies considerably, depending on the department.

だいかぐら 太神楽 **(1)**〖神道〗music and dance dedicated to the Ise Shrine. →神楽(かぐら); 伊勢神宮 **(2)**〖大道芸〗 a street performance including a lion dance and spinning plates in the Edo period.

だいかしょう 大迦葉 〖仏教〗 *Mahakasyapa*. One of the Ten Great Disciples of the Historical Buddha. Best at asceticism. →十大弟子

たいがどらま 大河ドラマ〖娯楽〗 a saga TV drama broadcast by NHK. Starts on the New Year's holidays and continues until the end of the year. Popular settings for its stories are the Warring States period in the 16th century and the period from the end of the Tokugawa shogunate to the Meiji Restoration in the 19th century.

たいかのかいしん 大化の改新 〖政治〗 Taika Reform. Prince Naka no Ooe, later Emperor Tenji, and NAKATOMI NO KAMATARI eliminated the Soga family and began to build a Chinese-style centralized state by weakening the power of other clans in 645. →天智天皇

だいかん 代官〖政治〗 a local administrator as deputy of the Tokugawa shogunate, or each feudal lord.

だいかん 大寒〖暦〗 one of the 24 seasonal nodes in the traditional calendar. Around January 20 in the current calendar. Means "the coldest day in a year." →二十四節気(にじゅうしせっき)

だいかんわじてん 大漢和辞典 〖言語・書名〗 *The Great Han-Japanese Dictionary*. Was compiled by Morohashi Tetsuji. Consists of 13 volumes. The first volume was published in 1943, and the last was published in 1960. Contains 49,946 kanji as entries.

だいきち 大吉〖神社・寺院〗 best fortune. A message on a fortune slip available at a Shinto shrine or Buddhist temple. ↔大凶 →お神籤(みくじ); 吉

だいきょう 大凶〖神社・寺院〗 worst fortune. A message on a fortune slip available at a Shinto shrine or Buddhist temple. ↔大吉 →お神籤(みくじ); 凶

だいぎんじょう 大吟醸 〖酒〗 a top-quality sake. Is brewed at low temperatures from rice polished to 50% or less of its original weight. →吟醸酒

だいぐうじ 大宮司〖神社〗 a chief priest of a major Shinto shrine,

such as the Ise Shrine, Atsuta Shrine, and Usa Shrine. →宮司(ぐうじ)

たいげん 体言 〖言語〗 an independent word with no inflection. Can be a subject of a sentence by itself. A noun or a pronoun.

たいこうき 太閤記 〖文芸・作品〗 the name of a biographical story written in 1625 by a Confucian scholar, Oze Hoan. Describes the entire life of TOYOTOMI HIDEYOSHI.

たいこうけんち 太閤検地 〖武士・政治〗 land surveys by TOYOTOMI HIDEYOSHI. Checked the land size and the productive capacity. Was conducted nationwide from 1582 to 1598 and led to the foundation of the early modern feudal system.

だいこくてん 大黒天 〖宗教〗 the deity of wealth. One of the Seven Deities of Good Fortune. Is usually depicted as standing on straw rice sacks, carrying a magical mallet and a bag full of treasure. Was originally a deity in the Indian mythology, *Mahakala*, was then introduced into Buddhism, and was later identified with OOKUNINUSHI NO KAMI in a Japanese mythology. →七福神

だいごくでん 大極殿 〖天皇・建築〗 the Main Hall of the Imperial Court in ancient times. Important ceremonies were held in this building. The last 'Daigokuden' was destroyed by fire in 1177. →朝堂(ちょうどう)院

だいこくひや 大国火矢 〖忍者〗 a fire arrow with gunpowder. Was used to set fire to an enemy's residence or camp. Some of them flew like rocket firework, using the powder for propelling power.

だいこくやこうだゆう 大黒屋光太夫 〖外交〗 1751-1828. The captain of a merchant ship, born in present Mie Pref. His ship was wrecked in 1782 and drifted ashore on the coast of the Aleutians. He lived in Russia for ten years, met Empress Ekaterina II, and came back to Japan in 1792.

だいごじ 醍醐寺 〖寺院〗 Daigoji Temple. The head temple of the Daigoji school of the Shingon sect located in Kyoto City. Was founded in 874 by a priest Shoubou. Has been known as a wonderful spot for cherry blossom viewing since TOYOTOMI HIDEYOSHI had a flower-viewing party in 1598. Possesses many National Treasures including its buildings, sculptures, and paintings. Was designated a World Heritage Site in 1994.

だいごのはなみ 醍醐の花見 〖政治・娯楽〗 Cherry Blossom Viewing in Daigo-ji Temple. Was held in 1598 by TOYOTOMI HIDEYOSHI.

たいこばし 太鼓橋 〖建築〗 an arched bridge. Examples can be seen at Tsurugaoka Hachimanguu Shrine in Kamakura, Kanagawa Pref., Sumiyoshi Grand Shrine in Osaka, Dazaifu-Tenmanguu Shrine in Fukuoka, and other Shinto shrines.

たいこむすび 太鼓結び 〖服飾〗 ⇨お太鼓

たいこもち 太鼓持ち〖娯楽〗 a jester for banquet. Enlivens the atmosphere and entertains the guests. Sometimes shows artistic skills. Was popular in the Edo period. Only a few survive at present.

たいこやき 太鼓焼き〖食べ物〗 ⇨今川焼

だいこん 大根〖食べ物・植物〗 a mooli, or giant white radish. *Raphanus sativus*. The root is used for a variety of cuisine such as pickles, hotpot, or a garnish for sashimi. The grated root is used as a condiment. The leaves are eaten stir-fried or as pickles. →沢庵(ﾀﾞｸ);おでん;鰤(ﾌﾞﾘ)大根;切り干し大根;風呂吹き大根;大根卸し

だいこんおろし 大根卸し〖調味料〗 grated mooli. Is used as a condiment for grilled fish or for a one-pot dish of chicken and vegetables. →焼き魚;水炊き

だいざ 台座〖仏教〗 a pedestal for a Buddhist image. There are various types such as a lotus flower, mountain, rock, or animal. →蓮華座;裳懸(ﾓｶﾞｹ)座

だいさんのびいる 第3のビール〖酒〗 new beer-taste alcoholic drink. Literally means "the third beer" because it was introduced after real beer and beer-taste alcoholic drink, called 'happoushu.' Cheaper than the two precursors. Soy beans or corn is sometimes used instead of malt.

だいし 大姉〖仏教〗 a title attached to a woman's posthumous Buddhist name. ↔居士(ｺﾞ)

だいじざいてん 大自在天〖仏教〗 *Mahesvara*. The Buddhist name for *Siva*, the deity of destruction and production in the Hindu religion.

たいししんこう 太子信仰〖仏教〗 faith in Prince Shoutoku. Although 'taishi' is a general noun that means "prince," it sometimes refers to Prince Shoutoku because he made a great effort to spread Buddhism in Japan. →聖徳太子

だいししんこう 大師信仰〖仏教〗 faith in the priest KUUKAI, who is also called Koubou daishi. Although 'daishi' is a general noun that means "great teacher of Buddhism," it sometimes refers to Kuukai because he is one of the most prominent priests in Japanese Buddhism.

たいしどう 太子堂〖仏教〗 the Prince Shotoku Hall. Enshrines the image of Prince Shotoku, who strived to spread Buddhism in the 5th and 6th centuries.

だいしどう 大師堂〖仏教〗 the Great Master Hall. Enshrines the image of Kuukai, who established the Shingon sect of esoteric Buddhism.

たいしゃ 大社〖神道〗 a grand Shinto shrine. Although the shrine ranking system was abolished after World War II, some shrines are still using the names with taisha, such as Kasuga Taisha. In a narrow sense, it only means Izumo Taisha.

たいしゃくてん 帝釈天〖仏教〗 a

guardian deity of Buddhism. *Indra*. The deity of thunder or war in the Indian mythology. Guards the east as one of the Twelve Devas. Is also said to reside at the top of Mt. Sumeru. Is often paired with *Brahman*, BON-TEN. →須弥山(しゅみせん)

たいしゃづくり　大社造り〘神社・建築〙 the Taisha style of Shinto architecture, which is the oldest Shinto style. The entrance is on the right hand of the gable side, and the central pillar is inside. The main sanctuary building of the Izumo Grand Shrine has this style. →本殿；出雲大社

たいしょ　大暑〘暦〙 one of the 24 seasonal nodes in the traditional calendar. Around July 23 in the current calendar. Means "the hottest day in a year." →二十四節気(にじゅうしせっき)

だいじょ　大序〘歌舞伎・文楽〙 the first part of the first act of a historical drama. Often refers to that of KANADEHON-CHUUSHINGURA.

たいしょう　大将　(1)〘武術〙 the last fighter in a five-member team competition of martial arts such as judo. →先鋒；次鋒；中堅；副将 **(2)**〘武士・軍事〙 a supreme commander of the army.

だいじょうかん　太政官〘行政〙 the Grand Council of State. The central organ of the administration system in ancient times. →律令制

だいじょうきょう　大乗経〘仏教〙 Mahayana sutras. Examples include the Lotus Sutra and Heart Sutra. →大乗仏教

たいしょうごと　大正琴〘音楽〙 a Taishou harp. Was invented in Nagoya in the early 20th century. Has two strings and keys indicating scales, like a typewriter.

だいじょうさい　大嘗祭〘天皇・祭礼〙 the great Imperial festival of rice harvest. The new Emperor offers newly cropped rice to heavenly deities and genii loci and himself eats it. It is held only once after a new Emperor has ascended to the throne. →新嘗(にい なめ)祭

たいしょうじだい　大正時代〘時代〙 the Taishou period, from 1912 to 1926. Taishou Democracy developed, and the Great Kanto Earthquake happened during this period.

たいしょうしんしゅうだいぞうきょう　大正新脩大蔵経〘仏教・書名〙 *Taishou Tripitaka*. The complete collection of Buddhist Scriptures published in Tokyo from 1924 to 1934.

だいじょうだいじん　太政大臣〘官位〙 the grand minister of state. The chief officer of the Grand Council of State in ancient times. No one was appointed when there was no suitable person. This title was created in 671 by Emperor Tenji for his son, Prince Ootomo. →太政官

たいしょうでもくらしい　大正デモクラシー〘思想〙 Taishou Democracy. Political ideas and movements asking for democratic reformation in the early 20th century.

たいしょうてんのう 大正天皇 〖天皇〗 Emperor Taishou. 1879-1926. The 123rd, on the throne from 1912 to 1926. Because of his poor health, appointed his eldest son as the regent in 1921. This son, Hirohito, was enthroned after Emperor Taishou died.

だいじょうてんのう 太上天皇 〖天皇〗 ⇨太上(だじょう)天皇

だいじょうぶっきょう 大乗仏教 〖仏教〗 Mahayana Buddhism. Arose around the first century in India. Mahayana means "great vehicle" because its goal is not only to enlighten oneself but to save all other people. Mahayana Buddhism spread in the Far East while its opposite party, Theravada Buddhism, spread in South and Southeast Asia. ↔小乗仏教

だいじんぐう 大神宮 〖神社〗 Another name for the Inner Shrine of Ise. Or a generic name for the Inner and Outer Shrine of Ise. →伊勢神宮；内宮(ないくう)；外宮(げくう)

だいす 台子 〖茶道〗 a stand for tea utensils. Is set in front of the tea host or hostess. A portable stove, a kettle, a pitcher, and other tools are placed on it.

だいず 大豆 〖食べ物・植物〗 soybeans. *Glycine max.* Were introduced from China in ancient times. Are used for a variety of food and seasoning such as tofu, MISO, and soy sauce. →醤油；豆腐

たいせいほうかん 大政奉還 〖政治〗 Return of Political Rule to the Emperor. The Tokugawa shogunate had political power since 1603, but the 15th shogun, TOKUGAWA YOSHINOBU, returned it to the Emperor in October 1867.

たいせつ 大雪 〖暦〗 one of the 24 seasonal nodes in the traditional calendar. Around December 7 in the current calendar. Means "heavy snow." →二十四節気(にじゅうしせっき)

たいせつざん 大雪山 〖山岳〗 ⇨大雪(だい)山

だいせつざん 大雪山 〖山岳〗 the Daisetsu Mountains. Are located in the center of Hokkaido. Consist of mountains above 2,000 m in height, stretching 15 km from east to west and 10 km from south to north. Some of them are volcanic. Are part of the Daisetsu-zan National Park. On the top of the mountains, snow remains even in summer.

だいせん 大山 〖山岳〗 Mt. Daisen. Is also called Houki Daisen or Houki Fuji. A volcano located in western Tottori Pref. Is 1,729 m high, making it the highest in the Chuugoku region. The Buddhist temple Daisen-ji has been the center of worship since the Heian period, and people could not climb the mountain without the temple's permission until the Edo period.

だいせんこふん 大仙古墳 〖天皇・史跡〗 ⇨仁徳天皇陵

たいぞういん 退蔵院 〖寺院〗 Taizo-in. A subsidiary temple of MYOUSHIN-JI Temple in Kyoto. Was founded in 1404. The India ink painting, *Catching a Catfish with a Gourd*, by Josetsu is a National Treasure.

たいぞうかいまんだら 胎蔵界曼荼羅〖仏教〗 Mandala of the Womb Realm. The Great Sun Buddha sits in the center, surrounded by 8 lotus leaves with Buddhas and Bodhisattvas on them. The central square is surrounded by several layers of rectangles containing many deities. The Womb Realm represents the reason of the Great Sun Buddha. ↔金剛界曼荼羅

だいぞうきょう 大蔵経〖仏教〗 the comprehensive collection of Buddhist scriptures. Includes Buddha's teachings, precepts, theology, and commentaries.

たいそうきょうぎ 体操競技〖スポーツ〗 gymnastics. Was introduced to Japan at the beginning of the 20th century. After Ono Takashi won the first gold medal at the Melbourne Olympics in 1956, Japan won more than 30 gold medals, in individual and team competitions.

だいそうじょう 大僧正〖仏教〗 the highest position in the priest's official hierarchy. →僧正；僧都(ずう)；律師

たいそうのれい 大喪の礼〖天皇〗 a funeral for an Emperor. Is held as a state ceremony.

だいだい 橙〖植物〗 a bitter orange, or a sour orange. *Citrus aurantium*. Is used as ornament for New Year's holidays. The peel is used for traditional Chinese medicine.

だいだいり 大内裏〖天皇〗 Palace Grounds of the Heijou and Heian Castles. The Imperial Palace and the government offices and ministries were located here. Its south gate is called SUZAKU-MON. →内裏(だいり)

だいだらぼっち だいだら法師〖妖怪〗 a legendary huge giant. It is said that he created some mountains with his hands and that his footprints became ponds.

だいとう 大刀〖武器〗 a generic term for a long sword. →太刀(たち)

だいとうあきょうえいけん 大東亜共栄圏〖政治〗 the Greater East Asia Co-Prosperity Sphere. Japan tried to rationalize its Asian invasion on the pretext of this idea during the Pacific War.

だいとうあせんそう 大東亜戦争〖戦争〗 the Greater East Asia War. The Japanese government called the Pacific War by this name on the pretext of building the Greater East Asia Co-Prosperity Sphere. →太平洋戦争；大東亜共栄圏

だいとくじ 大徳寺〖寺院〗 Daitoku-ji Temple. The head temple of the Daitoku-ji school of the Rinzai sect, located in Kyoto. Was founded in 1325 by a priest Shuuhou Myouchou and was revived by Ikkyuu after the Ounin War from 1467 to 1477. Has had close association with the tea ceremony. Consists of several subsidiary temples, called TACCHUU, and possesses many National Treasures including its buildings and paintings.

たいないくぐり 胎内潜り 〖仏教〗 walking through the inside of a big Buddhist sculpture or a sacred cave. A person who has passed is said to be purified.

たいないぶつ 胎内仏 〖仏教〗 a Buddhist sculpture stored in a larger sculpture. It was popular in and after the Heian period.

だいなごん 大納言 〖官位〗 a vice-minister of the Grand Council of State in ancient times. Ranked next to the minister and before CHUUNA-GON. →太政官

だいにちきょう 大日経 〖仏教〗 the Great Sun Sutra. A fundamental sutra for esoteric Buddhism. Describes sermons by the Great Sun Buddha.

だいにちにょらい 大日如来 〖仏教〗 the Great Sun Buddha. The central Buddha of the Shingon sect, which represents the ultimate reality of the universe. The Great Sun Buddha in the Mandala of the Diamond Realm makes the knowledge-fist mudra. The Great Sun Buddha in the Mandala of the Womb Realm makes the mudra for meditation.

だいにほんし 大日本史 〖人文学・書名〗 *Great History of Japan*. Began to be compiled in 1657 under the supervision of TOKUGAWA MITSUKUNI and was completed in 1906. Covers the history from the first Emperor Jinmu to Emperor Gokomatsu (1377-1433) in 397 volumes.

だいにほんていこくけんぽう 大日本帝国憲法 〖法律〗 Constitution of the Empire of Japan. Was promulgated in 1889 and was replaced by the present constitution in 1947. Prescribes that the Emperor has the sovereignty and that the people are his subjects.

だいねんぶつじ 大念仏寺 〖寺院〗 Dainenbutsu-ji. The head temple of the Yuuduu nenbutsu sect. Was founded in Osaka in 1127 by a priest Ryounin.

たいのうら 鯛の浦 〖魚・地名〗 Bay of Sea Breams. The sea coast of Kamogawa City, Chiba Pref. Has a legend that large sea breams gathered when the priest NICHIREN was born. Famous as a habitat of sea breams. A Special Natural Monument.

だいはちぐるま 大八車 〖交通〗 a two-wheeled wooden cart. Is pulled by men or an ox. Was used to carry loads from the 17th to 20th centuries.

たいふう 台風 〖自然〗 a typhoon. Usually forms from June to October. Three typhoons hit the Japan proper in a year on average.

だいふくちょう 大福帳 〖ビジネス〗 a traditional account book. Was used from the 17th to 19th centuries by merchants.

だいふくもち 大福餅 〖食べ物〗 a soft rice cake with sweet adzuki paste inside. There are several variations such as ones with strawberries, soy beans, or mugworts (YOMOGI).

だいぶつ 大仏 〖仏教〗 a great image of Buddha. Usually refers to an image whose height is more than 4.8 m (JOUROKU). →奈良大仏; 鎌倉大仏

だいぶっし 大仏師 〖仏教〗 a chief sculptor of Buddhist images. Led a group of sculptors in creating a large sculpture. →仏師(ᵇᵘ)

だいぶつよう 大仏様 〖仏教・建築〗 the Great Buddha style of architecture. Was introduced from southern China in the 12th century by a priest named CHOUGEN. Typical examples are the Southern Gate of TOUDAI-JI Temple in Nara and a hall of JOUDO-JI Temple in Hyougo Pref. Is also called 'tenjiku-you,' which literally means "Indian style" though it does not have a direct association with India. ↔禅宗様(ᵇᵘ)

たいへいき 太平記 〖文芸・作品〗 *Record of Great Peace.* A war chronicle written in the late 14th century. Authorship is attributed to Kojima Houshi. Describes political conflicts in the 14th century.

たいへいようせんそう 太平洋戦争 〖戦争〗 the Pacific War. The war fought between the Allies and Japan as part of World War II. Started with the attack on Pearl Harbor in 1941 and ended with Japan's acceptance of the Potsdam Declaration in 1945.

たいほう 大鵬 〖相撲〗 1940-2013. A sumo wrestler born in Hokkaido.

His real name is Naya Kouki. Became the 48th grand champion, yokozuna, at age 21.

だいほうおんじ 大報恩寺 〖寺院〗 Daihouon-ji Temple. Is also called Senbon Shaka-dou. Affiliated with the Shingon sect and is located in Kyoto. Was founded in 1221 by a priest named Gikuu. The main hall that survived multiple disasters such as the Ounin War from 1467 to 1477 is the oldest temple building in Kyoto and is designated a National Treasure. Also possesses Buddhist images created by sculptors of the Kei school. →応仁の乱; 慶派

たいほうりつりょう 大宝律令 〖法律〗 Taihou Code. Was compiled by Prince Osakabe, FUJIWARA NO FUHITO, and other aristocrats and was promulgated in 701 as Japan's first full-blown statute book. Contains 6 volumes of criminal law called 'ritsu' and 11 volumes of administrative law called 'ryou.'

だいほんえい 大本営 〖軍事〗 Imperial General Headquarters. The highest military council directly under the Emperor. Was abolished at the end of World War II.

だいほんざん 大本山 〖仏教〗 **(1)** a main temple of a Buddhist sect. Supervises branch temples and is supervised by the head temple. **(2)** the head temple of a sect or sub-sect in Zen Buddhism. →総本山

たいまでら 当麻寺 〖寺院〗 Taima-dera Temple. Affiliated with the Shingon and Pure Land sects and is located in northwestern Nara Pref. Is said to have been founded in 612 by a younger brother of Prince Shoutoku, Maroko. A mandala and three buildings are National Treasures. →中将姫；聖徳太子

たいまのけはや 当麻蹴速 〖相撲〗 the name of a legendary person said to have lived in Yamato, present Nara Pref. Boasted of the technique and power of sumo, but was kicked to death in a sumo match with NOMI NO SUKUNE.

たいみつ 台密 〖仏教〗 esoteric Buddhism of the Tendai sect. ↔東密

だいみょう 大名 〖武士〗 (1) a feudal lord in the Edo period. Was classified into three groups: Tokugawa relatives (SHINPAN), a hereditary feudal lord (FUDAI DAIMYOU), and outside feudal lords (TOZAMA DAIMYOU). Governed his domain called HAN, observed Laws for the Military Houses (BUKE-SHOHATTO), and had several duties imposed by the Tokugawa shogunate such as periodic residence in Edo (SANKIN-KOUTAI). (2)⇨戦国大名 (3)⇨守護大名

だいみょうぎょうれつ 大名行列 〖武士・交通〗 a feudal lord procession. A feudal lord had to live in Edo and his own feudal domain in alternate years and went to and came back from Edo every two years, making such a procession. →参勤交代

だいみょうじん 大明神 〖神道〗 Great Bright Deity. Is added as the honorific suffix after the names of Shinto deities or shrines. →明神

だいみょうびけし 大名火消し 〖災害・職業〗 a fire brigade under a feudal lord in the Edo period. Was in charge of preventing fire at Edo Castle, large temples, residences of feudal lords, and other significant places.

だいみょうやしき 大名屋敷 〖武士・建築〗 a mansion of a feudal lord in Edo. Was given to each feudal lord by the Tokugawa shogunate. A feudal lord lived there for one year and lived in his own feudal domain for the next year. The official wife and the heir had to live in Edo while the lord was back in his domain. →参勤交代

たいめし 鯛飯 〖食べ物〗 rice cooked with sea bream.

だいもく 題目 〖仏教〗 a title. However, in the Nichiren sect, it means the ritual phrase of 'Namu Myou-hou Renge-kyou,' which means "I put my faith in the Lotus Sutra of the Wonderful Law." Repeating aloud this phrase is emphasized in the Nichiren sect. →法華経；日蓮宗

だいもん 大門 〖仏教・建築〗 a large outermost gate of a Buddhist temple. Often the location is referred to as NANDAIMON, which means "the south main gate."

だいもんじやき 大文字焼き 〖仏教・祭礼〗 Great Bonfire Festival of Mt.

Daimonji. Is held on August 16 in Kyoto, to send off the ancestors' souls. Fire is lit in the shape of a kanji, 'dai,' which means "big," on the side of Mt. Daimonji. Four other fires are lit on other mountains almost at the same time.

たいやき 鯛焼き〘食べ物〙 a sea-bream-shaped hot pancake stuffed with sweet adzuki paste. Custard cream is sometimes used instead of adzuki paste.

たいやく 大厄〘宗教・通過儀礼〙 ⇨厄年

たいよう 太陽〘自然・精神性〙 ⇨日(ひ)

たいようれき 太陽暦〘暦〙 the solar calendar. Has been applied in Japan since 1873. ↔太陰暦

たいらのきよもり 平清盛〘武士〙 1118-1181. A military commander and stateman born in Kyoto. Established the administration of the Taira clan by defeating the Minamoto clan in the Heiji War. Made his daughter, KENREIMON-IN, marry Emperor Takakura and promoted trade with the Sung dynasty in China. But the Taira clan provoked the antipathy of warriors and bureaucrats, and Kiyomori died from a disease during the war against the Minamoto clan. →平治の乱；平氏；源氏

たいらのまさかど 平将門〘武士〙 ?-940. A warrior in present Chiba Pref. Rose in rebellion against the central government, temporarily governed the Kantou region, and was suppressed by Taira no Sadamori and FUJIWARA NO HIDESATO. This rebellion in 939 is called the Tengyou Rebellion. His spirit is enshrined at Kanda Shrine in Tokyo. →神田明神

たいらんずもう 台覧相撲〘天皇・相撲〙 sumo bouts watched by a member of the Imperial family.

だいり 内裏〘天皇〙 the Imperial Palace. Was located on the Palace Grounds of the Castle. →大内裏(だいだいり)

だいりびな 内裏雛〘天皇・人形〙 dolls of the Emperor and Empress Consort. Wear costumes from the Heian period and are placed on the top shelf of a tiered stand at the Girls' Festival on March 3 of every year.

たいろう 大老〘武士・官位〙 the interim super prime minister of the Tokugawa shogunate. Ranked highest above the Council of Prime Ministers.

たうえ 田植え〘農業〙 transplantation of rice sprouts. Rice sprouts are transplanted from nursery beds into a rice field around June.

たうえうた 田植え歌〘農業・音楽〙 a worksong sung while transplanting rice sprouts.

たうと タウト〘建築〙 ⇨ブルーノ・タウト

たおやめぶり 手弱女ぶり〘文芸〙 the feminine and delicate style of poetry. KAMO NO MABUCHI claimed in the 18th century that this style was found in the *Collection of*

Ancient and Modern Japanese Poetry (KOKINWAKASHUU) and later works. The opposite concept is the masculine style, MASURAOBURI.

たかあしだ 高足駄 〖履物〗 ⇨高下駄(たかげた)

たかおさん 高尾山 〖山岳〗 Mt. Takao. Is located in western Tokyo. Although it is not very high, with the peak being 599 m, it attracts many tourists, worshippers, climbers, and even trail runners, with its natural scenic beauty and well-maintained climbing routes. Is a location of mountain worship at Takao-san Yakuou-in. Today it is one of the most frequently visited mountains in the world. Can be accessed within an hour by the Keio Line train from central Tokyo.

たかがり 鷹狩 〖娯楽〗 falconry. Hunting by letting a hawk catch a bird or hare. Was done by the Imperial family or high-ranking samurai. Became obsolete in and after the Meiji era.

たかげた 高下駄 〖履物〗 a pair of rectangular wooden sandals with two high supports under the soles. Used to be worn by sushi cooks, but are now obsolete. →下駄

たかさご 高砂〖能・作品〗 *Takasago*. The name of a Noh song. Was sung in the wedding ceremony in olden times.

たかさごぞく 高砂族 〖少数民族〗 Gaoshan people. The Japanese term to refer to the indigenous tribes of Taiwan, when Japan colonized Taiwan.

たかしまだ 高島田 〖髪〗 a traditional hairstyle with a high hair knot for an unmarried woman. A bride arranges her hair in this style at present.

だがしや 駄菓子屋〖食文化・ビジネス〗 a store that sells cheap sweets and snacks for children. The number is now decreasing rapidly.

たがじょう 多賀城 〖城郭〗 Fort Taga. Was constructed in the central part of present Miyagi Pref. in 724 to administer local people, EMISHI, in this area.

たかすぎしんさく 高杉晋作 〖武士〗 1839-1867. A samurai in the Choushuu domain, born in present Yamaguchi Pref. Organized Irregular Militia, called KIHEITAI, in 1863. Unified the Choushuu domain to fight against the Tokugawa shogunate and defeated the shogunate forces in 1866.

たかせぶね 高瀬舟 **(1)**〖交通〗 a river boat. Was small with a deep bottom in medieval and ancient times, but large with a shallow bottom in early-modern times. **(2)**〖文芸・作品〗 *A Boat on Takase Canal*. A short novel published in 1916 by MORI OUGAI. Refers to the issue of euthanasia.

たがたいしゃ 多賀大社〖神社〗 Taga Grand Shrine. Is located in eastern Shiga Pref., and enshrines IZANAGI NO MIKOTO and IZANAMI NO MIKOTO, which have been worshipped as deities of longevity. →伊弉諾(いざなぎ)神宮

たかだやかへえ 高田屋嘉兵衛 〖経済〗 1769-1827. A shipping agent born in Awaji Island of Hyougo Pref. Gained a huge profit in trading with Hokkaido and explored Iturup Island. Was captured by Russia and was released in exchange for a Russian naval officer, Golovnin.

たかちほ 高千穂 〖神話・地名〗 the name of an area in northwestern Miyazaki Pref. It is said the grandson of the Sun Goddess descended from the High Celestial Plain to here. Has several place names related to the Japanese mythology such as TAKAMAGAHARA or AMA NO IWATO. →瓊瓊杵尊(ににぎの みこと)

たかつき 高坏 〖食器〗 a small-footed plate to hold food. Was made of clay in and for some time after the Joumon period, but came to be made of wood in and after the Heian period.

たかな 高菜 〖食べ物〗 leaf mustard. *Brassica juncea* var. *integrifolia*. Is often pickled in salt. Is also used for a variety of cuisines such as stir-fried rice, Japanese-style pilaf, ramen, and local sushi.

たかのちょうえい 高野長英 〖思想〗 1804-1850. A scholar of Dutch learning, born in present Iwate Pref. Studied medicine and the Dutch language under Philipp Franz von Siebold in Nagasaki. Criticized the diplomatic policy of the Tokugawa shogunate.

たかはしこれきよ 高橋是清 〖政治〗 1854-1936. A statesman born in Tokyo. Economic and fiscal policies were his strong points. After serving as prime minister, worked as minister of finance for several cabinets. In the financial crisis of 1927, ordered the Bank of Japan to make a large number of one-side-printed bills and provided them to commercial banks, to calm down the public sentiment.

たかはまきょし 高浜虚子 〖文芸〗 1874-1959. A haiku poet and novelist born in Ehime Pref. A disciple of MASAOKA SHIKI. Edited a haiku magazine, *Hototogisu*, after his teacher died.

たかはりぢょうちん 高張り提灯 〖生活〗 a paper lantern hung on a high stand.

たかふだ 高札 〖行政〗 ⇨高札(こう さつ)

たかまがはら 高天原 〖神話〗 High Celestial Plain. The heavenly land where the Sun Goddess and other deities dwell. →根の国；葦原(あしはら)の中つ国

たかまきえ 高蒔絵 〖美術〗 a decoration technique for lacquerware with embossed patterns using dust of gold, silver, or tin.

たかまくら 高枕 〖家具・髪〗 a high pillow. Is high enough to prevent a traditional female hairdo from being disarranged while sleeping.

たかまつし 高松市 〖地名〗 Takamatsu City. The capital of Kagawa Pref., located in its central part. In its eastern part is Yashima Island, which was the battlefield in the war between the Minamoto and Taira clans toward the end of the 12th century. In its central part is Ritsurin Park, which has a landscape garden with a circular path.

たかまつづかこふん 高松塚古墳〖考古〗 Takamatsuduka Tumulus. A round burial mound, dated to the 7th or 8th century. Is located in Asuka Village, Nara Pref. Colorful wall paintings, designated a National Treasure, decorate its inside.

たかみむすびのかみ 高皇産霊神〖神話〗 the second-born deity who appeared in the creation of the world. Had the power of creation.

たかむらこううん 高村光雲〖彫刻〗 1852-1934. A sculptor born in Edo. The father of TAKAMURA KOUTAROU. His works include *Statue of Saigou Takamori* at Ueno Park and *Aged Monkey* at the Tokyo National Museum.

たかむらこうたろう 高村光太郎〖文芸〗 1883-1956. A poet and sculptor born in Tokyo. The son of TAKAMURA KOUUN. His works of poetry include *Chieko's Sky* (CHIEKOSHOU). His sculptures include *Statue of Girlhood* on the shore of Lake Towada in Aomori Pref. and *Hand* at The National Museum of Modern Art in Tokyo.

たかやまし 高山市〖地名〗 Takayama City. Is located in northern Gifu Pref. and is the largest city in Japan in terms of area. Is called a Little Kyoto in Hida. Old houses,

temples, and streets have been preserved, and especially during the Takayama Festivals in April and October they attract many visitors.

たかやままつり 高山祭〖祭礼〗 Takayama Festival. The generic term for two festivals in Takayama City in northern Gifu Pref.: the Sannou Festival on April 14 and 15 at Hie Shrine and the Hachiman Festival on October 9 and 10 at Hachiman Shrine. Famous for the procession of gorgeous floats.

たかゆか 高床〖建築・考古〗 a raised floor. Raised-floor style architecture appeared around 2000 B.C. Raised-floor buildings are restored in some ruins. Is thought to be the prototype of Shinto architecture such as the Ise Shrine.

たからくじ 宝籤〖娯楽〗 a public lottery. One piece is 100 to 500 yen. The highest prize is 700 million yen.

たからぶね 宝船〖宗教〗 a treasure boat. A sailboat carrying the Seven Deities of Good Fortune, straw rice bags, and treasures. It is said that placing the picture of this boat under a pillow brings a pleasant first dream of the year, at the night of January 1st or 2nd. →七福神; 初夢

たきあわせ 炊き合わせ〖食べ物〗 mixture of simmered ingredients. For example, mixture of boiled fish and vegetables.

たきぎのう 薪能〖能〗 outdoor evening Noh. Is performed on a torchlit stage in the temple or shrine precincts.

たきこみごはん 炊き込みご飯 〔食べ物〕 Japanese-style pilaf. Rice is boiled with vegetables and meat, usually seasoned with soy sauce. Ingredients vary such as carrot, mushrooms, chicken, and seafood.

たきざわばきん 滝沢馬琴 〔文芸〕 ⇨ 曲亭馬琴

たくあん 沢庵 (1) 〔仏教〕 1573-1645. A Zen priest born in present Hyougo Pref. Became a chief priest of DAITOKU-JI Temple, challenged the Tokugawa shogunate and was exiled to present Yamagata Pref. Later was forgiven and came back to Edo. Is said to have invented yellow pickles of mooli. (2) 〔食べ物〕 ⇨沢庵漬け

たくあんづけ 沢庵漬け 〔食べ物〕 mooli pickled yellow in salt and rice bran. Is made by drying mooli and pickling it in a barrel. Is served with plain rice or DONBURI-MONO, rice with toppings. Is named after TAKUAN, a Buddhist priest who invented it in the 17th century.

だくてん 濁点 〔言語〕 a voiced mark. When two dots are added in the upper right corner of a KANA, the pronunciation becomes voiced. For example, さ is pronounced as 'sa,' while ざ is pronounced as 'za.'

たくはつ 托鉢 〔仏教〕 religious mendicancy. A monk or nun, chanting a sutra, stands in front of lay people's houses with a bowl to receive food or money.

だぐらすまっかあさあ ダグラス・

マッカーサー 〔戦争〕 ⇨マッカーサー

たくわん 沢庵 〔食べ物〕 ⇨沢庵漬け

たけ 竹 〔植物〕 a bamboo. *Bambuseae*. Has been used in various ways such as making buildings, walls, furniture, weapons, musical instruments, daily necessities, and tea utensils. Bamboo shoots are edible, and a bamboo grove is sometimes a theme of an India ink painting. An American inventor, Thomas Edison, used Kyoto bamboo as a filament in an incandescent light in 1882.

たけうま 竹馬 〔遊び〕 a pair of bamboo stilts.

たけかんむり 竹冠 〔言語〕 a crown radical in the shape of 竹, which means "bamboo." Is used in kanji such as 箱(box), 籠(basket), and 筍 (bamboo shoot). →偏; 部首

たけぐし 竹串 〔食文化〕 a bamboo skewer. Is used for a bite-size cutlet or grilled chicken. →串カツ; 焼き鳥

たけくらべ たけくらべ 〔文芸・作品〕 *Child's Play*. A short novel published in parts from 1895 to 1896 by HIGUCHI ICHIYOU. Describes the romance between a young boy and girl who lived in a red-light district.

たけすみ 竹炭 〔生活〕 bamboo charcoal. Is used as deodorant or a purifier for water or air.

たけだかつより 武田勝頼 〔武士〕 1546-1582. A warlord in present Nagano and Yamanashi Prefs. and parts of Shizuoka and Aichi Prefs.

A son of TAKEDA SHINGEN. Was defeated at the Battle of Nagashino by the allied forces of ODA NOBUNAGA and TOKUGAWA IEYASU. Consequently the Takeda clan was ruined.

たけだじょうあと 竹田城跡 〖城郭〗 Takeda Castle Ruins. Takeda Castle was constructed on a mountain at the height of 353 m in present central Hyougo Pref. Since the castle ruin looks as if it's floating in the sky when wrapped in a fog, it is called "Castle in the Air" or "Japanese Machu Picchu."

たけだしんげん 武田信玄 〖武士〗 1521-1573. A feudal lord governing around present Yamanashi and Nagano Prefs. Fought several times with UESUGI KENSHIN in present Niigata and Toyama Prefs. The Battles of Kawanaka-jima from 1553 to 1564 are famous. Died from disease after defeating TOKUGAWA IEYASU at Mikatagahara on the way to Kyoto.

たけとりものがたり 竹取物語 〖文芸・作品〗 "The Tale of the Bamboo Cutter." Was written in the early Heian period. The author is unknown. A princess named Kaguya-hime, born from a bamboo stem, is proposed marriage by five young gentlemen, but she refuses their offers. After she confesses that she came from the moon, she goes back home on the full moon night in August.

たけとんぼ 竹蜻蛉 〖玩具〗 a bamboo-copter. A children's toy that rotates a propeller by rolling a bamboo stick attached to it with both hands.

たけのうちのすくね 武内宿禰 〖神話〗 the name of a legendary minister who served five Emperors (Keikou, Seimu, Chuuai, Oujin, and Nintoku). A descendant of the 8th Emperor, Kougen, and the ancestor of the Soga and other powerful clans. Accompanied Empress Consort Jinguu to attack Silla.

たけのこ 筍 〖食べ物〗 a bamboo shoot. Literally means "child of bamboo." Eaten in various ways: simmered with seaweed, boiled with rice, as an ingredient of soup, and as a kind of salad called AEMONO.

たけのじょうおう 武野紹鴎 〖茶道〗 1502-1555. A tea master born in present Sakai City, Osaka Pref. Created the design of a tiny tea room using only three or two and half straw mats. The teacher of SEN NO RIKYUU.

たけみかづちのおのかみ 建御雷之男神 〖神話〗 the deity of thunder and martial arts. Born when IZANAGI NO MIKOTO killed HINOKAGUTSUCHI NO KAMI with a sword. The Sun Goddess dispatched him, together with Futsunushi no kami from the High Celestial Plain to the Central Land of Reeds to make OOKUNINUSHI NO KAMI waive his sovereignty over the land.

たけみつ 竹光 〖剣術〗 a fake sword

made of bamboo.

たけみなかたのかみ　建御名方神
〖神話〗 the deity of water, and a son of OOKUNINUSHI NO KAMI. When opposing his father submitting to heavenly deities, he was defeated by TAKEMIKADUCHI NO ONOKAMI and driven away to Suwa in the center of Nagano Pref. →諏訪大社

たけやらい　竹矢来 〖建築〗 a temporary bamboo fence.

たこ　凧 〖玩具〗 a kite. Was introduced from China in the 12th century. Is usually flown during the New Year's holidays.

たこ　蛸, 章魚 〖食べ物・魚〗 an octopus. Eaten as sashimi, sushi, or vinegared after boiling. Is also contained in an octopus ball called TAKOYAKI.

たこあげ　凧揚げ 〖遊び〗 kite-flying. Is popular as child's play during the New Year's holidays.

たこつぼ　蛸壺 〖漁業〗 an octopus pot. A fisherman sets it at the sea bottom and waits until an octopus enters it.

たこやき　蛸焼き 〖食べ物〗 an octopus ball. Is made of a wheat flour-based batter and chopped octopus and fried on a special hot plate with semispherical pits. The toppings are Worcester sauce, powder of dried sea lettuce, and sometimes mayonnaise.

だざいおさむ　太宰治 〖文芸〗 1909-1948. A novelist born in Aomori Pref. Wrote novels about self-destructive characters and killed himself by leaping into an aqueduct. His works include *The Setting Sun* (Shayou) in 1947 and *No Longer Human* (Ningen shikkaku) in 1948.

だざいふ　大宰府 〖政治〗 the remote government office of the Imperial Court. Was placed in present Fukuoka Pref. in ancient times. Was in charge of foreign affairs with China and Korea and administered the Kyushu region.

だざいふてんまんぐう　太宰府天満宮 〖神社〗 Dazaifu Tenmangu Shrine. One of the two head shrines of the Tenmanguu Shrines throughout Japan, together with Kitano Tenmangu Shrine. Is located in central Fukuoka Pref. Enshrines SUGAWARA NO MICHIZANE, worshipped as a deity of study. The legend of the flying plum tree is famous.

たざわこ　田沢湖 〖湖沼〗 Lake Tazawa. A caldera lake located in Akita Pref. The area is 26 km^2. The deepest point is 423 m, which makes it the deepest of all lakes in Japan. There is a legend that a beautiful girl named Tatsuko became a dragon and lived in the lake. A statue of Tatsuko stands at the edge of the lake.

だし　山車 〖祭礼〗 a festival float. Is elaborately decorated and towed by parishioners in a festival. The term differs from region to region, such as 'yamaboko' in Kyoto, 'yamagasa' in Hakata, 'yatai' in Takayama, and 'danjiri' in Kishiwada.

だし 出汁〘調味料〙 dashi, or soup stock that serves as the base of many dishes. Is prepared from one or more of kelp, dried bonito, and dried anchovies, all of which add UMAMI flavor. →昆布；鰹節；煮干し

だしこんぶ 出し昆布 〘調味料〙 kombu for making DASHI, or dried kelp for making soup stock. →昆布

だしじる 出し汁〘調味料〙 ⇨出汁

だしのもと 出汁の素〘調味料〙 soup stock powder or granules.

たじま 但馬〘旧国名〙 the old name of northern Hyougo Pref.

だしまき 出汁巻〘食べ物〙 a rolled omelette flavored with soup stock.

だじょうだいじん 太政大臣〘官位〙 ⇨太政(だいじょう)大臣

だじょうてんのう 太上天皇 〘天皇〙 a retired Emperor. The term, JOUKOU, was also used in and after the Heian period.

たすき 襷 **(1)**〘生活〙 a cord to tuck up kimono sleeves. **(2)**〘政治〙 a broad sash with the name of an election candidate. Is diagonally hung from the neck to the side. **(3)**〘スポーツ〙 a cloth sash used instead of a baton during a long-distance relay race called EKIDEN.

たたあるかいきょう タタール海峡〘海洋〙 ⇨間宮海峡

ただいまかえりました 只今帰りました〘言語〙 a greeting phrase uttered by a person who has just returned. Equivalent to the English "I'm home." Its abbreviated form, 'tadaima,' is usually uttered. ↔お帰りなさい

たたき 叩き〘食べ物〙 a cooking method to prepare fish, beef, or chicken, or food prepared in this way. 'Tataki' is a noun form of a verb 'tataku,' which means "to beat, to hit." **(1)** raw fish with seasonings such as ginger and green onion, chopped together to make the seasoning spread into every part of the flesh. An example is 'aji no tataki,' chopped raw horse mackerel. **(2)** slightly roasted fish, beef, or chicken, with its inside still raw. Sometimes hit with hands or knife to blend condiments well into its meat. An example is 'katsuo no tataki,' lightly roasted bonito.

たたき 三和土〘建築〙 a hardened earth floor. Cement is used these days, instead of earth. The floor of an entrance hall is often composed of this type of material.

たたみ 畳〘建築〙 a tatami mat. Straw is stuffed inside, its surface is covered with dried grass-like marsh plants, and its longer edges are hemmed with cloth. The size is 180 cm long by 90 cm wide.

たたみいと 畳糸〘建築〙 a thread to stitch a tatami mat.

たたみいわし 畳鰯〘食べ物〙 dried baby anchovies flattened like a sheet. Eaten lightly toasted.

たたみおもて 畳表〘建築〙 the surface of a tatami mat. Is made of grass-like marsh plants. →藺草(いぐさ)

たたみがえ 畳替え〘建築〙 renewing tatami mats or their surface.

たたみばり 畳針〘建築〙 a needle to

stitch a tatami mat. Is longer and thicker than an ordinary needle.

たち 太刀〚武器〛 a long sword. Is longer than 60 cm. Sometimes refers to a sword that is hung with its blade downward. →刀

たちあい 立ち合い〚相撲〛 the moment for wrestlers to stand up from the crouching position at the beginning of a bout.

たちかけ 太刀掛〚武器〛 ⇨刀掛け

たちからおのみこと 手力男命〚神話〛 a deity with Herculean strength. Opened the Gate of the Celestial Rock Cave and dragged AMATERASU OOMIKAMI out of it when she hid herself in the cave. Is enshrined at Togakushi Shrine in northern Nagano Pref.

たちぐい 立ち食い〚食文化〛 stand-and-eat style restaurant. There are a lot of buckwheat noodle restaurants with this style in railroad stations.

たちさばき 太刀捌き〚剣術〛 sword handling.

たちすぐりいすぐり 立ちすぐり居すぐり〚忍者〛 a technique to find an enemy spy who has sneaked into one's camp under the guise of one's colleague. A ninja uttered a password, and other colleague ninjas stood up or sat down, one at a time. The enemy spy who did not know the password responded late and was found. It is said that FUUMA NINJA used this technique.

たちのみや 立ち飲み屋〚酒・ビジネス〛 a stand-up bar. Serves alcohol and food at reasonable prices.

たちばな 橘〚植物〛 a tachinaba orange. *Citrus tachibana*. Native to Japan. Is depicted as a family crest.

たちばなのみちよ 橘三千代〚政治〛 ?-733. A wife of FUJIWARA NO FUHITO and the mother of TACHIBANA NO MOROE and Empress Consort Koumyou. Obtained the power in the Imperial Palace as a nursemaid of Emperor Monmu. Laid the foundation for the prosperity of the Fujiwara and Tachibana clans.

たちばなのもろえ 橘諸兄〚政治〛 684-757. A statesman. The son of TACHIBANA NO MICHIYO and the half-brother of Empress Consort Koumyou. Exercised political authority as the minister of the left, joining hands with KIBI NO MAKIBI and GENBOU, before FUJIWARA NO NAKAMARO rose to power.

たちまわり 立ち回り〚歌舞伎〛 a stylized fighting action by several actors. Usually uses swords with music.

たちもち 太刀持ち〚相撲〛 a sword bearer. Accompanies a yokozuna at the ring-entering ceremony called DOHYOU-IRI, carrying a sword.

たちもの 断ち物〚民間信仰〛 abstention of a food or beverage as prayer. A person avoids having a specific food or beverage such as sweets or tea until his or her wish is realized.

たちやく 立ち役〚歌舞伎〛 a general name for male roles as good guys. Does not include the role of a child, an elderly person, a villain, or a woman played by a male actor.

たつ 辰 〖干支〗 the fifth of the Chinese zodiac signs. Means "dragon." Recently the years 1988, 2000, and 2012 were dragon years. Indicates the east-southeast in direction and around 8 a.m. for hours.

だつあにゅうおう 脱亜入欧 〖外交・精神性〗 "Out of Asia and Into Europe." The trend of the times after the Meiji Restoration. The term originated with a thinker and educationist, FUKUZAWA YUKICHI.

だっかつかんしつ 脱活乾漆 〖仏教・彫刻〗 a sculpture technique of hollow dry lacquer. Was popular in the 8th century. The procedure is as follows: first, the basic form is made of clay; second, linen soaked in lacquer is wrapped around the clay form in many layers; third, the details are depicted on the lacquer; and finally, after the lacquer is dried, the clay is removed from the inside. Examples using this technique include Fukuukensaku at TOUDAI-JI Temple and Asura at KOUFUKU-JI Temple, both in Nara. ↔ 木心乾漆；阿修羅

だつかんしつ 脱乾漆 〖仏教・彫刻〗 ⇨脱活乾漆(だっかつかんしつ)

たづくり 田作り 〖食べ物〗 ⇨ごまめ

だっこう 奪口 〖忍者〗 **(1)** to speak the dialect fluently when a ninja visited an enemy country for reconnaissance. **(2)** a ninja in the duty of reconnaissance in an enemy country.

たつたあげ 竜田揚げ 〖食べ物〗 deep-fried chicken or fish coated in dogtooth violet starch (KATAKURIKO). Is flavored with soy sauce and mirin before fried. Is named after the Tatsuta River, which is famous for autumnal tints because the color of 'tatsuta-age' is reddish brown.

たっち タッチ 〖漫画〗 *Touch*. A high school baseball manga, written and illustrated by Adachi Mitsuru. Was published serially in a boy's magazine, *Weekly Shonen Sunday*, from 1981 to 1986.

たっちゅう 塔頭 〖仏教〗 a subsidiary temple. An individual temple building in a large temple. In a Zen temple, a small pagoda as a grave of a great priest or a hermitage near the pagoda is sometimes called this term.

たつのおとしご 竜の落とし子 〖動物〗 a sea horse. *Hippocampus coronatus*. About 10 cm long. A dried sea horse used to be a talisman for safe child birth.

たつのきんご 辰野金吾 〖建築〗 1854 -1919. An architect born in Saga Pref. After graduating from the Imperial College of Engineering, studied in the United Kingdom and became a professor at Tokyo Imperial University. His works include the headquarters of the Bank of Japan, the Tokyo Station, and the sumo stadium at Ryougoku.

だっぱん 脱藩 〖武士・政治〗 a samurai's leaving his feudal domain and being masterless, in the Edo period.

たっぴざき 竜飛崎〚地名〛 ⇨竜飛岬

たっぴみさき 竜飛岬〚地名〛 Cape Tappi. Is located at the northern end of the Tsugaru Peninsula in northwestern Aomori Pref. Across from the cape, the southern end of Hokkaido, Cape Shirakami, can be seen beyond the Tsugaru Channel. A song *Tsugaru Kaikyou Fuyugeshiki*, which means "Winter Scene of the Tsugaru Channel," made the name of the cape popular after it was released in 1977.

たつみ 巽〚干支〛 the southeast. The direction between TATSU (dragon) and MI (snake).

たて 殺陣〚武士・芸能〛 performance of a sword fight in a movie or play. Actors use fake swords.

たてあなしきじゅうきょ 竪穴式住居〚考古〛 a pit dwelling in the Joumon, Yayoi, and Tumulus periods. The floor was about 50 cm underground. A structure over it was supported with columns and beams and was thatched with grass or reeds.

たてえぼし 立烏帽子〚服飾〛 a traditional high black cap with its upper part unfolded. Was worn by adult noblemen or warriors. Is worn by Shinto priests at present.

たてがき 縦書き〚言語〛 writing vertically. Official documents were traditionally written from the top to bottom. Though horizontal writing is popular at present, vertical writing is usually used in novels, books on Japanese history or culture, dictionaries of the Japanese language, and paperback libraries. ↔横書き

たてぎょうじ 立行司〚相撲〛 one of the highest-rank sumo referees. Wears a dagger on the waist and judges the last bout of the day.

たてぐ 建具〚建築〛 the generic term for sliding partitions such as sliding doors and sliding screens. →障子(しょうじ); 襖(ふすま)

たてぐし 建具師〚建築・ビジネス〛 a joiner, or a carpenter of sliding partitions.

たてしなこうげん 蓼科高原〚地名〛 Tateshina Hills. A resort in the mountains in eastern Nagano Pref. Has three lakes—Shirakaba, Tateshina, and Megami—and several hot springs, as well as tourist ranches. Visitors can enjoy camping in summer and skiing in winter. Can be accessed by bus from Chino Station on JR Chuuou Line.

たてしゃかいのにんげんかんけい タテ社会の人間関係〚精神性・書名〛 *Japanese Society*. Was written in 1967 by a social anthropologist, Nakane Chie. Discusses human relationships in the group-oriented Japanese society.

たてまえ 建て前〚精神性〛 the public stance, or facade principle. It is often said that a Japanese has a public stance (tatemae), which is different from a true feeling (HONNE).

だてまき 伊達巻〚食べ物〛 a sweet rolled omelette containing ground fish. Eaten during New Year's holidays or on auspicious occasions.

だてまさむね 伊達政宗 〖武士〗 1567
-1636. A feudal lord born in present
Yamagata Pref. Conquered a large
area of the Tohoku region but surrendered to TOYOTOMI HIDEYOSHI
in 1590. Fought on the side of
TOKUGAWA IEYASU in the Battle of
Sekigahara in 1600. Dispatched
his vassal, HASEKURA TSUNENAGA,
to Rome in 1613. Was nicknamed
'Dokuganryuu,' which means "sin-
gle-eyed dragon" because he lost
his right eye in childhood.

たてみつ 立て褌 〖相撲〗 the verti-
cal part of a wrestler's loincloth. To
grasp that part is a foul.

たてやま 立山 〖山岳〗 Mt. Tateyama, or Mt. Tate. Is located in
southeastern Toyama Pref., in the
Hida Mountains. Consists of three
peaks, namely, Mt. Oonanji (3,015
m), Mt. Oyama (3,003 m), and Mt.
Fuji-no-oritate (2,999 m). One of
Japan's Three Holy Mountains,
along with Mt. Fuji and Mt. Haku.

たなかかくえい 田中角栄 〖政
治〗 1918-1993. A politician born
in Niigata Pref. Normalized diplomatic relations with mainland
China in 1972 and proposed "the
Plan for Remodeling the Japanese
Archipelago." Was notorious for
money politics and arrested for the
Lockheed Scandal in 1976.

たなかひさしげ 田中久重 〖科学技
術〗 1799-1881. An engineer and
inventor born in present Fukuoka
Pref. Made a clock, a miniature lo-
comotive, a cannon, and others. His
factory later became Toshiba Corp.
Was also called 'Karakuri Giemon.'
'Karakuri' means "mechanism,"
and 'Giemon' is his other name.

たなだ 棚田 〖農業〗 terraced rice
fields. Are constructed on a rather
steep slope, which look like stairways. Ones at Koushoku in Nagano
Pref. and at Wajima in Ishikawa
Pref. are famous.

たなばた 七夕 〖暦〗 the Star
Festival on July 7 in the traditional
or current calendar. It depends on
the region which calendar is used.
According to a Chinese legend, two
stars, a male star called 'HIKOBOSHI'
(Altair) and female star called
'ORIHIME' (Vega), fell in love and
were allowed to meet each other,
crossing the Milky Way only on this
day. People write their wishes on
colored paper strips, attach them to
bamboo branches, and wash them
down the river or into the sea.

たなべさくろう 田辺朔郎 〖科学技術〗
1861-1944. A civil engineer born
in Edo. Managed the construction
of a canal between Kyoto and Lake
Biwa, named BIWAKO SOSUI.

たにかぜかじのすけ 谷風梶之助 〖相
撲〗 1750-1795. A sumo wrestler
born in present Miyagi Pref. The
4th yokozuna. Won 63 bouts in row.

たにがわ たにがわ 〖鉄道〗 the express train of Joetsu Shinkansen. Is
named after Mt. Tanigawa on the
border between Gunma and Niigata
Prefs. Stops at most stations on

its route, and connects Tokyo and Echigo-Yuzawa in Niigata Pref. in 1.5 hours.

たにざきじゅんいちろう 谷崎潤一郎 〖文芸〗 1886-1965. A novelist born in Tokyo. Was first called a novelist of aestheticism. After moving to the Kansai area owing to the Great Kanto Earthquake in 1923, aspired to portray classical Japanese beauty. His works include *Naomi* (CHIJIN NO AI) in 1925, *A Portrait of Shunkin* (SHUNKINSHOU) in 1933, and *The Makioka Sisters* (SASAMEYUKI) in 1948. →関東大震災

たにぶんちょう 谷文晁 〖絵画〗 1763-1840. A painter born in Edo. Applied the techniques of Japanese, Chinese, and Western style paintings and developed his unique style. MATSUDAIRA SADANOBU was his patron.

たにまち 谷町〖相撲・地名〗 a financial supporter of a sumo wrestler. Is called so because there was a doctor who took care of wrestlers free of charge in Tanimachi, Osaka.

たにんどん 他人丼〖食べ物〗 a bowl of rice with soy sauce and sugar-seasoned beef or pork, egg, and vegetables on top. 'Tanin' means "having no relation in the kinship." Is named after the two ingredients: meat and egg. They have no relation to each other, unlike OYAKO-DON, "parent-child bowl," whose ingredients are chicken and egg.

たぬき 狸〖動物〗 a raccoon dog.

Nyctereutes procyonoides. in Japanese fairy tales, it often bewitches a human, but sometimes does foolish things.

たぬきそば 狸蕎麦 〖食べ物〗 **(1)** buckwheat noodles with deep-fried batter balls. **(2)** hot buckwheat noodles with thin deep-fried tofu. Is called so in the Kansai area.

たぬきばやし 狸囃子〖妖怪〗 mysterious festive music. Was said to be played by raccoon dogs.

たぬまおきつぐ 田沼意次 〖政治〗 1719-1788. A prime minister of the Tokugawa shogunate, born in Edo. Displayed his skill in restoring the shogunate's budget. However, bribery was prevalent during his tenure, and sometimes he was criticized as a typical corrupt politician.

たねがしま 種子島 **(1)**〖武器〗 another name of a harquebus. Was called so because it was first introduced into Tanegashima Island in 1543 by the Portuguese. **(2)**〖島名〗 Tanegashima Island, in Kagoshima Pref. Its area is 446 km^2. In 1543, a gun was first brought in to Japan by the Portuguese on this island. The largest rocket-launch complex in Japan, Tanegashima Space Center, is located here.

たねださんとうか 種田山頭火 〖文芸〗 1882-1940. A haiku poet born in Yamaguchi Pref. Became a monk and wandered around Japan, composing free-verse haiku. →自由律

たのかみ 田の神〖宗教〗 the deity of rice fields. The deity of the mountain goes down from the mountain to become the deity of rice fields in spring, and he goes back to the mountain in fall. The way of worship varies among areas.

たのもしこう 頼母子講 〖経済〗 a system for mutual financial support. Members provide money to the system, and one of them receives the total amount in turn. When all members had received money, the system would be dissolved. Started in the Kamakura period and became popular in the Edo period. Still exists in some local areas.

たび 足袋 〖服飾〗 a pair of split-toed socks. Is worn together with a kimono. The formal ones are white.

たびまくら 旅枕 〖忍者〗 the technique to prevent the enemy from stealing a sword. When sleeping, a ninja bound together the sword straps of a long and short swords and laid himself on the straps. One of the seven techniques of using a sword strap. →下げ緒七術

たべあわせ 食べ合わせ 〖食文化〗 bad combination of foodstuffs. For example, eel and pickled plum are considered a bad combination when they are eaten together, but there are no scientific grounds for this belief.

たほうとう 多宝塔 〖仏教・建築〗 a multi-treasure pagoda, or a two-storied pagoda. The lower layer is square-shaped while the upper layer is circular. The Historical Buddha and Abundant Treasure Buddha are enshrined. →多宝如来

たほうにょらい 多宝如来 〖仏教〗 Abundant Treasure Buddha. *Prabhuta-ratna*. Appeared up from the ground, in a pagoda called TAHOU-TOU, to prove the truth of the Historical Buddha's words when he was preaching the Lotus Sutra.

たま 多摩 〖地名〗 the name of a residential area to the west of Tokyo city proper. Was designed as a new town in 1965 in the hills of Tama City, western Inagi City, northern Machida City, and southern Hachiouji City. With a population of 200,000, it is the largest residential development in Japan as of 2017.

たまいれ 玉入れ 〖スポーツ〗 a ball throwing-in game. On a field day, two teams throw red or white balls into a basket for each team that is attached at the top of a high pole. The team that has thrown in more balls wins the match.

たまおくり 霊送り 〖仏教〗 to send off the ancestor's spirit at the end of the Bon Festival. →盂蘭盆会(うらぼんえ)

たまがき 玉垣 〖神道〗 the fence around a Shinto shrine or its main sanctuary building. Sometimes means the fence of the Imperial Palace.

たまがわ 多摩川 〖河川〗 Tama River. Flows from Mt. Kasatori located on the border of Saitama and Yamanashi Prefs., through the Tokyo-Kanagawa prefectural border, into Tokyo Bay near Haneda Airport. Its length is 138 km. On the border between Tokyo and Yamanashi Prefs. is the Ogouchi Dam and Lake Okutama, which play an important role in supplying water to Tokyo. On its upper stream, fishing, kayaking, and bouldering are popular. On its banks downstream are many parks and sport fields, as well as a bicycle path and running track.

たまがわじょうすい 玉川上水 〖河川〗 Tamagawa Aqueduct. Runs for 43 km in northern Tokyo from Hamura to Yotsuya. The Tokugawa shogunate ordered brothers, who were given the family name Tamagawa later, to build an aqueduct to supply water to Edo for drinking and in case of fire. The brothers started to construct it in 1653, taking water from the Tama River, and completed it within 2 years.

たまぐし 玉串 〖神道〗 a sprig of a sacred evergreen, 'SAKAKI,' with a zigzag-shaped white paper strip. Is offered to a god in Shintoism. → 紙垂(し)

たまぐしりょう 玉串料 〖神道〗 cost for a Shinto ritual. The worshipper pays it to a Shinto shrine. The price varies depending on the ritual or the shrine, but usually at least 5,000 yen is necessary.

たまごかけごはん 卵かけ御飯 〖食べ物〗 raw egg and rice. Is seasoned with soy sauce and sometimes topped with sesame, chopped green onion, or dried bonito flakes. Is sometimes called TKG, the abbreviation for 'tamago-kake gohan.'

たまござけ 卵酒 〖医療〗 eggnog without milk. Hot sake mixed with sugar and beaten egg yolk. Is said to have been effective against a cold.

たまごどうふ 卵豆腐, 玉子豆腐 〖食べ物〗 savory egg custard with soup stock. Although the name suggests it is a kind of tofu, it doesn't contain soy beans as an ingredient, different from Chinese-style egg tofu.

たまごとじ 卵綴じ, 玉子綴じ 〖食べ物〗 soft scrambled egg with soup. Is usually mixed with other food.

たまごどん 玉子丼 〖食べ物〗 a bowl of rice topped with egg and vegetables.

たまごやき 卵焼き, 玉子焼き 〖食べ物〗 a rectangular-shaped plain omelette. Is sometimes flavored with sugar or soy sauce.

たますだれ 玉簾 〖生活〗 a blind screen made of beads. →簾(すだれ)

たまてばこ 玉手箱 〖民話〗 a magic box that Otohime, the princess of the Sea God's palace, presented to URASHIMA TAROU. When he opened the box, mysterious smoke rose, and he became a gray-haired old man.

たまへん 玉偏 〖漢字〗 a left-side radical meaning "jewel." Is used in kanji such as 珍 (rare), 珠 (pearl), and 球 (ball). →偏; 部首

たまむし 玉虫 〘動物〙 a jewel beetle, or a metallic woodboring beetle. *Chrysochroa fulgidissima*. About 3 to 4 cm long. The wings have been used for ornaments.

たまむしのずし 玉虫の厨子 〘仏教〙 Beetle-wing Shrine. Was created in the Asuka period. A small palace-shaped shrine is on a rectangular base, and the total height is 233 cm. Wings of jewel beetles were placed under the open-work metal for decoration. Has been kept at HOURYUU-JI Temple in northwestern Nara Pref. A National Treasure.

たまものまえ 玉藻の前 〘妖怪〙 the name of a woman who is said to have been an imaginary fox with nine tails. She was a favorite mistress of Ex-emperor Toba, but was exposed by an exorcist and became a rock.

たまよりひめ 玉依毘売, 玉依姫 〘神話〙 a daughter of OOWADATSUMI NO KAMI, the wife of UGAYAFUKIAEZU NO MIKOTO, and the mother of Emperor Jinmu.

たまりじょうゆ 溜まり醤油 〘調味料〙 rich soy sauce. Is often used for sashimi or sushi.

ためいけ 溜め池 〘農業〙 an artificial pond for irrigation. There are more than 200 thousand of them throughout Japan. Hyougo, Hiroshima, Kagawa, and Osaka Prefs. have more than 10 thousand each.

たもと 袂 〘服飾〙 a sleeve of a kimono. Can be used as a pocket.

たもんてん 多聞天 〘仏教〙 One of the Four Guardian Kings, *Vaisravana*. Brings a small pagoda and defends the north. Is called BISHAMON-TEN when worshipped independently.

たやまかたい 田山花袋 〘文芸〙 1871 -1930. A novelist born in Gunma Pref. Promoted naturalistic literature. His works include *Futon* in 1907 and *Country Teacher* (Inaka kyoushi) in 1909.

たゆう 太夫 〘芸能・娯楽〙 the honorific title for the head of a Noh school, the narrator of a puppet drama, a top-rank female impersonator in kabuki, or a top-rank prostitute in the Edo period.

たらこ 鱈子 〘食べ物〙 salted cod roe, or salted roe of Alaska pollack. →介党鱈(すけとうだら)

たらしこみ たらし込み 〘絵画〙 a bleeding technique. To let paint run by dripping it on another paint that is still wet.

だらに 陀羅尼 〘仏教・言語〙 long magic words in esoteric Buddhism. *Dharani*. This original Sanskrit means "memorization." →真言

たりきほんがん 他力本願 〘仏教〙 salvation by faith in Amitabha Buddha. A term or idea in Pure Land Buddhism.

たるざけ 樽酒 〘酒〙 sake in a barrel. The surface of the barrel is covered with a straw mat, and auspicious words or a brand name is written on it. At a celebratory banquet, people open it by hitting the top lid with wooden hammers. A large one contains 72 liters, while a miniature one containing 1.8 liters is also available.

だるま　達磨〖人形〗a doll of Bodhidharma, or a round papier-mâché good-luck doll without limbs. Is usually red and has no eyes. A person with wish paints one eye first and paints the other eye when the wish is fulfilled.

だるまさんがころんだ　達磨さんが転んだ〖遊び〗a children's game similar to "red light, green light." One person is it, and all other players are set on the starting line. While it is uttering 'daruma-san ga koronda,' which means "Bodhidharma fell down," other players run close to it. When it stops uttering, the rest of the players have to stop moving. If a player moves, he or she becomes a captive of it. If a player succeeds to come to it while it is uttering, the captives are released. The details and the name of the game are different from region to region.

だるますとおぶ　達磨ストーブ〖家具〗a potbelly stove. Burns coal.

だるまだいし　達磨大師〖仏教〗⇨菩提達磨

たれ　垂れ　(1)〖武術〗a waist protector. Hangs from the breastplate. **(2)**〖漢字〗the upper-to-left radical of a KANJI. Literally means "dangling." There are a few 'tare' radicals such as MA-DARE in 広 (wide), GAN-DARE in 厚 (thick), and YAMAI-DARE in 病 (sick). **(3)**〖調味料〗thick sauce for dipping. Is made from soy sauce, sake, mirin, and other condiments.

たわら　(1)　俵〖食文化〗⇨米俵　**(2)**〖相撲〗straw barrels forming the circle of the sumo ring. Contain clay and are half-buried.

たわらのとうた　俵藤太〖武士〗⇨藤原秀郷

たわらやそうたつ　俵屋宗達〖絵画〗?-? A painter born in Kyoto around the 17th century. Created the style of the Rin school. Marked by his heavy use of gold and silver. His works include *Wind and Thunder Gods* at the KENNIN-JI Temple and *Waterfowls in Lotus Pond* at the Kyoto National Museum. →琳派（りんぱ）

たん　～反　(1)〖服飾・単位〗a unit of length of cloth. About 10.6 m. Corresponds to the cloth necessary to make a kimono for one person. →反物　**(2)**〖農林水産・単位〗a unit to measure land area. About 10 acres. One 'tan' equals 10 'se.' Ten 'tan' equal one CHOU.

だん　～段〖武術〗a grade above KYUU. The first grade, SHODAN, is lowest, and above the first grade is the second dan, called 'ni-dan.' The number before '-dan' such as 'ni,' 'san,' or 'yon' indicates the grade, which becomes higher as the skill improves.

だんおつ　檀越〖仏教〗a lay adherent of Buddhism. *dana-pati*. Offered food or clothes to a monk or a temple.

たんか 短歌〚文芸〛 a short rhyming poem with five lines of 5, 7, 5, 7, and 7 syllables each. Appeared in the 7th century and became the typical style of Japanese poetry in and after the Heian period. Is still composed by many people, including the Imperial family.

だんか 檀家〚仏教〛 a supporting family of a specific temple. *dana*. Usually the temple holds funerals or memorial services for the supporting family.

だんかいのせだい 団塊の世代〚生活〛 the baby-boom generation. Born from 1947 to 1949.

たんご 丹後〚旧国名〛 the old name of northern Kyoto Pref.

だんご 団子〚食べ物〛 a small ball of rice flour. Is sometimes coated with sweet adzuki paste or sweet soybean powder called KINAKO. Three balls are often skewered.

だんごう 談合〚経済〛 a prior secret agreement among construction companies in bidding for public works. Illegal but is said to have been common in the construction industry.

たんごのせっく 端午の節句〚暦〛 the Boys' Festival on May 5. Is celebrated by hoisting a carp-shaped streamer and putting a samurai doll or a miniature set of armor on display. People often eat a stick-type rice dumpling wrapped in bamboo leaves and a rice cake wrapped in an oak leaf. This day is now designated a national holiday, Children's Day. →節句; 子供の日

たんさい 淡彩〚絵画〛 weak coloring. Is sometimes used on India ink painting.

たんざく 短冊〚文芸・暦〛 a paper strip. Is used to write poetry or to draw a picture. In the Star Festival, people write their wish on it and hang it from a bamboo branch.

たんざんじんじゃ 談山神社〚神社〛 Tanzan-Jinja Shrine. Is located in central Nara Pref. Enshrines a forefather of the Fujiwara clan, FUJIWARA NO KAMATARI, who played an important role in the Taika Reform. A good spot for cherry blossom viewing.

たんじょうぶつ 誕生仏〚仏教・彫刻〛 a statue of the Historical Buddha at birth. Points at the heaven with the right hand and points at the earth with the left hand. This posture means that "only I am holy throughout heaven and earth." →灌仏(かんぶつ)会; 天上天下唯我独尊

だんじょこようきかいきんとうほう 男女雇用機会均等法〚法律〛 Equal Employment Opportunity Law for Men and Women. Was established in 1985.

だんじり 檀尻〚祭礼〛 a festival float. Is elaborately decorated and towed by parishioners in a festival. This term is mainly used in Western Japan. →山車(だし)

たんしんふにん 単身赴任〚企業・組織〛 to live alone, separated from one's family due to the transfer of workplace.

たんす 箪笥〖家具〗 a chest of drawers. A high-quality one is made of wood of very expensive trees.

たんぜん 丹前 〖服飾〗 a padded kimono for cold weather. Is often available for free at a traditional inn.

だんぞう 檀像 〖仏教・彫刻〗 a Buddhist image of white sandalwood or chinaberry. This type of image was carved very elaborately because of the hardness of the wood. It was not gilded or colored, to appreciate the fragrance of the wood. Popular in the 9th century.

たんちょうづる 丹頂鶴 〖動物〗 a Japanese crane, or a red-crowned crane. *Grus japonensis*. Can be seen in eastern Hokkaido.

たんにしょう 歎異抄〖仏教〗 *Lamentations of Divergences*. Is said to have been written in the Kamakura period by a priest named Yuien, a disciple of SHINRAN, the founder of the True Pure Land sect. Contains quotations from Shinran's words and criticizes the challenges by some of his disciples or adherents. →悪人正機説

だんのうらのたたかい 壇ノ浦の戦い 〖戦争〗 Battle of Dan-no-ura. In 1185, the Minamoto troops led by MINAMOTO NO YOSHITSUNE, defeated the Taira clan at Dan-no-ura near Shimonoseki City, Yamaguchi Pref. During the battle, many members of the Taira clan, including seven-year-old Emperor Antoku, died, and the clan was ruined.

たんば 丹波 〖旧国名〗 the old name of central Kyoto Pref. and eastern Hyougo Pref.

だんぱつしき 断髪式〖相撲〗 a hair-cutting ceremony for a retiring wrestler. The wrestler sits in the center of the ring, and his topknot is cut off by people involved such as the boss of his sumo stable, his family, and his friends.

たんぼああと 田んぼアート 〖農業・絵画〗 rice paddy art. To form a picture in a rice field by planting rice with various colors. Was first started in Aomori Pref. in 1993 to revitalize the village.

たんもの 反物 〖服飾〗 a long enough textile to tailor an adult kimono. About 34 cm wide and 10.6 m long. →～反

だんりんは 談林派 〖文芸〗 the Danrin school of haiku. Was popular in the late 17th century. Had an unrestrictive and witty style. Declined when the style of MATSUO BASHOU became popular.

ち

ちえこしょう 智慧子抄 〔文芸・作品〕 *Chieko's Sky*. An anthology of TAKAMURA KOUTAROU published in 1941. Contains 29 poems and 6 TANKA, in which he describes love and life with his wife, Chieko, who had passed away.

ちえんしょうめいしょ 遅延証明書 〔交通〕 a delay certificate. Is issued by a railroad company when the train operation is extremely behind schedule.

ちおんいん 知恩院 〔寺院〕 Chion-in Temple. The head temple of the Pure Land sect located in Kyoto City. Was started with a hermitage built by the priest HOUNEN in 1175, where Hounen spent last half of his life and passed away. One of his disciples, Genchi, built the temple buildings in 1234. The current buildings were rebuilt in 1639 by the third Tokugawa shogun, TOKUGAWA IEMITSU. The main gate, the main hall, and the picture scroll describing the life of Hounen are National Treasures.

ちがいだな 違い棚 〔建築〕 different-levelled shelves in a traditional style room. A short post connects the upper shelf with the lower shelf. Small ornaments are sometimes placed on them.

ちがいほうけん 治外法権 〔外交〕 extraterritorial rights. Diplomatic privilege for diplomats or heads of states to evade legal responsibility in a foreign country.

ちかてつさりんじけん 地下鉄サリン事件 〔犯罪〕 Tokyo subway sarin attack. Occurred on March 20, 1995. Members of the cult, then called Aum Shinrikyou, released sarin, the highly toxic chemical substance, in five trains on the present Tokyo Metro lines. 13 people died.

ちかまつもんざえもん 近松門左衛門 〔文芸〕 1653-1724. A playwright for KABUKI and JOURURI born in Fukui Pref. Is sometimes called a Japanese Shakespeare. His works include *The Love Suicide at Sonezaki* (Sonezaki shinjuu), *The Courier for Hell* (Meido no hikyaku), and *The Battles of Coxinga* (Kokusen'ya Kassen).

ちからいし 力石 〔神社〕 an oval-shaped stone for lifting competition. Is usually placed in a Shinto shrine. It is said that it was used to determine divine will.

ちからうどん 力饂飩 〔食べ物〕 hot thick wheat noodles with rice cake.

ちからがみ 力紙 〔相撲〕 power paper. Is used by a sumo wrestler to purify himself or wipe his lips before a bout.

ちからみず 力水 〔相撲〕 power water. Is put in a wooden pail beside the sumo ring. A sumo wrestler rinses his mouth with it before a bout.

ちぎ 千木〖神社・建築〗 an X-shaped ornament or projecting rafters on a Shinto shrine roof. →鰹木(かつお)

ちぎ 地祇〖神道〗 ⇨国つ神

ちぎょうち 知行地〖政治〗 a fief. Land that the shogunate or a feudal lord gave the vassals as stipends in the Edo period.

ちきんらあめん チキンラーメン 〖食べ物〗 Chicken Ramen. The world's first instant ramen invented in 1958 by a businessman named ANDOU MOMOFUKU.

ちきんらいす チキンライス〖食べ物〗 stir-fried rice with chicken, seasoned with tomato ketchup. Also includes minced onions.

ちくご 筑後〖旧国名〗 the old name of southern Fukuoka Pref.

ちくごがわ 筑後川〖地名〗 the Chikugo River. Its length is 143 km, making it the longest river in Kyushu. Flows from the north of Mt. Aso in Kumamoto Pref. through Ooita and Fukuoka Prefs. to the Ariake Sea in Saga Pref. Has played an important role for forestry in its upper reaches, and for growing rice in its lower reaches. Is also called Tsukushi Jirou.

ちくしょうどう 畜生道〖仏教〗 the Realm of Beasts in reincarnation. Souls in this realm live a life as animals or insects and act on instinct. →六道；輪廻

ちくぜん 筑前〖旧国名〗 the old name of northwestern Fukuoka Pref.

ちくぜんに 筑前煮〖食べ物〗 stir-fried and boiled chicken and vegetables. Is seasoned with soy sauce and sugar. Originally a local cuisine of Chikuzen, present Fukuoka Pref.

ぢぐち 地口〖落語〗 ⇨地口(じぐち)

ちくわ 竹輪〖食べ物〗 steamed and grilled fish paste in a cylindrical shape. Is sliced or cut short before eating.

ちくわぶ 竹輪麩〖食べ物〗 a cylindrical-shaped wheat gluten bread. Eaten in light soy-flavored stew called ODEN.

ちけんいん 智拳印〖仏教〗 the knowledge-fist mudra. Is signaled by the Great Sun Buddha in the Diamond Realm. The right hand grasps the upright forefinger of the left hand in front of the chest. A ninja in fictitious stories sometimes forms this mudra when performing ninjutsu. →印相；大日如来

ちご 稚児〖宗教・セックス〗 **(1)** a young child wearing a special costume in a festival procession. **(2)** a boy servant at a temple in olden times. Often practiced sex with a male monk.

ちしまかいきょう 千島海峡〖地名〗 First Kuril Strait. Is also simply called the Kuril Strait in English. Separates Shumshu Island of the Kuril Islands from the Kamchatka Peninsula in Russia. Connects the Sea of Okhotsk with the Pacific Ocean. Is 13 km wide at its narrowest point. Up until the end of World War II, it marked the border between Japan and the Soviet Union.

ちしまかいりゅう 千島海流〖海洋〗
⇨親潮

ちしまれっとう 千島列島〖島名〗
the Kuril Islands, or the Chishima
Islands. Consist of more than 50
islands including Kunashiri and
Etorofu. Stretch 1,200 km from the
east of Hokkaido to the south of
the Kamchatka Peninsula. Divide
the Sea of Okhotsk and the Pacific
Ocean. Have many volcanoes.

ちしゃくいん 智積院〖寺院〗 Chi-
shakuin Temple. The head temple
of the Chisan school of the Shingon
sect, located in Kyoto. *Maple Tree,
Cherry Blossoms*, and other works
painted by HASEGAWA TOUHAKU are
National Treasures.

ちしょうだいし 智証大師〖仏教〗 ⇨
円珍

ちじんのあい 痴人の愛〖文芸・作品〗
Naomi. A novel published in parts
from 1924 to 1925 by TANIZAKI
JUN'ICHIROU. The Japanese title literally means "a fool's love." The
term "Naomism," was coined after
the name of the novel's heroine,
whose lifestyle was wild and unre-
strained.

ちそかいせい 地租改正〖政治〗
Land Tax Reform. Was conducted
from 1873 to 1881 by the Meiji
government to lay a financial foundation. The tax rate was 3%, which
caused peasants' uprisings in several regions.

ちちかえる 父帰る〖文芸・作品〗
Return of the Father. A drama published in 1917 by KIKUCHI KAN. In
the play, a father abandons his family but returns home 20 years later.

ちちぶ 秩父〖地名〗 the name
of a mountainous area in western Saitama Pref., consisting of
Chichibu City and Chichibu County.
Japan's first coin, WADOUKAICHIN,
was made of copper from Chichibu
in 708. Later the area became
famous for the production of silk
textile materials in the Edo period
and cement production in the Meiji
period. Today its many festivals and
outdoor activities like camping and
rafting attract visitors.

ちてん 地天〖仏教〗 ⇨地天(じん)

ぢとう 地頭〖官位〗 ⇨地頭(じとう)

ちとせあめ 千歳飴〖食べ物〗 a lon-
gevity candy stick. Literally means
"one-thousand-year candy." Is usually colored red and white and sold
at a shrine during a children's rites-
of-passage event, called SHICHI-GO-
SAN.

ちとせくうこう 千歳空港〖交通〗 ⇨
新千歳空港

ちばけん 千葉県〖都道府県〗 Chiba
Pref. Is located in Eastern Japan,
neighboring Tokyo to the west,
facing the Pacific Ocean and Tokyo
Bay. Is 5,158 km^2 in area. Much
of its area is flat, and it is the only
prefecture in Japan that has no
mountain higher than 500 m. Its
capital is Chiba City, an ordinance-
designated city. Its industrial and
residential areas spread mainly
along Tokyo Bay, in cities such
as Funabashi, Chiba, Ichihara,

and Kisaradu. Spiny lobsters are caught, and canola flowers and peanuts are produced in abundance. Has Narita Airport, the Bousou Peninsula, Kujuukuri Beach, Cape Inubou, and Tokyo Disney Resort. Used to be Awa, Kazusa, and part of Shimousa.

ちばし 千葉市 〖地名〗 Chiba City. An ordinance-designated city and the capital of Chiba Pref. Is located in its central part, facing Tokyo Bay. Largely consists of residential and industrial areas around central Chiba, and the new waterfront business district in Makuhari in its northwest. Chiba Urban Monorail is the world's longest suspended monorail system. In its east is the Kasori Shell Midden, one of the largest shell mounds in the world.

ちばしゅうさく 千葉周作 〖剣術〗 1793-1855. A swordsman born in present Miyagi Pref. Founded a school called Hokushin Ittou-ryuu and opened a dojo called Genbu-kan in Kanda, Tokyo.

ちまき 粽 〖食べ物〗 a stick-type rice dumpling wrapped in bamboo leaves. Is often eaten around the Boys' Festival on May 5.

ちゃあはん チャーハン, 炒飯 〖食べ物〗 stir-fried rice. Was originally a Chinese cuisine, "chaofan." Has become popular enough to be served at various types of restaurants and eateries, not only Chinese. Tremendously varied ingredients include beef, pork, chicken, fish, onion, carrot, ginger, mushroom, and other edible things.

ちゃいれ 茶入れ 〖茶道〗 a ceramic tea caddy with a lid. Tea powders for formal strong tea are put it in.

ちゃいろ 茶色 〖色〗 brown. Literally means "the color of tea."

ちゃうけ 茶請 〖食文化〗 sweets or pickles to eat when drinking tea.

ちゃかい 茶会 〖茶道〗 a meeting for the tea ceremony. There are various types of meetings, depending on the hours, size, and formality. → 茶事(ちゃ)

ちゃかいせき 茶懐石 〖茶道〗 ⇨懐石料理

ちゃがけ 茶掛け 〖茶道〗 a hanging scroll to be hung in a decorative alcove of a tea room. An India ink painting or calligraphy is depicted on it. →茶室

ちゃがし 茶菓子 〖茶道・食べ物〗 sweets served before drinking tea in the tea ceremony.

ちゃがま 茶釜 〖茶道〗 a kettle used for the tea ceremony. Is round-shaped and has a small opening on top. Is usually made of iron.

ちゃき 茶器 〖茶道・工芸〗 ⇨茶道具

ちゃきん 茶巾 〖茶道〗 a linen cloth to wipe tea bowls. Is wet and folded small when used.

ちゃきんずし 茶巾寿司 〖食べ物〗 egg-wrapped sushi. Contains vinegared rice and ingredients such as chopped SHIITAKE mushroom or conger eel.

ちゃくたい 着帯 〖生活・服飾〗 the ceremony for an expectant mother

to wear a maternity belt in the fifth month of pregnancy. Its purpose is to preserve the mother's body temperature and to keep the fetus in the normal position.

ちゃぐちゃぐうまっこ チャグチャグ馬っこ 〖祭礼〗 Horse Parade Festival. Is held in Iwate Pref. on June 15. Children in festive costume ride on decorated horses and proceed from Onikoshi-souzen Shrine in Takizawa City to Morioka Hachiman Shrine.

ちゃこし 茶漉し (1)〖生活〗 a tea strainer. Is used to make ordinary tea. **(2)**〖茶道〗 a tea sifter. Is used to make powdered tea finer.

ちゃじ 茶事 〖茶道〗 a formal meeting for the tea ceremony. Special cuisine called KAISEKI RYOURI is served. Visitors drink both thick and thin tea. →茶会；濃茶(ﾉ)

ちゃしつ 茶室〖茶道・建築〗 a room for the tea ceremony. Has a decorative alcove and a sunken hearth. The standard one is square-shaped with four and half tatami mats. The guest entrance is very small. →床の間；炉(ﾛ)；躙(ﾆ)り口

ちゃしゃく 茶杓 〖茶道〗 a tea scoop. Is usually made of bamboo. Is used to scoop powdered tea from a tea caddy to a tea bowl.

ちゃじん 茶人 〖茶道〗 an expert of the tea ceremony. Should be a professional or have equivalent skills and knowledge of the tea ceremony.

ちゃせん 茶筅 〖茶道〗 a tea whisk. Is made of bamboo and is used to make green tea from powdered tea.

ちゃせんとおし 茶筅通し 〖茶道〗 the ceremonial checking and cleaning of a tea whisk. Is done before making tea, using water in a tea bowl.

ちゃそば 茶蕎麦 〖食べ物〗 buckwheat noodles containing tea powder.

ちゃたく 茶托 〖食文化〗 a saucer for a teacup. Is used when serving ordinary tea, not powdered tea.

ちゃだち 茶断ち〖宗教〗 abstinence from tea. Is done by a person to realize his or her wish.

ちゃだんす 茶箪笥 〖家具〗 a cupboard for tableware and tea utensils.

ちゃづけ 茶漬け 〖食べ物〗 cooked rice in tea. Hot water or broth is sometimes poured instead of tea. Eaten with savory toppings such as edible seaweed, pickles, or salmon.

ちゃつぼ 茶壺 〖茶道〗 a tea jar. A ceramic container to preserve tea leaves.

ちゃつみ 茶摘み〖農業〗 tea plucking. Tea shoots or young tea leaves are picked. This term also refers to a tea picker.

ちゃてい 茶庭〖茶道・庭園〗 a garden adjacent to or a pathway connected to a teahouse. Is equipped with a stone lantern, a stone washbasin, and stepping stones.

ちゃどう 茶道〖茶道〗 ⇨茶道(ﾄﾞｳ)

ちゃどうぐ 茶道具〖茶道・工芸〗 tea utensils. Include not only utensils for making tea but also peripheral articles such as room ornament and kitchen tools.

ちゃにわ 茶庭〚茶道・庭園〛 ⇨茶庭（ちゃてい）

ちゃのま 茶の間〚建築〛 a traditional-style living room. Is becoming less popular in cities these days.

ちゃのゆ 茶の湯〚茶道〛 ⇨茶道（さどう）

ちゃばしら 茶柱〚飲み物〛 a tea stalk. It is said that a tea stalk floating upright is a good omen.

ちゃばな 茶花〚茶道・華道〛 a flower arranged at a decorative alcove in a tea room. A flower of the season is used.

ちゃぶだい 卓袱台〚家具〛 a low, round dining table. In a family life drama on TV, an angry father sometimes dumps it over.

ちゃみせ 茶店〚食文化・ビジネス〛 a tea stall. Is often located at a tourist site or beside a walking trail and serves tea and sweets, sometimes snacks and other beverages. Tourists can take a break while eating and drinking.

ちゃめし 茶飯〚食べ物〛 (1) rice boiled in tea, instead of water. Is seasoned with salt.　(2) rice boiled with soy sauce and sake.

ちゃや 茶屋〚娯楽〛 (1) a teahouse to entertain a guest. The guest eats and drinks, enjoying conversation with a geisha. The operation of 'chaya' is permitted only at some specific areas such as Gion in Kyoto. (2)⇨茶店

ちゃりば 茶利場〚歌舞伎・文楽〛 a

comical scene in KABUKI or BUNRAKU.

ちゃわん 茶碗 (1)〚茶道〛 a tea bowl. Is used at the tea ceremony. (2)〚食器〛 a rice bowl. Is used to eat rice.

ちゃわんむし 茶碗蒸し 〚食べ物〛 cup-steamed savory custard. Contains shrimp, chicken, mushrooms, vegetables, gingko nuts, and sliced fish-paste.

ちゃん ～ちゃん〚言語〛 a suffix to show friendship by adding it to one's name. Is usually added to the first name such as 'Minoru-chan.' Is also added to a term referring to a superior relative. For example, 'oba,' which means "aunt," can be 'oba-chan.'

ちゃんこなべ ちゃんこ鍋〚食べ物・相撲〛 a hodgepodge stew for sumo wrestlers. Ingredients such as fish, meat, and vegetables are all simmered together in a large pot.

ちゃんちゃんこ ちゃんちゃんこ〚服飾〛 a long vest. Is often padded with cotton. A red one is worn for celebration when a person reaches the age of 60.

ちゃんぷるう チャンプルー〚食べ物〛 stir-fried tofu and vegetables. A local cuisine of Okinawa. →ゴーヤチャンプルー

ちゃんぽん ちゃんぽん〚食べ物〛 Chinese-style noodles with various ingredients such as pork, steamed fish paste, and vegetables. A specialty of Nagasaki.

ちゅうあいてんのう 仲哀天皇〚天皇〛 Emperor Chuuai. ?-? The

14th. The second prince of YAMATO TAKERU NO MIKOTO, and the husband of Empress Consort Jinguu. →神功皇后

ちゅうおうこうぞうせん 中央構造線〖自然〗 Median Tectonic Line. A fault line running from around Lake Suwa in Nagano Pref., along the Tenryuu River, through the Kii Peninsula, to Yatsushiro in Kumamoto Pref. Was found by a German geologist, Edmund Naumann. →ナウマン

ちゅうかそば 中華そば〖食べ物〗 ⇨ ラーメン

ちゅうかまんじゅう 中華饅頭〖食べ物〗 a Chinese-style bun. One containing minced pork and vegetables is called NIKUMAN, and one containing sweet adzuki beans is called ANMAN. There are several other types such as 'karee-man' or 'piza-man.' Is said to have been invented in Japan, imitating Chinese baos.

ちゅうきち 中吉〖神社・寺院〗 moderate good fortune. A message on a fortune slip available at a Shinto shrine or Buddhist temple. Chuukichi is better than KICHI at some shrines or temples while kichi is better than chuukichi at others. →お神籤(くじ); 大吉

ちゅうぐう 中宮〖天皇〗 **(1)** a grandmother, the mother, or the official wife of an Emperor in the ancient centralized administration system called RITSURYOU-SEI. **(2)** a wife of an Emperor in and after the Heian period.

ちゅうけん 中堅〖武術〗 the third fighter in a five-member team competition of martial arts such as judo. →先鋒; 次鋒; 副将; 大将

ちゅうげん 中元〖年中行事〗 ⇨お中元

ちゅうげん 中間〖武士〗 a lower class servant of a feudal lord. Attended a samurai from the Kamakura to Edo periods.

ちゅうけんはちこう 忠犬ハチ公〖動物・精神性〗 Loyal Hachi. A dog named Hachi-kou waited for his master in front of Shibuya Station, Tokyo, every day. Even after the sudden death of his master, Hachi kept waiting for almost 10 years. Based on this true story, the statue of Hachi was placed in front of Shibuya Station. A 2009 British-American film, *Hachi: A Dog's Tale*, comes from this story.

ちゅうこ 中古〖時代〗 early medieval times. Usually refers to the Heian period in literature history.

ちゅうごくさんち 中国山地〖山岳〗 the Chuugoku Mountains. Run from Hyougo Pref. in the east to Yamaguchi Pref. in the west for 500 km, along the border between Tottori and Okayama Prefs., and between Shimane and Hiroshima Prefs. The highest peak is Mt. Daisen (1,729 m) in Tottori Pref.

ちゅうごくざんりゅうこじ 中国残留孤児〖戦争・政治〗 Japanese orphans left behind in China after World War II. Mainly children of Japanese living in Manchuria. Were adopted by Chinese families.

ちゅうごくちほう 中国地方 〚地名〛 the Chuugoku region. Consists of five prefectures, namely, Tottori, Shimane, Okayama, Hiroshima, and Yamaguchi.

ちゅうしゅう 中秋 〚暦〛 August 15 in the traditional calendar. Its night is called JUUGO-YA.

ちゅうしゅう 仲秋 〚暦〛 mid-autumn. Another name for August in the traditional calendar.

ちゅうしゅうのめいげつ 中秋の名月 〚自然・暦〛 the harvest moon. The moon on August 15 in the traditional calendar. People enjoy moon viewing on this day. →月見

ちゅうしゅん 仲春 〚暦〛 mid-spring. Another name for February in the traditional calendar.

ちゅうしょう 中称 〚言語〛 a demonstrative referring to the intermediate relation. Its first letter is 'so,' such as 'sore' (that), 'sono' (that), and 'sochira' (there). →近称；遠称；不定称

ちゅうじょうひめ 中将姫 〚仏教〛 Princess Chuujou. A legendary woman. Is said to have become a nun at TAIMA-DERA Temple in the 8th century and to have woven a mandala from lotus thread at one night.

ちゅうしんぐら 忠臣蔵 〚武士〛 the generic term for a drama whose theme is the revenge of forty-seven masterless samurai from the Akou feudal domain. →赤穂浪士

ちゅうせい 中世 〚時代〛 medieval times. Consists of the Kamakura (1185-1333) and Muromachi (1333-1573) periods in Japanese chronology.

ちゅうそん 中尊 〚仏教〛 the central Buddhist image of a triad. For example, Amitabha Buddha is the central image of the Amitabha triad.

ちゅうそんじ 中尊寺 〚寺院〛 Chuson-ji Temple. A main temple of the Tendai sect located in southern Iwate Pref. Was founded in 850 by a priest, Ennin. Golden Hall is a National Treasure. →金色堂

ちゅうどう 中道 〚仏教〛 the Middle Way. Although avoiding two extremes has been a conventional motto of Buddhism since the Historical Buddha, the interpretation varies depending on the sects.

ちゅうとろ 中トロ 〚食べ物〛 slightly fatty meat of tuna. Is taken from the dorsal and rearward ventral sections. →大トロ

ちゅうなごん 中納言 〚官位〛 an assistant secretary of the Grand Council of State in ancient times. Ranked next to DAINAGON and prior to SHOUNAGON.

ちゅうにん 中忍 〚忍者〛 a medium-skilled ninja. According to *The Book of Ninja* (BANSENSHUUKAI), ninjas were divided into three ranks: high, medium, and low. In modern fiction, 'chuunin' is ranked at the middle level of a ninja organization and worked under a high-ranked ninja while administrating low-ranked ninjas. →上忍；下忍

ちゅうはい チューハイ 〖酒〗 a cocktail of Japanese spirits and flavored soda water. The alcohol content is not very high. →焼酎

ちゅうぶこくさいくうこう 中部国際空港 〖交通〗 Chubu Centrair International Airport. Is located on an artificial island in Ise Bay, off the Chita Peninsula, in Aichi Pref. Was opened in 2005. The word Centrair is an abbreviation of Central Japan International Airport Co., Ltd., the owner and operator of the airport. Its IATA code is NGO, an abbreviation of Nagoya, a nearby mega city. Around 10 million people use it every year. Can be accessed by a Meitetsu Mu-Sky limited express, which connects central Nagoya with the airport within 30 minutes.

ちゅうぶちほう 中部地方 〖地名〗 the Chuubu region. Consists of nine prefectures, namely, Niigata, Toyama, Ishikawa, Fukui, Yamanashi, Nagano, Gifu, Shizuoka, and Aichi. Occasionally, Mie Pref. is included.

ちゅうもん 中門〖仏教・建築〗 an inner gate. Is placed in the center of the south edge of a cloister. People see the inner gate right in front when entering through the south main gate. →南(なん)大門

ちゅうれい 昼礼〖ビジネス・教育〗 a lunch-time short meeting. Is held for clerical communication at an office or school, which has no morning short meeting. →朝礼

ちゅらうみすいぞくかん 美ら海水族館 〖魚・博物館〗 Okinawa Churaumi Aquarium. Was founded in 2002. Is located in northern Okinawa Pref. Its name 'churaumi' means "beautiful sea" in the Okinawa dialect.

ちょう ～丁 〖食べ物・助数詞〗 the counting suffix for tofu. Is also used to count the number of each dish in a restaurant.

ちょう ～町 〖距離・単位〗 (**1**) a unit of length. About 109 m. Sixty KEN equal one 'chou.' (**2**) a unit of area. About 99.18 acres. One 'chou' equals ten TAN.

ちょうか 長歌 〖文芸〗 a long rhyming poem of alternating 5- and 7-syllable lines, ending with a final line of 7 syllables. Many poems in this style are contained in the *Anthology of Myriad Leaves* (MAN'YOUSHUU). Waned during and after the Heian period. ↔短歌

ちょうがん 彫眼 〖仏教・彫刻〗 carved eyes. A technique for depicting eyes of a wooden Buddhist sculpture. Was popular before the technique of inlaid crystal eyes appeared in the 12th century. ↔玉眼(ぎょくがん)

ちょうけいてんのう 長慶天皇 〖天皇〗 Emperor Choukei. 1343-1394. The 98th, on the throne from 1368 to 1383. The 3rd Emperor of the Southern Court. →南北朝時代

ちょうげん 重源 〖仏教〗 1121-1206. A priest of the Pure Land sect. Visited the Sung dynasty three times. After coming back to Japan, made an effort to revive the Toudai-ji Temple destroyed by fire in 1180. →快慶

ちょうし 銚子 〖酒〗 a small ceramic bottle for warmed sake. Its nominal capacity is 180 or 360 cc, but actually 150 or 260 cc of sake is contained in most cases. Sake is poured from this bottle to a small cup called CHOKO.

ちょうじ 弔辞 〖冠婚葬祭〗 words of condolence. One of the relatives or close friends of the dead person reads a memorial message at the funeral.

ちょうしし 銚子市 〖地名〗 Choushi City. Is located in eastern Chiba Pref. Cape Inubou is the eastern tip of the Kantou region. Famous for soy sauce production. Has a large seaport, and its catch of fishes such as sardines, bonito, and tuna is among the largest in Japan. However, the size of the catch has been declining.

ちょうじゅうじんぶつぎが 鳥獣人物戯画 〖絵画〗 *Scrolls of Frolicking Animals and Humans*. Is said to have been drawn around the 12th to 13th centuries by Priest Toba and other painters. Consists of four volumes and is preserved at Kouzan-ji Temple in Kyoto.

ちょうしゅうせいばつ 長州征伐 〖戦争〗 Choushuu Expeditions. The Tokugawa shogunate tried to attack the Choushuu domain in 1864 and 1866. Choushuu signaled its

allegiance in the first expedition, and the shogunate withdrew its troops without fighting. In the second expedition, the shogunate was defeated and withdrew its troops. Owing to this battle, the shogunate drastically lost its authority.

ちょうしゅうはん 長州藩 〖政治〗 the Choushuu domain. Governed present Yamaguchi Pref. Its feudal lords were from the Mouri clan. Played the leading role together with the Satsuma domain in the Meiji Restoration in the late 19th century. Produced Yoshida Shouin, Takasugi Shinsaku, and Katsura Kogorou.

ちょうしん 朝臣 〖官位〗 a courtier. A retainer of the Imperial Court.

ちょうず 手水 〖生活〗 **(1)** to purify one's hands and face with water. **(2)** a lavatory.

ちょうずばち 手水鉢 〖生活〗 a washbasin.

ちょうずや 手水舎 〖宗教・建築〗 a hut for washing hands. People wash their hands and rinse their mouths, using water in a stone washbasin, before prayer in a Shinto shrine or Buddhist temple.

ちょうせんかいきょう 朝鮮海峡 〖海洋〗 Korea Strait. Is located between Tsushima Island and the Korean Peninsula. The Tsushima Current flows from the East China Sea to the Sea of Japan. →対馬海峡

ちょうせんつうしんし 朝鮮通信使 〖外交〗 the diplomatic corps from Korea in the Edo period. Came to

Japan in 1607 for the first time and in 1811 for the last, for a total of 12 times.

ちょうそ 重祚〖天皇〗 re-enthronement. Empress Saimei (594–661) and Empress Shoutoku (718–770) ascended to the throne again after they once dethroned.

ちょうそかべもとちか 長宗我部元親 〖武士〗 1539–1599. A warlord born in present Kouchi Pref. Governed the entire Shikoku but surrendered to TOYOTOMI HIDEYOSHI and joined Hideyoshi's invasion to Korea.

ちょうちょうまげ 蝶々髷 〖髪〗 a butterfly-shaped hair for a young girl.

ちょうちん 提灯，提燈 〖生活〗 a foldable paper lantern with a candle inside. There are various types, depending on its use. A family crest is sometimes painted on it.

ちょうちんぎょうれつ 提灯行列 〖政治・娯楽〗 a lantern procession. Is formed for a celebration, for example, when Emperor Shouwa was enthroned.

ちょうてい 朝廷 〖政治〗 the Imperial Court. The political system with the Emperor at its center. Was established in ancient times, but the Emperor him/herself gradually lost actual power after the rise of the aristocracy, and the establishment of the shogunate system by the warriors in medieval times.

ちょうてき 朝敵 〖政治〗 an enemy of an Emperor. This term was used by a political group when it tried to insist on its legitimacy and blame its opponent.

ちょうどういん 朝堂院 〖天皇・建築〗 the building complex of the Imperial Court offices. Its main building is DAIGOKU-DEN, and the main gate is Outen-mon.

ちょうないかい 町内会 〖生活・行政〗 a neighborhood association. An autonomous organization of a local community. Also functions as the smallest unit of the administrative organization.

ちょうにん 町人 〖政治・職業〗 merchants and artisans in the Edo period. Officially refers to those living in a city. Although they were ranked in the lower class in the hierarchy, merchants came to obtain strong economic power.

ちょうめ 丁目 〖行政〗 a division number of an area in an address. → 番地

ちょうようのせっく 重陽の節句 〖暦〗 the Chrysanthemum Festival on September 9. 'Chouyou' literally means "double yang," because nine is a yang number in the Yin-Yang Way. This festival is obsolete at present. →節句

ちょうれい 朝礼 〖ビジネス・教育〗 a morning short meeting. Is held for clerical communication at an office or school. →昼礼

ちよがみ 千代紙 〖遊び〗 colorful patterned paper. Is usually square and has been made in a traditional way. Is used to make various objects by folding paper. →折り紙

ちょきぶね 猪牙船〖交通〗 a small slender boat. Was used on a river in Edo, often to visit a red-light district.

ちょくおん 直音〖言語〗 a straight syllable. Its pronunciation can be expressed with one KANA, different from YOUON and SOKUON.

ちょくがん 勅願〖天皇〗 prayer held as an Imperial command.

ちょくがんじ 勅願寺〖仏教・天皇〗 a temple established at the behest of an Emperor. Examples include Yakushi-ji by Emperor Monmu and Toudai-ji by Emperor Shoumu.

ちょくし 勅使〖天皇〗 a direct messenger from an Emperor.

ちょくしもん 勅使門〖建築〗 a temple gate for a direct messenger from an Emperor.

ちょくしょ 勅書〖天皇〗 a document to pass an Imperial order.

ちょくせんわかしゅう 勅撰和歌集〖天皇・文芸〗 an anthology of poems compiled at the command of an Emperor. Twenty-one anthologies were issued from the *Collection of Ancient and Modern Japanese Poetry* (KOKINWAKASHUU) in the 10th century, to the *New Collection of Ancient and Modern Japanese Poetry* (SHIN-KOKINWAKASHUU) in the 13th century.

ちょくだい 勅題〖天皇・文芸〗 the subject in the Imperial New Year's Poetry Reading. →歌会始

ちょくれい 勅令〖天皇〗 an Imperial ordinance. Is prescribed under the Constitution of the Empire of Japan.

ちょこ 猪口〖酒・食器〗 a tiny cup for sake. Most of them are ceramics, but some are glassware. It holds about 20 to 40 cc. →銚子

ちょっかつりょう 直轄領〖武士・政治〗 a domain directly governed by the Imperial Court, the shogunate, or sometimes a feudal lord. →天領

ちよのふじ 千代の富士〖相撲〗 1955 –2016. A sumo wrestler born in Hokkaido. His real name is Akimoto Mitsugu. The 58th grand champion, YOKODUNA. Was nicknamed "Wolf." In 1990 became the first wrestler to win 1,000 bouts.

ちょんまげ 丁髷〖髪〗 a topknot hairstyle for men in the Edo period. The forehead and top were shaved.

ちらしずし 散らし寿司〖食べ物〗 uncaked sushi, or scattered sushi. Is not shaped into a bite-sized lump of rice like ordinary sushi. Rice is topped or mixed with ingredients such as slices of fish, shiitake mushroom, egg, sweetened mashed fish, and green peas.

ちりちょうず 塵手水〖相撲〗 wrestler's ritual clapping of hands in a squat position on a ring before a bout. A wrestler rubs his hands together, opens his arms, claps his hands, extends his arms to both sides, rotates the palms up, and puts down the arms. Is done to ritually show that he has no weapons.

ちりなべ ちり鍋〖食べ物〗 one-pot dish of white-flesh fish, tofu, and vegetables. Is dipped into a mixture of soy sauce and citrus juice, called PONZU, before eating.

ちりましほ 知里真志保 〔少数民族〕 1909-1961. A linguist born in Hokkaido. A professor at Hokkaido Univ. Was an Ainu and studied the language and culture of Ainu.

ちりめん 縮緬〔服飾〕 a silk crepe used to make a kimono. Is produced in Kyoto, Shiga, and Niigata Prefs.

ちりめんじゃこ 縮緬雑魚 〔食べ物〕 baby anchovies boiled in salt water and dried hard.

ちろり 銚釐〔酒〕 a sake warmer. Is made of copper or brass and has a spout and a handle.

ちんきん 沈金〔工芸〕 hairline gilding for lacquerware. Expresses a pattern with carved lines or grooves on the lacquerware surface that are filled with gilt.

ちんごこっか 鎮護国家 〔仏教〕 pacification and protection of the nation by Buddhism. This ideology was active in the Nara and Heian periods, and a provincial temple was built in each province. →国分寺

ちんじゅ 鎮守〔神社〕 a tutelary shrine, or a shrine for local deities.

ちんすこう ちんすこう〔食べ物〕 an Okinawan cookie. Does not contain egg and is a bit easy to break.

ちんそう 頂相〔仏教・美術〕 a portrait of a high-ranking Zen priest. Was given to his disciple as a token of full understanding of his teaching.

ちんどんや チンドン屋 〔ビジネス〕 a marching musical band for publicity. In colorful costume, parades through the streets while bringing small signboards of newly opened stores or coming events. Consists of drums, saxophones, and other instruments.

つ

ついじべい 築地塀〔建築〕 a roofed earth fence. A few horizontal lines are sometimes drawn on the fence to indicate the social rank of the resident. Roof tiles are sometimes inserted for reinforcement.

ついぜんくよう 追善供養〔仏教〕 a memorial service. People chant a sutra or make an offering to pray for the dead soul.

つうきんじごく 通勤地獄〔交通〕 a commuters' hell. Many business people commute more than one hour to the office by crowded train, especially in and around Tokyo.

つうてんかく 通天閣〔建築〕 the Tsuutenkaku Tower. Is located in Osaka City. The original one was built in 1912 and was dismantled during World War II. The current tower was built in 1956 by Naitou Tachuu, who also designed the Tokyo Tower. The height is 100 m.

つうやくあんないし 通訳案内士〔旅〕 a guide interpreter. Has an official license and guides international sightseers. Guides who speak English, French, Spanish, German, Chinese, Italian, Portuguese, Russian, Korean, and Thai are available.

つうやくがいど 通訳ガイド 〔旅〕 ⇨通訳案内士

つか 柄〔武器〕 the hilt, or the handgrip of a sword.

つかいすてかいろ 使い捨て懐炉〔生活〕 a disposable pocket-sized body warmer. Gets warm by use of chemicals, not fire.

つかはらぼくでん 塚原卜伝〔剣術〕 1489-1571. An expert swordsman. Was born in present Ibaraki Pref. as a son of a Shinto priest at Kashima Shrine. Taught swordsmanship to Ashikaga shoguns. →鹿島神宮；室町幕府

つがる 津軽 **(1)**〔地名〕 the old name of western Aomori Pref. **(2)** 〔文芸・作品〕 the name of a novel by DAZAI OSAMU, published in 1944. The setting of the story was Tsugaru, where Dazai was born and raised.

つがるかいきょう 津軽海峡〔地名〕 Tsugaru Channel. Is located between the Honshuu and Hokkaido Islands and connects the Pacific Ocean with the Sea of Japan. On the Hokkaido side is Hakodate City, and on the Honshuu side are the Shimokita and Tsugaru Peninsulas in Aomori Pref. Two islands are connected by an underground tunnel for trains, called the Seikan Tunnel. →青函トンネル

つがるじゃみせん 津軽三味線〔音楽〕 a local shamisen in the Tsugaru area of Aomori Pref., or its performance. Its performance is noted by a powerful driving rhythm, played in solo or ensemble. →三味線

つき 突き〖剣術〗a kendo technique to thrust at the throat. Junior high school students or younger are prohibited from using this technique because of its danger.

つきじいちば 築地市場 〖食文化〗The Tsukiji Market, or Tokyo Metropolitan Central Wholesale Market. Opened on the Tokyo Bay coast in 1935 and plans to move to Toyosu. Deals both marine products and vegetables and fruits. General people can observe the market business.

つきたおし 突き倒し〖相撲〗a technique to push down the opponent by thrusting at him from the front.

つきだし 突出し （1）〖食文化〗⇨ お通し （2）〖相撲〗a technique to thrust the opponent out of the ring from the front.

つきなみえ 月次絵〖絵画〗pictures of monthly subjects. Depicts annual events or manners and customs against a background of a natural scene in each month. Originated at the end of the 9th century.

つきにほえる 月に吠える〖文芸・作品〗*Howling at the Moon*. An anthology of poems published in 1917 by HAGIWARA SAKUTAROU. His poems have the musical beauty of colloquial language.

つきのわぐま 月の輪熊〖動物〗an Asian black bear, a moon bear, or a white-chested bear. *Selenarctos thibetanus*. Its height is about 1.5 m. Inhabits Honshuu and Shikoku.

つきびと 付き人 （1）〖相撲〗an attendant to a professional sumo wrestler. （2）〖芸能〗a personal assistant for an actor or actress, singer, or comedian.

つきへん 月偏〖漢字〗a left-side or right-side radical with two meanings: "moon" and "body." Is used in kanji such as 肌(skin), 肘(elbow), 朧(hazy), and 朝(morning).

つきみ 月見〖自然・酒〗moon viewing. People admire the moon on the night of August 15 and September 13 in the traditional calendar. Rice dumplings and vegetables are offered to the moon, with pampas grasses placed beside them.

つきみうどん 月見饂飩 〖食べ物〗thick white noodles with a raw egg in hot broth. Literally means "moon viewing thick white noodles" because the yolk on the noodle looks like the moon.

つきみざけ 月見酒〖酒〗drinking sake while viewing the moon. Usually in September.

つきみそう 月見草〖植物〗an evening primrose. *Oenothera tetraptera*. Grows to about 50 cm. A white flower blooms in the evening and withers and becomes red next morning.

つきみそば 月見蕎麦 〖食べ物〗buckwheat noodles with a raw egg in hot broth. Literally means "moon viewing buckwheat noodles" because the yolk on the noodle looks like the moon.

つきみだんご 月見団子〖食べ物〗a rice dumpling offered to the harvest moon. Its ingredients, shape, and taste are different from area to area. →月見

つきめいにち 月命日〖仏教〗 the same day in the month on which a person passed away. →祥月命日

つきやま 築山〖庭園〗 an artificial miniature mountain in a traditional garden.

つきよみのみこと 月読命〖神話〗 ⇨ 月読命(つくよみのみこと)

つくし 筑紫〖地名〗 the old name of Fukuoka Pref., except for its eastern part. Was divided into Chikuzen and Chikugo in the 7th century. Having the regional government in Dazaifu, it served as the main gateway to Japan from China and Korea in ancient times.

づくし ～尽くし〖食文化〗 cuisine containing an identical ingredient for all dishes or consisting of the same type of recipe. For example, 'maguro-dukushi' means a set meal with dishes of tuna prepared in various ways.

つくしじろう 筑紫二郎〖地名〗 a personified name of the Chikugo River. 'Tsukushi' refers to northern Kyushu, and 'Jirou' literally means the second son.

つくだに 佃煮〖食べ物〗 simmered seafood. A kind of preserved food thickly seasoned with soy sauce and sugar. Shellfish and seaweed are popular ingredients.

つくつくぼうし ツクツクボウシ〖動物〗 a Walker's cicada. *Meimuna opalifera*. Sings late summer to fall.

つくね 捏ね〖食べ物〗 a meatball of chicken, pork, or fish. Chicken meatballs are popular at a YAKITORI restaurant.

つくばい 蹲〖茶道〗 a stone washbasin placed in a tea garden. The tea guest purifies the hands before entering the tea room.

つぐみ 鶫〖動物〗 a dusky thrush. *Turdus eunomus*. Used to be eaten, but it is now prohibited to capture it.

つくもがみ 付喪神〖妖怪〗 an old tool with a spirit dwelling in it. It is said that a tool used for one hundred years would be possessed by a spirit, and its shape might be transformed. For example, a lute with a human body and four limbs is depicted in a picture scroll painted in the 17th century.

つくよみのみこと 月読命〖神話〗 the deity of the moon. Was born when IZANAGI NO MIKOTO purified himself after coming back from the Land of Darkness. A younger brother of the Sun Goddess (AMATERASU OOMIKAMI) and an elder brother of the God of Storms (SUSANOO NO MIKOTO).

つくり 旁〖漢字〗 the right-side radical of a kanji. The left-side radical is called HEN.

つくり 造り〖食べ物〗 a term referring to SASHIMI. Was originally a Kansai dialect.

つくりざかや 造り酒屋〖酒・ビジネス〗 a sake brewery. Sells sake at wholesale to retailers.

つげ 柘植 〖植物〗 a Japanese box-wood, or a little-leaf box. *Buxus microphylla* var. *japonica*. Its wood is used for combs, shogi pieces, and seals.

つけめん つけ麺 〖食べ物〗 a dipping-style ramen. Eaten after dipping into soup. Has a rather strong taste.

つけもの 漬け物 〖食べ物〗 pickles. There are many types of 'tsukemono' throughout Japan. Ingredients are mainly vegetables such as giant white radish, Chinese cabbage, cucumber, and eggplant. The seasonings include salt, miso, soy sauce, vinegar, and sake lees.

つけやき 付け焼き 〖食べ物〗 food grilled after being dipped in sauce.

つし 津市 〖地名〗 Tsu City. The capital of Mie Pref., and is located in its northern-central part, facing Ise Bay. Developed as a castle town of the Toudou clan and as a post town on the Ise Road.

つじぎり 辻斬り 〖剣術・犯罪〗 a street murder in the Edo period. Some samurai killed a chance passerby with a sword just to examine sharpness of their own swords or to try their fencing technique.

つじせっぽう 辻説法 〖仏教・言語〗 street preaching. A legendary example is that a priest in the 13th century, Nichiren, preached on a street in Kamakura, present Kanagawa Pref.

つしま 対馬 〖島名〗 Tsushima Island, in Nagasaki Pref. in the Korea Strait. Is 696 km^2 in area, and the 10th largest island in Japan. Has been divided into two islands by a waterway since the 17th century, with Kami-jima in the north and Shimo-jima in the south. With other small islands, they constitute the Tsushima Islands. Due to its location close to the Korean Peninsula, it served as a gateway to Japan in ancient times.

つしまかいきょう 対馬海峡 〖海洋〗 Tsushima Strait. Is located between Tsushima and the Iki Islands near Kyushu. The Tsushima Current flows from the East China Sea to the Sea of Japan. After the immigration from China and Korea to Japan in ancient times, it was the stage for some historical events such as the Mongol Invasions of Japan in the 13th century and Toyotomi Hideyoshi's invasions of Korea in the 16th century, both of which eventually failed. Is best-known for the Battle of Tsushima in 1905 during the Russo-Japanese War.

つしまかいりゅう 対馬海流 〖海洋〗 the Tsushima Current. Separates from the Japan Current toward the west of Kyushu and flows northward through the Tsushima Strait into the Sea of Japan.

つしまじんじゃ 津島神社 〖神社〗 a Tsushima Shrine. There are about 3,000 Tsushima or related shrines, mainly in the Kantou and Tohoku regions. The head shrine is located in western Aichi Pref. and en-shrines the God of Storms.

つだうめこ 津田梅子〔教育〕 1865-1929. A diplomat and Christian educator, born in Edo. Participated in the Iwakura Mission, lived in and visited the U.S. several times, and taught ITOU HIROBUMI's children back in Japan. In 1900, founded Joshi Eigaku Juku in Tokyo, originally a school to teach English to young women and now called Tsuda Univ., still a women's institution. Also established the first branch of the YWCA in Japan.

つたやじゅうざぶろう 蔦屋重三郎〔芸術〕 1750-1797. A publisher born in Edo. Published story books by SANTOU KYOUDEN and KYOKUTEI BAKIN and UKIYO-E by KITAGAWA UTAMARO, KATSUSHIKA HOKUSAI, and TOUSHUUSAI SHARAKU.

つちいばんすい 土井晩翠〔文芸〕 ⇨ 土井晩翠(どいばんすい)

つちぐも 土蜘蛛〔政治・妖怪〕 a derogatory name for local indigenous clans disobedient to the Yamato Court in ancient times. Literally means "earth spider" because they were said to live in caves and to be regarded as a kind of monster.

つちのえ 戊〔干支〕 the fifth item of JIKKAN. Literally means "yang of soil" or "the elder brother of soil." Its Chinese-style pronunciation is 'bo.'

つちのこ 槌の子 〔妖怪〕 a brown snake with fat trunk. An Unidentified Mysterious Animal.

Is said to jump high. Is also called 'bachihebi.'

つちのと 己〔干支〕 the sixth item of JIKKAN. Literally means "yin of soil" or "the younger brother of soil." Its Chinese-style pronunciation is 'ki.'

つちへん 土偏〔漢字〕 a left-side radical meaning "soil." Is used in kanji such as 地(earth), 坂(slope), and 埋(bury).

つっこみ ツッコミ 〔芸能〕 the straight man. One of the pair in a comic duo. Talks with common sense from a conventional viewpoint and follows the plot in the dialogue. ↔ボケ →漫才

つつじ 躑躅 〔植物〕 an azalea. *Rhododendron*. There are many varieties.

つっぱり 突っ張り〔相撲〕 a technique to thrust at the opponent's chest or shoulder.

つづみ 鼓〔音楽〕 a hand drum. The cylinder is made of wood, and its middle part is narrow. →大鼓; 小鼓

つづら 葛籠〔生活〕 a clothes basket woven with thin slips of bamboo or cypress, with a lid. Is usually painted with persimmon tannin or lacquer.

つなみ 津波〔自然・災害〕 a tsunami, or a tidal wave. Is caused by an earthquake or an eruption of a submarine volcano. When it is likely to occur, a tsunami warning is issued by the Meteorological Agency.

つのかくし 角隠し〔冠婚葬祭・服飾〕 a headdress worn by a bride at a

traditional wedding. The surface is white, and the back is red.

つのだる 角樽 〖酒〗 a two-handled keg. Is lacquered red or black and contains SAKE. Is presented on an auspicious occasion.

つのへん 角偏 〖漢字〗 a left-side radical meaning "horn." Is used in kanji such as 解 (solve) and 触 (contact).

つば 鍔 〖武器〗 a sword guard. Was often decorated minutely in the Edo period.

つばき 椿 〖植物〗 a camellia. *Camellia japonica*. Bears red flowers in early spring.

つばさ つばさ 〖鉄道〗 the express train on the Tohoku and Yamagata Shinkansen. Literally means "a wing." Most Tsubasa trains connect Tokyo with Yamagata in 2 hours 40 minutes, and Yamagata with Shinjou in 45 to 50 minutes.

つばす ツバス 〖食べ物・魚〗 a young yellowtail. This term is used in the Kansai region when the fish is shorter than 40 cm. →鰤(ぶり); メジロ; 鰤(はまち)

つばめ つばめ 〖鉄道〗 the express train on Kyushu Shinkansen. Literally means "a swallow." The Tsubame express connects Hakata with Kumamoto in 50 to 60 minutes, and Hakata with Kagoshima within 2 hours, stopping at every station on its route.

つぶあん 粒餡 〖食べ物〗 chunky sweet adzuki paste. After being boiled, adzuki beans are not sieved but are added to with sugar. ↔漉し餡(こしあん)

つぶらやえいじ 円谷英二 〖映画〗 1901-1970. A film director born in Fukushima Pref. Shot many monster movies and TV dramas using special effects, including a movie *Godzilla*, which was highly evaluated.

つぶらやこうきち 円谷幸吉 〖スポーツ〗 1940-1968. A long-distance runner born in Fukushima Pref. Won a bronze medal for the marathon race in the Tokyo Olympic Games in 1964. Received damage to his legs, lost self-confidence, and committed suicide.

つぼ ツボ 〖医療〗 an acupuncture point, a moxibustion point, or a SHIATSU point. Connects with internal organs through meridians called KEIRAKU. It is said that a human body has more than 300 such points.

つぼ 〜坪 〖建築・単位〗 a unit of measurement for the area of land or a house. One 'tsubo' is about 3.3 square meters.

つぼうちしょうよう 坪内逍遥 〖文芸〗 1859-1935. A novelist, literature critic, and playwright, born in present Gifu Pref. His works include a literature critique, *The Essence of the Novel* (SHOUSETSU SHINZUI), and a translation of *Julius Caesar* by Shakespeare.

つぼきり 坪錐 〖忍者〗 a two-pronged drill. Was used when a ninja opened a round hole on a soft earthen wall to make his way. The ninja stabbed one of the prongs and rotated the other prong to cut a circle in the wall.

つぼにわ 坪庭〖建築〗 a small courtyard. Is created mainly to enjoy its scenery or as a place for meditation, not as a place for physical activities.

つぼね 局 **(1)**〖建築〗 a private room for a court lady in the Imperial Court. **(2)**〖行政〗 a high-ranking woman serving a shogun or the Imperial Court.

つぼやき 壺焼き〖食べ物〗 a turban shell broiled in its shell.

つま (刺身の)妻〖食べ物〗 garnish for sashimi. Often thinly shredded white radish.

つまご 妻籠〖交通・地名〗 Tsumago post town. Is also called 'Tsumago-juku.' Was the 42nd relay station on NAKASENDOU, located in the Kiso Valley in the south of present Nagano Pref. Was one of Japan's first towns to aim at restoring historical sites and structures, as early as in the 1960s. Can be accessed by bus, with a 10-minute ride from JR Nagiso Station.

つまみ 摘み〖酒・食べ物〗 food to stimulate the appetite for alcohol. For example, salted fish guts, dried squid, or cucumber with unrefined soy sauce go well with sake, while boiled green soy beans, fried chicken, and French fried potatoes go well with beer.

つまもの 妻物〖食文化〗 **(1)** decora-

tion for a traditional dish. Flowers or leaves are used. **(2)** garnish, or small decorative side food such as buds of perilla or a young flowered cucumber.

つみれ 摘入〖食べ物〗 a dumpling of ground fish mixed with egg and flour. Eaten boiled, often in broth.

つむぎ 紬〖服飾〗 a textile woven with spun silk thread. Is a little strong but less smooth, compared with other silk fabric. Famous examples include OOSHIMA TSUMUGI, YUUKI TSUMUGI, and KIHACHIJOU.

つむぎいと 紬糸〖服飾〗 spun silk thread. Is thick and has some knots.

つめ 詰め〖茶道〗 the finishing guest at a tea ceremony. Enters the tea room last and plays an important role such as returning the tea bowl to the host after observing it. Is also called 'o-tsume.'

つめばら 詰め腹〖武士〗 compelled hara-kiri. To be forced to commit suicide by cutting the stomach with a sword, without agreeing with the reason.

つや 通夜〖冠婚葬祭〗 a wake, or a vigil for a dead person. Is usually held on the very day when the person has died.

つやもの 艶物〖文楽〗 a dramatic narrative whose theme is a love affair. →義太夫

つゆ 梅雨〖気象〗 the rainy season from June to July. It is said that Hokkaido has no such rainy season.

つゆあけ 梅雨明け〖気象〗 the end

of the rainy season. Usually in July. The exact day varies from region to region.

つゆいり 梅雨入り〖気象〗 the real beginning of the rainy season. Usually in June. The exact day varies from region to region. ↔梅雨明け；入梅

つゆざむ 梅雨寒〖気象〗 chill during the rainy season.

つゆのごろべえ 露の五郎兵衛〖落語〗 1643-1703. A comic storyteller born in Kyoto. Is said to be one of the two founders of comic storytelling, RAKUGO, in the Kansai region. This name was revived by Tsuyu no Gorobee II (1932-2009).

つゆはらい 露払い〖相撲〗 an attendant that precedes the yokozuna into the ring before the ring-entering ceremony. Literally means "dew-sweeper." →土俵入り

つゆばれ 梅雨晴れ〖気象〗 **(1)** a clear period during the rainy season. **(2)** nice weather after the rainy season.

つりかいだん 吊り階段〖忍者〗 a suspended stairway. Is used at a ninja mansion. Can be stored upstairs.

つりがき 釣書き〖冠婚葬祭〗 personal information for a marriage interview called MIAI. Contains personal history and family background.

つりがたな 吊り刀〖忍者〗 hanging a sword. After climbing up to a high place by using a sword for footing, a ninja lifted up the sword with a sword strap. One of the seven techniques of using a sword strap. →下げ緒七術

つりがね 釣鐘〖仏教〗 a temple bell. Is usually made of bronze and has a diameter of 1 to 2 m. Has no clapper inside and is tolled with a large wooden bar called SHUMOKU. Is hung in a belfry of a Buddhist temple.

つりこうこく 吊り広告〖ビジネス〗 a hanging advertisement. Is suspended above passengers from the ceiling of a train.

つりせんとれえ 釣り銭トレー〖ビジネス〗 a small tray for change. In payment, a customer places the bill or coins in the tray, and the shop clerk places the change in it.

つりだし 吊り出し〖相撲〗 a technique to lift up the opponent from the front and carry him out of the ring.

つりてんじょう 吊り天井〖建築〗 a suspended ceiling. Was used to crush to death the person who had entered the room by cutting the suspension.

つりどうろう 釣灯籠〖家具・建築〗 a lantern hung under the eaves. Is often ornamented with openwork.

つりどの 釣殿〖庭園〗 a small garden hut without walls located over or beside a pond.

つりばな 吊り花〖華道〗 a flower or flowers arranged in a container hung from the ceiling.

つりやね 吊り屋根〖相撲〗 a suspended roof above the ring. The roof is in the Shinto-shrine style and originally had four pillars, which were removed because they blocked the spectators' view.

つる 鶴 〔動物〕 a crane. *Gruidae.* Has been considered as a symbol of longevity, together with a tortoise. →丹頂鶴；鶴亀

つるがおかはちまんぐう 鶴岡八幡宮 〔神社〕 Tsurugaoka Hachimangu. Was established in 1063 by Minamoto no Yoriyoshi, an ancestor of Minamoto no Yoritomo, who moved the original precinct to the present location in Kamakura City, Kanagawa Pref. Enshrines Emperor Oujin, Empress Consort Jinguu, and Princess Ookami. A sword named Masatsune, a vermilion-lacquered bow, etc. are National Treasures.

つるがじょう 鶴ヶ城 〔城郭〕 the nickname of Aizu Castle. →会津城

つるかめ 鶴亀 〔動物〕 a crane and a tortoise. Both are considered as auspicious animals, and it is said that a crane lives for a thousand years and a tortoise lives for ten thousand years.

つるぎ つるぎ 〔鉄道〕 the short-distance express train on Hokuriku Shinkansen. Is named after Mt. Tsurugi in Toyama Pref. Connects Toyama with Kanazawa in Ishikawa Pref. in 22 to 23 minutes.

つるぎ 剣 〔武器〕 a double-bladed sword.

つるにょうぼう 鶴女房 〔民話〕 "The Crane Wife" or "Crane's Return of a Favor." A poor young man saved a crane's life. The crane turned into a beautiful girl and repaid his kindness by weaving a kimono with her feathers to sell.

つるのおんがえし 鶴の恩返し 〔民話〕 ⇨鶴女房

つるはせんねんかめはまんねん 鶴は千年、亀は万年 〔精神性〕 "A crane lives for one thousand years, and a tortoise lives for ten thousand years." Cranes and tortoises were symbols of longevity in esoteric Taoism, which was introduced into Japan.

つるやなんぼく 鶴屋南北 〔文芸〕 1755-1829. A playwright for kabuki, born in Edo. His works include *The Ghost Story of Tokaido Yotsuya* (Toukaidou Yotsuya kaidan).

つるれいし 蔓茘枝 〔食べ物・植物〕 ⇨ゴーヤ

つれ 連れ 〔能〕 a supporting actor. An actor who supports a main character is called 'shite-dure,' and an actor who supports the second-main character is called 'waki-dure.'

つれづれぐさ 徒然草 〔文芸・作品〕 *Essays in Idleness*. An essay collection written around 1330 by Yoshida Kenkou. Includes a wide variety of topics such as philosophy, Buddhism, nature, residence options, and hobbies.

つわのちょう 津和野町 〔地名〕 Tsuwano Town. Is located at the western tip of Shimane Pref. Developed as a castle town of the Kamei clan in the Edo period. Is known for its castle, traditional atmosphere, and Gion festival, and is sometimes called a little Kyoto. The novelist MORI OUGAI is from this town.

て

てい 丁 〔干支〕 ⇨丁(ひのと)

ていきんおうらい 庭訓往来 〔教育・書名〕 the name of a popular textbook at a private school in the Edo period. The title literally means "Letters for Home Education," and the content is a collection of letters. It is said to be compiled in the Muromachi period.

ていこくぎかい 帝国議会 〔政治〕 Imperial Diet. Was established in 1890 under the Constitution of the Empire of Japan and dissolved in 1947. Consisted of the House of Representatives and the House of Peers.

ていこくだいがく 帝国大学 〔教育〕 An imperial university before the end of World War II. The University of Tokyo became the first imperial university in 1886, and there were eight other imperial universities, including Kyoto, Tohoku, Kyushu, Hokkaido, Osaka, Nagoya, Seoul, and Taipei. In the new education system after 1947, two universities in colonies were abolished, and the other seven universities became national universities.

ていしゅ 亭主 〔茶道〕 the host or hostess of a formal tea ceremony. Usually wears a kimono.

ていねいご 丁寧語 〔言語〕 an honorific expression to show courtesy to the listener or reader. The honorific expression of a verb is made by conjugating the word end and adding an auxiliary 'desu' or 'masu.'

ていねん 定年 〔職業〕 mandatory retirement age. Most organizations define it at age 60 so far, but many companies are begining to extend it until 65.

ていはつ 剃髪 〔髪〕 to shave one's head. Especially for being a Buddhist monk.

てうち 手討ち 〔武士〕 to kill a lower-ranking person with a sword. A samurai did it in the Edo period, for example, when the person was discourteous, failed at a task, or made a mistake.

てうちうどん 手打ち饂飩 〔食べ物〕 handmade thick white noodles. Flour dough is kneaded and rolled out by hands.

てうちそば 手打ち蕎麦 〔食べ物〕 handmade buckwheat noodles. Buckwheat dough is kneaded and rolled out by hands.

でがいちょう 出開帳 〔仏教〕 exhibition of a secret Buddhist image, away from the home temple. ↔居開帳 →開帳

てかぎ 手鉤 〔忍者〕 a hand key. Was used to climb a wall.

てがきゆうぜん 手描友禅 〔服飾〕 the Yuzen-style textile with hand-drawn patterns.

てがたな 手刀 〔礼儀作法・相撲〕 This

term is usually used in the collocation, 'tegatana wo kiru.' It refers to a gesture of chopping the air with one hand, with the thumb and fingers outstretched but without space between them. A person uses this gesture when passing through a crowd, and a winning sumo wrestler uses this gesture before receiving the prize money.

でがたり 出語り〖文楽・歌舞伎〗 a performance by a narrator and shamisen player who appears in front of the audience in bunraku or kabuki.

てがら 手絡〖服飾〗 a decorative piece of cloth worn on a traditional chignon hairdo for women.

てきじゅく 適塾〖教育〗 the name of a private school of Dutch learning founded in Osaka in 1838 by OGATA KOUAN. Was also called Tekitekisai-juku. Taught medical science and produced many people active in the Meiji Restoration, such as FUKUZAWA YUKICHI and Oomura Masujirou. Developed into Osaka University.

てきや 的屋〖祭礼・ビジネス〗 ⇨香具師(ﾙ)

てこう 手甲〖服飾・忍者〗 ⇨手甲(ﾙ)

てごま 手駒〖将棋〗 a piece in hand. After a player captures the opponent's piece, he or she can put the piece at any vacant square on the board.

でし 弟子〖精神性〗 a disciple, or an apprentice. This term has been widely used in various fields, such

as martial arts, craftsmanship, tea ceremony, religion, and science.

てしおがわ 天塩川〖河川〗 the Teshio River. Flows from Mt. Teshio in northern Hokkaido to the Sea of Japan. Is 256 km long, making it the fourth longest river in Japan.

でじま 出島〖外交・地名〗 the name of a fan-shaped piece of reclaimed land in the port of Nagasaki. Was established in 1633 by the Tokugawa shogunate to segregate the Portuguese because of the national isolation policy. Functioned as the sole window to introduce European culture until the end of the Edo period.

てじめ 手締め〖精神性〗 a ceremonial hand-clapping. People clap hands in unison accompanied by shouting, sometimes at the end of a business banquet. There are several forms. →一本締め；三本締め；大阪締め

でぞめしき 出初式〖年中行事〗 the New Year's ceremony of fire brigades. In addition to the exhibition of firefighting, traditional acrobatics on a ladder are demonstrated.

てだい 手代〖職業〗 a middle-rank shop clerk in the Edo period. Was above DECCHI and under BANTOU. The age was usually from the twenties to thirties.

でづかい 出遣い〖文楽〗 to manipulate a puppet on the condition that the main puppeteer, called OMODUKAI, does not wear a hood to conceal his face.

てづかおさむ 手塚治虫 〖漫画〗 1928-1989. A manga artist born in Osaka. The pioneer of story manga. His works include *Black Jack*, *Buddha*, *Astro Boy* (Tetsuwan Atomu), and *The Stories of Three Adolfs* (Adorufu ni tsugu).

てつがくのみち 哲学の道 〖地名〗 Philosopher's Path, or Philosopher's Walk. Is located along a small canal at the foot of eastern mountains in Kyoto. It is said that a philosopher, Nishida Kitarou, took a walk there in contemplation.

てっかどん 鉄火丼 〖食べ物〗 a bowl of rice topped with sliced raw tuna. Small pieces of dried purple laver are sprinkled on it. Rice is often vinegared.

てっかまき 鉄火巻き 〖食べ物〗 a sushi roll containing raw tuna. Is covered with a sheet of purple laver.

てっけん 鉄拳 〖忍者〗 iron knuckle-dusters. Were worn on the hands when fighting without a sword.

てっこう 手甲 〖服飾・忍者〗 a cover of the wrist and the back of a hand. Was made of leather or cloth and protected the hand from dirt, injury, and solar radiation. Was worn in farmwork, during a journey, or when a samurai or ninja was under arms.

てっこうかぎ 手甲鉤 〖忍者〗 a hand claw. Is equipped with a circle and four long nails and looks like the head of a rake. The user grasps the circle so that the nails aim forward like the nails of Wolverine, who appears in the movie, *X-men*. Was used to block the enemy's sword or to hurt the enemy.

てっさ てっさ 〖食べ物〗 sashimi of pufferfish. This term is mainly used in the Kansai region.

てつじんにじゅうはちごう 鉄人28号 〖漫画〗 *Gigantor*, or *Super Robot 28*. A robot manga and anime. The manga was written and illustrated by Yokoyama Mitsuteru and was published serially in a boys' manga magazine, *Shounen*, from 1956 to 1966.

てっせん 鉄扇 〖武士〗 **(1)** a folding fan with iron ribs. **(2)** an iron stick, whose appearance resembles a folded fan.

てっそうせっこん 鉄双節棍 〖忍者〗 a pair of iron nunchakus.

でっち 丁稚 〖職業〗 an apprentice boy. Lived and worked for a merchant or craftsman in the Edo period.

てっちり てっちり 〖食べ物〗 a one-pot dish of pufferfish, tofu, and vegetables. Eaten after dipping in a mixture of soy sauce and citrus juice. →鉄砲；ポン酢

てっぱんやき 鉄板焼き 〖食べ物〗 teppanyaki. Meat and vegetables are roasted on a hot steel plate at the table.

てつびん 鉄瓶 〖食文化〗 an iron kettle. The area around Morioka City in Iwate Pref. is famous for its production.

てっぽう 鉄砲 **(1)** 〖相撲〗 an exercise of strongly thrusting at a wooden pillar, alternatively with one hand and then the other. **(2)** 〖食べ物〗 the nickname of a pufferfish. Is called so because a person who encounters the poison of a pufferfish may die, like being hit by 'teppou,' meaning "a gun." →河豚(ふぐ)

てっぽうかじ 鉄砲鍛冶 〖武器・科学技術〗 a gunsmith from the 16th to 19th centuries. After being introduced in 1543, guns spread rapidly, and gunsmith guilds formed mainly in the Kyushu and Kansai regions. Examples are Sakai in Osaka, Kunitomo in present Shiga Pref., and Negoro in present Wakayama Pref.

てっぽうでんらい 鉄砲伝来 〖武器・外交〗 the introduction of guns in 1543. Portuguese who were cast up on the coast of TANEGASHIMA Island sold two guns to the local feudal lord.

てっぽうまき 鉄砲巻き 〖寿司〗 a thin sushi roll containing dried strips of a bottle gourd (KANPYOU). →細巻

てっぽうやき 鉄砲焼き 〖食べ物〗 **(1)** grilled squid stuffed with chopped vegetables and its chopped arms. **(2)** spicy grilled pork gut.

てつまり 鉄毬 〖忍者〗 a three-dimensional pointed dagger for throwing. Is said to have been carried in a leather bag.

てつわんあとむ 鉄腕アトム 〖漫画〗 *Astro Boy*. A robot manga and anime. The manga was written and il-

lustrated by TEDUKA OSAMU and was published serially in a boys' manga magazine, *Shounen*, from 1951 to 1967.

てながあしなが 手長足長 〖妖怪〗 Long Arms and Long Legs. A pair of two monsters, sometimes a couple: one has very long arms and the other has very long legs. Different stories about them still exist in different regions such as the Tohoku and Kyushu regions.

てならい 手習い **(1)** 〖書道〗 ⇨習字 **(2)** 〖教育〗 learning.

てぬぐい 手拭い 〖生活・落語〗 a thin cotton hand towel. Is used as a tool to depict the image of everyday goods such as a wallet or a letter in a comic storytelling.

てのめ 手の目 〖妖怪〗 a bugbear with its eyes on the palms. Looks like a blind monk.

てばさき 手羽先 〖食べ物〗 a chicken wing. Eaten deep-fried, grilled, or simmered. The deep-fried type is popular in the Nagoya area.

でぱちか デパ地下 〖食文化・ビジネス〗 a deli and confectionery floor in a department store basement.

でばやし 出囃子 **(1)** 〖歌舞伎〗 on-stage musical accompaniment of kabuki. **(2)** 〖落語〗 a music played when a comedian appears on the stage.

てびねり 手びねり 〖陶磁器〗 to form pottery without using a wheel or cast.

てへん 手偏 〖漢字〗 a left-side radical meaning "hand." Is used in kanji such as 打 (hit), 技 (technique), 抗 (resist), and 押 (push).

てまえ 点前 〖茶道〗 a procedure of making tea in a tea ceremony. There are several ways to serve tea, depending on the guest, the situation, or type of tea itself.

でまえ 出前 〖食文化・ビジネス〗 food delivery. This term implies the food is an a la carte dish, not a course cuisine. →仕出し

でまえばこ 出前箱 〖食文化〗 a delivery box for food delivery.

てまきずし 手巻き寿司 〖食べ物〗 hand-rolled sushi. Is roughly rolled by hand in a cone of purple laver. At a home party, people select ingredients to make hand-rolled sushi for themselves.

てまり 手毬 〖玩具〗 a traditional small handball. A girl would bounce it on the ground while singing.

てみず 手水 〖食文化〗 water to wet rice. When pounding steamed rice into cake, an assistant wet the rice with this water.

てみずや 手水舎 〖宗教・建築〗 ⇨手水舎（ちょうず や）

てみやげ 手土産 〖生活〗 a small present when visiting someone. Usually food or drink. Bringing such a gift is considered to be polite, especially when visiting one's superior or senior.

てやきせんべい 手焼き煎餅 〖食べ物〗 a hand-grilled rice cracker. Is seasoned with soy sauce.

てら 寺 〖仏教・寺院〗 a Buddhist temple. Its origin is said to be the Jetavana Monastery (GION SHOUJA) donated to the Historical Buddha in India. The earliest examples in Japan include the SHITENNOU-JI Temple constructed in Osaka in 593 and the HOURYUU-JI Temple in Nara in 607. There are more than 70,000 temples throughout Japan. A Buddhist image is enshrined, and its architecture usually includes a main hall, a lecture hall, a pagoda, and a residential building for monks. →仏像；七堂伽藍（しちどう がらん）

てらうけせいど 寺請け制度 〖仏教・行政〗 certification system by a temple in the Edo period. A Buddhist temple issued an ID document to certify that its parishioner was not Christian.

てらこや 寺子屋 〖教育〗 a private elementary school in the Edo period. Taught reading, writing, and calculation to children of common people.

てらせん 寺銭 〖ギャンブル〗 a rental fee for a gambling house.

てらだとらひこ 寺田寅彦 〖科学技術〗 1878-1935. A physicist and essayist born in Tokyo. Wrote unique science essays.

てりやき 照り焼き 〖食べ物〗 teriyaki. Chicken or fish grilled after being marinated in the mixture of soy sauce and MIRIN.

てるてるぼうず 照る照る坊主 〖生活〗 a simple small doll to pray for fine weather on the next day. Is made of paper or cloth, has no limbs or hair, and is hung outside under the eaves.

てれびげえむ テレビゲーム〚玩具〛 a video game, or a computer game.

でわ 出羽〚旧国名〛 the old name of Akita and Yamagata Prefs. Was divided into Ugo and Uzen at the Meiji Restoration.

でわさんざん 出羽三山〚山岳〛 Three Mountains of Dewa. Mt. Gassan, Mt. Haguro, and Mt. Yudono. Are located in central Yamagata Pref. Famous as the holy place of mountaineering asceticism.

でわさんち 出羽山地〚山岳〛 the Dewa Mountains. Are located in the Tohoku region, parallel to the Ouu Mountains to the east. Extend from the Shirakami Mountains in the north to Three Mountains of Dewa in the south. The highest peak is Mt. Choukai (2,236 m). Cedar and beech trees grow in abundance.

てん 天〚仏教・美術〛 ⇨天部

てん 点〚言語〛 ⇨読点(とうてん)

てんえ 天衣〚仏教〛 ⇨天衣(てんね)

でんか 伝花〚華道〛 the form and method passed down in each school.

てんかい 天海〚仏教〛 1536-1643. A priest of esoteric Buddhism born in present Fukushima Pref. Had a strong influence on politics and diplomacy of the Tokugawa administration in the early Edo period and founded the KAN'EI-JI Temple in Edo. A political rival of KONCHI-IN SUUDEN. →黒衣(こくえ)の宰相

てんがい 天蓋〚仏教〛 a canopy. An ornament above a Buddhist image.

Is attached on or hung from the ceiling.

てんがいてんにん 天蓋天人〚仏教〛 a heavenly being on the canopy. Twenty-four heavenly beings were engraved on the canopy in the main hall of HOURYUU-JI Temple in Nara Pref. Some of them played instruments such as a lute or a recorder.

でんがく 田楽 **(1)**〚芸能〛 folk dance and music from the Heian to early Muromachi periods. Was originally dance and music for rice planting festivals. **(2)**〚食べ物〛 ⇨田楽豆腐

でんがくどうふ 田楽豆腐〚食べ物〛 skewed grilled tofu with miso. Is also called 'toufu dengaku.'

てんかす 天滓〚食べ物〛 batter flakes remaining after tempura is deep-fried. Are often sprinkled on traditional noodles such as UDON or SOBA. →揚げ玉

てんかとういつ 天下統一〚政治〛 unification of entire Japan. It was an ultimate goal for warlords in the 16th century, who fought against one another to accomplish it. ODA NOBUNAGA had partial success, TOYOTOMI HIDEYOSHI continued the process, and TOKUGAWA IEYASU completed it.

てんかのだいどころ 天下の台所〚地名〛 Nation's Kitchen. The nickname of Osaka in the Edo period because the city was a distribution center of rice and various commodities gathered from all over Japan.

でんぎょうだいし 伝教大師〚仏教〛

⇨最澄

てんぎょうのらん　天慶の乱〚戦争〛 the Tengyou Rebellion. A warrior, TAIRA NO MASAKADO, led the rebellion against the central government and temporarily governed the Kantou region in 939.

てんきんぞく　転勤族〚ビジネス〛 an employee who is frequently transferred to another location.

てんぐ　天狗〚妖怪〛 a monster with a human body, red face, long nose, and wings. Wears the costume of a mountain ascetic, lives deep in the mountain, and can fly. Creates mysterious phenomena in the mountain, but sometimes helps humans.

てんくうのしろ　天空の城〚城郭〛 ⇨ 竹田城跡

てんぐさ　天草〚植物〛 an agar weed. *Gelidium*. The raw material of agar-agar. →寒天

てんぐとびきりのじゅつ　天狗飛切りの術　**(1)**〚剣術〛 the technique of jumping high and cutting down the opponent.　**(2)**〚妖怪〛 the flying technique of a monster called TENGU. A legend says there was a human who had mastered it.

てんぐのつぶて　天狗の礫〚妖怪〛 fafrotskies. A stone or stones flying from somewhere in a mountain. Is said to be thrown by a monster called TENGU.

てんげん　天元〚碁〛 Center Position of Go Board. One of the seven titles in professional GO. The best-of-five title match, 'Tengen-sen,' takes place annually from October to December.

てんざる　天笊〚食べ物〛 chilled buckwheat noodles with tempura, usually topped with shredded laver. Eaten by dipping into special sauce. →笊蕎麦(ざるそば)；天婦羅蕎麦(てんぷらそば)；天盛り

てんし　天子〚言語・天皇〛 an old term for the Emperor.

てんじく　天竺〚国名〛 India. This name had been used from ancient times until the Meiji period.

てんじくよう　天竺様〚仏教・建築〛 ⇨大仏様

てんじてんのう　天智天皇〚天皇〛 Emperor Tenji. 626–671. The 38th, on the throne from 668 to 671. The second prince of Emperor Jomei and Empress Kougyoku, an elder brother of Emperor Tenmu, and the father of Empress Jitou. Destroyed the Soga clan and conducted the Taika Reform of 645 in cooperation with NAKATOMI NO KAMATARI. Dispatched troops to assist Paekche in 661 but was defeated in 663. Relocated the capital to present Shiga Pref. Laid the foundation for the centralized administration system called RITSURYOU-SEI. →大化の改新

てんじぶろっく　点字ブロック〚交通〛 a braille block system. Studded zones in a walkway or railroad station guide visually impaired people. Was invented in Japan in 1965.

てんじゃ　点者〚文芸〛 an evaluator of traditional rhyming poems such as HAIKU or TANKA.

てんしゅかく 天守閣〖建築〗 a donjon. Functioned not only as an observation tower but also as a symbol of the power of a feudal lord.

てんしゅきょう 天主教 〖キリスト教〗 the term to refer to Roman Catholicism in and before the early 20th century in Japan.

てんしゅどう 天主堂〖キリスト教〗 a cathedral of Roman Catholicism.

てんしょう 天正 〖時代〗 an era name from 1573 to 1592. In the Azuchi-Momoyama period.

てんしょういがのらん 天正伊賀の乱〖忍者・戦争〗 Tenshou Iga War, or Attack on Iga in Tenshou. ODA NOBUNAGA destroyed a self-governing ninja province, Iga, in present Mie Pref. in 1581.

てんしょうけんおうしせつ 天正遣欧使節〖外交・キリスト教〗 Tenshou Mission to Europe of 1582. Three Christian feudal lords in Kyushu dispatched four boys aged 14 or 15 to see Pope Gregory XIII. They returned in 1590. →キリシタン大名

てんじょうてんげゆいがどくそん 天上天下唯我独尊〖仏教〗 "Only I am holy throughout heaven and earth." It is said that the Historical Buddha uttered these words after taking seven steps immediately after his birth. →誕生仏; 灌仏会(かんぶつえ)

てんしん 点心 **(1)**〖禅〗 refreshments at a Zen temple. **(2)**〖茶道〗 a light meal served after a tea ceremony.

てんじん 天神〖神道〗 **(1)** the deified spirit of SUGAWARA NO MICHIZANE, or a Shinto shrine dedicated to the spirit. Sugawara no Michizane, an aristocrat, scholar, and poet in the 9th century, was exiled to Dazaifu in present Fukuoka Pref. and died there. After his death, the government honored his vengeful spirit as a deity. →天満宮 **(2)**⇨天(あま)つ神

てんじんばしすじしょうてんがい 天神橋筋商店街〖地名〗 Tenjinbashi-suji Shopping Street. Japan's longest shopping street located in Osaka. Stretches 2.6 km from north to south. There are approximately 600 shops such as bars, restaurants, apparel stores, bookstores, and other variety of business.

てんじんまつり 天神祭り 〖祭礼〗 Tenjin Festival. Is held on July 24 and 25 at Tenmanguu in Osaka. On the second day, portable shrines are carried on the river by the fleet of about 100 decorative boats. One of the Three Great Festivals of Japan. →大阪天満宮

てんすいおけ 天水桶〖生活〗 a rainwater barrel. Reserved rainwater for fire prevention in olden times.

てんそんこうりん 天孫降臨 〖神話〗 the advent of the grandson of the Sun Goddess. The Sun Goddess gave her grandson named NINIGI NO MIKOTO the Three Sacred Treasures of the Imperial Family and dispatched him to rule the Central Land of Reeds, namely Japan. He descended from the High Celestial Plain to Mt. Takachiho, located in

Hyuuga, the southwestern part of present Miyazaki Pref. →天照大神(あまてらすおおみかみ)；三種の神器；高天原(たかまがはら)；葦原(あし)のはら)の中つ国

てんだいしゅう　天台宗〖仏教〗 the Tendai sect. Was originally founded in China in the 6th century by Zhi-yi, based on the Lotus Sutra. A priest named SAICHOU introduced it to Japan in 806 and founded the Japanese Tendai sect by combining Zen and esoteric Buddhism. The head temple is ENRYAKU-JI Temple on Mt. Hiei, Shiga Pref.

てんだいみっきょう　天台密教〖仏教〗 ⇨天台宗

てんちかいびゃく　天地開闢〖神話〗 the beginning of the world. The chaos separated into the heavens and the earth, and the first three deities appeared. Namely, AME-NO MINAKANUSHI NO KAMI, TAKAMIMUSUHI NO KAMI, and KAMIMUSUHI NO KAMI.

てんちじん　天地人〖精神性〗 heaven, earth, and humans. Three elements forming the cosmos. This idea is applied to various fields, from flower arrangement to mahjong.

てんちゃ　点茶〖茶道〗 to make green tea by whipping hot water and tea powder.

てんちゅう　天誅〖思想〗 punishment by humans on behalf of heaven. This concept was employed when masterless samurai killed their political enemies, mainly in Kyoto, at the end of the Edo period.

でんちゅう　殿中〖武士・政治〗 the residence of a shogun in the Edo period. To draw a sword in such a place was prohibited.

てんちょうせつ　天長節〖暦・天皇〗 the old name of the Emperor's Birthday. This term was changed to TENNOU TANJOUBI in 1948.

てんつゆ　天つゆ〖調味料〗 dipping sauce for tempura. Is made of soy sauce, MIRIN, and DASHI.

でんでんだいこ　でんでん太鼓〖玩具〗 a small rotating toy drum. Consists of two heads, two balls attached on the sides with strings, and a handle. When the handle is rotated, two balls beat the two heads almost at the same time.

てんどう　天道〖仏教〗 the Realm of Heavens. The top realm among the Six Realms of Existence. Heavenly beings dwell in this realm. The realm where a person is reborn is decided according to deeds in the previous life. →六道；輪廻(りん)ね)；天人(てんにん)

でんとうてきけんぞうぶつぐん　伝統的建造物群〖法律〗 Groups of Traditional Buildings. Include groups of traditional buildings with historic value and scenery. Are defined by the Law for the Protection of Cultural Properties.

でんとうてきけんぞうぶつぐんほぞんちく　伝統的建造物群保存地区〖法律〗 Important Preservation Districts for Groups of Traditional Buildings. Are classified by the national government and can get financial assistance and technical instruction from the national and local governments.

てんとじ 天綴じ 〖食べ物〗 hot buckwheat noodles or thick wheat noodles with shrimp tempura and soft scrambled eggs.

てんどん 天丼 〖食べ物〗 a bowl of rice topped with tempura. A little thick sauce is sprinkled over it. The ingredients of tempura are often shrimp and vegetables.

てんにょ 天女 〖仏教〗 a heavenly maiden. Dwells in the heaven of the Six Realms of Existence and can fly.

てんにん 天人 〖仏教〗 a heavenly being. Dwells in the heaven of the Six Realms of Existence and can fly. Is often depicted as a woman.

てんね 天衣 〖仏教〗 a long cloth hung from the shoulder by a Bodhisattva or heavenly being. → 菩薩；天人(にん)

てんねんきねんぶつ 天然記念物 〖法律〗 a Natural Monument. As of August 1, 2016, 1,021 items, including animals, plants, and geological and mineral formations of high scientific value, have been designated by the Agency for Cultural Affairs.

てんのう 天皇 〖天皇〗 an Emperor. Its kanji means "heavenly sovereign." The first was Emperor Jinmu, and the current Emperor Akihito is the 125th. The *Chronicles of Japan* (NIHONSHOKI) mentions the events from Emperor Jinmu to the 41st Emperor Jitou,

of which the earlier ones are said to be legendary. The Emperor's political power and authority have been changing throughout Japanese history. The present Constitution of Japan considers the Emperor to be the symbol of the nation. Has been called various names or titles such as 'ookimi,' 'sumeramikoto,' 'mikado,' and 'tenshi.'

てんのうきかんせつ 天皇機関説 〖天皇・政治〗 Emperor-as-Organ-of-the-State Theory. Says that the state has sovereignty and the Emperor is an organ of the state. Was advocated by a jurist, Minobe Tatsukichi, and was popular in the Taishou era, but was dismissed in the Shouwa era after the ultra-nationalists gained power.

てんのうせい 天皇制 〖天皇・政治〗 the Emperor system of Japan. In the modern system before the end of World War II, the Emperor was sacred and had sovereignty. In the present system, the Emperor is the symbol of the state and of the unity of the people.

てんのうたんじょうび 天皇誕生日 〖祝日・天皇〗 Emperor's Birthday. December 23. A national holiday to celebrate the birthday of current Emperor Akihito.

てんのうはい 天皇杯 〖スポーツ〗 the Emperor's Cup. Is given to the national champion of several sports such as soccer, basketball, and judo.

てんぴょう 天平 〖時代〗 an era name from 729 to 749. In the Nara

period.

てんぴょうしょうほう 天平勝宝〔時代〕 an era name from 749 to 757. In the Nara period.

てんぴょうのいらか 天平の甍〔文芸・作品〕 *The Roof Tile of Tempyo*. A historical novel published in 1957 by INOUE YASUSHI. Describes the struggle and success of a Tang priest, GANJIN, and his disciples when they came to Japan in the 8th century.

てんぴょうぶんか 天平文化〔時代〕 the Tenpyou culture in the 8th century. Developed under the powerful centralized administration system and influence from the Tang culture, and had strong Buddhist features. Provincial temples in local areas and their head temple, TOUDAI-JI, in Nara, were established, and many Buddhist sculptures, including the original Great Buddha, were created. Several works of classic literature, including *Records of Ancient Matters* (KOJIKI), *Chronicles of Japan* (NIHONSHOKI), and *Anthology of Myriad Leaves* (MAN'YOUSHUU), were compiled.

てんびんぼう 天秤棒〔ビジネス〕 a yoke, or a shouldering pole. Was used to carry two equal loads in olden times.

てんぶ 天部〔仏教〕 a deva. The generic term for celestial beings including SHITENNOU, BON-TEN, TAISHAKU-TEN, or BENZAI-TEN. They were originally ancient deities in India and were incorporated into Buddhism as guardians.

でんぶ 田麩〔食べ物〕 mashed pale-fresh fish seasoned with sugar, mirin, and soy sauce. Fish is first boiled, the boiled fish is mashed, the mashed fish is roasted with sugar, mirin, and soy sauce, and then it is dried.

てんぶくろ 天袋〔建築〕 a small storage space above different-levelled shelves. Is attached on the ceiling and has sliding doors. ↔地袋 →違い棚

てんぷら 天麩羅, 天婦羅〔食べ物〕 tempura. Fish and vegetables deep-fried in a mixture of flour, egg, and water. Eaten with salt, or after dipping into a special sauce with grated white radish or ginger. Is said to have developed from European deep-fried food introduced to Japan in the 16th century.

てんぷらそば 天婦羅蕎麦〔食べ物〕 hot buckwheat noodles topped with shrimp tempura. Chilled variation is called TEN-ZARU.

てんぽう 天保〔時代〕 an era name from 1830 to 1844. In the late Edo period. →天保山; 天保銭; 天保の改革

てんぽうざん 天保山〔山岳〕 Mt. Tenpou. Is located in Minato Ward, Osaka City. Was man-made in the 1830s during the Tenpou era in the Edo period. Was known as the lowest mountain in Japan, with its peak only 4.5 m above the sea level. But in 2014, Mt. Hiyori in Miyagi

Pref. was recognized as the lowest mountain (3 m), and Mt. Tenpou became the second lowest.

てんぽうせん 天保銭 〖経済〗 an oval-shaped copper coin. Began to be minted in 1835 and was circulated until 1891.

てんぽうのかいかく 天保の改革 〖政治〗 Tenpou Reform. Was conducted from 1841 to 1843 by MIZUNO TADAKUNI. Forbade luxury, controlled publication, tried to lower the commodity prices by dissolving guilds called KABU-NAKAMA, and recommended that those who had moved from a rural area to Edo should go home. Also attempted to confiscate the feudal lords' land around Edo and Osaka and to offer other land instead. However, feudal lords and direct vassals opposed it, and Mizuno lost his position.

てんぽうりんいん 転法輪印 〖仏教〗 the *mudra* when the Historical Buddha preached the dharma for the first time. Both hands are placed in front of the chest.

てんません 伝馬船 〖交通〗 a small barge in early modern or modern times. Usually a single person pulled an oar.

てんまんぐう 天満宮 〖神社〗 a Tenmangu shrine, also called TENJIN. Enshrines SUGAWARA NO MICHIZANE, who is worshipped as a deity of study. The two head shrines are KITANO TENMANGUU in Kyoto and DAZAIFU TENMANGUU in Fukuoka.

てんむす 天むす 〖食べ物〗 a rice ball with shrimp tempura. Was invented in Tsu City, Mie Pref., in the 1950s, but it is now especially popular in Nagoya.

てんむてんのう 天武天皇 〖天皇〗 Emperor Tenmu. ?-686. The 40th, on the throne from 673 to 686. The third prince of Emperor Jomei and Empress Kougyoku, a younger brother of Emperor Tenji, and the husband of Empress Jitou. After the death of Emperor Tenji, killed Crown Prince Ootomo and was enthroned in 673 after the Jinshin War in 672. Reinforced the centralized administration system called RITSURYOU-SEI. →壬申(じん)の乱

てんめいのききん 天明の飢饉 〖災害〗 Tenmei Famine. From 1781 to 1789, unseasonable weather, cold rains, and the eruption of Mt. Asama caused a severe famine. Killed more than 900 thousand people, triggered riots everywhere, and became one of the causes for the fall of TANUMA OKITSUGU, the then prime minister, from power.

てんめいのたいか 天明の大火 〖災害〗 Conflagration at Tenmei. Occurred in Kyoto in 1788. Most urban areas of Kyoto were destroyed, including the Imperial Palace.

てんもくぢゃわん 天目茶碗 〖茶道〗 an iron-glazed, shallow conical tea bowl with a low bottom rim. Is named after Mt. Tenmoku, a holy place of Zen Buddhism in China, from which a priest brought back a tea bowl in the Kamakura period.

てんもり 天盛り 〖食べ物〗 chilled buckwheat noodles with tempura. Eaten by dipping into special sauce. →盛り蕎麦(もり); 天婦羅蕎麦(てんぷらそば); 天笊(てんざる)

てんもんかた 天文方 〖科学技術・行政〗 an astronomical officer, or astronomical bureau in the Tokugawa shogunate. Duties included astronomical observation, topographical surveys, calendar compilation, and translation of Dutch documents.

てんらんじあい 天覧試合 〖スポーツ・天皇〗 a game or match in front of the Emperor.

てんりきょう 天理教 〖宗教〗 Tenri-kyo, or Religion of the Divine Wisdom. One of the oldest new religions in Japan. Was founded in 1838 by Nakayama Miki, a farmer's wife who came to be viewed as a living deity. She composed hymns, scripture, and dances that are still central to the religion. Tenri-kyo combines Shinto beliefs with simple values of peasant living, along with the obligation to achieve social good in one's life. Has a strong organization, many followers, diverse facilities that include a university, and thousands of shrines throughout the world. Boasts about two million believers as of 2018, according to its Internet site.

てんりゅうがわ 天竜川 〖河川〗 the Tenryuu River. Flows from Lake Suwa in Nagano Pref. to the Pacific Ocean in Hamamatsu City, Shizuoka Pref. Its length is 213 km, which makes it the 9th longest river in Japan. The thrilling boat tours are famous.

てんりゅうじ 天龍寺 〖寺院〗 Tenryu-ji Temple. A main temple of the Tenryuu-ji school of the Rinzai sect, ranked first among the Five Zen Temples of Kyoto. Was founded in 1345 by MUSOU SOSEKI with financial support from ASHIKAGA TAKAUJI to pray for the soul of Emperor Godaigo. The garden is a special historic site, and the whole temple was designated a World Heritage Site in 1994. →臨済宗

てんりゅうじぶね 天龍寺船 〖交通・寺院〗 a Tenryuu-ji trading vessel. Was dispatched to the Yuan dynasty of China in 1342 to earn the construction costs for the Tenryuu-ji Temple.

てんりょう 天領 〖行政〗 a domain directly governed by the shogunate in the Edo period. Did not belong to any feudal domains, called 'han.' Examples were Osaka, Kyoto, Sakai, Nagasaki, and several important areas with harbors or mines.

と

と 都 〖行政〗 a prefecture. A local autonomous public entity containing cities or villages. Tokyo is the only 'to.' →都道府県

と ～斗 〖単位〗 A unit of liquid or rice. About 18 liters. Ten SHOU equal one 'to.' Ten 'to' equal one KOKU.

どいたけお 土居健郎 〖人文学〗 1920-2009. A psychiatrist born in Tokyo. His works include *The Anatomy of Dependence* (AMAE NO KOUZOU).

どいばんすい 土井晩翠 〖文芸〗 1871-1952. A poet and scholar of English literature born in Miyagi Pref. Translated the works of Homer and Byron and wrote the words of a song, "Koujou no Tsuki."

とう 唐 〖国名〗 Tang. A Chinese dynasty from 618 to 907. Had great cultural and political influence on Japan through envoys.

とう 塔 〖仏教・建築〗 a pagoda. Developed from a stupa that contained Buddha's ashes. There are several types of pagodas including two-, three-, five-, and thirteen-story ones. →多宝塔；三重塔；五重塔；十三重塔

とう 籘 〖植物〗 a cane palm, or a rattan. *Calameae*. Is used to make chairs and baskets.

どう 胴 〖剣術〗 **(1)** a torso protector used in kendou. Protects only the front part of the wearer. **(2)** a kendo technique to strike the opponent's torso.

どう 道 〖行政〗 a prefecture. A local autonomous public entity containing cities or villages. Hokkaido is the only 'dou.' →都道府県

どう ～道 〖精神性〗 Literally means "way," "route," or "road." An attempt to master the ultimate skills and mentality by practicing something. For example, KENDOU (Japanese-style fencing) is "sword-way," SHODOU (calligraphy) is "writing-way," and SADOU (tea ceremony) is "tea-way."

とういつしらぎ 統一新羅 〖国名〗 Unified Silla. After conquering Paekche in 660 and Koguryo (KOUKURI) in 668, Silla governed the entire Korean Peninsula. Was destroyed in 935 by Koryo (KOURAI).

とうえい 東映 〖映画・企業名〗 Toei Co., Ltd. A motion picture company established in 1951. Its works include many samurai, yakuza, and war films.

とうえいうずまさえいがむら 東映太秦映画村 〖映画〗 Toei Kyoto Studio Park. Visitors can observe the shooting of scenes in historical dramas and can walk around the film set that simulates streets in the Edo period.

どうおんいぎご 同音異義語 〖言語〗 a homonym. The Japanese

language has a great number of homonyms. For example, 'koukai' can be interpreted as "navigation," "regret," "renewal," "opening," or "high sea." 'Ishi' can be "doctor," "stone," "will," or "suicide by hanging."

とうか 刀架〖武器〗 ⇨刀掛け

とうかいどう 東海道　**(1)**〖地名〗 the name of an administrative district before the Meiji Restoration in 1868. Consisted of present Aichi, Shizuoka, Yamanashi, Kanagawa, Tokyo, Saitama, Chiba, and Ibaraki Prefs., and central to northern Mie Pref.　**(2)**〖交通〗 the Toukaidou Highway in the Edo period. Connected Edo with Kyoto, with 53 relay stations. Went through present Kanagawa, Shizuoka, Aichi, Mie, and Shiga Prefs.

とうかいどうごじゅうさんつぎ 東海道五十三次〖絵画・作品〗 *Fifty-Three Relay Stations of the Tokaidou Highway*. A woodblock painting produced by Andou Hiroshige around 1832 to 1834. Contains 55 pieces including the starting point, Nihon-bashi in Edo, and the final point, Sanjou in Kyoto.

とうかいどうしんかんせん 東海道新幹線〖鉄道〗 Tokaido Shinkansen. Connects Tokyo with Shin-Osaka in Osaka Pref. Started service in 1964 to assist transportation needs for Japan's most densely populated areas such as Tokyo, Kanagawa, Aichi, Kyoto, and Osaka Prefs., and for the Tokyo Olympics

in the same year. The busiest Shinkansen route in terms of the numbers of passengers and trains. The fastest super express, Nozomi, takes 2 hours 30 minutes from Tokyo to Shin-Osaka. Other express trains are named Hikari and Kodama.

とうかいどうちゅうひざくりげ 東海道中膝栗毛〖文芸・作品〗 *Shank's Mare*. A comic travel novel published in parts from 1802 to 1809 by Jippensha Ikku. In the novel, two Edoites, Yajirobee and Kitahachi, walk to Osaka along the Toukaidou Highway.

とうかいどうよつやかいだん 東海道四谷怪談〖歌舞伎・作品〗 *The Ghost Story of Tokaido Yotsuya*. A kabuki play written by Tsuruya Nanboku and first performed in 1825. A masterless samurai, Iemon, killed his wife, Oiwa, by poison, and she became a revengeful ghost.

とうがらし 唐辛子〖調味料・植物〗 a red pepper. *Capsicum annuum*. Was introduced into Japan in the 16th century.

とうがん 冬瓜〖食べ物・植物〗 a wax gourd. *Benincasa cerifera*. Eaten boiled.

どうがんじ 渡岸寺〖寺院〗 Douganji Temple. Is located in northeastern Shiga Pref. Enshrines the Eleven-headed Bodhisattva of Mercy, which is a National Treasure. → 十一面観音

とうき 陶器〖陶磁器〗 pottery. Is fired at 800 to 1,200 degrees

Celsius. Is water-absorbent and glazed. Harder than earthenware (doki) and softer than porcelain (JIKI).

とうき　登器 〖忍者〗 the generic term of tools for climbing walls or fences. Includes iron hook with rope (KAGINAWA), an extendable rake (SHINOBI KUMADE), and a ladder. →忍器(にん)

どうぎ　道着 〖武術〗 a garment for martial arts.

とうきゅう　東急 〖鉄道〗 ⇨東京急行電鉄

とうぎゅう　闘牛 〖娯楽〗 bullfighting. Different from the Spanish one in that two bulls fight against each other. Is held in Ehime, Niigata, Okinawa, and Shimane Prefs.

どうきょう　道教 〖宗教〗 Taoism. Influenced Japanese religious traditions such as the yin-yang way (ONMYOU-DOU) and KOUSHIN SHINKOU, though it is not clear when and how it was introduced to Japan.

どうきょう　道鏡 〖仏教〗 ⇨弓削道鏡(ゆげの どうきょう)

どうきょう　銅鏡 〖考古〗 a round-shaped bronze mirror in ancient times. Its back is ornamented with reliefs of deities or imaginary animals. Many of them were excavated from tumuli.

とうきょうおりんぴっく　東京オリンピック 〖スポーツ〗 the Tokyo Olympic Games. **(1)** Was held in 1964. The first Olympic Games held in Asia. Included 20 sports and 163 events, in which 5,586 athletes from 94 countries participated. **(2)** Will be held in August 2020. **(3)** Was planned to be held in 1940, but was cancelled because of World War II.

とうきょうきゅうこうでんてつ　東京急行電鉄 〖鉄道〗 Tokyu Corporation. One of the 16 major private railway operators of Japan. With its seven lines, it mainly serves in the south of Tokyo city proper, Kawasaki, and Yokohama. Some trains on the Touyoko Line (Shibuya to Yokohama), Meguro Line (Meguro to Den'en-choufu, both in Tokyo), and Den'en-toshi Line (Shibuya to Chuuou Rinkan in Kanagawa) go directly to other suburban railways, through the Tokyo Metro lines.

とうきょうこくさいくうこう　東京国際空港 〖交通〗 Tokyo International Airport. Is commonly known as Haneda Airport (HND). Is located in the southeast of Tokyo city proper. Started operation in 1931, and after the period of the U.S. Occupation from 1945 to 1952, it developed extensively as an international hub airport. Handles 70 million passengers annually, which makes it the fifth busiest airport in the world. Has three terminals, and only the international terminal is open 24 hours a day. From the airport, passengers can get to the metropolitan area and tourist spots by Tokyo Monorail, Keikyu train, bus, or taxi.

とうきょうこくりつはくぶつかん
東京国立博物館 〔博物館〕 the Tokyo National Museum. Was founded in 1872 and moved to the Ueno area of Tokyo in 1882. Stores fine art and crafts, historical archives, archaeological relics, and folk material. The collection contains more than 1,170 thousand items including 88 National Treasures, as of March 2016.

とうきょうさいばん
東京裁判 〔戦争〕 ⇨極東国際軍事裁判

とうきょうしょうけんとりひきじょ
東京証券取引所〔ビジネス〕 Tokyo Stock Exchange. Was established in 1949. Is located in Kabuto-chou, Tokyo. Lists more than 3,000 companies in total, as of 2018.

とうきょうすかいつりい
東京スカイツリー 〔娯楽〕 Tokyo Skytree. Is a broadcasting tower, with commercial and entertainment facilities, located in Sumida City in the northeast part of central Tokyo. Reaches 634 m in height, making it the tallest tower in the world, and the second tallest construction after Burj Khalifa. Since it was completed and opened to public in 2012, it has attracted visitors with the view of Mt. Fuji and much of the Kantou Plain from its 350 and 450 m-high observation decks. At night, the tower can be seen with its illumination patterns. Is within walking distance from the subway and Tobu line stations.

とうきょうだいがく
東京大学 〔教育〕 University of Tokyo. A leading national university in Japan. Was founded in 1877, and is now at the highest level with respect to education, research, difficulty of admission, and production of human resources, among all Japanese universities.

とうきょうだいくうしゅう
東京大空襲 〔戦争〕 the Great Tokyo Air Raid. Occurred on March 10th, 1945. About 300 Boeing 29s attacked Tokyo, and approximately 100,000 people died.

とうきょうたわあ
東京タワー 〔娯楽〕 Tokyo Tower. Was built in 1958 by Naitou Tachuu. The height is 333 m. The main observation deck is 150 m-high, and the special observation deck is 250 m-high.

とうきょうちかてつ
東京地下鉄〔鉄道〕 **(1)**⇨都営地下鉄 **(2)**⇨東京メトロ

とうきょうでぃずにいりぞおと
東京ディズニーリゾート〔娯楽〕 Tokyo Disney Resort. Is located in Urayasu City, Chiba Pref. Includes Tokyo Disneyland, which opened in 1983, and Tokyo Disney Sea, which opened in 2001. Is operated by Oriental Land Co., Ltd.

とうきょうと
東京都 〔都道府県〕 Tokyo Metropolis. Is also called Tokyo Pref. or Tokyo Metropolitan Pref. Is located on the Kantou Plain, facing Tokyo Bay. Its area, 2,191 km^2, is relatively small, but it has by far the largest population of Japanese prefectures, 13,700,000,

as of 2017. The metropolitan government office is in Shinjuku City. Can be roughly divided into three parts: the administrative, industrial, and commercial areas in Tokyo city proper in the east, the residential areas in the middle, and the hilly forested areas in the west. The Izu and Ogasawara Islands also belong to the Tokyo Metropolis. Since TOKUGAWA IEYASU started his shogunate in Edo in 1603, it has been practically the seat of government. In 1869, soon after the Meiji Restoration, Emperor Meiji moved from Kyoto, and Edo was renamed Tokyo and officially became the capital of Japan. Used to be part of Musashi.

とうきょうとちょう　東京都庁 〖行政〗　Tokyo Metropolitan Government. Administers Tokyo Metropolis, employing approximately 160,000 staff, including officials for police, firefighting, and education. The budget size exceeds 6 trillion yen, only to include general expenses. It has no national function at all, but a leading politician often becomes the governor because of its huge scale.

とうきょうにじゅうさんく 東京23区 〖地名〗　Tokyo city proper. Consists of 23 special cities, which are Adachi, Arakawa, Bunkyou, Chiyoda, Chuuou, Edogawa, Itabashi, Katsushika, Kita, Koutou, Meguro, Minato, Nakano, Nerima, Oota, Setagaya, Shibuya, Shinagawa, Shinjuku, Suginami, Sumida, Taitou, and Toshima.

とうきょうびじゅつがっこう　東京美術学校 〖美術・教育〗　Tokyo Fine Arts School. The present Faculty of Fine Arts at Tokyo University of the Arts. Was established in 1887. The first president was OKAKURA TENSHIN.

とうきょうぶんかざいけんきゅうしょ　東京文化財研究所 〖人文学・研究機関〗　the National Research Institute for Cultural Properties, Tokyo. An independent administrative institution. Was founded in 1930 in Ueno, Tokyo.

とうきょうめとろ　東京メトロ 〖鉄道〗　Tokyo Metro. One of the 16 major private railway operators of Japan, and one of the two subway systems in Tokyo, along with the Toei Subway. Of its nine lines, seven lines adopt through-line service on both ends. For example, Tokyo Metro Hanzomon Line connects Shibuya with Oshiage, but many trains go on via Tokyu Den'en-toshi Line to Kanagawa Pref. and via Tobu Skytree Line to Saitama Pref. In 1927, it started operation between Ueno and Asakusa as Japan's first subway system.

とうきょうものれえる　東京モノレール 〖鉄道〗　Tokyo Monorail. Connects Haneda Airport with Hamamatsucho Station of Japan Railway in the east of Tokyo city proper. Its length is 18 km.

とうきょうわん 東京湾 〖湾〗　Tokyo

Bay. Is located in the southeast of Tokyo, surrounded by the Bousou Peninsula in Chiba Pref. and the Miura Peninsula in Kanagawa Pref. Is connected to the Pacific Ocean to its south. Along the coast are the two industrial areas, namely, the Keiyou Industrial Zone in the east, and the Keihin Industrial Zone in the west.

とうぐう 東宮 〖天皇〗 another term for the Crown Prince. →皇太子

とうぐうごしょ 東宮御所 〖天皇〗 the palace of the Crown Prince. When the Imperial Palace was in Kyoto, the palace of the Crown Prince was toward the east of the Imperial Palace.

どうぐはいけん 道具拝見 〖茶道〗 appreciation of the tea utensils after drinking tea. The main guest asks some standardized questions about topics such as the type of tea caddy or the person who made the tea scoop, while other guests are observing the utensils.

どうくんいじ 同訓異字 〖漢字〗 two or more kanji with the same pronunciation and similar but different meanings. For example, 聞 and 聴 both have a pronunciation of 'kiku,' but the former is translated "to hear" and the latter is "to listen."

とうけい 闘鶏 〖娯楽〗 cockfighting. Has been held from ancient times in Japan. Was legally prohibited several times but still exists at present.

とうげい 陶芸 〖陶磁器〗 ceramic art. →陶器；磁器

とうけいじ 東慶寺 〖寺院〗 Tokeiji. Was founded in 1285 by a nun Kakusan-ni, wife of HOUJOU TOKIMUNE, after her husband's death. Is located in Kamakura, Kanagawa Pref. Has been best known as a refuge temple for women for 600 years, where men could not enter until 1902. →縁切寺

とうけん 闘犬 〖娯楽〗 dogfighting. Was popular in the Kamakura period.

どうけん 銅剣 〖考古〗 a bronze sword in ancient times. There were two types: one for a battle and the other for a ritual.

どうげん 道元 〖仏教〗 1200-1253. A Zen priest born in Kyoto and the founder of the Soutou sect. Visited the Sung dynasty from 1223 to 1228. After coming back to Japan, founded EIHEI-JI Temple in present Fukui Pref. in 1244. →曹洞宗

とうこう 刀工 〖武器〗 ⇨刀鍛冶

とうごうへいはちろう 東郷平八郎 〖軍事〗 1847-1934. A naval director born in Kagoshima Pref. Defeated the Russian Baltic Fleet in the Sea of Japan in 1905. →日本海海戦

どうごおんせん 道後温泉 〖温泉〗 the name of a hot spring in Matsuyama, Ehime. One of the oldest hot springs in Japan. Prince Shoutoku is said to have visited here in the 6th century. Is the location of Natsume Souseki's novel *Botchan* (1905). In and around the hot spring, visitors can see things derived from the novel and people disguised as characters in it. Is accessible from central Matsuyama by tram in 20 minutes.

とうさんどう 東山道 **(1)**〖地名〗 the name of an administrative district before the Meiji Restoration in 1868. Consisted of all the six prefectures in the present Tohoku region and present Tochigi, Gunma, Nagano, Gifu, and Shiga Prefs. **(2)** 〖交通〗 Tousandou Highway. The main route from Kyoto to the Tohoku region before the Meiji Restoration. Went through present Shiga, Gifu, Nagano, Gunma, Tochigi, Fukushima, Miyagi, Iwate, Yamagata, and Akita Prefs. The section between Kyoto and Gunma overlaps with NAKASENDOU Highway.

とうじ 冬至 〖暦〗 the winter solstice. One of the 24 seasonal nodes. Around December 22 in the current calendar. People take a citron bath and eat squash. →二十四節気（にじゅうしせっき）

とうじ 東寺 〖寺院〗 Toji. The head temple of the Shingon sect, located in Kyoto. The official name is Kyouougokoku-ji. Was founded in 794 by Emperor Kanmu and was bestowed to a priest, KUUKAI, in 823 by Emperor Saga. Possesses many National Treasures including the main hall, the five-story pagoda, mandalas, and statues. Was designated a World Heritage Site in 1994. →真言宗；桓武天皇

とうじ 湯治 〖温泉・医療〗 a hot-spring cure, or recuperation by hot springs. To heal disease or injury, by staying at a spa for a while.

どうし 動詞 〖言語〗 a verb. The dictionary form ends with an 'u' sound, such as 'hashiru' (to run), 'kaku' (to write), and 'taberu' (to eat).

どうし 導師 〖仏教〗 the leading priest of a Buddhist rite.

どうじ 童子 〖仏教〗 a servant boy at a temple. Is also used to refer to an attendant of a Buddha, Bodhisattva, or Wisdom King, such as SEITAKA DOUJI, or to refer to a demon, such as OOEYAMA SHUTEN DOUJI.

とうじき 陶磁器 〖陶磁器〗 ceramics. The generic term for pottery and porcelain.

どうしゃくが 道釈画 〖絵画〗 a human-figure painting related to Taoism or Buddhism.

とうしゅうさいしゃらく 東洲斎写楽 〖絵画〗 ?-? An ukiyo-e painter in the 18th century. Was good at bust portraits. It is inferred that he painted about 140 works in only 10 months, from 1794 to 1795. It is also said that he served a feudal lord in Awa, present Tokushima Pref. However, the details are unknown. →大首絵（おおくびえ）

どうじょう 道場 〖武術〗 **(1)** a training gym for martial arts. **(2)** a hall for religious training.

とうしょうかぶかしすう 東証株価指数 〖経済〗 Tokyo Stock Price Index, or TOPIX. Is calculated by dividing the current market capitalization of all companies, listed in the First Section of the Tokyo Stock Exchange, by that of the capitalization figure for January 4, 1968. →日経平均株価

とうしょうぐう 東照宮〔神社〕 a Toushouguu Shrine. Enshrines TOKUGAWA IEYASU, the founder of the Tokugawa shogunate. There are more than 100 Toushouguu Shrines throughout Japan. The most famous one is in Nikko. →日光東照宮

どうじょうじ 道成寺〔寺院〕 Dojoji Temple. Affiliated with the Tendai sect. Was founded in 701 by a priest Gien. Is located in Wakayama Pref. Possesses several National Treasures. Famous for the legend of a love story between Anchin and Kiyohime. →安珍・清姫

とうしょうだいじ 唐招提寺〔寺院〕 Toshodai-ji Temple. The head temple of the Ritsu sect, founded in 759 by GANJIN and located in Nara City. Possesses several National Treasures and is designated a World Heritage Site.

とうじょうひでき 東条英機〔戦争〕 1884-1948. A military officer and politician born in Tokyo. Became prime minister in 1941, was largely responsible for ordering the attack on Pearl Harbor, and was executed as a Class-A war criminal after the war in 1948.

どうしん 同心〔犯罪・武士〕 a lower-ranking officer under a feudal commissioner in the Edo period. Reported to a commander called YORIKI.

とうじんぼう 東尋坊〔自然・地名〕 Toujinbou Basaltic Cliffs. Are located in Sakai City, Fukui Pref., on the coast of the Sea of Japan. The 20-meter-high cliffs with columnar joints stretch for 1 km. The name Toujinbou is derived from a vicious Buddhist monk in the Heian period, who was disliked by the local people and was pushed off the cliffs.

とうす 東司〔禅・建築〕 a lavatory in a Zen temple. The oldest example exists at TOUFUKU-JI Temple in Kyoto.

どうそじん 道祖神〔宗教〕 a guardian deity of a local community. Is represented in a stone monument, such as in a relief of a man and woman. Usually stands at the entrance of the community or the corner of an intersection.

とうだいじ 東大寺〔寺院〕 Todaiji. A main temple of the Kegon sect, located in Nara City. One of the Seven Great Temples of Nara. In 741, Emperor Shoumu issued an Imperial order to establish the provincial temple system, called the KOKUBUN-JI System. Then Kinkoumyou-ji Temple, the predecessor of Todaiji, was founded as the head temple of the system. In 743, the Emperor issued an Imperial order to produce the Great Buddha, which was completed in 752. Possesses many National

Treasures including architecture, sculptures, paintings, and calligraphies. Was designated a World Heritage Site in 1998. →奈良大仏; 華厳宗; 東大寺大仏殿

とうだいじだいぶつでん 東大寺大仏殿〖仏教〗 the Great Buddha Hall of Toudai-ji Temple. The largest wooden building in the world. The original hall was built after the Great Buddha was completed. The present one was built in 1709.

とうだいじびるしゃなにょらい 東大寺毘盧舎那如来〖仏教・彫刻〗 ⇨ 奈良大仏

どうたく 銅鐸〖考古〗 a bell-shaped ritual tool made of bronze. Was used mainly in the present Kansai, Chuugoku, and Shikoku regions, in the Yayoi period. Is about 20 to 150 cm tall and adorned with patterns on its surface.

どうちゅうざし 道中差し〖武器〗 a short sword for traveling. Was brought for self-defense by merchants and artisans in the Edo period.

どうちょう 道庁〖行政〗 the Hokkaido government, or its office. Is located in Sapporo.

どうていしゅうげつ 洞庭秋月〖絵画〗 Harvest Moon over Lake Dongting. One of the Eight Views of Xiaoxiang. →瀟湘(しょうしょう)八景

とうてん 読点〖言語〗 a comma. Is represented as 、 and is often called 'ten,' which means "a point." Though equivalent to an English comma, its usage rules are less strict. ↔句点

どうとく 道徳〖教育〗 a class for ethical training. Is taught as a subject in elementary and junior high schools.

とうにゅう 豆乳〖飲み物〗 soybean milk. Is used as an ingredient of tofu and also is drinkable.

とうにゅうなべ 豆乳鍋〖食べ物〗 a hot-pot dish cooked in soybean milk.

とうば 塔婆〖仏教〗 ⇨卒塔婆(そとば)

とうばく 倒幕〖政治〗 the political idea to overthrow the Tokugawa shogunate in the 19th century. Was combined with the concept of "Revere the Emperor and expel the barbarians." ↔佐幕 →尊皇攘夷

とうふ 豆腐〖食べ物〗 tofu, or bean curd. Is made from soybeans by adding bittern to congeal. Is said to have been invented in China about 2,000 years ago and introduced into Japan in the Nara period. Eaten in a great variety of ways such as cold tofu (HIYA-YAKKO), skewed grilled tofu with miso (DENGAKU-DOUFU), one-pot dish (NABEMONO), salad, and even curry and rice.

とうふくじ 東福寺〖寺院〗 Tofukuji Temple. The head temple of the Toufuku-ji school of the Rinzai sect, ranked fourth among the Five Zen Temples of Kyoto. Was founded in 1236 by a priest, Enni, with financial support of a Court noble, Kujou Michiie. Consists of 25 subsidiary temples. Famous for colored leaves in fall. The front gate is a National

Treasure. →臨済宗；京都五山

とうぶてつどう 東武鉄道 〔鉄道〕
Tobu Railway. One of the 16 major
private railway operators of Japan.
Serves Tokyo, Saitama, Chiba,
Tochigi, and Gunma Prefs. Its
length is 463 km, which makes it
the second largest private railway
company after KINTETSU. Has two
terminal stations in Tokyo City
proper, in Asakusa and Ikebukuro.
In addition to commuter trains, limited express trains for Nikko and
Kinugawa Hot Spring in Tochigi
Pref. start from Asakusa. Ikebukuro
mainly serves for commuters between central Tokyo and southwestern Saitama. Tobu Isesaki
Line and Tobu Toujou Line adopt
through-line service with four Tokyo Metro subway lines.

とうふでんがく 豆腐田楽 〔食べ物〕
⇨田楽豆腐

とうぶんけん 東文研 〔人文学・研究機
関〕 ⇨東京文化財研究所

とうほう 東宝 〔映画・企業名〕 Toho
Co., Ltd. A motion picture company established in 1943. Has
produced and distributed a great
number of films. Toho films include
Godzilla, *Your Name*, and several
Kurosawa's works.

どうぼうしゅう 同朋衆 〔芸術〕 a
curator and art advisor for the
shogun or a feudal lord in the
Muromachi period. Usually had a
name including '-ami' of Amitabha
Buddha and the appearance of a
Buddhist monk. NOUAMI, GEIAMI,

and SOUAMI are famous.

とうほうるりこうじょうど 東方瑠
璃光浄土 〔仏教〕 the Eastern Pure
Land of Lapis Lazuli. The world of
the Healing Buddha. ↔西方極楽浄
土 →薬師如来

とうほくさんだいまつり 東北三大
祭り 〔祭礼〕 Three Great Festivals
in the Tohoku region. The Nebuta
Festival in Aomori City, the Kantou
Festival in Akita City, and the
Tanabata Festival in Sendai City. →
青森佞武多 (ねぶた) 祭り；秋田竿灯祭り；
仙台七夕祭り

とうほくしんかんせん 東北新幹線
〔鉄道〕 Tohoku Shinkansen. Connects Tokyo with Shin-Aomori in
Aomori Pref. Started service in
1982 between Oomiya in Saitama
Pref. and Morioka in Iwate Pref.
The route was extended to Tokyo
in 1991, and to Shin-Aomori in
2010. The fastest express, HAYA-
BUSA, takes 3 hours from Tokyo to
Shin-Aomori. Other express trains
are named HAYATE, YAMABIKO, and
NASUNO. Part of its route is shared
by Joetsu, Hokuriku, Yamagata,
and Akita Shinkansen, but not by
Tokaido Shinkansen.

とうほくちほう 東北地方 〔地名〕
the Tohoku region. Is located in
northeastern Japan, facing the
Pacific Ocean and the Sea of Japan.
Consists of Aomori, Iwate, Miyagi,
Akita, Yamagata, and Fukushima
Prefs.

とうほくよんだいまつり 東北四大
祭り 〔祭礼〕 Four Great Festivals

in the Tohoku region. The Nebuta Festival in Aomori City, the Kantou Festival in Akita City, the Tanabata Festival in Sendai City, and the Hanagasa Festival in Yamagata City. →青森佞武多(ねぶた)祭り；秋田竿灯祭り；仙台七夕祭り；山形花笠祭り

どうほこ 銅矛 〖考古〗 a bronze double-bladed spear. Was also used for rituals in ancient times.

どうまき 胴巻き 〖服飾〗 a waist-band that held money and valuables during a journey in olden times.

とうみつ 東密 〖仏教〗 esoteric Buddhism of the Shingon sect. ↔台密

とうみょう 灯明 〖宗教〗 a votive light offered to Buddhist or Shinto deities.

とうみょう 豆苗 〖食べ物・植物〗 edible pea sprouts.

どうみょうじ 道明寺 **(1)**〖寺院〗 Domyo-ji Temple. A nunnery of the Shingon sect. Is said to have been founded by the Haji clan and to have been named so by Prince Shoutoku. The Eleven-headed Bodhisattva of Mercy is a National Treasure. **(2)**〖食文化〗 powder made of dried glutinous rice. Was invented by a nun at (1).

どうも どうも 〖言語〗 a word literally meaning "very" or "very much." For example, 'doumo arigatou' means "thank you very much," and 'doumo sumimasen' means "I'm very sorry." However, 'doumo' is often used by itself in different occasions to mean "thank you,"

"sorry," "hello," "bye," etc.

とうようかんじ 当用漢字 〖漢字〗 kanji for daily use. In 1946, 1,850 kanji were designated for daily use by the government. In 1981, 1,945 kanji were designated JOUYOU KANJI for common use, and the limitation of 'touyou kanji' was abolished.

とうようのまじょ 東洋の魔女 〖スポーツ〗 Oriental Witches. The nickname of the Japanese women's volleyball team that won the gold medal at the Tokyo Olympics in 1964.

とうりょう 投了 〖碁・将棋〗 to resign from a game. As in western chess, professional go or shogi players do not usually continue until the last possible move, or until one of the kings is checkmated. Some resign even when it seems to be a close game to amateurs.

とうりょう 棟梁 〖建築〗 a master carpenter, or a carpenter's leader. The two kanji literally mean "the ridge of a roof" and "a beam."

とうろう 灯篭 〖建築・庭園〗 a traditional lantern. There are many variations in form, size, material, and purpose. →石灯籠；雪見灯籠；釣灯籠

とうろうながし 灯籠流し 〖仏教〗 a Bon event of floating a tiny boat on a river or sea. People place a paper lantern or votive offerings on the boat to see off the spirits of the dead on the last day of the Bon Festival. →盂蘭盆会(うらぼんえ)

どうわきょういく 同和教育 〖教育〗

the social integration education. Aims to eliminate social discrimination against outcaste communities called 'HISABETSU BURAKU.' Though at first it also is intended to improve academic abilities of students from these communities, its aim shifted to focus on human rights education from around 1970.

どうわたいさく 同和対策 〔行政〕 social integration measures, or measures against social discrimination.

どうわちく 同和地区 〔行政〕 the government term for a former outcaste community. →被差別部落

とえいちかてつ 都営地下鉄 〔鉄道〕 the Toei Subway. Is operated by the Tokyo Metropolitan Bureau of Transportation, which is an agency of the Tokyo Metropolitan Government. Is one of the two subway systems in Tokyo, along with the Tokyo Metro. These two subway systems complement each other in terms of the areas served, providing roughly the same types of service. Some trains on the Asakusa Line go to Narita Airport via Keisei lines and the Narita Sky Access Line, and to Haneda Airport via Keikyu lines. The other three lines are the Mita, Shinjuku, and Ooedo Lines.

とおかえびす 十日戎 〔祭礼〕 an Ebisu festival held on January 10. Ones at Imamiya Ebisu Shrine in Osaka and Nishinomiya Shrine in Hyogo Pref. are famous.

とおしきょうげん 通し狂言 〔歌舞伎〕 presentation of a whole play from the first to the last scene.

とおしや 通し矢 〔武術〕 an archery contest held at SANJUUSANGEN-DOU Temple in Kyoto in the Edo period. Literally means "shooting arrows through." Archers tried to shoot as many arrows as possible through the veranda of the temple within 24 hours. The record holder, Wasa Daihachirou successfully shot 8,133 arrows in 1686.

とおとうみ 遠江 〔旧国名〕 old name for western Shizuoka Pref.

とおのものがたり 遠野物語 〔人文学・書名〕 *The Legends of Tono*. A collection of folk tales, popular beliefs, and records of annual events in Toono, Iwate Pref., published in 1910 by YANAGITA KUNIO.

とおやまきんしろう 遠山金四郎 〔武士〕 ?-1855. A feudal commissioner of Edo. Also is popular as a character in fiction, who serves as a judge.

とかち 十勝 〔地名〕 the name of an area in eastern Hokkaido. Produces various vegetables and dairy products such as beans, potatoes, cheese, and beef.

どかべん ドカ弁 〔食文化〕 a thick lunch box, or a lunch in this box.

とがりいしいせき 尖石遺跡 〔史跡〕 the Togariishi Ruins. An archaeological site from the mid-Joumon period, located in central Nagano Pref. Thirty-three pit dwellings were excavated.

とかんむり 戸冠 〖漢字〗 a crown radical which means "door." Is also called 'to-dare.' Is used in kanji such as 扉 (door), 戻 (return), and 房 (room).

とき とき 〖鉄道〗 the fastest express train on Joetsu Shinkansen. Is named after the endangered Japanese crested ibis, TOKI, the last of which survived on Sado Island, Niigata Pref. Connects Tokyo with Niigata in 2 hours.

とき 朱鷺 〖動物〗 a Japanese crested ibis. *Nipponia nippon*. The wing length is about 40 cm, and the body length is about 75 cm. The wing is white. Was designated internationally protected bird in 1960. Artificial propagation succeeded in 1999, but the wild species became extinct in 2003.

とき ～刻 〖単位〗 a unit to count time in olden times. One 'toki' was one sixth of duration from sunrise to sunset in the Edo period; therefore, it was approximately two hours, though it changed from season to season.

どきょう 読経 〖仏教〗 to read a sutra aloud. A sutra is written only in Chinese characters and is read aloud in Chinese-style pronunciation, so most Japanese do not understand the contents when listening to a sutra reading.

ときわず 常磐津 〖音楽〗 a shamisen ballad. Accompanies dance in a kabuki play.

ときん と金 〖将棋〗 a promoted pawn. Moves like a KINSHOU.

ときん 兜巾 〖宗教・服飾〗 a small headgear with a chin strap, worn by a mountain ascetic. →修験道

どぐう 土偶 〖考古〗 a clay figurine. Was made in the Joumon period. The height is from 10 to 30 cm. Many of them represent a woman and may have been used for religious purposes.

とくがわいえなり 徳川家斉 〖武士〗 1773-1841. The 11th Tokugawa Shogun, from 1787 to 1837. Assigned MATSUDAIRA SADANOBU to implement the Kansei Reform. But after Sadanobu retired, Ienari lifted the strict regulations of the Reform, and eventually the Kasei culture flourished among townspeople of Edo. →化政文化

とくがわいえみつ 徳川家光 〖武士〗 1604-1651. The 3rd Tokugawa Shogun, from 1623 to 1651. The second son of TOKUGAWA HIDETADA. Amended the Laws for the Military Houses (BUKE-SHOHATTO) and established the system of periodical residence of feudal lords in Edo (SANKIN-KOUTAI). Completed the national isolation policy (SAKOKU) and strongly prohibited Christianity. Under his regime, the Edo Castle was constructed, and a firm foundation for the Tokugawa shogunate was established.

とくがわいえやす 徳川家康 〖武士〗 1542-1616. The 1st Tokugawa Shogun, from 1603 to 1605, born in present Aichi Pref. Was allied with ODA NOBUNAGA and obtained Mikawa, the eastern part of present Aichi Pref. After Nobunaga died, fought with TOYOTOMI HIDEYOSHI in 1584, and made peace temporarily afterwards. After Hideyoshi died, won a victory at the Battle of Sekigahara in 1600 and established the Tokugawa shogunate in 1603. Destroyed the Toyotomi clan at the Summer Campaign in Osaka in 1615 and completely unified the country. →関ヶ原の戦い; 大坂夏の陣; 徳川幕府

とくがわごさんけ 徳川御三家 〖武士・政治〗 the three branches of the Tokugawa clan. Descended from three sons of TOKUGAWA IEYASU: Yoshinao in Owari, Yorinobu in Kii, and Yorifusa in Mito. Assisted the shogun in the highest rank as feudal lords and had a privilege to let a son be adopted into the shogunate family if the shogun had no heir. Actually, the 8th shogun, TOKUGAWA YOSHIMUNE, came from the Kii family, and the 15th shogun, TOKUGAWA YOSHINOBU, came from the Mito family.

とくがわつなよし 徳川綱吉 〖武士〗 1646-1709. The 5th Tokugawa Shogun, from 1680 to 1709. The 4th son of TOKUGAWA IEMITSU. Minted bad coins and issued "Edicts on Compassion for Living Things." His governance terribly tortured common people.

とくがわなりあき 徳川斉昭 〖武士〗 1800-1860. The feudal lord of the Mito domain. Sympathized with the idea of "Revere the Emperor and expel the barbarians." Conflicted with the interim super prime minister, II NAOSUKE, and was placed under house arrest in the Ansei Purge in 1859. →尊皇攘夷; 安政 の大獄

とくがわばくふ 徳川幕府 〖武士・政治〗 the Tokugawa shogunate. Is also called 'Edo bakufu.' Was established at present Tokyo in 1603 by TOKUGAWA IEYASU and returned its political power to the Emperor in 1867. The Tokugawa clan retained its authority through the Edo period, unlike two weaker previous shogunates, Kamakura and Muromachi.

とくがわびじゅつかん 徳川美術館 〖美術〗 The Tokugawa Art Museum. Was established in Nagoya in 1935. Stores fine art and archives descending from the Tokugawa clan in Owari, present Aichi Pref.

とくがわひでただ 徳川秀忠 〖武士〗 1578-1632. The 2nd Tokugawa Shogun, from 1605 to 1623. The 3rd son of TOKUGAWA IEYASU. Was late for the Battle of Sekigahara in 1600. After becoming a shogun, reinforced the administration by the Tokugawa shogunate, carrying out several policies such as establishing Laws for the Military Houses (BUKE-SHOHATTO), prohibiting Christianity, and controlling overseas trade. →関ヶ原の戦い

とくがわみつくに 徳川光圀 〖武

土〗 1628-1700. A feudal lord of the Mito domain. Started to compile the *Great History of Japan*. After his death, became a legend and was a character in much fictional writing. →大日本史

とくがわよしのぶ 徳川慶喜 〖武士〗 1837-1913. The last, 15th, Tokugawa Shogun, from 1866 to 1867. Gave back the administrative power of the Tokugawa shogunate to the Emperor.

とくがわよしむね 徳川吉宗 〖武士〗 1684-1751. The 8th Tokugawa Shogun, from 1716 to 1745. First became the feudal lord of Wakayama in 1705 and then Shogun in 1716. Implemented the Kyouhou Reforms. →享保の改革

どくがんりゅう 独眼竜〖武士〗 the nickname of a warlord in the 16th to 17th centuries, DATE MASAMUNE. Literally means "one-eyed dragon." Masamune lost the sight of his right eye in his childhood.

とくしまけん 徳島県 〖都道府県〗 Tokushima Pref. Is located in eastern Shikoku, facing the Kii Channel. Its area is 4,145 km². Its capital is Tokushima City. Is connected with Awaji Island by the Oonaruto Bridge. Famous for the Awa Bon Dance and two gorges along the Yoshino River, named OOBOKE KOBOKE. Used to be called Awa. →大鳴門橋；阿波踊り

とくしまし 徳島市 〖地名〗 Tokushima City. The capital of Tokushima Pref. Is located in its eastern part, facing the Kii Channel. Developed as a castle town of the Hachisuka clan. Famous for the Awa Bon Dance. → 阿波踊り

とくせいれい 徳政令 〖法律〗 an order of debt remission in medieval times. Was first issued to save vassals from poverty during the Kamakura shogunate. The Muromachi shogunate often issued it, responding to the public demand expressed by repetitive uprisings.

どくだみ ドクダミ〖植物〗 a lizard tail, a chameleon plant, a heart leaf, or a poison-blocking plant. *Houttuynia cordata*. Is used to make herb tea or medicine.

とくだわら 徳俵 〖相撲〗 one of the four straw bales, called TAWARA, that are half buried slightly outside the circle line of the ring. A wrestler under pressure could escape to the point before being pushed out of the ring.

とくべつしせき 特別史跡〖法律〗 a Special Historic Site. As of August 1, 2016, 61 items, including shell mounds, tumuli, sites of fortified capitals, sites of forts or castles, and monumental houses of high historical or scientific value, have been designated by the Agency for Cultural Affairs.

とくべつてんねんきねんぶつ 特別天然記念物〖法律〗 a Special Natural Monument. As of August 1, 2016, 75 items, including animals, plants, and geological and mineral formations of high scientific value, have been designated by the Agency for Cultural Affairs.

とくべつはいかん 特別拝観 〖仏教〗 special exhibit at a temple. A garden, hall, or Buddhist image that are usually not open to public can be seen.

とくべつめいしょう 特別名勝 〖法律〗 a Special Place of Scenic Beauty. As of August 1, 2016, 36 items, including gardens, bridges, gorges, seashores, mountains, and other places of scenic beauty or of high artistic or scenic value, have been designated by the Agency for Cultural Affairs.

とくり 徳利 〖酒・食器〗 ⇨銚子(ちょうし)

どくりつぎょうせいほうじん 独立行政法人 〖行政〗 an independent administrative institution. Around the year 2000, various national organizations such as universities, museums, research institutes, and hospitals became this sort of institution.

どげざ 土下座 〖精神性〗 deep bow while kneeling and touching both hands on the ground or floor. Is done to express sincere apology.

とこがまち 床框 〖建築〗 the front edge beam of a decorative alcove.

とこだな 床棚 〖建築〗 shelves beside a decorative alcove.

とこなめやき 常滑焼 〖陶磁器〗 Tokoname ware. Ceramics produced in southwestern Aichi Pref. Started around the 9th century and was popular in medieval times.

Includes various products from tea bowls in the 16th century style to modern industry ware such as earthenware pipes, tiles, and stools. Famous for its reddish-brown color.

とこのま 床の間 〖建築〗 a decorative alcove with a low platform in a traditional room. Ornaments such as a flower arrangement or hanging scrolls are displayed.

とこばしら 床柱 〖建築〗 an ornamental pillar beside a decorative alcove called TOKONOMA.

とこぶし 常節 〖食べ物・動物〗 a Japanese ormer, or a small abalone. *Haliotis japonica*. Eaten boiled or steamed.

とこやま 床山 **(1)**〖歌舞伎〗 a wig manager for actors. Makes, maintains, and repairs wigs. **(2)**〖相撲〗 a hairdresser for sumo wrestlers.

とこよのくに 常世の国 〖宗教〗 a country of eternal life. Was thought to exist beyond the horizon in ancient times. Was also thought to be equal to the Land of Darkness. →蓬莱(ほうらい)山; 黄泉(よみ)の国

ところてん 心太 〖食べ物〗 noodle-like agar. Eaten with vinegar and soy sauce or dark syrup.

とこわきだな 床脇棚 〖建築〗 ⇨床棚

とさ 土佐 〖旧国名〗 the old name of Kouchi Pref.

とさいぬ 土佐犬 〖動物〗 **(1)**a Japanese mastiff, or Tosa fighting dog. A hybrid of native Japanese dogs and European dogs such as bulldog or mastiff. **(2)**a Shikoku dog, or a Japanese wolfdog. Native to Japan. A Natural Monument.

とさじょうゆ　土佐醤油　〖調味料〗 bonito-flavored soy sauce. Is used for sashimi or cold tofu.

とさず　土佐酢　〖調味料〗 bonito-flavored vinegar.

とさにっき　土佐日記　〖文芸・作品〗 *The Tosa Diary*. The first travel diary, written in KANA characters in 935 by KI NO TSURAYUKI. Though the author was male, he pretended to be a woman because a man usually used KANJI and a woman used kana in those days. Describes events during the 55-day trip from Tosa, the southern part of SHIKOKU, to Kyoto. Played an important role in the growth of kana characters and diary literature.

とさは　土佐派　〖絵画〗 the Tosa school of paintings. Is said to have started when the founder, Fujiwara Yukimitsu, was employed by the Imperial Palace. Had the traditional style before Chinese-style India ink painting was introduced around the 13th century. Rivaled the Kanou school, which employed the Chinese style.

とさはん　土佐藩　〖政治〗 the Tosa domain. Governed present Kouchi Pref. Its feudal lords were from the Yamanouchi clan since the Chousokabe clan had its fiefs expropriated after the Battle of Sekigahara. Playing a significant role in the Meiji Restoration. Produced SAKAMOTO RYOUMA and ITAGAKI TAISUKE.

とさぶし　土佐節　〖調味料〗 dried bonito produced in Kouchi Pref. →鰹節

とざまだいみょう　外様大名　〖武士・政治〗 an outside feudal lord. Became subordinate to the Tokugawa shogunate after the Battle of Sekigahara in 1600. Their domains were generally large but far from Edo. They could not hold important posts in the Tokugawa shogunate. →譜代大名

とさみつのぶ　土佐光信　〖絵画〗 ?-1522? A painter. Obtained a high position as a painter in the Imperial Palace and established the Tosa school. His works include *Legends about the Origin of Kiyomizu-dera Temple* stored in the Tokyo National Museum.

とさみなといせき　十三湊遺跡　〖史跡〗 the Tosaminato ruins. An archaeological site of a port from the 13th to 15th centuries, located along the western coast of Aomori Pref. The port was prosperous as a base of the Andou clan, which was powerful in this region.

とさわん　土佐湾　〖湾〗 Tosa Bay. Is located on the southern coast of Kouchi Pref., between Cape Muroto in the east and Cape Ashizuri in the west. Famous for bonito fisheries and whale watching.

どさんこ　道産子　〖動物〗 **(1)** 〖動物〗 a horse produced in Hokkaido. **(2)** 〖言語〗 a person born in Hokkaido.

としいわい 年祝〖通過儀礼〗 a ceremony to celebrate that a person reaches a specific age. In the traditional approach to age counting, usually the ages of 61, 70, 77, 80, 88, 90, and 99 are celebrated. →還暦；古希；喜寿；傘寿(さんじゅ)；米寿；卒寿；白寿

としおとこ 年男〖宗教〗 a man whose Chinese zodiac sign corresponds to those of the current year. Since there are twelve zodiac signs, for example, a man who has seen his 24th birthday in the year is 'toshi-otoko.' →十二支

としおんな 年女〖宗教〗 a woman whose Chinese zodiac sign corresponds to those of the current year. Since there are twelve zodiac signs, for example, a woman who has seen her 24th birthday in the year is 'toshi-onna.' →十二支

としがみ 年神〖暦・神道〗 the deity of the New Year. Descends from the auspicious direction to KADO-MATSU in front of the house gate at the beginning of the year. →恵方

としこし 年越し〖暦〗 to see the old year out and the new year in. On New Year's Eve, people decorate their houses with special ornaments such as KADOMATSU, SHIMEKAZARI, and KAGAMI-MOCHI to welcome the deity of the New Year. A Buddhist temple tolls a bell 108 times, which is the number of human earthly desires.

としこしそば 年越し蕎麦〖食べ物〗 buckwheat noodles eaten on New Year's Eve. People eat it to wish for longevity.

としだな 年棚〖暦・神道〗 ⇨歳徳棚(としとくだな)

としだま 年玉〖暦〗 ⇨お年玉

としとくじん 歳徳神〖宗教〗 ⇨年神

としとくだな 歳徳棚〖暦・神道〗 a New Year's home altar. Is hung toward the auspicious direction of each year. Rice cakes are offered.

どじょうすくい 泥鰌掬い〖芸能〗 the loach-scooping dance accompanied by a traditional folk song of Yasugi, eastern Shimane Pref.

どじょうなべ 泥鰌鍋〖食べ物〗 ⇨柳川鍋

とそ 屠蘇〖正月・酒〗 spiced sake for New Year's Day. Is said to expel evil spirits and prolong life span. →屠蘇散(とそさん)

どぞう 土蔵〖建築〗 a storehouse with plastered or earthen walls for fire resistance. Precious goods or commodities were stored in a merchant house, while agricultural products were stored in a farmhouse.

とそさん 屠蘇散〖正月・酒〗 one of the traditional Chinese medicines including prickly ash (SANSHOU), citrus peel ('chinpi'), root of balloon flower (KIKYOU), saposhnikovia root ('boufuu'), and cinnamon. Is used to add flavor to New Year's sake called TOSO.

とそつてん 兜率天〖仏教〗 the Tusita Heaven. According to Buddhist mythology, the Buddha-to-be, or Maitreya Bodhisattva, currently resides there to preach to heavenly beings and will descend to this world 5.67 billion years from now. The Historical Buddha also trained himself in the Tusita Heaven before his birth in this world.

とだれ 戸垂れ〖漢字〗 ⇨戸冠(とかんむり)

とちぎけん 栃木県〖都道府県〗 Tochigi Pref. Is located in Eastern Japan, on the northern edge of the Kantou Plain. Its area is 6,408 km^2. Its capital is Utsunomiya City. Famous sightseeing spots include the shrines, temples, and waterfalls in Nikko, Nasu Hills, and Kinugawa hot springs. The group of shrines and temples in Nikko was designated a World Heritage Site in 1999. Milk, rice, strawberries, and dried gourd shavings (KANPYOU) are produced in large quantities. Used to be Shimotsuke.

とちもち 栃餅〖食べ物〗 rice cake favored with horse chestnut.

とちょう 都庁〖行政〗 ⇨東京都庁

どちりなきりしたん ドチリナ・キリシタン〖キリスト教〗 Japanese versions of *Doctrina Christiana*, published at the end of the 16th century. A book on the Roman Catholic Catechism. Two of four existing versions were written in Japanese in the Roman alphabet to help foreigners learn the Japanese language. Two others were written in KANJI and KANA to teach the Catechism to the Japanese people.

どっきょう 読経〖仏教〗 ⇨読経(どきょう)

とっくり 徳利〖酒〗 ⇨銚子(ちょうし)

とっこうけいさつ 特高警察 〖行政〗 the Special Higher Police. A government unit that existed from 1911 to 1945 to suppress thought, expression, and political activities that were against the government.

とっこうたい 特攻隊〖軍事〗 ⇨神風特別攻撃隊

とったり 取ったり〖相撲〗 an arm bar throw. The technique to hold the opponent's arm and swing him out of the ring or let him down.

とっとりけん 鳥取県〖都道府県〗 Tottori Pref. Is located in Western Japan, facing the Sea of Japan. Its area is 3,507 km^2. Its capital is Tottori City. Famous for the Tottori Sand Dunes, Misasa hot springs, and snow resorts around Mt. Daisen. 20th century pears are produced and snow crabs (ZUWAI-GANI) are caught in large quantities. Used to be Inaba and Houki.

とっとりさきゅう 鳥取砂丘〖地名〗 Tottori Sand Dunes. Is the only sand dune in Japan. Is located along the coast of the Sea of Japan in eastern Tottori Pref. Visitors can enjoy the camel ride and the donkey cart ride. Is accessible from central Tottori City by bus, taking 20 minutes.

とっとりし 鳥取市〖地名〗 Tottori City. The capital of Tottori Pref. Is located in its eastern part, facing the Sea of Japan. Developed as a castle town of the Ikeda clan. Has the Tottori Sand Dunes.

どてなべ 土手鍋 〖食べ物〗 a miso-flavored hot-pot dish of oysters, vegetables, and tofu. Miso is spread on the rim of an earthen pot.

どてやき どて焼き 〖食べ物〗 beef muscle simmered with miso or mirin. Is popular in Osaka.

どてら 褞袍 〖服飾〗 ⇨丹前(ﾃﾞﾝ)

どどいつ 都々逸 〖音楽〗 a popular love song with 7-7-7-5 syllables accompanied by shamisen. Developed in the late 18th century.

とどうふけん 都道府県 〖行政〗 a prefecture. The administrative division of Japan. Consists of one 'to' (Tokyo-to), one 'dou' (Hokkai-dou, commonly written as Hokkaido), two 'fu' (Kyoto-fu and Osaka-fu), and 43 'ken.' Thus there are 47 prefectures in all.

どとん 土遁 〖忍者〗 escape technique using dirt or sand. One of the five major techniques. Involves hiding in a pit or hole or under fallen leaves and throwing dirt or sand into the enemy's eyes to blind him or her.

どなべ 土鍋 〖食器〗 an earthen flat pot with a lid. Is used to eat a one-pot dish called NABEMONO or thick wheat noodles called UDON.

となりぐみ 隣組 〖生活〗 a neighbor association. Around 10 households in a neighborhood were compulsorily incorporated into a nationwide network of a neighbor association in 1940, so that the government could easily control the civil society. The system was abolished in 1947.

とねがわ 利根川 〖地名〗 the Tone River. "Tone" here is pronounced like "toe nay." Flows from the Mikuni Mountains on the border between Gunma and Niigata Prefs. through the Kantou Plain to the Pacific Ocean on the border between Ibaraki and Chiba Prefs. Is 322 km long, which makes it the second longest river in Japan after the Shinano River. Its drainage area, 16,840 km^2, is the largest of all the rivers in Japan. Is also called BANDOU TAROU.

とねり 舎人 〖政治〗 a low-ranking official in the ancient government system. Attended to an Emperor or a member of the Imperial family.

とねりしんのう 舎人親王 〖政治〗 676-735. The third prince of Emperor Tenmu and the father of Emperor Junnin. Supervised the compilation of the *Chronicles of Japan* (NIHONSHOKI)

とのさまがえる 殿様蛙 〖動物〗 a leopard frog. *Rana nigromaculata*.

とはずがたり とはずがたり 〖文芸・作品〗 *The Confessions of Lady Nijo*. A diary written from 1271 to 1306 by a daughter of Kuga Tadamasa, who served Ex-emperor Gofukakusa. The first three volumes describe her love for the Emperor, and the last two volumes describe her life as a nun and pilgrim.

とばそうじょう 鳥羽僧正 〖仏教〗 1053-1140. A priest of the Tendai

sect. Is also called Kakuyuu. Is said to have drawn the *Scrolls of Frolicking Animals and Humans*. →鳥獣人物戯画

とばつびしゃもんてん 兜跋毘沙門天 〚仏教〛 a variation of BISHAMON-TEN, the Guardian King of the north. Is said to originate in Central Asia. A famous example of the image is kept at TOU-JI Temple in Kyoto.

とばてんのう 鳥羽天皇 〚天皇〛 Emperor Toba. 1103-1156. The 74th, on the throne from 1107 to 1123. The first prince of Emperor Horikawa. Had the political power as Ex-emperor from 1123 to 1141. Helped Emperor Goshirakawa to the throne and started the Hougen Rebellion. →院政；保元の乱

とばふしみのたたかい 鳥羽伏見の戦い 〚戦争〛 Battle of Toba-Fushimi. The initial battle in the Boshin Civil War. The new government defeated the former Tokugawa shogunate in the south suburban area of Kyoto in 1868. Since the Imperial Court issued an order to hunt down and kill the 15th shogun, Tokugawa Yoshinobu, he was regarded as an Imperial enemy, and many domains followed the new government.

とび 鳶 **(1)**〚動物〛 a black kite. *Milvus migrans*. Inhabits flat, coastal, and low mountain areas throughout Japan. **(2)**〚職業〛⇨鳶職 **(3)**〚神話・動物〛⇨金鵄(きん)

とびいし 飛び石 〚庭園〛 stepping stones. A visitor to a garden can walk without treading on the dirt.

とびうお 飛び魚 〚食べ物・魚〛 a flying fish. *Exocoetidae*. About 30 cm long and edible. Lives in the temperate and tropical zones. Flies more than 200 m, using the pectoral fins as wings.

とびうめ 飛梅 〚神社・植物〛 Flying Plum Tree. A plum tree in Dazaifu Tenmanguu Shrine in Fukuoka Pref. Legend has it that SUGAWARA NO MICHIZANE loved this tree in Kyoto, and it flew to Dazaifu after he was exiled from Kyoto.

とびぐち 鳶口 〚建築・道具〛 a fireman's hook, or an iron hook with a wooden handle. Is used to pull timber or a log.

とびくない 飛び苦無 〚忍者〛 a small double-bladed knife for throwing. Is probably fictitious because no literature refers to it, except fiction.

とびこ 飛子 〚食べ物・魚〛 roe of flying fish. Eaten as sushi.

とびしょく 鳶職 **(1)**〚災害・職業〛 ⇨町火消し **(2)**〚建築・職業〛 a scaffolding worker. Usually wears knickerbocker-style pants.

とぴっくす TOPIX 〚経済〛 ⇨東証株価指数

どひょう 土俵 〚相撲〛 a sumo ring. A circle that is 455 cm in diameter and that rests on a square earthen foundation that is 554 cm on each side. The ring is partitioned with 20 half-buried bales from the outside.

どひょういり 土俵入り 〚相撲〛 a

sumo wrestlers' ring-entering ceremony. There are two types of ceremony. In one ceremony, all wrestlers in the highest and second-highest divisions, except champions, enter the ring and clap their hands together. In the other ceremony, a grand champion, yokozuna, enters the ring with two subordinates, claps his hands, and stomps on the ground.

どびん 土瓶 〔食文化〕 an earthen kettle, or an earthen teapot.

どびんむし 土瓶蒸し 〔食べ物〕 matsutake mushroom and fish or chicken in clear broth steamed in a small earthen pot. The juice of a small sour citrus is squeezed on it before eating. Popular in autumn.

とぶくろ 戸袋 〔建築〕 a flat case for storm shutters. Is set beside the window or door and contains storm shutters in normal weather.

どぶろく 濁酒 〔酒〕 ⇨濁り酒

どま 土間 〔建築〕 a dirt floor inside the house. A person does not have to take off the shoes to walk on it. Is used mainly as an entrance or a kitchen.

とみおかせいしじょう 富岡製糸場 〔科学技術〕 Tomioka Silk Mill. Was established in Gunma Pref. in 1872 by the Meiji government. Introduced machinery and technology from France and brought up female technicians. Was designated a World Heritage Site in 2014.

とみくじ 富くじ 〔ギャンブル〕 a lottery in the Edo period. Was mainly promoted by a temple or shrine which tried to collect money for restoration.

とめそで 留め袖 〔服飾〕 a formal kimono for married women. Is attached with five family crests and decorated with elaborate gold and silver patterns on the lower part, usually on a black background.

とめわん 止め椀 〔食文化〕 a closing soup. Is served with rice and pickles at the end of the traditional-style course cuisine.

とも 供 〔能〕 a supporting actor who plays a minor role as one of TSURE.

ともえごぜん 巴御前 〔武士〕 ?–? A sub-wife of a warlord, KISO YOSHINAKA. Fought together with her husband in the battlefield. Is said to have become a nun in present Niigata Pref. after Yoshinaka died.

ともえなげ 巴投げ 〔柔道〕 a circle throw, or a stomach throw. The procedure is as follows: [1] Fall backward while grasping the opponent, [2] put a leg on the opponent's stomach, and [3] throw the opponent over and behind the head by stretching the knee in a rolling motion.

ともえり 共襟 〔服飾〕 a collar of a kimono, which is made of the same cloth as the body part.

ともしらが 共白髪 〔精神性〕 a condition that a couple live long together until their hair both turns gray. Has a kind of auspicious nuance.

ともちょこ 友チョコ 〖食べ物・精神性〗 chocolate casually given to a friend by a woman on Valentine's Day. →バレンタインデー

ともながしんいちろう 朝永振一郎 〖科学技術〗 1906-1979. A physicist born in Tokyo. Constructed the super-many-time theory and the renormalization theory and won the Nobel Prize in 1965.

ともびき 友引 〖暦〗 a day of "luring a friend" in the unofficial six-day calendar. The latter part of the Japanese in this term, 'biki,' has many meanings such as "pulling," "drawing," and "luring." Is said a match or game ends in a draw on this day. If a funeral is held, it is thought that the dead person will lure one of his or her friends toward death. If a wedding ceremony is held, the happiness of the married couple affects their friends. → 六曜(ろくよう)

ともぶた 友蓋 〖茶道〗 a lid whose material is identical with the container such as a tea kettle or a water vessel.

どもんけん 土門拳 〖芸術〗 1909-1990. A photographer born in Yamagata Pref. Took photos related to traditional Japanese culture as well as social issues.

とや 鳥屋 〖歌舞伎〗 a small room at the end of the runway elevated passage, called HANAMICHI, which kabuki actors use to reach stage. Actors wait, and some stage properties such as a boat or palanquin are placed in this room.

とやまけん 富山県 〖都道府県〗 Toyama Pref. Is located in central Japan, facing the Sea of Japan. Is 4,247 km² in area. Its capital is Toyama City. The Tateyama Kurobe Alpine Route is famous as a sightseeing spot. Used to be ECCHUU.

とやまし 富山市 〖地名〗 Toyama City. The capital of Toyama Pref., located in its central part and facing Toyama Bay. The Jinzuu River runs through it. Has been famous for medicine production since the 17th century. More recently, the abundant electricity supplies from hydro power stations in the North Alps and water supplies led to the development of agricultural, manufacturing, and chemical industries. The popular festival called Kaze no Bon is held annually in early September.

とやまわん 富山湾 〖湾〗 Toyama Bay. Is located on the coast of Toyama Pref. Is very deep, and there are few islands. The mirage, an optical phenomenon, can be seen in winter. Good fisheries for firefly squid and yellowtail.

とよ 臺与 〖政治〗 ⇨壱与(いよ)

とよあしはらのみずほのくに 豊葦原の瑞穂の国 〖国名〗 the Land of Abundant Reed Plains and Rice Fields. A eulogistic name for Japan in mythology.

どよう 土用 〖暦〗 18 days immediately before RISSHUN, RIKKA, RISSHUU, or RITTOU, which are four of the 24 seasonal nodes in the traditional calendar, called NIJUUSHI-SEKKI. Usually refers to the one before 'risshuu,' which is also called DOYOU NO USHI NO HI.

とようのうしのひ　土用の丑の日 〖暦〗 the Midsummer Day of the Cow. Around the end of July in the current calendar. People customarily eat grilled eel on this day. → 丑 (?); 十二支

とよださきち　豊田佐吉 〖科学技術・企業〗 1867-1930. An inventor and entrepreneur born in Shizuoka Pref. Invented an automatic weaving machine and established the foundation of Toyota Motor Corporation.

とよたまひめ　豊玉姫 〖神話〗 the wife of HOORI NO MIKOTO, and a daughter of OOWADATSUMI NO KAMI, the great deity of oceans. Asked her husband not to look inside the delivery room when bearing her son, UGAYAFUKIAEZU NO MIKOTO, but Hoori broke the taboo, and Toyotama went back to the ocean.

とよとみひでよし　豊臣秀吉 〖武士〗 1537-1598. A warlord born in present Nagoya, Aichi Pref. Was active as a vassal of ODA NOBUNAGA. After Nobunaga was killed by AKECHI MITSUHIDE, succeeded to Nobunaga's position by defeating Mitsuhide in 1582 and an ex-colleague, Shibata Katsuie, in 1583. Fought with TOKUGAWA IEYASU in 1584, but made peace temporarily afterwards. Conquered Shikoku and Kyushu and unified Japan by destroying the Houjou clan in present Kanagawa Pref. in 1590. Dispatched troops to Korea in 1592 and 1597 but failed and died from a disease the next year, leaving a very young son, TOYOTOMI HIDEYORI.

とよとみひでより　豊臣秀頼 〖武士〗 1593-1615. A warlord born in Osaka. The son of TOYOTOMI HIDEYOSHI and YODO-DONO. Though his father unified Japan, was downgraded to a mere feudal lord when TOKUGAWA IEYASU grasped the political power after the Battle of Sekigahara in 1600. Lived in Osaka Castle with his mother and married Ieyasu's granddaughter, SEN-HIME, in 1603. Was attacked in the Summer Campaign in Osaka by Ieyasu and committed suicide together with his mother.

とら　寅 〖干支〗 the third of the Chinese zodiac signs. Means "tiger." Recently the years 1986, 1998, and 2010 were tiger years. Indicates the east-northeast in direction and around 4 a.m. for hours.

どら　銅鑼 〖茶道〗 a gong. Is rung to inform the guest that the tea room is prepared.

どらいかれえ　ドライカレー 〖食べ物〗 dry curry. **(1)** curry-flavored dried minced meat and vegetables with rice. **(2)** fried rice with curry flavor. Though (2) is the original meaning of the term, people today mostly use the term to mean (1).

とらいじん 渡来人〖外交〗 Chinese or Korean Japanese in ancient times. Were nationalized to live in Japan and contributed to cultural development by their advanced knowledge and technology.

どらえもん ドラえもん〖漫画・アニメ〗 *Doraemon*. A manga and anime for young children. The manga was written and illustrated by Fujiko Fujio and was published serially in pupil's magazines from 1969 to 1986. The series was also adapted into animation films, which are still created every year.

どらごんぼおる ドラゴンボール〖漫画〗 *Dragon Ball*. An adventure kung-fu manga by Akira Toriyama. The series was published in a weekly magazine, *Weekly Shonen Jump*, from 1984 to 1995.

とらさん 寅さん〖映画〗 ⇨男はつらいよ；フーテンの寅

とらぴすちぬしゅうどういん トラピスチヌ修道院〖キリスト教〗 Trappistine Convent. A convent for Trappistine nuns. Is located in Hakodate City in southern Hokkaido. Was founded in 1898 as Japan's first Catholic convent that allowed only women on the premises. Tourists can enjoy the church building in the mixed style of Gothic and Romanesque.

とらぴすとしゅうどういん トラピスト修道院〖キリスト教〗 Our Lady of the Lighthouse Abbey, or Tobetsu Trappist Monastery. A monastery for Trappist monks. Is located in Hokuto City in southern Hokkaido. Was founded in 1896 as a Catholic monastery that allowed only men on the premises. Produces Trappist butter and cookies.

とらふぐ 虎河豚〖食べ物・魚〗 a Japanese pufferfish, or tiger puffer. *Takifugu rubripes*. Is considered to be the best material for pufferfish cuisine. →河豚(ふぐ)

どらやき 銅鑼焼き〖食べ物〗 adzuki pancakes. Sandwich made from a pair of pancakes and chunky sweet adzuki paste.

とり 酉〖干支〗 the tenth of the Chinese zodiac signs. Means "cock." Recently the years 1993, 2005, and 2017 were cock years. Indicates the west in direction and around 6 p.m. for hours.

とり 取り〖落語〗 a headliner. The last performer in a traditional vaudeville show. Is usually an experienced comic storyteller.

とりあわせ 鳥合わせ〖娯楽〗 ⇨闘鶏

とりい 鳥居〖神道〗 a gateway to a Shinto shrine. Is sometimes placed at a key point in the precinct. Consists of two columns and two crossbars, often with a vertical strut between the crossbars. Though a torii is a kind of symbol of Shinto shrine, its origin is unknown. →神社；明神(みょうじん)鳥居；神明(しんめい)鳥居

とりいきよなが 鳥居清長〖絵画〗 1752-1815. An ukiyo-e painter born in Edo. Invented his own stylistic figure of a beautiful woman, who looks healthy and tall in stature.

とりがい 鳥貝 〖食べ物・動物〗 a heart clam, an egg cockle, or a Japanese cockle. *Fulvia mutica*. Eaten dried or as sushi.

とりかぶと 鳥兜 〖忍者・植物〗 Chinese aconite, or Japanese monkshood. *Aconitum japonicum*. Its root can be the material of either deadly poison or traditional Chinese medicine.

とりかわ 鳥皮 〖食べ物〗 chicken skin. Eaten grilled or parboiled. → 焼き鳥; 湯引き

とりくち 取り口 〖相撲〗 the technique or tactics of sumo wrestling.

とりくみ 取組 〖相撲〗 a bout. The combination of two sumo wrestlers to fight each other.

とりこぼし 取りこぼし 〖相撲〗 to lose a bout that should have been won.

とりたてし 取り立て詞 〖言語〗 a focusing particle. Focuses an object in the context, adding the meaning of "too," "only," "even," and so on.

とりなおし 取り直し 〖相撲〗 to have the same bout again. Is done if the result of a bout was unclear or if a bout took too much time.

とりのいち 酉の市 〖祭礼〗 Cock Fairs. Are held at an Ootori Shrine in each region in November. Ornamental bamboo rakes are sold as good luck charms. →大鳥神社; 熊手

とりのこ 鳥の子 (1) 〖生活〗 high-quality traditional paper. Is made from ganpi trees. Light yellow like egg. Was used for painting, calligraphy, and sliding screens. (2) 〖忍者〗 a grenade to create a smoke screen. Fire powders and chemical agents are set in a ball made of (1). Is thrown after lighting a fuse.

とりのこもち 鳥の子餅 〖食べ物〗 a pair of red and white oval-shaped flat rice cakes.

とりのぶ 鳥の部 〖漢字〗 a right-side or lower-part radical meaning "bird." Is used in kanji such as 鳩 (pigeon), 鶏 (fowl), and 鷲 (eagle).

とりばし 取り箸 〖食器〗 serving chopsticks. Are used when diners take shared food on a large plate to a small plate for each person.

とりふだ 取り札 〖娯楽〗 a pick-up card in a traditional matching card game, called KARUTA. One player reads aloud a text on a reading card, and other players pick out the matching card among pick-up cards spread on the floor. ↔読み札

とりぶっし 止利仏師 〖仏教〗 ⇨鞍作止利(くらつくりのとり)

とりめし 鶏飯 〖食べ物〗 rice cooked with chicken.

とりものちょう 捕り物帳 〖文芸〗 a detective story. Its background is usually the life of ordinary people in the Edo period.

とろ とろ 〖食べ物〗 fatty meat of tuna. Less fatty meat is called CHUU-TORO, and more fatty meat is called OO-TORO. The latter is more expensive than the former. Both are good for SUSHI and SASHIMI.

とろいせき 登呂遺跡 〖史跡〗 the Toro ruins. An archaeological site of around the 1st century, located in Shizuoka City, Shizuoka Pref. Remains of residences, storehouses, rice fields, and woodenware were found in the mid-20th century. A National Historic Site.

どろたぼう 泥太坊 〖妖怪〗 a one-eyed muddy goblin like a monk. Appears from a rice field.

とろろ 薯蕷 〖食べ物〗 grated yam. Is used for soup or noodles.

とろろいも 薯蕷芋 〖食べ物〗 a generic term for yams that are eaten after grating, including Japanese and Chinese yams. →長芋；山芋

とろろこんぶ とろろ昆布 〖食べ物〗 vinegared and thinly scraped kelp. Is sometimes put into a clear hot soup.

とろろじる 薯蕷汁 〖食べ物〗 grated yam soup.

とろろそば 薯蕷蕎麦 〖食べ物〗 buckwheat noodles with grated yam. Raw quail egg is often added.

とわずがたり 問わず語り 〖文芸・作品〗 ⇨とはずがたり

とわだこ 十和田湖 〖湖沼〗 Lake Towada. A caldera lake located on the border of Aomori and Akita Prefs. The area is 61 km². The maximum depth is 327 m, and the surface is 401 m above sea level. The Oirase River, parts of which are designated a Special Place of Scenic Beauty and a Natural Monument, flows out of it. Sockeye salmon began to be cultivated at the beginning of the 20th century, and now people can enjoy fishing for and eating them.

とんかつ 豚カツ 〖食べ物〗 a deep-fried breaded pork cutlet. Is sometimes used as a topping of curry and rice or DONBURI-MONO. One of the most popular Japanized Western cuisine.

とんかつそおす とんかつソース 〖調味料〗 Japanese-style barbecue sauce, or Japanese-style thick Worcestershire sauce. Goes well with Japanese-style pork cutlets called TONKATSU.

とんこつ 豚骨 〖調味料〗 pork bones. Is used for soup stock of ramen.

とんじる 豚汁 〖食べ物〗 miso soup with pork, tofu, and vegetables. Popular in the winter season.

どんす 緞子 〖服飾〗 damask, or satin with patterns. Was introduced from China in the 16th century. Is used for kimono, sashes, bags, and futon.

どんたく どんたく 〖祭礼〗 ⇨博多どんたく

どんでんがえし どんでん返し 〖忍者〗 a hidden revolving door at a ninja mansion. The axis is in the center of the door, and the door revolves to open when one side is pushed. Was used to hide oneself or to escape from the enemy.

とんでんへい 屯田兵 〖政治〗 a farmer-soldier. Was recruited mainly among former samurai by the Meiji Governmet, to develop and defend Hokkaido. The system started in 1874 and ceased in 1904.

どんどやき どんど焼き 〔祭礼〕 a bonfire festival in mid-January. New Year's decorations are gathered from neighboring households and burned. It is said that one will be healthy if he or she eats rice cake grilled with the festival's fire.

とんふぁ トンファ 〔武器〕 a pair of side-handle batons. A weapon used in Okinawa karate.

とんぶり とんぶり 〔食べ物・植物〕 fruits of broom-goosefoot. Have a diameter of 1 to 2 mm and are called "field's caviar."

どんぶり 丼 〔食文化〕 ⇨丼鉢; 丼物

どんぶりばち 丼鉢 〔食器〕 a big bowl. Is often used when eating rice or noodles.

どんぶりもの 丼物 〔食べ物〕 rice with toppings, served in a bowl. The varied toppings includes egg, chicken, cutlet, tempura, sashimi, etc. →親子丼; カツ丼; 天丼

ないえん 内苑〖神道・庭園〗 the inner garden of the Imperial Palace or a Shinto shrine. ↔外苑

ないかくかんぼう 内閣官房〖政治〗 Cabinet Secretariat. Arranges cabinet meetings, controls and adjusts significant issues discussed in the meetings, and gathers intelligence.

ないかくそうりだいじん 内閣総理大臣〖政治〗 the prime minister. Is selected among members of the Diet. The position and authority is prescribed in the Constitution of Japan. →日本国憲法

ないかくふ 内閣府〖政治〗 the Cabinet Office. Processes clerical work for the prime minister and plans, proposes, and coordinates significant national policies, together with the Cabinet Secretariat. →内閣総理大臣

ないくう 内宮〖神社〗 the Inner Shrine of Ise. Enshrines the Sun Goddess (AMATERASU OOMIKAMI) and contains a mirror called YATA NO KAGAMI, one of the Three Sacred Treasures of the Imperial Family. Is also called 'Koutaijinguu.' →伊勢神宮；外宮(げくう)；三種の神器

ないじん 内陣〖宗教・建築〗 the inner sanctum in the main building of a Buddhist temple or Shinto shrine. The principal image of a temple (HONZON) or the sacred object of a shrine (SHINTAI) is enshrined. ↔外陣(げじん)

ないしんのう 内親王〖天皇・行政〗 (**1**) a legitimate princess, or a daughter of the eldest legitimate prince, according to the Imperial House Act. (**2**) a princess, or a sister of an Emperor, in ancient times. ↔親王

なうまん ナウマン〖考古〗 Edmund Naumann. 1854-1927. A German geologist. Was hired by the Meiji government in 1875 to teach geology at Tokyo Imperial University and to conduct geological research related to Japan. Traveled widely during his 10 years in Japan to make geological surveys of the country, and named the large depressed land zone in the middle of Honshu the Fossa Magna. Was instrumental in compiling Japan's geological history and studying its fossil record. Had an elephant fossil named after him that was found in Japan.

なうまんぞう ナウマン象〖動物〗 a Naumann elephant. *Palaeoloxodon naumanni*. Lived about 400,000 years ago and declined about 20,000 years ago. Its height was 2 to 3 m. Was reported early in the Meiji era by a German geologist, Edmund Naumann.

なおえかねつぐ 直江兼続〖武士〗 1560-1619. A warlord born in present Niigata Pref. Served UESUGI KENSHIN and Uesugi Kagekatsu and was known as a great chief retainer.

なおきさんじゅうご 直木三十五〖文芸〗 1891-1934. A popular novelist born in Osaka. Started a literary magazine, BUNGEI SHUNJUU, in 1923, together with KIKUCHI KAN. Mainly wrote period novels. →直木賞

なおきしょう 直木賞〖文芸〗 Naoki Prize. A biannual prize for popular literature. Was established by KIKUCHI KAN in a magazine, BUNGEI SHUNJUU, in 1935 to commemorate the life of NAOKI SANJUUGO. The Akutagawa Prize was established at the same time. →芥川賞

なおらい 直会〖神道・食文化〗 a feast after a Shinto ritual. Originally it was meant to be a kind of holy communion; in these days, however, participants just enjoy sake and food previously offered to the deity in the ritual.

なかい 仲居〖食文化・旅〗 a waitress at a traditional high-class restaurant or inn.

ながいかふう 永井荷風〖文芸〗 1879 -1959. A novelist born in Tokyo. His works include *American Stories* in 1908 and *Rivalry: A Geisha's Tale* (Udekurabe) in 1917.

ながいも 長芋〖食べ物・植物〗 a Chinese yam. *Dioscorea oppositifolia* or *Dioscorea batatas Decne*. Has a stick-shaped root. Is grown often in Hokkaido and Aomori Pref. Is grated to be eaten with sashimi of tuna, buckwheat noodles, or thin wheat noodles, or is sliced into thin rectangles to be eaten with soy sauce and dried bonito flakes.

なかいり 中入り〖芸能・相撲〗 an interlude during a show or sumo bouts. Better performers or stronger sumo wrestlers usually appear after the intermission. →寄席

ながうた 長唄〖音楽〗 an epic song or ballad chanted to the accompaniment of a shamisen. Was originally begun as accompaniment for kabuki dances in the 18th century but developed on its own in the 19th century.

なかうちいさお 中内功〖ビジネス〗 1922-2005. A businessman born in Osaka. Founded a supermarket chain, The Daiei, Inc., in 1957 and acquired a professional baseball team, Fukuoka Daiei Hawks, in 1988.

なかうみ 中海〖湖沼〗 Naka Inlet. A brackish lake near the mouth of the Hii River in northwestern Tottori Pref. and northeastern Shimane Pref. The area is 86 km^2, making it the 5th largest lake in Japan. Famous for bird watching. Was designated a Ramsar site in 2005, together with a neighboring Lake Shinji in Shimane Pref. →宍道(しんじ)湖

なかえちょうみん 中江兆民〖人文学〗 1847-1901. A philosopher born in present Kouchi Pref. Laid philosophical foundation for the Freedom and People's Rights Movement of the Taishou era. Translated *The Social Contract* by Jean-Jacques Rousseau into

Japanese. His works include *A Discourse by Three Drunkards on Government* (Sansuijin keirin mondou) in 1887.

ながおかきょう 長岡京 〔政治〕 the Imperial Capital from 784 to 794. Was located to the southwest of present Kyoto. The capital was relocated from HEIJOU-KYOU in present Nara to here. However, several inauspicious events occurred one after another, and the capital was relocated again to HEIAN-KYOU in present Kyoto.

なかおび 中帯 〔服飾〕 an under sash used to tie up a short sleeve kimono, called KOSODE, under the outerwear.

ながさきくんち 長崎くんち 〔祭礼〕 Is held at Suwa Shrine in Nagasaki City on October 7th to 9th. Famous for the snake dance. 'Kunchi' comes from 'ku-nichi,' which means the 9th day, because this festival used to be held on September 9th in the traditional calendar.

ながさきけん 長崎県 〔都道府県〕 Nagasaki Pref. Is located in the northwest of Kyushu Island, facing the East China Sea, the Ariake Sea, and the Tsushima Strait. Is 4,105 km^2 in area, including many islands such as Iki, Tsushima, and Goto Islands. Its capital is Nagasaki City. Has a very long irregular coastline called ria. Potatoes, carrots, onions, lettuce, Japanese plums, beef, and pearls are produced in large quanti-

ties. Its territory on Kyushu Island used to be part of Hizen. →雲仙岳；島原の乱；平戸市

ながさきげんばくしりょうかん 長崎原爆資料館 〔戦争・博物館〕 Nagasaki Atomic Bomb Museum. Was founded in Nagasaki City in 1996. Exhibits the materials which demonstrate the damage by the atomic bomb on August 9, 1945.

ながさきし 長崎市 〔地名〕 Nagasaki City. The capital of Nagasaki Pref., located in its southern part. In the latter half of the 16th century, it developed under the influence of Catholic and Portuguese cultures. During the period of the national isolation policy from the mid-17th to mid-19th centuries, it was the only seaport where trading with China and the Netherlands was allowed. Consequently, it became the center of Dutch studies. During World War II, the U.S. dropped an atomic bomb on the city on August 9, 1945. It completely destroyed the north of the city and killed 35,000 people. Ooura Church, also known as OOURA TENSHUDOU, and two buildings in Soufuku-ji Temple have been designated National Treasures. Other tourist spots include Glover Garden, Siebold Memorial Museum, Dejima Museum of History, Nagasaki Atomic Bomb Museum, and Megane Bridge. The sponge cake called castilla is sold as a souvenir, and a Chinese-style hotchpotch noodle called CHANPON is a local favorite.

ながさきぶぎょう 長崎奉行 〔行政〕 a feudal commissioner of Nagasaki, Kyushu. Exercised jurisdiction over Nagasaki, which was directly governed by the Tokugawa shogunate.

ながしそうめん 流し素麺 〔食べ物〕 to pick up and eat very thin wheat noodles, called SOUMEN, which are flowing down into water on a small flume. Is also called 'soumen-nagashi.'

ながしののたたかい 長篠の戦 〔戦争〕 Battle of Nagashino. Took place in present Aichi Pref. in 1575. ODA NOBUNAGA and TOKUGAWA IEYASU defeated TAKEDA KATSUYORI. Oda and Tokugawa systematically used firearms against Takeda's cavalry.

ながしびな 流し雛 〔暦〕 Doll Floating Ceremony. People transfer their own filth or impurity to paper dolls and float the dolls on a small boat down a river. The ceremony is held after the Girls' Festival on March 3rd.

なかじまひこうき 中島飛行機 〔軍事・企業名〕 Nakajima Aircraft Co. The first aircraft manufacturer in Japan. Was established in 1917, produced an fighter aircraft during World War II, named Nakajima Ki-43 or HAYABUSA, and also produced the engine for a Zero fighter. Was dissolved in 1946, but its technology was handed down to present

Fuji Heavy Industries Ltd. and other corporations. →ゼロ戦

ながじゅばん 長襦袢 〔服飾〕 long underwear for kimono. Is worn over next-to-skin underwear called HADA-JUBAN.

ながすねひこ 長脛彦 〔神話〕 the name of the chief of an ancient local clan in present Nara Pref. Resisted Emperor Jinmu but was killed by NIGIHAYAHI NO MIKOTO.

なかせんどう 中山道 〔交通〕 the Nakasendou Highway in the Edo period. Extended, with 69 relay stations, from Edo through Oomiya in present Saitama Pref., Takasaki in present Gunma Pref., Karuizawa and Shiojiri in present Nagano Pref., and Nakatsugawa in present Gifu Pref. to Kusatsu in present Shiga Pref.

なかだち 中立ち 〔茶道〕 a break after eating pre-ceremony cuisine. The guests wait at the garden while the host makes up the room. →懐石料理

ながつき 長月 〔暦〕 September in the traditional calendar. Means "long month" or "long moon." There are several opinions on its etymology. One of them says that the night begins to get longer in September, so "long moon." →旧暦

ながと 長門 〔旧国名〕 the old name of the northwestern half of Yamaguchi Pref. Is commonly called Choushuu.

なかとみのかまたり 中臣鎌足 〔政治〕 another name for FUJIWARA

NO KAMATARI. Was given this name after his death in 669 by Emperor Tenji. →天智天皇

ながねぎ 長葱 〘食べ物・植物〙 the term to distinguish a common NEGI (green onion) from a 'tamanegi' (onion).

なかのうみ 中の海 〘湖沼〙 ⇨中海(なかうみ)

なかのおおえのおうじ 中大兄皇子 〘政治〙 Prince Naka no Ooe. The name of Emperor Tenji before his enthronement. →天智天皇

ながのおりんぴっく 長野オリンピック 〘スポーツ〙 the Nagano Olympics. The 18th Winter Olympics held from February 7 to 22, 1998. 72 nations participated, and 68 events were contested in 7 sports. Japan won 5 gold medals: 2 each in ski jumping and speed skating and 1 in freestyle skiing. Japan also won 1 silver and 4 bronze medals. A new bullet train line was constructed from Tokyo to Nagano for this Olympics.

ながのけん 長野県 〘都道府県〙 Nagano Pref. Is located in central Japan, surrounded by eight prefectures such as Niigata, Gunma, and Shizuoka. Is 13,562 km^2 in area, the 4th largest in Japan. Its capital is Nagano City. Famous for apple production and high mountains. Used to be Shinano.

ながのし 長野市 〘地名〙 Nagano City. The capital of Nagano Pref. Is located in its northern part and has developed as a town in front

of ZENKOU-JI Temple. Hosted the Winter Olympic Games in 1998.

ながのしんかんせん 長野新幹線 〘鉄道〙 Officially a part of Hokuriku Shinkansen. Connects Takasaki in Gunma Pref. with Nagano. Started service in 1997, to assist transportation needs for the Winter Olympics in Nagano in 1998.

ながはまじょう 長浜城 〘城郭〙 Nagahama Castle. Was built in northern Shiga Pref. in 1575 by TOYOTOMI HIDEYOSHI. Was dismantled after the Toyotomi clan fell, and its parts were used to construct nearby Hikone Castle. Present Nagahama Castle was rebuilt in 1983 and is used as a history museum. →彦根城

なかはままんじろう 中浜万次郎 〘外交〙 John Mung. 1827-1898. A fisherman, navigation expert, and English translator, born in Kochi Pref. After being shipwrecked at age 14, Manjiro and four shipmates were rescued by an American whaler. Manjiro was brought to the United States in 1843, where he worked and was educated. Returned to Japan in 1851, where he was initially interrogated since Japan was employing the seclusion policy at that time. However, owing to his excellent English skills, he was soon employed as a samurai and high-level interpreter. Served as an interpreter during Commander Perry's visit to Japan and for the 1860 delegation to the United States to conclude the U.S.-Japan Treaty of Amity and Commerce. Produced a Japanese translation of Boditch's *American Practical Navigation*, wrote a Japanese-English phrase book, and taught navigation and interpretation in Japan.

ながひばち 長火鉢 〔家具〕 a rectangular wooden brazier with drawers. Is rarely seen in a modern house.

なかみせ 仲見世 〔ビジネス〕 a shopping street in the precinct of a temple or shrine. One at Sensou-ji Temple in Tokyo is famous.

なかむらかんざぶろう 中村勘三郎 〔歌舞伎〕 the stage name of a kabuki actor. Has been handed down from the 17th century.

ながもち 長持ち 〔家具〕 a large wooden rectangular clothing chest with a cover. Used to be one of the bride's typical household effects.

ながや 長屋 〔建築〕 a row house, or tenement house. A long house under one roof that is divided into several apartments. Most residents are of modest economic means.

ながやおう 長屋王 〔政治〕 684-729. The grandson of Emperor Tenmu. Had the political power in the early 8th century, but he was slandered by the Fujiwara clan and killed himself.

ながやもん 長屋門 〔建築〕 an entrance to a mansion that extends through a row house. A row house, which was built on the edge of an estate owned by a rich farmer or samurai, served as a home for estate workers

ながれづくり 流れ造り 〔神社・建築〕 Nagare style of Shinto architecture. The entrance is on the side parallel to the ridge of the roof, and the roof sweeps forward and down to cover the stairs leading to the entrance. The main sanctuary buildings of the Shimogamo Shrine was built in this style. →本殿；下鴨神社

ながれまんじしゅりけん 流れ卍手裏剣 〔忍者〕 a four-pointed throwing star with curved blades.

ながわきざし 長脇差 〔武器〕 a long secondary sword.

なきじんぐすく 今帰仁城 〔城郭〕 Nakijin Castle. The ruins are located in Okinawa Pref. and were designated a World Heritage Site in 2000.

なぎなた 薙刀 〔武器〕 a single-blade halberd, or a billhook with a long handle. The blade is a little wide and slightly curved. Had been used from the 12th to 17th centuries. Became a weapon for women in the Edo period after the use of the double-blade spears called 'yari' had spread among men.

なきりゅう 鳴き竜 〔建築〕 a reverberation following multiple echoes. Literally means "roaring dragon." Occurs when one claps his or her hands between two parallel flat surfaces. This phenomenon is famous at a hall of Toushouguu Shrine in Nikko, whose ceiling is painted with a dragon.

なけいようし ナ形容詞〖言語〗 na-type adjective. The infinitive form ends with 'na,' like 'shizukana' (quiet) or 'tashikana'(certain). Is also called 'keiyou-doushi,' which literally means "adjectival verb." Behaves as a noun when used before an auxiliary verb 'da.'

なげいれ 投げ入れ〖華道〗 thrown-in-style flower arrangement. Looks natural as if the flowers are just thrown into the container.

なげし 長押〖建築〗 a horizontal bar between vertical pillars. Its purpose is not structural but ornamental.

なげわざ 投げ技 〖柔道・相撲〗 a throwing technique. Throwing techniques of judo include the shoulder throw (SEOI-NAGE) and circle throw (TOMOE-NAGE). Those of sumo include the overarm throw (UWATE-NAGE) and armlock throw (KOTE-NAGE).

なこうど 仲人〖冠婚葬祭〗 a matchmaker. He or she usually becomes a witness, along their spouse, in the wedding ceremony. Since a marriage was thought of as a link between two families in olden times, a matchmaker played an important role. →媒酌(ばいしゃく)人

なこく 奴国〖国名〗 Na. A small country that existed in present Fukuoka Pref. around the 1st century. Sent an envoy to the Han dynasty in 57 and was presented with a gold seal. Is also called 'Na no kuni.'

なごみ 和み〖精神性〗 to calm down, to relax oneself, to become friendly, or to be healed emotionally. This word is usually used as the verb form, 'nagomu.' However, many restaurants, shops, retirement homes, and companies use the noun form, 'nagomi,' as part of their names such as Izakaya Nagomi, Ramen Nagomi, and Nagomi-no-sato.

なごやおび 名古屋帯〖服飾〗 a casual obi for women. Is designed to be easy to tie.

なごやし 名古屋市〖地名〗 Nagoya City. An ordinance-designated city, and the capital of Aichi Pref. Has developed as a castle town governed by Owari branch of the Tokugawa clan. Famous for flat wheat noodles (KISHIMEN), a breaded pork cutlet with miso sauce, toast with sweet adzuki paste, and chopped grilled eel on rice (HITSUMABUSHI). Has many sightseeing spots such as Nagoya Castle, Atsuta Shrine, and the Tokugawa Art Museum.

なごやじょう 名古屋城 〖城郭〗 Nagoya Castle. Was constructed in 1610 by TOKUGAWA IEYASU. Was destroyed in World War II and restored in 1959.

なごやてつどう 名古屋鉄道〖鉄道〗 Nagoya Railroad. Is abbreviated to Meitetsu. One of the 16 major private railway operators of Japan. Holds 20 railway lines and 275 stations in the central, southern, and western parts of Aichi Pref., and in the southwest of Gifu Pref. Connects Nagoya with Central Japan International Airport within 30 minutes by the Airport Limited Express train called μ-Sky. Three Meitetsu lines provide the through-line service with the Nagoya subway lines. Its total length is 444 km, which makes it the third largest private railway company in Japan.

なごやばしょ 名古屋場所 〔相撲〕 the July Grand Sumo Tournament. Is held at Aichi Prefectural Gymnasium in Nagoya City.

なし 梨〔食べ物・植物〕 a pear. *Pyrus pyrifolia*. There are two types: one that is juicy and slightly sour with a brown skin and one that is sweeter with a green skin. Since 'nashi' also means "no" or "nothing," it is sometimes called 'ari no mi,' which means "fruit of being."

なしじまきえ 梨子地蒔絵 〔工芸〕 lacquer technique that produces a surface similar to the skin of a pear. Flat, fine flakes of gold or silver are sprinkled over the lacquer

なすでんがく 茄子田楽 〔食べ物〕 grilled eggplant topped with sweet miso. Goes well with sake.

なずな 薺 〔植物〕 a shepherd's purse. *Capsella bursa-pastoris*. One of the seven herbs of spring in a lunar calendar. →春の七草

なすの なすの〔鉄道〕 the express train on Tohoku Shinkansen. Is named after the hills in northern Tochigi Pref. Connects Tokyo with Kooriyama in Fukushima Pref. in 1.5 hours, stopping at every station on its route.

なだ 灘 〔酒・地名〕 the Nada area. The southeastern part of Hyougo Pref. Covers parts of Kobe and Nishinomiya Cities. Famous for sake brewing because of its good water. →宮水(ﾐﾔﾐ)

なたね 菜種 〔植物〕 **(1)** a colza. *Brassica rapa* var. *nippo-oleifera*. Is also called 'aburana.' Grows to about 1 m high and bears many yellow blossoms. Young stems and leaves are edible as a boiled vegetable or tempura. Oil is extracted from its seeds. **(2)** rapeseed. →菜の花

なたねづゆ 菜種梅雨 〔気象〕 a short rainy season from late March to early April. Is named after colza (NATANE), whicd blooms in this season.

なたぼり 鉈彫り 〔彫刻〕 the hatchet-carving technique. The chisel marks are intentionally left on the surface of a sculpture, which is neither painted nor covered with gilt. This technique was popular in the Kantou and Tohoku regions in the 11th to 12th centuries.

なちのたき 那智の滝〔地名〕 Nachi Waterfall. Is located in Nachi Katsuura Town in southeastern Wakayama Pref. The Nachi River flows through the waterfall. The height of its main drop, 133 m, is the greatest of all the single waterfalls in Japan. Is regarded as one of the three most beautiful waterfalls in Japan, together with Kegon Falls in Tochigi Pref. and Fukuroda Falls in Ibaraki Pref. Can be accessed by bus, with a 30-minute ride from JR Kii Katsuura Station.

なづけ 菜漬け 〖食べ物〗 salted pickles of leaves of green vegetables such as leaf mustard (TAKANA) or potherb mustard (MIZUNA).

なっとう 納豆 〖食べ物〗 fermented brown soybeans. Sticky and have a characteristic odor. Are often served with soy sauce and raw egg at breakfast. Are sold in small white plastic containers.

なっとうきん 納豆菌 〖食文化〗 natto bacteria. Is normally sprayed directly on soy beans to produce NATTOU.

なっとうまき 納豆巻き 〖寿司〗 a sushi roll containing fermented soybeans, NATTOU.

なつばしょ 夏場所 〖相撲〗 the Summer Sumo Tournament. Is held at KOKUGIKAN in Tokyo in May.

なつみかん 夏蜜柑 〖植物・食べ物〗 a Japanese summer grapefruit, or Watson pomelo. *Citrus natsudaidai*. The rind is relatively thick, and the flesh tastes very sour. Eaten raw or as marmalade.

なつめ 棗 〖茶道〗 a lacquered tea caddy for thin powdered green tea. Was invented in the Muromachi period.

なつめそうせき 夏目漱石 〖文芸〗 1867-1916. A prominent fiction writer, scholar of English literature, and haiku poet, born in Edo. After earning a degree in English literature from Tokyo Imperial University, he studied in England from 1903-1905. Returned to Japan to teach literature and later to work as an editor of a major newspaper, Asahi Shimbun. Best known as a novelist and short story writer whose works emphasize the loneliness of humans, especially in the context of friction between Western and Japanese cultures. Some of his fiction works include *I am a Cat* in 1905, *The Grass Pillow* and *Botchan* in 1906, *The Poppy* in 1907, *The Poor Hearts of Men* in 1914, and *Grass by the Roadside* in 1915.

なでしこ 撫子 〖植物〗 a fringed pink, or a large pink. *Dianthus superbus*. One of the seven flowers of autumn in a lunar calendar. →秋の七草

なでしこじゃぱん なでしこジャパン 〖スポーツ〗 the nickname of the women's Japanese national football or soccer team.

なとり 名取り 〖芸道〗 an accredited master of traditional dancing.

なないろ 七色 〖色〗 seven colors. Violet, indigo, blue, green, yellow, orange, and red. Sometimes means "various."

ななかいき 七回忌 〖仏教〗 the 6th anniversary of a person's death. A memorial service is held. The first part of the Japanese expression 'nana' means seven because the day of the person's death is counted as the first. →〜回忌

ななくさ 七草〚植物〛 ⇨秋の七草；春の七草

ななくさがゆ 七草粥 〚暦・食べ物〛 rice porridge containing seven spring herbs. The seven ingredients are SERI (dropwort), NAZUNA (shepherd's purse), GOGYOU (Jersey cudweed), HAKOBERA (chickweed), HOTOKE-NO-ZA (nipplewort), SUZUNA (turnip), and SUZUSHIRO (mooli).

ななつぼし 七つ星〚鉄道〛 Cruise Train Seven Stars in Kyushu. One of Japan's most luxurious cruise trains, operated by JR Kyushu. The 2- and 4-day courses start from Hakata in Fukuoka Pref. and go through many historical and scenic spots in Kyushu. The seven stars indicate not only the seven prefectures on Kyushu Island, but also the seven sightseeing features and the seven cars of the train.

なにわ 難波，浪速，浪花〚地名〛 the old name of the area of Osaka City and its vicinity.

なにわのみや 難波宮 〚政治〛 Naniwa Capital. Was located in Osaka City. Emperor Nintoku established 'Naniwa Takatsu no miya' first, but its location is unknown. Emperor Koutoku established 'Naniwa no Nagara no Toyosaki no miya' to the south of present Osaka Castle in 645. Emperor Shoumu established 'Naniwa no miya' at the same place in 744.

なにわぶし 浪花節 〚音楽〛 narrative and singing accompanied by a shamisen. Was begun in Osaka in the Edo period. The themes are often about the socially expected duty, called GIRI, and the natural human emotion, called NINJOU.

なぬし 名主〚農業〛 a village mayor in the Edo period. This name was mainly used in Eastern Japan. →庄屋

なのくに 奴の国〚国名〛 ⇨奴国(き)

なのはな 菜の花〚植物〛 a blossom of a colza. →菜種

なはし 那覇市 〚地名〛 Naha City. The capital of Okinawa Pref. Is located in its southern part. Developed as the port of the capital of Ryuukyuu Kingdom. Restored Shuri Castle was designated a World Heritage Site in 2000.

なぶんけん 奈文研 〚人文学・施設〛 ⇨奈良文化財研究所

なべ 鍋〚食べ物〛 ⇨鍋物

なべしまかんそう 鍋島閑叟 〚武士〛 1815-1871. The lord of the Saga domain. Rebuilt the finances of the Saga domain, created the first reverberatory furnace in Japan, and installed state-of-the-art military equipment. The Saga domain was reluctant to take part in the battle to destroy the Tokugawa shogunate, but it took full advantage of the new weapons at the time of the Boshin War.

なべしまそうどう 鍋島騒動〚政治・妖怪〛 the internal trouble of the Hizen domain in northern Kyushu in the late 16th century. Was dramatized in the story of a goblin cat. →化け猫

なべしまなおまさ 鍋島直正〖武士〗⇨鍋島閑叟(かん)

なべづる 鍋鉉〖食文化〗 a handle for a pan. Some pans have two handles.

なべぶぎょう 鍋奉行〖食文化〗 a director of a one-pot dish. A person who decides when ingredients should be put in the pot and when people should eat them is called by this term. →鍋物

なべぶた 鍋蓋〖漢字〗 a crown radical in the shape of "pot lid." Has no specific meaning. Is used in kanji such as 文(sentence), 六(six), and 市(city).

なべもの 鍋物〖食べ物〗 a one-pot dish cooked at the table. People sit around the pot while the food is cooking, pick up their favorite cooked ingredients from the pot, and place them in their individual bowls. A special dipping sauce is sometimes used. →すき焼き；水炊き；寄せ鍋

なべやきうどん 鍋焼き饂飩〖食べ物〗 thick wheat noodles served in a small casserole. Contain a variety of ingredients such as vegetables, chicken, fish paste, and egg.

なまあげ 生揚げ〖食べ物〗⇨厚揚げ

なまがし 生菓子〖食べ物〗 a no-bake traditional cake. Its design changes in accordance with each season. Is often served at the tea ceremony.

なまこ 海鼠〖食べ物・動物〗 a sea cucumber. *Holothuroidea*. Is about 20 to 30 cm long and has many projections on the surface. When eaten, its meat is vinegared and its entrails are salted.

なまこかべ なまこ壁〖建築〗 a latticed wall. The square parts are made of tiles while the lines between squares are made of plaster.

なまこもち 海鼠餅〖食べ物〗 a flat hemicylindrical rice cake. Eaten sliced and grilled.

なまざけ 生酒〖酒〗 raw sake. Is not pasteurized after the fermented mash is filtered. →醪(もろ)

なます 膾〖食べ物〗 thin strips of carrots and white radishes seasoned in vinegar. Is commonly served in traditional New Year's cuisine. Sliced fish or meat is sometimes used as an ingredient, and this type of namasu is called 'nuta-namasu.'

なまず 鯰〖魚〗 a catfish. *Silurus asotus*. Lives in fresh water. About 50 cm long. There was a superstition that an earthquake occurs when a gigantic catfish rampages underground.

なまずえ 鯰絵〖絵画・災害〗 a catfish painting. The motif is based on the old belief that a big catfish under the ground causes an earthquake. This type of painting was popular after the Ansei Great Earthquake in Edo in 1855.

なまはげ なまはげ〖暦・妖怪〗 a demon who remonstrates children's laziness. In the Oga Peninsula of Akita Pref., young men wear a mask and costume of 'namahage' with a fake knife, visit village houses to admonish young children, and receive hospitality on January 15th. Due to the diminishing number of children in rural areas, the number of local communities that undertake such an event is decreasing, and 'namahage' is becoming more of a tourist icon.

なまやつはし 生八つ橋〚食べ物〛 an unbaked cinnamon dumpling. Is made from rice flour, sugar, and cinnamon and often contains sweet adzuki paste. Besides cinnamon, some modern versions have a variety of flavors, such as green tea and chocolate. A specialty of Kyoto. → 八つ橋

なまりぶし 生り節 〚調味料〛 steamed and half-boiled bonito. Is used for simmered food, vinegared food, or salad.

なみきりふどう 波切不動 〚仏教〛 Wave-cutting Immovable Wisdom King. It is said that KUUKAI carved a sculpture of the Immovable Wisdom King when the ship was in danger of having a wreck on his way back from China, and the Immovable Wisdom King cut the waves to guide the ship securely. → 不動明王

なみだあめ 涙雨〚精神性・気象〛 a gentle rain that occurs when someone is heartbroken. Literally means "tear rain."

なむあみだぶつ 南無阿弥陀仏 〚仏教〛 "I put my faith in Amitabha Buddha." This phrase is repeatedly chanted in Pure Land Buddhism. → 浄土宗；浄土真宗

なむたいしへんじょうこんごう 南無大師遍照金剛 〚仏教〛 "I put my faith in KUUKAI and Great Sun Buddha." This phrase is used in esoteric Buddhism, especially on a pilgrimage to eighty-eight temples in Shikoku. →遍路

なむみょうほうれんげきょう 南無妙法蓮華経〚仏教〛 "I put my faith in the Lotus Sutra of the Wonderful Law." This phrase is repeatedly chanted in the Nichiren sect. → 日蓮宗

なめこ 滑子〚植物・食べ物〛 nameko mushroom. *Pholiota nameko*. Eaten in miso soup or with grated white radish.

なめし 菜飯〚食べ物〛 rice boiled with green vegetables.

なら 楢 〚植物〛 a Japanese oak tree. *Quercus serrata*. Its fruits are acorns. The wood is used for furniture and architecture.

ならえほん 奈良絵本〚絵画・文芸〛 a picture book containing popular short stories, OTOGI-ZOUSHI. Was made from the 15th to 17th centuries. Is said to have been painted by a priest at KOUFUKU-JI Temple in Nara, but this point has not been verified.

ならけん 奈良県〚都道府県〛 Nara Pref. Is located east of Osaka and south of Kyoto in Western Japan. Is 3,691 km^2 in area. Its capital is Nara City. Has many temples and shrines such as the HOURYUU-JI Temple and the Kasuga Grand Shrine. Several ancient capitals such as FUJIWARA-KYOU (694-710) and HEIJOU-KYOU (710-784) were situated in Nara Pref. Used to be YAMATO.

ならこくりつはくぶつかん 奈良国立博物館〖博物館〗 Nara National Museum. Was founded in Nara City in 1895. Mainly stores Buddhist art. The Exhibition of SHOUSOU-IN Treasures is held every fall.

ならし 奈良市〖地名〗 Nara City. The capital of Nara Pref. Is located in its northern part. The Imperial Palace was relocated to here in 710 and moved to NAGAOKA-KYOU in 784. Has many temples and shrines including TOUDAI-JI, KOUFUKU-JI, YAKUSHI-JI, TOUSHOUDAI-JI Temples and Kasuga Grand Shrine, which were designated a World Heritage Site in 1988. Produces brushes and India ink sticks for calligraphy, flat plane carving called ITTOU-BORI, and Akahada ware. Its specialties include vegetables pickled in sake lees, called NARADUKE.

ならじだい 奈良時代〖時代〗 the Nara period, from 710 to 794. The capital was placed in HEIJOU-KYOU, in present Nara City. The ritsuryo system was well-developed, exchange with China and Korea was active, and Buddhism influenced political affairs. →天平時代；律令制

ならだいぶつ 奈良大仏〖仏教〗 the Great Buddha in Nara. Sits at TOUDAI-JI Temple. Is 15 m high. The original one was produced in 752 as the result of a vow made by Emperor Shoumu but was destroyed later several times. The existing one was reproduced in 1709.

ならづけ 奈良漬け〖食べ物〗 vegetables preserved in sake lees. Was invented in Nara Pref. but now is called 'naraduke' even if it is produced outside Nara.

ならにんぎょう 奈良人形〖玩具〗 a Nara doll. Is carved from wood in flat planes and colored. Started in the 19th century.

ならぶんかざいけんきゅうしょ 奈良文化財研究所〖人文学・研究機関〗 Nara National Research Institute for Cultural Properties. An independent administrative institution. Was founded in 1952 in Nara City.

なりたえくすぷれす 成田エクスプレス〖鉄道〗 Narita Express. Connects Narita Airport with major stations in the Tokyo metropolitan area such as Tokyo, Shinagawa, Shibuya, Shinjuku, Ikebukuro, and Yokohama. The trains operate every 30 minutes from early morning untill late at night. Takes 1 hour from Narita Airport to Tokyo, and 1 hour and 25 minutes from Narita Airport to Shinjuku. Abbreviated to N'EX.

なりたくうこう 成田空港〖交通〗 ⇨ 成田国際空港

なりたこくさいくうこう 成田国際空港〖交通〗 Narita International

Airport (NRT). Is also known as Tokyo Narita Airport, and was formerly called the New Tokyo International Airport. Shoud not be confused with Tokyo International Airport, also known as Haneda Airport (HND). Is located in Narita City in northern Chiba Pref. Amidst the violent protests by left-wing activists in the 1960s and 70s, it started operation in 1978. Handles 40 million passengers annually, mostly international travelers. Includes three terminal buildings. From the airport, passengers can get to the metropolitan area by JR Narita Express, Keisei Sky Liner, or direct bus services. Some train and bus services go beyond the metropolitan area to tourist spots such as Kamakura, Lake Kawaguchiko, Nikko, and even Kyoto.

なりたさんしんしょうじ 成田山新勝寺 〚寺院〛 Naritasan Shinshoji Temple. A main temple of the Chizan school in the Shingon sect, located in Narita City, Chiba Pref. Was founded in 940. Is also called Narita Fudou. Has branch temples in cities such as Tokyo, Yokohama, and Sapporo.

なりもの 鳴物 〚芸能・相撲〛 instruments other than the shamisen in kabuki. Namely percussion and wind instruments.

なるたきじゅく 鳴滝塾 〚学校〛 Narutaki School. A private school founded in 1824 by a German doctor, Philipp Franz von Siebold. Taught medicine, botany, and the Dutch language.

なると ナルト 〚漫画・作品〛 *Naruto*. A ninja manga, written and illustrated by Kishimoto Masashi. Was published serially in a boys' magazine, *Weekly Shonen Jump*, from 1999 to 2014.

なると 鳴門 〚食べ物〛 steamed fish paste with a spiral whirlpool-like pattern. Is mainly served with noodles in soup.

なるとかいきょう 鳴門海峡 〚地名〛 Naruto Strait. Is located between Awaji and Shikoku Islands. Connects the Inland Sea with the Kii Channel. Is only 1.4 km wide at its narrowest point. Japan's fastest current can be observed, flowing at 20 km/h. Famous for its swirling whirlpools.

なれずし 熟れ鮨 〚食べ物〛 preserved food of fermented rice and salted fish. Has a characteristic odor and sourness. Examples include FUNA-ZUSHI in Shiga Pref. and hatahata-zushi in Akita Pref.

なわしろ 苗代 〚農業〛 a nursery bed for rice seedlings. After being grown for about 50 days, the rice seedlings are transplanted into a rice field. →田植え

なわのれん 縄暖簾 **(1)**〚ビジネス〛a rope curtain. **(2)**〚酒〛a traditional-style pub. A rope curtain is hung down at the entrance. →居酒屋

なわばしご 縄梯子 〚忍者〛 a rope ladder. The two sides are made of

ropes, and the rungs are made of wood.

なんが 南画 〖絵画〗 a picture in the amateur-like style. After being influenced by BUNJIN-GA in China, the original Japanese style was established by IKE NO TAIGA and YOSA BUSON around the 18th century.

なんかいでんきてつどう 南海電気鉄道 〖鉄道〗 Nankai Electric Railway. One of the 16 major private railway operators of Japan. Serves southern Osaka and northern Wakayama Prefs. Connects its terminal Nanba in Osaka City with the residential areas such as Sakai, Kishiwada, and Wakayama Cities, Kansai Airport, and Mt. Kouya. Also operates a cable car system on Mt. Kouya. Runs all-reserved limited express trains such as "rapi:t" for Kansai Airport and "Koya" for Gokurakubashi on Mt. Kouya.

なんかいどう 南海道 〖地名〗 the name of an administrative district before the Meiji Restoration in 1868. Consisted of present Wakayama Pref., southern Mie Pref., Awaji Island in Hyougo Pref., and all the four prefectures in Shikoku.

なんかいとらふ 南海トラフ 〖自然〗 Nankai Trough. Stretches from Suruga Bay of Shizuoka Pref. to approximately 100 km offshore to the south of Shikoku. The Philippine Sea Plate sinks below earth here. Several great earthquakes in the past were related to the subduction of this plate.

なんきんたますだれ 南京玉簾 〖玩具〗 street performance using bamboo sticks. A performer creates various shapes with bamboo sticks connected loosely by threads, while chanting and dancing.

なんこう 楠公 〖武士〗 ⇨楠正成 (くすのきまさしげ)

なんしきてにす 軟式テニス 〖スポーツ〗 soft tennis. Uses a soft rubber ball. Was invented in Japan around 1890.

なんしきやきゅう 軟式野球 〖スポーツ〗 rubber ball baseball. Was invented for boys in Japan in 1919. Is played by almost all junior-high school baseball teams.

なんしゅうが 南宗画 〖絵画〗 ⇨文人画

なんせいしょとう 南西諸島 〖島名〗 the Southwest Islands. Extend from the south of Kyushu to Taiwan, separating the East China Sea from the Pacific Ocean.

なんぜんじ 南禅寺 〖寺院〗 Nanzenji Temple. A main temple of the Rinzai sect located in Kyoto. Was founded in 1291 by a priest, Daimin Kokushi. Was ranked the best among the Five Zen Temples of Kyoto. The living quarters of the chief priest (HOUJOU) are a National Treasure.

なんそうさとみはっけんでん 南総里見八犬伝 〖文芸・作品〗 *The Eight Dog Chronicles*, or *Satomi and the Eight "Dogs."* A fantasy novel published serially from 1814 to 1842 by

KYOKUTEI BAKIN. The Satomi clan in present Chiba Pref. was revived, owing to the help of eight warriors, who were associated with the mysterious connection between a human princess and a heroic dog.

なんだいもん 南大門 〖仏教・建築〗 the south main gate of a Buddhist temple. →中門(ちゅう)

なんちょう 南朝 〖政治〗 Southern Court. When ASHIKAGA TAKAUJI helped Emperor Koumyou to the throne in 1336, Emperor Godaigo escaped to Yoshino in present Nara Pref., bringing the Three Sacred Treasures of the Imperial Family, and established the Southern Court. It reconciled with the Northern Court in Kyoto when Emperor Gokameyama in the Southern Court bestowed the Sacred Treasures on Emperor Gokomatsu in 1392. →後醍醐天皇; 三種の神器

なんてん 南天 〖植物〗 a nandina, a heavenly bamboo, or a sacred bamboo. *Nandina domestica*. Bears small red spherical fruits in autumn, which are used in traditional Chinese medicine.

なんとしちだいじ 南都七大寺 〖寺院〗 Seven Great Temples of Nara. TOUDAI-JI, SAIDAI-JI, GANGOU-JI, DAI-AN-JI, YAKUSHI-JI, KOUFUKU-JI, and HOURYUU-JI.

なんとほくれい 南都北嶺 〖仏教・政治〗 KOUFUKU-JI Temple in Nara and ENRYAKU-JI Temple in Kyoto. The founder of the Tendai sect, SAICHOU,

used this term for the first time to contrast his sect with the Six Sects of Nara. Later this term came to indicate the monk army of Koufuku-ji and Enryaku-ji. →天台宗; 南都六宗; 僧兵

なんとやきうち 南都焼討ち 〖仏教・政治〗 Attacking and Burning of Nara in 1180. Was commanded by Taira no Shigehira, a son of TAIRA NO KIYOMORI. The TOUDAI-JI and KOUFUKU-JI temples were burned out.

なんとろくしゅう 南都六宗 〖仏教〗 the Six Sects of Nara. Were all introduced from China during the 7th and early 8th centuries and promoted as state Buddhism. Although titled "sects," they were divided as philosophical schools rather than religious sects, different from those in later periods. Include Joujitsu, Sanron, Hossou, Kusha, Kegon, and Ritsu sects. →法相(ほっそう)宗; 華厳宗; 律宗

なんばんえ 南蛮絵 〖絵画〗 a Western painting brought to Japan, or a Western-style painting influenced by it, in the 16th to 17th centuries. Declined because of the prohibition of Christianity and the seclusion policy.

なんばんじ 南蛮寺 〖キリスト教〗 a Christian church built in the 16th century.

なんばんじん 南蛮人 〖外交〗 the generic term for Portuguese and Spaniards visiting Japan in the 16th and 17th centuries as Christian missionaries or on business. They usually came through Southeast Asia.

なんばんせん 南蛮船〔外交・交通〕 a Portuguese or Spanish ship visiting Japan in the 16th and 17th centuries.

なんばんづけ 南蛮漬け 〔食べ物〕 deep-fried fish or chicken pickled in vinegar and seasoned with red pepper. Horse mackerels (AJI) and pond smelts (WAKASAGI) are popular as ingredients.

なんばんとらいのしな 南蛮渡来の品〔外交〕 an article imported from Europe in the 16th and 17th centuries.

なんばんに 南蛮煮〔食べ物〕 meat or fish and vegetables simmered with red pepper.

なんばんびじゅつ 南蛮美術〔美術〕 European-style fine arts in the 16th to 17th centuries. Were influenced by European products brought by the Portuguese and Spanish.

なんばんびょうぶ 南蛮屏風〔絵画〕 a pair of folding screens depicting visiting Europeans. Was popular in the 16th to 17th centuries, and there exist more than 60 works at present. Though the theme is European, the painting style is Japanese. →南蛮人

なんばんぶんか 南蛮文化 〔外交〕 European culture imported in the 16th and 17th centuries by Christian missionaries and traders.

なんばんぼうえき 南蛮貿易 〔外交・経済〕 trade with Spain and Portugal from the mid-16th century until the national seclusion policy was employed in 1639. Japan imported silk, guns, gunpowder, leather, and spices, and it exported silver, copper, swords, and lacquerware.

なんばんやき 南蛮焼き〔工芸〕 pottery imported from Southeast Asia in the 16th and 17th centuries.

なんぶてつびん 南部鉄瓶〔工芸〕 an iron kettle made in the area around Morioka, Iwate Pref.

なんぼくちょうじだい 南北朝時代 〔時代〕 the period of Northern and Southern Courts. Started in 1336 when Emperor Godaigo moved to Yoshino in present Nara Pref., and ended in 1392 when Emperor Gokameyama returned to Kyoto. The first one third of the Muromachi period. →後醍醐天皇；室町時代

に

にいがたけん　新潟県　〔都道府県〕 Niigata Pref. Its capital is Niigata City. Is located in central Japan, on the coast of the Sea of Japan between Yamagata and Toyama Prefs. Its area is 12,584 km², the 5th largest prefecture. Has many snow resorts such as Myoukou, Naeba, and Yuzawa. Famous for high-quality rice production. Its prefectural bird, TOKI, is designated an endangered species. Used to be Echigo.

にいがたし　新潟市〔地名〕 Niigata City. The capital of Niigata Pref. and the largest city on the coast of the Sea of Japan. Is located in the central part of the prefecture and has developed as a port town.

にいじまじょう　新島襄　〔教育〕 Joseph Hardy Neesima. 1843-1890. A Protestant educator, born in Edo to a samurai family. Was among early Christian converts in Meiji Japan. Stowed away to the U.S. in 1864, attended Amherst College, and served as an interpreter for the Iwakura Mission. Returned to Japan to help found a school that would later become Doshisha University in Kyoto.

にいなめさい　新嘗祭　〔天皇・祭礼〕 the Imperial festival of the rice harvest. The Emperor offers newly cropped rice to the deities and protective spirits and also eats it himself. Has been held on November 23 each year, which is now a national holiday, Labor Thanksgiving Day. →勤労感謝の日

にいにいろくじけん　二二六事件〔政治〕 ⇨二二六（ﾆﾆﾛｸ）事件

にいぼん　新盆〔仏教〕 the first Bon Festival after a person has died.

においぶくろ　匂袋〔服飾〕 a sachet. Contains perfume such as white sandalwood (BYAKUDAN), musk (JAKOU), and clove tree (CHOUJI). Is carried personally or put in a chest of drawers.

におう　仁王　〔仏教〕　 the Two Guardian Kings. *Vajrapani*. Are enshrined at many temple gates. One opens the mouth and is called A-GYOU, and the other closes the mouth and is called UN-GYOU. Most of the king figures are stripped to the waist. Two famous examples of the figures are located at the TOUDAI-JI Temple and the HOURYUU-JI Temple.

におうもん　仁王門〔仏教・建築〕　a temple gate with the statue of the Two Guardian Kings.

にがうり　苦瓜〔植物〕　⇨ゴーヤ

にがり　苦汁　〔食文化〕　 bittern. A bitter liquid left when salt is separated out from seawater. Is used to solidify tofu.

にかわ　膠〔科学技術〕　 glue. Is extracted from skin or bones of animals.

にきさく　二期作　〔農業〕　 double

cropping of rice. →二毛作

にぎはやひのみこと 饒速日命 〔神話〕 the ancestral deity of the Mononobe clan. Came down to earth by the flying stone ship before the advent of the grandson of the Sun Goddess, NINIGI NO MIKOTO.

にぎみたま 和御霊 〔神道〕 a peaceful divine spirit. ↔荒御霊(あらみたま)

にぎりずし 握り寿司 〔食べ物〕 hand-formed sushi with a topping of seafood. Typical sushi.

にぎりでっぽう 握り鉄砲 〔忍者〕 a small simple handgun.

にぎりめし 握り飯 〔食べ物〕 ⇨お握り

にくうどん 肉饂飩 〔食べ物〕 thick wheat noodles with sliced beef or pork in hot broth.

にくけい 肉髻 〔仏教〕 ⇨肉髻(にっけい)

にくけいしゅ 肉髻朱 〔仏教〕 ⇨肉髻(にっけい)朱

にくじゃが 肉じゃが 〔食べ物〕 meat, potatoes, and onions stewed in sweetened soy sauce. Sometimes includes KONNYAKU noodles, carrots, and other vegetables.

にくづき 肉月 〔漢字〕 ⇨月偏

にくまん 肉饅 〔食べ物〕 a Chinese-style meat bun. Contains minced pork and vegetables and is steamed when served. Is said to have been invented in Japan, imitating Chinese baos. →中華饅頭

にこごり 煮凝り 〔食べ物〕 jellied broth. The broth in which fish or meat has been simmered coagulates and becomes 'nikogori.'

にこみ 煮込み 〔食べ物〕 a stewed dish. →味噌煮込み饂飩(うどん)；もつ煮込み

にこみうどん 煮込み饂飩 〔食べ物〕 thick wheat noodles stewed with various ingredients.

にごりえ にごりえ 〔文芸・作品〕 *Troubled Waters*. A short novel published in 1895 by HIGUCHI ICHIYOU. Describes lower society by focusing on the life of a barmaid.

にごりざけ 濁り酒 〔酒〕 unrefined sake. Is made from rice without straining the lees. White, thick, and a little muddy.

にころがし 煮転がし 〔食べ物〕 ⇨煮っ転がし

にざかな 煮魚 〔食べ物〕 fish simmered with soy sauce, mirin, and sugar.

にしかた 西方 〔相撲〕 west side in sumo wrestling. A wrestler on the west side enters the ring from the west, while a wrestler on the east side enters the ring from the east. Each side has a wrestler in the same rank, but the status of the one in the west is lower than that of the one in the east. ↔東方

にしき 錦 〔服飾〕 gorgeous silk-woven fabric with colorful patterns.

にしきえ 錦絵 〔絵画〕 colorful wood-block ukiyo-e. Has multiple colors in the details, different from prior ukiyo-e. Was popular at the end of the 18th century.

にしきごい 錦鯉 〔魚〕 a variously colored carp. Was selectively bred in Japan as an ornamental fish.

にしきのみはた 錦の御旗 〔軍事・

政治』 the Imperial standard. The 16-petal chrysanthemum is embroidered in gold threads on a red background.

にしじんおり 西陣織 『服飾』 high-quality yarn-dyed fabrics produced in Nishijin, Kyoto.

にしだきたろう 西田幾多郎 『人文学』 1870-1945. A philosopher and professor at Kyoto University, born in Ishikawa Pref. Fused Occidental philosophy into Oriental thought. His works include *An Inquiry into the Good* (Zen no kenkyuu)．

にしにっぽんてつどう 西日本鉄道 『鉄道』 Nishi-Nippon Railroad. One of the 16 major private railway operators of Japan, which serves western Fukuoka Pref. Its main line connects its terminal Tenjin in central Fukuoka City with residential areas such as Chikushino, Kurume, Yanagawa, and Oomuta Cities. Its Dazaifu Line is the only railway line that leads to Dazaifu Tenmangu Shrine. →太宰府天満宮

にしにほんかざんたい 西日本火山帯 『自然』 West Japan Volcanic Belt. Used to be divided into Hakusan and Kirishima Volcanic Belts. Known for its alkaline volcanic products.

にじのまつばら 虹ノ松原 『植物・地名』 the name of a black pine forest in Karatsu City in northern Saga Pref. Literally means "Pine Forest of the Rainbow." Stretches for 4.5 km along the coast of Karatsu Bay. In the 17th century, the feudal lord,

Terazawa Hirotaka, planted trees to create a windbreak along the coast. Has become a popular tourist spot, within walking distance from a JR Nijinomatsubara Station.

にしのみやじんじゃ 西宮神社 『神社』 Nishinomiya Shrine. The head shrine of the Ebisu Shrines throughout Japan, located in southeastern Hyogo Pref. Enshrines HIRUKO no ookami, who is identified with EBISU, the deity of business and fishing, and three other deities.

にしほんがんじ 西本願寺 『寺院』 Hongwanji. The head temple of the Hongwanji school of the True Pure Land sect, located in Kyoto. Was founded in 1591 by a priest, Junnyo, the third son of KENNYO. The main hall, the founder's hall, and the gate are National Treasures. Was designated a World Heritage Site in 1994. ↔東本願寺 →浄土真宗

にじます 虹鱒 『魚』 a rainbow trout. *Salmo gairdneri*. Originally came from North America. Lives in fresh water. About 50 cm long. Eaten fried or grilled with salt.

にしまわりこうろ 西回り航路 『交通』 the westward sea route during the Edo period. Products from the Tohoku and Hokuriku regions were carried to Kyoto and Osaka on vessels called KITAMAE-BUNE via the Sea of Japan and Lake Biwa, or via the Sea of Japan, the Kanmon Strait, and the Inland Sea.

にしめ 煮染め 『食べ物』 dish of vegetables, mushroom, tofu, and other ingredients simmered in soy sauce and water until the liquid is almost gone. Is often used for New Year's cuisine.

にじゅうかぎかっこ 二重鉤括弧〖言語〗『 』. Encloses text that is said by someone in an utterance by another person, like「あの時彼は『嫌だ』って言ったのよ」("At that time, he said 'No.'"), or refers to a book title.

にじゅうごぼさつ 二十五菩薩〖仏教〗 Twenty-five Bodhisattvas. Come for a dying person as attendants of the Amitabha Buddha to take his or her soul to the Western Pure Land. →阿弥陀来迎(あみだらいごう)

にじゅうしせっき 二十四節気〖暦〗 the 24 seasonal nodes in the traditional calendar. →立春；雨水(うすい)；啓蟄(けいちつ)；春分の日；晴明(せいめい)；穀雨(こくう)；立夏；小満(しょうまん)；芒種(ぼうしゅ)；夏至(げし)；小暑(しょうしょ)；大暑(たいしょ)；立秋；処暑(しょしょ)；白露(はくろ)；秋分の日；寒露(かんろ)；霜降(そうこう)；立冬；小雪(しょうせつ)；大雪(たいせつ)；冬至(とうじ)；小寒；大寒

にじゅうばし 二重橋〖橋〗**(1)** Imperial Palace Main Gate Iron Bridge. Literally means "double bridge." Was originally built in 1614 as part of the Edo Castle. Was reconstructed in 1964, but its double girders disappeared. Is located on the east side of the Imperial Palace. **(2)** the generic name for (1) and a stone bridge with two arches next to (1). Accessible on foot from Nijuubashi-mae Station on the Tokyo Metro Chiyoda Line.

にじゅうはちぶしゅう 二十八部衆〖仏教〗 Twenty-eight Devas. Guard the Thousand-armed Bodhisattva of Mercy. Famous examples are in Sanjuusangen-dou in Kyoto. →千手観音

にじょうじょう 二条城〖城郭〗 Nijo Castle. Was constructed in Kyoto in 1603 by Tokugawa Ieyasu. Was used as a lodging of a shogun in the Edo period. The last shogun, Tokugawa Yoshinobu, decided to return political power to the Emperor in 1867. Was designated a World Heritage Site in 1994.

にじりぐち 躙り口〖茶道・建築〗 the small entrance to a room for the tea ceremony. Guests crouch down and crawl through the entrance, which is about 60 cm square. →茶道口

にしん 鰊〖魚〗 a Pacific herring. *Clupea pallasi*. Eaten dried, smoked, or salted. Its roe called kazunoko are eaten as New Year's cuisine.

にしんごてん 鰊御殿〖ビジネス・建築〗 a herring mansion. These mansions were built in Hokkaido by wealthy fishermen when the herring industry boomed. Some existing mansions are designated cultural properties.

にしんそば 鰊蕎麦〖食べ物〗 hot buckwheat noodles with dried herring. The head, tail, gills, guts, and bones have been removed, and the remaining part has been sliced into two or three portions and simmered down in soy sauce, mirin, and sugar. A specialty of Kyoto.

にせこ ニセコ 〔地名〕 the name of a popular snow resort in western Hokkaido, at the foot of Mt. Niseko-Annupuri. Another snow resort, Rusutsu, is located nearby. Can be accessed by bus from JR Niseko, Kutchan, or Sapporo Stations. There is also a direct bus service from New Chitose Airport, taking 3 hours.

にせたいじゅうたく 二世帯住宅 〔生活〕 a two-family house. Two families of three generations sometimes live in the same house, the inside of which is clearly divided into two parts. Each part has an entrance, a kitchen, and a bathroom for each family.

にそう 尼僧 〔仏教〕 ⇨尼(½)

にちえいどうめい 日英同盟 〔外交〕 Anglo-Japanese Alliance. Was built in 1902 to oppose Russia's southward expansion. On the pretext of this alliance, Japan participated in WW I. Was disbanded in 1923.

にちぎんたんかん 日銀短観 〔経済〕 a Short-Term Economic Survey of Enterprises in Japan. Is published quarterly by the Bank of Japan. The survey is based on statistical data and queries to about 10,000 companies.

にちどくいさんごくどうめい 日独伊三国同盟 〔外交〕 Tripartite Pact. Was concluded in 1940 by Germany, Italy, and Japan for military cooperation. The three nations

agreed to mutually respect each other's leading positions in Europe and Asia, respectively.

にちぶ 日舞 〔芸能〕 ⇨日本舞踊

にちぶんけん 日文研 〔人文学・施設〕 ⇨国際日本文化研究センター

にちべいあんぜんほしょうじょうやく 日米安全保障条約 〔外交〕 U.S.-Japan Security Treaty. Was concluded in 1951 and amended in 1960. Stipulates that Japan and the United States will cooperate with each other for their mutual security. Under this treaty, the U.S. military troops are stationed in Japan. The termination of the treaty is possible by the unilateral announcement of one of either party, but it will be automatically extended unless it is not terminated.

にちべいしゅうこうつうしょうじょうやく 日米修好通商条約 〔外交〕 Harris Treaty, or U.S.-Japan Treaty of Amity and Commerce. Was concluded in 1858 without Imperial authorization. Forced Japan to open five ports: Hakodate, Kanagawa, Nagasaki, Niigata, and Hyougo, to exempt U.S. citizens staying at those ports from the jurisdiction of Japanese law, to exchange diplomatic agents and consuls, and to agree on the principles of free trade.

にちべいぼうえいきょうりょくしん 日米防衛協力指針 〔外交〕 Guidelines for U.S.-Japan Defense Cooperation. Agreement on concrete methods of defense cooperation based on the U.S.-Japan Security Treaty. Defines the role of each nation in case of an emergency in or for Japan. When amended in 1997, the response to the case of a Korean Peninsula emergency was added. When amended in 2015, the support of the U.S. military by the Japan Self-Defense Forces was expanded to include an international context.

にちべいわしんじょうやく　日米和親条約〖外交〗 Kanagawa Treaty, or Treaty of Peace and Amity between the U.S. and the Empire of Japan. Was concluded in 1854 when Commodore Perry visited Japan. Though not referring to trade, it became the first step for Japan to open the country to commerce.

にちれん　日蓮〖仏教〗 1222-1282. A priest born in present Chiba Pref. and the founder of the Nichiren sect. Was exiled twice because he severely criticized Zen and Pure Land Buddhism and predicted national crisis. →日蓮宗

にちれんしゅう　日蓮宗〖仏教〗 the Nichiren sect. Was founded by Nichiren in the Kamakura period. Emphasizes the teaching of the Lotus Sutra. Its adherents repeatedly chant the prayer, 'Namu myouhou renge kyou,' which means "I put my faith in the Lotus Sutra of the Wonderful Law."

にちろせんそう　日露戦争〖戦争〗 Russo-Japanese War. Started in 1904, with Japan struggling for dominance over Korea and Manchuria, and ended in 1905 through the mediation of the U.S.A. Under the Treaty of Portsmouth, Japan won southern Sakhalin, the Liaodong Peninsula, and the South Manchuria Railway.

にっかじへん　日華事変〖戦争〗 ⇨日中戦争

にっかんきほんじょうやく　日韓基本条約〖外交〗 Korea-Japan Basic Treaty. Was concluded in 1965 to establish diplomatic relations between Japan and South Korea, including Japanese economic contributions of about 1.1 billion USD to Korea. By concluding this treaty, the treaty about the previous annexation of Korea to Japan became invalid, and the two countries did not determine the territorial dispute over the Liancourt Rocks, 'Takeshima.'

にっかんへいごう　日韓併合〖外交〗 ⇨韓国併合

にっきぶんがく　日記文学〖文芸〗 diary literature. Was popular from the 10th to 14th centuries and mainly written in kana by women. Examples include *The Tosa Diary*, *The Gossamer Years*, *As I Crossed a Bridge of Dreams*, and *The Confessions of Lady Nijo*. →土佐日記; 蜻蛉(かげろう)日記; 更級(さらしな)日記; とはずがたり

にっきょうそ　日教組〖教育・団体名〗 ⇨日本教職員組合

につけ　煮付け〖食べ物〗 fish simmered with soy sauce until the liquid is almost gone.

にっけい 肉髻〔仏教〕 a protruding head of a Buddha. Is said to depict the wisdom of Buddha. One of the 32 major physical characteristics of Buddha. →三十二相八十種好

にっけいしゅ 肉髻朱〔仏教〕 the red circle in front of the protruding head of a Buddha. Red crystal is often inserted. →肉髻

にっけいへいきんかぶか 日経平均株価〔経済〕 Nikkei Stock Average. A stock price index calculated with 225 issues in the first section of the Tokyo Stock Exchange by a newspaper publisher, *Nikkei*. →日本経済新聞

にっこう 日光〔地名〕 Nikko. Is located in northwestern Tochigi Pref., and has many popular sightseeing spots such as the Toushouguu Shrine, Kegon Waterfalls, Lake Chuuzenji, and Mt. Nantai. Its shrines and temples were designated a World Heritage Site in 1999.

にっこうかいどう 日光街道〔交通〕 Nikko Highway. One of the five highways radiating from Edo in the Edo period. Starting from Nihon-bashi, Edo, it ran through present Saitama and Ibaraki Prefs., and terminated in Nikko in Tochigi Pref. Takes roughly the same route as present Route 4, from Tokyo to Utsunomiya in Tochigi Pref., and present Route 119 from Utsunomiya to Nikko.

にっこうとうしょうぐう 日光東照宮〔神社〕 Nikko Toshogu Shrine. Was established in Nikko, present Tochigi Pref., in 1617. Enshrines TOKUGAWA IEYASU, the founder of the Tokugawa shogunate. Some buildings including two gates are National Treasures. Was designated a World Heritage Site in 1999. →陽明門

にっこうぼさつ 日光菩薩〔仏教〕 Bodhisattva of Sunlight. *Surya-prabha*. An attendant to the Healing Buddha on the left in a triad. Is not worshipped independently. →薬師如来；月光(がっ)菩薩

にっころがし 煮っ転がし〔食べ物〕 taros or potatoes simmered to dry in broth.

にっしょうき 日章旗〔外交〕 the sun disc flag. The national flag of Japan. The sun disc is placed in the center of the white background. The diameter of the disc is three-fifth of the length of the vertical side. The ratio of the vertical and horizontal sides is 7 to 10.

にっしんしゅうこうじょうき 日清修好条規〔外交〕 Sino-Japanese Amity Treaty. Was concluded in 1871 and was abolished when the Sino-Japanese War started in 1894.

にっしんせんそう 日清戦争〔戦争〕 Sino-Japanese War from 1894 to 1895. After struggling for dominance over Korea, Japan and China concluded the Shimonoseki Peace Treaty in 1895, under which China agreed on the independence of Korea, and Japan won the Liaodong Peninsula, Taiwan, and the Pescadores Islands and the payment of 200 million taels as war reparations. →三国干渉

にっそうかん 日想観〘仏教〙 mental training to envision the Western Pure Land by looking at the setting sun.

にっそきょうどうせんげん 日ソ共同宣言〘外交〙 Soviet-Japan Joint Declaration. Was exchanged between Japan and the Soviet Union in 1956. Since the Soviet Union did not sign the San Francisco Peace Treaty, the two nations issued this declaration to normalize mutual diplomatic relations. In this declaration, the territorial issue was postponed, but the Soviet Union agreed to return the Habomai Islands and Shikotan Island to Japan when the Peace Treaty was concluded between the two countries.

にっそちゅうりつじょうやく 日ソ中立条約〘外交〙 Soviet-Japan Neutrality Treaty. Was concluded between Japan and the Soviet Union in 1941. Prescribed mutual inviolability and the neutrality of one nation if the other was targeted by the military action of a third nation. At the end of World War II, the Soviet Union abandoned this treaty and participated in the war against Japan.

にったよしさだ 新田義貞〘武士〙 1301-1338. A warlord born in present Gunma Pref. As a friendly force of the Kamakura shogunate, attacked KUSUNOKI MASASHIGE in 1331 but destroyed the shogunate in cooperation with Emperor Godaigo and ASHIKAGA TAKAUJI in 1333. When Emperor Godaigo and Takauji had a conflict with each other, took the side of the Emperor. →後醍醐天皇

にっちゅうきょうどうせいめい 日中共同声明〘外交〙 China-Japan Joint Statement. Was signed to normalize mutual diplomatic relations between Japan and China in 1972. China announced that Taiwan was part of China, and Japan expressed its respects for China's position. As a result of this statement, diplomatic ties between Japan and Taiwan were broken.

にっちゅうせんそう 日中戦争〘戦争〙 Sino-Japanese War from 1937 to 1945. Started without the declaration of war, triggered by the encounter between Japanese and Chinese troops at the Marco Polo Bridge, called 'Rokou-kyou' in Japanese, in Beijing. Developed into the Pacific War, as part of World War II. →太平洋戦争

にっちゅうへいわゆうこうじょうやく 日中平和友好条約〘外交〙 China-Japan Peace and Friendship Treaty. Was concluded for the development of diplomatic relations between Japan and China in 1978, based on the China-Japan Joint Statement of 1972. At that time, China was quite antagonistic toward the Soviet Union, so it took six years from the joint statement to the conclusion of the treaty, due to the complications of international politics. →日中共同声明

にってん 日天〔仏教〕 Deva of the Sun. *Surya*. One of the Twelve Devas. Guards the sun. →十二天

にっとうぐほうじゅんれいこうき 入唐求法巡礼行記〔仏教・作品〕 *The Record of a Pilgrimage to China in Search of the Law*. Was written in the 9th century by a priest named ENNIN. Consists of four volumes and describes his travel to Tang from 838 to 847. Was translated into English by Edwin Reischauer.

にっぽじしょ 日葡辞書〔言語・作品〕 *Vocabvlario da Lingoa de Iapam*. A Japanese-Portugese dictionary compiled in 1630 by a Christian missionary to Japan. Has entries of about 32,000 words.

にっぽんえいたいぐら 日本永代蔵〔文芸・作品〕 *The Eternal Storehouse of Japan*. Was written in 1688 by IHARA SAIKAKU. Contains stories of successful and unsuccessful businessmen. Some of them are based on actual events.

にっぽんぎんこう 日本銀行〔経済〕 Bank of Japan. The central bank of Japan. Was founded in Tokyo in 1882. Issues paper money, functions as the bank of banks, and is in charge of devising financial policies.

にっぽんばし 日本橋〔地名〕 Nippon Bridge. A bridge over the Doutonbori River, and its neighborhood area to the south of the bridge in the central part of Osaka City. After World War II, the area became a large electric town and is now a center of manga, anime, and game culture, comparable to Akihabara in Tokyo. Not to be confused with NIHONBASHI in Tokyo.

にっぽんりゅう 日本竜〔動物〕 *Nipponosaurus sachalinensis*. A dinosaur whose fossil was discovered in Sakhalin. About 2 m high.

にとうりゅう 二刀流〔剣術〕 two-sword fencing. A swordsman holds two swords, one in each hand. Is said to have been invented by MIYAMOTO MUSASHI.

にとべいなぞう 新渡戸稲造〔外交〕 1862-1933. A Protestant minister, educator, writer, and diplomat, born in Morioka, Iwate Pref. Studied English and agricultural techniques at Sapporo Agricultural College. Became a Christian in 1884, traveled widely in the U.S. and elsewhere, returned to Japan, and took a teaching position. Later went back to the U.S. and wrote *Bushido: The Soul of Japan*, which exposed Westerners to Bushido theory and practice. Attended the Peace Conference in Versailles and served as under-secretary-general of the League of Nations.

にないだいこ 担い太鼓〔音楽〕 a portable drum. Is beaten while carried by two people.

ににぎのみこと 瓊瓊杵尊〔神話〕 a grandson of the Sun Goddess (AMATERASU OOMIKAMI). According to her order, descended from the High Celestial Plain (TAKA-MAGAHARA) to rule the Central Land of Reeds, namely Japan, and married KONOHANA NO SAKUYA HIME. The first emperor Jinmu was his great-grandson.

ににろくじけん 二二六事件 〖政治〗 February 26th Incident. A failed coup d'etat attempted by young army officers in 1936. Requesting direct administration by the Emperor, they shot senior statesmen including TAKAHASHI KOREKIYO. However, Emperor Shouwa refused to employ direct administration, and the coup troops were suppressed and treated as rebels.

ににんばおり 二人羽織 〖娯楽〗 two people in one kimono. A traditional party game. One person sits in front, and the other person sits just behind him or her. These two people together put on one kimono. The rear person slips the arms into the sleeves, while the front person's head appears. This quasi-one person tries to eat or drink.

にぬり 丹塗り 〖工芸〗 to be painted vermilion or to be red-lacquered. The buildings of a Shinto shrine or a Buddhist temple are often painted vermilion partly because the color is associated with divinity and partly because the pigment protects the building from insect damage and erosion.

にぬりやでんせつ 丹塗矢伝説 〖神話〗 Legend of a red arrow. A deity has transformed into a red arrow had a sexual relationship with a human female.

にねんざか 二年坂 〖地名〗 Ninen Slope. Is located in the Higashi-yama area of Kyoto. Traditional shops line the path. Leads to the Sannen Slope and is good for strolling. →三年坂

にのぜん 二の膳 〖食文化〗 the second-served set of dishes in a traditional full-course cuisine. Is placed on the right side of the first-served tray. →本膳料理; 一の膳; 三の膳

にのまる 二の丸 〖城郭〗 the second outer section of a castle. Encloses the innermost section. →本丸; 三の丸

にはいず 二杯酢 〖調味料〗 a mixture of vinegar and soy sauce, or a mixture of vinegar and salt.

にはいにはくしゅいっぱい 二拝二拍手一拝 〖神道〗 ⇨二礼二拍手一礼

にはちそば 二八蕎麦 〖食べ物〗 soba noodles made from 80 percent buckwheat flour and 20 percent wheat flour as a thickener. Is considered to be a low-ranking soba.

にばんだいこ 二番太鼓 〖歌舞伎・落語〗 drum beating to inform the guests that the performance soon will begin in the theater. →一番太鼓

にびたし 煮浸し 〖食べ物〗 grilled and simmered fish or vegetables. Eaten after the broth has soaked well into the ingredient.

にひゃくとおか 二百十日 〖暦〗 the 210th day from the beginning of spring in the traditional calendar.

Around September 1 in the current calendar. Typhoons frequently come to Japan around this time.

にひゃくはつか 二百二十日 〖暦〗 the 220th day from the beginning of spring in the traditional calendar. Around September 11 in the current calendar. Typhoons frequently come to Japan around this time.

にべ 鮸 〖食べ物・動物〗 a blue drum, or a Honnibe croaker. *Nibea mitsukurii*. About 60 cm long. Its flesh is used for fish paste, and its air bladder is used for fish glue.

にぼし 煮干し 〖調味料〗 boiled and dried young anchovies. Are used to make soup stock.

にほんあるぷす 日本アルプス 〖山岳〗 the Japanese Alps. Consist of the three very high mountain ranges: namely, the Northern Alps, originally known as the Hida Mountains; the Central Alps, known as the Kiso Mountains; and the Southern Alps, known as the Akaishi Mountains. The English archaeologist William Gowland coined the name "the Japanese Alps" in 1881, referring only to the Hida Mountains. Later, the English clergyman Walter Weston made recreational mountaineering popular in Japan. He has been called the father of the Japanese Alps, or the father of mountaineering in Japan, and his bronze statue stands in Kamikouchi in the Northern Alps.

にほんえいたいぐら 日本永代蔵 〖文芸・作品〗 ⇨日本(にっぽん)永代蔵

にほんえいほう 日本泳法 〖スポーツ〗 ⇨古式泳法

にほんおおかみ 日本狼 〖動物〗 a Japanese wolf. *Canis lupus hodophilax*. The body length was about 1 m. Was captured last in 1905 and is thought to be extinct.

にほんが 日本画 〖絵画〗 traditional Japanese paintings. Use traditional styles and techniques. This term is often used when contrasted with modern Western paintings. →大和絵

にほんかい 日本海 〖地名〗 the Sea of Japan. The sea between Japan, Russia, and the Korean Peninsula. The Tsushima Current flows from southwest to northeast off the coast of Japan.

にほんかいかいせん 日本海海戦 〖戦争〗 Battle of Tsushima. The Combined Fleet of Japan defeated the Russian Baltic Fleet on May 27 and 28 in 1905, during the Russo-Japanese War. →日露戦争

にほんかいこう 日本海溝 〖海洋〗 Japan Trench. A part of the Pacific Ring of Fire, located off Eastern Japan. Is 10,554 m deep at its deepest point.

にほんかいりゅう 日本海流 〖海洋〗 ⇨黒潮

にほんがみ 日本髪 〖髪〗 a generic term for traditional hairstyles for women. Include SHIMADA-MAGE, MOMOWARE, and SUBERAKASHI.

にほんかもしか 日本羚羊 〖動物〗 a Japanese serow. *Capricornis crispus*. Lives in mountainous areas that are 500 to 2,000 m high throughout Japan except Hokkaido.

にほんきいん 日本棋院〚碁〛 Japan Go Association. Organizes the go tournaments for the professionals and issues grades for the amateur players. Was founded in 1924 in Tokyo. Unlike the Japan Shogi Association, it is not the only go association in Japan. The Kansai Kiin was founded in 1950 in Osaka, and professionals in Western Japan belong to it. →日本将棋連盟

にほんきょうさんとう 日本共産党 〚政治〛 Communist Party of Japan. Was established in 1922 and has experienced oppression at times. Has changed its political stance, corresponding to various situations and events.

にほんきょうしょくいんくみあい 日本教職員組合　　〚教育・団体名〛 Japan Teachers' Union. The federation of teachers' unions in each prefecture. Was established in 1947. Members are mainly teachers at elementary and junior high schools, but some are teachers at high schools or colleges.

にほんぎんこう 日本銀行〚経済〛 ⇨ 日本(にっ)銀行

にほんぎんこうけん　　日本銀行券 〚経済〛　　a Bank of Japan note. Currently the 1,000-yen bill, 2,000-yen bill, 5,000-yen bill, and 10,000-yen bill are issued.

にほんけいざいしんぶん　　日本経済新聞〚経済・マスコミ〛　*Nikkei*. Literally means "Japan economic newspaper." Started publication in 1876. Has a circulation of about 2.4 million as of 2018.

にほんけいざいだんたいれんごうかい 日本経済団体連合会〚経済〛 ⇨ 日本経団連

にほんけいだんれん 日本経団連〚経済〛　　Japan Business Federation. An organization mainly composed of companies listed in the First Section of the Tokyo Stock Exchange. The Japan Federation of Economic Organizations (former Keidanren) turned into the Japan Business Federation (present Keidanren) in 2002, integrated with the Japan Federation of Employers' Associations (Nikkeiren). The Keidanren chairman once had a great influence on the political world and economic circles and was called "Prime Minister of the Business World," but the influence of the person in the position has declined in recent years.

にほんご　　日本語　　〚言語〛　　the Japanese language. Is spoken throughout Japan by more than 120 million people, including Korean Japanese and the Ainu. Features open syllables phonetically and agglutination grammatically. KANJI were introduced from China around the 3rd century. People use four kinds of characters at present: HIRAGANA, KATAKANA, kanji, and the alphabet.

にほんこうき 日本後紀〚政治・書名〛 *Later Chronicle of Japan*. One of the

Six National Histories. Was compiled in 840. Covers from 792 to 833. →六国(??)史

にほんこうぎょうきかく　日本工業規格〔科学技術・経済〕 Japanese Industrial Standards. Are often abbreviated as JIS. Were established in 1949 to maintain industrial qualities. A product that satisfies the standards is allowed to carry the JIS mark.

にほんこうくう　日本航空〔交通・企業名〕 Japan Airlines. The flag air carrier for Japan. Was established in 1951.

にほんごがく　日本語学〔言語〕 Japanese linguistics. Used to be called 'kokugo-gaku,' which means "research of national language."

にほんごがっこう　日本語学校〔言語・教育〕 a Japanese language school. Many of them are open to foreign people who have come to Japan, besides the Japanese language courses offered at universities.

にほんごきょういくのうりょくけんていしけん　日本語教育能力検定試験〔言語・教育〕 Japanese Language Teaching Competency Test. Is conducted annually by a public service corporation named the Japan Educational Exchanges and Services. Can be taken only in Japan.

にほんこくけんぽう　日本国憲法〔法律〕 the Constitution of Japan. The current constitution consisting of the preface and 103 articles in eleven chapters. Was made public on November 3, 1946 and became effective on May 3, 1947. Prescribes the sovereignty of the people, the Emperor as a symbol of the state, the renunciation of war, the fundamental human rights, and so on.

にほんこくゆうてつどう　日本国有鉄道〔鉄道〕 Japanese National Railways. Was established in 1949 as a state-owned public corporation. Successfully constructed four SHINKANSEN routes. However, due to its huge debt, was privatized and divided into 7 Japan Railways (JR) companies in 1987.

にほんごけんてい　日本語検定〔言語・教育〕 Japanese Language Examination. Is conducted biannually, mainly for Japanese native speakers. Offers seven levels and examines the ability in the field of vocabulary, grammar, kanji, and honorifics.

にほんごのうりょくしけん　日本語能力試験〔言語・教育〕 Japanese-Language Proficiency Test. Is conducted biannually for non-native speakers of Japanese. Offers five levels and examines the ability in the field of Japanese characters, vocabulary, grammar, and communication.

にほんざし　二本差し〔武士〕 euphemism for samurai in the Edo period. Literally means "to bring two swords." Only samurai were permitted to carry a long sword and a short sword. ↔一本差し

にほんざる 日本猿〖動物〗 a Japanese monkey, or a Japanese macaque. *Macaca fuscata*. Has the northernmost habitat of any monkeys in the world. Monkeys soaking in a hot spring at Jigokudani in northern Nagano Pref. are popular among tourists.

にほんさんけい 日本三景〖旅〗 the Three Famous Views of Japan. MATSUSHIMA in Miyagi Pref., AMA-NO-HASHIDATE in Kyoto Pref., and MIYAJIMA in Hiroshima Pref.

にほんさんだいがっかり 日本三大がっかり〖旅〗 the Three Great Disappointments of Japan. Three tourist spots that are famous but are disappointing to visitors. The Harimaya Bridge in Kouchi, the Clock Tower in Sapporo, and either the Shureimon Gate in Okinawa or the Oranda Slope in Nagasaki.

にほんさんだいじつろく 日本三代実録〖政治・書名〗 *Veritable Record of Three Generations of Japan*. One of the Six National Histories. Was compiled in 901. Covers from 858 to 887. →六国(⁇)史

にほんさんだいまつり 日本三大祭り〖祭礼〗 the Three Great Festivals in Japan. The Gion Festival in Kyoto (GION-MATSURI), the Tenjin Festival in Osaka (TENJIN-MATSURI), and the Kanda Festival in Tokyo (KANDA-MATSURI).

にほんさんめいえん 日本三名園〖庭園〗 the Three Most Beautiful Gardens in Japan: KAIRAKU-EN in Ibaraki Pref., KENROKU-EN in Ishikawa Pref., and KOURAKU-EN in Okayama Pref.

にほんさんめいせん 日本三名泉〖温泉〗 the Three Most Famous Hot Springs in Japan. ARIMA ONSEN in Hyougo Pref., GERO ONSEN in Gifu Pref., and KUSATSU ONSEN in Gunma Pref. Were listed by a scholar HAYASHI RAZAN around the 17th century.

にほんしゅ 日本酒〖酒〗 sake. ⇨酒 (**1**)

にほんしゅど 日本酒度〖酒〗 the sake meter value. Indicates dryness or sweetness. Usually ranges from −6 to +6: the higher the value, the drier the sake.

にほんしょうぎれんめい 日本将棋連盟〖将棋〗 Japan Shogi Association. Deals with professional shogi in Japan through activities such as negotiating sponsorships to organize title matches and supervising apprentice professionals. Describes its aims as "to contribute to the development of Japanese traditional culture ..., and to establish friendly exchanges with people of other countries through shogi." Founded in 1924, it has been run by both active and retired professionals.

にほんしょき 日本書紀〖政治・書名〗 *Chronicles of Japan*. Japan's second oldest chronicle of 30 volumes. Began to be compiled at the behest of Emperor Tenmu and was completed in 720 by TONERI SHINNOU, OONO YASUMARO, and so on. Covers events from the creation of heaven and earth to the time of Empress Jitou. It is said that its articles are more detailed, rational, and objective, compared with those in *Records of Ancient Matters* (KOJIKI).

にほんしりいず　日本シリーズ 〖スポーツ〗 Japan Baseball Championship Series. The champions of the Central and Pacific Leagues play seven-game series for the annual championship. Is usually held in October or November.

にほんじんがっこう 日本人学校 〖教育・外交〗 an educational facility to give compulsory education to Japanese children who live overseas. Has a full-time schooling system equivalent to those inside Japan. Is authorized by the Minister of Education, Culture, Sports, Science and Technology and is distinguished from other supplementary schools.

にほんじんとゆだやじん　日本人とユダヤ人 〖人文学・書名〗 *The Japanese and the Jews*. Was published in 1970 by Izaya Bendasan.

にほんしんわ　日本神話 〖神話〗 Japanese mythology. Is recorded in the *Records of Ancient Matters* (KOJIKI), the *Chronicles of Japan* (NIHONSHOKI), official records of geographical descriptions, called FUDOKI, and other ancient archives. Describes the creation of the world, births of deities, the advent of the Imperial ancestors, and other legendary events. Major deities include ZOUKA SANSHIN, IZANAGI NO MIKOTO, AMATERASU OOMIKAMI, SUSANOO NO MIKOTO, and OOKUNINUSHI NO KAMI. →高天原(たかまがはら); 天孫降臨(てんそんこうりん)

にほんすもうきょうかい　日本相撲協会 〖相撲〗 Japan Sumo Association. Deals with professional sumo wrestling in Japan, including the regular tournaments, while taking care of the active wrestlers, referees, hairdressers, and ushers. Founded in 1925, it has been run by elders called 'toshiyori,' who are mainly retired high-ranking wrestlers.

にほんだいら　日本平 〖地名〗 the name of a plateau in southern Shizuoka City. Its peak is Mt. Udo (307 m). Produces oranges and green tea leaves. Provides a view of Mt. Fuji beyond Suruga Bay and a night view of Shizuoka City. On its south is Kunouzan Toushouguu Shrine, where TOKUGAWA IEYASU was originally buried. Nihondaira is accessible by bus in 35 minutes from Shizuoka Station on Tokaido Shinkansen. It takes another 5 minutes from Nihondaira to Kunouzan Toushouguu Shrine by ropeway.

にほんちんぼつ　日本沈没 〖文芸・作品〗 *Japan Sinks*. A science fiction novel published in 1973 by KOMATSU SAKYOU. The Japanese Archipelago is sinking into the ocean because of crustal movements, and Japanese people are forced to escape from their mother country.

にほんていえん 日本庭園 〔庭園〕 a Japanese-style garden. Often depicts a natural landscape or a Buddhist idea.

にほんとう 日本刀〔武器〕 a Japanese sword. The major weapon of a samurai. Usually refers to a long and single-edged sword after the 10th century. Can be classified in several ways depending on the manufacturer, the size, the purpose, or the period of production.

にほんばし 日本橋 〔交通・地名〕 Japan Bridge. A bridge over the Nihonbashi River, and its neighborhood area of Chuuou City in central Tokyo. The starting point of the Five Highways in the Edo period. Not to be confused with NIPPONBASHI in Osaka.

にほんひょうじゅんじ 日本標準時 〔時刻〕 Japan Standard Time. JST. Adopts the local time of Akashi City, Hyougo Pref. on the meridian line of 135 degrees east longitude. Nine hours ahead of Greenwich Mean Time.

にほんぶよう 日本舞踊〔芸能〕 a generic term for traditional dance accompanied by songs and shamisen.

にほんぷろさっかありいぐ 日本プロサッカーリーグ〔スポーツ〕 ⇨ Jリーグ(じえい)

にほんぶんがく 日本文学〔文芸〕 ⇨ 国文学

にほんぼうえきしんこうかい 日本貿易振興会〔経済〕 ⇨ JETRO(じえとろ)

にほんみんげいかん 日本民藝館 〔工芸・博物館〕 Japan Folk Crafts Museum. Was established in Tokyo in 1936 by YANAGI MUNEYOSHI. Collects folkcrafts from all over the world in addition to works by KAWAI KANJIROU, Bernard Leach, and MUNAKATA SHIKOU.

にほんもんとくてんのうじつろく 日本文徳天皇実録 〔政治・書名〕 *Veritable Record of Emperor Montoku of Japan.* One of the Six National Histories. Was compiled in 879. Covers from 850 to 858. →六国(??)史

にほんらいん 日本ライン 〔自然〕 Japan Rhine. The 13 km valley of the Kiso River on the border between Gifu and Aichi Prefs., named after the Rhine River in Europe because of their similar landscapes. Used to be popular for boating tours, but it has been discontinued since 2013.

にほんりょういき 日本霊異記 〔仏教・書名〕 *Miraculous Stories from the Japanese Buddhist Tradition.* The oldest narrative literature in Japan. Was written in Japanese-style Chinese texts in the 9th century by a priest named Kyoukai. Consists of three volumes and contains 116 stories with morals based on Buddhism.

にほんりょうり 日本料理 〔食文化〕 Japanese cuisine. In addition to traditional cuisine called WASHOKU, also refers to all other food newly created in Japan, such as OKONOMIYAKI, GYUUDON, OMURAISU, and Japanese-style pasta.

にほんれっとう　日本列島〔自然〕 Japanese Archipelago. Consists of four main islands: Honshuu, Shikoku, Kyushu, and Hokkaido, and other islands such as Okinawa, Sado, Awaji, and Amami Ooshima. Is placed at the collision point of four tectonic plates: the Eurasian Plate, North American Plate, Pacific Plate, and Philippine Plate. Consequently, earthquakes and volcanic activities occur very frequently.

にほんろうどうくみあいそうれんごうかい　日本労働組合総連合会〔政治・経済〕 Japanese Trade Union Confederation. Was established as the national center of labor unions in 1989 by unifying several federations of labor unions. Is often called 'Rengou.'

にまいびょうぶ　二枚屏風〔生活・絵画〕 a double-leaf folding screen. → 屏風

にもうさく　二毛作〔農業〕 double cropping of rice and other product. →二期作

にもの　煮物〔食文化〕 a generic term for simmered food. Includes vegetables, fish, and meat.

にゅうがくしき　入学式〔教育〕 an entrance ceremony. Is held at all school levels such as elementary schools, junior and senior high schools, and universities. Parents often participate as well as students.

にゅうどう　入道 **(1)**〔仏教〕 to become a Buddhist monk. **(2)**〔仏教〕 a Buddhist monk. **(3)**〔髪〕 a shaven-headed man.

にゅうとうおんせんきょう　乳頭温泉郷〔温泉〕 the name of a group of hot springs in eastern Akita Pref., near Lake Tazawa, deep in the Ouu Mountains. Famous for its seven hot springs with different effects, and Japanese-style inns with thatched roofs. Can be accessed by bus, with a 50-minute ride from Tazawako Station on Akita Shinkansen.

にゅうばい　入梅〔気象〕 the calendrical beginning of the rainy season. Around June 11 in the current calendar, when the sun is on the 80 degree line of celestial longitude.

にゅうまく　入幕〔相撲〕 the promotion of a wrestler to the top division of professional sumo.

にゅうみゅうじっく　ニューミュージック〔音楽〕 New Music. Japanese pop music in the 1970s and early 1980s.

にゅうめつ　入滅〔仏教〕 the death of the Historical Buddha or an important priest. →涅槃(ねん)

にゅうめん　煮麺〔食べ物〕 very thin wheat noodles in soy-flavored broth or miso soup. →素麺(そうめん)

によい　如意〔仏教〕 a slightly waved stick for a priest. Is held when a priest chants a sutra or preaches.

にょいほうじゅ　如意宝珠〔仏教〕 a wish-fulfilling jewel. In Sanskrit, *cintamani*. Is held by Nyoirin-kannon, Kisshou-ten, or Jizou-

BOSATSU. The shape is sometimes like a short and thick teardrop and sometimes three balls in fire.

にょいりんかんのん 如意輪観音〖仏教〗 Omnipotent Bodhisattva of Mercy. *Cintamani-cakra*. Usually has six arms, one of which holds a wish-fulfilling jewel (NYOI-HOUJU) and another of which holds a dharma ring (HOURIN). Is said to save those who reside in the Realm of Heavens in esoteric Buddhism. Famous examples include the one at KANSHIN-JI Temple in Osaka Pref. →観音；天道

にょう 繞〖漢字〗 a left to lower part of a kanji. For example, the 辶 part of a kanji 進 (advance).

にょうぼう 女房〖行政〗 a high-ranking court lady. Was given a residential room in the Imperial Palace.

にょうぼうことば 女房言葉〖言語〗 the language of women at the Imperial Court in the Muromachi period. Mainly words about eating and living. One typical form is the combination of 'o' and an abbreviation. For example, the latter part of the word ODEN is the abbreviation of 'dengaku.' Another typical form is the combination of an abbreviation and 'moji.' For example, the former part of the word SHAMOJI is the abbreviation of 'shakushi'

にょぜがもん 如是我聞〖仏教〗 Thus have I heard. Often the first phrase used in Buddhist sutras. After this phrase, the contents start. The word "I" in this phrase refers to the compiler of sutras, ANANDA.

にょにんきんせい 女人禁制〖仏教〗 no admittance to women. Some sanctuaries of Buddhism or mountain asceticism used to be closed to women.

にょにんこうや 女人高野 〖仏教〗 another name for MUROU-JI Temple in Nara Pref. or JISON-IN Temple in Wakayama Pref. Literally means "Mt. Kouya for women" because women visited one of these temples instead of KONGOUBU-JI Temple in Mt. Kouya, which used to be closed to women.

にょらい 如来 〖仏教〗 a Buddha, Enlightened One, or Thus-Come One. *Tathagata*. Has attained enlightenment. There are several Buddhas such as the Historical Buddha (Shaka nyorai), the Buddha of Infinite Light (AMIDA NYORAI), the Healing Buddha (YAKUSHI NYORAI), and the Great Sun Buddha (DAINICHI NYORAI).

にらいかない ニライカナイ〖宗教〗 the Paradise which was believed to exist beyond the horizon in the Okinawa and Amami areas.

にらめっこ 睨めっこ〖遊び〗 a staring game. Two people stare at each other to make the other laugh. The one who laughs loses the game.

にれいにはくしゅいちれい 二礼二拍手一礼〖神道〗 the way of worshipping at a Shinto shrine. [1] put money into an offertory box.

[2] ring a bell by pulling a rope, if there is one. [3] bow twice. [4] clap hands twice. [5] make a wish. [6] bow once again.

にわばん 庭番〖忍者〗 ⇨御庭番

にんき 忍器〖忍者〗 the generic term for ninja gadgets. Include opening tools (KAIKI), fire-related tools (KAKI), water-related tools (SUIKI), and climbing tools (TOUKI).

にんぎょ 人魚〖妖怪〗 a mermaid. It was believed that those who had eaten the flesh of a mermaid could prolong their life. The legend of the Eight-hundred-year Old Priestess, named YAO-BIKUNI, is famous.

にんきょうえいが 任侠映画〖映画〗 ⇨やくざ映画

にんぎょうじょうるり 人形浄瑠璃〖文楽〗 traditional puppet theater accompanied by a dramatic narrative and three-stringed instrument called a SHAMISEN.

にんぎょうつかい 人形遣い〖文楽〗 a puppeteer in BUNRAKU. In the olden days, one puppet was operated by one person. However, operation by three people, called SANNIN-DUKAI, was devised in 1734, and that style has become popular.

にんぎょうやき 人形焼〖食文化〗 a face-shaped cake. Is made from flour, egg, sugar, and honey and stuffed with sweet adzuki paste. A specialty of Tokyo.

にんげんぎょらい 人間魚雷〖武器〗 ⇨回天

にんげんこくほう 人間国宝〖芸術〗 ⇨重要無形文化財保持者

にんげんどう 人間道〖仏教〗 the Realm of Humans. The second from the top among the Six Realms of Existence. The realm into which a person is born depends on his or her deeds in previous lives. →六道; 輪廻(りん)

にんじゃ 忍者〖忍者〗 ninja. A spy, sometimes an assassin, using NIN-JUTSU in the Warring States and Edo periods. Was originally called 'shinobi,' but was also called different names in different areas such as RAPPA, SUPPA, and NOKIZARU. Ninjas from Iga and Kouka were employed by feudal lords in other domains. ODA NOBUNAGA severely destroyed the community of IGA NINJA in 1581, but TOKUGAWA IEYASU hired Iga and KOUKA NINJA because they helped him escape at the Honnou-ji Incident in 1582. The 8th Tokugawa shogun, TOKUGAWA YOSHIMUNE, set up a ninja system called ONIWABAN. →本能寺の変

にんじゃしょく 忍者食〖忍者〗 field rations, or a packed meal for ninja. Mainly includes round-shaped small pills such as SUIKATSUGAN to control thirst and KIKATSUGAN to stave off hunger.

にんじゃとう 忍者刀〖忍者〗 ⇨忍び刀

にんじゃのさんびょう 忍者の三病〖忍者〗 three mental conditions to be avoided: fear, underrating an enemy, and too much thought.

にんじゃはくぶつかん 忍者博物館〖忍者・博物館〗 ⇨伊賀流忍者博物館

にんじゃやしき 忍者屋敷〔忍者〕 ⇨ 伊賀流忍者博物館；甲賀流忍術屋敷

にんじゅつ 忍術〔忍者〕 ninjutsu. Literally means "art of stealth." Actually, comprehensive techniques for espionage and survival, based on communication and negotiation skills, mnemonics, knowledge of medicine, astronomy, and meteorology, skills of infiltration and escaping, use of gunpowder, and martial arts. Though two ninjutsu books, *Secret Ninja Tradition* (NINPIDEN) and *The Book of Ninja* (BANSENSHUUKAI), refer to the origin of ninjutsu in ancient China, it really developed in the Warring States period. →忍者

にんじょう 人情〔精神性〕 natural human emotion. Is sometimes contrasted with GIRI, which is the duty based on human relationships.

にんじょうぼん 人情本〔文芸〕 a book about human feelings in the 19th century. Contains realistic love stories of townspeople. Derived from witty books, SHAREBON.

にんせい 仁清〔工芸〕 ⇨野々村仁清

にんそくよせば 人足寄場〔行政〕 a housing facility for the homeless and former convicts in the Edo period. Was founded at Ishikawa Island in Edo in 1790, according to a proposal by HASEGAWA HEIZOU.

にんとくてんのう 仁徳天皇〔天皇〕 Emperor Nintoku. ?-? The 16th, in the 5th century. A son of Emperor Oujin. Is said to have learned that people suffered from poverty because he had seen, from the palace, no smoke coming up from the kitchen stoves of the masses. A tumulus attributed to his grave is the largest in Japan. →仁徳天皇陵

にんとくてんのうのうりょう 仁徳天皇陵〔天皇・史跡〕 the Tumulus of Emperor Nintoku. Is located in Sakai City, Osaka Pref., and dates back to the 5th century. Its length is 486 m, and its height is 33 m, making it the largest keyhole-shaped burial mound in Japan. Is surrounded by three moats, with the outer one being almost 3 km around. Is also called 'Daisen kofun' in Japanese.

にんなじ 仁和寺〔寺院〕 Ninnaji Temple. The head temple of the Omuro school of the Shingon sect, located in Kyoto. Was founded in 888 by Emperor Uda. The main hall and the Amitabha Triad are National Treasures. Famous for cherry blossoms. Was designated a World Heritage Site in 1994. →真言宗；阿弥陀三尊

にんぴでん 忍秘伝〔忍者〕 *Secret Ninja Tradition*, or *The Ninja Scroll*. One of the three major ninjutsu books. Had been handed down in the samurai family of Hattori Hanzou in Iga, present Mie Pref. Was given to HATTORI HANZOU MASANARI by his father Yasunaga in 1560. Consists of 4 volumes and describes the history, techniques, and tools of ninja.

にんべつちょう 人別帳 〔政治〕 a family registration book in the Edo period.

にんべん 人偏 〔漢字〕 a left-side radical meaning "person." Is used in kanji such as 仲(relationship), 住 (living), and 俺(me).

にんみょうてんのう 仁明天皇 〔天皇〕 Emperor Ninmyou. 810-850. The 54th, on the throne from 833 to 850. The first prince of Emperor Saga.

ぬ

ぬえ 鵺〔妖怪〕 a monster with a head like a monkey, a trunk like a raccoon dog, a tail like a snake, limbs like a tiger, and the voice of a thrush. Was exterminated by MINAMOTO NO YORIMASA in *The Tale of the Heike* (HEIKE MONOGATARI).

ぬか 糠〔食文化・生活〕 ⇨米糠

ぬかたのおおきみ 額田王 〔文芸〕 ?–? A poet in the 7th century. Contributed 13 poems to the *Anthology of Myriad Leaves* (MAN'YOUSHUU). Was once a lover of Prince Ooama, who later became Emperor Tenmu, and then became a concubine of Emperor Tenji, the elder brother of Ooama. →天武天皇；天智天皇

ぬかぶくろ 糠袋〔生活〕 a rice-bran bag. Was used to smooth one's skin in the bath.

ぬかみそ 糠味噌〔調味料〕 fermented rice-bran paste with salt. Is used to pickle vegetables.

ぬきて 抜き手〔スポーツ〕 a traditional swimming stroke similar to a face-up crawl. The legs are kicked in the same way as with the breaststroke.

ぬさ 幣〔神道〕 a short rod with zig-zag-shaped paper strips. Is placed in the main sanctuary building of a Shinto shrine as an object to which a deity descends. →紙垂(しで)

ぬし 塗師〔芸術〕 ⇨塗り師

ぬしま 沼島 〔島名〕 Nushima Island. Is located 4 km offshore and to the south of Awaji Island. Is said to correspond to Onokoro Island in Japanese mythology, which IZANAGI NO MIKOTO and IZANAMI NO MIKOTO created at the first among Japanese islands.

ぬすみぐみ 偸組〔忍者〕 a term referring to ninja, used by the Maeda clan in present Ishikawa Pref. in the Edo period. It is said that they were offspring of those who had survived the TENSHOU IGA NO RAN in 1581.

ぬた 饅〔食べ物〕 seafood or vegetables flavored with a mixture of miso, vinegar, and sugar.

ぬひ 奴婢〔政治〕 male and female slaves. The first letter 奴 'nu' is male and 婢 'hi' is female in the centralized administration system in ancient times, called RITSURYOU-SEI. This slave system was abolished in the 10th century.

ぬらりひょん 滑瓢〔妖怪〕 Slippery Gourd. A monster with the appearance of an old man and a gourd-shaped head, wearing a Buddhist-monk costume. Is often depicted as the leader of all traditional Japanese monsters (YOUKAI) in current fiction, but its source is unknown.

ぬりかべ 塗り壁〔妖怪〕 an invisible wall monster. If a person walks a deserted street late at night and cannot proceed by any means, that is believed to be the manifestation of 'nurikabe.'

ぬりげた 塗り下駄 〔履物〕 a lacquered wooden sandals.

ぬりし 塗り師 〔工芸〕 a lacquerware artisan. Paints lacquer on unfinished ware that has been created by a woodcraft smith called KIJIYA.

ぬりばし 塗り箸 〔食器〕 a pair of lacquered chopsticks.

ぬりべ 漆部 〔工芸・美術〕 a tribe that demonstrated lacquer techniques in ancient times. Belonged to the national government. The lacquer skills descended from generation to generation.

ぬりもの 塗り物〔工芸〕 ⇨漆器

ぬりわん 塗り腕 〔食器〕 a lacquered wooden bowl. Is usually used to eat traditional soup.

ぬるかん ぬる燗 〔酒〕 mildly warmed sake. The temperature is around 40 degrees centigrade. →燗酒；銚子；猪口(ちょこ)

ぬるで 白膠木〔植物〕 a Chinese sumac, or a nutgall tree. *Rhus javanica*. It is said that Prince Shoutoku made Buddhist sculptures with this wood to pray for victory at the battle against the Mononobe clan. →聖徳太子；物部氏

ぬれえん 濡れ縁 〔建築〕 an open porch. Is placed outside sliding storm shutters. →縁側；雨戸

ぬれぼとけ 濡れ仏 〔仏教〕 a Buddhist sculpture placed in the open air.

ね

ね 子 〖干支〗 the first of the Chinese zodiac signs. Means "rat." Recently the years 1984, 1996, and 2008 were rat years. Indicates the north in direction and around midnight for hours.

ねぎ 葱 〖食べ物・植物〗 a green onion, or a Welsh onion. *Allium fistulosum.* Is used as ingredients or garnish in many kinds of cuisine, including miso soup, buckwheat noodles, and a savory pancake called OKONOMIYAKI.

ねぎ 禰宜 〖神道〗 an assistant priest of a Shinto shrine. →神主；宮司(ぐじ)

ねぎしやすもり 根岸鎮衛 〖武士〗 1737-1815. A feudal commissioner for governance of Edo. Held the position for 18 years. Wrote an essay collection called MIMIBUKURO.

ねぎとろ ねぎとろ 〖食べ物〗 minced fatty tuna with chopped green onion. Eaten as sushi.

ねぎま 葱間 〖食べ物〗 broiled chicken with green onion. Consists of three or four chicken pieces, usually thigh meat, skewered with chopped green onion in between. One of the most popular types of YAKITORI.

ねぎま 葱鮪 〖食べ物〗 a hot-pot dish with fatty tuna and green onion.

ねこだまし 猫だまし 〖相撲〗 a fake-out. A sumo technique of confusing the opponent by slapping hands in front of the face, usually before initial contact in the bout.

ねこて 猫手 〖忍者〗 cat claws, or metal fingerstalls with sharp claws. Are attached on the finger tips to scratch the enemy.

ねこまた 猫又 〖妖怪〗 an old cat with a forked tail. When it turns 40 or older, a cat acquires supernatural powers, and its tail is split into two. Stands on its hind legs, licks lamp oil, understands human language, and controls the body of a person who has died recently.

ねごろじ 根来寺 〖寺院〗 Negoro-ji Temple. The head temple of the Shingi school in the Shingon sect, located in northern Wakayama Pref. Was originally founded at Mt. Kouya in 1130 by a priest named Kakuban, and then moved to the present location in 1286. Possessed many monk soldiers in the Warring States period, but was severely attacked in 1585 by TOYOTOMI HIDEYOSHI. The two-storied pagoda, called TAHOU-TOU, is a National Treasure.

ねごろしゅう 根来衆 〖仏教・軍事〗 a group of monk soldiers at Negoro-ji Temple in present Wakayama Pref. in the Warring States period. Were good at gunnery and sometimes were hired as mercenary soldiers. Were destroyed in 1585 by TOYOTOMI HIDEYOSHI.

ねざめのとこ 寝覚ノ床 〖地名〗 a

scenic spot in Agematsu Town in southern Nagano Pref. Literally means "Bed of Awakening." It is said that the hero of a folktale, URASHIMA TAROU, awoke here. Eroded granites along the Kiso River create scenic beauty. A bus service connects it with JR Agematsu Station in 25 minutes.

ねじりはちまき 捩じり鉢巻き 〖精神性・服飾〗 a twisted towel worn as a headband. Figuratively means "very eagerly."

ねずみがえし 鼠返し 〖建築・考古〗 a rat stop. A wooden board is attached to a pillar under a storehouse to protect harvested grains.

ねずみこぞうじろきち 鼠小僧次郎吉 〖犯罪〗 1795-1832. A chivalrous robber born in Edo. Appeared as a hero in kabuki and storytelling.

ねつけ 根付け 〖服飾・美術〗 a small ornament to suspend articles from the sash of a kimono. It is decoratively carved in ivory or wood and was popular among townsmen in the Edo period.

ねつさましいと 熱さまシート 〖医療〗 Koolfever. The trademark of a fever relief pad. A product of Kobayashi Pharmaceutical Co., Ltd.

ねったいや 熱帯夜 〖自然〗 A tropical night. Its temperature is 25 degrees centigrade or higher.

ねづびじゅつかん 根津美術館 〖美術・博物館〗 the Nezu Museum. Was founded in 1940 and is located in Aoyama, Tokyo. Contains Japanese and East Asian fine art,

including seven National Treasures and 87 Important Cultural Properties. A painting on a pair of folding screens, *Irises* by OGATA KOURIN, and a painting, *Nachi Waterfall*, are famous.

ねのくに 根の国 〖神話〗 ⇨黄泉(よみ)の国

ねはん 涅槃 〖仏教〗 *nirvana*. The condition of enlightenment in which selfhood is extinct, so there is no earthly desire. Is thought of as the goal of Buddhism. Cannot be explained logically and can only be experienced. Also means the death of the Historical Buddha. →涅槃図

ねはんえ 涅槃会 〖仏教〗 the memorial service for the Historical Buddha. Is held on February 15 in the traditional calendar, when he passed away.

ねはんず 涅槃図 〖仏教〗 a picture depicting the death of the Historical Buddha. The Buddha lies with his head toward the north, his face toward the west, and his right side downward. Around his body are several Bodhisattvas, disciples, ordinary people, and animals, which are all mourning over his death. Two sal trees grow in each of the four directions, the north, south, east, and west.

ねはんぞう 涅槃像 〖仏教〗 a sculpture of the Historical Buddha immediately after his death. →涅槃図

ねぶかじる 根深汁 〖食べ物〗 miso soup with green onion. Shimonita green onion produced in Gunma

Pref. is commonly used. Mainly eaten in the Kantou region.

ねぶたまつり 佞武多祭り〔祭礼〕 ⇨ 青森佞武多祭り

ねぶたまつり 佞武多祭り〔祭礼〕 ⇨ 弘前佞武多祭り

ねぶりばし 舐り箸〔食文化〕 to lick one's chopsticks while eating. Is regarded as bad etiquette, known as KIRAI-BASHI.

ねぼとけ 寝仏〔仏教〕 ⇨涅槃像

ねまわし 根回し〔企業・組織〕 to negotiate or make a decision behind the scene. Sometimes a decision about a critical subject will have been made, among people who are concerned, even before an official business or political meeting is held.

ねむりねこ 眠り猫〔彫刻〕 *Sleeping Cat*. A wood carving by HIDARI JINGOROU, a legendary carpenter in the Edo period. Is set on the cloister of Toushouguu Shrine in Nikko, Tochigi Pref. A National Treasure.

ねりあん 練り餡〔食べ物〕 kneaded sweet adzuki paste.

ねりうめ 練り梅〔食べ物〕 kneaded paste of pickled plum flesh. Pickled leaves of beefsteak plant or dried bonito flakes are often added.

ねりきり 練り切り〔食べ物〕 a non-baked traditional cake made from white bean paste, yam or rice flour, and sugar. Usually has an artistic shape and is often eaten at a tea ceremony.

ねりべい 練塀〔建築〕 a roofed fence of clay and tiles. The fence includes alternate layers of clay and tiles.

ねりもの 練り物〔食べ物〕 salted and heated fish paste. Includes KAMABOKO and CHIKUWA.

ねりようかん 練り羊羹〔食べ物〕 a rectangular bar of sweet adzuki paste.

ねわざ 寝技〔柔道〕 a groundwork technique of judo. A player gains a half point when pinning the opponent for 10 seconds and a full point for 20 seconds.

ねんが 年賀〔正月〕 New Year's greetings. People visit relatives, friends, teachers, bosses, and customers, or send post cards. →年賀状

ねんがじょう 年賀状〔正月〕 a New Year's greeting card. Since it is not a Christmas card, it does not have Christmas greetings, only those for New Year's. People send it in time to be delivered on January 1. →年賀

ねんがはがき 年賀はがき〔正月〕 a New Year's postcard with a lottery number. A winning number can get a prize. Although the top prize is different from year to year, the lowest one is usually special New Year's postage stamps. →年賀状

ねんき 年季〔ビジネス〕 a period in olden times when a person contracted to work for a shop as an apprentice.

ねんきほうよう 年忌法要〔仏教〕 a memorial service on an anniversary of a person's death. →〜回忌

ねんきん 年金 〔生活・経済〕 pension. The pension system has been a severe social issue in Japan, partly because some people do not receive a sufficient amount after retirement, partly because the age at which people begin to receive a pension is being raised, and partly because some people do not pay the premiums. However, the main problem is the rapid aging of Japanese society, which means there is an increasing number of people receiving pensions, while the number of people paying into the system is decreasing. →高齢化社会

ねんぐまい 年貢米 〔農業・行政〕 rice as land tax. Was paid to the feudal lord by peasants.

ねんごう 年号 〔暦〕 ⇨元号

ねんこうじょれつ 年功序列 〔企業・組織〕 the seniority system. Is used by most Japanese organizations. Since it is apt to lower the motivation of young talented people, many companies are reconsidering the efficacy of salary and promotion guidelines that are based on the seniority system.

ねんじぶつ 念持仏 〔仏教〕 a personal Buddhist sculpture. The owner kept it at his or her side and worshipped it every day. Was usually compact in size and was sometimes contained in a special chest.

ねんしまわり 年始回り 〔正月〕 New Year's greeting visits to one's superiors, customers, or relatives.

ねんねこ ねんねこ 〔服飾〕 a short padded coat worn by a person carrying a baby on his or her back.

ねんぶつ 念仏 〔仏教〕 prayer to the Buddha. Was originally related to any Buddha but came to refer only to Amitabha, as Pure Land Buddhism became popular after the Kamakura period. The chanted phrase is NAMU AMIDA-BUTSU, meaning "I put my faith in Amitabha." → 阿弥陀如来(あみだにょらい)

の

のう 能 〔能〕 Noh. A traditional theatrical art with mime, dance, and songs. The theater consists of three parts: actors, backing singers, and instrumentalists. The main actor, called SHITE, wears a mask. It began to be developed from medieval performing art, called SARUGAKU, and was fully developed by KAN'AMI and ZEAMI in the 14th and 15th centuries.

のうあみ 能阿弥 〔絵画〕 1397-1471. A painter, curator, and art advisor for the Ashikaga shogunate. Also a poet of linked poems, called RENGA. His works include *White Robed Kannon*, possessed by the Tokiwayama Bunko Foundation. His son, GEIAMI, and his grandson, SOUAMI, were also in the same position for the shogunate. →室町幕府

のうがく 能楽 〔能・狂言〕 Noh and Noh farce.

のうがくし 能楽師 〔能〕 a professional Noh performer. There are several groups such as protagonists called SHITE-kata, deuteragonists called WAKI-kata, farce actors called KYOUGEN-kata, and instrumental accompanists called HAYASHI-KATA.

のうがくどう 能楽堂 〔能〕 a building that houses a Noh theater. The first one was built in Tokyo in 1881.

のうかん 能管 〔能〕 a bamboo flute for Noh music. Has seven finger holes.

のうかんし 納棺師 〔冠婚葬祭〕 a coffinman. As his job, he prepares a body for a coffin, sometimes including embalming, and then places it in the coffin.

のうかんしき 納棺式 〔冠婚葬祭〕 the rite of placing a body in a coffin.

のうきょうげん 能狂言〔芸能〕 ⇨狂言

のうこつ 納骨 〔冠婚葬祭〕 to put one's ashes in an urn, or to place the urn in the grave or charnel house.

のうこつどう 納骨堂〔冠婚葬祭〕 a charnel house, or an ossuary. The ashes of dead people are placed there.

のうさつ 納札 〔宗教〕 to offer a slip to a Buddhist temple or Shinto shrine for a pilgrim token or prayer. The pilgrim's name is written on the slip.

のうしょうぞく 能装束 〔能・服飾〕 Noh costume. Does not include a mask. Varies according to the role.

のうちかいかく 農地改革 〔農業・政治〕 Agricultural Land Reform. Was carried out in 1947 by the Japanese government, under the direction of the Supreme Commander for the Allied Powers (SCAP). The farmland was forcibly bought by the government at a low price, and it was sold to peasants who had actually cultivated it. Since this reform produced a large number of independent farmers, rural areas were strong constituencies for conservative parties for a long time.

のうぶたい 能舞台 〖能〗 a Noh stage. The three sides are open, the rear wall is painted with a pine tree, and the floor is boarded. The stage is connected with the dressing room through a passageway.

のうめん 能面 〖能〗 a Noh mask. Is classified into several groups such as deities, men, women, and demons. Its expression is vague on purpose, in order to look either glad, angry, sad, or pleasant.

のうやくしゃ 能役者 〖能〗 a Noh actor. Includes protagonists called SHITE and deuteragonists called WAKI.

のうりょうゆか 納涼床 〖食文化・娯楽〗 a platform built over the river bank during the summer. People enjoy eating and drinking on it. The one along the Kamo River in Kyoto is famous. Is also called 'kawayuka.'

のうりんすいさんしょう 農林水産省 〖行政機関〗 Ministry of Agriculture, Forestry and Fisheries. The former Ministry of Agriculture and Forestry was renamed as such in 1958.

のかみ ～の守 〖官位〗 ⇨～守

のきざる 軒猿 〖忍者〗 a term referring to ninja. Literally means "eaves monkey" because ninja hid themselves in the shade of eaves like a monkey. Though it is said that this term refers to ninja under the Uesugi clan in present Niigata Pref., its source is unknown.

のぎへん ノ木偏 〖漢字〗 a left-side or upper radical meaning "rice" or "cereal." Is used in kanji such as 利 (profit), 季 (season), and 稔 (ripen).

のぎまれすけ 乃木希典 〖戦争〗 1849-1912. An army officer born in Tokyo. Was internationally acclaimed, for leading the attack on Port Arthur in the Russo-Japanese War and for treating the surrendered Russian soldiers generously. Committed suicide after Emperor Meiji died.

のぐちひでよ 野口英世 〖科学技術〗 1876-1928. A physician and specialist in infectious diseases, born in Fukushima Pref. Moved to the United States in 1900 and had research positions first at the University of Pennsylvania and later at the Rockefeller Institute for Medical Research. Was nominated three times for the Nobel Prize. His main contributions include work on the causes of syphilis and yellow fever and on the use of snake venom in serums. However, some of his research findings were questioned or proved false after his death. Died in Africa of yellow fever, when he was conducting research on the disease.

のさっぷみさき 納沙布岬 〖地名〗 Cape Nosappu. Is located in Nemuro City, on the easternmost end of Hokkaido. Hokkaido's oldest lighthouse and the Tower of Peace stand at its tip, where visitors can enjoy the view of Kunashiri Island, Shikotan Island, and the Habomai Islands.

のざわな 野沢菜 〔食べ物・植物〕 a leaf vegetable like turnip greens. *Brassica campestris* var. *hakabura*. Is usually pickled. A specialty of Nagano Pref.

のし 熨斗 〔生活〕 red and white paper folded into a long hexagon, containing a thin strip of dried abalone. Is attached on gift wrapping as an auspicious symbol.

のしあわび 熨斗鮑 〔生活〕 a thin strip of dried abalone. Was originally eaten in a ceremony, but is now attached to a congratulatory gift.

のしがみ 熨斗紙 〔生活〕 auspicious gift wrapping paper. The picture of a decorative folded paper, called NOSHI, and paper cords, called MIZUHIKI, are printed on it.

のしぶくろ 熨斗袋 〔生活〕 an envelop for a money gift. The picture of a decorative folded paper, called NOSHI, and paper cords, called MIZUHIKI, are printed on it.

のしめ 熨斗目 〔服飾〕 a formal kimono with a partly striped pattern around the waist. Was worn under a formal costume, called KAMISHIMO, by samurai in the Edo period. Is sometimes worn on an auspicious occasion by a male child at present.

のしもち 伸し餅 〔食べ物〕 a long flat rice cake. Is sliced to eat.

のじりこ 野尻湖 〔湖沼〕 Lake Nojiri. Is located on the hill of 654 m in height in Shinano Town in northern Nagano Pref. Since the discovery of a tooth of Naumann's Elephant, excavation has been proceeding. The Lake Nojiri Naumann Elephant Museum provides information on the excavation and other events.

のぞみ のぞみ 〔鉄道〕 the name of the fastest super express train on Tokaido and San'yo Shinkansen. Literally means "hope." Most Nozomi trains run between Tokyo and Shin-Osaka, Hiroshima, or Hakata in Fukuoka Pref. Connects Tokyo and Shin-Osaka in 2 hours 30 minutes, and Tokyo and Hakata in 5 hours.

のだて 野点 〔茶道〕 an outdoor tea ceremony. It is said that SEN NO RIKYUU prepared tea for TOYOTOMI HIDEYOSHI in the open air in 1587.

のちじて 後仕手 〔能〕 the main character for the latter half, when the drama of a Noh or Noh farce consists of two parts. ↔前仕手

のっぺいじる 濃餅汁 〔食べ物〕 slightly thick soup containing chicken, fried tofu, mushrooms, yam, carrot, and white radish. Is flavored with soy sauce, salt, and mirin.

のっぺらぼう のっぺらぼう 〔妖怪〕 a faceless phantom. Has no eyes, nose, or mouth. Just frightens a person, with no harm. Is sometimes said to be the transformation of a fox, a raccoon dog, or an otter.

のと 能登 〖旧国名〗 the old name of northern Ishikawa Pref.

のとはんとう 能登半島 〖半島〗 the Noto Peninsula. Is located in Ishikawa Pref., surrounded by the Sea of Japan and Noto Bay. Famous for lacquerware and the morning market in Wajima City, Hot Spring of Wakura, and terraced rice fields along its northern coast. →輪島塗; 棚田

のどわ 喉輪 〖相撲〗 a thrust on the throat. The attacker aligns and slightly bends four fingers, with a thumb open, and thrusts them onto the opponent's throat.

のなかのじんばり 野中の陣張り 〖忍者〗 the technique to set up a quasi-tent by stretching a sword strap between branches and covering it with a coat. One of the seven techniques of using a sword strap. →下げ緒七術

ののむらにんせい 野々村仁清 〖陶磁器〗 ?–? A potter in the 17th century, born in present Kyoto Pref. Mainly produced tea utensils. Is said to have perfected the style of the Kyou ware. →京焼

のび 野火 〖文芸・作品〗 *Fires on the Plain*. A war novel published in 1951 by Oooka Shouhei. Depicts situations under extremely harsh conditions, based on his own experience in the Philippines as a soldier in World War II.

のべおくり 野辺送り 〖冠婚葬祭〗 to send off a dead person to the crematory or cemetery. Was once done on foot as a part of a funeral rite, but it is done by car these days.

のぼとけ 野仏 〖仏教〗 a stone Buddha image in a field. Usually small. The most popular 'nobotoke' is Jizou Bodhisattva.

のぼり 幟 〖軍事・ビジネス〗 a banner. Was hoisted in the battlefield in olden times. Is now hoisted to indicate the place of an event or a shop, or the name of a group or person participating in the event.

のぼりがま 登り窯 〖工芸〗 a climbing kiln. Has several connected chambers on a hillside, with a fire mouth at the bottom chamber and a chimney at the top. Was introduced from Korea in the 16th century.

のぼりべつおんせん 登別温泉 〖温泉〗 the name of a hot spring in the south of Hokkaido. One of the largest and most popular hot springs in Hokkaido, with nine different types of spring constituents. Has been well-known since the late-Edo period but became more popular when it was designated as the place for healing soldiers wounded in the Russo-Japanese War (1904–05). Noboribetsu Bear Park is nearby.

のみのすくね 野見宿禰 〖相撲・考古〗 ?–? A legendary person, from present Shimane Pref. Came to Yamato, present Nara Pref., to have a sumo match with Taima no Kehaya. Won the match by kicking Kehaya to death and acquired Kehaya's land.

Is also said to have devised clay figures, called HANIWA, to bury in the tumulus when Empress Consort Hihasu-hime died.

のむうつかう 呑む・打つ・買う〖娯楽・精神性〗 to drink, to gamble, and to buy a woman. Traditional pastimes for men in the past, but it is said they are getting less popular.

のむらこどう 野村胡堂〖文芸〗 1882 –1963. A novelist and music critic born in Iwate Pref. Published *Coin-Throwing Detective, Zenigata Heiji*, issued in parts from 1931 to 1957.

のもんはんじけん ノモンハン事件〖戦争〗 Nomonhan Incident, or Battles of Khalkhyn Gol. This conflict between Japan and the Soviet Union occurred in 1939 on the border between Manchuria and the Mongolian People's Republic. It had long been thought that the Soviet Union defeated Japan overwhelmingly in this incident, but the collapse of the Soviet Union revealed that the reported victory was based on information manipulated by the Soviet Union.

のり 海苔〖食べ物・植物〗 purple laver. *Porphyra tenera*. An edible seaweed grown near the coast. Is often cultivated. A sheet of dried laver is used for various foods such as a rice ball or a sushi roll. →おにぎり；巻き寿司

のりちゃづけ 海苔茶漬け〖食べ物〗 cooked rice in tea, topped with dried purple laver.

のりと 祝詞〖神道・言語〗 a prayer in a Shinto ritual. Is written in old style Japanese and offered to deities by a Shinto priest.

のりのつくだに 海苔の佃煮〖食べ物〗 purple laver simmered down in soy sauce. Goes well with boiled rice.

のりまき 海苔巻き〖食べ物〗 ⇨巻き寿司

のるでぃっくふくごう ノルディック複合〖スポーツ〗 Nordic combined. Japan first joined the Nordic combined event of the Winter Olympics at St. Moritz in 1928. As of 2018, Japan has won two gold medals by teams at Albertville in 1992 and at Lillehammer in 1994.

のれん 暖簾〖ビジネス〗 (**1**) a split curtain for a shop or restaurant. Is hung at the entrance during business hours. The name and crest of the shop or restaurant are printed on it. (**2**) goodwill of a shop or restaurant.

のれんわけ 暖簾分け〖ビジネス〗 to help an employee be independent and open a new shop or restaurant in the same business field. The ex-employee is permitted to use the same name of the shop or restaurant by which he or she used to be employed.

のろ のろ〖宗教〗 a female priest of the traditional religion in Okinawa.

は

ばあなあどりいち バーナード・リーチ 〖工芸〗 Bernard Leach. 1887-1979. A British potter born in Hong Kong. Lived in Japan from 1909-1920 and returned many times thereafter. Learned pottery technique together with Tomimoto Kenkichi under a potter, Ogata Kenzan VI, and earned the title of Ogata Kenzan VII. In England, was influential in introducing Asian motif and techniques to British pottery-making. When revisiting Japan, helped an art critic and philosopher, YANAGI MUNEYOSHI, and other artists to establish the Japan Folk Crafts Museum in Tokyo. His publications include *A Potter's Book* in 1940 and *Between East and West* in 1978. Among his honors is the Order of the Sacred Treasures in 1966, the highest honor a foreigner can receive from the Japanese government. →尾形乾山(けん); 日本民藝館; 瑞宝(ずいほう)章

ぱあふぇくとりばてぃいきょうだん パーフェクト・リバティー教団 〖宗教〗 Church of Perfect Liberty. Was established in 1946. Its headquarters is located in Osaka Pref.

はあん ハーン 〖文芸〗 ⇨小泉八雲

ばいう 梅雨 〖気象〗 the rainy season. Occurs from early June to mid-July because of a stationary front between the Okhotsk high pressure system and the Ogasawara high pressure system. Hokkaido does not have this rainy season.

はいかい 俳諧, 誹諧 〖文芸〗 the term to refer to HAIKU in the Edo period.

はいから ハイカラ 〖精神性〗 to be modern and stylish. Comes from "high collar" because politicians or bureaucrats who followed Western fashion wore costumes with high collars in the Meiji period. →蛮カラ

はいかん 拝観 〖寺院〗 to view the precincts of a temple, the inside of a temple building, or a Buddhist image. Usually the fee is required.

はいく 俳句 〖文芸〗 a haiku, a short rhyming poem with three lines of 5, 7, and 7 syllables each. Appeared in the 17th century and became popular in the Edo period. Always contains a word implying a season.

はいけい 拝啓 〖言語〗 an initial greeting word in a letter. Equivalent to "Dear Sir or Madam." When a letter begins with this word, the conclusive word should be KEIGU.

ばいしゃくにん 媒酌人 〖冠婚葬祭〗 a pair of wedding witnesses. Matchmakers, called NAKOUDO, usually carry out this duty in the wedding ceremony for an arranged marriage. In an ordinary marriage ceremony, one of the bridegroom's superiors often play this role.

はいじん 俳人 〖文芸〗 a HAIKU poet.

ばいしん 陪臣 〖武士〗 a vassal of a vassal. A feudal lord, DAIMYOU, was an immediate vassal of a SHOUGUN in the Edo period, but vassals of a feudal lord were 'baishin' for a shogun. ↔直臣(じき)

はいだん 俳壇 〖文芸〗 the community of HAIKU poets.

はいでん 拝殿 〖神社・建築〗 the oratory of a Shinto shrine. Is located in front of the main sanctuary building. Is used by worshippers to send up prayers or by priests to conduct rituals. →本殿

ばいにく 梅肉 〖食べ物〗 pulp of pickled plum. Is added to vegetables, chicken, or other ingredients as a condiment.

はいはんちけん 廃藩置県 〖政治〗 the abolition of feudal domains and the establishment of prefectures. The feudal system was abolished, and the administrative power was centralized in 1871. That year, 305 prefectures were established, but the number was reduced to 75 the same year.

はいぶつきしゃく 廃仏毀釈 〖仏教・神道〗 movements to abolish Buddhism. Temples, sculptures, sutras, and utensils were destroyed in many places in the early Meiji period, based on the government's policy to promote Shintoism as the state religion. →神仏分離；国家神道

はいまつ 這松 〖植物〗 a dwarf stone pine. *Pinus pumila*. Grows in high mountains. Its trunk usually crawls near the ground.

はうた 端唄 〖音楽〗 a short popular song accompanied by a shamisen. Popular in Edo in the 19th century.

はおり 羽織 〖服飾〗 a traditional short coat worn over a kimono. Is tied by cords at the front. A traditional 'haori' bears the family crest. →紋付

はおりはかま 羽織袴 〖服飾〗 a traditional short coat, called HAORI, and loose-legged, long, and pleated trousers, called HAKAMA. Traditional male formal costume.

はかい 破戒 〖文芸・作品〗 *The Broken Commandment*. A novel published in 1906 by SHIMAZAKI TOUSON. Describes the mental agony of the hero who comes from an outcaste community. His father told him that he should conceal his background, but he broke the father's commandment.

ばかがい 馬鹿貝 〖食べ物・動物〗 a trough shell. *Mactra chinensis*. Lives on the shallow sand sea floor of China, Japan, and Korea. Is used for various cuisines such as sushi or tempura.

はがくれ 葉隠 〖武士・書名〗 *Hagakure: The Book of the Samurai*. A self-improvement book of the samurai code written in 1716. A speech by Yamamoto Tsunemasa is transcribed. Preaches the conscience and readiness that a samurai should always keep in mind. Contains a famous phrase, "the way of the samurai is found in death."

はがじ 羽賀寺 〔寺院〕 Haga-ji Temple. Is affiliated with the Shingon sect and is located in Obama City, Fukui Pref. Was founded in 716 by GYOUKI. The Eleven-headed Bodhisattva of Mercy is an Important Cultural Property.

はかた 博多 〔地名〕 the name of a cultural and historical area in Fukuoka City. Also a ward name. Includes headquarters of many Kyushu-based companies, as an economic hub of the city. The name of three major stations in central Fukuoka City is Hakata, not Fukuoka. Namely, the Hakata Station of Shinkansen, JR Kyushu lines, and the subway line. The traditional dolls called HAKATA NINGYOU have been produced since the 17th century. Famous foods include spicey pollock roe (MENTAIKO) and ramen with pork bones broth. Three popular festivals are Hakata Dontaku in early May, Hakata Gion Yamakasa in early July, and Hakata O-kunchi in late October.

はかたおり 博多織 〔服飾〕 a yarn-dyed silk fabric produced in Hakata, Kyushu. Is used for OBI, HAKAMA, or bags.

はかたぎおんやまかさ 博多祇園山笠 〔祭礼〕 Hakata Gion Yamakasa Festival. Is held at Kushida Shrine in Fukuoka City from July 1 to July 15. Famous for the float race on the last day.

はかたどんたく 博多どんたく 〔祭礼〕 Dontaku Festival. Is held in Fukuoka City on May 3 and 4. People parade the streets in various costumes. The word 'Dontaku' comes from a Dutch word "Zontag," which means "holiday."

はかたにんぎょう 博多人形 〔人形〕 a Hakata doll. Is made from baked clay. Not glazed but is elaborately colored.

はかま 袴 〔服飾〕 a loose-legged long pleated trousers, or a long pleated skirt worn over a kimono. Is worn on a formal occasion.

はかまいり 墓参り 〔仏教・冠婚葬祭〕 a visit to a grave. Many people visit their ancestors' grave during the Bon Festival or an equinoctial week or on the anniversary of a person's death.

はかまだれ 袴垂 〔犯罪〕 a legendary robber in the Heian period. Appeared in *Tales of Times Now Past* (KONJAKU MONOGATARI) and other archives.

はぎ 萩 〔植物〕 a bush clover. *Lespedeza*. One of the seven flowers of autumn in a lunar calendar. →秋の七草

はぎし 萩市 〔地名〕 Hagi City. Is located in northern Yamaguchi Pref., facing the Sea of Japan. The private school SHOUKASON-JUKU, headed by YOSHIDA SHOUIN, produced many great figures in the late 19th to early 20th centuries, including the former prime ministers, ITOU HIROBUMI and Yamagata Aritomo. Produces Hagi pottery.

はぎやき 萩焼 〔陶磁器〕 Hagi pottery. Mainly a white-glazed tea bowl. Is produced in Hagi City, Yamaguchi Pref. Was started by Korean potters who were fetched by Mouri Terumoto after TOYOTOMI HIDEYOSHI invaded Korea in the 16th century.

はぎわらさくたろう　萩原朔太郎　〖文芸〗　1886-1942. A poet born in Gunma Pref. Expressed the melancholy and loneliness of modern people in colloquial language. His works include *Howling at the Moon* in 1917 and *Cat Town* in 1923.

ばく　獏　**(1)**〖動物〗a tapir.　**(2)**〖妖怪〗an imaginary animal that eats human nightmares. Has a bear-like body, an elephant-like nose, rhinoceros-like eyes, tiger-like legs, and a bull-like tail.

はくさい　白菜　〖食べ物・植物〗　a Chinese cabbage, or a napa cabbage. *Brassica rapa pekinensis*. Was introduced from China in the Meiji period. Is now widely used as an ingredient in pickles or boiled food.

はくさん　白山　〖山岳〗　Mt. Haku. A volcano on the border between Ishikawa and Gifu Prefs. 2,702 m high. Has been an object of worship since ancient times.

はくさんじんじゃ　白山神社　〖神社〗 a Hakusan Shrine. There are about 2,700 Hakusan Shrines throughout Japan. Most of them enshrine Shirayama-hime, IZANAGI NO MIKOTO and/or IZANAMI NO MIKOTO. It is said that Shirayama-hime, whose other name is Kukuri-hime, arbitrated

the conflict between Izanagi and Izanami, who were a married couple.

はくじ　白磁　〖陶磁器〗　white porcelain. The first example in Japan is Arita ware, which was created by a Korean potter who had been brought back to Japan after TOYOTOMI HIDEYOSHI invaded Korea in the late 16th century. →有田焼

はくじゅ　白寿　〖通過儀礼〗　the age of 99 in the traditional approach to age counting. People usually celebrate when a person turns 98, in the modern approach to age counting. 'Hakuju' literally means "white age" for the following reason. One hundred is written as 百 in KANJI, and one is written as 一. Ninety-nine is 100 minus 1, namely '百 minus 一.' Since the top part of 百 has the same shape of 一, the top part should be deleted from 百 to make ninety-nine. Then, it becomes 白, and this kanji reads 'haku' and means "white." →数え年

ばくしん　幕臣　〖武士〗　⇨直参(ﾁ̆ょ̆ん)

はくすきのえのたたかい　白村江の戦い　〖戦争〗　⇨白村江(はくそんこう)の戦い

はくそんこうのたたかい　白村江の戦い　〖戦争〗　Battle of Baekgang-gu. The allied forces of Tang and Silla defeated the allied forces of Paekche and Japan. After this battle, Japan withdrew its military forces from the Korean Peninsula and devoted itself to the domestic affairs. →百済(ﾀ̆だ̆ら); 新羅(ﾚ̆ぎ̆); 唐

はくたか　はくたか　〖鉄道〗　the

express train on Hokuriku Shinkansen. Literally means "White Hawk," a legendary bird in the Northern Alps. Runs between Tokyo and Kanazawa in Ishikawa Pref. via Joetsu and Hokuriku Shinkansen, in 3 hours.

はくば 白馬 〖地名〗 the name of a village in northwestern Nagano Pref. Has a popular ski resort, Happou-One, with a 6 km-long slope. 'One' here is pronounced like "on nay," meaning a mountain ridge. When Nagano City hosted the Winter Olympics in 1998, Hakuba was the main competition venue for alpine and cross-country races and ski jumping.

はくばい 白梅 〖植物〗 a Japanese plum tree with white flowers. A painting by OGATA KOURIN that depicts 'hakubai' and a red-flowering plum, KOUBAI, is a National Treasure, which is stored at the MOA Museum of Art in Shizuoka Pref.

ばくはんたいせい 幕藩体制 〖武士・政治〗 a feudal system consisting of the Tokugawa shogunate and feudal domains during the Edo period. → 徳川幕府；大名

はくびょうが 白描画 〖絵画〗 monochrome India ink drawing. Lines are thin and constant in width mainly to draw contours or outlines, different from an India ink painting (SUIBOKU-GA), in which the stroke of the brush is sometimes powerfully emphasized. Examples

include *Scrolls of Frolicking Animals and Humans* (CHOUJUU JIN-BUTSU GIGA) at Kouzan-ji Temple in Kyoto.

ばくふ 幕府 〖武士・政治〗 shogunate, warrior's administration, or military government based on a feudal system. The Kamakura shogunate from 1185 to 1333, the Muromachi shogunate from 1336 to 1573, and the Tokugawa shogunate from 1603 to 1867. →鎌倉幕府；室町幕府；徳川幕府

ばくふちょっかつりょう 幕府直轄領 〖武士・政治〗 ⇨天領

はくぶん 白文 〖漢字〗 Chinese classics without reading marks. →訓点

はくほうぶんか 白鳳文化 〖時代〗 the Hakuhou culture from the latter 7th to the early 8th centuries. Was influenced by the culture of early Tang and marked by fresh and energetic feelings. Representative works in this era include the East Pagoda and the Triad of the Healing Buddha at the YAKUSHI-JI Temple, the Five-storied Pagoda at the HOURYUU-JI Temple, and wall paintings in the Takamatsuduka Tumulus. →高松塚古墳

はくまい 白米 〖食べ物〗 polished white rice, or milled rice. Rice bran and germs have been removed. →玄米

ばくまつ 幕末 〖時代〗 the last stage of the Tokugawa shogunate. Usually from 1854, when the Kanagawa treaty was concluded, to 1867, when the Tokugawa shogunate returned political rule to the Emperor.

はくろ 白露 〖暦〗 one of the 24 seasonal nodes in the traditional calendar. Around September 8th in the solar calendar. Means "white dew" because dew begins to form on plant leaves in this season. → 二十四節気(にじゅうしせっき)

ばけねこ 化け猫 〖妖怪〗 a goblin cat. A famous episode is based on the internal trouble of the Nabeshima family in the Hizen domain in northern Kyushu in the late 16th century. A person who was involved in the trouble was killed. His or her cat licked the blood oozing from the body and became a goblin cat. There are several variations of the story.

はごいた 羽子板 〖玩具〗 a wooden racket for traditional badminton during the New Year's holidays. Some of them are artistically ornamented with embossed pictures. → 羽根突き

はこがき 箱書き 〖美術・書道〗 a note of authentication on a box. To certify that the work contained in the box is an authentic work, the author or a connoisseur writes the title or the author's name on the box, together with a seal.

はこずし 箱寿司 〖寿司〗 ⇨押し寿司

はこせこ 箱迫 〖服飾〗 a flat-box-type tissue pouch made of fabric. Was carried by a woman in formal wear in the Edo period. Is now used on an auspicious occasion by a bride or a female child.

はこだてし 函館市 〖地名〗 Hakodate City. Is located in southern Hokkaido and facing the Tsugaru Channel. In 1868, at the end of the war for the Meiji Restoration, the ex-shogunate army entrenched themselves in a pentagonal fortress, GOROUKAKU, in this city. →戊辰(ぼしん)戦争；榎本武明；ハリストス正教会；函館山

はこだてせんそう 箱館戦争 〖戦争〗 Battle of Hakodate. The last part of the Boshin Civil War from January 1868 to May 1869. Ex-shogunal vassals, led by ENOMOTO TAKEAKI, resisted the new government, placing the headquarters at a Western-style star-shaped fortress called GOROUKAKU, and surrendered.

はこだてやま 函館山 〖山岳〗 Mt. Hakodate. Is located in Hakodate City in Hokkaido. The height is 334 m. Famous as a spot for enjoying night views of Hakodate City.

はこね 箱根 〖地名〗 the name of a scenic resort in southwestern Kanagawa Pref. Famous for hot springs, museums, Lake Ashi, and the view of Mt. Fuji. Popular hot springs are located in areas such as Yumoto, Tounosawa, Miyanoshita, and Kowakien. Around Lake Ashi is Hakone Shrine, and the Oowakudani geysers and Hakone Botanical Garden of Wetlands are nearby. The inter-collegiate relay race called HAKONE EKIDEN takes place annually on January 2 and 3, between

Tokyo and Lake Ashi. Yumoto hot spring is accessible by train, with a 100-minute ride on the Odakyu limited express "Hakone." Visitors can travel from Yumoto to Lake Ashi by train, cable car, and rope-way. Tourists can enjoy boarding a pirate-style ship to cross the lake.

はこねえきでん 箱根駅伝〖スポーツ〗 Hakone Ekiden. Officially called Tokyo-Hakone Round-Trip College Ekiden Race. The 217 km relay race, divided into 10 sections, takes place annually on January 2 and 3. The participants are students from universities in the Kantou region. It started in 1920, and the 94th competition took place in 2018, with interruption in the 1940s due to World War II. The following universities have achieved four or more consecutive victories: Nihon University (1935-1938), Chuo University (1959-1964), Nippon Sport Science University (1969-1973), Juntendo University (1986-1989), Komazawa University (2002-2005), and Aoyama Gakuin University (2015-2018). Chuo University also holds a record of 14 victories.

はこべ 繁縷〖植物〗 a chickweed. *Stellaria media*. One of the seven herbs of spring in a lunar calendar. →春の七草

はこべら 繁縷〖植物〗 ⇨繁縷(はこべ)

はこまくら 箱枕〖生活〗 a box-type pillow. A small cushion stuffed with buckwheat chaff is set on a wooden box. Was placed under the neck to retain the top-knot hair style while sleeping in the Edo period.

はこみや 箱宮〖神道〗 a miniature shrine. Is placed on a home Shinto altar. →神棚

はごろもでんせつ 羽衣伝説〖伝説〗 a legend of a flying robe. While a heavenly maiden was bathing in the sea, a man stole her robe of feathers. She was not able to fly back to heaven and became his wife. After getting back the robe, she returned to heaven. This legend can be found throughout Japan.

はざくら 葉桜〖植物〗 a cherry tree when blossoms have fallen and fresh young leaves have come out.

ばさし 馬刺し〖食べ物〗 sashimi of raw horse meat. Is popular in Kumamoto and Nagano Prefs.

はさみしょうぎ 挟み将棋〖将棋〗 a piece-capturing board game, using a shogi board and 18 pawns. A player can capture and take off the opponent's pawn by sandwiching it with two of his or her own pawns. The player who captures more pawns than the opponent is the winner.

はし 箸〖食器〗 a pair of chopsticks. Is made of wood, bamboo, or plastic. Rarely metal or ivory. At home, people usually use chopsticks to eat almost all dishes including noodles and soup. A disposable type is called WARIBASHI, and one to be used for cooking is called SAIBASHI. There are several bad manners to avoid, called KIRAI-BASHI.

はしあらい 箸洗い〖食文化〗 lightly seasoned soup served in traditional course cuisine. Literally means "chopstick washer."

はしおき 箸置き〖食器〗 a chopstick rest. The thin ends of chopsticks are placed on it.

はしがかり 橋掛かり〖能〗 the bridge between the stage and the green room. Extends from the stage to the left.

はじき 土師器〖考古・陶磁器〗 Haji ware. Unglazed reddish-brown earthen ware used from the 4th to the 12th centuries. Was fired at around 800 degrees centigrade. Was derived from Yayoi ware.

はしたて 箸立て〖食器〗 a chopstick stand. Is sometimes placed at a cheap Japanese-style restaurant. A number of chopsticks are stood in it with their tips below.

はしはかこふん 箸墓古墳〖考古〗 Hashihaka Tumulus. One of the oldest keyhole-shaped burial mounds, dating from the later 3rd century. Is located in Sakurai City, Nara Pref. Has not been researched academically because it is under the control of the Imperial Agency.

はしひめ 橋姫〖橋・妖怪〗 a bridge princess. Guards a bridge. Becomes jealous when someone praises a bridge other than the one she guards. There are several bridges a bridge princess haunts, including Uji Bridge in Kyoto and Kara Bridge in Shiga.

ぱしふぃっくりいぐ パシフィック・リーグ〖スポーツ〗 Pacific League. One of the two professional baseball leagues. Was established in 1949. Includes six teams: Buffalos, Fighters, Golden Eagles, Hawks, Lions, and Marines.

はしまくら 箸枕〖食器〗 ⇨箸置き

はしもとがほう 橋本雅邦〖絵画〗 1835-1908. A painter born in Edo. Studied in the Kanou school, was recognized by OKAKURA TENSHIN and Ernest Fenollosa, and was influential in establishing a new style of Japanese painting. Taught YOKOYAMA TAIKAN at the Tokyo Fine Arts School. His works include *White Clouds and Autumn Leaves* at Tokyo University of the Arts.

ばしゃく 馬借〖交通〗 a horse transporter in medieval times.

はしやすめ 箸休め〖食文化〗 a side dish served between the main dishes. There are several types such as vinegared vegetables, cold soup, and pickles.

ばしょ ～場所〖相撲〗 a sumo grand tournament. Literally means "a place," but refers to one of the six tournaments in professional sumo.

ばしょう 芭蕉 **(1)**〖文芸〗⇨松尾芭蕉 **(2)**〖植物〗 a Japanese fiber banana. *Musa basjoo*. A foliage plant native to China. Its fruit is not edible.

はしら ～柱〖宗教・助数詞〗 a counting suffix for Shinto deities, spirits of the dead, or memorial tablets.

はしらえ 柱絵〖絵画〗 **(1)** painting on a pillar in a temple building.

Examples are seen at Byoudou-in Temple and Daigo-ji Temple in Kyoto. ⑵ an ukiyo-e on a vertically long screen, usually 76 cm by 13 cm. Is hung on a pillar.

はす 蓮 〖植物・仏教〗 a lotus. *Nelumbo nucifera*. A water plant native to India. About 1 to 2 m high. Its root is edible. A lotus has a close connection with Buddhism; for example, lotus flowers bloom in a pond in the Wesern Pure Land. → 蓮根(れんこん); 西方極楽浄土; 蓮華(れんげ); 蓮台(れんだい)

ばすたしんじゅく バスタ新宿 〖交通・施設〗 Shinjuku Expressway Bus Terminal. Is abbreviated to Buster Shinjuku. Opened in 2016 next to the JR Shinjuku Station in the center of Tokyo city proper. Passengers can get on the airport buses to and from Narita Airport or Haneda Airport, and on the expressway buses for many places including the Tohoku, Kansai, Shikoku, and Kyushu regions.

はすのうてな 蓮の台 〖仏教〗 ⇨ 蓮台(れんだい)

ぱすも PASMO 〖交通〗 PASMO. A contactless, credit-card-sized smart card. Costs 2,000 yen, is rechargeable, and operates on a prepay basis. When it was launched in 2007 by the major private railway companies in the Kantou region, its use was restricted to riding their trains. But it came to be usable in many other areas, and for many other purposes like shopping.

はぜ 沙魚 〖魚〗 a goby. *Gobiidae*. Eaten caramelized or as tempura.

はせがわとうはく 長谷川等伯 〖絵画〗 1539-1610. A painter born in present Ishikawa Pref. Established the Hasegawa school in rivalry with the Kanou school. His works include *Pine Trees*, a National Treasure at the Tokyo National Museum, and *Old Trees and Monkeys*, at the Kyoto National Museum. → 狩野(かのう)派

はせがわへいぞう 長谷川平蔵 〖武士〗 1745-1795. A direct shogunal vassal born in Edo. Became the chief of special police, called HITSUKE TOUZOKU ARATAME, in Edo. Is described as a hero in a samurai novel, *Onihei Hankachou*, by IKENAMI SHOUTAROU.

はせがわまちこ 長谷川町子 〖漫画〗 1920-1992. A manga artist born in Saga Pref. Serialized *Sazaesan* in newspapers from 1946 to 1974. Received the People's Honor Award after her death.

はせくらつねなが 支倉常長 〖外交〗 1571-1622. A vassal of the Date clan in Sendai, present Miyagi Pref. Was dispatched to Europe in 1613 by DATE MASAMUNE but failed in his trade negotiations. Was baptized a Catholic while in Europe. However, when he returned to Japan in 1620, Christianity had become strictly forbidden by the Tokugawa shogunate.

はせでら 長谷寺 〖寺院〗 Hasedera Temple. The head temple of the

Buzan school of the Shingon sect, located in Sakurai City, northern Nara Pref. Was established in the 7th century by the priest Doumyou. The main hall, a bronze plaque, a sutra case, and a sutra are National Treasures.

はたきこみ はたき込み〖相撲〗 a slap down. To dodge the opponent's rush and then to knock him in the ring with a slap to the neck, shoulder, or back.

はたご 旅籠〖旅〗 an inn in the Edo period. Served two meals.

はたさしもの 旗指物〖軍事〗 a banner to indicate the name of the clan or unit in a battlefield in the Warring States period. Some banners were attached on the back of armor, and others were brought by hands.

はだしのげん はだしのゲン〖漫画〗 *Barefoot Gen*. An antinuclear history manga, written and illustrated by Nakazawa Keiji. The story is based on his personal experience as a victim of the atomic bomb in Hiroshima. Was published serially in a boys' magazine, *Weekly Shonen Jump*, from 1973 to 1974.

はだじゅばん 肌襦袢〖服飾〗 next-to-skin underwear for a kimono.

はたじるし 旗印〖軍事〗 the crest or characters on a banner, which was hoisted as a mark on a battlefield.

はたはた はたはた〖食べ物・魚〗 a sailfin sandfish. *Arctoscopus japonicus*. Lives along the coast of Northern Japan. Has no scales and is about 20 cm long. Eaten boiled, grilled, or dried.

はたもと 旗本〖武士〗 a direct vassal of the Tokugawa shogun. Had the privilege to see the shogun. Received an annual stipend of 10,000 KOKU or less of rice. ↔御家人〖武〗

ばち 桴〖音楽〗 a pair of drumsticks. However, some drums are beaten with the hands.

ばち 撥〖音楽〗 a plectrum. Is used to play the SHAMISEN or BIWA, a Japanese lute with four or five strings.

はちこう ハチ公〖精神性・動物〗 ⇨ 忠犬ハチ公

はちごろう 八五郎〖落語〗 a hasty and careless man in a traditional comic storytelling, RAKUGO. Only partly listens to what another person says and causes funny events to occur.

はちじゅうはちや 八十八夜〖暦〗 the 88th day from the beginning of spring in the traditional calendar. Around May 2 in the current calendar. Farmers begin to be busy planting rice seeds, picking tea leaves, and raising silkworms.

はちじゅうはっかしょめぐり 八十八か所巡り〖仏教・旅〗 pilgrimage to 88 holy places. Although there are several pilgrimage courses of this type, the one in Shikoku is the most famous. →四国八十八カ所

はちじょうま 八畳間〖建築〗 a room with eight TATAMI mats. The term

often refers to a room that will fit eight tatami mats, even if mats are not there.

はちだいじごく 八大地獄 〖仏教〗 Eight Great Hells of Buddhism. Deeds in one's lifetime determine which hell he or she enters.

はちだいりゅうおう 八大竜王 〖仏教〗 Eight Great Dragon Deities. In a Buddhist legend, listened to a lecture by the Historical Buddha about the Lotus Sutra. They control the rain. →法華経

はちぶしゅう 八部衆 〖仏教〗 Eight Devas. Eight guardians of Buddhism. Include Ashura, Karura, Kendatsuba, and other deities that vary from temple to temple. Famous examples are at Koufuku-ji Temple in Nara.

はちまき 鉢巻き 〖服飾・精神性〗 a headband. A long piece of cloth is tied around the head to show his or her determination.

はちまんぐう 八幡宮 〖神社〗 a Hachiman Shrine. Enshrines Emperor Oujin. It is said that there are about 25,000 Hachiman Shrines throughout Japan, and the head shrine is Usa Hachiman in Ooita Pref. →応神天皇; 八幡神

はちまんじん 八幡神 〖神道・仏教〗 the guardian deity of samurai. Is identified as Emperor Oujin and also called Hachiman Bodhisattva because this Shinto deity was incorporated into Buddhism. →八幡宮

はちまんづくり 八幡造り 〖神社・建築〗 Hachiman style of Shinto architecture. The front building and the rear building are connected so that the roofs touch along the eaves. The main sanctuary building of the Usa Shrine has this style. →本殿; 宇佐神宮

はちろうがた 八郎潟 〖湖沼〗 Lake Hachirou-gata. A lagoon located in central Akita Pref., connected to the Sea of Japan. Used to be the second largest lake in Japan, but for rice production, much of the lake was reclaimed in the 1950s and 60s. The water area is now 28 km^2. However, the reclamation was criticized as a mistake in agricultural planning, since Japan did not need such a vast rice field or so much rice after the 1960s. Nowadays, it is famous for pond smelt (wakasagi) and black bass fishing.

ぱちんこ パチンコ 〖娯楽〗 pachinko. An upright-type pinball machine game. Very popular among adults. People can get prizes or can earn money indirectly when winning.

ぱちんこや パチンコ屋 〖娯楽〗 a pachinko parlor. Those under 18 are prohibited from entering by law.

はつ ハツ 〖食べ物〗 grilled heart. Cardiac muscles of cattle, pigs, or chickens are grilled on a skewer. The origin of the word is "heart" in Japanized pronunciation.

ばつ × 〖言語〗 An x-shaped mark, which means "bad," "impossible," "error," or "divorce." ↔○(まる)

はつうま 初午 〖暦〗 the first

"horse" day of the year in the Chinese zodiac signs. A festival is held at a shrine of the cereals deity. →十二支；稲荷神社

はつおん 撥音〚言語〛 the syllabic nasal. Is spelled as 'n' in the alphabet and as ん or ン in KANA.

ばっかく 幕閣〚政治〛 a cabinet minister of the Tokugawa shogunate.

はつがつお 初鰹〚食べ物〛 the first bonito of the season. Eaten in early summer.

はつがま 初釜〚茶道〛 New Year's tea ceremony.

はづき 葉月〚暦〛 August in the traditional calendar. Means "leaf month," but there are several hypotheses about its etymology. One of them says that tree leaves begin to fall in this month. →旧暦

はっけい ～八景〚地名〛 eight beautiful scenes of a province. Originated from eight beautiful scenes in the Xiao-Xiang area of China. In Japan, several areas boast their own eight scenes such as KANAZAWA HAKKEI or OUMI HAKKEI. →瀟湘(しょうしょう)八景

はっけよい 八卦良い〚相撲〛 a phrase shouted by a referee, like "Fight" in boxing, either when both wrestlers are ready to start their bout, or when both have stopped moving during their bout. Is said to mean "Fortune is good," or "Raise the spirit higher."

はっさく 八朔 **(1)**〚暦〛 August 1 in the traditional calendar. Farmers used to have an annual event to pray for an abundant harvest. **(2)**〚食べ物・植物〛 a thick-skinned yellowish orange. *Citrus hassaku*. Was discovered in Hiroshima Pref. in the Edo period. Was named because it becomes edible around the day of (1).

はっすん 八寸〚食文化〛 a set of several kinds of small food for drinking sake. Usually served cold. Is served on a 24-cm wooden square plate in the traditional course cuisine. 'Hassun' literally means 8 SUN, equivalent to 24 cm.

はつぜっく 初節句〚通過儀礼〛 the first seasonal festival after childbirth. The Girls' Festival is on March 3, and the Boys' Festival is on May 5. →節句

はっちょうぼり 八丁堀〚犯罪・地名〛 the name of an area in present central Tokyo. The officers, called YORIKI or DOUSHIN, who worked for a feudal commissioner, called MACHIBUGYOU, lived around this area in the Edo period.

はっちょうみそ 八丁味噌〚調味料〛 dark-brown miso produced in Okazaki City, Aichi Pref. A little strong and salty.

ばってら バッテラ〚寿司〛 pressed sushi with mackerel. The name 'battera' comes from "bateira" in Portuguese, which means "boat," because its shape used to resemble a boat.

はっとう 法堂〚仏教・建築〛 the lecture hall of a Zen temple. Corresponds to KOUDOU in some other sects.

はつどひょう 初土俵 〔相撲〕 the debut of a professional sumo wrestler. A sumo wrestler has to pass the physical examination by the Japan Sumo Association.

はっとりはんぞうまさなり 服部半蔵正成 〔忍者〕 1542-1596. A vassal of TOKUGAWA IEYASU. When the Honnou-ji Incident occurred in 1582, AKECHI MITSUHIDE blocked the retreat line of Ieyasu. Hanzou Masanari commanded ninja to help Ieyasu escape to his own castle in Okazaki, present Aichi Pref.

はつに 初荷 〔正月・交通〕 the first shipment in the New Year. The goods were sent with an adorned cart or horse on January 2 in the Edo period.

はつねみく 初音ミク 〔音楽〕 the name of a piece of singing synthesizer software, which is called Vocaloid. The virtual pop idol character portrayed as a 16-year-old girl with a long bluish-colored pigtails. Was developed by Crypton Future Media.

はつばしょ 初場所 〔相撲〕 New Year Sumo Tournament. Is held at KOKUGIKAN in Tokyo in January.

はっぴ 法被 〔服飾〕 a traditional short coat for a craftsman. Carries the crest or name of the employer on the back.

はっぴいまんでえ ハッピーマンデー 〔暦〕 the happy Monday floating holidays. Some national holidays were moved from their original day to a Monday to create three consecutive holidays. Coming-of-Age Day on January 15 was moved to the second Monday in January, Marine Day on July 20 was moved to the third Monday in July, Respect-for-the-Aged Day on September 15 was moved to the third Monday in September, and Health Sports Day on October 10 was moved to the second Monday in October. →成人の日；海の日；敬老の日；体育の日

はつひので 初日の出 〔正月・自然〕 the sunrise on January 1. Some people climb mountains or go to the seaside to watch the sun rise from the horizon.

はっぴゃくびくに 八百比丘尼 〔妖怪〕 ⇨八尾比丘尼（やおびくに）

はっぴゃくやちょう 八百八町 〔生活〕 a term to express that Edo consisted of many streets in the Edo period. Literally means "eight-hundred and eight streets."

はっぴゃくやばし 八百八橋 〔生活〕 a term to express that Osaka had many bridges in the Edo period. Literally means "eight-hundred and eight bridges."

はっぽうしゅ 発泡酒 〔酒〕 beer-taste alcoholic drink. Cheaper than beer. The percentage of malt is lower than 67% in the ingredients excepting water while the percentage of malt in the ingredients of beer is 67% or higher. →第3のビール

はっぽうしゅりけん　八方手裏剣 〖忍者〗 a throwing star with eight striking points. →手裏剣

はつぼん　初盆 〖仏教〗 ⇨新盆(にいぼん)

はつもうで　初詣で 〖正月・宗教〗 to visit a shrine or temple during the New Year's holidays. People pray for good fortune in the new year and buy a fortune slip. →御神籤(おみくじ)

はつもの　初物 〖食文化〗 the first produce or fish of the season. Some people attach importance to it.

はつゆめ　初夢 〖正月〗 one's first dream of the year. The dream on the night of January 1 or 2. Tells one's annual fortune. It is said that a dream about Mt. Fuji is the best omen, a hawk is second, and an eggplant is third. →宝船

はつわらい　初笑い 〖正月・マスコミ〗 the first laugh during the New Year's holidays. Is said to bring people happiness for the whole year. The titles of TV comedy programs during the New Year's holidays often include the word 'hatsu-warai.'

ばてれん　伴天連 〖キリスト教〗 a Portuguese Catholic father from the late 16th to the 17th centuries. Also refers to Christianity or Christians in a broader sense.

ばてれんついほうれい　伴天連追放令 〖キリスト教・政治〗 the order to expel Christian missionaries. Was issued in 1587 by Toyotomi Hideyoshi.

ばとうかんのん　馬頭観音 〖仏教〗 Horse-head Bodhisattva of Mercy. Wears a horse-headed crown and has an angry expression. Often has three faces and eight arms. Is said to save those who reside in the Realm of Beasts in esoteric Buddhism. Famous examples include the one at Joururi-ji Temple in Kyoto Pref. →観音；畜生道

はとぶえ　鳩笛 〖音楽〗 a pigeon-shaped earthen whistle. Makes sounds like pigeons cooing.

ばどみんとん　バドミントン 〖スポーツ〗 badminton. Is said to have begun to be played in the 1930s in Japan. Japan won the first gold medal in women's doubles at the Rio de Janeiro Olympics in 2016.

はとむぎ　鳩麦 〖植物・食文化〗 an adlay, or Job's tears. *Coix lachryma-jobi* var. *ma-yuen*. Is used for medicine or drunk as tea.

はな　鼻 〖文芸・作品〗 *The Nose*. A novel published in 1916 by Akutagawa Ryuunosuke. Describes the psychology of a priest who has a large nose. Is based on a story in the *Tales of Times Now Past* in the early 12th century. →今昔(じゃく)物語

はないた　花板 〖食文化〗 a chef, or the best cook, at a traditional Japanese restaurant.

はないちもんめ　花一匁 〖遊び〗 a traditional children's game. The children are separated into two teams. The members of each team make a line with hand in hand and face each other. One team steps forward, singing a special song, while the other walks backward. After repeating the process, the representatives from each team do rock-paper-scissors (JANKEN). The winner gets a member of the opponents and adds him or her to the winner's own team. When one team loses all members, the game ends.

はなお 鼻緒 〔履物〕 clog thongs, or straps attaching the sole to the foot. Are used for ZOURI and GETA.

はなおかせいしゅう 花岡青洲 〔医療〕 1760-1835. A surgeon born in present Wakayama Pref. Learned both traditional and Western medicine and developed anesthetic drugs. Successfully removed breast cancer in an operation under a general anesthesia for the first time in the world in 1804.

はながさ 花笠 〔祭礼・服飾〕 a sedge hat decorated with flowers. Is worn at a festival.

はながさまつり 花笠祭り 〔祭礼〕 Yamagata Hanagasa Festival. Is held in Yamagata City from August 5 to 7. People wear a sedge hat decorated with flowers and parade while dancing.

はながつお 花鰹 〔食べ物〕 flakes of dried bonito. Dried bonito is usually shaved into flakes. →鰹節

はながるた 花歌留多 〔遊び〕 ⇨花札

はなさかじじい 花咲爺 〔民話〕 "The Old Man Who Made the Dead Trees Blossom." A folk tale. An honest old man dug out gold coins from the earth, following the in-struction of his dog. A neighboring evil-minded old man imitated it but failed. The evil-minded man killed the dog in anger. The honest man constructed a wooden grave for the dog. The wooden grave grew into a big tree. The honest man made a mortar and pounded rice in the mortar. The rice became gold coins. The evil-minded man imitated it but failed again and burned the mortar. The honest man sprinkled the ash of the mortar onto a dead tree. Then it bore blossoms.

はなしか 噺家 〔落語〕 ⇨落語家

はなしょうぶ 花菖蒲 〔植物〕 a Japanese iris. *Iris ensata.* Is cultivated at the waterside as an ornamental plant. The colors of flowers are various such as purple, pink, and white.

はなずもう 花相撲 〔相撲〕 bouts and exhibitions outside the regular tournaments. Include charity bouts, retirement bouts, and the wrestlers' chorus. The results do not influence the rank or salary of wrestlers.

はなだい 花代 〔娯楽〕 ⇨玉代（ぎょくだい）

はなどめ 花留め 〔華道〕 a flower holder. Fixes the position of flowers to arrange easily.

はなばさみ 花挟み 〔華道〕 scissors for trimming flowers.

はなび 花火 〔娯楽〕 fireworks. Were introduced to Japan in the 16th century and became popular in the Edo period. Great exhibitions are held at many places in summer.

はなびし 花菱〖文様〗 a diamond design consisting of flower petals.

はなぶさいっちょう 英一蝶 〖絵画〗 1652-1724. A painter born in Kyoto. Was good at urban-style genre paintings. Also learned haiku under MATSUO BASHOU. Was exiled to Miyake Island from 1693 to 1709 for an unknown reason. His works include *Waiting the Season's Sunrise* at the Idemitsu Museum of Arts.

はなふだ 花札 〖遊び〗 a flower matching card game. Each card includes a picture of one of 12 flowers, which represent 12 months. Four cards are illustrated with the same flowers, though the point of each card is different. A card with the combination of a flower and another object has high points.

はなふぶき 花吹雪〖気象〗 a shower of falling cherry blossoms.

はなまち 花街〖娯楽〗 a red-light district in olden times. Prostitution is forbidden by law at present.

はなまつり 花祭り〖仏教〗 ⇨灌仏会(かんぶつえ)

はなみ 花見〖娯楽〗 cherry-blossom viewing. People usually hold a party under cherry trees in the daytime or evening from early April to May. The season varies from region to region. →桜前線

はなみざけ 花見酒〖娯楽・酒〗 sake in cherry-blossom viewing. People drink not only sake but also beer and other alcoholic beverages. →花見

はなみち 花道〖歌舞伎〗 an elevated passage at the same level with the stage. Leads from the left side of the stage through the audience at a right angle. The entrances, exits, and performances of actors look more impressive owing to this passage.

はなみどう 花御堂〖仏教〗 a small hut decorated with flowers. A statue of the Historical Buddha at birth is placed in it at his Birthday Festival on April 8. →誕生仏; 灌仏会(かんぶつえ)

はなむすび 花結び〖生活〗 a rosette using a cord, or a flower-shaped knot.

はなれ 離れ〖建築〗 a small annex of a large residence. ↔母屋(おもや)

はなわほきいち 塙保己一 〖人文学〗 1746-1821. A scholar of Japanese classics, born in present Saitama Pref. Lost his eyesight at 7. Studied Japanese classics under KAMO NO MABUCHI. Compiled the archive collection named *Gunsho-ruijuu*.

はにわ 埴輪〖考古〗 a clay image. Unglazed earthenware placed on or around a burial mound in ancient times. Takes several shapes such as a cylinder, human, horse, and house.

はねだくうこう 羽田空港〖交通〗 ⇨東京国際空港

はねつき 羽根突き〖遊び〗 traditional Japanese badminton on the New Year's holidays. Is played with a shuttlecock and a racket called HAGOITA. The loser has some India ink put on his or her face as a penalty.

ははこぐさ 母子草〖植物〗 a Jersey cudweed. *Gnaphalium affine*. Is also called 'gogyou' when counted as one of the seven herbs of spring in a lunar calendar. →春の七草

はばへん 巾偏〖漢字〗 a radical meaning "cloth." Is used in kanji such as 布 (cloth), 帆 (sail), and 帯 (belt).

はぶ 波布〖動物〗 a habu snake. *Trimeresurus flavoviridis*. About 2 m long and poisonous. Inhabits the Okinawa and Amami Islands.

はぶたえ 羽二重〖服飾〗 a glossy pure white silk fabric woven from untwisted high-quality yarn. Is used for lining material of a kimono or traditional formal wear.

はぶたえもち 羽二重餅〖食べ物〗 a smooth soft rectangular cake made from rice flour. A specialty of Fukui City.

ばぶるけいざい バブル経済〖経済〗 Bubble Economy. The economic boom in the latter half of the 1980s. The real estate and stock prices soared up too much because of speculation, compared with the situation of the real economy.

はへん 歯偏〖漢字〗 a left-side radical meaning "tooth." Is used in kanji such as 齢 (age) and 齬 (bite).

はぼうき 羽箒〖茶道〗 a feather duster. Is used to clean around the hearth in the tearoom.

はぼく 破墨〖絵画〗 a technique of India ink painting to depict solidity, using a shade of ink.

はぼまいぐんとう 歯舞群島〖島名〗 the Habomai Islands. Are located off the coast of eastern Hokkaido, at the southern tip of the Kuril Islands. Have been under Russian rule since 1945.

はまがり 刃曲〖忍者〗 a folding saw. Was used to enter a place secretly.

はまぐり 蛤〖食べ物・動物〗 an Asian hard clam, or a common orient clam. *Meretrix lusornia*. The length of the shell is about 8 cm. Is put into clear soup. The shell powder, called GOFUN, is used as white paint in traditional fine arts.

はまぐりごもんのへん 蛤御門の変〖政治〗 Forbidden Gate Incident, or Imperial Palace Gate Incident. Broke out in the vicinity of the Imperial Palace in 1864. The allied forces, mainly consisting of the Aizu and Satsuma domains, had excluded the Choushuu domain from Kyoto. After this battle, the defeated Choushuu domain was regarded as the "Emperor's enemy" because it fired toward the Imperial Palace. This incident was used as the pretext for the First Choushuu Expedition by the Tokugawa shogunate. →長州征伐

はまち 飯〖食べ物・魚〗 **(1)** a young yellowtail. This term is used in the Kansai region when the fish is about 20 to 40 cm. →鰤(ｽﾞ); メジロ; ツバス **(2)** a farmed yellowtail.

はまちどり 浜千鳥〖工芸〗 plovers on the beach. Is sometimes used as an ornamental subject of handicraft such as an inkstone case or a small dish.

はまなこ 浜名湖 〔湖沼〕 Lake Hamana. A brackish lake located in Shizuoka Pref. Its area is 65 km², and the deepest point is 13 m. Famous for farming eels.

はまや 破魔矢 〔神道〕 a talisman arrow. Is sold at a Shinto shrine during the New Year's holidays. In the next year, people bring it to the shrine to have it burned. →どんど焼き

はまやき 浜焼き 〔食べ物〕 grilled seafood fresh from the sea. People often enjoy it on the seashore.

はも 鱧 〔食べ物・魚〕 a pike conger. *Muraenesox cinereus*. A grown-up male is about 70 cm long, while a female grows to around 2 m long. One from Kii Channel or the Inland Sea is famous. Eaten in various ways such as tempura or sushi. Is eaten lightly boiled in Osaka and Kyoto in summer.

はもん 破門 〔武術・華道・茶道〕 expulsion from a school of arts. This term is used in various traditional fields such as martial arts, performing arts, flower arrangement, tea ceremony, and academic study.

はやかご 早駕籠 〔交通〕 an express palanquin. Though an ordinary palanquin was carried by 2 bearers, the express one was carried and pulled by 8 to 10 bearers.

はやがわり 早替わり 〔歌舞伎〕 to change costumes quickly when an actor plays more than one role in one scene.

はやざし 早指し 〔将棋〕 **(1)** a quick game of shogi, or lightning Japanese chess. The time limit is short. For example, the total time limit of each player is less than one hour, or each player has to move a piece less than 30 seconds after the other player's move. A quick game of go is called 'haya-go' rather than 'haya-zashi.' **(2)** a shogi player who considers the next move quickly.

はやし 囃子 〔音楽〕 musical accompaniment for performing arts such as Noh, Noh farce, kabuki, and comic storytelling. Include shamisen, drums, and flutes.

はやしかた 囃子方 〔歌舞伎・能〕 a band of the instrumentalists accompanying kabuki and Noh plays. Includes flutes, small hand drums, large hand drums, and stick drums. →小鼓；大鼓

はやしふみこ 林芙美子 〔文芸〕 1903-1951. A novelist born in Yamaguchi Pref. Her works include autobiographical novels such as *Diary of a Vagabond* (Hourou-ki) in 1948 and *Floating clouds* (Ukigumo) in 1951.

はやしらざん 林羅山 〔人文学〕 1583-1657. A Confucianist born in Kyoto. Served four Tokugawa Shoguns: Ieyasu, Hidetada, Iemitsu, and Ietsuna. Founded a private school in 1630, which later became SHOUHEIKOU.

はやて はやて 〔鉄道〕 the second fastest super express train

on Tohoku Shinkansen. Its name means a "gale." Connects Tokyo with Sendai in 2 hours, and Tokyo with Shin-Aomori in 3 hours 20–50 minutes. Most Hayate trains are reservation-only.

はやと 隼人〖少数民族〗 an ancient tribe in southern Kyushu. Was subjugated by the Yamato Court in the 8th century.

はやびきゃく 早飛脚〖通信〗 an express courier in the Edo period. → 飛脚

はやひと 隼人〖少数民族〗 ⇨隼人（はやと）

はやぶさ はやぶさ　(1)〖鉄道〗 the fastest express train on the Tohoku and Hokkaido Shinkansen. Literally means a "falcon," a very fast-flying bird. Runs at the maximum speed of 320 km/h. Many Hayabusa trains run between Tokyo and Shin-Hakodate-Hokuto. Connects the two stations in 4 to 4.5 hours. Most Hayabusa trains are reservation-only.　**(2)**〖科学技術〗 the name of an unmanned asteroid explorer. MUSES-C. Was launched in 2003 and returned to the earth in 2010. Hayabusa 2 was launched in 2014 and will return in 2020.

はやぶさ 隼〖軍事〗 Nakajima Ki-43 Oscar. A fighter aircraft during World War II. The Japanese name means "Peregrine Falcon." Was manufactured by Nakajima Aircraft Co. and was used by the Japanese army while a Zero fighter was used by the navy. →中島飛行機；ゼロ戦

はらい 祓い〖神道〗 ⇨お祓い

はらがけ 腹掛け〖服飾〗 a traditional apron worn by a workman or a shop-boy. Has a large pocket in front.

はらきり 腹切り〖武士〗 ⇨切腹

はらこ 腹子〖食べ物〗 seasoned hard roe. Include SUJIKO, TARAKO, and TOBIKO.

ばらずし バラ寿司〖寿司〗 ⇨五目寿司

はらたかし 原敬〖政治〗 1856-1921. A statesman born in Iwate Pref. After leading the Mainichi Shimbun company as its president, served as prime minister from 1918 to 1921, but was assassinated by a railroad worker. His cabinet is said to have been the first full-fledged political party cabinet in Japan. Since he continued to decline to accept the title of nobility, he was nicknamed "Commoner Prime Minister."

はらまき 腹巻き〖服飾〗 **(1)** a belly warmer, or a stomach band. Is usually made of wool or cotton and worn on the abdomen. **(2)** a torso protector. A kind of a simple armor in medieval times.

はり 鍼〖医療〗 acupuncture. A traditional method to treat disease by sticking special thin needles onto vital points of the skin.

ぱりいぐ パ・リーグ〖スポーツ〗 ⇨ パシフィック・リーグ

はりくよう 針供養〖神道・仏教〗 the memorial ceremony for needles. Is held to thank old or broken needles on February 8th or December 8th.

People stick the needles in tofu or gelatinous paste, called KONNYAKU, and offer them to a shrine or temple.

はりす ハリス 〔外交〕 Townsend Harris. 1804-1878. An American diplomat and merchant who served as the first American counsel to Japan in 1856. In 1858, negotiated the first U.S. trade treaty with Japan, called the U.S.-Japan Treaty of Amity and Commerce, or Harris Treaty. It opened six ports to U.S. trade and helped Japan expand its international trade. Yet it contained some provisions that were unpopular in Japan and led to later conflicts.

はりすとすせいきょうかい ハリストス正教会 〔キリスト教〕 Orthodox Church in Japan, abbreviated to OCJ. Is officially called 'Nihon Harisutosu Seikyoukai' in Japanese. Is under the patronage of the Russian Orthodox Church. They call Christ 'Harisutosu,' based on the Greek pronunciation. Started their mission in 1861, when their first church was founded in Hakodate in southern Hokkaido, and St. Nicholai started to preach there. Its chapel is an Important Cultural Property, which tourists can visit.

はりせん 張り扇 〔芸能〕 a slapping paper slip with a handle. Is used by a professional storyteller called KOUSHAKU-SHI to make sounds by hitting a table. Is self-made by the storyteller.

はりだしよこづな 張出横綱 〔相撲〕 an extra yokozuna, or an associate yokozuna. Though the number of yokozuna is limited to four at present, it used to be just two. At that time, a wrestler whose performance was great enough could be promoted to 'haridashi yokozuna,' which was ranked below the principal yokozuna. The second highest position, oozeki, had the same system. This system was abolished in 1994.

はりて 張り手 〔相撲〕 slapping on the opponent's cheek or neck side.

はりま 播磨 〔旧国名〕 the old name of central and western Hyougo Pref.

はるか はるか 〔鉄道〕 JR Airport Express Haruka. Connects Kansai-airport Station with major stations in Osaka, Kyoto, and Shiga Prefs., such as Tennouji, Shin-Osaka, Kyoto, Ootsu, and Maibara Stations. Does not stop at Osaka Station. Unlike Narita Express, non-reservation seats are available.

はるさめ 春雨 **(1)**〔気象〕 spring drizzle, or light rain in spring. **(2)** 〔食べ物〕 thin noodles made from bean starch. Are used in stir-fried dishes, soups, and particularly hot-pot dishes. Recently have been regarded as an ingredient to help lose weight.

ばるちっくかんたい バルチック艦隊 〔戦争〕 Russian Baltic Fleet. Was destroyed at the Battle of Tsushima in 1905 by the Combined Fleet of

Japan during the Russo-Japanese War. →日露戦争

はるのおと ハルノート 〖外交〗 Hull note. Informal term for the November 26, 1941, proposal from the United States to Japan concerning the two nations' differences. Was delivered by the Secretary of State Cordell Hull and included various concessions from both nations. Mainly, it required Japan's withdrawal from Indochina and China. Though it did not intend to halt negotiations, the note was viewed as a final warning by some people in Japan. The fleet intending to attack Pearl Harbor, which had already set sail, was not called back, and the attack took place on December 7. →太平洋戦争

はるのななくさ 春の七草 〖植物〗 the seven herbs of spring in a lunar calendar. SERI (dropwort), NAZUNA (shepherd's purse), GOGYOU (Jersey cudweed), HAKOBERA (chickweed), HOTOKE-NO-ZA (nipplewort), SUZUNA (turnip), and SUZUSHIRO (mooli). ↔ 秋の七草

はるばしょ 春場所 〖相撲〗 Spring Sumo Tournament. Is held at Edion Arena Osaka in Osaka in March.

はれ 晴れ 〖精神性〗 the concept of a special occasion or celebration. Is related to either public events such as festivals or personal celebrations such as weddings. On the day of 'hare,' people wear special costumes and eat special cuisine. Was contrasted against the con-

cept of daily life, KE, by a folklorist, YANAGITA KUNIO.

ばれえぼおる バレーボール 〖スポーツ〗 volleyball. Was introduced to Japan in 1913 by an American, Franklin H. Brown. The women's team won the gold medal at the Tokyo Olympics in 1964 and the Montreal Olympics in 1976. The men's team won the gold medal at the Munich Olympics in 1972.

ばれんたいんでえ バレンタインデー 〖暦・精神性〗 St. Valentine's Day. February 14. In Japan, women give chocolate to men on this day. Sometimes as confession of love, and sometimes as a token of friendship or a kind of obligatory gift.

はろおきてぃ ハロー・キティ 〖服飾・玩具〗 Hello Kitty. A character for children's clothes, stationaries, and fancy goods by Sanrio Co., Ltd. Her fictional background is that her real name is Kitty White, she was born in England on November 1, and she has a twin sister.

はん 藩 〖武士・政治〗 a feudal domain in the Edo period. All Japan was divided into around 250 han, including large and small ones, under the control of the Tokugawa shogunate.

ばん 幡 〖仏教〗 a pennant to express the virtue and power of the Buddha. The head part is triangular, the body part is rectangular, and the tail part consists of long slips.

ばん 盤 〖碁・将棋〗 ⇨碁盤; 将棋盤

はんえり 半襟 〖服飾〗 a decorative

collar sewn on underwear for a kimono. Also has a function to prevent a kimono from being dirty.

はんがえし 半返し〚冠婚葬祭〛 to reciprocate with a gift worth half the price of the original gift. For example, if receiving a gift worth 10,000 yen, a person gives back a gift worth 5,000 yen. This custom prevails on an auspicious occasion or a funeral.

ばんがさ 番傘〚生活〛 an oil-paper umbrella. The frame is made of bamboo.

はんかしい 半跏思惟〚仏教〛⇨半跏思惟(はんか
じゆい)

はんかしゆい 半跏思惟〚仏教〛 half-cross-legged pose in meditation. The image sits on a chair with the right foot resting on the left thigh, the left leg hanging down, and the right hand softly touching the cheek. Sculptures of Maitreya Bodhisattva produced in ancient times all adopt this posture. →弥勒(み
ろく)菩薩

はんかふざ 半跏趺坐〚仏教〛 the half lotus position for sitting. A meditator places one of his or her feet on the opposite thigh. Is considered acceptable practice if the full lotus position, KEKKA-FUZA, is too difficult.

ばんから 蛮カラ〚精神性〛 to be wild and unrefined, sometimes on purpose. Was coined by parodying its antonym, HAIKARA, which means "modern and stylish." Usually refers to male students, often im-

plying the context of the good old days.

ばんぎ 板木〚茶道・仏教〛 a wooden board for making a sound to serve as a signal. Is hit by a wooden hammer. Is used in the tea ceremony or at a temple.

はんきゅうでんてつ 阪急電鉄〚鉄道〛 Hankyu Corporation. One of the 16 major private railway operators of Japan, which serves the three mega cities, Kyoto, Osaka, and Koube. Holds ten lines with 90 stations, which extend to Takaraduka Spa in Hyougo Pref. and Arashiyama, a tourist spot in Kyoto. Adopts a through-line service with the Osaka Municipal Subway. Also operates Takaraduka Revue, which has two theaters in Tokyo and Takaraduka City.

はんぎょく 半玉〚娯楽〛 an apprentice geisha, or a geisha trainee. The charge to a customer is half-price.

はんげしょう 半夏生〚暦〛 the 11th day from the summer solstice. Around July 2 in the solar calendar. Farmers would finish transplantation of rice sprouts by this day.

はんこ 判子〚生活〛⇨印鑑

はんこう 藩校〚武士・教育〛 an official school of a feudal domain in the Edo period. The major academic subject was Chinese classics, especially Confucianism, but some of them were teaching martial arts and medical science by the end of the Edo period.

ばんこやき 万古焼〚陶磁器〛 Banko

ware. Was first made in present Mie Pref. in the 18th century by a businessman named Nunami Rouzan. Red-brown teapots called KYUUSU are popular.

ばんざい 万歳 〔言語・精神性〕 Hurrah. Is shouted with both arms raised, often three times, to express celebration or joy. Although 'banzai' has become a loan word in English, its meaning has changed from the original one.

はんさつ 藩札 〔武士・経済〕 paper currency issued by a feudal domain in the Edo period. Circulated only within the domain. The permission of the shogunate was necessary for issuing it.

はんし 半紙 〔書道〕 traditional paper for calligraphy. About 25 cm long and 33 cm wide.

はんし 藩士 〔武士・政治〕 a vassal of a feudal lord in the Edo period.

はんしゅ 藩主 〔武士・政治〕 the lord of a feudal domain in the Edo period. Is also called DAIMYOU.

ばんしゅう 播州 〔地名〕 ⇨播磨（はりま）

ばんしょ 番所 〔犯罪・行政〕 a guard station in the Edo period.

はんしょう 半鐘 〔災害〕 a fire alarm bell. Was installed at the top of the fire watchtower, called HINOMI YAGURA, and was rung when a fire was found.

はんしんあわじだいしんさい 阪神淡路大震災 〔災害〕 the Great Hanshin and Awaji Earthquake. Occurred at 5:46 on January 17, 1995, and struck southern Hyougo Pref. The epicenter was northern Awaji Island, Hyougo Pref. The magnitude was 7.3, and the maximum seismic intensity was 7. The number of the dead was 6,434. → 震度

はんしんでんきてつどう 阪神電気鉄道 〔鉄道〕 Hanshin Electric Railway. One of the 16 major private railway operators of Japan, which serves the industrial and residential areas between Osaka and Koube Cities. Holds four lines and 51 stations. Adopts a through-line service with KINTETSU Railway and Sanyo Electric Railway. Owns the popular professional baseball team, the Hanshin Tigers.

はんぜいてんのう 反正天皇 〔天皇〕 Emperor Hanzei. ?-? The 18th. The third son of Emperor Nintoku. Is said to be one of the Five Kings of Wa. →倭の五王

はんせきほうかん 版籍奉還 〔政治〕 Return of Domain Registers in 1869. The political reform as part of the Meiji Restoration, in which all feudal domains returned their land and people to the Emperor. After that, 285 feudal lords and 142 court nobles were bestowed titles, and the Meiji aristocratic system was established.

ばんせんしゅうかい 萬川集海 〔忍者・書名〕 *The Book of Ninja.* One of the three major ninjutsu books. Was compiled in 1676 by Fujibayashi Yasutake, born in Iga, present Mie Pref. A kind of ninjutsu encyclopedia. Consists of 22 volumes and describes the philosophy, techniques, and tools of ninja. Is said to have been used as a textbook at a military training school for secret agents before World War II.

ばんだい 番台〔風呂〕 an elevated seat at the entrance of a public bath to collect the fee. →銭湯

ばんだいさん 磐梯山〔山岳〕 Mt. Bandai. An active volcano in northern Fukushima Pref. Is 1,816 m high. Is also called Mt. Aizu Bandai, or Aizu Fuji, as it is shaped like Mt. Fuji. Is located in the old province of Aizu.

はんだくおん 半濁音〔言語〕 a p-sound syllable, such as "pa," "pi," "pu," "pe," and "po." →半濁点

はんだくてん 半濁点〔言語〕 a p-sound mark. When a small circle is added in the upper right corner of kana in the 'ha' column, like ぱ, the pronunciation becomes a p-sound such as "pa" or "pi."

ばんち 番地〔行政〕 a block number or a lot number in an address. →丁目

ばんちゃ 番茶 〔飲み物〕 coarse green tea, or low-quality green tea. Is made from slightly hard leaves. Is brewed with boiling water. →煎茶

ばんづけ 番付〔相撲〕 an official ranking list for the sumo tournament. Is announced by the Japan Sumo Association two weeks prior to each tournament. →日本相撲協会

はんてい 藩邸〔武士・政治〕 ⇒江戸屋敷

はんてん 半纏, 袢纏〔服飾〕 a traditional short coat without lapels. Has been worn mainly by craftspeople and merchants since the Edo period. A padded type is also worn to keep out the cold.

はんでんしゅうじゅのほう 班田収授法〔法律〕 Land Allotment System. Rice fields were granted to peasants, who paid the tax in return. Started under the centralized administration system, called RITSURYOU-SEI, in the 7th century and was abolished in 902.

はんとう 半東〔茶道〕 the assistant to the host at a tea ceremony. Brings sweets and tea. Sometimes plays a role like an MC.

ばんとう 番頭〔職業〕 a head shop clerk in the Edo period. Directed other clerks and apprentices such as TEDAI and DECCHI. A large merchant firm had a general manager, called OOBANTOU, above 'bantou.'

ばんどうたろう 板東太郎〔河川〕 a personified name of the Tone River. 'Bandou' refers to the Kantou region, and 'Tarou' literally means the first son. →利根川

はんとき 半刻〔時刻〕 about an hour. Literally means "a half of one TOKI," which was a unit to count time in olden times. One toki was one sixth of the duration from the sunrise to sunset.

はんにゃ 般若 **(1)**〔能〕 the mask

of a female demon. Has two horns and an extended mouth. Is worn to express the anger and jealousy of a woman. **(2)**〖仏教〗true wisdom. *prajna*. Wisdom to intuitively grasp the true aspect of existence in the universe.

はんにゃしんぎょう 般若心経 〖仏教〗 Heart Sutra. *Prajnaparamita-hridaya-sutra*. Briefly summarizes the contents of the huge Great Perfection of Wisdom Sutra. The version translated by the priest Xuan-zang in the Tang dynasty is used in Japan. The phrase, "all materialistic objects are nothing but emptiness," is famous. →色即是空

はんにゃとう 般若湯 〖仏教・酒〗 priest jargon to refer to sake. Literally means "hot water of wisdom."

はんばつせいじ 藩閥政治 〖政治〗 politics by cliques of specific feudal domains. After the Meiji Restoration in 1868, the government was dominated by politicians who came from SATSUMA-HAN, CHOUSHUU-HAN, TOSA-HAN, and HIZEN-HAN, which greatly contributed to the success of the restoration. However, politicians from Tosa and Hizen were gradually excluded, and those from Satsuma and Choushuu came to possess dominant power. This political situation lasted until the 1920s.

はんはばおび 半幅帯 〖服飾〗 a half-width obi used for a casual kimono such as YUKATA.

はんぺん はんぺん 〖食べ物〗 a white, flat, and puffy fish cake. Has a puffier feel in the mouth than other fish cakes because it contains yams. Is mainly used in a stew in a broth lightly flavored with soy sauce, called ODEN.

ひ

ひ 日〖自然・精神性〗 the sun. Plays an important role in Japanese culture. Prince Shoutoku called Japan "the land of sunrise" when he sent the first letter to the emperor of Sui in the 7th century. The nation's name, 'Nippon' or 'Nihon,' can also be read 'Hi no moto,' which literally means "the origin of the sun." The national flag, HINOMARU, is the sun disc flag. The central figure of Japanese mythology is the Sun Goddess, and people celebrate the first sunrise, HATSU-HINODE, on January 1.

ぴいえるきょうだん PL教団〖宗教〗 ⇨パーフェクトリバティー教団

びいきゅうぐるめ B級グルメ〖食文化〗 B-grade gourmet food. Casual and frugal, but tasty.

びいしいしいだぶるじぇい BCCWJ 〖言語〗 Balanced Corpus of Contemporary Written Japanese. →現代日本語書き言葉均衡コーパス

びいだま ビー玉〖遊び〗 **(1)** a small glass ball. About 1.5 cm in diameter. **(2)** marbles. A game using (1) on the ground.

びいちさんだる ビーチサンダル 〖履物〗 a pair of beach sandals. Is said to have been devised in Japan around 1952.

びいにじゅうく B-29〖軍事〗 B-29 Superfortress. A four-engine, propeller-driven bomber developed in the early 1940s by Boeing and used by the U.S. in the war against Japan and in the Korean War. Among other innovations, it was the first bomber with a pressurized pilot's cabin. B-29s inflicted heavy damage on Japan targets starting in 1944. Then, on August 6 and 9, 1945, two B-29s were used to drop atomic bombs on Hiroshima and Nagasaki. The two bombers have been restored and are on display in the United States. The Enola Gay is at the Smithsonian Institute, and the Bockscar is at the National Museum of the U.S. Air Force.

ひいらぎ 柊〖植物〗 a false holly, or a holly olive. *Osmanthus heterophyllus*. Is said to have a magical power to expel evil spirits. Its twig is set together with a sardine head at the entrance of one's home on February 3, the day of SETSUBUN.

びいるけいいんりょう ビール系飲料〖酒〗 the generic term for beer, beer-taste alcoholic drink, and new beer-taste alcoholic drink. →発泡酒; 第3のビール

ひいろ 緋色〖色〗 scarlet. A term that is rarely used nowadays.

びいわんぐらんぷり B1グランプリ〖食文化〗 B1 Grand Prix. Is held once a year to revitalize towns by drawing attention to their specialty foods. Specialties are evaluated in the competition, and the gold, silver, or bronze prize is awarded to the winners. B here stands for "local brand," not "B-class gourmet."

ひうお　氷魚〔魚〕 a young sweet fish. About 2 or 3 cm long.

ひえ　稗〔食べ物・植物〕 a Japanese barnyard millet. *Echinochloa utilis*. Has been cultivated as a hardy crop. Is also used to feed birds.

ひえいざん　比叡山〔仏教・山岳〕 Mt. Hiei. Is located on the border of Kyoto and Shiga Prefs. 848 m high. ENRYAKU-JI Temple is on its top.

ひえじんじゃ　日枝神社　〔神社〕 Hie Shrine. Is located in Chiyoda City in central Tokyo. Enshrines Ooyamakui no kami, the guardian deity of Mt. Hiei. A sword named Norimune is a National Treasure. Famous for the Sannou Festival. → 日吉大社；比叡山；山王祭

ひえだのあれ　稗田阿礼〔文芸〕 ?–? An attendant to Emperor Tenmu. Recited the imperial genealogy and mythology, and in 711 OONO YASUMARO wrote the *Records of Ancient Matters* (KOJIKI), based on his oral recitations. →天武天皇

ひおうぎ　檜扇〔生活〕 a fan made of Japanese cypress. Is made by binding 20 to 40 slats of cypress. Was used when an aristocrat wore formal wear in the Heian period.

ひかえりきし　控え力士〔相撲〕 a sumo wrestler seated at ringside. Is either waiting to fight in the next bout or watching the last bout of the day after his own second-to-last bout. Is entitled to challenge the judgment of the referee.

ひかくさんげんそく　非核三原則〔政治〕 the three non-nuclear principles, which were initiated by the then Prime Minister Satou Eisaku in 1967. One of Japan's fundamental defence policies: not to possess nuclear weapons, not to make nuclear weapons, and not to allow nuclear weapons to enter Japan. However, some people point out that the U.S. forces stationed in Japan possess nuclear weapons. The Japanese government doesn't ask the U.S. government about the matter, making it vague whether by intention or not.

びかご　美化語〔言語〕 a polite word. Usually add 'o' or 'go' to a word. For example, 'o-sake,' 'o-sushi', and 'go-hon'(book).

ひがし　干菓子〔茶道〕 a dry confectionery. Takes various shapes such as a cherry blossom, maple leaf, whirlpool, and chrysanthemum. Is often served in a succinct tea ceremony.

ひがしいんどがいしゃ　東インド会社〔ビジネス〕 East India Company. European nations established their companies from the 17th to 18th centuries. Japan only traded with the Dutch East India Company during the period of the national seclusion.

ひがしおおさかし　東大阪市〔地名〕 Higashioosaka City. Is located in central Osaka Pref. Famous for many small factories with high technical skills and the Hanazono

Stadium, the first rugby field in Japan.

ひがしかた 東方 〖相撲〗 the east side in sumo wrestling. A wrestler on the east side enters the ring from the east, while a wrestler on the west side enters the ring from the west. Each side has a wrestler in the same rank, and the status of the one in the east is higher than the other in the west. →西方

ひがしにほんかざんたい 東日本火山帯 〖山岳〗 East Japan Volcanic Belt. Used to be divided into Chishima, Nasu, Choukai, Fuji, and Norikura Volcanic Belts, but experts came to regard it as pointless to divide the East Japan Volcanic Belt according to the area. Many of the volcanoes in it consist of basalts and andesites.

ひがしにほんだいしんさい 東日本大震災 〖災害〗 the Great East Japan Earthquake. Struck East Japan at 14:46 on March 11 in 2011, caused a tsunami, destroyed the Fukushima Daiichi Nuclear Power Plant, and killed approximately 16,000 people. Its magnitude was 9.0.

ひがしほんがんじ 東本願寺 〖寺院〗 Higashi Honganji. Is also called 'Shin-shuu honbyou.' The head temple of the Ootani school of the True Pure Land sect, located in Kyoto. Was founded in 1602 by the priest Kyounyo, the eldest son of KENNYO. ↔西本願寺 →浄土真宗

ひがしまわりこうろ 東回り航路 〖交通〗 the eastward sea route during the Edo period. Products from the Tohoku region were carried to Edo on vessels via the Pacific Ocean.

ひがしやまかいい 東山魁夷 〖絵画〗 1908-1999. A painter born in Yokohama. Graduated from the Tokyo Fine Arts School. His works include *Road* and *Polar Summer Night*, both at The National Museum of Modern Art in Tokyo.

ひがしやまぶんか 東山文化 〖時代〗 the Higashiyama culture in the late 15th century. Was named after the Higashiyama area in Kyoto. The 8th Muromachi Shogun, ASHIKAGA YOSHIMASA, tried to construct the Silver Pavilion, but silver leaves were not applied because he died before they could be applied. The cultures of court nobles, warriors, and Zen Buddhism were fusing into one under the influence of Chinese culture at the Sung dynasty. India ink paintings, architecture, tea ceremony, and flower arrangement flourished during this period. ↔北山文化 →銀閣

ぴかちゅう ピカチュー 〖アニメ〗 the name of a pocket monster. One of the most popular characters. →ポケットモンスター

ひかり ひかり 〖鉄道〗 the super express train of Tokaido and San'yo Shinkansen. Literally means "light," the fastest-travelling substance. Thus the train has used the name "light" since 1964, when Japan's first Shinkansen started operation, until the super express Nozomi started service in 1992. Takes 3 hours from Tokyo to Shin-Osaka, and another 3 hours from Shin-Osaka to Hakata in Fukuoka Pref.

ひかりもの 光り物〚寿司〛 sushi of silver-blue glossy fish. Examples are mackerel (SABA), horse mackerel (AJI), and young dotted gizzard shad (KOHADA).

ひかるげんじ 光源氏〚文芸〛 the hero of *The Tale of Genji* (GENJI MONOGATARI).

ひかわじんじゃ 氷川神社 〚神社〛 Hikawa Shrine. The head shrine of about 300 Hikawa Shrines in the Kantou region, located in eastern Saitama Pref. Enshrines the God of Storms (SUSANOO NO MIKOTO) and two other deities.

ひがん 彼岸 **(1)**〚暦〛 an equinoctial week. A week around March 20 and around September 23. People hold a Buddhist service or visit the ancestors' graves. **(2)**〚仏教〛 the state of enlightenment, or the world of nirvana. Literally means "the other shore," regarding this world as "this shore." ↔此岸(しがん)

ひがんえ 彼岸会〚仏教〛 a Buddhist memorial service held in an equinoctial week. →彼岸**(1)**

ひがんざくら 彼岸桜〚植物〛 a rosebud cherry, or a winter-flowering cherry. *Prunus subhirtella*. Bears light pink flowers around the vernal equinoctial week.

ひがんのちゅうにち 彼岸の中日

〚仏教〛 a mid-day of an equinoctial week. The Vernal Equinox Day in March or the Autumnal Equinox Day in September.

ひがんばな 彼岸花〚植物〛 a red spider lily, or a naked lily. *Lycoris radiata*. Bears red flowers around an autumnal equinoctial week. Is also called MANJUSHAGE.

ひがんまいり 彼岸参り〚仏教〛 a visit to a temple or family grave during an equinoctial week.

ひきおとし 引き落とし〚相撲〛 a hand pull-down. The technique to pull down the opponent by the shoulder, arm, or belt called MAWASHI.

ひきこもり 引きこもり〚医療・生活〛 the social withdrawal. It is said that about 540 thousand people of age 15 to 39 are socially withdrawn in Japan as of 2015.

ひきぞめ 引染〚服飾〛 the technique of dyeing a fabric by applying the dye liquor using a brush.

ひきちゃ 挽き茶〚茶道〛 ⇨抹茶

ひきでもの 引き出物〚冠婚葬祭〛 a gift to guests at a ceremonial party, especially a wedding reception. The gift used to be a horse led into the garden.

ひきまく 引幕 〚歌舞伎・文楽〛 a vertical-striped tricolor curtain at the front of the stage. Is opened and closed by pulling sideways.

ひきめかぎばな 引目鉤鼻 〚絵画〛 one-stroke eyes and a hooked nose. A technique of Japanese-style painting to represent faces of a court noble in the Heian period. Is shown in *Illustrated Handscroll of The Tale of Genji* at the Tokugawa Art Museum in Nagoya.

ひきや 曳き家 〖科学技術・建築〗 a technique of moving a building without taking it apart. The whole building is jacked up and towed to the desired destination.

ひきゃく 飛脚 〖通信〗 a courier in olden times. The courier system started in ancient times and developed in the Edo period. Delivered documents and parcels on foot or horseback.

びく 比丘 〖仏教〗 an officially ordained monk who has vowed to observe the precepts of Buddhism. A phonetic transliteration of *bhikshu* in Sanskrit.

びく 魚籠 〖農林水産〗 a creel, or a basket for fish. Was hung from the waist in olden times.

ひぐちいちよう 樋口一葉 〖文芸〗 1872-1896. A novelist and poet born in Tokyo. Her portrait was placed on the former 5,000 yen bill. Her works include *Troubled Waters* (Nigorie) and *Child's Play* (Takekurabe).

びくに 比丘尼 〖仏教〗 an officially ordained nun who has vowed to observe the precepts of Buddhism. A phonetic transliteration of *bhikshuni* in Sanskrit.

ひぐらし 蜩 〖動物〗 an evening cicada. *Tanna japonensis*. Sings in the early morning and early evening in summer.

ひけし 火消し 〖職業〗 a fireman, or a fire brigade in the Edo period. There were three types: JOU-BIKESHI, DAIMYOU-BIKESHI, and MACHI-BIKESHI.

ひご 肥後 〖旧国名〗 the old name of Kumamoto Pref.

ひごい 緋鯉 〖魚〗 a red carp, a white carp, or a spotted carp. Its colors and patterns vary.

ひこにゃん ひこにゃん 〖ゆるキャラ〗 the name of a relaxing mascot character of Hikone Castle in Shiga Pref. A white cat wearing a red warrior's helmet.

ひこねじょう 彦根城 〖城郭〗 Hikone Castle. Began to be built in 1604 by Ii Naotsugu and was completed in 1622 by his younger brother, Ii Naotaka. Faces Lake Biwa and uses its water for moats. A National Treasure.

ひこぼし 彦星 〖伝説〗 Altair. In a Chinese legend, fell in love with Vega and was allowed to meet her, crossing the Milky Way, only on the day of the Star Festival. →七夕(たなばた)

ひこほほでみのみこと 彦火火出見尊 〖神話〗 ⇨山幸彦(やまさちひこ)

ひざかくし 膝隠し 〖落語〗 a small wooden screen placed in front of a comic storyteller in the Kansai region.

ひさべつぶらく 被差別部落 〖政治〗 an outcaste community. Was inhabited by those who belonged to the lowest class, called 'ETA' or 'HININ,' in a feudal caste system in early-modern times. Some say that there still exists social discriminations against those who come from this community.

ひざまくら 膝枕 〖精神性〗 to rest one's head on somebody's lap. Usually a husband or a boyfriend rests his head on his wife's or girlfriend's lap.

ひさめ 氷雨 〖気象〗 a freezing rain in late fall or early winter. This term is often used in a literary context.

ひじかたとしぞう 土方歳三 〖武士〗 1835-1869. The vice commander of special police for Kyoto, called SHINSENGUMI, born in present Tokyo. After being defeated in the Battle of Toba and Fushimi, died in the Battle of Hakodate. →戊辰(ぼしん)戦争

ひじき 肘木 〖建築〗 a horizontal short bar to support a beam or an eave.

ひじき 鹿尾菜 〖食べ物・植物〗 hijiki seaweed. *Hizikia fusiforme*. Edible brown algae.

びじねすほてる ビジネスホテル 〖旅〗 a budget hotel for business people. Many rooms are for single use.

ひしまきのき 菱撒き退き 〖忍者〗 to escape by scattering caltrops on the enemy's path. →撒き菱

ひしもち 菱餅 〖食べ物〗 a rhombus-shaped rice cake. Has three layers in red, white, and green. Is eaten to celebrate the Girls' Festival on March 3rd.

ひしゃ 飛車 〖将棋〗 a rook. The

promoted rook, RYUUOU, is considered to be the strongest piece.

ひしゃく 柄杓 〖茶道〗 a wooden ladle. Is used to spoon up water by a tea host or hostess.

びしゃもんてん 毘沙門天 〖仏教〗 the Guardian King of the north. *Vaisravana*. One of the Seven Deities of Good Fortune. Holds a spear and a small pagoda. Also one of the Four Guardian Kings, with the name Tamonten, in Buddhism. →七福神；多聞天

びじんが 美人画 〖絵画〗 a portrait of a beautiful woman, especially that of ukiyo-e. The models include prostitutes, geisha, waitresses, and ordinary ladies. Examples are *Beauty Looking Back* by Hishikawa Moronobu and *Courtesans of Edo, Kyoto, and Osaka* by Okumura Masanobu. Both of them are stored at the Tokyo National Museum.

ひぜん 肥前 〖旧国名〗 the old name of Saga and Nagasaki Prefs., excepting Iki and Tsushima Islands.

びぜん 備前 〖旧国名〗 the old name of southeastern Okayama Pref.

ひぜんはん 肥前藩 〖政治〗 the Hizen domain. Governed present Saga Pref. Its feudal lords were from the Nabeshima clan since the clan was bestowed this fief by TOYOTOMI HIDEYOSHI. NABESHIMA KANSOU reformed the political system of the domain, obtained stronger military power than any other domain, and played a significant role in the Meiji Restoration. →鍋

島騒動

びぜんやき 備前焼〔陶磁器〕 Bizen ware. Unglazed brown pottery produced in southeastern Okayama Pref. Originally developed from Sue ware. →須恵器(すえき)

ひだ 飛騨〔旧国名〕 the old name of northern Gifu Pref.

ひだかさんみゃく 日高山脈〔山岳〕 the Hidaka Mountains. Are located in southern Hokkaido, near Cape Erimo. The highest peak is Mt. Poroshiri at 2,052 m.

びだくおん 鼻濁音〔言語〕 a nasal voiced syllable. A g-sound syllable became nasal when it is not in the beginning of a word. For example, 'ga' in 'ogawa'(stream) is nasal.

ひださんみゃく 飛騨山脈〔山岳〕 the Hida Mountains. Are located mainly on the border between Nagano and Gifu Prefs., and partly on the border between Niigata and Toyama Prefs. The highest peak is Mt. Oku Hotaka at 3,190 m. Are also called the Northern Alps.

ひだたかやま 飛騨高山〔地名〕 ⇨高山市

ひたたれ 直垂〔服飾〕 a samurai suit. Was everyday clothes for a samurai in the Kamakura period and became formal wear in later periods. Is now worn by a sumo umpire.

ひたち 常陸〔旧国名〕 the old name of Ibaraki Pref.

びだつてんのう 敏達天皇〔天皇〕 Emperor Bidatsu. 538?-585. The 30th, on the throne from 572 to 585. The second prince of Emperor Kinmei. Under his reign, the Soga and Mononobe clans fought over the introduction of Buddhism into Japan.

ひだら 干鱈〔食べ物〕 salted dried cod.

ひだりじんごろう 左甚五郎〔工芸・建築〕 ?-? A shrine carpenter and sculptor born in present Hyougo Pref. Is said to have participated in building Toushouguu Shrine in Nikko and Kan'ei-ji Temple in Ueno, Tokyo. Many legends about him remain. →日光東照宮

ひだりづかい 左遣い〔文楽〕 a left-arm puppeteer. Operates the left arm of a puppet. →三人遣い

ひちりき 篳篥〔音楽〕 a wind instrument with double reeds. Is made of bamboo, is about 18 cm long, and has nine finger holes. Is used in court music called GAGAKU.

ひつ 櫃〔食器〕 ⇨御櫃(おひつ)

ひつけとうぞくあらため 火付け盗賊改め〔犯罪・職業〕 special police under the Tokugawa shogunate. Kept surveillance over arson and robbery. The most famous figure is HASEGAWA HEIZOU, who led the police in the late 18th century.

ひっこしそば 引っ越し蕎麦〔食文化〕 buckwheat noodles as a gift for moving in. Traditionally, those who moved in presented buckwheat noodles to new neighbors as a token of friendship. This custom is now obsolete.

ひつじ 未〔干支〕 the eighth of

the Chinese zodiac signs. Means "sheep." Recently the years 1991, 2003, and 2015 were sheep years. Indicates the south-southwest in direction and around 2 p.m. for hours.

ひつじさる 坤 〔干支〕 the south-west. The direction between HI-TSUJI (sheep) and SARU (monkey). Is sometimes called urakimon, which means "opposite demon's gate," because 'hitsujisaru' is the opposite direction of USHITORA, namely the northeast, or KIMON, which means "demon's gate."

ひつじゅん 筆順 〔言語〕 the order of strokes in writing a kanji or kana. Most people do not care, but it is important in calligraphy.

びっちゅう 備中 〔旧国名〕 the old name of western Okayama Pref.

ひつまぶし 櫃まぶし 〔食べ物〕 rice topped with chopped eel fillets. Is served in a lacquered container called HITSU. Eel fillets are cooked over charcoal with soy-sauce-flavored sauce. A specialty of Nagoya.

ひてん 飛天 〔仏教〕 a heavenly being flying around the main image in a Buddhist art. Is often depicted as a relief on a halo or canopy of a sculpture.

ひでん 秘伝 〔武術・食文化〕 an inherited secret skill. Often refers to a skill in martial arts or cooking, but this term is sometimes used in other fields such as architecture or medical treatment.

ひとえ 単衣 〔服飾〕 a kimono with-out lining. Is usually worn during summer.

ひとがた 人形 〔神道〕 ⇨形代(かた)

ひとことぬしのかみ 一言主神 〔神話〕 the deity of one word. Gives an oracle, whether good or bad, in one word. Dwells in Mt. Katsuragi on the border between Osaka and Nara Prefs.

ひとつめこぞう 一つ目小僧 〔妖怪〕 a one-eyed goblin. One legend says that it came from a custom that a person who served deities at a festival had an eye removed.

ひとばしら 人柱 〔宗教・建築〕 a human sacrifice for construction. Is said that sometimes people were buried under the ground during the construction of a castle, bank, or bridge.

ひとはだ 人肌 〔酒〕 lukewarm sake. Literally means "human skin." The name suggests the temperature of sake is around 40 degrees centigrade. →燗酒(かん); 銚子; 猪口(ちょ)

ひとめぼれ ヒトメボレ 〔食べ物・植物〕 a sort of hybrid rice, improved by selective breeding. Tasty and has resistance against the cold weather.

ひとりづかい 一人遣い 〔文楽〕 to operate a puppet with one person. Is not popular at present.

ひなあられ 雛霰 〔食べ物〕 bite-sized sweetened rice crackers for the Girls' Festival. Include white and red ones.

ひなかざり 雛飾り 〔祭礼・人形〕 to display a set of dolls for the Girls'

Festival.

ひなだん 雛壇〚祭礼・人形〛 a tiered stand for displaying dolls on the Girls' Festival. Is covered with a red carpet.

ひなにんぎょう 雛人形〚祭礼・玩具〛 a set of dolls for the Girls' Festival. Consists of the Imperial couple, three court ladies-in-waiting, five court musicians, and two guards. All dolls wear court costume of the Heian period. Their accessories include paper peach branches and miniatures of table lamps, a palanquin, and a clothing chest.

ひなまつり 雛祭り〚暦〛 the Dolls' Festival, or Girls' Festival. Is held on March 3. A family that has a girl puts a set of dolls on display, offering peach blossoms, white sake, rhombus-shaped rice cakes, and bite-sized rice crackers. →雛人形；白酒(しろ・ざけ)；菱餅(ひし・もち)；雛霰(あられ)

ひなわじゅう 火縄銃〚武器〛 a harquebus, or a matchlock. An early type of gun with a fuse cord. Was invented in Spain in the 15th century and was introduced into Japan in 1543 by the Portuguese. Was also called TANEGASHIMA, on which the Portuguese landed.

ひにん 非人〚政治・職業〛 an outcaste group in medieval and early modern times. Was mainly engaged in begging, performing arts, and chores of a prison or an execution site. Was severely discriminated against. The Meiji government abolished the caste system in 1871.

→被差別部落

ひのえ 丙〚干支〛 the third item of JIKKAN. Literally means "yang of fire" or "the elder brother of fire." Its Chinese-style pronunciation is 'hei,' which was used to refer to the third rank in grading because 'hinoe' is the third item among 'jikkan.'

ひのえうま 丙午〚干支〛 the 43rd year of 60 combinations of 10 trunks with 12 branches, called ETO. The combination of "the elder brother of fire" with "horse." It was said that many fires occur in this year and that the husband of a woman who has been born in this year dies earlier. The years of 1966 and 2026 are 'hinoe-uma.'

ひのかぐつちのかみ 火之迦具土神 〚神話〛 the deity of fire. At birth, the fire burned his mother, IZANAMI NO MIKOTO, after which his angry father, IZANAGI NO MIKOTO, killed him with a sword.

ひのき 檜〚植物〛 a hinoki cypress, or a sun tree. *Chamaecyparis obtusa*. Grows 30 to 40 m high and 1 to 2 m in diameter. Is considered valuable timber.

ひのと 丁〚干支〛 the fourth item of JIKKAN. Literally means "yin of fire" or "the younger brother of fire." Its Chinese-style pronunciation is 'tei,' which used to refer to the fourth rank in grading because 'hinoto' is the fourth item among 'jikkan.'

ひのとみこ 日野富子〚政治〛 1440 -1496. The wife of ASHIKAGA

YOSHIMASA, the 8th Muromachi Shogun. Interfered in the shogunate succession and caused the Ounin War from 1467 to 1477. → 応仁の乱

ひのとり 火の鳥〖漫画〗 *Phoenix.* An incomplete science fiction manga written and illustrated by TEDUKA OSAMU. A person who has drunk the blood of the phoenix becomes immortal. The published 12 volumes provide separate stories at different places and times, all of which deal with the topic of immortality.

ひのまる 日の丸〖外交〗 ⇨日章旗

ひのまるべんとう 日の丸弁当〖食文化〗 a "sun disc" lunch. A boxed lunch with a pickled plum in the center of boiled white rice. Looks like the sun disc flag.

ひのみやぐら 火の見櫓〖災害〗 a fire watchtower. When a fire was found, an alarm bell at the top of the tower was rung. Is rarely seen nowadays.

ひばし 火箸〖茶道〗 a pair of long metal chopsticks to pick up charcoal. Was used together with a floor-level brazier called HIBACHI.

ひばち 火鉢〖家具〗 a floor-level brazier. Is rarely seen in a modern house.

ひぶつ 秘仏〖仏教〗 a secret Buddhist image. Is usually housed in an ornamented double-door chest and only shown to the public on fixed days. →開帳

ひへん 火偏〖漢字〗 a left-side radical meaning "fire." Is used in kanji such as 灯 (light), 炊 (boil), and 炉 (hearth).

ひへん 日偏〖漢字〗 a radical meaning "sun" or "day." Is used in kanji such as 昇 (rise), 昔 (past), and 明 (bright).

ひまつり 火祭り〖祭礼〗 a fire festival. Is held at various Buddhist temples and Shinto shrines such as Kurama-dera in Kyoto, Sengen Shrine in Shizuoka Pref., and Kumano Nachi Shrine in Wakayama Pref.

ひまわり ひまわり〖科学技術〗 the nickname for a stationary meteorological satellite. The official name of a current one is Multifunctional Transport Satellite. The first Himawari was launched from the Kennedy Space Center in 1977. Current Himawari 6, launched from the Tanegashima Space Center in 2005, is also used for air-traffic control.

ひみこ 卑弥呼〖政治〗 ?–? A queen of an ancient nation named YAMATAI-KOKU in the 3rd century. Was not married and implemented a theocracy as a shaman, assisted by her younger brother. Sent an envoy to the Wey dynasty in 239. Could be the woman who appeared in the *Records of Ancient Matters* (KOJIKI) or *Chronicles of Japan* (NIHONSHOKI), but there is no accepted thesis on this point.

ひめじじょう 姫路城〖城郭〗 Himeji Castle. Was originally constructed in 1346 by Akamatsu Sadanori. Was enlarged and repaired by Toyotomi Hideyoshi, Ikeda Terumasa, and Honda Tadamasa. Four donjons and a turret are National Treasures. Was designated a World Heritage Site in 1993.

ひめます 姫鱒 〖食べ物・魚〗 a kokanee, or a sockeye salmon. *Oncorhynchus nerka*. Native to lakes in Hokkaido such as Lake Akan. Now lives also in Lake Towada in Aomori Pref., Lake Chuuzenji in Tochigi Pref., and other lakes in the Honshuu Island. About 30 cm long and edible. →紅鮭(255)

ひめゆりのとう ひめゆりの塔 〖戦争〗 the Tower of Himeyuri. A small memorial tower erected outside an air-raid shelter in Itoman City in the south of Okinawa Island. Along with Japanese soldiers, many local students serving as military nurses were killed there during the Battle of Okinawa in 1945.

ひもかわうどん 紐皮饂飩 〖食べ物〗 ⇨きしめん

ひもの 干物 〖食文化〗 dried seafood. Includes SURUME, MEZASHI, and MIGAKI NISHIN.

びゃくごう 白毫 〖仏教・彫刻〗 the three white curly bristles between the eyebrows of a Buddha. Are often represented by crystal on a sculpture.

ひゃくしょういっき 百姓一揆 〖政治〗 a peasant uprising against feudal lords in the Edo period. Was mainly caused by severe taxation and occurred about 3,000 times.

びゃくだん 白檀 〖彫刻・植物〗 white sandalwood. *Santalum album*. Native to Indonesia. The wood emits a strong fragrance and is used for sculptures, fans, and perfumes.

ひゃくどまいり 百度参り 〖神社・寺院〗 one-hundred-time prayer. A worshipper goes back and forth one hundred times between the main building and the short stone pillar in a shrine or temple, praying at the entrance of the building each time. This style of prayer was popular in the Edo period. The stone pillar is called 'hyakudo-ishi,' which literally means "one-hundred-time stone."

ひゃくにんいっしゅ 百人一首 〖文芸・娯楽〗 *Single Verses by a Hundred People*, or *One Hundred Poets, One Poem Each*. An anthology compiled in the 13th century by FUJIWARA NO TEIKA. Is sometimes called 'Ogura hyakunin isshu' because Teika compiled it at Mt. Ogura in Kyoto. The oldest poem was composed in the 7th century by Emperor Tenji. As a card game, 100 cards, YOMIFUDA, carry the full poems, while the other 100 cards, TORIFUDA, carry the second half only. When playing, the poem reader reads aloud a 'yomifuda' at random, and other players take the 'torifuda' corresponding to the read poem. The player who has taken the most 'torifuda' wins the game.

ひゃくまんとう 百万塔 〔仏教・政治〕 the one-million tiny pagodas. Were created as part of a vow made by Empress Shoutoku after the rebellion by FUJIWARA NO NAKAMARO in 764. Each pagoda is about 21 cm high and contains a sutra. Some of them exist at HOURYUU-JI Temple.

ひゃくみだんす 百味箪笥 〔医療・家具〕 a medicine chest of a traditional medical doctor. Contains traditional Chinese medicines in small drawers. →漢方薬

ひゃくものがたり 百物語 〔妖怪〕 a meeting for one-hundred ghost stories. One hundred candles were lit, and each participant told a ghost story in turn. After one participant told a story, one candle was put out. When the last candle was put out and it turned deadly dark, it was said that a monster would appear.

ひゃくやっつ 百八つ 〔仏教〕 one hundred and eight. It is said in Buddhism that a human has 108 earthly desires, called BONNOU. To dissolve the desires, a temple bell was rung 108 times at midnight on New Year's Eve.

ひやざけ 冷や酒 〔酒〕 unwarmed sake. ↔燗酒(かんざけ) →冷酒(れいしゅ)

ひやしそうめん 冷やし素麺 〔食べ物〕 chilled thin wheat noodles. Eaten after being dipped in soy-sauce based broth with chopped green onion and grated ginger. Popular in summer.

ひやしちゅうか 冷やし中華 〔食べ物〕 cold ramen. Is seasoned with soy sauce, vinegar, and sesame oil, and topped with shredded ham, plain omelet, and cucumber.

ひやじる 冷や汁 〔食べ物〕 cold soup flavored with miso and dashi. Contains vegetables and fish. One in Miyazaki Pref. is famous.

ひゃっきやこう 百鬼夜行 〔妖怪〕 a monster procession. Various monsters and goblins hold a parade at night. Is referred to in *Tales of Times Now Past* (KONJAKU MONOGATARI).

びゃっこ 白虎 〔宗教・動物〕 the white tiger. The animal deity that symbolizes the west. →四神(しん); 青竜(せいりゅう); 朱雀(すざく); 玄武(げんぶ)

びゃっこたい 白虎隊 〔戦争〕 White Tiger Battalion. Was organized by the Aizu domain for the Aizu War in 1868, composed of young samurai from 16 to 17 years old. 19 soldiers in a unit despaired of victory and committed suicide at Mt. Iimoriyama near Aizu Castle. One of them, who survived alone, wrote a memoir, and 'Byakkotai' became well-known.

ひやむぎ 冷や麦 〔食べ物〕 chilled medium-thin white wheat noodles. Eaten after being dipped in soy-sauce based broth with chopped green onion and grated ginger. Popular in summer.

ひややっこ 冷奴 〔食べ物〕 cold tofu. Eaten with chopped green onion, shaved flakes of dried bonito, and soy sauce. Grated ginger is often added.

ひゅうが 日向〖旧国名〗 the old name for Miyazaki Pref. and a part of Kagoshima Pref.

ひょういもじ 表意文字〖言語〗 an ideogram. Each character has a meaning. KANJI is one of them.

ひょうぐし 表具師〖家具・職業〗 a craftsman who makes and repairs hanging scrolls or paper screens.

ひょうごけん 兵庫県〖都道府県〗 Hyougo Pref. Is located in Western Japan and consists of the Honshuu part in the north and Awaji Island in the south. Is 8,395 km^2 in area. Its capital is Koube City. On the coast of the Inland Sea are large cities with seaports, factories, and residential areas, such as Amagasaki, Nishinomiya, Koube, Akashi, and Himeji, from east to west. Akashi Municipal Planetarium stands at 135 degrees east longitude, determining Japan Standard Time. Himeji Castle was designated a World Heritage Site in 1993. In its central and northern parts are farming and fishing areas, with tourist spots like Kinosaki with hot springs and Asago with Takeda Castle, locally called "Machu Picchu of Japan." Used to be Tajima, Harima, Awaji, part of Settsu, and part of Tanba.

ひょうしぎ 拍子木〖災害・芸能〗 a pair of wood sticks to make a high-pitched sound. Are beaten as an opening or closing signal at a theater or as a warning of a night patrol.

ひょうじょうしょ 評定所〖行政〗 the supreme court of the Tokugawa shogunate. According to the importance of the case, highest-ranking ministers (ROUJUU), censors (METSUKE), or feudal commissioners (BUGYOU) took part.

ひょうたん 瓢箪〖植物〗 a bottle gourd, or a calabash. *Lagenaria siceraria* var. *gourda*. Its tough outer skin was dried hard and used for a sake bottle in olden times.

びょうどういん 平等院〖寺院〗 Byodoin Temple. Affiliated with both the Tendai and Pure Land sects. Is located in southern Kyoto Pref. Was founded by a regent, FUJIWARA NO YORIMICHI, in 1052. In the following year, Phoenix Hall, 'Houou-dou,' was completed. Was designated a World Heritage Site in 1994.

びょうどういんほうおうどう 平等院鳳凰堂〖寺院・建築〗 Phoenix Hall at BYOUDOU-IN Temple. Was built in 1053. Enshrines the Amitabha Buddha created by a sculptor, JOUCHOU. Consists of the center hall, the right and left wings, and the tail corridor, whose combination shapes a phoenix with the wings spread. The front view of Phoenix Hall is used for the design of the present 10-yen coin. The building itself, the paintings on the walls and doors, the Amitabha Buddha, and its attendants are all National Treasures.

びょうぶ 屏風〖建築〗 a folding

screen. Consists of two, four, or six panels. Although its original function had been to partition a room or to block the wind, it later came to be used for decoration with paintings or calligraphy. Usually two screens are placed in a pair.

びょうぶえ 屏風絵 〖絵画〗 a picture on a folding screen. Often a theme forming a pair is depicted such as spring and autumn or a dragon and a tiger. →屏風；龍虎(りゅうこ)

ひょうろうがん 兵糧丸 〖忍者〗 a small ball of food. Was made from rice, yam, lotus fruit, coix seed, ginseng, cinnamon, and sugar. It was said that a ninja did not have to have a lunch or supper if he or she took seven 'hyourougan' when eating morning rice porridge. It also had the effect of maintaining good physical condition.

ひょこまわり ひょこ周り 〖将棋〗 ⇨ 周り将棋

ひよしじんじゃ 日吉神社 〖神社〗 a Hiyoshi Shrine. Enshrines Ooyamakui no kami, the guardian of Mt. Hiei. There are many Hiyoshi Shrines throughout Japan. The head shrine is Hiyoshi Grand Shrine in Shiga Pref. →日吉大社； 比叡山(ひえいざん)

ひよしたいしゃ 日吉大社 〖神社〗 Hiyoshi Grand Shrine. The head shrine of approx. 3,800 Hie, Hiyoshi, and Sannou Shrines throughout Japan. Is located in southwestern Shiga Pref. Consists of the East Shrine, which enshrines

Ooyamakui no kami, the deity of Mt. Hiei, and the West Shrine, which enshrines Oonamuchi no kami, another name of OOKUNINUSHI NO KAMI. The west and east main buildings are National Treasures. Monkeys are said to be messengers from this shrine. →比叡山

ひょっとこ ひょっとこ 〖芸能〗 a mask of a funny-faced man with protruding lips. Some open both eyes widely while others half-close an eye. Appears on the stage of a musical comedy for a Shinto ritual and plays the fool together with a round-faced woman, OKAME. Is said to have come from an expression related to when a man blows on a spark to kindle a fire.

ひらいずみ 平泉 〖地名〗 the name of a historic site in southern Iwate Pref. In the 11th to 12th centuries, the Fujiwara clan was based here and constructed CHUUSON-JI and MOUTSUU-JI Temples. These two temples, gardens, and archeological sites were designated a World Heritage Site in 2011.

ひらがげんない 平賀源内 〖科学技術〗 1728-1779. A scientist, doctor, painter, and playwright, born in Kagawa Pref. Invented several items such as a generator with friction and a thermometer.

ひらがな 平仮名 〖言語〗 a rounded letter to represent a syllable, or the writing system using it. Was invented from a cursive kanji. Is mainly used to write particles, inflections, or indigenous Japanese words.

ひらかんむり 平冠〖漢字〗 ⇨ワ冠

ひらたあつたね 平田篤胤〖人文学〗 1776-1843. A scholar of Japanese classics, born in present Akita Pref. Advanced the ideas of MOTOORI NORINAGA, advocated Restoration Shinto, and influenced the idea of "Revere the Emperor and expel the barbarians." →復古神道; 尊皇攘夷

ひらちゃわん 平茶碗〖茶道〗 a flat tea bowl. Is used in summer.

ひらでまえ 平手前〖茶道〗 the basic procedure of making tea in a tea ceremony.

ひらど 平戸市〖地名〗 Hirado City. Is located in northwestern Nagasaki Pref. Was prosperous as a trading port with Portugal, the Netherlands, and the U.K. in the 16th to 17th centuries.

ひらにわ 平庭〖庭園〗 a traditional flat garden. Is not equipped with an artificial miniature mountain called TSUKIYAMA.

ひらまく 平幕〖相撲〗 another name for MAEGASHIRA. Is ranked below KOMUSUBI.

ひらめ 平目〖動物・食べ物〗 an olive flounder, a bastard halibut, or Japanese flatfish. *Paralichthys olivaceus*. Eaten in various ways such as sashimi, sushi, grilled, and fried. →縁側

びりけん ビリケン〖宗教〗 a Billiken. Was introduced from the U.S. in the early 20th century. The one at the TSUUTENKAKU Tower in Osaka is famous.

ひるこ 蛭子〖神話〗 the first child of the divine couple, IZANAGI NO MIKOTO and IZANAMI NO MIKOTO. Was washed out to sea on a reed boat because he could not stand by himself at the age of three. Is sometimes identified with EBISU, and the kanji 蛭子 is also read as 'ebisu.'

びるしゃなぶつ 毘盧舎那仏〖仏教〗 Vairocana Buddha, or the Solar Buddha. *Vairocana*. The central Buddha of the Kegon sect. Is considered to be identified with the Great Sun Buddha in esoteric Buddhism. Famous examples are the one at the TOUDAI-JI Temple and the TOUSHOUDAI-JI Temple. →大日如来

ひるせき 昼席〖落語〗 the daytime performance at traditional vaudeville. ↔夜席

ひれざけ 鰭酒〖酒〗 hot sake served with a grilled pufferfish fin soaked in it. →河豚(⚠)

ひろ ～尋〖単位〗 a fathom. A unit to measure a length of rope or the depth of water. About 1.5 to 1.8 meters. One 'hiro' equals 5 or 6 SHAKU. The origin of 'hiro' is the length of a man's outstretched arms, as is the origin of "fathom."

ひろうえん 披露宴〖冠婚葬祭〗 ⇨結婚披露宴

ひろうす 飛竜頭〖食べ物〗 ⇨がんもどき

ひろえん 広縁〖建築〗 a wide porch, or a wide verandah. →縁側

ひろこうじ 広小路〖交通〗 a boulevard also used as a firebreak belt. Was constructed after the Meireki Conflagration in 1657, but only remains as a place name at present. →明暦の大火

ひろさきじょう　弘前城　〖城郭〗 Hirosaki Castle. Is located in Hirosaki City, western Aomori Pref. Was originally constructed in 1611 and burned down in 1627. The current donjon was constructed in 1810. Famous for its beautiful cherry blossoms.

ひろさきねぷたまつり　弘前佞武多祭り〖祭礼〗 Lantern Float Festival in Hiroshima from August 1 to 7. Parade includes many large fan-shaped lantern floats, on which historical heroes are depicted.

ひろしげ　広重〖絵画〗 ⇨安藤広重

ひろしまけん　広島県　〖都道府県〗 Hiroshima Pref. Is located in Western Japan, facing the Inland Sea. Is 8,479 km² in area. Its capital is Hiroshima City. Has sightseeing spots such as Hiroshima Peace Memorial Park and Atomic Bomb Dome, Hiroshima Castle, Shukkei-en Garden, Itsukushima Shrine, Kure Maritime Museum (also known as Yamato Museum), and Taishaku Valley in the Chuugoku Mountains. Farmed oysters and Hiroshima-style savory pancake (OKONOMIYAKI) are famous. Used to be Bingo and Aki.

ひろしまし　広島市〖地名〗 Hiroshima City. An ordinance-designated city, and the capital of Hiroshima Pref., located in its southwestern part. Has the largest population in the Chuugoku-Shikoku region. On August 6, 1945, the world's first atomic bomb was dropped in the center of the city, killing 100,000 people by the end of the year. After World War II, Peace Park was opened with the Atomic Bomb Dome and Hiroshima Peace Memorial Museum. Today Hiroshima is known as a City of Peace, and its government advocates the abolition of nuclear weapons.

ひろしまふうおこのみやき　広島風お好み焼き〖食べ物〗 a Hiroshima-style savory pancake. Different from the Kansai style, its ingredients are not mixed but placed in layers. →お好み焼き

ひろしまへいわきねんしりょうかん　広島平和記念資料館　〖戦争・博物館〗 Hiroshima Peace Memorial Museum. Was founded in Hiroshima in 1955. Displays materials related to the dropping of the atomic bomb.

ひろそで　広袖〖服飾〗 a sleeve with its edge not sewn up. Underware for a kimono and a padded kimono have this type of sleeve.

びわ　枇杷〖食べ物・植物〗 a loquat. *Eriobotrya japonica*. Its fruit is edible. Its lumber is used to make a wooden sword.

びわ　琵琶〖音楽〗 a Japanese lute with four or five strings. Is played with a plectrum and accompanies a narrative. Is said to have been introduced to Japan in the Nara period.

びわこ 琵琶湖 〖湖沼〗 Lake Biwa. A depression lake, located in Shiga Pref. Its area is 670 km^2, making it the largest lake in Japan. The deepest point is 104 m. The Yodo River runs from its southmost end to Osaka Bay. Since ancient times, Lake Biwa has been a significant waterway between the coast of the Sea of Japan and Kyoto or Osaka. Tourists can enjoy Eight Views of Lake Biwa along the lakeside. →近江八景

びわこそすい 琵琶湖疏水 〖科学技術〗 Lake Biwa Canal. Runs from Lake Biwa to Kyoto. Has two routes, the first being completed in 1890 and the second in 1912. Some points on its banks provide good sightseeing spots.

ひわだぶき 檜皮葺 〖建築〗 a thatching technique using the bark of a sun tree (HINOKI). Is used for the buildings of a palace, shrine, or temple.

ひわたり 火渡り 〖宗教〗 walking on fire. Is conducted as a practice of mountain asceticism. Ordinary people can experience it at some temples.

びわほうし 琵琶法師 〖音楽〗 a blind minstrel with a Japanese lute in medieval times. Had the appearance of a Buddhist monk and recited narratives of stories such as *The Tale of the Heike* (HEIKE MONOGATARI).

びんがた 紅型 〖服飾〗 traditional stencil printing in Okinawa. Features lively and colorful patterns.

ひんきゅうもんどうか 貧窮問答歌 〖文芸・作品〗 "Dialogue on Poverty." A pair of poems, one a long rhyming poem and the other a short rhyming poem, composed by YAMANOUE NO OKURA, in the 8th century. Are contained in the 5th volume of the *Anthology of Myriad Leaves* (MAN'YOUSHUU). Describe the difficulty of living with a poverty in the form of a question and an answer.

びんご 備後 〖旧国名〗 the old name of eastern Hiroshima Pref.

びんずるそんじゃ 賓頭盧尊者 〖仏教〗 *Pindola Bharadvaja*. The first of Sixteen Arhats. His sculpture is sometimes placed at a temple building. It is said that one's disease or injury is cured if a person strokes the diseased or injured part of the image.

びんちょうたん 備長炭 〖食文化〗 high-quality charcoal produced in Wakayama Pref. Was invented in the Edo period by Bicchuu-ya Chouzaemon.

びんぼうがみ 貧乏神 〖宗教・妖怪〗 the deity of poverty. Looks like a thin old man in shabby clothes and haunts a household or person to reduce them to poverty. His favorite food is MISO.

ふ 歩〖将棋〗 a pawn. Unlike a pawn in Western chess, it only moves one square ahead. When it is promoted to TOKIN, by entering the opponent's area, it moves like a KINSHOU.

ふ 府〖都道府県〗 a prefecture. A local autonomous public entity where cities or villages are located. Osaka and Kyoto are the only two 'fu.' → 都道府県

ふ 麩〖食べ物〗 small, round, wheat gluten bread. Eaten in miso soup, SUKIYAKI, and other dishes.

ぶ ～分〖経済・単位〗 a unit of money in the Edo period. One 'bu' is worth 12,000 to 30,000 present yen, depending on the era and method of calculation.

ふぁっとまん ファットマン 〖武器〗 Fat Man. A plutonium-type atomic bomb dropped on Nagasaki on August 9, 1945. About 3.5 m in length, 1.5 m in diameter, and 4.5 t in weight.

ふぁみりいれすとらん ファミリーレストラン〖食文化〗 a family restaurant. Serves a wide variety of cuisine from traditional Japanese to Western-style meals, including kids' meals. Most family restaurants are incorporated into a restaurant chain.

ふぃぎゅあすけえと フィギュアスケート〖スポーツ〗 figure skating. Japan first joined the figure skating event of the Winter Olympics at Lake Placid in 1932. As of 2018 Japan has won three gold medals: Arakawa Shizuka at Torino in 2006 and Hanyuu Yuzuru at Sochi in 2014 and at PyeongChang in 2018.

ふううたいまつ 風雨松明〖忍者〗 a torch for wind and rain. Can be used in wind or rain.

ふうしかでん 風姿花伝 〖能・書名〗 *The Flowering Spirit: Classic Teachings on the Art of No*. Was written around 1400 by ZEAMI.

ふうじて 封じ手〖碁・将棋〗 the sealed move to keep fairness in terms of the time limitation in an overnight game. Is used as the initial move of a game being continued on the second day. At the end of the first day, the player considering the next move should write the next move and put it in an envelope, seal it, and hand it to the judge.

ふうじん 風神〖仏教〗 Wind God. Carries a balloon to produce wind and is usually paired with the Thunder God (RAIJIN).

ふうせんばくだん 風船爆弾 〖武器〗 a balloon bomb. Was invented to attack the U.S. mainland during World War II. About 9,000 balloons that hung bombs were launched so that they could be transported by the prevailing westerlies.

ふうちん 風鎮〖絵画・書道〗 a pair

of weights for a hanging scroll. Are hung at the both lower end of the hanging scroll to prevent swinging.

ふうてん 風天 〖仏教〗 Wind Deva. *Vayu.* One of the Twelve Devas. Guards the northwest. →十二天

ふうてんのとら フーテンの寅 〖映画〗 the nickname of the hero in the movie series, *It's Tough Being a Man* (OTOKO WA TSURAIYO).

ふうまにんじゃ 風魔忍者 〖忍者〗 a ninja group who worked around present Kanagawa Pref. Was named after its leader, Fuuma Kotarou. Served the Houjou clan in Odawara. Is said to have been good at handling information.

ふうりん 風鈴 〖生活〗 a wind chime. Tinkles when the paper strip catches the wind and the clapper swings. Is hung at a window early in summer.

ふうりんかざん 風林火山 〖武士・精神性〗 Wind, Forest, Fire, Mountain. The motto of a feudal lord, TAKEDA SHINGEN, in the 16th century. Originally were words of the Chinese strategist Sunzi. Means "swift like a wind, quiet like a forest, intrusive like a fire, immovable like a mountain."

ふうろ 風炉 〖茶道〗 ⇨風炉(る)

ふぇのろさ フェノロサ 〖美術〗 ⇨ アーネスト・フェノロサ

ふえばしら 笛柱 〖能〗 the rear-right pillar on a Noh stage.

ふぉっさまぐな フォッサマグナ 〖自然〗 Fossa Magna. A large belt zone from north to south in the center of Japan proper. Geologically divides Japan proper into the northeastern and southwestern regions. Its western edge is the Itoigawa-Shizuoka Tectonic Line, but the eastern edge is not clear. Was named by a German geologist, Edmund Naumann. →ナウマン

ふかあみがさ 深編笠 〖服飾〗 a full-face cylindrical straw hat. Was worn to hide the face by a samurai or a monk called KOMUSOU.

ふかがわめし 深川飯 〖食べ物〗 littleneck clam rice. There are two types: rice in miso soup of littleneck clams and chopped long onion, or flavored rice boiled with littleneck clams.

ぶがく 舞楽 〖音楽・芸能〗 court music with dancing, or dance accompanied by court music. Is performed at some Shinto shrines and Buddhist temples such as the Kasuga Shrine and Shitennou-ji Temple.

ふがくさんじゅうろっけい 富嶽三十六景 〖絵画・作品〗 *Thirty-six Views of Mt. Fuji.* A series of woodblock paintings, depicting landscapes of Mt. Fuji seen in several regions. Was produced by KATSUSHIKA HOKUSAI in the Edo period.

ぶかん 武鑑 〖武士・文書〗 a samurai Who's Who in the Edo period. Was first published in the 17th century. Contains information on feudal lords and direct vassals of the Tokugawa shogunate.

ふき 蕗 〖食べ物・植物〗 a butterbur. *Petasites japonicus*. Eaten boiled or stewed. Tasty in spring.

ふぎ 溥儀 〖政治〗 Pu-yi. 1906-1967. The last emperor of the Qing dynasty (1908-1912) and then the emperor of Manchukuo (1934-1945). →満州国

ふきながし 吹き流し 〖年中行事〗 a tube-shaped streamer. Is hoisted together with carp-shaped streamers before and on May 5, to celebrate the Boys' Festival. →鯉のぼり

ふきばりじゅつ 吹き針術 〖忍者〗 an attack by shooting a needle with a blowpipe.

ふきやじゅつ 吹き矢術 〖忍者〗 an attack by shooting a dart with a blowpipe. Was used for assassination by poisoning the dart. A dart was also used for illumination by setting fire to gun powder or combustible paint in a dark room.

ぶぎょう 奉行 〖武士・官位〗 a feudal commissioner in the Edo period. There were several positions such as one for administration of temples and shrines, one for governance of townspeople, and one for finance. →町奉行; 寺社社奉行; 勘定奉行

ぶぎょうしょ 奉行所 〖行政機関〗 the office of a feudal commissioner.

ふぐ 河豚 〖食べ物・動物〗 a pufferfish, or a globefish. *Tetradontidae*. Fills itself with air when in danger. Poisonous parts have to be removed before eating, so a profes-

sional cook needs a special license. Eaten as sashimi (TESSA) or a one-pot dish (TECCHIRI).

ふくいけん 福井県 〖都道府県〗 Fukui Pref. Is located in central Japan on the coast of the Sea of Japan, between Ishikawa and Kyoto Prefs. Is 4,190 km² in area. Its capital is Fukui City. Famous for a silk fabric called HABUTAE, eye-glass production, EIHEI-JI Temple, and a sea cliff called TOUJINBOU. Has 15 nuclear reactors.

ふくいけんいち 福井謙一 〖科学技術〗 1918-1998. A chemical researcher born in Nara Pref. Advocated the frontier orbital theory in 1952. Received the Nobel Prize in Chemistry in 1981.

ふくいし 福井市 〖地名〗 Fukui City. The capital of Fukui Pref., located in its central part on the coast of the Sea of Japan. The castle of a feudal lord, ASAKURA YOSHIKAGE, existed there.

ふくうけんさくかんのん 不空羂索観音 〖仏教〗 Never-Empty-Rope Bodhisattva of Mercy. *Amoghapasa*. Usually has 3 eyes and 8 arms. Has a lotus flower, a jingling rod, a lasso, and a rosary in each hand. A famous example is the one at Hokkedou of TOUDAI-JI Temple in Nara. →観音

ふくおかくうこう 福岡空港 〖交通〗 Fukuoka Airport (FUK). An international airport in Fukuoka City, Kyushu. The fourth busiest airport in Japan, and the fourth busiest single-runway airport in the world, as of 2017. Was founded as Mushiroda Airfield in 1944 during World War II. After the war, the U.S. Air Force used it until 1972 as Itaduke Air Base, particularly during the Korean War (1950-1953), because it was close to Korea. Boasts quick access from the city center; it takes only five minutes to travel from the airport to the business district of Fukuoka City by subway.

ふくおかけん 福岡県 〖都道府県〗 Fukuoka Pref. Is located at the northern end of Kyushu. Is 4,986 km^2 in area. Its capital is Fukuoka City. Has long been the gateway to China and Korea. The most densely populated prefecture in Kyushu, having two ordinance-designated cities, Fukuoka and Kitakyuushuu. Covers old Chikuzen, Chikugo, and a part of Buzen.

ふくおかし 福岡市〖地名〗 Fukuoka City. An ordinance-designated city, and the capital of Fukuoka Pref. Is located in its northwestern part on the coast of GENKAINADA. Famous for Hakata doll, ramen noodles, spicy cod roe (KARASHI-MENTAIKO), and the Hakata Gion Yamagasa Festival.

ふくさ 袱紗 〖茶道〗 a square silk cloth with sides of about 28 cm. Is used to handle tea utensils.

ふくさずし 袱紗寿司 〖寿司〗 egg-wrapped sushi. Contains vinegared rice and other chopped ingredients such as vegetables, mushrooms, and seafood.

ふくさばさみ 袱紗挟み 〖茶道〗 a portable flat case for tea ceremony accessories. Its purpose is to carry items such as a square silk cloth (FUKUSA), paper napkins (KAISHI), short wooden sticks (KUROMOJI), and a folding fan (SENSU).

ふくざわゆきち 福沢諭吉 〖教育〗 1834-1901. A philosopher and educator, born in Osaka. Studied Western sciences through the Dutch language at a private school in Osaka, TEKIJUKU, and visited Western countries several times. Founded Keio Gijuku in 1858, which later became Keio University. His works include *An Encouragement of Learning* and *Conditions in the West*. →慶應義塾大学; 学問のすすめ; 西洋事情

ふくしまけん 福島県 〖都道府県〗 Fukushima Pref. Is located in Northern Japan, extending from the coast of the Pacific Ocean to the other side of Japan's dividing ridge. Is 13,784 km^2 in area, the 3rd largest of all the prefectures. Its capital is Fukushima City. The Fukushima Daiichi Nuclear Disaster occurred in its coastal area in 2011, following the Great East Japan Earthquake. Famous for peach and pear production and snow resorts. Used to be part of Mutsu (1) and covered Iwaki and Iwashiro. →東日本大震災

ふくしまし 福島市 〖地名〗 Fukushima City. The capital of Fukushima Pref. Is located in its central part. Developed as a castle and post town along the highway from Edo to Aomori.

ふくしまだいいちげんぱつ 福島第一原発 〔災害〕 Fukushima Daiichi Nuclear Power Plant. Is located on the coast of the Pacific Ocean in Fukushima Pref. Was damaged by a tsunami in March 2011, caused by the Great East Japan Earthquake, and polluted the vicinity. →東日本大震災

ふくじゅそう 福寿草 〔植物〕 a pheasant's-eye, or an Amur adonis. *Adonis amurensis*. Bears a yellow flower and is often potted during the New Year's holidays. The root is used for medicine.

ふくしょう 副将 〔武術〕 the second-to-last fighter in a five-member team competition of martial arts such as judo. →先鋒; 次鋒; 中堅; 大将

ふくじょし 副助詞 〔言語〕 an adverbial particle. Each adverbial particle functions differently. For example, 'sae' means "even," 'nado' means "and so on," and 'dake' means "only." →助詞

ふくじんづけ 福神漬け 〔食べ物〕 pickles of seven kinds of chopped vegetables. Usually include mooli, eggplant, lotus root, ginger, perilla seeds, sword beans, and mushrooms. Goes well with curry and rice.

ふくすけ 福助 〔人形〕 a male doll with a big head, a childlike face, and a topknot. Wears a formal samurai costume and kneels on the floor. Is said to bring good luck.

ふくちゃ 福茶 〔飲み物〕 good luck tea. Contains black soybeans (KURO-MAME), kelp (KONBU), pickled plum (UMEBOSHI), and prickly ash (SAN-SHOU). Is drunk on auspicious occasions.

ふぐちり 河豚ちり 〔食べ物〕 ⇨てっちり

ふくのかみ 福の神 〔宗教〕 a deity of good fortune. Examples are the Seven Deities of Good Fortune. →七福神

ふくはうちおにはそと 福は内！鬼は外！〔年中行事・言語〕 "Come in, good luck! Get out, evil!" People shout this prayer while scattering beans on February 3. →節分; 豆撒き

ふくはち 覆鉢 〔仏教・建築〕 an inverted bowl. Is placed at the top of a pagoda roof.

ふくぶくろ 福袋 〔ビジネス〕 a lucky bag, a mystery bag, or a grab bag. Contains various items whose combined individual prices are higher than the price of the bag, but the purchaser has no way of knowing what items are in it. Is sold during the New Year's holidays.

ふくまめ 福豆 〔年中行事・食べ物〕 parched beans thrown on February 3, the day just before the beginning of spring in the traditional calendar. →節分; 豆撒き

ふくみばりじゅつ 含み針術 〔忍者〕 an attack by blowing a needle with the mouth. To hold a needle in the mouth and blow it at the enemy within a point-blank range. If it hit an eye, it seriously damaged the enemy.

ふくろおび 袋帯 〖服飾〗 a double-layered obi for a formal kimono. Easy to fasten because it does not need thick cotton cloth called OBI-SHIN.

ふくろくじゅ 福禄寿 〖宗教〗 the deity of wealth and longevity. One of the Seven Deities of Good Fortune. Is usually depicted as an old man with a long bald head. Was worshipped as a manifestation of the southern polar star and originally was identical to the deity JUROUJIN in China. →七福神

ふくろだのたき 袋田の滝 〖地名〗 Fukuroda Falls. Is located in Daigo Town in northern Ibaraki Pref. Has four drops, with a total height of 120 m. Is considered to be one of the three most beautiful waterfalls in Japan, together with Kegon Falls in Tochigi Pref. and Nachi Falls in Mie Pref. Accessible by bus, with a 10-minute ride from JR Fukuroda Station. →華厳の滝；那智の滝

ふくわらい 福笑い 〖暦・遊び〗 a blinded face-parts-arranging game. One of the traditional games played in the New Year's holidays. The blinded player places the eyes, nose, and mouth made of thick paper on a girl's face drawn on another paper. The girl is usually a young, jolly-faced, unattractive woman, called OKAME.

ぶけ 武家 〖武士〗 (**1**) a samurai, or a warrior. (**2**) a family of samurai.

ぶげいじゅうはっぱん 武芸十八般 〖武士〗 18 martial arts. Include fencing, archery, gunnery, horsemanship, swimming, jujitsu, skills of a single-blade halberd (NAGINATA), and one-motion sword attack (IAI). There are several variations with other martial arts among the 18.

ぶけしょはっと 武家諸法度 〖武士・法律〗 Laws for the Military Houses. Was issued in 1615 by the Tokugawa shogunate so that it could control feudal lords. Provided the rules about marriage, castle repairing, and the periodic residence of feudal lords in Edo, called SANKIN-KOUTAI. Some feudal lords who violated them had their fiefs expropriated.

ふけそう 普化僧 〖仏教〗 ⇨虚無僧 (こむそう)

ぶけやしき 武家屋敷 〖武士・建築〗 a samurai mansion. Was provided to samurai in a castle town by their lord. Examples are seen in several sightseeing areas such as Kakunodate in Akita Pref., Matsue in Shimane Pref., Aizu-wakamatsu in Fukushima Pref., and Sakura in Chiba Pref.

ふげんぼさつ 普賢菩薩 〖仏教〗 Bodhisattva of Practice. *Samantabhadra*. One of the two attendants of the Historical Buddha. Often rides on a white elephant with six tusks.

ふこくきょうへい 富国強兵 〖政治〗

A policy to develop the national economy and to expand military power. The Tokugawa shogunate had recognized the necessity of its implementation at the end of the Edo period, and the Meiji government made this a basic policy.

ふさ　房〔相撲〕 four tassels hung at the four corners of a suspended roof above the sumo ring. →青房；赤房；黒房；白房

ふじ　藤〔植物〕 Japanese wisteria. *Wisteria floribunda*. Bears purple flowers in May.

ふじ　～富士〔山岳〕 a Mt. Fuji. A word component to refer to a beautiful high mountain in a local area. Since Mt. Fuji is the highest and considered the most beautiful in Japan, a mountain nicknamed with a suffix '-Fuji' is the representative mountain of a local area. For example, Aizu-Fuji is Mt. Bandai in Fukushima Pref., Akita-Fuji is Mt. Choukai in Akita Pref., Satsuma-Fuji is Mt. Kaimon in Kagoshima Pref., and so on.

ぶし　武士〔武士〕 a samurai, a warrior, or a military person. Emerged around the 10th century and came to guard noblemen with their military power. The Minamoto clan established the first shogunate in the late 12th century, and 'bushi' remained the ruling class until the Meiji Restoration.

ふじいでら　葛井寺〔寺院〕 Fujiidera Temple. A temple affiliated with the Shingon sect, located in cen-

tral Osaka Pref. Is said to have been founded in 725 by GYOUKI and revived from 806 to 810 by Prince Abo. The Thousand-armed Bodhisattva of Mercy is a National Treasure.

ふじこう　富士講〔宗教・旅〕 a mutual financing group for funding a pilgrimage to Mt. Fuji. Was popular in the Edo period. Members saved up money and dispatched their representatives to Mt. Fuji.

ふじごこ　富士五湖〔湖沼〕 Fuji Five Lakes. Namely, Lake Yamanaka, Lake Kawaguchi, Lake Saiko, Lake Shouji, and Lake Motosu. Are located at the foot of Mt. Fuji on its north side in Yamanashi Pref.

ふじさん　富士山〔山岳〕 Mount Fuji. An active stratovolcano. Japan's highest mountain with its peak at 3,776 m. Is located on the border between Yamanashi and Shizuoka Prefs. Was designated a World Heritage Site in 2013.

ふじさんほんぐうせんげんたいしゃ　富士山本宮浅間大社〔神社〕 Fujisan Hongu Sengen Shrine. The head shrine of Sengen Shrines, located in eastern Shizuoka Pref. Enshrines KONOHANA NO SAKUYA HIME, the deity of Mt. Fuji. →浅間(せん)神社

ふじたびじゅつかん　藤田美術館〔美術・博物館〕 Fujita Museum. Was founded in Osaka in 1954. Contains Eastern fine arts collected by the Fujita family, including nine National Treasures. Examples are the *Illustrated Diary of Murasaki Shikibu* and *Newly Risen Moon above the Brushwood Gate*.

ぶしどう 武士道〔武士・精神性〕 the warrior's morals, the samurai code, or Japanese chivalry. Emphasizes the loyalty to the lord and the value of honor even above life. In the Edo period, was strongly influenced by Confucianism and became a unique ideology for the ruling class. →葉隠れ

ふじのきこふん 藤の木古墳 〔考古〕 Fujinoki Tumulus. A round burial mound, dated to the later 6th century. Is located in northern Nara Pref. Two male bodies in a red-painted house-shaped stone coffin, bronze horse gear, and earthenware were excavated during the surveys in 1985 and 1988.

ふじばかま 藤袴〔植物〕 a thoroughwort, or a Japanese boneset. *Eupatorium japonicum*. One of the seven flowers of autumn in a lunar calendar. →秋の七草

ふじびたい 富士額〔髪〕 a forehead with a hairline shaped like Mt. Fuji. Was once considered as a prerequisite of a beautiful girl.

ふしみ 伏見〔酒・地名〕 the southern part of Kyoto. Famous for sake brewing because of its good water.

ふしみいなりたいしゃ 伏見稲荷大社〔神社〕 Fushimi Inari Grand Shrine. The head shrine of the Inari Shrines throughout Japan, located in Kyoto City. Enshrines Ukano mitama no ookami and other deities.

It is said that the Hata clan founded this shrine on the first day of Horse, HATSUUMA, in February 711. Famous for passages under about 10,000 yellowish-red torii gates.

ふしみにんぎょう 伏見人形〔玩具〕 Fushimi Doll. An earthen doll produced in Fushimi, Kyoto Pref.

ぶしゅ 部首〔漢字〕 a radical of kanji. Forms a component and gives a basic meaning to the kanji. Can be broadly classified by its position in the kanji. For example, the upper radical is called KANMURI, meaning "crown," while the left-side radical is called HEN, meaning "imbalance." Is also used to classify kanji characters in a kanji dictionary.

ぶしゅう 武州〔旧国名〕 ⇨武蔵

ぶしゅうぎぶくろ 不祝儀袋〔冠婚葬祭〕 an envelope for a money gift at a funeral or memorial service. Tied on it are white cords, along with either a silver or black cord called MIZUHIKI.

ぶしゅさくいん 部首索引 〔漢字〕 the index of kanji radicals. Is used to retrieve a kanji in a kanji dictionary.

ぶじゅつしなんやく 武術指南役〔武士〕 an instructor of martial arts. Was hired by a feudal domain in the Edo period.

ぶしょう 武将〔武士〕 a warlord, or a military commander. This term usually refers to a samurai general from the 12th to 17th centuries, not in other periods.

ふじわらきょう 藤原京 〔政治〕

Fujiwara Capital. Was located in present Kashihara City, Nara Pref. from 694 to 710. The first capital that imitated the plan of a castle town in Tang.

ふじわらし 藤原氏 〖氏族〗 the Fujiwara clan. The name started when Nakatomi no Kamatari was given the family name and became FUJIWARA NO KAMATARI. Reached its zenith in the 11th century when FUJIWARA NO MICHINAGA promoted the regency government called SEKKAN-SEIJI.

ふじわらのかまたり 藤原鎌足 〖政治〗 614-669. An aristocrat born in present Nara Pref. Executed the Taika Reform of 645, in cooperation with Prince Nakano Ooe, who later became Emperor Tenji. Was given the clan name 'Fujiwara' by Emperor Tenji when dying and became the ancestor of the Fujiwara clan. →大化の改新; 天智天皇; 藤原氏

ふじわらのさだいえ 藤原定家 〖文芸〗 ⇨藤原定家（ていか）

ふじわらのすみとも 藤原純友 〖政治〗 ?-941. A local officer dispatched from Kyoto to present Ehime Pref. After finishing his tenure, did not come back and rose in revolt in the Inland Sea. Was defeated by the government force and killed in 941. →天慶（てんぎょう）の乱

ふじわらのていか 藤原定家 〖文芸〗 1162-1241. A poet laureate born in Kyoto. One of the six anthologists of the *New Collection of Ancient and Modern Poems*. Is also said to have compiled *Single Verses by a Hundred People*. →新古今和歌集; 百人一首

ふじわらのなかまろ 藤原仲麻呂 〖政治〗 706-764. An aristocrat and nephew of Empress Consort Koumyou. Obtained power by driving off his political rivals in 757 and was given another name 'Emi no Oshikatsu' by Emperor Junnin in 758. Failed to get rid of the priest DOUKYOU from political circles and was killed. →光明皇后; 淳仁天皇

ふじわらのひでさと 藤原秀郷 〖武士〗 ?-? A military commander in the Kantou region in the Heian period. Suppressed the Tengyou Rebellion together with Taira no Sadamori. Is said to have exterminated a giant centipede named Tawara Touta in legend. →天慶（てんぎょう）の乱

ふじわらのひでひら 藤原秀衡 〖政治〗 ?-1187. The leader of a powerful clan in northwestern Japan, born in present Iwate Pref. Gave refuge to a warlord, MINAMOTO NO YOSHITSUNE, who was pursued by MINAMOTO NO YORITOMO after exterminating the Taira clan. Hidehira's mummy is stored at the Golden Hall of CHUUSON-JI Temple in Iwate Pref.

ふじわらのふひと 藤原不比等 〖政治〗 659-720. An aristocrat and leader of the Fujiwara clan, born in present Nara Pref. The second son of FUJIWARA NO KAMATARI and the father of Empress Consort Koumyou. Took part in the compilation of the Taihou and Yourou Codes. Built the foundation of the prosperity of the Fujiwara clan. →光明皇后；大宝律令；養老律令

ふじわらのみちなが 藤原道長 〖政治〗 966-1027. An aristocrat and leader of the Fujiwara clan. The father of FUJIWARA NO YORIMICHI. Became the maternal relative of three Emperors by marrying his daughters to them. Became the regent of his grandson, Emperor Goichijou in 1016, and the grand minister in 1017. His glory is depicted in *The Great Mirror*. →藤原氏

ふじわらのやすひら 藤原泰衡 〖政治〗 1155-1187. The leader of a powerful clan in northwestern Japan, born in present Iwate Pref. A son of FUJIWARA NO HIDEHIRA. Was forced by MINAMOTO NO YORITOMO to kill a warlord, MINAMOTO NO YOSHITSUNE, to whom his father gave refuge. Was later destroyed by Yoritomo.

ふじわらのよりみち 藤原頼通 〖政治〗 992-1074. An aristocrat and leader of the Fujiwara clan. The eldest son of FUJIWARA NO MICHINAGA. Occupied the position as a regent and supreme adviser for Emperors Goichijou, Gosuzaku, and Goreizei. Founded the BYOUDOU-IN Temple at Uji, Kyoto Pref. in 1052.

ふじわらぶんか 藤原文化 〖時代〗 ⇨ 国風文化

ふしんぶぎょう 普請奉行 〖武士・行政〗 a commissioner in charge of construction and architecture under the shogunates from the 14th to 19th centuries.

ふすま 襖 〖建築〗 a removable sliding screen made of paper and a wooden frame. All sliding screens are removed when converting several smaller rooms into one large one. Was invented around the Kamakura period.

ふすまえ 襖絵 〖絵画〗 a picture on a sliding screen. Often two to four screens are used to depict a large picture.

ふせ 布施 〖仏教〗 ⇨御布施

ふせき 布石 〖碁〗 the arrangement of stones in the initial stage of GO. As in shogi and Western chess, there are some opening patterns in 'go' that have been considered effective by many professionals.

ぶぜん 豊前 〖旧国名〗 the old name of eastern Fukuoka Pref. and northern Ooita Pref.

ふそう 扶桑 〖地名・伝説〗 another name of Japan. Chinese mythology says that there is a land to the east, where a gigantic divine tree grows. That land corresponds to Japan.

ふだいだいみょう 譜代大名 〖武士・政治〗 a hereditary feudal lord. Had served the Tokugawa family since before the Battle of Sekigahara in 1600. Their domains were rather small compared with those of outside feudal lords, called TOZAMA DAIMYOU, but they were located in strategically critical places. Some hereditary lords also held powerful posts in the Tokugawa shogunate. →親藩

ふたえいぶき 二重息吹〔忍者〕 a breathing technique when a ninja ran a long distance. To repeat the respiration in the rhythm of "in-out-out-in-out-in-in-out." It is said that the concentration on this pattern made the runner empty his mind and prevented him from feeling tired.

ふたおき 蓋置〔茶道〕 a rest for a teakettle lid. A ladle is also placed there.

ぶたきむち 豚キムチ〔食べ物〕 fried sliced pork with kimchee. Goes well with beer.

ふたくちおんな 二口女〔妖怪〕 Two-mouth Lady. A character in legends. Looks like a normal woman, but has a second mouth on the back of the head, hidden under the hair. Some of her hairs form like a snake and move to bring food to the second mouth.

ぶたしゃぶ 豚しゃぶ〔食べ物〕 parboiled thin-sliced pork and vegetables slightly cooked in hot soup for just several seconds. Eaten after dipping it in a mixture of soy sauce, citrus juice, and grated mooli.

ふだしょ 札所〔仏教〕 a temple to dedicate a pilgrimage tag. People offered the temple a tag as a token of the pilgrimage. On the tag, their wish, their name, and the visiting date were written since medieval times. However, it is popular these days that a pilgrim obtains the signature and seal of the temple on a special notebook called SHUINCHOU. →四国八十八カ所; 西国三十三カ所

ぶたじる 豚汁〔食べ物〕 ⇨豚汁(ﾄﾝじる)

ぶたたま 豚玉〔食べ物〕 a Japanese-style savory pancake containing egg and sliced pork. The most common among savory pancakes called OKONOMIYAKI.

ふたつめ 二つ目〔落語〕 a middle-ranked comic storyteller in the Tokyo area. A 'futatsume' storyteller is promoted to the highest rank, SHIN'UCHI, according to his or her skills. The rakugo community in the Osaka area does not have this system.

ぶたどん 豚丼〔食べ物〕 a pork bowl. Is topped with richly tasting sliced pork on top of a bowl of rice. A specialty of eastern Hokkaido.

ぶたのかくに 豚の角煮〔食べ物〕 a simmered chunk of pork. Is seasoned with soy sauce, mirin, and ginger.

ふたばていしめい 二葉亭四迷〔文芸〕 1864-1909. A novelist and translator born in Edo. His works include a novel, *Drifting Clouds* (Ukigumo), and a translation of a Russian novel, *A Sportsman's Sketches* (Ahibiki).

ぶたまん 豚饅〔食べ物〕 ⇨肉饅

ふち 扶持〔武士・経済〕 a stipend of a samurai in the feudal age. Was paid with rice.

ふちゃりょうり 普茶料理〔食文化〕

Chinese-style Buddhist vegetarian cuisine. A Chinese Zen priest, Yinyuan, introduced it in the 17th century. Is served at MANPUKU-JI Temple in Uji, Kyoto Pref.

ふちょう 府庁 〖行政機関〗 a prefectural government of Osaka or Kyoto. Other prefectural governments are called KENCHOU.

ぶつえん 仏縁 〖仏教〗 the personal religious connection between a Buddha or Buddhist deity and a living thing.

ぶつが 仏画 〖仏教〗 a Buddhist picture. Includes a mandala, a picture of Buddhist deities, or a picture depicting a story in Buddhism.

ぶっかい 仏界 〖仏教〗 the Pure Land, or the Buddha's Realm.

ぶっかく 仏閣 〖仏教〗 ⇨寺

ふづき 文月 〖暦〗 ⇨文月(ふみづき)

ぶっきょう 仏教 〖仏教〗 Buddhism. Was founded in India around the 5th century B.C. by Gautama Siddhartha, spread to China, and was introduced through Korea to Japan in 538 or 552. Its holy place is a Buddhist temple called TERA. On the official reception of Buddhism, the Soga clan conflicted with the Mononobe clan. After the victory of Soga in 587, Prince Shoutoku implemented policies based on Buddhism. Emperor Shoumu built national temples in provinces throughout Japan in the 8th century. Two priests, KUUKAI and SAICHOU, brought back esoteric Buddhism in the 9th century.

New sects such as the Pure Land, Rinzai, and Nichiren sects were born in the 12th and 13th centuries. From the 13th to 16th centuries, Zen Buddhism had a great influence on culture such as in literature, paintings, architecture, and the tea ceremony. Immediately after the Meiji Restoration in the 19th century, Buddhism was prosecuted by the government, which tried to establish Shinto as the national religion, but this trend did not last long. Several new religous groups related to Buddhism were born after the Meiji Restoration. The popularity of such groups reached a high point in the 1960s.
→釈迦牟尼; 聖徳太子; 国分寺; 五山文学; 詩画軸; 廃仏毀釈

ぶつぐ 仏具 〖仏教〗 a utensil for Buddhist rituals. Includes ornaments for an altar and tools for service.

ふづくえ 文机 〖家具〗 ⇨文机(ふづくえ)

ふっこしんとう 復古神道 〖神道〗 Restoration Shinto. In the 18th to 19th centuries, MOTOORI NORINAGA, HIRATA ATSUTANE, and other scholars insisted on reviving the pure ancient Japanese spirit described in the classic literature and mythology and also abandoning foreign influences such as Buddhism and Confucianism. Had a great influence on Shinto-oriented policies such as SONNOU JOUI and HAIBUTSU-KISHAKU.

ぶつざ 仏座 〖仏教〗 ⇨蓮台

ぶっし　仏師〖仏教〗 a sculptor of Buddhist images. →鞍作止利 (くらつくりの とり)；定朝(じょう ちょう)；運慶

ぶつじ　仏事〖仏教〗 a Buddhist ritual or event.

ぶっしゃり　仏舎利〖仏教〗 ⇨舎利

ぶっしゃりとう　仏舎利塔〖仏教〗 ⇨ 舎利塔

ぶつぜん　仏前〖仏教〗 ⇨御仏前 (ごぶつぜん)

ぶつぜんけっこん　仏前結婚〖仏教・結婚〗 a Buddhist-style wedding. Is held at a temple. Not very popular these days.

ぶつぞう　仏像〖仏教〗 a Buddhist image, or a Buddhist sculpture. Buddha was not depicted in any way for a few centuries after the Historical Buddha died in the 4th century B.C. His sculpture began to be created in northeastern India at the end of the 1st century A.D. With the development and expansion of Buddhism, a wide variety of Buddhist images were produced. Buddhist images existing in Japan include AMIDA NYORAI, YAKUSHI NYORAI, KANNON BOSATSU, JIZOU BOSATSU, FUDOU MYOUOU, SHITENNOU, and other various works. →三十二相 八十種好

ぶっそくせき　仏足跡〖仏教〗 a stone with the impression of the Buddha's footprints.

ぶっだ　仏陀〖仏教〗 **(1)**⇨釈迦牟尼 **(2)**a Buddha. *Tathagata*. An enlightened one. Is also called NYORAI in Japanese. Examples include Amitabha Buddha (AMIDA NYORAI),

the Healing Buddha (YAKUSHI NYORAI), and the Great Sun Buddha (DAINICHI NYORAI).

ぶつだん　仏壇〖仏教〗 a family Buddhist altar. Contains a small Buddhist image, memorial tablets inscribed with deceased people's names, the death register, and other ornaments such as a flower vase, a candle stand, and a censer. Its design and contents vary from sect to sect, region to region. →位 牌；過去帳

ぶってん　仏典〖仏教〗 literature on Buddhism, including sutras.

ぶつでん　仏殿〖禅・建築〗 the main hall containing the principal image at a Zen temple. →本堂

ふつぬしのかみ　経津主神〖神話〗 a deity of military arts. AMATERASU OOMIKAMI dispatched him, together with TAKEMIKADUCHI NO ONOKAMI, from the High Celestial Plain to the Central Land of Reeds to make OOKUNINUSHI NO KAMI waive his sovereignty over the land. Is enshrined at Katori Shrine in Chiba Pref. →高 天原(たかまが はら)；香取神宮

ぶっぽうそう　仏法僧〖仏教〗 Buddha, dharma, and monks. Are regarded as the three treasures in Buddhism. →三宝(さん ぼう)

ぶつま　仏間〖仏教・建築〗 a room with a family Buddhist altar. Usually a traditional-style room.

ぶつめつ　仏滅〖暦〗 a day of "Buddha death" in the unofficial six-day calendar. Everything is awful on this day. Most people avoid this day for weddings. Its origin actually has no relation to the death of the Buddha. →六曜(るく)

ぶつもん 仏門 〖仏教〗 the monastic society of Buddhism. The expression 'butsumon ni hairu' means "to become a Buddhist priest."

ふていしょう 不定称 〖言語〗 a demonstrative pronoun referring to an indefinite relation. Its first letter is 'do' such as in 'dore' (which), 'dono' (which), and 'dochira' (where). →近称；中称；遠称

ぶどう 武道 〖武術〗 the generic term for martial arts. Since Japanese martial arts lay emphasis not only on skillfullness but also on spirituarity of its practitioners, most of them include the word DOU, which means "way," in its name, such as KENDOU and AIKIDOU. This term began to be used in the Meiji period.

ふとうこう 不登校 〖教育〗 nonattendance at school. The state in which a student does not or cannot go to school, even though there are no financial or physical obstacles. Public statistics do not include students who are absent because of sickness or financial reasons.

ふどうみょうおう 不動明王 〖仏教〗 the Immovable Wisdom King. *Acala*. The central figure of the Five Wisdom Kings. Was originally a Hindu deity that was absorbed into Buddhism. Was introduced to Japan in the 9th century, together with esoteric Buddhism. Is con-

sidered to be an incarnation of the Great Sun Buddha to exorcise evil spirits in and out of people's minds. Has a furious face, a sword in the right hand, and a rope in the left hand, with a burning flame on the back. Is sometimes accompanied by two boys, KONGARA DOUJI and SEITAKA DOUJI. Sculptures can be seen at TOU-JI Temple in Kyoto and at Ganjouju-in Temple in Shizuoka Pref. Paintings can be seen at SHOUREN-IN Temple in Kyoto and the MOA (Mokichi Okada Association) Museum of Art in Shizuoka Pref.

ふどき 風土記 〖書名〗 an official record of geographical descriptions. In 713, Empress Genmei ordered each province to record its natural features, oral traditions, and origins of place names and to submit them. The only extant examples are those of Izumo (present western Shimane Pref.), Hitachi (present Ibaraki Pref.), Harima (part of present Hyougo Pref.), Bungo (present Ooita Pref.) and Hizen (present Nagasaki and Saga Prefs.).

ふところ 懐 〖服飾〗 the space between the breast and the kimono. Is used as a pocket.

ふとざお 太棹 〖音楽〗 a shamisen with a thick neck. Is used for dramatic narratives called GIDAYUU-BUSHI, or a local shamisen performance in Aomori Pref. called TSUGARU-JAMISEN.

ふとまき 太巻き 〖寿司〗 a thick

sushi roll. Vinegared rice is wrapped with purple laver (NORI) and contains an omelet, strips of a bottle gourd (KANPYOU), and freeze-dried tofu. Is sliced when eaten.

ふともの 太物〖服飾〗 a fabric made of thick yarn such as cotton or hemp, in contrast to thin yarn such as silk.

ふとん 布団, 蒲団〖家具〗 a futon. Contains cotton or down. People spread out a bottom futon on the tatami mat, lie on it, and cover themselves with a top futon.

ふとん 蒲団〖文芸・作品〗 *Futon.* A novel published in 1907 by TAYAMA KATAI. Describes a novelist's love for his female pupil. Is based on the author's experience.

ふな 鮒〖魚〗 a crucian carp. *Carassius.* Is 20 to 25 cm long. Lives throughout Japan in lakes, ponds, and rivers that are on plains.

ぶな 橅〖植物〗 a Japanese beech. *Fagus crenata.* Native to Japan. Is used for architecture and pulp.

ふながたこうはい 舟形光背 〖仏教〗 a pointed oval-shaped halo of a Buddhist image. The Triad of the Historical Buddha at Houryuu-ji Temple has this type of halo.

ふなずし 鮒寿司〖食べ物〗 crucian carp fermented with rice and salt. A specialty of Lake Biwa.

ふなっしい ふなっしー〖ゆるキャラ〗 the name of a mascot character of Funabashi City, Chiba Pref. The fairy that represents the pear fruit.

ふなもり 船盛り〖食文化〗 sashimi served on a wooden plate in the shape of a traditional boat.

ふなやど 船宿 **(1)**〖交通〗 an accommodation for ship sailors in the Edo period. Also mediated between ship owners and sailors, sold cargo to wholesalers, and provided necessities for voyages. **(2)**〖娯楽〗 an agent to arrange a boat for recreational fishing or a lovers' rendezvous.

ふなゆうれい 船幽霊〖妖怪〗 a sea phantom, or Davy Jones. A spirit of one who died by drowning at sea. Appears often in a group and asks the encounterer for a ladle. The spirits ladle the sea water into the encounterer's boat and sink it. To avoid sinking, the encounter should hand a ladle without the bottom.

ふねへん 船偏〖漢字〗 a left-side radical meaning "ship." Is used in kanji such as 船(ship) and 航(cross).

ふまわり 歩周り〖遊び〗 ⇨周り将棋

ふみいし 踏み石 **(1)**〖生活〗 a stone on which shoes are placed after being taken off when entering a house. **(2)**〖庭園〗 ⇨飛び石

ふみえ 踏絵〖政治・キリスト教〗 a tablet with an image of Christ or the Virgin. People were forced to walk on the image, showing their disregard for the Christian figures. Was said to have been devised in 1629 by a feudal commissioner who governed Nagasaki. Was abolished in 1858 when the Harris Treaty was concluded. →隠れキリシタン;

日米修好通商条約

ふみぐるま 踏み車 〖農林水産〗 a treadwheel, or a treadmill. A water lifting device for a rice field. Is said to have been invented in the Edo period.

ふみづき 文月 〖暦〗 July in the traditional calendar. Means "letter month." Is said to come from a custom of the Star Festival, in which people wish to improve their ability at calligraphy by writing a poem or letters on a paper slip. →旧暦

ふみづくえ 文机 〖家具〗 a low desk for reading or writing. A person sits in front of it, directly on the floor without a chair.

ふゆふにゅう 不輸不入 〖政治〗 the privileges of a manor owner to refuse tax and inspection. →荘園

ぶらきすとん ブラキストン 〖科学技術〗 Thomas Wright Blakiston. 1832-1891. A British explorer and naturalist who moved to Hokkaido in 1861 and studied the birds of Japan. Observed that animals in Hokkaido were related to species in northern Asia, unlike those on Honshuu that were similar to those in southern Asia. The strait between Hokkaido and Honshuu was known as "Blakiston's Line," an imaginary line separating the fauna of southern and northern Asia. Went back to England in 1884.

ぶらきすとんせん ブラキストン線 〖動物・植物〗 Blakiston's Line. The border of the geographical distribution of animals, located between Honshuu and Hokkaido. Was named after a British zoologist, T. W. Blakiston.

ぶらく 部落 〖政治〗 ⇨被差別部落

ぶらくかいほうどうめい 部落解放同盟 〖政治〗 Buraku Liberation League. Aims at putting an end to discrimination against members from a former outcaste community called HISABETSU BURAKU.

ぶらっくばす ブラックバス 〖魚〗 a black bass. *Micropterus*. About 50 cm long. Was introduced from North America in 1925 for fishing. Eats native species of Japan.

ふらんくろいどらいと フランク・ロイド・ライト 〖建築〗 Frank Lloyd Wright. 1867-1959. An American architect who was influenced by, and also influenced, Japanese art and architecture. First visited Japan in 1905 and later designed the Imperial Hotel in Tokyo, built between 1919 and 1922. The hotel reflects Wright's belief that a structure should fit organically within its natural setting. Although this well-built hotel was not destroyed by the 1923 earthquake nor by World War II bombings, it was razed in the 1960s to make way for the current New Imperial Hotel. Its main entrance hall and lobby are preserved in the Museum Meiji-mura, Aichi Pref.

ふらんしすこざびえる フランシスコ・ザビエル 〖キリスト教〗 Saint Francis Xavier. 1506-1552. A Spanish missionary. Came to Japan in 1549 to introduce Christianity for the first time. Died in China.

ふり ～振り 〚助数詞〛 a counting suffix for swords.

ぶり 鰤 〚食べ物・魚〛 a yellowtail, or Japanese amberjack. *Seriola quinqueradiata*. About 1 to 1.5 m long. Eaten in various ways, such as sushi, teriyaki, grilled, and simmered with white radish. Has different names as it grows. →鰤大根；出世魚

ふりいたあ フリーター 〚職業・教育〛 a "freeter." A Japanese-English term. Means "a permanent part-timer."

ふりかえきゅうじつ 振替休日 〚暦〛 a substitute national holiday. When a national holiday falls on Sunday, the next Monday becomes a holiday.

ふりかけ 振り掛け 〚食文化〛 rice topping. A mixture of various ingredients such as chopped purple laver, sesame seeds, dried salmon, and dried cod roe. Is sprinkled on rice when eating.

ふりがな 振り仮名 〚漢字〛 small-sized kana added above a kanji to show its pronunciation. Is also called RUBI.

ぷりくら プリクラ 〚遊び〛 Print Club. The trademark of a photo sticker machine. The user can add an ornamental background or outline.

ふりこめさぎ 振り込め詐欺 〚犯罪〛 bank transfer fraud. There are four types: impersonation, fictitious charging, fictitious investment, and fictitious refunding.

ふりそで 振り袖 〚服飾〛 a formal kimono for a young unmarried woman. Has sleeves with a length of about one meter. Generally worn at a coming-of-age ceremony or a wedding ceremony. Was devised in the early Edo period. The sleeves were lengthened later as it became more popular among young women as a formal outfit. Some people say that the longer sleeves make its wearer look more beautiful on the stage when performing Japanese dances.

ふりそでかじ 振袖火事 〚災害〛 Furisode Fire. Another name for the Meireki Conflagration in 1657. →明暦の大火

ぶりだいこん 鰤大根 〚食べ物〛 white radish simmered with yellowtail. Is seasoned mainly with soy sauce, mirin, and ginger.

ふるいちこふんぐん 古市古墳群 〚考古〛 Furuichi Burial Mounds. Are located in central Osaka Pref. Consists of about 100 tumuli, including the Tumulus of Emperor Oujin, the second largest keyhole-shaped burial mound. →応神天皇陵

ぶるうのたうと ブルーノ・タウト 〚建築〛 Bruno Taut. 1880-1938. A German architect and city planner. Fled Nazi Germany and moved to Japan in 1933. As an admirer of simplicity of form in Japanese art and architecture, he published works on this topic while in Japan.

He especially appreciated, and wrote and spoke about, the Ise Shrine and the Katsura Detached Palace in Kyoto. On the latter, he depicted it as "a completely isolated miracle in the civilized world." Moved to Turkey in 1936 to become a professor there.

ふるたおりべ 古田織部 〖茶道〗 1544 -1615. A warlord and tea master, born in present Gifu Pref. Served ODA NOBUNAGA and TOYOTOMI HIDEYOSHI. Learned the tea ceremony under SEN NO RIKYUU and devised the Oribe-style pottery. Taught tea ceremony to TOKUGAWA HIDETADA, KOBORI ENSHUU, and HON'AMI KOUETSU. After the Battle of Sekigahara, became a feudal lord under TOKUGAWA IEYASU. During the Summer Campaign in Osaka, communicated secretly with the Toyotomi clan and was ordered to commit suicide. →織部焼

ふるづけ 古漬け 〖食べ物〗 vegetables pickled for a long time.

ふるな 富楼那 〖仏教〗 *Purna*. One of the Ten Great Disciples of the Historical Buddha. Foremost among the disciples in preaching the dharma. →十大弟子

ぶれいこう 無礼講 〖酒・精神性〗 a casual party without any formal features. The status or hierarchy of participants can be disregarded.

ふれだいこ 触れ太鼓 〖相撲〗 a drum announcing the sumo tournament beginning on the next day.

ぶれつてんのう 武烈天皇 〖天皇〗

Emperor Buretsu. ?-? The 25th. The *Chronicles of Japan* (NIHON-SHOKI) describes him as a violent person.

ふろ 風呂 〖風呂〗 a bath. In a Japanese-style bath, a bath-taker washes one's body outside the bathtub and then soaks oneself in the hot water of the bathtub. One should not soak one's towel in the tub, and the water of the tub should not be drained after each person finishes bathing. The current style of bathing started in the Edo period. Before that, a kind of a steam bath was popular. →銭湯; 温泉

ふろ 風炉 〖茶道〗 a portable stove. The tea host or hostess puts a kettle on it to boil water for the tea ceremony. From May to October, is used instead of a sunken hearth called RO.

ふろいす フロイス 〖キリスト教〗 ⇨ ルイス・フロイス

ふろおけ 風呂桶 〖風呂〗 ⇨湯船; 湯桶(ゆおけ)

ふろがま 風炉釜 〖茶道〗 a kettle used for a portable stove called FURO.

ふろしき 風呂敷 〖生活〗 a square wrapping cloth. The side is usually about 70 cm to 1 m long. People used to spread it on the floor when going to a public bath in olden times.

ふろしきづつみ 風呂敷包み 〖生活〗 a parcel wrapped in a square cloth called FUROSHIKI.

ふろふきだいこん 風呂吹き大根〖食

べ物〗 soft-boiled white radish with miso.

ふろや 風呂屋〖生活〗 ⇨銭湯

ぶんえい 文永〖時代〗 an era name from 1264 to 1275 in the Kamakura period. The Mongolian troops attacked northern Kyushu during this time.

ぶんえいのえき 文永の役〖戦争〗 ⇨元寇

ぶんかくんしょう 文化勲章〖政治〗 the Order of Culture. Is bestowed on people in academic and artistic fields. Was established in 1937.

ぶんかざい 文化財〖法律〗 a cultural property. Cultural properties include Tangible Cultural Properties, Intangible Cultural Properties, Folk Cultural Properties, Monuments, Cultural Landscapes, and Groups of Traditional Buildings.

ぶんかざいほごほう 文化財保護法〖法律〗 the Law for the Protection of Cultural Properties. Was enacted in 1950 and has regulated cultural properties such as National Treasures (KOKUHOU), Important Cultural Properties (JUUYOU BUNKAZAI), Historic Sites (SHISEKI), Natural Monuments (TENNEN KINENBUTSU), and Intangible Cultural Properties (MUKEI BUNKAZAI).

ぶんかちょう 文化庁〖行政機関〗 Agency for Cultural Affairs. An external bureau of the Minister of Education, Culture, Sports, Science and Technology. Promotes cultural activities, protects and utilizes cultural properties, and deals with administrative affairs of religions.

ぶんかてきけいかん 文化的景観〖行政〗 Cultural Landscapes. Include landscapes that help one understand the lifestyles and livelihoods of the people. Are defined by the Law for the Protection of Cultural Properties.

ぶんかのひ 文化の日〖祝日〗 Culture Day. November 3. A national holiday to appreciate freedom and peace and to develop culture. The present constitution was promulgated on this day in 1946.

ふんかわん 噴火湾〖海洋〗 ⇨内浦湾

ぶんけ 分家〖生活〗 a branch family. Before World War II, the eldest son usually succeeded his father as the head of the family, and any other sons became independent to have their own new family, 'bunke,' which was thought of as subordinate to the original family. ↔本家

ぶんげいしゅんじゅう 文藝春秋〖文芸〗 a magazine that means "literature around the year." Was first published as a literary magazine in 1923 by KIKUCHI KAN. Became a general magazine in 1926. Established the Akutagawa and Naoki Prizes in 1935. Is still being published. →芥川賞；直木賞

ぶんご 豊後〖旧国名〗 the old name for the largest part of Ooita Pref.

ぶんごすいどう 豊後水道〖地名〗 Bungo Channel. Is located between Shikoku and Kyushu. Connects the Inland Sea with the Pacific Ocean. Its narrowest part is called the

Houyo Strait, 14 km wide, between Cape Sada in Ehime Pref. and Cape Seki in Ooita Pref. Famous for the catches of fishes such as horse mackerel (AJI) and chub mackerel (SABA).

ぶんごたい 文語体 〚言語〛 the old style of written Japanese. Was based on the language in the 10th to 11th centuries and was used until the 19th century. ↔口語体

ぶんじんが 文人画 〚絵画〛 a picture in the amateur style by literati. Is often called Nanshuu-ga. This style originated in China, emphasized subjective and poetic expression rather than techniques. Mainly depicted landscapes with India ink and was introduced to Japan around the 18th century.

ぶんしんのじゅつ 分身の術 〚忍者〛 a body-doubling technique. A typical ninja skill depicted in fiction. Though its details are unknown, a ninja might have made the enemy hallucinate that there existed more than one ninja by hypnotizing the enemy or inducing a hallucination with a drug.

ぶんせつ 文節 〚言語〛 the smallest unit in a Japanese sentence. A speaker or writer of the Japanese language can pause or insert a comma only immediately after 'bunsetsu.'

ぶんちん 文鎮 〚書道〛 a paperweight. Is used in calligraphy.

ふんどし 褌 **(1)** 〚服飾〛 a loincloth. A traditional men's underwear made of cotton. **(2)** 〚相撲〛 a thick belt worn by a sumo wrester.

ふんどしかつぎ 褌担ぎ 〚相撲〛 a lower-ranking sumo wrestler. Literally means "a carrier of a loincloth." Takes care of a higher-ranking wrestler in his daily life.

ぶんぶくちゃがま 分福茶釜 〚民話〛 the title of a folktale about a raccoon dog's transformation. The story at Morin-ji Temple in Gunma Pref. says that a priest named Shukaku brought a tea kettle, which kept sufficient hot water no matter much water was used. Later Shukaku had his true identity as a raccoon dog revealed. In another story, after the true identity of the kettle as the raccoon dog was revealed, the raccoon dog exhibited a dance on a tightrope.

ぶんぶりょうどう 文武両道 〚精神性〛 excellence in both learning and martial arts. Is said to have been the ideal for a samurai. This expression is figuratively applied to students nowadays, to refer to excellence in both study and sports.

ぶんめいかいか 文明開化 〚精神性〛 Western-oriented civilization after the Meiji Restoration. Japan rapidly tried to become a Westernized country in the late 19th century, copying European and American cultures.

ふんやのやすひで 文屋康秀 〚文芸〛 ?-? One of the Six Immortal Poets. His five tanka are contained in the *Collection of Ancient and Modern*

Japanese Poetry (KOKINWAKASHUU). His biographical details are unknown. →六歌仙

ぶんらく 文楽 《文楽》 Osaka-style traditional puppet theater. Is accompanied by a dramatic narrative and three-stringed instrument called SHAMISEN. Originally the name of a theater where the puppet drama was performed.

ぶんらくにんぎょう 文楽人形 《文楽》 a puppet used in BUNRAKU. Its size is about two thirds of a human. One puppet is moved by three puppeteers who are working together. →三人遣い

ぶんろくけいちょうのえき 文禄・慶長の役 〔戦争〕 Bunroku-Keichou War. Japan unsuccessfully invaded Korea in 1592 and 1597 under the command of TOYOTOMI HIDEYOSHI. 'Bunroku' and 'Keichou' refer to the era names in which the invasions occurred.

ぶんろくのえき 文禄の役 〔戦争〕 ⇨ 文禄・慶長の役

へい 丙〘干支〙 ⇨丙(ひのえ)

へいあんきょう 平安京 〘政治〙 Heian Capital. Was located in present Kyoto from 794 to 1869. Measured about 5.3 km north-south and about 4.5 km east-west. Lost its political function when the Kamakura shogunate was established in the 12th century.

へいあんじだい 平安時代 〘時代〙 the Heian period, from 794 to 1185. The capital was placed in present Kyoto. In the early period, the centralized administration system based on laws, called RITSURYOU-SEI, was maintained. In the middle period, the regency government, called SEKKAN-SEIJI, was strong. In the late period, a retired emperor ruled the government (INSEI), and warriors began to obtain political power.

へいあんじんぐう 平安神宮〘神社〙 Heian Jingu Shrine. Is located in Kyoto City and enshrines Emperor Kanmu and Emperor Koumei. Was founded in 1895 by Kyoto City to commemorate the 1,100th anniversary since the capital was relocated from Nara to Kyoto. Famous for the Festival of Ages. →桓武天皇；孝明天皇；時代祭

へいか 瓶花〘華道〙 arranging flowers in a deep container such as a vase or jar.

へいきんじゅみょう 平均寿命 〘生活〙 the average life span. That of Japanese is 86.8 years for women and 80.5 years for men as of 2017.

べいぐんきち 米軍基地〘軍事・外交〙 ⇨在日米軍基地

へいけ 平家〘武士〙 ⇨平氏

へいけものがたり 平家物語〘文芸・作品〙 *The Tale of the Heike*. A war chronicle whose author and year written are unknown. Describes the glory and the fall of the Taira clan in the 12th century, based on a Buddhist view of life as transient and empty.

べいごま 貝独楽〘玩具〙 a small top without a stem. Was originally made from a seashell.

へいさらくがん 平沙落雁〘絵画〙 Wild Geese Descending on a Sandbank. One of the Eight Views of Xiaoxiang. →瀟湘(しょうしょう)八景

へいし 平氏〘武士〙 the Taira clan. The offspring of Emperor Kanmu. Defeated the Minamoto clan in the Hougen and Heiji Rebellions of 1156 and 1159 and established the first warrior administration, led by TAIRA NO KIYOMORI. After Kiyomori died, was destroyed in 1185 by the surviving members of the Minamoto clan. ↔源氏

へいじ 平治〘時代〙 an era name from 1159 to 1160 in the late Heian period. The Taira clan reached its zenith.

へいじのらん 平治の乱 〘政治〙 Heiji Rebellion in 1159. After

the Hougen Rebellion, TAIRA NO KIYOMORI and a priest Shinzei, who was an aide to Ex-emperor Goshirakawa, extended their power. Minamoto no Yoshitomo and Fujiwara no Nobuyori, who opposed to them, confined the Ex-emperor and killed Shinzei while Kiyomori was out of Kyoto. After returning in haste, Kiyomori defeated Yoshitomo and Nobuyori. This event led to great prosperity of the Heike clan. →保元の乱

へいじものがたり 平治物語 〖文芸・作品〗 *The Tale of Heiji.* A war chronicle probably written in the 13th century. The author is unknown. Describes the events of the Heiji Rebellion of 1159. →平治の乱

べいじゅ 米寿 〖通過儀礼〗 the age of 88 in the traditional approach to age counting. People usually celebrate when a person turns 87, in the modern approach to age counting. 'Beiju' literally means "rice age," because when 88(八十八) is written vertically in kanji, it looks like 米, which means "rice." →数え年

へいじょうきゅうし 平城宮址 〖史跡〗 Heijo Palace, or Nara Palace Site. Is located in Nara City. Several buildings are restored, and the museum exhibits archaeological materials, photographs, and a diorama.

へいじょうきょう 平城京 〖政治〗 Heijou Capital. Was located in Nara from 710 to 784. Measured about 4.8 km north-south and about 4.3 km east-west. →平城宮跡

へいせいじだい 平成時代 〖時代〗 the Heisei period, beginning in 1989. Since Emperor Heisei is to abdicate the throne to his son in 2019, the Heisei period will end in 2019. After the collapse of the so-called bubble economy, witnessed a depression and three big earthquakes: the Great Hanshin and Awaji Earthquake in 1995, the Great East Japan Earthquake in 2011, and the Kumamoto Earthquakes in 2016. The consumption tax was introduced in 1989, and Japan hosted the Nagano Winter Olympic Games in 1998.

へいそく 幣束 〖神道〗 ⇨幣(へい)

へいのうぶんり 兵農分離 〖職業・政治〗 the separation between warriors and peasants from the 16th to 17th centuries. Before it, warriors were farmers in peacetime, and peasants were armed when necessary. →刀狩り

へいはく 幣帛 〖神道〗 the generic term for votive offerings for deities worshipped in a Shinto shrine. Includes clothes, food, drink, and money.

へいみん 平民 〖政治〗 a commoner. Was ranked below the nobility (KAZOKU) and the former samurai (SHIZOKU). This term was used from 1869 to 1947.

へいわきねんしきてん 平和記念式典 〖戦争〗 **(1)** Hiroshima Peace Memorial Ceremony. Is held on

August 6th. **(2)** Nagasaki Peace Memorial Ceremony. Is held on August 9th.

へそくり 臍繰り〖生活〗 secret personal savings. Usually not a very large amount of money.

べついん 別院〖仏教〗 **(1)** an associated head temple of a sect. **(2)** a branch temple.

べっこう 鼈甲〖工芸〗 tortoiseshell. Is used for combs or accessories.

べったらづけ べったら漬け〖食べ物〗 white radish lightly picked with salt, sugar, and mold-covered rice.

べったん べったん〖遊び〗 ⇨めんこ

べっぷおんせん 別府温泉〖温泉〗 the name of a group of eight hot springs in central Ooita Pref. One of the largest spa resorts in Japan.

べっぷし 別府市〖地名〗 Beppu City. Is located in central Ooita Pref., at the west end of Beppu Bay. Is well-known for hot springs.

べっぷわん 別府湾〖湾〗 Beppu Bay. Is located off the central coast of Ooita Pref. and surrounded by the Kunisaki and Saganoseki Peninsulas. The southwestern end of the Inland Sea.

べにざけ 紅鮭〖食べ物・魚〗 a red salmon. *Oncorhynchus nerka*. Lives in the northern Pacific Ocean. About 60 cm long and edible. The landlocked type of this species is called HIMEMASU.

べにしょうが 紅生姜〖調味料〗 red pickled ginger. Is served in thin strips or in chopped form, often on a beef bowl (GYUUDON) or fried noodles (YAKISOBA).

べにばな 紅花〖植物〗 safflower. *Carthamus tinctorius*. Native to the Middle East. Is said to have been introduced from Korea in the 6th or 7th century. Its flowers are used for dyestuff and rouge for lips. Cooking oil is extracted from its seeds. The chief producing district is Yamagata Pref.

べねでぃくと ベネディクト〖人文学〗 ⇨ルース・ベネディクト

へのへのもへじ へのへのもへじ〖遊び〗 an easy face-drawing with hiragana characters. Two へ(he) make the eyebrows, two の(no) make the eyes, one も(mo) makes the nose, one へ(he) makes the mouth, and one じ(ji) makes the outline of the face. Another version is he-no-he-no-mo-he-no.

へび 蛇〖動物〗 the generic term for snakes. Common snakes in Japan include rat snakes (AODAISHOU), striped snakes (SHIMAHEBI), and pit vipers (MAMUSHI). It was said in olden times that a snake lived in a human house as a guardian. In the Japanese myth, the God of Storms (SUSANOO NO MIKOTO) exterminated a monster serpent (YAMATA NO ORO-CHI), and the deity enshrined into OOMIWA JINJA was transformed into a snake. →巳(み)

へぼん ヘボン〖言語〗 James Curtis Hepburn. 1815-1911. An American missionary doctor. Came to Japan in 1859 and left in 1892. Invented the Hepburn system of writing

Japanese in the alphabet and compiled the first Japanese-English dictionary, *A Japanese and English Dictionary: with an English and Japanese Index*, in 1867. →和英語林集成

へぼんしきろおまじ ヘボン式ローマ字 〔言語〕 the Hepburn system of writing Japanese in the Roman alphabet. Some sounds are expressed in different ways from the statutory system. For example, ち is written as 'chi' in the Hepburn system while it is written as 'ti' in the statutory system. ↔訓令式ローマ字

ぺりい ペリー 〔外交〕 Matthew C. Perry. 1794–1858. An American naval officer who led a four-ship fleet that arrived in Japan in July 1853. Was instructed by U.S. President Millard Fillmore to begin trade with Japan. Forced shogunal authorities to sign in 1854 a document that came to be known as the Kanagawa Treaty. It triggered Japan to open its door to the world after over two hundred years of virtual isolation.

べるさいゆのばら ベルサイユの薔薇 〔漫画〕 *Rose of Versailles*. A history manga, written and illustrated by Ikeda Riyoko. Describes the life of Lady Oscar and Princess Marie Antoinette in France. Was published serially in a girls' magazine, *Margaret*, from 1972 to 1973.

へん 偏 〔漢字〕 the left-side radical of a KANJI. Literally means "imbalance." There are many 'hen,' each

of which usually suggests the main meaning of the kanji. Includes SAN-ZUI-HEN, meaning "water," and KI-HEN, meaning "tree." ↔旁(つくり)

へんか 返歌 〔文芸〕 a short rhyming poem composed in reply to another person's poem.

べんがら 紅殻 〔美術・建築〕 Indian red, or iron oxide red. Its name comes from the Bengal region.

べんけい 弁慶 〔武士〕 ?–1189. A priest and a retainer of MINAMOTO NO YOSHITSUNE, born in present Wakayama Pref. Although he is depicted as a strong soldier in some documents, his actual existence is not clear.

べんざいてん 弁財天, 弁才天 〔宗教〕 the goddess of water and music. One of the Seven Deities of Good Fortune. Is usually depicted as playing a lute. The origin was the goddess of the Saravasti River in Indian mythology. Was introduced into Buddhism as the goddess of music, eloquence, fortune, and wisdom. →七福神

へんじょう 遍照 〔文芸〕 ⇨僧正遍照

ぺんしょん ペンション 〔旅〕 a Western-style tourist home. Many are located in mountainous resorts. The accommodation charge is more reasonable than an ordinary hotel or a traditional-style inn called RYO-KAN.

へんたいがな 変体仮名 〔言語〕 an unorthodox form of HIRAGANA. Was used until the end of the 19th century.

へんたいかんぶん 変体漢文 〚言語〛
quasi-classical Chinese. Is written
by Japanese with only kanji. Looks
like classical Chinese, but it has a
unique vocabulary and usage patterns that real Chinese does not
have.

べんてん 弁天 〚宗教〛 ⇨弁財天

べんとう 弁当 〚食文化〛 **(1)** portable
lunch. People usually prepare it
in a box at home and go out with
it. **(2)** a set meal in a box. Is sold at
a takeout food shop, convenience
store, or supermarket, is served at
a restaurant, or is delivered by a
caterer.

べんとうばこ 弁当箱 〚食器〛 a
lunch box. One for repeated daily
use is made of plastic, while some
more elaborate types are lacquered.
A paper lunch box is disposable.

へんろ 遍路 〚仏教〛 a pilgrimage,
or a pilgrim. Usually refers to a pilgrimage to eighty-eight temples in
Shikoku, where the priest KUUKAI
is said to have walked around as
part of his ascetic practices. →四国
八十八カ所

ほ

ぼ 戊〖干支〗 ⇨戊(つち)

ぼいん 拇印 〖ビジネス・生活〗 a thumbprint, or a thumbmark. Can be put on a document instead of a seal.

ほうい 法衣〖仏教・服飾〗 ⇨法衣(ほうえ)

ほういん 法印 〖仏教・医療・技術〗 the highest title of a priest. Was given to a priest according to his wisdom, virtue, or achievement. Was also given to a doctor, a painter, or a poet in medieval and early-modern times. →法眼；法橋

ほうえ 法会〖仏教〗 a Buddhist rite. Not only memorial services for the dead but also various Buddhist meetings in which sutra is chanted and lecture given.

ほうえ 法衣〖仏教・服飾〗 a costume of a Buddhist priest. Varies in some ways, depending on the sect and the priest's rank.

ほうえいじしん 宝永地震 〖災害〗 Houei Earthquake. Occurred in October 1707. Its magnitude is estimated to have been 8.6. Devastated the TOUKAIDOU area, the coast of Ise Bay, and the Kii Peninsula. Killed about 20,000 people. After the earthquake in the same year, Mt. Fuji erupted.

ほうえいしょう 防衛省〖行政機関〗 Ministry of Defense. Was estab-lished in 2007 by raising the status of the Defense Agency.

ほうおう 法皇〖天皇〗 a monastic Ex-emperor. The formal title for a retired Emperor who became a Buddhist priest. Emperor Uda became the first monastic Ex-emperor after retiring in 897. Some monastic Ex-emperors continued to have political power in the 12th and 13th centuries. Emperor Reigen became the last monastic Ex-emperor in 1687.

ほうおう 鳳凰〖宗教・動物〗 a phoe-nix, or an imaginary bird of luck in ancient China. Has been thought of as an auspicious sign.

ほうがく 邦楽 〖音楽〗 Japanese music. In a broad sense, includes Japanese modern music.

ほうかん 幇間〖娯楽〗 ⇨太鼓持ち

ほうき 伯耆〖旧国名〗 the old name for western Tottori Pref.

ほうきょう 法橋〖仏教〗 ⇨法橋(ほっきょう)

ほうきょういんとう 宝篋印塔 〖仏教〗 a small stone pagoda storing a sutra called Houkyouin Darani. Was used as a grave post.

ほうぐ 法具〖仏教〗 ⇨仏具

ぼうぐ 防具〖剣術〗 a set of protec-tive gear in Japanese-style fencing, KENDOU. Consists of a helmet (MEN), two gauntlets (KOTE), a torso pro-tector (DOU), and a waist protector (TARE).

ぼうくうずきん 防空頭巾〖戦争〗 an air-raid hood. Was used toward the end of World War II. →防災頭巾

ほうげん 保元 〖時代〗 an era name

from 1156 to 1159 in the late Heian period. The Hougen Rebellion occurred, and warriors began to obtain political power.

ほうげん　法眼〖仏教・医療・芸術〗 the second highest title of a priest. Was given to a priest based on his wisdom, virtue, or achievement. Was also given to a doctor, painter, or poet in medieval and early-modern times. →法印；法橋

ほうけんせいど　封建制度〖政治〗 a feudal system. The lord gives land to the vassals, and the vassals are obliged to offer tributes or military service to the lord. In Japan, was established by the Kamakura shogunate and continued until the end of the Edo period. The governance of the lord was usually inherited by one of his children.

ほうげんのらん　保元の乱〖戦争〗 Hougen Rebellion in 1156. The conflict over the succession arose in Kyoto between Ex-emperor Sutoku and Emperor Goshirakawa. Both sides tried to draw military support from the two warrior clans: Taira and Minamoto. Both clans also broke up into two subgroups and fought against each other. The Goshirakawa side won. This event triggered the warrior class's advance into political power.

ほうげんものがたり　保元物語〖文芸・作品〗 *The Tale of Hogen*. A war chronicle written in the early 13th century. The author is unknown. Describes the events of the Hougen Rebellion of 1156. →保元の乱

ぼうさいずきん　防災頭巾〖災害〗 a padded hood to protect the head in disasters. Originated as an air-raid hood during World War II. Is now considered to be a kind of emergency supply.

ほうじ　法事〖仏教〗 a memorial service. Is held on the 7th day, the 49th day, the first anniversary, the second anniversary, and in the year when a specific number of years have passed after a person's death.

ほうじちゃ　焙じ茶〖飲み物〗 roasted low-quality green tea. Low in caffeine. →番茶

ぼうしゃ　坊舎〖仏教・建築〗 ⇨僧坊

ほうじゅ　宝珠〖仏教〗 ⇨如意(にょい)宝珠

ぼうしゅ　芒種〖暦〗 one of the 24 seasonal nodes in the traditional calendar. Around June 6 in the current calendar. Means "the season for casting seeds." →二十四節気(にじゅうしせっき)

ぼうじゅつ　棒術〖武術〗 traditional martial arts with a staff weapon. Uses a long stick that is 180 cm long or a short stick that is 90 cm long.

ぼうしゅりけん　棒手裏剣〖忍者〗 a small throwing knife. About 12 to 20 cm long. There are several shapes, such as a wedge or a pen.

ほうしょう　褒章〖政治〗 Medals of Honor. The system is administered by the Cabinet Office. →紅綬(こうじゅ)褒章；黄綬(おうじゅ)褒章；藍綬(らんじゅ)褒章；

緑綬(りょくじゅ)褒章；紫綬(しじゅ)褒章

ほうじょう 方丈 〖禅・建築〗 the living quarters of the chief priest of a Zen temple. 'Jou' is a unit of length equivalent to 3 m. Namely, 'houjou' literally means "a square room with sides of 3 m each." Comes from a legend that the living quarters of Yuima-koji, an ideal lay adherent of Buddhism, was 3 m^2.

ほうじょううじやす 北条氏康 〖武士〗 1515-1571. A feudal lord born in present Kanagawa Pref. After fighting with TAKEDA SHINGEN and IMAGAWA YOSHIMOTO, concluded peace with them and ruled present Kanagawa and Saitama Prefs., the Izu Peninsula, and Tokyo.

ほうじょうえ 放生会 〖仏教〗 a ritual of releasing living things. Is implemented on August 15 of the lunar calendar, following the precept of not killing living things.

ほうじょうき 方丈記 〖文芸・作品〗 *An Account of My Hut*. An essay collection written in 1212 by KAMO NO CHOUMEI. Discusses a Buddhist view that everything is transient by describing social upheavals and natural disasters.

ほうじょうし 北条氏 〖武士・政治〗 **(1)** the Houjou clan in the Kamakura period. HOUJOU TOKIMASA helped MINAMOTO NO YORITOMO establish the Kamakura shogunate in the 1180s, and after Yoritomo's death, he and his descendants grasped political power as shogunal regents called SHIKKEN. The clan

was overthrown with the fall of the Kamakura shogunate. **(2)** the Houjou clan in the Warring States period. Had power around present Kanagawa Pref., but was destroyed in 1590 by TOYOTOMI HIDEYOSHI.

ほうじょうそううん 北条早雲 〖武士〗 1432-1519. A feudal lord who laid the foundation of the Houjou clan at Odawara, present Kanagawa Pref.

ほうじょうときまさ 北条時政 〖武士〗 1138-1215. The 1st shogunal regent (SHIKKEN) for the Kamakura shogunate, born in present Shizuoka Pref. The father-in-law of the 1st Kamakura shogun, MINAMOTO NO YORITOMO. Helped his son-in-law establish the Kamakura shogunate in the 1180s, and after Yoritomo's death, he and his descendants grasped political power.

ほうじょうときむね 北条時宗 〖武士〗 1251-1284. The 8th shogunal regent (SHIKKEN) for the Kamakura shogunate, from 1268 to 1284. Administered the defense against the Mongol Invasions in 1274 and 1281. Had strong faith in Zen and invited the priest Mugaku Sogen from Sung to found ENGAKU-JI Temple. →元寇

ほうじょうまさこ 北条政子 〖武士〗 1157-1225. The prime wife of MINAMOTO NO YORITOMO, the 1st Kamakura shogun, and a daughter of HOUJOU TOKIMASA, the 1st shogunal regent (SHIKKEN).

ほうしょがみ 奉書紙 〖生活〗 traditional Japanese paper made from the paper mulberry (KOUZO). Is pure white, thick, and soft.

ぼうず 坊主 〖仏教〗 ⇨僧侶

ぼうずし 棒寿司 〖寿司〗 bar-like sushi. Rice is shaped and pressured into a short and fat rod and is topped with ingredients such as mackerel. Is thickly sliced when eaten.

ぼうずめくり 坊主めくり 〖遊び〗 Turning up Bonze. A game using the cards for *One Hundred Poets, One Poem Each* (HYAKUNIN ISSHU). The one hundred cards consist of three types: one with a picture of a bonze, one with a picture of a lady, and one with a picture of a gentleman. Each player picks up a card from the top of one of two card stacks with the picture face down. Each stack includes about 50 cards. If the player picks up a gentleman card, he or she gets the card. If the player picks up a bonze card, he or she has to give up his or her own cards. If the player picks up a lady card, he or she gets cards other players have given up.

ほうせいきょく 法制局 〖行政機関〗 Cabinet Legislation Bureau. Writes the draft of a bill and examines laws. Resides in the House of Representatives, the House of Councilors, and the Cabinet.

ぼうたおし 棒倒し 〖スポーツ〗 pole toppling, or pole pull-down. A dangerous game played on an athletic meet at school. Each of two teams fights to pull down the opponent's pole which is defended by the other team. The one at the National Defense Academy is famous.

ぼうだら 棒鱈 〖食べ物〗 dried fillet of cod. Was produced as preserved food in Northern Japan and was mainly transported to the Kansai region.

ほうとう 餺飥 〖食べ物〗 flat wheat noodles with vegetables in miso broth. A specialty of Yamanashi Pref.

ほうねん 法然 〖仏教〗 1133–1212. A priest born in present Okayama Pref. Studied the doctrine of the Tendai sect at ENRYAKU-JI Temple and founded the Pure Land sect. His teaching focuses on chanting the phrase, NAMU AMIDA-BUTSU, which means "I put my faith in Amitabha Buddha." One of his disciples was SHINRAN. →浄土宗

ぼうねんかい 忘年会 〖娯楽〗 a year-end party. Literally means "forget-the-year party." Is usually held in December by friends, colleagues, or other social groups.

ほうのうずもう 奉納相撲 〖相撲〗 a sumo wrestling event dedicated to deities in Shinto or Buddhism.

ほうふん 方墳 〖考古〗 a square or rectangular burial mound. Was constructed around the 7th century. The biggest existing 'houfun' is the Masuyama Tumulus in Nara Pref.

ほうみょう 法名 〖仏教〗 **(1)** a dharma name, or a Buddhist religious name given to an ordained monk or nun. **(2)** a posthumous name.

ほうむしょう 法務省 〖行政機関〗 Ministry of Justice. Was established in 1952.

ほうもつかん 宝物館〖寺院・神社〗 a treasure hall, or small museum of a temple or shrine.

ほうもつでん 宝物殿 〖寺院・神社〗 ⇨宝物館

ほうもんぎ 訪問着〖服飾〗 a semi-formal women's kimono for visiting.

ほうよう 法要 〖仏教〗 ⇨法会(ほうえ)

ぼうよしょとう 防予諸島 〖地名〗 the Bouyo Islands. The islands in the Inland Sea between Yamaguchi and Ehime Prefs. Consist of some 40 islands, the largest of which is Suou Ooshima, also called Yashiro Island. Oranges are produced on many of the islands.

ほうらいさん 蓬莱山 〖宗教〗 Mountain of Eternal Life. A divine mountain in ancient Chinese legend. Was thought to exist to the east of the ocean, and to be inhabited by a hermit who was producing an elixir of life.

ほうりき 法力 〖仏教〗 the supernatural power obtained through Buddhist asceticism.

ほうりひや 抛火矢 〖忍者〗 ⇨焙烙(ほうろく)火矢

ほうりゅうじ 法隆寺〖寺院〗 Horyu Temple. The head temple of the Shoutoku sect located in northern Nara Pref. Was founded in 607 by Empress Suiko and Prince Shoutoku according to the will of Emperor Youmei. Has much Buddhist art and many buildings registered as National Treasures. Was designated a World Heritage Site in 1993. →聖徳太子

ほうりゅうじしゃかさんぞん 法隆寺釈迦三尊 〖仏教・彫刻〗 the Triad of the Historical Buddha at HOURYUU-JI Temple. Was produced in 623 by Kuratsukuri no Tori to pray for the soul of Prince Shoutoku, who passed away in 622. The masterpiece representing the style of sculptures in the Asuka culture. Wears a so-called archaic smile. →聖徳太子

ほうりん 法輪〖仏教〗 the dharma wheel, or the wheel of law. *dharmacakra*. The symbol of the teachings of the Buddha.

ほうれき 邦暦〖暦〗 ⇨和暦

ほうろく 俸禄〖武士・経済〗 ⇨扶持(ふち)

ほうろくひや 焙烙火矢〖忍者・武器〗 a grenade. Gun powder and iron pieces are sandwiched between two earthen pans. Is thrown after igniting the fuse.

ぼおかろいど ボーカロイド 〖アニメ・音楽〗 a Vocaloid. The trademark of a program to create a song when a melody and words are input into a computer. Was developed by Yamaha.

ほおずき 酸漿 **(1)**〖植物〗 a Chinese lantern, or a winter cherry. *Physalis alkekengi* var. *francheti*. Bears yellow flowers in summer and red spherical fruits in early autumn. **(2)**〖玩具〗a toy for making simple sounds in the mouth. Is made of a fruit of (1).

ぽおつますじょうやく ポーツマス条約〖外交〗Treaty of Portsmouth. Ended the 1904–1905 Russo-Japanese War, in which Japan defeated Russia. Was negotiated in August 1905 in Portsmouth, New Hampshire, in the United States. Though not present at Portsmouth, President Theodore Roosevelt mediated the treaty and received the 1906 Nobel Peace Prize for doing so. The treaty gave Japan control over Korea and required Russia to give up various territorial claims, including the southern half of Sakhalin Island. Yet Japan did not receive all that it had hoped for, such as reparation payments from Russia.

ぽおなす ボーナス〖経済〗a bonus. Is paid to an employee usually twice a year. The amount depends on the economic climate, the company's profits, and the employee's personal performance.

ほおりのみこと 火遠理命 〖神話〗the youngest son of NINIGI NO MIKOTO, and the grandfather of the first Emperor Jinmu. In mythology, was born from fire together with HODERI NO MIKOTO and HOSUSERI NO MIKOTO. Also known as YAMASACHIHIKO.

ほくえつせんそう 北越戦争〖戦争〗Hokuetsu War. A collective term of a series of battles fought around the present central Niigata Pref. during the Boshin Civil War from 1868 to 1869. The Meiji government forces defeated the alliance of feudal domains, including the Nagaoka domain, in northeastern Japan. Though defeated, the Nagaoka domain gained the reputation by fighting well, employing the latest weapons of the time.

ぼくが 墨画〖美術〗⇨水墨画

ほくぎ 北魏 〖国名〗 Bei-wei. A Chinese dynasty from 386 to 534. The style of Buddhist sculptures influenced the ones at HOURYUU-JI Temple.

ほくさい 北斎〖美術〗⇨葛飾北斎

ぼくじゅう 墨汁〖書道〗 ready-to-use fluid of India ink. Is sold in a bottle. The user does not have to rub an ink stick to make the ink.

ほくちょう 北朝〖天皇〗 Northern Court. When ASHIKAGA TAKAUJI helped Emperor Koumyou to the throne in 1336, Emperor Godaigo escaped to Yoshino in present Nara Pref., bringing the Three Sacred Treasures of the Imperial Family, and established the Southern Court. Consequently, the remaining court in Kyoto became the Northern Court. The two courts reconciled with each other when Emperor Gokameyama in the Southern Court bestowed the sacred treasures on Emperor Gokomatsu in 1392. →後醍醐天皇；三種の神器

ぼくとう 木刀〖剣術〗 a wooden

sword. Is often made of oak or loquat. Is used to practice Japanese-style fencing, KENDOU.

ほくりくしんかんせん　北陸新幹線　〖鉄道〗 Hokuriku Shinkansen. Connects Takasaki in Gunma Pref. with Kanazawa in Ishikawa Pref. Started service between Takasaki and Nagano in 1997. The extended route between Nagano and Kanazawa started service in 2015. The fastest super express, KAGAYAKI, connects Tokyo with Kanazawa in 2.5 hours without stopping at Takasaki. Otherexpress trains are named HAKUTAKA, ASAMA, and TSURUGI.

ほくりくちほう　北陸地方　〖地名〗 the Hokuriku region. The coastal area along the Sea of Japan in central Honshuu. Consists of Niigata, Toyama, Ishikawa, and Fukui Prefs. Is known for the production of high-grade rice and for snowy weather in winter.

ほくりくどう　北陸道　〖地名〗 the old name of the Hokuriku region before the Meiji Restoration. Consisted of Wakasa, Echizen, Kaga, Noto, Etchuu, Echigo, and Sado.

ぼけ　ボケ　〖芸能〗 the fool. One of the pair of a comic duo. Talks with puns, jokes, and sarcasm and goes off the main track in the dialogue. ↔ツッコミ →漫才

ほけきょう　法華経　〖仏教〗 the Lotus Sutra. The abbreviated name of the Lotus Sutra of the Wonderful Law. One of the most important sutras in Mahayana Buddhism. The Tendai and Nichiren sects are grounded on this sutra. →天台宗；日蓮宗

ぽけっともんすたあ　ポケットモンスター　〖ゲーム〗 Pocket Monsters, or Pokémon. Mixed media entertainment in which a player trains a pocket monster to let them fight each other in an imaginary universe. Each pocket monster has unique powers and features. A smartphone app called "Pokémon Go" is popular worldwide.

ほこ　鉾　〖武器〗 a double-blade halberd. The blade is slightly wide and not sharply pointed, different from a spear. A bronze type was introduced to Japan in the Yayoi period. Was used for religious services in and after the Kamakura period.

ほこへん　矛偏　〖漢字〗 a left-side radical meaning "halberd." Is used in kanji such as 矛 (pike) and 務 (serve).

ほこら　祠　〖神道〗 a small shrine. Not an official Shinto shrine, and not equipped with a torii gate. Sometimes enshrines a Buddhist deity.

ぼさつ　菩薩　〖仏教〗 a Buddhist saint. *Bodhisattva*. Trains himself or herself to attain enlightenment. There are several Bodhisattvas such as the Bodhisattva of Mercy (KANNON BOSATSU), the Bodhisattva of Wisdom (MONJU BOSATSU), and the Bodhisattva of Sunlight (NIKKOU

BOSATSU).

ほしうお 干し魚 〖食べ物〗 a dried fish. Horse mackerel (AJI) and right-eye flounder (KAREI) are popular.

ほしがき 干し柿 〖食べ物〗 a dried persimmon. An astringent persimmon is used.

ほししいたけ 干し椎茸 〖食べ物〗 dried shiitake mushroom. Is mainly produced in the Kyushu region.

ほしとりひょう 星取り表 〖相撲〗 the scoresheet of a sumo tournament. A white circle indicates a win, and a black circle indicates a loss.

ほしひゅうま 星飛雄馬 〖漫画〗 a hero in a baseball manga, *Star of the Giants*. Was a left-handed fastball pitcher in the first series but became a right-handed pitcher in the sequel.

ほじょどうし 補助動詞 〖言語〗 an auxiliary verb. Adds supplementary meaning to other verbs. Examples are 'iru' in 'tabete-iru,' which means "be eating," or 'shimau' in 'tabete-shimau,' which means "have eaten."

ぼしんせんそう 戊辰戦争 〖戦争〗 the Boshin Civil War. A part of the Meiji Restoration. The new government forces defeated the ex-shogunate forces. Started with the Battle of Toba-Fushimi in 1868 and ended with the Battle of Hakodate in 1869.

ほすせりのみこと 火須勢理命 〖神話〗 the second son of NINIGI NO MIKOTO. In mythology, was born from fire together with HODERI NO MIKOTO and HOORI NO MIKOTO.

ほそかわがらしゃ 細川ガラシャ 〖キリスト教〗 1563-1600. The second daughter of a warlord, AKECHI MITSUHIDE, and the wife of Hosokawa Tadaoki. Was baptized and got the Christian name, Gracia. Killed herself when ISHIDA MITSUNARI tried to force her to enter Osaka Castle as a hostage immediately before the Battle of Sekigahara.

ほそまき 細巻 〖寿司〗 a thin sushi roll. Vinegared rice is wrapped with purple laver (NORI) and contains several types of ingredients. TEKKA-MAKI and KAPPA-MAKI are popular examples.

ぼだいじ 菩提寺 〖仏教〗 a family temple. The graves of ancestors are located here, and the priest of the temple performs memorial services for the ancestors.

ぼだいじゅ 菩提樹 〖仏教・植物〗 a bo tree, a peepul, or a pipal. *Ficus religiosa*. Native to India. It is said that the Historical Buddha attained enlightenment under a bo tree. 'Bodaiju' growing in Japan is called *Tilia miqueliana*, which is different from a bo tree. It is native to China and sometimes planted as a substitute for a bo tree in a temple.

ぼだいだるま 菩提達磨 〖仏教〗 Bodhidharma. ?-528. An Indian priest and the founder of Zen Buddhism. Came to China and built the Shaolin Temple. Is also often depicted in pictures in Japan. The legend of his nine-year meditation facing a wall produced DARUMA doll.

ほたかだけ 穂高岳 〘山岳〙 Mt. Hotaka. The highest in the Hida Mountains, on the border between Nagano and Gifu Prefs. The highest peak is 3,190 m.

ぼたもち 牡丹餅 〘食べ物〙 a glutinous rice ball coated with sweet adzuki paste. Some are covered with sesame or soybean flour. The same food used to be called 'ohagi' in the vernal equinoctial week and 'botamochi' in the autumnal equinoctial week.

ほたるいか 蛍烏賊 〘食べ物・動物〙 a firefly squid, or a sparkling enope squid. *Watasenia scintillans*. About 5 cm long. Lights up in the dark like a firefly. Eaten as sashimi or with a mixture of miso and vinegar. Is caught abundantly in Toyama Bay.

ほたるがり 蛍狩り 〘娯楽〙 firefly catching. Is enjoyed on summer evenings.

ほたるのひかり 蛍の光 〘音楽・精神性〙 Auld Lang Syne. A Scottish folk song. The writer of the Japanese words is unknown. Is sung at a graduation ceremony. Only the melody is played at the closing time of department stores or supermarkets.

ぼたん 牡丹 **(1)**〘植物〙 a tree peony. *Paeonia suffruticosa*. Native to China and is used for Chinese medicine. **(2)**〘食文化〙 meat of a wild boar.

ぼたんなべ 牡丹鍋 〘食べ物〙 a one-pot dish with wild boar meat. Is seasoned with miso. →鍋物

ぽちぶくろ ぽち袋 〘生活〙 a small envelope for a money gift.

ほっかいどう 北海道 〘地名〙 Hokkaido. The name of an island, a prefecture, and a region in Northern Japan. The second largest island in Japan, after Honshuu, and the largest prefecture, with an area of 83,400 km^2. Its capital is Sapporo City. Produces a great deal of fish and seafood in the coastal areas, and dairy products in the farming areas. A great number of horses, cows, and sheep are raised on farms, and wild bears, foxes, and deer live in the rural areas. Tourists can find numerous hot springs and snow resorts all over Hokkaido. The coastline along the Sea of Okhotsk is the only place in Japan with a view of drift ice. The Shiretoko Peninsula in its east part was designated a World Heritage Site in 2005. Fifteen other places, including Kushiro Wetland, Lake Kutcharo, Lake Akan, and Sarobetsu Plain, were registered as Ramsar sites. Used to be called Ezo. →登別温泉；宗谷岬

ほっかいどうかいたくきねんかん
北海道開拓記念館 〘博物館〙 Historical Museum of Hokkaido. Was founded in Sapporo City in 1971 and renewed as Hokkaido Museum in 2015. →北海道博物館

ほっかいどうかいたくのむら 北海道開拓の村 〖博物館〗 Historical Village of Hokkaido. An open-air museum to exhibit architecture in the frontier period of Hokkaido from the mid-19th to early 20th centuries. People's daily lives and local industry at that time is reproduced for exhibition, including a horse-drawn trolley in summer and a horse-drawn sleigh in winter.

ほっかいどうしんかんせん 北海道新幹線 〖鉄道〗 Hokkaido Shinkansen. Started service in March 2016. Connects Shin-Aomori in Aomori Pref. with Shin-Hakodate-Hokuto in Hokkaido through the Seikan Tunnel under the sea. The express trains, HAYABUSA and HAYATE, connect the two stations in 60–70 minutes. It is expected that it will be extended to Sapporo in 2031.

ほっかいどうはくぶつかん 北海道博物館 〖博物館〗 Hokkaido Museum. Was founded in Sapporo, Hokkaido, in 2015, integrating the Historical Museum of Hokkaido and the Hokkaido Ainu Culture Research Center. Exhibits items about the nature, history, and culture of Hokkaido.

ほっきがい 北寄貝 〖食べ物・動物〗 ⇨姥(うば)貝

ほっきょう 法橋 〖仏教・医療・芸術〗 the third highest title of a priest. Was given to a priest based on his wisdom, virtue, and achievement. Was also given to a doctor, painter, or poet in medieval and early-modern times. →法印；法眼

ほづきょう 保津峡 〖地名〗 Hozukyou Ravine. Part of the upper stream of the Katsura River in northwestern Kyoto City. Famous for a two-hour sightseeing whitewater boat tour, which has been in operation since 1885. Tourists can also enjoy a nice view of the ravine from the Sagano Romantic Train for 20 minutes.

ほっく 発句 〖文芸〗 the first three lines in a linked poem, RENGA. Contains seventeen syllables. ↔挙句(あげく)

ほっけ 𩸽 〖食べ物・魚〗 an Okhotsk Akta mackerel, or an Arabesque greenling. *Pleurogrammus azonus*. About 40 cm long. Eaten grilled or dried.

ほっけじ 法華寺 〖寺院〗 Hokkeji. A nunnery of the Shingon-Ristu sect, located in Nara City. Was founded in the early 8th century as the head nunnery by Empress Consort Koumyou. The statue of the Eleven-headed Bodhisattva of Mercy is a National Treasure. →国分尼寺；光明皇后

ほっす 払子 〖仏教〗 a brush with long white hair, or a white tuft with a handle. One of the utensils for Buddhist rituals. Was originally used to chase away flies and mosquitos in daily life in India. Has the connotation of driving off earthly desires (BONNOU) in Zen Buddhism.

ほっそうしゅう 法相宗 〖仏教〗 the Hossou sect. One of the Six Sects

of Nara. Was introduced from China in 653 by the priest Doushou. Is based on the theory that all phenomena exist only in the mind, called YUISHIKI. The head temples are KOUFUKU-JI and YAKUSHI-JI Temples in Nara. →南都六宗

ぽつだむせんげん ポツダム宣言 〔外交〕 Potsdam Declaration. Was issued on July 26, 1945, by the U.S.A., the UK, and China to urge Japan to surrender. The Soviet Union joined the declaration on August 8, and Japan accepted it on August 14.

ぼっちゃん 坊っちゃん 〔文芸・作品〕 *Botchan*. A novel published in parts in the magazine HOTOTOGISU in 1906 by NATSUME SOUSEKI. Describes the life of a young Tokyoite teacher in Matsuyama, Ehime Pref., based on the author's experience.

ほっぽうりょうど 北方領土 〔外交・地名〕 Northern Territories. Have been ruled by Russia since World War II. Include the Kunashir, Habomai, Shikotan, and Iturup islands.

ほてい 布袋 〔宗教〕 Bu-dai. ?-916. An actual priest in the Tang dynasty of China. Has been considered one of the Seven Deities of Good Fortune in Japan, while being worshipped as a manifestation of the Maitreya Bodhisattva in China. Is depicted as a potbellied middle-aged man carrying a big bag. →七福神; 弥勒菩薩

ぼてふり 棒手振り 〔ビジネス〕 a hawker carrying goods with a shoulder pole in olden times.

ほでりのみこと 火照命 〔神話〕 the eldest son of NINIGI NO MIKOTO. In mythology, was born from fire together with HOSUSERI NO MIKOTO and HOORI NO MIKOTO. Known as UMISACHIHIKO.

ほとけ 仏 **(1)** 〔仏教〕 Buddha, especially the Historical Buddha. →如来 **(2)** 〔生活〕 a dead person.

ほとけのざ 仏の座 〔植物〕 a nipplewort. *Lapsana apogonoides*. One of the seven herbs of spring in a lunar calendar. →春の七草

ほととぎす ホトトギス 〔文芸〕 the name of a haiku magazine. First published in 1897 and is still being issued. The first editor was MASAOKA SHIKI, and the second was TAKAHAMA KYOSHI. Was temporarily a literary magazine from 1906 to 1912, to which NATSUME SOUSEKI contributed a novel, *I am a Cat*.

ほねつぎ 骨接ぎ 〔医療〕 a rather dated name for an osteopathic clinic. →整骨院

ほねへん 骨偏 〔漢字〕 a left-side radical meaning "bone." Is used in kanji such as 骸(dead bone) and 髄(marrow).

ほばくにもちいるほう 捕縛に用いる法 〔忍者〕 the technique to bind the captured enemy with a sword strap. One of the seven techniques of using a sword strap. →下げ緒七術

ほや 海鞘 〔食べ物・動物〕 a Japanese

ascidian, a sea squirt, or a sea pine-apple. *Halocynthia roretzi*. Eaten dressed with vinegar mixture of soy sauce and citrus juice, or in soup.

ぼら 鯔 〖魚〗 a striped mullet. *Mugil cephalus*. About 80 cm long and edible. Has different names at different stages of growth: 'haku,' 'oboko,' 'ina,' and 'todo.' Its roe is a delicacy, called KARASUMI.

ほらがい 法螺貝 〖動物・軍事〗 a trumpet shell, a conch shell, or a trumpet triton. *Charonia tritonis*. Was used for a signal in a battle-field or to drive off wild animals in mountains.

ほり 濠 〖軍事・建築〗 a moat. Was dug and filled with water to prevent an enemy from invading a castle.

ほりごたつ 掘り炬燵 〖建築〗 a low table with a heating device over a pit in the floor. Since this posture relaxes its users, some Japanese-style bars utilize 'horigotatsu' type tables over pits though they have no heating devices.

ほりたつお 堀辰雄 〖文芸〗 1904-1953. A novelist born in Tokyo. His works include *The Wind Has Risen* in 1936.

ほりもの 彫り物 〖服飾〗 ⇨刺青

ほりものし 彫り物師 〖職業〗 a tat-tooer.

ほるもんやき ホルモン焼き 〖食べ物〗 barbecued internal organs of pigs or cattle.

ほわいとでい ホワイトデー 〖暦・精神性〗 White Day. March 14. Boys give sweets to their girlfriends if they have received chocolate on St. Valentine's Day, February 14.

ぼん 盆 〖仏教〗 ⇨盂蘭盆会(うらぼんえ); 盆休み

ほんあみこうえつ 本阿弥光悦 〖芸術〗 1558-1637. A multi-talented artist born in Kyoto. Excellent in calligraphy, pottery, lacquer art, and tea ceremony. Managed an art vil-lage in the northern part of Kyoto. His works include *Writing Box with Boat and Reed Motif in Mother-of-Pearl Inlay* at the Tokyo National Museum.

ほんいんぼう 本因坊 〖碁〗 One of the seven titles in professional GO. Named after the Hon'inbou family who in the 16th century started serving ODA NOBUNAGA, TOYOTOMI HIDEYOSHI, and TOKUGAWA IEYASU. The best-of-seven title match, 'hon'inbou sen,' takes place annu-ally from May to June or July.

ぼんおどり 盆踊り 〖祭礼・遊び〗 Bon Festival dancing. People wear informal thin kimono (YUKATA) and dance around a high stage on which a singer sings. Is thought of as a custom to welcome and then send back the spirits of ancestors who come home. →盂蘭盆会(うらぼんえ)

ほんかどり 本歌取り 〖文芸〗 an ad-aptation of a classic poem or story, sometimes a Chinese classic. Was used as a technique in composing a traditional poem.

ほんがん 本願 〖仏教〗 a vow sworn by a Buddha or a Bodhisattva to save strayed living things.

ぼんかん ポンカン〚食べ物〛 a ponk-an mandarin, or tangerine. *Citrus reticulata*. Native to India. Is mainly produced in Kyushu.

ほんがんじ 本願寺〚寺院〛 **(1)**⇨石山本願寺 **(2)**⇨西本願寺 **(3)**⇨東本願寺

ほんぐう 本宮〚神社〛 **(1)** a head shrine. When a divine spirit at a shrine is newly enshrined at another shrine, the former is called 'honguu,' and the latter is called 'SHINGUU.' **(2)** an abbreviation of KUMANO HONGUU TAISHA.

ほんけ 本家〚生活〛 a head family. Before World War II, the eldest son usually succeeded his father as the head of the family, and other son(s) became independent and started a new family, called 'bunke,' which was thought of as subordinate to the head family, 'honke.' ↔分家

ぼんけい 盆景〚自然・娯楽〛 a miniature landscape on a tray. Stones, sands, and plants are arranged to express a landscape.

ぼんさい 盆栽〚娯楽〛 a bonsai, or a potted dwarf tree. To grow a miniature tree in a container by pruning and wiring roots and branches.

ぼんじ 梵字〚仏教・言語〛 Sanskrit characters. Are also called Brahmi, which means the writing system invented by Brahma, who is the creator of the world in ancient Indian mythology.

ほんじすいじゃくせつ 本地垂迹説 〚神道・仏教〛 the theory of original

reality and manifested traces. In this theory, a Shinto deity is considered to be a manifestation of a Buddhist divinity. For example, the Sun Goddess is regarded as the manifestation of the Great Sun Buddha, though the pairings are different among sects, temples, and shrines. This theory developed in the Heian period and continued until the Meiji government issued a decree for separation of Shintoism and Buddhism in the 19th century. →神仏分離

ほんしゃ 本社 **(1)**〚神社〛 ⇨本宮 **(2)**〚ビジネス〛 the headquarters of a company.

ほんしゅう 本州〚地名〛 Japan proper. The main island of Japan, shaped like an arc, which divides the Sea of Japan from the Pacific Ocean. Its area is 228,000 km^2, taking up more than half of Japan, which makes it the seventh largest island in the world. Most of Japan's ordinance-designated cities are on this island, from Sendai, Tokyo, and Yokohama in the east, through Nagoya in the middle, to Kyoto, Osaka, Koube, and Hiroshima in the west. Used to be called Akitsu-shima.

ほんしゅうしこくれんらくきょう 本州四国連絡橋 〚橋〛 Honshu-Shikoku Bridges. Include three routes: Nishi-Seto Expressway, Seto-Chuo Expressway, and Kobe-Awaji-Naruto Expressway. →しまなみ海道; 瀬戸大橋; 明石海峡大橋; 大鳴門橋

ぼんしょう 梵鐘〖仏教〗 ⇨釣鐘

ほんじょうぞうしゅ 本醸造酒〖酒〗 a good-quality sake. Is brewed from rice polished to 70% or less of its original weight. Brewing alcohol is added, but it should be 120 liters or less per one ton of rice.

ほんじん 本陣〖旅〗 an accommodation for high-ranking travelers such as court nobles, feudal lords, and shogunate officers in the Edo period. Was placed in a post station, called 'shukuba,' along the highways.

ぽんず ポン酢〖調味料〗 a mixture of soy sauce and citrus juice. Is used as a dip for a one-pot dish such as CHIRI-NABE or MIZUTAKI.

ぼんせき 盆石〖芸術〗 a miniature rock garden on a tray. Depicts a landscape with small stones and sand.

ほんぜん 本膳〖食文化〗 ⇨一の膳

ほんぜんりょうり 本膳料理〖食文化〗 traditional formal course cuisine. Is served at a ceremonial occasion. Three or five sets of dishes come to each guest on square trays. This style was established in the Edo period. → 一の膳；二の膳；三の膳

ほんぞうがく 本草学〖医療〗 herbalism. The study of herbs, animals, and minerals for medical purposes. Was introduced from China in the Nara or Heian period.

ほんぞうわみょう 本草和名〖医療〗 the oldest dictionary of traditional medicines. Was written around 918 by Fukane Sukehito. Contains about 1,000 entries, and each entry shows Chinese and Japanese names, name variations, and its producing centers in Japan.

ほんぞん 本尊〖仏教〗 the principal image of a temple. Is sometimes housed in an ornamented double-door chest, called ZUSHI, and shown to the public on special days only.

ぼんでまえ 盆手前〖茶道〗 the simplest procedure of making tea in a tea ceremony. Tea is made on a tray.

ぼんてん 梵天〖仏教〗 Deva of Heaven. *Brahman*. The deity of creation in Indian mythology. Guards the upward direction as one of the Twelve Devas. Is often paired with *Indra*, TAISHAKU-TEN.

ほんでん 本殿〖神道・建築〗 the main sanctuary building of a Shinto shrine. Is located behind the oratory and contains the sacred object wherein a deity or deities dwell. → 神体；拝殿

ほんどう 本堂〖仏教・建築〗 the main hall of a Buddhist temple. Contains the principal image of the temple. Several sects use different terms such as KONDOU in esoteric Buddhism and BUTSUDEN in Zen.

ぽんとちょう 先斗町〖地名〗 the name of an entertainment area on the west bank of the Kamo River in Kyoto. Restaurants line both sides of a narrow street. It is said that its name comes from "ponto" in Portuguese.

ほんね 本音 〖精神性〗 true feeling, or personal idea. It is often said that the 'honne' of a Japanese person is different from his or her public stance (TATEMAE).

ぼんのう 煩悩 〖仏教〗 earthly desires, disturbing emotions, evil passions, or mind poisons. Include persistence, hatred, anger, doubt, fear, self-conceit, jealousy, and so on. A Buddhist can attain enlightenment by escaping from these earthly desires. Though there are various ways of classification, it is often said that a person has 108 'bonnou.' →除夜の鐘

ほんのうじのへん 本能寺の変 〖戦争〗 the Honnou-ji Incident in 1582. ODA NOBUNAGA was attacked by his vassal, AKECHI MITSUHIDE, and committed suicide at Honnou-ji Temple in Kyoto. Only 11 days later, Mitsuhide was defeated at the Battle of Yamazaki in present Osaka Pref. by TOYOTOMI HIDEYOSHI.

ほんぱしきえもん 翻波式衣紋 〖彫刻〗 a rolling-wave technique to depict drapery on a sculpture. Round waves and sharp waves are carved alternatively to depict drapery. This style was popular in the 9th century. Examples are shown on the Healing Buddha at JINGO-JI Temple in Kyoto and the Eleven-headed Bodhisattva of Mercy at HOKKE-JI Temple in Nara.

ほんばしょ 本場所 〖相撲〗 a regular sumo tournament. There are six regular tournaments a year: January, May, and September in Tokyo, March in Osaka, July in Nagoya, and November in Fukuoka.

ほんぶたい 本舞台 〖歌舞伎〗 the main stage in a kabuki theater. Does not include the elevated passage, called HANAMICHI.

ぼんぼり 雪洞 〖生活〗 a paper-covered lamp with a leg.

ほんまぐろ 本鮪 〖食べ物・魚〗 ⇨黒鮪

ほんまる 本丸 〖軍事・建築〗 the innermost section of a castle. Usually includes a donjon. →二の丸；三の丸；天守閣

ほんやく 本厄 〖宗教・通過儀礼〗 ⇨厄年

ぼんやすみ 盆休み 〖暦〗 Bon holidays in mid-August. Usually from three or four days to nine days. Many people return to their hometowns or go travelling.

ぼんりゃくてまえ 盆略手前 〖茶道〗 ⇨盆手前(ぼんでまえ)

ほんわり 本割 〖相撲〗 a regular bout of a sumo tournament. The play-off for deciding the champion is not included.

ま

ま 間〔武術・芸能〕 a temporal vacuum between actions. Is very significant in performing or martial arts.

まいこ 舞妓〔娯楽〕 a geisha trainee in Kyoto. A girl under 18 is not permitted to serve at a banquet by law.

まいぞうぶんかざい 埋蔵文化財〔法律〕 Buried Cultural Properties. Those who try to excavate them have to submit notice to the Agency for Cultural Affairs.

まいたけ 舞茸〔食べ物・植物〕 Hen of the Woods. *Grifola frondosa*. An edible mushroom. Literally means "the dancing mushroom" because it is said that those who found it danced for joy.

まいどありがとうございます 毎度有難う御座います 〔精神性〕 "Thank you for continuous support." The full phrase is not commonly uttered; abbreviated phrases such as "maido arii" in the Tokyo area or "maido ookini" in the Kansai area are used more often, mainly at modestly priced restaurants.

まいにちしんぶん 毎日新聞〔マスコミ〕 The Mainichi Newspapers. One of the five major newspapers. Was founded in 1872 and had circulation of over three million as of 2017.

まいひめ 舞姫〔文芸・作品〕 *The Dancing Girl*. A short novel published in 1890 by MORI OUGAI. Describes the love between a Japanese government official and a German dancer.

まいわし 真鰯〔食べ物・魚〕 a sardine, or pilchard. *Sardinops melanostictus*. Lives near Japan and the Kamchatka Peninsula. About 20 cm long and edible. Eaten in several ways such as deep-fried or stir-fried, grilled, stewed, marinated, and as sashimi or sushi.

まえがしら 前頭〔相撲〕 a sumo wrestler at the fifth rank in the Grand Sumo Tournament. Namely, the lowest rank in the top division. Next to KOMUSUBI, and above JUU-RYOU. Is also called 'hiramaku.'

まえさばき 前捌き〔相撲〕 the struggle to take an advantageous position in the first moment of a bout.

まえじて 前仕手〔能〕 the first main character when the drama of a Noh or Noh farce consists of two parts. ↔後仕手(のちじて)

まえずもう 前相撲〔相撲〕 bouts between newly recruited apprentice wrestlers. Are held in the beginning of the program. Wrestlers who fight in these bouts are not listed in a ranking chart called BAN-DUKE.

まえだてもの 前立て物〔武器〕 an ornament attached to a warrior's helmet. →兜(かぶと)

まえのりょうたく 前野良沢〔科学技

術〗 1723-1803. A physician and scholar of Dutch learning, born in Edo. Translated *Ontleedkundige Tafelen* together with SUGITA GENPAKU and other scholars under the title *KAITAI SHINSHO*.

まえばしし 前橋市 〖地名〗 Maebashi City. The capital of Gunma Pref., located in its southern part. Developed as the center of the silk industry but is now famous for stock farming. Is often compared with the neighboring city of Takasaki to the southwest. While it is the political and cultural center of Gunma, Takasaki plays an important role in commerce and public transport.

まえはたひでこ 前畑秀子 〖スポーツ〗 1914-1995. A swimmer born in Wakayama Pref. The first gold medalist in the Olympic Games as a Japanese woman. Won the gold medal in the breaststroke in the Berlin Olympics of 1936.

まえみごろ 前身頃 〖服飾〗 the front cloth of the main part of a kimono. ↔後ろ身頃

まえみつ 前褌 〖相撲〗 the front part of a wrestler's loincloth, on the abdomen.

まえやく 前厄 〖宗教〗 the year before an unlucky age. In the traditional approach to age counting, these ages include 24 and 41 for men and 18 and 32 for women. →厄年; 後厄

まがいぶつ 磨崖仏 〖仏教〗 a Buddhist image carved in the niche of a cliff. Many of them are reliefs. →臼杵石仏(うすきせきぶつ); 大谷(おおや)磨崖仏

まかかしょう 摩訶迦葉 〖仏教〗 *Mahakasyapa*. One of the Ten Great Disciples of the Historical Buddha. Foremost among the disciples in renouncing desires. Led a group of monks after the death of the Historical Buddha. →十大弟子

まがたま 勾玉 〖考古〗 a comma-shaped jewel in ancient times. Was used as a necklace by passing a thread through the hole in the rounded part. The materials were agate, jade, crystal, and amber.

まがりや 曲り屋 〖建築〗 a private house with an L-shaped plan. A stable is attached to the end of the main building at a right angle. Examples are seen in Iwate Pref.

まきえ 蒔絵 〖美術〗 a decoration technique for lacquerware using the dust of gold, silver, or tin. Was invented in Japan in the Nara period and developed in the Heian period. Examples are *Writing Box with Eight Bridges* by Ogata Kourin and *Toiletry Case with Cart Wheels in Stream* whose author is unknown. Both of them are National Treasures stored at the Tokyo National Museum.

まきおとし 巻き落とし 〖相撲〗 a twisting-down technique. A technique to grab the opponent's torso, not grasping the loincloth, and to throw him down.

まきす 巻き簾 〖寿司〗 a bamboo mat to make a sushi roll.

まきずし 巻き寿司〔寿司〕 a sushi roll. Is usually wrapped with purple laver and contains a wide variety of ingredients such as rolled fried egg, vegetables, shiitake mushroom, and bottle gourd. →鉄火巻き；かっぱ巻き；軍艦巻き

まきのとみたろう 牧野富太郎〔植物〕 1862-1957. A botanist born in Kouchi Pref. Contributed to the development of plant taxonomy in Japan by collecting sample plants all over Japan and finding more than 500 species. Published *Makino's Illustrated Flora of Japan* (Makino Nihon Shokubutsu Zukan) in 1940.

まきびし 撒菱〔忍者・武器〕 a caltrop. A ninja scattered several of them on an escape route in advance, or just when trying to escape, to injure pursuers on their soles. Has a spike on each of four apexes of a regular tetrahedron so that one spike always points up vertically. Some of them were dried water chestnuts, and others were made of iron or wood.

まきもの 巻物〔絵画・文書〕 a hand scroll. Includes pictures or documents. The contents unfolded from right to left as the scroll unrolled. →絵巻物

まくあい 幕間〔芸能〕 an interlude. The interval between two acts in a play.

まくうち 幕内〔相撲〕 the top division in professional sumo wrestling. The ranks in this division are YOKODUNA, OOZEKI, SEKIWAKE, KOMUSUBI, and MAEGASHIRA.

まくした 幕下〔相撲〕 the third division in professional sumo wrestling. Next to JUURYOU and above SANDANME.

まくのうちべんとう 幕の内弁当〔食べ物〕 a variety box lunch. The most popular box lunch. Contains sesame-sprinkled rice and several other foods such as grilled fish, rolled fried egg, fish cake, and a pickled plum. Was originally invented for a theatergoer to eat during an intermission.

まくはりめっせ 幕張メッセ〔ビジネス〕 Makuhari Messe. An international convention complex located in Chiba Pref. Contains exhibition halls, conference rooms, and a multi-purpose arena.

まくま 幕間〔芸能〕 ⇨幕間(まくあい)

まくら 枕〔落語〕 a short narrative before the main story. The topic is sometimes unrelated to the main story, such as a current event or a private issue of the storyteller.

まくらえ 枕絵〔絵画〕 ⇨春画(しゅんが)

まくらことば 枕詞〔言語・文芸〕 a conventional adjectival phrase used in classical poems. Usually has five syllables and no concrete meaning. Each 'makura kotoba' exclusively modifies a specific word. For example, 'tarachineno' always modifies 'hama'(mother).

まくらざきたいふう 枕崎台風〔災害〕 the 16th typhoon in 1945. Attacked Western Japan on September 17 and 18. The lowest air pressure was 916.6 hPa, and the maximum wind speed was 30.2 m/s. The number of dead and missing people was 3,756.

まくらぞうし 枕草紙〖美術〗 a book of pornographic pictures.

まくらのそうし 枕草子 〖文芸・作品〗 *The Pillow Book.* An essay collection written around 1000 by Seishounagon. Describes nature and human affairs, based on her acute sensitivity and talent. Had a great influence on later literature as one of the two greatest female works in the Heian period, together with *The Tale of Genji* by Murasaki Shikibu. →源氏物語

まくらびょうぶ 枕屏風〖生活〗 a bedside folding screen. The height is less than 1 m, lower than an ordinary folding screen.

まぐろ 鮪〖食べ物・魚〗 a tuna. Especially a bluefin tuna. *Thunnus.* About 3 m long. One of the most popular fish for food. Eaten as sushi, sashimi, or teriyaki.

まげ 髷〖髪〗 a topknot. The form was different between men and women. Only sumo wrestlers have this hairstyle at present.

まけこし 負け越し〖相撲〗 losing more times than winning. In the top division of the Grand Sumo Tournament, sumo wrestlers have 15 bouts. If a wrestler loses 8 times, he may be demoted. ↔勝ち越し

まげもの 髷物〖文芸・芸能〗 a ge-

neric term for popular stories set in the Edo period. 'Mage' means "topknot hair style," which was popular in the Edo period.

まこ 真子〖食べ物・魚〗 roe. ↔白子(しらこ)

まごい 真鯉〖魚〗 a black carp. This term is often used to contrast with a red carp called HI-GOI, especially when talking about carp-shaped streamers called KOI-NOBORI.

まごのて 孫の手〖生活〗 a back scratcher. About 30 to 50 cm long and made of wood or bamboo. Literally means "grandchild's hand" because its end is like a baby's hand so that the user can easily scratch the back.

まさおかしき 正岡子規〖文芸〗 1867–1902. A haiku and tanka poet born in Ehime Pref. Insisted on the innovation that haiku and tanka should be brief and sketchy, thus aspiring to the simplistic style of the *Anthology of Myriad Leaves* (MAN'YOUSHUU). Edited a haiku magazine, *Hototogisu.* His disciples include a haiku poet, Takahama Kyoshi, and a tanka poet, Itou Sachio. Also loved baseball, which was introduced into Japan in 1873.

まさむね 正宗 **(1)**〖武器〗1264?–1343? A swordsmith lived in present Kanagawa Pref. **(2)**〖武器〗a sword forged by Masamune (1). There exist only a few swords with his inscription. **(3)**〖酒〗a brand name of sake. Was named around 1840 by a brewer in Nada, Hyougo

Pref. The brewer intended to call the brand 'Seishuu,' which is similar to 'seishu' in sound, meaning "sake." However, people read 正宗 as 'Masamune,' which became the name. Since 'Masamune' was very popular, many brewers mimicked the name and called their own brand '-masamune,' such as Kikumasamune and Sakura-masamune.

まさめ 柾目 〖建築〗 lumber whose wooden grain is straight and parallel. ↔板目

ましこやき 益子焼 〖陶磁器〗 the Mashiko ware. Pottery manufactured in Mashiko, southwestern Tochigi Pref. Is said to have been made first in 1853 by Ootsuka Keizaburou.

ましゅうこ 摩周湖 〖湖沼〗 Lake Mashuu. A caldera lake located in eastern Hokkaido. The area is 19.2 km². The surface is 351 m above sea level, and the maximum depth is 211 m. Famous for a high degree of transparency and frequent fogs.

ます 枡 〖食文化〗 a wooden square-shaped container to measure liquid or grains, including rice. The capacity is usually 90 cc, 144 cc, 180 cc, 900 cc, or 1.8 litters.

ます 鱒 〖食べ物・魚〗 **(1)**⇨桜鱒 **(2)** ⇨虹鱒

ますかがみ 増鏡 〖文芸・作品〗 *The Clear Mirror*. A chronicle written in the mid-14th century. Authorship is attributed to a statesman and poet, Nijou Yoshimoto. Describes historical facts from the birth of Emperor Gotoba in 1180 to the return of Emperor Godaigo from Oki Island in 1333. One of the Four Mirrors, four historical stories whose names include "mirror." →後鳥羽天皇；後醍醐(だいご)天皇；四鏡(しきょう)）

ますけっとじゅう マスケット銃 〖武器〗 a musket. A muzzle-loading gun. Was developed in Spain in the 16th century and was introduced to Japan in the 19th century.

ますざけ 升酒 〖酒〗 sake served in a square wooden cup. The cup is sometimes placed on a plate, or a small glass sometimes in the cup. In either case, sake is poured beyond the cup or glass brims.

ますせき 升席 〖芸能・相撲〗 a box seat for watching sumo wrestling or traditional performing arts.

ますらおぶり 益荒男ぶり 〖文芸〗 the masculine and placid style of poetry. KAMO NO MABUCHI claimed in the 18th century that this style was ideal and was found in the ancient *Anthology of Myriad Leaves* (MAN'YOUSHUU). The opposite concept is the feminine style, TAOYAMEBURI.

またぎ マタギ 〖職業〗 a professional hunter in the Tohoku region.

またたびもの 股旅物 〖旅・文芸〗 a generic term for stories of wandering gamblers in the Edo period.

またもの 又者 〖武士〗 ⇨陪臣(ばいしん)

まだれ 麻垂れ 〖漢字〗 an upper-to-left radical meaning "hemp." Is used in kanji such as 広 (broad), 麻 (hemp), and 磨 (polish).

まちあい 待合 〔茶道〕 a small hut without walls for waiting for the tea ceremony. Is built in a tea garden.

まちしゅう 町衆 〔行政〕 people of commerce and industry in the Muromachi period. Started autonomous organization in the urban area and created their original customs and culture.

まちどしより 町年寄 〔官位〕 a high-ranking townsman engaged in municipal administration in the Edo period. His job was different from region to region.

まちびけし 町火消 〔災害・職業〕 a fire brigade for townspeople in the Edo period.

まちぶぎょう 町奉行 〔官位〕 a feudal commissioner for governance of townspeople under the Tokugawa shogunate. Was in charge of judicature, administration, and police in big cities such as Edo, Kyoto, and Osaka.

まちや 町家 〔建築〕 a traditional merchant house. Was built along a town street. Merchants lived and worked there. Nowadays, examples of them can be observed in several areas such as Kawagoe in Saitama Pref. and Takayama in Gifu Pref.

まちやくにん 町役人 〔政治〕 a townsman engaged in municipal administration in the Edo period. Was supervised by a feudal commissioner called MACHI-BUGYOU.

まつ 松 〔植物〕 a pine. *Pinus*. Several species are grown in Japan, including red pine (AKA-MATSU), black pine (KURO-MATSU), and dwarf stone pine (HAI-MATSU). Is sometimes the subject of a painting.

まつえし 松江市 〔地名〕 Matsue City. The capital of Shimane Pref. in its northeastern part. Has two lakes, NAKA-UMI in its eastern part, and SHINJI-KO in its western part. Is rich in historic sites of ancient times such as tumuli and a provincial temple. The main sanctuary building of Kamosu Shrine and the donjon of Matsue Castle are National Treasures. Patrick Lafcadio Hearn lived in the city from 1890 to 1891.

まつえじょう 松江城 〔城郭〕 Matsue Castle. Was built in 1611 by Horio Yoshiharu. Is also called Chidori-jou. A National Treasure.

まつおばしょう 松尾芭蕉 〔文芸〕 1644-1694. A haiku poet, born in Ise of present Mie Pref. Abandoned his status as a samurai and studied haiku in Kyoto. Moved to Edo, walked around Japan, and died in Osaka. His works include *The Narrow Road to the Interior*. →奥 の細道

まっかあさあ マッカーサー 〔外交〕 Douglas MacArthur. 1880-1964. An American five-star general with long experience in Asia. Accepted the surrender of Japan on September 2, 1945. After the War, served as first head of the Supreme Commander for the Allied Powers (S.C.A.P.). Was well regarded by the Japanese and led the reform and recovery effort in post-war Japan.

まつかざり 松飾り〖暦〗⇨門松(かど)

まつごのみず 末期の水〖冠婚葬祭〗 water to moisten the mouth of a dying person. It is said that this custom came from the episode when the Historical Buddha asked for water when dying.

まつさかうし 松阪牛〖食べ物・動物〗 Japanese cattle for beef, produced in Matsusaka, central Mie Pref. Their meat is shipped throughout Japan as high-quality beef.

まつしたこうのすけ 松下幸之助〖ビジネス〗 1894-1989. A businessman born in Wakayama Pref. Invented a two-way socket and founded his own company in Osaka, which later became Panasonic. Also founded PHP Institute and the Matsushita Institute of Government and Management.

まつしま 松島〖地名〗 one of the Three Famous Views of Japan, and a Special Place of Scenic Beauty in Miyagi Pref. Matsushima Bay is dotted with more than 260 small islands where pine trees grow thick. A haiku poet, Matsuo Bashou, visited here in 1689 and referred to it in his travel diary, *The Narrow Road to the Interior*. →日本三景；奥の細道；瑞巌(ずいがん)寺

まっしゃ 末社〖神社〗 a subordinate shrine. Enshrines a deity invited from another shrine or a deity related to a deity of the head shrine. →本宮(ほんぐう)；摂社(せっしゃ)

まつだいらさだのぶ 松平定信〖武士〗 1759-1829. The feudal lord of the Shirakawa domain in present southern Fukushima Pref. Executed the Kansei Reforms as a prime minister under the 11th Shogun, Tokugawa Ienari.

まつだいらし 松平氏〖武士〗 the former name of the Tokugawa clan in present Aichi Pref. TOKUGAWA IEYASU first called himself a Tokugawa. In the Edo period, some feudal lords of Tokugawa relatives had the name of Matsudaira.

まつたけ 松茸〖植物・食べ物〗 a pine mushroom, or a matsutake mushroom. *Tricholoma matsutake*. Literally means "pine mushroom" because it grows at the foot of a Japanese red pine. Eaten grilled or as an ingredient of a clear hot soup. Smells very good and tastes wonderful, but it is quite expensive.

まつたけごはん 松茸ご飯〖食べ物〗 pine mushroom rice. Is boiled with MATSUTAKE mushrooms.

まっちゃ 抹茶〖飲み物〗 powdered green tea. Is drunk not only in the tea ceremony but also at a traditional-style teahouse. Ice cream and Western-style cake with tea flavor are also popular.

まっちゃあいす 抹茶アイス〖食べ物〗 an ice cream with green-tea flavor.

まつのうち 松の内〖暦〗 the first seven or fifteen days of the New year. After this period, New Year's decorations are removed.

まつばがに 松葉蟹〖食べ物・動物〗 a champagne crab. *Hypothalassia ar-*

mata. About 15 cm wide and in a shell. Edible.

まっぽうしそう 末法思想 〖仏教〗 the belief of the Dharma Ending Age. Was popular from the 12th to 13th centuries. According to this belief, the influence of the Buddha's teachings would diminish through three stages. In the first stage, the Age of True Dharma, people would follow the teachings of Buddha and could attain enlightenment. In the second stage, the Age of Semblance Dharma, people would practice Buddha's teaching but no one could attain enlightenment. In the third stage, the Dharma Ending Age, no one would bother to practice the Buddha's teachings. It was said that the third stage had begun in 1052. This belief triggered the establishment of new Buddhism in the Kamakura period.

まつまえずし 松前寿司 〖寿司〗 pressed and kneaded sushi with mackerel and kelp. 'Matsumae' is the old name of Hokkaido because the kelp used for this sushi comes from Hokkaido.

まつまえはん 松前藩 〖政治〗 Matsumae domain. Governed southeastern Hokkaido in the Edo period.

まつもとじょう 松本城 〖城郭〗 Matsumoto Castle. Was built in 1504 by Shimadachi Sadanaga. Is located in Matsumoto, Nagano Pref. A National Treasure.

まつもとせいちょう 松本清張 〖文芸〗 1909-1992. A novelist born in Fukuoka Pref. Wrote many detective stories based on social problems and also wrote historical novels and essays. His works include *The Legend of the Kokura Diary* (Aru Kokura-Nikki-den) in 1952, *Points and Lines* (Ten to Sen) from 1957 to 1958, and *Inspector Imanishi Investigates* (Suna no Utsuwa) from 1960 to 1961.

まつやまし 松山市 〖地名〗 Matsuyama City. The capital of Ehime Pref., and is located in its central part, facing the Inland Sea. Famous for the Dougo Hot Spring and Matsuyama Castle. Is the setting for Natsume Souseki's masterpiece *Botchan*.

まつらせいざん 松浦静山 〖武士〗 1760-1841. A feudal lord of the Hirado domain in present Nagasaki Pref. Wrote an essay collection, *Kasshiyawa*.

まつり 祭り 〖祭礼〗 a festival. Many Shinto shrines hold festivals throughout Japan. Famous examples include the Nebuta Festival in Aomori, the Kantou Festival in Akita, the Kanda Festival in Tokyo, the Gion Festival in Kyoto, the Tenjin Festival in Osaka, and the Hakata Gion Yamakasa in Fukuoka.

まつりばやし 祭り囃子 〖祭礼・音楽〗 festive music. Is played on an elaborately decorated float. The main instruments are flutes and drums.

まてがい 馬刀貝 〖食べ物・動物〗 a

razor shell, or a jackknife clam. *Solen strictus*. About 12 cm long and edible.

まな 真名〔言語〕 kanji. Literally means "formal character."

まながつお 真魚鰹〔魚・食べ物〕 a silver pomfret, or a harvest fish. *Pampus argenteus*. About 60 cm long. Eaten as teriyaki, grilled fish, or simmered fish.

まなつび 真夏日〔気象〕 a midsummer day. The daily maximum temperature is 30 degrees centigrade or higher.

まねきねこ 招き猫〔ビジネス・宗教〕 a beckoning cat figure. The figure raises its front paw to the ear just like it is inviting good luck. Is placed in the entrance of a shop.

まふゆび 真冬日〔気象〕 an ice day. The daily maximum temperature is below 0 degrees centigrade.

まほろば まほろば〔言語〕 an ancient term meaning "a great place." Is still sometimes used for a name of a restaurant, hotel, train, or project.

ままちゃり ママチャリ〔生活〕 a daily-use bicycle. Literally means "mommy's bicycle." Is equipped with a basket for shopping in front and often a child seat in the rear and is often used by a housewife. Its crossbar is low enough for a lady in a skirt to ride easily.

まみやかいきょう 間宮海峡〔海洋〕 Strait of Tartary. Is the strait between the Asian Continent and the Russian island of Sakhalin.

Connects the Sea of Okhotsk and the Sea of Japan. Despite its length of 660 km from north to south, it is only 7 km wide at its narrowest point, near the mouth of the Amur River. It is called 'Mamiya kaikyou' (Mamiya Strait) in Japan because the Japanese explorer Mamiya Rinzo discovered in 1808-1809 that Sakhalin was not a peninsula but an island.

まみやりんぞう 間宮林蔵〔科学技術〕 1780-1844. An explorer, born in present Ibaraki Pref. Learned land surveying from INOU TADATAKA and discovered that Sakhalin is an island.

まむし 蝮〔動物〕 a pit viper. *Agkistrodon blomhoffi*. Grayish brown and about 50 cm long. Ranges from Hokkaido to Kagoshima.

まむしざけ 蝮酒〔医療・酒〕 pit viper spirits. Are produced by soaking the snake alive in spirits. Is thought of as a tonic.

まめごはん 豆ご飯〔食べ物〕 rice boiled with peas. Soy beans can be used instead of peas.

まめしぼり 豆絞り〔文様〕 a spotted pattern. Is used for a hand towel or a light summer kimono called YUKATA.

まめたん 豆炭〔生活〕 an oval block of pressed coal dust. Was used for a low table with a heater called KOTATSU. Is now obsolete.

まめへん 豆偏〔漢字〕 a left-side radical meaning "beans." Is used in kanji such as 頭 (head) and 豌 (pea). →偏；部首

まめまき 豆撒き〖暦・宗教〗 bean scattering. People throw parched soybeans outward to expel evil spirits and inward to invite good luck while shouting "Get out demons, come on good luck." After scattering the beans, they eat the remaining beans in the same number as their age. →節分

まめもやし 豆萌やし〖食べ物〗 a beansprout with its seed remaining. A beansprout without the seed is called MOYASHI.

まもりぶくろ 守り袋〖宗教〗 a talisman case. A colorful cloth pouch with a drawstring.

まゆだま 繭玉〖年中行事〗 New Year's ornament of a twig attached to rice cakes shaped like cocoons.

まよいばし 迷い箸〖食文化〗 to move chopsticks back and forth over dishes, hesitating to choose which food to eat. Is regarded as bad etiquette, known as kirai-bashi.

まらそん マラソン〖スポーツ〗 a marathon. The first race titled "marathon" in Japan was held in 1909. Takahashi Naoko won the gold medal in the Sydney Olympic Games in 2000. A great number of fun run marathons are held throughout Japan.

まりあかんのん マリア観音〖キリスト教・仏教〗 Bodhisattva of Mercy worshipped by hidden Christians as a substitute for the Virgin Mary in the Edo period.

まりしてん 摩利支天〖仏教〗 the deity of heat haze. *Marici*. Was a daughter of the deity Brahman in ancient India. In Japan, was worshipped as a guardian deity of the samurai. Is said to possess a power to hide herself.

まりも 毬藻〖植物〗 a moss ball, or a round green alga. *Cladophora sauteri*, or *Aegagropila linnaei*. Grows in freshwater and forms a green ball. The one in Hokkaido is a Special Natural Monument.

まる 丸〖言語〗 **(1)** a circle meaning correct or all right. Is used in a school exam. **(2)**⇨句点

まるおび 丸帯〖服飾〗 a formal broad sash for a women's kimono.

まるぼし 丸干し〖食べ物〗 a white radish or fish dried whole.

まるほんもの 丸本物〖歌舞伎・文楽〗 a kabuki play whose story has been introduced from a traditional puppet theater called NINGYOU JOURURI.

まるまげ 丸髷〖髪〗 a traditional hairdo for married women. The hair is curved toward the back of the head.

まるやまおうきょ 円山応挙〖絵画〗 1733-1795. A painter born in present Kyoto Pref. Invented his unique style by synthesizing the Western perspective technique and the Japanese decorative technique. His works include *Pine Trees in Snow* at the Mitsui Memorial Museum in Tokyo.

まるやままさお 丸山真男〖人文学〗 1914-1996. A researcher of

political science and history of political philosophy. His works include *Studies in the Intellectual History of Tokugawa Japan* (Nihon Seijishisou-shi Kenkyuu) in 1952.

まわし 回し〘相撲〙 a loincloth. A sumo wrestler's belt. →化粧回し

まわりしょうぎ 周り将棋〘遊び〙 a go-around game using a Japanese chessboard. A piece moves on the outermost squares, as in backgammon. If a piece stops at one of the four corners, it is promoted to the next rank.

まわりどうろう 回り灯籠〘生活〙 a revolving lantern. Heated air from a candle inside rotates a cylinder with several paper cuts, and pictures that are projected on the translucent outer cover move.

まわりぶたい 回り舞台〘歌舞伎〙 a revolving stage. A part of the stage is a circle that turns around to change the scene.

まんいんおんれい 満員御礼〘芸能・相撲〙 "House Full, Thank you." The sign is put up at a theater of traditional performing arts or a sumo stadium.

まんが 漫画 〘漫画〙 manga. Cartoons or comics. Current manga covers various topics such as sports, school life, love, history, business, war, and social issues. Its readers range from preschool children to middle-aged business people.

まんがきっさ 漫画喫茶〘漫画〙 a coffee house with a manga library.

The fee is paid, based on time spent there.

まんざい 漫才〘芸能〙 a comic dialogue. Is usually performed by two comedians. Started in Osaka in the early 20th century.

まんざいし 漫才師〘芸能〙 a pair of comic dialogists, or comic duo.

まんじ 卍〘仏教・文様〙 a swastika. Is used as a symbol of Buddhism or a Buddhist temple. Has no connection to the Nazis.

まんじしゅりけん 卍手裏剣〘忍者〙 a swastika-shaped throwing weapon. Is not realistic and only appears in a TV ninja drama.

まんじゅう 饅頭 〘食べ物〙 a steamed bun stuffed with sweet paste. Although a typical 'manjuu' is made from flour and contains adzuki paste, there are several other variations such as SOBA-MAN-JUU (buckwheat bun), KURI-MANJUU (chestnut bun), SAKA-MANJUU (sake bun), and CHUUKA-MANJUU (Chinese-style bun).

まんじゅうがさ 饅頭笠〘服飾〙 a round piece of headgear with a chin strap. A driver of a human-powered rickshaw often wears a black one.

まんしゅうこく 満州国 〘国名〙 Manchukuo. Japan established it in 1932, appointing the last emperor of the Qing dynasty, Pu-yi, as its emperor. When Japan surrendered in World War II, it collapsed.

まんしゅうじへん 満州事変 〘戦争〙 Manchurian Incident. With the explosion of the South Manchuria

Railway on September 18, 1931, Japan invaded Manchuria, the northeastern area in China, and established Manchukuo. This incident led to the Sino-Japanese War of 1937 to 1945.

まんじゅしゃげ 曼珠沙華 〖植物・仏教〗 **(1)**⇨彼岸花 **(2)** *manjusaka*. A white flower in heaven. A person who has seen this flower can clear away his or her bad karma.

まんだら 曼荼羅 〖仏教〗 a mandala. Represents a Buddhist universe by aligning many Buddhas and Bodhisattvas. Is used for religious rituals. There are several kinds of mandala such as the Womb World Mandala and the Diamond World Mandala. →胎蔵界(たいぞうかい)曼荼羅；金剛界曼荼羅

まんだん 漫談 〖芸能〗 a comic chat, or stand-up comedy. Different from traditional storytelling called RAKUGO, often takes up current topics and social satire, not based on a fixed story.

まんちゅういん 満中陰 〖仏教〗 ⇨ 四十九日

まんどう 万灯 〖仏教〗 rows of votive lanterns for a Buddhist service or a Shinto festival.

まんどうろう 万灯篭 〖神社〗 Lantern Festival. Is held at Kasuga Grand Shrine on the night of February 3. About three thousand lanterns are lit in the precinct. →春日大社

まんどころ 政所 〖武士・政治〗 **(1)** a home management office at the residence of a prince or a court noble in the Heian period. **(2)** a political office of the Kamakura and Muromachi shogunate.

まんのういけ 満濃池 〖湖沼〗 Mannou Pond. A large irrigation pond constructed in the 8th century. Is located in southern Kagawa Pref. Is said to have been repaired in the 9th century by the priest KUUKAI.

まんはったんけいかく マンハッタン計画 〖戦争〗 Manhattan Project. A secret research program of the United States that led to development of the first atomic bomb. Its code name "Manhattan Project" was given in 1942. It first was centered in several American research universities but soon had its own major facilities, such as those at Los Alamos, New Mexico. Just a month after the first successful test of a bomb in New Mexico on July 16, 1945, two atomic bombs were dropped on Japan in August 1945. The project continued until 1947, when the United States Atomic Energy Commission was established and became the center of nuclear research. →原子爆弾

まんぷくじ 萬福寺 〖寺院〗 Mampuku-ji Temple. The head temple of the Oubaku sect. Was founded in 1661 by Ingen, a priest from Ming, sponsored by Tokugawa Ietsuna, the fourth shogun of the Tokugawa shogunate. Is located in Uji, Kyoto Pref. Famous for Chinese-style vegetarian cuisine.

→黄檗(おうばく)宗；普茶(ふちゃ)料理

まんまく 幔幕 〖冠婚葬祭・武士〗 a curtain to indicate that a place is special. For example, a party space for a picnic, or also a temporary headquarters during the Warring States period, was surrounded by 'manmaku.' 'Manmaku' is also half hung at the entrance when a wedding ceremony or funeral is held, though its design varies. →鯨幕(くじらまく)

まんようがな 万葉仮名 〖言語〗 a writing system in which KANJI were used as phonograms. Was applied in the *Anthology of Myriad Leaves* (MAN'YOUSHUU). Some of the characters later developed into HIRAGANA or KATAKANA.

まんようしゅう 万葉集 〖文芸〗 *Anthology of Myriad Leaves*. The oldest collection of Japanese poetry. In 20 volumes. Was compiled in the 8th century, mainly by Ootomo no Yakamochi. Contains 4,536 poems, not only by people in high society but also by ordinary people living in rural areas or soldiers dispatched to northern Kyushu. The poetry style is simple and frank. →東歌(あずまうた)；防人の歌

まんりきぐさり 万力鎖 〖忍者・武器〗 chain with weights at both ends.

み

み 巳〔干支〕 the sixth of the Chinese zodiac signs. Means "snake." Recently the years 1989, 2001, and 2013 were snake years. Indicates the south-southeast in direction and around 10 a.m. for hours.

みあい 見合い〔冠婚葬祭〕 an arranged meeting for marriage. Is usually held at a restaurant or hotel through the intermediation of relatives or acquaintances as a matchmaker. →仲人

みあいけっこん 見合い結婚〔冠婚葬祭〕 an arranged marriage. In Japan, the majority of couples used to be united by arranged marriage, not by love marriage. However, the trend changed and the ratio shifted in the 1960s. As of 2014, 88% of couples were in love marriages. ↔ 恋愛結婚

みいでら 三井寺〔寺院〕 ⇨園城(おんじょう)寺

みうけ 身請け〔娯楽〕 ransoming to relieve a prostitute. In the Edo period, a prostitute usually had a debt on the brothel and had to work to redeem it. A rich sponsor paid off her debts to make her his mistress.

みうらあんじん 三浦按針〔外交〕 Williams Adams. 1564-1620. An English captain who piloted the Dutch ship Liefde that was shipwrecked on the Japanese coast in 1600. Remained in Japan for the rest of his life, and was treated favorably by the shogunate. Provided the shogunate with information on shipbuilding, navigation, and trade. Was known as Miura Anjin in Japan. Died in the northern part of present Nagasaki Pref. The novel *Shogun* (1976) by James Clavell includes a fictionalized version of his life.

みうらおり 三浦折り〔科学技術〕 the Miura fold. Was devised by a scientist, Miura Kouryou, so that a solar power panel of an artificial satellite could open and close. A sheet can easily fold or unfold by pushing or pulling the opposite angles. Is also utilized for a map or leaflet.

みえ 見得〔歌舞伎〕 a powerfully exaggerated pose in kabuki. An actor pauses his action in the middle of a performance to express heightened emotions.

みえいどう 御影堂〔仏教〕 ⇨祖師堂

みえけん 三重県〔都道府県〕 Mie Pref. Is located in central Japan, facing Ise Bay, between Aichi and Nara Prefs. Famous for the production of high-quality Matsusaka beef, lobsters, green tea, and pearls. The Ise Shrine is located in the eastern part of the prefecture, and a homeland of ninja, Iga, is located in the northern part. Used to be Ise, Iga, Shima, and part of Kii.

みがきにしん 身欠き鰊 〖食べ物〗 gutted and dried herring. The head, tail, gills, and bones have been removed, and the remaining body has been filleted.

みかさ 三笠 〖軍事・船名〗 ⇨戦艦三笠

みかじめりょう 見ヶ〆料 〖ヤクザ〗 protection money. Is forcefully exacted by YAKUZA from restaurants, bars, massage parlors, etc. in their territory.

みかたがはらのたたかい 三方原の戦い 〖戦争〗 Battle of Mikatagahara. TAKEDA SHINGEN defeated TOKUGAWA IEYASU at Mikatagahara, present Shizuoka Pref., in 1572. Ieyasu fled into Hamamatsu Castle.

みかど 御門 〖天皇〗 an old honorable term for the Emperor.

みかわ 三河 〖旧国名〗 the old name of eastern Aichi Pref.

みかん 蜜柑 〖食べ物・植物〗 the generic term for oranges. Includes UNSHUU-MIKAN, NATSU-MIKAN, and DAIDAI.

みくじ 神籤 〖宗教〗 ⇨お神籤

みくだりはん 三行半 〖結婚〗 a letter of divorce from a husband to a wife in the Edo period. Was written in three and half lines.

みけねこ 三毛猫 〖動物〗 a tortoiseshell cat. In most cases, female because of a genetic reason.

みこ 巫女 〖宗教〗 (**1**) a Shinto shrine maiden. Usually, a young woman in a white kimono and a red pleated skirt called HAKAMA. Dances in a ritual or sells talismans. (**2**) a female shaman, or a psychic medium.

みこし 神輿、御輿 〖神道〗 a portable shrine. Literally means "deity's palanquin." Has a phoenix on the top of the roof and rests on two long bars for people to carry on their shoulders. Goes around the local community during festival days. Its history began when the deity of the Usa Shrine in Kyushu was carried to TOUDAI-JI Temple in Nara to protect the construction of the Great Buddha in 749. →大仏

みことのり 詔 〖天皇・政治〗 an official imperial order, or the document containing it.

みごろ 身頃 〖服飾〗 the main part of a kimono, excepting sleeves, collars, and front gussets.

みささおんせん 三朝温泉 〖温泉〗 a hot spring in central Shimane Pref. Helpful in treating rheumatism, asthma, and neuralgia.

みざるきかざるいわざる 見ざる、聞かざる、言わざる 〖精神性〗 ⇨三猿（さんえん）

みしまゆきお 三島由紀夫 〖文芸〗 1925-1970. A novelist and playwright born in Tokyo. Tried to stage a coup at a Self Defense Forces base in Tokyo but failed and committed hara-kiri. His works include *Confessions of a Mask* (Kamen no Kokuhaku) in 1949, *The Temple of the Golden Pavilion* (KINKAKU-JI) in 1956, and *The Sea of Fertility* (Houjou no Umi) in 1970.

みしょうりゅう 未生流 〖華道〗 Misho School of Ikebana. Was

founded in Osaka in the early 19th century by Mishousai Ippo. Features the symbolic and formalistic style.

みす 御簾 〔建築〕 a bamboo blind used by noble people. The edges are decorated with cloth. →簾(すだれ)

みずあげ 水揚げ〔華道〕 treatment to help a flower draw in water by burning the cut end or soaking the cut end in hot water.

みずいり 水入り〔相撲〕 a break during a long bout. If a bout is not decided for four or five minutes, the referee declares a break. When the bout is restarted, the sumo wrestlers take the exact positions they had immediately before the interruption.

みずかがみ 水鏡〔文芸・作品〕 *The Water Mirror*. Authorship is attributed to a statesman, Nakayama Tadachika. A chronicle written in the latter half of the 12th century. Describes historical facts from the first Emperor Jinmu to Emperor Ninmyou in the 9th century. One of the Four Mirrors. →神武天皇; 四鏡(きょう)

みずがき 瑞垣〔神社〕 ⇨玉垣

みずかぜ 瑞風 〔鉄道〕 Twilight Express Mizukaze. One of Japan's most luxurious cruise trains, operated by JR West. Travels around the San'in and San'you areas, stopping at several sightseeing spots. Has two- or three-day courses.

みずき 水城〔軍事〕 Water Fortress. A long, low embankment with a moat was constructed in 664 in present western Fukuoka Pref. to defend the remote office of the Imperial Court against a possible invasion from China or Korea. It was 1.2 km long and 10 m high and partly remains.

みずきり 水切り〔華道〕 to cut the flower stem in water. Prevents air from entering the stem.

みずぐも 水蜘蛛〔忍者〕 a floating instrument, literally meaning "water spider." Four fan-shaped wooden boards surround a rectangular wooden board, forming a doughnut shape. There are several explanations about its purpose. The most likely theory says that a ninja sat on the center board and moved across the water like rowing a boat. Fins might have been worn. Another theory says that a ninja wore them on both feet and walked in a marshy place.

みずこくよう 水子供養〔仏教〕 a memorial service for a miscarried or aborted baby. Some temples specialize in such services.

みずさかずき 水杯〔精神性・戦争〕 a farewell toast with a cup of water. People exchanged small cups of water when they thought they would never see each other, such as in the case of the Kamikaze Special Attack Force.

みずさし 水指〔茶道〕 a water vessel. The tea host or hostess scoops water from it to add to a teakettle, or to rinse a tea bowl or a tea whisk.

みずたき 水炊き 〔食べ物〕 a one-pot dish of chicken, vegetables, and tofu. Is dipped into a mixture of soy sauce and citrus juice when eaten. Chopped green onion, grated white radish, or red peppers are often added.

みずち 蛟 〔妖怪〕 a river dragon, a sea serpent, a water deity, or a poisonous imaginary animal with four legs and horns. Its definition is unclear.

みずちゃや 水茶屋 〔食文化〕 a casual tea house in the Edo period. Stood along the street or in the precincts of a shrine or temple.

みずな 水菜 〔食べ物・植物〕 **(1)** a pot-herb mustard. *Brassica nipposinica* var. *oblanceolata*. Eaten as pickles or as an ingredient of soup. Is also called 'kyouna.' **(2)** *Elatostema umbellatum* var. *majus*. The young stem is edible.

みずなす 水茄子 〔食べ物・植物〕 a watery eggplant. Usually eaten lightly pickled. A specialty of southwestern Osaka Pref.

みずのえ 壬 〔干支〕 the ninth item of JIKKAN. Literally means "yang of water" or "the elder brother of water." Its Chinese-style pronunciation is 'jin.'

みずのただくに 水野忠邦 〔政治〕 1794-1851. The feudal lord of the Hamamatsu domain. Implemented the Tenpou Reforms as a prime minister under the 12th Shogun, Tokugawa Ieyoshi.

みずのと 癸 〔干支〕 the tenth item of JIKKAN. Literally means the "yin of water" or "the younger brother of water." Its Chinese-style pronunciation is 'ki.'

みずばしょう 水芭蕉 〔植物〕 a white skunk-cabbage. *Lysichiton camtschatcense*. Grows in the wetlands of Eastern and Northern Japan.

みずひき 水引 〔生活〕 decorative paper cords on an envelope for a money gift. The color and the knotting style are different, depending on the occasion. Gold and red are used on an auspicious occasion, while silver and black are used in a funeral or memorial service. In most cases, white cords are used with colored ones.

みずほ みずほ 〔鉄道〕 the fastest super express train on the San'yo and Kyushu Shinkansen. Refers to the ancient and poetic name of the nation of Japan. Most Mizuho trains run between Shin-Osaka and Kagoshima-Chuuou within 3 hours 50 minutes.

みずほのくに 瑞穂の国 〔国名〕 ⇨豊葦原(とよあしはら)の瑞穂の国

みずもち 水餅 〔食べ物〕 to preserve rice cake in water to prevent it from cracking and getting moldy.

みずや 水屋 〔茶道〕 a small kitchen for the tea ceremony. Tea utensils are kept, and the tea host, hostess, or their assistants prepare for and clear up after the tea ceremony.

みずようかん 水羊羹 〔食べ物〕 soft,

sweet, adzuki-bean paste jelly. Contains more water than ordinary YOUKAN.

みぜんけい 未然形 〔言語〕 the imperfective form. In the verb conjugation, precedes a negative auxiliary 'nai' or a volitional auxiliary 'u.' In the adjective conjugation, precedes a volitional auxiliary 'u.'

みそ 味噌〔調味料〕 miso. Brown fermented paste made from soybeans, salt, and malt called KOUJI. Is used as flavoring for a great variety of dishes such as soup and ramen. Several types of miso, including red, white, spicy, and sesame ones, are available.

みそか 三十日〔暦〕 the last day of a month. →大晦日(おおみそか)

みそかつ 味噌カツ 〔食べ物〕 a breaded pork cutlet with miso sauce. A specialty of Nagoya.

みそぎ 禊〔神道〕 a rite of ablutions. Purifying oneself by bathing in a river or sea when one is impure or before a Shinto ceremony. Originated from a story in the myth in which IZANAGI NO MIKOTO purified himself after coming back from the Land of Darkness to see his deceased wife.

みそしる 味噌汁〔食べ物〕 miso soup. A kind of soul food for Japanese people. Goes very well with boiled rice and is available at any traditional dining place, from a cheap diner to a high-class restaurant. Its ingredients greatly vary from family to family, restaurant to

restaurant, and region to region. Contains green onion, onion, white radish, eggplant, mushroom, seaweed, clam, or tofu. Since miso soup has a simple taste, the soup stock is important and has variations such as a kelp base, dried-bonito base, or dried-anchovy base. →出汁

みそづけ 味噌漬け〔食文化〕 vegetables, fish, or meat pickled in miso.

みそに 味噌煮〔食文化〕 food boiled in miso. Mackerel is popular, but other fish, meats, or vegetables are also used.

みそにこみうどん 味噌煮込み饂飩 〔食べ物〕 thick wheat noodles boiled in miso broth. Are served in an earthen flat pot with a lid. Popular in Aichi Pref.

みそひともじ 三十一文字 〔文芸〕 another term for a short rhyming poem, TANKA. Literally means "31 letters" because a tanka consists of 31 syllables.

みそらひばり 美空ひばり 〔音楽〕 1937-1989. A singer born in Yokohama, Kanagawa Pref. Her real name was Katou Kazue. Produced many hit songs. The People's Honor Award was bestowed on her after her death.

みぞれあえ 霙和え〔調味料〕 ⇨おろし和え

みだいどころ 御台所 〔武士・政治〕 the prime wife of a shogun, a minister, or other high-ranking officials.

みたけ 身丈〔服飾〕 the length of a

kimono.

みたましろ 御霊代〔宗教〕⇨神体

みたまや 御霊屋〔宗教〕 a mausoleum. Enshrines the spirit of the nobility.

みたらしだんご 御手洗団子 〔食べ物〕 a dumpling covered with sweet soy sauce. Is made from rice flour. Usually three or four balls are stuck to a skewer.

みだれがみ みだれ髪 〔文芸・作品〕 *Tangled Hair*. An anthology of TANKA love poems composed by YOSANO AKIKO, published in 1901. Contains 399 poems.

みちのえき 道の駅〔交通〕 a roadside rest area. Sells food and local specialties and provides tourist information. There were 1,117 roadside rest areas throughout Japan, as of 2017.

みちのく 陸奥〔旧国名〕the old name of present Aomori, Iwate, Miyagi, and Fukushima Prefs. This term is still sometimes used these days.

みついざいばつ 三井財閥 〔企業名〕 Mitsui business conglomerate. One of the three major zaibatsu along with Mitsubishi and Sumitomo. Was established by MITSUI TAKATOSHI at the end of the 17th century. From the 19th to 20th centuries, expanded its business to various fields, centering on banking, trading, and coal mining. After World War II, was liquidated by the order of the Supreme Commander for the Allied Powers.

みついたかとし 三井高利 〔経済〕

1622-1694. Born in Ise, present Mie Pref. Built the foundation of present Mitsui group by merchandizing kimono and exchanging money in Edo. →三井財閥；両替屋

みっきょう 密教〔仏教〕 esoteric Buddhism. Was established in India around the 7th century, by absorbing the elements of other religions. Was introduced from the Tang dynasty to Japan in the 9th century by KUUKAI and SAICHOU. The former founded the Shingon sect, and the latter founded the Tendai sect, in Japan. →真言宗；天台宗

みつぐそく 三つ具足〔仏教〕 three utensils for ornaments on a Buddhist altar. A flower vase, a candle stand, and a censer are placed in or in front of the altar.

みっどうぇえかいせん ミッドウェー海戦 〔戦争〕 Battle of Midway. A major World War II naval battle in June 1942 between Japan and the United States. Occurred at Midway Island, which Japan had intended to capture. The U.S. discovered the invasion plans and defeated the Japanese fleet under Admiral Nagumo. Was considered by many to be a turning point in the war.

みつば 三つ葉〔食べ物・植物〕 a Japanese hornwort. *Cryptotaenia japonica*. Literally means "three leaves" because its leaf consists of three small leaves. Eaten in various ways such as an ingredient in soup or a one-pot dish.

みつびしざいばつ 三菱財閥〔企業名〕 Mitsubishi business conglomerate. One of the three major zaibatsu along with Sumitomo and Mitsui. Was established by IWASAKI YATAROU and monopolized the marine transportation business of Japan with the help of the Meiji Government. Established the Mitsubishi Joint-stock Company in 1893, expanding its business to various fields. After World War II, was liquidated by the order of Supreme Commander for the Allied Powers.

みつまた 三椏〔植物〕 a paper bush, or paper plant. *Edgeworthia papyrifera*. Native to China and was introduced to Japan in ancient times. Is used to make traditional paper.

みつまめ 蜜豆〔食べ物〕 a mixture of agar cubes and cut fruits in syrup.

みつめこぞう 三つ目小僧〔妖怪〕 a three-eyed goblin. A folktale says that a raccoon dog transformed itself into a three-eyed goblin.

みとこうもん 水戸黄門〔武士〕 another name for TOKUGAWA MITSUKUNI. This term is popular because of the title of a TV drama.

みとし 水戸市〔地名〕 Mito City. The capital of Ibaraki Pref., and is located in its eastern part, facing the Pacific Ocean. Famous for Japanese apricot flowers in Kairaku-en Park, which attracts around two million visitors a year. Developed as a castle town of the Mito Tokugawa family, one of the three branches of the Tokugawa clan.

みとめいん 認印〔生活〕 an unregistered seal. Is used in Japanese daily life. A person can easily purchase several seals at stationery shops. ↔実印 →印鑑

みどりのひ 緑の日〔暦〕 Greenery Day. May 4. Originally April 29 was enacted as Greenery Day in 1989 when Emperor Shouwa passed away. Was moved to May 4 in 2007.

みどりのまどぐち みどりの窓口〔鉄道〕 a JR Ticket Office. Marked with the green logo indicating a seated person, where reservation tickets for Shinkansen and other limited express trains can be purchased. Available at most major stations, especially in large cities.

みなかたくまぐす 南方熊楠〔科学技術〕 1867-1941. A botanist and folklorist born in Wakayama Pref. Temporarily worked for the British Museum and contributed to *Nature* magazine about 50 times. His work included a collection of botanical samples, research in mucus fungi, and preservation of shrine forests.

みなづき 水無月〔暦〕 June in the traditional calendar. Means "water month" because much water is necessary for transplantation of rice sprouts during this month. →旧暦

みなまたびょう 水俣病〔公害〕 Minamata disease. A kind of organic mercury poisoning. Occurred around Minamata Bay, Kumamoto

Pref., in 1953, because of water contamination by factory wastes. In 1968 patients were officially recognized by the government as sufferers of a pollution-caused disease.

みなみあるぷす 南アルプス〔山岳〕 the Southern Alps. Another name for the Akaishi Mountains. Was named by a British climber, Walter Weston. →赤石山脈

みなみまちぶぎょう 南町奉行〔武士・政治〕 the southern feudal commissioners in the Edo period. There were two feudal commissioners to govern the Edo commoners, and they were alternately on duty for a month. One whose office was in the south was called 'Minami machi-bugyou.' ↔北町奉行 →江戸町奉行

みなもとのさねとも 源実朝〔武士〕 1192-1219. The third shogun of the Kamakura shogunate from 1203 to 1219. The second son of MINAMOTO NO YORITOMO and HOUJOU MASAKO. Was not eager to pursue political career because the real power already had passed into the hands of the Houjou clan, which for generations had acceded to the position as regent. Loved aristocratic culture in Kyoto, composed many tanka, and compiled his private edition, *The Golden Pagoda-Tree Collection of Japanese Poetry* (KINKAI-WAKASHUU). Was killed by his nephew, Kugyou, when visiting Tsurugaoka Hachiman-guu in Kamakura.

みなもとのよしいえ 源義家〔武士〕 1039-1106. A warlord born in present Osaka. Helped his father defeat the Abe clan in the Earlier Nine Years' War from 1051 to 1062. Destroyed the Kiyohara clan in the Later Three Years' War from 1083 to 1087. Through these events, solidified the foundation of the expansion of the Minamoto clan in later years. →前九年の役; 後三年の役

みなもとのよしつね 源義経〔武士〕 1159-1189. A military commander. After the Heiji Rebellion of 1159, entered Kurama-dera Temple in Kyoto and moved to Hiraizumi in present Iwate Pref., where he was put under the protection of FUJIWARA NO HIDEHIRA. Helped his elder brother, MINAMOTO NO YORITOMO, by defeating his cousin, KISO YOSHINAKA, and winning at several battles with the Heike clan at Ichinotani in present Hyougo Pref., Yashima in present Kagawa Pref., and Dan-no-ura in present Yamaguchi Pref. After conflicting with Yoritomo, escaped to Hidehira. After Hidehira's death, was killed by Hidehira's son, who submitted to Yoritomo's pressure.

みなもとのよしとも 源義朝〔武士〕 1123-1160. A warlord. The father of Minamoto no Yoritomo and Yoshitsune. Took the side of Emperor Goshirakawa in the Hougen Rebellion and won. Started the Heiji Rebellion, together with Fujiwara no Nobuyori, but was defeated.

みなもとのよりいえ 源頼家 〚武士〛 1182-1204. The second shogun of the Kamakura shogunate from 1202 to 1203. The eldest son of MINAMOTO NO YORITOMO and HOUJOU MASAKO. Opposed the council system of the Houjou clan and tried to exterminate the clan but failed. Was confined in Shuzen-ji Temple of Izu, present Shizuoka Pref., and was killed by the Houjou clan.

みなもとのよりとも 源頼朝 〚武士〛 1147-1199. The first shogun of the Kamakura shogunate. Was exiled to Izu in present Shizuoka Pref. in the Heiji Rebellion of 1159. Married HOUJOU MASAKO, a daughter of the leader of the Houjou clan, which had political power in Izu. Raised an army against the Taira clan in 1180. In 1184, dispatched his younger brother, MINAMOTO NO YOSHITSUNE, to destroy his cousin, KISO YOSHINAKA, who defeated a troop of the Taira clan in Kyoto. Completely destroyed the Taira clan by dispatching Yoshitsune to Dan-no-ura in present Yamaguchi Pref. in 1185. Became the shogun in 1192.

みなもとのよりまさ 源頼政 〚武士〛 1104-1180. A warlord and poet. Took the side of Emperor Go-shirakawa in the Hougen War and took the side of TAIRA NO KIYOMORI in the Heiji War. Afterward planned to destroy the Taira clan but failed. Famous for a legend of exterminat-ing a monster called NUE in the Hall for Imperial Ceremonies named SHISHINDEN.

みなもとのよりみつ 源頼光 〚武士〛 948-1021. A warlord. Was favored by the powerful Fujiwara clan and accumulated wealth. Famous for a legend of exterminating the leader of demons living in Mt. Ooe. →大江山酒呑童子(おおえやましゅてんどうじ)

みねうち 峰打ち 〚剣術〛 to hit the opponent with the back of a sword without cutting him.

みの 蓑 〚服飾〛 a rain cape made of straw or sedge. Was often used to-gether with a lampshade headgear called KASA.

みの 美濃 〚旧国名〛 the old name of the most part of Gifu Pref., except for its northern part which used to be called HIDA.

みのやき 美濃焼 〚陶磁器〛 Mino ware. Ceramics produced in the Mino area centering on Tajimi, Gifu Pref. Started around the 7th century and prospered in the 16th century with its unique glazing and teabowls. At present, one of the largest production areas for ceram-ics for daily use.

みぶのただみね 壬生忠岑 〚文芸〛 ?-? A poet in the early Heian period. Compiled the *Collection of Ancient and Modern Japanese Poetry* (KOKIN-WAKASHUU) in 905, together with Ki no Tsurayuki and two other poets. One of the Thirty-six Immortal Poets. →三十六歌仙

みほのまつばら 三保の松原 〚植物・

地名〗 a seashore lined with pine trees in Shizuoka City. Famous for its great view of Mt. Fuji and for the legend of a flying robe. →羽衣伝説

みまさか 美作 〖旧国名〗 the old name of northeastern Okayama Pref.

みまな 任那 〖国名〗 Imna. The vassal nation(s) of Japan in south Korea from the 4th to 6th centuries. Was destroyed in 562 by Silla. →新羅(ら)

みみなしほういち 耳なし芳一 〖妖怪・文芸〗 Earless Houichi. The story of an excellent blind lute player named Houichi, was called to a meeting of ghosts. To protect him, a priest wrote Buddhist sutras on the whole body of Houichi, excepting ears. A ghost who came to Houichi did not see him, except for his ears, and brought Houichi's ears back. Houichi was left, losing both his ears.

みみぶくろ 耳袋 〖文芸・作品〗 *Bag of Ears*. An essay collection by Negishi Yasumori, who was a feudal commissioner of Edo in the 18th to 19th centuries. Contains transcriptions of about 1,000 oral stories on samurai, Buddhism, ghosts, medicine, and funny anecdotes, which were told on the streets.

みみへん 耳偏 〖漢字〗 a left-side radical meaning "ear." Is used in kanji such as 聴 (listen), 職 (occupation), and 取 (take). →偏；部首

みやぎけん 宮城県 〖都道府県〗 Miyagi Pref. Is located in northeastern Japan. Is 7,286 km^2 in area. The capital is Sendai City, located on the coast of Ishinomaki Bay. Tourists can enjoy MATSUSHIMA, which is one of the Three Famous Views of Japan, several spas in its mountainous area, and Aobayama Castle built by DATE MASAMUNE, who governed this area from the 16th to 17th centuries. The Sendai Tanabata Festival in August is also famous. Was severely damaged in 2011 by the Great East Japan Earthquake and gigantic tsunami. Used to be a part of Mutsu.

みやげ 土産 〖精神性・生活〗 a souvenir. People often buy souvenirs, not only for family or friends but also for colleagues.

みやざきけん 宮崎県 〖都道府県〗 Miyazaki Pref. Is located in southeastern Kyushu in Western Japan. Is 7,735 km^2 in area. The capital is Miyazaki City, located on the coast of the Pacific Ocean. Is said to be the land most related to the founding of the nation and has more than 2,000 tumuli, including Saitobaru Burial Mounds. A sea-eroded rock formation named "Devil's Washboard" (Oni no Sentakuita) is famous for its scenic beauty. Used to be called Hyuuga.

みやざきし 宮崎市 〖地名〗 Miyazaki City. The capital of Miyazaki Pref. and is located in its southeastern part, facing the Pacific Ocean. The Ooyodo River runs through it.

Famous for tourist spots such as Miyazaki Shrine, Aoshima Island, and the Peace Tower.

みやさま 宮様 〖天皇〗 an Imperial prince or princess.

みやざわけんじ 宮沢賢治 〖文芸〗 1896-1933. A poet, writer of children's stories, and agricultural engineer born in Iwate Pref. His works include *Strong in the Rain* (Ame nimo Makezu) in 1931, *Matasaburo of the Wind* (Kaze no Matasaburou) in 1934, and *Night on the Galactic Railroad* (Ginga-tetsudou no Yoru) in 1941.

みやじま 宮島 〖地名〗 Miyajima Island, located in southwestern Hiroshima Pref. One of the Three Famous Views of Japan, designated a Special Place of Scenic Beauty and a Special Historic Site. Itsukushima Shrine (a World Heritage Site) is located in the north, and a big red torii stands in the water. Is also called Itsukushima. →日本三景；厳島神社

みやだいく 宮大工 〖建築〗 a shrine and temple carpenter. Not only constructs new buildings but also repairs old structures such as National Treasures.

みやのうらだけ 宮之浦岳 〖山岳〗 Mt. Miyanoura. Is located in Yaku Island, Kagoshima Pref. The height is 1,936 m, making it the highest mountain in the Kyushu region. Primitive forests of Japanese cedar spread out halfway up the mountain.

みやまいり 宮参り 〖暦・神道〗 a baby's first visit to a Shinto shrine. Parents take their newborn baby, dressed in festive clothes, to a local shrine about 30 days after birth.

みやまにしき 美山錦 〖酒・植物〗 rice for brewing sake. A chief producing area is Nagano Pref. →酒米（さかまい）

みやみず 宮水 〖酒〗 good water for sake brewing. Literally means "shrine water." Is drawn from wells in the NADA area of Koube and Nishinomiya Cities, Hyougo Pref.

みやもとむさし 宮本武蔵 **(1)**〖剣術〗 1584?-1645. An expert swordsman born in present Okayama Pref. Is said never to have been defeated in about 60 duels including a famous one with Sasaki Kojirou. Served the Kumamoto feudal domain in his later years. **(2)**〖文芸・作品〗 *Musashi*. A historical novel published in parts from 1935 to 1939. Describes the life of (1).

みゆき 行幸 〖天皇〗 ⇨行幸（ぎょうこう）

みょうおう 明王 〖仏教〗 a Wisdom King. *Vidyaraja*. Protects Buddhism with a ferocious face, as a manifestation of the Great Sun Buddha, Dainichi Nyorai. There are several Myouous, such as Fudo, Aizen, and Kujaku. →不動明王；愛染（あいぜん）明王；孔雀（くじゃく）明王；五大明王

みょうが 茗荷 〖食べ物・植物〗 a Japanese ginger. *Zingiber mioga*. It was once said that a person who ate myouga would become forgetful.

みょうこうこうげん 妙高高原 〔地名〕 a highland in southwestern Niigata Pref. Tourists can enjoy hot springs and skiing.

みょうこうにん 妙好人 〔仏教〕 a deeply pious Buddhist, especially in the True Pure Land sect. Their stories were compiled as books named *Myoukounin-den* in the 19th century.

みょうしゅ 名主 〔農業〕 ⇨名主(なぬし)

みょうじょう 明星 〔文芸〕 a poetry magazine influenced by European Romanticism movement. Was first published in 1900 by YOSANO TEKKAN. Its final issue was published in 1908.

みょうじん 明神 〔神道〕 Bright Deity. Is added as the honorific term after the names of Shinto deities or shrines. Buddhists called some Shinto deities by this term, based on syncretism between Shintoism and Buddhism. →神仏習合；大明神

みょうしんじ 妙心寺 〔寺院〕 Myoshin-ji Temple. A main temple of the Myoshin-ji school in the Rinzai sect located in Kyoto City. The Imperial villa of Retired Emperor Hanazono was converted into a Zen temple in 1337. The layout of the temple buildings is a notable example of Early Modern Zen style. Consists of 46 sub-temples. The temple bell and calligraphies are National Treasures. →臨済宗；花園天皇

みょうじんとりい 明神鳥居 〔神道・建築〕 a Myoujin-style gateway to a Shinto shrine. Consists of two slightly inclined columns, two horizontal bars, and a vertical strut between the bars. The upper bar curves gently upward toward the ends. It is the most popular style among several TORII styles. ↔神明(しんめい)鳥居

みょうつうじ 明通寺 〔寺院〕 Myotsuu-ji Temple. Was founded in 808 and is located in western Fukui Pref. Is said to have been founded by a military commander, SAKANOUE NO TAMURAMARO. The main building and the three-story pagoda are National Treasures.

みょうほうれんげきょう 妙法蓮華経 〔仏教〕 ⇨法華経

みりん 味醂 〔調味料〕 sweet sake used for seasoning. The alcohol content is about 15%, but most of the alcohol burns off during cooking.

みりんぼし 味醂干し 〔食べ物〕 dried fish with soy sauce and MIRIN flavor. A horse mackerel or sardine is often used.

みるがい ミル貝 〔食べ物・動物〕 a surf clam, or a Japanese horse clam. *Tresus keenae.* About 14 cm long. A portion of the water pipe is edible.

みるくいがい ミルクイ貝 〔食べ物・動物〕 ⇨ミル貝

みろくにょらい 弥勒如来 〔仏教〕 Maitreya Buddha. The Future Buddha. *Maitreya Tathagata.* Though he is not a Buddha yet, he will attain Buddhahood 5.67 billion years after the Historical Buddha has passed away. →弥勒菩薩

みろくぼさつ 弥勒菩薩 〔仏教〕 the Buddha-to-be. *Maitreya Bodhisattva*. Is now preaching for heavenly beings in the Tusita Heaven. Will descend to save people in this world and will attain Buddhahood 5.67 billion years after the Historical Buddha has passed away. The most famous example of the Miroku sculpture is the one at the Kouryuu-ji Temple. →兜率天(とそつ); 弥勒如来

みわやま 三輪山 〔神道・山岳〕 Mt. Miwa. Is located in northern Nara Pref. The height is 467 m. The entire mountain is worshipped as the sacred object of Oomiwa Shrine. Appeared in several poems of the *Anthology of Myriad Leaves* (MAN'YOUSHUU). →大神(おおみわ)神社

みん 明 〔国名〕 Ming. A Chinese dynasty from 1368 to 1644. Had an official tally trade system with Japan.

みんげい 民芸 〔美術・工芸〕 folkcraft. Is local, unsophisticated, and practical, originating from daily life of the common people. The word 'mingei' was coined in the folk-arts movement by YANAGI MUNEYOSHI.

みんしゅく 民宿 〔旅〕 a boarding house, or tourist home. The facilities are small and often in a traditional style. The accommodation charge is more reasonable than RYOKAN, a traditional-style inn, because 'minshuku' is usually family-run.

みんぞくぶんかざい 民俗文化財 〔行政〕 Folk Cultural Properties. Include manners and customs, folk performing arts, folk skills, and their related clothes, tools, and houses, which help one to understand the transition of the daily lives of Japanese. Are defined by the Law for the Protection of Cultural Properties.

みんちょうたい 明朝体 〔言語〕 a Japanese serif typeface. Is generally used in Japanese books, magazines, and newspapers. It is said that this typeface was used in the Ming dynasty of China.

みんぱく 民博 〔博物館〕 ⇨国立民族学博物館

みんよう 民謡 〔音楽〕 a traditional folk song. Includes lullabies and festive songs. The composer or songwriter may not be specified.

む

むえんぼとけ 無縁仏〔仏教〕 a deceased person for whose soul nobody prays.

むかえがね 迎え鐘〔仏教〕 a bell to ring to receive the spirits of the dead in the Bon Festival. →盂蘭盆会(うらぼんえ)

むかえび 迎え火〔仏教〕 a fire to welcome the spirits of the ancestors. Is lit at the house gate on the first evening of the Bon Festival. ↔送り火 →盂蘭盆会(うらぼんえ)

むかえぼん 迎え盆〔仏教〕 the first day of the Bon Festival. People receive the returning spirits of the dead. →盂蘭盆会(うらぼんえ)

むかえみず 迎え水〔仏教〕 water for welcoming ancestors' spirits. Is prepared on a Buddhist altar in the Bon Festival. →盂蘭盆会(うらぼんえ)

むかご 零余子〔食べ物・植物〕 a bulbil or brood bud of a Japanese yam. Is often boiled with rice.

むかで 百足〔妖怪〕 a centipede. Appears as a monster in several folk tales or legends. A famous story is that a military commander, Fujiwara no Hidesato, exterminated a giant centipede in present Shiga Pref. in the Heian period.

むぎちゃ 麦茶〔飲み物〕 barley tea. Is usually drunk cold in summer.

むぎとろ 麦とろ〔食べ物〕 rice boiled with barley, topped with grated yam.

むぎめし 麦飯〔食べ物〕 **(1)** rice boiled with barley. **(2)** boiled barley.

むけいぶんかざい 無形文化財〔法律〕 Intangible Cultural Properties. Include "drama, music and craft techniques," embodied by individuals or groups who have special skills. Are defined by the Law for the Protection of Cultural Properties.

むけんじごく 無間地獄〔仏教〕 ⇨阿鼻(び)地獄

むげんじごく 無間地獄〔仏教〕 ⇨阿鼻(び)地獄

むこうじょうめん 向こう正面〔相撲〕 the south side of the sumo ring. The opposite side of the main seats in the sumo arena.

むこうづけ 向付〔食文化〕 sashimi or vinegared food in a traditional-style banquet cuisine, called KAISEKI RYOURI. Is placed at the far side on an individual tray for the diner.

むさし 武蔵 **(1)**〔旧国名〕 the old name of Tokyo and Saitama Prefs., and eastern Kanagawa Pref. **(2)**〔軍事〕 ⇨戦艦武蔵

むさべつきゅう 無差別級〔柔道〕 an open-weight division. Has no weight restrictions of the participants. This division was abolished after the 1984 Olympics.

むしきかい 無色界〔仏教〕 the world of formless beings. Consists only of minds, without desires or forms. Exists on top of the three worlds. →三界

むしこまど 虫籠窓〔建築〕 a window divided by several posts. Is set on the plaster wall upstairs in a traditional-style townhouse.

むしずし 蒸し寿司 〔食べ物〕 steamed sushi. Includes vinegared rice, SHIITAKE mushroom, bottle gourd strips, and broiled conger eel. Is mainly eaten in Western Japan. →干瓢(かんぴょう); 穴子

むじな 貉〔妖怪〕 a badger or raccoon dog. Though these two animals are of different species, they were confused when appearing as a goblin in folk tales because of their similar appearance. Some 'mujina' are just mischievous while some kill people.

むしへん 虫偏〔漢字〕 a left-side radical meaning "insect" or "worm." Is used in kanji such as 蚊 (mosquito), 蛾(moth), 蛤(clam), 蛙 (frog), and 蛇(snake).

むしもの 蒸し物〔食文化〕 steamed food. Includes cup-steamed savory custard, called CHAWAN-MUSHI, and littleneck crams steamed with sake, called 'asari no saka-mushi.'

むしゃえ 武者絵〔武士・絵画〕 a picture depicting an armed warrior.

むしゃしゅぎょう 武者修行〔武士〕 samurai's errantry. A samurai traveled around to improve his sword skills. Began in the 15th century and was popular in the Edo period.

むしゃにんぎょう 武者人形〔武士・人形〕 a samurai doll. Is displayed at the Boys' Festival on May 5.

むしゃのこうじさねあつ 武者小路実篤〔文芸〕 1885-1976. A novelist born in Tokyo. Started the literary magazine *SHIRAKABA*, together with SHIGA NAOYA. His works include *Friendship* (YUUJOU) in 1919.

むじゅうじ 無住寺〔寺院〕 a temple without a live-in priest. It is said that there are more than 20,000 uninhabited temples throughout Japan as of 2015.

むしゅく 無宿〔生活・行政〕 a person removed from a family registration book in the Edo period. Did not have a residence or occupation. The reasons were various; for example, running away from home, being disinherited, or being exiled from a village.

むじょうかん 無常観〔仏教〕 a Buddhist view that everything is transient.

むじんこう 無尽講〔経済〕 ⇨頼母子講(たのもしこう)

むすびのいちばん 結びの一番〔相撲〕 the last bout of the day. Usually at least one of the wrestlers is a grand champion.

むすびばしご 結び梯子〔忍者〕 a knot ladder. A ninja can climb it by holding a rope on its knots with the big toes and the second toes.

むせんまい 無洗米〔食文化〕 wash-free rice. Bran is removed in advance by machine so that the rice does not have to be washed.

むそうこくし 夢窓国師〔仏教〕 ⇨夢窓疎石(むそうそせき)

むそうそせき 夢窓疎石〔仏教〕 1275

-1351. A Zen Buddhist priest born in present Mie Pref. Was respected by Emperor Godaigo and ASHIKAGA TAKAUJI, founded TENRYUU-JI Temple, and designed several gardens. →後醍醐(ﾟﾞ)天皇

むそうまど 無双窓 〖建築〗 a horizontal-type "hit-and-miss" window. Is made of narrow slats, with open space between each slat equal to the width of the slat.

むそくにん 無足人 〖武士〗 a samurai who did not have his own land.

むちゃく 無著 〖仏教〗 an Indian Buddhist priest. His name in Sanskrit is *Asanga*. About 310-390. Established "consciousness only" theory, YUISHIKI, together with his younger brother, SESHIN. His statue is at KOUFUKU-JI Temple.

むつ 陸奥 〖旧国名〗 **(1)** the old name of Aomori, Iwate, Miyagi, and Fukushima Prefs. At the Meiji Restoration, was divided into Mutsu (2), RIKUCHUU, RIKUZEN, IWAKI, and IWASHIRO. **(2)** the old name of Aomori Pref. and northern Iwate Pref. in the Meiji era.

むつき 睦月 〖暦〗 January in the traditional calendar. Means "communication month." Is said to derive from the cultivation of friendships at banquets during the New Year's holidays. →旧暦

むっくり ムックリ 〖音楽〗 a jaw harp, or Jew's harp. Has been played among indigenous people of Hokkaido, AINU, especially by women.

むつごろう ムツゴロウ 〖動物〗 a great blue-spotted mudskipper. *Boleophthalmus pectinirostris*. Lives only in the Ariake Sea and Yatsushiro Sea on Kyushu. Can breathe through the skin and crawls on mud at low tide. Edible.

むつむねみつ 陸奥宗光 〖政治〗 1844 -1897. A diplomat and statesman, born in present Wakayama Pref. Made an effort to revise unfair treaties with Western countries. Also signed the Shimonoseki Treaty for the Emperor, thus ending the Sino-Japanese War.

むつわん 陸奥湾 〖湾〗 Mutsu Bay. Is located between the Shimokita Peninsula and the Tsugaru Peninsula in Aomori Pref. Scallops are cultivated in large quantities. Is named after Mutsu (2).

むなかたさんじょしん 宗像三女神 〖神話〗 the Three Goddesses of Munakata: Ichikishima-hime, Tagitsu-hime, and Tagori-hime. Born when the Sun Goddess and the God of Storms opposed each other and took an august oath. They all guard the sea navigation.

むなかたしこう 棟方志功 〖美術〗 1903-1975. A woodblock-print artist born in Aomori Pref. Was colleagues with a folkcraft researcher, YANAGI MUNEYOSHI, and a potter, KAWAI KANJIROU. Received the International Woodblock Print Award at the Venice Biennial in 1956 and other international prizes. Munakata Shiko Memorial Museum of

Art is located in Aomori City.

むなかたたいしゃ 宗像大社〔神社〕 Munakata Grand Shrine. Consists of three sub-shrines: Hetsumiya, Nakatsumiya, and Okitsumiya, and enshrines the Three Goddesses of Munakata, who are all sea deities. Hetsumiya, located on the coast of Fukuoka Pref., enshrines Ichikishima-hime; Nakatsumiya, located on Ooshima Island, enshrines Tagitsu-hime; and Okitsumiya, located on Okinoshima Island, enshrines Tagori-hime.

むねあげ 棟上げ〔建築〕 the term for completing the framework of a house and raising the ridge beam on it.

むねあげしき 棟上げ式〔建築〕 a ceremony connected with raising a house ridge beam. Is held when the framework of a new house is completed, sometimes even though the house is not wooden and has no ridge beam. Began in the Heian period and is still conducted today.

むねわりながや 棟割長屋〔建築〕 ⇨ 長屋

むびょうそくさい 無病息災〔医療・宗教〕 perfect health. People pray for their health in a local religious event usually during the New Year's holidays.

むらさき 紫〔寿司〕 sushi jargon meaning "soy sauce." Literally means "purple" because of the color of soy sauce. →醤油

むらさきしきぶ 紫式部〔文芸〕 973? -1014? A novelist. After the death of her husband, wrote *The Tale of Genji* and *The Diary of Lady Murasaki*. Worked under a wife of Emperor Ichijou, named Shoushi. →源氏物語；一条天皇

むらさきしきぶにっき 紫式部日記〔文芸・作品〕 *The Diary of Lady Murasaki*. Was written from 1008 to 1010 by a female novelist, MURA-SAKI SHIKIBU. Describes her life in the court service.

むらじ 連〔政治・言語〕 a title given to a high-ranking clan in ancient times. Was attached after the clan name, like 'Mononobe no muraji.'

むらはちぶ 村八分〔組織〕 ostracism in the Edo period. As private punishment, the whole village cut relations with a family that broke a village rule.

むらまさ 村正〔武器〕 the name of a swordsmith who lived in present Mie Pref. The name was handed down from the 14th to 16th centuries. It was said that a sword with this inscription haunted its owner.

むりょうこうにょらい 無量光如来〔仏教〕 the Buddha of Infinite Light. *Amitabha Tathagata*. Another name of AMIDA NYORAI.

むりょうじゅにょらい 無量寿如来〔仏教〕 the Buddha of Infinite Life. *Amitayus Tathagata*. Another name of AMIDA NYORAI.

むろうじ 室生寺〔寺院〕 Murou-ji Temple. A main temple of the Shingon sect, located in northeastern Nara Pref. Is said to have been founded in 681 by EN NO ODUNU. Is sometimes called 'Nyonin Kouya,' meaning "Women's Mt. Kouya," because Murou-ji allowed women to enter the temple, whereas the center of the Shingon sect, Mt. Kouya, did not. The five-story pagoda, the main building, the statue of the Historical Buddha, etc., are National Treasures. →高野山

むろとたいふう 室戸台風 〖災害〗 the Muroto Typhoon. Landed at Cape Muroto in Kouchi Pref. and devastated the Kansai region in 1934. The minimum air pressure was 911.9 hPa. The number of the dead and lost was 3,036.

むろとみさき 室戸岬 〖地名〗 Cape Muroto. Is located in southeastern Kouchi Pref., facing the Pacific Ocean. Is often hit by typhoons. Japan's largest lighthouse stands at the tip of the cape. Sperm whales and dolphins can be seen there.

むろまちじだい 室町時代 〖時代〗 the Muromachi period, from 1333 to 1573. Ashikaga Takauji established the shogunate in Kyoto and acquired political power. Sometimes the period until 1392 is called the period of the Northern and Southern Courts, and the period after the Ounin War from 1467 to 1477 is called the Warring States period. →室町幕府; 南北朝時代; 応仁の乱; 戦国時代

むろまちばくふ 室町幕府 〖武士・政治〗 the Muromachi shogunate. Was established at present Kyoto in 1336 by ASHIKAGA TAKAUJI and collapsed in 1573 because ODA NOBUNAGA exiled the 15th shogun, Ashikaga Yoshiaki.

めあかし 目明し〖犯罪・行政〗 a low-ranking criminal investigator in the Edo period. Was privately hired by an official detective called YORIKI or DOUSHIN. Often used to be a criminal himself.

めいげつ 名月〖自然〗 ⇨仲秋の名月

めいじいしん 明治維新 〖政治〗 Meiji Restoration. Political, economic, and social reformation in the latter 19th century. Includes Matthew Perry's arrival in 1853, the opening of the country in 1854, the Return of Political Rule to the Emperor and the Restoration of Imperial Rule in 1867, the Boshin Civil War from 1868 to 1869, and the Abolition of Feudal Domains and the Establishment of Prefectures in 1871. The Tokugawa shogunate collapsed, and the modern Imperial nation was established. → ペリー；開国；大政奉還；王政復古；戊辰(ぼん)戦争；廃藩置県

めいじじだい 明治時代〖時代〗 the Meiji period, from 1868 to 1912. The new government was established in Tokyo, and Japan developed to a modern nation, and won two external wars against China and Russia during this period.

めいじじんぐう 明治神宮 〖神社〗 Meiji Jingu. Was founded in Tokyo in 1920 and enshrines Emperor Meiji and his wife, Empress Dowager Shouken. The Outer Precinct includes baseball stadiums and other sports facilities.

めいじてんのう 明治天皇 〖天皇〗 Emperor Meiji. 1852-1912. The 122th, on the throne from 1867 to 1912. Was supported by the anti-shogunate group and issued the edict of the Restoration of Imperial Rule in 1867.

めいじむら 明治村〖博物館〗 The Museum Meiji-mura. Was founded in Inuyama, Aichi Pref., in 1965. Exhibits more than 60 buildings from the Meiji period in the open air.

めいしゅ 銘酒〖酒〗 high-quality sake with a special brand.

めいしょう 名勝〖行政〗 a Place of Scenic Beauty. As of August 1, 2016, 398 items, including gardens, bridges, gorges, seashores, mountains, had been other places of scenic beauty of high artistic or scenic value, have been designated by the Agency for Cultural Affairs.

めいじん 名人 **(1)**〖碁〗 Grandmaster of Go. One of the seven titles in professional go. Literally means "grandmaster." The best-of-seven title match, 'meijin-sen,' takes place annually from September to October or November. **(2)** 〖将棋〗 Grandmaster of Shogi. One of the eight titles in professional shogi. The best-of-seven title match takes place annually from

April to May or June.

めいせん 銘仙〔服飾〕 reasonably priced and strong silk textile. Was produced in the Kantou region.

めいてつ 名鉄〔鉄道〕 ⇨名古屋鉄道

めいど 冥土〔仏教〕 the underwold. Includes Realms of Hells, Hungry Ghosts, and Beasts. →地獄; 餓鬼; 畜生道

めいとう 銘刀〔武器〕 a sword inscribed with the name of the swordsmith. →正宗; 村正

めいどかふぇ メイドカフェ〔娯楽〕 a maid café. Young waitresses in maid costumes serve customers as if they were their masters or mistresses. Started in Akihabara, Tokyo, at the beginning of this century, is getting popular, and has now expanded overseas.

めいにち 命日〔仏教〕 ⇨祥月(しょうつき)命日 →月命日

めいめいざら 銘々皿〔食文化〕 a small plate for each person at a table. The food is distributed onto the plates.

めいれいけい 命令形〔言語〕 the imperative form. Adjectives do not have this form.

めいれきのたいか 明暦の大火〔災害〕 Meireki Conflagration. Occurred in Edo in 1657 and killed over 100,000 people. Its origin was said to be FURISODE, a long-sleeved kimono, which was burned for a Buddhist service, so that it is also called Furisode Fire.

めえどきっさ メード喫茶〔娯楽〕 ⇨ メイドカフェ

めおといわ 夫婦岩〔神道・地名〕 Husband-and-wife rocks. Are located about 700 m off the coast of Ise City, Mie Pref. The husband rock is 9 m high above the sea, while the wife rock is 4 m high. A sacred straw rope is hung between the rocks, which are considered to be the gate to a holy rock in the sea. The sunrise can be seen between the two rocks from May to July.

めおとぢゃわん 夫婦茶碗〔食器〕 a pair of large and small rice bowls. Literally means "husband and wife bowls." The large one is for the husband, and the small one is for the wife.

めかけ 妾〔法律・セックス〕 a mistress. Had been recognized by law from the Meiji Restoration until 1882. Is not so recognized today.

めがねばし 眼鏡橋〔建築〕 a double-arched bridge. Looks like a pair of eyeglasses because of the water's reflection.

めきき 目利き〔美術〕 a connoisseur of fine arts, crafts, and swords.

めくらじま 盲縞〔服飾〕 dark-blue cotton textile with very narrow stripes.

めざし 目刺し〔食べ物〕 salted and dried sardines. Several sardines are joined with a straw or bamboo skewer that penetrates the sardines' eyes.

めし 飯〔食文化〕 **(1)** boiled rice. Is sometimes mixed with barley or beans. **(2)** a meal. Breakfast is 'asa-meshi,' lunch is 'hiru-meshi,' and dinner is 'ban-meshi,' which literally means "morning meal," "midday meal," and "evening meal," respectively.

めしぢゃわん 飯茶碗〔食器〕a bowl for boiled rice.

めしびつ 飯櫃〔食器〕⇨お櫃

めしもりおんな 飯盛り女 〔娯楽・セックス〕a waitress at an inn along a highway in the Edo period. Also worked as a prostitute.

めじろ メジロ〔食べ物・魚〕a young yellowtail. This term is used in the Kansai region when the fish is about 40 to 80 cm long. →鰤(ﾌﾞﾘ); 飯(はまち); ツバス

めだい 目鯛〔食べ物・魚〕a Japanese butterfish. *Hyperoglyphe japonica*. Eaten grilled or as sashimi.

めだか 目高〔魚〕a Japanese killifish, or Japanese rice fish. *Oryzias latipes*. About 3 cm long. Has big eyes and lives in a pond, small stream, or rice field of a plain.

めつけ 目付〔官位〕an inspector or censor in the Tokugawa shogunate. Oversaw and evaluated direct vassals of a shogun under a councilor called WAKADOSHIYORI. Each feudal domain also had a similar position for internal control.

めつけばしら 目付柱〔能〕the front-left pillar on a Noh stage.

めつぶし 目つぶし〔忍者〕a blinding missile. Contained peppers, limes, and other substances in an easily torn sac and was thrown to an enemy.

めばる 眼張〔魚〕a dark-banded rockfish, or a sea-perch. *Sebastes inermis*. About 20 cm long. Eaten often boiled.

めびな 雌雛〔人形〕a doll of an Empress Consort. Is displayed side by side with an Emperor doll on the top tier of a platform during the Girls' Festival.

めへん 目偏〔漢字〕a left-side radical meaning "eye." Is used in kanji such as 眼 (eye), 眠 (sleep), and 眺 (see). →偏; 部首

めやすばこ 目安箱〔政治〕an appeal box. Was placed in front of the supreme court of the Tokugawa shogunate. Common people posted a complaint and request in it, and the shogun personally read the contents. The system was established in 1721 by the eighth shogun, TOKUGAWA YOSHIMUNE.

めん 面 **(1)**〔剣術〕a helmet used in kendo. The front part consists up of small metal bars. **(2)**〔剣術〕a kendo technique to strike the helmet. **(3)**〔能〕⇨能面

めんきょかいでん 免許皆伝〔剣術・芸術〕full mastership. Means that a disciple receives the secret of all techniques from the master in martial arts, performing arts, or practical arts.

めんこ 面子〔遊び〕a flip-over cardboard game for boys. Players place their cards on the ground, and each of them attempts to turn over one of the others' cards by throwing his own card at it.

めんたいこ 明太子〔食べ物〕⇨辛子

明太子

めんつゆ 麺汁 〖調味料〗 noodle broth, or dipping sauce for noodles. Is made by mixing soy sauce, mirin, and soup stock.

めんぼう 麺棒 〖食器〗 a rolling pin. Is used to extend noodle dough to make thick wheat noodles called UDON or buckwheat noodles called SOBA.

めんま メンマ 〖食べ物〗 fermented bamboo shoot. Originally a Chinese food. Is formed into a stick shape and used as a topping on ramen. Is also called 'shinachiku,' which means "Chinese bamboo."

めんるい 麺類 〖食文化〗 noodles. Include UDON, SOBA, and ramen.

もうこしゅうらい 蒙古襲来〔外交〕 ⇨元寇

もうこしゅうらいえことば 蒙古襲来絵詞〔絵画〕 Scrolls of the Mongol Invasions of Japan. Were painted around 1293. A warrior, Takezaki Suenaga, had someone paint them. It is said that the painters were Tosa Nagataka and his son, but that theory has not been verified. The Imperial Household Agency possesses the original work.

もうこはん 蒙古斑〔医療・自然〕 a Mongolian spot. A blue mark around the buttocks of an infant. Is most common in darker-skinned babies. Usually disappears before adolescence.

もうしょび 猛暑日〔気象〕 an extremely hot day. The daily maximum temperature is 35 degrees centigrade or higher.

もうせん 毛氈〔生活〕 a felt rug made of animal hair. Is usually red.

もうつうじ 毛越寺〔寺院〕 Motsuji Temple. Affiliated with the Tendai sect. Is located in southern Iwate Pref. Was founded by the priest Ennin in 850 and became a cultural center of that area alongside the Chuuson-ji Temple. The existing garden made in the Heian period is designated a Special Historic Site.

もうひつ 毛筆〔書道〕 a writing brush used for traditional calligraphy called SHODOU. Different from a writing instrument with a hard tip, such as a pen or pencil. ↔硬筆

もうりもとなり 毛利元就〔武士〕 1497-1571. A warlord born in present Hiroshima Pref. Governed present Hiroshima, Yamaguchi, Tottori, Shimane, part of Okayama, part of Ooita, and part of Ehime Prefs. An anecdote about three arrows is famous though probably not a historical fact. He is said to have told his three sons that "one arrow is easy to break, but three arrows are not. So, you three have to cooperate with one another."

もえきゃら 萌えキャラ〔アニメ・ゲーム〕 a cute girl character. Appears in an anime or a computer game. Is also used as a mascot character of an event, organization, or product.

もおす モース〔科学技術〕 Edward Sylvester Morse. 1838-1925. An American zoologist who became an expert on features of Japanese culture such as its pottery, architecture, archaeology, anthropology, and natural history. Visited Japan several times, first in 1877 to study brachiopods. Was hired to teach at Tokyo Imperial University. Discovered and excavated the Oomori Shell Mound and developed his theory on Japan's natural history based on his findings. Back in the United States he was appointed director of the Peabody Academy of Sciences and lectured widely on Japan. Some of his works include *Japanese Homes and Their Surroundings* in 1886, and *Japan Day by Day* in 1917. Received the Order of the Rising Sun Third Class in 1898, and the Order of the Sacred Treasures Second Class in 1923. →大森貝塚; 旭日章; 瑞宝(ずいほう)章

もおら モーラ 〔言語〕 a mora. A phonetical unit to indicate the time length corresponding to one KANA.

もかけざ 裳懸座 〔仏教・美術〕 a robe-hanging pedestal. Depicts the state in which Buddha sits on a pedestal, with his long robe hanging at the end of the pedestal. →台座

もがみがわ 最上川 〔河川〕 the Mogami River. Flows from the foot of Mt. Azuma to Sakata City, both in Yamagata Pref. Its length is 229 km, making it the seventh longest river in Japan. Is known as one of the three fastest-flowing rivers, and MATSUO BASHOU wrote a haiku about its rapid flow.

もぎ 裳着 〔服飾〕 a ceremony for a Coming-of-Age woman to wear a traditional skirt in the Heian period. Was usually conducted when a girl became twelve to sixteen years old.

もぎげんばく 模擬原爆 〔武器〕 a dummy atomic bomb. Pumpkin bombs were dropped at 49 places in July and August of 1945, as a practice for dropping atomic bombs.

もくぎょ 木魚 〔仏教〕 a wooden slit drum for sutra chanting. Literally means "wooden fish," and patterns of fish scales are carved on the surface. Is said to have developed from a fish-shaped wooden gong, GYOBAN.

もぐさ 艾 〔医療〕 moxa. Is made from dried leaves of mugwort. Is burned for moxibustion. →蓬(よもぎ)

もくじき 木喰 〔彫刻〕 1718-1810. A priest and sculptor, born in present Yamanashi Pref. Lived on nuts and edible wild plants without eating cereals, traveled all over Japan, and carved more than 1,000 Buddhist images. His works feature round shapes and gentle smiles.

もくしんかんしつ 木心乾漆 〔仏教・彫刻〕 a sculpture technique of wood-core dry lacquer. Was popular in the 9th century. The procedure is as follows: first, the basic form is made of wood; second, linen soaked in lacquer is wrapped around the wood form in many layers; finally, the details are depicted on the lacquer. Examples using this technique include the Eleven-headed Bodhisattva of Mercy at Shourin-ji Temple in Nara. ←脱活乾漆(だっかつ)

もくとん 木遁 〔忍者〕 escape technique using wood. One of the five major techniques. Examples include hiding on or behind a tree and felling timbers to disturb pursuers.

もくもくれん 目目連 〔妖怪〕 Countless eyes on a sliding paper screen. Appeared to peep at a sleeping person when a traveler stayed at a deserted house. Is said to be related to the concept of a phrase "the walls have ears, and the sliding screens have eyes."

もくれん 木蓮〔植物〕 a lily magnolia. *Magnolia liliflora*. Bears purple flowers in spring.

もこし 裳階〔仏教・建築〕 a pent roof. The double-roof structure with a pent roof is seen at the main hall of HOURYUU-JI Temple and the pagodas of YAKUSHI-JI Temple.

もしゅ 喪主〔冠婚葬祭〕 a chief mourner. The eldest son or spouse of the dead person often does this duty.

もずく 水雲〔食べ物〕 a brown slimy seaweed. *Nemacystus decipiens*. Eaten seasoned with vinegar.

もずこふんぐん 百舌鳥古墳群〔考古〕 Mozu Burial Mounds. Are located in Sakai City, Osaka Pref. Consist of more than 100 tumuli, including the Tumulus of Emperor Nintoku, the largest keyhole-shaped burial mound. →仁徳天皇陵

もすら モスラ〔映画・動物〕 Mothra. A monster like a gigantic moth in Toho films. Debuted in 1961 and has appeared in several monster series. Though a monster, it usually fights against other evil monsters to help humans.

もだんやき モダン焼き〔食べ物〕 a savory pancake with stir-fried noodles. One of the Osaka-style OKONOMIYAKI.

もち 餅〔食べ物〕 a rice cake. Is made from glutinous rice. Eaten seasoned with soy sauce or sweetened soybean flour. Or is put into a soup, very often during the New Year's holidays.

もちごめ 糯米〔食べ物〕 glutinous rice. Is used to make rice cakes.

もちつき 餅つき〔食文化〕 to pound steamed glutinous rice into sticky dough, from which rice cakes are made.

もちねた 持ちネタ〔落語〕 a standard story in the individual repertoire of a comic storyteller.

もちゅう 喪中〔冠婚葬祭〕 the mourning period. One year after a person's death. His or her family do not send New Year's greeting cards during this period. →忌中(きちゅう)

もちゅうはがき 喪中葉書き〔年中行事〕 a mourning-notification card. Is sent to tell receivers that the sender is in mourning and will not send the New Year's cards.

もつ モツ〔食べ物〕 the internal organs of chicken, pigs, and cows. In a narrow sense, guts.

もっかん 木簡〔文書・考古〕 a thin wooden strip on which a document was written. About 3 cm wide and 20 cm long. Was used in ancient China and Japan.

もっけんれん 目犍連〔仏教〕 *Mogallana*. One of the Ten Great Disciples of the Historical Buddha. Foremost among the disciples in supernatural powers. →十大弟子

もったいない もったいない〔精神

性〗 an adjective meaning "wasteful," implying "pity, love, or fear of Mother Nature." →ワンガリ・マータイ

もつにこみ モツ煮込み 〖食べ物〗 stewed internal organs. Are often flavored with miso.

もと 酛〖酒〗 ⇨酒母(ぼ°)

もと (〜の)素〖調味料〗 convenient seasoning and ingredients. For example, 'chaahan no moto,' which literally means "base for Chinese-style stir-fried rice," contains seasoned pork and chopped green onion.

もとおりのりなが 本居宣長〖人文学〗 1730-1801. A scholar of Japanese classics and a poet, born in present Mie Pref. Researched traditional literature and philology and wrote a commentary book on *Records of Ancient Matters* (KOJIKI). A disciple of KAMO NO MABUCHI. His works include an essay collection, *Jeweled Comb Basket* (Tamakushige).

もとゆい 元結〖髪〗 a paper string to make a traditional hairstyle.

もなか 最中〖食べ物〗 a wafer cake filled with sweet adzuki paste.

ものいい 物言い〖相撲〗 a challenge to the referee's judge. Is submitted by a committee member or a waiting wrestler. The committee has a discussion in the ring as to whether the original judge should be kept or reversed. When it is reversed, the same bout is fought again.

ものだち 物断ち〖宗教〗 ⇨断ち物

もののあわれ 物の哀れ 〖精神性〗 an aesthetic sense in the Heian period. Compassion a person feels when appreciating the existence of an object.

もののけ 物の怪〖妖怪〗 an evil spirit of either a living or dead person that haunts another person. Appeared in classic literature or folk tales. Sometimes refers to a monster or bugbear.

もののふ 武士〖武士〗 an elegant term for a samurai.

もののべし 物部氏〖氏族〗 the Mononobe clan. Was mainly in charge of military and police affairs in the Imperial Court from the 5th to 6th centuries. Opposed to the reception of Buddhism and conflicted with the Soga clan.

もののべのもりや 物部守屋〖政治〗 ?-587 A head of a powerful clan. A top administrator for Emperor Bidatsu. Opposed to Buddhism and conflicted with SOGA NO UMAKO. After Emperor Youmei died, tried to let Prince Anahobe ascend to the throne but failed and was killed by Umako.

もふく 喪服 〖冠婚葬祭・服飾〗 mourning clothes. Most men wear Western costumes, while some women wear a special black kimono called TOMESODE.

もみがら 籾殻〖農林水産〗 rice chaff, or rice hulls.

もみじ 紅葉 **(1)**〖植物〗 autumnal red leaves. Since the most popular tree is maple, this term sometimes refers to "maple." **(2)**〖食べ物〗

venison. Is called so because a deer is depicted on a card of autumnal red maples in the flower matching card game, called HANAFUDA.

もみじおろし 紅葉おろし 〖調味料〗 grated mooli of red color. Is named so because 'momiji' means "autumnal red leaves." One type is the mixture of grated white radish with red pepper. The other type is the mixture of grated white radish with grated carrots.

もみじがり 紅葉狩り 〖年中行事〗 autumnal red leaves viewing. People usually enjoy autumnal leaves while walking, different from cherry blossom viewing while drinking sake.

もみじまんじゅう 紅葉饅頭 〖食べ物〗 a maple-shaped cake. Is made from flour, egg, sugar, and honey and stuffed with sweet adzuki paste. A specialty of Hiroshima Pref.

もみのり もみ海苔 〖調味料〗 small pieces of dried purple laver. Are sprinkled on rice as a topping.

もめんどうふ 木綿豆腐 〖食べ物〗 firm tofu. Literally means "cotton tofu" because a cotton cloth is used to strain off the water from the tofu. ↔絹ごし豆腐

もも 桃 〖植物・食べ物〗 a peach. *Prunus persica.* Native to China.

ももいろ 桃色 〖色〗 pink, or pale rosy. Literally means "peach color" but not a pinkish-orange color. Is sometimes associated with sex play.

ももたろう 桃太郎 〖民話〗 "Peach Boy." The hero of a folk tale. An old lady picked up a large peach floating on a river. When she cut the peach, a baby boy was born from it. After he had been raised by the lady and her husband, he left on an expedition to exterminate demons living in an island. On the way to the island, he gave millet dumplings to a monkey, a dog, and a pheasant to take them into his service. After defeating the demons, he brought back the treasures that demons had collected.

もものせっく 桃の節句 〖年中行事〗 the Peach Festival or Girls' Festival on March 3. Is celebrated by decorating special dolls, thus it is also called the Dolls Festival. →節句; 雛祭り

ももひき 股引 〖服飾〗 (**1**) tight underpants against the cold. (**2**) working pants for artisans in the Edo period.

ももやまぶんか 桃山文化 〖時代〗 the Momoyama culture. Features magnificence, gorgeousness, and freedom, reflecting the domestic unification by ODA NOBUNAGA and TOYOTOMI HIDEYOSHI and the exchange with European countries. Examples include gorgeous pictures on walls or sliding doors, genre paintings, completion of the tea ceremony, and the development of Noh. →安土桃山時代

ももわれ 桃割れ 〖髪〗 a chignon with a bun like a split peach. Was worn by teenaged girls from the late 19th to the early 20th centuries.

もやし 萌やし〚食べ物〛 a beansprout without seeds. A beansprout with seeds is called MAME-MOYASHI.

もりあわせ 盛り合わせ〚食べ物〛 an assorted food set. Several kinds of food can be used. For example, 'moriawase' of sashimi includes tuna, sea bream, and shrimp, and 'moriawase' of grilled chicken includes skin, heart, and liver.

もりおうがい 森鴎外〚文芸〛 1862 –1922. A novelist and army doctor, born in present Shimane Pref. After graduating from the Tokyo Imperial University and studying in Germany as a doctor, began to write novels. His works include *The Dancing Girl* (MAIHIME) in 1890, *The Boat on the Takase River* (TAKASEBUNE) in 1916, *Sansho the Steward* (SANSHOU-DAYUU) in 1915, and *Vita Sexualis* (WITA-SEKUSUARISU) in 1909.

もりおかし 盛岡市〚地名〛 Morioka City. The capital of Iwate Pref., located in its central part. Its main festival, Morioka Sansa Dance, is held for four days every August, with dancers and other participants marching with more than 10,000 portable Japanese drums. The Chagu-chagu Umakko Festival, a marching ceremony with horses, has been held every June for more than 200 years. It symbolizes the area's reliance on horses since the Heian period. The former Prime Minister HARA TAKASHI, the poet ISHIKAWA TAKUBOKU, and the linguist and folklorist KINDAICHI KYOUSUKE are from the city.

もりじお 盛り塩〚食文化〛 a small mound of salt. Is placed at the entrance of a traditional restaurant or a performing theater for purification and good fortune.

もりそば 盛り蕎麦〚食べ物〛 cold plain buckwheat noodles on a bamboo tray. Are dipped into sauce when eaten.

もりそんごうじけん モリソン号事件〚外交〛 Morrison Incident. An 1838 event during which an American merchant ship, the *Morrison*, attempted to bring seven shipwrecked Japanese back to their home country, in an effort to gain trading privileges for the United States. The ship faced cannon fire at two different ports and was kept from landing, in line with the Tokugawa shogunate's prohibition against foreign ships. →鎖国；異国船打払令

もりつけ 盛り付け〚食文化〛 to dish out food on a plate. Is important because Japanese cuisine puts a high value on appearance. For example, vegetables are cut into beautiful shapes such as flowers or maple leaves. This technique is called KAZARI-GIRI.

もりばな 盛花〚華道〛 arranging many flowers in a shallow container with a wide opening.

もろきゅう もろキュー〚食べ物〛

cucumber with unrefined soy sauce called MOROMI. Miso is sometimes used instead of unrefined soy sauce.

もろこ 諸子 〔食べ物・動物〕 a Biwa gudgeon, or a field gudgeon. *Gnathopogon elongatus*. Lives in fresh water. Edible.

もろざし 両差し 〔相撲〕 a position in which a wrestler has thrusted both of his arms under the opponent's arms.

もろはしてつじ 諸橋轍次 〔言語〕 1883-1982. A scholar of the Chinese classics born in Niigata Pref. Compiled *The Great Han-Japanese Dictionary* (DAI-KANWA JITEN) in 1960.

もろみ 醪, 諸味 〔酒・調味料〕 fermenting or fermented mash of the ingredients of sake or soy sauce. After being fermented, is filtered to become sake or soy sauce. →麹(ﾞ); 酵母

もん 紋 〔生活・文様〕 ⇨家紋

もん ～文 〔単位〕 a unit of money in the Edo period. A coin called KAN'EI TSUUHOU is worthy of one 'mon,' and 4,000 'mon' equal one RYOU.

もんがく 文覚 〔仏教〕 ?-? A priest of esoteric Buddhism in the 12th to 13th centuries. Originally a samurai, but became a priest, regretting having killed his friend's wife accidentally. Helped MINAMOTO NO YORITOMO raise an army against the Heike clan, and reestablished JINGO-JI temple.

もんじゃやき もんじゃ焼き 〔食べ物〕 a soft savory pancake with shredded cabbage and other ingredients. A specialty of Tokyo.

もんしゅ 門主 〔仏教〕 (**1**) the head priest of a sect. (**2**) a member of the Imperial family or a noble court, who serves as the chief priest of a temple.

もんじゅぼさつ 文殊菩薩 〔仏教〕 Bodhisattva of Wisdom. *Manjusri*. One of the two attendants of the Historical Buddha. Often has a sword on the right hand and rides on a lion. Is sometimes depicted as a figure crossing the sea or debating with an ideal image as a lay adherent of Buddhism, YUIMA-KOJI.

もんぜきじいん 門跡寺院 〔寺院〕 a temple whose chief priest was a member of the Imperial family or of a noble court. Examples include SHOUREN-IN, SANZEN-IN, and NINNA-JI, all of which are located in Kyoto.

もんぜんまち 門前町 〔宗教・経済〕 a town developed around a large shrine or temple. For example, Nagano City in front of Zenkou-ji Temple, or Ise City in front of the Ise Shrine.

もんちゅうじょ 問注所 〔武士・政治〕 (**1**) a court of justice in the Kamakura shogunate. (**2**) an archive office in the Muromachi shogunate.

もんつき 紋付き 〔服飾〕 a crested formal kimono. Bears one, three, or five family crests, the last of which is the most formal.

もんと 門徒〖仏教〗 a devotee of a Buddhist sect, especially the True Pure Land sect. →浄土真宗

もんどころ 紋所〖精神性・文様〗 ⇨ 家紋

もんぶかがくしょう 文部科学省 〖行政機関〗 the Ministry of Education, Culture, Sports, Science and Technology. MEXT. Was started in 2001 by unifying the Ministry of Education, Science and Culture with the Science and Technology Agency.

もんぺ もんぺ〖服飾〗 baggy work pants for women. Are gathered at the ankles. Was worn during World War II.

もんめ ～匁〖単位〗 a unit to measure weight. About 3.75 g. One KAN equals 1,000 'monme.'

やいづし 焼津市〚地名〛 Yaizu City. Is located in central Shizuoka Pref. Has a base port associated with the ocean fishery for tuna and skipjack. It is said that a mythical hero, YAMATOTAKERU NO MIKOTO, escaped dangers by cutting down grasses with the Sacred Sword, named AME-NO MURAKUMO-NO TSURUGI, when he was surrounded by fire lit by his enemies in his eastern campaign.

やえざくら 八重桜〚植物〛 a multi-petal cherry tree. *Prunus lannesiana*. Blooms a little later than other cherry trees.

やおびくに 八尾比丘尼〚妖怪〛 Eight-hundred-year Old Female Priest. It is said that she had lived long because she ate the flesh of a mermaid. Her legend remains in the Wakasa area of Fukui Pref.

やおやおしち 八百屋お七〚犯罪〛 1668–1683. A young girl at a vegetable shop. When a large fire occurred in Edo in 1682, fled to a temple, met a young monk, and fell in love. Desperately wanted to see the monk again the next year, committed arson, and was arrested to be executed. This story became a motif of KABUKI and BUNRAKU.

やおよろずのかみがみ 八百万の神々〚神道〛 myriads of deities. In Shintoism, deities exist everywhere, not only in heaven but also in places such as mountains, oceans, houses, and even kitchen stoves.

やかずはいかい 矢数俳諧〚文芸〛 performance during which a poet simultaneously created and presented a large number of haiku in a set time period, in the Edo period. For example, Ihara Saikaku generated 23,500 haiku in one day, at a rate even too fast for them to be recorded.

やがすり 矢絣〚文様〛 the pattern of arrow feathers. Is used for a kimono.

やかたぶね 屋形船〚食文化〛 a roofed pleasure boat. People enjoy sightseeing, eating, and drinking on the ship.

やきいも 焼き芋〚食べ物〛 a roasted sweet potato. Popular in winter.

やきうどん 焼き饂飩〚食べ物〛 stir-fried thick white noodles. Cooked with meat and vegetables.

やきおにぎり 焼きおにぎり〚食べ物〛 a grilled rice ball. The surface is covered with soy sauce or miso and is grilled until the surface is browned.

やきざかな 焼き魚〚食べ物〛 grilled fish. Many kinds of fish, such as salmon, sea bream, and yellow tail, are used as ingredients.

やきそば 焼きそば〚食べ物〛 stir-fried noodles. Ingredients include vegetables, mushrooms, pork or beef, and squid. There are several types of yakisoba. The popular ones are the Worcester sauce flavored style and the Chinese style. The latter is called chow mein in English.

やきだんご 焼き団子 〔食べ物〕 a toasted small ball of rice flour. →団子

やきどうふ 焼き豆腐 〔食べ物〕 grilled tofu. Firm tofu is usually used.

やきとり 焼き鳥〔食べ物〕 grilled chicken on a skewer. Several parts of chicken are used, including the meat, heart, skin, and gizzard. Is seasoned with teriyaki sauce or salt. Goes well with beer or sake.

やきなす 焼き茄子 〔食べ物〕 a grilled eggplant. Is often cut into bite-sized pieces. Eaten with soy sauce and shaved dried bonito.

やきにく 焼き肉〔食べ物〕 grilled beef. The Korean style is popular. Sirloin, rib, diaphragm, and tongue are eaten.

やきのり 焼き海苔〔食べ物〕 toasted dried laver. Is not seasoned. Is often dipped in soy sauce before being eaten. ↔味付け海苔

やきはまぐり 焼き蛤 〔食べ物〕 grilled hard clam on the shell. A specialty of Kuwana, Mie Pref.

やきめし 焼き飯〔食べ物〕 ⇨チャーハン

やきもち 焼き餅 (**1**)〔食べ物〕 a grilled rice cake. Is often seasoned with soy sauce or sweetened soybean flour. (**2**)〔言語〕 the state of getting jealous. The term is coined as such because the shape of a blown cheek in anger seems similar to that of a blown rice cake when grilled.

やきもの 焼き物 (**1**)〔工芸〕 the generic term for porcelain, pottery, and earthen ware. (**2**)〔食べ物〕 grilled, toasted, or lightly fried food.

やきゅう 野球〔スポーツ〕 baseball. Was introduced to Japan in 1873 and has become one of the most popular sports. Professional baseball in Japan began in 1934, and the national tournament of high-school baseball began in 1915.

やぎゅうじゅうべえ 柳生十兵衛〔剣術〕 1607-1650. An expert swordsman born in present Nara Pref. The eldest son of YAGYUU MUNENORI. Taught swordsmanship to the third Tokugawa shogun, TOKUGAWA IEMITSU. Frequently appears in historical fiction as a one-eyed swordsman, though there is no evidence that he lost one eye.

やぎゅうみつよし 柳生三厳〔剣術〕 ⇨柳生十兵衛

やぎゅうむねのり 柳生宗矩〔剣術〕 1571-1646. An expert swordsman born in present Nara Pref. The fifth son of YAGYUU MUNEYOSHI. Taught swordsmanship to the second and third Tokugawa shoguns, Tokugawa Hidetada and TOKUGAWA IEMITSU. Systematized the theory of the Yagyuu school. Became good friends with a priest, TAKUAN.

やぎゅうむねよし 柳生宗厳 〖剣術〗 1527-1606. An expert swordsman born in present Nara Pref. Learned swordsmanship of the Shinkage school under KAMIIZUMI HIDETSUNA and founded the Yagyuu school.

やぎゅうりゅう 柳生流 〖剣術〗 the Yagyuu school of swordsmanship. Was founded by YAGYUU MUNEYOSHI. Some masters in this school served Tokugawa shoguns as instructors of swordsmanship.

やく 厄 〖宗教〗 ⇨厄年

やくおとし 厄落とし 〖宗教〗 ⇨厄除け

やくざ 八九三 〖犯罪〗 a gangster. Literally means "8, 9, and 3," which was the worst combination in a popular card game, called OICHO-KABU, in the Edo period.

やくざえいが やくざ映画 〖映画〗 a yakuza movie. Was popular from the 1960s to 1980s. Famous examples include *Battles Without Honor and Humanity* (Jingi-naki tatakai) in 1973, *The Yakuza Wives* (Gokudou no tsuma-tachi) in 1986, and *Violent Cop* (Sono otoko, kyo-ubou ni tsuki) in 1989,

やくしさんぞん 薬師三尊 〖仏教〗 the Triad of the Healing Buddha. Combination of the Healing Buddha and the two attendant bodhisattvas: the Bodhisattva of Sunlight on the left, and the Bodhisattva of Moon-light on the right. →薬師如来；日光菩薩；月光(がっこう)菩薩

やくしじ 薬師寺 〖寺院〗 Yakushiji Temple. A main temple of the Hossou sect located in Nara City. One of the Seven Great Temples of Nara. Was founded in 698 by Emperor Tenmu, who prayed for his wife's recovery. Has several National Treasures including the Triad of the Healing Buddha, the Holy Bodhisattva of Mercy, a picture of Goddess of Beauty, and the East Pagoda. →天武天皇；南都七大寺

やくしにょらい 薬師如来 〖仏教〗 the Healing Buddha. *Bhaisajya-guru*. Vowed to heal illness of people and resides in the Eastern Pure Land of Lapis Lazuli. Usually has a medicine pot on his left palm. The most famous example is at Yakushiji Temple in Nara.

やくしま 屋久島 〖島名〗 Yakushima Island, or Yaku Island, in Kago-shima Pref. Its area is 503 km^2, and its shape is close to a circle. Has much rain throughout the year. The forests of wild Yaku cedars are designated a World Heritage Site in 1993.

やくしゃえ 役者絵 〖絵画〗 a portrait of a kabuki actor in the Edo period. One of the popular themes in UKIYO-E.

やくすぎ 屋久杉 〖自然〗 a wild Japanese cedar growing on Yaku Island, Kagoshima Pref. Some are 1,000 years old. Are designated a Special Natural Monument.

やくどし 厄年 〖宗教・通過儀礼〗 an unlucky age. In the traditional approach to age counting, ages 25 and

42 are unlucky for men and ages 19 and 33 are unlucky for women, based on the theory of the Yin-Yang Way. →数え年；陰陽(おんよう)道

やくばらい 厄払い〖宗教〗 ⇨厄除け

やくびょうがみ 疫病神〖妖怪〗 a deity of plagues. Was believed to come from the outside of a village community in olden times. Some festivals or annual events are related to the belief in such deities.

やくみ 薬味〖食べ物〗 condiments. Popular ones are wasabi, ginger, giant white radish, prickly ash, sesame, green onion, and dried bonito. Are usually grated, chopped, or shaved.

やくみざら 薬味皿〖食器〗 a small plate for seasoning and condiments.

やくみだんす 薬味箪笥〖医療〗 ⇨百味箪笥(ひゃくみだんす)

やくよけ 厄除け〖宗教〗 exorcism. People at unlucky ages visit Shinto shrines or Buddhist temples to get purified. →厄年

やぐら 櫓 **(1)**〖建築〗a turret of a castle. **(2)**〖祭礼〗a high stage for singing songs or playing instruments at a festival.

やぐらだいこ 櫓太鼓〖相撲〗 a traditional drum to announce the beginning and ending of sumo bouts. Is beaten on a high stage before the first bout begins and after the last bout has ended.

やぐるま 矢車〖年中行事〗 an arrow windmill. Is placed on the top of a pole for carp streamers. →鯉のぼり

やげん 薬研〖医療〗 a ship-shaped pharmacist's mortar. Is used to grind medical materials into smaller pieces or powder by rolling a disk on the material.

やごう 屋号〖ビジネス〗 the name of a store. A suffix '-ya' is often added such as 'matsuzaka-ya' or 'yoshino-ya.'

やさかじんじゃ 八坂神社〖神社〗 Yasaka Shrine. The head shrine of the Yasaka Shrines throughout Japan, located in Kyoto City. Enshrines the God of Storms and other deities. Famous for the Gion Festival. →須佐之男命(すさのおのみこと)；祇園祭

やさかにのまがたま 八尺瓊勾玉〖神話・天皇〗 the Comma-shaped Sacred Jewel. One of the Three Sacred Treasures of the Imperial Family. Was used when deities prayed that the Sun Goddess would reappear after she had hidden herself in the Celestial Rock Cave. →三種の神器；天岩戸

やし 香具師〖祭礼・ビジネス〗 a street vendor at a festival. Their varied businesses include selling food, providing a prize game, and producing a cheap show. They form a group, of which a single boss controls the entire business. Some of them are related to YAKUZA.

やじきた 弥次喜多〖文芸〗 ⇨弥次さん・喜多さん

やじさんきたさん 弥次さん・喜多さん〖文芸〗 Yajirobee and Kitahachi. Two heroes in a comic travel novel, *Shank's Mare*, written in

1809 by JIPPENSHA IKKU. Walked from Edo to Osaka along the Toukaidou Highway.

やしゃ　夜叉〖仏教〗 an ancient Indian demon. *Yaksha*. Was introduced into Buddhism and became an attendant of the Guardian King of the north, called BISHAMON-TEN.

やしろ　社〖神社〗 a building of a Shinto shrine. Sometimes means a Shinto shrine itself.

やじろべえ　弥次郎兵衛　(1)〖玩具〗 a balance toy. Has a short body and two long curved arms with counterweights. When the body is supported on a finger, the toy stands, keeping its balance while swinging. **(2)**〖文芸〗⇨弥次さん・喜多さん

やすくにじんじゃ　靖国神社〖神社〗 Yasukuni Shrine. Was established in Tokyo in 1879. Enshrines the spirits of almost 2.5 million people who died in wars. Since war criminals are also enshrined there, visiting by a prime minister or other Cabinet members has long been debatable.

やすだざいばつ　安田財閥〖ビジネス〗 Yasuda business conglomerate. The fourth largest ZAIBATSU after Mitsui, Mitsubishi, and Sumitomo. Was established in the 19th century by Yasuda Zenjirou. After World War II, was liquidated by the order of the Supreme Commander for the Allied Powers.

やたい　屋台〖祭礼・娯楽〗 a street vendor's stall. Many stalls stand in a row within the precincts, or in front of a shrine or a temple on a festival day. Some sell junk food such as TAKOYAKI, IKAYAKI, and TAIYAKI. Others provide amusements such as quasi-shooting and goldfish scooping.

やたがらす　八咫烏〖神道・スポーツ〗 Sacred Tripodal Crow. Guided Emperor Jinmu to Nara in the Japanese myth. The icon of Yatagarasu is used as the emblem of Japan Football Association.

やたて　矢立　(1)〖武器〗 a portable long case for carrying arrows. **(2)**〖文具〗 a portable set of India ink and a writing brush. Is seldom used at present.

やたのかがみ　八咫の鏡〖神道〗 the Sacred Mirror. One of the Three Sacred Treasures of the Imperial Family. Was used to lure the Sun Goddess out after she had hidden herself in the Celestial Rock Cave. →三種の神器；天岩戸

やたらづけ　矢鱈漬け〖食べ物〗 mixed pickles of various vegetables. A specialty of Yamagata Pref.

やつがたけ　八ヶ岳〖山岳〗 the Yatsugatake Mountains. A volcanic mountain range, located on the border between Yamanashi and Nagano Prefs. Its highest peak, Mt. Aka, is 2,899 m high. The mountains in its southern half are generally high and steep and popular for rock climbing and ice climbing. At its foot are popular resorts such as Tateshina, Kiyosato, and Nobeyama Hills, where lettuce and cabbage are grown in large quantities.

やつくち 八つ口 〖服飾〗 the opening between the sleeve and main part of a women's kimono.

やっこ 奴 〖武士〗 a samurai's footman. Carried a spear or a traveling box on foot at the head of his master's procession.

やっこだこ 奴凧 〖玩具〗 a kite in the shape of a samurai's footman with his arms open.

やっこどうふ 奴豆腐 〖食べ物〗 ⇨冷奴

やつはし 八つ橋 〖食べ物〗 a warped cinnamon cookie. Is made from rice flour, sugar, and cinnamon, in the shape of a 13-stringed zither, called KOTO. Is said to be named after a composer and 'koto' player, Yatsuhashi Kengyou (1614-1685). A specialty of Kyoto. →生八つ橋

やながわなべ 柳川鍋 〖食べ物〗 a pot of loaches boiled with shaved burdock root and beaten egg.

やなぎ 柳 〖植物〗 a willow. *Salix*. Was sometimes associated with a ghost in paintings.

やなぎごうり 柳行李 〖生活〗 a wicker box for clothes.

やなぎたくにお 柳田國男 〖人文学〗 1875-1962. A folklorist, born in Hyougo Pref. Pioneered the study of Japanese folklore. His major works include *The Legends of Tono* (TOONO MONOGATARI) and *The Birth of Momotaro* (Momotarou no tanjou).

やなぎだる 柳樽 〖酒〗 a sake cask with two long handles. Is often lac-

quered red. Is used for auspicious occasions.

やなぎばし 柳箸 〖食器〗 willow chopsticks. Are used during the New Year's holidays. Are said to be auspicious because a willow is not easily broken.

やなぎばぼうちょう 柳刃包丁 〖食器〗 a long, thin kitchen knife to slice sashimi.

やなぎむねよし 柳宗悦 〖美術〗 1889-1961. An art critic and philosopher born in Tokyo. Noticed the beauty of miscellaneous ware in daily life and coined the word 'mingei,' which means "folk art" or "folk craft." Established the Japan Folk Crafts Museum in Tokyo in 1936, together with KAWAI KANJIROU, Bernard Leach, and other artists and art critics.

やなせたかし やなせたかし 〖漫画・アニメ〗 1919-2013. A cartoonist born in Kouchi Pref. His most famous work is *Anpanman*.

やなり 家鳴り 〖妖怪〗 house rambling. It was said that small goblins would shake the house mischievously. Might be scientifically said to be related to resonance with something underground.

やばけい 耶馬溪 〖地名〗 a group of gorges northwest of Ooita Pref., along the Yamakuni River and its branches. Famous for its high cliffs, a tunnel named AO NO DOUMON, and bridges such as Yabakei Bridge, which is Japan's longest stone-built arch bridge. It is 116 m in length.

Can be accessed by bus, with a 20-minute ride from JR Nakatsu Station.

やはず 矢筈 〔武器〕 the notch of an arrow. Is put on a bowstring for shooting.

やぶいり 藪入り 〔ビジネス〕 New Year's and mid-August holidays for servants and apprentices in olden times. They lived in their employer's or master's house and did not have weekly holidays.

やぶさめ 流鏑馬 〔武術〕 horseback archery. An archer shoots at targets while riding at a gallop. Was popular as training for worriers in the Kamakura period. Is now held as a Shinto ceremony at some shrines.

やぶそば 藪蕎麦 〔食べ物〕 light-green buckwheat noodles. When making buckwheat powder, buckwheat nuts are ground without removing the chaff.

やぶみ 矢文 〔通信〕 a letter attached to an arrow. Was sent by shooting the arrow.

やへん 矢偏 〔漢字〕 a left-side radical meaning "arrow." Is used in kanji such as 知 (knowledge) and 短 (short). →偏；部首

やぼ 野暮 〔精神性〕 being unsophisticated, dumb, inconsiderate, rigid, and insensitive to other people's needs. The antonym of 'yabo' is IKI in Japanese.

やまいだれ 病垂れ 〔漢字〕 an upper-to-left radical related to "sickness." Is used in kanji such as 病 (disease), 疫 (epidemic), and 症 (symptom).

やまいも 山芋 〔食べ物・植物〕 a Japanese yam. *Dioscorea japonica.* The root is eaten sliced or grated. The bulbils, called MUKAGO, are also edible.

やまいもたんざく 山芋短冊 〔食べ物〕 rectangular-sliced yam. Eaten with shredded dried laver and soy sauce. Sometimes wasabi, dried shaved bonito, or raw egg is added.

やまうば 山姥 〔妖怪〕 ⇨山姥（やまんば）

やまおかてっしゅう 山岡鉄舟 〔武士〕 1836-1888. A samurai and statesman born in Edo. As a vassal of the Tokugawa shogunate, arranged the meeting of KATSU KAISHUU and SAIGOU TAKAMORI for capitulation of the Edo Castle without resistance in 1868.

やまかけ 山掛け 〔食べ物〕 sashimi of tuna topped with grated yam. Is usually seasoned with soy sauce and wasabi.

やまがたけん 山形県 〔都道府県〕 Yamagata Pref. Is located in northeastern Japan, facing the Sea of Japan. Is 9,323 km^2 in area. Its capital is Yamagata City. Its inland basins have a great difference in temperature between summer and winter. The Yamagata Basin recorded 40.8 degrees Celsius in July 1933, making it the highest temperature in more than 70 years. Yamagata-ken produces about 70 percent of all the cherries in Japan. Tendou City in its eastern part is famous for the production of SHOUGI pieces. Each city, town, or village in this prefecture has its own hot spring. Used to be Uzen and part of Ugo.

やまがたし 山形市 〖地名〗 Yamagata City. The capital of Yamagata Pref., located in its eastern part. Developed as a castle town of the Mogami clan during and after the 14th century. Famous for RISSHAKU-JI Temple and the ZAOU spa and snow resort.

やまがたしんかんせん 山形新幹線 〖鉄道〗 Yamagata Shinkansen. Connects Fukushima Station with Shinjou Station in Yamagata Pref. Started service in 1992. The only express train running on the line is TSUBASA.

やまかんむり 山冠 〖漢字〗 a crown radical meaning "mountain." Is used in kanji such as 岩 (rock), 岸 (shore), 崖 (cliff), and 崩 (collapse).

やまくぐり 山潜り 〖忍者〗 the ninja group in Satsuma, present Kagoshima Pref.

やまくずし 山崩し 〖将棋〗 knock-down-the-mountain. All shogi pieces are roughly piled up like a mountain, and players try to take out pieces one by one, only using an index finger. If the player makes a noise, even though very slight, while moving a piece, he or she loses the chance, and the next player tries.

やまぐちけん 山口県 〖都道府県〗 Yamaguchi Pref. Is located in Western Japan, at the western tip of Honshuu, facing the Sea of Japan and the Inland Sea. Is 6,112 km² in area. Its capital is Yamaguchi City. Has a mild climate. Famous for the production of seafood such as blowfish, horse mackerels, and squids, and industrial products such as cement and Hagi ware. Popular sightseeing spots include Hagi castle town and a private school named SHOUKASON-JUKU in its north, Kintai-kyo Bridge in its east, and AKIYOSHI-DAI Plateau and AKIYOSHI-DOU Caves in its central part. Historically, Dannoura was the final battlefield in the Heiji Rebellion between the Minamoto and Taira clans in 1185. Produced many prominent politicians and scholars in the late Edo period to lead the Meiji Restoration. Used to be Suou and Nagato.

やまぐちし 山口市 〖地名〗 Yamaguchi City. The capital of Yamaguchi Pref., located in its central southern part. Yuda Hot Springs, Funakata Farm, and Oouchi Dolls are famous. The Yamaguchi Gion Festival in July and the Yamaguchi Tanabata Lantern Festival in August attract many tourists. Among the many temples and shrines, the five-storied pagoda of the Rurikou-ji Temple is a National Treasure. Yamaguchi Xavier Memorial Church was rebuilt in 1998 in honor of St. Francis Xavier, the first Christian to preach in Japan in the mid-16th century.

やまごえあみだ 山越阿弥陀〖仏教・絵画〗 Amitabha Coming over the Mountain. A popular theme of a Buddhist painting in the Kamakura period. Amitabha Buddha comes to bring a dead soul to the Western Pure Land. →阿弥陀如来; 西方極楽浄土

やまざきとよこ 山崎豊子 〖文芸〗 1924-2013. A novelist born in Osaka. Wrote socially concerned novels such as *The Barren Zone* (Fumou-chitai) in 1976 and *Two Homelands* (Futatsu no sokoku) in 1983.

やまざくら 山桜〖植物〗 a mountain cherry tree. *Prunus jamasakura*. Was popular for cherry blossom viewing before a species called SOMEI-YOSHINO appeared.

やまさちひこ 山幸彦 〖神話〗 another name of HOORI NO MIKOTO or Hikohohodemi no mikoto. Lived by hunting in the mountains, but borrowed a fishing hook from his brother, Umisachihiko, and lost it. He visited the palace of Oowadatsumi no kami to look for the hook and got married to his daughter, TOYOTAMA HIME.

やましたきよし 山下清 〖絵画〗 1922-1971. A painter born in Tokyo. Had a mental disability. Escaped from a protective institution in 1940 and traveled all over Japan. His diary later became a movie, *Travel Log of a Naked Artist* (Hadaka no taishou hourou-ki).

やましろ 山城 〖旧国名〗 the old name of the southeastern end of Kyoto Pref.

やましろのおおえのおう 山背大兄王〖政治〗 ?-643. A member of the Imperial family. The son of SHOUTOKU TAISHI and the grandson of SOGA NO UMAKO. Was forced to kill himself by SOGA NO IRUKA, in the battle for the succession to the Imperial Throne.

やませ 山背〖自然〗 a wind blowing from behind the mountains. Especially the cold and wet wind blowing from the northeast in the Hokkaido and Tohoku regions in summer.

やまたいこく 邪馬台国〖国名〗 an ancient nation ruled by Queen Himiko around the 3rd century. Its location is ambiguously written in "The Record of Japan" in the *History of Wei* and has been a major issue in the research of Japanese ancient history.

やまだながまさ 山田長政〖外交〗 ?-1630. A diplomat and businessman in present Thailand, born in present Shizuoka Pref. Went to Siam, settled in its capital, Ayutthaya, and became the head of the Japanese community there. Obtained the confidence of the king, but was poisoned to death after the king died.

やまだにしき 山田錦〖酒・植物〗 the most popular rice for brewing sake. A chief producing area is Hyougo Pref. →酒米(さかまい)

やまたのおろち 八岐大蛇 〖神道〗 an eight-headed and eight-tailed

serpent in the myth. Had eaten daughters of an old couple living in Izumo and was exterminated by the God of Storms, SUSANOO NO MIKOTO. A sacred sword, named AME-NO MURAKUMO-NO TSURUGI, was found in its tail.

やまてせん 山手線〘鉄道〙 ⇨山手(やまの)て線

やまでら 山寺〘寺院〙 ⇨立石(りっしゃく)寺

やまと 大和 **(1)**〘地名〙 a name for present Nara or for Japan in ancient times. **(2)**〘旧国名〙 the old name for Nara Pref. **(3)**〘軍事〙 ⇨戦艦大和

やまとえ 大和絵〘絵画〙 **(1)** a painting depicting Japanese landscape or customs. The term 'yamato-e' was used in this sense from the 9th to 13th centuries. ↔唐絵(からえ) **(2)** a Japanese-style painting. The term referred to the traditional-style painting, contrasted with Chinese-style India ink painting that was introduced around the 13th century. ↔漢画 **(3)** a Tosa-style painting. Sometimes also refers to a Rin-style painting or ukiyo-e. 'Yamato-e' came to have this meaning after the Tosa school presided over the Imperial painting studio in the 15th century. →土佐派；琳派

やまとことば 大和言葉〘言語〙 an indigenous Japanese word. Was used before Chinese or other foreign languages were introduced. Many basic Japanese words have one or two syllables, like 'te' meaning "hand" or 'umi' meaning "sea."

やまとさんざん 大和三山〘地名〙 three famous mountains in Nara: Mt. Kagu, Mt. Unebi, and Mt. Miminashi. Appear in several poems in the *Anthology of Myriad Leaves* (MAN'YOUSHUU).

やまとじ 大和路〘地名〙 a road in or to Nara. YAMATO is the old name of Nara.

やまとせいけん 大和政権〘政治〙 Yamato administration. A coalition government from the 4th to 7th centuries. Was based in the present Nara area. The Emperor was the leader of confederate clans. After the Taika Reform of 645, shifted to the centralized administration called RITSURYOU-SEI. →大化の改新

やまとたけるのみこと 倭建命〘神話〙 a legendary hero and a son of Emperor Keikou. Was called 'Ousu no mikoto' when young. The Emperor sent him on campaigns against KUMASO in Kyushu and EMISHI in Eastern Japan. On his way back, he became ill near Mt. Ibuki in present Shiga Pref. and passed away in Mie Pref. After his death, his soul turned into a swan and flew away. His story is described in the *Records of Ancient Matters* (KOJIKI) and the *Chronicles of Japan* (NIHONSHOKI).

やまとだましい 大和魂〘精神性〙 the Japanese spirit. Includes characteristics of being brave and determined. Was used as propaganda for extreme patriotism during World War II.

やまとちょうてい 大和朝廷 〔政治〕 ⇨大和政権

やまとに 大和煮 〔食べ物〕 beef simmered with soy sauce, sugar, and ginger.

やまどり 山鳥 〔動物〕 a copper pheasant. *Phasianus soemmerringii*. The male bird has a long tail.

やまなかこ 山中湖 〔湖沼〕 Lake Yamanaka. One of the Fuji Five Lakes located in southeastern Yamanashi Pref. The area is 6.5 km^2, which makes it the largest of the five lakes. The surface is at 982 m above sea level, and the maximum depth is 14 m. Boating, water skiing, wind surfing, and fishing are popular. Visitors can enjoy a nice view of the lake and Mt. Fuji at the viewing spot called 'Panorama Dai.' Is accessible from central Tokyo by a direct bus service, with a 2.5-hour ride. →富士五湖

やまなかしかのすけ 山中鹿之助 〔武士〕 1545-1578. A warlord born in present Shimane Pref. Served the Amako clan and fought against the Mouri clan. Famous for an anecdote in which he prayed to a crescent moon for "seven difficulties and eight sufferings" to test his own competency.

やまなしけん 山梨県 〔都道府県〕 Yamanashi Pref. Is located on the north of Mt. Fuji in central Japan and has no seacoast. Is 4,465 km^2 in area. Its capital is Koufu City. Produces grapes and wine. Used to be called Kai.

やまのいも 山の芋 〔食べ物・植物〕 ⇨山芋

やまのうえのおくら 山上憶良 〔文芸〕 660-733? An aristocrat and poet who might have come from Paekche on the Korean Peninsula. Contributed 90 poems to the *Anthology of Myriad Leaves* (MAN'YOUSHUU). Composed many ideological poems such as "Dialogue on Poverty" (HINKYUU MONDOU KA).

やまのうちかずとよ 山内一豊 〔武士〕 1546-1605. A warlord born in present Aichi Pref. Served ODA NOBUNAGA and TOYOTOMI HIDEYOSHI. In the Battle of Sekigahara, took the side of TOKUGAWA IEYASU and became the feudal lord of Tosa, present Kouchi Pref. An anecdote about his wife's assistance is famous.

やまのうちようどう 山内容堂 〔武士〕 1827-1872. A feudal lord of Tosa, present Kouchi Pref. Promoted the union of the Imperial Court and the Tokugawa shogunate. Petitioned the 15th shogun, TOKUGAWA YOSHINOBU, to return political power to the Emperor. The petition was approved and power was returned. →公武合体

やまのてせん 山手線 〔鉄道〕 the Yamanote Line, or the Tokyo Loop Line. Is operated by JR East. Is 34.5 km long and connects 29 stations including Tokyo, AKIHABARA, UENO, Ikebukuro, Shinjuku, Shibuya, and Shinagawa.

やまのひ 山の日 〔祝日〕 Mountain

Day. August 11. A national holiday to commune with the mountains and to be thankful for them. Was ordained in 2016.

やまのべのみち 山の辺の道 〘交通〙 an ancient road from present Nara City to present Sakurai City in eastern Nara Pref. Along it are several old temples, shrines, and tumuli.

やまびこ やまびこ〘鉄道〙 the express train on Tohoku Shinkansen. Literally means "echo through the hills." Connects Tokyo with the Sendai Station in Miyagi Pref. in 2 hours, and Tokyo with Morioka Station in Iwate Pref. in 3 hours 20 minutes.

やまびこ 山彦〘自然・宗教〙 an echo in the mountain. It was believed that the mountain deity mimicked the human voice.

やまびらき 山開き〘自然・娯楽〙 the beginning of the climbing season. A religious ceremony used to be held to allow ordinary people to climb a sacred mountain.

やまぶき 山吹〘植物〙 a Japanese rose, or a kerria. *Kerria japonica*. Golden flowers bloom in early summer.

やまぶし 山伏〘宗教・忍者〙 a mountain ascetic. Has trained himself to attain supernatural power in the mountains. Wears a special costume including a small cap and a jingling rod, carries a portable box called OI on his back, and blows a conch-shell horn. →修験道

やまべのあかひと 山部赤人〘文芸〙 ?-? A poet laureate in the 8th century. Contributed 50 poems to the *Anthology of Myriad Leaves* (MAN'YOUSHUU). Famous for descriptive poems of nature.

やまへん 山偏〘漢字〙 a left-side radical meaning "mountain." Is used in kanji such as 岬 (promontory), 峡 (gorge), and 峠 (mountain pass).

やまぼこ 山鉾〘祭礼〙 ⇨山車〘祭〙

やまめ 山女〘魚〙 cherry salmon, or brook trout. *Oncorhynchus masou*. About 20 cm long. Popular as a target of fishing in a small river.

やまもとかんすけ 山本勘助〘武士〙 1493?-1561? A warlord and strategist under TAKEDA SHINGEN. Was said to be one-eyed and one-legged.

やまもとしちへい 山本七平〘人文学〙 1921-1991. A publisher and social critic born in Tokyo. Is said to have written *The Japanese and the Jewish* (Nihonjin to Yudayajin) under the pseudonym of Izaya Bendasan, but he himself denied it.

やまんば 山姥〘妖怪〙 a mountain crone. Lives deep in the mountains. Appears in several folk tales such as KINTAROU.

やみいち 闇市〘経済〙 a black market. Appeared throughout Japan immediately after World War II.

やよい 弥生〘暦〙 March in the traditional calendar. Means "plants grow thickly." →旧暦

やよいしきどき 弥生式土器〘考古〙 ⇨弥生土器

やよいじだい 弥生時代 〔時代〕 the Yayoi period. From around the 4th century B.C. to the 3rd century A.D. The use of bronze and iron ware and rice cultivation began. The social hierarchy was born, and small tribal states appeared. →弥生文化; 縄文時代

やよいどき 弥生土器 〔考古〕 Yayoi earthenware. Is called so because it was excavated in the Yayoi area of Tokyo in 1884. Was calcinated at 600 to 800 degree Celsius. Reddish-brown and unglazed. Often has geometrical patterns on the surface.

やよいぶんか 弥生文化 〔時代〕 the Yayoi culture. From around the 4th century B.C. to the 3rd century A.D. The use of bronze and iron ware and rice cultivation began. →弥生土器

やらい 矢来 〔建築〕 a temporary fence made of logs or bent bamboo strips.

やり 槍 〔武器〕 a spear. Was used from the Joumon period until the Edo period.

やり 香車 〔将棋〕 ⇨香車(きょうしゃ)

やりいか 槍烏賊 〔食べ物・動物〕 a spear squid. *Loligo bleekeri*. About 40 cm long. Eaten as sashimi or dried squid.

やりがたけ 槍ヶ岳 〔山岳〕 Mt. Yari. Is located on the border between Nagano and Gifu Prefs. Its height is 3,180 m. Is called so because the summit is like a spear, 'yari' in Japanese.

やりてばばあ 遣り手婆 〔セックス・娯楽〕 the madam of a brothel. Managed prostitutes and provided a prostitute for a guest in the Edo period.

やりどめ 槍止め 〔忍者〕 the technique to tightly fasten the enemy's spear and to stop the motion. One of the seven techniques of using a sword strap. →下げ緒七術

やりみず 遣り水 〔庭園〕 a small stream that led into a traditional garden. Was popular in the Kamakura and Heian periods.

やるたきょうてい ヤルタ協定 〔戦争〕 Yalta Agreement. An agreement made at the Yalta Conference, held at the resort area of Yalta in Crimea in February 1945. Was attended by British Prime Minister Winston Churchill, U.S. President Franklin D. Roosevelt, and Soviet Premier Joseph Stalin. The main parts of the agreement supported unconditional surrender of Germany, outlined post-war plans for Europe, and required the Soviet Union to enter the war against Japan after Germany surrendered. As a condition of the Soviets entering the war, land lost in the 1904-1905 Russo-Japanese War would be returned to the Soviet Union.

やんばるくいな 山原水鶏 〔動物〕 an Okinawa rail. *Rallus okinawae*. Wading bird that rarely flies but runs fast. Was discovered in 1981. A Natural Monument.

やんよおすてん ヤン・ヨーステン

〖ビジネス〗　1560-1623. A Dutch navigator who was an officer on the De Leifde, which wrecked off the Japanese coast in 1600. Along with his friend and shipmate, William Adams, he was employed by the shogun, Tokugawa Ieyasu, to provide military advice and to enhance Japan's relationship with Holland. Was permitted to develop a thriving trading business, to have a Japanese family, and to adopt a Japanese name. Was made a samurai, in direct service to the shogun. It is said that a district called Yaesu near Tokyo Station was named after him. →三浦按針

ゆ

ゆいいつしんめいづくり 唯一神明造 〖神社・建築〗 Genuine Shimmei style of Shinto architecture. Is used for the main building of the Ise Shrine. →神明(しんめい)造り

ゆいしき 唯識 〖仏教〗 the idea of consciousness only, or mind only. *Yogacara*. The fundamental doctrine of the Hossou sect. Says only consciousness exists, and every object results from being realized by consciousness. →法相(ほっそう)宗

ゆいしょうせつ 由井正雪 〖政治〗 1605-1651. A military scientist born in present Shizuoka Pref. Tried to overthrow the Tokugawa shogunate, failed, and killed himself.

ゆいなわ 結縄 〖忍者〗 rope communication. A ninja knotted a rope and hung it under an eave. An allied ninja would know the meaning by the shape of the knot.

ゆいのう 結納 〖冠婚葬祭〗 ceremonial exchange of engagement gifts or money. Is said to have been conducted in the Heian period. Is often omitted these days.

ゆいのうきんはんがえし 結納金半返し 〖冠婚葬祭〗 to return half the value of engagement gifts. In the tradition of some regions, the family of the prospective gloom gave gifts to the family of the bride, and the latter gave back gifts of half the value.

ゆいまきょう 維摩経 〖仏教〗 the *Vimalakirti Nirdesa* Sutra. Depicts discussions in which a lay adherent, named YUIMA-KOJI, won arguments with disciples of the Historical Buddha. Is considered significant in Zen Buddhism.

ゆいまこじ 維摩居士 〖仏教〗 *Vimalakirti*. A fictional hero in a sutra. Was depicted as an ideal lay adherent of Buddhism, who criticized disciples of the Historical Buddha and later held discussions with MONJU BOSATSU (*Manjusri*).

ゆうえすじぇい USJ 〖娯楽・施設〗 abbreviation for Universal Studio Japan.

ゆうかく 遊郭 〖娯楽・セックス〗 a red-light district authorized by the Tokugawa shogunate. Examples are YOSHIWARA in Edo, Shinmachi in Osaka, Shimabara in Kyoto, and Maruyama in Nagasaki.

ゆうから ユーカラ 〖少数民族〗 Yukar. Epic poetry for recreation, handed down among AINU, the indigenous people of Hokkaido.

ゆうきつむぎ 結城紬 〖服飾〗 a robust textile produced in the Yuuki area, Ibaraki Pref. →紬(つむぎ)

ゆうけいぶんかざい 有形文化財 〖法律〗 Tangible Cultural Properties. Include buildings, paintings, sculptures, crafts, calligraphy, ancient documents, and archeological artifacts, which have historical, artistic, or scientific value. Are defined by the Law for the Protection of Cultural Properties.

ゆうげん 幽玄 〚精神性〛 soft and elegant beauty with mysterious and profound quietness. This term has been used in theories of Noh or poetry, though the meaning varies depending on the periods or scholars.

ゆうこう 有効 〚柔道〛 an effective offense in a judo match. In the old rule, getting 'yuukou' was advantageous when the match was decided by a judge's decision. In the new rule revised in 2017, 'yuukou' was abolished.

ゆうじょう 友情 〚文芸・作品〛 *Friendship*. A novel published in 1919 by MUSHANOKOUJI SANEATSU. Describes the friendship and conflict between two young men who loved the same girl.

ゆうせんざせき 優先座席〚交通〛 a priority seat for the elderly, passengers with disabilities, pregnant women, and passengers accompanying small children on a train or bus.

ゆうせんせき 優先席〚交通〛 ⇨優先座席

ゆうぜんぞめ 友禅染め〚服飾〛 textile dyed in the Yuuzen style. Is characterized by elegant pictures of human figures, birds, and flowers. Was named after a painter, Miyazaki Yuuzen-sai, around the late 17th century.

ゆうだち 夕立〚気象〛 a shower on a summer afternoon.

ゆうづうねんぶつしゅう 融通念仏宗 〚仏教〛 the Yuuzuu nenbutsu sect. Part of Pure Land Buddhism. Was founded by Ryounin at the end of the Heian period. Its main teaching is that people can share the merit of prayer to Amitabha and can be reborn together in the Western Pure Land. A concept somewhat similar to "one for all, all for one." The head temple is Dainenbutsu-ji Temple in Osaka City. →念仏；極楽往生

ゆうひつ 祐筆〚武士・行政〛 a secretary samurai. Wrote documents as their job. Each of the shogunate systems and feudal lords had their own 'yuuhitsu.'

ゆうやく 釉薬〚陶磁器〛 ⇨上薬

ゆうりゃくてんのう 雄略天皇 〚天皇〛 Emperor Yuuryaku. ?–? The 21st, on the throne in the later 5th century. Is identified as 'Bu,' one of the Five Kings of Wa, which were described in a historical document of Sung. Is said to have composed the first poem in the *Anthology of Myriad Leaves* (MAN'YOUSHUU). → 倭の五王

ゆおけ 湯桶〚生活〛 a washbowl for bathing. Is used to scoop hot water from a bathtub or to wash a hand towel.

ゆかた 浴衣〚服飾〛 informal thin kimono. People wear yukata on the occasion of festivals in summer or at a Japanese-style inn.

ゆかたおび 浴衣帯〚服飾〛 a sash

for an informal thin kimono, called YUKATA.

ゆかわひでき 湯川秀樹 〔科学技術〕 1907–1981. A physicist born in Tokyo. Developed the meson theory and got the first Nobel Prize in Japan.

ゆきおんな 雪女 〔妖怪〕 a snow lady, or a snow ghost. Appears as a beautiful young lady who looks very pale, dressed in white attire within snowy provinces at night.

ゆきぐに 雪国 〔文芸・作品〕 *Snow Country*. A novel published in parts from 1935 to 1947 by KAWABATA YASUNARI. Describes the romance between a GEISHA girl and a dilettante at a snowy spa.

ゆきづり 雪吊り 〔生活〕 snow suspenders. Ropes suspended over a tree from a tall pole protect its branches from heavy snow. Are popular in Kanazawa, Ishikawa Pref.

ゆきひら 行平 〔食器〕 (**1**) a pottery pan with a handle and a lid. (**2**) a metal pan with a handle.

ゆきまつり 雪祭り 〔祭礼〕 a snow festival. Is held at several snowy areas, where snow or ice statues are exhibited. One in Sapporo is the most famous. →札幌雪祭り

ゆきみざけ 雪見酒 〔酒〕 drinking sake while appreciating a snowy scenery.

ゆきみしょうじ 雪見障子 〔建築〕 a sliding screen with a movable lower part. One can raise the lower part to see out of the glass window behind it.

ゆきみどうろう 雪見灯籠 〔庭園〕 a snow-viewing stone lantern. An ornament in a traditional garden. Is usually about 30 cm to 1 m tall and has a large shade and three legs.

ゆぎょうしゅう 遊行宗 〔仏教〕 ⇨時宗(じしゅう)

ゆげのどうきょう 弓削道鏡 〔仏教〕 ?–772. A Buddhist priest born in present Osaka Pref. Was favored by Empress Shoutoku and got into political circles, but fell out of power after the death of the Empress. →称徳天皇

ゆしませいどう 湯島聖堂 〔宗教・教育〕 Confucian Sacred Hall at Yushima. Was founded in 1690 by TOKUGAWA TSUNAYOSHI, the fifth shogun of the Tokugawa shogunate, and became a school for samurai in 1797. Was burned down as a result of the Great Kanto Earthquake and was rebuilt in 1935.

ゆず 柚子 〔調味料・植物〕 a small aromatic citron. *Citrus junos*. Is used to add aroma and a refreshing flavor to cooking.

ゆずがま 柚子釜 〔食べ物〕 a hollow, small aromatic citron, containing food such as fish, roe, and vegetables. The citrus aroma is added. Is sometimes grilled.

ゆずこしょう 柚子胡椒 〔調味料〕 seasoning paste made of ground green pepper and the peel of small aromatic citron, called YUZU, with salt. Is used as a seasoning or condiment.

ゆずみそ 柚子味噌〔調味料〕 fermented soybean paste mixed with a small aromatic citron called YUZU. →味噌

ゆずゆ 柚子湯〔生活〕 a hot bath scented with a small aromatic citron called YUZU. People take it on the day of the winter solstice. It is said that taking a citron bath prevents one from catching a cold.

ゆた ゆた〔宗教〕 a female shaman in Okinawa. Tells a fortune about the private matters of people while she is possessed.

ゆたん 油単〔生活〕 **(1)** a cloth cover on a chest of drawers. Usually has a family crest. **(2)** oiled cloth or paper. Was used to cover furniture or as a floor covering in olden times.

ゆたんぽ 湯湯婆〔家具〕 a hot water bottle. Used to warm feet in bed. Is becoming outdated because people nowadays tend to use electric devices.

ゆとう 湯桶〔食器〕 a small wooden lacquered pitcher. Contains the hot water that has been used for boiling buckwheat noodles. After eating cold buckwheat noodles, people mix the remaining dipping sauce with the hot water served in 'yutou' and drink the mixture.

ゆどうふ 湯豆腐〔食べ物〕 boiled tofu served in a pot. Eaten after being dipped in a special sauce. Vegetables or mushrooms are often added.

ゆとうよみ 湯桶読み〔漢字〕 reading a two-kanji compound in a Japanese-style pronunciation for the first kanji and in a Chinese-style pronunciation for the second kanji. For example, in the word 湯桶, which means "a small wooden pitcher for hot water," the first kanji 湯 is pronounced as 'yu,' which is the Japanese-style pronunciation of the kanji, called KUN'YOMI. On the other hand, the second kanji 桶 is pronounced as 'tou,' which is the Chinese-style pronunciation of the kanji, called ON'YOMI. ↔重箱読み

ゆどの 湯殿〔風呂・建築〕 the old term for a bathroom.

ゆとりきょういく ゆとり教育〔教育〕 more relaxed education. Was adopted as an education policy, from 2002 to 2010, to reduce the amount of learning and to promote voluntary learning. Actually, however, students' academic abilities went down, and the policy was abolished in 2011.

ゆな 湯女〔風呂・セックス〕 a prostitute at a public bath in the Edo period. Washed the guest, served sake, and gave him bed service.

ゆにばあさるすたじおじゃぱん ユニバーサル・スタジオ・ジャパン〔娯楽・施設〕 Universal Studio Japan. A movie theme park, located in Osaka City. Opened in 2001.

ゆねすこむけいぶんかいさん ユネスコ無形文化遺産〔行政〕 UNESCO Intangible Cultural Heritage. As of 2016, 21 Japanese items, including Noh, KABUKI, BUNRAKU, GAGAKU, WASHOKU, and WASHI, have been registered.

ゆのはな 湯の華 〔風呂〕 sinter, or mineral deposits of hot spring water.

ゆのみぢゃわん 湯呑茶碗 〔食器〕 a teacup without a handle. Is usually ceramic. The sizes and textures vary.

ゆば 湯葉 〔食べ物〕 skin of soybean milk, or a tofu sheet. Is used in various ways in traditional cuisine. Is mainly produced in Kyoto and Nikko.

ゆびき 湯引き 〔食べ物〕 parboiled meat. Examples include chicken, pike conger, sea bream, and pufferfish.

ゆびきり 指切り 〔遊び・精神性〕 to cross little fingers as a token of a firm promise. The two individuals sing a song beginning with a phrase 'yubikiri genman' in unison. The words of the song mean "If you should tell a lie, I will make you swallow one thousand needles."

ゆびつめ 指詰め 〔ヤクザ〕 to cut off a finger as penalty or for apology. The first knuckle of a little finger is usually cut.

ゆふいん 由布院 〔温泉・地名〕 a hot spring in the center of Ooita Pref. Surrounded by rivers and forests, has developed as part of Beppu hot spring resort since the early 20th century. To preserve the pastoral scenic beauty, the local people defeated the plans of building a dam and a golf resort in Yufuin Town. Because of the regulations on de-

velopment activities, there is no huge hotel or entertainment area.

ゆぶね 湯船 〔生活〕 a bathtub. People soak in it but should not wash themselves or put a towel in the water.

ゆべし 柚餅子 〔食べ物〕 rice cake with the flavor of a small aromatic citron called YUZU. Ingredients usually are rice flour, sugar, miso, walnuts, and yuzu, though they vary by region.

ゆみとりしき 弓取り式 〔相撲〕 the bow-twirling ceremony. Is held after the final bout each day by a designated wrestler.

ゆみはりぢょうちん 弓張り提灯 〔生活〕 a paper lantern with a bow-shaped handle.

ゆみへん 弓偏 〔漢字〕 a left-side radical meaning "bow." Is used in kanji such as 引 (pull), 弦 (bowstring), and 強 (strong).

ゆめどの 夢殿 〔仏教〕 the Hall of Visions. The main building in the eastern precinct of the Horyuji Temple. Is said to have been built at the residence site of Prince Shoutoku. Yumedono itself is a National Treasure, and several Buddhist images are kept there, including Guze Kannon, also a National Treasure.

ゆめぴりか ゆめぴりか 〔食べ物・植物〕 a new brand of rice. Began to be developed in Hokkaido in 1997. Is very tasty.

ゆるきゃら ゆるキャラ 〔ゆるキャラ〕 a relaxing mascot character. Is

not fashionable, but it is cute and relaxes people. Is used to promote a place, event, or organization that it represents. Often appears as a real-life figure, with a human wearing its costume, at promotional events. Famous examples include Kumamon at Kumamoto Pref., Funasshii at Funabashi City, Chiba Pref., and Hikonyan at Hikone Castle, Shiga Pref.

ゆわり 湯割り 〖酒〗 mixture of distilled alcohol and hot water. Usually uses Japanese spirits called SHOU-CHUU.

よ

よあけまえ 夜明け前 〔文芸・作品〕 *Before the Dawn*. A historical novel published in parts from 1929 to 1935 by SHIMAZAKI TOUSON. Describes the life of a scholar of the Japanese classics from the end of the Edo period to the Meiji Restoration in the 19th century.

よいやま 宵山 〔祭礼〕 a pre-festival. Usually refers to the eve of the Gion Festival in Kyoto. →祇園祭

ようおん 拗音 〔言語〕 a contracted sound. Is spelled as 'y' in the alphabet, except for 'h' in 'sha,' 'shu,' and 'sho.' Is spelled with a small や, ゅ, or ょ in hiragana and a small ャ, ュ, or ョ in katakana. Since a contracted sound is a phoneme, its presence affects the meaning of a word. For example, 'inkyo' with a contracted sound means "a retired person," while 'inko' without a contracted sound means "a parakeet."

ようかい 妖怪 〔妖怪〕 a generic term for monster, goblin, and ogre in folklore. Some are horrifying and harmful, while others are just mischievous and sometimes humorous. Still others are even helpful to humans. Usually are said to appear at a specific location and time.

ようかん 羊羹 〔食べ物〕 a rectangu-

lar bar of sweet adzuki paste jelly. Is about 20 cm long and sliced into about 2 or 3 cm thick pieces when eaten. Goes well with green tea.

ようきょく 謡曲 〔音楽〕 ⇨謡(うたい)

ようげん 用言 〔言語〕 a content word with inflectional endings. Can be a predicate independently. Includes verbs, i-adjectives, and na-adjectives. ↔体言

ようさい 栄西 〔仏教〕 ⇨栄西(えいさい)

ようじがくれ 楊枝隠れ 〔忍者〕 the hiding technique with a toothpick. A ninja flipped away a toothpick and, while the opponent's attention was distracted to it, concealed himself.

ようじゅつ 妖術 〔忍者・宗教〕 witchcraft. In some fictional stories, a ninja is described as a supernatural magician; however, they were actually not, even though their physical and psychological abilities were remarkable.

ようしょく 洋食 〔食文化〕 Western-style cuisine. This term refers to both real Western dishes and quasi-one. For example, "curry and rice" and "ketchup fried rice wrapped in a thin omelette" are categorized as 'youshoku,' though they were invented in Japan. ↔和食

ようじんなわ 用心縄 〔忍者〕 the device to trap an enemy by stretching a strap at the entrance of a room. One of the seven techniques of using a sword strap. →下げ緒七術

ようぜいてんのう 陽成天皇 〔天皇〕

Emperor Youzei. 868-949. The 57th, on the throne from 876 to 884. Was dethroned because of several eccentric behavior.

ようにん 用人〖武士〗 a household manager of a high-ranking samurai family including a shogun and feudal lords in the Edo period.

ようにん 陽忍〖忍者〗 the visible tactics. To show oneself to fulfill one's duty while concealing one's identity. For example, he or she intruded upon enemies by disguising oneself. A ninja conducted either visible or invisible tactics according to the situation. ↔陰忍(にん)

ようめいがく 陽明学〖人文学〗 the teaching of Wang Yang-ming. A school of Confucianism. Preaches that knowledge must be accompanied by practice. Was studied in the Edo period.

ようめいてんのう 用明天皇〖天皇〗 Emperor Youmei. ?-584. The 31st, on the throne from 585 to 587. The father of Prince Shoutoku. During his reign, two powerful clans, Soga and Mononobe, had conflicts with each other about the introduction of Buddhism. →聖徳太子

ようめいもん 陽明門〖神社・建築〗 Yomeimon Gate. A gate of Toshogu Shrine in Nikko, Tochigi Pref. A National Treasure. Is also called 'Higurashi no mon,' which means "all-day-long gate," because its decoration is too elaborate to appreciate in a short time. →日光東照宮

ようらく 瓔珞〖仏教〗 jewelry ornaments for Buddhist images or temples. Bodhisattvas (BOSATSU), Wisdom Kings (MYOUOU), or Devas (TEN-BU) wear them while Buddhas (NYORAI), excepting the Great Sun Buddha, do not.

ようろうのたき 養老の滝〖自然〗 the Yourou Falls. Is located in southwestern Gifu Pref. A spring near the falls has a legend that sake gushed out of it. A budget pub chain, 'Yourou no Taki,' is named after this legend.

ようろうりつりょう 養老律令〖政治〗 Yourou Code. Was compiled in 718 by FUJIWARA NO FUHITO, based on a modification of the Taihou Code. →大宝律令

よおすてん ヨーステン〖ビジネス〗 ⇨ヤン・ヨーステン

よがんいん 与願印〖仏教・美術〗 the mudra for fulfilling a wish. Usually, the left hand hangs down or is placed on the thigh. Its palm is turned toward the front, and its fingers are stretched or slightly bent. Is usually combined with the mudra of the right hand for soothing fear, SEMUI-IN.

よくかい 欲界〖仏教〗 ⇨欲界(かい)

よこいしょういち 横井庄一〖戦争〗 1915-1997. An ex-army soldier born in Aichi Pref. Hid himself in a jungle of Guam Island for 28 years after World War II, not knowing that the war was over. Was found in 1972.

よこがき 横書き〖言語〗 to write

a text horizontally. Letters and characters used to be written from the right to left, but the opposite direction, namely the same way as English and other European languages, became popular after World War II. ↔縦書き

よこづな 横綱 〖相撲〗 a grand champion of sumo. Once a sumo wrestler becomes a yokozuna, he is not supposed to be demoted. It means he has to keep strong or retire when weak.

よこづなしんぎいいんかい 横綱審議委員会 〖相撲〗 Yokozuna Deliberation Council. An advisory committee of the Japan Sumo Association. Was established in 1950. Consists of 15 or fewer members. Discusses and reports various issues including the promotion of a wrestler to a grand champion, yokozuna.

よこづなどひょういり 横綱土俵入り 〖相撲〗 yokozuna's ceremonial entrance to the ring. Wearing a thick white rope and a decorative apron, the grand champion claps his hands and stomps on the ground in one of two styles: UNRYUU-GATA or SHIRANUI-GATA.

よこはまし 横浜市 〖地名〗 Yokohama City. Is an ordinance-designated city, and the capital of Kanagawa Pref., located in its eastern part. Since the opening of the port in 1859, rapidly developed and has become the second largest city in Japan. Has many sightsee-

ing spots and historical landmarks which were constructed after the Meiji Restoration. Many tourist spots are scattered around its bay area, such as Yokohama Landmark Tower (296 m high), Yamashita Park, Chinatown, and the Red Brick Warehouse. Sankeien Park and Souji-ji Temple (the head monastery of the Soutou sect) are also popular.

よこみつりいち 横光利一 〖文芸〗 1898-1947. A novelist born in Fukushima Pref. His works include *The Fly* in 1923, *Machine* in 1930, and *Shanghai* in 1931.

よこやまたいかん 横山大観 〖絵画〗 1868-1958. A painter born in Ibaraki Pref. Was taught by OKAKURA TENSHIN and Hashimoto Gahou. Invented the vague style with blurred outlines. Painted many pictures of Mt. Fuji. His works include *Metempsychosis* (Seisei-ruten) at the National Museum of Modern Art, Tokyo.

よさのあきこ 与謝野晶子 〖文芸〗 1878-1942. A tanka poet born in Osaka. The wife of YOSANO TEKKAN. Her works include a tanka collection *Tangled Hair* (Midaregami) in 1901, and an antiwar poem "Beloved, You Must Not Die" (Kimi, shinitamou-koto nakare) in 1904.

よさのてっかん 与謝野鉄幹 〖文芸〗 1873-1935. A poet born in Kyoto. The husband of YOSANO AKIKO. Started a poetry magazine, *Myou-*

jou, in 1900.

よさぶそん 与謝蕪村〚芸術〛 1716
-1783. A painter and haiku poet
born in present Osaka Pref. After
studying painting and haiku in Edo,
settled down in Kyoto. His works
as a painter include *Album of Ten
Conveniences and Ten Pleasures*
(Juuben-juugi), which was a collaboration with IKE NO TAIGA. His
works as a poet include *Dawn Crow*
(Akegarasu).

よしかわえいじ 吉川英治 〚文芸〛
1892-1962. A writer of historical
novels born in Kanagawa Pref. His
works include *Musashi* (Miyamoto
Musashi) in 1939 and *The Heike
Story* (Shin-Heike-monogatari) in
1957.

よじじゅくご 四字熟語〚漢字〛 a
four-kanji compound word. Some
of them are based on Chinese classics or historical events, and others
come from Buddhism.

よしず 葦簀〚生活〛 a reed screen.
Is used to block the sunlight in
summer.

よしだけんこう 吉田兼好 〚文芸〛
1283-1352? A poet and essayist born in Kyoto. His father was
a Shinto priest, but he became a
Buddhist priest around the age
30. His works include *Essays in
Idleness* (Tsureduregusa).

よしだしげる 吉田茂〚政治〛 1878
-1967. A statesman born in Tokyo.
Was appointed as a prime minister five times. Concluded the San
Francisco Peace Treaty in 1951 to

end World War II.

よしだしょういん 吉田松陰〚教育・
人文学〛 1830-1859. A thinker and
educator born in Yamaguchi Pref.
At a school called SHOUKASON-JUKU
in Hagi, educated significant figures
of the Meiji Restoration such as
TAKASUGI SHINSAKU, ITOU HIROBUMI,
Yamagata Aritomo, and Kusaka
Genzui.

よしだみつよし 吉田光由〚科学技術〛
1598-1672. A mathematician born
in Kyoto. Wrote *Jingouki*, a best-
selling textbook of mathematics in
the Edo period.

よしど 葦戸〚建築〛 a sliding door
with a reed screen. Blocks the
sunlight and permits the breeze to
come in.

よしの 吉野〚地名〛 the area in central Nara Pref. Produces Japanese
cedars and sweet fish. Politically,
Prince Ooama, later Emperor Tenmu, temporarily retired here and
started the Jinshin War in 672.
Emperor Godaigo moved here from
Kyoto in 1336, after which time the
period of the Northern and Southern Courts started. →壬申(じん)の乱；
南北朝時代

よしのがりいせき 吉野ヶ里遺跡
〚史跡〛 the Yoshinogari Ruins. Is
located in eastern Saga Pref. Remains of residences, storehouses,
and graves in the Yayoi period have
been excavated. The outer moat is
about 2.5 km long. Several facilities
have been restored.

よしのがわ 吉野川 〚河川〛 the

Yoshino River. Flows from Mt. Ishizuchi in Ehime Pref. into the Kii Channel between Wakayama and Tokushima Prefs. Its length is 194 km, making it the longest river in SHIKOKU. Two gorges along it, named OOBOKE KOBOKE, are famous as scenic spots. Is also called 'Shikoku Saburou.'

よしのすぎ 吉野杉 〖植物〗 a cedar produced in the YOSHINO area, Nara Pref. Is mainly used to make sake casks.

よじょうはん 四畳半 〖建築〗 a room with four and a half TATAMI mats. Its floor is square and about 7.5 m² in area.

よしわら 吉原 〖娯楽・セックス〗 the prostitution area in Edo, which was authorized by the Tokugawa shogunate. Was first located in present Nihonbashi, but relocated in the 17th century to the area near Asakusa.

よせ 寄席 〖落語〗 traditional vaudeville. Contains comic storytelling (RAKUGO), rhythmical storytelling of historical episodes or fictions (KOUDAN), comic dialogue (MANZAI), magic, and other performing arts.

よせぎづくり 寄木造り 〖彫刻〗 carving technique for a sculpture, using joined blocks of wood. Made the processes more productive by permitting multiple people to work on the sculpture. Was developed in the 10th century by a sculptor called Jouchou. Examples include the Amitabha Buddha at Byoudouin

Temple in Kyoto and the Two Guardian Kings at the south main gate of Toudai-ji Temple in Nara. ↔ 一木造り

よせげいにん 寄席芸人 〖芸能〗 a vaudevillian.

よせなべ 寄せ鍋 〖食べ物〗 a one-pot dish with a variety of ingredients such as vegetables, mushrooms, tofu, seafood, and meat. People sit around one pot and take their favorite food to their plate while the food is cooking. Dipping sauce is not used.

よせばし 寄せ箸 〖食文化〗 to pull a dish closer to oneself using chopsticks. Is regarded as bad etiquette, known as KIRAI-BASHI.

よせむねづくり 寄棟造り 〖建築〗 a building style with a hip roof. An example is seen on the Great Buddha Hall of TOUDAI-JI Temple in Nara Pref. →入母屋(いりもや)造り；切妻(きりづま)造り

よたか 夜鷹 〖娯楽・セックス〗 an unofficial prostitute in the Edo period. Looked for clients on the street.

よたろう 与太郎 〖落語〗 a stupid young man in a traditional comic storytelling called RAKUGO. Literally takes what another person says, without understanding the context, and causes funny events to occur.

よっかい 欲界 〖仏教〗 the world of desires. Namely this world. Exists under the world of beings with form, called SHIKIKAI.

よっかいちぜんそく 四日市喘息 〖公害〗 Yokkaichi Asthma. A pollution

disease that occurred in Yokkaichi City in Mie Pref. around 1960. The cause was air pollution let out by a petrochemical complex.

よつずもう 四つ相撲 〖相撲〗 a bout or a state in which both wrestlers grasp the opponents' loincloth with both hands.

よつめがき 四つ目垣 〖建築〗 a fence of bamboo lattice. Artificial bamboo is sometimes used.

よつやかいだん 四谷怪談 〖歌舞伎・作品〗 ⇨東海道四谷怪談

よどどの 淀殿 〖政治〗 1567-1615. An official sub-wife of TOYOTOMI HIDEYOSHI, born in present Shiga Pref. The eldest daughter of AZAI NAGAMASA, and the mother of TOYOTOMI HIDEYORI. After the death of Hideyoshi, intervened in political affairs, living in Osaka Castle. Was attacked in the Summer Campaign in Osaka by TOKUGAWA IEYASU and committed suicide together with Hideyori.

よどやたつごろう 淀屋辰五郎 〖ビジネス〗 ?-? A wealthy merchant in the 17th to 18th centuries, born in Osaka. Had his property confiscated and was exiled from Osaka because of his overtly luxurious lifestyle.

よなきそば 夜鳴き蕎麦 〖食文化〗 noodles sold at a street vendor's stall at night.

よなぐにじま 与那国島 〖島名〗 Yonaguni Island. The westernmost island of Japan. Is located at 122 degrees 56 minutes east. Its area is 29 km^2.

よねざわひこはち 米沢彦八 〖落語〗 ?-1714. The father of Osaka-style comic storytelling called RAKUGO. Performed at the Ikukunitama Shrine in Osaka.

よばい 夜這い 〖セックス〗 night crawling. An old custom that a young unmarried man sneaked into a woman's room at night to make love.

よびこう 予備校 〖教育〗 a private preparatory school mainly for university entrance examinations. Provides not only ordinary lectures but also trial exams, course consultation, and video lectures.

よびだし 呼び出し 〖相撲〗 an usher. Calls wrestlers' name in the ring before each bout.

よぶこ 呼子 〖妖怪〗 ⇨山彦

よみうりしんぶん 読売新聞 〖マスコミ〗 *The Yomiuri Shimbun*. One of the five major newspapers. Started in 1874 and had a circulation of about nine million as of 2016.

よみがな 読み仮名 〖漢字〗 ⇨振り仮名

よみくだし 読み下し 〖言語〗 to read Chinese classics as the Japanese language. Is possible by adding some kana characters as grammatical aids and some numbers to show the reading order.

よみせ 夜店 〖祭礼・ビジネス〗 a night fair. Various stalls such as food sellers, prize game stands, and goldfish scooping are lined up in rows.

よみのくに 黄泉の国 〖神話〗 Land

of Darkness. The world where dead souls are dwelling. The wife of the first couple in the mythology, IZANAMI NO MIKOTO, dwelt here after bearing the deity of fire and being burned to death. Its concept is different from the hell in Buddhism, where sinful souls are punished.

よみふだ 読み札〖娯楽〗 a reading card in a traditional matching card game, called KARUTA. One player reads aloud a text on a reading card, and other players pick out the matching card among pick-up cards spread on the floor. ↔取り札

よみほん 読み本〖文芸〗 books for reading from the 18th to 19th centuries. Were so called because their purpose was for reading, different from illustrated books, kusa-zoushi. Mainly contain imaginary, fantasy, or historical novels. Examples include *The Eight Dog Chronicles* (Nansou Satomi Hakkenden) by Takizawa Bakin and *Tales of Moonlight and Rain* (Ugetsu Monogatari) by Ueda Akinari. →南総里見八犬伝; 雨月物語

よめいりどうぐ 嫁入り道具〖結婚〗 personal effects brought by a bride to her husband's household.

よもぎ 蓬〖植物〗 a mugwort. *Artemisia indica*. Grows wild all over Japan, and has a characteristic odor. Is sometimes made into a paste and is mixed with a rice cake. The crude material for moxa.

よもぎもち 蓬餅〖食べ物〗 ⇨草餅

よもつひらさか 黄泉平坂〖神話〗 a slope or a tunnel between this world and the Land of Darkness. The husband of the first couple in mythology, IZANAGI NO MIKOTO, blocked its exit after he escaped from the Land of Darkness so that his demonized wife, Izanami, could not catch him.

よりき 与力〖武士・官位〗 a platoon commander under a feudal commissioner in the Edo period. Headed a patrol and guard unit of lower-level officers called DOUSHIN.

よりきり 寄り切り〖相撲〗 a frontal force-out. A technique to hold the opponent's loincloth by both hands and to drive him out of the ring.

よりしろ 依代〖神道〗 an object for a deity to descend upon. Various objects such as a rock, tree, or animal can be a 'yorishiro.'

よりつき 寄り付き〖茶道〗 a small room for a guest to prepare for the tea ceremony. A guest ready for the tea ceremony moves on to a hut or an anteroom called MACHIAI.

よるせき 夜席〖落語〗 the evening performance at traditional vaudeville called YOSE.

よろい 鎧〖武器〗 a suit of armor. Protects the torso, shoulders, arms, and legs.

よろしくおねがいします 宜しくお願いします〖精神性・言語〗 "I look forward to your interest." This phrase is used in various scenes or documents. For example, when people meet each other for the first time, or when a person asks another person to do something.

よろずや　万屋　〚ビジネス〛　a small general shop. Sells daily necessities. Is decreasing in number because of the expansion of supermarkets and convenience store chains.

よんかこくじょうやく　四か国条約 〚外交〛　Four-Power Treaty. A December 1921 treaty that resulted from the Washington Conference and that was signed by France, Great Britain, Japan, and the United States. Signatories agreed that (a) all four would be consulted if there was any issue related to the East Asia region that concerned any two of them, and (b) all four would respect each other's interests in the region. The treaty later was considered to be too vague to prevent aggression by Japan.

よんごうびん　四合瓶　〚酒〛　a 720 cc bottle for sake. One of the most popular sizes when buying sake at a liquor shop. →一升瓶; ～合

よんこままんが　四コマ漫画　〚漫画〛　a four-frame comic strip. Often applies the four-phase structure in Chinese classic poems: introduction, development, turn, and conclusion. Is mainly serialized in a newspaper. →起承転結

ら

らあめん ラーメン〔食べ物〕 ramen. Chinese-style noodles in broth. Its varied tastes include soy sauce, salt, and miso. Toppings include sliced roast pork, pickled bamboo shoots, and chopped green onions. One of the most popular foods in Japan. The instant type without ingredients is sold in a plastic bag, while the precooked type with ingredients is sold in a cup of foaming polystyrol.

らあめんさらだ ラーメンサラダ〔食べ物〕 a ramen salad. Combination of vegetable salad and ramen noodles, without broth. Originated in Hokkaido.

らいごう 来迎〔仏教〕 ⇨阿弥陀来迎

らいさんよう 頼山陽〔人文学〕 1780-1832. A Confucianist, poet, and historian born in Osaka. Wrote the 22-volume *Nihon Gaishi*, which means "an unofficial history of Japan." His historical view stimulated those who tried to revere the Emperor and expel the foreigners.

らいしゃわあ ライシャワー〔人文学〕 Edwin Reischauer. 1910-1990. An American diplomat and scholar, born in Japan when his parents were missionaries there. Served as U.S. ambassador to Japan in the 1960s. Taught Asian studies at Harvard and wrote many books on Japan, such as *Japan, Past and Present* (1946), *The United States and Japan* (1950), *Japan: The Story of a Nation* (1970), and *The Japanese* (1977). Strong proponent of Japan throughout his life. As a member of the so-called "Chrysanthemum Club," he is regarded by some scholars as being an apologist and uncritical observer of Japan.

らいじゅう 雷獣〔妖怪〕 a thunder beast. An imaginary creature that comes down to the ground with a thunderbolt and strikes trees or buildings.

らいじん 雷神〔宗教〕 Thunder God. Brings small drums and sticks and is usually paired with the Wind God. This image was probably introduced to Japan together with Buddhism because the thunder deity in Japanese mythology, named TAKEMIKADUCHI NO ONOKAMI, did not have drums. →風神

らいちょう 雷鳥〔動物〕 a rock ptarmigan, or snow grouse. *Lagopus mutus*. Lives in mountainous areas of central Japan, higher than 3,000 m. Its feathers are brown in summer and white in winter. Is designated a Special Natural Monument.

らいでん 雷電〔軍事〕 Thunderbolt, or Mitsubishi J2M3. A fighter plane developed for World War II. The code name among the Allies was "Jack."

らいでんためえもん 雷電為右衛門 〖相撲〗 1767–1825. A sumo wrestler born in present Nagano Pref. Is said to have been the strongest in sumo history, with 254 wins and only 10 defeats in 17 years.

らいと ライト 〖建築〗 ⇨フランク・ロイド・ライト

らかん 羅漢 〖仏教〗 ⇨阿羅漢

らくいちらくざ 楽市楽座 〖経済〗 the economic policy of a free market and an open guild. Was enacted by a feudal lord in the 16th century to govern commerce in his domain. Abolished the monopolistic privilege of existing guilds and allowed newly rising business people to sell products or commodities.

らくがん 落雁 〖食べ物〗 a small, hard, dry confection made from rice flour and sugar. Is usually flower-shaped or has a relief of a picture or letters. Sometimes eaten at the tea ceremony.

らくご 落語 〖落語〗 traditional comic storytelling. A storyteller sits on a square floor cushion and acts out several roles by turning different directions and changing wording and voice tones. The tools used by a storyteller are usually only a folding fan and hand towel. Storytellers also sometimes use small clappers, called KOBYOUSHI, in the Kansai region.

らくごか 落語家 〖落語〗 a professional comic storyteller. It is said that there are about 800 professionals as of 2016.

らくしゅ 落首 〖文芸〗 an anonymous satiric verse. →落書(らくしょ)

らくしょ 落書 〖文芸〗 an anonymous satire. Was popular from medieval to early-modern times. Some of them still exist. A verse type is called RAKUSHU.

らくすまん ラクスマン 〖外交〗 Adam Kirilovich Laksman. 1766–1803? A Russian envoy. Visited Hokkaido in 1792, together with DAIKOKU-YA KOUDAYUU, a Japanese captain who drifted to Russia. Negotiated to establish a commercial relationship with Japan but was refused.

らくちゅうらくがいず 洛中洛外図 〖絵画〗 a painting of scenes in and around Kyoto. Famous tourist spots, festivals, and ordinary life of the common people are depicted in detail with a bird's-eye view. Is often painted on a pair of folding screens. Was popular from the 16th to 17th centuries.

らくやき 楽焼 〖陶磁器〗 Raku ware. Soft grazed pottery baked at a low temperature. Is made without using a wheel. Was invented in the 16th century in Kyoto by Choujirou. The method is usually used to make tea bowls.

らごら 羅睺羅 〖仏教〗 *Rahula*. One of the Ten Great Disciples of the Historical Buddha. Also his son. Foremost among the disciples in esoteric practices. →十大弟子

らじおたいそう ラジオ体操 〖教育・スポーツ〗 radio gymnastic exercises. Originally people did light exercises accompanied by a music broadcast on radio. In 1928, the government began to broadcast such program but stopped it for a while after World War II. The program restarted in 1951, and the exercises spread mainly in schools.

らしょうもん 羅生門　**(1)**〖文芸・作品〗 "Rashomon." A short story published in 1915 by AKUTAGAWA RYUUNOSUKE. Describes human egoism based on an episode in *Tales of Times Now Past*, a collection of narratives written in the early 12th century. →今昔物語　**(2)**〖映画・作品〗 *Rashomon*. A psychological thriller produced in 1950. Was directed by KUROSAWA AKIRA and starred Mifune Toshirou and Kyou Machiko. The story is based on a short story by AKUTAGAWA RYUUNOSUKE, "In a Grove."

らじょうもん 羅城門　〖天皇・建築〗 the main gate of the Heijou Castle or Heian Castle. Was located at the southern end of the main street.

らせつ 羅刹　〖仏教〗 an ogre. *Raksasa*. A devil in Indian mythology that eats humans. Was incorporated into Buddhism. →羅刹天

らせつてん 羅刹天　〖仏教〗 Ogre Deva. *Raksasa*. One of the Twelve Devas. Guards the southwest.

らっかん 落款　〖絵画・書道〗 a signature and a seal of a painter or calligrapher. Is placed at the corner of the work. The date or location of completion, or the title, is some-times added.

らっきょう ラッキョウ　〖食べ物〗 a Chinese scallion, or a Japanese shallot. *Allium chinense*. Eaten as pickles.

らっぱ 乱破　〖忍者〗 a generic term for ninja in the present Kantou region. Among them, ninja who served the Houjou clan around present Kanagawa Pref. were called FUUMA NINJA.

らでん 螺鈿　〖美術〗 mother-of-pearl inlay. Is fixed into lacquer or a wooden surface to decorate accessories, furniture, or a building's interior.

らぬきことば ラ抜き言葉　〖言語〗 an auxiliary verb to indicate potentiality, omitting 'ra.' Some auxiliary verbs to indicate potentiality include the sound 'ra,' which is sometimes missing. For example, 'mirareru' that means "can look," sometimes becomes 'mireru' by omitting 'ra.' Those who are strict about grammar hate this trend.

らふかでぃおはあん ラフカディオ・ハーン　〖文芸〗 ⇨小泉八雲

らぶほてる ラブホテル　〖セックス・娯楽〗 a love hotel. A short-stay hotel specializing in offering couples the opportunity to sleep together.

らほつ 螺髪　〖仏教〗 short spiral curly hair on Buddha's head. One of the thirty-two major physical characteristics of Buddha. →三十二相八十種好

らむさあるじょうやくとうろくしっち ラムサール条約登録湿地　〖自

然・政治〛 Ramsar site. A wetlands location considered to be important by the Ramsar Wetlands Convention, an international environmental treaty signed in Ramsar, Iran, in 1971. Over 2,000 Ramsar sites have been designated around the world.

らんがく 蘭学〚人文学〛 Dutch learning. Its contents were the study of Western science and culture written in the Dutch language, because the only Western language that was allowed to be studied during the national seclusion was Dutch. Dutch learning developed in the 18th century and had a great influence on medical, natural, and social science in Japan.

らんがくしゃ 蘭学者〚人文学〛 a scholar of Dutch learning.

らんじゃたい 蘭奢待〚香道〛 piece of high-quality aloeswood kept at the SHOUSOU-IN warehouse of Toudai-ji Temple. Is said to have come from China in ancient times and to have been stored at the Toudai-ji Temple in the 8th century. Is said to have been cut partly by ASHIKAGA YOSHIMITSU, ODA NOBUNAGA, TOKUGAWA IEYASU, and other power holders in history. Is 153 cm long and 130 kg in weight. →伽羅(きゃら)

らんじゅほうしょう 藍綬褒章〚政治〛 the Medal with Blue Ribbon. Is "awarded to individuals who have made prosperous efforts in the areas of public welfare and education," says the Cabinet Office. →褒章

らんしんぐいしいきょうてい ランシング・石井協定〚外交〛 ⇨石井・ランシング協定

らんどせる ランドセル〚教育〛 a backpack for an elementary school child. Traditionally, black for boys and red for girls, but one can choose from a variety of colors nowadays.

らんどり 乱取り〚武術〛 free practice in judo. Two players fight each other as if it is a match.

らんぽうい 蘭方医〚医療〛 a doctor of Western medicine. This term was used to distinguish a Western medical doctor from a doctor of Chinese medicine in the Edo period. ↔漢方医

らんま 欄間〚建築〛 an opening between the ceiling and a lintel for sliding screens. Its original purpose was ventilation and lighting, but later the opening was developed to include openwork.

り ～里〚単位〛 a unit of distance. One 'ri' is about 4 km.

りいち リーチ〚工芸〛 ⇨バーナード・リーチ

りかがくけんきゅうじょ 理化学研究所〚科学技術・研究機関〛 RIKEN. An institute of physical and chemical research founded in 1917. Was reorganized as an independent administrative institution in 2003. Produced great scientists such as TERADA TORAHIKO, YUKAWA HIDEKI, and TOMONAGA SHIN'ICHIROU.

りきし 力士 **(1)**〖相撲〗⇨相撲取り **(2)**〖仏教〗⇨金剛力士

りきどうざん 力道山 〖スポーツ〗 1924-1963. A professional wrestler born in Korea. His real name was Kim Sin-rak in Korean and Momota Mitsuhiro in Japanese. After retiring from sumo, established the first promotional association of professional wrestling. Giant Baba was his disciple. →ジャイアント馬場

りきゅう 利休〖茶道〗⇨千利休

りきゅう 離宮〖天皇・建築〗 a Detached Palace. There are two detached palaces: KATSURA RIKYUU and SHUGAKUIN RIKYUU, both in Kyoto. →御用邸

りきゅうばし 利休箸〖茶道〗 chopsticks with both ends sharpened. Are made of cedar and often used for tea-ceremony cuisine.

りくぎえん 六義園〖庭園〗 a landscape garden with a circular path, located in Bunkyou-ku, Tokyo. Was completed in 1702 under the order of Yanagisawa Yoshiyasu, a favorite retainer of the 5th Tokugawa shogun, TOKUGAWA TSUNAYOSHI.

りくじょうきょうぎ 陸上競技〖スポーツ〗 track and field. Was introduced to Japan at the beginning of the Meiji period. Oda Mikio won the first gold medal for Japan in the triple jump at the Amsterdam Olympics in 1928.

りくぜん 陸前〖旧国名〗 the name in the early Meiji era of central and northern Miyagi Pref. and southeastern Iwate Pref.

りくちゅう 陸中〖旧国名〗 the name in the early Meiji era of Iwate Pref., except its southeastern part.

りくとう 陸稲〖農業・植物〗 ⇨陸稲（おかぼ）

りけん 理研〖科学技術・施設〗⇨理化学研究所

りちゅうてんのう 履中天皇〖天皇〗 Emperor Richuu. ?-? The 17th, in the early 5th century. The eldest son of Emperor Nintoku. Is sometimes identified as 'San,' one of the Five Kings of Wa, which were described in a historical document of Sung.

りつ 律 **(1)**〖法律〗⇨律令 **(2)**〖音楽・単位〗 the unit of a pitch. One 'ritsu' corresponds to a halftone in Western music.

りっか 立夏〖暦〗 one of the 24 seasonal nodes in the traditional calendar. Around May 6 in the current calendar. Means "the summer season begins." →二十四節気（にじゅうしせっき）

りっか 立華〖華道〗 the vertical arrangement of flowers in a vase.

りっけんかいしんとう 立憲改進党〖政治〗 Constitutional Reform Party. Was established in 1882 by OOKUMA SHIGENOBU to promote British-style constitutional monarchy. Was disbanded in 1896 to establish the Progressive Party (Shinpo-tou).

りっこくし 六国史 〖政治・書名〗 Six National Histories. Official chronicles compiled from the 8th to 12th centuries. *NIHONSHOKI, SHOKU NIHON-GI, NIHON-KOUKI, SHOKU NIHON-KOUKI, NIHON MONTOKU TENNOU JITSUROKU,* and *NIHON SANDAI JITSUROKU.*

りっし 律師 〖仏教〗 the title of the third class of an official priest. →僧正; 僧都(そうづ)

りっし 律詩 〖文芸〗 a Chinese-style classic poem, made up of eight lines. ↔絶句 →五言律詩; 七言律詩

りっしゃくじ 立石寺 〖寺院〗 Risshaku-ji Temple. Is commonly called 'Yamadera.' Affiliated with the Tendai sect. Is located in eastern Yamagata Pref. Was founded in 860 by the priest Ennin. Famous for a haiku by Matsuo Basho: deep silence - / the shrill of cicadas / seeps into rocks (translated by Robert Hass).

りっしゅう 立秋 〖暦〗 one of the 24 seasonal nodes in the traditional calendar. Around August 8 in the current calendar. Means "the autumn season begins." →二十四節気(にじゅうしせっき)

りっしゅう 律宗 〖仏教〗 the Ritsu sect. One of the Six Sects of Nara. Was introduced from China in 754 by a Chinese priest, *GANJIN.* Emphasizes the observance of monastic discipline. The head temple is *TOUSHOUDAI-JI* Temple in Nara. →南都六宗

りっしゅん 立春 〖暦〗 one of the 24 seasonal nodes in the traditional calendar. Around February 4 in the current calendar. Means "the spring season begins." →二十四節気(にじゅうしせっき)

りっしょうこうせいかい 立正佼成会 〖宗教〗 Rissho Kosei-kai. A new Buddhist organization which follows the teaching of Nichiren. Was founded in 1938 by Niwano Nikkyou and Naganuma Myoukou, once members of *REIYUUKAI.*

りっしんべん 立心偏 〖漢字〗 a left-side radical meaning "heart." Is used in kanji such as 忙 (busy), 快 (comfortable), and 性 (sex).

りつぞう 立像 〖彫刻〗 a standing sculpture. →座像; 椅像(いぞう)

りっとう 立冬 〖暦〗 one of the 24 seasonal nodes in the traditional calendar. Around November 7 in the current calendar. Means "the winter season begins." →二十四節気(にじゅうしせっき)

りっとんちょうさだん リットン調査団 〖外交〗 Lytton Commission. A five-person group established by the League of Nations to investigate Japan's military activity in Manchuria in the early 1930s. Was led by Count Lytton. The commission's report concluded that Japan had been the aggressor. The acceptance of the report by the League of Nations was followed by Japan's withdrawal from the League in 1933.

りつりょう 律令 〖法律〗 fundamental laws in ancient times. Were

formulated in the 7th and 8th centuries, modeling on the example of Chinese dynasties. 'Ritsu' corresponded to the criminal codes, and 'ryou' corresponded to the administrative laws.

りつりょうせい 律令制 〔政治〕 the centralized administration system based on laws in ancient times. Was established in the 7th century, modeled on the examples of Chinese dynasties. →律令

りつれいしき 立礼式 〔茶道〕 ⇨立礼 (りゅうれい)式

りとるぼおい リトルボーイ 〔武器〕 Little Boy. A uranium-type atomic bomb dropped on Hiroshima on August 6, 1945. About 3 m long, 71 cm in diameter, and 4 t in weight.

りまんかいりゅう リマン海流 〔海洋〕 the Liman current. A cold current around Japan. Starts in the Tatar Strait and flows along the coast of Siberia to the Korean Peninsula. It is thought that the Tsushima Warm Current turns around and gets cool. →対馬海流

りゅう 竜 〔宗教・動物〕 a dragon. In legend, has a snake-like long body covered with scales, four legs, and two horns. Usually lives in water and sometimes flies in the sky. Unlike a dragon in Western cultures, is worshipped as a deity of water. →四神(しん)

りゅうおう 竜王 〔将棋〕 **(1)** a dragon king. The promoted rook, HISHA. Is commonly called 'ryuu.' Is considered to be the strongest piece in shogi. **(2)** Dragon King. One of the eight titles in professional shogi. Is named after ryuuou (1). The best-of-seven title match, 'Ryuuou-sen,' takes place annually between October and January. The winner of this title match gets a prize of over ¥40,000,000, the highest of all the shogi titles.

りゅうおうせん 竜王船 〔忍者〕 a dragon boat. Was shaped like a dragon and traveled under water. Probably fictional.

りゅうきゅうおうこく 琉球王国 〔国名〕 Ryuukyuu Kingdom. Was established in 1429. Was invaded and came to be governed in 1609 by a Japanese feudal domain, SATSUMA-HAN. Was incorporated as a prefecture into the modern Japanese administrative system in 1879.

りゅうきゅうしょとう 琉球諸島 〔島名〕 the southern half of the Southwest Islands, which stretches between Kyushu and Taiwan. Consist of the Okinawa Islands and the Sakishima Islands. →南西諸島

りゅうきゅうほうげん 琉球方言 〔言語〕 Ryukyuan. The dialect in the Okinawa area. Some researchers consider it to be an independent language, though belonging to the same family as Japanese. Is also called 'uchinaaguchi' in Okinawa.

りゅうぐうじょう 竜宮城 〔民話〕 the Sea God's Palace. Is visited by URASHIMA TAROU, the hero of a fairy tale similar to Rip van Winkle. Is home to a beautiful princess,

Otohime.

りゅうこ 龍虎 〖動物・絵画〗 a dragon and a tiger. Refers to two great rivals. Originally was the following pair: the blue dragon symbolizing the east and the white tiger symbolizing the west. It is said that a dragon creates a cloud and a tiger controls a wind. Is a popular theme for India ink paintings. Examples are contained at the Nezu Museum in Tokyo and the Tokugawa Art Museum in Nagoya. →四神(じん)

りゅうず 竜頭 〖仏教〗 an ear of a temple bell. Is usually shaped like dragons' heads. →釣鐘

りゅうぜんこう 竜涎香 〖香道〗 ambergris. A perfume like pine resin. Is generated in the intestines of a sperm whale.

りゅうぞう 立像 〖彫刻〗 ⇨立像(りゅうぞう)

りゅうどすい 竜吐水 〖災害〗 a pump to extinguish a fire in the Edo period.

りゅうは 流派 〖芸道・武術〗 a school related to the tea ceremony, flower arrangement, martial arts, etc. Techniques and manners are often different from school to school.

りゅうれいしき 立礼式 〖茶道〗 a tea ceremony at tables and chairs. The host and guests both sit on chairs, not TATAMI mats. Was devised for international guests at an exposition in 1871.

りょう 〜両 〖貨幣・単位〗 a unit of money in the Edo period. One 'ryou' is worth 50,000 to 100,000 in present yen, depending on the era and the way of calculation.

りょうあんじ 龍安寺 〖寺院〗 Ryoanji Temple. Affiliated with the Myoushin-ji school of the Rinzai sect. Was founded in Kyoto in 1450 by a warlord, Hosokawa Katsumoto. Famous for the rock garden, named 'Tora-no-ko watashi,' where fifteen rocks are placed but a visitor can see only fourteen at a time. Was designated a World Heritage Site in 1994.

りょうかいまんだら 両界曼荼羅 〖仏教・絵画〗 Mandalas of the Two Realms. Mandala of the Womb Realm and Mandala of the Diamond Realm. Although they had different origins, two mandalas were combined in Chinese esoteric Buddhism and were introduced to Japan in the 9th century by KUUKAI. Several temples, including TOU-JI or JINGO-JI, possess them. →胎蔵界曼荼羅；金剛界曼荼羅

りょうがえや 両替屋 〖貨幣・ビジネス〗 a money changer in the Edo period. Exchanged gold coins with silver coins, or gold or silver coins with copper or iron coins. Took commissions on each exchange and also operated banking business.

りょうかん 良寛 〖仏教〗 1758-1831. A priest and poet born in present Niigata Pref. After making a pilgrimage throughout Japan, he came back to his home village and created Japanese and Chinese poetry and calligraphy, without belonging to a temple.

りょうげのかん 令外官〔行政〕an additional post in the centralized administration system in ancient times, called RITSURYOU-SEI. Is not prescribed in administrative laws called 'ryou.' Examples include KANPAKU, CHUUNAGON, and KEBIISHI.

りょうごくこくぎかん 両国国技館〔相撲・施設〕⇨国技館

りょうしゅ 領主〔政治〕**(1)** a feudal lord in the Edo period. **(2)** an owner of a manor in the Heian period.

りょうじんひしょう 梁塵秘抄〔文芸〕*Songs to Make the Dust Dance.* An anthology of popular songs compiled in the late 12th century by Monastic Ex-emperor Goshirakawa. Was originally in 20 volumes, but only four of them now exist. →後白河法皇

りょうてい 料亭〔食文化〕a high-class traditional restaurant. The guest eats and drinks in a private room and can ask for a GEISHA to be sent to the room.

りょうぶしんとう 両部神道〔神道・仏教〕Dual Shinto. A Shinto teaching promoted by esoteric Buddhists who tried to merge Shintoism into the doctrine of dual realms of the Great Sun Buddha: the Diamond Realm and the Womb Realm. →神仏習合；本地垂迹（ほんじすいじゃく）説；両界曼荼羅（りょうかいまんだら）

りょうまがゆく 竜馬が行く〔文芸・作品〕*Ryoma Goes His Way.* A historical novel published in parts from 1962 to 1966 by SHIBA RYOUTAROU. Describes the life of an ambitious and business-minded samurai, SAKAMOTO RYOUMA, in the 19th century.

りょうみん 良民〔政治〕citizens, except for the untouchables, in the centralized administration system in ancient times. →律令制

りょうめんすくな 両面宿儺〔妖怪〕a double-faced and four-handed monster. Was said to live in present northern Gifu Pref. in ancient times. The *Chronicles of Japan* (NIHONSHOKI) describe him as a traitor, while local legends say he slew a dragon or founded a temple.

りょかん 旅館〔旅〕a traditional-style inn. A guest stays in a traditional-style room, wears an informal kimono called YUKATA, is served with traditional-style cuisine for dinner and breakfast, takes traditional-style large public bath provided for guests, and sleeps on a real Japanese futon. All costs, except for drinks, are included in the accommodation fee.

りょくじゅほうしょう 緑綬褒章〔政治〕the Medal with Green Ribbon. Is "awarded to morally remarkable individuals who have actively taken part in serving society," says the Cabinet Office. →褒章

りょくちゃ 緑茶〔飲み物〕green tea. Rich in caffeine and vitamin C. Has several types and grades such as MACCHA, GYOKURO, SENCHA, and BANCHA.

りょじゅん 旅順〔地名〕Lushun, or Port Arthur in China. Was leased

by Japan after the Russo-Japanese War that took place from 1904 to 1905. Was returned to China in 1955. →日露戦争

りん ～厘〖単位〗 a unit of length. About 3 mm. One hundred 'rin' equal one SUN.

りんかいがっこう 臨海学校〖教育〗 a seaside summer school. Is held during summer vacation. Basically, all students participate when they are in an elementary or a junior high school.

りんかんがっこう 林間学校〖教育〗 a school camp. Is held in highland areas during summer vacation. Basically, all students participate when they are in an elementary or a junior high school.

りんぎ 稟議〖ビジネス〗 a bottom-up proposal in a company or government office. It may be circulated among related personnel so that a meeting can be avoided. Sometimes no particular person is responsible for its contents.

りんざいしゅう 臨済宗〖仏教〗 the Rinzai sect of Zen Buddhism. Was introduced from China in 1191 by EISAI. Considers the KOUAN to be most important, as opposed to the Soutou Zen, which considers the meditation to be most important. Is now divided into 14 schools: TENRYUU-JI, SHOUKOKU-JI, KENNIN-JI, NANZEN-JI, MYOUSHIN-JI; KENCHOU-JI, TOUFUKU-JI, DAITOKU-JI, ENGAKU-JI, Eigen-ji, Houkou-ji, Kokutai-ji, Buttsuu-ji and Kougaku-ji.

りんず 綸子〖服飾〗 satin with subdued patterns. Is used for a formal kimono or obi.

りんね 輪廻〖仏教〗 reincarnation. In Sanskrit, *samsara*. All living things repeatedly die and are reborn in the Six Realms of Existence: Hells, Starving Ghosts, Beasts, Bellicose Spirits, Humans, and Heavens, according to the sum of good and bad actions in their lives, which is called karma. Living things can escape from the cycle only by attaining Buddhahood. →地獄；餓鬼；畜生道；修羅道；業(ｺﾞｳ)

りんぱ 琳派〖絵画〗 Rin School. Famous for its decorative style. Painters in this school include TAWARAYA SOUTATSU, OGATA KOURIN, and HON'AMI KOUETSU.

りんぴょうとうしゃかいじんれつざいぜん 臨兵闘者皆陣列在前〖宗教〗 magic words chanted by a mountain ascetic or a monk of esoteric Buddhism to protect himself. The person praying draws four vertical and five horizontal lines in the air with his fingers while chanting. Means that soldiers in a row are preparing for a fight in front of him. Is also called 'kuji' because these words consist of nine kanji characters.

る

るいじゅうこくし 類聚国史 〖政治・書名〗 *Classified History of Japan*. Classifies the articles in Six National Histories (RIKKOKUSHI) for retrieval. Was compiled by SUGAWARA NO MICHIZANE.

るいすふろいす ルイス・フロイス 〖キリスト教〗 Luis Frois. 1532–97. A Portuguese missionary and writer who was a member of the Society of Jesus (Jesuits). Served in Japan for about 30 years. Met two major leaders, first the shogun Ashikaga Yoshiteru and later the daimyo ODA NOBUNAGA, who supported him as a patron. Moved to Macau for several years when missionaries were expelled from Japan but returned and died in Japan. Main works include *The First European Description of Japan* in 1585, and *History of Japan* in 1594.

るいべ ルイベ 〖食べ物〗 thin-sliced frozen salmon. A local food of Hokkaido.

るうすべねでぃくと ルース・ベネディクト 〖人文学〗 1887–1948. A well-known American anthropologist who wrote *The Chrysanthemum and The Sword* (1946), which asserted that Japan has a "shame" or 'haji' culture rather than a "guilt" or 'tsumi' culture. Never visited Japan but based her book on research conducted during World War II for the Office of War Information. Also, was a professor at Columbia University and president of the American Anthropological Association.

るうずべると ルーズベルト 〖外交〗 ⇨セオドア・ルーズベルト

るしゃなぶつ 盧舎那仏 〖仏教〗 ⇨毘盧遮那（びるしゃな）仏

るすい 留守居 〖武士・政治〗 **(1)** a diplomat from a local feudal domain. Lived in Edo and was in charge of communication with the Tokugawa shogunate and other feudal domains. **(2)** a castle-defense officer when a shogun was away from Edo Castle. Was also in charge of controlling the inner palace called OOOKU.

るび ルビ 〖漢字〗 small kana showing the pronunciation of kanji. Originally meant "the letter size of 5.5 points," which was called ruby.

るりこうじ 瑠璃光寺 〖寺院〗 Rurikou-ji Temple. Affiliated with the Soutou sect of Zen Buddhism. Is located in Yamaguchi City, Yamaguchi Pref., though originally founded in another place with a different name. Its five-story pagoda is a National Treasure.

るりこうじょうど 瑠璃光浄土 〖仏教〗 ⇨東方瑠璃光浄土

れ

れいきん 礼金 〔生活〕 key money. Is paid to the landlord by a tenant when moving into a house or apartment, in addition to the rent. →敷金

れいげん 霊験 〔宗教〕 the effect of supernatural power in responding to a wish.

れいしきかんじょうせんとうき 零式艦上戦闘機 〔軍事〕 a Zero fighter. Is usually called 'zero-sen' in Japanese. The principal combat plane of the Japanese Navy during World War II. The maximum speed was about 500 km/h. About 10,000 planes were manufactured. Toward the end of the war, Zero fighters were used for suicide bombing called 'kamikaze.'

れいしゃぶ 冷しゃぶ 〔食べ物〕 sliced pork or beef dipped into hot water and then cooled. Is served with special sauce and vegetables.

れいしゅ 冷酒 〔酒〕 (1) unwarmed sake. (2) sake to be drunk cold.

れいじょう 霊場 〔宗教〕 a spiritual place, or a sacred place. Some old Buddhist temples or Shinto shrines are called 'reijou.'

れいゆうかい 霊友会 〔宗教〕 Reiyukai. A new Buddhist organization that follows the teaching of Nichiren. Was founded in 1923 by Kubo Kakutarou.

れきししょうせつ 歴史小説 〔文芸〕 a historical novel. Describes a historical event in ancient to early-modern times, though it is fiction based on actual events. →時代小説

れきしてきかなづかい 歴史的仮名遣い 〔言語〕 the historical orthography for kana. Was abolished when the modern orthography was introduced in 1946. In this system, kana were written based on literature around or before the 11th century. ↔現代仮名遣い

れきはく 歴博 〔博物館〕 ⇨国立歴史民俗博物館

れざのふ レザノフ 〔外交〕 Nikolai Petrovich Rezanov. 1764–1807. A Russian entrepreneur and envoy. Visited Nagasaki in 1804 and requested commercial relations with Japan but was refused. As retaliation, attacked KARAFUTO and Etorofu Islands in 1806 and 1807.

れすりんぐ レスリング 〔スポーツ〕 wrestling. Was introduced to Japan in 1931. Ishii Shouhachi won the first gold medal in the bantamweight class at the Helsinki Olympics in 1952. Since then, Japanese men and women have won a total of more than 30 gold medals.

れんあいけっこん 恋愛結婚 〔冠婚葬祭〕 a love marriage. Most marriages are based on love in Japan at present, but this term has been used as the antonym of an arranged marriage, which was very common in olden times. ↔見合い結婚

れんが 連歌〔文芸〕 a linked poem. To make this tanka-form poem, one person composes the first three lines with seventeen syllables, and another composes the last two lines with fourteen syllables. The two sets of lines are alternatively repeated by two or more people. Was popular in the Kamakura and Muromachi periods.

れんげ 蓮華〔仏教・植物〕 a lotus flower. Is regarded as the symbol of Buddhism because the flower is beautiful though a lotus grows in a slough. Represents sublime teaching in a filthy world. →蓮(はす)

れんげざ 蓮華座〔仏教・美術〕 ⇨蓮台(れんだい)

れんごう 連合〔政治・経済〕 ⇨日本労働組合総連合会

れんごうこくぐんさいこうしれいかんそうしれいぶ 連合国軍最高司令官総司令部〔戦争・外交〕 General Headquarters of the Supreme Commander for the Allied Powers (SCAP). Ruled Japan from the end of World War II until 1952. Is usually called GHQ in Japan.

れんごうせきぐん 連合赤軍〔政治・犯罪〕 Allied Red Army. A terrorist organization active in the early 1970s.

れんこん 蓮根〔食べ物・植物〕 a lotus root. Often eaten boiled, fried, or stirred. Has a slightly crisp texture.

れんじまど 連子窓〔建築〕 a window with wooden square lath strips. The section of each lath strip is square, and its edge side faces front.

れんじゅ 連珠〔娯楽〕 ⇨五目並べ

れんだい 蓮台〔仏教・美術〕 a lotus flower pedestal. A Buddhist image sits or stands on it. In a painting called the Descent of Amitabha Buddha, the Bodhisattva of Mercy (KANNON) often carries it, on which a deceased soul is supposed to ride. →阿弥陀来迎(あみだらいごう)

れんたいけい 連体形〔言語〕 the continuative form of a verb or adjective to nouns or pronouns. In all conjugations, it takes the same form as it appears in a dictionary.

れんたいし 連体詞〔言語〕 a prenoun modifier. Examples are 'aru' meaning "a certain" and 'ironna' meaning "various."

れんだく 連濁〔言語〕 sequential voicing. The beginning sound of the second word gets voiced in a compound word. For example, in a word, 冷や酒, which is pronounced as 'hiyazake' and means "cold sake," the beginning sound of the second word, 's,' becomes 'z,' and 'sake' changes to 'zake.'

れんにょ 蓮如〔仏教〕 1415-1499. A priest born in Kyoto. Restored the True Pure Land sect and built ISHIYAMA HONGAN-JI Temple in Osaka. Organized followers of the sect by teaching them in easily understandable vernacular language. Thanks to his efforts, the True Pure Land sect became the largest Buddhist sect in Japan. →浄土真宗

れんようけい 連用形〚言語〛 the continuative form of a verb or adjective to verbs or adjectives. In the verb conjugation, precedes a polite auxiliary 'masu' or a conjunctive particle 'te.' In the i-adjective conjugation, precedes a conjunctive particle 'te' or a past auxiliary 'ta.' In the na-adjective conjugation, precedes a conjunctive particle 'te' or takes the te-form or adverbial form.

ろ

ろ 炉〚茶道・建築〛 a square sunken hearth. The host or hostess boils water here to use in the tea ceremony. A part of a tatami mat is cut off, and the hearth is placed under the floor. When the room is not used for the tea ceremony, a small square tatami covers the opening.

ろう 〜浪〚教育・単位〛 a counting suffix for years until a high-school graduate successfully goes into a university. For example, a student who has spent two years until he or she enters a university after graduation from high school is called 'ni-rou,' in which 'ni' means "two."

ろうきょく 浪曲〚芸能〛 ⇨浪花節 (なにわ ぶし)

ろうし 浪士〚武士〛 a masterless but politically ambitious samurai. Usually refers to the forty-seven masterless samurai from the Akou feudal domain, called AKOU ROUSHI, or the masterless samurai who tried to intervene in political matters at the end of the Edo period.

ろうじゅう 老中〚武士・官位〛 a highest-rank minister of the Tokugawa shogunate. Four or five hereditary feudal lords of large domains were appointed and supervised political issues of the shogunate.

ろうじょ 老女〚武士・政治〛 the leader of waiting maids in a samurai family.

ろうじょう 籠城〚戦争〛 to entrench themselves in a castle. Several warlords took this tactic to wait until the allied army came or the enemy gave up, in the Warring States period.

ろうどうきじゅんほう 労働基準法〚法律〛 Labor Standards Law. Was promulgated in 1947 to protect workers.

ろうどうくみあい 労働組合〚経済〛 a labor union. In Japan, it is usually organized within a corporation. Some corporate labor unions in the same industry cooperate for wage negotiation in the spring, called SHUNTOU.

ろうにん 浪人 (1)〚武士〛 a masterless samurai. It is said that there were about 400,000 of them in the early Edo period because the shogunate broke up several feudal clans. 'Rounin' were permitted to carry swords though they were not official warriors. (2) 〔教育〕 a high-school graduate who has failed in university entrance exams and is preparing for the next year. The number of 'rounin' is decreasing because the number of high-school students are decreasing, and the number of universities and colleges has increased.

ろうべん 良弁 〔仏教〕 689-773. A priest born in present Shiga or Kanagawa Pref. It is said that he was carried off by an eagle at two years of age, was left at a tree in Kasuga Shrine in Nara, and was brought up by a priest, Gien. He made a great contribution in founding TOUDAI-JI Temple. →春日大社

ろうもん 楼門 〔建築〕 a two-story gate for a temple, shrine, or castle. The first floor usually does not have a roof.

ろおまじ ローマ字 〔言語〕 the system of writing Japanese in the Roman alphabet. There are several types, such as the Hepburn and statutory systems. →ヘボン式ローマ字; 訓令式ローマ字

ろくおんじ 鹿苑寺 〔寺院〕 Rokuon-ji Temple. The official name of KINKAKU-JI, the Temple of the Golden Pavilion, located in Kyoto. ASHIKAGA YOSHIMITSU built the Golden Pavilion in 1397 and used it as a villa. After his death, the site became a temple with MUSOU SOSEKI as the founder. Now a subsidiary temple of SHOUKOKU-JI Temple.

ろくかんのん 六観音 〔仏教〕 Six Bodhisattvas of Mercy. SHOU-KANNON, SENJU-KANNON, BATOU-KANNON, JUUICHIMEN-KANNON, JUNTEI-KANNON, and FUKUUKENSAKU-KANNON. Save the straying people in the Six Realms of Existence, called ROKU-DOU. →観音

ろくさんさんよんせい 六三三四制 〔教育〕 the 6-3-3-4 year school system. The first 9 years are the period for compulsory education, consisting of elementary and junior high schools. Has been in operation since 1947.

ろくじぞう 六地蔵 〔仏教〕 six transformation of Jizou Bodhi-sattva. Each Jizou saves the straying people in the Six Realms of Existence, called ROKUDOU. →地蔵

ろくしゃくふんどし 六尺褌 〔服飾〕 a 1.8 m-loincloth for men. Is made of bleached cotton.

ろくじょうま 六畳間 〔建築〕 a room with six TATAMI mats. The term often refers to a room that will fit six tatami mats, even if the room has no mats.

ろくだか 禄高 〔武士〕 the amount of the stipend for samurai in the Edo period. The salary was paid in rice in those days.

ろくどう 六道 〔仏教〕 the Six Realms of Existence. Hells, Starving Ghosts, Beasts, Bellicose Spirits, Humans, and Heavens. →地獄; 餓鬼; 畜生道; 修羅道; 輪廻

ろくどうりんね 六道輪廻 〔仏教〕 ⇨ 輪廻

ろくはらたんだい 六波羅探題 〖官位〗 a local agency under the Kamakura shogunate to watch the Imperial Court, guard the town of Kyoto, and administer military affairs in Western Japan. Was established in Rokuhara, Kyoto, in 1221 and abolished in 1333.

ろくまいびょうぶ 六枚屏風 〖絵画・建築〗 a six-paneled folding screen. →屏風

ろくめいかん 鹿鳴館 〖政治・建築〗 Deer Cry Pavilion. A Western-style building proposed by Inoue Kaoru and completed by a British architect, Josiah Conder, in 1883. As a symbol of the Westernization of Japan, parties and balls were held there. Was destroyed in 1941.

ろくよう 六曜 〖暦〗 the unofficial six-day calendar cycle. Came from China and includes superstitions about good and bad fortune associated with certain days. →先勝；友引；先負；仏滅；大安；赤口(しゃっこう)

ろくろ 轆轤 〖陶磁器〗 a potter's wheel. Has been used since ancient times. The modern type is electric-powered.

ろくろくび 轆轤首 〖妖怪〗 **(1)** a young lady with an extendable neck. Licks the oil in a paper-covered lamp called ANDON at night by extending her neck. **(2)** a flying-head man or woman. The head is separated from the body and flies at night.

ろざのだいぶつ 露座の大仏 〖仏教〗 the outdoor-seated Great Buddha.

The Great Buddha at KOUTOKU-IN Temple in Kamakura, Kanagawa Pref.

ろさんじん 魯山人 〖陶磁器〗 ⇨北大路魯山人

ろじ 露地 〖茶道・庭園〗 a garden adjacent to, or a pathway connected to, a teahouse. Is equipped with a stone lantern, a stone washbasin, and stepping stones.

ろっかせん 六歌仙 〖文芸〗 Six Immortal Poets. Ariwara no Narihira, Soujou Henjou, Kisen houshi, Ootomo no Kuronushi, Fun'ya no Yasuhide, and Ono no Komachi. Their names are listed as six great poets in the preface of the first imperial anthology, the *Collection of Ancient and Modern Japanese Poetry* (KOKINWAKASHUU), compiled in 905.

ろっきょくいっそう 六曲一双 〖絵画・書道〗 a pair of folding screens with six panels. →屏風(びょうぶ)

ろっこんしょうじょう 六根清浄 〖仏教〗 to purify six roots of perception: seeing, hearing, smelling, tasting, touching, and consciousness. This phrase is repeatedly recited when climbing a spiritual mountain.

ろっぷ 六腑 〖医療〗 six digestive organs in Chinese medicine: large intestines, small intestines, stomach, gallbladder, and 'sanshou,' which is unknown. →五臓六腑

ろっぽうしゅりけん 六方手裏剣 〖忍者〗 a throwing star with six striking points. →手裏剣(しゅりけん)

ろてんぶろ 露天風呂 〖風呂〗 an

open-air bath. Some open-air baths have a roof, without walls.

ろばた 炉端 〖建築〗 the fireside area around an open sunken hearth at a traditional-style residence. → 囲炉裏(いろり)

ろばたやき 炉端焼き 〖食文化〗 a traditional-style pub where foods are grilled in front of customers and served on a large wooden spatula.

ろばん 露盤 〖仏教・建築〗 a square-shaped dew basin at the bottom of a SOURIN, which is the decorative part on the top of a pagoda roof. →伏鉢(ふくばち); 請花(うけばな); 九輪(くりん); 水煙(すいえん); 竜舎; 宝珠(ほうじゅ)

ろんご 論語 〖人文学・書名〗 *The Analects of Confucius*, or *Lun-yu*. Is said to have been introduced through Paekche in ancient times. Has been an important textbook in education. Many references on this book were published in Japan.

ろんどんかいぐんぐんしゅくじょうやく ロンドン海軍軍縮条約 〖外交・軍事〗 London Naval Treaty. An April 1930 treaty, known formally as the Treaty for the Limitation and Reduction of Naval Armaments, that was signed by France, Italy, Great Britain, Japan, and the United States. Was considered an extension of the Five-Power Treaty and set limits on the number, size, and firepower of submarines of the signatories.

わ

わ 和 〖精神性〗 peace, friendship, and harmony. Regarded as the most important guideline in the Seventeen-Article Constitution in the 7th century, 'wa' is a fundamental feature of the Japanese mentality. Thus a Japanese person as an individual or Japan as a nation usually tends to avoid conflict, even in argumentative situations. →十七(じっ)条憲法

わいえすじゅういち YS-11 〖科学技術〗 YS-11. An airplane developed in Japan that had twin turbopropped engines. Was first placed in service in 1965 and was retired from domestic airlines in 2006. 182 planes were manufactured, of which 72 were exported to the U.S., Canada, Brazil, etc.

わいはんないかく 隈板内閣 〖政治〗 Waihan Cabinet formed in 1898. Was the first party cabinet and was named after OOKUMA SHIGENOBU and ITAGAKI TAISUKE. Ookuma was appointed as both the prime minister and the foreign minister while Itagaki as the interior minister. Was organized to counter the political situation dominated by cliques of specific feudal domains, but it lasted only for 4 months. →藩閥政治

わえいごりんしゅうせい 和英語林集成 〖言語・書名〗 *A Japanese and English Dictionary: with an English and Japanese Index*. The first Japanese-English dictionary, compiled in 1867 by J. C. Hepburn. The second edition was published in 1872 and the third in 1886.

わか 和歌 〖文芸〗 a traditional rhyming poem with a fixed form. Literally means "Japanese song," to be distinguished from Chinese poems, KANSHI. The most popular type is called tanka and includes 31 syllables. Other types are CHOUKA, SEDOUKA, and KATAUTA.

わかくさやま 若草山 〖山岳〗 Mt. Wakakusa, or Mt. Mikasa. Is located in Nara City. The height is 342 m. The whole hill is covered with grass. In January, dead grass on the entire hill is burned to get rid of harmful insects.

わかさ 若狭 〖旧国名〗 the old name of southwestern Fukui Pref.

わかさぎ 公魚 〖魚・食べ物〗 a pond smelt. *Hypomesus olidus*. Lives in a pond or lake. About 15 cm long and edible. People enjoy fishing for smelt in a frozen pond.

わかさわん 若狭湾 〖湾〗 Wakasa Bay. Is located off the western coast of Fukui Pref., facing the Sea of Japan, surrounded by Cape Echizen in the north of Fukui Pref. and Cape Kyouga-misaki at the northern tip of Kyoto Pref. Has a sawtooth coastline with many seaports, where mackerel has been unloaded for centuries. Famous for natural scenic beauties such as AMA-NO-HASHIDATE and Kehi-no-Matsubara. Several nuclear power plants are located along the coast.

わがし 和菓子〔食べ物〕 traditional-style confectionery. Major ingredients are rice and adzuki. Is classified into several categories such as NAMA-GASHI, HI-GASHI, and yaki-gashi. Examples include OKOSHI, RAKUGAN, MANJUU, YOUKAN, and DORAYAKI.

わかたけに 若竹煮〔食べ物〕 simmered bamboo shoots with edible brown seaweed called WAKAME.

わかどしより 若年寄〔武士・政治〕 a councilor in the Tokugawa shogunate. The second-highest position next to a minister called ROUJUU. Three to five hereditary feudal lords of small domains were appointed to the position to supervise direct vassals of the shogun.

わかとの 若殿〔武士・政治〕 a young lord. This term was usually used to distinguish the son from the father, whether the father had retired or not. ↔大殿

わがはいはねこである 吾輩は猫である〔文芸・作品〕 *I am a cat.* A novel published in parts from 1905 to 1906 by NATSUME SOUSEKI. Satirically describes a human life, viewed from the perspective of a cat.

わかみず 若水〔年中行事〕 the first water drawn from a well on the morning of January 1. Is said to eliminate evil spirits in the year. Is offered to the deity of the New Year. →歳神(としがみ)

わかめ 若布〔食べ物・植物〕 an edible brown seaweed. *Undaria pinnitifida.* Grows 50 to 150 cm long. Is used for various traditional dishes such as miso soup and vinegared salad. →味噌汁；酢の物

わかやまけん 和歌山県〔都道府県〕 Wakayama Pref. Is located south of Osaka and forms part of the Kii Peninsula. Is 4,726 km^2 in area. Its capital is Wakayama City. Famous for production of oranges and pickled plums. Used to be a major part of KII.

わかやまし 和歌山市〔地名〕 Wakayama City. The capital of Wakayama Pref., and is located in its northwestern part. Developed as a castle town of the KII Tokugawa family, one of the three branches of the Tokugawa clan.

わかやまぼくすい 若山牧水〔文芸〕 1885-1928. A TANKA poet born in Miyazaki Pref. Composed many poems related to traveling and drinking. Was influenced by naturalism.

わかんこんこうぶん 和漢混淆文〔言語〕 a text written in a mixed style of literary Japanese and Chinese classics. Works written in this style include *Tales of Times Now Past* (KONJAKU MONOGATARI) and *The Tale of the Heike* (HEIKE MONOGATARI).

わかんむり ワ冠〔漢字〕 a crown radical in the shape of ワ (wa). Originally means "cover." Is used in kanji such as 写 (copy), 軍 (military), and 冠 (crown).

わかんろうえいしゅう 和漢朗詠集 〚文芸・作品〛 *Collection of Japanese and Chinese Verses*. Was compiled around 1013 by Fujiwara Kintou. Contains 588 Chinese poems and 216 Japanese poems.

わき ワキ 〚能〛 a deuteragomist, or a second main character in a Noh play. Does not wear a mask. Plays the role of a real human being, while the main character, SHITE, is a supernatural being.

わきざし 脇差 〚武器〛 a short sword. Was carried together with a long sword by a samurai.

わきじ 脇侍 〚仏教〛 an attendant to a central Buddhist image in a triad. A particular central image always has the same two attendants in multiple settings. For example the attendants of Amitabha Buddha are always KANNON BOSATSU and SEISHI BOSATSU. →三尊

わきばしら 脇柱 〚能〛 the front-right pillar on a Noh stage.

わぎゅう 和牛 〚食べ物・動物〛 a Japanese breed of cattle. Its meat is tender and marbled and is usually said to be high-grade, compared with imported beef.

わくん 和訓 〚言語〛 ⇨訓読み

わけいせいじゃく 和敬清寂 〚茶道〛 the mind of the tea ceremony. Literally means "harmony, respect, purity, and elegant simplicity." The first half expresses the mutual manners of a host or hostess and guests. The last half expresses the manner when handling the utensil and using the setting such as a room and garden.

わけぎ 分葱 〚食べ物・植物〛 a small, thin variety of green onion. *Allium fistulosum* var. *caespitosum*. Is put into soup or eaten dressed with vinegar and miso. →葱(ねぎ)

わけのきよまろ 和気清麻呂 〚政治〛 733–799. A court noble born in present Okayama Pref. Had a conflict with a politically ambitious priest named DOUKYOU and was exiled to present Kagoshima Pref. After Doukyou lost his position, served Emperor Kanmu.

わご 和語 〚言語〛 ⇨大和言葉

わこう 倭寇 〚外交・犯罪〛 Japanese pirates in the 13th to 16th centuries. Mainly attacked coastal areas of Korea and China.

わこく 倭国 〚政治〛 ancient Japan. Japan was called 'Wa' by ancient China. 'Koku' means "nation."

わごと 和事 〚歌舞伎〛 the feminine style of kabuki play. The hero is usually a good-looking young man and performs love scenes, using a tender gesture, words, makeup, and costume.

わこんようさい 和魂洋才 〚精神性〛 Japanese mentality with Western knowledge. A motto in the 19th century when high waves of Western knowledge surged into Japan.

わざあり 技有り 〚柔道〛 a half-point offense in a judo match. In the old rule, a player would win the match when getting waza-ari twice. This provision was temporally abolished in 2017, only to be revived in the rule change effective in 2018.

わさび 山葵〖調味料・植物〗 wasabi, or Japanese horseradish. Is used as a condiment for sushi, sashimi, and cold buckwheat noodles.

わさびじょうゆ 山葵醤油〖調味料〗 soy sauce with wasabi. Some people do not like mingling wasabi with soy sauce when eating sashimi. Also good with avocado.

わさん 和算〖科学技術〗 traditional Japanese mathematics. Was introduced from China in ancient times and developed in the Edo period, separately from European mathematics.

わさんぼん 和三盆〖調味料〗 light-yellow, fine-grained, high-quality sugar. Is used for making a traditional high-grade confection. A specialty of Kagawa and Tokushima Prefs.

わし 和紙〖生活〗 traditional paper. It is said that the way of making paper was introduced from China through Korea to Japan in the early 7th century. Is made from a paper bush (MITSUMATA), paper mulberry (KOUZO), or *Wikstroemia sikokiana* (GANPI).

わじ 和字〖言語〗 ⇨国字

わしつ 和室〖建築〗 a Japanese-style room. Its floor is covered with TATAMI mats.

わじまし 輪島市〖地名〗 Wajima City. Is located in northern Ishikawa Pref. Famous for its morning market and lacquerware called WAJIMA-NURI.

わじまぬり 輪島塗〖漆器〗 Wajima lacquerware. Is produced by a complicated process in Wajima City, Ishikawa Pref. Is considered to be high-quality.

わじゅう 輪中〖科学技術・行政〗 an area surrounded by a wall to protect the area against a river flooding. The community hemmed in Kiso, Nagara, and Ibi Rivers is famous.

わしょ 和書〖生活〗 a book bound in the traditional Japanese style. Is bound on the right side because the Japanese text is usually written vertically and read from right to left.

わじょう 和上, 和尚〖仏教〗 a senior priest. Although the pronunciation is the same, the Hossou and Shingon sects use different kanji, 和尚, while the Ritsu sect uses different kanji, 和上. →和尚(おしょう)

わしょく 和食〖食文化〗 traditional-style cuisine. Eaten with chopsticks. This term usually implies food with a long history, such as SASHIMI, SUSHI, tempura, and grilled eel with thick sauce. Some people may say that rather new food such as SUKIYAKI, OYAKO-DON, or OKONOMI-YAKI are also 'washoku,' but others may disagree. Western-taste dishes such as "curry and rice" and "ketchup fried rice wrapped in a thin omelette," called OMURAISU, are not categorized into 'washoku' though they are unique to Japanese food culture. ↔洋食

わしんとんかいぎ　ワシントン会議
〖外交〗 Washington Conference. November 1921–February 1922 military conference held in Washington, D.C., and associated with the League of Nations. Was organized by Warren G. Harding, President of the United States, to discuss issues related to East Asia and the Pacific region, especially the armaments race. Was attended by nine nations: Belgium, China, France, Great Britain, Italy, Japan, the Netherlands, Portugal, and the United States. Three main treaties resulted from the conference: the Four-Power Treaty, the Five-Power Treaty, and the Nine-Power Treaty. It triggered the cancellation of the 1902 Anglo-Japanese Alliance.

わせいえいご　和製英語　〖言語〗 Japanese English. An English-like word or phrase coined in Japan. For example, 'back mirror,' which means "rearview mirror," or 'sharp pencil,' which means "mechanical pencil."

わせん　和船〖交通〗 a traditional-style wooden ship. Is propelled by a single oar attached to the stern or a sail. Lacks a Western-style keel.

わたあめ　綿飴〖食べ物〗 ⇨綿菓子

わだいこ　和太鼓〖音楽〗 a traditional drum. Is beaten with two thick sticks. The edge is also beaten to produce different tones.

わたいれ　綿入れ〖服飾〗 a wadded garment to protect against the cold.

わたがし　綿菓子〖食べ物〗 cotton candy. Is usually sold at a street vendor's stall at a festival.

わたしばし　渡し箸〖食文化〗 to rest one's chopsticks across the top of one's bowl. Is regarded as bad etiquette, known as kirai-bashi.

わたせせん　渡瀬線〖自然〗 the Watase line. A boundary line of geographical fauna and flora. Is drawn between Yaku and Tanegashima Islands and Amami-ooshima Island in Kagoshima Pref. Was discovered by a zoologist, Watase Shouzaburou.

わたつみ　海神〖神道〗 a deity of the ocean. There are several deities of the ocean in Japanese mythology, such as OOWADATSUMI NO KAMI and SUMINOE NO KAMI.

わたなべかざん　渡辺崋山〖絵画・人文学〗 1793–1841. A scholar of Dutch learning and painter, born in Edo. Studied Western affairs, criticized the shogunate system, and killed himself during his house arrest. His works as a painter include *Portrait of Takami Senseki* at the Tokyo National Museum.

わたなべのつ　渡辺の津〖海洋・交通〗 Watanabe Harbor. Existed at a river mouth in Osaka from ancient to medieval times. When visiting Shitennou-ji Temple, Sumiyoshi Grand Shrine, Mt. Kouya, or the Kumano area, people from Kyoto departed from a ship at this harbor to travel on land.

わたなべのつな　渡辺綱〖武士〗 953–1025. One of the four great warriors under MINAMOTO NO YORI-MITSU. Is said to have cut off an arm of a demon, which lived at the main gate of Heian Castle, and to have joined in the extermination of demons in Mt. Ooe in present northern Kyoto Pref. →大江山酒呑童子（おおえやましゅてんどうじ）

わたぼうし 綿帽子 〖冠婚葬祭・服飾〗 a white floss veil for a bride. Is worn with a traditional bridal costume.

わだんす 和箪笥〖家具〗 a traditional chest of drawers. A high-class chest made of paulownia and very airtight.

わつじてつろう 和辻哲郎 〖人文学〗 1889-1960. A philosopher born in Hyougo Pref. His works include *Pilgrimages to the Ancient Temples in Nara* (Koji junrei) in 1919 and *Climate and Culture: A Philosophical Study* (Fuudo) in 1935.

わどうかいちん 和同開珎〖経済〗 a coin minted in Japan in 708. Is 2.4 cm in diameter, is round-shaped, and has a square hole. Four kanji characters 和同開珎 are embossed on it. There are two types: silver and copper.

わどうかいほう 和同開寳〖経済〗 ⇨ 和同開珎（わどうかいちん）

わとじ 和綴じ 〖生活〗 Japanese-style binding of a book. Binds the right side of a book, using a thread. →和書

わにぐち 鰐口〖寺院〗 a flat gong with a slit. Literally means "alligator mouth" because of its shape. Is hung in front of a main building of a temple, sometimes a shrine. People ring it before worshipping.

わにゅうどう 輪入道〖妖怪〗 Wheel Monster. A monk's face with a heavy beard and whiskers is on the hub of a blazing wheel. It is said that a person who looks at a Wanyuudou loses his or her soul.

わのごおう 倭の五王〖天皇〗 Five Kings of Wa. When Japan was named 'Wa' in the 5th century, five kings were referred to in a historical document of Sung as San, Chin, Sei, Kou, and Bu. It is said that San is Emperor Oujin, Nintoku, or Richuu, Chin is Emperor Nintoku or Hanzei, Sei is Emperor Ingyou, Kou is Emperor Ankou, and Bu is Emperor Yuuryaku.

わのなのこくおういん 倭奴国王印 〖考古〗 ⇨漢倭奴国王印

わび 侘び〖精神性〗 quiet simplicity, or beauty through a sense of austerity. A term for haiku or tea ceremony.

わびちゃ 侘び茶 〖茶道〗 tea ceremony pursuing the beauty of austerity.

わふう 和風〖精神性〗 traditional Japanese style, or Japanese taste. Often refers to architecture, interior design, gardens, costumes, and cuisine.

わふうぱすた 和風パスタ 〖食べ物〗 Japanese-style pasta. Usually flavored with soy sauce, though sometimes with white sauce or just salt. Ingredients are varied such as salmon, cod roe, clam, purple laver, fermented soybeans, and mushrooms.

わふく 和服〖服飾〗 ⇨着物

わよう 和様〖芸術〗 Japanese style. Often refers to architecture and calligraphy, usually contrasted with the Chinese style, in and before early-modern times.

わようせっちゅう 和洋折衷〖精神性〗 blending of Japanese and Western styles. Often refers to architecture, interior design, and cuisine.

わらいえ 笑絵〖絵画〗 ⇨春画(しゅんが)

わらじ 草鞋〖履物〗 a straw sandal. Had a clog thong and a kind of shoelace, with which the foot was fixed on the flat sole. Good for a long-distance walk in olden times. →藁草履(わらぞうり)

わらぞうり 藁草履〖履物〗 a simple straw sandal. Has only a clog thong on a flat sole. →草鞋(わらじ)

わらにんぎょう 藁人形〖宗教〗 a straw figure. Was used to curse an enemy to death in the Edo period. The petitioner stuck long nails of about 15 cm into a straw figure of the enemy in a Shinto shrine around 2 am. →丑(うし)の刻参り

わらびもち 蕨餅〖食べ物〗 a bracken-starch dumpling. Sweetened soybean flour is often sprinkled on it.

わらぶき 藁葺き〖建築〗 a term for thatching with straw. There remain some houses with this type of roof.

わりげいこ 割り稽古〖茶道〗 practice of each step in the tea ceremony. The whole process of making tea can be divided into several steps, each being exercised separately.

わりした 割り下〖調味料〗 stock for a one-pot dish such as SUKIYAKI. Consists of soy sauce, mirin, and sugar.

わりばし 割り箸〖食器〗 disposable chopsticks. Some are wooden, and others are made of bamboo. Since the upper parts of two chopsticks are connected, people split them before eating.

わりふ 割符〖忍者・ビジネス〗 a tally. Two parties identified each other by putting together two pieces of a broken wooden tag on which a character or a picture was drawn.

われき 和暦〖暦〗 the traditional Japanese calendar. Also refers to era names. →旧暦；元号

われただたるをしる 吾唯足知〖精神性・仏教〗 a phrase in Zen Buddhism, which means "I am just content with what I am." Is inscribed on a stone-water basin at Ryouan-ji Temple.

わをもってとうとしとなす 和を以て尊しとなす〖精神性〗 "Harmony is to be valued." The first phrase of Article 1 in the Seventeen-Article Constitution. →十七(じゅうしち)条憲法

わん 椀〖食器〗 a wooden soup bowl. Is often called 'o-wan,' with the polite prefix, 'o,' to distinguish a bowl for rice, CHAWAN. A high-grade soup bowl is usually lacquered.

わんがりまあたい ワンガリ・

マータイ〚精神性〛 1940-2011. A Kenyan environmental activist and political leader. Is best known for starting the Green Belt Movement in 1977, which stresses the planting of trees and other efforts for environmental sustainability. Came across the Japanese word 'mottainai' when she visited Japan in 2005, and initiated the Mottainai environmental campaign. 'Mottainai' superficially means "wasteful," but it also implies "pity, love, or fear of Mother Nature." The Mottainai campaign is quite popular in Japan. Received the Nobel Peace Prize in 2004 and Japan's Grand Cordon of the Rising Sun in 2009. →旭日章

わんぎり ワン切り 〚生活・犯罪〛 one-ring hang-up call. Is usually used to communicate mutual numbers of a cellular phone.

わんこそば 椀子蕎麦 〚食べ物〛 buckwheat noodles served in small bowls. Mouthfuls of noodles are continuously served with a dipping sauce until the customer signals that he or she is done. A specialty of Iwate Pref.

わんせん 腕釧〚仏教〛 a bracelet of a Buddhist image.

ゐ ゐ〚言語〛 a hiragana that had a similar pronunciation to い. Is not used at present.

ヰ ヰ〚言語〛 a katakana that had a similar pronunciation to い. Is not used at present.

ゐたせくすありす ヰタ・セクスアリス〚文芸〛 *Vita Sexualis*. A novel published in 1909 by MORI OUGAI. Describes adolescent sexual desire. Was prohibited from being sold. The title is Latin, meaning "sexual life."

ゑ ゑ〚言語〛 a hiragana that had a similar pronunciation to え. Is not used at present.

を を〚言語〛 a hiragana that has a similar pronunciation to お. Is mostly used at present to spell a postpositional particle to indicate the objective case.

ヲ ヲ〚言語〛 a katakana that has a similar pronunciation to お.

度量衡一覧

【長さ Length】

ミリメートル (millimeter)	1 mm = 0.001m	インチ (inch)	1 in.
センチメートル (centimeter)	1 cm = 0.01m	フィート (foot, feet)	1 ft. = 12 in.
メートル (meter)	1 m	ヤード (yard)	1 yd. = 3 ft.
キロメートル (kilometer)	1 km = 1000m	マイル (mile)	1 mi. = 1760 yd.

［換算表］

	cm	m	in.	ft.	yd.
1 cm	1	0.01	0.393700787	0.032808399	0.010936133
1 m	100	1	39.37007874	3.280839895	1.093613298
1 in.	2.54	0.0254	1	1/12	1/36
1 ft.	30.48	0.3048	12	1	1/3
1 yd.	91.44	0.9144	36	3	1

	m	km	yd.	mi.
1 m	1	0.001	1.093613298	0.000621371
1 km	1000	1	1093.613298	0.621371192
1 yd.	0.9144	0.0009144	1	0.000568182
1 mi.	1609.344	1.609344	1760	1

【面積】

平方センチメートル (square centimeter)	$1 \text{ cm}^2 = 0.0001 \text{ m}^2$	平方インチ (square inch)	1 sq.in.
平方メートル［平米］(square meter)	1 m^2	平方フィート (square foot)	1 sq.ft. = 144 sq.in.
アール (are)	1 a = 100 m^2	平方ヤード (square yard)	1 sq.yd. = 9 sq.ft.
ヘクタール (hectare)	1 ha = 100 a	エーカー (acre)	1 ac = 4840 sq.yd.
平方キロメートル (square kilometer)	$1 \text{ km}^2 = 100000 \text{ m}^2$	平方マイル (square mile)	1 sq.mi. = 640 ac

畳	1 畳 = 1.6562 m^2 = 17.827 sq.ft.	坪	1 坪 = 3.3124 m^2 = 35.654 sq.ft. = 2 畳

［換算表］

	cm^2	sq.in.	sq.ft.	sq.yd.	m^2
1cm^2	1	0.15500031	0.001076391	0.000119599	0.0001
1sq.in.	6.4516	1	1/144	0.000771605	0.00064516
1sq.ft.	929.0304	144	1	1/9	0.09290304
1sq.yd.	8361.2736	1296	9	1	0.83612736
1m^2	10000	1550.0031	10.76391042	1.195990046	1
1ac.	—	—	43560	4840	4046.856422

	ac.	sq.mi.	km^2
1ac.	1	1/640	0.004046856
1sq.mi.	640	1	2.58998811
1km^2	247.1053815	0.386102159	1

【体積 Volume】

立方センチメートル (cubic centimeter)	1 cm^3 [cc] = 0.000001 m^3	立方インチ (cubic inch)	1 cu.in.
立方メートル (cubic meter)	1 m^3	立方フィート (cubic foot)	1 cu.ft. = 1728 cu.in.
		立方ヤード (cubic yard)	1 cu.yd. = 27 cu.ft.

［換算表］

	cm^3	cu.in.	cu.ft.	cu.yd.	m^3
1cm^3	1	0.061023744			
1cu.in.	16.387064	1	1/1728	1/46656	
1cu.ft.	28316.84659	1728	1	0.037037037	0.028316847
1cu.yd.	764554.858	46656	27	1	0.764554858
1m^3	1000000	61023.74409	35.31466672	1.307950619	1

【容積 Capacity】

ミリリットル (milliliter)	1 ml. = 1 cm^3 [cc]	カップ (cup)	1 cp. = 1/2 pt.
デシリットル (deciliter)	1 dl. = 100 ml.	パイント (pint)	1 pt. = 2 cp.
リットル (liter)	1 l.	クオート (quart)	1 qt. = 2 pt.
キロリットル (kiloliter)	1 kl. = 1000 l.	ガロン (gallon)	1 gal. = 4 qt.
		ブッシェル (bushel)	1 bu. = 8 gal.

[換算表]		ml. (US)	ml. (UK)
	1 cp.	236.5882365	284.130625
	1 pt.	473.176473	568.26125
	1 qt.	946.352946	1136.5225
	1 gal.	3785.411784	4546.09
	1 bu.	30283.29427	36368.72

【重さ Weight】

グラム (gram)	1 g	オンス (ounce)	1 oz.
キログラム (kilogram)	1 kg = 1000 g	ポンド (pound)	1 lb. = 16 oz.

[換算表]		g	oz.	lb.
	1 g	1	0.035273962	0.002204623
	1 oz.	28.34952313	1	1/16
	1 lb.	453.59237	16	1

メートル・トン (metric ton)	1 t [m.t.] = 1000 kg	ショート・トン (short ton)（米）	1 t [s.t.] = 2000 lb.
		ロング・トン (long ton)（英）	1 t [l.t.] = 2240 lb.

[換算表]		kg	m.t.	s.t.	l.t.
	1 kg	1	0.001	0.001102311	0.000984207
	1 m.t.	1000	1	1.102311311	0.984206528
	1 s.t.	907.18474	0.90718474	1	0.892857143
	1 l.t.	1016.046909	1.016046909	1.12	1

【温度】

摂氏 degree Celsius（℃）　　C＝(F − 32)/1.8
華氏 degree Fahrenheit（℉）　F＝C×1.8 + 32

℃	−40	−30	−20	−10	0	10	20	30	40	50	60	70	80	90	100
℉	−40	−22	−4	14	32	50	68	86	104	122	140	158	176	194	212

℉	−30	−10	0	10	30	50	70	90	110	130	150	170	180	190	210
℃	−34.4	−23.3	−17.8	−12.2	−1.1	10.0	21.1	32.2	43.3	54.4	65.6	76.7	82.2	87.8	98.9

688

【体温】

℃	35	35.5	36	36.5	37	37.5	38	38.5	39	39.5	40	40.5	41	41.5	42
°F	95	95.9	96.8	97.7	98.6	99.5	100.4	101.3	102.2	103.1	104	104.9	105.8	106.7	107.6

【身長】

身長(cm)を30.48で割った1の位がフィート，小数点以下に12をかけた値がインチになる.
(例) 身長160cmの場合 :
$160 \div 30.48 = 5.249$ $0.249 \times 12 = 2.988 (\fallingdotseq 3)$ $\therefore 160cm = 5'3''$ (5 feet 3 inches)

cm	150	155	160	165	170	175	180	185	190	195	200
ft.'in.''	4'11''	5'1''	5'3''	5'5''	5'7''	5'9''	5'11''	6'1''	6'3''	6'5''	6'7''

【体重】

体重(kg)×2.2046 ＝体重(lb.)

kg	40	45	50	55	60	65	70	75	80	85	90	95	100
lb.	88.2	99.2	110.2	121.3	132.3	143.3	154.3	165.3	176.4	187.4	198.4	209.4	220.5

【速度】

km → mile: 1 km = 0.62137 miles   mph = miles per hour

km/h	40	50	60	80	100	120	140	160
mph	24.9	31.1	37.3	49.7	62.1	74.6	87.0	99.4

mile → km: 1 mile = 1.60934 km

mph	30	40	50	60	70	80	90	100
km/h	48.3	64.4	80.5	96.6	112.7	128.7	144.8	160.9

主な参考文献

Sandra Buckley, ed., *Encyclopedia of Contemporary Japanese Culture* (2009: Routledge)

Donn F. Draeger, *Ninjutsu* (1989: Tuttle)

H. Byron Earhart, *Japanese Religion*, 3rd edition (1982: Wadsworth)

John Gauntner, *The Sake Handbook* (2002: Tuttle)

Richard Hosking, *A Dictionary of Japanese Food* (1995: Tuttle)

Christmas Humphreys, *Buddhism*, 3rd edition (1962: Penguin Books)

Kodansha, *Japan: An Illustrated Encyclopedia* (1993: Kodansha)

Robert T. Paine and Alexander Soper, *The Art and Architecture of Japan* (1974: Penguin Books)

Michel Random, *The Martial Arts* (1984: Peerage Books)

Statistic Bureau, *Statistical Handbook of Japan 2014* (2014: Ministry of Internal Affairs and Communications, Japan)

The University of Chicago, *The Chicago Manual of Style*, 15th edition (2003: The University of Chicago Press)

Hiroko Yoda and Matt Alt, *Yokai Attack! The Japanese Monster Survival Guide* (2012: Tuttle)

秋山虔，猪野謙二，西尾実『新版・日本文学史』(1971: 秀英出版)

秋山裕一『日本酒』(1994: 岩波書店)

安部直文『対訳ビジュアル双書：全図解・日本のしくみ』(2012: IBC パブリッシング)

飯倉晴武『日本人のしきたり』(2003: 青春出版社)

大谷光男『旧暦で読み解く日本の習わし』(2003: 青春出版社)

小西友七・監修, 岸野英治・編『ウィズダム和英辞典』第2版 (2013: 三省堂)

CR & LF 研究所『日本の神様』(2014: マイナビ)

新潮社『新潮世界美術辞典』(1985: 新潮社)

戸部新十郎『忍者と忍術』(1996: 毎日新聞社)

友田晶子, ギャップ・ジャパン編集部『世界に誇る「国酒」日本酒』(2013: ギャップ・ジャパン)

中村元・編『仏教語源散策』(1976: 東京書籍)

中村元・編著『新・仏教語源散策』(1986: 東京書籍)

西海コエン『日英対訳　日本の歴史』(2015: IBC パブリッシング)

松本美江『英語で日本紹介ハンドブック』改訂版 (2014: アルク)

南出康世, 中邑光男・編『ジーニアス和英辞典』第3版 (2011: 大修館書店)

山口百々男・編『和英　日本の文化・観光・歴史辞典』改訂版 (2014: 三修社)

山田雄司『忍者の歴史』(2016: KADOKAWA)

歴史群像編集部『図説・忍者と忍術　忍器・奥義・秘伝集』(2007: 学研)

和英対照日本美術用語辞典編集委員会『和英対照日本美術用語辞典』
　(1990: 東京美術)

渡邉敏郎, E. Skrzypczak, P. Snowden・編『研究社和英大辞典』第5版
　(2003: 研究社)

その他, 官公庁, 地方自治体, 寺社, 博物館など, 各種ホームページなど多数

［編著者］

森口 稔 （もりぐち・みのる）

1958 年，大阪生まれ。北海道大学卒，Southern College of Technology（現 Southern Polytechnic State University）大学院修士課程修了。高校英語教師，英文雑誌記者，機械翻訳開発担当，テクニカルライター，実務翻訳者，大学教員などを経験。通訳ガイド資格保持者。現在は，大学非常勤講師として英語や日本語や日本文化を教えながら，辞書執筆や実務翻訳などに携わる。

著書に，『テクニカルコミュニケーションへの招待』『日本語を書くトレーニング』（共著）『日本語を話すトレーニング』（共著）『基礎からわかる話す技術』（共著）『基礎からわかる日本語表現法』（共著）。

執筆・校閲等に関わった辞書に，『ウィズダム英和辞典』『ジーニアス和英辞典第3版』『三省堂国語辞典第7版』『ジーニアス英和辞典第5版』『ベーシックジーニアス英和辞典第2版』『最新英語学・言語学用語辞典』。

「コミュニケーションの情と理」「段階的コミュニケーション力と学校教育」「日本テクニカルコミュニケーション史の可能性」「TC的観点から見た電子辞書UIの比較」「翻訳における読者分析の重要性」「情報検索における索引の重要性について」などの論文を執筆。

［英文校閲］

William S. Pfeiffer （ウィリアム・S・ファイファー）

1947 年，米国オハイオ州生まれ。Amherst College 卒業，Kent State University 大学院博士課程修了，Ph.D. 取得。Southern Polytechnic State University 教授，Warren Wilson College 学長などを経験。テクニカルコミュニケーション，英文学，国際論が専門。

著書に，*Technical Communication: A Practical Approach* (Pearson, 8th ed.), *Pocket Guide to Technical Communication* (Pearson, 5th ed.), *Proposal Writing: The Art of Friendly and Winning Persuasion* (Pearson) など。
日本文化，特に，新興宗教や日本におけるキリスト教についての論文多数。

2018年7月10日　初版発行

英語で案内する
日本の伝統・大衆文化辞典

2020年1月10日　第2刷発行

編著者	森口 稔 (もりぐち・みのる)
英文校閲	William S. Pfeiffer (ウィリアム・S・ファイファー)
発行者	株式会社 三省堂　代表者 北口克彦
印刷者	三省堂印刷株式会社
発行所	株式会社 三省堂

〒101-8371　東京都千代田区神田三崎町二丁目22番14号
電話　編集　(03) 3230-9411
　　　営業　(03) 3230-9412
https://www.sanseido.co.jp/

〈日本伝統大衆文化辞典・704pp.〉

落丁本・乱丁本はお取り替えいたします。
ISBN978-4-385-10489-8

本書を無断で複写複製することは，著作権法上の例外を除き，禁じられています。また，本書を請負業者等の第三者に依頼してスキャン等によってデジタル化することは，たとえ個人や家庭内での利用であっても一切認められておりません。